THE OXFORD HANDBOOK OF

EMPLOYMENT RELATIONS

THE OXFORD HANDBOOK OF

EMPLOYMENT

RELATIONS

COMPARATIVE EMPLOYMENT SYSTEMS

Edited by

ADRIAN WILKINSON,
GEOFFREY WOOD,
and
RICHARD DEEG

OXFORD
UNIVERSITY PRESS

OXFORD
UNIVERSITY PRESS

Great Clarendon Street, Oxford, OX2 6DP,
United Kingdom

Oxford University Press is a department of the University of Oxford.
It furthers the University's objective of excellence in research, scholarship,
and education by publishing worldwide. Oxford is a registered trade mark of
Oxford University Press in the UK and in certain other countries

First Edition published in 2014

Impression: 1

Published in the United States of America by Oxford University Press
198 Madison Avenue, New York, NY 10016, United States of America

British Library Cataloguing in Publication Data
Data available

Library of Congress Control Number: 2013954457

ISBN 978-0-19-969509-6

Printed and bound in Great Britain by
CPI Group (UK) Ltd, Croydon, CR0 4YY

To

Erin and Aidan

Vicky and Alice

Claudia, Anna, and Wesley

ACKNOWLEDGEMENTS

THANKS to our editor David Musson and to Emma Booth for their assistance, patience, and insights.

Contents

PART IV SUBSTANTIVE THEMES

PART V REFLECTIONS

LIST OF FIGURES

LIST OF TABLES

About the Contributors

The Editors

Adrian Wilkinson is Professor and Director of the Centre for Work, Organization, and Wellbeing at Griffith University, Australia. Prior to his 2006 appointment, Adrian worked at Loughborough University in the UK where he was Professor of Human Resource Management. Adrian has also worked at the University of Manchester Institute of Science and Technology. He holds Visiting Professorships at Loughborough University, Sheffield University, and the University of Durham, and is an Academic Fellow at the Centre for International Human Resource Management at the Judge Institute, University of Cambridge.

Adrian has authored/co-authored/edited 20 books and over 140 articles in academic journals. His books include *Managing Quality and Human Resources* (Blackwell, 1997); *Managing with TQM: Theory and Practice* (Macmillan, 1998); *Understanding Work and Employment: Industrial Relations in Transition* (Oxford University Press, 2003); *The Sage Handbook of Human Resource Management* (Sage, 2009); *The Oxford Handbook of Organisational Participation* (Oxford University Press, 2010); *The Research Handbook on the Future of Work and Employment Relations* (Edward Elgar, 2011); *New Directions in Employment Relations* (Palgrave Macmillan, 2011); *The Research Handbook of Comparative Employment Relations* (Edward Elgar, 2011); *The International Handbook of Labour Unions* (Edward Elgar, 2011); *HRM at Work: People Management and Development*, 5th edition (CIPD, 2012).

Adrian was appointed as a British Academy of Management Fellow in 2010. In 2011 he was elected as an Academician of the Academy of Social Sciences as recognition of his contribution to the field. In 2012 he was shortlisted by *HR* magazine for the award of HR (Most Influential International Thinker. <http://www.hrmostinfluential.co.uk/results/hr-most-influential-2012-shortlist-international-thinkers>.

Geoffrey Wood is Professor of International Business, University of Warwick. Previously, he was Professor and Director of Research at Middlesex University Business School and before that, taught at Rhodes University, South Africa (where he attained the rank of Associate Professor) and Coventry University, Coventry, UK (where he attained the rank of Reader). He has also held visiting fellowships at Cranfield University, Victoria University of Wellington (New Zealand), and the American University in Cairo, Cornell University, and Rhodes University. He currently is Overseas Research Associate of the University of the Witwatersrand. Geoffrey Wood has served as Commissioned

Researcher for the South African Truth and Reconciliation Commission. He has authored/co-authored/edited 12 books and over 100 articles in peer-reviewed journals (including journals such as *Work and Occupations, Work, Employment and Society, Organization Studies, British Journal of Industrial Relations, Human Relations, Economy and Society, Human Resource Management* (US)). He has had numerous research grants including from funding councils, the European Union, government departments (e.g. US Department of Labor), charities (e.g. Nuffield Foundation) and the labour movement (e.g. the ITF). He was the winner of the ECGI 2012 prize (with Marc Goergen and Noel O'Sullivan) for the best working paper in finance. Geoff's research interests centre on the relationship between national institutional setting, corporate governance, firm finance, and firm-level work and employment relations. While much of the contemporary comparative institutional literature draws distinctions between national contexts based on stylized ideal types, macroeconomic trends, and/or limited panels of case studies, his work brings to bear systematic comparative firm level evidence.

Richard Deeg is Professor and Chair of the Department of Political Science at Temple University. He received his Ph.D. from MIT and has been a Postdoctoral Fellow and Visiting Scholar at the Max Planck Institute for the Study of Societies in Cologne, Germany. He has written extensively on financial market regulation, institutional theory, and varieties of capitalism. His publications include *Finance Capitalism Unveiled: Banks and the German Political Economy* (University of Michigan, 1999) and dozens of articles on German and European political economy in various journals, including *Comparative Political Studies, Economy and Society, Journal of European Public Policy, Journal of International Business Studies, Publius: The Journal of Federalism, Small Business Economics, Socio-Economic Review, West European Politics*, and *World Politics*. His current research focuses on causes and mechanisms of institutional change in financial systems.

The Contributors

Jose Aleman Associate Professor of Political Science, Fordham University

Matthew M. C. Allen Senior Lecturer in Organization Studies, University of Manchester

Sabina Avdagic Research Fellow University of Sussex

Lucio Baccaro Professor of Sociology, University of Geneva

Franco Barchiesi Associate Professor of African-American and African Studies, Ohio State University

Michael Barry Associate Professor, Griffith University

Robert Boyer Economist, associated at the Institute of the Americas, Vanves (France)

Chris Brewster Professor of International Human Resource Management, University of Reading

Harald Conrad Sasakawa Lecturer in Japan's Economy and Management, University of Sheffield

Fang Lee Cooke Professor of Human Resource Management and Chinese Studies, Monash University

Colin Crouch Emeritus Professor, University of Warwick

Niall Cullinane Lecturer in Management, Queen's University

Richard Deeg Professor of Political Science, Temple University

Jimmy Donaghey Reader in Industrial Relations, University of Warwick

Peter Fairbrother Professor of International Employment Relations, RMIT University

Michele Ford Professor of Southeast Asian Studies, University of Sydney

Marc Goergen Professor of Finance, Cardiff University

Paul J. Gollan Professor of Management, Macquarie University

Heidi Gottfried Associate Professor at Wayne State University

Michel Goyer Senior Lecturer, Department of Management, Birmingham Business School, University of Birmingham

Samanthi J. Gunawardana Lecturer in Gender and Development in the School of Political and Social Inquiry, Monash University

Bob Hancké Reader in European Political Economy, London School of Economics and Political Science

Marco Hauptmeier Senior Lecturer in International Human Resource Management, Cardiff University

Frank Horwitz Professor of International Human Resource Management, Cranfield University

Gregory Jackson Professor of Management, Freie Universität Berlin

Senia Kalfa Lecturer in Management, Macquarie University

Harry Katz Dean and Professor of Collective Bargaining, ILR School, Cornell University

Anja Kirsch Research Fellow, Freie Universität Berlin

Gilton Klerck Professor of Sociology, Rhodes University

Christel Lane Professor of Economic Sociology, University of Cambridge

Johann Maree Emeritus Professor of Sociology, University of Cape Town

Cathie Jo Martin Professor of Political Science, Boston University

Guglielmo Meardi Professor of Industrial Relations, University of Warwick

Lindah Mhando Professor Penn State University

Glenn Morgan Professor of International Management, Cardiff University

Martin Myant Head of Unit for European Economic, Employment and Social Policy, European Trade Union Institute, Brussels

Kristine Nergaard Research Coordinator, Fafo, Institute for Labour and Social Research

Barbara Pocock Professor of Work, Employment, and Industrial Relations, University of South Australia

Juliane Reinecke Associate Professor of Organisational Behaviour, University of Warwick

Nick Wailes Professor at the Australian Graduate School of Management, The University of New South Wales

Adrian Wilkinson Professor of Employment Relations, Griffith University

Geoffrey Wood Professor of International Business, Warwick Business School, University of Warwick

CHAPTER 1

COMPARATIVE EMPLOYMENT SYSTEMS

ADRIAN WILKINSON, GEOFFREY WOOD,
AND RICHARD DEEG

INTRODUCTION

CERTAIN events—most notably the 2008 financial crisis—have led to a reassessment in the study of employment relations. It is apparent that the worsening of the terms and conditions of employment in liberal market economies (LMEs) has led to a persistent crisis of demand, with the rupturing of the virtuous Kaldorian circle being only temporarily compensated through debt-fuelled demand. A sustainable recovery is at least in part contingent on a more durable basis for demand, which, in turn, involves a fundamental retrospection and rethinking of the dominant trends in employment relations since the early 1970s. With respect to the latter, much of the debate in contemporary human resource management (HRM) has focused on a false dichotomy between hard/instrumental and soft/cooperative HRM, when it is clear that many firms employ 'mix and match' policies that are best distinguished through a scrutiny of core terms and conditions of employment, rather than through an exploration of trends in people management.

There has been a proliferation of accounts exploring the relationship between institutions and firm practices. However, much of this literature tends to be located in distinct theoretical-traditional 'silos', such as national business systems, social systems of production, regulation theory, or varieties of capitalism, and with limited dialogue between different approaches to understanding institutional effects. Again, evaluations of the relationship between institutions and employment relations have tended to be of a broad-brushstroke nature, often founded on macro-data, and with only limited attention being accorded to internal diversity and details of actual practice. Our hope was to produce a definitive book and one relevant to the present condition, but at the same time, bringing together an assembly of work that will be comprehensive and of sufficiently high quality so as to be of value to future scholars wishing to understand changes in employment relations since the early 1970s. At a theoretical level this book brings together accounts linking varieties of capitalism, business systems, and different modes of regulation to the specific practice of employment relations. This includes recent accounts on internal diversity and change within varieties of capitalism (cf. Lane and Wood 2009), and the role of social action and innovation in redefining paradigms (cf. Sorge 2005). We include attempts to explicitly link this literature to earlier industrial relations (IR) theoretical approaches and traditions (Ackers and Wilkinson 2003, 2008).

At both theoretical and applied levels, the collection is explicitly comparative, providing frameworks and empirical evidence for understanding trends in employment relations in different parts of the world; indeed one of the major shortfalls of the existing literature on comparative capitalism is its lack of attention to the developing world (cf. Wood and Frynas 2006), and this collection seeks, at least in part, to address this lacuna. In short, this collection has theoretical rigour, and an explicitly comparative focus, the two components being closely related. Most notably, we will seek to incorporate at a theoretical level regulationist accounts and recent work that links bounded internal systemic diversity with change, and, at an applied level, a greater emphasis on recent applied evidence, specifically dealing with the employment contract, its implementation and related questions of work organization. What is new about this book is that recent developments and extensions within these traditions have explored questions of diversity, continuity, and change, but often at the levels of sectoral or national governance and inter-firm relations; this collection seeks to bring these new insights to bear in exploring more closely the implications for understanding the employment relationship. In the remainder of this introduction we discuss first some of the broader societal factors shaping the evolution of employment relations. We then discuss how firms and firm-level institutions are evolving within this broader context. Finally, we summarize the key findings of each chapter in this volume.

SOCIETAL LEVEL ISSUES AND INSTITUTIONS

Across OECD economies there is a broad trend towards decommodification of labour, broadly construed. The political conditions—and Fordist production model—that made decommodification in the mid-twentieth century possible seem no longer present, or are greatly weakened (e.g. strong labour movements and labour-oriented political parties). This process feeds directly into the weakening of the Fordism-based Kaldorian circle and the protracted search for a new production model that could reproduce that virtuous circle. A feature recognized by much of the literature on contemporary political economy is that long periods of growth—such as the Fordist era—are interposed with similar periods of downturns or recession, in line with economic long waves (Kelly 1998; Jessop 2001b). Given that the global economy has been characterized by recession interposed with volatile growth since the 1970s, the 2008 financial crisis may be seen as simply the latest episode in a longer period of economic disorder. This raises the question as to what will define the next period of growth. Much of the early regulationist literature concerned itself with the likely possible successors, with debates centring on whether Fordism would be succeeded by a more advanced and inherently superior post-Fordist growth regime (Jessop 2001b). From a rather different starting point, Piore and Sabel's (1984) work on the *Second Industrial Divide* also predicted that classic Fordism would be supplanted by a superior production paradigm but a highly decentred one.

On the one hand, we believe that such accounts were correct in their underlying proposition that the post-1970s crisis was of broad historical significance and the Fordist/welfare state paradigm that had propelled a virtuous circle of production and demand had broken down. On the other hand, it can be argued that, with the wisdom of hindsight, such accounts failed to take full account of the weight of historical evidence. The last long economic crisis—from roughly 1900 to 1945—was not characterized by one production paradigm supplanting another on an orderly basis, but rather a long, messy, and contested transition marked by fascism and war. In focusing on a key feature of the human condition—production and consumption—such accounts neglected another key feature: the centrality of disorder, bitter social conflict and divisions, and war during key periods of societal formation and institution building or reconstruction (see Gumplowicz 2013). It could be argued that, given the Iraq, Afghanistan, and Libya conflicts militarists within global elites have overplayed their hand (Priestland 2012), and that, in any event, distant military adventures have little relevance for understanding the relationship between societal features and workplace practice within the developed world. But long economic transitions are also characterized by societal dislocations, the national and transnational movement of peoples, and struggles over resource allocations. The tendency of elites to experiment with war as a means of mobilizing mass support behind them, and to resolve or at least diminish the importance of internal structural problems, is a feature of historical economic crises, even if such experiments can ultimately undermine or destroy them (Mann 1984). We are sceptical of the argument that present wars represent simply a mechanism for expropriating resources (see Harvey 2004). However, the present protracted wars have proved very lucrative for insider firms and have, up until recently, been effective in diverting mass attention away from structural economic difficulties closer to home.

A further issue is that in focusing on production and the decline of production regimes, it can be argued that consumption was somewhat neglected, with the assumption that a superior future production regime would result in better rewarded workers. More postmodernist accounts did accord due attention to consumption, but this was seen as part of a more fluid societal condition where material concerns became diluted as the edges of reality blurred (see Baudrillard 1999). A great irony here is that the present long crisis has been characterized by both the rise of mindless consumerism fuelled by dreams and aspirations rather than need—for once, the postmodernists were proven correct—and, owing to rising wage inequality with stagnant or declining wages experienced by the bulk of society, a real crisis of consumption. Within liberal market economies, this problem was 'solved' through a combination of increasing consumer debt made possible through the over-inflation of property markets (Boyer 2012), increased working hours by households, primarily by women entering the labour force in greater numbers (Pontusson 2006), and—perversely—by capital flows from emerging to developed economies that financed both consumer and sovereign debt (Schwartz 2009). On the supply side, the resolution was again temporary and speculative, with the rise of large low-cost supermarkets (often reliant on Taylorist forms of work organization) being matched by more traditional specialized retail chains adopting a completely different business paradigm: as opportunities for leveraging property assets rather than selling goods to customers. Independent landlords took similar advantage of the property bubble to similarly over-acquire debt to be precariously paid off through unrealistic rents. Both the latter paradigms are increasingly proving unsustainable. As customers have diminishing means of spending, low-cost supermarkets have increasingly squeezed suppliers, leading to successive food quality scandals, reminiscent of the excesses outlined in Upton Sinclair's *The Jungle*, an exposé of the Chicago meatyards during the last economic long crisis. In the UK, on the high street/main street, the debt leverage model has been subject to unwinding: the need to service excessive debt or pay excessive rents has rendered many shops/chains uncompetitive against both supermarkets and online retailers. As increasing numbers of traditional high street chains and independent retailers have been forced into bankruptcy, this has led to a proliferation of vacant properties, making a further debt crisis inevitable.

This raises the question as to why all this is happening. There are, of course, many explanations, ranging from technology advances to the emergence of new producer nations causing a crisis of over-production. A political lens sees the current crisis as resulting from an economically (and eventually politically) unsustainable shift in economic and political power from labour to capital, and along with that a shift in the accumulation and consumption of resources from those with less to those with more: excessive debt enabled an overcoming of the inherent contradictions within this trend by facilitating excess consumption, but this process was bound to reach its limits and most likely end up in crisis. One may also advance a structural view of the crisis focusing on a long energy transition which is relevant as the basis for future sustainable growth, a growth model that must also solve the fundamental social and economic challenge of balancing resources across social groups in a sustainable fashion. Structural changes in the availability and relative cost of energy resources are, of course, intimately bound up with technological advances, but, it can be argued that it is easier to make advances in the realm of ideas than in the material world. The increased scarcity and direct cost of hydrocarbons (any temporary 'fracking' revolution notwithstanding), and the indirect and delayed costs of their usage (in terms of run-away global warming) has created coterminous economic and environmental crises that will be difficult to solve through any technological fix. As argued by Wood and Lane (this volume) such transitions are particularly costly for those with physical or human capital tied up in particular regions or processes, notably patient investors and workers. In contrast, speculative interests are relatively advantaged; however, an irony is that, as their power and influence increases, the crisis is likely to worsen. In other words, while the crisis may not have been caused by owners of highly fungible assets, they make it more difficult to solve.

Two further features of the present condition mitigate against major technological advances, either in terms of energy extraction and usage, or indeed, other areas of design and production, that might lead to a new sustainable growth model. First, as Jessop (2012) notes, under neo-liberalism, there has been an intensified enclosure of the intellectual commons. Patenting and the protection of intellectual property have been taken to absurd levels, even encompassing naturally occurring substances (including human genes). In turn, this makes it very different for innovators to build on and consolidate previous ideas from a range of sources (Boyle 2003); earlier advances that relied on this range from powered flight to the internal combustion engine. Second, an obsession with short-term shareholder returns discourages the type of investment that makes open-ended R&D tinkering possible, which often, again, led to major advances in the past. It is perhaps telling that technological advances in industries that have thrived in liberal market economies, such as pharmaceuticals, have diminished (Scannell et al. 2012; Drews and Ryser 1996); this has occurred at the same time as the intensification of both short-termism and the protection of intellectual property rights.

Returning to the theme of shifting political power, there are few or hard to discern sources for any Polanyian counter-movement to turn the tide against decommodification, employment insecurity, and decline of collective rights of workers and unions, i.e. the erosion of labour standards (Gottfried this volume). Any such counter-movement would have to confront structural factors that favour capital over labour, financial capitalism over industrial capitalism, those with fungible assets over those with less fungible ones. Fundamental shifts in the costs of resources inputs, the proliferation of low-cost labour, and the erosion of meaningful politics mitigate against a dilution of the power of the former. Broad swaths of most OECD societies rely more than ever on financial markets to secure their own future and guard against life risks (which have been successfully re-individualized in many societies, especially LMEs but even in many social market economies, albeit to a lesser degree). Again, a problem with predictions of Polanyian double movements is that they are somewhat ahistorical; there is an assumption that a new period of greater and more effective state mediation will be on the lines of—or, at least, as beneficial as—the welfare state of the 1950s and 1960s. Of course, Polanyi himself cautioned that statism is not necessarily benign, as borne out by the rise of fascism in the 1920s and 1930s. As Wood and Wilkinson (this volume) suggest, we may already have entered a period of new statism, characterized not by social mediation and redistribution, but rather by the active reallocation of accumulated state resources to insider economic interests and repression. In the case of the USA and the UK, this has encompassed bloated military industrial and penal complexes, hi-tech and pharmaceutical industries heavily dependent on R&D by the state (university and regional development authority) and non-profit sectors, handouts for the financial services industry, and an increased intolerance of domestic dissent. This process is not without contradiction: cutbacks in core state spending in areas such as education serve to undercut, for example, the reliance of key industries on taxpayer-funded university R&D.

If the state will not redistribute, then a counter-movement is likely to arise within society itself. And while there has been a steady growth of politically engaged societal organizations (non-governmental organizations—NGOs) since the 1970s, these organizations are different from the collective actors and social movements—now much weakened—that produced the mid-century economic models favourable to labour (Gall et al. 2011). The last three decades have witnessed the individualization of political behaviour and the decline of old collective actors and their replacement by more citizen-driven social movements (Dalton 2008). These groups are smaller and more fragmented; moreover they are driven by educationally privileged individuals who generally enjoy greater access to politics but also benefit from higher incomes and security. Such groups also tend to focus on specific issues framed around postmodernist conceptualizations like corporate social responsibility and sustainability. Thus it remains an open question as to whether the working and much of the middle class can be successfully organized in this new organizational environment into a broad socio-political coalition for change. In short, the political representation and capacity of the lower classes is probably weaker than at any other time since the early twentieth century. The emergence of such a political coalition is further obstructed by the structural power of business (Culpepper 2011) that has grown with globalization and the increased lobbying power of business in many polities (notably in the USA with the explosion of corporate campaign finance arising from the *Citizens United* decision; this decision ruled that governments could not restrict spending on political campaigns by corporations, holding that corporations represented associations of individuals).

If the domestic political conditions for reinvigorating the strength of labour are not favourable, can a regional organization, such as the European Union (EU), be a vehicle to 'remedy' the erosion of worker rights and political power? In some ways the EU has moved the UK towards coordinated market economy (CME)-like labour regulation (see Gottfried, this volume)—e.g. the Works Councils directive. But mostly what we see with the EU is middle-ground Directives that seek to accommodate the preferences of LMEs and CMEs by leaving room to adapt EU-mandated rules (institutions) to national preferences. Moreover, the EU does little to affect domestic wage-setting institutions or systems that are a big factor in the eurozone crisis and rising differences within Europe. The German response to the euro crisis also places greater pressure on southern European members to deregulate their labour markets, and there has been some movement in that direction. Given the lack of institutional requisites for coordinated wage bargaining in southern Europe, any labour market deregulation is likely to yield rising wage inequality and job insecurity (Hancke, this volume).

Three issues emerge here. The first is that the Europeanization process has greatly contributed not only to continental trade relations and historically unprecedented levels of peace which are commonly taken for granted, but also to democratization and social reforms in both southern and eastern Europe. Second, although it has become common in the Anglophone popular media to blame economic difficulties in the continent on the euro and on broader economic integration, many of the problems experienced are less with institutions and institutional design, and more with weak institutional coupling both at the supra- and subnational levels. Third, and, related to this, is that there persist great imbalances in Europe that are characterized less by positive symbiosis and more by pathology: debtor nations and creditor nations, producer nations and consumer ones. Homogeneous policy reforms are likely to worsen the situation: ironically, a closer and more effective Europe is contingent on recognizing diversity. Many of these imbalances depend on rectifying, once more, a structural problem of consumption, in turn due to a lack of good jobs, especially on the European periphery.

There is also a question of what a new, sustainable growth model could be that is neither a Fordist production model nor a finance capitalism model. In the 10–15 years before the 2008–9 crisis (i.e. under a finance capitalism model) leverage was a key source of growth in many economies, notably the USA, UK, and other European countries; this bolstered aggregate demand in face of declining or stagnant real wages/household income. But what is the new growth model? Here, again—even if somewhat disturbing—it may be worth taking a historical long view. Prior to the birth of the modern, all preceding societies have ultimately run up against physical resource constraints, and, as noted above, it cannot be presumed that technological fixes will preclude this happening again. It is possible that there will be no new growth model to replace the finance capitalism model, and we will simply enter a period of long decline, as characterized by Europe during the periods of the dark and middle ages. However, on a more optimistic note, it is worth noting that a number of European societies, from Germany to Spain, have made great advances in moving beyond hydrocarbons. A feature of alternative energy sources is high initial investment but ultimately lower running costs; in turn, this may ultimately tilt the balance in favour of more patient investors, workers with skills tied in specific industries, and states that prioritize long-term growth and environmental concerns over the immediate wants of oligarchs.

The latter raises an important issue. If the origins of the crisis are economic, at least part of the solution is political. Again, from a broad historical perspective, it is worth noting that almost all societies were founded on labour coercion (including capitalism), and, in historical terms, the relative empowerment and prosperity of workers across the advanced societies—recent setbacks notwithstanding—is quite unusual. The rise of a global class of oligarchs—weakly rooted to any national locale, their deft usage of petty nationalism to bolster up their power notwithstanding—poses a challenge to this working- and middle-class prosperity. This would suggest that we need, as suggested by Wood and Wilkinson (this volume) to consider the role of elites more carefully. As is the case with any social formation, elites are composed of different segments, although speculative interests and militarists may have gained the upper hand over more altruistic elite components in recent years (Priestland 2012). On a different plane, the policy community has essentially become increasingly monochromatic, reflecting the ecological dominance of neo-liberalism (see Jessop 2012). Although it would be unfair to dismiss policy elites as uniformly corrupt, there is little doubt that, as is the case with war, the ubiquity of corruption under any advanced economic order cannot be underestimated. As Engelen et al. (2011) note, in many national contexts, there has been a revolving door situation, with senior politicians, civil servants, and army officers moving on to lucrative sinecures in the financial services and security industries. Not only does this mean that decisions while in political office or public service may be partially moulded by future career concerns, but also that even honest and altruistic individuals may be infected by dominant viewpoints. In other words, even the uncorrupt may become drawn into espousing particular points of view, given the lack of interest in or support for alternatives. Again, the solution to this is political; while the immediate fix would be to impose on senior politicians and civil servants restraint of trade agreements on future high-level economic and security private sector roles (somewhat akin to that commonly agreed to by small business owners on selling their enterprise), such a solution would have to be imposed by pressures from below.

Höpner (2007) argues that, in Germany at least, macro-social organization has declined while sectoral coordination is maintained. But this coordination is based on almost purely voluntaristic and self-interested behaviour by firms—securing a core workforce with requisite skills (i.e. dualism is entrenched). This contributes to the much noted and cited dualization of labour markets. Given that nearly all advanced economies have increased non-standard and flexible employment, it would appear that this dualization is a functional necessity under current conditions of global competition. Yet, there are big differences across countries in the degree and conditions for non-standard employment—the level of insecurity associated with non-standard employment varies. This raises the question of whether more flexible, non-standard employment can be provided in ways more favourable to workers and with better macroeconomic effects. Can the security gap between standard and non-standard employment be narrowed? Although it has become fashionable to promote the Danish/Dutch style flexicurity model, it is worth highlighting the extent to which it depends on a well-developed welfare state with a high degree of social protection—mitigating weak job protection—and adherence by employers to informal norms restraining managerial power (Houwing et al. 2011). In short, flexicurity cannot be promoted hand-in-hand with broader liberalization; rather it must be part of a substitute for liberal market reforms. This may explain the limited impact of flexicurity measures in other European countries, where liberalization is more advanced.

This raises a much broader question. The present imbalances within and between nations point to a very real shift in the relative competitiveness of particular industrial players. The rise of China and Germany as mega-exporters has made it very difficult for manufacturers in other areas of the world to compete; even traditional exporting nations such as Japan now run a balance of trade deficit. Indeed, most developed societies now are characterized by balance of trade deficits, while, other than Germany and China and a few other notable exceptions, nations with great balance of trade surpluses are primary commodity exporters. In short, even if many nations retain competitive advantages in particular areas, their relative importance has diminished, with lower value-added areas of economic activity serving as a poor substitute. In other words, the specific sets of complementarities which characterized many advanced societies have diminished in importance. Therefore, rather than focusing on the nature of complementarity (see Crouch 2005), perhaps a more salient concern is their relative decline. This, of course, is bound up with the present long economic crisis. Here it is worth noting that although there remain possibilities for both serendipitous discovery and active institutional rebuilding or reconstruction, a powerful segment of global policy elites has ruthlessly pursued a path of institutional breakage, precisely to preclude this happening. Although the most spectacular example would be the degeneration of Yeltsin's Russia into a dysfunctional kleptocracy, many other examples can be found both in liberal market economies and economies undertaking liberal market reforms. As Klein (2007) notes, the 'shock doctrine' of imposed confusion to enable elite expropriation has gained wide currency.

There are other trends at work as well. High primary commodity prices have allowed many nations—obvious examples being Australia and South Africa—to escape having to deal with the crises of diminishing competitiveness in many industrial sectors, at least in the short term. This has led to elites neglecting the re-examination of what is needed in institutional supports to underpin diverse economies, even if the latter are very necessary to offset external shocks in a volatile global environment.

A central debate in comparative institutional analysis has been the nature and extent of convergence and divergence (Barry and Wilkinson 2011). However, given that institutional arrangements in coordinated markets are inherently denser and more closely intermeshed than in liberal markets, a process of de-coordination will be longer and more uneven than further liberalization in settings where regulation is already weaker and institutional mediation more tenuous. Hence, as suggested by the literature on variegated capitalism, ecosystemically dominant ideologies (neo-liberalism) and trends (expropriation and enclosure of commons resources) has gone hand-in-hand with persistent unevenness within and between countries (Jessop 2012). It has been argued that as coordinated markets liberalize, so do liberal market ones, so the gap between them remains the same (Streeck 2009). This is, perhaps, too orderly an assumption. The LME/CME distinction was largely conceived based on evidence compiled in the 1980s and 1990s, when, it can be argued, the differences were very much less pronounced in the 1950s. Although the USA never developed a proper welfare state, there were certainly strong checks and balances on the excessive power of short-termist financial interests up until the 1980s. What evidence we have from the 2000s is that change has been uneven and disorderly, and that as some economies have become more like CMEs (e.g. Slovenia and, to some extent, Slovakia), the CME model within the core of Europe has become frayed. In short, one is more likely to see greater—but bounded—diversity within categories previously deemed coherent units, and drifts to and from limited coordination. However, it is likely that the great experiments in market coordination of preceding decades will be repeated without a major political realignment not only nationally, but globally as well.

The return to growth in Africa, and the strong social outcomes associated with progressive governments in central and southern America suggest that these may be contexts where the relative position of workers—and their bargaining power—might represent a powerful counter-tendency against a worldwide trend to union decline. However, right-wing coups in Paraguay and Honduras, and persistent destabilization by oligarchs in Venezuela and elsewhere highlight the tenacity of reactionary elites and the extent to which social gains in Latin America remain uneven and contested. In Africa, much of the growth has been on the back of resurgent prices for primary commodities, raising the spectre of the resource curse.

In a world of uneven institutional coverage and inequality, improvement in the relative position of women is again an ambivalent process. On the one hand, a growing emphasis on individual rights opens the possibility for fairer treatment under the law and in practice, and indeed, real gains have been made in many of the advanced societies. On the other hand, among the global precariat, the position of women is particularly vulnerable (Standing 2011).

Chapter Overviews

In this book, perspectives on comparative employment systems from leading scholars in the field, briefly summarized below, will be discussed. The book is organized into five parts and contains thirty-one chapters. In the first section we define the field. Geoffrey Wood and Adrian Wilkinson review key strands of comparative institutional analysis from the economic, socio-economic, and industrial relations traditions. More specifically, this chapter links recent controversies and advances in comparative institutional theory to the study of work and employment relations. It argues for real trends in firm-level work and employment relations to be placed more centrally in comparative institutional thinking. It further locates current trends in the relative position of workers in broader historical context.

Harry Katz and Nick Wailes review some common arguments for employment relations convergence, from the logic of industrialism, to globalization and varieties of capitalism. They find most explanations of convergence overly deterministic, and that empirical evidence tends to support a conclusion of increasing divergence. While they find some convergence across advanced capitalist economies on certain workplace practices (e.g. decentralization), the relative portion of these different workplace patterns (and the role of unions within them) varies considerably as a result of larger institutional differences. They believe that explaining convergent and divergent tendencies requires a less rigid conception of institutions—one that allows for greater degrees of change resulting from the changed preferences and power of key actors such as multinational corporations (MNCs). They conclude by noting that the recent financial crisis accelerated convergence in the erosion of labour standards, or the 'low road' to competitiveness.

Part II provides new theoretical insights in the area. In Chapter 4, Cathie Jo Martin explores the contributions and deficiencies of the varieties of capitalism (VOC) framework for understanding employment relations. Her analysis starts with the claim that there are three basic systems of employer organization and associated patterns of coordination—macrocorporatist, sectoral, and segmentalist—associated with differences in skill formation regimes. When combined with greater attention to the role of labour and the state, these three systems can help explain divergent patterns of institutional change in capitalist systems: macrocorporatist regimes, for example, may be better able to resist neo-liberal policy changes and dualism, because the historical co-evolution of a multiparty political system and centralized associational structures facilitates collective problem solving that is more likely to bind all actors to a jointly determined solution.

In the next chapter, Matthew M. C. Allen discusses the contribution of the business systems framework to our understanding of employment relations across different countries. He draws out important distinctions between the business systems framework and the related VOC paradigm. Individual business systems, as well as the employment relations that are associated with them, are discussed in detail. He highlights the importance, within the business systems framework, of linking firms' strategic priorities, the organizational capabilities they (seek) to develop, the types of employment relations policies that they adopt, and their specific institutional context in analyses. Consequently, the ways in which the internationalization of product, capital, and some labour markets affect any particular firm's institutional setting are likely to become increasingly important within such analyses.

Robert Boyer develops and extends the regulationist project to more fully take account of the consequences of the interlinkage of work and employment relations on the one hand, and capitalist growth regimes on the other. He argues that spillover between the two is most likely to be the abiding source of economic crises. Boyer suggests that the heterogeneity of work regimes that is an abiding feature of the present condition not only makes it difficult for a new stable model to replace the post-Fordist one to emerge, but also reflects the ongoing search for a new viable growth regime. The complex variety of employment forms, in turn, mirrors the shifting of risk by many employers on to employees, changes in skills, and national institutional realities. With regard to the latter, national alternative employment models remain viable, even as the information and communications technology (ICT) revolution has contributed to greater individualization.

In looking at diversity and change within national capitalist archetypes, Geoffrey Wood and Christel Lane argue that national institutions are neither tightly coupled, nor do they make for coherent outcomes. There is much, albeit bounded, diversity in socio-economic relations within and between firms. This diversity may reflect specific sectoral or regional dynamics, the uneven consequences of social action, and governmental partiality to specific players. It also reflects broader changes in the global capitalist ecosystem—which, they believe, are the product of a long energy transition—and the uneven manner in which national institutions seek to accommodate themselves to this.

In the following chapter, Chris Brewster, Marc Goergen, and Geoffrey Wood argue that particularly influential in the economics, finance, and neo-liberal policy community have been approaches that link the law to firm-level work and employment relations, macroeconomic outcomes, and the consequences of particular traditions and associated bodies of law: these approaches favour the stronger private property rights associated with the common-law tradition. However, the evidence marshalled to support the common-law superior macroeconomic outcomes thesis is highly selective. A further limitation is that the firm is primarily seen as a transmission belt: the effect of institutional environment is explored primarily in terms of possible macroeconomic outcomes. In other words, for a theory of, and debate around, corporate governance, there is remarkably little about the firm.

In Chapter 9, Glenn Morgan and Marco Hauptmeier explore four variants of institutionalism and what they can tell us about the nature and evolution of employment relations. Rational choice institutionalism's strength in explaining stable institutional equilibria helps us understand why employment relations systems evolve slowly in a path-dependent fashion. Historical institutionalism takes a more actor-centric approach that attributes greater latitude to actors in interpreting how institutions are to be applied and in reshaping those institutions along with their shifting preferences. Sociological institutionalism moves further away from rational choice conceptions by positing that actors are guided by a 'logic of appropriateness'. This approach seems particularly useful in understanding how certain practices diffuse from one setting to another. Constructivist institutionalism gives greater explanatory weight to the substantive content of ideas themselves in shaping actor behaviour and institutional change. In conclusion the authors suggest some ways that comparative employment research can profit from engaging with all four variants of institutionalism.

In Chapter 10, Niall Cullinane notes that institutions have remained central to industrial relations analysis in terms of understanding the behaviour of actors and the outcomes of processes. Within the IR tradition, the most influential accounts on institutional effects have dovetailed with a broadly functionalist sociology. The purpose of this chapter is to consider the functionalist legacy in institutional IR analysis with particular reference to Durkheim. In this regard, the classical work of the 'institutional pluralists' and the 'radical/sociological institutionalists' is considered alongside the contemporary formulation of neo-pluralism and the varieties of capitalism literatures.

In the following chapter, Franco Barchiesi shows how transformations in collective bargaining systems, the decline of trade unionism, and global economic instability have challenged theories of employment relations predicated upon institutionalized interactions involving states and representatives of employers and employees. This chapter provides first an overview of classical debates in industrial relations, emphasizing the early centrality of order and stability in competing pluralist paradigms. It then analyses the emergence of radical approaches explaining changes in employment relations as a result of social and labour conflicts and critical ruptures in Fordist production regimes. It finally discusses theories of change that, since the early 1980s, have emphasized, in opposition to epoch-defining categories like 'post-Fordism', recurring patterns or long waves within capitalism. Barchiesi questions the potentials and limitations of long-wave theories in light of recent sociological debates on precarious employment and shifting labour politics and identities.

In the next section we review the comparative evidence. Jackson and Kirsch review changes in employment relations in six countries broadly recognized as liberal market economies. They compare these cases on numerous indictors, including wages and inequality, collective bargaining, unions and employers' associations, and employee voice institutions. While they find a common direction towards liberalization in all these cases, there remains substantial and often unrecognized diversity across these cases. Moreover, low levels of regulation in most of these domains translate into considerable internal diversity within these cases, since actors (corporations) have much greater latitude to choose employment relations strategies that suit their preferences.

Kristine Nergaard examines the Nordic systems of industrial relations distinguished by high rates of organization among workers and employers, centralized bargaining coordination, low wage dispersion, and a strong company tier of negotiations and participation. Universal, income-related, and relatively generous income protection schemes and state-funded educational systems are other characteristics of the Nordic labour market models. Over the last decades, Nordic labour and employment relations have adapted to internal and external challenges. More decentralized bargaining coordination at sector level and more stringent requirements for job-seeking activity have been introduced, partially followed by reduced compensation rates in labour market-related benefits. The countries with the strongest trade unions have seen declining union membership, and increased labour migration has put wage floors and collective agreements under pressure in some sectors.

In Chapter 14, Bob Hancké argues that Europe can be divided into two basic employment relations systems. Northern European coordinated market economies are characterized by strong labour unions and employer associations who link wages to productivity gains and propagate these wage rates to the rest of the economy. The mixed market economies (MMEs) of southern Europe are associationally weaker and the state compensates by intervening in wage determination and labour market protections. Within the same monetary regime, the employment systems of northern Europe were better at maintaining competitive unit labour costs. Hancké argues that these structural differences are the key contributing factor to growing current account imbalances within Europe and, directly and indirectly, to the sovereign debt crisis. Given the political resistance to radical labour market deregulation in MMEs, and the near impossibility of constructing centralized wage setting systems à la CMEs, the eurozone's long-term solutions lie not in fiscal austerity but in a macroeconomic policy that equalizes growth and inflation rates across the zone (e.g. through fiscal union).

In Chapter 15, Harald Conrad explores changes in institutional mediation and the practice of work and employment relations in the three most developed East Asian countries: Japan, South Korea, and Taiwan. In all three countries, long-term approaches to employment and seniority-based pay have eroded; these similar trends, however, do not entail convergence. There are growing in-country variations, and a greater diversity in approaches to people management within organizations. However, the overall nature of organized labour has not changed noticeably in the last two decades. Finally, reforms have sometimes gone hand-in-hand with the preservation of traditional welfare benefits. This means that innovations are combined with long-standing practices in a manner that is distinct from other capitalist archetypes.

In looking at the broader socio-economic and employment relations systems in the post-state socialist countries of central and eastern Europe, Martin Myant argues that previously very similar systems have in many respects diverged, and that raises questions as to whether they can still be lumped together into a single analytical category. Some common features include the wide role of informal practices, and specific legal traditions; key differences emerge in relative will and capabilities for law enforcement, and the role of actors in propping up the system. Although there is generally more respect for the law than in the immediate period following transitions, in many countries employers are now experimenting with legal mechanisms to promote individualization, including the conversion of employees to independent contractors. However, where collective bargaining is deeply entrenched, there has been a tendency towards the further institutionalization of collectivism. Finally, politics matters, and during periods of right-wing rule, even in countries such as Slovenia, greater liberalization has been promoted.

In looking at the relationship between context and employment relations across Africa, in Chapter 17, Johann Maree ties the relative fortunes of organized labour to the relative effectiveness of democratic institutions. While democracy does not necessarily make for effective unionism, trade unions are likely to be more effective when democratic institutions are effective. However, organized labour is also more vulnerable in less balanced economies, especially those heavily dependent on primary commodity exports. On the one hand, there has been a long process of democratization across Africa that is beneficial for the prospects of organized labour. On the other hand, many African countries have regressed to a greater dependence on primary exports, which has the potential to undermine any gains.

In Chapter 18, Jose Aleman investigates what effects progressive governments have had on employment relations in Latin America since 1999. The chapter shows that compared to their conservative counterparts, left governments have reduced precarious employment, while requiring firms to set aside more funds to cover social insurance charges and contributions. Differences between left and conservative governments are to be expected given the ideology of these governments and the perceived need to address some of the continent's long-standing problems, but they do not primarily emanate from diffusion of a model of employment relations unique to these governments. Progressive governments have instead maintained or expanded previous policies in some countries facilitated by a more accommodating international environment.

In Chapter 19, Michele Ford examines the factors influencing employment relations structures and practices in the export-oriented economies of developing Southeast Asia. She begins with a discussion of historical legacies affecting the employment relations systems of developing Asia as a whole before moving on to case studies of Indonesia, Vietnam, and Malaysia. The chapter then reflects on the negative complementarities that account for the ongoing weakness of trade unions in all three settings, despite Malaysia's emerging high road production strategy and Indonesia's recent democratization. The chapter concludes that—while not necessarily representing a discrete 'variety of capitalism'—colonial legacies, Western support for authoritarian regimes in capitalist

Southeast Asia during the Cold War, and the competitive imperatives of export-oriented production are responsible for similarities in these otherwise very different national contexts.

In the following chapter, Frank Horwitz compares and assesses employment relations in the BRICS countries, a growing global economic grouping which reflects a shift in economic power from mature economies to emerging markets. These countries are Brazil, Russia, India, China, and South Africa. The chapter focuses on employment relations in these countries by comparing similarities and differences in their employment relations institutions, regulations, labour markets, and workplace practices. The findings show the diversity and complexity of employment relations and labour markets in these emerging economies. The chapter discusses collective bargaining, trade unions, workplace flexibility, and the changing nature of work. The development of informal or casual work through outsourcing and subcontracting in these economies varies but is important.

The fourth section provides a new lens by looking at various substantive themes. In Chapter 21 Michel Goyer, Juliane Reinecke, and Jimmy Donagchey discuss globalization. They note that there is little doubt that globalization has had profound effects on the governance of employment relations with destabilization of national institutional frameworks taking place in the absence of coherent transnational systems. Nevertheless, these destabilized institutional configurations are shaping new emerging institutional arrangements. The authors explore this phenomenon in the context of the globalization of finance and the emergence of global labour standards and conclude by arguing that, despite globalization, actor strategies in the globalized context are shaped by pre-existing institutional experience.

Barbara Pocock explores gender and employment issues in Chapter 22. She points to long historical legacies and continuities in work and gender, despite the changes brought about by neo-liberal reforms and broader associated processes of globalization. First, women do more unpaid domestic or 'private work', while many perform more 'public' paid work. Second, even in workplaces where the overwhelming majority of workers are male or female, gender issues manifest themselves in sexualized practices or culture. Third, the nature of social reproduction affects labour market participation of both genders. Fourth, dense fabrics of gender relations within institutions construct and reconstruct hierarchies on gender lines. Finally, institutions make for persistently uneven outcomes in work and employment according to gender. The gendered fortunes of those in the north and south have become increasingly interlinked, however; inequality can only be dealt with through concerted global resolve and action.

In Chapter 23, Michael Barry, Adrian Wilkinson, Paul J. Gollan, and Senia Kalfa review the literature on employee voice. The authors examine various types of voice arrangements looking at the purpose of voice arrangements from both employee and management perspectives. It is suggested that employee-initiated voice is typically broader than the management schemes because the latter have as their core concern issues of efficiency and productivity, whereas employee-initiated voice sees employee interests as often compatible, but nevertheless separate from those of management. In examining voice arrangements across the globe, special attention is focused on the regulatory context, and the chapter draws on the varieties of capitalism literature to show how and why voice arrangements vary in different national settings.

In Chapter 24, Heidi Gottfried explores the spread since the 1990s of insecure and non-standard employment that now comes close to one quarter of employment in nearly all OECD countries. Gottfried argues that conventional explanations such as globalization or risk society theory cannot explain the *uneven* growth and distribution of non-standard employment across OECD countries. Instead, Gottfried fuses the VOC and worlds of welfare capitalism institutional theories with an understanding of how each national welfare and production regime also embodies a distinct *reproductive bargain* determining the extent to which care work and social reproduction are carried out by private households or shifted to the market or state. The evolution of these distinct bargains, plus changes in gender relations, tell us much about the relative inclusion and exclusion of different groups in non-standard employment. These theoretical arguments are developed through a contextualized comparison of two coordinated market economies (Japan and Germany) with two liberal market economies (UK and USA).

In the subsequent chapter, Samanthi J. Gunawardana and Lindah Mhando explore the interplay of the migration–development nexus, unskilled women's migration patterns, and the transitions taking place in and around global and local labour markets and employment relations. Although states have sought to both facilitate migration into precarious employment positions and to step in to protect workers, migration has exposed the limitations of extant paradigms that take nation-states as a unit of analysis for development and employment relations. The state's role is underscored by the existence of a complex and textured field of gendered and socially embedded institutions and governance mechanisms, which has made migrant workers particularly vulnerable to precarious conditions.

In Chapter 26, Colin Crouch examines changes in state policies impacting employment relations, including macroeconomic policy as it impacts the labour market; the state's relation to employees' individual rights; and the state's policies on the role of collective actors in the labour market. The most consistent evidence of a turn to neo-liberalism across all the countries examined is found in the decline of employment protection laws. A second clear inference is that in countries where unions' industrial strength is weak and there is a strong neo-liberal ideology, governments have made little effort to sustain social partnership institutions, though they have typically avoided complete liberalization of labour markets by imposing statutory minimum wages. Third, a clear turn towards neo-liberal policies only occurred in the mid-1990s. In sum, the turn towards neo-liberalism is substantiated in all of the countries, but the timing, extent, and dimensions of that turn vary quite substantially

In our final section we examine actors in the field. Guglielmo G. Meardi looks at the relationship between the state and employment relations. In contrast to predictions of globalization theories, it is clear that the state remains central in moulding the nature of work and employment relations in particular national contexts. At the same time, the political nature of employment relations makes the latter an important source of transformation at state level. Hence, for example, trade union decline and shifts in the nature of collective bargaining paved the way for governmental reforms towards further labour market deregulation.

In Chapter 28, Peter Fairbrother focuses on the challenges facing trade unionism, particularly over the last three decades. He begins the analysis with the observation that unions face challenges relating to organization, capacity, and purpose. In the context of change in capitalist economies, some unions are beginning to renew themselves. However, this process is uneven. Unions face difficulties when the class composition and the politics associated with it changes, often in dangerous and forbidding ways. The chapter discusses the prospects for a progressive and active form of unionism, characterized as social movement unionism. Nonetheless, the tensions between material concerns and alternative views about the ways in which society could be organized remain in the forefront of union concern and purpose.

In Chapter 29, Gilton Klerck evaluates dichotomous understandings of managerial practice, highlights the extent to which firms combine different forms of employee representation, control, and tenure, and explores the foundations of this 'hybridization'. Institutional approaches are a key component of recent theoretical developments dealing with the systemic diversity of managerial practices. Making sense of hybridization requires an explicit focus on the articulation of scales of governance, locating managerial practices in terms of wider patterns of uneven development and the forms of conflict and accommodation at various scales. The path-dependency of the processes of labour regulation—stemming from their rootedness in diverse contexts, their co-evolution with opposing modes of coordination, and their (partially) regularized forms of articulation and institutionalization—suggests that they are conjuncturally specific phenomena, which only coalesce under certain spatio-temporal conditions, and that a determinate variegation is one of their necessary and persistent features.

In Chapter 30, Fang Lee Cooke and Geoffrey Wood note that the growing inadequacy of the traditional institutional actors in defending workers' rights has created both the space and the need for 'new' actors (international coalitions, grassroots organizations, and activists, etc.). Some of the actors are not necessarily new but are playing a stronger or taking on new role in (re)shaping employment relations at the workplace level and beyond; in some contexts, these actors interact and permeate each other's sites and spatial boundaries in recognition of and to complement each other's resource/capacity constraints. Empirical evidence suggests there is indeed increasing scope for the emergence of new actors, whose presence is generally, though not always, beneficial to those whom they seek to organize and represent, against a universal trend of deteriorating employment security and workforce well-being.

In the final chapter, Sabina Avdagic and Lucio Baccaro review changes in employment relations institutions in 25 capitalist countries from the 1990s. They find there is a common and unmistakable decline in employment relations institutions in all countries. Yet, the pattern varies significantly, and there is no convergence on any single model of employment relations. The authors root the primary structural cause in the decline of Fordism and the employment relations systems that created the aggregate demand that undergirded that particular regime of accumulation. A reversal of this decline is conceivable, but it would take considerable political will by the state and partisan actors to rebuild employment relations institutions which capture positive externalities. Given the declining organizational strength of the unions and ideological shifts among traditionally left-leaning parties, this too seems improbable. The ability of unions to organize more workers also seems in doubt, and building transnational capacities for collective action are even more doubtful.

CONCLUSION

A common theme running through the contributions in this volume is that ongoing developments and crises in the macroeconomy are closely bound up with changes in the workplace. While there has been a global trend towards more insecure and contingent employment, a decline of collectivist institutions, and stagnation of pay for the bulk of employees, these broad trends combine with persistent diversity. The latter encompasses variations in relative competitiveness, with liberal market economies being particularly associated with a hollowing-out of productive areas of economic activity in favour of low-end service sector work and speculative activity. While many other nations face their own crises, the global ecosystem is characterized not so much by homogeneity as by great imbalances and 'pathological complementarities': between mega importers and exporters, debtor and creditor nations, and between those that have become increasingly dependent on primary commodity exports and those that have not. This raises broader questions of economic long waves and epochalism. First, it is remains unclear whether the virtuous circle of the 1950s and 1960s, characterized by wage and productivity rises, and the general bettering of material conditions for the bulk of the workforce represented a historical anomaly; almost all complex societies are characterized by great inequality and labour repression of some sort or another. Second, given increasing competition for, and scarcity of, primary commodities, and looming ecological catastrophe, it is unclear whether renewed growth on a sustainable basis is possible without a fundamental reordering of social life and the nature of production. This could suggest a long decline, on a scale unprecedented since the birth of the modern. Finally, this leads to the question of politics. While it could be argued that superior production paradigms, and broader types of economic regulation, will inevitably supplant inferior ones, this assumes perfect competition for ideas. As noted by Wilkinson and Wood (this volume), the dominance of a global elite with highly fungible assets whose light commitment to productive areas of national economies is matched with a durable one to ideologies that reaffirm the value of speculation and weak regulation, means that meaningful changes in regulation and practice will have to come through politics. A paradox here is that, again while the need for political solutions has become more pressing, within many national contexts politics has become rather enmeshed with oligarchic interests. We hesitate to end our introduction on such a pessimistic note: What also characterizes the contributions to this volume is a focus on the creativity and dynamic process of institution building, and evidence that, in many national contexts, employees and more long-term orientated property owners have indeed forged mutually beneficial compromises, even if at times these are confined to specific enclaves of broader economies. Hence, while the solutions of the past cannot be transposed, there remains the possibility for creative new mechanisms for societal mediation and workplace regulation.

REFERENCES

Ackers, P. and Wilkinson, A. (eds.) (2003). *Understanding Work and Employment: Industrial Relations in Transition*. Oxford and New York: Oxford University Press.

—— (2008). 'Industrial Relations and the Social Sciences', in P. Blyton, N. Bacon, J. Firito, and E. Heery (eds.), *The Sage Handbook of Industrial Relations*. London: Sage, 53–68.

Barry, M. and Wilkinson, A. (eds.) (2011). *Research Handbook of Comparative Employment Relations*. Cheltenham: Edward Elgar.

Baudrillard, J. (1999). *Revenge of the Crystal*. London: Pluto.

Boyer, R. (2001). 'The Eighties: The Search for Alternatives to Fordism', in B. Jessop (ed.), *Regulationist Perspectives on Fordism and Post-Fordism: Regulation Theory and the Crisis of Capitalism Volume 3*. Cheltenham: Edward Elgar, 106–32.

—— (2012). 'The Four Fallacies of Contemporary Austerity Policies', *Cambridge Journal of Economics*, 36(1): 283–312.

Boyle, J. (2003). 'The Second Enclosure Movement and the Construction of the Public Domain', *Law and Contemporary Problems*, 66(33): 33–74.

Crouch, C. (2005). 'Three Meanings of Complementarity', *Socio-Economic Review*, 3(2): 359–63.

Culpepper, P. (2011). *Quiet Politics and Business Power*. Ithaca: Cornell University Press.

Dalton, R. (2008). *Citizen Politics: Public Opinion and Political Parties in Advanced Industrial Democracies*, 5th edition. Washington: CQ Press.

Drews, J. and Ryser, S. (1996). 'Innovation Deficit in the Pharmaceutical Industry', *Therapeutic Innovation and Regulatory Science*, 47(2): 97–108.

Engelen, E., Ertürk, I., Froud, J., Johal, S., Leaver, A., Moran, M., Nilsson, A., and Williams, K. (2011). *After the Great Complacence: Financial Crisis and the Politics of Reform*. Oxford and New York: Oxford University Press.

Gall, G., Wilkinson, A., and Hurd, R. (eds.) (2011). *The International Handbook of Labour Unions: Responses to Neo-Liberalism*. Cheltenham: Edward Elgar.

Gumplowicz, L. (2013). *The Outlines of Sociology*. London: Forgotten Books.

Harvey, D. (2004). *The New Imperialism*. Oxford and New York: Oxford University Press.

Höpner, M. (2007). *Coordination and Organization: The Two Dimensions of Nonliberal Capitalism*. MPIfG Discussion Paper No. 07/12. Cologne: Max Planck Institute.

Houwing, H., Keune, M. J., Pochet, P., and Vandaele, K. (2011). 'Comparing Flexicurity Arrangements in Belgium and the Netherlands', in M. Barry and A. Wilkinson (eds.), *Research Handbook of Comparative Employment Relations*. Cheltenham: Edward Elgar, 260–85.

Jessop, B. (2001a). 'Series Preface', in Jessop (ed.), *Regulationist Perspectives on Fordism and Post-Fordism: Regulation Theory and the Crisis of Capitalism Volume 3*. Cheltenham: Edward Elgar, ix–xxiv.

Jessop, B. (2001b). 'Introduction', in Jessop (ed.), *Regulationist Perspectives on Fordism and Post-Fordism: Regulation Theory and the Crisis of Capitalism Volume 3*. Cheltenham: Edward Elgar, xxv–xlii.

—— (2012). 'Rethinking the Diversity and Variability of Capitalism: On Variegated Capitalism in the World Market', in C. Lane and G. Wood (eds.), *Capitalist Diversity and Diversity within Capitalism*. London: Routledge, 209–37.

Kelly, J. (1998). *Rethinking Industrial Relations: Mobilization, Collectivism and Long Waves*. London: Routledge.

Klein, N. (2007). *The Shock Doctrine: The Rise of Disaster Capitalism*. New York: Metropolitan.

Lane, C. and Wood, G. (2009). 'Diversity in Capitalism and Capitalist Diversity', *Economy and Society*, 38(4): 531–51.

Mann, M. (1984). 'Capitalism and Militarism', in M. Shaw (ed.), *War, State and Society*. London: Macmillan, 25–46.

Piore, M. and Sabel, C. (1984). *The Second Industrial Divide*. New York: Basic Books.

Pontusson, J. (2006). *Inequality and Prosperity: Social Europe vs. Liberal America*. Ithaca: Cornell University Press.

Priestland, D. (2012). *Merchant, Soldier, Sage: A New History of Power*. London: Penguin.

Scannell, J., Blanckley, A., Bolden, H., and Warrington, B. (2012). 'Diagnosing the Decline in Pharmaceutical R&D Efficiency', *Nature Reviews Drug Discovery*, 11: 191–200.

Schwartz, H. (2009). *Subprime Nation: American Power, Global Finance and the Housing Bubble*. Ithaca: Cornell University Press.

Sorge, A. (2005). *The Global and the Local*. Oxford and New York: Oxford University Press.

Standing, G. (2011). *The Precariat: The New Dangerous Class*. London: Bloomsbury.

Streeck, W. (2009). *Reforming Capitalism*. Oxford: Oxford University Press.

Wood, G. and Frynas, G. (2006). 'The Institutional Basis of Economic Failure: Anatomy of the Segmented Business System', *Socio-Economic Review*, 4(2): 239–77.

PART I

DEFINING THE FIELD

CHAPTER 2

···

INSTITUTIONS AND EMPLOYMENT RELATIONS

···

GEOFFREY WOOD AND ADRIAN WILKINSON

Introduction

While the marginalization of unions and the hegemony of neo-liberalism in many the advanced societies has challenged the raison d'être of industrial relations, the revival of institutional approaches to political economy has underscored the relevance of a field of study where institutions have always been central. Although generated through failures in market regulation, the recent economic crisis has, ironically, led both to pressures for a further paring back of governmental capabilities for regulation and enforcement, and a renewed interest in the possibilities for meaningful institutional redesign. This chapter highlights main currents in contemporary institutionalist thinking and their relevance for the study of industrial relations.

Institutions and the Industrial Relations Tradition

In studying work and employment relations, there has been a historical division into two distinct streams (Kaufman 1993). The first, that of broad personnel management, argued that any labour issues were mostly about poor management and associated misunderstandings between players. The second, institutional labour economics, was concerned with the manner in which imperfectly operating markets disadvantaged employees, and the persistence of an (ultimately premodern) master and servant relationship, which denied employees procedural and democratic rights (Kaufman 1993). These problems could only be solved at the institutional level through legislation, systemically embedded unions, full employment policies, and adequate social protection (Kaufman 1993). Institutional labour economics gradually infused elements of sociology and political studies, and law, and 'drifted away from the parent discipline' (Kaufman 1993).

Dunlop (1958) posited that industrial relations were about embedded rules; institutions provided stability, order, and continuity. Critics such as Hyman (2002: 52) argued that this focus on order reflects an inherently conservative orientation that ignores the possibility of conflict and contradictions. In Dunlop's defence, it should be noted that he was writing at a time when, within most advanced societies, there was a political consensus on the need for institutional mediation between competing interests, and when, even in liberal markets, genuine social trade-offs were more the norm than the exception. More salient is the criticism that his systems approach focuses on organization, when there has been a growing individualization of employment relations (Hyman 2002: 52). Again, a focus on formal rules ignores the importance of informal conventions (Jessop 2001a; Sisson 2010). A further limitation is that much is said about the role of institutions as underpinning order, but little about the often traumatic historical circumstances under which institutions are bedded down, and indeed, when they are remade (Ackers and Wilkinson 2008). Additionally there is a considerable gap between saying that institutions matter, and generating testable hypotheses as to what, and where, their precise effects may be (Kelly 1998: 42).

RATIONAL CHOICE APPROACHES AND INSTITUTIONS

As Peters (2005: 20) notes, rational choice approaches see institutions as giving rules and inducements, informing the choices of utility-maximizing individuals. From a neo-classical economics perspective, institutions would be seen as distorting the smooth operation of markets. Neo-institutional rational choice accounts share this concern, that inappropriate institutions may prompt 'wrong' or sub-optimal choices. However, they also hold that institutions can be efficient, reflect rationality, and provide the sort of incentives necessary to make optimal choices; in other words, rationality combines with setting, making for outcomes that are dependent on the context (Djelic 2010: 25–9). This may suggest a 'watering down' of the focus on rational actors encountered in mainstream economics (Djelic 2010: 29). However, in practice, rational choice accounts have centred on the extent to which institutions protect private property rights, or fail to do so (North 1990; La Porta et al. 1998, 2000). What characterizes this approach is an emphasis on strong path dependence, and on the existence of institutional ideal types worth emulating; more specifically, the liberal market framework, centring on the common law legal tradition (La Porta et al. 1998, 2000). Such work assumes that institutions 'work'; in other words, that compliance and adaption of behaviour is more common than outright evasion. Particularly influential has been the work of La Porta and colleagues, focusing on legal origin, owner rights, and economic performance.

This work was later broadened to explore the impact of worker rights, which were depicted as incompatible with, and inherently weakening, owner rights; in practice, nations tended to be distinguished by relative variations of both, but with strength in one area being associated with a weakness in the other (Botero et al. 2004). In short, worker rights are bad for firms. Indeed, it was argued that workers would ultimately benefit from stronger owner rights, as firms would prosper, and those most productive and effective workers would gain their due rewards, or reap benefits elsewhere through the efficient operation of deregulated external labour markets (Botero et al. 2004). This, of course, is anathema to the bulk of mainstream industrial relations scholars, who point to the fact that many firms found their competitiveness on sustained labour repression (Gall et al. 2011). Moreover, the assumptions of sustained systemic functionality, and the view that the 'most rational' institutional frameworks are stable and immune from contestation, ignore both the great volatility of the most lightly regulated markets, and the mobilization and resistance that are associated with long-term changes in capitalism (see Kelly 1998). But, if this perspective has been contested by scholars with an interest in industrial relations (Cooney et al. 2011; Deakin and Sarkar 2008), it has had considerable policy and practical influence. More specifically, the World Bank *Doing Business Project* has aggressively promoted the notion that weak worker rights make for a good environment to do business: that countries should accordingly roll back labour law (Cooney et al. 2011). Thus while industrial relations scholars may dispute the theoretical foundations of this approach, its impact on industrial relations practice is likely to be considerable, particularly within those countries dependent on international financial institutions (IFIs).

ORGANIZATIONAL–SOCIETAL APPROACHES

In a particularly influential essay, DiMaggio and Powell (1983) argued that actors choose to follow institutional rules for legitimation rather than for profit-maximizing reasons. Organizations reproduce 'taken for granted' and embedded cognitive assumptions as to what is desirable (Whitley 1999: 13). Within the employment relationship, it is desirable for managers and owners to at least have some legitimacy in the eyes of their workforce: outright coercion is inefficient and with uncertain outcomes. From the side of employees, acting within broad rules and conventions that are seen as 'reasonable' and 'fair' makes them better equipped to enforce mutually agreed rights. Again, in their interactions with other firms and actors, cooperation is facilitated through mutual notions of legitimacy. Hence, within a particular social context, industrial relations practices within individual firms (whether locals or multinationals) will become 'isomorphic' within dominant institutional frameworks.

In seeking to understand institutional building and change, DiMaggio and Powell argue that this takes place when actors have a strong interest in a particular institutional framework (DiMaggio and Powell 1988). Critics have argued that this juxtaposes external institutional constraints and theories of rational strategic resource mobilization (Djelic 2010: 681). Streeck (2010: 681) argues that seeking to rewrite the rules for one's own interest is likely to undermine existing solidarities and ties, and be an 'act in bad faith'. In other words, if players require legitimacy, rewriting the rules to favour their interests is likely to undermine this: in short, in seeking to legitimize certain types of behaviour, the basis of their existing and potential legitimacy is undermined. Or, as Jackson (2010: 70) notes, actors are depicted by rational choice economics as rule makers, enacting institutions in order to optimize choices and outcomes. The structuralist sociological tradition has tended to see actors as rule takers, in other words, following conventions, norms, and rules (Jackson 2010). DiMaggio and Powell's work rather conflates this approach.

VARIETIES OF CAPITALISM APPROACHES

The early varieties of capitalism (VOC) literature sought to explain the relatively superior performance of Germany and Japan when compared to liberal market economies (LMEs), such as Britain and the United States in the 1980s; particularly when it came to manufacturing and the export of manufactured goods (see Lincoln and Kalleberg 1990). It was argued that this reflected specific institutional frameworks that encouraged cooperative work and employment relations (Lincoln and Kalleberg 1990). The recovery of liberal markets by the early 2000s—even if they were still associated with poor performance in manufacturing—led to a shift in much of the literature to a rather more neutral position. While Dore (2000) made the case for the intrinsic superiority—both in performance and moral grounds—of stakeholder capitalism and associated cooperative work and employment relations over shareholder capitalism, a particularly influential collection by Hall and Soskice (2001) suggested that no system is intrinsically superior. Rather specific sets of national configurations make for specific sets of complementarities in both rules and practices, favouring certain types of economic activity over others. Thus, for example, within liberal markets, good generic tertiary education and weak tenure enable skills and knowledge to be diffused across organizations that would not otherwise be possible in a situation of adversarial competition (Thelen 2001); highly mobile investor capital enables innovative start-ups. Again, within coordinated market economies (CMEs) many firms found their competitiveness from regulations that underpin co-specific assets shared with workers, such as industry-specific skills bases and knowledge (Hall and Soskice 2001). Hall and Soskice held that firms will seek to hang on to or restore the institutional basis of their competitive advantage after external shocks; in most cases, coordination can be restored (Hall and Soskice 2001: 65).

In short, what characterized this literature was both an emphasis on continuity and parsimony in analysis. Ultimately, within advanced societies, most countries fell into or close to the LME or CME archetype. The Hall and Soskice (2001) collection owed its particular influence to the fact that not only did it allow for simplicity in analysis, but it also emphasized the relative durability and viability of the CME model in the face of neo-liberal attacks. In terms of the specific industrial relations features associated with each model, Hall and Soskice (2001) concentrated on broad brushstrokes, but specific contributors to the collection highlighted specific characteristics of work and employment relations, and of labour markets that were particularly associated with one capitalist archetype or another.

A number of criticisms can be advanced against this approach. Firstly, it fails to take account of the internal diversity encountered in many contexts. For example, in the USA, an archetypical LME, one can identify at least two archetypical work and employment paradigms. The first, encountered in the hi-tech sector, is about contingent working, but also about high levels of generic knowledge, the linking of individual fortunes to organizational fortunes through share offerings, individual bargaining where the employee has meaningful skills and knowledge to bargain, and relatively good wages (see Wright and Dwyer 2006). The second, encountered in the low-end sector, is characterized by poor wages, contingent working interposed with periods of unemployment or sub-employment, wages being set at the legal minimum or subsistence level, and highly unequal individual bargaining (Wright and Dwyer 2006).

Secondly, the VOC approach assumes that both LMEs and CMEs are intrinsically viable, owing to the strong nature of the complementarities encountered in each context. In more mixed or diluted systems, such complementarities are likely to work less well, and hence, other systems will be impelled to one or other archetype (Hancké et al. 2007). However, it is evident that each of the two main models has performed better than the other at specific times (Allen 2012); this suggests that neither model is intrinsically effective or immune from pressures to change. Thirdly, this approach assumes a strong path dependence; countries generally progress on incremental and linear lines. However, in reality, the evolution of national systems is an uneven process, with periods of orderly progression readily being broken through ruptures, which represent significant departures from previous models (Hollingsworth 2006).

HISTORICAL INSTITUTIONALISM

Historical institutionalism suggests that institutions are structural frames, which are bedded down and entrenched at specific times (Djelic 2010). In short, a formative event, trauma, or crisis leads to institution building then consolidation. The resultant coordination is a political process that requires constant nurturing, renegotiation, or simply patching up (Thelen 2010). This reflects conflict inherent in the system, not only between employers and employees, but also between firms and other associations, and between different firm types. Institutions do not reflect a single, but rather many different logics and principles of rationality (Jackson 2010). The latter reflect historical compromises. Given that institutions are likely to face constant strains and pressures, their reconstitution is a political process. While it would be incorrect to say institutions have a specific shelf life, the longer institutional arrangements remain in place, the more likely they are to be overturned.

In his classic 'old institutionalist' writings, Polanyi (1944) talked of a double movement. At specific times, unrestrained capitalist interests gain the upper hand; this leads to a reaction in order to rein in the destructive features of markets. In turn, comprehensive regulation will bring with it tensions of its own, leading to a counter-movement back to the deregulation of markets. Where contemporary historical institutionalism differs from this is in regarding this process as both meandering and temporarily specific (Streeck 2010). The move from one pole to the other is not linear, and markets and regulations assume different forms at different times. In other words, it is not possible to rebuild or recapture the social compromises of the past, while in different settings, markets introduce both specific pathologies and strengths. What does this mean for the study of industrial relations? One can neither assume that great systemic distortions or failures will right themselves, nor that once broken down, historical compromises cannot be reconstituted. A progressive double movement *deus ex machina* will not automatically arise out of the failures of neo-liberalism, but neither is neo-liberalism indefinitely sustainable in the face of persistent market failure. New compromises are certainly possible, but so is a sustained period of contestation, of disorder or meandering prior to the bedding down of a new compromise.

REGULATION THEORY

Of all the institutional approaches, the mainstream regulationist approach devoted the most specific attention to the articulation between institutions and firm-level work and employment relations practice. Regulationist theory concerns itself with both an accumulation regime and a dominant associated mode of regulation (i.e. the institutions that mediate, stabilize, and make growth possible), both of which are temporarily specific, mediated by class conflict, and endow specific stages of capitalism with their own patterns and structural crises (Jessop 2001a: xiv). Accumulation regimes not only embody the dominant production paradigm, but also wage distribution and relative inequality, demand and the time horizons of investment decisions (Boyer 2001: 106). A major criticism of early regulation theory is that, in its concern with the structural crises of Fordism, it neglected the nature of diversity of the latter, and the importance not only of temporal, but also of spatial specificality. As Jessop (2001b: 55) notes, Fordist regional economies and clusters of other types of production paradigm can be encountered within the same national setting, while in some national contexts, 'purer' forms of Fordism were encountered during the long boom.

What does this mean in practice? To regulationists, classic Fordism was associated not only with mass production, but also involved a relatively fairer distribution of wages and incomes than would be encountered in much of the contemporary world. The limits of such a relatively homogenized view of the past notwithstanding (limits now acknowledged by mainstream regulationist theorists), this does still underscore the point that, in many contexts, wages, tenure, and working conditions have deteriorated or stagnated for a large component of the workforce, and this is bound up with the inherent instability of the global economy over the past forty years. Indeed, this has led some writers to argue that neo-liberalism is not a functional accumulation regime at all (Wolfson 2003). A possible critique of contemporary regulationist theory is that a concern with the crisis of Fordism has led to analysis shifting away from the point of production to the wider political economy; hence, it could be inferred that work and employment have become somehow less important.

More recent regulationist concerns have shifted to the issue of systemic change. More specifically, change may be about institutional substitution, hybridization, or experimentation (Boyer 2006). There is much common ground between this and contemporary historical institutionalism (Streeck 2010), and points to the extent to which both the reality of, and changes to, dominant work and employment relations paradigms and associated institutions is a messy, complex, and contested process. In contrast, the VOC approach has emphasized systemic coherence and parsimony in defining features (Jessop 2012).

Jessop (2012) argues that rather than historical institutionalism or the varieties of capitalism approach, the contemporary order may best be understood as variegated capitalism. By this it is meant that while there are many nationally specific different forms of capitalism, one type of order assumes predominance within the global capitalist ecosystem at any particular time. This would explain why there are common trends in contemporary work and employment to less secure and contingent working, greater social inequality, and weaknesses in organized labour. Many developed societies are neither liberal nor neo-liberal markets, but all have experienced some contagion from neo-liberalism. Reflecting this, central concerns of the mainstream industrial relations literature have been with union decline, instability, and rising inequality within and beyond the workplace. Drawing on the Marxist tradition, Jessop adds that 'within rational capitalism, only the expenditure of socially necessary labour power in commodity production generates value (and hence the potential for profit) for capital as a whole' (Jessop 2012: 214). This highlights the vital distinction between the activities of rentiers and productive capital, and the extent to which the relative enhancement of the power of the former within the global ecosystem is likely to be a symptom of crisis and decay, rather than the basis for stable and sustainable growth.

MULTI-ARCHETYPICAL MODELS

Whitley (1999) shares the view of Hall and Soskice (2001) that contractual relations depend on embedded formal and informal rules. Business systems theory sets out to be an explicitly firm-centred analysis, and hence makes somewhat stronger predictions as to how firm-level work and employment practices are likely to differ from context to context.

More specifically, Whitley (1999) argues that one of the defining features of distinct business systems is employer–employee interdependence and delegation. The former involves variations in security of tenure, and in investments in skills and developments. The latter, meanwhile, concerns employee voice (Whitley 1999). Based on this, a very much wider range of national archetypes is identified: in addition to the continental West European/liberal market distinction, the Italian industrial districts model is seen as an archetype in its own right, as are two different categories of far Eastern economies. The main criticism that can be levelled at this approach (in addition to the omnipresent question as to the desirable number of capitalist archetypes) is how the other defining features of capitalism are identified, and the empirical foundations of differentiation. Despite a firm-level focus, very little actual evidence is presented on real distinctions in practice: as with the VOC literature, much of this approach is centred on stylized ideal types.

Recently, authors working on business systems theory have turned their attention to the multinational firm, a player commonly ignored in the varieties of capitalism literature. Whitley (2010) argues that firms will vary their approach according to the specific dynamics of the country of domicile, without necessarily opting for homogeneity with their local counterparts. When attracted, for example, through the possibility of access to a particularly rich market, they may be especially sensitive to local conditions, as would be the case when seeking the benefits conferred by a specific local production regime. In contrast, when simply seeking to access cheap labour, they may be rather more opportunistic and short-termist (Whitley 2010). Alternatively, they may seek to remake the dominant institutional regime in their host country to more closely suit their own specific requirements (Morgan 2012). Indeed, they may serve as norm entrepreneurs (cf. Dore 2008), challenging existing ways of doing things through introducing new practices. For example, recent evidence from Japan has highlighted the extent to which changes in the Japanese model have indeed partially stemmed from takeovers of domestic firms by US multinational corporations (MNCs) (Sako and Kotosaka 2012).

Another particularly influential multi-archetype approach has been the social systems approach of Amable (2003), which draws on both regulation theory and aspects of historical institutionalism. Amable (2003) bases his country categorization on empirical analysis of a range of different national characteristics, largely based on macroeconomic indices external to the firm. More specifically, he explores, inter alia, specific features of the industrial relations environment, encompassing issues such as variations in collective bargaining and unionization, and in social protection, and derives his different country categories via cluster analysis. The categories derived, in addition to the normal liberal market and (coordinated) 'continental European capitalism', include a developed Far Eastern paradigm, a Mediterranean model, and Scandinavian 'social democracy'. Empirical evidence on actual firm-level industrial relations practices confirms that the Scandinavian social democracies do indeed differ from their continental European counterparts (Goergen et al. 2012). However, a closer examination of individual national economies throws up some important nuances. For example, the Dutch 'polder model' may have more in common with other 'flexicurity economies', such as Denmark. And northern Italy has little in common with more peripheral Mediterranean economies such as Portugal and Greece.

RECENT DEVELOPMENTS

Greater volatility within individual national economies has led to increased interest in both internal variety and the nature of systemic change. This has led to a growing realization that institutions are fluid, subject to both incremental change and rupture, and somewhat less closely coupled than commonly presumed. Indeed, there has been increasing recognition that, reflecting internal diversity within national contexts, not one but several dominant industrial relations paradigms may be encountered within a particular setting (Barry and Wilkinson 2011; Wilkinson 2008).

Given, as noted above, institutions are subject to evolution and change, it is likely that they will operate in a manner somewhat removed from what was intended at the time of their original design (Wood and Lane 2012; Lane and Wood 2009). The latter represents both the choices of social actors, and external forces, which can range from technical innovations, through changes in extractable resources, to shifts in the global balance of power.

A challenge of contemporary institutionalist thinking has been reconciling spatial and temporal analysis. Early regulationist theory focused on the crisis of Fordism, the latter being seen as a phenomenon that was encountered across all the advanced societies. While there were later attempts to inject a spatial dimension, contemporary regulationist concerns with financialization suggested again that a dominant way of doing things had come to characterize world capitalism. Meanwhile, the literature on comparative capitalism initially concerned itself with spatial difference, the two archetypical systems each being characterized by seemingly immutable features. Late critics pointed out the extent to which at specific times one system has performed very much better than the other (Allen 2012). As noted above, this could lead to strong pressures at specific times to import features from one to the other. While historical institutionalism is intrinsically a theory of both space and scale, in recent years, there has been a strong focus on the possible decay of more coordinated contexts (see Streeck 2010). Although historical institutionalists may have good grounds for pessimism, the relatively good performance of northern European coordinated economies since the onset of the 2008 economic crisis might suggest that there are strong counter-pressures towards the retention of core features of these models.

Internal Diversity within Contexts

Wood and Lane (2012) argue that internal diversity within national institutional systems reflects four factors: social action, complementarity, systemic change, and sub- and supranational configurations. They develop their arguments more fully in a chapter in this volume, but some key features here merit review. As noted above, 'norm entrepreneurs' may challenge existing orders, pioneering changes which then diffuse across an economy (Dore 2008). In making such interventions, they are guided both by reality and experience, and by their subjective reinterpretations thereof (Simmel 1981). In practice, such processes are characterized by deliberate intention and experimentation, serendipitous discoveries, and failures (Boyer 2006). The failure of particular sets of institutions to continue to provide the basis for growth is likely to result in ongoing rounds of such experiments. While an individual firm rarely can shape an entire contextual environment, regulation notwithstanding, they have considerable room for manoeuvre in terms of their work and employment relations practices. Hence, it could be argued that changes in the latter serve as something of a barometer for broader systemic change.

Secondly, there is the nature of complementarity. Complementarity represents the introduction and clustering of rules and practices both to build on systemic strengths and to compensate for weaknesses (Crouch 2005): this process of adjustment may assume a regional and/or sectoral dimension. What is important to note is that there are complementarities not only within, but also between nations, and they may be not only compensatory, but in some instances, essentially pathological. An example would be a heavy reliance on outsourcing which may cut labour costs, but ultimately reduces the pool of consumers within the most developed markets, although the latter may, in turn, benefit from cheaper goods.

Thirdly, there are important regional and sectoral differences, reflecting not only formal regulation, but also embedded ties. Importantly, in countries where political power is devolved, local regulation may run counter to the dominant political discourse in the core: an example would be the partial departure of Scotland and Wales on more socially democratic trajectories when compared to the intensifying neo-liberalism of the English core. Again, within Spain, Catalonia remains very much more committed to social democracy than within the national polity. This will impact on the structure of the job market, and indeed, the relative extent to which pubic sector jobs are provided directly by the state, devolved to privatized services or simply done away with. At a sectoral level, some local production networks may be more durable—and hence effective—in safeguarding good jobs than others. An example would be northern Italy, where the clothing and textile industry has proven more vulnerable and subject to outsourcing than, say, the production networks encountered within the motor and machine tool industries.

In terms of the implications for work and employment relations, three issues are worth considering. Firstly, while neo-liberalism may indeed have ecosystemic dominance (Jessop 2012), there are important counter-tendencies on regional and sectoral lines. This is likely to result in further reforms continuing to be uneven, episodic, and in some cases even contested by elite segments. Secondly, trade union renewal drives are likely to continue to be context-specific; while it is possible for unions to adopt innovative practices from elsewhere, relative successes cannot be divorced from context. Thirdly, pathological complementarities allow for structural imbalances to be shored up for very much longer than would otherwise be the case: it cannot be presumed that just because conditions are worsening, adjustments are inevitable.

Financialization

The literature on financialization is undeniably diverse. What lies at its heart is the assumption that the increased focus on shareholder value since the 1980s reflects structural changes in capitalism, characterized by the rise of financial intermediaries who increasingly make inroads into the value traditionally accruing to other stakeholders, most notably workers and long-term savers (Folkman et al. 2007). Central to financialization has been the rupturing of the virtuous Kaldorian circle; a situation of stagnant or declining wages for workers has created a real crisis of demand, which has been temporarily resolved through debt-fuelled consumption (Folkman et al. 2007).

In short, financialization is about the heightened power of financial intermediaries, bound up with structural changes in the banking industry, a process that has brought with it great speculative bubbles (Froud et al. 2007: 340). The process has been marked by the globalization of financial markets, strong emphasis on short-term value release by firms, and increasingly complex financial investment vehicles (Stockhammer 2004: 722). As such it entails the dominance of capital market finance, and structural changes in the balance of power between financial services and other industries (Epstein 2007). Again, there has been an increasing divide between those large investors who enjoy close ties to specific financial institutions, and the bulk of small and medium savers whose interests are treated as 'passive and subordinate' (Dumenil and Levy 2004: 132).

While some of the early literature on financialization saw it as partially a cultural or even postmodern phenomenon, in recent years the focus has shifted back to more orthodox political economy concerns. Notably, Arrighi (2005: 85) has argued that financialization represents little more than a recurrent phenomenon in capitalism: in response to the over-accumulation of capital at key stages in its development, rentiers have become increasingly powerful. In other words, financialization both represents a response to crisis, and embodies crisis tendencies of its own. More specifically, it requires endless bailouts to sustain speculative bubbles, which in turn sucks capital away from more productive sectors of society, leading to worsening inequality and crisis (Arrighi 2005: 85), an undeniably prescient statement given the continuous bank bailouts that have characterized the post-2008 crisis period. Ultimately, however, these contradictions will lead to a resurgence in the power of more productive sectors of capital (Arrighi 2005).

A limitation of the literature on financialization is that it has tended to assume strong homogenizing pressures in global capitalism, when important differences remain between heavily financialized societies such as the UK, and many of the economies of northern Europe; in many continental European countries, the mainstay of the economy remains more orthodox sectors of industry, and, in key competitive areas, high labour standards. Again, a distinction needs to be drawn between 'vulture' investors and, for example, sectors of venture capital that provide invaluable support to new start-ups.

Other political economy approaches have argued that financialization does not merely represent a long-term cyclical shift of power to rentiers, but indeed, the resurgence of more primitive features of capitalism. For example, Harvey (2004: 145) suggests that a key feature of contemporary capitalism has been accumulation by dispossession, most notably the attempted expropriation of mineral rights in key Middle Eastern economy through ongoing neo-imperial wars. However, while the violent dimensions of capitalism are not to be underestimated, it is worth noting that recent imperial adventures have proved extremely costly, and have failed to yield anticipated bonanzas; the main beneficiaries have been traditional manufacturers in the USA's bloated military–industrial complex and mercenary contractors.

The New Statism

Although neo-liberalism is commonly held up as the triumph of lightly regulated markets, it is worth noting that many supposedly liberal markets are heavily statist. Most notably, as Weiss (2010) notes, whilst the USA is held up as the quintessential LME, in many areas, the US state is highly interventionist. More specifically, the hi-tech and defence industries rely heavily on state protection, support, and in the case of the latter, highly beneficial government contracting (Weiss 2010). The R&D base of these sectors is partially underwritten by the state and not-for-profit university sectors. Indeed, it could be argued that the other archetypical area of economic activity encountered in the USA, the low value-added service sector, also bears the imprint of statism. Workfare policies help secure and discipline low-cost unskilled labour (Peck 2001). The penalization of over two million of the poor helps both to underpin social order and to mask unemployment; the large military also helps mop up excessive numbers of the redundant poor. In short, liberal markets may be characterized by a great deal of formal and informal regulation, while still being internally diverse. Although traditional industrial relations approaches have suggested that governments may seek to promote best practices in work and employment relations, there is no sign of such an agenda under the new statism. Lavish defence spending and a wide range of hidden subsidies may prop up traditional defence contractors that employ large numbers of manufacturing workers who enjoy relative good terms and conditions of service. However, it has also led to the proliferation of private military companies employing large numbers of mercenaries. While the latter may enjoy relatively good pay, they also bear large personal risks and are readily laid off when their services are no longer required: again, private military companies have been equally ready to outsource their labour requirements to subcontractors, who engage very much cheaper manpower in the developing world. Again, the use of workfare and prison labour leads to the destruction of conventional jobs in favour of neo-slavery.

The Rise of the Precariat

While a large number of poorly paid workers has been a characteristic of various stages of capitalist development, a feature of the present condition is the rise of a global precariat who are neither occupationally nor spatially rooted (Standing 2011). This new underclass is forced to move within and across national boundaries, engaging in a wide range of poorly paid jobs. Ever more stringent border controls have failed to stem this movement, but rather facilitated wholesale labour coercion: if an illegal immigrant has no hope of legal status, he or she may be condemned to lifelong peonage, locked in debt to human smugglers, labour brokers, and slumlords, with complaints being dealt with by physical violence and/or being exposed to the authorities. In turn, neo-peons are likely to systematically undercut unskilled legal workers. The rising inequality that has characterized liberal markets since the early 1980s has led to the ranks of vulnerable workers being swelled by downwardly mobile sections of the middle classes, who themselves no longer enjoy occupational and pensions security and whose savings face expropriation by financial intermediaries. In turn this has led to essentially reactionary horizontal struggles over the crumbs from the neo-liberal table, the ultimate losers being those who are weakest, with the winners being little better off, leading to further conflict (Davis 2006). Such conflicts have been enthusiastically stoked by the right-wing media, and by particularly reactionary segments of capital. While it is correct to state that the destabilizing effects of large-scale downward social mobility have indeed been alleviated by such means, it is worth noting that the most fertile recruiting grounds for proto-fascist causes has to date been the same as was the case for classic fascism in its heyday in the 1920s and 1930s: the downwardly mobile middle class, rather than the long-term working class.

Structural Crisis and Change—Causality and Directions

As noted in chapter 7, there is a case to be made that the rising power of speculative sections of capital is more a consequence than a cause of ongoing crisis. Indeed, it can be argued that the present condition has firmly material roots, in a long-term energy transition that has fundamentally changed the nature of input costs. While oil and gas demand may be rising, this form of energy is no longer cheap, and its share of the energy mix has begun to decline. As was the case with the long energy transition of the early twentieth century, such a transition greatly favours the interests of owners of highly fungible assets over those with less fungible ones, such as workers, who have skills and capabilities tied to specific industries and locales. However, unlike the crisis of the 1920s, the present owners of highly fungible actors include statist and quasi-statist actors, most notably sovereign wealth funds. This may serve to stay some of the excess associated with rootless rentiers, but it also challenges the basis of political power within and between national boundaries, and may bring with it new political conflicts within and between countries.

For some time, optimistic progressives have comforted themselves with the possibility of a new Polanyian double movement that will lead a swing back from market excess to greater state regulation. However, state mediation is not necessarily progressive, and indeed, the new statism encountered within the USA may indeed be such a regressive double movement (see Chapter 7 by Lane and Wood). A further limitation of neo-Polanyian approaches is that they may lead to overly functionalist conclusions. It could be argued that, given endless speculative bubbles and bailouts, ultimately the system will exhaust itself and collapse, leading to more progressive alternatives being constructed. In other words, as systems cease to work, they will be replaced with an order that does, allowing for renewed growth. However, even if many of the features of global capitalism in general, and liberal markets in particular, are undeniably dysfunctional in objective terms, they continue to work extremely well in serving the interests of insiders. The latter may even be unconcerned about questions of growth, as long as they can expropriate an ever increasing proportion of resources. Indeed, they may prioritize short-term destructive extraction over longer-term growth, given the latter requires a degree of restraint. As Singer (2000) notes, a limitation of neo-liberal thinking is that it is very poor in accurately costing long-term value and costs. Or as Diamond (2005) notes, as supposedly rational individuals, people are notoriously unwilling to deal with bad news, and tend to prioritize short-term incentives over more abstract long-term costs.

This raises an important question regarding the long-term evolution of social systems. There has been a tendency for theories of long waves to depict the process as a broadly level one. Yet, a long-term historical view suggests that there have been times—from the birth of the modern to the present day—when economic long waves less represented a standing wave, and more steps on an ascending staircase. At other times, such as during the periods of the dark and middle ages, the process was more akin to a descending one. It cannot be assumed that, because there has been an exponential increase in the size of the global economy since the late middle ages, this process will inevitably persist. As Diamond (2005) notes, the downfall of many previous societies has been human needs outstripping resource constraints. We are cautious of neo-Malthusianism—the decay of societies is not purely a product of excess population simply overwhelming nature. Indeed, predatory elites may accelerate the process of societal decline, and social equity may allow for fairer and more efficient distributions of existing or even diminishing resource pools. However, the growing global environmental crisis has highlighted the limitations of viewing the planet as a provider of infinite resources. The reluctance of elites to face up to visible 'bad news', and the continued prioritization of short-term benefit over long-term costs may mean that meaningful action will only come when it is too late (Diamond 2005).

What does this mean in terms of work and employment relations? Here it is worth noting that the story of most large-scale organized societies has been one of wholesale labour coercion. While the latter persists to the present day, it is no longer an inevitable feature of the human condition: dignified and well-rewarded work is widely encountered. Any long decline may lead to a diminishment of the latter, as elites ruthlessly expropriate larger slices of a dwindling pie.

While the problems of the global economy are likely to be at least in part ultimately due to natural resources and the associated usage of specific technologies, there is little doubt that politics has both exacerbated problems, and represents the vehicle for a meaningful solution. As Gourevitch and Shinn (2005) note, the manner in which firms are governed is both intensely political and inevitably the subject of political contestation. Yet, as global elites have become convinced as to the necessity for more neo-liberalism, in many contexts electoral politics is largely devoid of meaningful alternatives. Both progressive and proto-fascist movements have undeniably benefited from this political crisis, but high abstention rates in many contexts suggest that the concerns of many remain unarticulated. The present dominance by oligarchic elites has been shored up through a wide range of mechanisms ranging from aggressively partisan media disinformation through to, at least within the USA, the incarceration and disenfranchisement of large numbers of the criminalized poor. Potentially more serious has been the extent to which due to security paranoia, leading politicians have in many contexts increasingly isolated themselves from everyday life. Sandel (2012) argues that the common life represents a vital underpinning of social solidarity; there is little doubt that the withdrawal of economic and political elites into closed private and privately secured spaces is fundamentally corrosive. Indeed, negotiated compromises between capital and labour are likely to become increasingly difficult if the former are increasingly in a position to opt out, rather than be daily confronted with the consequences of their choices.

CONCLUSIONS

It has become fashionable for progressive industrial relations scholars to be pessimistic, given the present 'dark times' of worsening global inequality, and while it can be argued that no understanding of work and employment is complete without taking account of the interplay of practice with institutions, the linkages are by no means always closely articulated (Wilkinson and Townsend 2011). From within the radical political economy tradition, the relationship between the physical and social process of production and wider societal institutions is central. However, as Thompson and Smith (2010: 22) note, much of the labour process literature has remained focused on a 'plant based' approach, with 'some sensitivity' to the wider socio-economic framework. Within regulation theory, while again there is an implicit connection drawn between work and employment relations, and institutions, much recent regulationist literature has focused on macro-societal issues, drawing implicit, rather than explicit connections to changes and continuities in the employment relationship.

Again, the early literature on comparative capitalism specifically drew links between particular work and employment relations paradigms, and wider institutional realities (Lincoln and Kalleberg 1990; Dore 2000). However, from Hall and Soskice (2001) onwards, there has been a focus on broad trends, and the often anecdotal presentation of case study evidence, but with a stronger emphasis on the political rather than broader crises within the global capitalist economy (Thompson and Vincent 2010: 58).

It is perhaps Bob Jessop's recent work on variegated capitalism that comes closest to resolving this issue, through the above-mentioned distinction between the wider capitalist ecosystem and what takes place within specific national contexts. However,

Jessop's work is closer to the regulationist tradition; his primary engagement with the varieties of capitalism literature is at the level of critique.

Business systems theory does make very implicit connections between the key dynamics of work and employment and context (Whitley 1999), although in recent years this focus has shifted towards issues such as the multinational corporation (cf. Morgan 2012). Historical institutionalists have sought to resolve this concern, albeit through a stronger focus on social action (Thompson and Vincent 2010), which in practice remains often at the level of formal association rather than discussing the contradictions and contestations that characterize working life, whether unionized or not.

What this book seeks to do is bring back institutions into how we understand work and employment relations, and vice versa, through focusing more closely on the articulations.

ACKNOWLEDGEMENTS

This chapter adapts material from Wilkinson and Wood (2012), courtesy of Wiley-Blackwell.

REFERENCES

Ackers, P. and Wilkinson, A. (2008). 'Industrial Relations and the Social Sciences', in P. Blyton, N. Bacon, J. Firito, and E. Heery (eds.), *The Sage Handbook of Industrial Relations*. London: Sage, 53–68.

Allen, F. (2012). 'Financing Firms in Different Countries', in G. Wood and M. Demirbag (eds.), *Handbook of Institutional Approaches to International Business*. Cheltenham: Edward Elgar, 41–64.

Amable, B. (2003). *The Diversity of Modern Capitalism*. Oxford and New York: Oxford University Press.

Arrighi, G. (2005). 'Hegemony Unravelling', *New Left Review*, 33: 83–116.

Barry, M. and Wilkinson, A. (eds.) (2011). *Research Handbook of Comparative Employment Relations*. Cheltenham: Edward Elgar.

Botero, J., Djankov, S., La Porta, R., Lopez-de-Silanes, S., and Shleifer, A. (2004). 'The Regulation of Labor', *Quarterly Journal of Economics*, 119: 1339–82.

Boyer, R. (2001). 'The Eighties: The Search for Alternatives to Fordism', in B. Jessop (ed.), *Regulationist Perspectives on Fordism and Post-Fordism: Regulation Theory and the Crisis of Capitalism Volume 3*. Cheltenham: Edward Elgar, 164–92.

—— (2006). 'How do Institutions Cohere and Change? The Institutional Complementarity Hypothesis and Its Extension', in G. Wood and P. James (eds.), *Institutions, Production, and Working Life*. Oxford and New York: Oxford University Press, 13–61.

Cooney, S., Gahan, P., and Mitchell, R. (2011). 'Legal Origins, Labour Law and the Regulation of Employment Relations', in M. Barry and A. Wilkinson (eds.), *Research Handbook of Comparative Employment Relations*. Cheltenham: Edward Elgar, 75–97.

Crouch, C. (2005). 'Three Meanings of Complementarity', *Socio-Economic Review*, 3(2): 359–63.

Davis, M. (2006). *Planet of Slums*. London: Verso.

Deakin, S. and Sarkar, P. (2008). 'Assessing the Long-Run Economic Impact of Labour Law Systems: A Theoretical Reappraisal and Analysis of New Time Series Data', *Industrial Relations Journal*, 39: 453–87.

Diamond, J. (2005). *Collapse*. London: Penguin.

DiMaggio, P. J. and Powell, W. (1983). 'The Iron Cage Revisited: Institutional Isomorphism and Collective Rationality in Organizational Fields', *American Sociological Review*, 48: 147–60.

—— (1988). 'Interest and Agency in Institutional Theory', in L. Zucker (ed.), *Institutional Patterns and Organizations*. Cambridge, MA: Ballinger, 3–21.

Djelic M.-L. (2010). 'Institutional Perspectives—Working towards Coherence or Irreconcilable Diversity?', in G. Morgan, J. Campbell, C. Crouch, O. K. Pedersen, and R. Whitley (eds.), *The Oxford Handbook of Comparative Institutional Analysis*. Oxford: Oxford University Press, 15–40.

Dore, R. (2000). *Stock Market Capitalism: Welfare Capitalism*. Cambridge: Cambridge University Press.

—— (2008). 'Best Practice Winning Out?', *Socio-Economic Review*, 6(4): 779–84.

Dumenil, G. and Levy, D. (2004). 'Neoliberal Income Trends', *New Left Review*, 30: 105–33.

Dunlop, J. (1958). *Industrial Relations Systems*. New York: Holt-Dryden.

Epstein, G. (2007). 'Introduction: Financialization and the World Economy', in Epstein (ed.), *Financialization and the World Economy*. Cheltenham: Edward Elgar, 3–16.

Folkman, P., Froud, J., Johal, S., and Williams, K. (2007). 'Working for Themselves: Financial Intermediaries and Present Day Capitalism', *Business History*, 49(4): 552–72.

Froud, J., Leaver, A., and Williams, K. (2007). 'New Actors in a Financialised Economy and the Remaking of Capitalism', *New Political Economy*, 12(3): 339–47.

Gall, G., Wilkinson, A., and Hurd, R. (eds.) (2011). *The International Handbook of Labour Unions: Responses to Neo-Liberalism*. Cheltenham: Edward Elgar.

Goergen, M., Brewster, C., Wood, G., and Wilkinson, A. (2012). 'Varieties of Capitalism and Investments in Human Capital', *Industrial Relations*, 51 (Suppl.): 501–27.

Gourevitch, P. and Shinn, J. (2005). *Political Power and Corporate Control*. Princeton: Princeton University Press.

Hall, P. A. and Soskice, D. (2001). 'An Introduction to Varieties of Capitalism', in Hall and Soskice (eds.), *Varieties of Capitalism: The Institutional Foundations of Comparative Advantage*. Oxford and New York: Oxford University Press, 1–68.

Hancké, B., Rhodes, M., and Thatcher, M. (2007). 'Introduction', in B. Hancké, M. Rhodes, and M. Thatcher (eds.), *Beyond Varieties of Capitalism: Conflict, Contradiction, and Complementarities in the European Economy*. Oxford: Oxford University Press, 1–48.

Harvey, D. (2004). *The New Imperialism*. Oxford and New York: Oxford University Press.

Hollingsworth, R. (2006). 'Advancing our Understanding of Capitalism with Niels Bohr's Thinking about Complementarity', in G. Wood and P. James (eds.), *Institutions and Working Life*. Oxford: Oxford University Press, 62–82.

Hyman, R. (2002). 'What is Industrial Relations?', in J. Kelly (ed.), *Industrial Relations: Critical Perspectives on Business and Management*. London: Routledge, 50–68.

Jackson, G. (2010). 'Actors and Institutions', in G. Morgan, J. Campbell, C. Crouch, O. K. Pedersen, and R. Whitley (eds.), *The Oxford Handbook of Comparative Institutional Analysis*. Oxford and New York: Oxford University Press, 63–86.

Jessop, B. (2001a). 'Series Preface', in Jessop (ed.), *Regulationist Perspectives on Fordism and Post-Fordism: Regulation Theory and the Crisis of Capitalism Volume 3*. Cheltenham: Edward Elgar, ix–xxiv.

—— (2001b). 'Introduction', in Jessop (ed.), *Regulationist Perspectives on Fordism and Post-Fordism: Regulation Theory and the Crisis of Capitalism Volume 3*. Cheltenham: Edward Elgar, xxv–xlii.

—— (2012). 'Rethinking the Diversity and Variability of Capitalism: On Variegated Capitalism in the World Market', in C. Lane and G. Wood (eds.), *Capitalist Diversity and Diversity within Capitalism*. London: Routledge, 209–37.

Kaufman, B. (1993). *The Origins and Evolution of the Field of Industrial Relations in the United States*. Ithaca: ILR Press.

Kelly, J. (1998). *Rethinking Industrial Relations: Mobilization, Collectivism and Long Waves*. London: Routledge.

Lane, C. and Wood, G. (2009). 'Diversity in Capitalism and Capitalist Diversity', *Economy and Society*, 38(4): 531–51.

La Porta, R., Lopez-de-Silanes, F., Shleifer, A., and Vishny, R. (1998). 'Law and Finance', *Journal of Political Economy*, 106: 1113–55.

—— (2000). 'Investor Protection and Corporate Governance', *Journal of Financial Economics*, 58: 3–27.

Lincoln, J. and Kalleberg, A. (1990). *Culture, Control and Commitment: A Study of Work Organization in the United States and Japan*. Cambridge: Cambridge University Press.

Morgan, G. (2012). 'International Business, Multinationals and National Business Systems', in G. Wood and M. Demirbag (eds.), *Handbook of Institutions and International Business*. Cheltenham: Edward Elgar, 18–40.

North, D. C. (1990). *Institutions, Institutional Change and Economic Performance*. Cambridge: Cambridge University Press.

Peck, J. (2001). *Workfare States*. New York: Guilford Press.

Peters, G. (2005). *Institutional Theory in Political Science*. New York: Continuum.

Polanyi, K. (1944). *The Great Transformation: The Political and Economic Origins of Our Time*. Boston: Beacon Press.

Sako, M. and Kotosaka, M. (2012). 'Institutional Change and Organizational Diversity in Japan', in C. Lane and G. Wood (eds.), *Capitalist Diversity and Diversity within Capitalism*. London: Routledge, 69–96.

Sandel, M. (2012). *What Money Can't Buy: The Moral Limits of Markets*. New York: Farrar, Straus and Giroux.

Simmel, G. (1981). *On Individuality and Social Forms*. Chicago: University of Chicago Press.

Singer, P. (2000). *Writings on an Ethical Life*. New York: Ecco.

Sisson, K. (2010). 'Employment Relations Matters'. Available at <http://www2.warwick.ac.uk/fac/soc/wbs/research/irru/erm/>.

Standing, G. (2011). *The Precariat: The New Dangerous Class*. London: Bloomsbury.

Stockhammer, E. (2004). 'Financialisation and the Slowdown in Accumulation', *Cambridge Journal of Economics*, 28: 719–41.

Streeck, W. (2010). 'Institutions in History: Bringing Capitalism Back In', in G. Morgan, J. Campbell, C. Crouch, O. K. Pedersen, and R. Whitley (eds.), *The Oxford Handbook of Comparative Institutional Analysis*. Oxford: Oxford University Press, 659–86.

Thelen, K. (2001). 'Varieties of Labor Politics in the Developed Democracies', in P. A. Hall and D. Soskice (eds.), *Varieties of Capitalism: The Institutional Foundations of Comparative Advantage*. Oxford and New York: Oxford University Press, 71–103.

—— (2010). 'Beyond Comparative Statics', in G. Morgan, J. Campbell, C. Crouch, O. Pedersen, and R. Whitley (eds.), *The Oxford Handbook of Comparative Institutional Analysis*. Oxford: Oxford University Press, 41–62.

Thompson, P. and Smith, C. (2010). 'Labour Process Theory in Retrospect and Prospect', in Thompson and Smith (eds.), *Working Life: Renewing Labour Process Analysis*. Basingstoke: Palgrave Macmillan, 1–12.

Thompson, P. and Vincent, S. (2010). 'Labour Process Theory and Critical Realism', in Thompson and C. Smith (eds.), *Working Life: Renewing Labour Process Analysis*. Basingstoke: Palgrave Macmillan, 47–69.

Weiss, L. (2010). 'The State in the Economy', in G. Morgan, J. Campbell, C. Crouch, O. Pedersen, and R. Whitley (eds.), *The Oxford Handbook of Comparative Institutional Analysis*. Oxford: Oxford University Press, 183–210.

Whitley, R. (1999). *Divergent Capitalisms: The Social Structuring and Change of Business Systems*. Oxford and New York: Oxford University Press.

—— (2010). 'Changing Competition in Market Economies: The Effects of Internationalization, Technological Innovations, and Academic Expansion on the Conditions Supporting Dominant Economic Logics', in G. Morgan, J. Campbell, C. Crouch, O. Pedersen, and R. Whitley (eds.), *The Oxford Handbook of Comparative Institutional Analysis*. Oxford and New York: Oxford University Press, 363–98.

Wilkinson, A. (2008). 'Industrial Relations', in S. Clegg and J. Bailey (eds.), *Encyclopedia of Organizational Studies*. London and New York: Sage, 652–3.

Wilkinson, A. and Townsend, K. (eds.) (2011). *The Future of Employment Relations: New Paradigms, New Developments*. Basingstoke: Palgrave Macmillan.

Wilkinson, A. and Wood, G. (2012). 'Institutions and Employment Relations: The State of the Art', *Industrial Relations: Journal of Economy and Society*, 51(2): 373–88.

Wolfson, M. (2003). 'Neo-liberalism and the Social Structure of Accumulation', *Review of Radical Political Economics*, 35(3): 255–63.

Wood, G. and Lane, C. (2012). 'Institutions, Change, and Diversity', in Lane and Wood (eds.), *Capitalist Diversity and Diversity within Capitalism*. London: Routledge, 1–31.

Wright, E. and Dwyer, R. (2006). 'The Patterns of Jobs Expansions in the United States: A Comparison of the 1960s and the 1990s', in G. Wood and P. James (eds.), *Institutions, Production, and Working Life*. Oxford and New York: Oxford University Press, 275–314.

CHAPTER 3

CONVERGENCE AND DIVERGENCE IN EMPLOYMENT RELATIONS

HARRY KATZ AND
NICK WAILES

INTRODUCTION

ONE of the most profound debates in the study of employment relations concerns whether employment systems and practices are converging to a common form across countries. This convergence debate questions whether there are inevitable trends and outcomes in employment system evolution. Perhaps even more importantly, debates about convergence assess whether, and if so under what circumstances, particular employment systems grow or decline due to their effects on economic performance or have differing effects on income distribution and social well-being, in other words, whether certain employment systems perform better than others. Researchers have concluded that there are 'complementarities' between employment systems and other key aspects of national political economies, such as corporate governance structures and the relationships that exist between firms and financial systems. Other researchers claim that key complementarities arise at the workplace level in the ways various employment practices and policies interact with and reinforce one another resulting in the existence of common employment 'patterns'. Consideration of complementarities, whether at the broad or workplace level, builds on the core question within modern comparative research, namely, the interplay between, and relative strength of, market and institutional (legal, historical, and political) factors.

Given the dramatic effects of the financial crises that began in 2008 and the subsequent economic downturn it is fitting to consider both the short- and long-term relationship between the present economic crisis and national patterns of employment relations. Our assessment of the available evidence is that, despite some enduring differences between national patterns of employment relations, it is possible to identify a common pattern of *converging divergences* in employment relations across developed market economies. In the short run, the impact of the recent global financial crisis has to some extent accelerated this pattern.

This chapter is structured as follows. The first section briefly reviews a variety of arguments that predict convergence in national patterns of employment relations in one form or another (the logic of industrialism, workplace patterns, the simple globalization thesis, and the varieties of capitalism approach). The next part of the chapter reviews research that, contrary to these convergence arguments, finds evidence of continued diversity and divergence in national patterns of employment relations but at the same time also points to a common trend of increasing diversity *within* national employment relations patterns, or *converging divergences*. Drawing on the comparative capitalisms literature, in the third section of this chapter we draw a link between converging divergences and the emerging concept of institutional plasticity and focus, in particular, on the extent to which increasing diversity within national patterns of employment relations is associated with multinational corporations. The chapter concludes by examining the relationship between converging divergences in employment relations and the global financial crisis.

ARGUMENTS FOR CONVERGENCE

Over the past 50 years there have been a number of arguments in the comparative employment relations literature that predict convergence of national patterns of employment relations. The original *convergence* hypothesis was developed by Kerr, Dunlop, Harbison, and Myers in their book *Industrialism and Industrial Man* (1960). Their core proposition is that there is a global tendency for technological and market forces associated with industrialization to push national employment relations systems towards uniformity or 'convergence'. This conclusion is based on the view that there is a *logic of industrialism* and that as more societies adopted industrial forms of production and organization, this logic would create 'common characteristics and imperatives' across these societies. To accommodate these imperatives, Kerr et al. (1960: 384–92) argue that industrial societies had to develop a means of developing a consensus and employment relations systems which embodied the 'principles of pluralistic industrialism' which played a central role in establishing this consensus.

Some accused Kerr et al. of *technological determinism*, arguing that even though there may have been strong pressures associated with industrialism and modernization, this did not necessarily imply that there would be convergence on a single set of societal institutions (Cochrane 1976; Doeringer 1981; Berger 1996: 2–4). Others questioned the notion of industrialism itself. *Industrialism and Industrial Man* was one of a number of books, including Daniel Bell's (1960) *The End of Ideology* and W. W. Rostow's (1960) *The Stages of Economic Growth*, written during the Cold War which presented the American social, political, and economic system as superior to Soviet communism and as a model for other countries. To this extent the links drawn between industrialism and a particular set of social and political institutions were prescriptive. The implication was that countries needed to adopt social and political institutions like those of the United States to be able to benefit from modernization and industrialism (Goldthorpe 1984).

A second set of arguments that predict convergence of employment relations focuses on workplace practices. Dore (1973) suggested that while there may be a tendency towards convergence in national patterns of employment relations, the tendency is towards convergence on Japan and not the USA (the implicit model that underpinned Kerr et al.'s analysis). He argues that as a late developer, Japan had been able to adopt organizational forms and institutions more suited to industrialization than those of countries that industrialized relatively early. Later analysis of Japanese employment relations practices went on to argue that these workplace practices are linked to Japanese manufacturing (and organizational) practices which together produce superior economic performance through their heightened attention to quality and flexibility, and their relatively low cost. Favourable performance outcomes are said to derive from continuous improvement efforts, low inventories, and other features of the Japanese production system that are facilitated by Japanese employment practices (Womack et al. 1990; MacDuffie 1995). This view led to predictions that Japanese-style employment practices would diffuse widely throughout advanced economies.

The net effect of this Japanization of employment relations is alleged to be a movement towards more enterprise-oriented employment relations including very decentralized bargaining structures, team-oriented work practices, and lifetime employment (at least for a core of the workforce). It is worth noting, however, that in a major study of the adoption of lean production in automobile assembly, Kochan et al. (1997) found evidence that a lean type of production system was consistent with a range of employment relations patterns across countries. Interestingly, among those who see a Japanization of employment relations occurring there are some, such as Dore (1992), who are attracted to the increased organizational orientation in Japanese practices and others, such as Parker and Slaughter (1988) and Babson (1995), who claim these practices increase employee stress and union subservence.

Given the strong employment growth experienced in the United States in the 1990s, especially when compared to the high unemployment rates that characterized the labour markets in most European countries from the early 1980s on, other observers have claimed that a new international convergence towards US-style flexible labour markets (and deregulated product markets) was underway (Krugman 1996). A related claim in this line of argumentation was that a key competitive advantage emerged in the USA through the early and heavy re-engineering of managerial practices that helped create an American model of lean management (Hammer and Champy 1993). While put in very different terms, it is interesting to note the common claim of American superiority found in this school of thought and the earlier convergence notions of Kerr et al.

There were also debates that focused on US and Japanese comparisons including concern over whether distinctive Japanese employment practices were eroding and being replaced by US-style practices. Jacoby (2005), for example, argued that Japan continued to possess distinctive employment practices even in the face of some incremental movement towards more market-oriented and less organizationally oriented employment relations within Japan. The contributions to Aoki et al. (2007), on the other hand, suggest the emergence and coexistence of three distinct patterns of corporate governance, each with its own distinctive employment relations model. We return to this notion of increased diversity *within* national systems later in this chapter.

Neither American-style managerial autocracy or Japanese organizationally oriented and enterprise focused employment systems had much of a role for strong independent unionism. As a result, many observers concluded that the declining strength of unions in the USA and other advanced industrial economies was consistent with a new convergence to a world of employment relations where management gained unilateral authority either through advanced personnel practices and heightened sensitivity to the needs of the workforce, or through the exercise of brute market power.

Indeed some even argued that by the early 1990s international economic activity had become so interconnected that the conditions for persistent national differences in the organization of market economies, including the regulation of the labour market, had all but eroded (Ohmae 1990, 1995; Friedman 2005). In its extreme form, globalization theorists predicted a universal 'race to the bottom' in terms of wages and other labour standards across most economies and the erosion of nationally specific labour market regimes, including those which may provide for union security or encourage the pursuit of equity as well as efficiency (Tilly 1995).

Interestingly, and somewhat ironically, it is also possible to identify a convergence logic in the varieties of capitalism (VOC) approach that has become increasingly influential in comparative employment relations scholarship. Conceived as a counter to the overly simplistic arguments about globalization, Hall and Soskice (2001) reject the notion that there is one best way to organize capitalism and identify at least two institutional equilibria that resolve the coordination problems faced by market societies in an economically efficient manner: liberal market economies (LMEs), in which firms rely on markets and hierarchies to resolve coordination problems, and coordinated market economies (CMEs), in which firms are more likely to use non-market mechanisms to coordinate external and internal relationships.

Although some have interpreted the VOC approach as introducing an element of contingency into the comparative analysis of market economies, an alternative view is that the model replaces convergence on one model with a prediction of *dual convergence* in employment relations (Hay 2004). Central to Hall and Soskice's argument, and of particular significance for understanding the dual convergence logic of the VOC approach, is the concept of *institutional complementarities*. Hall and Soskice (2001: 18) argue that 'nations with a particular type of coordination in one sphere in the economy should tend to develop complementary practices in other spheres as well' (see also Amable 2003: 54–66). As Gospel and Pendleton (2005) have recently demonstrated, there appear to be close relationships between forms of firm financing and labour management practices. Hall and Gingerich (2004) provide evidence that not only is there a strong relationship between corporate governance arrangements and employment practices across countries, but also that levels of economic growth are closely associated with the extent to which corporate governance and employment practices are institutionally aligned.

The implication is that to compete successfully in the global economy, countries that have institutional arrangements that resemble those of CMEs need to pursue employment relations practices that are consistent with this institutional matrix to achieve the benefits of non-market coordination, while countries with institutional arrangements that resemble those liberal market economies, over time find it difficult to sustain employment relations practices that deviate from the short-term, market-based practices typical of LMEs. In CMEs, which are characterized by patient capital, insider forms of corporate governance, and production strategies based on exploiting firm-specific skills developed over long periods of time, and therefore labour-management practices that encourage long-term commitment and elicit worker contribution to decision-making and work design, are likely to be more common than those which reduce the relationship to short-run, market exchanges (Aoki 1988; Streeck 1987).

In LMEs, where there is a heavy reliance on equity markets for firm finance and outsider forms of corporate governance, the implication is that labour-management practices and production systems tend to be market-based and short-term in character and thus less likely to be able to sustain industrial relations practices that imply a long-term commitment by employers to employees. Lacking certainty in the long-term financial commitment of investors, and unwilling to provide employees with the commitment necessary to encourage investment in firm-specific human capital, the competitiveness of firms in LMEs is less likely to be based on the development of firm-specific assets and more likely to be derived from innovation and experimentation (Lehrer and Darbishire 1997).

In our view this prediction of 'dual convergence', in part, reflects the highly *determinist* model of social action that underpins the VOC approach as it was originally presented (Wailes 2007). As Crouch (2005: 1) notes:

> The main emphasis of the [VOC approach]...was that there was no single form of capitalism...But I was increasingly struck by the paradoxical determinism behind this ostensibly liberating message: There were two but only two viable forms of capitalism. Nation-states possessed one or the other of these, the institutions appropriate to which extended in a coherent way across a wide range of economic, political and social areas, determining their economic capacities over most products and types of production. And once a country had a particular set of such institutions, there was very little it could do to change it.

It is worth noting that, while the VOC approach may help explain differences in employment relations patterns across different types of market economies, it implies that the influence of the institutional context in which firms in a national economy operate is so strong that they will adopt the same set of employment relations practices irrespective of their market strategy, the industry in which they operate, and the production technologies they adopt (Morgan 2007; Lane and Wood 2009). As such it provides very little insight into the circumstances under which employment relations practices within national economies may become more diverse (a theme that we return to later in this chapter).

EMPLOYMENT SYSTEM DIVERGENCES RATHER THAN CONVERGENCES?

Despite various predictions of convergence much of the empirical research on employment practices from the 1970s on suggests that national patterns of employment relations were increasingly *diverging*. Following the Second World War there was a prolonged period of economic growth, normally referred to as the 'long boom'. As the long boom came to an end during the 1970s, development in the third world slowed, conflict between employers and employees began to increase and differences between market societies became more evident (Cammack 1997; Katzenstein 1978; Crouch and Pizzorno 1978). In an influential analysis, Goldthorpe (1984) identified the development of two distinct national patterns of employment relations during this period. Some countries, like Norway, Austria, Germany, and Sweden, he argued, attempted to increase economic growth and reduce inflation through *corporatist* policies that involved centralized negotiations between employers, unions, and, in some cases, the state. In countries like Britain and the USA, in contrast, the traditional labour market institutions (e.g. collective bargaining) were being undermined in an effort to eliminate perceived rigidities in the market. Goldthorpe argued that this was producing a *dualism* in employment relations in these countries with the workforce separated into core and peripheral employees. The former remained unionized and within the collective bargaining framework, albeit in a more decentralized mode, while the latter were employed under more individualistic work arrangements characterized by contractual forms of control.

In a similar vein, Freeman (1989) identifies evidence of divergent trends in union membership and density across developed market economies during the 1980s. He argues that 'far from converging to some modal type, trade unionism... traditionally the principal worker institution under capitalism developed remarkably differently among Western countries in the 1970s and 1980s' (Freeman 1989: 9). Since the 1980s union density increased or at least was maintained at high levels in the Scandinavian countries, but declined significantly in the UK, Australia, and the USA. This divergence in density occurred despite common factors such as increasing trade, technological transfer, and capital flows between countries, which might have been expected to exert pressures for similarities (see also Visser 1996).

Both these analyses draw attention to the potential role that national-level institutions play in producing cross-national diversity in employment relations systems. Since the early 1990s, there has been a growing body of literature that explicitly attributes diversity in employment relations policies and outcomes to institutions. As Locke and Thelen (1995: 338) put it, according to this view, 'international trends are not in fact translated into common pressures in all national economies but rather are mediated by national institutional arrangements and refracted into divergent struggles over particular national practices'. Because differences in national-level institutions are relatively enduring, this approach suggests that pressures associated with globalization are unlikely to lead to a general convergence in national patterns of employment relations (Locke et al. 1995). Rather, the institutionalist approach predicts continuity and even increased divergence between national patterns of employment relations.

Both Turner (1991) and Thelen (1991), for example, argue that the 'dual system' of industrial relations in Germany enabled German unions to withstand the pressures of globalization better than their counterparts in the USA and Sweden. Turner (1991) compares the involvement of unions in industrial restructuring in Germany and the USA and places heavy emphasis on the role that differences in institutional arrangements have played in determining the reaction of employers and workers to international economic pressures (Doellgast 2012). Similarly, Thelen (1991) argues that the German system, with national- and industry-level bargaining plus separate legally enriched rights for workers at the workplace level, allowed pressures for decentralized bargaining to be accommodated within the existing institutional configuration. In Sweden, by contrast, the absence of institutionalized rights for workers at the workplace, and the divisions created between blue-collar and white-collar workers by the centralized bargaining system, meant that pressures for decentralized bargaining could not be accommodated within the existing structure of bargaining.

The importance of differences in national-level institutions for explaining differences in patterns of employment relations is also emphasized by Ferner and Hyman (1998). In particular, they point to the re-emergence of 'societal corporatism' in some European economies during the 1990s as evidence that 'states possess a key role in the reconfiguration of the relations between social regulation and markets (including labour markets)' (Ferner and Hyman 1998: xxi). They also develop the notion that some forms of labour market institutions can adapt to international economic changes better than others. Similarly Traxler et al. (2001) show evidence of considerable diversity in employment relations across developed market economies and argue this is because 'market pressures affect labour relations institutions indirectly, in that they are processed and filtered by institutions' (2001: 289).

While institutions clearly play an important role in shaping how international economic pressures impact on national patterns of employment relations, in our view there are a number of limitations to this approach. First, there are common developments of 'process changes' in employment relations across countries that are often obscured by analyses that focus on institutions and emphasize difference. For example, since the mid-1980s there has been a noticeable decentralization of bargaining taking place in many countries.

This has generally involved the locus of bargaining shifting downwards from a national or industry level, to an enterprise or workplace level. However, the degree of decentralization and the means by which changes in bargaining structures occurred have varied between countries. Based on a comparison of experiences in six countries (Australia, Germany, Italy, Sweden, Britain, and the USA), Katz (1993) reports many similarities in the process of decentralization. In each country except Germany, there was a shift towards decentralization in the formal structure of bargaining initiated by employers, and a consequent reduction in the extent of multi-employer bargaining. With the exception of Australia (where there was an Accord between the unions and the then Labor government) most central union organizations opposed decentralization of bargaining.

Katz (1993) evaluates three hypotheses which have been suggested to explain the trend towards decentralized bargaining: first, shifts in bargaining power from unions to employers; second, the emergence of new forms of work organization which put a premium on flexibility and employee participation; and, third, the decentralization of corporate structures and diversification of worker preferences. Katz concludes that the second hypothesis is the most convincing on the grounds that certain groups of labour and management appear to have gained distinct advantages from the work restructuring which accompanied decentralization. However, shifts in bargaining power, as well as the diversification of corporate and worker interests are also important contributing factors to the decentralization process.

In a more recent study of 12 European countries Baccaro and Howell (2011) find that globalization has led to a reshaping of centralized bargaining, which in their view had been the lynchpin of the 'negotiated capitalism' characteristic of European social democracies. This reshaping of the functions associated with bargaining structures is, according to their research, occurring in a 'convergent direction'. Excessive focus on the institutional differences between these countries tends to obscure this more fundamental similarity in terms of the direction of change taking place and in the nature of the outcomes the different institutions are producing.

A second limitation of the institutionalist approach is that it assumes that while differences in national institutional arrangement produce differences across countries, within countries institutional effects are so strong that employment relations patterns are relatively homogeneous. Drawing on research examining the changes occurring in employment relations in Italy in the 1980s, Richard Locke (1992) noted that within-country diversity in employment relations has increased so much that it may no longer be meaningful to compare national employment systems. In analysing developments in automobile and telecommunications industries in seven advanced industrial economies Katz and Darbishire (2000) arrived at very similar conclusions. Their analysis identified four sets of employment patterns that were spreading across all of the cases that they looked at. These four patterns and their key features are summarized in Table 3.1.

In the low wage pattern, work practices give management considerable discretion and power, are typically applied informally, and have little or no role for unions. This pattern contrasts with the human resource management (HRM) pattern that is characterized by individualized reward and career development and a strong emphasis on corporate

Table 3.1 Growing patterns of workplace practices

Low wage	HRM	Japanese-oriented	Joint team-based
Managerial discretion with informal procedures	Corporate culture and extensive communication	Standardized procedures	Joint decision-making
Hierarchical work relations	Directed teams	Problem solving teams	Semi-autonomous work groups
Low wages with piece rates	Above average wages with contingent pay	High pay linked to seniority and performance appraisals	High pay with pay-for-knowledge
High turnover	Individualized career development	Employment stabilization	Career development
Strong anti-union animus	Union substitution	Enterprise unionism	Union and employee

Source: Katz and Darbishire (2000: 10).

culture. Katz and Darbishire note that while the HRM pattern as it developed in the USA was often non-union, there is evidence in other countries that this pattern can complement rather than replace traditional collective bargaining. The third and fourth work patterns that Katz and Darbishire identify, the Japanese-oriented and joint team-based patterns, differ mainly in regard to the extent to which jobs are standardized, teams have discretion, and the extent to which workers take on traditional supervision roles.

Their analysis showed that there were differences in the extent to which each of the four patterns were spreading across different countries and the implications of these different patterns for different groups of workers. They attributed these differences to institutional differences in the countries. Nonetheless, despite differences in the prevalence of these patterns, the analysis did demonstrate that there was evidence of each employment pattern in each of the countries that they looked at and that, as a result, increasing within-country diversity was common to all of the cases that they looked at across both manufacturing and service industries. In other words, Katz and Darbishire found evidence of *converging divergences* in employment relations across developing market economies.

CONVERGING DIVERGENCES AND INSTITUTIONAL PLASTICITY

We have reviewed arguments for convergence and divergence in the comparative employment relations literature and have argued that, rather than simple convergence or divergence, there is evidence of converging divergences, or increased within-country diversity across countries. In this section we explore the connection between the emerging concept of institutional plasticity in the comparative capitalism literature and converging divergences.

The growing prevalence of within-country diversity in employment patterns suggests the need for an alternative view of institutions to the one that has informed recent debates about convergence and divergence in employment relations. In particular we would argue that the assumption of homogeneity in intra-national patterns of employment relations reflects the dominance of what Hall and Taylor (1996) describe as the 'culturalist' view of institutions in much of the literature. The culturalist view suggests that existing institutional arrangements not only shape the range of options that social actors have, but also determine how they define their interests (Pontusson 1995). The implication is that if they are operating in the same institutional regime, social actors will pursue the same outcomes and hence, while there might be diversity between different national forms of capitalism, there is unlikely to be diversity within national forms of capitalism.

In a recent review of the comparative capitalism literature, Deeg and Jackson (2007: 157) suggest that

> important limits have been reached to the notion of national varieties of capitalism as institutionally complete, coherent and complementary sets of institutions, which achieve and maintain stable sets of characteristics. A growing wealth of empirical literature has shown national forms of capitalism to be more institutionally fragmented, internally diverse and display greater 'plasticity' with regard to the combinations of institutional forms and functions.

Importantly they note the emergence of an alternative view of institutions, one that treats institutions as less determinate of social action and recasts them as *resources* that social actors can use in pursuit of their interests. Put simply, this approach suggests that faced with a particular set of institutional constraints social actors may choose to accept the existing rules of the game, alter how these institutions function, go outside existing institutional patterns, or indeed replace existing institutional arrangements with others than more closely align with their interests (Streeck and Thelen 2005).

Drawing on the notion of institutional plasticity, Howell and Kolins Givan (2011) examine the process of institutional change in industrial relations in Britain, France, and Sweden over the past 25 years. They argue that while each of these countries experienced different patterns of institutional change, these changes produced broadly similar outcomes. While in Sweden existing institutions came to play very different roles, the UK witnessed the 'wholesale destruction and reconstruction of institutions'. Industrial relations in France on other hand have been characterized by the introduction of new sets of institutions and changes in the role played by existing institutions. Despite these differences in patterns of institutional change, Howell and Kolins Givan (2011: 250) conclude:

> the trajectory of industrial relations development has been broadly in the same direction: toward decentralized, individualized, firm-centered industrial relations institutions offering much greater flexibility, and autonomy in the determination of

pay and conditions at the firm level. That has not necessarily meant institutional convergence... but it does mean that different institutions have mutated so as to function in similar ways.

Recent research on Germany also provides evidence of the strength of convergent tendencies including the weakening of union power along with a growth of non-union and contingent employment practices in part spurred by increased outsourcing and corporate 'de-verticalization' (Doellgast 2012). There is also evidence of increased decentralization within German collective bargaining. At the same time, Doellgast's research reveals a continuing influence of German co-determination and related labour market institutions that are constraining, or at least modifying, employment practices and processes that in other countries operate in a more market-oriented manner and produce outcomes even more unfavourable to employees and unions than is taking place in Germany. A number of industry studies show similar converging trends while at the same time demonstrating a continuing critical role for national institutions, in other words convergent and divergent tendencies (Batt et al. 2009).

The concept of institutional plasticity helps explain not only patterns of institutional change in national economies, but also the emergence of diversity in national patterns of employment relations. Lane and Wood (2009) point to three sets of factors that are likely to result in increased national diversity. First they argue that the adoption of neo-liberalism and policies of deregulation, to the extent that erodes 'the power of unions... to uphold and defend employment and industrial relations norms... has further expanded the space for the adoption of diverse solutions, particularly in the realm of employment relations' (Lane and Wood 2009: 536). Second, they point to increasing firm internationalization as a source of increased diversity, both in terms of the experiences and practices they can draw on and in terms of the factors that shape their interests. Third, Lane and Wood argue that an uneven pace of change in institutional domains can result in increased diversity within national capitalisms. In particular they point to the differential effect that the transformation of German corporate governance has had on employment relations practices in that economy. While in some sectors of the economy changes in corporate governance have been associated with significant employer-led changes in employment relations practices and outcomes, in other sectors employers have been content to operate within the traditional institutional context (see for example Fiss and Zajac 2004).

Increasing diversity in patterns of employment relations within countries, in our view, reflects the complex interplay of interests and institutions in the context of significant changes in the international economy. These themes also emerge from Sato's (2007) discussion of increased organizational diversity in Japan since the late 1990s. She argues that in both financial and labour markets the layering of new institutional forms (new stock exchanges and temporary work) and the conversion of existing institutions (venture capital and the Shunto spring wage offensive) produced the conditions for increased organizational diversity as Japanese firms sought to respond to changing market conditions.

Multinational Corporations as Drivers of Within-Country Diversity

The preceding discussion suggests that comparative employment relations scholars need to be much more attentive to the potential sources of diversity that can exist within as well as between national economies. In this section we focus in more detail on one potentially important driver of within country diversity—multinational corporations (MNCs). Deeg and Jackson (2007) argue that national economies are becoming increasingly 'institutionally incomplete' by which they mean that the institutional constraints that shape social actors' behaviour do not necessarily emanate from within the confines of a particular national economy. They argue that the increasing size and significance of MNCs are one of the major drivers of this process of institutional incompleteness. As Morgan and Kristensen (2006) put it, to a significant extent MNCs act as a bridge across different institutional domains and are likely to introduce significant amounts of change.

Another strand of this literature suggests that the desire of MNCs to standardize employment relations practices across their operations is less a reflection of influence of the institutional context of their home country, and more closely related to their desire to reproduce work practices associated with firm-specific sources of competitive advantage. Thus, for example, in a study of human resources practices of US, German, and Japanese multinationals, Pudelko and Harzing (2008) found little evidence to suggest that these companies were seeking to reproduce distinctive sets of practices that reflect the traditions of their home country. Rather they found strong evidence that MNCs from the USA, Germany, and Japan were seeking to adopt broadly similar sets of human resources policies, which they describe as global best practice, and to limit the extent of localization of human resources practices across their operations.

Given the growing size, scale, and spread of MNCs, and the extent to which these firms attempt to reproduce similar employment relations practices across their global operations, MNCs can be viewed as a convergent force—driving out traditional local or country-specific practices (Hall and Wailes 2009). As MNCs regionalize or globally coordinate internally within a company, this also serves as a convergent pressure by standardizing practices and eliminating or at least reducing the frequency of local (within-country) or country-specific practices.

Nonetheless, the pressures for decentralization have led many corporations to shift area management or business unit structures to gain flexibility in industrial relations administration and in some cases, bargaining power advantages. Yet, globalization pressures are leading to potentially cross-cutting shifts in the internal operations of MNCs. A special dilemma for industrial relations managers in MNCs arises from the fact that culture, law, and institutions retain much of their international diversity at the same time that globalization has increased the premium on coordination and central control.

Cross-national differences in culture, law, and institutions have long created control and coordination problems for multinational firms. Traditionally, multinational firms responded to this problem by maintaining a high degree of local control (decentraliza-tion) in the internal direction of industrial relations (Kujawa 1980). Previous analysis of multinational firms generally showed that the administration of industrial relations was more decentralized than other management functions such as finance or marketing. Multinationals found that there were substantial benefits to be gained from the decentrali-zation of industrial relations. These benefits include the ability to respond flexibly to various kinds of diversity. By allowing local managers in each country to fashion industrial rela-tions policies, these managers create policies and procedures that fit with local conditions and events. Yet, there is accumulating evidence that shifts are underway in multinational corporate strategy and structure due to the pressures of globalization (Katz et al. 2008).

Although corporations might still prefer to keep the everyday conduct of collective bargaining localized, in order to better respond to local differences and avoid potentially uplifting employment condition comparisons, more extensive coordination of labour policies and work practices is emerging within multinational corporations. For exam-ple, so-called centres of excellence give MNCs the capability to take greater advantage of scale economies and more continuous operation of advanced process technologies. In this environment, labour disputes that in the past would have effects in only one coun-try now potentially affect a multinational corporation's regional or global 'supply chain'. This in turn is stimulating greater corporate concern for labour relations and human resources practices in regional production centres and is creating a push for regionaliza-tion in corporate labour relations and human resources activities, which in turn leads to convergent pressures on MNC work policies and practices.

Further pressure for greater corporate involvement in labour relations and stand-ardization comes from the fact that MNCs see advantage in the coordination of work reorganizations occurring around their global operations in order to take advantage of successful and innovative cases. The similarities in work restructuring concerning teams and participatory work systems and contingent pay practice or continuous operations stimulate the need for mechanisms through which MNCs can transfer information and learning across operating sites and national boundaries. These factors are leading to the formation of a new regional level of human resource management and greater corporate coordination and standardization of labour relations policies and practices in MNCs (Katz et al. 2008).

Other parts of the MNC human resources literature add an institutional perspective by providing evidence and theory as to why national institutions constrain the influ-ence and spread of MNC practices as MNCs find that they have to conform to national, or in some cases local, institutional constraints and/or pressures. So, instead of MNCs bringing standardization in workplace practices across countries, some of the literature suggests that it is MNCs that have to bend and modify their practices to fit institutional constraints and pressures rather than the other way around. One component of this lit-erature suggests that the intersection of MNC and country-specific institutions leads to 'hybridization'—organizational forms and practices that are blends between the home country practices of the MNC and the practices common in the country where the MNC is operating.

At the same time, studies of the employment relations practices of MNCs consistently reveal a strong country of origin effect. Ferner (1997) rejects the notion that this 'country of origin' effect stems primarily from cultural differences between countries and argues instead that the tendency of MNCs to diffuse key employment relations practices across their subsidiaries reflects the extent to which MNCs and their management are embedded in the institutional context of their home countries. Studies of US MNCs operating in Europe, for example, have shown the tendency of these firms to adopt highly centralized human resources policies with an emphasis on performance management, workplace diversity, and anti-unionism (e.g. see Ferner et al. 2001). Thus, while the transfer of employment relations practices across US MNCs is in part shaped by institutional arrangements in the host country and power relations between corporate headquarters and the subsidiary, they are also influenced by distinctive features of the US national business system, including the structure of capital markets and the dominant form of corporate governance (Clark and Almond 2006).

What are the implications of the growth of MNCs and some of the developments we have summarized here for the diversity of employment relations within and across countries? It is possible to draw three broad conclusions. First, the employment relations practices of MNCs are increasingly less likely to be influenced solely by the local institutional factors of the host countries in which they are operating. Second, while debate continues on whether the national business system of MNCs' country of origin or how they are structured or how they choose to compete are more important in shaping their approach to employment relations, it is reasonable to suggest that MNCs contribute significantly to within-country diversity in employment relations patterns. Indeed it would be interesting to examine in more detail whether the increases in diversity in employment relations are related to growth in the size and significance of MNC activity. Third, the extent to which employment relations diversity associated with MNCs is likely to continue to increase or diminish can be said to depend on (a) the extent to which MNCs from different countries remain distinct or converge on a model of best practice and (b) the extent to which different MNCs see firm-specific employment relations practices as part of their competitive advantage. Both these issues deserve more empirical attention.

Implications of the Recent Financial Crises for Employment Relations and Economic System Convergence

There are both short-term and long-term implications of the financial crises that have plagued advanced economies across the globe in recent years in terms of employment systems. As we clarify those implications, in this section we contrast potential convergent and divergent tendencies.

The financial crises led to sharp economic downturns in nearly all economies (China stands out as an important exception). The crisis first appeared in the USA with the bursting of the housing market bubble and the collapse of Lehman Brothers, AIG, and a number of other large financial services firms. The rapid spread of the crisis to other economies and the often common character of the crisis—a housing bubble and excessively leveraged banks—were themselves a convergent pressure. It could be argued that the increased role of highly leveraged, and often common, banks and other financial institutions across countries created interconnections between countries and their employment systems. Through a common and ever more global financial system, economic systems are thereby becoming more similar and more interconnected, whether national governments like it or not.

The recent crisis also clarified that financial and other economic events that start in one country now have ripple effects and perhaps even more importantly, move directly very quickly across countries and that this fast movement itself is producing convergent tendencies across countries. This convergence is, in turn, reducing the role of national-specific institutional factors. This transforms what first appeared as a common short-term problem, a common financial crisis, into a long-term issue, a common (convergent?) global economic system.

Another short-term consequence of the financial crises involved the policies adopted by firms in response to the economic crises. There is evidence that firms chose a particular, and seemingly common set of means to respond to the economic downturn, namely, a cost-cutting 'low road' approach that involved employee pay cuts, union concessions, lay-offs and other reductions in employment security, and greater use of non-regular and contingent employees. It could be argued, therefore, that the financial crisis accelerated or enhanced the race to the bottom that was already underway as a result of globalization, but importantly, accelerated the pace of the deterioration in employment conditions and standards.

At the same time, although there were many reports of specific firms adopting low road strategies, it is not clear that the low road was inevitable or even, in fact, what the distribution of firm strategies actually was. Given the logic of employment patterns discussed above, and the absence of evidence that a low road approach is in fact superior on economic performance grounds, it might have been just as sensible for firms to move 'upscale' in the face of the economic downturn and some, perhaps many, did so. A key future research question is identification of the distribution of various employment relations strategies within firms and across countries.

There is some evidence (and frequent claims) that Germany and other countries that would be classified by VOC adherents, as coordinated market economies, either recently faced less of a financial crisis or recovered better from whatever economic downturn they did face. The claim is that because Germany and other CMEs experienced a smaller role of highly leveraged banks and private equity, they thereby faced a less significant financial crisis as compared to the USA and other LMEs. In addition, there is some evidence that Germany experienced a smaller and shorter rise in unemployment as German firms made use of internal adjustments (such as training and reductions in work hours and work sharing) rather than external adjustments to cope with sales declines and economic slowdown. If so, then this lends some credence to the VOC framework, and also raises the possibility that a world of heightened financial speculation and volatility may give CMEs a new source of comparative economic advantage. The latter would raise the possibility of a new convergent pressure towards the CME economic system type. However, the pattern of converging divergences that is common across LME- and CME-type economies also suggests an uncoupling of key institutional dimensions of many national capitalisms. It may be that one of the consequences of the financial crisis is to undermine the possibility of complementarity between institutional domains in all forms of national capitalism required to achieve optimal economic performance.

The recent financial crisis also may illustrate a long-term acceleration in the pace of globalization leading some to conclude that globalization and the associated homogenizing effects are ever more inevitable. Along with this claim the crisis clearly illustrated that financial and other economic trends spread very quickly across national borders given the integrated way that financial markets increasingly operate and the increasing role of a common set of banks and other related financial institutions and actors. In that way, it could be argued that the crisis reveals the powerful convergent force of financial globalization and the rapid ongoing pace of financial and economic system integration. In the face of financial and economic system integration it is unlikely that meaningful differences in employment relation and employment practices could persist for long, leading in turn to convergence in employment systems. One could easily add these convergent tendencies to the race-to-the-bottom claims and end up with a rather gloomy forecast.

A very different long-term forecast follows if one concludes that the recent financial crisis illustrates the limits and unsustainable nature of deregulated and unbridled markets. This conclusion follows from the fact that it seems clear that one of the causes of the crisis was the prior relaxation of financial regulations, in the USA and other countries, often justified at the time by the claim that the market inherently can respond to any economic fluctuations and effectively be self-regulating. The contradictory evidence regarding the ability of financial markets to be self-regulating and stable generated by the crises lends credence to claims that institutions matter on positive grounds and should be strengthened on normative grounds to provide more favourable economic and social outcomes. This defence of economic institutions can, of course, be extended to institutions that operate in the labour market and in this way, one of the long-term effects of the financial crises might be the political and intellectual support it provides to those who believe that employment system-related institutions matter.

References

Amable, B. (2003). *The Diversity of Modern Capitalism*. Oxford and New York: Oxford University Press.

Aoki, M. (1988). *Information, Incentives and Bargaining in the Japanese Economy*. Cambridge: Cambridge University Press.

Aoki, M., Jackson, G., and Miyajima, H. (eds.) (2007). *Corporate Governance in Japan: Institutional Change and Organizational Diversity*. Oxford: Oxford University Press.

Babson, S. (1995). 'Whose Team? Lean Production at Mazda U.S.A.', in Babson (ed.), *Lean Work: Empowerment and Exploitation in the Global Auto Industry*. Detroit: Wayne State University Press, 235–46.

Baccaro, L. and Howell, C. (2011). 'A Common Neoliberal Trajectory: The Transformation of Industrial Relations in Advanced Capitalism', *Politics and Society*, 39(4): 521–63.

Batt, R., Holman, D., and Holtgrewe, U. (2009). 'An Introduction to the Globalization of Service Work: Comparative Institutional Perspectives on Call Centers', *Industrial and Labor Relations Review*, 62(4): 453–88.

Bell, D. (1960). *The End of Ideology: On the Exhaustion of Political Ideas in the Fifties*. New York: Free Press.

Berger, S. (1996). 'Introduction', in S. Berger and R. Dore (eds.), *National Diversity and Global Capitalism*. Ithaca, NY: Cornell University Press, 1–27.

Cammack, P. (1997). *Capitalism and Democracy in the Third World: The Doctrine for Political Development*. London: Leicester University Press.

Clark, I. and Almond, P. (2006). 'Overview of the US Business System', in P. Almond and A. Ferner (eds.), *American Multinationals in Europe: Managing Employment Relations Across National Borders*. Oxford and New York: Oxford University Press, 37–56.

Cochrane, J. L. (1976). 'Industrialism and Industrial Man in Retrospect: A Preliminary Analysis', in J. L. Stern and B. D. Dennis (eds.), *Proceedings of the Twenty-ninth Annual Winter Meetings, Industrial Relations Research Association Series*. Madison, WI: IRRA, 274–87.

Crouch, C. (2005). *Capitalist Diversity and Change: Recombinant Governance and Institutional Entrepreneurs*. Oxford and New York: Oxford University Press.

Crouch, C. and Pizzorno, A. (eds.) (1978). *The Resurgence of Class Conflict in Western Europe since 1968*. New York: Holmes & Meier.

Deeg, R. and Jackson, G. (2007). 'Towards a More Dynamic Theory of Capitalist Diversity', *Socio-Economic Review*, 5(1): 149–79.

Doellgast, V. (2012). *Disintegrating Democracy at Work*. Ithaca, NY: ILR Press.

Doeringer, P. B. (1981). 'Industrial Relations Research in International Perspective', in P. B. Doeringer, P. Gourevitch, P. Lange, and A. Martin (eds.), *Industrial Relations in International Perspective: Essays on Research and Policy*. London: Macmillan, 1–21.

Dore, R. (1973). *British Factory, Japanese Factory: The Origins of National Diversity in Industrial Relations*. London: Allen & Unwin.

—— (1992). 'Japan's Version of Managerial Capitalism', in T. A. Kochan and M. Useem (eds.), *Transforming Organizations*. Oxford and New York: Oxford University Press, 17–27.

Ferner, A. (1997). 'Country of Origin Effects and HRM in Multinational Companies', *Human Resource Management Journal*, 7(1): 19–37.

Ferner, A. and Hyman, R. (1998). 'Introduction: Towards European Industrial Relations?', in Ferner and Hyman (eds.), *Changing Industrial Relations in Europe*, 2nd edn. Oxford: Blackwell, xi–xxvi.

Ferner, A., Quintanilla, J., and Varul, M. (2001). 'Country of Origin Effects, Host Country Effects and the Management of HR in Multinationals: German Companies in Britain and Spain', *Journal of World Business*, 36(2): 107–27.

Fiss, P. and Zajac, E. (2004). 'The Diffusion of Ideas Over Contested Terrain: The (Non) Adoption of a Shareholder Value Orientation Among German Firms', *Administrative Science Quarterly*, 49(4): 501–34.

Freeman, R. B. (1989). *On the Divergence in Unionism among Developed Countries*. Discussion Paper No. 2817. Boston: National Bureau of Economic Research.

Friedman, T. (2005). *The World Is Flat*. New York: Farrar, Straus and Giroux.

Goldthorpe, J. H. (1984). 'The End of Convergence: Corporatist and Dualist Tendencies in Modern Western Societies', in Goldthorpe (ed.), *Order and Conflict in Contemporary Capitalism: Studies in the Political Economy of Western European Nations*. Oxford: Clarendon Press, 315–43.

Gospel, H. and Pendleton, A. (2005). 'Corporate Governance and Labour Management: An International Comparison', in H. Gospel and A. Pendleton (eds.), *Corporate Governance and Labour Management: An International Comparison*. Oxford and New York: Oxford University Press, 1–32.

Hall, P. A. and Gingerich, D. (2004). *Varieties of Capitalism and Institutional Complementarities in the Macro-Economy*. MPIfG Discussion Paper 04/5. Cologne: Max Plank Institute for the Study of Societies.

Hall, P. A. and Soskice, D. (eds.) (2001). *Varieties of Capitalism: The Institutional Foundations of Comparative Advantage*. Oxford and New York: Oxford University Press.

Hall, P. A. and Taylor, R. (1996). 'Political Science and the Three New Institutionalisms', *Political Studies*, 44: 936–57.

Hall, R. and Wailes, N. (2009). 'International and Comparative Human Resource Management', in A. Wilkinson, N. Bacon, T. Redman, and S. Snell (eds.), *The Sage Handbook of Human Resource Management*. London: Sage, 115–32.

Hammer, M. and Champy, J. (1993). *Re-engineering the Corporation: A Manifesto for Business Revolution*. New York: Harper Business.

Hay, C. (2004). 'Common Trajectories, Variable Paces, Divergent Outcomes? Models of European Capitalism Under Conditions of Complex Economic Interdependence', *Review of International Political Economy*, 11(2): 231–62.

Howell, C. and Kolins Givan, R. (2011). 'Rethinking Institutions and Institutional Change in European Industrial Relations', *British Journal of Industrial Relations*, 49(2): 231–55.

Jacoby, S. (2005). *The Embedded Corporation: Corporate Governance and Employment Relations in Japan and the United States*. Princeton: Princeton University Press.

Katz, H. C. (1993). 'The Decentralization of Collective Bargaining: A Literature Review and Comparative Analysis', *Industrial and Labor Relations Review*, 47(1): 1–22.

Katz, H. C. and Darbishire, O. (2000). *Converging Divergences: Worldwide Changes in Employment Systems*. Ithaca, NY: Cornell University Press.

Katz, H. C., Kochan, T. A., and Colvin, A. J. S. (2008). *An Introduction to Collective Bargaining and Industrial Relations*, 4th edn. New York: Irwin-McGraw Hill.

Katzenstein, P. (ed.) (1978). *Between Power and Plenty: Foreign Economic Policies of Advanced Industrial States*. Madison, WI: University of Wisconsin Press.

Kerr, C., Dunlop, J. T., Harbison, F. H., and Myers, C. A. (1960). *Industrialism and Industrial Man: The Problems of Labour and Management in Economic Growth*. London: Penguin.

Kochan, T. A., Lansbury, R. D., and MacDuffie, J. P. (eds.) (1997). *After Lean Production: Evolving Employment Practices in the World Auto Industry*. Ithaca, NY: Cornell University Press.

Krugman, P. (1996). *Pop Internationalism*. Cambridge, MA: MIT Press.

Kujawa, D. (1980). *The Labour Relations of United States Multinationals Abroad: Comparative and Prospective Views*. Geneva: International Institute of Labour Studies.

Lane, C. and Wood, G. (2009). 'Capitalist Diversity and Diversity within Capitalism', *Economy and Society*, 38(4): 531–51.

Lehrer, M. and Darbishire, O. (1997). *The Performance of Economic Institutions in a Dynamic Environment: Air Transport and Telecommunications in Germany and Britain.* Wissenschaftzentrum Berlin Discussion Paper FSI 97-301.

Locke, R. M. (1992). 'The Decline of the National Union in Italy: Lessons for Comparative Industrial Relations Theory', *Industrial and Labor Relations Review*, 45(2): 229–49.

Locke, R. M., Kochan, T. A., and Piore, M. (1995). *Employment Relations in a Changing World Economy.* Cambridge, MA: MIT Press.

Locke, R. and Thelen, K. (1995). 'Apples and Oranges Compared: Contextualized Comparisons and the Study of Comparative Politics', *Politics and Society*, 23(3): 337–67.

MacDuffie, J. P. (1995). 'Human Resource Bundles and Manufacturing Performance: Organizational Logic and Flexible Production Systems in the World Auto Industry', *Industrial and Labor Relations Review*, 48(2): 197–221.

Morgan, G. (2007). 'National Business Systems Research: Progress and Prospects', *Scandinavian Journal of Management*, 23(2): 127–45.

Morgan, G. and Kristensen, P. H. (2006). 'The Contested Space of Multinationals: Varieties of Institutionalism, Varieties of Capitalism', *Human Relations*, 59(11): 1467–90.

Ohmae, K. (1990). *The Borderless World: Power and Strategy in the Interlinked Economy.* New York: Harper Business.

—— (1995). *The End of the Nation State.* New York: Free Press.

Parker, M. and Slaughter, J. (1988). *Choosing Sides: Unions and the Team Concept.* Boston: South End Press.

Pontusson, J. (1995). 'From Comparative Public Policy to Political Economy: Putting Political Institutions in their Place and Taking Interests Seriously', *Comparative Political Studies*, 28(1): 117–48.

Pudelko, M. and Harzing, A.-W. (2008). 'The Golden Triangle for MNCs: Standardization towards Headquarters Practices, Standardization towards Global Best Practices and Localization', *Organizational Dynamics*, 37(4): 394–404.

Rostow, W. W. (1960). *The Stages of Economic Growth: A Non-Communist Manifesto.* Cambridge: Cambridge University Press.

Sako, M (2007) 'Organizational Diversity and Institutional Change: Evidence from Financial and Labor Markets in Japan' In M. Aoki, G. Jackson, and H. Miyajima (eds.), *Corporate Governance in Japan: Institutional Change and Organizational Diversity.* Oxford: Oxford University Press, 399–426.

Streeck, W. (1987). 'The Uncertainty of Management in the Management of Uncertainty: Employers, Labour Relations and Industrial Adjustments in the 1980s', *Work, Employment and Society*, 1(3): 281–308.

Streeck, W. and Thelen, K. (2005). 'Introduction: Institutional Change in Advanced Political Economies', in W. Streeck and K. Thelen (eds.), *Beyond Continuity: Institutional Change in Advanced Political Economies.* Oxford and New York: Oxford University Press, 1–39.

Thelen, K. A. (1991). *Labor Politics in Postwar Germany.* Ithaca, NY: Cornell University Press.

Tilly, C. (1995). 'Globalization Threatens Labor's Rights', *International Labor and Working-Class History*, 47: 1–23.

Traxler, F., Blaschke, S., and Kittel, B. (2001). *National Labour Relations in Internationalized Markets: A Comparative Study of Institutions, Change and Performance.* Oxford and New York: Oxford University Press.

Turner, L. (1991). *Democracy at Work: Changing World Markets and the Future of Labour Unions.* Ithaca, NY: Cornell University Press.

Visser, J. (1996). 'Interest Organizations and Industrial Relations in a Changing Europe', in J. Van Ruysseveldt and J. Visser (eds.), *Industrial Relations in Europe: Traditions and Transitions*. London: Sage, 1–41.

Wailes, N. (2007). 'Globalization, Varieties of Capitalism and Employment Relations in Retail Banking', *Bulletin of Comparative Labour Relations*, 64: 1–14.

Womack, J., Jones, D., and Roos, D. (1990). *The Machine that Changed the World*. New York: Rawson-Macmillan.

PART II

INSTITUTIONS AND EMPLOYMENT RELATIONS—ALTERNATIVE ACCOUNTS, NEW INSIGHTS

....

CHAPTER 4

GETTING DOWN TO BUSINESS

Varieties of Capitalism and Employment Relations

....

CATHIE JO MARTIN

INTRODUCTION

....

ACADEMIC writings on diverse types of capitalism are anchored by a seminal work, aptly entitled 'Varieties of Capitalism', edited by Peter Hall and David Soskice (2001). The editors' introduction constructs an elegant and parsimonious model of employers' strategic choices for economic production and social protections: these business choices are shaped by institutions regulating national political economies and, in turn, they determine the path for continuing economic development. This meditation on capitalism tends towards optimism, in suggesting that in some corners of the world (tiny though they may be) the ravages of capitalist competition can be held at bay. Our grasping, avaricious, barbaric selves can be conquered, won over by promises of peace and prosperity through coordination, and by joint efforts to secure collective goods. Although individuals might be tempted to defect from the mutually beneficial path, they are kept in line by the interconnected labour market institutions that shape the strategic choices of both employers and workers. Thus, institutions governing the employment contract are causally important to the differentiation of various capitalist forms.

The varieties of capitalism (VOC) model has been hugely influential and widely cited, yet its parsimony has also made it a target for criticism. One argument suggests that the model is a bit too muscular to allow for the extensive diversity of corporate strategy at the national, regional, sectoral, and firm levels. Indeed, the celebration of national industrial institutions feels suspect at a moment in which life seems so vulnerable to global financial flows and international crises. Another argument charges that the model underestimates the crucial impact of agency and the organization of labour and the state on the evolution of diverse political economies, as well as on employers' strategic preferences. Moreover, the model posits employers' strategic interests as evolving from static political-economic institutions, yet this stasis gives little insight into the dynamics of institutional change.

What, then, can this categorization of diverse forms of national capitalism teach us? Although the model certainly cannot account for the extensive diversity in the competitive and social strategies of individual firms, a more political and historically attuned investigation of comparative capitalism illuminates how national systems of industrial relations and concerns about skills delimit policy choices and shape socio-economic outcomes. Recent work in the VOC tradition recognizes the importance of accidents of history and the agency of other social actors and seeks to untangle the reciprocal impacts of political structures and modes of coordination on the evolution and reinvention of comparative capitalisms. For example, Martin and Swank (2004, 2008, 2012) investigate the political origins of diverse modes of regulation and the subsequent feedback effects of market competition or non-market coordination on employers' preferences, national policy outcomes, and institutional change.

This chapter reflects on the strengths, weaknesses, and trends in the study of capitalist varieties. First, I present a quick synopsis of the VOC model and its implications for the employment relationship. The second part of the chapter evaluates the criticism that the model fails to account for the extensive diversity within models and considers the other types of business institutions that matter at each level to the employment relationship. The third part of the chapter recognizes that labour and the state are undervalued in the original theory and suggests how the agency and organization of other social actors matters to the evolution of diverse political economies. Finally, I reflect on the implications for theories of institutional change.

VARIETIES OF CAPITALISM

The literature on 'varieties of capitalism' espouses the belief that the skills of a nation's workforce define the competitive strategies available to employers and that a defined set of political economic institutions create possibilities for diverse types of worker skills. The VOC literature sorts advanced, industrial nations roughly into two ideal types—coordinated market economies (CMEs) and liberal market economies (LMEs)—and suggests that the distinctive type of workforce skills found in each category drives both the strategic choices in economic production and the political preferences of business. CMEs tend to produce a blue-collar workforce with specific skills (which are largely relevant only to a single firm or industry and are produced through intensive vocational training programmes). In CME countries, skills formation is at the heart of the employment relationship; employers take a leadership role in advancing workforce development and engage in extensive negotiations with workers over this issue area. LME countries nurture workers with general skills (which are delivered through high schools and other general education programmes); here, apart from narrow in-house training efforts, employers largely leave skills development to formal education institutions and have little interaction with labour over skills. These skill formation processes are directly related to the competitive strategies of firms, to employers' preferences for welfare state services, and to the balance of power between business and labour. Employers in coordinated market economies compete in high-skill market niches and are motivated to enhance their competitive positions with institutional arrangements that encourage skills development and information exchange; therefore, they are willing to foster cooperative labour relations—avoiding lay-offs and strikes—in order to secure sufficient skills. Because firms in liberal market economies are more likely to use price competition, workers with lower skills, and market rather than non-market mechanisms for coordination, they are less conciliatory towards organized labour and less favourably disposed towards welfare state benefits (Hall and Soskice 2001; Whitley 1999; Hemerijck and Visser 1997; Huber and Stephens 2001).

These skills regimes are reinforced by complementarities among the institutions that give rise to diverse types of political economies, including industrial relations systems, vocational training systems, corporate governance regimes, organizations for inter-firm relations, and intra-firm practices (such as in human resources) for reconciling the diverse interests of management and labour. The deep linkages among these institutional structures mean that one cannot be altered independently of change in the other spheres (Hall and Soskice 2001). For example, alternative systems of social protection create different types of skills. Coordinated market economies with high levels of protection to secure employment (i.e. regulations to prevent lay-offs) and/or to ward off unemployment (i.e. benefits after termination of work) make workers more willing to invest in skills that are highly specific to their firms or industries. These investments in specific skills are risky, making workers vulnerable to lay-offs and market fluctuations; but high levels of social protection enable workers to take the gamble. In liberal market economies without high levels of social or employment protection, workers will choose instead to invest only in general skills that enable rapid retooling. Employers in countries with high levels of social protection, thereby, can more easily compete in market niches with high value-added products that rely on a highly skilled workforce (Estevez-Abe et al. 2001). Other types of social programmes also contribute to worker productivity: pensions help to ease older, less productive workers out of the labour force, and quality childcare and flexible family leave policies expand support for working women, curb absenteeism, and improve retention rates (Martin 1995, 2000; Ebbinghaus 2010; Immergut et al. 2007; Hassel 2007; Mares 2003).

The varieties of capitalism literature shares much with other meditations on comparative capitalist economies in recognizing that industrial development does not merely follow a natural evolutionary path grounded in economic structure. Thus, the French Regulation School importantly observes that economies are governed by overarching regimes of accumulation that allocate productive assets between consumption and accumulation. Modes of regulation are necessary to bring about the reproduction of these regimes: to guide capital investment, to allocate economic surplus between wages and profits, and to shape patterns of consumption (Lipietz 1987: 14; Jessop 2002). Streeck's (1992) crucial theory of 'diversified quality production' recognizes the important linkages between skills and competitive strategies, and traces the 'German model' to a distinctive set of institutions enabling high levels of coordination. Piore and Sabel (1984) offer penetrating insight into the problems of American manufacturing from a comparative perspective in their portrayal of Fordism versus flexible specialization. Ashton and Green (1996) perceptively recognize the complicated relationship between education, skills, and industrial performance: skill formation and the expansion of human capital do not automatically lead to higher levels of economic production; rather, the institutional context of the employment relationship pushes firms along a high skills versus low skills avenue of economic competition. Esping-Andersen's significant portrayal of three major welfare state regimes suggests that each has diverse implications for skills, economic competition, and class formation (Esping-Andersen 1990; see also Scharpf and Schmidt 2000). Recent fascinating work expands the theory beyond its initial focus on skills to the linkages between capitalist regimes and higher education systems (Ansell 2008; Jensen 2011; Busemeyer and Trampusch 2011b).

While Hall, Soskice, and their co-authors certainly gained much from these other explorations, the varieties of capitalism model has become a foundational work in comparative politics due to its elegance, parsimony, breadth, employer-centred theory of action, and preferential focus on the structural features of the political economy as determinants of cross-national variation. As often seems the case, however, the strengths of the work—its beauty and asceticism—have opened the door to criticisms. The model masks the enormous diversity of employment relations and strategic competition at the national, regional, sectoral, and firm levels. The original formulation of the model explains institutional stability more readily than institutional change and does not attempt to explain the historical evolution of comparative capitalisms. It neglects the agency and institutions of the state and labour. Institutional change should be viewed as a contested process and actors experiment with diverse forms of institutional complementarities (see also Deeg and Jackson 2007; Lane and Wood 2009, 2011).

BALANCING PARSIMONY AND DIVERSITY

This highly stylized rendition of coordinated and liberal economies offers insights into the important links between social protections and skills, yet it tends to overestimate the homogeneity of models, nations, industries, or even firms. This section considers some of the institutional determinants of diversity that are overlooked by the varieties of capitalism model. Thus I consider varieties of coordination at the national level, varieties of regional and sectoral production, and varieties of employment relations and management strategies within firms.

First, each of the two distinctive varieties of capitalism encompasses countries that appear profoundly different at the national level on various dimensions: France,

Germany, and Sweden, for example, have very diverse types and levels of labour organization. Thus, in a survey of human resources (HR) practices in 22 countries, Goergen (2007) finds that CMEs vary dramatically in their approaches to vocational training and workplace development, and that these differences do not seem much affected by the constraints imposed by other institutions defining the varieties of capitalism. Moreover, countries with high levels of employment security look very different from those with few employment regulations; yet the CME model encompasses both.

Amable (2003; see also Schmidt 2002) tries to make sense of the within-model differences by reflecting on how institutions interact in different countries. Thus he agrees with Hall and Soskice that institutional complementarities position models on distinctive paths, but suggests that diverse types of complementarities are characteristic of five ideal types of capitalism—the social democratic, continental, Mediterranean, Asian, and liberal models. Institutional change can and does happen in his model, but it is likely to happen in realms in which the hegemonic political coalitions have the most limited vested interests in preserving the status quo. In this way, Amable seeks to introduce greater dynamism and politics into the notion of institutional complementarities.

Martin and Swank (2012) and Martin and Thelen (2007) explore variations in modes of coordination, and suggest that particularly sharp differences separate the national, state-led coordinating institutions of Scandinavia and the essentially private, sectoral-led types of coordination found in Christian democratic countries. The VOC literature recognizes crucial differences in the liberal and coordinated ideal types, which operate according to wholly different logics relying on market competition versus non-market coordination; however, this distinction misses the crucial differences in the *level* and *form* of coordination. Drawing on the older literature on corporatism, we suggest that the coordinated market economy model encompasses several types of cooperation that do not necessarily appear in all countries, and suggest three systems of employer organization and associated patterns of coordination.

Macrocorporatist coordination constitutes the sustained interaction between densely organized, nationally centralized labour unions, employers' associations, and the state through national collective bargaining and tripartite policy-making forums to produce social and labour market policies. Peak employers' associations and unions are highly centralized (with a high level of power by peak federations over members), highly coordinated among collective bargaining units, and highly integrated in national policy forums. National macrocorporatist coordination carries out the processes of coordination through broader and more encompassing networks and associations, usually with high levels of involvement by the state, and complements the economic logic of individual firms by binding them into a more macro-societal perspective. With coordination led by the state, the social partners often focus on broad collective concerns and make deals about broad aspects of the employment relationship that have an impact on workers well beyond the employment contract. Thus, the social partners may negotiate the contours of the public childcare system, arrive at uniform rules about part-time work that apply equally to the public and private sectors, or negotiate programmatic solutions for coping with the long-term unemployed and others largely outside of the employment contract.

Sectoral and/or regional coordination (also called 'meso-corporatism') predominantly entails cooperation between firms and/or workers at a more intermediate level and may include cooperation across enterprises that is less national in focus and that evolves without sustained state participation (Hicks and Kenworthy 1998). Sectoral coordination includes tightly coordinated connections among firms and investors, cooperation among competing firms within the same industrial sector for training or for research and development, long-term relations between purchasers and suppliers, and enterprise-based labour–management cooperation. Sectoral coordination is more disorganized than macrocorporatism, as it happens through cooperative relations between economic actors in smaller corners of the economy, and may operate according to a relatively narrow microeconomic logic. Moreover, the content of cooperation is more likely to be restricted to the labour market needs of the workers within the sector rather than of the broader citizenry. Thus, whereas macrocorporatist or state-led coordination cooperation occurs through collective bargaining and formal tripartite channels for interest intermediation in the policy-making process, sectoral coordination constitutes the cooperation among private firms and/or their unions, suppliers, purchasers, etc.

One even finds some cooperation under 'pluralism', in the strategies of some individual firms' to cooperate with and attract labour with company social policies, works councils, and shopfloor production teams. Yet these 'segmentalist' strategies are seldom found above the firm level, employers remain very divided in their political representation, and market-based coordination of economic production is pervasive. Thus, what we often think of as 'coordinated capitalism' may be either organized by the state at the national level or a bit more disorganized in transpiring between largely private, sectoral groups, and the two dimensions of interaction that we usually associate as being together—coordination and organization—can, in fact, appear separately (Martin and Thelen 2007; Martin and Swank 2012; Höpner 2006; Hicks and Kenworthy 1998; Palier and Thelen 2010).

The coordinated market economy model also encompasses rather diverse types of vocational training systems. Countries differ with respect to the types of portable specific skills produced; for example, while German workers gain firm-specific skills, Danish ones gain specific skills that can be carried to other firms within the industry (Estevez-Abe et al. 2001). Countries relying on a dual vocational training model differ in the relative importance of firm-based apprenticeships and school-based instruction: thus while the firm apprenticeships are of primary importance to the training of skilled workers in the German system, dual-system countries such as Denmark and Austria have relied relatively more on school-based instruction (Greinert 2005; Busemeyer and Trampusch 2011a). Countries differ according to how firms, associations, and the state allocate the tasks of educating workers (Busemeyer and Trampusch 2011a) and on the oversight mechanisms for reconciling the school- and work-based apprenticeship training: for specifying the content of educational instruction in both realms and for making adjustments in response to broad changes in the political economy.

To some extent, the type of coordinating associations, discussed above, shaped the early political struggles over key decisions about vocational training systems. Encompassing associations in macrocorporatist countries were more successful than those in countries with sectoral coordination in helping employers to overcome their sectoral divisions, to engage in associational oversight of the content of skills training in both apprenticeships and school-based instruction, and to produce industry-specific, portable skills. In countries with highly coordinated macrocorporatist employers' associations, the social partners were given a crucial role in the oversight and credentialling of vocational training comparatively early, while in collectivist countries with sectoral coordination, individual firms or industry-level bodies retained greater control. Macrocorporatist countries—in comparison to ones with sectoral coordination—were more likely to retain a role for the state through social partnerships with business and labour, to rely to a greater extent on school-based training, and to create industry-level rather than firm-level specific skills. Employers in countries with national encompassing associations were also more willing to tolerate high levels of spending on vocational training, because they had significant input into the process and trusted that policy outcomes would satisfy their business needs (Martin 2011).

A second flaw in the notion of institutionally coherent varieties of capitalism models consists of the significant economic disparities at the sectoral and regional levels. For example, the model underestimates the importance of specific skills to some firms in liberal countries; indeed, industrial relations in the United States exhibit strong tendencies towards dualism rather than encompass a singular strategy of economic competition (Deeg and Jackson 2007; Morgan 2007; Whitley 2005; Herrigel 1996; Martin 1995, 2000; Ackers and Wilkinson 2003). Sub-national institutional domains may be quite varied, reflecting alternative, historically specific economic orders, uneven impacts of regulation, or incompletely implemented institutional projects; thus, national internal diversity also constitutes grounds for intra-model permutations. Sometimes, alternative patterns of economic competition and organizational development are wholly unexpected, given our preconceived notions of each type of capitalist model (Lane and Wood 2009; Schneiberg 2007). For example, the Grange, a prominent agricultural organization, led an anti-corporate social movement against the dominant mode of industrial production in the nineteenth century; ultimately, this struggle resulted in an important role for dairy cooperatives in the American economy (Schneiberg et al. 2008).

A third source of diversity within VOC models is provided at the level of individual firms: companies cultivate unique profiles of economic competition and political participation, and these vary enormously within nations and even within sectors. Firms have multiple goals and may choose from a range of preferences, especially because decision-making occurs under conditions of bounded rationality; therefore, companies with similar industrial structures often take divergent positions on public policy both cross-nationally and even within countries. Companies' constructed preferences may reflect their position within broader social networks (Fligstein 1990; DiMaggio and

Powell 1991; Mizruchi 1992; Fioretos 2011). But the strategic competitive and political postures assumed by firms may also reflect unique path dependencies arising from a company's historical development (Penrose 1959; Jacoby 1998; Jones 2005; Allen 2004; Brewster et al. 2006). Firm-centric views of employer preference hold a profoundly different conception of the primary causal agent for cooperation from views that emphasize distinctive national systems of economic coordination: patterns of cooperation, according to the firm-centric view, emerge from the distinctive constellations of the participating firms' historical legacies and capacities (Morgan 2005).

Political and economic strategies of individual firms may also reflect their own internal organizational capacities for gathering information and deliberating about public policy. Companies with in-house public policy experts have different preferences from those firms lacking the internal capabilities for evaluating public policy, because policy experts within the firm share both language and perspective with policy analysts in government, labour, and academic sectors. These corporate technocrats expose their colleagues to technical arguments, when they bring ideas from the external community of policy-makers back to others within the firms, a process referred to as 'boundary spanning' (DiMaggio and Powell 1991; Dobbin 2004; Martin 1995, 2000). For example, while government affairs departments were developed, in part, to fight the new social legislation of the 1970s, these departments later became primary locations for intercourse with government. In a randomly selected sample of large US firms, the presence of a government affairs office significantly expanded a company's support for national health reform during the Clinton administration (Martin 1995, 2000).

Yet, while firm-level institutions are crucial to the evolution of firms' strategic choices and preferences, it would appear that these institutions may also co-vary with diverse types of capitalism. For example, in a study of 107 randomly selected companies in Denmark and Great Britain, the presence of a large human resources department was a significant determinant of a firm's participation in active labour market programmes in Britain but not in Denmark. Alternatively, Danish companies were significantly more likely to participate when they belonged to a corporatist employers' association, whereas this was not the case in Britain. Qualitative interview data confirmed that the British firms were more likely to identify their own internal HR department as their most significant source of information about the programmes, while Danish firms learned from their associations (Martin and Swank 2012). This suggests that firms are brought to participate through different processes across systems and perhaps explains why British and American scholars have increasingly turned to firm-level institutional factors to explain firm preference, while scholars of Europe have paid greater attention to national political institutions.

Fourth, the firm-centric perspective takes on added weight as national economies increasingly come to be dominated by large multinational concerns. Multinationals operating in several countries may choose from multiple institutional models and strategies for employment relations. Globalization also accelerates institutional change. Thus, whereas the global economy can be traced back centuries, there has been significantly more institution building at the multinational level in recent years. This proliferation of transnational rules, structures, and standardization also may influence firms' competitive environments and strategic choices (Morgan 2005; Djelic and Quack 2003; Hancké et al. 2007; Sorge 2005). For example, shifting patterns of corporate governance have made for higher levels of internal diversity within national models of capitalism in Europe, as a small but important number of large firms have embraced international practices in firm financing. Thus while many companies continue to adhere to traditional practices specific to their countries, the internationalization of these key firms is creating a new source of internal diversity (Deeg 2009).

Finally, countries exhibit diversity across time. Recent writings in business history, institutional sociology, and comparative political economy suggest shifts between periods of liberalism and coordination within the historical experience of many countries. Considerable economic coordination existed even within now-liberal countries during the nineteenth century and these periods of coordination created legacies that persisted long after the hegemonic turn towards liberalism (Wiebe 1967; Schneiberg 2007). Berk (2009) draws a sharp line between nineteenth-century small-scale capitalism and twentieth-century large-scale capitalism, in his fascinating intellectual history of Brandeis's vision of the American political economy. An alternative competitive strategy, 'regulated competition', coexisted alongside neo-liberal market competition, built on the legacies of the nineteenth-century and republican anti-monopolist ideology, and espoused increasing efficiency and profits without increasing economies of scale. The German political economy and institutions for coordination have also varied tremendously across epochs. To grasp fully the ongoing revisions of the German model, one must explore the specific historical context at critical junctures, emergent political coalitions that capture and convert older forms for shifting purposes, and the evolution of German managerial control. After the cartel movement produced high levels of concentration in some parts of German industry, firms in the monopoly capital sector became less interested in a statist-welfare solution than employers in less concentrated sectors and even than their British counterparts. Indeed, looking at Germany before the First World War, one would hardly have predicted that the country would emerge as a poster-child for corporatist coordination (Fear 2005; Herrigel 1996; see also Fellman et al. 2008 on Scandinavia).

THE STATE AND SOCIAL PARTNERS IN CAPITALISM AND PUBLIC POLICY

Another core criticism of VOC theory is its relative neglect of labour and the state in the workings of diverse political economies. Whereas VOC self-consciously placed employers' strategic choices at the centre of the theory, these choices are embedded in a broader political context; consequently, one must include other social actors to grasp fully the dynamics embedded in a nation's characteristic processes of collective political engagement.

An initial critique is that the VOC model pays insufficient attention to the importance of organized labour in negotiating the terms of the employment relationship. The model presupposes that employers in coordinated market economies favour social programmes that enhance skills, labour market stability, and productivity. To its credit, the model shows how firms' attitudes towards social investment influence both workers' decisions to invest in firm-specific skills, and company patterns of skills attainment (i.e. whether firms get skilled workers through labour poaching, internal skills training, or contributions to external skill-building institutions) (Mares 2003). But scholars criticize the theory for making a less significant contribution to the evolution of national welfare state policies, with claims that specific programmes are often forced upon business and that labour unions take the lead in many welfare state initiatives (Paster 2011; Emmenegger and Marx 2011; Stephens 1980; Schrank 2009). Because welfare states alter the balance of power between capital and labour, countries with a high degree of union organization and a longer tenure of working-class participation in government through social democratic party control should produce a larger commitment of national resources to social spending. Social democratic governments have championed high levels of universally available social services and long-term party control enables these governments to take action without business interference (Korpi 2006; Stephens 1980; Huber and Stephens 2001; Swank 2002).

Unfortunately, debates over the relative contributions of business and labour power to welfare state development sometimes become polarized; yet higher levels of labour organization and social democratic party control need not rule out complementary support from employers. The development of institutions for coordinating employers and labour has often been closely connected, with both spheres shaping the motivations and actions of the other. Both organized business and organized labour can pursue several different types of interests. Hyman (2001) perceptively tells us that unions may potentially be promoters of their members' economic interests, social partners in the development of public policy, and agents for class struggle. These functions are combined in diverse ways across time and space.

A more serious criticism, perhaps, is that the theory neglects the profound influence of the structures and agency of the state on firms' preferences for social benefits and regulation, on processes of institutional change, and on the origins of diverse capitalist forms. This initial gap has been remedied, to some extent, by recent work on the role of partisan politics in bolstering forms of coordination and the role of the state in the evolution of political economic institutions.

On complementarities between party politics and forms of coordination, Cusack et al. (2007) suggest that both proportional representation (PR) electoral rules and coordinated market economies encourage long-term investments in highly specific skills. Employers in countries with a tradition of strong guilds became highly organized to sustain the high level of workforce skills inherited from pre-industrial days, and sought the evolution of PR electoral arrangements as a way to defend their minority interests against the centre-left. Parties in PR systems came to represent well-organized economic interests, did not poach voters from other parties, and participated in coalition governments; therefore, they were less inclined to focus solely on short-term electoral interests and were better positioned to work towards longer-term goals and to urge capitalists to do the same (see also Swank 2002). Thus, both high levels of coordination and PR party systems fostered the evolution of high-skills equilibrium economies, because both economic and state actors had incentives to pursue their long-term interests.

On the impact of state structures and agency in the evolution of political economic institutions, Duane Swank and I (2008, 2012) suggest that the structure of political competition mattered deeply to the consolidation of national forms of coordination in its significant impact on the formation of peak employers' associations. We agree that party and industrial relations systems have strong complementarities (Martin and Swank 2008); however, we see national economic models as much less formed at the end of the nineteenth century, as many countries had regional pockets of coordination. The emergence of strong national systems of labour market coordination only occurred with the development of highly centralized encompassing employers' and labour associations. This evolution of strong associations did not arise naturally from pre-industrial legacies of coordination (for example, from guilds) but was an artefact of political struggle and leadership by state agents.

At the end of the nineteenth century, employers and their government supporters across the Western world shared an interest in industrial development policies and struggled in parallel fashion to develop highly coordinated forms of business peak associations to push their industrial policy agenda. National employers' associations were (in fact and often secretly) created at the behest of right party leaders because politicians sought business aid in struggles over industrialization; therefore, the early trajectories for national business organization were deeply influenced by the structure of party competition. Employers became more strongly organized in countries with multiparty systems than they did in those with two-party systems, and centralized governments tended to produce more highly organized employers' associations than did federal governments. While skills and other legacies from pre-industrial and early industrial production had an impact on associational development, agency, contingency, and political struggle over industrialization contributed mightily to the emergence of social institutions and to their subsequent impact on the political economy.

The characteristics of party systems shape employer organization, because multiparty systems are more likely to include most employers in a single party, to inspire cooperation among social actors, and to delegate policy-making power to associations of social actors. Parties largely inclusive of employers inspire coordination because they focus attention on common goals among their business constituents, do not compete for the median voter, and make credible promises that enhance members' trust in government. Most importantly, leaders of business parties at the end of the nineteenth century had an incentive to delegate policy-making authority to private channels, because faced with expanding democratization, they recognized that they were unlikely to win electoral majorities and their constituents may well secure more favourable policy outcomes in direct negotiations with workers than through parliamentary processes. In two-party systems, employers are often dispersed between parties and employers trust the state and government regulation less; party leaders are less willing to delegate policy-making authority to private actors because they have hopes of winning outright electoral victories (Martin and Swank 2008, 2012).

Centralization of government matters because federal party systems tend to vary across regions and to be less ideologically consistent; employers organize to intervene at lower levels of government and exhibit regional diversity. A centralized party system is more likely to produce political cleavages divided along class lines, while a federal party system is more likely to divide the electorate along regional or ethnic lines. Thus, centralized, multiparty systems tend to produce highly coordinated macrocorporatist associations with a high level of state involvement. Federal, multiparty systems tend to produce corporatist employers' organizations with high levels of coordination but without significant involvement of the state. Federal, two-party systems tend to produce pluralist employers' associations and competitive strategies that largely rely on market competition (Martin and Swank 2008, 2012).

These structures did not *determine* the outcomes, but rather set the boundaries of contestation and, in this way, influenced the incentives of both politicians and managers. This was decidedly not a functionalist process: while both party leaders and social partners sometimes took measures to achieve policy ends, they almost always acted to maximize their power and control. Thus, these models evolved less because party leaders and employers pursued functional solutions to their needs for certain types of skills than for political reasons, although the positive impacts of these political economic arrangements became more apparent with time.

MODELS OF COORDINATION AT MOMENTS OF CHANGE

Finally, the varieties of capitalism approach is criticized for being too rigid and muscular to account for significant institutional change. According to the model, complementarities among institutions for labour market coordination are an essential ingredient, as these restrain erosion of the distinctive models, sustain business commitment to the chosen path, and bolster resistance to exogenous shocks. Thus, the vocational training systems that produce highly skilled workers in CMEs could not exist without consensual industrial relations, and change in one institution would have a negative impact on the other (Hall and Soskice 2001; Berger and Dore 1996; Whitley 1999; Swank 2002). Yet critics remain uneasy about the concept of institutional complementarities: they point to various possibilities for institutional integration, which permit the diversity of experience within models, and view institutions as potential resources for (rather than as absolute determinants of) strategic action. All complementarities are not created equal and the particular rule-making processes that govern institutional reform are, in a sense, more important than the institutional impacts (Morgan 2005; Deeg and Jackson 2007).

In particular, questions abound about the current capacity of labour market coordination to resist the disorienting impacts of deindustrialization, global financial crisis, and neo-liberal rants. While defenders of VOC theory see persistence, critics note an erosion of coordination and drift towards 'liberalization' among coordinated countries in response to the pressures of deindustrialization and globalization (Hall and Gingerich 2009; Pontusson 1997; Howell 2003). Thus, Campbell and Pedersen (2007) identify a hybridization of models, as countries struggle to adjust to threats such as deindustrialization and globalization. Undoubtedly, the model's theoretical difficulties in accounting for institutional change contribute to the lack of consensus about what has been happening to diverse types of capitalism.

To some extent, questions about the persistence of non-market coordination can be rather simply answered with better specified *categories of countries*; yet better categories tell us little about *processes* of institutional change unless we also explore countries' capacities to rework their modes of coordination in response to shifting exogenous threats or endogenous erosion. To understand why some countries can make adjustments more easily than others, we must consider the processes of political engagement that are associated with diverse types of national models. Within the VOC's list of interlocking institutions that govern the political economy, the institutions that bring actors together in collective negotiation will be those that are most essential to processes of institutional change. Institutions governing industrial relations and inter-firm relations are—together with political parties—the core mechanisms by which citizens and major social groups come together to solve new policy problems. Thus, the political economic institutions for coordination may be more significant as a venue for processes for collective political engagement than as a source of specific labour market and competitive practices and strategies (Martin and Swank 2012).

Processes for collective political engagement play an essential role in both abrupt and gradual institutional change. The dominant theories of institutional change fall into two categories: punctuated equilibria models and slow processes of incremental institutional change. First, scholars of institutional change utilizing punctuated equilibria models suggest that the resolution of political conflicts at critical junctures creates enduring path dependencies and analyse the specific political issues and agency at the points of institutional and policy creation. Moments of economic and political upheaval permit a broad repertoire of response and outcomes are often unpredictable. Yet choices taken at critical junctures establish paths with increasing returns and the path dependencies clearly lay down a track for future policy incarnations (Capoccia and Ziblatt 2010).

A second theory of institutional change focuses on the incremental shifts responding to endogenous decay: new coalitions of actors arise to seize control of institutions with new priorities and new purposes; and institutions adjust through an erosion of their initial functions, conversion to new purposes, and layering of new goals on the prior ones (Streeck and Thelen 2005). Thelen (2004) describes a process of incremental institutional change in her treatment of the historical development of vocational training systems. For Thelen, pre-industrial patterns of collectivism (and most importantly, the presence of guilds) led employers and workers in some countries to engage in non-wage competition and reinforced the linkages between high-skilled and low-skilled workers. Government leaders accorded privileges to the handicraft sectors (with close links to the former guilds) because they wished to restrain the power of other social actors, but over time labour was able to gain control of skill-building institutions and convert these to new, egalitarian purposes. In comparison, craft unions in other countries were more likely to limit the provision of skills than industrial unions; consequently, employers in countries with craft unions scaled back their reliance on skilled labour and developed more confrontational relations with unions (Thelen 2004).

Both types of institutional change have great merit, yet variations in the collective processes of political engagement have an impact on each type of change process—in shaping the manner in which policy legacies are reinterpreted at critical junctures and delimiting the range of political coalitions that might contribute to incremental institutional change. Certainly, agency at critical junctures establishes new paths and new political coalitions capture existing institutions for their own political purposes, yet political structures of engagement constrain strategic action. Countries have characteristic ways of solving social and economic problems, and these reflect the ways that social actors come together with government actors to negotiate new policies. These rules of political engagement also exert a strong influence on institutional adaptation.

The VOC literature pays more attention to the material incentives created by complementary political economic institutions than to the processes by which economic actors rework these institutions in response to shifting threats and needs. But the antecedent work on macrocorporatism—from which the VOC literature draws—offers some insights into comparative processes of collective political engagement (Streeck 1992; Crouch 1993; Katzenstein 1985). Countries with national, state-led macrocorporatist coordination have greater resources for resisting the erosion of non-market coordination than countries that rely on sub-national sector coordination that often transpires beyond the purview of the state due to political economic, collective action, and cognitive effects. In terms of the *political economic effects*, centralized collective bargaining produces wage compression, which motivates employers to eliminate low-skilled jobs and to support social programmes that motivate investments in skills. Macrocorporatist coordination has *collective action effects*, because powerful peak associations may bind firms to negotiated decisions and bring members to trust that they will not be punished for commitment to longer-term goals. When the provision of skills is left up to private firms, only some employers will perform this task (as free-riding companies may poach trained employees). High levels of labour market coordination have *cognitive* effects in educating their members about the benefits of social policies, focusing on broad shared concerns and, thereby, shaping preferences. Finally, while in pluralist systems, social partners provide input primarily through the legislative process, employers are more likely in corporatist settings to influence policies through collective bargaining or tripartite advisory commissions, and these iterative patterns of interaction create a positive-sum game for all participants. In comparison, pluralist systems of interest representation have fragmented, decentralized, and competing groups, limited collective bargaining and wage compression, minimal capacities for collective action, and less favourable views by employers of social programmes (Martin and Swank 2012; Katzenstein 1985; Streeck 1992; Crouch 1993; Hemerijck and Visser 1997; Wallerstein and Golden 1997; Martin 2000; Traxler 2000; Huber and Stephens 2001; Anthonsen and Lindvall 2009).

Processes of collective political engagement tell us much about how countries are responding to the challenges of post-industrial manufacturing and the global economic crisis. Faced with globalization and the transition to a post-industrial economy in the late twentieth century, a wide range of countries considered very similar neo-liberal policy prescriptions to reduce employment and unemployment protections that threatened to erode consensual employee relations. Yet some (largely social democratic) countries sustained high levels of coordination, relative equality, and economic growth, even while changing their public policies to adjust to the new economic era; another (largely liberal) group significantly scaled back the welfare state. A third (largely Christian democratic) group of countries sustained labour market cooperation in some core sectors but reduced social investments in economically marginal actors.

Empirical evidence confirms that countries with macrocorporatist coordination and centralized peak business and labour organizations have been better able to resist the penetration of neo-liberal ideas, market inequality, and dualism than countries with sector coordination or with pluralist organization of the labour market partners. Duane Swank and I use cross-national, quantitative analyses to document the positive impact of employer organization and macrocorporatism on direct fiscal redistribution by the state, wage equality, and features of labour market dualism such as irregular employment. We also find clear evidence that coordination, for all its importance in maintaining solidaristic policies and outcomes, does not impede economic growth (Martin and Swank 2012).

High levels of macrocorporatist coordination ease government policy entrepreneurs' efforts to fold employers into solidaristic political coalitions to address the needs of low-skilled workers, because these associations bring managers to participate in forums joining diverse sectors in discussions about the potential labour market contributions of low-skilled workers. Thus, politicians in macrocorporatist countries can entice employers into political coalitions to adopt policies that minimize negative impacts on marginal groups—even labour market actors in the Danish export sector have participated in efforts to skill and employ marginal workers—and this sustains higher levels of equality, employment, and economic growth. Countries with large and capacious public sectors, somewhat surprisingly, sustained higher levels of labour market coordination, as large public sectors create higher levels of employment, tend to provide more vocational training, and move welfare recipients back into the workforce (thus diminishing distributional conflicts between skilled and unskilled labour). Moreover, private employers and workers become more willing to cooperate to preserve their jurisdiction against the intrusion of a large state: they are loath to lose their own policy-making authority, and tend to participate in these state campaigns to stay in charge. In this vein, a representative of a Danish peak association told me that 'business and labour are like Siamese twins' in seeking to preserve their jurisdictional authority against the state. Countries with sectoral coordination have less luck in rallying business to the aid of marginal workers and in maintaining relative equality; for example, employers and workers in the German export sector agreed to political strategies that largely shunted ageing and low-skilled workers into the unemployment system (Martin and Thelen 2007).

Finally, more coordinated countries have largely maintained higher levels of social solidarity and responded more robustly in the wake of the global financial crisis. Although the financial crisis has had a quite powerful negative impact on economic growth, social partners in countries that maintained high levels of labour market coordination and a large welfare state have struggled to sustain coordination and to support somewhat solidaristic solutions to economic malaise. Highly coordinated countries with larger public sectors have surprisingly waged the best defence against budgetary deficits, as these countries largely enjoyed budget surpluses before the crisis (OECD 2012). While employment has declined in coordinated countries such as Denmark, there has been less pain than one might have predicted, as unemployed citizens have gone into training programmes (indeed, just as the 'flexicurity' model was intended to work) and Danes have been more optimistic about getting another job than citizens of other countries (Hansen 2010).

CONCLUSION

To conclude, the theory of varieties of capitalism offers an elegant and parsimonious explanation for the cross-national divergence of employers' preferences, social protections, and policy outcomes among advanced, industrialized countries. The theory certainly cannot capture all diversity at the national, regional, sectoral, and firm levels, and its static categories have difficulty explaining institutional change. Yet the model—particularly in its later renditions—does shed light on the ways in which the sphere of industrial coordination engages with national systems of political representation to delimit the choices of employers and other actors. The characteristic ways of bringing groups and individuals together—what I refer to as the structures for collective political engagement—have an impact on the ways that firms characteristically engage with the policy environment and on social and economic outcomes, on the scope and evolution of regulatory regimes, and on institutional change.

Strong complementarities exist between these public and private spheres, particularly between proportional representation party systems and coordinated market economies. Political economists root these complementarities in the strong motivations of both politicians and the social partners to restrain short-term preferences for electoral victory and rent-seeking rewards in favour of longer-term interests in the production of highly specific skills that are necessary to a high-growth equilibrium (Garrett 1998; Swank 2002; Cusack et al. 2007; Martin and Swank 2008). But following sociologists, one must also recognize the collective action and cognitive impacts of diverse institutional arrangements that facilitate the realization (or not) of longer-term economic interests. Granted, the political and industrial structures *constrain* rather than *determine* motivations and case histories are idiosyncratic directions that have profound feedback effects on future action. Yet, the institutional design characteristics of party systems and encompassing labour market associations for the social partners have a substantial impact on the probabilities of groups constructing and realizing their material interests in various ways. Coordinated countries produce a more favourable balance between growth and equality, in part, because the world-views of well-organized social partners are moulded by their representative organizations. Highly coordinated associations resist rent-seeking behaviour by both individual capitalists and the state. Thus, while the various models of capitalism cannot account for all diversity at the firm and sectoral levels, national systems of representation and collective bargaining have a special impact on the provision of collective social goods.

Capacities for reinvention are shaped by the institutional arrangements connecting the social partners which influence the types and range of adaptation; ultimately these different processes of adaptation and adjustment—delimited by societal patterns of engagement—shape whether a country is capable of profound redirection or whether it is must be satisfied with a more limited set of responses. For example, in the wake of the global financial crisis, liberalism has been the default option and the one chosen by countries lacking the state and societal power to pursue a more imaginative route to regime transformation. In the highly coordinated Nordic countries, by comparison, the crisis prompted a resurgence of governmental controls, coordinated efforts by the social partners to manage the economic malaise, and a redirection of investment into emergent green technologies. The ultimate significance of the social democratic course remains to be seen and it is too early to predict what this middle way entails for the future of capitalist regulation. The challenges of global contradictions in capitalist competition may simply swamp national solutions of all ilk, and there is a plausible case to be made that global processes of engagement are necessary for coping with the international contradictions in capitalist production (Ryan and Worth 2010). Yet to date, the social democratic model—with a large public sector and high degrees of coordination—has flourished rather than unravelled in the wake of the financial decline; and it behoves us to delve deeper into these pockets of resistance to liberalism in our search for a new regulatory order.

References

Ackers, P. and Wilkinson, A. (eds.) (2003). *Understanding Work and Employment: Industrial Relations in Transition*. Oxford and New York: Oxford University Press.

Allen, M. (2004). 'The Varieties of Capitalism Paradigm: Not Enough Variety?', *Socio-Economic Review*, 2(1): 87–108.

Amable, B. (2003). *The Diversity of Modern Capitalism*. Oxford and New York: Oxford University Press.

Ansell, B. (2008). 'Traders, Teachers, and Tyrants: Democracy, Globalization, and Public Investment in Education', *International Organization*, 62: 289–322.

Anthonsen, M. and Lindvall, J. (2009). 'Party Competition and the Resilience of Corporatism', *Government and Opposition*, 44(2): 167–87.

Ashton, D. and Green, F. (1996). *Education, Training and the Global Economy*. Cheltenham: Edward Elgar.

Berger, S. and Dore, R. (eds.) (1996). *National Diversity and Global Capitalism*. Ithaca, NY: Cornell University Press.

Berk, G. (2009). *Louis D. Brandeis and the Making of Regulated Competition, 1900–1932*. Cambridge: Cambridge University Press.

Brewster, C., Brookes, M., and Wood, G. (2006). 'Varieties of Capitalism and Varieties of Firm', in Wood and P. James (eds.), *Institutions, Production, and Working Life*. Oxford and New York: Oxford University Press, 217–34.

Busemeyer, M. and Trampusch, C. (2011a). 'Introduction', in Busemeyer and Trampusch (eds.), *The Political Economy of Collective Skill Formation*. Oxford and New York: Oxford University Press, 3–38.

—— (2011b). 'Review Article: Comparative Political Science and the Study of Education', *British Journal of Political Science*, 41: 413–43.

Campbell, J. and Pedersen, O. K. (2007). 'The Varieties of Capitalism and Hybrid Success', *Comparative Political Studies*, 40(3): 307–42.

Capoccia, G. and Ziblatt, D. (2010). 'The Historical Turn in Democratization Studies: A New Research Agenda for Europe and Beyond', *Comparative Political Studies*, 43(8–9): 931–68.

Crouch, C. (1993). *Industrial Relations and European State Traditions*. Oxford and New York: Oxford University Press.

Cusack, T., Iversen, T., and Soskice, D. (2007). 'Economic Interests and the Origins of Electoral Institutions', *American Political Science Review*, 101(3): 373–91.

Deeg, R. (2009). 'The Rise of Internal Capitalist Diversity? Changing Patterns of Finance and Corporate Governance in Europe', *Economy and Society*, 38(4): 552–79.

Deeg, R. and Jackson, G. (2007). 'Towards a More Dynamic Theory of Capitalist Diversity', *Socio-Economic Review*, 5(1): 149–80.

DiMaggio, P. and Powell, W. (1991). 'Introduction', in Powell and DiMaggio (eds.), *The New Institutionalism in Organizational Analysis*. Chicago: University of Chicago Press, 1–38.

Djelic, M.-L. and Quack, S. (eds.) (2003). *Globalization and Institutions: Redefining the Rules of the Economic Game*. Cheltenham: Edward Elgar.

Dobbin, F. (2004). *The Sociology of the Economy*. New York: Russell Sage Foundation.

Ebbinghaus, B. (2010). 'Reforming Bismarckian Corporatism: The Changing Role of Social Partnership in Continental Europe', in B. Palier (ed.), *A Long Goodbye to Bismarck? The Politics of Welfare Reform in Continental Europe*. Amsterdam: Amsterdam University Press, 255–78.

Emmenegger, P. and Marx, P. (2011). 'Business and the Development of Job Security Regulations: The Case of Germany', *Socio-Economic Review*, 9(4): 729–56.

Esping-Andersen, G. (1990). *The Three Worlds of Welfare Capitalism*. Cambridge: Polity Press.

Estevez-Abe, M., Iversen, T., and Soskice, D. (2001). 'Social Protection and the Formation of Skills', in P. A. Hall and Soskice (eds.), *Varieties of Capitalism: The Institutional Foundations of Comparative Advantage*. Oxford and New York: Oxford University Press, 145–83.

Fear, J. (2005). *Organizing Control: August Thyssen and the Construction of German Corporate Management*. Cambridge, MA: Harvard University Press.

Fellman, S., Iversen, M., Sjögren, H., and Thue, L. (eds.) (2008). *Creating Nordic Capitalism: The Business History of a Competitive Periphery*. New York: Palgrave Macmillan.

Fioretos, O. (2011). *Creative Reconstructions: Multilateralism and European Varieties of Capitalism after 1950*. Ithaca, NY: Cornell University Press.

Fligstein, N. (1990). *The Transformation of Corporate Control*. Cambridge, MA: Harvard University Press.

Garrett, G. (1998). *Partisan Politics in the Global Economy*. New York: Cambridge University Press.

Goergen, M. (2007). 'Corporate Governance Regimes, Investments in Human Capital and Economic Growth'. European Corporate Governance Institute. Finance Working Paper No. 188/207.

Greinert, W.-D. (2005). *Mass Vocational Education and Training in Europe*. Luxembourg: CEDEFOP.

Hall, P. A. and Gingerich, D. (2009). *Varieties of Capitalism and Institutional Complementarities in the Political Economy*. MPIfG Discussion Paper 04/5. Cologne: Max Planck Institute for the Study of Societies.

Hall, P. A. and Soskice, D. (2001). 'An Introduction to Varieties of Capitalism', in Hall and Soskice (eds.), *Varieties of Capitalism: The Institutional Foundations of Comparative Advantage*. Oxford and New York: Oxford University Press, 1–68.

Hancké, B., Rhodes, M., and Thatcher, M. (eds.) (2007). *Beyond Varieties of Capitalism: Conflict, Contradictions, and Complementarities in the European Economy*. Oxford and New York: Oxford University Press.

Hansen, M. B. (2010). 'Danskerne frygter ikke at miste jobbet', *Agenda*, 8 (6 April).

Hassel, A. (2007). 'What Does Business Want? Labour Market Reforms in CMEs and its Problems', in B. Hancké, M. Rhodes, and M. Thatcher (eds.), *Beyond Varieties of Capitalism: Conflict, Contradictions, and Complementarities in the European Economy*. Oxford and New York: Oxford University Press, 253–77.

Hemerijck, A. and Visser, J. (1997). '*A Dutch Miracle*': Job Growth, Welfare Reform, and Corporatism in the Netherlands. Amsterdam: Amsterdam University Press.

Herrigel, G. (1996). *Industrial Constructions: The Sources of German Industrial Power*. New York: Cambridge University Press.

Hicks, A. and Kenworthy, L. (1998). 'Cooperation and Political Economic Performance in Affluence Democratic Capitalism', *American Journal of Sociology*, 103: 1631–72.

Höpner, M. (2006). 'What is Organized Capitalism? The Two Dimensions of Nonliberal Capitalism'. Workshop on Institutional Emergence, Stability and Change, 1–2 June, Copenhagen.

Howell, C. (2003). 'Varieties of Capitalism: And Then There was One?', *Comparative Politics* 36(1): 103–24.

Huber, E. and Stephens, J. D. (2001). *Development and Crisis of the Welfare State: Parties and Policies in Global Markets*. Chicago: University of Chicago Press.

Hyman, R. (2001). *Understanding European Trade Unionism: Between Market, Class & Society*. London: Sage.

Immergut, E., Anderson, K., and Schulze, I. (eds.) (2007). *The Handbook of West European Pension Politics*. Oxford and New York: Oxford University Press.

Jacoby, S. (1998). *Modern Manors: Welfare Capitalism since the New Deal*. Princeton: Princeton University Press.

Jensen, C. (2011). 'Capitalist Systems, Deindustrialization, and the Politics of Public Education', *Comparative Political Studies*, 44(4): 412–35.

Jessop, B. (2002). *The Future of the Capitalist State*. Cambridge: Polity Press.

Jones, G. (2005). *Renewing Unilever: Transformation and Tradition*. Oxford and New York: Oxford University Press.

Katzenstein, P. (1985). *Small States in World Markets: Industrial Policy in Europe*. Ithaca, NY: Cornell University Press.

Korpi, W. (2006). 'Power Resources and Employer-Centered Approaches in Explanations of Welfare States and Varieties of Capitalism: Protagonists, Consenters, and Antagonists', *World Politics*, 58(2): 167–206.

Lane, C. and Wood, G. (2009). 'Capitalist Diversity and Diversity within Capitalism', *Economy and Society*, 38(4): 531–51.

—— (eds.) (2011). *Capitalist Diversity and Diversity within Capitalism*. London: Routledge.

Lipietz, A. (1987). *Mirages and Miracles: Crisis in Global Fordism*. New York: Verso.

Mares, I. (2003). *The Politics of Social Risk: Business and Welfare State Development*. Cambridge: Cambridge University Press.

Martin, C. J. (1995). 'Nature or Nurture? Sources of Firm Preferences for National Health Care Reform', *American Political Science Review*, 89(4): 898–913.

—— (2000). *Stuck in Neutral: Business and the Politics of Human Capital Investment Policy*. Princeton: Princeton University Press.

—— (2004). 'Reinventing Welfare Regimes: Employers and the Implementation of Active Social Policy', *World Politics*, 57(1): 39–69.

—— (2011). 'Political Institutions and the Origins of Collective Skill Formation Systems', in M. R. Busemeyer and C. Trampusch (eds.), *The Political Economy of Collective Skill Formation*. Oxford and New York: Oxford University Press, 41–67.

Martin, C. J. and Swank, D. (2004). 'Does the Organization of Capital Matter? Employers and Active Labor Market Policy at the National and Firm Levels', *American Political Science Review*, 98(4): 593–611.

—— (2008). 'The Political Origins of Coordinated Capitalism: Business Organizations, Party Systems, and State Structure in the Age of Innocence', *American Political Science Review*, 102(2): 181–98.

—— (2012). *The Political Construction of Business Interests: Coordination, Growth, and Equality*. New York: Cambridge University Press.

Martin, C. J. and Thelen, K. (2007). 'The State and Coordinated Capitalism: Contributions of the Public Sector to Social Solidarity in Postindustrial Societies', *World Politics*, 60(1): 1–36.

Mizruchi, M. (1992). *The Structure of Corporate Political Action: Interfirm Relations and their Consequences*. Cambridge, MA: Harvard University Press.

Morgan, G. (2005). 'Introduction', in Morgan, R. Whitley, and E. Moen (eds.), *Changing Capitalisms? Internationalization, Institutional Change, and Systems of Economic Organization*. Oxford and New York: Oxford University Press, 1–18.

—— (2007). 'The Theory of Comparative Capitalisms and the Possibilities for Local Variation', *European Review*, 15(3): 353–72.

OECD (2012). 'General Government Fiscal Balances', *Economic Outlook*, 91: Table #27.

Palier, B. and Thelen, K. (2010). 'Institutionalizing Dualism: Complementarities and Change in France and Germany', *Politics & Society*, 38(1): 119–48.

Paster, T. (2011). *German Employers and the Origins of Unemployment Insurance*. MFIfG Discussion Paper 11/5. Cologne: Max Planck Institute for the Study of Social Sciences.

Penrose, E. (1959). *The Theory of the Growth of the Firm*. Oxford: Basil Blackwell.

Piore, M. and Sabel, C. (1984). *The Second Industrial Divide: Possibilities for Prosperity*. New York: Basic Books.

Pontusson, J. (1997). 'Between Neo-Liberalism and the German Model: Swedish Capitalism in transition', in C. Crouch and W. Streeck (eds.), *Political Economy of Modern Capitalism: Mapping Convergence & Diversity*. London: Sage, 55–70.

Ryan, B. and Worth, O. (2010). 'On the Contemporary Relevance of Left Nationalism', *Capital & Class*, 34(1): 54–9.

Scharpf, F. and Schmidt, V. (eds.) (2000). *Welfare and Work in the Open Economy: From Vulnerability to Competitiveness*. Oxford and New York: Oxford University Press.

Schmidt, V. (2002). *The Futures of European Capitalism*. Oxford and New York: Oxford University Press.

Schneiberg, M. (2007). 'What's on the Path? Path Dependence, Organizational Diversity, and the Problem of Institutional Change in the US Economy, 1900–1950', *Socio-Economic Review*, 5(1): 47–80.

Schneiberg, M., King, M., and Smith, T. (2008). 'Social Movements and Organizational Form: Cooperative Alternatives to Corporations in the American Insurance, Dairy, and Grain Industries', *American Sociological Review*, 73(4): 635–67.

Schrank, A. (2009). 'Understanding Latin American Political Economy: Varieties of Capitalism or Fiscal Sociology?', *Economy and Society*, 38(1): 53–61.

Sorge, A. (2005). *The Global and the Local: Understanding the Dialectics of Business Systems*. Oxford and New York: Oxford University Press.

Stephens, J. (1980). *The Transition from Capitalism to Socialism*. Atlantic Highlands, NJ: Humanities Press.

Streeck, W. (1992). *Social Institutions and Economic Performance: Studies of Industrial Relations in Advanced Capitalist Economies*. London: Sage.

—— (2009). *Re-Forming Capitalism: Institutional Change in the German Political Economy*. Oxford and New York: Oxford University Press.

Streeck, W. and Thelen, K. (eds.) (2005). *Beyond Continuity: Institutional Change in Advanced Political Economies*. Oxford and New York: Oxford University Press.

Swank, D. (2002). *Global Capital, Political Institutions, and Policy Change in Developed Welfare States*. New York: Cambridge University Press.

Thelen, K. (2004). *How Institutions Evolve: The Political Economy of Skills in Germany, Britain, the United States and Japan*. Cambridge: Cambridge University Press.

Traxler, F. (2000). 'Employers and Employer Organisations in Europe: Membership Strength, Density and Representativeness', *Industrial Relations Journal*, 31(4): 308–16.

Wallerstein, M. and Golden, M. (1997). 'The Fragmentation of the Bargaining Society: Wage Setting in Nordic Countries, 1950–1992', *Comparative Political Studies*, 30(6): 699–731.

Whitley, R. (1999). *Divergent Capitalisms: The Social Structuring and Change of Business Systems*. Oxford and New York: Oxford University Press.

—— (2005). 'How National Are Business Systems? The Role of States and Complementary Institutions in Standardizing Systems of Economic Coordination and Control at the National Level', in G. Morgan, Whitley, and E. Moen (eds.), *Changing Capitalisms? Internationalization, Institutional Change, and Systems of Economic Organization*. Oxford and New York: Oxford University Press, 190–232.

Wiebe, R. H. (1967). *The Search for Order, 1877–1920*. New York: Hill & Wang.

....

CHAPTER 5

BUSINESS SYSTEMS THEORY AND EMPLOYMENT RELATIONS

....

MATTHEW M. C. ALLEN

INTRODUCTION

....

In the wake of the increasing internationalization of product, capital, and some labour markets, understanding the ways in which companies in different locations create and sustain competitive advantages has become ever more important for policy-makers, company managers, union officials, entrepreneurs, and employees. The 'business systems' framework represents a highly influential contribution in this area. It seeks to explain the links between institutionalized systems of economic coordination and control, on the one hand, and firms' routines, organizational capabilities and competitiveness, on the other. The framework has been most closely associated, but not exclusively so, with various publications by Richard Whitley (1990, 1992a, 1992b, 1994, 1999, 2000, 2003, 2005, 2007, 2010). While the business systems framework shares some common ground with the varieties of capitalism (VOC) paradigm, it differs in significant ways.

This contribution is structured as follows. The next section sets out the business systems framework. The distinctions between it and the VOC approach are then examined and important developments in the framework are identified and discussed. Subsequent sections examine individual business systems in detail. The growing importance of internationalization to business systems, in general, and multinational companies, in particular, is discussed. Finally, conclusions are drawn and suggestions about the possible future development of the framework are put forward. This contribution focuses on issues relating to employment relations (for a related review, see Wilkinson and Wood 2012); however, it should not be forgotten that other aspects of the business systems framework, such as ownership and control structures, corporate governance, the role of political authorities, public science systems, and inter-firm networks, could also be scrutinized. It is also worth noting at the outset that, although the term 'business systems' is often prefaced by the adjective 'national', the country level is not necessarily the most pertinent unit of analysis for the study of organizations and, indeed, business systems, as more than one business system may exist within one country (Allen and Whitley 2012; Morgan 2007a, 2007b; Whitley 2007, 2009; Whitley and Morgan 2012; see also Wood et al. 2009).

The 'Business Systems' Framework

The cardinal contention behind the business systems framework is that the institutionalized rules of the game—both formal and informal ones—constitute and shape the types of firms that exist, their priorities, the interconnections between them, and, consequently, the kinds of routines, organizational capabilities, and strategies that they can implement successfully (Whitley 1999, 2007, 2010). As a result, companies are likely to be more successful in some sub-sectors than others, as, firstly, the types of market, technological, managerial and organizational challenges that firms will encounter will vary from sub-sector to sub-sector and, secondly, the ability of companies to surmount those challenges will be shaped by their institutional setting (Allen and Whitley 2012; Casper and Whitley 2004; Whitley 2007: 147). In order to show these links more concretely, with an especial emphasis on employment relations, it will be necessary to examine 'business systems' and the characteristics of sub-sectoral competitiveness and innovation in more detail.

Business systems can be defined as the distinctive and dominant (or usual) ways in which economic activities are coordinated and controlled within a given territory that is governed by particular kinds of institutions. Those involved in that process can cover owners, managers, employees, experts, state representatives, and unions. The ways in which those groups interact will, importantly, reflect the extent to, and means by, which economic activities are authoritatively coordinated and controlled. That authority could be exercised through organizational hierarchies, contracts, informal commitments, or personal ties (Whitley 1999: 33). Therefore, in order to understand the different types of business systems and the key ways in which they vary, it is first necessary to examine the institutions that structure them. The key institutional systems underpinning business systems are: the state, the financial system, the skill development and control system, and norms governing trust and authority relationships.

The state can influence business system characteristics by stipulating the conditions under which firms can be incorporated; by regulating which organizations can or cannot operate in certain markets; by determining bankruptcy rules; by encouraging or discouraging the presence and importance of intermediary bodies, such as employers' associations and unions; and by intervening directly in the economy by sharing investment costs and risks with companies. Together these factors shape product, capital, and labour markets in terms of their segmentation, competitive rivalry, resource mobility, and firm flexibility (Whitley 1999: 49). In other words, the state can, amongst other things, influence the degree to which firms compete or cooperate with one another; the ability of unions to play a role in skill formation systems and wage bargaining; the availability of funds; and the willingness of firms to undertake investments in risky technological innovations.

The financial system, too, has various aspects; however, a crucial distinction is drawn in the area of corporate financing. In particular, the relative importance within economies of capital markets or banks in funding companies provides a key means to differentiate business systems. If capital is provided through equity markets by institutional investors, such as pension funds and unit trusts, those owners will have a relatively narrow, profit-oriented interest in the firms that they invest in. This is especially so if a market for corporate control exists; that is, if firms can be acquired relatively easily and price premiums are paid to existing shareholders to acquire their shares. By contrast, if capital is provided by banks, which act as intermediaries between savers and companies, then direct links between firms and lenders are likely to be established. Consequently, banks may become locked into the commercial futures of the firms that they have lent to. Although this dichotomy between business systems is not as distinct in practice, both within territories and over time, as it is in theory (Goyer 2006, 2011; Tylecote and Ramirez 2006), it forms a useful basis on which to classify countries and many of the companies within them. The reason for this is that the ownership and control of firms have significant implications for their ability, firstly, to invest for the long term and, secondly, to forge obligational long-term, trust-based relationships with, for example, suppliers and employees. This, in turn, has ramifications for the types of capabilities that firms are able to develop and their ability to become competitive in certain sectors (Whitley 1999: 49–50; Whitley 2007).

The skill development and control system covers, firstly, the education and training system and, secondly, important aspects of labour markets. These two elements can, in turn, be disaggregated further. For instance, from a business systems perspective, there are two highly important features of the education and training system: firstly, the extent to which employers, state agencies, and unions collaborate to determine the content of training programmes and to certify skills; and, second, the degree to which practical training within firms is complemented by theory-based courses within educational establishments. In terms of labour markets, the critical elements are, firstly, the involvement of unions and professional associations in controlling skills and the deployment of skilled workers; secondly, the degree to which unions and professional associations are organized according to expertise, the enterprise, the sector, or the country; and, finally, the extent to which wage bargaining is centralized. These factors influence the mobility of workers between firms (and between sectors), organizational career structures, and collaboration not only between employers and employees, but also between different firms. This, once again, has implications for the type of activities that firms will be able to carry out competently and their subsequent ability to compete successfully in certain product markets (Whitley 1999, 2007).

Inter-firm cooperation is also influenced by the norms and values governing trust and authority relations. Trust in formal rules, regulations, and the agencies that enforce legislation and contractual agreements has important implications for the governance of economic activities, and, hence, the types of firms that emerge as well as the capabilities that they are likely to have (Whitely 1999, 2007). For instance, if investors do not trust the relevant agencies to enforce legislation and commercial agreements, they are unlikely to delegate any authority or decision-making powers to those to whom they do not have strong family or personal ties. Consequently, firms may well be small and alliances between firms very difficult to forge. If trust is high, however, owners are more likely to share authority with some employees and business partners. As a result, career structures for some employees are likely to emerge within large firms. Thus, under contrasting levels of trust in formal rules and legal agencies, different types of firm are likely to become more common; their priorities will vary, as will their capabilities and ability to compete successfully in different markets.

It is important to note that it is not just the individual elements that contribute to the characteristics of business systems, but also their interdependencies or complementarities (Whitley 1999: 53–4; see also Crouch et al. 2005). For instance, the ability of firms to adopt a long-term perspective on investment decisions and employment relations, *inter alia*, can be promoted by owners, such as families with a controlling stake or banks, who are committed to the business. In terms of employment relations, such a long-term perspective is likely to complemented—or reinforced—if other institutions also exert a similar influence. For example, labour-market institutions that grant employee representatives a say in strategy decisions or the organization of work within establishments are likely to restrain companies' abilities to decrease the size of the workforce or to change rapidly the activities that are carried out by workers. This can encourage employers yet further to adopt a long-term approach to employees. Consequently, the mutual commitment between employers and employees is likely to increase; this, in turn, may then enable the company to encourage employees to invest in firm-specific skills that can aid competitiveness in certain sectors.

Although particular types of business systems have been linked to countries or regions within countries (Whitley 1999, 2007), the business systems framework is best treated as a collection of ideal types in the Weberian sense (Morgan 2007a). In other words, Whitley (1999, 2007) does not claim that the different business systems capture and reflect the complexities of countries or regions as they exist in reality. Therefore, the business systems framework should not be assessed on the extent to which any particular business system corresponds completely to any country or region. Similarly, the framework did not, initially, seek to provide a detailed analytical tool to assess the dynamics of capitalist systems.

Rather, Whitley claims that the types of business systems that he puts forward are logically consistent abstractions of socio-economic phenomena. Two important corollaries follow from this claim. Firstly, the discussion of business systems is limited to those that are not undermined by logical inconsistencies (Whitley 1999: 41; 2007: 11–12; cf. Wood and Frynas 2006). For instance, in one sense, given the number of institutional domains that Whitley identifies as being important, it is possible that numerous business systems could exist—even if those domains are treated in just a dichotomous way. However, many of these would suffer from severe tensions between particular institutional domains. For example, finding a business system that combines a developmental state with strong unions and business associations that can pursue strategies that are independent of those of the state will be unlikely. Similarly, large vertically integrated firms are unlikely to form long-term alliances with other firms, as such companies will be able to draw on internally generated complementary assets and capabilities. In short, the theoretical business system associated with an empirically implausible firm type is not considered in the framework.

The second corollary relates to the analytical use of the framework. Arguably, the business systems approach should be used not just to identify the ways in which exist-ing countries or locations do or do not conform to one or other business system (which forms part of the analysis by, for instance, Morgan and Kubo 2005; Schneiberg 2007), but also to examine how—and with what consequences—firms, regions, and coun-tries do not conform to the posited, logically consistent ideal types (Morgan 2007a). This can, for instance, involve an analysis of the conditions under which firms can draw on international resources to overcome institutional deficiencies to be competitive in particular industries (Allen and Whitely 2012). Alternatively, it could cover a close examination of the ways in which firms and other actors are able to shape their local institutional settings in ways that do not necessarily adhere closely to the ideal type, but that are designed to enhance competitiveness (Becker-Ritterspach et al. 2010; Casper and Whitley 2004; Crouch et al. 2009).

DIFFERENCES TO THE 'VARIETIES OF CAPITALISM' FRAMEWORK AND DEVELOPMENTS WITHIN THE BUSINESS SYSTEMS FRAMEWORK

The key difference between the business systems framework and the VOC paradigm lies, arguably, in the analytical focus that is placed on the firm. Despite claims to the contrary, the VOC paradigm places relatively little emphasis on the firm as a separately constituted collective actor that has varying autonomy (Allen 2004; Crouch 2005; cf. Hancké et al. 2007). Indeed, it could be argued that, within the VOC perspective it is not necessary to examine the specific managerial and organizational challenges that firms face, because the strategic objectives and associated organizational routines can be understood by analysing the national institutional setting of companies (Allen 2004). In other words, firms within any one country are, within the VOC framework, construed as being homogeneous. This is not the case in the business systems approach.

Although it will not be possible to go into details here, the business systems frame-work builds on contentions from the resource-based view of the firm (Whitley 2007: 147–8; Whitley 2010) and the 'sectoral systems of innovation' approach (Casper and Whitley 2004; Whitley 2007: 204–6). For instance, with the former, the business systems perspective shares an emphasis on explaining the detailed ways in which firms and the managers within them create collective competitive competencies (Dosi et al. 2000; Penrose 1959; Teece et al. 1997). This focuses the analysis on the key activities that are carried out within firms, the routines that are used to create and develop core competencies, and the typical problems organizations are likely to face when implementing particular routines. This approach can be contrasted to those that place greater emphasis on factors outside the firm in their analyses. For instance, transaction cost economics emphasize the advantages or disadvantages associated with using the market or the firm—that is, hierarchically ordered processes within an organization—to perform economic activities. It highlights the costs that firms incur, if they use the market, to search for appropriate suppliers/customers, to draw up contracts, to monitor performance, and to enforce those agreements if the other company fails to deliver the product or service in the right quantity or quality (Williamson 1985). Similarly, some strategy frameworks, such as Porter's (1979) five forces model, focus on factors that are outside the company to help firms devise appropriate responses.

In common with the 'sectoral systems of innovation' approach, the business systems approach seeks to anticipate the managerial and organizational challenges that firms face given the technological, knowledge, and competition characteristics associated with particular economic sub-sectors (Malerba 2002; Malerba and Orsenigo 1997). The ability to overcome these challenges will depend upon the establishment and development of a set of appropriate routines and capabilities. For instance, in firms that are attempting to overcome technological and market risks to develop radically new technologies, managers must be able to encourage employees to invest in skills that could become redundant if the firm were to fail. In other words, managers must be able to overcome the challenges associated with competence destruction. This can be done by offering employees relatively large stakes in the organization or by offering them substantial bonuses if the firm succeeds. By contrast, in firms in which employees face lower competence destruction risks, managers may need to encourage employees to invest in firm-specific skills that, by definition, cannot easily be sold to other employers. This challenge may be met by making credible commitments to workers in the form of employment guarantees that are supported by strong legal rights for employee representatives (Casper and Whitley 2004).

Yet, the business systems framework is distinct from the resource-based view of the firm and the sectoral systems of innovation perspective: it stresses the importance of the interdependencies between firms' abilities to compete successfully by overcoming key organizational challenges through the creation and development of routines and capabilities, on the one hand, and the external institutional setting of firms, on the other (Casper and Whitley 2004; Whitley 2007). For example, the ability of employers to make credible commitments to employees about their employment and the use of their skills will be influenced by the presence of works councils, whose existence and powers do not depend upon employers, but on legislation, to monitor managers' behaviour (Croucher et al. 2012; Harcourt and Wood 2007; Whitley 1999). It is these links that recent research has analysed (Allen and Whitley 2012; Casper 2007; Crouch and Voelzkow 2009; Schneiberg 2007; Sako and Jackson 2006; Wilkinson and Fay 2011).

A number of corollaries follow from this analytical focus. Firstly, the specific institutional settings of firms become part of the research, as these cannot be inferred directly from the national or macro-level framework (Allen 2004, 2013; Allen et al. 2011; Casper and Whitley 2004; Morgan and Kubo 2005). Indeed, the particular institutional settings of firms can be shaped by the increasing internationalization of product, capital, and some labour markets (Allen 2013; Allen and Whitley 2012; Almond 2011; Casper 2009; Lange 2009; Whitley and Morgan 2012), so that it is not just the national institutional framework of the country that the firm is located in that is important, but those abroad, potentially, as well. Secondly, and consequently, this highlights the ways in which specific institutional settings may contain elements or resources that diverge from those within archetypal institutional regimes (Lane and Wood 2012; Schneiberg 2007; Wood et al. 2009). Thirdly, it draws attention to the role of actors in shaping institutions, and, hence, how institutions may become the subject of contestation (Becker-Ritterspach et al. 2010; Crouch and Voelzkow 2009; Djelic and Quack 2003; Morgan 2007b; Streeck 2009; Whitley 2007). Finally, as the primary unit of analysis within much of the recent business systems literature is the firm or the industry level rather than the national institutional setting, the approach, arguably, opens up a richer depiction of firms and the challenges that they face compared to the portrayal of firms in the VOC perspective (Casper and Whitley 2004; Morgan 2007a).

Where the business systems literature may be lacking in comparison to the VOC approach is in the systematic application of the analytical framework to countries beyond Japan and those in Western Europe and North America. Although the business systems framework has been used to analyse the development of economies in Central and Eastern Europe (Czaban et al. 2003; Whitley and Czaban 1998), recent research in this area has tended to draw on the VOC paradigm (see, for instance, Allen and Aldred 2011; Bohle and Greskovits 2007; Lane and Myant 2007; Nölke and Vliegenthart 2009). Only a limited number of studies has attempted to apply and extend the business systems framework systematically to other countries and regions (Wood and Frynas 2006; Wood et al. 2011).

EMPLOYMENT RELATIONS WITHIN BUSINESS SYSTEMS

This contribution sets out five ideal types of business systems. It then discusses the evidence on the links between employment relations and firm capabilities that can be interpreted from a business systems perspective; that is, evidence that, in general, combines an analysis of firms' employment strategies, organizational objectives, and institutional settings. To be sure, not all of the research reviewed here has been conducted explicitly within a business systems approach; it can, however, contribute to that strand of the literature. As noted above, the socio-economic reality of firms should not be expected to conform completely to any ideal type of business system. Table 5.1 summarizes the key

Table 5.1 Ideal firm types and associated business systems, employment relations, and organizational capabilities

	Type of firm				
	Opportunistic	Specialized network	Isolated hierarchy	Centralized hierarchy	Collaborative hierarchy
Business system associated with	Fragmented	Coordinated industrial districts, and project networks	Compartmentalized	State organized	Collaborative and highly coordinated
Examples	Informal economy in Nigeria	Emilia-Romagna, Italy; Baden-Württemberg, Germany; Silicon Valley, US	US and UK	South Korea before c.1990, Russia	Germany and Japan
Characteristics					
Owner control type	Direct	Direct/Market	Market	Direct	Committed
Employee constraint	Low	Considerable	Limited to managers	Limited to top managers	Considerable
Degree of authority sharing	Low	Considerable	Some	Limited	Considerable
Scope of authority sharing	Low	Considerable	Limited to managers	Limited	Considerable
Longevity and scope of organizational careers	Low	Low	Some for managers	Limited	Considerable
Capabilities					
Strength of coordinating capabilities	Restricted to personal control	Restricted to specialized firms and limited in scope	Considerable	Considerable	High
Strength of organizational learning capabilities	Limited	Limited to teams	Limited to managers	Limited to top managers	Considerable
Strength of reconfigurational capabilities	High for entrepreneurs	Limited in industrial districts; high in professional project networks	Considerable	Considerable	Limited

Source: adapted from Whitley (2010: 463; cf. Whitley 1999: 75)

characteristics of those five ideal firm types that are discussed here, the associated business system, the anticipated employment relations within the firms, and their organizational capabilities.

Fragmented

Fragmented business systems develop in environments that are characterized by low levels of trust and by unreliable formal institutions (Whitley 1999: 59). In other words, the rule of law is very limited or non-existent. Consequently, this makes predicting the outcomes of any legal process exceedingly difficult. The limited applicability of the rule of law is likely to reflect either a weak or a predatory state. As a result of these characteristics, commercial risks will be difficult to share. This, in turn, will mean that firms are likely to be small, be independent of political elites (cf. the situation in China and South Korea), and rely on their own, limited resources and capabilities to be competitive. These capabilities are likely, because of the low-trust and weak legal environment within which firms operate, to be confined to the owner-manager's competencies. Where links to other companies exist, these are likely to be based upon familial or strong personal ties. Similarly, within companies, owner-managers will be reluctant to share any authority with employees and employees will, because they do not have the opportunity to develop any substantive skills, not represent a constraint on the firm's decision-making. Finally, the generally low skill levels of employees within opportunistic firms as well as the dearth of opportunities for workers to develop new skills will mean that employees carry out a limited range of simple tasks within such firms.

The capabilities that such firms develop are likely to be restricted to those of the owner-manager. Thus, opportunistic firms will only be able to coordinate economic activities that are within the purview of the owner-manager. The range of that coordination may be extended by familial or strong personal ties, but it is still likely to be limited in scope. As a consequence, most employees in opportunistic firms will not have any real discretion or ability to develop their skills, organization learning will be limited, and the propensity of the firm to acquire new capabilities will depend upon the learning of the owner-manager or a very small number of trusted managers within the firm. However, because opportunistic firms are not constrained by any employees, they will, theoretically, be able to reconfigure their capabilities quickly if they operate in markets that enable or require them to do so. In practice, of course, if the owner-manager does not possess the requisite skills both to adapt the business and to make it a success in the changed environment, the company will fail.

The informal economy in Nigeria matches many of these characteristics (Fajana 2008; see also Wood and Frynas 2006 and Wood et al. 2011 for related studies). For instance, although employment in the informal economy in Nigeria is estimated to account for 50% or more of total employment, most of the enterprises in the sector are small in terms of the number of employees. In addition, such enterprises often form and then disband relatively rapidly. The formation of enterprises frequently depends upon the acquisition of new skills by the owner-manager or a small amount of capital from family or friends. Owner-managers often pay their employees relatively low wages, invest little in the development of their employees' skills, and do not countenance unions within their workplaces. The capabilities that such firms possess are restricted to the owner-manager's skills and knowledge. The survival of the enterprise, therefore, depends upon that of the owner-manager or the owner-manager continuing to take an active interest in the business or the owner-manager possessing the skills to adapt the enterprise to a changed business environment (Fajana 2008).

Specialized Network

Specialized networks cover two distinctive ideal types of business system: coordinated industrial districts and project networks. The variation within the actual forms that adhere relatively closely to those ideal types can be quite great. Despite this, specialized networks share certain characteristics that can be used to distinguish them from other types of business systems. The most pertinent distinguishing features are the typical ownership and control patterns of firms within the network and their employment relations. These result in distinctive capabilities.

In terms of ownership, many firms within specialized networks are owned and controlled directly by either the company's founders (or their heirs), venture capital backers, or partners. Most firms within such networks tend to be relatively small. Within both types of specialized networks, firms are constrained to a considerable degree by employees, as it is they who have the crucial skills and knowledge that form the foundations of the firm's competitiveness. A corollary of this is that companies must also share a considerable amount of authority with their employees across a relatively wide range of issues. However, the longevity of organizational careers is likely to be limited for many employees in specialized networks. For those in coordinated districts, this is because workers may seek new employment to ensure that their skills are constantly upgraded; for those in project networks, because the project has been completed or because the 'project', such as developing a new biotechnology-based therapeutic treatment or a novel piece of standard applications-based software, was unsuccessful. The scope of organizational careers is likely to be low, as employees with highly valued, specialized skills and knowledge will, *ipso facto*, lack the necessary experience and expertise to conduct other activities within the organization.

These characteristics are likely to result in firms that, because of their small size and specialization, will find it difficult to coordinate with a wide variety of other companies. This may be because firms fear the loss of key knowledge to potentially larger, more diversified competitors (Allen and Whitley 2012) or because they lack the resources to coordinate economic activities beyond those that are similarly specialized. Such firms are also likely to have limited organizational learning capabilities, as it is the members of teams who have the expertise and who interact with one another. Consequently, learning may be embedded within individuals and teams rather than within the organization, *sensu stricto*. While project networks that operate in fluid labour markets and in high-technology sectors are likely to be able to reconfigure their capabilities quickly, those specialized networks that resemble coordinated industrial districts are likely to have more limited reconfigurational capabilities, as a result of the slower pace of technological and knowledge evolution and more stable labour markets (Whitley 2010: 464).

Many of these characteristics can be observed in different countries and regions around the world. Denmark, for instance, has, alongside large companies that are often controlled by foundations, such as the A.P. Moller-Maersk Group, Carlsberg, and Leo Pharma, numerous highly successful small companies. In these latter firms, founding families frequently maintain a controlling stake in the business (Kristensen 2006: 298). In Germany, many of the country's *Mittelstand* or small and medium-sized enterprises that are significant exporters are family-owned and -controlled businesses (Simon 2007: 330). Similarly, high-technology firms in their initial stages will be owned and controlled by the founding entrepreneur. Even when such firms grow and stakes in the company are sold to private equity investors, those backers will often assume managerial responsibilities within the firm and they could be construed as direct owners who exert control over the enterprise. Even when high-tech companies become large, as, for instance, Google has done, the company can be structured in a way that provides the founders and key personnel with a controlling stake in the firm.

In terms of authority sharing, Kristensen (2006: 301) has noted that for small manufacturing firms in Denmark to remain or become competitive, they must be attractive to highly skilled workers. In order to do this, firms seek to specialize in certain processes rather than perfecting a particular product. This reduces the chances that repetitive jobs are created within the company, as a push to become more efficient in delivering a particular product is likely to result in a desire to increase volumes and, hence, to standardize certain activities. For workers who are accustomed to conducting ever more challenging jobs and who can readily access high-quality training courses, standardized, de-skilled jobs will not be attractive. As a result, they are likely to leave the company and the firm may well lose its reputation and its competitiveness, as it will no longer be able to meet the requirements of sophisticated customers (Kristensen 2006, 2011).

This clearly illustrates, firstly, the degree of authority sharing with employees and, secondly, how firms in coordinated industrial districts are constrained by their employees, as the loss of key employees will have a detrimental effect on competitiveness. The scope of authority sharing in many Danish companies is also considerable, as hierarchies are often flat (Kristensen 2006). Authority is shared with employees across a range of activities as a result. Although it is possible for skilled workers to become supervisors, engineers, and production managers within companies (Kristensen 2006: 303), it would appear that this is unlikely to be achieved within the same company, as the Danish labour market is a highly fluid one (Croucher et al. 2012; Kristensen 2006; Nielsen and Lundvall 2006) that encourages workers to learn by moving from firm to firm (Lundvall and Lorenz 2006). This means that the longevity and scope of organizational careers are likely to be low, as suggested by the ideal typical 'specialized network'.

Although fluid labour markets and the limited length of organizational careers will mean that there is a high turnover of personnel within Danish firms, this will not lead to reconfigurational capabilities that enable companies to alter radically and rapidly their organizational competencies. As noted above, Danish firms often seek, firstly, to increase the depth of their specialization and, secondly, to apply their capabilities to new, yet related, areas; consequently, the ability of such firms to depart from that specialization and develop expertise in radically new areas is likely to be limited.

A fluid labour market is also a characteristic of coordinated industrial districts in Italy. For instance, in the production of specialized machinery in Italy, it has been found that, due to a dearth of appropriately skilled employees, poaching is commonplace (Farrell and Holten 2004). The companies that recruit workers are able to draw on the knowledge and skills of production methods of their new employees to upgrade their organization's capabilities; while this may have benefits for the sector as a whole, it may deter company investments in activities that cannot be patented (Farrell and Holten 2004). The presence of poaching within the industry is one indication that there are limits to inter-firm cooperation. Thus, the ability to coordinate activities across the industry will be limited (cf. McCaffrey 2013). Where coordination does take place, it occurs vertically within production chains and horizontally between firms that provide complementary rather than competing goods (Farrell and Holten 2004).

By contrast, specialized networks that more closely resemble professional project networks than they do coordinated industrial districts are more likely to have greater reconfigurational capabilities. To be sure, this will be bounded by the variety of tasks that such networks are asked to carry out. However, the ability of professional project networks to recruit specialists in a range of areas and then integrate them to ensure that the required activities are completed means that they will be more flexible—or, to put it a different way, will be capable of 'being reconfigured' in more diverse ways—than networks more commonly found in coordinated industrial districts. This is because the latter networks are built around key skills and organizational capabilities for a certain economic sector (Whitley 2007; see also Morgan and Quack 2005, on 'reciprocity-based' professional networks).

Start-ups in therapeutic biotechnology in Silicon Valley resemble professional project networks in many respects (Whitley 2007: 14). Such firms are often owner-managed either by the original entrepreneurs and founders or, more commonly, by private equity investors who have bought a stake in the company with a view to selling it on in an initial public offering (IPO). These companies are often heavily constrained by key groups of employees, such as researchers, as it is they who underpin the company's ability to come up with new treatments before rivals. Once protected by patents, these new treatments will be the firm's source of profits. As this group of workers have advanced knowledge and skills, managers must be willing to share authority with them in meaningful ways across a number of areas. For instance, researchers must be able to use their discretion to decide which experiments to conduct in the future. This, in turn, may have wide-ranging implications for the use of the company's financial and material resources that may prevent the firm from conducting alternative projects.

However, the longevity and scope of organizational careers are likely to be low: if rivals beat the company to a new therapeutic treatment, the organization may cease to exist or managers may decide to make researchers redundant (Casper 2007). Similarly, if a different approach to the development of a new drug looks more promising than the firm's current techniques, the company may decide to make researchers redundant if that new approach requires a different set of hard-to-learn skills.

Compartmentalized

The key feature of compartmentalized business systems is the presence of large companies under a unified ownership structure that can coordinate and control activities within production chains and across related sectors that are based on common skills, knowledge, and capabilities, and that can offer economies of scope and scale (Whitley 2007: 15–16). Such firms are largely self-sufficient and do not, on the whole, collaborate with other firms, and employers display little commitment to employees. These crucial features reflect ownership and control structures as such companies are owned and controlled, in an indirect way, by institutional investors and financial markets (Whitley 1999: 43; see also Gospel and Pendleton 2003). These ownership patterns may not be sufficient to lead to the privileging of short-term financial objectives by firms. However, if they are coupled with a strong market for corporate control—that is, if firms can be acquired or taken over relatively easily—then these pressures will be more pronounced (O'Sullivan 2000; Tylecote and Ramirez 2006).

Consequently, this pressure to maintain or increase short-term profitability limits the commitments that senior managers can make to both lower-level employees and other organizations, including suppliers and rival firms in the same industry (Dyer and Nobeoka 2000; Lane 1989). In the case of employees, senior managers may decide that the most appropriate way to surmount any looming profitability problems is to make workers redundant (Gospel and Pendleton 2003). Indeed, employers will be cautious about not only sharing significant authority with employees, but also granting them discretion across a range of the company's activities. If they were to share authority with employees, the organization and senior managers would, in part, become dependent on those employees, and, hence, constrained by them. This would, in turn, make dismissing such employees more difficult. Thus, many employees will lack the opportunity to extend their skills across a range of the firm's activities (Harcourt and Wood 2007). The key resources in isolated hierarchies are, therefore, likely to be embodied within a senior tier of managers.

The consequences of this approach to employment relations for the firm's capabilities are, firstly, that the ability of the organization to learn will be confined to managers, as they are the ones who have the discretion and knowledge of the company's business activities. Secondly, as most employees do not contribute significantly to the competitiveness of isolated hierarchies, the firm is not dependent upon, or constrained by, them. Therefore, managers will be able to reconfigure the organization relatively easily. Finally, because a defining characteristic of isolated hierarchies is their 'self-reliance', they will be able to orchestrate a number of activities, potentially across a number of related sectors. In other words, they will possess considerable coordinating capabilities (Whitley 2010: 463–5).

However, the incentives of employees to invest time and effort in developing cross-functional and cross-divisional skills will be low. Consequently, attempts to implement competition strategies based on incremental innovation will be severely limited in isolated hierarchies. Indeed, employees in such firms are likely to have strong incentives to increase those skills that increase their chances of finding employment elsewhere, as the firm's commitment to them is low. They need, in short, to ensure that they have employment opportunities with other companies. It is only relatively senior managers in such companies who are likely to have a deep commitment to the company. However, the ownership and control structures of such companies and markets for corporate control can reduce even their job tenures.

It should also be noted, though, that the compartmentalized business system affords companies greater room for manoeuvre than other systems. As a result, managers may seek to introduce forms of 'welfare capitalism' (Jacoby 1997) into the company; this is intended to grant employees a status within the firm and to protect them, to a certain extent, from commercial risks. In concrete terms, US firms that pursued a policy of welfare capitalism introduced healthcare schemes and training programmes for employees. However, the types of firms that are able to implement such policies successfully are those that are sheltered from short-term financial pressures either by family ownership or by the separation of ownership and control (Jacoby 1997).

Centralized Hierarchy

Centralized hierarchies are associated with state-organized business systems, which are, in turn, linked with environments in which the state is prevalent in economic decision-making and exerts a powerful influence over intermediary organizations. In such business systems unions are either weak or controlled by the state. As a consequence, wage bargaining, if it is conducted in any meaningful way, is likely to be decentralized. The reluctance of such states to forbear the presence of unions is likely to be extended to business associations if these act as an impediment to the state's direction of the economy (Whitley 2007: 43). Indeed, individual companies will be heavily dependent on state agencies and officials, as these are likely to control access to funding, permits to operate in certain markets, and the use of crucial resources. A corollary of these characteristics is that the centralized, hierarchical firms that operate in such states will not grant much discretion to employees. Relatedly, employers will see few advantages in offering employees long and extensive careers. Similarly, long-term commitments to business partners or competitors will be difficult to establish, as firms' cardinal relationships are with the state and its agencies rather than other companies (Whitley 1999: 61–2; Whitley 2007: 43). Indeed, centralized hierarchies are likely to remain under the control of founding families even if shares are owned by institutional investors. This is, perhaps, most clearly illustrated by the appointment (or attempted appointment) of family members to senior management positions within Samsung. Samsung is a listed company, but it is, through cross-shareholdings, a family-controlled one.

In terms of capabilities, centralized hierarchies are, as an extension of the ability of the state to direct economic activities, likely to have considerable coordinating capabilities. Similarly, such firms are likely to possess significant reconfigurational capabilities if this is required by the state. This latter capability also reflects centralized hierarchies' ability to take decisions free from any constraints imposed by employees, except top managers. Centralized hierarchies' independence from most employees will mean their capability to learn as an organization will be minimal. Indeed, any organizational learning that does take place is likely to be confined to senior managers.

Employment relations within Hyundai Motor Company, which forms part of Hyundai, one of South Korea's oldest and largest family-owned conglomerates or *chaebol*, closely resemble those outlined within the ideal type of a centralized hierarchy. For instance, the company used the dormitory system to enable workers to be closely supervised and controlled (Cho 1999, cited in Lansbury et al., 2006). This indicates that little authority was shared with employees. Research by Lansbury et al. (2006: 138) reveals that, despite Hyundai Motor Company adopting certain employment practices in its South Korean facilities from Mitsubishi Motor Company, the firm did not involve its employees in some aspects of decision-making at the plant level, maintained high-status differentials between workers and managers in factories, and did not enable shopfloor employees to be promoted to higher positions. This reinforces the idea that little authority sharing occurs within the company. It also indicates that organizational careers are limited in scope for non-managerial employees.

These aspects conform to the ideal type of centralized hierarchy outlined above. Although Lansbury et al. (2006) did not examine organizational performance, other evidence indicates that South Korean companies have found it easier to reach the same productivity levels as local competitors in sectors in which crucial knowledge is explicit rather than tacit and in which knowledge is embodied in machinery or equipment (Jung and Lee 2010). This, too, is consistent with the above framework, as organizational learning is likely to be limited to top managers in centralized hierarchies. Lower-level employees do not contribute to organizational learning. As a result, the ability to generate new knowledge to improve existing products or create new ones is limited. However, the success of South Korean firms in the mobile-phone industry, to which they were relative latecomers, suggests that their ability to coordinate different capabilities across different economic activities is considerable (Hu and Hsu 2008).

Although there are, clearly, many differences between South Korea and Russia, the term centralized hierarchy can be applied to companies in Russia, too. In general, employers are free to determine the style of employment relations within such companies (Croucher and Cotton 2009). This often results in a lack of trust between managers and employees (Domsch and Lidokhover 2007). In addition, the longevity and scope of organizational careers are low (Linz and Semykina 2008). These conditions suggest that organizational learning in Russian companies will be confined to senior managers.

Indeed, evidence from Dixon et al. (2007) indicates that those Russian oil companies that they analysed and that exhibited these characteristics had weak organizational learning capabilities in the areas of exploitation and exploration. In addition, and in contrast to South Korean companies, the Russian firms that conformed relatively closely to the centralized hierarchy ideal type also lacked extensive coordinating capabilities.

Collaborative Hierarchy

Collaborative hierarchies develop in collaborative and highly coordinated business systems, which are characterized by institutional supports for cooperation between collective economic actors. These institutional supports can, *inter alia*, be provided by the state, which plays a coordinating, but not a directive role in the economy. In order to achieve this, the state may encourage the development of intermediary bodies to aid the formulation and implementation of (para-)public policies (Whitley 1999: 62). The importance of banks, as opposed to stock markets, in providing credit to companies also facilitates this cooperation, as banks are often closely connected to their debtors, and they cannot easily withdraw their funding if market conditions change. This results, to a certain extent, in the success of banks and their debtor companies becoming intertwined (Whitley 1999: 62). This funding enables company owners to be committed to their enterprises; unlike institutional investors, they are unlikely to sell their stakes if short-term difficulties are encountered.

Partly as a result of this commitment to firms by their owners, managers are able to adopt a longer-term approach to the business. Consequently, employers will be able to share authority with employees in terms of both depth and breadth, as the pressures to reduce staffing levels as a result of a downturn in profits will be less than they are in companies owned by a number of institutional investors. In addition, employees who form part of the core workforce will be less wary about investing in firm-specific skills, as the company will be under less pressure to make them redundant in response to decreases in profitability. In other words, the length of job tenures will be increased; this will enable companies to create a workforce with firm-specific skills. Consequently, internal labour markets will be important and any vacant positions within the firm are likely to be filled by existing employees. A corollary of these factors is that collaborative hierarchies will be constrained by their employees.

In terms of organizational capabilities, collaborative hierarchies will possess strong coordinating abilities, as employees are encouraged to develop firm-specific skills and employees, especially those in highly coordinated business systems, are moved between departments; this gives them greater insights into the firm's various functions and divisions. Hence, coordination should be easier to achieve (Whitley 2010: 466). The emphasis on firm-specific skills and internal labour markets within collaborative hierarchies will mean that they will have considerable organizational learning capabilities, as, firstly, credible employment commitments will lessen workers' concerns about sharing knowledge and, secondly, employees will have strong incentives to deepen their firm-specific knowledge to improve their organizational career prospects. However, radical reconfigurational capabilities are likely to be severely hindered precisely because of these commitments (Whitley 2010).

Germany is, perhaps, the archetypal collaborative business system. Despite the increase in the presence of foreign institutional investors on the German stock market, such investors are far less prevalent than they are in the UK, as Table 5.2 shows. Moreover, this change in the ownership profiles of large German firms has not heralded

Table 5.2 Stock market capitalization and stock ownership distribution in Germany and the UK, selected years 1992–2007

Country	Year			
	2007	2002	1997	1992
GERMANY				
Stock market capitalization (% GDP)	63.5	34.3	38.2	16.9
SHARE OWNERSHIP				
Foreign investors	21.3	14.8	10.1	10.4
Domestic investors	78.7	85.2	89.9	89.6
Comprising:				
Private financial enterprises	24.2	31.5	29.8	23.3
Private non-financial companies/orgs	39.3	36.6	37.6	42.2
Individual investors/households	13.3	14.0	17.3	18.8
Public sector	1.9	3.1	5.2	5.3
UK	2006	2002	1997	1992
Stock market capitalization (% GDP)	157.9	117.8	149.4	85.9
SHARE OWNERSHIP				
Foreign investors	40.0	35.9	28.0	13.1
Domestic investors	60.0	64.1	72.2	86.9
Comprising:				
Private financial enterprises	44.4	47.8	52.5	61.1
Private non-financial companies/orgs	2.7	1.9	3.1	3.6
Individual investors/ households	12.8	14.3	16.5	20.4
Public sector	0.1	0.1	0.1	1.8

Notes: The years vary slightly for Germany and the UK; this reflects the availability of the FESE (2008) data; rounding errors may prevent appropriate figures equalling 100% cent.
Sources: Stock market capitalization: World Development Indicators (Edition: September 2009); all other values: Federation of European Stock Exchanges (2008).

an emphasis on shareholder value in company decision-making (Börsch 2007). Many shares in German companies are held by non-financial firms; this indicates a degree of cross-shareholding amongst German companies. Such owners can be expected to be committed and so will not sell their stakes in another company if profits in that other company decline. It is also worth noting that the data on stock-market capitalization as a percentage of gross domestic product indicate that the stock market and, hence, institutional investors play a much greater role in financing companies' activities in the UK than they do in Germany.

The ownership characteristics of many German companies enable them to adopt a long-term perspective on the development of the company. This is complemented by labour market institutions, such as works councils and sectoral collective agreements. Although not as widespread as they once were and although sometimes functioning in ways that run counter to archetypical ones (Brewster et al. 2007; Hassel 1999; Streeck and Hassel 2003), these institutions still play an important role in many German firms (Allen 2006). They have, in general, helped to create cooperative employment relations in German companies (Haake 2002; Streeck 1992). These collaborative employment relations are associated with other outcomes that are likely to be beneficial to firms that rely on a relatively high proportion of their workforce for their competitiveness. For instance, works councils and collective wage agreements are linked to fewer difficulties recruiting and retaining employees, lower levels of absenteeism, and reduced quit rates (Allen 2006).

These outcomes strongly suggest that firms are in a position to build upon their employees' high commitment levels to increase their firm-specific skills. Such skills are likely to be of particular value in sectors that are characterized by relatively limited competence destruction risks. This could be because products are improved incrementally and knowledge is cumulative; that is, new knowledge builds upon existing knowledge. For instance, in the automobile sector, product improvements in general require, *inter alia*, production employees who, firstly, have a deep understanding of how their activities fit into the rest of the manufacturing process and, secondly, put forward suggestions to improve productivity as well as the quality of the finished vehicles (Crouch et al. 2009). In the enterprise-software sector, products are customized to the client firm's demands. In order to compete in this sector, firms must be able to draw on the skills and knowledge of employees who, firstly, have a strong understanding of the firm's products and, secondly, can comprehend and cater to client firms' evolving demands. In other words, employees have firm-specific knowledge that must be upgraded in an incremental fashion to improve the firm's service to customers (Casper and Whitley 2004).

In the latter sector in Germany, sectoral collective wage bargaining eases employees' fears over possible exploitation by employers. Such fears are increased if employees have firm-specific skills that severely limit their ability to change employers. Corporate governance regulations grant employee representatives a say in major decisions within large companies. Employment-protection legislation hinders dismissals. Works councillors within individual establishments must be consulted on matters relating to work organization. These factors have led to cooperative workplace employment relations (Casper and Whitley 2004). This has, in turn, created the conditions under which investments in cumulative, firm-specific knowledge can be undertaken. As a result, German companies are more competitive in the enterprise-software sector than their UK rivals (Casper and Whitley 2004).

In the automobile sector, the institutions of the archetypal 'German model', such as sectoral collective agreements, works councils, and the vocational training system, have helped German companies to remain competitive (Jürgens 2008). Although the ways in which these institutions operate have changed since the 1980s as a result of globalization, they are still present and the institutional change that has occurred within the industry has taken place in a cooperative and collaborative way (Jürgens 2008). (See Crouch et al. 2009 for more on changes within the German automobile sector.)

Japan is the paradigmatic example of a highly coordinated business system. However, once again, it would be incorrect to argue that all intra- and inter-organizational cooperation in Japan resembles a highly coordinated business system and that all firms are closely akin to collaborative hierarchies. For instance, small firms that offer limited job guarantees, if any, and that do not develop employees' skills form part of the Japanese manufacturing sector (Whitley 2005; see also Keizer 2008). These do not conform to the archetypal Japanese firm, but do complement more stereotypical ones (Morgan 2007b). In addition, foreign institutional investors have, collectively, acquired large stakes in Japanese companies. Their aim has often been to promote greater returns to shareholders (Jacoby 2007; Olcott 2009). Their success, however, is debatable, as, *inter alia*, corporate governance regulations and existing business linkages have hindered their efforts (Jackson 2009; Jacoby 2007; see also Keizer 2009).

In common with firms in collaborative business systems, those in highly coordinated business systems have committed owners. In *kereitsu*, or corporate networks that are underpinned by ownership ties, this can take the form of a major shareholding by the bank that forms part of the network as well as stakes held by other firms in the group (Jackson 2009; Vogel 2006). This facilitates a long-term perspective among senior managers within large companies, as the threat of being acquired or taken over is diminished. Consequently, the commitments that managers can give to employees about long-term employment security, as least for the firm's core workforce, are more credible. This, in turn, helps to create the conditions under which employers can devolve considerable discretion in both degree and scope to employees. However, for this to happen, employers must also be sanguine that employees will not 'hold up' the firm; that is, employees will not use their key position within the firm to increase their share of the firm's profits by threatening, for example, to delay or halt production. The presence of enterprise rather than industry unions in Japan encourages employees and their representatives to focus on their own firm's prospects rather than consider industry-wide developments (Whitley 1999). Similarly, established norms among large firms not to poach skilled workers as well as the sharing of information on wage rates limit the possibilities and incentives for such workers to change employer (Whitley 2007: 52; see also Sako and Kotosaka 2012). This is reinforced by seniority-based pay in large Japanese companies. As a result of these institutional factors, large Japanese companies are constrained to a significant extent by their employees.

This enables them to generate strong coordination capabilities of economic activities across the network (Dyer and Nobeoka 2000; Lam 2005). They also have considerable organizational learning capabilities. These can be related to the practice within many large Japanese companies of encouraging employees to have several areas of responsibility that may overlap with those of others; this encourages employees to develop a holistic and long-term understanding of the firm's activities and objectives. This contrasts with the situation in many large US companies that adopt a narrower perspective on employees' organizational responsibilities, which leads employees to focus on a restricted range of objectives. This, in turn, hinders organizational learning (Hamel 1991).

Internationalization, Business Systems, and Multinational Companies

As noted above, the heightened internationalization of product, capital, and some labour markets has reduced the homogeneity of national (and sub-national) business systems. It has also opened up, at least theoretically, the possibility that firms—in particular, multinational companies (MNCs)—will be able to develop distinctive capabilities that transcend national borders and that are independent of any particular institutional environment (Whitley 2010: 479). If MNCs can free themselves from their institutional environments, the business systems framework would be undermined (Allen 2013). This issue has been addressed within the business systems literature; it is somewhat downplayed in the VOC paradigm.

However, it is important to highlight that the effects of internationalization on firms' coordination mechanisms and competitive capabilities are likely to be significant only when important resources are located overseas; overseas subsidiary managers play a major role in decision-making and capability development; and domestic policies, including employment-related measures, are adapted to, and by, foreign sites (Whitley 2010: 479–80). In the absence of these, MNCs will, in general, find it difficult to develop transnational capabilities. If they fail to create and maintain such capabilities, MNCs will not differ, as strategic economic actors, from similar, yet purely domestic firms. To be sure, within a single MNC, domestic establishments and foreign locations may have capabilities that enable them to compete successfully within the markets they serve; however, their capabilities will remain separate unless organizational practices and routines are changed within the MNC to encourage transnational organizational learning. Learning within firms is likely to be characterized by the transfer of new ideas, skills, and knowledge from innovating subsidiaries to other parts of the organization (Whitley 2010).

A corollary of this is that the number of MNCs that develop distinctive transnational competitive capabilities—as opposed to those that rely on a collection of discrete competencies located within national subsidiaries—is likely to be low (Whitley 1998, 2010). This is particularly so, as the development of transnational organizational learning is likely to be characterized by employees making investments in firm-specific skills. This, in turn, will require employees and the MNCs' business partners to be committed to the creation and enrichment of its cross-border competencies.

A number of implications for MNCs' employment relations follow from this. Firstly, creating employee commitment across the organization will require authority to be shared with those employees. Employees in different locations will need to be able to contribute to, and make, important decisions within the firm. Secondly, the commitment to the firm of senior managers from across the MNC is likely to depend upon them being offered the credible prospect of lengthy organizational careers, including head-office positions, if they contribute significantly to organizational learning. In other words, very senior positions within the firm should not be the preserve of those from the MNC's home country (Whitley 2010).

As noted above, the willingness of owners and employers to grant decision-making powers to lower-level employees and to provide organizational careers will be shaped significantly by institutions. Consequently, the ability of subsidiaries of an MNC that are based in varying types of institutional setting to share authority with employees will differ as will their ability to offer organizational careers (Whitley 2010). Indeed, even MNCs from countries, such as Japan, that have been able to offer credible long-term employment commitments to their core workforce may find it difficult to operate in the same way abroad (see much of the evidence cited in Morgan et al. 2003). For instance, Japanese manufacturing subsidiaries in the UK were unable to offer long-term employment commitments to British workers (Morgan et al. 2003); this is likely to have reduced their ability to learn from the UK. In addition, MNCs may struggle to adapt organizational routines to foreign locations. For instance, subsidiaries of Japanese MNCs that sought to gain access to external sources of knowledge often found it difficult because the MNCs were centralized and authority was not shared with subsidiary managers (Lam 2003). By contrast, US MNCs were able to tap into overseas sources of knowledge to a greater extent as they were less centralized and more authority was shared with subsidiary managers. If knowledge and skills in specific areas are becoming increasingly dispersed across the world, the country of origin of the MNC may play an important role in the extent to which the company can draw on foreign competencies and integrate them across the whole of the firm.

Conclusions

This contribution has put forward evidence to corroborate the links between business systems, firm types, employee relations, and organizational capabilities within the business system framework. However, there are relatively few studies that attempt to detail the institutional setting of firms; the technological and market risks associated with different sub-sectors of the economy; the resultant organizational capabilities needed to surmount those challenges; the employment practices and routines required to create, maintain, and develop those competitive competencies; and the ways in which firms' institutional settings help or hinder companies to implement those routines successfully. This is, perhaps, not surprising. However, from a business systems perspective, analyses that focus on, say, the links between firms' institutional settings and employee turnover halt the analysis too early. From a business systems perspective, the analysis should be extended to encompass the links between employee turnover and the ability, or otherwise, of firms to compete in their relevant product markets. Similarly, those analyses that, for example, examine the links between organizational routines, such as the ways in which work is organized and careers are structured, and organizational capabilities should be deepened so that they incorporate the influence of institutions on the ability of firms to pursue certain routines and, hence, their ability to compete successfully.

To be sure, this is no easy task. Recent developments in the international economy will make it even more arduous. The internationalization of product, capital, and some labour markets means that the opportunities that firms have to overcome domestic institutional constraints have been increased. However, the ability of companies to draw on these institutional resources is likely to depend on the nature of those resources, including their 'transferability'. Thus, some sources of finance may be available to companies in many more locations than was previously the case: Kazakhmys, a Kazakh mining company, is, for instance, listed on the London Stock Exchange, potentially making its owners a dispersed group of investors. By contrast, certain forms of knowledge may be embedded within public science systems, which may hamper the ability of foreign companies to gain access to that knowledge (Allen and Whitley 2012). Thus, the internationalization of certain markets means that firms' institutional settings must be specified rather than inferred from any macro-level framework. For instance, Kazakhmys may have a dispersed ownership structure and be subject to UK regulations on publicly quoted companies, but it is still embedded within the Kazakh business system, as some of its most influential owners and many of its senior managers are Kazakh and its main assets are there. Employment relations are, therefore, likely to be shaped most strongly by the Kazakh and not the British employment system.

In addition to the increasing internationalization of certain institutional resources, some countries have seen heightened institutional diversity at the sub-national level. For instance, the UK has witnessed moves to devolve certain policy-making responsibilities to Scotland, Northern Ireland, and Wales. Consequently, institutions, such as public funding related to industrial policies, have become increasingly varied (Allen and Whitley 2012). Thus, diversity has increased even within states that may once have been regarded as offering a homogeneous institutional setting to companies. This requires researchers to take heterogeneity into account in their analyses.

This enhanced diversity in the institutional settings of firms that has been wrought by increasing internationalization and heightened sub-national variation also draws attention to the role of actors. In particular, it highlights the ways in which they can select institutional resources to enhance their competitive positions. This, in turn, has implications for our understanding of the perceptions of collective actors, such as firms, employers' associations, and unions, in the process of institutional displacement, layering, conversion, and drift (Streeck and Thelen 2005). This implies that institutions are not static, but are subject to contestation by a range of actors with varying levels of autonomy (see, for example, Kristensen and Zeitlin 2005; Mahoney and Thelen 2010; Morgan 2007b). These issues are ones that are likely to be at the heart of analyses that draw on the business systems framework in the future. By doing so, future studies will extend a framework that has already provided key insights into the systematic variation in firms, their priorities, their capabilities, their employment relations, and their levels of competitiveness across a range of countries.

REFERENCES

Allen, M. M. C. (2004). 'The Varieties of Capitalism Paradigm: Not Enough Variety?', *Socio-Economic Review*, 2(1): 87–107.

—— (2006). *The Varieties of Capitalism Paradigm: Explaining Germany's Comparative Advantage?* Basingstoke: Palgrave Macmillan.

—— (2013). 'Comparative Capitalisms and the Institutional Embeddedness of Innovative Capabilities', *Socio-Economic Review*, 11(4): 771–94.

Allen, M. M. C. and Aldred, M. L. (2011). 'Varieties of Capitalism, Governance, and High-Tech Export Performance: A Fuzzy-Set Analysis of the New EU Member States', *Employee Relations*, 33(4): 334–55.

Allen, M. M. C., Tüselmann, H.-J., and Aldred, M. L. (2011). 'Institutional Frameworks and Radical Innovation: An Analysis of High- and Medium-High-Technology Industries in Germany', *International Journal of Public Policy*, 7(4–6): 265–81.

Allen, M. M. C. and Whitley, R. (2012). 'Internationalization and Sectoral Diversity: The Roles of Organizational Capabilities and Dominant Institutions in Structuring Firms' Responses to Semiglobalization', in C. Lane and G. T. Wood (eds.), *Capitalist Diversity and Diversity within Capitalism*. London: Routledge, 97–120.

Almond, P. (2011). 'The Sub-National Embeddedness of International HRM', *Human Relations*, 64(4): 531–51.

Becker-Ritterspach, F., Saka-Helmhout, A., and Hotho, J. J. (2010). 'Practice Transfer in MNEs as the Socially-Embedded Translation of Practices', *Critical Perspectives on International Business*, 6(1): 8–37.

Bohle, D. and Greskovits, B. (2007). 'The State, Internationalization, and Capitalist Diversity in Eastern Europe', *Competition and Change*, 11(2): 89–115.

Börsch, A. (2007). *Global Pressure, National System: How German Corporate Governance is Changing*. Ithaca, NY: Cornell University Press.

Brewster, C., Croucher, R., Wood, G., and Brookes, M. (2007). 'Collective and Individual Voice: Convergence in Europe?', *International Journal of Human Resource Management*, 18(7): 1246–62.

Casper, S. (2007). *Creating Silicon Valley in Europe: Public Policies towards New Technology Industries*. Oxford and New York: Oxford University Press.

—— (2009). 'Can New Technology Firms Succeed in Coordinated Market Economies? A Response to Herrmann and Lange', *Socio-Economic Review*, 7(2): 209–15.

Casper, S. and Whitley, R. (2004). 'Managing Competences in Entrepreneurial Technology Firms: A Comparative Institutional Analysis of Germany, Sweden and the UK', *Research Policy*, 33(1): 89–106.

Cho, H. J. (1999). 'The Employment Adjustment of Hyundai Motor Company: A Research Focus on Corporate-Level Labour Relations', *Korean Journal of Labour Studies*, 5(1): 63–96.

Crouch, C. (2005). *Capitalist Diversity and Change: Recombinant Governance and Institutional Entrepreneurs*. Oxford and New York: Oxford University Press.

Crouch, C., Schröder, M., and Voelzkow, H. (2009). 'Regional and Sectoral Varieties of Capitalism', *Economy and Society*, 38(4): 654–78.

Crouch, C., Streeck, W., Boyer, R., Amable, B., Hall, P. A., and Jackson, J. (2005). 'Dialogue on Institutional Complementarity and Political Economy', *Socio-Economic Review*, 3(2): 359–82.

Crouch, C. and Voelzkow, H. (eds.) (2009). *Innovation in Local Economies: Germany in Comparative Context*. Oxford and New York: Oxford University Press.

Croucher, R. and Cotton, E. (2009). *Global Unions, Global Business*. London: Middlesex University Press.

Croucher, R., Wood, G., Brewster, C., and Brookes, M. (2012). 'Employee Turnover, HRM and Institutional Contexts', *Economic and Industrial Democracy*, 33(4): 605–20.

Czaban, L., Hocevar, M., Jaklic, M., and Whitley, R. (2003). 'Path Dependence and Contractual Relations in Emergent Capitalism: Contrasting State Socialist Legacies and Inter-Firm Cooperation in Hungary and Slovenia', *Organization Studies*, 24(1): 7–28.

Dixon, S. E. A., Meyer, K. E., and Day, M. (2007). 'Exploitation and Exploration Learning and the Development of Organizational Capabilities: A Cross-Case Analysis of the Russian Oil Industry', *Human Relations*, 60(10): 1493–1523.

Djelic, M.-L. and Quack, S. (eds.) (2003). *Globalization and Institutions: Redefining the Rules of the Economic Game*. Cheltenham: Edward Elgar.

Domsch, M. and Lidokhover, T. (2007). 'Introduction: The Broader Historical, Social and Economic Context of the Current Situation in Russia', in Domsch and Lidokhover (eds.), *Human Resource Management in Russia*. Aldershot: Ashgate, 1–22.

Dosi, G., Nelson, R., and Winter, S. (eds.) (2000). *The Nature and Dynamics of Organizational Capabilities*. Oxford and New York: Oxford University Press.

Dyer, J. H. and Nobeoka, K. (2000). 'Creating and Managing a High-Performance Knowledge-Sharing Network: The Toyota Case', *Strategic Management Journal*, 21(3): 345–67.

Fajana, S. (2008). 'The Nigerian Informal Economy: Instigating Decent Work and Pay, and National Development through Unionisation', *Employee Relations*, 30(4): 372–90.

Farrell, H. and Holten, A.-L. (2004). 'Collective Goods in the Local Economy: The Packaging Machinery Cluster in Bologna', in C. Crouch, P. Le Galès, C. Trigilia, and H. Voelzkow (eds.), *Local Production Systems in Europe: Reconstruction and Innovation*. Oxford and New York: Oxford University Press, 23–45.

Federation of European Stock Exchanges (FESE) (2008). *Share Ownership Structure in Europe*. Available at <http://www.bourse.lu/contenu/docs/commun/societe/Actualites/2008/FESE_SHARE_OWNERSHIP_SURVEY_2007.pdf>.

Gospel, H. and Pendleton, A. (2003). 'Finance, Corporate Governance and the Management of Labour: A Conceptual and Comparative Analysis', *British Journal of Industrial Relations*, 41(3): 557–82.

Goyer, M. (2006). 'Varieties of Institutional Investors and National Models of Capitalism: The Transformation of Corporate Governance in France and Germany', *Politics & Society*, 34(3): 399–430.

—— (2011). *Contingent Capital: Short-term Institutional Investors and the Evolution of Corporate Governance in France and Germany*. Oxford and New York: Oxford University Press.

Haake, S. (2002). 'National Business Systems and Industry-Specific Competitiveness', *Organization Studies*, 23(5): 711–36.

Hamel, G. (1991). 'Competition for Competence and Inter-Partner Learning within International Strategic Alliances', *Strategic Management Journal*, 12(2): 83–103.

Hancké, B., Rhodes, M., and Thatcher, M. (eds.) (2007). *Beyond Varieties of Capitalism: Conflict, Contradictions, and Complementarities in the European Economy*. Oxford and New York: Oxford University Press.

Harcourt, M. and Wood, G. (2007). 'The Importance of Employment Protection for Skill Development in Coordinated Market Economies', *European Journal of Industrial Relations*, 13(2): 141–59.

Hassel, A. (1999). 'The Erosion of the German System of Industrial Relations', *British Journal of Industrial Relations*, 37(3): 483–505.

Hu, J.-L. and Hsu, Y.-H. (2008). 'The More Interactive, the More Innovative? A Case Study of South Korean Cellular Phone Manufacturers', *Technovation*, 28(1–2): 75–87.

Jackson, G. (2009). 'The Japanese Firm and its Diversity', *Economy and Society*, 38(3): 605–28.

Jacoby, S. M. (1997). *Modern Manors: Welfare Capitalism since the New Deal*. Princeton: Princeton University Press.

—— (2007). 'Principles and Agents: CalPERS and Corporate Governance in Japan', *Corporate Governance*, 15(1): 1–15.

Jung, M. and Lee, K. (2010). 'Sectoral Systems of Innovation and Productivity Catch-Up: Determinants of the Productivity Gap between Korean and Japanese Firms', *Industrial and Corporate Change*, 19(4): 1037–69.

Jürgens, U. (2008). 'Gobalization and Employment Relations in the German Auto Industry', in R. Blanpain and R. D. Lansbury (eds.), *Globalization and Employment Relations in the Auto Assembly Industry*. Alphen: Kluwer Law International, 49–72.

Keizer, A. B. (2008). 'Non-Regular Employment in Japan: Continued and Renewed Dualities', *Work, Employment and Society*, 22(3): 407–25.

—— (2009). 'Transformations in- and outside the Internal Labour Market: Institutional Change and Continuity in Japanese Employment Practices', *International Journal of Human Resource Management*, 20(7): 1521–35.

Kristensen, P. H. (2006). 'Business Systems in the Age of the "New Economy": Denmark Facing the Challenge', in J. L. Campbell, J. A. Hall, and O. K. Pedersen (eds.), *National Identity and the Varieties of Capitalism: The Danish Experience*. Montreal: McGill-Queen's University Press, 295–320.

—— (2011). 'Developing Comprehensive, Enabling Welfare States for Offensive Experimentalist Business Practices', in Kristensen and K. Lilja (eds.), *Nordic Capitalisms and Globalization: New Forms of Economic Organization and Welfare Institutions*. Oxford and New York: Oxford University Press, 220–58.

Kristensen, P. H. and Zeitlin, J. (2005). *Local Players in Global Games: The Strategic Constitution of a Multinational Corporation*. Oxford and New York: Oxford University Press.

Lam A. (2003). 'Organizational Learning in Multinationals: R&D Networks of Japanese and US MNEs in the UK', *Journal of Management Studies*, 40(3): 673–703.

—— (2005). 'Work Roles and Careers of R&D Scientists in Network Organisations', *Industrial Relations*, 44(2): 242–75.

Lane, C. (1989). *Management and Labour in Europe*. Cheltenham: Elgar.

Lane, C. and Wood, G. T. (eds.) (2012). *Capitalist Diversity and Diversity within Capitalism*. London: Routledge.

Lane, D. and Myant, M. (eds.) (2007). *Varieties of Capitalism in Post-Communist Countries*. Basingstoke: Palgrave Macmillan.

Lange, K. (2009). 'Institutional Embeddedness and the Strategic Leeway of Actors: The Case of the German Therapeutical Biotech Industry', *Socio-Economic Review*, 7(2): 181–207.

Lansbury, R. D., Kwon, S.-H., and Suh, C.-S. (2006). 'Globalization and Employment Relations in the Korean Auto Industry: The Case of the Hyundai Motor Company in Korea, Canada and India', *Asia Pacific Business Review*, 12(2): 131–47.

Linz, S. and Semykina, A. (2008). 'How Do Workers Fare during Transition? Perceptions of Job Insecurity among Russian Workers, 1995-2004', *Labour Economics*, 15(3): 442–58.

Lundvall, B.-Å. and Lorenz, E. (2006). 'Welfare Systems and National Systems of Innovation', in Lorenz and Lundvall (eds.), *How Europe's Economies Learn: Coordinating Competing Models*. Oxford and New York: Oxford University Press, 411–32.

McCaffrey, S. J. (2013). 'Tacit-rich Districts and Globalization: Changes in the Italian Textile and Apparel Production System', *Socio-Economic Review*, 11(4): 657–85.

Mahoney, J. and Thelen, K. (eds.) (2010). *Explaining Institutional Change: Ambiguity, Agency, and Power*. Cambridge: Cambridge University Press.

Malerba, F. (2002). 'Sectoral Systems of Innovation and Production', *Research Policy*, 31(2): 247–64.

Malerba, F. and Orsenigo, L. (1997). 'Technological Regimes and Sectoral Patterns of Innovative Activities', *Industrial and Corporate Change*, 6(1): 83–117.

Morgan, G. (2007a). 'National Business Systems Research: Progress and Prospects', *Scandinavian Journal of Management*, 23(2): 127–45.

—— (2007b). 'The Theory of Comparative Capitalisms and the Possibilities for Local Variation', *European Review*, 15(3): 353–71.

Morgan, G., Kelly, B., Sharpe, D., and Whitley, R. (2003). 'Global Managers and Japanese Multinationals: Internationalization and Management in Japanese Financial Institutions', *International Journal of Human Resource Management*, 14(3): 389–407.

Morgan, G. and Kubo, I. (2005). 'Beyond Path Dependency? Constructing New Models for Institutional Change: The Case of Capital Markets in Japan', *Socio-Economic Review*, 3(1): 55–82.

Morgan, G. and Quack, S. (2005). 'Internationalization and Capability Development in Professional Services Firms', in Morgan, R. Whitley, and E. Moen (eds.), *Changing Capitalisms? Internationalization, Institutional Change, and Systems of Economic Organization*. Oxford and New York: Oxford University Press, 277–311.

Nielsen, P. and Lundvall, B.-Å. (2006). 'Learning Organizations and Industrial Relations: How the Danish Economy Learns', in E. Lorenz and Lundvall (eds.), *How Europe's Economies Learn: Coordinating Competing Models*. Oxford and New York: Oxford University Press, 161–77.

Nölke, A. and Vliegenthart, A. (2009). 'Enlarging the Varieties of Capitalism: The Emergence of Dependent Market Economies in East Central Europe', *World Politics*, 61(4): 670–702.

O'Sullivan, M. (2000). *Contests for Corporate Control: Corporate Governance and Economic Performance in the United States and Germany*. Oxford and New York: Oxford University Press.

Olcott, G. (2009). *Conflict and Change: Foreign Ownership and the Japanese Firm.* Cambridge: Cambridge University Press.

Penrose, E. (1959). *The Theory of the Growth of the Firm.* Oxford: Blackwell.

Porter, M. E. (1979). 'How Competitive Forces Shape Strategy', *Harvard Business Review*, 57(2): 137–45.

Sako, M. and Jackson, G. (2006). 'Strategy Meets Institutions: The Transformation of Management–Labor Relations at Deutsche Telekom and NTT', *Industrial and Labor Relations Review*, 59(3): 347–66.

Sako, M. and Kotosaka, M. (2012). 'Institutional Change and Organizational Diversity in Japan', in C. Lane and G. T. Wood (eds.), *Capitalist Diversity and Diversity within Capitalism.* London: Routledge, 69–96.

Schneiberg, M. (2007). 'What's on the Path? Path Dependence, Organizational Diversity, and the Problem of Institutional Change in the US Economy, 1900–1950', *Socio-Economic Review*, 5(1): 47–80.

Simon, H. (2007). *Hidden Champions des 21. Jahrhunderts: Die Erfolgstrategien unbekannter Weltmarktführer.* Frankfurt am Main: Campus Verlag.

Streeck, W. (1992). *Social Institutions and Economic Performance: Studies of Industrial Relations in Advanced Capitalist Economies.* New York: Sage.

—— (2009). *Re-Forming Capitalism: Institutional Change in the German Political Economy.* Oxford and New York: Oxford University Press.

Streeck, W. and Hassel, A. (2003). 'The Crumbling Pillars of Social Partnership', *West European Politics*, 26(4): 101–24.

Streeck, W. and Thelen, K. (2005). 'Introduction: Institutional Change in Advanced Political Economies', in Streeck and Thelen (eds.), *Beyond Continuity: Institutional Change in Advanced Political Economies.* Oxford and New York: Oxford University Press, 1–39.

Teece, D. J., Pisano, G., and Shuen, A. (1997). 'Dynamic Capabilities and Strategic Management', *Strategic Management Journal*, 18(7): 509–33.

Tylecote, A. and Ramirez, P. (2006). 'Corporate Governance and Innovation: The UK Compared with the US and "Insider" Economies', *Research Policy*, 35(1): 160–80.

Vogel, S. K. (2006). *Japan Remodeled: How Government and Industry are Reforming Japanese Capitalism.* Ithaca, NY: Cornell University Press.

Whitley, R. (1990). 'Eastern Asian Enterprise Structures and the Comparative Analysis of Forms of Business Organization', *Organization Studies*, 11(1): 47–74.

—— (1992a). *Business Systems in East Asia: Firms, Markets and Societies.* London: Sage.

—— (ed.) (1992b). *European Business Systems: Firms and Markets in their National Contexts.* London: Sage.

—— (1994). 'Dominant Forms of Economic Organization in Market Economies', *Organization Studies*, 15(2): 153–82.

—— (1998). 'Internationalization and Varieties of Capitalism: The Limited Effects of Cross-National Coordination of Economic Activities on the Nature of Business Systems', *Review of International Political Economy*, 5(3): 445–81.

—— (1999). *Divergent Capitalisms: The Social Structuring and Change of Business Systems.* Oxford and New York: Oxford University Press.

—— (2000). 'The Institutional Structuring of Innovation Strategies: Business Systems, Firm Types and Patterns of Technical Change in Different Market Economies', *Organization Studies*, 21(5): 855–86.

—— (2003). 'From the Search for Universal Correlations to the Institutional Structuring of Economic Organization and Change', *Organization*, 10(3): 481–502.

—— (2005). 'How National Are Business Systems? The Role of States and Complementary Institutions in Standardizing Systems of Economic Coordination and Control at the National Level', in G. Morgan, Whitley, and E. Moen (eds.), *Changing Capitalisms? Internationalization, Institutional Change and Systems of Economic Organization*. Oxford and New York: Oxford University Press, 190–232.

—— (2007). *Business Systems and Organizational Capabilities: The Institutional Structuring of Competitive Competences*. Oxford and New York: Oxford University Press.

—— (2009). 'U.S. Capitalism: A Tarnished Model?', *Academy of Management Perspectives*, 23(2): 11–22.

—— (2010). 'The Institutional Construction of Firms', in G. Morgan, J. L. Campbell, C. Crouch, O. K. Pedersen, and Whitley (eds.), *The Oxford Handbook of Comparative Institutional Analysis*. Oxford and New York: Oxford University Press, 453–95.

Whitley, R. and Czaban, L. (1998). 'Institutional Transformation and Enterprise Change in an Emergent Capitalist Economy: The Case of Hungary', *Organization* Studies, 19(2): 259–80.

Whitley, R. and Morgan, G. (2012). 'Capitalisms and Capitalism in the Twenty-First Century: Introduction', in Morgan and Whitley (eds.), *Capitalisms and Capitalism in the Twenty-First Century*. Oxford and New York: Oxford University Press, 1–10.

Wilkinson, A. and Fay, C. (2011). 'New Times for Employee Voice?', *Human Resource Management*, 50(1): 65–74.

Wilkinson, A. and Wood, G. (2012). 'Institutions and Employment Relations: The State of the Art', *Industrial Relations*, 51(S1): 373–88.

Williamson, O. E. (1985). *The Economic Institutions of Capitalism*. New York: Free Press.

Wood, G., Croucher, R., Brewster, C., Collings, D. G., and Brookes, M. (2009). 'Varieties of Firm: Complementarity and Bounded Diversity', *Journal of Economic Issues*, 43(1): 239–58.

Wood, G., Dibben, P., Stride, C., and Webster, E. (2011). 'HRM in Mozambique: Homogenization, Path Dependence or Segmented Business System?', *Journal of World Business*, 46(1): 31–41.

Wood, G. and Frynas, G. (2006). 'The Institutional Basis of Economic Failure: Anatomy of the Segmented Business System', *Socio-Economic Review*, 4(2): 239–77.

CHAPTER 6

DEVELOPMENTS AND EXTENSIONS OF 'RÉGULATION THEORY' AND EMPLOYMENT RELATIONS

ROBERT BOYER

INTRODUCTION

EMPLOYMENT relations can be analysed according to a wide variety of viewpoints or paradigms within the diverse social sciences. The legal approach focuses upon the specificity of labour contracts between employees and employers, as opposed to typical commercial contracts. The specialists in business organization study the various incentives and constraints that contribute to the commitment of workers, with a special concern for the links between productive organization and remuneration system. Labour sociology is dedicated to understanding the role of values and norms in the balance between cooperation and competition in the workplace and the relation between fairness and economic efficiency.

The new microeconomics of labour emphasizes the role of asymmetric information in the extraction of effort from workers and it has shown how this feature drastically affects the clearing of the labour market, as soon as the remuneration become a tool for disciplining workers, unemployment being one of the possible consequence of this dilemma between a typical market relation and the specific subordination associated to the labour contract. By contrast, modern macroeconomic theories continue to consider that the wage should be the adjusting variable between the supply and demand of labour. Within such a framework, labour is a commodity among a whole set of other commodities. On another side of the spectrum, the renewal of institutional economics has insisted upon the choice between a commercial contract and an employment contract, in the context of different configurations for the organization of the production and degree of uncertainty.

The present chapter proposes a bridge between two usually disconnected research programmes, those of macroeconomics and institutional analysis. All markets are embedded into a set of rules, organizations, and institutions that make them sustainable. For instance, fair competition calls for clear and efficient public control and therefore various forms of competition can be implemented according to different regulatory regimes. The impact of the institutional context is still stronger concerning labour and employment relations, since they are highly contested fields. According to the nature of past conflicts and institutionalized compromises, a large diversity of forms of wage–labour nexus can be observed. Nevertheless, the institutions that govern private labour contracts are mainly analysed from a microeconomic point of view: they are rarely introduced into a macroeconomic context. One of the key specificities of French 'Régulation theory' is precisely to tentatively reconcile qualitative institutional approaches along with the search for macroeconomic regularities. This is not a variant of the American regulation school that studies how governments may control and monitor public utilities and services. By contrast, Régulation theory investigates the long-run institutional and organizational transformations of capitalism; state interventions are only a part of these transformations.

The present chapter is built upon this general hypothesis. The conceptual framework is first presented in order to explicate how this approach differs from the usual conception of economists who consider markets as the unique coordinating mechanism in modern economies. A special emphasis is put upon the wage–labour nexus, whose employment relation is discussed below. A vast majority of labour market economics only deals with micro and short-run adjustments, with few concerns about the long-term impact of labour institutions upon growth regimes. It is thus interesting to provide a brief synthesis about the major findings of the long-run analysis of the transformations of labour in American and French capitalisms. Basically, one finds a remarkable co-evolution between the wage–labour nexus and macroeconomic growth regimes from the early nineteenth century until the end of the post-Second World War Golden Age. There is no better introduction to a detailed analysis of the various employment relations that are coexisting and competing since the demise of the canonical Fordist wage nexus. The related taxonomy is then enlarged in order to prospectively analyse the employment relations that are potentially compatible with the transformations of regulation modes and growth regimes during this first part of the twenty-first century. A short conclusion wraps up the major findings and their implications for future research.

MIXING INSTITUTIONS AND MACROECONOMICS: A REFRESHER COURSE IN RÉGULATION THEORY

Three Methodological Principles

The research programme discussed here tries to combine *inductive* and *deductive methods*, in other words to build some bridges between the stylized facts highlighted by economic historians about capitalist development and the highly abstract growth theory. Second, and consequently, there is probably no grand theory able to explain synthetically the whole set of the relevant stylized facts: this is the Achilles' heel of conventional economic theories. By contrast, the regulation approach looks for *local and period dependent analyses* of macro-dynamics, by providing a set of intermediate concepts which describe the coordination mechanisms actually in use for a given economy and historical epoch. Finally, capital accumulation is supposed to be the driving force of capitalist society. But since accumulation is a fairly uneven and contradictory process, we have to investigate under what conditions the conflicts and disequilibria inherent to capital accumulation nevertheless deliver the possibility of periods of sustained growth.

The answer is simple indeed: cumulative growth will be possible if the four basic institutional forms which define a capitalist economy produce a productivity regime on one side and a demand regime on the other which ex-post are coherent, i.e. able to define a growth regime, with the property of self-equilibration with respect to internal dynamic as well as possible external shocks. Let us present briefly the broad relationships between the four institutional forms and long-term growth.

The Centrality of the Wage–Labour Nexus

The wage–labour nexus describes the configuration associated with a given state of division of labour, as well as income distribution. Following the seminal work by Adam Smith, and pushed a step forward by Karl Marx, the forms of internal productive organization within firms and their relations with the market are the key factors shaping a productivity regime. Briefly, each stage in the history of the division of labour is associated with definite factors of productivity increases, which combine in various proportions the impact of specialization, learning by doing, design of machines, and the sizes of minimum efficiency scale (Boyer and Schmeder 1990). An economy composed exclusively of craftsmen or pin manufacturers, or Fordist assembly line or Silicon Valley high tech firms would clearly exhibit contrasting productivity regimes. This distinction is crucial for macroeconomics: there is no natural and general form of production functions.

It is a Component of a Set of Other Institutional Forms

Conventional economic theories used to privilege the hypothesis of pure competition, just for simplicity's sake. But it is clear that in most economies imperfect competition prevails, whatsoever its origin: barriers to entry, uncertainty about quality, collusion among few producers, etc. Consequently, defining the *forms of competition* is important for price formation and of course investment decisions. The new theories of industrial organization convincingly argue that the dynamics of profit, investment, and price are highly sensitive to the institutional setting codifying the relations between firms (Tirole 1988). These differences can explain contrasted trajectories in terms of capacity utilization, investment, or even innovation.

The *state* has then to be inserted into the analysis. On one side, property right theoreticians have pointed to the role of the constitution and law in providing the prerequisites of any capitalist market economy. Under this general heading, the viability of any contract supposes not only laws and jurisdictions but a rather stable monetary system. Remember that in the writings of Adam Smith, specialization and deepening of labour division can only occur if stable market relations are warranted over a foreseeable future. On the other side, the modern state in advanced capitalist countries has largely extended its interventions towards the supply of many collective goods which are necessary for the efficiency and growth of a market economy: education, training, health, transport infrastructure, telecommunications, and credit and subsidy in favour of innovators. Consequently, state interventions contribute to both the productivity and the demand regime.

A fourth institutional form for any economy relates to its *insertion into the international regime*. At each historical epoch, there exists a set of institutions, explicit or implicit rules which define the rights and duties of any country, concerning external trade, short-run capital movement, exchange rate determination, foreign investment, property rights, and so on. Consequently, the constraints and opportunities created by a given international regime are to be taken into account in any analysis of long-term national growth (Mistral 1986; Keohane 1984). Similarly, within such a regime, the countries may experience varying degrees of openness, control over the price of exports, and of course contrasted specialization (primary or intermediary products, low or high quality consumer goods, equipment goods and patents, etc.). Therefore from a quasi-closed continental economy to a small open country, there is a whole spectrum of configurations, with a key influence upon growth and stability.

The Macro Compatibility of a Wage–Labour Nexus with an Institutional Configuration

The central issue at stake is then the following: do these different institutional forms define a viable socio-economic regime and sustain a viable growth regime or does their incoherence lead to structural instability and one form or another of crisis? In the new institutional economics, each organization or type of labour contract is analysed through its micro-foundations and the compatibility of a complete set of incentives. Sometimes one gets the impression that an optimal design could deliver the best practice in a fully decentralized manner with little or no consideration for other surrounding institutions. In contrast, the 'régulation' approach, without denying the importance of sound micro-foundations, stresses the *structural compatibility* of the major institutional forms (Fig. 6.1). There could be no Fordist wage formula without a permissive monetary system, a rather closed economy, or at least a stable international system. Conversely, what many economists attribute to an inherent flaw at the micro level (for example wage rigidity) might result from the inadequacy of the labour institutions given the new macroeconomic context and the occurrence of unprecedented shocks difficult to absorb in the present configuration, such as a decay of the international system, shift in the objective of economic policies, or consequences of global competition and financial deregulation.

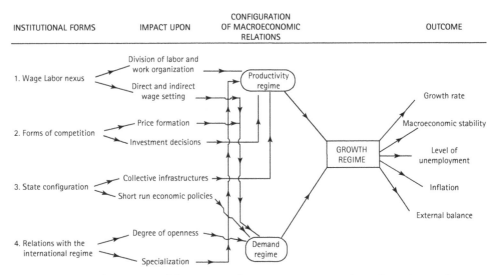

FIGURE 6.1 How does a wage–labour nexus fit into an institutional configuration and sustain a growth regime?

THE CO-EVOLUTION OF THE WAGE–LABOUR NEXUS AND MACROECONOMIC REGIMES

This framework has two major implications. First, there exists a priori a multiplicity of such viable configurations at odds with the search for an optimal wage–labour nexus typical of neo-classical theorizing but also with a benchmarking strategy that implies one best way for employment relations. Multiple cross-national comparisons have confirmed the diversity of capitalism brands (Schor and You 1995; Boyer 1995, 2001; Amable et al. 1997; Amable 2004; Baccaro and Howell 2010). Second, since capitalist economies are permanently evolving under the pressure of competition, a static analysis has to be replaced by a study of the historical transformations of a set of institutional forms. During some periods, they smoothly sustain a rather stable growth regime, but in others they lose their ability to efficiently coordinate the strategies of actors and they enter into a structural crisis, when the issue at stake is no less than the search for a new configuration, among a sharpening of conflicting interests and visions about the required properties of the emerging configuration.

The Long-Run Transformations in Labour Market Institutions

The recurring finding of Régulation theory is thus that long-run institutional changes have significantly or totally altered economic mechanisms (Table 6.1).

Table 6.1 In the long run, major changes in the wage–labour nexus and other institutional forms: the French case

PERIODS / INSTITUTIONAL FORMS	1789	1848	1873	1896	1914–1918	1929	1939–1952	1967	1973	1980
• WAGE-LABOUR NEXUS										
– Work organization	Manufacturers replace craftsmen	Work duration is extended but reaches crisis level	Limitations of malleability of work rules	Early scientific management	Massive use of Taylorist methods	...implemented for civilian goods. ...but workers oppose it	Industrial disruption and recovery	Fordism becomes dominant...but	hits some limits	The search for new forms
– Lifestyle	Basically out of the capitalist sector	Slight evolution in consumption norms		Slow insertion of wage-earners in society		Social wage is recognized as a principle	Launching of a complete • Welfare system • Workers benefit from mass consumption			The slowing down shakes welfare state financial stability
• COMPETITION										
– Concentration and centralization	Large plants are emerging....	...Tendency towards concentration		Finance capital is strengthening	Cooperation large firms/state	Industrial cartels and financial holdings	Basis for national planning	Concentration of markets...	...French holding becomes international...	...a new balance between home and international strategy
– Price formation	Controlled by guilds	Principle of free market	Price clear the market	Early monopolistic pricing	State price controls	First example of mark-up pricing	State controls	• Administered prices, public control • Medium-term strategy in pricing decisions		...the return to more price competition
• STATE										
– Budget & taxes	Limit to general functions	...even if regulations are important	Small size of budget/GDP	Significant economic interventions (railways)	Unprecedented margin	Budgetary cuts... Relative growth in the depression	New and high level for public spending/GDP	Slow growth of the size of state	stabilization growth	...tentative to curb down competition

(Continued)

Table 6.1 Continued

INSTITUTIONAL FORMS / PERIODS	1789	1848	1873	1896	1914–1918	1929	1939–1952	1967	1973	1980
– Money & credit	Metal reserves limit money creation		Credit is checked by external balance and interest variations		The war financed by pure money credit...	...so is the post-war boom / Return to gold standard		Credit money has now a leading role...	... periodic devaluations... / ... tentative monetary control	...crisis of economic policy
● INTERNATIONAL REGIME										
– Hegemonic country	England in the core of industrial revolution...			and the banker of the world United States and Germany are challenging British hegemony	British decline is reinforced	...surge of US might	US are now hegemonic, organize and stabilize the international regime...		...which is challenged by new competitors	Underlying crisis of US leadership
– Cohesive forces	Exchange of manufactured goods versus primary commodities			The relative stability devices from the position of England	The loss of competitiveness	...destabilizes the system	A new international order...	...allows OECD growth...	...until the crisis of Bretton Woods	A very unstable system

Sources: CEPREMAP-CORDES report *Approches de l'inflation* (1977); Boyer (1993).

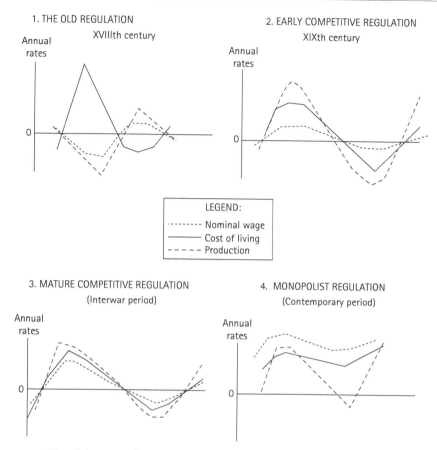

FIGURE 6.2 When labour market institutions change, so does wage formation

Source: Boyer (1979).

The formation of nominal wages in France gives a suggestive insight into the amplitude of these changes (Boyer 1979). Closely associated to the transformations of the wage–labour nexus, at least four wage patterns have been observed (Fig. 6.2).

During the eighteenth century, nominal wage was quite rigid, rather insensitive to labour market disequilibria, and not at all indexed with respect to price level. In 'régulation à l'ancienne', real wage fell rapidly during the inflationary crisis due to insufficient crops and this was the very consequence of the marginal role of wage-earners, totally embedded into an economy dominated by the agricultural sector, whereas wage formation was modelled by the conventions typical to craftsmanship (Fig. 6.2 (1)).

- When industrial revolution takes off, these mechanisms are slowly altered and local and urban labour markets progressively emerge, but are still largely disconnected due to the cost of transportation. Initially, workers' associations were forbidden by law, each labour contract was essentially individual with no collective bargaining involved. In addition, few employment contracts had long-term duration. All these institutional features might explain the genuine factors of wage formation in this epoch: large heterogeneity of wage across skills, sectors, and regions; absence of any clear meaning of the modern concept of average wage; strong competitive forces operating at the local level; inability of workers to pass on any consumer price increases into wage hikes. This is typical competitive 'régulation' (Fig. 6.2 (2)), which reminds us of some features of the pure labour market of neo-classical theory but does not have the same property of maintaining full employment nor does it provide an equal wage for the same skills, due to the local nature of most labour markets.

- As industrialization unfolds, from one business cycle to another the whole institutional setting evolves: the average size of plant increases, as do the size of the wage-earner population and consequently their ability to organize themselves and create unions defending their collective interests, to go on strike for better wages, to demand protective regulations and work duration limitation. Initially the impact is quite small indeed: for instance wages become somehow inert in response to cyclical downturns but still react positively in boom periods. Similarly, after the First World War the unprecedented high inflation made more necessary the indexing of wages and the specific political circumstances made such an innovation possible or even inescapable. Consequently, a new pattern emerges for wages. The larger integration of the various local markets, the implementation of careers, and the stratification of skills by collective agreements now give a central role to the average wage, since most individual wages tend to follow roughly the same increase rate. During the inter-war period, the evolution of nominal wage reacted both to the fluctuations of industrial production as used to be the case previously for local markets, and to the cost of living index, specially designed by state statisticians in order to track the evolution of the standards of living of wage-earners and so respond to the demands of unions (Figure 6.2 (3)). It is worthwhile to stress that a significant lag takes place between the changes in the institutional setting and their actual impact even if they are sufficiently large to potentially alter wage formation. Clearly, structural transformations only take place over several decades, for they often suppose the renewal of generations and the shaping of industrial structures by the new institutions and conversely.

- A fourth wage pattern progressively emerges from the political and social turmoil which took place during and after the Second World War: a large welfare state provided a minimum security to wage-earners, collective bargaining was rather disconnected from the direct pressure of unemployment, itself quite limited until the 1960s, and permanent inflation pushed towards a full and fast indexing of wages with respect to prices. This underlying deep transformation was not fully recognized until the two oil shocks which made apparent for everybody that wage formation had significantly changed with respect to the inter-war period (Fig. 6.2 (4)): in spite of a large increase in unemployment, nominal, and during a few years even real wages have kept growing, in accordance with previously

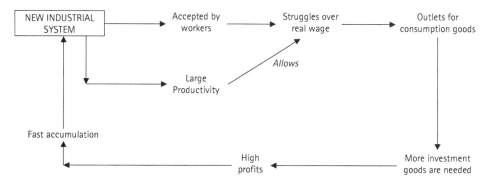

FIGURE 6.3 The determinant role of the wage–labour nexus in Fordism

Source: Boyer (1988).

negotiated pay systems. Note that this evolution supposed a prolonged boom of the world economy, the acceptance of an accommodating monetary policy, the sustainability of large public deficits, and the persistence of a buoyant investment in spite of poor profits and a deterioration of the financial stability of firms and banks (Fig. 6.2 (4)).

From a Subordinate to a Central Role in the Growth Regime: Fordism

It is noteworthy that at the heart of post-war growth lay the capital–labour compromise, whose impact was felt in all other institutional forms. Thanks to compromise on sharing productivity gains, demand for consumer goods was institutionally synchronized with the extension of production capacities, so that competition became oligopolistic, unlike that observed in the inter-war period, marked by price war (Fig. 6.3).

At the same time, the state was no longer restricted solely to providing the tradi-tional major functions of government, since it had also become a wage-earner state: the structure of public expenditure and of social protection recorded this major change. Short-term stabilization policy played a part in regularizing the economic dynamic, already strongly hemmed in by the Fordist compromise and the creation of relevant forms of social protection. Strict monetary constraint, which had previously provided the foundation for regulating competition, was weakened by the workings of infla-tion and the facility of exchange rate adjustment, which itself had become permissible through the stability of the international regime. It is not excessive to take the view that, at that time, the capital–labour compromise provided the foundation for 'régulation' in action. In theoretical terms, the wage–labour nexus was hierarchically superior to the other institutional forms that were redesigned in order to cope with its requirements and the sustainability of the Fordist growth regime (Fig. 6.4).

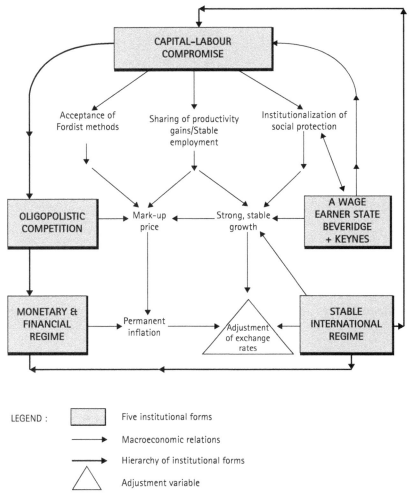

FIGURE 6.4 The capital–labour compromise at the heart of post-war growth

A Simultaneous Destabilization of the Wage–Labour Nexus and Growth Regime

In fact, this institutional configuration has finally been destabilized by its very success, since various disequilibria and contradictions have progressively matured. First, full employment gave wage-earners the advantage and favoured an inflationary outcome to conflicts over distribution of incomes; this was all the more serious because, in the United States, Fordist methods and the substitution of capital for labour came up against a sustained slowdown in productivity from the end of the 1960s until the mid-1990s. In North America, accumulation is no longer intensive and centred on mass consumption, but extensive and based on the differentiation of lifestyles and the reinforcement of inequalities. This change, which has gone unnoticed for a long time, is fundamental to an understanding of contemporary forms of capitalism (Juillard 1993; Boyer and Juillard 2001). *Mutatis mutandis*, it has spread to the majority of advanced capitalist economies, following the two oil crises and then the liberalization of finance and its expansion beyond territorial boundaries.

Since the mid-1960s, the division of labour principle, associated with Fordism and with the increasing returns to scale which it pursues, has led to a growing extraversion of national economies which were previously very largely autonomous. Thus, the freezing of the Fordist regime in the United States has finally spread across the majority of other countries, through the extension of world trade, variable exchange rates, and the increasing number of financial innovations with a mission to create more 'globalized' markets. There is an inherent tendency in capitalism, namely, its capacity to conquer new spaces using the adaptability and malleability of market relations and finance. In a sense, the current phase of internationalization is in keeping with the long-term rhythms of capitalist economies, even if it is particularly vigorous (Hirst and Thompson 1996) and brings into play more countries or geographical zones. But, since the mid-1980s, the dynamism of direct investment has supplanted that of trade, and, in its turn, financial capital is piloting the redeployment of productive capital, a tendency already analysed both by Karl Marx in the second half of the nineteenth century and by Keynes between the wars.

Finally, the freezing of the Fordist accumulation regime has led to the end of labour shortage in those industrialized economies which used to have recourse to immigration in order to satisfy the needs of accumulation. The rise in unemployment has eaten away at the bargaining power of wage-earners, and this has finally led to a change in the capital–labour compromise of the post-war period, even in social democratic regimes, such as Sweden, or state-driven regimes, such as France. The collapse of the Soviet regime has reinforced this movement, since the disappearance of this potential threat has shattered political coalitions based on the exclusion of communist parties. These events put the inheritance of the Golden Age in danger, and this is evidenced by the many reforms aiming to rationalize social protection, as the slowdown in growth makes it more and more difficult to finance. In the second half of the 1990s, this movement affected economies even as strong as that of Germany (Streeck 2009).

In fact, over and above the diversity of national trajectories, three series of factors combine to explain the generalized nature of this transformation of 'modes of regulation'.

- First, governments favourable to wage-earners, whether explicitly or implicitly, have given way to governments which put restoring firms to good health at the top of their agenda. This shift itself stems from the crisis in modes of 'régulation', which has been building up gradually since the Second World War: it is, therefore, very largely endogenous.
- It is more conventional to invoke the change in production paradigms: whereas mass production of standardized products favoured the homogeneity of

employment relations, competition based on quality and innovation assumes pay differentials and greater differentiation between contracts of employment, all the more so since uncertain economic circumstances call for the creation of new adjustment mechanisms. This movement is linked to the exhaustion of Fordist methods, itself linked to past success.

- Last but not least, internationalization of demand has been followed by burgeon-ing direct investment, then by extremely rapid growth in short-term capital flows. Modes of 'régulation' that were very largely autonomous have been increasingly subjected to the ups and downs of the international economy, over which national governments have little hold. This explains the radical change of the orientation of economic policies. However, it was not the primary factor which set the difficulties of the 1990s in motion, since modes of 'régulation' had begun to stall much earlier and, in many cases, the change of direction in economic policy took place several years—even a decade—after the destabilization of the institutional architecture of the Golden Age.

After the Crisis of Fordism, again a Hierarchical Domination by Competition

Analysis of the period 1973–1998 has shown the importance, among factors explaining the *coherence* of a group of institutional forms, of the *hierarchy* which governs their sys-tematic arrangement. In the Fordist period, the capital–labour compromise appeared to be hierarchically superior, in the sense that it imposed structural constraints on the configuration of other institutional forms (see Fig. 6.3). But a different definition of the hierarchy of institutional forms applies more particularly to periods in which the mode of 'régulation' is transformed. An institutional form may be said to be hierarchically superior to another if *its development implies a transformation of this other form*, in its configuration and its logic. Unlike the earlier definition, the latter does not imply that the mode of 'régulation' which emerges from this complex of transformations will be coherent.

In the light of these definitions, there is little doubt that the 1990s marked a major qualitative change in the structuring of institutional forms (Fig. 6.5). Integration into the international economy has played a cardinal role in the context of opening up to broader world trade, of increasing productive investment abroad, and, especially, of cre-ating particularly active globalized financial markets. The consequences have repercus-sions for all other institutional forms (Fig. 6.5).

- First of all, the previous form of nationally based *oligopolistic competition* has been strongly destabilized, as far as most of the products which formed the core of Fordist production are concerned. Because of this, new pricing mechanisms take into account the strategic aspects of competition. In addition, the growing

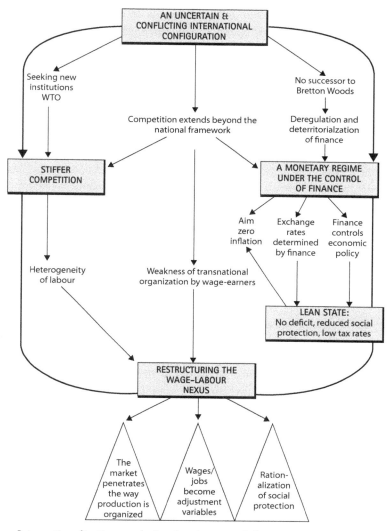

FIGURE 6.5 Internationalization and the dominance of finance over national institutional forms: the 1990s

influence of financial markets on the method of government of firms directly affects distribution of incomes, which in turn has repercussions for the management of labour and for employment relations.

- Next, *the monetary and financial regime* which enjoyed very broad national autonomy during the 1960s, because of weak mobility of capital, is now directly subject to evaluation by the international financial markets, in particular of the credibility of policies followed by the central bank, which in most cases has been made independent in order to better satisfy the demands of finance. Because of this, the exchange rate is a variable that is very widely determined by the financial markets and is no longer the result of political decisions. In many countries, the sole objective of the central bank has become to stabilize inflation, as opposed to previous policies which most often promoted growth and the stability of wage compromise, even if at the expense of inflation.

- *Relations between state and economy* have changed considerably: first because, as we have seen, monetary policy has tended to become autonomous, second and above all because budgetary and fiscal policy is itself affected by this shift in the international regime. The tax system has evolved in favour of the most mobile production factors, and public borrowing is immediately interpreted as a sign of bad management, so that budgetary policy has tended to become pro-cyclical and is no longer anti-cyclical. Over the 1990s, as interest charges on public borrowing came to occupy an increasingly large part of state budgets, the movement of international interest rates directly influenced national budgetary choices, most often to the detriment of expenditure on investment and social transfers. The idea has become current that inequality is a necessary ingredient in incentives to work and to save, as well as towards a spirit of enterprise, with the result that rates of taxation are far from progressive, with single or almost undifferentiated rates being favoured. Thus the Fordist, Keynesian, wage-earner state has been transformed into a lean, Schumpeterian state, in the sense that it seeks to encourage enterprise, foreign investment, and innovation.

- *The wage–labour nexus* is now subject to all the pressures brought by transformations of the other institutional forms. The hardening of competition brings in its wake developments that differ according to firm and sector, so that maintaining uniform and extremely codified employment relations becomes problematic, all the more so since it is the most heavily unionized sectors which are most directly subject to the impact of this industrial restructuring. The large variation in financial markets has repercussions for the investment and production decisions of firms. Under these conditions, the majority of arrangements provided for by collective agreements and labour law seem extremely 'rigid', when they are compared to the rapidity with which the price of financial assets is now formed. In saying this, we are forgetting that the time of finance will never lead that of production and still less that of technical change, for which the time scale is by definition much longer. Finally, the difficulties of financing expenditure on social issues bring the question of reforming social protection to the fore. Conceived in a period of strong growth and low unemployment, social protection has, of course, been destabilized throughout the 1990s, which were marked, as we know, by a growth rate generally lower than the real interest rate. This has led to the idea that social protection should take the financial market route towards privatization. Pensions, for example, have tended to move from a collective distribution system to an individualized, funded system.

Thus, employment relations have developed less under the impact of endogenous development than under the multiform pressures brought about by transformations of other institutional forms. Therefore, the wage–labour nexus is hierarchically dominated, as is evidenced by its position in the middle of Figure 6.5, compared to that in Figure 6.3.

In passing, we should note that this shift of institutional forms goes hand in hand with the overthrowing of past political coalitions. *The political is rarely absent from changes in mode of 'régulation'.* This is the converging conclusion of much contemporary research on the links between political coalitions, governance modes, and employment relations (Roe 1994; Gourevitch and Shinn 2007). A long-term view could even argue that workers have rarely been part of the ruling coalition, run by successive elites (Priestland 2012).

If we are not careful, we might conclude from this that capitalism has again taken up its long-standing tendencies to impoverish the weakest, accentuate inequalities, and put national spaces in a competitive situation, along with attempts on the part of financial circles to bring governments and public policies into line. However, contemporary economies are not identical to those of the nineteenth century. First, social protection systems continue to shape the expectations of wage-earners, who may rebel against budgetary cuts perceived as fundamentally unjust. Next, the expression of universal suffrage has often involved the overturning of governments which have wanted to call earlier compromises into question without finding new ones on a more universal and innovative basis. The conflict between democracy and market has then gone on to produce things which are very new by comparison with the nineteenth-century analyses proposed by Marx. Finally, the very bases of urban social life presuppose more extensive solidarity and public interventions than at the time when competitive capitalism was emerging from a rural society.

CONTEMPORARY CAPITALISMS IN SEARCH OF RELEVANT EMPLOYMENT RELATIONS

All these factors point to a core diagnosis about the period that opened at the end of the 1960s: most economies, especially the American and French ones, are not only facing a series of cyclical crises and a significant slowdown of growth, since they have entered a structural crisis. A last specificity of Régulation theory is to oppose two configurations and periods. When the institutional architecture sustains a coherent mode of regulation and growth regime, macroeconomic regularities can be detected and the causality runs from the institutional forms to the behaviours of agents, i.e. from the macro to the micro level. This was the case for the Golden Age. By contrast, when such an institutional order is decaying, some of the past macroeconomic regularities are eroded and consequently the agents face a major uncertainty about the likely evolution of the economy. During these periods, past determinisms are replaced by the conflicting strategies of firms, wage-earners, and banks and the lost coherence of the previous public interventions in terms of monetary, budgetary, and regulatory policies.

Thus, researchers have to focus their analyses where the action is really taking place, i.e. at the level of firms, unions, and the transformations of the legal system. Macroeconometric analyses have become less relevant and have to be replaced by case studies sufficiently rich to capture the diversity of the strategies followed by the different actors that shape employment relations. Within this framework, employment relations are observed at the micro or meso level, whereas the wage–labour nexus is assumed to characterize the regularities that emerge at the society-wide level.

A Trial and Error Process

Inspired by the process of institutionalization of Fordism, régulationist researchers have, since 1973, recurrently searched for the emergence of a canonical reconfiguration of the wage–labour nexus. Facing the long-term de-industrialization trend, some have forecast the progressive diffusion of a *service economy* and its related employment relations (Petit 1985), but the fragmentation according to the precise nature of the service provided has prevented the diffusion of a unique and typical employment relation. Taking into account the domination of competition over other institutional forms was a more promising avenue and the very hypothesis of institutional hierarchy was suggesting that several decades of opening to *international competition* should finally realign the institutional architecture. In a sense, the small, social democratic and open economies had explored such an employment relation, featuring the key role of the exporting sector in shaping the economy-wide wage–labour nexus (Mjøset 2001). Nevertheless, it appeared that other medium-sized economies have recurrently been unable to promote such a competition-led wage–labour nexus, and consequently the rise of unemployment has been simultaneously the disciplinary device to restore competitiveness and an obstacle to negotiating less detrimental employment relations (Schor and You 1995).

In the light of the emergence of a new industrial productive paradigm in Japan, other researchers have stated that the Fordist wage–labour nexus could be replaced by a Toyota-ist one, characterized by employment stability, internal mobility of labour within the *keiretsu*, in-house training, and retraining of workers (Coriat 1991). Actually, some of the productive management tools such as just-in-time production and *kaizen* have diffused all over the world without being associated with the same human resource management, since the very specific industrial organization and social values of Japan could not be transplanted (Boyer and Freyssenet 2002). Furthermore, a closer investigation of the Japanese case has shown that the complement to the Toyota-ist employment relation was a highly flexible form of labour contract within the service sector. This pointed to the central issue of *employment relation heterogeneity* within an identical industrial relation and legal system configuration. Retrospectively, labour sociologists and economists have shown that the Fordist employment relation was associated with a quite different approach in sectors outside manufacturing: for instance in the construction sector, the recurring fluctuations of the level of activity required labour contracts displaying large flexibility in terms of employment and hours worked, with possible compensation by higher remuneration. Similarly, in firms where production was largely, if not completely, automated, still other labour contracts were observed.

Thus, it was probably erroneous to try to detect the diffusion and domination of a single employment relation, since *the past had to be reinterpreted* as the shift in the statistical distribution of a series of labour contracts, in such a manner that the regularities observed at the macroeconomic level were basically a composite, even though with near full employment the dynamism of the Fordist growth regime had generalized a common wage formation, but not at all the conditions for hiring and firing workers. This teaching was useful when the rise in information and communication technologies (ICT) convinced a majority of analysts of a new convergence towards a wage–labour nexus in line with the emergence of a knowledge economy. Actually, not only was the related growth regime quite unbalanced but also it was only a part of other social and structural transformations of most sectors, including health, education, and leisure (Boyer 2004b). One could also mention that ecological constraints might well shape the next growth regime and call for a reconfiguration of employment relations and tax systems (Lane and Wood 2012).

These remarks about the reinterpretation of the past have thus suggested a shift from a *top-down* analysis, i.e. from the macro institutions to micro behaviours, to a *bottom-up* approach according which the interaction of heterogeneous individual strategies shapes macroeconomic outcomes.

A Taxonomy of the Contemporary Wage–Labour Nexus

This was precisely the methodology of a case study that investigated the transformations of the employment relations for a sample of large French companies (Beffa et al. 1999). This has led to a typology of ideal types of employment relationships (Box 6.1) that incorporates a number of independent variables (some of which coexist within one and the same firm) which may serve as a focal point for remuneration policies (Coutrot 1998: 175; Salais and Storper 1993).

The first employment relationship derives from the Fordist tradition, and emphasizes the *polyvalence* and *stability* of employment. The second, on the other hand, reflects the extreme mobility which *characterizes the professions that drive corporate innovation and dynamism*. The third also features a high level of mobility, but the types of know-how that it incorporates are more standardized, such that employees are subject to *market flexibility*. The operating principle at the heart of the fourth system is *risk-sharing*, a concept derived from the 'share economy' model (Weitzman 1985). Finally, the success of company profit plans, and in the Anglo-Saxon world, of pension funds, defines the existence, at least theoretical, of a fifth type of employment relationship, one that is based on the notion of *stakeholding* (Aglietta 1998; Aglietta and Rebérioux 2004). These categories have in common their transcendence of a Fordist-type logic that associated the polarization and complementarity of tasks, on one hand, with the use of collective agreements to determine pay ladders and average salary adjustments, on the other. However, it is possible to imagine *theoretical arguments* that could justify any one of these employment relationships—to the exclusion of all the others. Such constructs would allow us to home in on the theoretical foundations underlying each of these configurations.

- *Polyvalent stability* is based on the existence and reinforcement over time of firm-specific skills. This explains why employment stabilization is in the mutual interest of staff and management. Of course, this does not mean that the company

---

Box 6.1 Definitions of the five ideal types of employment relationships

- Polyvalent stability: based on employee versatility and stability. Typifies a category of job that already exists in certain industrial companies, as well as in the service sector (insurance, banking).
- Professional: concerns a small number of employees—individuals who reputedly possess a high degree of know-how, and who are therefore considered to be crucial to the firm's overall performance.
- Market flexibility: characterized by external mobility, and by the company paying its employees the going market rate. Driven by the diffusion of information and communication technologies (ICT) in sectors such as distribution, retail trade, food and drink, and hotels.
- Risk-sharing: involves profit-sharing—the company syndicates its risks as well as its rewards.
- Stakeholding: emphasizes financial and patrimonial considerations, co-opting employees as shareholders, and relying heavily on the performance of the financial markets to determine a significant part of total remuneration.

---

will not sometimes cut its levels of hours and employment in an attempt to adjust either to major technical changes or else to increased competition. In such a context, it is not surprising that pay systems translate the idiosyncrasies both of the firm's management systems, and of its past trajectories.

- A *professional* relationship is characterized by the wholesale transferability of employee competencies. This state of affairs allows *professionals* to respond to rising demand (a situation in which market and production paradigms change drastically) by using market mechanisms to leverage their mobility, whether real or invented, into higher earnings.
- *Market flexibility* involves a set of skills that are more basic, but which are still transferable. It refers to the externalization of the adjustments that are necessitated by extremely active job markets, and is modelled on analyses of certain Taylorist industries or services.
- *Risk-sharing* and *stakeholding* cannot be seen as dominant configurations—but in theory, they could attain this status one day. In the reality of the 1990s, these forms of remuneration could be used to *supplement* a system that featured both *polyvalent stability* (participation, performance-related pay) and a *professional* employment relationship (i.e. *stock-options*).

This study of the various types of modern pay systems demonstrates that within a given company or sector, more than one configuration can exist at any one time. For example, *risk-sharing* can be part of a model based on *polyvalent stability*, just as a *professional* relationship can be supplemented by *stakeholding* (Table 6.2). Contemporary human resource management techniques have optimized employment decisions and cleverly used this diversification of labour contracts. Not only are cost reductions

Table 6.2 The determinant of modern employment relations

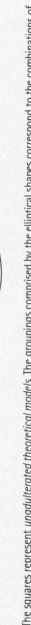

Organization of work Remuneration is determined by:	Polarization – but job specificities are still complementary	Job-specific skills – employment is stabilized	Skills are essential to one company, but can also be transferred to another	Little competence involved – high degree of transferability
• Collective agreements • "Market price" • Individualization of pay systems • Profit-sharing • Income from company profit plans	0. The Fordist employment relationship	1. "Polyvalent stability"	2. A "professional" employment relationship 4. "Risk-sharing" 5. "Stake-holding"	3. "Market flexibility"

Note: The squares represent *unadulterated theoretical models*. The groupings comprised by the elliptical shapes correspond to the combinations of *characteristics* observed in the case studies

Source: Beffa et al. (1999).

obtained, but the expression of social solidarity is made more difficult even within the same firm.

How they Differ from the Golden Age Configurations

The three main types of employment relations are reminiscent of the ways in which economists were already characterizing the 'modern' labour markets of the 1960s and 1970s. Economic literature had already started to contrast pay ladders in the larger companies (the *internal markets*) with ports of entry to (and exit from) the labour market— and usually averred that these latter factors had a correlative effect on the wage setting process (the *secondary market*). This dichotomy, which gave birth to the theory of segmentation, was criticized by authors who preferred to stress the importance of a third kind of market, which they called *professional* (Marsden 1990). This latter denomination was usually designed to describe the types of commercial or employment relationships underlying occupations such as chartered accountancy, the law, medicine, consultancy, etc. In most cases, vocational training and codes of conduct were controlled through entry quotas and professional associations. All of these distinctions are relatively true representations of the situation during the 1960s and 1970s.

The configuration that came to dominate the 1980s was, on the other hand, very different, specifically as a result of the transformations in firms' economic environment, but also because of companies' decisions to explore new organizational and productive paradigms (Table 6.3). This case study suggests that these evolutions design more than a mere dualization.

This pattern is probably not specific to France. A statistical study of the evolution of employment during the 1990s in the US shows a polarization in the quality of jobs: both high and low wage employment grow but intermediate levels are relatively stable, which implies also an increasing heterogeneity of employment relations (Wright and Dwyer 2006). Nevertheless, beneath some common trends, the precise distribution of employment relations varies largely from one national economy to another since globalization and neo-liberalism do show and even utilize these spatial variations (Jessop 2012). The rest of this chapter does not present the numerous comparative studies along 'regulation' or 'social structure of accumulation' theories (Amable 2004; Boyer 1995, 2001; Harada and Tohyama 2012; Mjøset 2001; Schor and You 1995) but focuses upon micro/meso/macro links of employment relations in France.

- During the 1960s, the *internal market* was based on the transposition to industrial companies of an organizational model that had been previously reserved for governmental administrations. The principal trend involved the institutionalization of career-long pay ladders (Kaukewitsch and Rouault 1998)—and inasmuch as the rapid and relatively stable economic growth that characterized this era had created a favourable regulatory environment, firms were on the whole willing to agree to their employees' demands. The differences with the current model of *polyvalent*

Table 6.3 A comparison of employment relationships in the 1960s and 1990s

1960s	1990s
Internal market: Employment status is paramount; career progression is based on seniority; standardized increases in base salary regardless of worker skill) Product of the institutional framework	**Polyvalent stability:** Skills are tied to a particular post; salaries are differentiated; in-house training) Shaped by the specifications of the particular job
Professional market: Entries into the branch are managed by a professional organization; initial training ensures the transferability of a well-defined set of skills	**Profession:** Provides the 'new skills' that will ensure the future competitiveness of the firm; competencies are transferable but in a constant state of flux (thus extending beyond pre-employment or vocational training)
Secondary market: Complements the internal market; absence of employment status (which in any event provides little protection); average market salary; little training	**Market flexibility:** Characterizes entire sectors; payment of going market salaries; standardization of jobs and equipment diminishes the need for the development of employee competency
Participation: State-run system with societal vocation; transplanted onto the other components of the total pay package	**Risk–sharing:** Left to the firm's discretion; purpose is economic, also to ensure that interests of employee and corporation mesh; economy (and society!) to revolve around 'stakeholders' rather than wage-earners
Stock–options: Scheme reserved for executives; allocated on an individual basis	**Stakeholding:** Available to most of the workforce; constitution of managed collective funds

stability are stark. First of all, decisions as to which employees are deemed to be the most effective, and therefore worthy of being offered a modicum of stability, are now being left up to the firms themselves. Companies can redefine professions as they see fit—and nowadays, their decisions are relatively independent of union demands for the generalization of a particular status. As a result, the exact organization of the employment relationship is no longer being funnelled through a previously agreed collective agreement, and specific pay systems are being developed within each establishment, firm, or group. In sum, firms now carry out a cost/benefit analysis before granting anyone a guaranteed status—and as a result, fewer employees now enjoy a security promise.

- *Professional markets*, such as they were at the time, were scrupulously supervised both by the professional associations and by the public institutions themselves, that is, by the organizations that were in charge of managing entry into an occupation, and also for ensuring that its rules of conduct were respected. As such, professionals rendered services that enhanced firms' added value, but they did not play a crucial role in the origination of corporate performances. In fact, the services that professionals offered were often provided under the auspices of a commercial rather than an employee contract. Inversely, during the 1990s, professionals often operated within the framework of an employment relationship, but the skills that they brought to a firm were often considered crucial for the added value which they provide, as well as for the commercial and managerial functions that such employees fulfil. In certain extreme cases (advertising, specialized financial advice, research, etc.), *professional* employees are responsible for creating more than half of a firm's added value, especially in those cases where the majority of assets are immaterial. *Professionals* have considerable bargaining power, as they can create their own company, or get recruited by competitor firms in the same sector. All in all, it is clear that this employee status shares certain attributes with the preceding one—but they are not the same.

• *The secondary market* was often seen as a complement to the *internal market*. This was because it forced employees to accept external flexibility on a permanent basis, thus helping firms to respond to market uncertainty and to organizational and technological innovation. What *market flexibility* and the preceding category have in common is that they both depend heavily on employee mobility, flexible working hours, and on the elasticity of wages to a company's current economic and financial situation. In all probability, the only real novelty of the past two decades is that entire sectors have tended to organize themselves according to the tenets of a model based on *market flexibility*. This is primarily due to the fact that a Taylorist standardization of tasks makes it easier for a company to adapt to market constraints by substituting one employee for another. In addition, and above all, the development of household services such as distribution, retailing, food and drink, and hotel accommodation has rendered this type of employment relationship all the more attractive. In fact, the new technologies have played a major role in the emergence of this form of employment, as they can, in certain instances, greatly simplify the management of the tasks and operations that are involved in the end product or service. Some formerly Fordist industries seem to be going down this road now.

• French authorities have long sought to create institutional mechanisms that encourage a modicum of cooperation between capital and labour—hence the birth, in that country at least, of various types of profit-sharing schemes. The objective was to strengthen a system that could function outside of the firms' competitive imperative. Since then, theoreticians have advanced the idea that profit-sharing is, in and of itself, a boon. This is because it allows levels of remuneration to vary in parallel to environmental changes; and because it supports the dynamics of job creation without impeding the goal of full employment. In France, profit-sharing was revitalized by a law that was passed in 1986, but it was not until the 1990s that firms themselves really began to build ongoing strategies around the concept of *risk-sharing*. It is true that a relatively insignificant proportion of total earnings is determined by this mechanism, and as such, it cannot be used to any great macroeconomic effect, i.e. to stabilize employment trends. However, the trend has been towards the generalization of this model, and there is little doubt but that the majority of the employment contracts that have been signed during the 1990s included an increased assumption of risk by the employee. For this reason, *risk-sharing* has become one element of the adjustment of employment and wage levels.

• *Stock-options* have long been part of the contracts offered to corporate executives and senior managers in American and British firms. The novelty of the past decade is that this mechanism has been offered to a wider group of employees, reaching well beyond the spheres of senior management. For example, one offshoot of the profit-sharing system has been the company or group profit plan, an in-house investment scheme in which employees reinvest part of their bonuses. Pension funds, whose increased role has been the topic of much discussion lately, can also be lumped together with these mechanisms, the sum total of which can be referred to as the elements that comprise a *stakeholder* system. It should be noted that this device, like its predecessor, is an attempt to find a compromise between the diverging objectives of the financial markets, corporate executives, and permanent employees whose skills are essential for the firm's continued success. For this reason, the present category is a complement to the *polyvalent stability* that has been observed in the processing industries which make intermediate products.

All in all, the classification that we have proposed is different from the one that was being commonly used during the 1960s and 1970s, for the very reason that it has been influenced by the multiform structural changes which have taken place in the meantime.

Why Collective Action and Labour Law are So Difficult

During the 1960s, mass production was the impetus behind a certain type of employment relationship. The logic underlying this configuration ended up by governing most of the work world, largely as a result of the way in which the average productivity of a given economy would affect the homogenization of its wage adjustments. The strike/negotiation sequence would lead to the conclusion of a collective agreement, and to an improvement in social welfare. This system was at the heart of the industrial relations that marked the era. However, since then, times have changed—the vehicles for expression, and the nature of the disputes, are quite different. On this score, it is useful to refer

Table 6.4 How industrial relations and union membership rates vary for each type of employment relationship

Industrial relations Employment relationship	Vehicle for expression	Seriousness of dispute	Type of labour union
Polyvalent stability	*Voice* strategies, including strikes	*Moderate to low*, despite union presence—labour and management have interests in common (the firm's specific capital)	Mostly company-level chapters, but possibility of an association with the branch-wide union
Profession	*Exit* strategies determine how demands are to be expressed	*Low*, as there is little (if any) union membership. In addition, employee mobility can be high	Difficult for unions to gain a foothold
Market flexibility	*Exit* strategies in which mobility is usually at the firm's behest	*Low*—however, there can be demands for legal or social guarantees	Appropriateness of representation either at the branch or else at the local level
Risk-sharing	*Voice* strategies are deployed in management committees	*Diminished* because employees identify, at least in part, with the firm's objectives	The union participates in a system of co-determination
Stakeholding	*Exit* strategies (purchase/sale of securities), but *voice strategies* can be deployed in the firm's or group's management committees	Altered by the fact that employees can hold assets—especially when these are the firm's own securities	The union manages the employees' savings

to the distinction that has been made between 'voice' and 'exit' strategies (Hirschman 1970) (Table 6.4).

- The relationships that *stable* employees—that is, those who possess skills that are primarily firm-specific—entertain with their personnel managers function along the lines of a *voice* strategy. When a problem occurs, *stable* employees seek to negotiate first and not so much to strike. This is not to say that all discord automatically leads to confrontation—after all, both parties are aware of the constraints of competition and internationalization. As such, both management and labour often underplay disputes, even when a union is present, since it is in the interest of both parties to share the surplus engendered by a company's 'specific capital'. *Exit* strategies are a very expensive option for both partners.

- *Professional* employees, i.e. individuals who possess skills that are both essential and transferable, find themselves in a totally different situation. They will often defend their own interests to the best of their ability by taking advantage of the *exit* mechanisms that characterize their particular market. In many cases, they are completely unprotected by the professional association—and when such a guild does exist, it is usually fairly weak. The resulting labour disputes are relatively innocuous, and social unrest is infrequent. In most cases, discord merely reflects this category's residual resistance to the Taylorization of design engineering—a function that used to be considered essential, but which has since become somewhat mundane.
- For employees operating within a system of *market flexibility*, the key to any *exit* strategy is mobility. This is the case both when turnover is voluntary (i.e. when the employee takes the initiative), and also when this is not the case (enforced mobility). This situation is different from the preceding one, insofar as the bargaining positions are reversed. There is also a lesser degree of conflict—but the tensions associated with this type of employment contract can lead to demands for greater legal guarantees.

The analysis can also be applied to the two remaining forms of employment relationships, despite the fact that they are, at least for the moment, less pervasive than the three preceding ones.

- When employees are prepared to *share risks*, they usually demand a right of *voice* alongside the firm's executive. Labour conflicts tend to be less acute, as the employees try to find a balance between a higher base salary and an increased participation in profits—after all, they know that company earnings will suffer if strikes break out, as the firm will be sanctioned by the financial markets. In circumstances such as these, it is not surprising that wage demands tend to be moderate (Jerger et al. 2007: 5). The interests of labour and of management start to converge, and this hearkens back, in France at least, to the rationale that had originally inspired the legislation governing profit-sharing schemes. In fact, in most countries across the world, this conception of the firm as a community has come back into fashion.
- Even though it functions according to a similar logic, *stakeholding* reserves a major role for *exit strategies*, defined here as the purchase and/or sale of the company's securities, or more generally, of any company's securities (when individual employees' savings are being managed collectively). Where stock portfolios are very diversified, employees' behaviour will be partially dictated by financial thinking, and will have little or no impact on their stake in the firm. If the portfolios are not diversified, employees have to make another trade-off between an immediate rise in their base salary and medium or long-term gains in their stock portfolios. The legal framework within which the collective funds are being managed can therefore induce employees to either cooperate with management—or not.

In any event, the break-up of the Fordist relationship has caused a diversification of industrial relations. This explains the problems that labour unions, employer associations, and lawmakers have had with work and social welfare issues. In addition, *union representation*, which, in France at least, is usually organized on a national or sectoral level, has been caught napping by the trend towards extremely differentiated corporate strategies, and by the reactions of local company union chapters, where they do exist. In a sense, the French legislation that covers this area of activity (les lois Auroux) has had a paradoxical effect. The laws had been designed to reinforce the labour movement by ring-fencing areas of sovereignty within the companies themselves; instead, they have accentuated the strategic problems that unions have to overcome. The net effect has been more divisive than unifying. Furthermore, the *worst disputes* have usually been observed in the public or nationalized sector: company-specific agreements increasingly cover working hours and jobs rather than salaries and bonuses alone.

For these reasons, each of these types of employment relationships should have a different effect on the nature and on the extent of unionization (Table 6.4).

- *Polyvalent stability* is compatible with the unionization of a firm. In this case, the union is the platform that allows employees to express their demands. A prerequisite is that a labour movement exists, and that it now defends this new form of employment—otherwise human resources departments will be taking back the initiative, using so-called 'ethical' codes (Mercier 1999) as a partial replacement for the regulations that the social partners should have been negotiating.
- The *professional* category is a major challenge for labour organizations. In the 1960s version of this model, professional associations were in charge of vocational training, access to a profession, and conflict resolution. In the modern version, each professional is tempted to negotiate the best possible deal for him- or herself—on an individual basis. This approach explains the lesser presence of labour organizations in the new professions—both in France and internationally.
- *Market flexibility* creates a paradoxical situation for labour organizations. On one hand, the smaller the firm, the more frequent its reorganizations, and the greater the degree of inter-company mobility—the lesser the employees' bargaining power. On the other hand, given how heterogeneous employment relations have become (in terms of the labour law that has been handed down from the Fordist period), and in light of the possibilities that *polyvalent stability* offers for increased unionization, it is very possible that this configuration will lead to the creation of union chapters that cater to local markets, or to specific occupations.
- *Risk-sharing* mobilizes a completely different type of unionism. French labour law has traditionally codified the trade-off that has to be made between the employee's subordination to the objectives of a firm, on one hand, and (short-term) job or wage security, on the other. However, profit-sharing schemes have been a great success, and the logical extension is that employees should be able to *participate in the firm's management* (or that they at least are kept abreast of major decisions)—after

all, they are sharing the risks. The feasibility of this sort of co-determination probably depends on the existence of appropriate social legislation (see the example of Germany).

- *Stakeholding* comprises a potential extension of unions' zone of influence. Company or group profit plans raise the question of how to manage the funds that have been collected. This gives unions different alternatives: they can either subcontract the management of these funds to traditional financial institutions; or else they can come up with original types of employee funds which could be run according to criteria other than the attainment of the maximum financial yield, in the strictest sense of this term (Aglietta 1998; Davanne et al. 1998; Aglietta and Rebérioux 2004).

All in all, the configuration that had been the legacy of the Fordist era has become obsolete—and both the unions as well as the institutions that oversee industrial relations need to integrate the new forms of employment relationships into their thinking. During a first stage, this has generally accelerated the decline of union density and it explains the growing complexity of labour codes that try to capture this diversity of employment relations.

What Could Be the Relevant Employment Relations for the Twenty-First Century?

If the past configurations for industrial relations are no longer viable, does the previous analysis help in imagining possible evolutions towards more coherent systems that would propagate again a synergy between labour institutions and growth regimes?

The Factors that Govern the Viability of Each Potential Reconfiguration

How can we use the conclusions that have been drawn from these case studies to develop a forward-looking approach? Current methodologies do not lend themselves to exhaustive analysis, much less to forecasting. There is, however, a certain constancy to the reasons underlying a pay system's appropriateness at any given moment in time. If we can explain the *microeconomic coherency* between an employment contract and a given business organization, we could then determine that particular firm's optimal pay system by choosing among those systems which have already proved their viability in other *leading firms*. Moreover, if we then study the principles underlying the diffusion of that pay system that we have selected (the market itself, collective bargaining, legislation, consulting, etc.), we may be able to calculate its chances of long-term survival. Of course, the employment relationship must also be coherent with the *macroeconomic dynamics* that mark the surrounding environment: depending on their main focus (the domestic market, export, price or quality-based competitiveness, etc.), regimes can vary widely from one another, and a priori, no one pay system can function ubiquitously. As a matter of fact, there was a sea change between the rationale behind the employment model that had epitomized the post-war boom years (Fordism) and the principles that were to serve as guidelines to its successors.

Examples of incompatibility should help us to illustrate this point. Let us suppose, for instance, that a company bases its competitiveness on the skills of its operators, considered to be the source of its products' quality and differentiation. On a *microeconomic* level, the payment of a market salary could be incompatible with the stability that is required of the workforce, that is, with a company's need for internal polyvalence. This is reflected in the absence of any equivalent configuration in either the theoretical matrix (Table 6.2) or, apparently, in French reality. In much the same way, an employment relationship can conflict with *a company's original cultural consensus*. If a group is mooting its intentions to take a cooperative approach to workshop relations even as it is carrying out mass dismissals; or if a group is increasing executive compensation at the same time that it is forcing its employees to make a range of concessions—then it is unlikely that the model will be viable. In fact, this is the probable explanation behind the problems that the British manufacturing sector experienced when it tried to introduce *polyvalent stability*. British firms' conceptions and management styles are quite incompatible with this type of employment relationship.

It is possible for an employment relationship to be viable in a given sector, even in several, yet not spread to the entire economy. This is primarily due to two factors: the microeconomic conditions that define competitiveness may vary from one sector to another; and the mode of regulation may undermine the generalization of this particular type of employment relationship. The patchy diffusion of profit-sharing schemes exemplifies the first explanation—despite legislative and fiscal incentives, such schemes have not yet reached a threshold that would justify shifting the entire configuration towards an employment system based on *risk-sharing*. In 1995, 36% of all French employees were covered by some profit-sharing scheme. Amongst this population, 44% worked in industry, 6% in construction, and 50% in the tertiary sector.

As pertains to the second explanation, it is clear that a system based on *polyvalent stability* would encounter grave difficulties if growth were to slow down, and if macroeconomic volatility started to hinder internal mobility to such an extent that this process became unable to fulfil its role. In such a scenario, the path is cleared for a system based on *market flexibility* (Boyer and Juillard 1997, 1998). Moreover, we can use these same evaluation criteria to envisage how the configurations that have appeared during the 1990s will turn out in the future.

A Synoptic View about Possible Futures for Employment Relations

Within any given employment system, there will always be some degree of microeconomic coherency between worker skills, job control, and pay. This coherency thus becomes a criterion in and of itself, and it will have certain consequences. The first is that it is highly unlikely that employment relationships will ever converge towards a unique model, especially since modern economies are permanently characterized by the coexistence of very different forms of productive organization: processing industries, hi-tech industries, large distribution networks, firms that specialize in corporate services. All of these sectors are linked to a specific type of employment relationship. Moreover, the progressive disappearance of the collective actors who are capable of creating homogeneous branch-wide collective agreements (i.e. the model that had typified the 1960s) will lead to the increased distinctiveness of each of these relationships (Table 6.5).

- In a sense, *polyvalent stability* is the heir to the Fordist employment relationship, as it emphasizes the differentiation of products, especially through quality, yet still conserves certain attributes of mass production. On the other hand, the progressive shift from a system of control based on the fulfilment of assignments to one that involves an appreciation of worker skills will create a situation in which pay systems are diversified according to each productive organization's own imperative, and each company's past social relations. The diffusion of *polyvalent stability* reflected the competitive pressures that had been affecting the product markets; the impact of the various methods of management; and the example of Japanese firms, including the transplants. Now, this employment relationship involves sectors of industry that are either in a state of maturity, or else which are subject to fierce international competition, and as such, it is the manufacturing companies that have been forced to make massive job cuts ever since the mid-1980s. These adjustments have been greatly facilitated by public monies (i.e. the state funding of early retirement programmes). For this reason, the principle of long-term contractualization of employment relations at an individual level has not been incompatible with job cuts on a company or sectoral level. On the other hand, in the modern tertiary sector, represented by insurance companies or even by certain distributors, employment trends have encouraged relations that are based on *polyvalent stability*—even though some of the industrial relations in this sector have been left untouched by the logic underlying this employment system.
- The *professional* model complements the preceding one, both for firms in the manufacturing sector, and also for service companies. It has been at work in the field of advertising since the very beginning, and seems to have been barely

Table 6.5 Which employment contract will dominate the early twenty–first century?

Configuration / Criteria	Coherency between the productive organization and the pay system	Quid pro quo? The fundamental compromise between companies and employees	The firm's or the sector's dynamics determine the principles of the system's diffusion	How the system is co-opted into current or emerging modes of regulation
1. Origination: *The Fordist employment relationship*	Mass production enables the institutionalization of collective agreements, law, and regulations; wage setting is homogenized	A division of labour is exchanged for the sharing of productivity gains.	Primacy of firms in the Parisian metalworker industry; diffusion via collective agreements; labour market later approaches full employment	The Fordist labour nexus, based on mass production and consumption, was one of the pillars of the post-war mode of regulation
2. The factors of change	Quality is at the heart of the shift from mass production to innovation and differentiation; firms that were hierarchical become 'networked'	Diversification of firms' situations and employees' expectations. Wider choice of possible compromises	Internal contradictions hurt the manufacturing sector; service sector performances are variable: unions lose influence as unemployment remains high	1. Increased international interdependence (trade, investment and finance) 2. Heterogeneity of lifestyles 3. Greater uncertainty at all levels (market, innovation, finance)
3. Emerging employment relationships				
• *Polyvalent stability*	Product differentiation and the search for quality lead firms to reward staff for versatility and personal performance	Job specifications are malleable, and 'insiders' trade off performance against employment stability	• Competitive pressures in the product markets • Role models (Japanese transplants and management styles)	Regime of growth is based on the advancement of mass production through greater differentiation—in a context of quasi-full employment.

• *Profession*	The emphasis on innovation and new technologies benefits those professionals that are seen as the catalysts for rising standards of management and performance	Trade-off between helping staff avail itself of know-how and negotiating benefits that satisfy each employee yet reflect economic reality	Competition in a primarily internationalized professional market	Model of growth is propelled by innovation and internationalization, with a high degree of geographic polarization
• *Market flexibility*	Tasks are simplified as a result of new technologies, increased mobility, and payment of the going market salary	Employment versus salary: a minimalist compromise	In the eldest industrialized societies, demand migrates towards the service sector, yet pay systems continue to be very heterogeneous	Model of growth based on the heterogenization of lifestyles, which often stems from rising inequality
• *Risk-sharing*	The uncertainty of modern markets explains the shift to a relationship that is based on a (profit-) sharing	Employment stabilization is meant to offset earnings variability	Public incentives (participation) and role models	Model of growth in which profitability drives investment and higher output
• *Stakeholding*	The idea is that if the employee is a shareholder, his or her interests will correspond to the firm's	Acceptance of a mode of corporate governance that is marked by the maximization of financial returns rather than by a participation in the corresponding patrimonial gains	This type of governance is diffused via the *financial markets* (note the role of pension funds and institutional investors)	Regime of growth that is based on the concept of stakeholding, and which is subject to the supreme judgement of the financial markets

affected by the events of the 1990s or even accelerated in the 2000s with its extension to finance, media, sport, and leisure. Moreover, as we have seen, the change has been significant for firms in the hi-tech sector. The individuals who have been the catalysts of technological and product innovations are very mobile, both nationally and internationally, and this has severely hampered the management of human resources. Companies tend to bid up earnings, but only for this category of personnel—it is evident that this model is not being applied to lower echelon employees. Even more fundamentally, the success of this type of employment relationship would require that the entire model of growth be governed by the twin factors of innovation and internationalization. However, given the strong geographic polarization of the various systems of innovation, this can only occur in a few regions within any given country (Amable et al. 1997; Amable 2004; Boyer et al. 2011). Note that this model is more or less diametrically opposed to the preceding one, and that it therefore implies a very different type of public intervention.

- *Market flexibility* characterizes a number of activities, both industrial and tertiary, that are run in situations in which the codification and simplification of tasks have allowed for a further development of Taylorist logic—for instance, intellectual occupations that had been previously amalgamated with a managerial status; or with a *professional* type of relationship. The telecommunications sector, or certain hi-tech activities, could also be included in this trend—but for the most part, an employment relationship of this sort is disseminated throughout the service and distribution sectors, in conjunction with the evolution of lifestyles and consumption patterns. External mobility becomes paramount, and affects earnings in a way that is reminiscent of certain attributes of *competitive* regulation, especially since unions are poorly represented, if at all. In theory, *market flexibility* is coherent with models of growth that mesh with the trend towards the increased heterogeneity of lifestyles—which depends, in turn, on the speed with which inequality widens. As such, an employment relationship based on market flexibility is distinct from the two preceding ones, as each belongs to a separate system of growth.

Of course, in practice, the three configurations are interrelated, and depending on the country or on the period in time, each will contribute to a varying degree to the dynamism of the job market. In the past, *stable* and *polyvalent* employees represented, in France, between 35 and 40% of the working population, but this proportion will probably decrease over the next 20 years. The *professional* employment relationship, which had first dropped to less than 5% of the total working population, has tended to expand along with the increase in the number of 'symbolic analysts' (Reich 1993), and now represents more than 10% of all wage-earners. This could explain why, in modern economies, employees who are subject to *market flexibility* now represent the majority, and why it is so important that employment law be restructured so as to take this category into account. In fact, it would be useful to monitor the way in which the legal environment contributes to the development of each type of employment relationship.

Is the Full Marketization of the Wage–Labour Nexus the Solution?

Nevertheless, the previous section has shown how the structural transformations of contemporary economies made quite difficult the collective action of wage-earners and the redesign of labour laws as well. Given the intrinsic difficulties of coordination by negotiated rules, the market mechanisms have a special appeal for policy-makers: if the process of political deliberation is unable to work out a consensus, why not delegate to anonymous markets the task of governing the extreme heterogeneity of employment relations? The logical consequence would be the progressive transformation of labour contracts into typical commercial transactions, in conformity with North American practices but at odds with the rules prevailing in continental Europe.

Three factors push towards this reconfiguration. First of all, it is more and more difficult to monitor *competition* at the domestic level, since it expresses itself at the continental or regional level (NAFTA, European Union, Asian economic integration). Consequently, the instability of the product market is more directly transmitted to labour, which calls for renewed flexibility strategies: any past labour institution is perceived as an obstacle to adaptation and economic performance, i.e. a rigidity that hurts efficiency and welfare. Second, nowadays the *financial markets* are dominant since the viability and legitimacy of any firm's strategy is assessed in real time. It has become common to observe that any deterioration of financial performance on the stock market triggers a restructuring of employment and production. The volatility of the stock market is therefore affecting quasi instantaneously decisions about firing or lay-off. Econometric studies confirm this new dependency between the structure of financing of French quoted firms and the speed of adjustment of employment and work hours (Perraudin et al. 2007). Third, the leading role of finance in contemporary economies affects also the evolution of *exchange rates*: they tend to equalize the rate of return of capital and they thus depend on interest rate differentials and expectations about economic prosperity of the domestic economy. Consequently, they might diverge drastically from the exchange rate that would deliver a long-term equilibrium of trade balance and in case of over-valuation of the domestic currency, firms have to slim down their production costs by wage cuts or productivity increases. This third channel defines another pressure towards labour flexibility and the adoption of more active labour market adjustments.

If for simplicity's sake, one follows a varieties of capitalism approach (VOC) (Hall and Soskice 2001) this would imply a clear premium to liberal market economies to the detriment of coordinated ones. *De facto*, Germany is one emblematic example of this second configuration, and the resilience of its economy is closely related to the domination of a polyvalent employment relation in the manufacturing exporting sector;

thus if new and different industries emerge and grow (biotech, ICT, professional business services) it is not that sure that they can be monitored within the same institutional and legal framework that has been promoting the machine tool or car industries for instance. In a sense, the successive reforms of German welfare and labour have taken into account this discrepancy and introduced more market mechanisms within this still coordinated economy. But in weakly competitive European economies, for instance France or Italy, the rise of structural unemployment has frequently been the cost to be paid due to the obsolescence of past industrial relations and the inability to work out new compromise to cope with the rising macroeconomic volatility (see Fig. 6.7).

The Lessons from the Flexicurity Model: Born Out of Conflict and Difficult to Emulate Elsewhere

Is this march to marketization of labour irreversible? Not necessarily if one follows the hopes raised by the resilience of the so-called flexicurity Danish model (Jorgensen and Madsen 2007; Campbell et al. 2006; Pedersen 2006; Barbier 2007). Basically, this oxymoron challenges the intrinsic and universal superiority of pure market mechanisms: an extended but carefully designed welfare system might be a trump card in the capacity of firms to respond to external competition and an unstable world economy. The famous flexicurity triangle is well known: firms are entitled to adjust employment quickly, but workers benefit from a generous unemployment compensation system... provided they accept being retrained in order to get access to a higher skill and higher wage jobs, possibly changing from one industry to another.

In this respect, the contribution of regulationist researches is twofold:

- On one side, this hybridization between collectively organized institutions and typical market adjustments was not at all the consequence of an *ex ante* rational design, but the unintended outcome of the response to deep and lasting unemployment. During the crisis of the Danish economy in the early 1990s, the radical opposition between the respective demands of firms and wage-earners was overcome by the invention of a third device that could make these two conflicting principles compatible *ex post*. In order to prevent the durable exclusion of workers with obsolete competencies, sophisticated procedures of control and training of the unemployed have been elaborated. After a while, this new configuration appeared to be able to reduce unemployment and provide a viable mechanism for adjusting the economic and social demands, respectively of firms and citizens (Fig. 6.6).

It has been a recurring theme for regulationists to point out that open conflicts between capital and labour have been *de facto* the origin of the Fordism compromise (Boyer and

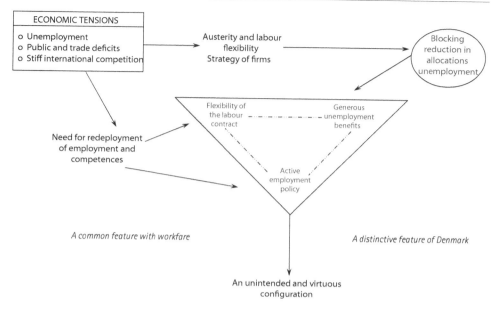

FIGURE 6.6 The flexicurity Danish model: the unintended consequence of an unemployment crisis and the conflict of opposite interests and rationales

Orléan 1991). An equivalent demonstration has been provided concerning the so-called Danish model (Boyer 2006).

- On the other side, it is a specific embodiment of a more general principle that is also implemented in many other Nordic social democratic economies under other configurations. The flexicurity triangle is only a particular example of a synergy between three usually disconnected features: first, the full acceptance of world competition without any protectionist temptation, second, a relentless effort for innovation from firms and public authorities, and last but not least the permanent reorganization of welfare in order to foster institutionalized competitiveness. The basic economic mechanism is simple enough: labour has to move from low to high value-added firms and sectors, which implies simultaneously employment mobility and the equivalent of lifelong learning, i.e. the permanent or periodic upgrading of skills (Boyer 2014).

Nevertheless, the French case shows that such a model is quite difficult to transplant in the absence of the socio-political conditions that make it acceptable for both firms and wage-earners, not to mention the major cultural differences in the system of values at the origin of the emergence of universal welfare state (Ostergard 2009). If the national tradition is built upon recurring and violent conflicts between capital and

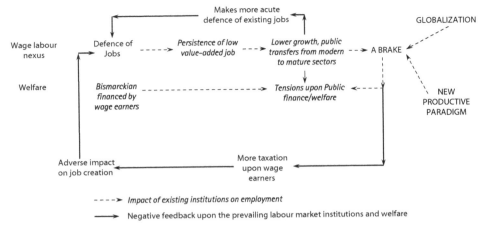

FIGURE 6.7 A counter model: the vicious circles of Bismarckian welfare and job defence and job protection

labour, if the idea of a long-lasting basic compromise exchanging performance of the firms against economic and social benefits for wage-earners is absent, and when successive governments have been unable to reform the financing and organization of the welfare inherited from the Golden Age (André 2003), then structural and long-lasting unemployment is the cost to be paid for not adjusting the domestic institutions to the new international regime, productive paradigms, and social demands from the citizens (Fig. 6.7).

Consequently, contrasted national trajectories continue to prevail in spite of a common inspiration by free market ideas concerning labour market and welfare (Boyer 2004a). The crisis of the eurozone which opened in 2010 reveals crudely how heterogeneous are the wage–labour nexus: on one side, Nordic countries and a significantly reformed German economy fare quite well in terms of competitiveness whereas Southern Europe suffers from a major institutional mismatch (Boyer 2012). The nation-state and domestic polity are still important in the evolution of institutional forms and the wage–labour nexus is not an exception.

CONCLUSION

The contribution of régulation theory to the analysis of employment relations can be summarized by the following propositions.

1. Social scientists and especially economists should resist the temptation to analyse labour in terms of a more or less perfect market configuration that leads to the conclusion that the rules that govern them are sources of rigidity, poor

economic performances, and structural unemployment. From a theoretical point of view, the capital–labour relation is so conflicting and contradictory that specific organizational devices and national institutions have to channel and shape the behaviour of employees and employers. It might be ruled by a specific branch of the legal system, as observed in continental Europe, or be the outcome of tripartite negotiations in Nordic societies and/or collective bargaining of the type observed after the Second World War for instance in the USA.

2. Historical long-term analyses and contemporary cross-national comparisons falsify the general vision of a convergence towards a canonical employment relation that would deliver optimal economic results. Given the complexity of the wage–labour nexus, many different institutional arrangements might govern the conditions for hiring and firing, the ability to extend working hours, the remuneration system in reaction to contrasted work organizations that span from the putting out system to the assembly line and more recently the financial traders' room. The core argument derived from regulation theory is simple but important: these organizational and institutional configurations are not mere frictions upon a more or less perfect labour market, but are constitutive of modern societies and economies.

3. A still more important result recurrently emerges from historical and comparative analyses: labour market institutions matter for macroeconomic dynamics. For instance, competitive capitalism was characterized by the serialization of workers, unable to fight against the disciplinary role of unemployment over work intensity and nominal wage flexibility. By contrast, the concentration of production and the collective defence by workers of their interests have favoured the emergence of totally new employment relations, whereby the implementation of collective bargaining agreements has progressively made the nominal wage less dependent on unemployment. The whole macroeconomic pattern has changed in the direction of a higher and stable growth.

4. Régulationist approaches have thus given different examples of a complementarity between a high degree of institutionalization of the wage–labour nexus and remarkable performances in terms of dynamic efficiency. The speed of adjustments of employment and wage might be lower but this negative effect is more than compensated by the dynamism of productivity, better living standards, and less violent social and political conflicts. Nevertheless, the Fordist configuration, observed in the USA and France, is not the only example. The so-called Danish flexicurity is the initially unintended outcome of the apparent incompatibility between the demand for security for workers and the requirements of the firms in their responses to competition and macroeconomic volatility. An active employment policy has proved able to make compatible high unemployment benefits and fast adjustments in employment. This alternative to workfare shows the potential diversity of viable employment relations.

5. Since the 1990s many structural changes have eroded the labour market institutions progressively built after the Second World War. A permanent deepening

of internationalization has propelled the two institutional forms, competition and integration into the world economy, as the drivers in the transformation and redesign of employment relations. More recently, the new norms imposed by international finance upon the rate of return of firms have triggered a higher reactivity of employment, an increasing sensitivity of wage to the health of the firms and the evolution of the national economy they belong to, but also a financialization of workers' remunerations and of some components of welfare, such as pensions. Last but not least, the pervasiveness of ICT, the transition towards a knowledge-based economy, and the related large differentiation of services have induced a trend towards decentralization and individualization of labour contracts.

6. As a consequence, various employment relations do coexist, but with a different mix according to the sector, the nature of the skills required, and the national style for industrial relations. Polyvalent stability coexists along with highly flexible labour, whereas the new sources of competitiveness related to innovation have promoted a totally different employment relation, restricted to a small number of individuals with highly idiosyncratic talents. Similarly, labour has now to bear a larger fraction of the economic risks that were traditionally borne by entrepreneurs via the volatility of their profits. In some high-tech and financial sectors, one finds the implementation of share economy principles that have been proposed to be more efficient than the traditional wage–labour nexus. Consequently, the distribution of various types of employment relations displays an unprecedented complexity.

7. This kaleidoscope of employment relations is here to stay, and many factors might explain why researches have been unable to find a convergence towards a canonical model that would be a follow-up of the Fordist wage–labour nexus. With the deepening of the division of labour, within and across sectors, work organizations evolve quite differently in the traditional manufacturing industries and the emerging science-based ones, such as the biotech industry, in the health and education system, and in the retailing sectors, just to give a few examples. The second reason for this heterogeneity of labour contracts is related to the uncertain search for viable growth regimes, which has not delivered any clear and sustainable configuration alternative to the Golden Age one.

This is more evidence for one of the major findings of this programme of research: employment relations and macroeconomic growth regimes do co-evolve, in such a way that the two related uncertainties spill over from one to another and probably explain the recurring economic financial crises.

REFERENCES

Aglietta, M. (1998). 'Le capitalisme de demain', *Note de la fondation Saint-Simon*, November.

Aglietta, M. and Rebérioux, A. (2004). 'Du capitalisme financier au renouveau de la social-démocratie', *Prisme* no. 5, Centre Saint Gobain pour la Recherche en Economie, Paris, October.

Amable, B. (2004). *The Diversity of Modern Capitalisms*. Oxford: Oxford University Press.

Amable, B., Barré, R., and Boyer, R. (1997). *Les systèmes d'innovation à l'ère de la globalisation*. Paris: Economica/OST.

André, C. (2003). 'Ten European Systems of Social Protection: An Ambiguous Convergence', in D. Pieters (ed.), *European Social Security and Global Politics*. London: Kluwer Academic Publishers, 3–44.

Baccaro, L. and Howell, C. (2010). 'Institutional Change in European Industrial Relations: Reformulating the Case for Neoliberal Convergence', Mimeograph prepared for the Council for European Studies, Seventeenth International Conference, Montreal, Canada, 15–17 April.

Barbier, J.-C. (2007). 'From Political Strategy to Analytical Research and Back to Politics: A Sociological Approach of "Flexicurity"', in J. Henning and K. Madsen (eds.), *Flexicurity and Beyond*. Copenhagen: DJOF Publishing, 155–88.

Beffa, J. L., Boyer, R., and Touffut, J.-P. (1999). 'Employment Relationships in France: The State, the Firms, and the Financial Markets', *Notes de la Fondation Saint Simon*, no. 107, June.

Boyer, R. (1979). 'Wage Formation in Historical Perspective: The French Experience', *Cambridge Journal of Economics*, 3(2): 99–118.

—— (1988). 'Technical Change and the Theory of "Régulation"', in G. Dosi, C. Freeman, G. Silverberg, and L. Soete (eds.), *Technical Change and Economic Theory: The Global Process of Development* (Part 1). London: Pinter, 67–94.

—— (1993). 'Labour Institutions and Economic Growth: A Survey and a "Regulationnist" Approach', *Labour*, 7(1): 25–72.

—— (1995). 'Capital–Labour Relations in OECD Countries: From the Fordist Golden Age to Contrasted National Trajectories', in J. Schor and J.-I. You (eds.), *Capital, the State and Labour: A Global Perspective*. Cheltenham: Edward Elgar, 18–69.

—— (2001). 'The Diversity and Future of Capitalisms: A *Régulationnist* Analysis', in G. M. Hodgson, M. Itoh, and N. Yokokawa (eds.), *Capitalism in Evolution: Global Contentions—East and West*. Cheltenham: Edward Elgar, 100–21.

—— (2004a). *The Future of Economic Growth*. Cheltenham: Edward Elgar.

—— (2004b). 'New Growth Regimes, But Still Institutional Diversity', *Socio-Economic Review*, 2(1): 1–32.

—— (2006). *La flexicurité danoise: quels enseignements pour la France?*, Opuscule CEPREMAP, no. 2. Paris: Éditions de l'ENS.

—— (2012). 'Overcoming the Institutional Mismatch of the Euro-Zone', paper prepared for 'Asian Economic Integration in Transition: Learning from European Experiences', Yokohama International Conference, 21–22 August.

—— (2014). 'The Welfare-Innovation Institutional Complementarity: Making Sense of Scandinavian History', in S. Borras and L. Seebrooke (eds.), *Sources of National Institutional Competitiveness: Sense-Making and Institutional Change*.

Boyer, R. and Freyssenet, M. (2002). *The Productive Models: The Conditions of Profitability*. Basingstoke: Palgrave Macmillan.

Boyer, R. and Juillard, M. (1997). 'Le rapport salarial japonais a-t-il atteint ses limites?', *Revue Économique*, 48(3): 731–9.

—— (1998). 'The Contemporary Japanese Crisis and the Transformations of the Wage Labor Nexus', *Couverture Orange CEPREMAP*, no. 9822.

—— (2001). 'The United States: Goodbye, Fordism!', in R. Boyer and Y. Saillard (eds.), *Régulation Theory: The State of The Art*. London: Routledge, 238–46.

Boyer, R. and Orléan, A. (1991). 'Les transformations des conventions salariales entre théorie et histoire. D'Henry Ford au fordisme', *Revue Économique*, 42(2): 233–72.

Boyer, R. and Schmeder, G. (1990). 'Un retour à Adam Smith', *Revue Française d'Economie*, 5(1): 125–59.

Boyer, R., Uemura, H., and Isogai, A. (eds.) (2011). *Diversity and Transformations of Asian Capitalisms*. London: Routledge.

Campbell, J., Hall, J., and Pedersen, O. K. (2006). *National Identity and the Varieties of Capitalism: The Danish Experience*. Montreal: McGill-Queen's University Press.

Coriat, B. (1991). *Penser à l'envers: Travail et Organisation dans la Firme Japonaise*. Paris: C. Bourgois.

Coutrot, T. (1998). *L'entreprise néo-libérale, nouvelle utopie capitaliste?* Paris: La Découverte.

Davanne, O., Lorenzi, J.-H., and Morin, F. (1998). 'Retraites et épargne', *Rapport du Conseil d'Analyse Économique*, no. 7. Paris: La documentation française.

Gourevitch, P. and Shinn, J. (2007). *Political Power and Corporate Control*. Princeton: Princeton University Press.

Hall, P. A. and Soskice, D. (eds.) (2001). *Varieties of Capitalism: The Institutional Foundations of Comparative Advantage*. Oxford and New York: Oxford University Press.

Harada, Y. and Tohyama, H. (2012). 'Asian Capitalisms: Institutional Configurations and Firm Heterogeneity', in R. Boyer, H. Uemura, and A. Isogai (eds.), *Diversity and Transformations of Asian Capitalisms*. London: Routledge, London, 243–63.

Hirschman, A. O. (1970). *Exit, Voice and Loyalty: Response to Decline in Firms, Organizations and States*. Cambridge, MA: Harvard University Press.

Hirst, P. and Thompson, G. (1996). *Globalization in Question*. Cambridge: Polity Press.

Jerger, J. and Michaelis, J. 2007. 'Why Profit Sharing is So Hard to Implement', Working Paper. University of Kassel.

Jessop, B. (2012). 'Rethinking the Diversity and Variability of Capitalism: on Variegated Capitalism in the World Market', in C. Lane and G. Wood (eds.), *Capitalist Diversity and Diversity within Capitalism*. London: Routledge, 209–37.

Jorgensen, H. and Madsen, P. K. (eds.) (2007). *Flexicurity and Beyond*. Copenhagen: DJOF Publishing.

Juillard, M. (1993). *Un schéma de reproduction pour l'économie des Etats-Unis: 1948–1980. Tentative de modélisation et de quantification*. Publications Universitaires Européennes. Paris: Peter Lang.

Kaukewitsch, P. and Rouault, D. (1998). 'La structure des salaires en France et en Allemagne en 1995: une analyse statistique comparative des hiérarchies salariales', *Économie et Statistique*, 315: 3–27.

Keohane, R. O. (1984). *After Hegemony*. Princeton: Princeton University Press.

Lane, C. and Wood, G. (eds.) (2012). *Capitalist Diversity and Diversity within Capitalism*. London: Routledge.

Marsden, D. (1990). 'Institutions and Labour Mobility: Occupational and Internal Labour Markets in Britain, France, Italy and West Germany', in R. Brunetta and C. Dell'Aringa (eds.), *Labour Relations and Economic Performance*. London: Macmillan, 414–38.

Mercier, S. (1999). *L'éthique dans les entreprises*. Repères. Paris: La Découverte.

Mistral, J. (1986). 'Régime internationale et trajectoires nationales', in R. Boyer (ed.), *Capitalismes fin de siècle*. Paris: Presses Universitaires de France, 167–202.

Mjøset, L. (2001). 'The Nordic Countries: A *Régulation* Perspective on Small Countries', in R. Boyer and Y. Saillard (eds.), *Régulation Theory: The State of the Art*. London: Routledge, 254–9.

Ostergard, U. (2009). 'Lutheranism, Nationalism and the Universal Welfare State'. Working Paper CBP. CBS, 26–27 November.

Pedersen, O. K. (2006). 'Corporatism and Beyond: The Negotiated Economy', in J. Campbell, J. Hall, and O. K. Pedersen (eds.), *National Identity and the Varieties of Capitalism: The Danish Experience*. Montreal: McGill-Queen's University Press, 245–70.

Perraudin, C., Petit, H., and Rebérioux, A. (2007). 'The Stock Market and Human Resource Management: Evidence from a Survey of French Establishments'. Mimeograph Ces Matisse, Université Paris 1, October.

Petit, P. (1985). *Slow Growth and the Service Economy*. London: Pinter.

Priestland, D. (2012). *Merchant, Soldier, Sage: A New History of Power*. London: Allen Lane.

Reich, R. (1993). *L'économie mondialisée*. Paris: Dunod.

Roe, M. (1994). *Strong Managers, Weak Owners: The Political Roots of American Corporate Finance*. Princeton: Princeton University Press.

Salais, R. and Storper, M. (1993). *Les mondes de production. Enquête sur l'identité économique de la France*. Paris: Éditions de l'EHESS.

Schor, J. and You, J.-I. (eds.) (1995). *Capital, the State and Labour: A Global Perspective*. Cheltenham: Edward Elgar.

SES (1992). '`L'introduction de l'intéressement et les hausses de salaires dans les entreprises', Première Synthèses, no. 18, June, Ministère du Travial de l'Emploi et de la Formation Professionnelle, Service des Études et de la Statistique.

Streeck, W. (2009). *Reforming Capitalism: Institutional Change in the German Political Economy*. Oxford: Oxford University Press.

Tirole, J. (1988). *The Theory of Industrial Organization*. Cambridge, MA: MIT Press.

Weitzman, M. L. (1985). *L'économie du partage. Vaincre la stagflation*. Paris: Hachette, Lattes.

Wright, E. O. and Dwyer, R. (2006). 'The Patterns of Job Expansions in the United States: A Comparison of the 1960s and the 1990s', in G. Wood and P. James (eds.), *Institutions, Production, and Working Life*. Oxford and New York: Oxford University Press, 275–314.

....

CHAPTER 7

CAPITALIST DIVERSITY, WORK AND EMPLOYMENT RELATIONS

....

CHRISTEL LANE AND GEOFFREY WOOD

INTRODUCTION

....

THE great value of the literature on comparative capitalism is its emphasis on the persistent viability of alternative models to market liberalism. Central to the viability of more heavily coordinated markets are specific production regimes, supported through cooperative work and employment relations, encompassing significant participation and involvement, strong industry and firm skills sets, and bargaining centralization (Hall and Soskice 2001; Estevez-Abe et al. 2001; Hancké et al. 2007). In contrast, the liberal market model is distinguished by less strong unions, decentralized bargaining, weaker worker rights, insecure tenure, and flexible labour markets. As such, this approach has considerable value as a theoretical starting point both for categorizing different national industrial relations regimes and in explaining the spatial concentration of specific sets of industrial relations practices. At the same time, while the nation-state remains an important level of analysis, there is considerable variety in practice both within nations and capitalist archetypes (Lane and Wood 2009, 2012). This would reflect the fact that institutions are rarely closely coupled, with distinct regional and sectoral dynamics. Moreover, supranational forces may not only erode national distinctiveness, but also reinforce difference between nations.

RETHINKING CAPITALIST DIVERSITY

....

In the early varieties of capitalism (VOC) literature, it was argued that firms opted in to specific institutional arrangements owing to the competitive advantages they conferred (Hall and Soskice 2001). As institutions solve problems, this will make for enduring differences between nations, an example being how, in some places, the law supports strong unions and more coordinated bargaining (Thelen 2010: 52). In other words, employers chose to fit in with, for example, national bargaining structures, owing to the benefits flowing from them in particular contexts; while the compromises this forces with organized labour may, at times, be unpalatable, the gains may greatly outweigh the costs (Hall and Soskice 2001). But, unlike the regulation theorists (cf. Jessop 2001), Hall and Soskice (2001) made no specific predictions that one form of capitalism was necessarily superior to another. Instead, they argued that two alternative models, the liberal market economy (LME) and coordinated market economy (CME), each had particular strengths and weaknesses. The former was distinguished by flexible labour and financial markets, particularly conducive to high technology/innovative industries (Hall and Soskice 2001; Amable 2003). In contrast, coordinated industrial relations institutions, strong vocational skills bases, and joint problem solving structures were, in turn, conducive to incrementally innovative production (Hall and Soskice 2001; Thelen 2001).

A key assumption was that each model conferred known advantages through mutually supportive rules, structures, and social ties, making for complementarities, that is, when specific systemic features yield superior outcomes when combined than the sum of their individual parts (Hall and Soskice 2001; Crouch 2005). Importantly, this would suggest that, as mutually supportive complementarities are not as developed, mixed systems will perform less well (Hancké et al. 2007; Hall and Gingrich 2004). This would discourage the emergence of hybrids between the two models, with other varieties of capitalism, most notably emergent market economies (EMEs, the post-state socialist economies of Eastern and Central Europe) and mixed market economies (MMEs, the Mediterranean European states) being impelled in one or the other direction (Hancké et al. 2007). Notably, MMEs are essentially bifurcated between large firms and the state sector on the one hand, and SMEs and the informal economy on the other hand; within the latter areas, regulatory coverage is uneven or absent. Again, as noted above, this would encourage firms within particular national settings to opt in to particular production paradigms and associated rules, owing to the clear advantages conferred by them (Hall and Soskice 2001).

In practice, however, the empirical evidence is somewhat mixed. LMEs remain characterized not only by highly innovative firms, but also by a large low value-added service sector, as well as, for example, significant numbers of more traditional manufacturing firms that have survived from the Fordist era (Wright and Dwyer 2006). Again, many smaller firms in CMEs make use of work, employment, and industrial relations practices that are somewhat removed from the CME ideal type (Streeck 2009). Moreover, there is no evidence of one type of firm or production paradigm largely driving out others. This raises the question as to what produces diversity within institutional arrangements and associated work and employment relations paradigms within national settings.

DEBATING COMPLEMENTARITY

In our earlier work, we noted that early thinking on complementarity as solely a synergistic building on strengths is no longer tenable. While synergistic relationships still are found they often have been replaced by one that is of a more compensatory nature (Lane and Wood 2009; Wood and Lane 2012; Crouch 2005). The latter would suggest that practices often are encountered together to make up for problems flowing from other dimensions of national institutional structures (Crouch 2005). This makes for a kind of hybridization that is not dysfunctional, but rather a sign of robustness (Crouch 2005). Hence, complementarity may make for diversity, with firms, rather than simply opting in or out, making more or less use of systemic features, as their own circumstances and that of their peers dictate.

On the one hand, this would explain the persistence of diversity. This would suggest that different parts of a system are each potentially functional in their own way, and what happens in one part may reinforce other parts and the whole in a beneficial manner (Crouch 2005). On the other hand, this discounts the possibility of pathological coexistence that might not necessarily be a sign of well-being, but rather of crisis (Jessop 2008). At a supranational level, the rise of mega exporters (Germany, China) is matched by heavily financialized mega importers (US, UK), with surplus capital generated by the former absorbed by the latter to fund renewed imports. Within countries, a comparable pathological dependence on one another by diverse players and sectors may similarly emerge. For example, with LMEs such as the US and the UK, the decline of traditional manufacturing work led to both wage squeezes by remaining manufacturing firms, and the replacement of such employment through new low-end jobs in the service sector (Wright and Dwyer 2006). However, declining standards of living were compensated for by the increased availability of credit from the financial services industry and successive housing price bubbles (Boyer 2010). The resulting period of growth proved unsustainable, despite increasingly desperate central bank attempts to prop it up, *inter alia*, through very low interest rates and quantitative easing.

What this would suggest is that rather than complementarity, the coexistence of bundles of rules and practices within and across nations is often more about coping. They may indeed be highly functional in working together, making up a broad 'growth regime' (Jessop 2001). However, they may simply persist owing to uncertainties as to the viability of alternative arrangements. They may also be cannibalistic, with one sector or actor feeding off the accumulated resources of another (Harvey 2004). An example would be the private pensions crisis in the UK. Historically, firms provided pensions as a form of deferred pay; in their absence, individuals purchased pensions or annuities through respected financial institutions, gaining a decent return on retirement. Their decline not only reflected (in the case of the former) firms taking pensions 'holidays', but also systematic failures of pension fund managers (Blackburn 2006,

2008). Long-term savings were diverted to fund short-term speculation and provided excessive incentives to engage in the latter (Blackburn 2006, 2008; Arrighi 2005). In turn, this has led to a growing class of ageing workers faced with the prospect of impoverished old age. Quite simply, the health of the pensions industry became dependent on the impoverishment of those working in other areas of the economy (Blackburn 2006, 2008). Again, this would reinforce the brittle strengths of the financial services industry, and the diffusion of cost-cutting production paradigms in manufacturing and retail. It also has immediate links with work and employment. The decline of occupational pensions has meant, in many instances, the abrogation of implicit contracts based on assumptions of deferred pay; in turn, this will effect the relative commitment of employees to firms.

REGIONAL DIFFERENCE: WORK AND EMPLOYMENT RELATIONS

Specific industries and associated forms of work and employment relations may do particularly well in some regions, owing to their natural or human resource endowments, geographic locale, or due to formative historical events. As resource endowments change, and/or due to external shocks, these advantages may decline or even evaporate (cf. Sewell 2008). Three issues are of importance here. First, archetypical industries within a particular region support an ecosystem of smaller, sometimes seemingly unrelated, firms. This means that a reduction in the job creating capacity of the former will have similar effects on the latter; in turn, overall higher unemployment may force down wages and encourage migration away from the region concerned. The converse would be true should archetypical firms prosper.

Second, the relative concentration of specific industries and particular regional traditions may make for a greater collectivism or individualism among workers. In turn, this is likely to impact on the relative strength of unions and the incidence of collective bargaining, and/or the viability of specific firm types, which, in turn, impact on other work and employment relations policies and practices. In some, but not all, instances, this may be structurally important. An example of the former would be the relative strength of cooperatives in some regions—for example, the Basque country, and parts of northeast England, which build on regional cultural traditions and associated solidarities. Another example would be the persistent strength of unions in the Eastern Cape, South Africa (despite very high unemployment), building on a particular political history. After a long period of adversarialism, this has translated into cooperative partnerships with management. These have spearheaded the transformation of the region's car plants from serving a small closed market through small batch production, into global export success stories.

Third, regional distinctiveness is bound up with politics. According to the geographic base of their constituents, and indeed, their own geographic origin and ties, politicians may direct resources towards or divert them from particular regions. However, the latter process may lead to popular backlashes, and/or such rapid regional decline as to force a reversion of such policies (Hudson 2012). This may even lead to politicians who are ideologically hostile to statism conceding to active industrial or regional regeneration policies in declining regions (Hudson 2012). Key actors may oppose or respond to central government initiatives in an uneven manner (Hudson 2012: 195). In turn, this will lead to renewed job creation, but with employment and growth often remaining contingent on continued state support.

Regional development may be affected by electoral systems. In 'first past the post' systems, politicians may be beholden to their immediate constituents. However, as elections are decided by ideologically uncommitted voters in marginal seats, this means that politicians can often afford to ignore the interests of particular classes, notably workers (Pagano and Volpin 2005), and/or even particular regions. In practice, in 'first past the post' systems, the interests of property owners are likely to assume predominance (Pagano and Volpin 2005). In highly proportional systems, politicians may lack the same close spatial connection to a particular locale, and they are forced to build coalitions with others. This makes for more inclusive political systems, characterized by cross-class compromises, and taking account of particular regional interests (Pagano and Volpin 2005). Not only does this mean that employees are likely to have more rights under the law in highly proportional systems, but the culture of compromise and coalition building is likely to diffuse beyond the political realm, to include work relations within the individual firm (Pagano and Volpin 2005). Again, there will be more attempts to reconcile the needs of different stakeholder groups, which may have distinct regional bases, under such systems. Broadly encompassing coalitions will reduce the chances of great imbalances between different regions and sectors.

Third, there is the issue of regional crisis and change. Should it not be possible to forge mutually satisfactory compromises within and between regions, it is possible for greater institutional layering to take place (Thelen 2010: 56). For example, Scottish, Welsh, and Irish devolution in the UK has led to the former two, and to some extent the latter, moving on to a more social democratic trajectory. Inevitably this will impact on firms, and work and employment relations in the regions concerned.

INDUSTRY EFFECTS

Much internal diversity in work and employment relations within national contexts is encountered in sectors. Two key issues are worth considering here. First, when sectors become concentrated in a specific geographical area, industrial districts may develop. These can be highly successful, yet were somewhat neglected in the early VOC literature. Within a particular sector and locale, firms may form close relations with each other that are distinct from others (Crouch and Voelzkow 2004). Crouch and colleagues argue that institutional arrangements are relatively fluid, with institutional fragments being creatively recombined at local level (Crouch et al. 2009). Within nation-states, local specialisms emerge and persist, with sets of alternative local, regional and/or sectoral institutional solutions being available within specific national contexts. Firms will opt for such arrangements if national institutions do not suit their specific needs (Crouch et al. 2009). This will allow specific types of firms to prosper in a particular sub-national space.

Trigilia and Burroni (2009) argue that there may be a lack of complementarity between coordination at national and regional levels; rather than part and parcel of national complementarities, industrial districts may simply coexist with other sectors and regions. This does suggest dislocation. The latter may well impact on national governance. Moreover, no matter how dense the ties are between firms within specific industrial districts, they are not self-contained and are likely to have close ties with other firms within and beyond the national context. Within CMEs, national-level legal regulation of industrial relations historically has reduced the chances of pronounced differences between industries.

However, while sectoral differences have always been pronounced in low-regulated LMEs the hitherto more homogeneous CME sectoral regimes have been diverging strongly in economies like the German one. The high-skill, high-security model in the core export-oriented industries continues but, since the early 2000s, has been supplemented by an extensive low-wage sector, particularly in service industries. In these sectors lower skill, low pay, and reduced employment security now provide employers with a flexible reservoir of labour. This development has been accompanied by a gradual shrinking of the previously encompassing system of labour representation and the emergence of many more separatist and individualized bargaining and pay determination processes at company level (Streeck 2009: 93f.). Although jobs in the low-pay economy still only form a large minority, this development nevertheless has created a strongly segmented and even polarized labour market, with recruitment from different social groups. Thus, in the German employment system we now find side by side totally different institutional arrangements, seemingly insulated one from the other by sectoral boundaries. However, complete insulation is impossible, and, as Streeck (2009) has noted, the disorganizing effects of the low-wage and low-organization sectors are seeping through into those still clinging to the traditional model.

State and Industry

A related issue to consider is the role of the state. When compared to the VOC approach, business systems theory accords rather more attention to its impact on shaping national development, an issue rather neglected by the former (Whitley 2007). However, the state generally does not act in an even-handed manner across industries. An obvious example would be the enormous (and objectively uncompetitive) interlocking military-industrial, security, and penal complexes in the USA. Private firms within these complexes may be propped up through opaque contracting that has more to do with political patronage and personal contacts than any market reality, either via direct government procurement or aid to foreign governments tied to spending on domestic military contractors (Hasik 2008; Mann 2003). Again, much of the competitive advantage of the high technology sector in the USA depends on lavish governmental spending on defence and security (Lane and Wood 2009; Mann 2003; Hasik 2008). In the UK, there has been very much less evidence of beneficial technological spillover between defence and other industries, and there have been significant budgetary cutbacks in this area. However, the pharmaceutical industry is heavily reliant on partially state-subsidized R&D conducted within the (quasi-state) university sector.

Within the USA, an interesting phenomenon that has reinforced diversity has been the emergence of new regional labour market institutions, such as sectoral partnerships and regional training consortia (Appelbaum et al. 2005: 303). However, tight sectoral labour markets do not always work to the benefit of workers; they may encourage greater outsourcing or relocation in the industries concerned, or lead to changes in work organization, all costing jobs (Appelbaum et al. 2005: 304).

Large-scale state bailouts and ongoing state support have been readily forthcoming to the financial services industry in both the USA and UK (Boyer 2010). The scale of these bailouts is indisputably enormous. Moreover, phenomenal amounts of money injected into the financial system in the form of quantitative easing, ostensibly to enhance the availability of credit, appears to have largely and mysteriously vanished to plug only partially known black holes and/or into offshore tax havens.

As Boyer (2010: 351) notes, this support has been matched by a willingness often (but with some notable exceptions) to leave conventional firms and workers to fend for themselves, no matter how adverse their circumstances. Saving bankers has meant saving their ideologies, in theory, lightly regulated markets, but in practice state support channelled into specific sectors at the expense of others. Given its volatile performance, and the clear bounds to its job creating abilities, the financial services industry cannot serve as a coherent basis for national growth (Wolfson 2003), and the role of other firms—no matter how marginalized—remains critical. On the one hand, the USA has clearly diverged from the archetypal LME model (Weiss 2010). On the other hand, the intervention is focused, uneven, and closely bound up with political processes and lobbying. While conventional firms making and selling non-financial goods and services have been damaged by the process, the system is dependent on significant numbers of them surviving. Again, this points to persistent diversity within such contexts, even if some industries operate on a sub-optimal level, owing to the adverse effects of others.

ACTION, THE LOCAL AND THE SUPRANATIONAL

Dore (2008) suggests that specific actors may play the role of norm entrepreneurs within particular settings. By introducing new practices, they challenge existing ways of doing things, which, over time, may gradually erode the established order. An example would be activist investors, such as private equity. Such investors have challenged the view that the dispassionate insights of a new managerial team can release more value (at least in the short term) than longer serving managers who would have a more intimate understanding of organizational process and the capabilities of its people. Another example in Japan would be that increasing foreign ownership has led to the diffusion of US-style practices (see Sako and Kotosaka 2012). However, this process has been a very uneven one, rather than a simple process of substitution. Rather, Streeck (2005: 580) suggests that within national systems, there occur both continuities and change, with specific practices being always open to re-evaluation and reformulation.

Diversity, of course, not only represents the product of social action at the national level, but also of supranational pressures. First, there is the role of supranational institutions, such as the European Union (EU) and international financial institutions (IFI). On the one hand, certain European bodies, such as the European Court of Justice, have done much to promote liberalization and individual rights. On the other hand, EU regional development funding may re-energize marginalized regions, without necessarily bringing them closer to either national norms, or an emerging neo-liberal order. Again, while the International Monetary Fund (IMF) has imposed neo-liberal reforms on those nations that have been forced to turn to it for assistance, this has not necessarily made for homogeneous outcomes. Cutbacks in government spending can reinforce difference, with economically weak regions and sectors of society being further marginalized through a self-reinforcing 'backwash' effect (Myrdal 1957).

Supranational actors may play a similar role in reinforcing diversity within national contexts. Two particular actors are worth considering here (Wood and Demirbag 2012). The first are multinational corporations (MNCs). They may challenge existing ways of doing things. An example would be the effect of Japanese MNCs on industrial relations in Britain: the direct effect has been to undermine traditions of multi-unionism within companies, and thus introduce significant diversity in the practices of union representation. However, rather than driving homogenization through importing perceived 'best practices' from abroad, MNCs may vary their practices according to setting. They may, for example, insert themselves into local production regimes owing to the competitive advantages they confer (Whitley 2010). This may simply be to gain access to cheap labour, but alternatively may occur to take advantage of the possibilities afforded by particular skills sets and embedded participative frameworks. In the case of the latter, innovations may result more in layering than transformation. Outsourcing production may also shore up existing ways of doing things within the area where production is domiciled, reinforcing tendencies to found competitiveness on cost cutting, encompassing labour repression. In short, while MNCs may indeed play the above-mentioned role of norm entrepreneurs, they may also reinforce localized or sector-specific ways of doing things. The latter would include buying into dominant local work and employment relations paradigms.

The second supranational actor is labour. As Standing (2011) notes, a feature of the contemporary world has been the rise of an underclass, the 'precariat', who are neither occupationally nor spatially rooted. This has potentially ambiguous implications, once more making for diverse outcomes within specific national contexts. On the one hand, one of the many contradictions of neo-liberalism is that dogged proponents of free markets are often equally forthright in advocating ever higher barriers to migration (MacEwan 1999). Growing employment insecurity within many developed societies, fanned by conservative media and politicians, has led to popular backlashes against immigrants, and a progressive tightening up on cross-border mobility (Standing 2011). On the other hand, the primary victims of the latter have been skilled migrants, and those seeking to enter countries via legal routes (for example, asylum seekers). Proponents of immigration restrictions are often silent when it comes to enforcing labour standards at home, and the extent to which the presence of large numbers of illegal workers may be used as a mechanism for depressing wages, and, indeed, labour coercion. Such migrants are often trapped between the Scylla of human traffickers, labour brokers, and their accomplices, and the Charybdis of the authorities, with constant fear of deportation (and thereafter being saddled with an unpayable debt to, and possible retaliation by, said traffickers). This makes for a reluctance to challenge even the most demeaning of working conditions and the lowest of pay (Standing 2011; Davis 2006). The outcome of all this are sectors of the economy characterized by relatively optimal conditions for skilled labour (with reduced possibilities for competition by immigrants) and others dominated by highly vulnerable workers, including large numbers of illegals (Standing 2011).

SYSTEMIC CHANGE

Actors and Change

As Crouch (2005: 22) notes, 'where there is institutional diversity there is potentially the possibility of recombination and, therefore, change and innovation'. The process of institutional change is an uneven one, and will, as noted above, further reinforce internal diversity. Institutional arrangements may change in a wide range of ways ranging from simply substitution to sedimentation (where new features progressively replace the old) (Boyer 2006: 48). This may include hybridization, that is, the 'adding of new elements to get a system that incorporates both old and new features' (Boyer 2006: 48). As noted above, foreign MNCs may pioneer new practices, which are absorbed by local structures, whose roles will not necessarily be completely transformed (Jürgens 2003).

While there always has been diversity in institutional arrangements and practices within nations (Trigilia and Burroni 2009), it can be argued that this process has been accelerated since the 1990s. This process has led to scepticism as to the persistence of familiar capitalist archetypes. Indeed, it can be argued that 'important limits have been reached to the notion of national varieties of capitalism as institutionally coherent and complementary sets of institutions' (Deeg and Jackson 2007: 157). This, of course, may reflect either plasticity in institutional arrangements or a new process of institutional transformation (Lane and Wood 2009).

The latter would be in line with contemporary regulationist authors who have abandoned early notions of a relatively smooth and short transition from Fordism to a new post-Fordist growth regime (Jessop 2001). Rather, it has been argued that the neo-liberal era, with its many dysfunctionalities, has not attained the characteristics of a growth regime. Instead, the present era is seen to constitute a sustained period of experimentation, volatile growth, and recession (Wolfson 2003; Boyer 2006).

Systemic change may be seen in actor-centred or class terms (Hancké et al. 2007), through the interaction of politically motivated actors and malleable institutions (Amable 2003; Höpner 2005; Jacoby 2005; Morgan and Kubo 2005; Streeck 2005; Boyer 2006; Deeg and Jackson 2007). The historical institutionalist approach emphasizes the tensions between systems that embody some logic of economic action, and actor creativity (Thelen 2010; Streeck 2009). Early institutional arrangements affect both subsequent arrangements and the direction of change (Rehberg 2006: 411). Decisions made in the early stages of institutional development will influence later ones. Even when existing systems are overturned, they will affect efforts to devise replacement structures (Rehberg 2006: 411).

What all these approaches have in common is a focus on change coming about primarily via societal arrangements, rather than stemming from specific problems or contestations arising within the firm. This is somewhat in contrast to early regulationist writings on the crisis of Fordism, which suggested that this could be superseded by a new post-Fordist production paradigm. However, current regulationist approaches have shifted their emphasis away from the workplace to concentrate on areas such as financial services (cf. Boyer 2010), which might suggest that work and employment relations have somehow become less important. However, whatever the starting point, it is clear that at societal level, the organized interests of workers, and especially unions are relatively weak today, particularly in LMEs, where this process has been matched by a reassertion of owner rights over those of other stakeholders in the firm (Dore 2000). Indeed, the direction of change has not been favourable to workers, as other more powerful players seek to rearrange institutional structures. In practical terms, within LMEs, this has led to an intensification of the negative dimensions of prior work and employment practices. This process has been detrimental to those firms which base their competitive advantages more on cooperative arrangements with workers, rather than pursuing shareholder value to the detriment of employees. As noted above, change within CMEs has perhaps been more pronounced, with the emergence of a low-wage pay sector in countries such as Germany. On the one hand, it could be argued that a revival of growth will re-strengthen the hand of workers (Kelly 1998). Owners of productive property will naturally resist this process, leading to a sustained period of conflict both within and beyond the workplace, forcing renewed attention to institutional mediation (Kelly 1998). On the other hand, a wide body of literature has suggested that the relative importance of workplace contestations varies according to time and place, and that the main challenges to the present order are likely to emerge within communities and the political domain (cf. Habermas 1993; Amable and Palambarini 2009).

Historical institutionalists believe that institutional arrangements become bedded down in times of crisis and trauma (cf. Sorge 2005). Over time, as other alternatives appear viable, arrangements will enter a period of decay or drift towards another model (Streeck 2009). Hence, for example, the class compromises that underpinned the 'golden age' from the early 1950s have gradually unwound, initially in LMEs, where they were always weaker, and gradually in the CMEs as well (Streeck 2009). This does not mean that systems will necessarily converge, but rather that both are drifting towards liberalization, even if the differences between them endure (Streeck 2009). Streeck (2005: 580) notes that all national types of capitalism embody continuity and change. Even if national economies remain distinct, patterns of behaviour and social relations within them are necessarily fragile and prone to reappraisal and adjustment on an ongoing basis. Again, this will make for diversity within national settings (Streeck 2005). Even archetypical CMEs such as Germany and Japan are characterized by complex and provisional institutional solutions, rather than representing coherent and homogeneous wholes.

Structuration theory—and indeed, some strands of the historical institutionalist literature—do highlight the link between agent and structure and see them as mutually constitutive (Jones 2001; Giddens 1984, 1990; Sorge 2005). As this interaction is spatially and temporally uneven, this will reinforce, but also constrain diversity within specific contexts (cf. Giddens 1990). However, this does not really answer the question as to where change comes from, and what is sufficiently powerful to disrupt any cycle of mutual constitution (Jones 2001: 824). We are cautious of the notion that institutional arrangements have a natural 'shelf life'. Rather, there is merit to the view that the admission of external or objective constraints permits accounting for objective factors 'external to the human consciousness' (Jones 2001: 824).

The Exogeneity of Change

Hence, what, other than the shifting balance of power between stakeholders through social action, impels institutional change? Diversity and change involve both objective pressures and subjective reinterpretations by actors (Simmel 1977, 1981). What makes an analysis of the interconnectedness of the subjective and the objective difficult is that it can lead to 'problems of confusion of behavior and outcomes' (Jones 2001: 825).

The literature on comparative capitalism makes repeated reference to exogenous shocks, which spur actors into promoting change (Hollingsworth 2006). Wood and Lane (2012) note that, just as was the case with the economic crisis of the first half of the twentieth century, the present condition is characterized by an energy transition. The former was marked by a shift from coal to oil; while the latter provided cheap, highly portable and relatively efficient energy, it also fundamentally changed the relative competitiveness of firms, industries and regions, and the allocation of capital (cf. Hackett

Fischer 1996). More specifically, industrial districts which had based their competitiveness at least partially on readily accessible coal reserves entered a long period of decline, which, in most instances, has continued to the present day. While demand for oil is increasing, the proportion of oil as part of the global energy mix has declined since the early 1970s (Jenkins 1989). Such processes greatly favour the owners of highly fungible capital, over those whose capital is committed to specific industries, processes, and locales (Wood and Lane 2012). Highly fungible capital has a partly statist element that distinguishes it from the concept of rentiers: it encompasses not only private speculative interests, but also sovereign wealth funds, with the latter, ironically, often accumulated by petro-states through oil exports.

Where do workers stand in this situation? The human assets and capabilities workers possess are very much less fungible than highly mobile investor capital. The former are often specific to a sector or region (Thelen 2001), and, indeed, their worth may be tied to the broader cognitive capabilities of a specific firm (Aoki 2010). As the competitiveness of firms and regions becomes more volatile, firms will naturally seek to offload as much of the risk onto workers: this would make for increasing insecurity, although the nature and extent of this will continue to vary from setting to setting (cf. Streeck 2009). And, as noted above, this process has been coterminous with the rise of a global precariat, whose great mobility is contingent on their ready substitutability (Standing 2011; cf. Appelbaum et al. 2005). In other words, the precariat may be able to take advantage of unforeseen upturns in the demand for labour—and cope better with downturns—by being spatially rootless. Their marketability depends on a willingness to accept inferior terms and conditions of service and to readily change occupation. In short, systemic crises may reinforce—and intensify—labour market segmentation, and diversity in work and employment relations practice within and across settings.

A caveat is in order here. We are very aware of the reductionist trap. A central strand in the new political economy literature has been long waves or cycles in capitalist development (Jessop 2001; cf. Polanyi 1944; Kelly 1998). While there is undeniable evidence of such fluctuations, their uneven duration, and persistent variations in the economic fortunes of nations not only on temporal but also spatial terms (whether due to regional dynamics or specific national political economies) reduce both their predictive and analytical power. Such fluctuations are undeniably due to complex and interconnected causes, of which energy availability is only one dimension. As Jones (2001: 822) notes, a truly satisfactory dissection of the roots of the present condition necessitates a thoroughgoing exploration of the complex interrelationship of the various components of cycles or waves; there is more to human and societal development than simply a shopping list of factors.

However, two issues are worth considering. First, energy availability, costing, and usage is bound up with technology (Diamond 2005). The emergence of the internal combustion engine, for example, paved the way for the transition to oil, and the continued lack of a single alternative means of locomotion that has the same beneficial features has made the present transition away from oil and gas particularly difficult despite declining reserves and increasing costs. Second, as with other energy sources and associated technologies, the usage of large amounts of oil and gas imposes indirect costs in terms of pollution and global warming that are easily offloaded from the individual and the firm onto the commons (see Jessop 2008; Diamond 2005). Given that contemporary economic theory prioritizes readily calculable present value over more abstract long-term costs (Singer 1995), and, indeed, that a persistent characteristic of human nature has been a reluctance to face up to discomforting social or environmental challenges, it is likely that environmental catastrophe will present itself prior to the general substitution of hydrocarbons for alternatives (Giddens 2009; Diamond 2005). Again, the costs of environmental crisis will be greatest for those who have invested skills and capabilities in particular locales and industries. Those most likely to benefit are those who can readily reallocate their capital, and/or hold scarce yet generic skills, with losers being increasingly driven down to the human fungibility of the precariat (Standing 2011; Davis 2006).

Given there is increasing consensus as to the existence of a great systemic crisis (cf. Amable and Palambarini 2009), the question emerges as to what form a new institutional order might assume. A comforting thought within progressive circles has been the Polanyian notion of double movement, whereby periods of market excess lead to a counter-movement, with a shift back to greater state mediation (Polanyi 1944). This has been associated with predictions of a possible revival in organized labour (Kelly 1998), and, indeed, of a possible return to the golden age of the welfare state. However, as Streeck (2009) notes, societal evolution is not simply on the lines of a swinging pendulum, but rather a winding path between differing forms of statism and market dominance. As Benjamin (1978; Wood and Lane 2012) notes, historical progress incorporates a destructive element, with the 'angel of history' leaving rubble behind. It may indeed be possible to piece together this rubble, and revive aspects of past institutional orders (Boyer 2006), yet the ultimate form will be very different to the past. Indeed, Polanyi (1944) cautioned that renewed drives for social security owing to the destructive consequences of unrestrained markets may be all too responsive to extremist agendas and right-wing authoritarianism. Indeed, across large areas of Europe, the immediate political winners of the present crisis have been extreme right-wing political parties, while in the USA, the formerly centre right Republican party has shifted towards an ever greater extremism. As noted earlier, leading LMEs incorporate some highly statist elements already: any Polanyian double movement may be leading towards a greater role for national military-industrial, security, and penal complexes, rather than towards a revival of social democracy and an associated systemic rebalancing of power within the workplace.

CONCLUSION

National institutions are neither tightly coupled, nor do they make for coherent outcomes. There is much, albeit bounded, diversity in socio-economic relations within and between firms. This diversity may reflect specific sectoral or regional dynamics, the uneven consequences of social action, and governmental partiality to specific players. It also reflects broader changes in the global capitalist ecosystem, and the uneven manner in which national institutions seek to accommodate themselves to this (Jessop 2012). While we may have entered a period of institutional drift, this does not necessarily mean that all previously beneficial arrangements have broken down, or that the rise of a coherent alternative order (either global or country-specific) is visible or even likely.

What does this mean for work and employment relations? On the one hand, labour power encompasses both readily substitutable (e.g. physical strength) and less fungible (e.g. human capital and associated collective capabilities—Aoki 2010) dimensions. Periods of sustained crisis are likely to reinforce diversity in work and employment relations practice, and the relative position of different categories of labour. Above all, this process involves the diminution of traditional 'good' jobs, tied to a particular skill or trade (Wright and Dwyer 2006). Work and employment relations paradigms have become trifurcated between labour repression centred on a disorganized precariat, traditional jobs associated with modified Fordist practices, and individualized jobs with high pay around scarce yet generic skills. This does not mean that this process has been a uniform one, with important differences remaining between LMEs and CMEs, even if there has been a common drift towards individualization (Streeck 2009). Socio-economic relations within the firm are interconnected with the broader external web of socio-economic ties enmeshing the firm and other players (Hancké et al. 2007). In other words, the internal elements of bounded regional and sectoral diversity are closely related to their external elements. However, both may be subject to further dislocation owing to the present and sustained nature of the current great systemic crisis.

References

Amable, B. (2003). *The Diversity of Modern Capitalism*. Oxford and New York: Oxford University Press.

Amable, B. and Palambarini, S. (2009). 'A Neorealist Approach to Institutional Change and the Diversity of Capitalism', *Socio-Economic Review*, 7(1): 123–43.

Aoki, M. (2010). *Corporations in Evolving Diversity: Cognition, Governance and Institutions*. Oxford and New York: Oxford University Press.

Appelbaum, E., Berhardt, A., Murname, R., and Weinberg, J. (2005). 'Low Wage Employment in America: Results from a Set of Industry Case Studies', *Socio-Economic Review*, 3(2): 293–310.

Arrighi, G. (2005). 'Hegemony Unravelling', *New Left Review*, 33: 83–116.

Benjamin, W. (1978). *Reflections*. New York: Harcourt Brace Jovanovich.

Blackburn, R. (2006). 'Finance and the Fourth Dimension', *New Left Review*, 39: 39–70.

—— (2008). 'Financialization and the Sub-Prime Crisis', *New Left Review*, 50: 63–106.

Boyer, R. (2006). 'How do Institutions Cohere and Change? The Institutional Complementarity Hypothesis and Its Extension', in G. Wood and P. James (eds.), *Institutions, Production, and Working Life*. Oxford and New York: Oxford University Press, 13–61.

Boyer, R. (2010). 'The Collapse of Finance, But Labour Remains Weak', *Socio-Economic Review*, 8(2): 348–53.

Crouch, C. (2005). 'Three Meanings of Complementarity', *Socio-Economic Review*, 3(2): 359–63.

Crouch, C., Schroeder, M., and Voelzkow, H. (2009). 'Regional and Sectoral Varieties of Capitalism', *Economy and Society*, 38(4): 654–78.

Crouch, C. and Voelzkow, H. (2004). 'Introduction', in Crouch, P. Le Galès, C. Trigilia, and Voelzkow (eds.), *Changing Governance of Local Economies: Responses of European Local Production Systems*. Oxford and New York: Oxford University Press, 1–10.

Davis, M. (2006). *Planet of Slums*. London: Verso.

Deeg, R. and Jackson, G. (2007). 'Towards a More Dynamic Theory of Capitalist Diversity', *Socio-Economic Review*, 5(1): 149–80.

Diamond, J. (2005). *Collapse: How Societies Choose to Fail or Succeed*. New York: Viking Books.

Dore, R. (2000). *Stock Market Capitalism: Welfare Capitalism*. Cambridge: Cambridge University Press.

—— (2008). 'Best Practice Winning Out?', *Socio-Economic Review*, 6(4): 779–84.

Estevez-Abe, M., Iverson, T., and Soskice, D. (2001). 'Social Protection and the Formation of Skills: A Reinterpretation of the Welfare State', in P. A. Hall and Soskice (eds.), *Varieties of Capitalism: The Institutional Foundations of Comparative Advantage*. Oxford and New York: Oxford University Press, 145–83.

Giddens, A. (1984). *The Constitution of Society*. Cambridge: Polity Press.

—— (1990). *The Consequences of Modernity*. Cambridge: Polity Press.

—— (2009). *The Politics of Climate Change*. Cambridge: Polity Press.

Habermas, J. (1993). *Moral Consciousness and Communicative Action*. Cambridge: Polity Press.

Hackett Fischer, D. (1996). *The Great Wave: Price Revolutions and the Rhythm of History*. Oxford and New York: Oxford University Press.

Hall, P. A. and Gingerich, D. (2004). *Varieties of Capitalism and Institutional Complementarities in the Macroeconomy*. MPIfG Discussion Paper 04/5. Cologne: Max Planck Institute for the Study of Societies.

Hall, P. A. and Soskice, D. (2001). 'An Introduction to Varieties of Capitalism', in Hall and Soskice (eds.), *Varieties of Capitalism: The Institutional Foundations of Comparative Advantage*. Oxford and New York: Oxford University Press, 1–68.

Hancké, B., Rhodes, M., and Thatcher, M. (2007). 'Introduction', in Hancké, Rhodes, and Thatcher (eds.), *Beyond Varieties of Capitalism: Conflict, Contradictions, and Complementarities in the European Economy*. Oxford and New York: Oxford University Press, 3–38.

Harvey, D. (2004). *The New Imperialism*. Oxford and New York: Oxford University Press.

Hasik, J. (2008). *Arms and Innovation: Entrepreneurship and Alliances in the Twenty-First-Century Defense Industry*. Chicago: University of Chicago Press.

Hollingsworth, J. Rogers (2006). 'Advancing our Understanding of Capitalism with Niels Bohr's Thinking about Complementarity', in G. Wood and P. James (eds.), *Institutions, Production, and Working Life*. Oxford and New York: Oxford University Press, 62–82.

Höpner, M. (2005). 'What Connects Industrial Relations and Corporate Governance? Explaining Institutional Complementarity', *Socio-Economic Review*, 3(2): 331–58.

Hudson, R. (2012). 'Regions, Varieties of Capitalism and the Legacies of Neoliberalism', in C. Lane and G. Wood (eds.), *Capitalist Diversity and Diversity within Capitalism*. London: Routledge, 189–208.

Jacoby, S. (2005). *The Embedded Corporation: Corporate Governance and Employment Relations in Japan and the United States*. Princeton: Princeton University Press.

Jenkins, G. (1989). *Oil Economists' Handbook*, 5th edn. London: Taylor & Francis.

Jessop, B. (2001). 'Series Preface', in Jessop (ed.), *Regulation Theory and the Crisis of Capitalism. Volume 4: Country Studies*. Cheltenham: Edward Elgar.

—— (2008). 'Polanyian, Regulationist and Autopoeiticist Reflections on States and Markets and their Implications for the Knowledge-Based Economy', in A. Ebner and N. Beck (eds.), *The Institutions of the Market: Organizations, Social Systems, and Governance*. Oxford and New York: Oxford University Press, 328–47.

—— (2012). 'Rethinking the Diversity and Variability of Capitalism: On Variegated Capitalism in the World Market', in C. Lane and G. Wood (eds.), *Capitalist Diversity and Diversity within Capitalism*. London: Routledge, 209–37.

Jones, B. (2001). 'International Political Economy', in Jones (ed.), *Routledge Encyclopedia of International Political Economy*. New York: Routledge, 813–29.

Jürgens, U. (2003). 'Transformation and Interaction: Japanese, U.S., and German Production Models in the 1990s', in K. Yamamura and W. Streeck (eds.), *The End of Diversity? Prospects for German and Japanese Capitalism*. Ithaca and London: Cornell University Press, 212–39.

Kelly, J. (1998). *Rethinking Industrial Relations: Mobilization, Collectivism and Long Waves*. London: Routledge.

Lane, C. and Wood, G. (2009). 'Diversity in Capitalism and Capitalist Diversity', *Economy and Society*, 38(4): 531–51.

—— (eds.) (2012). *Capitalist Diversity and Diversity within Capitalism*. London: Routledge.

MacEwan, A. (1999). *Neoliberalism or Democracy? Economic Strategy, Markets, and Alternatives for the 21st Century*. London: Zed Books.

Mann, M. (2003). *Incoherent Empire*. London: Verso.

Morgan, G. and Kubo, I. (2005). 'Beyond Path Dependency? Constructing New Models for Institutional Change: The Case of Capital Markets in Japan', *Socio-Economic Review*, 3(1): 55–82.

Myrdal, G. (1957). *Economic Theory and Underdeveloped Regions*. London: Duckworth.

Pagano, M. and Volpin, P. (2005). 'The Political Economy of Corporate Governance', *American Economic Review*, 95: 1005–30.

Polanyi, K. (1944). *The Great Transformation: The Political and Economic Origins of Our Time*. Boston: Beacon Press.

Rehberg, K.-S. (2006). 'Institutions', in A. Harrington, B. Marshall, and H-P. Müller (eds.), *Encyclopedia of Social Theory*. New York: Routledge, 280–2.

Sako, M. and Kotosaka, M. (2012). 'Institutional Change and Organizational Diversity in Japan', in C. Lane and G. Wood (eds.), *Capitalist Diversity and Diversity within Capitalism*. London: Routledge, 69–96.

Sewell, W. (2008). 'The Temporalities of Capitalism', *Socio-Economic Review*, 6(3): 517–37.

Simmel, G. (1977). *The Philosophy of History*. New York: Free Press.

—— (1981). *On Individuality and Social Forms*. Chicago: University of Chicago Press.

Singer, P. (1995). *Practical Ethics*. Cambridge: Cambridge University Press.

Sorge, A. (2005). *The Global and the Local*. Oxford and New York: Oxford University Press.

Standing, G. (2011). *The Precariat: The New Dangerous Class*. London: Bloomsbury Academic.

Streeck, W. (2005). 'Rejoinder: On Terminology, Functionalism (Historical), Institutionalism and Liberalization', *Socio-Economic Review*, 3(3): 577–88.

—— (2009). *Reforming Capitalism: Institutional Change in the German Political Economy*. Oxford and New York: Oxford University Press.

Streeck, W. and Thelen, K. (2005). 'Introduction: Institutional Change in Advanced Political Economies', in Streeck and Thelen (eds.), *Beyond Continuity: Institutional Change in Advanced Political Economies*. Oxford and New York: Oxford University Press, 1–39.

Thelen, K. (2001). 'Varieties of Labor Politics in the Developed Democracies', in P. A. Hall and D. Soskice (eds.), *Varieties of Capitalism: The Institutional Foundations of Comparative Advantage*. Oxford and New York: Oxford University Press, 71–103.

—— (2010). 'Beyond Comparative Statics: Historical Institutional Approaches to Stability and Change in the Political Economy of Labor', in G. Morgan, J. Campbell, C. Crouch, O. K. Pedersen, and R. Whitley (eds.), *The Oxford Handbook of Comparative Institutional Analysis*. Oxford and New York: Oxford University Press, 41–62.

Trigilia, C. and Burroni, L. (2009). 'Italy: Rise, Decline and Restructuring of Organized Capital', *Economy and Society*, 38(4): 630–53.

Weiss, L. (2010). 'The State in the Economy: Neoliberal or Neoactivist?', in G. Morgan, J. Campbell, C. Crouch, O. K. Pedersen, and R. Whitley (eds.), *The Oxford Handbook of Comparative Institutional Analysis*. Oxford and New York: Oxford University Press, 183–210.

Whitley, R. (2007). *Business Systems and Organizational Capabilities: The Institutional Structuring of Competitive Competences*. Oxford and New York: Oxford University Press.

—— (2010). 'Changing Competition Models in Market Economies: The Effects of Internationalization, Technological Innovations, and Academic Expansion on the Conditions Supporting Dominant Economic Logics', in G. Morgan, J. Campbell, C. Crouch, O. K. Pedersen, and R. Whitley (eds.), *The Oxford Handbook of Comparative Institutional Analysis*. Oxford and New York: Oxford University Press, 363–98.

Wolfson, M. (2003). 'Neoliberalism and the Social Structure of Accumulation', *Review of Radical Political Economics*, 35(3): 255–63.

Wood, G. and Demirbag, M. (2012). 'Institutions and Comparative Business Studies: Supranational and National Regulation', in Demirbag and Wood (eds.), *Handbook of Institutional Approaches to International Business*. Cheltenham: Edward Elgar, 3–17.

Wood, G. and Lane, C. (2012). 'Institutions, Change, and Diversity', in Lane and Wood (eds.), *Capitalist Diversity and Diversity within Capitalism*. London: Routledge, 1–31.

Wright, E. and Dwyer, R. (2006). 'The Patterns of Job Expansions in the United States: A Comparison of the 1960s and the 1990s', in G. Wood and P. James (eds.), *Institutions, Production, and Working Life*. Oxford and New York: Oxford University Press, 275–314.

CHAPTER 8

OWNERSHIP RIGHTS AND EMPLOYMENT RELATIONS

CHRIS BREWSTER, MARC GOERGEN, AND GEOFFREY WOOD

INTRODUCTION

THIS chapter explores the relationship between a single institutional feature, the law, and actual firm level practices. As many of the chapters in this book indicate, much of the variety of employment relations around the world can be understood through the lenses of theories that have attempted to encompass societal institutions as a web of interconnected influences or, alternatively, as structures that mould the choices of actors. Many of these theories give some importance to the relationships not only between firms (and between firms and governments and other players) but also to relationships within the firm, notably the hierarchical interactions between managers and employees. Particularly influential in the economics, finance and neo-liberal policy community have been approaches that link the law to firm practice and macroeconomic outcomes, and the consequences of particular traditions and associated bodies of law: these approaches centre on the stronger private property rights associated with the common law tradition. As a growing body of critics have pointed out, such approaches fail to take account of the diversity within national settings, while the evidence marshalled to support the civil-law superior macroeconomic outcomes thesis is highly selective (Cooney et al. 2010). However, a limitation with both these approaches and their critics is that the firm is primarily seen as a transmission belt: the effect of institutional environment is explored primarily in terms of possible macroeconomic outcomes. In other words, for a theory of, and debate around, corporate governance, there is remarkably little about the firm: rather, the concern is with exploring what particular inputs result in possible societal level macroeconomic outputs. There has been very little firm level evidence marshalled either way in this debate.

The Law and Comparative Institutional Analysis[1]

Teasing out antecedents of societal variations is a difficult task, largely because so many factors are involved and the likelihood of any real-world system fitting exactly into a parsimonious theoretical frame is unlikely. Nevertheless, such theoretical analyses are important because they indicate the relative strengths of layers of explanation. Fundamental to the Hall and Soskice (2001a, 2001b) distinction between liberal market economies (LMEs) and coordinated market economies (CMEs) is the degree of protection accorded to employees and, conversely, the relative position of shareholders. However, Hall and Soskice's (2001a, 2001b) theory is that of social relationships; hence, rather than looking at a single societal feature, what is important is how actors, in conjunction with each other, react to such rules, making choices and accommodations accordingly. Hence, the effect of the law will be diluted and mediated by other rules and relations.

In contrast, there have been long-standing attempts to proclaim that the law provides a central explanation for the way that society is organized. According to the classic writings on institutions by Emile Durkheim (1960: 28; cf. Cotterrell 1999: 33) law is the 'key' to understanding society: it unlocks a space that is otherwise closed to our understanding. Durkheim indeed argued that 'since law reproduces the main types of social solidarity, we only have to classify the different types of law in order to investigate what types of social solidarity correspond with them' (Durkheim 1960: 25; cf. Cotterrell 1999: 33). Law both reflects and reinforces social solidarity and, as such, is a touchstone for the way that individuals and organizations interact. Durkheim's (1960) classical theory was developed as an attempt to understand anomie in the modern industrial world and to encourage its substitution by what he saw as a historically socially cohesive society. He aimed to understand and argue for a system that allowed the individual pursuit of self-interest whilst ensuring that it did not undermine collective cooperation.

The question that this raises is who should be the immediate beneficiaries of the regulation. Should the regulation operate in a neo-liberal context, giving preference to the interests of owners? In the specific case of employment relations this means the owners of the businesses and in private sector organizations they will nearly always be founding families or shareholders. They are, after all, it is argued, the only stakeholders who actually have sunk funds into the firm (Djankov et al. 2003; La Porta et al. 1997; Shleifer and Vishny 1997) and there is therefore a sense of fairness and rationality in ensuring that their returns are maximized. Otherwise, there is no incentive to invest in firms and the system needs such incentives in order to survive. Such legal priority will encourage and enable the owners to ensure that the businesses are run in the most cost-effective way and will therefore allow the businesses to remain successful and profitable. From the economics and finance disciplines authoritative voices argued that, for these reasons, institutions provide the foundations for economic growth (La Porta et al. 1997; North

1990). A perhaps predictably conservative consensus emerged that a key institutional base concerned property rights: where these were stronger, success and growth were likely to be more robust. This—since profitable businesses are the core of the capitalist mode of production—will ensure that a business is able to pay taxes and that wealth is distributed through the society through these social contributions and through the trickle-through effects of the increased security and earnings of employees at all levels of the firm. Improving, for example, the rights of workers against their employers, since it is assumed that this is a zero-sum game (Botero et al. 2004; Roe 2003), will weaken the ability of firms to be successful and risk the efficient operation of the whole system, worsen the classic agency problem between the owners and the managers (Jensen and Meckling 1976), and constrain the possibilities of the business being run as effectively and efficiently as possible—to the longer-term disadvantage not only of the owners but also of the employees and society.

Or, by contrast, should the regulation operate to ensure a spread of responsibilities? Should the already immense powers of owners (their ability to locate in certain places, to source from anywhere in the world, to provide work in any location, and to control many aspects of working lives, and in some contexts the lives well beyond the work environment) be reined in so that other stakeholders, such as the firm's management, the workers, customers, suppliers, the local community, and the state, are given rights that will go some way towards balancing the owners' powers?

The answers that states have adopted to such questions vary, emphasizing the power of the institutional environment, classically defined as a nation's 'distinctive set of highly established and culturally sanctioned action patterns and expectations' (Lincoln et al. 1986: 340).

Durkheim's Classical Sociology and the Law

The importance of law in helping underpin social solidarity is central to Durkheim's vision of the way societies operate; he saw law as 'the key to sociology', a central tool for explanation (Cotterrell, 1999: 32). In talking about 'law' Durkheim wanted to include civil law, contract law, commercial law, procedural law, and constitutional law. His views were, inevitably, coloured by his experience of the continental European civil law systems—above all, French law—that place a strong emphasis on promoting social cohesion (1960: 371).

Durkheim understood that societies differ and noted the more minimalistic, less comprehensive legislation in countries such as Great Britain. He felt that this created imbalances in favour of the powerful and, presciently, noted that such approaches might undermine social inclusion and create 'huge disparities flowing from the market system' (Wilde 2007: 175). The emphasis on solidarity in certain continental European state traditions was aimed at restricting class antagonisms through a commitment to social progress for all (Wilde, 2007).

Durkheim believed that the quality of law provided an index of social solidarity (Prosser 2006: 371) and he rejected the notion of free exchange, typified by individual contracting, which he felt would ultimately make for social instability. Only when contracts, of any kind, are subject to a regulatory social force can the social interest be secured (Prosser 2006: 380). For Durkheim inequality could be superseded by social solidarity through legal mediation (Adair 2008): this fundamentally reflects the civil law tradition rather than the common law one.

Hence, Durkheim's interest was in the cohesion of society as a whole. Trade unions, for example, although they do seek to challenge the (too powerful) rights of property owners (Giddens 1971: 103; Durkheim 1960) and provide some protection, he saw as focused on the interests only of those who could be, are, were (or rely on) workers. Their interests are necessarily partial. Broader sets of role relations affect the relationship between employees and their bosses within the workplace. Despite their limits, unions in most countries are important representatives of workers' class interests, and they can act as a counter to excessive individualism (Stepan-Norris 1997; cf. Sverke and Hellgren 2001). The collectivism they articulate will mean that unions are likely to reduce anomie (McCaffrey et al. 1995). Beyond immediate terms and conditions of employment, trade unions also limit the ability of owners and managers to arbitrarily dispose of labour (Whitley 1999: 100). In many countries the legal environment and the activities of trade unions combine to make it harder for businesses to gain competitive advantage through labour cuts and other forms of employment-related cost cutting. So managers have to develop firm-specific competencies in order to make effective use of the firm's human capabilities.

RATIONAL-HIERARCHICAL ALTERNATIVES

This vision has been increasingly challenged by economists who see institutions as providers of incentives and disincentives to rational actors and argue that business works best when it is least trammelled by regulation. This stream of writing has sought to categorize societies according to the kind and the amount of legislation that restricts the owners of businesses from pursuing their own immediate ends. It distinguishes between countries according to the extent to which they protect individual property rights (North 1990). La Porta et al. (1997) distinguished, like Durkheim, between two main families of law: common law and civil law. Common law, the legal system of the UK, the USA, and most Commonwealth countries, accords an important role to judges. They pass judgments that become precedents for other courts. Later courts follow the precedents as much as the legislation. By contrast, civil law, the legal system of continental Europe and most of the rest of the world, is based on extensive codes of law—often having their origins in Roman law—and the role of judges is limited to interpreting these codes in the courts. The codes often explicitly privilege the rights of employees, social groups, consumers, etc. above those of the owners of businesses. La Porta et al. argue that, given its higher flexibility and better enforcement, common law provides stronger investor protection than civil law. Hence, Durkheim and those in the rational hierarchical economic traditions, make firm—but converse—judgements as to the desirability of specific legal traditions. To the former, civil law systems are superior on account of their ability to engender greater social solidarity and cohesion while, to the latter, common law systems are better, as they encourage rational actors to make optimal choices. This distinction as to the relative desirability of archetypical system aside, the shared interest in the consequences of legal origin provides an interesting starting point for comparative institutional analysis. The reasons are simple. First, legal origin approaches are easily extended to encompass the European transitional societies and the developing world, in contrast to the literature on comparative capitalisms, which requires the generation of fresh archetypes. Second, even if the law is not necessarily seen as the primarily deterministic institutional feature, an exploration of the consequences of legal tradition and the law is particularly salient, given strong global pressures on nation-states to deregulate their industrial relations systems.

Both Durkheim and later rational hierarchical approaches to the law suggest that there is a continuum between purer systemic variations, rather than the discrete categories envisaged by (at least, the early) literature on comparative capitalisms. Among the civil law family, La Porta and colleagues argue that French civil law provides the lowest levels of shareholder protection, followed by German civil law and Scandinavian civil law (La Porta et al. 1999).[2]

Directly relevant for our purposes here, La Porta and colleagues have argued that legal systems shape the way that markets are regulated and they specifically include labour markets in this (Botero et al. 2004: 1379). Civil law countries, they argue, are characterized, *inter alia*, by a more extensive involvement of direct government in labour markets as they have more extensive law relating to employment and industrial relations in contrast to common law countries where investors are provided with better protection. This, they argue, explains why common law countries tend to have more developed stock markets, a higher dispersion of ownership, and, at the time they were writing, higher growth in their economies. As this approach is about *legal origin*, this would suggest a very strong path dependence. Indeed, La Porta et al. (2008) primarily cast the East European changes in terms of a reactivation of earlier legal traditions (e.g. German civil law), rather than new ones.

As noted above, La Porta et al. argue that the most important feature distinguishing legal systems is the extent to which they protect private property rights. They argue that property and labour rights are a zero-sum game (Goergen et al. 2009) and that, therefore, employee labour rights act to weaken the rights of owners.

There are three immediate limitations with this approach. First, it fails to take account of internal diversity within national systems. Whilst it may seem that the law is the archetypical national institution, even within a liberal market economy such as the UK, there is much variation: English law is certainly common law, but Scottish law is hybrid, and incorporates strong civil law elements (see Siems and Deakin 2009). Second, and as noted above, this approach assumes strong path dependence; an interesting position, given that their arguments have often been deployed as a means of promoting or justifying labour market deregulation, most notably by the IMF and the World Bank (Cooney et al. 2010). Third, the approach makes very bold predictions as to the performance of firms (which is assumed generally to be stronger in common law systems), which are not borne out by reality. The evidence base marshalled by La Porta et al. and their imitators centres on the 1990s and early to mid-2000s, the height of the neo-liberal bubble era; their results are helped through the inclusion of the dysfunctional civil law countries of West Africa in their analysis, and their categorization of Scandinavia as somehow more neo-liberal than Germany. Why, then, bother with such approaches? First, there is their undeniable influence. Second, much comparative work on the effect of institutions on work and employment relations has confined itself to stylized ideal types or broad societal level indicators. This is true both with the literature on comparative capitalisms, and approaches that centre on the consequences of a single institutional feature such as the law. Even if one sees the law as not necessarily the most important feature, its impact is worth exploring in that differences encountered at firm level provide insights as to the impact of societal features on governance and firm level practice. And legal origin approaches greatly facilitate comparative analysis across a wider range of countries than that traditionally encompassed by the literature on comparative capitalisms.

EFFECTS OF THE LEGAL SYSTEM ON EMPLOYMENT RELATIONS

Given the ambition of the legal theories, we should not be surprised that they have obvious consequences for employment relations. In employment relations terms, a key dimension of the *interdependence* of businesses and their employees is continuity in relations and the deepening of ties through familiarity rather than through a narrow transactional relationship (Whitley 1999). Such continuity results in the socialization of the employee into the workplace and the embedding of habitual modes of thought (Giddens 1971: 102).

La Porta et al. (1997; Djankov et al. 2003) suggest that employee rights are stronger in civil law countries, for three linked reasons. First, individual (e.g. job protection) and collective (e.g. union and bargaining) employment rights tend to be stronger in civil countries. Second, since the rights of owners and shareholders are weaker, managers have more room to 'empire build', which, for interests of prestige and resource access, they have a natural inclination to do—what is referred to as the agency problem (Roe 2003). Empire building is likely to be more successful in collusion with employees, who also have an interest in working for larger entities (since they are associated with better terms and conditions of employment and greater job security) and who, in turn, will extract concessions from management. Third, legislation in common law countries tends to be more broadly drawn, and much is being left to the courts to interpret with case law and precedent 'filling in' the remainder. By contrast, rights and obligations in civil law systems are more clearly delineated (Wood et al. 2004). For employees, taking legal action against an employer is always an activity fraught with danger, particularly so in common law systems, but this may be the only legal option in those systems (though of course there are extra-legal options).

Empirical Evidence

As noted above, the empirical firm level evidence marshalled in supporting or interrogating comparative institutional approaches has been sparse. Our work with the Cranet survey (Wood et al. 2012; Goergen et al. 2012) has attempted to uncover some of the correlations. In this work we have been conscious of the impact of sector and size of firm on any results. Doellgast et al. (2009: 492) have pointed out that the sector may have pronounced effects on the nature of industrial relations and, we would argue, employment relations more generally. For example, they suggest that the service sector is less likely to be covered by collective bargaining and vocational training, while the limited substitutability of capital means that firms in this sector are likely to be under strong pressures to cut labour costs. In contrast, unions are likely to be stronger in manufacturing, for the converse reasons, and also in the public sector (Doellgast et al. 2009). Size effects are also likely to be substantial (Ferrer and Lluis 2009). In smaller firms employees can be monitored more closely and pay can be more accurately related to performance; in contrast, standardized contracting is more common in larger firms, in order to reap economies of scale. This standardization makes it easier to implement collective bargaining, while the presence of large numbers of workers in a single locale makes union organization easier and more cost effective.

The results of our work confirm the existing statistical trends regarding the changes in union fortunes, and variations in union growth and decline (see ILO 2001), and, hence, the amount of countervailing employee power. Trade unions have fared better in some national contexts than others, but most have battled to stem declining memberships, revitalization strategies notwithstanding (Kelly 1998; cf. Checchi and Visser 2005; Western 1993). We found that trade union penetration is lower in countries of the common law variety. However, contrary to the expectations of La Porta et al. (1997, 1998, 2000) and Botero et al. (2004), union membership is higher in countries with German and highest in those with Scandinavian law relative to the countries with French origin law. Furthermore, trade unions in the common law countries have suffered the largest drop in their influence over the past decade, closely followed by those in countries with German law. If anything, trade unions in countries of the Scandinavian law tradition have benefited from a slight increase in their influence. We do note, however, that the influence of trade unions varies across industries as well as across the various legal families; reflecting perhaps variations in work organization and the relative importance of centralized bargaining (Boyer and Hollingsworth 1997).

Size and sector have the expected effects but even taking them into account, the legal origin fits precisely with the broad prediction: all of the civil law categories have a significantly higher union impact that the common law ones. However, as common sense would suggest, employee countervailing power in the workplace in Scandinavia and Finland is rather more robust than that suggested by La Porta and colleagues (Botero et al. 2004). In other words, of the civil law sub-types the Nordic countries have a significantly greater union impact than the French or German ones, which is rather different from La Porta et al.'s expectations, given that Scandinavian law is a less 'pure' manifestation of civil law than its French counterpart. Hence, while legal origin is a clear predictor, it is not necessarily the case that 'purer' civil law makes for a greater trade union impact: rather, the evolution of a legal system reflects a specific historical experience and the changing nature of supportive social institutions. This would highlight the validity of Durkheim's sociological approach to the law, as adverse to the somewhat mechanistic, rational choice economic approach of La Porta et al.

The interdependence of firms and workers tends to be higher in unionized firms: trade union members are less likely to quit firms since the union gives them a vehicle to express their concerns and to impact on organizational life (Batt et al. 2001). The collective dimension of union membership propagates a solidaristic ideal (e.g. McLean Parks et al. 1995; McCaffrey et al. 1995; see also Krauss et al. 1984) which further enhances interdependence. Brown and Marsden (2011) argue that staff turnover and the relative use of compulsory redundancies are good measures of security and continuity on employment. We found that the civil law countries have significantly lower turnover rates than the common law ones (Goergen et al. 2009, 2012), although here it is the French and German origin countries, especially the German ones, that display the greatest difference from the common law countries. In terms of compulsory redundancies (Goergen et al. 2012), the results do not fit the models so neatly. Firm size is irrelevant to the likelihood of the organization having undertaken compulsory redundancies in the last three years and there is no significant difference between the Nordic countries and the common law ones here (the implications for individuals may, of course, be quite different). Firms in the other civil law countries, i.e. those of French and German legal origins, are much less likely to use compulsory redundancies.

In a different look at the same dataset, Brewster et al. (2011) confirmed the complex relationship between societal institutions, legal traditions, political parties and electoral systems, corporate governance, and the relative strength of unions and collective representation at workplace level. Clearly, there is more to understanding corporate governance than simply property relations. Law provides the basis for securing property rights but also provides rights for employees on a collective and individual basis, and these may overlap; more of one does not mean less of the other (Piore and Safford 2006). Furthermore, firms are constrained by the legal system in which they operate but it is apparent from the variation in the data that they have, and they do make, choices that vary between firms in similar institutional circumstances.

This raises a further question as to the relative interdependence of a firm and its people in contexts of strong property owner rights. It might seem that, when employee rights are stronger, firms are forced to be more committed to their workforce, and hence are more likely to invest in them; in contrast, when tenure is weak, firms can look to the external labour market for specific skills, offsetting the cost of training on the individual job seeker. In looking at the Cranet data, we did again find a relationship between legal origin and training spend, but once more encountered important differences between the Nordic countries and continental Europe that cannot be explained by La Porta et al.'s assumption that the former represents a diluted form of civil law (Goergen et al. 2012). However, the relationship between owner rights and relative training spend was not a converse one. Rather, firms in common law countries tended to spend a proportionately large amount on training; further analysis revealed that such training tended to be of short duration, a product of the need to provide more frequent basic induction training when tenure is weak (Goergen et al. 2012). In contrast, training in more cooperative national archetypes tended to be of longer duration, with the cost of sustained investments in people being spent over many years (Goergen et al. 2012).

Where does this leave multinational corporations (MNCs) whose activities straddle legal contexts? Although labour law will mediate practice in country of domicile, property owner rights in country of origin are likely to have a significant effect. Indeed, while early comparative accounts tended to concentrate on country of domicile effects, there has been an increasing realization that country of origin has a major influence (Brewster et al. 2008). This is particularly the case with US MNCs, reflecting the strong orientation towards shareholder rights. This has led writers such as Sako and Kotasaka (2012) to point to their effects in pioneering the dissemination of liberal-market practices into traditionally heavily coordinated markets. However, as Whitley (2010) notes, MNCs may be forced to amend their practices, according to whether they wish to access the competitive advantages of specific locally embedded production regimes and/or to fit in with onerous local rules in order to access particularly large or lucrative markets. However, firms will be in an easier position to make such choices if owner power is mediated by that of other stakeholders in country of origin. This would point to mixed country of origin/country of domicile effects, as confirmed by analysis of the Cranet data (Brewster et al. 2008).

Second, our empirical work has encountered much variation between civil law countries. Whilst this is recognized by La Porta et al. (1999), our analysis has also revealed considerable variation in common law countries. This is particularly true when it comes to union power and the nature and extent of firm investments in training and development. This points to the interrelated and mediating effects of different institutions on each other. Examples would include the influence of different electoral systems (e.g. Ireland's proportional system) or specific political dynamics (e.g. the need to reconcile competing ethnic interest groupings in Canada). Again, some liberal market economies, such as the USA, are highly statist in specific aspects, most notably the enormous penal, military-industrial, and security complexes, and the role of the state and not-for-profit sector in supporting R&D; this will make for a considerable degree of internal diversity.

GENERAL ISSUES

Our research suggests that there is some evidence that the 'legal family' theories, such as that advanced by La Porta et al. (1997), have some validity. There is a negative relationship between owner rights and levels of unionization, implying a direct link between law and investor protection and employment relations. We found a clear relationship between legal system and trade unionism, and, indeed, training and development activities, though less evidence of any relationship with other aspects of employment relations. However, the relationship was not one strictly on the lines predicted by La Porta et al. In practice, supposedly hybrid legal systems were more effective in promoting and protecting collective workplace activity than 'purer' French civil law ones. This would reflect the extent to which the legal system is interlocked with a range of other institutions, and the limits of focusing on a single institutional feature. Again, there is a difference between formal institutional structures and associated regulations, and how they work in practice; our analysis revealed this gap was particularly pronounced in the case of the Mediterranean world.

How are we to interpret the evidence that we found? It both supports and questions the La Porta et al. thesis. An emerging body of critical literature points to the limits of these measures (Cooney et al. 2010; Siems and Deakin 2009). Eight, overlapping, issues need to be noted before we can draw any final conclusions.

The La Porta et al. thesis rests on the assumption that one specific dimension (law, in this case) overrides others, imposing its effects on subsidiary institutions, corporate governance, managerial practice, and employment relations. While Durkheim may have been ready to accept such an assumption, in practice this may mean that the effects of law and the legal system on the behaviour of firms are exaggerated. Not only is what firms do mitigated—or exaggerated—through other institutional features, but there is implicit in the whole legal families discussion an assumption that organizations and the people who comprise them act rationally. Only brief experience of organizational life is needed for it to become apparent that while this may be a useful academic device, it bears little relationship to real life, where bounded rationality, limited information, emotion, self-interest, and error play a very real role. This does not mean that the legal system does not matter in employment relations, but the effects may be more contingent, more varied, and more open to contestation than these rational hierarchical approaches imply.

There must be concerns about the premise that owners have primacy because they are the only stakeholders with sunk capital in the enterprise. In practice this may be a fleeting commitment as investors move in and out of organizations. In other words, employees have at least as much or more to lose if the company underperforms: they may be dismissed, and may not readily find other jobs, especially during a time of recession (Goergen et al. 2009). And if they do find another post there are substantial transaction costs for the individual, so that even a new job under similar terms and conditions of service can still leave the individual worse off (Marsden 1999). In other words, the human assets of workers are relatively infungible, in contrast to highly fungible segments of capital (Lane and Wood 2012). In addition, a host of other stakeholders (suppliers, customers, and surrounding communities) will all have some interest in the prosperity of the firm. The argued primacy of the owners' rights cannot be defended on the grounds of sunk costs—it can only be argued on the grounds of increased success for the firm, and that has proven very difficult to establish. While La Porta et al. (1999, 2002) go on to argue that systems that prioritize private property rights yield better economic outcomes, this is only the case for a very limited range of years, and a specific panel of countries.

There is an assumption in La Porta et al. (1999), and Botero et al. (2004) that owner rights are incompatible with worker rights and tend to be a zero-sum affair; if the law accords greater power to one side then the interests of the other will necessarily suffer. In contrast, the literature on institutional complementarity suggests that sets of practices may work better together than on their own; this means that it is not necessarily the case that a limited pool of resources will simply be reallocated according to institutional configurations (Crouch 2005). Since our findings did not strictly follow the predictions of differences in owner rights made by La Porta and his colleagues (cf. Goergen et al. 2009) it is at least possible that owner rights and unionization are not necessarily incompatible, highlighting the relevance of Durkheim's emphasis on the importance of social compromises and reconciliation, and helping to explain the success of the economies in the Nordic legal family.

There are also some methodological issues. The equal weighting applied to different aspects of legislation such as works council rights and formal job protection in Botero et al. (2004) appears at best arbitrary (Cooney et al. 2010). The inclusion of some African states (but not others) might also be questioned, given that many are closely bound up with the vicissitudes of global commodity markets, with relative growth rates often having little to do with governance or the rule of law.

More seriously from a conceptual viewpoint, the legal families theorists tend to assume that institutions are relatively closely coupled. If legislation, from whatever source, is in place but is not rigorously applied, then the effect may be different from both contexts where it is and where regulation is absent. In cases of *partial institutional decoupling*, players may partially disengage, but still make demands on the system. We know, for example, that within many of the French legal origin countries of the Mediterranean world enforcement of the law, particularly but by no means only, within the family-owned business sector, is uneven or weak (Psychogios and Wood 2010); at the same time, such players have expectations which may be difficult to mediate.

The legal families theorists tend to discount the range of external pressures which work for and against homogenization. On the one hand, as Jessop (2012) notes, neo-liberalism has a degree of global ecosystemic dominance, and this has led to strong pressures towards commoditization and short-termism. On the other hand, there has been the rise of new statist investor categories, such as sovereign wealth funds, that often pursue agendas other than short-term shareholder value maximization. Moreover, company law and legally enforced securities regulation tend to be commonplace in all varieties of capitalism (Siems 2006)—as widely used in common law countries as in constitutional law countries; and jurisprudence tends to develop as a source of law even in civil law countries. A categorization based on legal families may be too simplistic.

The globalization point leads us to the wider issue of evolution and change. Despite the division into distinct legal families in terms of origin, all such systems are involved in a continuous process of evolution and adaptation. Laws, as Durkheim emphasized in his later writings, represent a 'living idea' embedded in social processes that should be seen in historical and comparative terms (Cotterrell 1999: 34). Current practice cannot be understood purely in terms of legal origin, but rather how law has evolved, contributes to, and 'lives in' such processes. This goes some way towards explaining why Nordic law is rather different in its relationship with workplace solidarities than the diluted civil law archetype (with diluted worker and somewhat strengthened owner rights) suggested by La Porta et al. (2000). Nordic economies have, since 1945, become heavily associated with social accords that are contingent on unions having broad social footprints (Olson 1982). Although support for union membership is underpinned legally (Olson 1982), these social accords are not an inevitable feature of civil law per se. Many other countries have hybrid systems as the examples of the UK (with its overlay of European Union legislation and the specific position of the different Scottish system) and South Africa illustrate. It is evident that, whatever the intentions of the early founders of specific legal traditions, legal systems represent the product of a developing range of pressures and compromises (Siems and Deakin 2009), including continuing adjustment and experimentation (Streeck 2005). It might indeed be the case that less pure or hybrid systems may work better for one or all parties (Crouch 2005). This would reflect the fact that hybridization may make for more workable compromises and complementarity than would be possible under more rigid and 'purer' contexts (Crouch 2005).

And that in turn takes us to the nature of complementarity; the concept that laws, rules, and practices can together yield better results than a scrutiny of their component parts would suggest: enhancing systemic strengths, compensating for inherent weaknesses, or imparting flexibility into systems that otherwise appear to be overly rigid or sclerotic (Crouch 2005; Lane and Wood 2009). This means that even when owner rights are weaker, alternative sets of complementarities may still make for outcomes equally beneficial to those situations where they are stronger. This means that owner–worker rights are not necessarily a zero-sum game. Complementarities may also be pathological, an obvious example being the relationship between mega-exporting and mega-importing nations, although others are possible at firm level.

Conclusions

Overall, and taking account of all these issues, what conclusions can be drawn from the study of law as an antecedent of employment relations? What is the relationship between studies of legal origin and the associated studies, in a different discipline, of comparative capitalisms (Deeg and Jackson 2008)? The legal origin literature is based on a uni-dimensional, coherent, and consistent set of visible institutions—the legal system and the way that it works. The different strands of the comparative capitalisms literature, by contrast, tend to draw their evidence somewhat eclectically and it is perhaps unsurprising that there are different strands—the range of options in terms of focus and evidence makes that inevitable. There are continuing debates about precisely how many and which forms of capitalism there are (see Hancké et al. 2007; Amable 2003); whether they are on a single continuum and/or whether societies can adopt or change form without moving closer to one or another particular archetype (Hancké et al. 2007; Amable 2003); and about the degree of variety within them as opposed to between them (Lane and Wood 2009, 2012).

Some of these criticisms apply less in the case of the more visible and observable legal origin school. Legal structures, laws, and cases can be easily identified. While there may be some discussion about the placing of societies between the poles and along the continuum, and the allocation of families of law in between the poles, there is more coherence about the argument and the effects. Owners' rights, and by extension the rights of employees and trade unions, constitute an important element of all the discussions of comparative capitalisms and their effects on employment relations. Clearly, despite the different bases and arguments, there is considerable overlap between the legal and comparative capitalisms sets of explanatory factors. Our empirical work confirms differences between setting and firm practices and that, contrary to predictions of global homogenization or diffuse diversity (Katz and Darbishire 2000), national differences persist. Despite very different starting points, there is much in common with legal origin theories and the literature on comparative capitalisms. The LMEs are broadly the same countries as those that have common law systems privileging the rights of owners of businesses. The CMEs are generally common law, i.e. constitutional law countries. Using Amable's (2003) more subtle categorization also has some common ground with legal origins approaches, but provides the basis for a more nuanced view. If the question of enforcement of legislation is added to the legal framework analysis, the Nordic states have less but more rigorously enforced legislation—in employment relations through trade unions, consultative bodies, and joint consultation arrangements, remembering that in these societies most managers are also trade union members and there are strong social pressures to conformity. The Mediterranean countries generally have legal systems with origins in the French law tradition but, with a preponderance of small firms, family-owned businesses, limited trade unionism, and weak state enforcement agencies, the law may be strictly applied in only relatively few cases. What this would suggest is that there is virtue in approaches that place countries in discrete categories rather than positioned on a continuum. This may also be a factor accounting for the degrees of variety within, as opposed to between, varieties of capitalism.

We may indeed conclude that the law, and variance in the form of different legal traditions, remains important in influencing the propensity for social solidarity in the workplace. The relative performance of countries in the aftermath of the financial crisis is rather different to that suggested by La Porta et al., which would highlight the folly of policy prescriptions based on the notion that labour market deregulation results in superior growth. It also suggests the superiority of Durkheim's classical sociological theory for understanding contemporary workplace dynamics over narrowly economistic approaches. However, whatever the theoretical origin, it is evident that legal origins do not determine workplace practices and social relations independent of other societal features and relations. In other words, it is not only legal tradition, but also the evolution of law and the associated social context in which it is enacted that matters.

NOTES

1. This discussion on Durkheim draws on the ongoing work of two of the authors with Phil Johnson, and the contribution of the latter to this is acknowledged (see Johnson et al. 2012).
2. There does seem to be a broad consensus that civil law contexts are profoundly different from common law ones; differences in detail do not detract from the relevance of broad trends (cf. Aoki 2010).

REFERENCES

Adair, S. (2008). 'Status and Solidarity: A Reformulation of Early Durkheimian Theory', *Sociological Enquiry*, 78(1): 97–120.

Amable, B. (2003). *The Diversity of Modern Capitalism*. Oxford and New York: Oxford University Press.

Aoki, M. (2010). *Corporations in Evolving Diversity: Cognition, Governance and Institutions*. Oxford and New York: Oxford University Press.

Armour, J., Deakin, S., Sarkar, P., Singh, A., and Siems, M. (2009). 'Shareholder Protection and Stock Market Development: An Empirical Test of the Legal Origins Hypothesis', *Journal of Empirical Legal Studies*, 6(2): 343–80.

Batt, R., Colvin, A., and Keefe, J. (2001). 'Employee Voice, Human Resource Management and Quit Rates', *Industrial and Labor Relations Review*, 55(4): 573–94.

Botero, J., Djankov, S., La Porta, R., and Lopez-de-Silanes, F. (2004). 'The Regulation of Labor', *Quarterly Journal of Economics*, 119(4); 1339–82.

Boyer, R. and Hollingsworth, J. R. (1997). 'From National Embeddedness to Spatial and Institutional Nestedness', in Hollingsworth and Boyer (eds.), *Contemporary Capitalism: The Embeddedness of Institutions*. Cambridge: Cambridge University Press, 433–84.

Brewster, C., Goergen, M., and Wood, G. (2011). 'Corporate Governance Systems and Industrial Relations', in A. Wilkinson and K. Townsend (eds.), *The Future of Employment Relations: New Paradigms, New Developments*. Basingstoke: Palgrave Macmillan, 238–53.

Brewster, C., Wood, G. and Brookes, M. (2008). 'Similarity, Isomorphism or Duality? Recent Survey Evidence on the HRM Policies of MNCs', *British Journal of Management*, 19(4): 320–42.

Brown, W. and Marsden, D. (2011). 'Individualization and Growing Diversity of Employment Relationships', in Marsden (ed.), *Employment in the Lean Years: Policy and Prospects for the Next Decade*. Oxford and New York: Oxford University Press, 73–86.

Checchi, D. and Visser, J. (2005). 'Pattern Persistence in European Trade Union Density', *European Sociological Review*, 21(1): 1–21.

Cooney, S., Gahan, P., and Mitchell, R. (2010). 'Legal Origins, Labour Law, and the Regulation of Employment Relations', in M. Barry and A. Wilkinson (eds.), *Handbook of Comparative Employment Relations*. Cheltenham: Edward Elgar, 75–97.

Cotterrell, R. (1999). *Emile Durkheim: Law in a Moral Domain*. Stanford: Stanford University Press.

Crouch, C. (2005). 'Three Meanings of Complementarity', *Socio-Economic Review*, 3(2): 359–63.

Deeg, R. and Jackson, G. (2008). 'Comparing Capitalisms: Understanding Institutional Diversity and its Implications for International Business', *Journal of International Business Studies*, 39: 540–61.

Djankov, S., Glaeser, E., La Porta, R., Lopez-de-Silanes, F., and Shleifer, A. (2003). 'The New Comparative Economics', *Journal of Comparative Economics*, 31: 595–619.

Doellgast, V., Holtgrewe, U., and Deery, S. (2009). 'The Effects of National Institutions and Collective Bargaining Arrangements on Job Quality in Front-Line Service Workplaces', *Industrial and Labor Relations Review*, 62(4): 489–509.

Durkheim, E. (1912/1960). 'The Elementary Forms of Religious Life', in K. Wolff (ed.), *Emile Durkheim et al.: Writings in Sociology and Philosophy*. New York: Harper & Row.

Ferrer, A. and Lluis, S. (2009). 'Should Workers Care About Firm Size?', *Industrial and Labor Relations Review*, 62(1): 104–25.

Giddens, A. (1971). *Capitalism and Modern Social Theory: An Analysis of the Writings of Marx, Durkheim and Max Weber*. Cambridge: Cambridge University Press.

Goergen, M., Brewster, C., and Wood, G. (2009). 'Corporate Governance Regimes and Employment Relations in Europe', *Industrial Relations/Relations Industrielles*, 64(6): 620–40.

Goergen, M., Brewster, C., Wilkinson, A. and Wood, G. (2012). 'Varieties of Capitalism and Investments in Human Capital', *Industrial Relations: A Journal of Economy & Society*, 51(S1): 501–27.

Hall, P. A. and Soskice, D. (2001a). 'An Introduction to Varieties of Capitalism', in Hall and Soskice (eds.), *Varieties of Capitalism: The Institutional Foundations of Comparative Advantage*. Oxford and New York: Oxford University Press, 1–68.

—— (eds.) (2001b). *Varieties of Capitalism: The Institutional Foundations of Comparative Advantage*. Oxford and New York: Oxford University Press.

Hancké, B., Rhodes, M., and Thatcher, M. (2007). 'Introduction', in Hancké, Rhodes, and Thatcher (eds.), *Beyond Varieties of Capitalism: Conflict, Contradictions, and Complementarities in the European Economy*. Oxford and New York: Oxford University Press, 3–38.

ILO (2001). *UNION: ILO Database on Union Membership*. Geneva: ILO.

Jensen, M. and Meckling, W. (1976). 'Theory of the Firm: Managerial Behavior, Agency Costs and Capital Structure', *Journal of Financial Economics*, 3: 305–60.

Jessop, B. (2012). 'Rethinking the Diversity and Variability of Capitalism: On Variegated Capitalism in the World Market', in C. Lane and G. Wood (eds.), *Capitalist Diversity and Diversity within Capitalism*. London: Routledge, 209–37.

Johnson, P., Brewster, C., Brookes, M. and Wood, G. (2012). 'Legal Origin and Workplace Social Solidarity', mimeo.

Kalleberg, A. L. 2009. 'Precarious Work, Insecure Workers: Employment Relations in Transition', *American Sociological Review*, 74: 1–22.

Katz, H. and Darbishire, O. (2000). *Converging Divergences: Worldwide Changes in Employment Systems*. New York: Cornell University Press.

Kelly, J. (1998). *Rethinking Industrial Relations: Mobilization, Collectivism and Long Waves*. London: Routledge.

Krauss, E., Rohlen, T., and Steinhoff, P. (eds.) (1984). *Solidarity in Japan*. Honolulu: University of Hawaii Press.

La Porta, R., Lopez-de-Silanes, F. and Shleifer, A. (1999). 'Corporate Ownership Around the World', *Journal of Finance*, 54(2): 471–517.

—— (2008). 'The Economic Consequences of Legal Origins', *Journal of Economic Literature*, 46(2): 285–332.

La Porta, R., Lopez-de-Silanes, F., Shleifer, A. and Vishny, R. (1997). 'Legal Determinants of External Finance', *Journal of Finance*, 52(3): 1131–50.

—— (1998). 'Law and Finance', *Journal of Political Economy*, 106: 1113–55.

—— (2000). 'Investor Protection and Corporate Governance', *Journal of Financial Economics*, 58: 3–27.

—— (2002). 'Investor Protection and Corporate Valuation', *Journal of Finance*, 57(3): 1147–70.

Lane, C. and Wood, G. (2009). 'Introducing Diversity in Capitalism and Capitalist Diversity', *Economy and Society*, 38(3): 531–51.

—— (2012). 'Institutions, Change, and Diversity', in Lane and Wood (eds.), *Capitalist Diversity and Diversity within Capitalism*. London: Routledge, 1–31.

Lincoln, J. R., Hanada, M., and McBride, K. (1986). 'Organizational Structures in Japanese and U.S. Manufacturing', *Administrative Science Quarterly*, 31(3): 338–64.

McCaffrey, D., Faerman, S., and Hart, D. (1995). 'The Appeal and Difficulties of Participative Systems', *Organization Science*, 6(6): 603–27.

McLean Parks, J., Gallagher, D., and Fullagar, C. (1995). 'Operationalizing the Outcomes of Union Commitment: The Dimensionality of Participation', *Journal of Organizational Behavior*, 16: 533–55.

Marsden, D. (1999). *A Theory of Employment Systems*. Oxford and New York: Oxford University Press.

North, D. C. (1990). *Institutions, Institutional Change and Economic Performance*. Cambridge: Cambridge University Press.

Olson, M. (1982). *The Rise and Decline of Nations: Economic Growth, Stagflation and Social Rigidities*. New Haven: Yale University Press.

Piore, M. and Safford, S. (2006). 'Changing Regimes of Workplace Governance, Shifting Axes of Social Mobilization and the Challenges to Industrial Relations Theory', *Industrial Relations*, 45(3): 299–325.

Prosser, T. (2006). 'Regulation and Social Solidarity', *Journal of Law and Society*, 33(3): 367–87.

Psychogios, A. and Wood, G. (2010). 'Human Resource Management in Greece in Comparative Perspective: Alternative Institutionalist Perspectives and Empirical Realities', *International Journal of Human Resource Management*, 21(14): 2614–30.

Roe, M. (2003). *Political Determinants of Corporate Governance*. Oxford and New York: Oxford University Press.

Sako, M. and Kotosaka, M. (2012). 'Institutional Change and Organizational Diversity in Japan', in C. Lane and G. Wood (eds.), *Capitalist Diversity and Diversity within Capitalism*. London: Routledge, 69–96.

Shleifer, A. and Vishny, R. (1997). 'A Survey of Corporate Governance', *Journal of Finance*, 52: 737–783.

Siems, M. (2006). 'Legal Origins: Reconciling Law & Finance and Comparative Law', ESRC Centre for Business Research, Working Paper 32. Available at <http://ssrn.com/abstract=920690>.

Siems, M. and Deakin, S. (2009). 'Comparative Law and Finance: Past, Present and Future Research', SSRN Working Paper. Available at <http://papers.ssrn.com/sol3/papers.cfm?abstract_id=1428247>.

Stepan-Norris, J. (1997). 'The Making of Union Democracy', Social Forces, 76(2): 475–510.

Streeck, W. (2005). 'Requirements for a Useful Concept of Complementarity', Socio-Economic Review, 3: 363–6.

Sverke, M. and Hellgren, J. (2001). 'Exit, Voice and Loyalty Reactions to Job Insecurity in Sweden', British Journal of Industrial Relations, 39(2): 167–82.

Western, B. (1993). 'Postwar Unionization in Eighteen Advanced Capitalist Countries', American Sociological Review, 58(2): 266–82.

Whitley, R. (1999). Divergent Capitalisms: The Social Structuring and Change of Business Systems. Oxford and New York: Oxford University Press.

—— (2010). 'The Institutional Construction of Firms', in G. Morgan, J. Campbell, C. Crouch, O. K. Pedersen, and R. Whitley (eds.), The Oxford Handbook of Comparative Institutional Analysis. Oxford and New York: Oxford University Press, 453–96.

Wilde, R. (2007). 'The Concept of Solidarity: Emerging from the Theoretical Shadows?', British Journal of Politics and International Relations, 9(1): 171–81.

Wood, G., Goergen, M., and Brewster, C. (2012). 'Institutions, Unionization and Voice: The Relative Impact of Context and Actors on Firm Level Practice', mimeo.

Wood, G., Harcourt, M., and Harcourt, S. (2004). 'The Effects of Age Discrimination Legislation on Workplace Practice', Industrial Relations Journal, 35(4): 359–71.

CHAPTER 9

VARIETIES OF INSTITUTIONAL THEORY IN COMPARATIVE EMPLOYMENT RELATIONS

GLENN MORGAN AND MARCO HAUPTMEIER

INTRODUCTION

IN this chapter, we explore the role of institutionalist analysis in the study of comparative employment relations. Institutionalism is one of the bedrock foundations not only of comparative employment relations, but more generally of the field of employment relations (Commons [1934] 1990). The focus of institutionalist analysis in this field has been on the pattern of formal rules that shape and structure the way in which actors coordinate the employment relationship. Much of this research is comparative between societies since it is through comparisons at this level that we can observe institutional differences and develop our understanding of how institutions structure work and employment relations. The study of comparative employment relations is therefore replete with research that links national formal laws and regulations to different national patterns of employment relations (e.g. Bamber et al. 2011; Martin and Ross 1999).

However, institutionalism as an approach is significant in a wide range of social science disciplines, beyond the study of employment systems. Disciplines such as economics, political science, and sociology have been strongly influenced by institutionalism and within these areas, the presuppositions of this approach have been widely debated. In our view, this variety and the debates which have been engendered have not been sufficiently recognized in comparative employment relations. The aim of this chapter, therefore, is to facilitate a dialogue between different institutional theories and comparative employment relations. We draw on these broader debates and contrasts within the discourse of institutionalism in order to illuminate the variety of ways in which issues of comparative employment systems can be considered (see Hall and Taylor 1996 for an initial early formulation of these differences). We seek to go beyond other contributions within employment relations which have noted this diversity (Godard 2004; Kaufman 2011; Wilkinson and Wood 2012) and provide a systematic overview of the contrasts between different types of institutionalism.

We look separately at each of four main varieties of institutionalism which are currently influential in the broader field of social sciences. These four variants are rational choice institutionalism, historical institutionalism, sociological institutionalism, and constructivist (or discursive) institutionalism. While we acknowledge that institutionalism as a theoretical perspective can be traced back to earlier in the twentieth century (in the works of Veblen, Commons, Selznick, Gouldner, etc.), we would argue that there has been a significant renewal and 'second wave' of institutionalism beginning around the late 1970s and it is on this which we concentrate. In relation to each form of institutionalism we ask a series of key questions. How do authors within these camps define the concept of 'institution', how do they explain the emergence of 'institutions', and how do they explain 'institutional change'? Within each variant of institutionalism, we then show how work on employment relations fits with these assumptions, either implicitly or explicitly, and we suggest how each variant of institutionalism can be further developed.

RATIONAL CHOICE INSTITUTIONALISM

Within the field of economics, the focus on institutions as shaping markets has a long history going back to Adam Smith's *Theory of Moral Sentiments*, perceived by Smith as a necessary adjunct to his more well-known discussions of markets and the wealth of nations (Smith 1976). However, as economics professionalized and shifted towards more systematic analysis of macro- and microeconomics, the relationship between institutions and economics was relatively under-explored until it was revived by the writings of Douglass North (1990), Elinor Ostrom (2005), and Avner Greif (2006) among others.

The Origins of Institutions

Rational choice institutionalism treats the origins of institutions from the perspective of rational agents making decisions that maximize their utility. Researchers emphasize that this process occurs under conditions of uncertainty, bounded rationality, and complexity. In other words, market mechanisms fail and other means of coordination may be required. Institutions are *shared patterns of action* that economic agents devise in order to overcome uncertainty and economize on search processes. Under certain circumstances, therefore, they lower transaction costs and enable actors to calculate and predict how others will behave in an interaction. Actors have stable sets of preferences that are pre-given and exogenous to the model. They design institutions that reduce uncertainty and enable them to overcome 'market failures'. Uncertainty is replaced with certainty, stability, and an equilibrium that becomes more powerful and self-reproducing over time.

The Reproduction of Institutions

Once institutions are established, actors become committed to them and may make investments, for example in companies or human resources, on the basis that the institutions will always exist. These investments are often asset-specific and if the institution dissolves or changes, then the assets will become worthless. This creates a process of lock-in, institutional inertia, and path dependency. Through elaborating on institutional inertia and path dependency, economists such as Arthur (1989) showed how the costs and benefits of institutions could change over time. At first, the more that social actors commit to the institution, the more likely it will bring increasing returns to them since coordination and information costs continue to fall. Actors who do not adhere to the institution find that others will not deal with them and therefore there is pressure to conform until the institution becomes commonly accepted. However, once this occurs, if other solutions to the original coordination problem emerge, they will not be judged solely on their technical efficiency because of the fixed costs which have now been incurred. Thus there is a time when increasing returns to the institution cease and the institution begins to be a drag on innovation and efficiency (see e.g. David's (1985) classic article on the QWERTY keyboard and its survival).

Rational choice institutionalists also argue that the interaction of two or more institutional patterns tends to generate greater returns because the productivity of any particular institution is increased by the presence of the other (Milgrom and Roberts 1990)—a situation described by the term 'institutional complementarity'. In such situations it is difficult to change any one institution without disrupting the complementarities and thus causing a large drop in productivity. This in turn strengthens the 'lock-in' effect, holding actors on a particular path and making it highly unlikely that they will deviate, since this will only reduce the relative efficiency of their operations. Once actors have made such investments, they are much more likely to look for incremental reform to the institution when conditions change rather than wholesale restructuring, not just because of potential losses in one sphere but also because of knock-on effects in other institutions.

Rational choice institutionalists tend to operate with a functionalist explanation of institutions, i.e. that the institution has emerged because it solves a particular problem for the actors and it is reproduced because it brings increasing returns. Actors are perceived as stable entities in themselves with fixed preferences that precede the development of the institution. Preferences do not alter as a result of the emergence of the institution but are rather deepened and reinforced by processes of institutional complementarity. The approach involves identifying the institution itself and working backwards to explain what problem it has solved for the actors—or what function it performs and how this leads to institutional complementarities and lock-ins. Hall and Taylor (1996: 954) state that this approach posits that 'actors have a fixed set of preferences or tastes, behave entirely instrumentally so as to maximize the attainment of these preferences and do so in a highly strategic manner that presumes extensive calculation'. As Djelic (2010: 25) states, this form of institutionalism 'has a tendency to propose, in the end, that existing institutional frames are efficient and reflect rationality'.

Institutional Change

Rational choice institutionalism emphasizes reproduction of existing arrangements under normal circumstances. Major change is unusual in this perspective because sunk costs and complementarities produce a considerable level of resistance to institutional change. Thus rational choice institutionalists tend to assume a 'punctuated equilibrium' model of change where the pressure to change is likely to come, if it appears at all, from exogenous shocks rather than endogenous processes. For the rational choice institutionalist, events of a large enough scale engulf a society quickly and cause previous calculations to be irrelevant. Continuing in the same old way no longer guarantees returns or benefits. Therefore actors abandon the old established institutions even though coordination costs will rapidly and massively increase. This is a moment of openness; old institutions have collapsed but new institutions are yet to be born. It is a moment that allows for institutional design again. The new designs may pick up on elements of the old institutions but they will organize them in new ways to resolve the new problems. At such moments of openness, there will be multiple options that arise; which institutional design gets picked up will not be predetermined and the costs and benefits of the option chosen will only become clearer over the longer term. However, the new route is likely to emerge quite quickly as actors try to control again coordination and information costs by re-establishing stable patterns of interaction. This dynamic therefore constitutes a phase of 'punctuated equilibrium' indicating that most of the time, institutions reproduce themselves for the reasons outlined but this is punctuated by massive change induced exogenously by developments in the wider environment.

Greif and Laitin (2004) have argued that it is possible within this framework to develop a theory of endogenous institutional change. Drawing in part on Pierson (2004) and responding to the points developed by historical institutionalists (as discussed in the following section), they suggest that, over time, institutional reproduction can alter what they describe as the quasi-parameters of an institution and make it self-undermining. In some cases, institutions are self-reinforcing; in other cases, however, the way the institution works causes certain incremental effects that reduce the number of actors and contexts in which the institution is relevant, until a point is reached when it collapses. They develop a series of contrasting case examples where the initial parameters of institutions are predominantly similar but vary in ways that are not necessarily clear to participants. The consequences of the differences become magnified over time as one set of institutions is self-reinforcing and the other self-undermining. They also reveal how actors may begin to perceive these consequences and seek to establish remedies but, because of bounded rationality and uncertainty, this 'redesign' process may fail or alter the path of reproduction in unexpected ways.

Applications in Employment Relations

Even though few employment relations studies explicitly refer to rational choice institutionalism, there is a certain affinity between important employment relations research, in particular in the USA, and rational choice institutionalism. For example, the influential strategic choice framework (Kochan et al. 1984, 1994) shares important assumptions with rational choice institutionalism. These authors explain the changes of American employment relations in the 1970s and 1980s. In a dynamically changing economic environment, managers sought to break free from collective bargaining and engaged in union-avoidance strategies, while other managers sought to implement new types of work organization. Throughout the post-war decades, managers preferred a unilateral right to manage and opposed labour unions, though they settled on an uncomfortable post-war political compromise with labour and engaged in collective bargaining. However, changes of markets unsettled this equilibrium in the 1970s and 1980s. Managements gained more power and strategically adapted to the changing environment, pushing for realizing their preferences and increasingly avoiding labour unions and collective employment relations. As in much rational choice institutionalism, actor preferences are kept constant and changes in actor behaviour are primarily conceptualized as a strategic adaptation to changes of the material context.

Other research uses game theory to examine work and employment relations. Golden, in her book *Heroic Defeats* (1997), compares union strike action in Britain, Italy, Japan, and the USA. She examines the question why unions resist jobs losses through large-scale strike action in some cases and countries but not in others, and answers this in terms of how actors respond to institutional settings in ways which maximize their utility. Golden assumes that union leaders act in an instrumental and rational fashion and develops a game-theoretical model—'the job-loss game'—which allows her to derive testable propositions. If union leaders and their broader activist network are not institutionally protected when facing redundancies, the rational choice of union leaders is to call for massive strike action in order to protect themselves and fellow activists. In contrast, if union leaders and the broader activist network are institutionally protected through worker rights or seniority rules in times of labour shedding, they do not engage in strike action as their position and that of fellow activists are not threatened. Golden argues that this model explains, for example, union strikes in Britain in contrast to greater labour quiescence in Japan. Other game theory-inspired research explains how social organizations built coalitions and pooled their resources during the World Trade Organization protest in Seattle (Levi and Murphy 2006). Levi and Murphy's model emphasizes pre-existing trust relationships and institutional arrangements and rules that make commitments credible. Such institutional rules exclude actors from resources if they are not abiding by the rules. Under these conditions, individual groups are willing to invest in the collective effort. This type of research maintains that actor behaviour can be best modelled and understood as a rational choice within a particular institutional context, even in highly charged social situations such as strikes and protests.

The widely cited collective action problem in employment relations is also directly based on rational choice theory. Olson (1965: 2) argued: '[U]nless there is coercion or some other special device [or benefits] to make individuals act in their common interest, rational, self-interested individuals will not act in their common interest.' The logic is that individuals gain from the provision of collective goods without being a member of a group, and therefore the rational choice for the individual is to free-ride without taking part in the collective effort. For example, workers can profit from higher wages negotiated by a labour union in a sector without being a member and having to pay membership dues. In line with his general position, Olson argues that unions overcome the collective action problem through coercion and benefits. Unions force workers to become a member, for example, through 'closed shop' rules. Another instrument of coercion is the picket-line during a strike that prevents non-union members from doing the work of union members. However, unions also provide a range of benefits to their members such as insurances, social and welfare benefits, grievance procedures, and seniority rights. Thus, workers have a special incentive to join a union. Olson's classic argument continues to provide insights into the fortune of labour unions nowadays. In Sweden, for example, unions take part in the administration of the unemployment insurance and workers receive benefits once they become a union member. This helps to explain the continuing high union membership in Sweden in contrast to unions in other countries that are not able to provide such attractive special incentives and benefits.

Assessment

These literatures in employment relations draw on at least three important assumptions within rational choice institutionalism. First, actors have far-reaching rational capacity to pursue the best course of action and maximize their interest. They do this through building institutions that reduce their costs and maximize their efficiencies. Preferences (which are broadly stated in economic terms and are in this perspective 'uncontaminated' by social values) come both logically and historically prior to institutions. Second, once established, actors conform to the rules of the institution because it is in their best (economic) interests to do so. Change would be expensive and cause asset losses. There is 'lock-in' and path dependency reinforced by institutional complementarities. Third, institutional change and changes in actor behaviour are linked to external shocks and changes of the material context; change follows the 'punctuated equilibrium' path. Overall, by its continued insistence on considering the economic costs and benefits of institutions, rational choice institutionalism provides some clear directions to researchers seeking to understand why national employment systems tend to change slowly.

HISTORICAL INSTITUTIONALISM

Issues identified by rational choice institutionalism such as inertia, path dependence, and lock-in had clear appeal to researchers outside the field of economics. However, by insisting on analysing institutions in terms of economic calculation and efficiencies, there was a limit to the degree to which this could be diffused more widely in the social sciences. This became clear in particular from the collection of essays published by Steinmo et al. (1992). This sought to formalize and identify an approach to institutionalism that drew on certain key concepts from rational choice institutionalism but placed them in a wider historical and political context. Steinmo et al. labelled this approach 'historical institutionalism'. It is worth noting that this approach grew directly out of debates on the degree of change in corporatism, the welfare state, and the role of labour that developed in the period from the 1970s to the growing dominance of neo-liberalism under Thatcher and Reagan in the 1980s (Crouch 1993; Goldthorpe 1984; Katzenstein 1985; Streeck 1984; Turner 1991). These analyses often considered how the position of labour was being undermined through changes in law, economic policy, and broader political and economic discourses emphasizing markets, the need for deregulation, and the impact of globalization. Thus historical institutionalism developed in a dialogue with studies of labour markets, trade unions, and employment systems and remains the dominant institutionalist approach in this field. However, it is also clear that within the historical institutionalist approach, there is a distinct tension reflecting how much rational choice institutionalism is drawn on. In the sections that follow, we will clarify the common presuppositions of historical institutionalists while showing the internal diversity of this approach.

Origins of Institutions, Institutional Reproduction, and Institutional Change

One interpretation of historical institutionalism which we associate here with Hall and Soskice's (2001) 'varieties of capitalism' (VOC) approach is quite close to the rational choice approach. It draws on a number of key concepts from that approach, such as path dependency and institutional complementarities, and derives from this a strongly determinist view in which institutions are very powerful shapers of actors and their orientations. As with rational choice institutionalism, it views institutions, once established, as self-reinforcing and relatively impervious to change. Institutions may adapt to challenges but institutional complementarities and path dependencies shape that process of adaptation. New institutions are created in those rare moments of crisis when externally induced change can release actors from the grip of these forces.

The VOC approach emphasizes the strategic interaction of actors within institutional contexts in which there is complementarity and path dependency. It therefore makes sense for the actors to continue to act in a particular way because in doing so they gain cost advantages, informational advantages, and calculative advantages. In coordinated market economies, actors will solve problems by using their abilities to engage in coordinative approaches whereas in liberal market economies, environmental changes will prompt actors to look for market solutions. Unlike rational choice institutionalists, therefore, the historical institutionalism of the VOC approach recognizes that the preferences of actors are not pre-given; rather they are formed by institutions and through the process of institutional reproduction and change. Institutions are not the outcome of an ahistorical form of rational choice and design where actors agree on resolving coordination problems by setting up institutional arrangements in order to enhance economic efficiency. Rather actors' preferences are social and path dependent, and even in situations of institutional breakdown, actors continue to carry these preferences forward. Where challenges to the existing order emerge, actors look for ways to deal with them within the constraints of the dominant institutional logic so they can sustain the value of their existing assets. This creates the path dependency/lock-in effect. Once a set of institutions are established and actors more invested in them, this has a determining effect on what comes next, on the sequencing of social processes (Pierson 2004). As Farrell and Newman (2010: 621–2) state: 'this means that at any particular moment, political actors' ability to adapt to a changing environment will be shaped, at least in part by previous institutional choices which may have been taken without any cognizance of what their later historical consequences would have been' (see also Drezner 2010).

This view of historical institutionalism and institutional reproduction has been challenged by a more 'actor-centric' view of institutions developed most recently by authors such as Streeck and Thelen (2005). This approach is more open to the idea that processes of incremental change can occur that over time lead to new institutional structures on the basis not of punctuated equilibrium but out of a more gradual process of adjustment (Mahoney and Rueschemeyer 2003; Pierson 2000, 2004). These processes of change can emerge from actors undertaking forms of activity that are not determined by existing institutions. In other words, institutions do not determine preferences; they may shape them in significant ways but actors can project a different future, leading them to act in new ways. Actors can also review the past, identify for themselves the origins of institutions in some specific set of conditions, and as a result decide, in the present, that these conditions no longer hold. They can therefore act, potentially successfully, against the inertial powers of existing institutions, creating new patterns of action.

In this perspective, the intended and unintended consequences of actions and institutions are explored. Thus on the one hand, actors have far-reaching cognitive capacities to figure out the best course of action in a given material and institutional structure. Their choices are conditioned by politics, power, and historical processes—including competition, markets, and economic performance—but they are not fully determined by existing institutions. New institutions emerge based on the power relations of different groups at particular moments and their abilities to impose certain rules and routines under particular economic and political conditions (Crouch 2005; Morgan 2005). This group of historical institutionalists have therefore been much more interested in the precariousness of institutional reproduction and defining different processes, mechanisms, and types of institutional change.

Streeck and Thelen (2005), for example, identified a number of mechanisms of gradual, endogenous institutional change where actors engage with path dependent existing institutions and the outcomes of these processes are determined by politics at various levels and not simply explicable in terms of the functionalist reproduction of existing arrangements. They describe these five forms of gradual institutional change as displacement, layering, drift, conversion, and exhaustion. In work with Mahoney, Thelen has sought to specify in more detail how institutional change emerges (Mahoney and Thelen 2010). They argue that key intermediary factors in the process are, first, the extent to which there exist powerful groups able to exercise a veto over change and, second, the extent to which institutions are tightly defined and monitored, or offer degrees of ambiguity and enforcement.

A number of authors have sought to bridge the gap between the more static analysis of the original VOC formulation in Hall and Soskice (2001) and the more open and political analysis of Thelen et al. The central dilemma here is whether it is possible to retain the original insight that institutions structure preferences while acknowledging that actors can use institutions as resources to further their own interests. In two related papers, Deeg and Jackson argue that it is necessary to develop a more dynamic theory of institutional change which takes into account the role of power and politics (Deeg and Jackson 2007; Jackson and Deeg 2008) while at the same time recognizing the variety of ways in which path dependency and institutional complementarity shape the terrain on which actors strategize (see also Hall and Thelen 2009). A key aspect in the development of this bridging analysis which has increasingly come to the fore both in Deeg and Jackson and in others (e.g. Amable 2003) is an effort to distinguish the roots of core elements in the underlying institutional logic from particular institutional manifestations. Thus as Hall and Thelen (2009) point out, what look to be relatively unchanged institutions can work in very different ways over time because actors have adapted them to new circumstances. Similarly, new institutions can be put in place by governmental reforms but because the underlying social formations remain little changed, the reforms have limited impact or are incorporated and implemented in ways rather different from the expectations of their supporters (Goyer 2011; Thelen 2004). This therefore points to the need to identify the forces of continuity in this underlying institutional logic, separate from the institutions themselves. Here the focus has moved strongly to the idea of long-term coalitional forces creating interdependencies between particular social groupings; as Hall and Thelen state: 'our perspective suggests promise in focusing on the political arrangements that support the institutional arrangements underpinning the coordination... (tracing) the genesis of important institutional configurations to specific sets of coalitions, formed either among producer groups or within the electoral arena, many of them cross-class coalitions' (Hall and Thelen 2009: 25; see e.g. the recent work of Soskice et al.: Soskice and Iversen 2006; Iversen and Soskice 2009; Cusack et al. 2010). Historical institutionalism therefore has evolved to place issues of politics, power, and institutional change more centrally into the analysis. However, it still maintains a strong focus on how path dependencies and institutional complementarities shape the possibilities for change. The roots of these institutional settlements are in turn related to earlier struggles to form coalitions across social groupings and to shape political institutions that can sustain and reproduce such coalitions. Therefore a key issue becomes the degree to which institutions are changing and evolving while the underlying logic of coalition remains intact or whether in situations of change, this coalition itself and its key supporting institutions are starting to break apart. This is a central issue for many analysts in terms of how systems of work and employment have been evolving under conditions of neo-liberalism and globalization as discussed in the following sections.

Applications in Employment Relations

It is clear that much employment relations research is conducted within an historical institutionalist frame of reference. In Streeck's (1984) book on German industrial relations, for example, he compares employment relations outcomes across two auto company cases, in which union and works council strategies differ radically. Despite vastly different union strategies, the employment relations outcomes are strikingly similar. The message of his case study is that union strategies led to varying processes, but substantive outcomes were foremost shaped by the German industrial relations institutions. Streeck (1997) went further when he argued that institutions like works councils, collective bargaining on the sectoral level, and a national training regime put 'beneficial constraints' on employer strategies, making it impossible to pursue a low-road business strategy and instead facilitating a diversified quality production regime with high quality, high price products manufactured by highly paid workers. This produced positive economic and social outcomes for companies and workers. However this process was not an outcome of 'institutional design' but an unexpected result of the way in which different actors used their powers to forge institutions which represented an acceptable compromise given the politics of Germany in the post-war period.

A related study is Thelen's (2004) comparison of skill regimes in the UK, Germany, and Japan. Thelen demonstrates that the central characteristics of the national training systems were formed in the nineteenth century and endured over time. However, the way in which these systems were reformed and changed, how they fitted with other institutions in society, and how they responded to challenges of economic change, war, and globalization, was historically emergent at the same time as it was path dependent. Central to Thelen's account is that institutions should be considered as reflecting the outcomes of power struggles and coalitions between actors and that, while these political processes may be temporarily suspended, they can reopen for a variety of reasons. Once they are reopened, further power conflicts and realignments of coalitions occur as actors seek to modify the institutions and their outcomes, a point developed further in Palier and Thelen (2010): they argue that the evolution of employment systems in France and Germany can be characterized in terms of the emergence of a dualism between core employment, where there are high levels of security, wages, and employment rights, and secondary/peripheral employment which is characterized by insecurity, part-time, temporary, and agency work, low wages and low skills. In both societies, this dualism emerged from a situation where there tended to be one dominant model of employment that arose during a particular historical juncture. However, as this juncture changed and in particular global competition increased pressure on large firms to reduce their costs and increase productivity, adaptations emerged. Since institutional characteristics in France and Germany meant that an outright attack on core employees would lead to massive social unrest, employers, some of the trade unions, and the government enabled the opening up of a secondary labour market with lower costs while sustaining the position of core employees. Palier and Thelen show how the intricate interplay of actions that lead to institutional change across a wide variety of spheres results in what is effectively, to return to the language of Streeck and Thelen, a 'layering' process. The secondary labour market is layered on top of the continued reproduction of the conditions of the core employees.

In similar research, Hancké (2002) shows how the basic structure of French industry, characterized by large firms with strong elite network-based relations to the state and finance, was modernized in the 1980s and 1990s under the pressure of global competition. The firms did this by a selective adaptation of labour market institutions that increased the degree of competitiveness of French industry while not changing the basic structure of control through the French elite. Goyer's (2006, 2011) recent work on Germany and France and the impact of international investors reinforces this point. Short-term international investors prefer to invest in France because they know that they can exert pressure on the French company which is highly centralized and controlled by the elite management cadre. In effect, they are working with the institutional grain in pressing for greater productivity and higher returns to shareholders and executives. By contrast, the German employment system means that decisions have to be based on much more consultation and incorporation of different interests. Investors cannot alter this process and thus their investments are necessarily going to be long-term compared to investments in France which can deliver short-term returns. Thus the basic institutional logic of each society is reproduced even in the face of growing international competition and the increased role of international investors.

More recently, Streeck has focused on the question of the degree of change in the German system since the 1970s. Streeck's (2009: 93) view is that 'institutional change in the German political economy after the Golden Age proceeded gradually, cumulatively and without dramatic disruptions of continuity in a variety of institutional settings along parallel trajectories'. In the sphere of collective bargaining and wage setting, this involved increasing fragmentation of the previously centralized system, a process reflected in the weakening of organized capital and organized labour and accompanied by a decline in the close relations of firms and banks (see also Martin and Swank 2012). In turn, these changes placed more pressure on the public finances to deal with the rising expenditure on social welfare and a reform in the labour market institutions that had sustained this equilibrium. Streeck argues that this was an endogenous process of change that involved Germany shifting from an organized form of capitalism to what he describes as 'disorganized' and a process of liberalization (see also Amable et al. 2010).

Such disorganization processes and uneven effects of institutions are also found in Doellgast's (2012) comparative work on call centres in the USA and Germany which operate in liberalized markets with strong competition. Managers in both countries have to respond to these pressures by restructuring operations and increasing efficiency. However, distinct national labour institutions pose varying constraints on management and lead to distinct workplace outcomes. Stronger participation and collective bargaining rights in Germany allow labour representatives to limit monitoring and discipline and to negotiate greater investment in skills and work place discretion in comparison to US workplaces (Doellgast 2010). The impact of institutions is, however, highly uneven across workplaces. Under competitive pressure German call centre managers outsource non-core employees into subsidiaries that are not covered by collective bargaining and do not have works council representation. These and other 'institutional avoidance' strategies by employers contribute to the segmentation of the German model and increasing inequality.

Other research on forms of coordinated capitalism also reveals a mixed picture in terms of institutional change and changes in work and employment, though there is generally more focus now on what Howell and Kolins Givan (2005)—in their analysis of industrial relations changes in the UK, Sweden, and Italy—identify as 'institutional plasticity' and particularly, following Streeck, a shift 'towards decentralised, individualised, firm-centred industrial relations institutions offering much greater flexibility and autonomy in the determination of pay and conditions at the firm level' (Howell and Kolins Givan 2005: 250). The authors identify this change as in part path dependent but also, again in common with Streeck, as driven by a broader process of liberalization. In the Nordic countries, however, there is evidence that coordinated market institutions have been adapted to maintain skills and a strong welfare state (Kristensen and Lilja 2011), both through bottom-up initiatives of actors and firms developing new patterns and through the facilitating action of local and national governments. In this context, liberalization in the global economy does not inevitably lead to deeper liberalizing tendencies in the national economies, though as Kristensen and Lilja show, this varies across the Nordic countries.

Assessment

These contributions illustrate the vitality and strength of historical institutionalism. Increasingly this approach treats institutions as contingent outcomes of political struggles. Although there is a path dependency, this is far from determining and instead is fragile and susceptible to change. While it is useful to explore institutional complementarities, these are treated as uncertain, matters not of design but of accident susceptible to change. Change can be gradual, but over the medium term consequential and significant. The ways in which institutions change vary, arising from drift, layering, etc., and these processes are likely to be accompanied by actors taking on different sorts of approaches to the institutional change dynamics.

In terms of potential criticisms, there are three which are relevant and link to the strengths of other forms of institutionalism. First, the role of economic incentives, increasing returns, and the broad framework of economic action and feedback loops from the market is uncertain (see Amable's comments in Amable et al. 2010). This can lead to high levels of indeterminacy and a tendency towards description and away from explanation particularly in the more 'actor-centric' versions of historical institutionalism. Second, institutions are defined in a relatively narrow way, focusing often on the role of the state and formal organizations. This results in a considerable underplaying of the role of informal norms and along with this the whole sphere of cultural meanings and ideational factors. Actors' identities and capacities are treated as pre-given by the positions which they have in society; and while historical institutionalists dissolve the unitary character of institutions, opening them up as ambiguous, subject to incoherence and potential to change, they still maintain a relatively unitary and static view of the collective actors involved in these processes. However, if institutions lack stability, it could also be argued that collective actors are subject to similar processes of reconstitution and re-formation, in which case issues of identity emerge more crucially as will be discussed in the following sections. Finally, historical institutionalists tend to focus on the national and generally neglect the embeddedness of national patterns in international regimes. They therefore pay limited attention to how processes of regulation and organization at the transnational level trickle down and impact on the national level (for obvious exceptions see Djelic and Quack 2003; Fioretos 2011).

SOCIOLOGICAL INSTITUTIONALISM

Sociological institutionalism distinguishes between the 'logic of consequences' and the 'logic of appropriateness'. In the former, actions are undertaken because of the consequences expected to follow. However, sociological institutionalists doubt that such a logic can ever be effective because of informational complexities and decision-making failures, leading to unanticipated outcomes. Thus while they agree that institutions emerge as ways of stabilizing social interactions, they reject the argument that they are rooted in rational assessments of how to solve coordination problems. Instead, they argue that social actors favour a 'logic of appropriateness' and the institutions which emerge do so because they are seen as 'natural, rightful, expected and legitimate' (March and Olsen 2006: 7; 1989). Thus sociological institutionalism is about how certain institutional forms get adopted and diffuse and the mechanisms and processes which facilitate diffusion.

The Origins of Institutions

Institutions themselves arise from efforts to find ways of stabilizing interactions among social actors. Central to this approach is that shared norms and cognitive structures, accompanied by regulative processes to sanction deviance, are the essential pillars of social order (Scott 2003). This gives rise to the concept of 'institutional logics' that 'shape individual preferences, organizational interests and the categories and repertoires of actions to attain those interests and preferences' (Thornton et al. 2012). The concept of *field* provides an important intermediary concept here. Sociological institutionalists have tended to be less interested in historical processes of social change within societies broadly defined and more focused on specific spheres within a particular social order. Drawing from Bourdieu, they have developed the concept of the field as a framing device to study how within a particular sphere of activity, specific institutionalized patterns of activity have emerged (Powell and DiMaggio 1991; Fligstein and McAdam 2012). Institutions are seen as embedded within particular fields, whether these are defined by types of organization (public/private, educational/medical/legal, etc.) or by types of economic activity (defined, for example, through industrial sectors) or by national/international/regional contexts. Actors learn what frames of meaning, cognitive schema, and normative templates are legitimate and expected in these particular fields and what sanctions exist for those unwilling to conform.

Reproduction of Institutions

Sociological institutionalists emphasize the multi-levelled nature of institutional reproduction. A central concept is 'institutional work', understood as 'the purposive action of individuals and organizations aimed at creating, maintaining and disrupting institutions' (Lawrence and Suddaby 2006: 215). In later work, they modify somewhat the 'purposive' nature of institutional work, distinguishing between situations where actors reproduce institutions with relatively little intentionality from those situations where actors are highly intentional and are 'working' to achieve a particular form of institutionalization within a field (Lawrence et al. 2009). The latter involves a lot more 'effort' and investment on the part of actors to build cognitive schema, normative structures, and regulatory mechanisms and to keep them functioning. A central part of this is the role of discourses and meaning structures in sustaining and reproducing institutions (as well as providing a means for changing and tracking changes in institutions). Discourses become embedded in organizational scripts, routines, and rules that are taken for granted.

As described, legitimation processes are central to this approach. Any building of institutions requires a base in a generally accepted structure of legitimacy. Therefore a central task of institutional work is to draw support from existing legitimate institutions: Scott, for example, refers to legitimacy as 'not a commodity to be possessed or exchanged but a condition reflecting cultural alignment, normative support or consonance with relevant rules or laws' (Scott 1995: 45). Legitimacy, as Suchman and Deephouse show (Deephouse and Suchman 2008; Suchman 1995), emerges from a wide variety of sources, ranging from pragmatic legitimacy (a practice seems to work and so can legitimately be followed elsewhere) through to normative legitimacy where something is deemed to be a 'good thing' in one field and can therefore be justifiably taken to another field. This has led sociological institutionalists to become very interested in what Brunsson describes as 'organizations of organizations' (Brunsson and Sahlin-Andersson 2000). These sorts of collective organizations play a central role in articulating, disseminating, and monitoring standards within and across borders, thus reinforcing institutionalization processes (see also Wedlin 2006; Djelic and Quack 2010; Djelic and Sahlin-Andersson 2006; Drori et al. 2006).

Institutional Change

Similar to historical institutionalism, particularly in its actor-centric form, sociological institutionalism suffers from what Battilana and D'Aunno refer to as the 'paradox of embedded agency', in other words, the conundrum that actors so thoroughly socialized in the field are still able to find ways of changing the field (Battilana 2006; Battilana and D'Aunno 2009). In contexts where identities are defined and sustained by institutions, how is it possible to break free and discuss institutional change? Sociological institutionalism resolves this problem partly through appealing to the coexistence of multiple logics across fields and arguing that this opens up the possibility for agency and for bricolage, i.e. taking bits from a variety of fields to create something new (Campbell 2004; Fligstein and McAdam 2012; Thornton et al. 2012). Because it is less interested in the national level, it has never developed any particular concern with the idea of institutional complementarities. Therefore the coexistence of different logics is not inherently problematic as it might be for rational choice institutionalism or historical institutionalism. Thus sociological institutionalism has been concerned to define a role for institutional entrepreneurship as something that emerges out of different logics and offers opportunities for change (Thornton and Ocasio 2008).

The concept of 'institutional entrepreneurship' alongside that of 'institutional work' has been important as a means of emphasizing the ability of actors to create institutional change even in contexts where there has been long-term stability. Maguire et al. refer to institutional entrepreneurship as the 'activities of actors who have an interest in particular institutional arrangements and who leverage resources to create new institutions or transform existing ones' (Hardy and Maguire 2008: 205; Maguire et al. 2004). A central aspect of this process is what is referred to as 'interpretive struggles', 'the complex, ongoing struggles over meaning among numerous actors, the outcomes of which are not necessarily predictable or controllable' (Hardy and Maguire 2008: 205). Institutional entrepreneurs seek to reshape meaning structures, reinterpret legitimation claims, and from these processes develop new institutions. In turn, this requires a combination of political activity and the use of power in specific situations together with the forma-tion of supportive networks. In this stream of research, linkages have been made to the social movements literature (Davis et al. 2005; Fligstein and McAdam 2012; Schneiberg and Lounsbury 2008) to show the role of such movements in the establishment of new institutions.

Applications in Employment Relations

As an approach, sociological institutionalism has not had a strong influence on the study of comparative employment relations. Nevertheless, a number of applications of sociological institutionalism can be found in the wider employment relations, sociology of work, and human resource management (HRM) literatures.

In an attempt to map the strategic behaviour of employers, Boxall and Purcell (2011) point to cost-efficiency, organizational flexibility, and performance as important HR goals, but they stress that successfully managing a company also requires social legiti-macy. Companies need to comply with prevailing norms and values in terms of how to treat people at the workplace. An interesting development of this argument examines the move, particularly in the UK and the USA, towards equal opportunities that aims to eliminate discrimination based on gender, race, sexual orientation, and physical ability. Dobbin (2009) shows how equal opportunities in the USA were developed particularly through professional personnel managers who created an 'equal opportunities' frame that was then diffused into legislation, resulting in a reinforcing process of institution-alization through large US companies. This combines an emphasis on the role of social movements together with the importance of changes in the self-definition of a profes-sion leading to the institutionalization of new expectations within organizations.

Such institutionalization processes can also be observed with respect to labour standards. Social movements and labour unions used the core labour standards out-lined by the International Labour Organization (ILO) to target companies that vio-lated labour rights. An example is the campaign against Nike in the late 1990s/early 2000s that revealed widespread child labour. While this was not in violation of laws in plants in some developing countries, it was not deemed acceptable by consumers in Western countries. These social pressures hurt the company in the product market and as a consequence Nike implemented a far-reaching social code of conduct, which has been monitored and enforced through regular labour inspections (Locke et al. 2007). Changing labour norms became institutionalized within Nike and its global supply net-work, which changed working standards.

Other employment relations research focused on multinational corporations (MNCs) has increasingly drawn on sociological institutionalism. Kostova and Roth (2002) developed the concept of institutional duality to describe the situation in MNC subsidiaries where managers and employees are subjected to a dual pressure; on the one hand, they are pressured to work according to the institutionalized practices of the head office. On the other hand, they are pressured to conform to local institutional expectations. This has given rise to a whole series of studies of multinationals examining this duality. Gooderham et al. (1999) found in a comparison of firms across Germany, France, Denmark, Norway, Spain, and the UK that HRM is 'particularly sensitive to nationally idiosyncratic institutional pressure'. The empirical data demonstrate variations in terms of collaborative and calculative HR practices across the examined countries. They also observe the diffusion of HR practices across countries within MNCs; however, this process is constrained through social and regulative norms embedded within national contexts. The work of Ferner and others on multinationals shows how institutional pressures are shaped by the powers exerted by various actors both within the organizational setting of the MNC and in the home and host societies (Almond and Ferner 2006; Dörrenbächer and Geppert 2011; Ferner et al. 2005; Kristensen and Zeitlin 2005; Morgan and Kristensen 2006; Tregaskis et al. 2010). As Edwards and Ferner (2004: 64) put it:' [a] practice may not operate in the same fashion in the donor unit, but rather, may undergo a transmutation as actors in the recipient seek to adapt to pre-existing models of behaviour, assumptions, and power relations'.

Sociological institutionalism has been used to look more broadly at how ideas and practices 'travel' across national boundaries and may in the process be translated (Czarniawska-Joerges and Sevon 2005) or adapted as a result of local opposition and political pressure (Halliday and Carruthers 2009), for example the spread of HRM as a culture and set of institutionalized practices globally (Luo 2006). Transnational communities of expertise and international agencies have been perceived as providing mechanisms through which these institutional processes can be diffused. Themes which are relevant to employment systems in these discussions include the diffusion of labour standards through international bodies and codes of conduct such as the UN Global Compact, the ILO, etc., and the role of trade unions, government bodies, and social movements in developing, monitoring, and enforcing these codes (Davis et al. 2005; Djelic and Quack 2010; Djelic and Sahlin-Andersson 2006; Simmons et al. 2008).

Assessment

Sociological institutionalists have developed a useful range of middle level concepts for examining how institutions reproduce and change. They have also been very open to the interaction between different levels of analysis and in particular the interactive nature of the global and the local. They have focused strongly on meaning structures, the way these become embedded in practices and cultures, and the possible ways in which institutions can be disrupted. By focusing primarily on 'fields', they are able to put boundaries around the object of study and provide plausible accounts of patterns of change within particular institutions. However, sociological institutionalism does not have a strong concept of 'society' with clearly defined boundaries or concomitantly the role of the state in institutional formation (Vidal and Peck 2012: 606), both of which remain central to comparative employment relations. It is therefore less able (as well as less concerned) to systematically analyse over time broad institutional change, such as in the organization of capital, labour, and employment. Similarly, although the issue of connections between fields is now of more concern (Thornton et al. 2012), there is no clear theoretical anchoring of these interconnections in the way that, for example, rational choice institutionalists focus on the centrality of the market or historical institutionalists on the interaction of the state and the market. The lack of such an anchoring framework reinforces this preference for a focus on rather narrowly defined 'fields'. On the other hand, an important advantage of sociological institutionalism is its focus on the spread of practices across borders, thus providing a distinctive way of addressing the convergence debate which continues to loom large in comparative employment relations (Doellgast 2012; Katz and Darbishire 2000).

CONSTRUCTIVIST INSTITUTIONALISM

Since Hall and Taylor's (1996) original formulation, there has emerged a 'fourth' form of institutionalist analysis labelled constructivist or discursive institutionalism which arises from, in Schmidt's (2010) words, 'taking ideas and discourse seriously'. Ideas refer to a wide range of ideational factors such as ideology, collective beliefs, values, norms, world-views, and identities. This ideational approach places a new emphasis on the level of meaning in terms of how institutions reproduce and change. Although norms, cognition, and discourse are familiar in sociological institutionalism as discussed in the previous section, Schmidt and others in the social sciences (Abdelal et al. 2010; Béland and Cox 2011; Blyth 2002; Hay 2006) have taken a different approach to this concept. Their focus is more explicitly on the ideational elements in institutional contexts, the mechanisms by which ideas change and how they become constituted into specific policies, programmes, practices, and institutions.

The Origins of Institutions

In one of the earliest expositions and developments of this approach in institutional research, Blyth (2002) questioned the direct link between institutions and actors and sought to capture this—in his view—less simplistic relationship with the phrase 'institutions do not come with instruction sheet'. While recent work in historical institutionalism makes the point that institutional rules are often ambiguous and need to be interpreted and enacted, Blyth is keen to emphasize the centrality of ideas and ideologies. He argues that when ideas become powerful and accepted they reduce uncertainty and offer new institutional blueprints (Blyth 2002: ch. 2). Blyth was seeking to understand what he described as the 'great transformations' and in particular the shift of ideas from Keynesianism to neo-liberal market economics.

For constructivist institutionalists, these broad shifts in ideology are an important focus for understanding institutional change (see also Hall 1989), a theme which was obviously central to the founders of sociology, e.g. in Weber's discussion of the impact of the Protestant Ethic (Weber 2002). Ideas have the capacity to change the identity of collective actors, to make individuals and groups look at their circumstances in different ways and to reorient their behaviour towards institutions or create new institutions. How ideas can have such a causal effect in shaping the economy is highlighted in Weber's famous switchmen quote: 'It is interests (material and ideal), and not ideas which have directly governed the actions of human beings. Yet frequently the "world views" that have been created by ideas, like switchmen, determined the tracks along which action has been pushed by the dynamic of interest' (Weber 2009: 63–4).

Reproduction of Institutions

However, it is important to note that ideas require material carriers. They have to be stabilized in texts of various levels of complexity and sustained in social networks of committed individuals, organizations, or social movements. These in turn utilize communicative mechanisms that carry the ideas from one setting to another and in the process translate and reshape them so that new audiences appreciate their relevance and can see them as meaningful to their own specific life. Diffusion in turn requires resources, not least financial support but also in terms of people. Ideas require translation into programmes and policies of political parties and social movements; this in turn depends on power and influence. Ideas also require in the contemporary world a panoply of technical expertise (and experts) that can define appropriate mechanisms, benchmarks, and monitoring procedures for policy-makers and governments. Campbell identifies an interconnected network of different sorts of actors who are engaged in these processes, ranging from theorists (academics and intellectuals who develop new ideas) to brokers (media organizations, management consultants, trade associations, epistemic communities, educational institutions) to framers (i.e. those actors who develop the sound-bites, the slogans, the images that give a public and political life to ideas). These actors in turn impact on both the decision-makers, i.e. politicians, bureaucrats, and corporate managers) and the public in their roles as voters, consumers, investors, etc. (Campbell 2004: ch. 4).

It is interesting to see how researchers are gradually filling in these processes with regard to the rise of neo-liberalism. This can be discerned at three levels. First, one stream of this research focuses strongly on maintenance of these ideas by a small group of economists led by Hayek even in the face of Keynesian dominance with the establishment of the Mont Pelerin society in the immediate post-war period. The Mont Pelerin society became a centre of free market thinking that influenced generations of economists and policy-makers from across the world (Mirowski and Plehwe 2009; Peck 2010; Stedman Jones 2012). Second, the impact of these ideas on the discipline of economics and through this on law, politics, and policy-making is another theme that has been developed through the empirical study of particular aspects of liberal market economies (Dezalay and Garth 2002a, 2002b; Fourcade

2006, 2009; Halliday and Carruthers 2009; Mirowski 2002; Van Horn et al. 2011). Third, a number of authors have looked at how these ideas have been received, translated, adapted, and resisted in various national contexts (e.g. Abdelal 2007; Blyth 2002; Campbell and Pedersen 2001; Fourcade-Gourinchas and Babb 2002; Schmidt 2002).

Constructivist institutionalists have also used the concept of path dependency to model the reproduction of institutions, although it differs from the concept used by historical institutionalists who focus mostly on formal institutions. Hay (2006) suggests, for example, focusing on ideational path dependency: 'Institutions are built on ideational foundations which exert an independent path dependent effect on their subsequent development' (Hay 2006: 65). The formation of ideologies and identities is crucially based on memories and past experiences, as well as the ideas that have become embedded within institutions. These 'imprints of the past' and 'collective memories' (Schmidt 2011: 111) inform the subsequent evolution and adaptation of ideologies and institutions to new circumstances and changing contexts.

Institutional Change

However, constructivist institutionalists also recognize that a dramatic departure from a path can take place at particular historical junctures. Similar to historical institutionalism and rational choice institutionalism, this line of inquiry focuses on dramatic changes such as war or economic depression. Constructivist institutionalists are interested in the far-reaching ideational changes such dramatic events can lead to over time, e.g. from Keynesianism to neo-liberalism. Previous economic paradigms get blamed for the crisis and lose legitimacy both among the policy elite and more generally. This leads to an exploration of and search for new ideas. Major historical shocks and junctures open up space for ideological change, but it requires political actors and social movements to exploit the void by constructing appropriate ideational discourses that are able to address the problems actors are facing and capable of communication to elites and mass populations (Hall 1989).

Like some historical institutionalists, constructivist institutionalists also focus on endogenous institutional change. Schmidt emphasizes the role of discourse for engineering institutional change, since ideas are conveyed through discourse. People have an 'ability to think and act outside the institutions in which they continue to act' (Schmidt 2008: 315). Social actors are able to deliberate and convince others of new ideas. Discourse is described as an interactive process, and it is through processes of communicative action that ideas and institutions change. Other constructivists argue that actors and institutions are mutually constitutive (Hay and Wincott 1998; see also Jackson 2010). In sociological and historical institutionalism it is well known how institutional environments shape actor practices and ideas, but constructivist institutionalists go further and argue that reflexive and pragmatic actors with changing ideologies and identities have the capacity to change their institutional environment. This type of institutional change can appear in different forms. Changing ideas can trigger policy reform and lead to changes of institutions, while other constructivist institutionalists emphasize the changing meaning of institutions. The latter point relates to the constructivists' insight that institutions are not objective structures and need to be interpreted (Blyth 2002). This looser correspondence between institutions and actor behaviour opens up some space for a varying enactment of institutions by actors with changing ideas and ideologies (Hauptmeier 2012).

Constructivist institutionalism offers itself as a way of developing a more dynamic view of change by focusing on how new ideas emerge, become embedded in policies, programmes, and techniques, and open up possibilities for institutional change. Some of this is similar to the actor-centric view of historical institutionalism, for example where Streeck and Thelen have emphasized the centrality of neo-liberal ideas to the transformations of capitalism (Streeck 2009; Streeck and Thelen 2005). Yet as Schmidt says in her critique of these authors:

> they tend more to describe *how* such change occurs through processes of layering, reinterpretation, conversion and drift rather than to explain *why* it occurs the *way* it occurs...Incrementalist discursive institutionalists are more focused on explaining the why and the wherefore of incremental change by reference to agents' own ideas and discourse about how they go about layering, reinterpreting, or converting those institutions. (Schmidt 2011: 108)

Why the changes occur the way that they occur is crucially down to how actors perceive and construct meanings using the discourses available to them.

Applications in Employment Relations

Most previous institutional literature in employment relations focuses on how institutions regulate and constrain the behaviour of actors and analyses the practices and patterns of employment relations actors; however, some literature goes further and shows how institutions shape ideologies and actor orientations. The case studies in Turner's (1991) comparison of employment relations in Germany, the USA, Sweden, Italy, and Japan provide evidence of how national institutions shape variation in union orientation and ideologies across countries. For example, in Germany co-determination rights on the shopfloor and supervisory boards provide workers with influence in management decision-making processes. Unions have veto power in key employment relations decisions (e.g. working time and work organization) and management needs to engage in collaborative negotiations with labour to move HR matters forward. In addition, labour has institutionally guaranteed rights to access key company information, which allows union representatives to assess independently management claims about, for example, company losses or the need for restructuring. This institutionally defined 'open-book' approach to employment relations and the fact that worker representatives have real responsibility in governing companies tends to facilitate an ideology of social partnership and cooperation between management and works councillors. In fact works councillors are regularly described as co-managers. The US case in Turner's study provides a very different picture of how institutions influence union ideologies. Beyond negotiating a collective bargaining agreement with management, unions have little influence in shaping employment relations and management decisions on a continuous basis, and this is why they tend to focus narrowly on defending norms of the collective bargaining agreement. Unions also have no institutionally guaranteed right to access company information and, since they cannot verify and therefore do not trust the information provided by management, unions tend to react defensively to proposed changes in work organization and company restructuring. The more limited institutionally defined rights do not enable unions to develop broader responsibilities in running companies productively. Instead unions tend to focus more narrowly on defending their jobs and the norms of collective bargaining, an ideology that has been described as 'job-control unionism' (Katz 1985). While there are certainly exceptions to these depictions of employment relations in both countries, this research highlights broad ideological differences between countries and how institutions influence ideas and actor ideologies.

Other research in employment relations focuses on the opposite relationship and examines how ideas and ideologies shape and influence institutions. Hauptmeier (2012), for example, analyses the varying impact of national institutions on the company level in Spain between the transition to democracy and the economic crisis in 2008/9. In the 1980s employment relations were contentious and strike prone. Two decades later employment relations look strikingly different and in two of the examined cases cooperative, market-oriented employment relations emerge. Leadership change, generational change, diffusion, and identity work are identified as the mechanisms for ideological change which shape the shift from paternalistic, authoritarian management ideologies and contentious union ideologies in the 1980s to more market-oriented, cooperative management, and union ideologies in the 2000s. Actors' ideas and ideologies are seen to evolve in ways which have the capacity to enact institutions on the company level in different ways, even if the formal rules of national institutions do not change. Thus, this account does not regard institutions as objective structures that shape uniform patterns of employment relations, but instead emphasizes that institutions are open to reinterpretation and a different construction by actors. To an important extent 'institutions are what actors make of them'.

Other research has examined how ideas transformed the transnational institution of the European Works Council (EWC). While in the vast majority of company cases EWCs do not have a significant effect on employment relations, the EWC at General Motors Europe negotiated collective agreements with GM's European management and developed far-reaching transnational worker cooperation and collective action, e.g. the EWC organized European work stoppages in which more than 40,000 workers took part (Greer and Hauptmeier 2012). The transformation of the EWC is explained through the 'identity work' of the EWC leadership that organized regular exchanges and plant visits across borders, built up close relationships between workers and union leaders from different countries, integrated representatives from peripheral countries into EWC leadership positions, engaged in transnational collective action, and gradually shaped common norms and values. These various elements of the EWC's leadership 'identity work' helped to develop and sustain transnational worker cooperation for more than a decade.

Locke and Thelen's (1995) comparison of labour politics in Italy, Sweden, the USA, and Germany also combines ideational and institutional analysis. The starting point of the analysis is the observation that unions in all examined countries are facing similar challenges such as international competition, the introduction of new work organization and technology, demands for increased working time and flexibility, and industrial restructuring. However, while the challenges for labour are similar, the specific manifestations of labour struggles and responses are distinct across countries. By drawing on insights in historical institutionalist research, the authors find that common pressures are translated and mediated through the institutional context. Different institutional arrangements create different sets of rigidities and sticking points. Where these are bound up with traditional union identities—and here the authors draw on the constructivist literature—the meaning of contentious issues amplifies and becomes the focus of labour politics. For example, unions in the USA had problems agreeing on new types of work organization, because this required the loosening or even abandoning of norms and job descriptions in the collective bargaining agreement that are so essential to the union project in the USA given the lack of other institutionalized protections and rights. In contrast, in Germany work organization was less of an issue for works councillors because the co-determination rights fully guaranteed a say in decision-making processes and the continuous development of work organization.

Assessment

Constructivist institutionalism provides a new approach to the study of change in employment relations. It captures the sense that there are alternative policy discourses and ideas available that are drawn upon by existing or new forms of actors to question institutional routines and to open up possibilities for change. The development of these arguments shows that this approach does not rely on the 'abstract' power of ideas but on the ways in which they are given material force and power in organizations, unions, etc. and how this material force is shaped by existing economic and political resources as well as by historical memories and the path dependent nature of ideational structures. Much in these arguments could be grafted on to historical institutionalism without detriment to either approach by using a more expansive, ideational foundation of actor behaviour. Constructivist institutionalism does run the danger though that it becomes too focused on ideas per se and not enough on the social processes through which ideas become effective and influential. It may also be associated with a radical subjectivism in which everything is discourse but this is something which its proponents have stoutly rejected. Certainly, it is in some respects difficult to disentangle ideas from institutions and to develop causal arguments that make sense and are not simply tautologies.

However, there is no reason why careful empirical study cannot achieve this (Jepperson et al. 1996).

CONCLUSION

There exists a certain empiricist undercurrent in comparative employment relations which focuses on detailed and rich empirical work but attempts to stay clear from overly theorizing research issues. It favours a straightforward approach to institutions. There is a clear link between formal institutions and actor behaviour, and actors seem to have the strategic capacity to figure out the best course of action in a given material and institutional context. However, these assumptions are often not spelled out, because these choices are assumed and presented as a natural and obvious approach to institutional research in comparative employment relations. While these implicit assumptions are legitimate choices for institutional research, they are not value-free and represent a particular brand of institutionalism distinct from other types of institutionalism discussed in this chapter. Comparative employment relations could profit from a further engagement with the debate on the different forms of institutionalisms in the social sciences. Innovations and tools of other types of institutionalism could advance comparative employment relations research. In return, the rich empiricist research tradition and inductive approach to theory building place comparative employment relations research in a strong position to contribute to institutional theory. This chapter sought to facilitate this dialogue by introducing and specifying different types of institutionalism and linking them to comparative employment relations research.

There exist direct connections between employment relations research and both rational choice and historical institutionalism. Rational choice institutionalism shares important assumptions with institutional labour economics, strategic choice literature, the collective action problem, and game theory-inspired research in comparative employment relations. Historical institutionalism directly grew out of research on employment relations issues and remains closely intertwined with research in comparative employment relations. Though there exist fewer links between comparative employment relations research and constructivist and sociological institutionalisms, we have highlighted comparative research on work and employment relations that draws on them.

How can employment relations research profit more from further engagement with the different types of institutionalism? First, the comparisons and depictions of national systems of employment relations have tended to be overly static. Tightly linking national employment relations patterns to the institutional context produces stable images of national models if institutions do not change. There is a vibrant debate in historical institutionalism and constructivist institutionalism underway that assumes a looser coupling between institutions and actors' behaviour, recognizes the capacity of actors to influence and enact institutions, and seeks to specify mechanisms of institutional change, all of which might be helpful to analyse the evolution of employment relations in national contexts. Second, while the national level will remain of primary importance in employment relations, the diffusion and spread of employment relations practices across borders can be observed in the current era. MNCs have begun to introduce global HRM systems and to implement various codes of conduct in relation to labour. Equal opportunity legislation has been introduced in a greater number of countries and the ILO promotes the adoption of (core) labour standards. The diffusion of employment relations practices has often been cast in the language of the convergence debate. The toolkit of sociological institutionalism could help to examine on a more specific level how employment relations practices and working standards travel across borders and, in the process, change and create new hybrid systems. Third, literature in comparative employment relations widely assumes rational or strategic actors with far-reaching cognitive capacities to figure the best course of action or best practices. Both sociological and constructivist institutionalism raise questions about these cognitive capabilities and suggest that actor behaviour is also crucially shaped by values, belief systems, and ideologies. As these ideas and values change, so will institutions.

We presented four distinct bodies of institutional work in this chapter, but we are aware that the boundaries between different types of institutionalism can be blurred and that boundaries could be relaxed or even collapsed. For example, using a richer concept of the actor in historical institutionalism by including a more systematic analysis of beliefs and ideology might bridge the divide with constructivist institutionalism. Recent contributions in historical institutionalism actually have moved in this direction (Mahoney and Thelen 2010). Similarly efforts to explore synergies between historical and rational choice institutionalism have become more common (Katznelson and Weingast 2005). It is clear that the more the focus is on institutional change and the more the conceptual framework moves from the parsimonious models, the looser the institutionalist framework becomes. There are many different variants in the definition of institutions, the way institutions evolve, and the role of individuals and ideas in institutional change and reproduction. Some researchers may be inclined to emphasize theoretical purity and to draw clean boundaries between the different forms of institutionalism. Others seem more willing to use a variety of concepts and approaches even while seeking to retain some form of coherence. Whichever approach is taken, there is no doubt that the institutionalist perspective is thriving and can continue to thrive in areas such as comparative employment relations for a long while yet.

REFERENCES

Abdelal, R. (2007). *Capital Rules: The Construction of Global Finance*. Cambridge, MA: Harvard University Press.

Abdelal, R., Blyth, M., and Parsons, C. (eds.) (2010). *Constructing the International Economy*. Ithaca, NY and London: Cornell University Press.

Almond, P. and Ferner, A. (eds.) (2006). *American Multinationals in Europe: Managing Employment Relations across National Borders*. Oxford and New York: Oxford University Press.

Amable, B. (2003). *The Diversity of Modern Capitalism*. Oxford and New York: Oxford University Press.

Amable, B., Eichorst, W., Fligstein, N., and Streeck, W. (2010). 'On Wolfgang Streeck: *Re-forming Capitalism*', *Socio-Economic Review*, 8(3): 559–80.

Arthur, W. B. (1989). 'Competing Technologies, Increasing Returns, and Lock-In by Historical Events', *Economic Journal*, 99(394): 116–31.

Bamber, G., Lansbury, R. D., and Wailes, N. (eds.) (2011). *International and Comparative Employment Relations: Globalisation and Change*, 5th edn. Los Angeles and London: Sage.

Battilana, J. (2006). 'Agency and Institutions: The Enabling Role of Individuals' Social Position', *Organization*, 13(5): 653–76.

Battilana, J. and D'Aunno, T. (2009). 'Institutional Work and the Paradox of Embedded Agency', in T. B. Lawrence, R. Suddaby, and B. Leca (eds.), *Institututional Work: Actors and Agency in Institutional Studies of Organizations*. Cambridge: Cambridge University Press, 31–58.

Béland, D. and Cox, R. H. (eds.) (2011). *Ideas and Politics in Social Science Research*. Oxford and New York: Oxford University Press.

Blyth, M. (2002). *Great Transformations: Economic Ideas and Institutional Change in the Twentieth Century*. Cambridge: Cambridge University Press.

Boxall, P. F. and Purcell, J. (2011). *Strategy and Human Resource Management*, 3rd edn. Basingstoke: Palgrave Macmillan.

Brunsson, N. and Sahlin-Andersson, K. (2000). 'Constructing Organizations: The Example of Public Sector Reform', *Organization Studies*, 21(4): 721–46.

Campbell, J. L. (2004). *Institutional Change and Globalization*. Princeton: Princeton University Press.

Campbell, J. L. and Pedersen, O. K. (eds.) (2001). *The Rise of Neoliberalism and Institutional Analysis*. Princeton: Princeton University Press.

Commons, J. R. ([1934] 1990). *Institutional Economics: Its Place in Political Economy*, 2 vols. New Brunswick, NJ: Transaction Publishers.

Crouch, C. (1993). *Industrial Relations and European State Traditions*. Oxford and New York: Oxford University Press.

—— (2005). *Capitalist Diversity and Change: Recombinant Governance and Institutional Entrepreneurs*. Oxford and New York: Oxford University Press.

Cusack, T., Iversen, T., and Soskice, S. (2010). 'Coevolution of Capitalism and Political Representation: The Choice of Electoral Systems', *American Political Science Review*, 104(2): 393–403.

Czarniawska-Joerges, B. and Sevon, G. (eds.) (2005). *Global Ideas: How Ideas, Objects and Practices Travel in a Global Economy*. Malmö, Sweden: Liber and Copenhagen Business School Press.

David, P. A. (1985). 'Clio and the Economics of QWERTY', *American Economic Review*, 75(2): 332–7.

Davis, G. F., McAdam, D., Scott, W. R., and Zald, M. N. (eds.) (2005). *Social Movements and Organization Theory*. Cambridge: Cambridge University Press

Deeg, R. and Jackson, G. (2007). 'Towards a More Dynamic Theory of Capitalist Variety', *Socio-Economic Review*, 5(1): 149–80.

Deephouse, D. L. and Suchman, M. (2008). 'Legitimacy in Organizational Institutionalism', in R. Greenwood, C. Oliver, K. Sahlin, and R. Suddaby (eds.), *The Sage Handbook of Organizational Institutionalism*. London: Sage, 49–78.

Dezalay, Y. and Garth, B. G. (eds.) (2002a). *Global Prescriptions: The Production, Exportation, and Importation of a New Legal Orthodoxy*. Ann Arbor: University of Michigan Press.

—— (2002b). *The Internationalization of Palace Wars: Lawyers, Economists, and the Contest to Transform Latin American States*. Chicago: University of Chicago Press.

Djelic, M.-L. (2010). 'Institutional Perspectives: Working Towards Coherence or Irreconcilable Diversity?', in G. Morgan, J. L. Campbell, C. Crouch, O. K. Pedersen, and R. Whitley (eds.), *The Oxford Handbook of Comparative Institutional Analysis*. Oxford and New York: Oxford University Press, 15–40.

Djelic, M.-L. and Quack, S. (eds.) (2003). *Globalization and Institutions: Redefining the Rules of the Economic Game*. Cheltenham: Edward Elgar.

—— (eds.) (2010). *Transnational Communities: Shaping Global Economic Governance*. Cambridge: Cambridge University Press.

Djelic, M.-L. and Sahlin-Andersson, K. (eds.) (2006). *Transnational Governance: Institutional Dynamics of Regulation*. Cambridge: Cambridge University Press.

Dobbin, F. (2009). *Inventing Equal Opportunity*. Princeton: Princeton University Press.

Doellgast, V. (2010). 'Collective Voice under Decentralized Bargaining: A Comparative Study of Work Reorganization in US and German Call Centres', *British Journal of Industrial Relations*, 48(2): 375–99.

—— (2012). *Disintegrating Democracy at Work: Labor Unions and the Future of Good Jobs in the Service Economy*. Ithaca, NY: ILR Press.

Dörrenbächer, C. and Geppert, M. (eds.) (2011). *Politics and Power in the Multinational Corporation: The Role of Institutions, Interests and Identities*. Cambridge: Cambridge University Press.

Drezner, D. W. (2010). 'Is Historical Institutionalism Bunk?', *Review of International Political Economy*, 17(4): 791–804.

Drori, G. S., Meyer, J. W., and Hwang, H. (eds.) (2006). *Globalization and Organization: World Society and Organizational Change*. Oxford and New York: Oxford University Press.

Edwards, T. and Ferner, A. (2004). 'Multinationals, Reverse Diffusion and National Business Systems', *Management International Review*, 44(1): 49–79.

Farrell, H. and Newman, A. L. (2010). 'Making Global Markets: Historical Institutionalism in International Political Economy', *Review of International Political Economy*, 17(4): 609–38.

Ferner, A., Almond, P., and Colling, T. (2005). 'Institutional Theory and the Cross-National Transfer of Employment Policy: The Case of "Workforce Diversity" in US Multinationals', *Journal of International Business Studies*, 36(3): 304–21.

Fioretos, O. (2011). *Creative Reconstructions: Multilateralism and European Varieties of Capitalism after 1950*. Ithaca, NY: Cornell University Press.

Fligstein, N. and McAdam, D. (2012). *A Theory of Fields*. Oxford and New York: Oxford University Press.

Fourcade, M. (2006). 'The Construction of a Global Profession: The Transnationalization of Economics', *American Journal of Sociology*, 112(1): 145–94.

—— (2009). *Economists and Societies: Discipline and Profession in the United States, Britain & France, 1890s to 1990s*. Princeton: Princeton University Press.

Fourcade-Gourinchas, M. and Babb, S. L. (2002). 'The Rebirth of the Liberal Creed: Paths to Neoliberalism in Four Countries 1', *American Journal of Sociology*, 108(3): 533–79.

Godard, J. (2004). 'The New Institutionalism, Capitalist Diversity, and Industrial Relations', in B. E. Kaufman (ed.), *Theoretical Perspectives on Work and the Employment Relationship*. Champaign, IL: Industrial Relations Research Association, 229–64.

Golden, M. (1997). *Heroic Defeats: The Politics of Job Loss*. Cambridge: Cambridge University Press.

Goldthorpe, J. H. (1984). *Order and Conflict in Contemporary Capitalism*. Oxford: Clarendon Press.

Gooderham, P. N., Nordhaug, O., and Ringdal, K. (1999). 'Institutional and Rational Determinants of Organizational Practices: Human Resource Management in European Firms', *Administrative Science Quarterly*, 44(3): 507–31.

Goyer, M. (2006). 'Varieties of Institutional Investors and National Models of Capitalism: The Transformation of Corporate Governance in France and Germany', *Politics & Society*, 34(3): 399–430.

—— (2011). *Contingent Capital: Short-Term Investors and the Evolution of Corporate Governance in France and Germany*. Oxford and New York: Oxford University Press.

Greer, I. and Hauptmeier, M. (2012). 'Identity Work: Sustaining Transnational Worker Cooperation at GM Europe', *Industrial Relations*, 51(2): 275–97.

Greif, A. (2006). *Institutions and the Path to the Modern Economy: Lessons from Medieval Trade*. Cambridge: Cambridge University Press.

Greif, A. and Laitin, D. (2004). 'A Theory of Endogenous Institutional Change', *American Political Science Review*, 98(4): 633–52.

Hall, P. A. (1989). *The Political Power of Economic Ideas: Keynesianism across Nations*. Princeton: Princeton University Press.

Hall, P. A. and Soskice, D. (2001). 'An Introduction to Varieties of Capitalism', in Hall and Soskice (eds.), *Varieties of Capitalism: Varieties of Capitalism: The Institutional Foundations of Comparative Advantage*. Oxford and New York: Oxford University Press, 1–68.

Hall, P. A. and Taylor, R. C. R. (1996). 'Political Science and the Three New Institutionalisms', *Political Studies*, 44(5): 936–67.

Hall, P. A. and Thelen, K. (2009). 'Institutional Change in Varieties of Capitalism', *Socio-Economic Review*, 7(1): 7–34.

Halliday, T. and Carruthers, B. (2009). *Bankrupt: Global Lawmaking and Systemic Financial Crisis*. Stanford: Stanford University Press.

Hancké, B. (2002). *Large Firms and Institutional Change: Industrial Renewal and Economic Restructuring in France*. Oxford and New York: Oxford University Press.

Hardy, C. and Maguire, S. (2008). 'Institutional Entrepreneurship', in R. Greenwood, C. Oliver, R. Suddaby, and K. Sahlin-Andersson (eds.), *The Sage Handbook of Organizational Institutionalism*. London: Sage, 198–217.

Hauptmeier, Marco (2012). 'Institutions Are What Actors Make of Them: The Changing Construction of Firm Level Employment Relations in Spain', *British Journal of Industrial Relations*, 50(4): 737–59.

Hay, C. (2006). 'Constructivist Institutionalism', in R. A. W. Rhodes, S. A. Binder, and B. A. Rockman (eds.), *The Oxford Handbook of Political Institutions*. Oxford and New York: Oxford University Press, 56–74.

Hay, C. and Wincott, D. (1998). 'Structure, Agency and Historical Institutionalism', *Political Studies*, 46(5): 951–7.

Howell, C. and Kolins Givan, R. (2011). 'Rethinking Institutions and Institutional Change in European Industrial Relations', *British Journal of Industrial Relations*, 49(2): 231–55.

Iversen, T. and Soskice, D. (2009). 'Distribution and Redistribution: The Shadow of the Nineteenth Century', *World Politics*, 61(3): 438–86.

Jackson, G. (2010). 'Actors and Institutions', in G. Morgan, J. L. Campbell, C. Crouch, O. K. Pedersen, and R. Whitley (eds.), *The Oxford Handbook of Comparative Institutional Analysis*. Oxford and New York: Oxford University Press, 63–86.

Jackson, G. and Deeg, R. (2008). 'From Comparing Capitalisms to the Politics of Institutional Change', *Review of International Political Economy*, 15(4): 680–709.

Jepperson, R. J., Wendt, A., and Katzenstein, P. J. (1996). 'Norms, Identity, and Culture in National Security', in P. J. Katzenstein (ed.), *The Culture of National Security: Norms and Identity in World Politics*. New York: Columbia University Press, 33–75.

Katz, H. C. (1985). *Shifting Gears: Changing Labor Relations in the U.S. Automobile Industry*. Cambridge, MA: MIT Press.

Katz, H. C. and Darbishire, O. (2000). *Converging Divergences: Worldwide Changes in Employment Systems*. Ithaca, NY: Cornell University Press.

Katzenstein, P. J. (1985). *Small States in World Markets: Industrial Policy in Europe*. Ithaca, NY: Cornell University Press.

Katznelson, I. and Weingast, B. R. (eds.) (2005). *Preferences and Situations: Points of Intersection between Historical and Rational Choice Institutionalism*. New York: Russell Sage Foundation.

Kaufman, B. E. (2011). 'Comparative Employment Relations: Institutional and Neoinstitutional Theories', in M. Barry and A. Wilkinson (eds.), *Research Handbook of Comparative Employment Relations*. Cheltenham: Edward Elgar, 25–55.

Kochan, T. A., Katz, H. C., and McKersie, R. B. (1994). *The Transformation of American Industrial Relations*. Ithaca, NY: ILR Press.

Kochan, T. A., McKersie, R. B., and Cappelli, P. (1984). 'Strategic Choice and Industrial Relations Theory', *Industrial Relations*, 23(1): 16–39.

Kostova, T. and Roth, K. (2002). 'Adoption of an Organizational Practice by Subsidiaries of Multinational Corporations: Institutional and Relational Effects', *Academy of Management Journal*, 45(1): 215–33.

Kristensen, P. H. and Lilja, K. (eds.) (2011). *Nordic Capitalisms and Globalization: New Forms of Economic Organization and Welfare Institutions*. Oxford and New York: Oxford University Press.

Kristensen, P. H. and Zeitlin, J. (2005). *Local Players in Global Games: The Strategic Constitution of a Multinational Corporation*. Oxford and New York: Oxford University Press.

Lawrence, T. B. and Suddaby, R. (2006). 'Institutions and Institutional Work', in S. Clegg (ed.), *The Sage Handbook of Organization Studies*, 2nd edn. London and Thousand Oaks, CA: Sage, 215–54.

Lawrence, T. B., Suddaby, R., and Leca, B. (eds.) (2009). *Institutional Work: Actors and Agency in Institutional Studies of Organizations*. Cambridge: Cambridge University Press.

Levi, M. and Murphy, G. H. (2006). 'Coalitions of Contention: The Case of the WTO Protests in Seattle', *Political Studies*, 54(4): 651–70.

Locke, R. M., Fei, Q. I. N., and Brause, A. (2007). 'Does Monitoring Improve Labor Standards? Lessons from Nike', *ILR Review*, 61(1): 3–31.

Locke, R. and Thelen, K. (1995). 'Apples and Oranges Revisited: Contextualized Comparisons and the Study of Comparative Labor Politics', *Politics & Society*, 23(3): 337–67.

Luo, X. (2006). 'The Spread of a "Human Resources" Culture: Institutional Individualism and the Rise of Personal Development Training', in G. S. Drori, J. W. Meyer, and H. Hwang (eds.),

Globalization and Organization: World Society and Organizational Change. Oxford and New York: Oxford University Press, 225–40.

Maguire, S., Hardy, C., and Lawrence, T. B. (2004). 'Institutional Entrepreneurship in Emerging Fields: HIV/AIDS Treatment Advocacy in Canada', *Academy of Management Journal*, 47(5): 657–79.

Mahoney, J. and Rueschemeyer, D. (eds.) (2003). *Comparative Historical Analysis in the Social Sciences.* Cambridge: Cambridge University Press.

Mahoney, J. and Thelen, K. A. (2010). 'A Theory of Gradual Institutional Change', in Mahoney and Thelen (eds.), *Explaining Institutional Change: Ambiguity, Agency, and Power.* Cambridge: Cambridge University Press, 1–37.

March, J. G., and Olsen, J. P. (1989). *Rediscovering Institutions: The Organizational Basis of Politics.* New York: Free Press.

—— (2006). 'Elaborating the New Institutionalism', in R. A. W. Rhodes, S. A. Binder, and B. A. Rockman (eds.), *The Oxford Handbook of Political Institutions.* Oxford and New York: Oxford University Press, 3–20.

Martin, A. and Ross, G. (1999). *The Brave New World of European Labor: European Trade Unions at the Millennium.* New York: Berghahn Books.

Martin, C. J. and Swank, D. (2012). *The Political Construction of Business Interests: Coordination, Growth and Equality.* Cambridge: Cambridge University Press.

Milgrom, P. and Roberts, J. (1990). 'The Economics of Modern Manufacturing: Technology, Strategy and Organization', *American Economic Review*, 80(3): 511–28.

Mirowski, P. (2002). *Machine Dreams: Economics becomes a Cyborg Science.* Cambridge: Cambridge University Press.

Mirowski, P. and Plehwe, D. (2009). *The Road from Mont Pèlerin: The Making of the Neoliberal Thought Collective.* Cambridge, MA: Harvard University Press.

Morgan, G. (2005). 'Institutional Complementarities, Path Dependency and the Dynamics of Firms', in G. Morgan, R. Whitley, and E. Moen (eds.), *Changing Capitalisms? Internationalization, Institutional Change and Systems of Economic Organization.* Oxford and New York: Oxford University Press, 415–46.

Morgan, G. and Kristensen, P. H. (2006). 'The Contested Space of Multinationals: Varieties of Institutionalism: Varieties of Capitalism', *Human Relations*, 59(11): 1467–90.

North, D. C. (1990). *Institutions, Institutional Change and Economic Performance.* Cambridge: Cambridge University Press.

Olson, M. (1965). *The Logic of Collective Action: Public Goods and the Theory of Groups.* Cambridge, MA: Harvard University Press.

Ostrom, E. (2005). *Understanding Institutional Diversity.* Princeton: Princeton University Press.

Palier, B. and Thelen, K. (2010). 'Institutionalizing Dualism: Complementarities and Change in France and Germany', *Politics & Society*, 38(1): 119–48.

Peck, J. (2010). *Constructions of Neoliberal Reason.* Oxford and New York: Oxford University Press.

Pierson, P. (2000). 'The Limits of Design: Explaining Institutional Origins and Change', *Governance: An International Journal of Policy and Administration*, 13(4): 475–99.

—— (2004). *Politics in Time: History, Institutions, and Social Analysis.* Princeton: Princeton University Press.

Powell, W. W. and DiMaggio, P. (eds.) (1991). *The New Institutionalism in Organizational Analysis.* Chicago: University of Chicago Press.

Schmidt, V. A. (2002). *The Futures of European Capitalism*. Oxford and New York: Oxford University Press.

—— (2008). 'Discursive Institutionalism: The Explanatory Power of Ideas and Discourse', *Annual Review of Political Science*, 11: 303–26.

—— (2010). 'Taking Ideas and Discourse Seriously: Explaining Change through Discursive Institutionalism as the Fourth "New Institutionalism" ', *European Political Science Review*, 2(1): 1–25.

—— (2011). 'Speaking of Change: Why Discourse is Key to the Dynamics of Policy Transformation', *Critical Policy Studies*, 5(2): 106–26.

Schneiberg, M. and Lounsbury, M. (2008). 'Social Movements and Institutional Analysis', in R. Greenwood, C. Oliver, K. Sahlin, and R. Suddaby (eds.), *The Sage Handbook of Organizational Institutionalism*. London: Sage, 650–72.

Scott, W. R. (1995). *Institutions and Organizations*. Thousand Oaks, CA: Sage.

—— (2003). *Organizations: Rational, Natural, and Open Systems,* 5th edn. Upper Saddle River, NJ: Prentice Hall.

Simmons, B. A., Dobbin, F., and Garrett, G. (eds.) (2008). *The Global Diffusion of Markets and Democracy*. Cambridge: Cambridge University Press.

Smith, A. (1976). *The Theory of Moral Sentiments*. Oxford: Clarendon Press.

Soskice, D. and Iversen, T. (2006). 'Electoral Institutions and the Politics of Coalitions: Why Some Democracies Redistribute More Than Others', *American Political Science Review*, 100(2): 165–81.

Stedman Jones, D. (2012). *Masters of the Universe: Hayek, Friedman and the Birth of Neoliberal Politics*. Princeton: Princeton University Press.

Steinmo, S., Thelen, K. A., and Longstreth, F. (1992). *Structuring Politics: Historical Institutionalism in Comparative Analysis*. Cambridge: Cambridge University Press.

Streeck, W. (1984). *Industrial Relations in West Germany: A Case Study of the Car Industry*. New York: St. Martin's Press.

—— (1997). 'Beneficial Constraints: On the Economic Limits of Rational Voluntarism', in J. R. Hollingsworth, and R. Boyer (eds.), *Contemporary Capitalism: The Embeddedness of Institutions*. Cambridge: Cambridge University Press, 197–219.

—— (2009). *Re-Forming Capitalism: Institutional Change in the German Political Economy*. Oxford and New York: Oxford University Press.

Streeck, W. and Thelen, K. A. (2005). 'Introduction: Institutional Change in Advanced Political Economies', in Streeck, and Thelen (eds.), *Beyond Continuity: Institutional Change in Advanced Political Economies*. Oxford and New York: Oxford University Press, 1–39.

Suchman, M. C. (1995). 'Managing Legitimacy: Strategic and Institutional Approaches', *Academy of Management Review*, 20(3): 571–610.

Thelen, K. A. (2004). *How Institutions Evolve: The Political Economy of Skills in Germany, Britain, the United States, and Japan*. Cambridge: Cambridge University Press.

Thornton, P. and Ocasio, W. (2008). 'Institutional Logics', in R. Greenwood, C. Oliver, K. Sahlin, and R. Suddaby (eds.), *The Sage Handbook of Organizational Institutionalism*. London: Sage, 99–129.

Thornton, P. H., Ocasio, W., and Lounsbury, M. (2012). *The Institutional Logics Perspective: A New Approach to Culture, Structure, and Process*. Oxford and New York: Oxford University Press.

Tregaskis, O., Edwards, T., Edwards, P., Ferner, A., and Marginson, P. (2010). 'Transnational Learning Structures in Multinational Firms: Organizational Context and National Embeddedness', *Human Relations*, 63(4): 471–99.

Turner, L. (1991). *Democracy at Work: Changing World Markets and the Future of Labor Unions*. Ithaca, NY: Cornell University Press.

Van Horn, R., Mirowski, P., and Stapleford, T. A. (eds.) (2011). *Building Chicago Economics: New Perspectives on the History of America's Most Powerful Economics Program*. Cambridge: Cambridge University Press.

Vidal, M. and Peck, J. (2012). 'Sociological Institutionalism and the Socially Constructed Economy', in T. J. Barnes, J. Peck, and E. S. Sheppard (eds.), *The Wiley-Blackwell Companion to Economic Geography*. Chichester and Malden, MA: Wiley-Blackwell, 595–611.

Weber, M. (2002). *The Protestant Ethic and the Spirit of Capitalism and Other Writings*. New York: Penguin Books.

—— (2009). *From Max Weber: Essays in Sociology*. London: Routledge.

Wedlin, L. (2006). *Ranking Business Schools: Forming Fields, Identities and Boundaries in International Management Education*. Cheltenham: Edward Elgar.

Wilkinson, A. and Wood, G. (2012). 'Institutions and Employment Relations: The State of the Art', *Industrial Relations: A Journal of Economy and Society*, 51(S1): 373–88.

CHAPTER 10

INSTITUTIONS AND THE INDUSTRIAL RELATIONS TRADITION

NIALL CULLINANE

INTRODUCTION

INSTITUTIONS have remained central to industrial relations (IR) analysis in terms of understanding the behaviour of IR actors and the outcomes of IR processes. Within the IR tradition, the most influential accounts on institutional effects have dovetailed with a broadly functionalist sociology. Historically, this inclination, in turn, has tended to generate an auto-critique broadly underpinned by various 'conflict' sociological theories. The purpose of this chapter is to consider the functionalist legacy in institutional analysis and the underlying, if not always self-consciously realized, sociological borrowings. The chapter considers the associated critiques of such postures and subsequent attempts to build upon and refine such analysis.

The argument of the chapter is as follows: it will open with a brief review of the early institutional-pluralist schema of IR offered by the US 'Berkeley–Harvard' tradition. A number of complementary, sociological parallels are found: chiefly the structural-functionalism of Talcott Parsons, itself leaning heavily on a particular reading of Durkheim. Yet for further sociological development of IR institutions, the chapter argues, it is not to the United States that one must look, where the field of IR was subsequently subsumed by neo-classical labour economics, but to Britain. In Britain, while a latent functionalism was often apparent in the work of Oxford scholars, explicit sociological anchoring in Durkheim was used to explain the 'inflationary disorder' that spawned the important Donovan Commission (Fox and Flanders 1969). As this tradition was seriously challenged by Marxist sociology and labour process analysis in subsequent years (Hyman 1975; Nichols and Beynon 1977), the

Durkheimian sociology of IR institutions was in turn reconstructed and elaborated by radical-institutionalists to explain 'disorder' as a product of liberal market societies (Goldthorpe 1969; Fox 1974; Gilbert 1986). While such sociological underpinnings eroded as the full effects of the 'monetarist counter-revolution' were felt throughout the 1980s and 1990s, a space for such thinking re-emerged in subsequent developments around Durkheimian neo-pluralist approaches to the employment relationship (Ackers 2002, 2012) and the varieties of capitalism (VOC) literature in particular (Frege and Kelly 2004). The VOC literature has been particularly influential in the IR world and the various linkages between the two, and their intertwining sociological aspects, are discussed.

Sociology and the Institutional-Pluralist Tradition

Institutions have long been central to IR analysis. Different regulatory institutions were recognized by the earliest pioneers of the field like Webb and Webb (1920), who notably distinguished between legal enactment and collective bargaining, and Commons (1950) and Perlman (1928), who attached primary importance to understanding the emergence of 'rules of occupancy and tenure'. Yet the first schematic attempt to trace out the centrality of institutions in IR may well derive from the 'Berkeley–Harvard' tradition in the United States. One of their chief scholars, John Dunlop (1958), treated IR as an 'analytical subsystem' of industrial society, in turn identifying three important actors within this system: workers, management, and the state. Through their interactions, these agents produced a web of substantive and procedural rules, regulating conflict and promoting social order. Complementing such rules were influences of a sociological nature: a broadly 'common ideology' about 'acceptable behaviour' within the system. The historical emergence of this system is portrayed in Kerr et al. (1973), on foot of a sociological theory around changing social structures in industrialized societies. This thesis argued that while worker militancy and social conflict peaked during the early course of industrialization, it progressively dissipated in intensity thereafter as organized labour habituated itself to industrialism and employers grew to accept the legitimacy of collective bargaining. Such development permitted the emergence of institutions for conflict containment, which, in turn, cultivated an ethic of compromise and piecemeal advancement. The latter held sway due to a widespread acceptance of the material wealth and degree of social liberty afforded by industrial society. A further 'logic' of this industrialism led to the formation of social structures punctuated by various social gradations. Thus 'class conflict' associated with early industrialism gave way to a conflict between pluralistic 'interest groups'. The crisis of industrialization was resolved, the working class were integrated into its structures, and all subsequent labour problems were principally technocratic matters or perhaps generated by recalcitrant minorities 'with a conflicting, exclusive ideological orientation' (Kerr 1964: 15). This was held to be a trend upon which all industrialized societies institutionally converged.

On review, the sociological assumptions behind this institutionalism appear closely bound up in Cold War liberalism. It was closely affiliated with the first wave of pluralist theorizing in the field of US political science (Dahl 1958), but also, more importantly, functionalist sociology (cf. Poole 1981). Central to functionalism was an interpretation of society as a structure with interrelated, constituent elements like norms, customs, traditions, and institutions. Each of these performed a particular role or 'function': the different parts acting as 'organs' that worked towards the proper functioning of the body (society) as a whole (Giddens 1984). Talcott Parsons is typically identified as the chief architect of this system in post-war sociology and indeed Dunlop (1958: 28–32), in constructing his IR sub-system, explicitly borrowed from his sociology. Parsons' (1951: 24) analysis starts from the problem of order in society: conflict was inevitable where a 'plurality of individual actors' pursued their ends in circumstances of scarcity. Since disorder was an omnipresent probability, Parsons sought to account for how order was actually obtained in the absence of obvious manifest conflict. This led him to emphasize the durable properties of societies which enabled stable maintenance and reproduction without being torn asunder. In this regard, Parsons concluded that social and cultural norms had a crucial role to play in reconciling the ends of individual actors and integrating them: what Lockwood (1993) elsewhere terms 'normative functionalism'. This was not sociological idealism, however, as norms interfaced with a distinct social structure or system of 'rule institutionalization'. As norms were deemed to be largely internalized by social actors, except for occasional 'deviants' (Parsons 1951: 250), the tendency was consequently towards a self-equilibrating system. Some modicum of 'social strain' was not wholly avoidable and taken as given due to the pluralistic multitude of associational structures. These latter bodies in any case impeded excessive concentrations of power.

The construction of such sociological foundations relied heavily upon a particular reading of Durkheim: indeed Parsons (1968, cited in Gouldner 1971: 163) freely admitted that his 'own inclination is to refer above all to Durkheim' in the construction of his sociology. The comparisons are, at one level, apt: Durkheim's sociology was similarly preoccupied with explaining how societies and social groups held together as structures. Parsonian interpretations of social and cultural norms echo Durkheim's (1982) external constraints of intangible 'social facts', while the aforementioned normative functionalism of industrial society is reflective of Durkheim's (1984) 'mechanical solidarity'. Yet in the American construction of the IR institutional framework Durkheim remains largely ignored, coming through only in reference to Parsons. This might be accounted for by the relatively limited sociological theorizing that characterized the field of study in the US where the parameters of the debate were between institutional and neo-classical labour economics and later social psychology (Godard 1994; Kaufman 2004). It is only when we turn to the British tradition of institutional analysis that we find Durkheimian sociology more fully elaborated.

Yet this is perhaps curious as, in contrast to Dunlop and Kerr, the main architects of British IR institutionalism, Hugh Clegg and Allan Flanders, had relatively little contact with sociology in the early part of their careers. Indeed the preface to *The System of Industrial Relations in Great Britain* displays some scepticism towards sociology, at least in its crude human relations guise (Flanders and Clegg 1954: v–vi). Both Clegg and Flanders would later thaw in their attitude to the discipline, primarily through their contact with the industrial sociologist Alan Fox and the Warwick Industrial Relations Research Unit, where a 'sociological wing' of IR emerged in the 1970s (Ackers 2011). Although sociological functionalism is not explicitly self-evident in the workings of the 'Oxford School', if we accept Fox's (1971: v) critical characterization of British institutionalists as those 'who concern themselves with what are currently defined…as "problems" which impede or threaten what they deem the orderly and "rational" working of the industrial relation system' then an underlying species of functionalism might be discerned. More pertinent is the summation offered by Martin (1999: 1213), who senses a 'functionalist tradition…dominat[ing] the field historically, although usually implicitly and without the theoretical apparatus often associated with functionalism in mainstream sociological theory'. Flanders (1970: 86), as is well known, asserted that 'a system of industrial relations is a system of rules' and that the 'study of industrial relations may therefore be described as a study of job regulation'. While Hyman (1975: 11) complained such rendering made the field of IR a bedfellow of 'conservative sociology' (cf. Blyton and Turnbull 2004), Clegg (1979: 451) openly approved the 'conservative implications' of words like 'regulation' and 'system' in the IR lingua franca. Further, the type of assumptions that underwrote Kerr's thesis on industrial society occasionally found voice in the analysis of the British institutionalists even if they came to similar conclusions through very different pathways. Clegg's (1960: 29) social philosophy, for example, appeared to rotate on a belief that the 'political and industrial institutions of the stable democracies already approach the best that can be realized', while it would appear that Flanders was not averse to such Whiggish evaluations either (Kelly 2010). The social-democratic project of moderate reform was seen to have been secured by the 1945 Labour government: the role of IR, in true functionalist fashion, was to simply perfect the post-war settlement and the various institutions that supported it. This rational, piecemeal liberal reform could be achieved for example through encouraging progressive management and responsible trade unionism (Flanders 1964: 248–56).

From a theoretical viewpoint, the institutional arrangements provided for collective bargaining were deemed the central pivot upon which workplace actors' behaviour ultimately rested. The seminal contribution in this regard is probably Clegg's (1976) *Trade Unionism Under Collective Bargaining*. Choosing six countries, Clegg set out to demonstrate that union behaviour was a function of the state and character of collective bargaining in these countries. High union density among private sector manual workers in Sweden, for example, was accounted for by the relatively easy and widespread recognition of unions extended by the central employers' organization. In France, by contrast, employer resistance to collective bargaining in the private sector, coupled with union preference for political action, led to lower rates of unionization. Clegg also claimed to identify the pervasive effects of the structuring of collective bargaining institutions upon several major facets of IR outcomes like union government, the distribution of power within union structures, and different strike rates. Thus the institution of collective bargaining was endowed with a functionalist property to shape a variety of complementary outcomes.

While this British tradition often echoed functionalist inclination in variously subtle ways, it is the open engagement with Durkheim where these tendencies become most manifest: in particular the emphasis on 'normative regulation for the maintenance of social order' (Fox and Flanders 1969: 156). It is here, in an influential paper by Fox and Flanders, that Durkheim is used to explain the roots of industrial disorder in Britain during the long boom. Trends such as a rising rate of unofficial strike action, wage drift, inflation, and low productivity were viewed as a reflection of institutional lag, inadequate grasp of the sources of disorder, and reluctance on the part of management and unions to depart from well-tried practices. As such, the understanding of the British institutionalists was that Durkheim's analysis complemented their own framework in the acknowledgement of autonomous interest groups and associated inter-group competition that marked out industrial societies. Other complementary points of analysis could also be found: Durkheim maintained that it was neither necessary nor possible for social life to be without conflict, it could therefore not be suppressed, only regulated (cf. Clegg 1975: 309 for a similar approach). Indeed much like the IR institutionalists, Durkheim could be found to hold a dual perspective on social conflict: as both an inevitable feature of social life, but as potentially disruptive of social order (Flanders 1970: 26; Fox and Flanders 1969: 158). Influenced by their own 'normative systems', interest groups in exchange with each other could collapse into a Hobbesian war of all against all, without due concern for social proportion (Fox and Flanders 1969: 156). In this regard, institutionalist analysis, as befitting a field concerned with the making and administration of rules regulating employment, emphasized 'collective bargaining' as then being the principal norm-creating institution which might keep conflict within socially tolerable bounds. This was achieved because the rules it produced were seen to be supported by a sufficiently high degree of consent among those whose interests were most affected by their application (Fox and Flanders 1969: 160). Nevertheless for various reasons, if the institutional fittings were not rightly inserted, *anomie* or disorder was held to result.

Confining their analysis to industry level, Fox and Flanders (1969: 176–7) identified institutional forms which could be implemented at different, but interrelated levels of industrial life. Specifically at enterprise level, normative integration was held attainable through productivity agreements and job evaluation schemes; industry-level guidelines devised by employer associations and trade unions could complement this as could inter-industry normative regulation for public bodies concerned with prices and incomes and good industrial relations. Thus, through a process of exclusively workplace and industry-level re-engineering, the functionalist equilibrium could be restored and the more vexed strains in the system could be smoothed out.

Sociology in the Radical-Institutionalist Tradition

Problematically, the institutional pluralist project occurred in a context where the conditions of the post-war settlement were progressively unravelling as a result of rising strike action, profit squeeze, and the stagflationary crisis of the 1970s (Glyn and Sutcliffe 1972; Armstrong et al. 1984). By the start of the 1970s, civil rights unrest, growing industrial conflict, and the persistence of inequality in liberal, or social-democratic, societies appeared to suggest flaws in the conceptual schema associated with functionalist analysis and the more benign readings of 'dispersed power' provided by classical pluralism. As the consensus deteriorated, elements of Western intellectual life became increasingly radicalized. Parsons's sociology, having reached the zenith of its influence in the 1940s and 1950s, was, by the late 1960s, in decline as its place in the academy was increasingly supplanted by more 'conflict oriented' approaches (Dahrendorf 1959). The first wave of pluralist political science, associated with the likes of Dahl and others, was progressively challenged by a range of alternative theoretical traditions that presented empirical and conceptual criticisms of the pluralist case (Domhoff 1967). Institutional IR was not immune to such influences. The rise of the Marxist academy and New Leftism in British IR (Allen 1971; Hyman 1975), and its attempt to re-shift the analytical lens away from stability and order towards class and conflict, reflected this trajectory. Sociologically, Braverman (1974), and associated labour process analysis, placed its store on conflict and control which appeared more germane to a radicalized climate keen to reject frameworks that sought a dissipating social order. In the United States, the dynamic in IR was different, but the institutionalists suffered a much greater, and unremitting, marginalization. As the hollowing out of the New Deal IR system steadily continued into the 1970s and 1980s, the institutionalist paradigm was eclipsed (Kochan et al. 1986). The strong labour economics tendency in IR began to dominate, particularly under the influence of neo-classical mathematical modelling, while the diffusing of non-unionism and human resource management (HRM) further accelerated the death-knell for Dunlop's system. This was not strictly the fate of IR institutionalism in Britain, where the challenges of the 1970s produced an element of self-reflection and critical engagement with radical thinking (Clegg 1975, 1979). It is this dialogue within the British IR tradition that we now turn to.

Radical IR scholarship deeply distrusted the 'conservative tradition' of institutionalist IR given its emphasis upon the search for order. The institutions of IR were seen mainly as vehicles for the 'management of discontent': useful mechanisms by which the capitalist class, with the aid of incorporated union bureaucrats, or wider ideological socialization, assuaged conflict down easily manageable channels of containment (Herding 1972; Hyman 1975). Concern was raised too over the bounding of IR into a self-contained sub-system of institutions, shorn of any wider socio-political context. This coexisted with criticisms of an associated tendency to cast human actors, particularly in the Dunlopian formula, as unreflexive carriers of the roles allocated to them by the system's 'functional imperatives'. Further, by appearing to emphasize the formal processes of institutional rule-making, such bias was claimed to ignore the role of informal work groups and shopfloor stewards, whose militancy posed a challenge from below to official IR institutions in many countries in the 1960s and 1970s. Analytically then, institutions appeared to play a secondary role in radical analysis, as the focus turned to consider social processes of conflict generation at the point of production.

Yet dissatisfaction with the institutionalist tradition also stemmed from an alternative sociological persuasion that was neither politically Marxist nor labour process inspired. An interesting exemplar of this tradition is the then view of the British sociologist, Alan Aldridge. Commenting on the institutionalist tradition in British IR, Aldridge noted that:

> [Institutionalist IR] is an inbred literature, the child of an over-eager division of labour. Their desire to remain in touch with the industrial world and to avoid being digested by the academic has had as its darker side a narrowness of focus and lack of ambition. . . It would, of course, be ridiculous to dream that the student of industrial relations should be a new Renaissance Man intimately acquainted with the intricacies and profundities of every social science: investigation has to end somewhere and human abilities are finite. Nevertheless, limited capacity is not the same thing as complacent abstemiousness. (Aldridge 1976: x)

Aldridge in particular identified how institutionalists deployed ostensively sociological concepts like 'consent' as explanatory sources in determining the way particular institutional arrangements, like collective bargaining, worked. Yet the concept of consent, long puzzling to political philosophers and sociologists, was used in the literature of institutional IR as though its meaning were self-evident. Such inclinations, Aldridge maintained, had effectively exposed the institutionalist pluralist's 'left flank to attack [by] radicals and Marxists'. Institutionalists were urged to engage with the sociological origins of such concepts, which they could do without putting on the strait-jacket of so-called 'authoritarian orthodoxies'. Aldridge's critique was not isolated and perhaps better known arguments were volleyed by the industrial sociologists Alan Fox (1973) and John Goldthorpe (1969, 1977). Indeed the latter's critique is of note, arising as it does from an argument that Durkheim's sociology had not been fully appreciated by the institutionalist tradition in their argument on disorder. Goldthorpe held that the institutionalists had failed to follow Durkheim in relating the problem of anomie to wider social inequalities and the necessity of a wider egalitarian restructuring of society if normative order was to follow. Notably, there is evidence of cross-fertilization between Fox and Goldthorpe in the construction of their respective sociologies of IR (Fox 1971: vi; Goldthorpe 1975: 135). Considered alongside the later efforts of the sociologist Michael Gilbert (1986), who sought to build upon Fox's and Goldthorpe's analysis, one can trace a particular 'school' of IR: one that emphasizes the anomic temperament of industrial relations and the dearth of normative constraints on distributional conflict within advanced industrial societies (cf. Heery 2008: 73). These scholars sought to attach sociology to institutional analysis so as to explain the ubiquitous problems of strikes, wage drift, inflation, and productivity lag. Institutions were given their due importance, but were cast in pre-institutional, sociological roots that were seen to structure a path-dependent logic to the trajectory of national IR systems. Like the institutional-pluralists, the disorder associated with the Donovan era was similarly a concern, but it was held to be a more intractable problem requiring what today might be termed 'institutional complementarities' across the socio-economic structure for it to be minimized (Howell 2003; Coates 2005). Such complementarities could only be secured through radical restructuring.

Specifically, institutional disorder arose from an unequal division of labour in the employment relationship, the particular variety of British capitalism based on a historical tradition of laissez-faireism and associated economistic sectionalism. Thus, in his study of the consequences of the employment relationship in industrial societies, Fox (1974) advanced how the historical imposition of such roles gave rise to a 'large proportion' of the population working in 'low-discretion' work tasks (Fox 1974: 16–20). This was said to bound employees to prescribed routines and, moreover, social inequality, based on income and social status, tended to vary directly with levels of job discretion. Fox maintained that those occupying low-discretion work roles were managed on the assumption that they were undeserving of trust and could not be relied upon to voluntarily act in accordance with the values of superordinates. This created reciprocal distrust: people who felt that they were not trusted responded in turn by distrusting those deemed to distrust them. The implications of this low-trust syndrome for workplace relations were held to be as follows: low-trust perceptions engendered, or accentuated, the characteristics of economic exchange where employees traded specific services, or quanta of effort, for tightly specified material rewards (Goldthorpe et al. 1968: 189–90). Both sides relied upon distributive bargaining and pressure tactics to determine the terms of the exchange.

Although this was held to be a long-run trajectory of industrialization more generally, it was proposed that such trends could vary and be mediated by national social values and historical institutional and economic arrangements which would reduce 'low-trust' tendencies (Fox 1985a: 49; Gilbert 1986: 36). In Britain, low-trust economism was held to be exacerbated by its particular arrangement of these dynamics (Goldthorpe 1978: 200–1; Fox 1985b: 191–9; Gilbert 1986: 64–6). As British industrialization had depended relatively little on government action, this translated into a cultural laissez-faireism which stressed individual rights and liberties rather than collectivist obligations and responsibilities. The values espoused by market relations, as they developed under British industrialization, demanded that contracting individuals be freed from all non-economic ties and obligations, while notions of government non-interference extended to the sphere of IR in the form of liberal-voluntarism. In the absence of any centralizing or corporatist tendencies, individual managements and employees were left to bargain over contracts that they entered into without, as in other countries, the government seeking to extensively regulate the terms of those contracts.

Under these circumstances British organized labour enacted the values of self-interested behaviour. Bargaining was confined to purely economic matters and British unionism revolved around groups of workers in sectional conflict with one another, warily guarding their differentials over lower paid groups or seeking to catch up with those who were just above (Fox 1974: 331; Goldthorpe 1978: 199; Gilbert 1986: 38). As existing market and social inequalities could no longer be legitimated by reference to norms of social superiority, as in pre-industrial societies, it was open to groups of employees to assert and maximize their market power to enhance their labour market standing (Gilbert 1986: 38). In the post-war context of supportive full employment and economic expansion, economistic striving was asserted to have increased in pervasiveness and intensity, as appetites were whetted by growing prosperity and a 'revolution of rising expectations' and 'increased worker pushfulness' (Goldthorpe 1978: 201). It was advanced that British workers felt no obligation to hold back on demands or aspirations that they might have as 'nothing in the culture surrounding them convinced them that there might be some higher good to which they should abrogate themselves; this was not part of the English individualist tradition' (Fox 1985b: 24). It was in this way that the 'low-trust dynamic' projected from the individual division of labour in the workplace to the society at large in the form of wage scrambles, strikes, and rising inflation (Fox 1974: 322).

While the sociological foundations for their analysis were frequently diverse, drawing upon Marxist and Weberian ideas, there was nonetheless again a strong Durkheimian element to this core argument in that its treatment of disorder in British IR closely correlates with Durkheim's own treatment of anomie (cf. Lockwood 1993). For Durkheim, anomie operated at three levels: first, anomie was derived from the loss of social cohesion engendered by the intensified division of labour in industrial societies as 'the individual hemmed in by his task becomes isolated...[and] no longer feels the idea of a common work being done by those who work side by side' (Durkheim 1984: 357). This was held to detach the individual worker from the wider community as 'the peculiar scope of his special activity...constantly links him to his own private interest whose true relation with the public interest he perceives but very vaguely' (Durkheim 1984: 357-8). Second, anomie arose from the free play of laissez-faire market forces and the disordering effects they were seen to sponsor: 'Production becomes unbridled and unregulated...From this comes the crisis which periodically disturbs economic functions' (Durkheim 1984: 366-7). Third, anomie was attributed to the tendency of market societies to cultivate 'excessive individualism' (Durkheim 1952: 217). Whereas pre-industrial societies were claimed to have provided a normative status order offering a glue of consensual values about the relative worth of different groups of people, industrialization, and the emergence of market forces, were seen to have relaxed such social bonds. The commercialization of exchange relationships, and the spread of the cash nexus, undermined previously accepted notions of obligations and responsibility. Industrialization was seen to engender an abrupt growth in wealth and 'with increased prosperity, desires increase' (Durkheim 1959: 242). As status began to depend more on individual achieve-ments in market exchange and less on localized interactions, 'unrestrained' and 'exces-sive appetites' arose which could not be reconciled by traditional sources of authority. The absence of moral order led to 'unlimited desires' expressed behaviourally through various interest groups attempting to assert their power so as to enhance their material rewards:

> Some particular class especially favoured by the crisis is no longer resigned to its for-mer lot, and, on the other hand, the example of its great fortune arouses all sorts of jealously below and about it. (Durkheim 1952: 252–3)

All three sources of anomie were mutually reinforcing: if anomie in social life was to be curtailed, all three variants would need to be tackled (Durkheim 1959: 243–4; 1984: 37). This could be achieved through reconstituting a 'corporative reorganisation of modern society' (Durkheim 1959: 30–1). Similarly for Fox, Goldthorpe, and Gilbert the unbri-dled pluralism of British society was seen to frustrate macroeconomic management: the putative 'disorder' could be resolved only by moving away from pluralism towards a concerted arrangement. The labour market would need to be organized in a way to ensure social integration and involvement of workers through moving beyond a wholly contractual order and building institutions that forged a social compromise between capital and labour (Fox 1985b: 119–28; Gilbert 1978: 749–50; Goldthorpe 1984: 323–9).

The Sociological Tradition in Contemporary Institutional Analysis

As these radical sociologists suspected, a fundamental overhaul of British IR institu-tions towards social corporatism was unlikely, particularly in light of the emergence of Thatcherism: its associated advancement of economistic free-for-all was seen as more consonant with the British individualist tradition. Yet Thatcherite politics was regarded as likely to stoke, rather than tame, disorder: its application to British IR was expected to exacerbate traditional patterns of adversarial relations and institutional mistrust, which, in time, would inevitably be renewed by organized labour during an economic upswing (Fox 1985a: 429; Gilbert 1986: 80–9). Yet Thatcherism, and the eco-nomic and social changes it engendered, in time displaced the labour problem, margin-alized trade unions, and hollowed out the voluntarist system of collective bargaining. The IR paradigm more generally, whatever its particular sociological casting, as well as associated normative traits, appeared progressively out of sync as non-unionism and individualistic human resource management took hold. Where sociology had any influ-ence it continued to be heavily anchored, not in Durkheim's search for cohesion, but in Marxist labour process theory (Thompson 1982) and the continued study of job controls

(Edwards and Scullion 1982; Terry and Edwards 1988). Much of this sociological tra-dition fell from grace, however, as Marxism suffered political and ideological setback in the late 1980s while the manufacturing economy, which held host to such investi-gations, was subject to neo-liberal shock therapy. To a lesser extent, and more in the field of political science than classical IR, sociological interpretations of institutions remained evident in the macro-examination of formal arrangements at national level (Schmitter 1974). As the long post-war boom faltered in the 1970s and as mass unem-ployment re-emerged, attention switched to the factors influencing national economic performance. There was a growth of research on corporatism and the systems of IR in Northern Europe that coordinated wage bargaining and generated relatively low infla-tion and low unemployment (Goldthorpe 1984). For the most part, however, sociol-ogy in IR, as Wood (2000) observed, gave way to economics. Increasingly this took the form, as Kelly (1998: 16) notes, of a 'large-scale quantitative survey of establishments and companies with sophisticated sampling procedures and instrument design and the use of statistical analysis... the Warwick survey of 1977/88... inaugurated a veritable flood of sequels and offshoots'.

In time, however, sociology and institutional analysis would be rejoined. Admittedly some of this dynamic has occurred without reference to mainstream IR in the form of sociological neo-institutionalism (Scott 2001). While this has received some attention in IR (Ackers and Wilkinson 2008) it has, as Jackson and Muellenborn (2012) note, made slow inroads. Rather where sociology finds its voice in contemporary IR insti-tutional analysis is through the integration of concepts like the employment relation-ship with the institutions that surround this dynamic (Edwards 2003; Ackers 2012). Commentators increasingly stress that national 'IR systems' be sensitive to a broader political sociology which understood IR as embedded in the wider society of different 'national business systems'. Institutions remained central to this because the employ-ment relationship, while holding many consistent and durable features across time and space, was seen to express itself in different institutional configurations, themselves products of history, culture, and political development. Thus Godard (2004: 243) has emphasized the core of IR to be 'institutional arrangements... which tend to reflect eco-nomic, political and social traditions that have become embedded in rules, norms and expectations'. Hyman's (2004: 270) consideration of IR theory, although starting with the capitalist labour process and employment relationship, observes that the institutions of industrial relations must be understood as elements in this apparatus alongside the 'role of ideas, beliefs, social norms and indeed language in shaping industrial relations'. Similarly Ackers (2005, 2012) has noted that the employment relationship, while central, can be over-extended into an explanatory meta-narrative. In reality, the employment relationship can only hint at tensions and tendencies:

Once we start asking important questions, such as why are there more strikes in manufacturing than in retail, or more in France than in the UK, the employment relationship per se can tell us little, the labour process not so much more. Instead, we turn to institutions (in their broadest sense) for explanation. And were these institutions grown from the seed of an employment relationship? Well, yes, in a certain very generic sense, as with trade unions and employer associations, but they grew on very different soil, in traditional societies that existed before capitalism, and shaped its local development. The employment relationship is a useful ideal type to build IR around, but institutions are the historical forces that pour life into it. (Ackers 2005: 540)

The link between institutions and matters of an underlying sociological currency find expression in two avenues associated with contemporaneous IR analysis. The first is in the attempt to reconstitute IR institutionalism under the rubric of 'neo-pluralism'. Initiated by Ackers (2002), neo-pluralism has sought to reconnect institutionalist analysis with traditions of sociological functionalism and the search for social order. This work has sought to move the trajectory of institutional pluralism away from its presumed associations with some strain of conflict theory towards an appreciation of its normative and functionalist heritage. Notably, Durkheim again reappears as the underlying sociological foundations. Although the neo-pluralist architecture deliberately traces its legacy to the Oxford School, the aforementioned thesis of the radical-institutionalists, linking the problem of order at the workplace to wider societal conditions, is perhaps the more natural intellectual antecedent for aspects of this thesis. Ackers (2002: 5), in particular, refers to the 'the wider economic and social dynamics of society' and the need to consider the 'new problem of order' as evident in the destabilizing effects of social discord, rampant individualism, and unregulated market forces on IR and its institutions. The disordering effects of neo-liberalism are seen to pervade the whole of society and then recoil back on to the employment relationship. Where neo-pluralism diverges from the sociological lineage in IR is in its scepticism towards what it perceives as the ahistoricism, and generality of, the employment relationship (Ackers 2012: 5–11). Arguably this scepticism appears ensconced in ideological as much as analytical concerns about the real-world implications of 'Marxian sociology' and a normative preference for Popperian piecemeal social engineering (Ackers and Wilkinson 2008: 65). Many of the neo-pluralist criticisms directed at radical sociology could be reconciled into an empirical and historically institutional method without absence of policy implication (for a classic defence of such method, see Goldthorpe 1977).

In any event the neo-pluralist argument is not incompatible with a second influential strand based around the notion of 'varieties of capitalism' (Soskice 1994; Hopner 2005). While VOC is an updated version of the aforementioned scholarship on corporatism, Wilkinson and Wood (2012) note that interest in the latter had waned as the performance of once successful economies faltered. While the focus on national institutions survived, the focus became less partisan in favouring corporatist economies over more liberalized models. Thus firms in liberal market economies were seen to have greater capacity for innovation, while in coordinated market economies, long-term high trust relations between firms' investors and employees were seen to underpin a strategy of high value added in mature manufacturing. Although this literature has originated from outside the realm of traditional IR, it has been a source of great interest to

IR scholarship. It has also served to attune the traditional IR analysis to a wider set of influences not directly linked with employment institutions. Central to the VOC analysis is that an interconnected configuration of political, economic, and social arrangements across different levels can combine to produce a range of dynamic effects such as stable and predictable patterns of social relations based on shared understandings and social compromises which lessen the effects of economic uncertainty. The degree of 'fit' between institutional and productive structures, themselves a product of past economic specialization, social traditions, and political choices, is seen to be important.

It is not surprising that the VOC literature has held such appeal to contemporary IR institutionalists trained in the aforementioned classical school of 'Berkeley–Harvard' or 'Oxford'. In many respects the VOC approach partly resonates with the earlier endeavours of the IR institutionalists. Like classical IR, the VOC literature lays emphasis on the integrated and mutually reinforcing character of different system elements. Similarly, institutions are seen to play a central role in creating particularized and regularized patterns. However, unlike Dunlop's system or Clegg's study of collective bargaining, the VOC literature extends beyond the sphere of IR narrowly construed. Thus it is not collective bargaining that has central functionality, but typically the organization of the business system as a whole. Similarly VOC has fallen foul of many of the same criticisms previously levelled by radical critics of institutional IR. The most obvious is the accusation of a revived functionalism, given that much like the Dunlopian approach, actors merely enact the roles required of them by 'the system' (Crouch 2005). Noteworthy too is that the emphasis on 'institutional complementarities' and 'isomorphic processes' in the VOC literature has often been held to downgrade elements of national systems that do not fit the core characteristics of the model. This hearkens back to radical criticisms around classical IR for privileging sources of stability and order rather than conflict and change and the need for considering contradiction and complexity in appropriate frameworks. Both the classical institutional pluralists and the VOC approach, with their emphasis on synergies between institutions, have tended to run shy of such factors. In this regard, it might be said that later theoretical innovations in IR, like the American strategic choice approach, are perhaps superior (Kochan et al. 1986). This at least offers scope for conflictual agency, through the lens of ideology and values, which provides opportunities for managers to actively circumvent and transform institutional pressures to suit their own ends.

Yet despite criticisms of VOC, it has chimed with the radical strain of IR analysis which has sought to embed institutions in 'the wider society'. The adoption of VOC into the IR fold has served to erode the boundary between IR and other fields of analysis, a key goal of the old IR radicals, and situates IR as an integral part of a national business system rather than as a distinct sub-system sufficient unto itself as the classical institutional-pluralists sought. Thus, the impact of business financing and corporate governance on IR has been one fruitful outcome of this integration (Gospel and Pendleton 2003). In other ways too, the VOC literature has perhaps reinvigorated the classical institutional ardour to civilize the market order (Flanders 1970). Particularly for IR institutionalists in liberalized settings, there is evidence that alternative types of capitalism, more amenable to workers' concerns or which sponsor less conflictual work-places, have been attractive (Adams 1995). Institutions like German works councils for example have been acknowledged as one reformist vehicle to fashion 'mutual gains' in liberal market economies.

Similarly, while the language of Durkheim is not immediately present in the VOC literature, there is resonance with the aforementioned radical Durkheimian analysis on the need for integration across a number of levels to alleviate anomic mal-integration (Durkheim 1959: 30–1). Specifically, minimizing the three types of anomie which Durkheim held to be predominant in laissez-faire markets required mutually reinforc-ing initiatives to introduce order into economic life. Although the language is frequently opaque, the task of 'moralizing' economic relationships, even if a principled distribution of rewards could be established, was for Durkheim unlikely to be accomplished unless the economic system as a whole was rationally regulated. Organic solidarity at the work-place was unlikely to occur unless work was perceived to be a purposeful part of the whole, and this was unlikely to occur unless the wider economic system was perceived in some sense as 'rational' and 'ordered'.

There is also a broader alignment with existing IR concerns around the structuring of national employment relations systems and their capacity for generating equitable and socially just outcomes and the Durkheimian thesis on the anomic consequences of the division of labour, laissez-faireism, and the atomistic individualism of liberal market societies. For example, evidence would suggest that workers in Nordic countries have greater job autonomy and discretion than workers in the liberal market economies of the United States, Canada, and Australia. It appears that where national systems are oriented towards rule-governed work, job discretion will be low, whereas those sys-tems oriented to skill-governed work, tend to demonstrate higher levels of autonomy (Dobbin and Boychuk 1999; Gallie 2007). Furthermore, liberal market economies tend, *ceteris paribus*, to be more vulnerable to severe economic shock and downturn (Reich 2009). Not only do liberal market economies produce more income inequality but they tend to be 'socially dysfunctional' across a number of outcomes in terms of more teen-age pregnancies, lower literacy scores, more obesity, worse mental health, more crime and higher proportions of the population incarcerated in prisons (Wilkinson and Pickett 2009). An aside to this is that there is some evidence to suggest that levels of trust between members of the public are lower in countries where income differences are larger (Ulsaner 2002). People trust each other most in what are frequently termed the 'collectivist' Scandinavian countries, while in those termed 'individualist' countries, like the United States, trust is found to be much lower: a trend replicated internally, with trust being lower in those US states where income is more unequally distributed. Echoing Durkheim's (1952: 244) thesis that disorganized economies 'rouse appetites' and excessive acquisitiveness, recent evidence suggests that there are linkages between income disparities and economic crisis: huge gaps in income create perverse incentives that put national economies at risk (Rajan 2010). The source of the global financial crisis of 2008 is an exemplar of this, partly resulting from those at the bottom of the income ladder indulging in cheap credit and home equity loans in order to maintain their stagnating living standards, while those at the top have excess surpluses invested in risky mortgage-backed securities and credit derivatives for quick profit. The anomic consequences of this inequality in income, long rumbling beneath the surface, became most plain with the collapse of the mortgage industry but also in the social riots and unrest that have spread across the West in recent years. In this regard, the previous concerns of the Durkheimian imbued IR sociology appear dated in form but not content: 'privatised Keynesianism' (Crouch 2012), itself a product of the neo-liberal organization of employment, rather than striking unions and inflation, has become the new source of disorder.

CONCLUSION

Institutions and their impacts have remained central to IR analysis, with many of the more influential accounts on institutional effects being imbued with a broadly functionalist flavour. That is, institutions, and their effects, have been traditionally interpreted in terms of their capacity to generate or maintain 'order' or stability in the employment relationship. Institutions have been viewed as playing a particular role in ensuring interest group exchanges do not break down or descend into conflagration. Of course, institutions were not privileged exclusively because they secured 'order': stability was only of interest to the institutionalist insofar as it preserved what were perceived to be the best features of the democratic polity. In this regard, the institutionalist IR project was a normative device even if it sought to occasionally cloak such influences in the language of sceptical empiricism (cf. Clegg 1975). As such it is difficult to discount the idea that a strong influence in the construction of the institutionalist tradition was opposition to the perceived totalitarianism of communism as much as it was a commitment to liberal or social democracy. Sociologically then, it is no surprise that these scholars sought explanatory tools in the functionalist sociology of Talcott Parsons in the USA and Émile Durkheim in Britain. As interpretative frameworks of industrial society, both sought to understand how interest groups, competing over scarce resources, might be integrated into cohesive social institutions that would avoid the worst excesses of 'disorder'. Yet such discourse became decidedly unfashionable in the academy by the 1970s, as various forms of radical and conflict-orientated social theories emerged, notably in the form of Marxism. At the same time, the Durkheimian associations within IR analysis were not entirely sidelined. The search for 'high trust' workplaces remained evident (Fox 1974), but this was embedded in a broader awareness of the limitations of institutional reform at workplace or even industry level. 'Anomie' at this level was held insurmountable in the face of the wider disordering effects resulting from social inequalities and laissez-faire market societies and their associated possessive individualism. These were structural rather than institutional problems. Although a well-regarded thesis of disorder, it was, however, never entirely of the mainstream. Rather the trajectory of IR analysis in the subsequent years of the monetarist counter-revolution was institutional empiricism, economics, or partial integration into the new field of HRM. Institutions at national level, particularly in corporatist arrangements, became a source of interest in seeking out organized responses to stagflationary crisis. Yet institutional IR has over time proven relatively durable. The conceptual importance of the employment relationship and the regulatory institutions that surround this dynamic have been maintained. While in some quarters this has continued to be shaped more by Marx and the materialist labour process (Edwards 2003; Blyton and Turnbull 2004), Durkheimian functionalism has explicitly re-emerged in a strain of neo-pluralism (Ackers 2002). While the former in particular has sought to trace a link back to the Durkheimianism of the Oxford School, by noting the problem of order not just in the workplace, but in the wider relationship between work and society, it is, analytically, if not normatively, closer to the sociological radicalism of Fox, Goldthorpe, and Gilbert. Although long recognized in Durkheimian sociology, and evident in the radical-institutionalist analysis of IR, the link between work and the wider institutional configuration of market societies is now centrally recognized through the influence of the VOC approach. While the VOC literature emerged autonomously from classical IR, there are, as noted, many areas of intellectual similarity. It also points to key lessons for the mainstream institutionalist tradition of IR. In being cognizant of wider societal context, by implication it would suggest that the inherent reformist inclinations of the institutionalist tradition must be willing to consider, in the words of Fox (1985a: 171), a wider 'assault on gross inequalities of wealth, income and privilege' if the contemporary disorder afflicting many contemporary liberalized market societies is to be adequately addressed.

Acknowledgement

I would like to thank the editors for helpful comments and guidelines on an earlier draft of this chapter.

References

Ackers, P. (2002). 'Reframing Employment Relations: The Case for Neo-Pluralism', *Industrial Relations Journal*, 33(1): 2–19.

—— (2005). 'Theorizing the Employment Relationship: Materialists and Institutionalists', *British Journal of Industrial Relations*, 43(3): 537–42.

—— (2011). 'The Changing System of British Industrial Relations, 1954–1979: Hugh Clegg and the Warwick Sociological Turn', *British Journal of Industrial Relations*, 49(2): 306–30.

—— (2012). 'Rethinking the Employment Relationship: Neo-Pluralist Critique of British Industrial Relations Orthodoxy', *International Journal of Human Resource Management*, iFirst: 1–18.

Ackers, P. and Wilkinson, A. (2008). 'Industrial Relations and the Social Sciences', in P. Blyton, N. Bacon, J. Fiorito, and E. Heery (eds.), *The Sage Handbook of Industrial Relations*. London: Sage, 53–69.

Adams, R. J. (1995). *Industrial Relations Under Liberal Democracy: North America in Comparative Perspective*. Columbia, SC: University of South Carolina Press.

Aldridge, A. (1976). *Power, Authority and Restrictive Practices*. Oxford: Blackwell.

Allen, V. I. (1971). *The Sociology of Industrial Relations*. London: Longman.

Armstrong, P., Glyn, A., and Harrison, J. (1984). *Capitalism Since World War II: The Making and Breakup of the Great Boom*. London: Fontana.

Blyton, P. and Turnbull, P. (2004). *The Dynamics of Employee Relations*. Basingstoke: Palgrave Macmillan.

Braverman, H. (1974). *Labor and Monopoly Capital: The Degradation of Work in the Twentieth Century*. New York: Monthly Review Press.

Clegg, H. A. (1960). *A New Approach to Industrial Democracy*. Oxford: Blackwell.

—— (1975). 'Pluralism in Industrial Relations', *British Journal of Industrial Relations*, 13(1): 309–16.

—— (1976). *Trade Unionism Under Collective Bargaining*. Oxford: Blackwell.

—— (1979). *The Changing System of Industrial Relations in Great Britain*. Oxford: Blackwell.

Coates, D. (ed.) (2005). *Varieties of Capitalism, Varieties of Approach*. Basingstoke: Palgrave Macmillan.

Commons, J. R. (1950). *The Economics of Collective Action*. New York: Macmillan.

Crouch, C. (2005). 'Models of Capitalism', *New Political Economy*, 10(4): 441–56.

—— (2012). 'Beyond the Flexibility/Security Trade Off: Reconciling Confident Consumers with Insecure Workers', *British Journal of Industrial Relations*, 50(1): 1–22.

Dahl, R. (1958). 'A Critique of the Ruling Elite Model', *American Political Science Review*, 52(2): 463–9.

Dahrendorf, R. (1959). *Class and Class Conflict*. London: Routledge & Kegan Paul.

Dobbin, F. and Boychuk, T. (1999). 'National Employment Systems and Job Autonomy: Why Job Autonomy is High in the Nordic Countries and Low in the United States, Canada and Australia', *Organization Studies*, 20(2): 257–91.

Domhoff, G. W. (1967). *Who Rules America?* Englewood Cliffs, NJ: Prentice Hall.

Dunlop, J. T. (1958). *Industrial Relations Systems*. New York: Henry Holt and Co.

Durkheim, E. (1952). *Suicide*. London: Routledge.

—— (1959). *Socialism*. London: Routledge.

—— (1982). *The Rules of Sociological Method*. New York: Free Press.

—— (1984). *The Division of Labour in Society*. New York: Free Press.

Edwards, P. K. (2003). 'The Employment Relationship and the Field of Industrial Relations', in Edwards (ed.), *Industrial Relations: Theory & Practice*. Oxford: Blackwell, 1–36.

Edwards, P. K. and Scullion, H. (1982). *The Social Organization of Industrial Conflict: Control and Resistance in the Workplace*. Oxford: Blackwell.

Flanders, A. (1964). *The Fawley Productivity Agreements*. London: Faber.

—— (1970). *Management and Unions*. London: Faber.

Flanders, A. and Clegg, H. A. (eds.) (1954). *The System of Industrial Relations in Great Britain*. Oxford: Blackwell.

Fox, A. (1971). *A Sociology of Work in Industry*. London: Collier-Macmillan.

—— (1973). 'Industrial Relations: A Social Critique of Pluralist Ideology', in J. Child (ed.), *Man and Organization*. London: George Allen & Unwin, 185–233.

—— (1974). *Beyond Contract: Work, Power and Trust Relations*. London: Faber and Faber.

—— (1985a). *Man Mismanagement*. London: Hutchinson.

—— (1985b). *History and Heritage*. London: George Allen & Unwin.

Fox, A. and Flanders, A. (1969). 'The Reform of Collective Bargaining: From Durkheim to Donovan', *British Journal of Industrial Relations*, 7(2): 151–80.

Frege, C. M. and Kelly, J. (eds.) (2004). *Varieties of Unionism: Strategies for Union Revitalization in a Globalizing Economy*. Oxford: Oxford University Press.

Gallie, D. (2007). 'Welfare Regimes, Employment Systems and Job Preference Orientations', *European Sociological Review*, 23(3): 279–93.

Giddens, A. (1984). *The Constitution of Society*. Cambridge: Polity Press.

Gilbert, M. (1978). 'Neo-Durkheimian Analyses of Economic Life and Strife: From Durkheim to the Social Contract', *Sociological Review*, 26: 729–54.

—— (1986). *Inflation and Social Conflict*, Sussex: Wheatsheaf Books.

Glyn, A. and Sutcliffe, R. B. (1972). *British Capitalism, Workers and the Profit Squeeze*. London: Penguin.

Godard, J. (1994). 'Beyond Empiricism: Towards a Reconstruction of IR Theory and Research', *Advances in Industrial and Labor Relations*, 6(1): 1–35.

—— (2004). 'The New Institutionalism, Capitalist Diversity and Industrial Relations', in B. E. Kaufman (ed.) *Theoretical Perspectives on Work and the Employment Relationship*. Ithaca: Cornell University Press, 229–64.

Goldthorpe, J. H. (1969). 'Social Inequality and Social Integration in Modern Britain', *Advancement of Science*, 26: 190–202.

—— (1975). 'Book Reviews: Beyond Contract', *British Journal of Industrial Relations*, 13(1): 135–48.

—— (1977). 'Industrial Relations in Great Britain: A Critique of Reformism', in T. Clarke and L. Clements (eds.), *Trade Unions Under Capitalism*. London: Fontana, 184–224.

—— (1978). 'The Current Inflation: Towards a Sociological Account', in F. Hirsch and J. H. Goldthorpe (eds.), *The Political Economy of Inflation*. London: Martin Robertson, 186–214.

—— (1984). 'The End of Convergence: Corporatist and Dualist Tendencies in Modern Western Societies', in Goldthorpe (ed.), *Order and Conflict in Contemporary Capitalism*. Oxford: Clarendon Press, 315–43.

Goldthorpe, J. H., Lockwood, D., Bechhofer, F., and Platt, J. (1968). *The Affluent Worker: Industrial Attitudes and Behaviour*. Cambridge: Cambridge University Press.

Gospel, H. and Pendleton, A. (2003). 'Finance, Corporate Governance and the Management of Labour: A Conceptual and Comparative Analysis', *British Journal of Industrial Relations*, 41(3): 557–82.

Gouldner, A. W. (1971). *The Coming Crisis of Western Sociology*. London: Heinemann.

Heery, E. (2008). 'System and Change in Industrial Relations Analysis', in P. Blyton, N. Bacon, J. Fiorito, and Heery (eds.), *The Sage Handbook of Industrial Relations*. London: Sage, 69–91.

Herding, R. (1972). *Job Control and Union Structure*. Rotterdam: Rotterdam University Press.

Hopner, M. (2005). 'What Connects Industrial Relations and Corporate Governance? Explaining Institutional Complementarity', *Socio-Economic Review*, 3(2): 331–58.

Howell, C. (2003). 'Varieties of Capitalism: And Then There Was One?', *Comparative Politics*, 36(1): 103–24.

Hyman, R. (1975). *Industrial Relations: A Marxist Introduction*. London: Macmillan.

—— (2004). 'Is Industrial Relations Theory Always Ethnocentric?', in B. E. Kaufman (ed.), *Theoretical Perspectives on Work and the Employment Relationship*. Ithaca: Cornell University Press, 265–92.

Jackson, G. and Muellenborn, T. (2012). 'Understanding the Role of Institutions in Industrial Relations: Perspectives from Classical Sociological Theory', *Industrial Relations*, 51(1): 472–500.

Kaufman, B. (2004). *The Global Evolution of Industrial Relations*. Geneva: ILO.

Kelly, J. (1998). *Rethinking Industrial Relations: Mobilization, Collectivism and Long Waves*. London: Routledge.

—— (2010). *Ethical Socialism and the Trade Unions: Allan Flanders and British Industrial Relations Reform*. London: Routledge.

Kerr, C. (1964). 'Industrial Relations and the Liberal Pluralist', in C. Kerr (ed.), *Labour and Management in Industrial Society*. New York: Anchor, 8–14.

Kerr, C., Dunlop, J. T., Harbison, F. H., and Myers, C. A. (1973). *Industrialism and Industrial Man*. London: Penguin.

Kochan, T. A., Katz, H. C., and McKersie, R. (1986). *The Transformation of American Industrial Relations*. New York: Basic Books.

Lockwood, D. (1993). *Solidarity and Schism: The Problem of Disorder in Durkheimian and Marxist Sociology*. Oxford: Oxford University Press.

Martin, R. (1999). 'Mobilization Theory: A New Paradigm for Industrial Relations', *Human Relations*, 52(9): 1205–16.

Nichols, T. and Beynon, H. (1977). *Living With Capitalism: Class Relations and the Modern Factory*. London: Routledge & Kegan Paul.

Parsons, T. (1951). *The Social System*. Chicago: Free Press.

—— (1968). *The Structure of Social Action*, Volume II. Chicago: Free Press.

Perlman, S. (1928). *A Theory of the Labor Movement*. Philadelphia: Porcupine.

Poole, M. (1981). *Theories of Trade Unionism: A Sociology of Industrial Relations*. London: Routledge & Kegan Paul.

Rajan, R. (2010). *Fault Lines: How Hidden Fractures Still Threaten the World Economy*. Princeton: Princeton University Press.

Reich, M. (2009). 'The Current Crisis of Capitalism: Insights from Social Structure of Accumulation Theory', paper presented to the Annual Meeting of SASE Conference, Paris, July.

Schmitter, P. C. (1974). 'Still the Century of Corporatism?', *Review of Politics*, 36(1): 85–131.

Scott, W. R. (2001). *Institutions and Organizations*. Thousand Oaks, CA: Sage.

Soskice, D. (1994). 'Reconciling Markets and Institutions: The German Apprenticeship System', in L. Lynch (ed.), *Training and the Private Sector: International Comparisons*. Chicago: University of Chicago Press, NBER Conference Volume, 25–60.

Terry, M. and Edwards, P. K. (1988). *Shopfloor Politics and Job Controls: The Post-War Engineering Industry*. Oxford: Blackwell.

Thompson, P. (1983). *The Nature of Work: An Introduction to Debates on the Labour Process*. Basingstoke: Macmillan.

Ulsaner, E. M. (2002). *The Moral Foundations of Trust*. Cambridge: Cambridge University Press.

Webb, S. and Webb, B. (1920). *Industrial Democracy*. London: Longman.

Wilkinson, A. and Wood, G. (2012). 'Institutions and Employment Relations: The State of the Art', *Industrial Relations*, 51(1): 373–88.

Wilkinson, R. and Pickett, K. (2009). *The Spirit Level: Why Equality is Better for Everyone*. London: Penguin.

Wood, S. (2000). 'The BJIR and Industrial Relations in the New Millennium', *British Journal of Industrial Relations*, 38(1): 1–5.

CHAPTER 11

···

CONFLICT, ORDER, AND CHANGE

···

FRANCO BARCHIESI

INTRODUCTION: CAPITALISM, CRISIS, AND THE PROBLEM OF HISTORICAL CHANGE IN EMPLOYMENT RELATIONS

DURING the last two decades of the twentieth century and at the beginning of the twenty-first, a major theme in the scholarship on employment relations has been the global decline of organized labour and workers' protections. Empirical studies have identified several concomitant factors as possible causes. Trade liberalization and the globalization of investment flows have placed new pressures on enterprises. Governmental policies and reforms proposed by international organizations have shifted towards 'market regulation' (Standing 1997; Esping-Andersen and Regini 2000), which subordinates interest representation and societal mediations to the need of attracting transnational investments and augmenting corporate competitiveness. The new global climate has benefited employers, who have aggressively advanced organizational and technological restructuring that sidesteps trade unions through the individualized setting of wages and working conditions and management-initiated participation schemes (Deery and Mitchell 1999). Firm strategies geared to greater flexibility in functions and headcounts have fragmented workplace-based collective identities and helped the proliferation of temporary and contingent jobs (Streeck 1987). Finally, labour market changes have facilitated the expansion of flexible occupations as the youth and growing numbers of women entering employment often prefer schedules that allow a better balancing of work with specific everyday life obligations (Kalleberg 2000; Lombard 2001; Blossfeld et al. 2008).

In a variety of national employment relations contexts, the balance of power has shifted in favour of employers to an extent that questions the institutional location of organized labour. The process presents important theoretical challenges. The institutionalization of trade unions at various levels of bargaining was in fact not only central to the experience of post-war industrial capitalism but also provided a central tenet for the study of industrial and employment relations. John Dunlop's (1958) pioneering work proposed that interactions among key actors—employers, workers, and government— be structured around systems of tripartite bargaining geared to consent. Subsequent contributions, influenced by modernization theory (Kerr et al. 1960) or pluralist paradigms of interest intermediation (Barbash 1984), added temporal dynamism to Dunlop's static institutional analysis (see also Müller-Jentsch 2004: 15). The emerging consensus praised the capacity of industrial relations systems to recognize the legitimacy of contesting interests and achieve mutual trust as workers relinquished claims to workplace control and managers abandoned unilateral decision-making (Fox 1974). Such views presented order as the virtuous outcome of societal interactions, regarded conflict as a pathology to be minimized, and understood change as a process of adaptation and convergence of diverse cultural, social, and political national realities around the imperatives of productive efficiency.

The theoretical framework of early industrial relations theories reflected policy approaches and institutional arrangements variously influenced in Western economies by Fordist productivity pacts, Taylorist rationalization of production, Keynesian demand-driven approaches to growth, and welfarist macro-social compacts. All these elements underpinned the expectation that trade unions could be incorporated, without losing their independence as representatives of the working class, in the management of capitalist systems. It was, in a sense, the culmination of policy debates that since the late nineteenth century had accompanied the access of the working class to political rights and representation. Ruling elites have in fact faced the problem of how to channel labour's political power away from demands and mobilizations that threatened the established order of things (Flora and Heidenheimer 1981). As major capitalist economies experienced a prolonged crisis in the 1970s, the recognition by scholars and policy-makers that actors in production have legitimate, diverse, and independent interests opened the way to neo-corporatist approaches, which aspired to a joint management of capitalist crises through societal bargaining, mediated by state institutions, between strongly organized workers' and employers' constituencies (Korpi 1983; Rothstein 1987).

The return to growth in capitalist countries passed therefore through processes of institutionalization of class conflict that foreground the crucial importance of employment relations. It is in this sphere, Gøsta Esping-Andersen (1990) insisted, that working-class consent is elicited through different 'welfare regimes' that 'decommodify' labour by reducing the vulnerabilities arising from market relationships. He famously defined three regimes of social protection—which include unemployment insurance, retirement provisions, and public assistance—that are highly contingent upon specific trajectories of class struggle, party alignments, ideological frameworks, and juridical traditions. The 'liberal' regime, evident in the United States, the United Kingdom, and 'Anglo-Saxon' capitalism broadly understood, amounts to a limited decommodification through residual and strongly selective social provisions. The 'corporatist' regimes of much of continental Europe envisage robust systems of social protection whose decommodifying potential depends on occupational status and agreements in specific industries. The 'social democratic' regimes prevalent in Scandinavian countries have decommodifying policies that stress redistribution and universalism rather than the capacity of different occupational categories to negotiate benefits within their sector.

In the 1970s radical critics, often inspired by Marxism, started to target early industrial relations theory. Richard Hyman (1975) attacked pluralist paradigms that promoted tripartite consensus, accusing them of normatively assuming that capital and labour share in the final analysis similar or complementary goals. As an alternative he proposed a view of capitalist relations of employment as inherently unstable, whereas change is the product of struggles constantly arising from a reality of domination in which employees contest their employers' determination of rules on workplace interactions, working conditions, and work effort. Rather than being a pathological and undesirable outgrowth, conflict is for Hyman both an obvious result of the existing socio-economic order and the propulsive force for its transformation.

Further impetus to radical approaches was provided in the 1970s by studies on the capitalist labour process following Harry Braverman's classic *Labor and Monopoly Capital* (1974). Labour process theory aimed to provide a comprehensive method for the study of work, breaking the disciplinary barriers that separated labour sociology, organization studies, and industrial relations. The Taylorist workplace was for most labour process scholars a contested terrain defined by shifting boundaries of control over job design, systems of remuneration, authority, and skills. They saw managerial rationalization and bureaucratization as ways to fragment and deskill production tasks so that corporate rationality could appropriate the employees' knowledge while minimizing possibilities for collective resistance and workers' control (Thompson 1989). An important result of labour process debates was to transcend polarized alternatives that in industrial relations literature had opposed 'unitarist' perspectives prioritizing managerial prerogatives to 'pluralists'—focused on the convergence of workers' and employers' distinct interests— and 'radicals', which stressed the ultimate antagonism of capital and labour. Instead, labour process theory came to see workers' subjectivity on the one hand as an autonomous repository of demands—workplace control, autonomy, job security—essentially incompatible with capitalist authority. On the other hand, however, such demands and their ensuing conflicts could be harnessed into what Edwards (1986) called 'structured antagonisms', meaning that corporate bureaucracies could give selected groups of 'core' workers autonomy and stable employment to enable cooperation and interdependence, which are also constantly subject to conflict and renegotiation.

Marxist-inspired analyses thus grappled with conflict in multifaceted ways, seeing in it a force that simultaneously threatens capitalist accumulation but could also be turned through appropriate mixes of organizational, technological, ideological, and legal interventions into a source of support for accumulation. They concomitantly ceased to represent the profit motive as the sole engine of the labour process, which crucially came to rely on inherently unstable, conflict-prone strategies to elicit workers' consent.

Michael Burawoy (1985) offered important radical insights into work and the labour process with his sequential framework based on the succession of 'regimes' of production. Burawoy's analysis transcended the boundaries of the workplace by placing the labour process within complex interactions underpinned by socio-economic policies and state-supported social wage. Institutional interventions thus facilitate workers' consent and the legitimacy of the capitalist workplace discipline. Fordist mass production represented for Burawoy a shift towards a 'hegemonic' production regime that reproduced managerial authority through social provisions and consumerism, which replaced the despotic employers' unilateralism during early industrialization. State policies took care of removing the reproduction of the working class from the domain of inherently exploitative and precarious wage relations. Far from being a merely superstructural element, politics is for Burawoy essentially implicated in the labour process, defining it as a terrain of workers' claims and cooperation out of which some degree of stability can emerge to assuage a conflict-ridden capitalist system. Post-Fordist liberalization constitutes instead a new phase where the negotiated consent of hegemonic Fordism comes under attack as employers roll back workers' collective power and the state subordinates social inclusion to the private sector's competitive success rather than tying it to redistributive interventions. The hegemony of corporate values is therefore reproduced through the aggressive and authoritarian imposition of market discipline, which Burawoy terms 'hegemonic despotism'.

Following the resurgence of Marxist studies of work and industrial relations, theorists who rejected radical anti-capitalism became nonetheless more attentive to the impacts of economic uncertainty and started to emphasize change and adaptation in industrial relations rather than order and stability. Debates in the 1980s and early 1990s echoed the rise of neo-liberalism as a globally hegemonic paradigm in economic and social policy as well as sociological concerns with a shift to post-Fordism and post-industrialism in older capitalist democracies and emerging East Asian economies. Part of that intellectual conversation, which was connected to broader meditations on 'globalization' and 'lean production', was a growing awareness that Western Europe and North America were deindustrializing. The shrinkage of historically unionized working classes and the growth of service sectors hiring large numbers of women and youth in 'flexible' employment contracts accompanied and encouraged the replacement of 'industrial relations' with 'employment relations' in academic parlance. The works of Kochan et al. (1986) and Locke et al. (1995) marked the inclusion of globalization as a crucial problem for employment relations scholarship (see also Kaufman 2011: 20–2). Their emphasis was on managerial strategy and choice, which they regarded as both embedded in legal, cultural, and socio-economic contexts as well as evolving in response to changing global competitive scenarios, comparative advantages, and environmental uncertainties. As the power of employers grew within neo-liberal settings, these scholars turned their attention to the decline of established patterns of trade union representation and collective bargaining.

Locke et al. (1995), in particular, regarded firm-level decision-making as the core driver of change in employment relations. The imperatives of adjusting to the pressures of the global economy resulted for them in the adoption of flexible productive and working arrangements that facilitate the decentralization of collective bargaining and a growing individualization of relationships between employers and employees. Flexible remunerations are particularly decisive to nurture and reward critical skills. Locke and colleagues finally envisaged two alternative ways for pursuing competitive advantage: a 'low road'—centred on cost reduction, managerial unilateralism, adversarialism between labour and capital, and the erosion of job security—and a 'high road' prioritizing value added, labour–capital cooperation, and employees' participation. Organized labour's potential for change was thus diverted from class conflict towards a definition of the unions' role as partners in human resource management, which is conducive to a 'win–win' high-road performance. The 'high road' concept proved hugely influential among those labour scholars who foresaw in the unions' embrace of workplace cooperation and flexible employment an opportunity for a worker-friendly globalization. For them the 'functional' flexibility of multi-skilled, highly motivated, career-orientated workers could counterbalance pressures towards a merely 'numerical' flexibility premised on multi-tasked, disposable, casualized employees.

Sceptics of the 'high road' approach have problematized its ambition to draw universal prescriptions. For Müller-Jentsch (2004: 22–3) the focus on managerial strategic choice in Kochan et al. (1986) is in fact deeply steeped in ideas, typical of English-speaking countries, of minimal state intervention, workplace-centred industrial relations, dominance of human resource functions, and individual contracts. They would, conversely, underestimate the relevance of institutional actors, broad societal compacts, and policy differences, which are important factors of change in the employment relations systems of continental Europe (see Albert 1993).

Opponents of capitalism were meanwhile also busy conceptualizing the rise of neo-liberalism as a long-term historical shift. In the 1970s the 'regulation school' had updated the Marxian approach to capitalist crises and restructuring through a periodization based on 'regimes of accumulation' and 'modes of regulation'. The former defined the organization of production, social wage, distribution, and consumption, while the latter identified the concomitant institutional settings, legal paradigms, and policy frameworks. Following Alain Lipietz's analysis of Fordism, the regulation school had seen in the arrangements of post-war industrial capitalism the triumph of what Robert Boyer termed a 'monopolist mode of regulation' revolving around mass production and Keynesian demand management, welfare states and productivity deals (Boyer 1990). The liberalization of trade and investment in the context of the 1970s economic slowdown and 'stagflation' had announced a new age of globalization by reasserting the prerogatives of management in response to workers' wage demands. As a consequence, Keynesian compacts, crucially premised on collective bargaining and the inclusion of trade unions in the formulation of income policies, had become dysfunctional to accumulation. Neo-liberal policies, automated technologies, and lean production thus announced, according to regulationists, the advent of post-Fordism.

Bob Jessop (2001: xiii) has stressed that the initial interest of the regulation approach was in 'how long waves of capitalist expansion and contraction are mediated through particular institutions and practices which modify the general laws and crisis tendencies of capitalism'. It was, in other words, a theory of capitalist change that bridged the gap between empirical descriptions of localized historical processes and a general conceptualization of the movements and phases that characterize capitalism as a system. To that end, regulationists emphasized the importance of social actors, interactions, and institutions to explain change in a non-determinist way, as the result of experimentations, trials, and errors, which nonetheless congealed into relatively coherent 'modes of regulation' capable of turning economic crises and market disequilibria into the growth phase of a new 'wave'. It was a view deeply influenced by theorists of capital accumulation as a wave-like dynamics, not only Marx as a precursor but also Antonio Gramsci, Joseph Schumpeter, and Karl Polanyi. Long waves, Jessop continues, provided a crucial tool to early regulationist analyses. They are as such distinguished from 'long cycles', which respond to single causal mechanisms while long waves place multiple causes, complex interactions, contestations, and indeterminacy as core explanatory categories for temporal change.

In their later debates, regulationists recognized that the complexities and local variations of Fordist crises defy a rigid periodization based on the Fordism/post-Fordism dichotomy. Rather than assuming post-Fordism as inevitable, they thus became more interested in the factors that shaped or delayed the post-Fordist transition, not only in older industrial countries but also in East Asia, Latin America, and South Africa. The regulation approach therefore addressed the study of conflict, order, and change towards explaining spatial discrepancies and convergences between capitalisms or the articulation of different scales—local, regional, and national—within capitalisms.

The regulation approach maintained nonetheless that neo-liberalism was a significantly new mode of regulation, which advanced a type of state intervention that Jessop called 'Schumpeterian workfare state' (Jessop 2002; see also Peck 2001), based on cutbacks of public programmes, the removal of employees' statutory protections, and a growing emphasis on individual initiative in the labour market as conditions to access social benefits and public safety nets. Somewhat related to these discussions were the contributions of labour process and employment relations scholars influenced by Michel Foucault. They saw in neo-liberalism a transformation in the way power is exercised in capitalist societies, whereby employees are required to become what Foucault termed 'entrepreneurs of the self', or agents for whom the alignment of individual choice with corporate requirements for human capital is the main avenue to socio-economic inclusion (Knights 1989; Clegg 1994). In a different vein, postmodernists detected in the individualization of employment relations and the fragmentation of workers' identities evidence of a broader decay of collective solidarities premised on the class politics of social transformation (Hancock and Tyler 2001). Underpinning those debates was the sense that a decisive discontinuity was taking place from industrialism to a 'post-industrial' society characterized not merely by market liberalization and the erosion of workers' power but also by a reorientation of production towards knowledge-based activities in what Manuel Castells (2000) saw as an emerging global and networked 'information society'. Parallel to such economic and productive realignments, Castells argued, a general displacement was occurring at the level of collective identities, which moved away from class and towards social movement politics. More pessimistic views understood the decline of manufacturing and the growing importance of service sectors as paths to the proliferation of low-level, poorly paid, insecure occupations, for example in retail and restaurants (Ritzer 2000), which undermine established workers' identities in a perpetual, increasingly globalized 'race to the bottom'.

FROM HISTORICAL RUPTURES TO LONG WAVES: RETHINKING CONTINUITY AND CHANGE

In the late 1990s an important Marxist reassessment of conflict and change under capitalism responded to the sense, shared by various competing theoretical approaches, that neo-liberalism was a profound historical rupture. John Kelly (1998) rejected the idea of post-Fordism as an epoch-making, essentially new modality of industrial relations that allegedly replaces adversarialism with social partnership and collectivism with individualism in bargaining dynamics. Although he especially targeted postmodernism, his argument also clearly departs from crucial aspects of the regulation school. In general, he deprecates what he regards as the unquestioning adoption by employment relations scholars of a corporate viewpoint preoccupied with the stability of capitalism and orderly human resource management. As an alternative, Kelly reclaims a research agenda focused on conflict and power relations, which in his view underscores the continuous relevance of collectivism and labour organizing. His aim is to place recent capitalist restructuring within a long-term historical perspective, which, often neglected by advocates of post-Fordism, should instead allow a sound balance of continuities and changes. At the core of Kelly's methodology is thus the attempt to connect cycles of organized labour's activity—which he conceptualizes in terms of a 'mobilization theory' derived from the social movement studies of Charles Tilly and Doug McAdam—to long waves of economic growth and decline. He explicitly refers in this regard to the classical theorization of long waves by Nikolai Kondratieff, who saw the development of capitalism as shaped by regular, 50-year patterns, each of which were characterized by economic 'upswings' and 'downswings' of approximately equal length:

> If we assume the existence of Kondratieff long waves in the economy then it can be demonstrated that the periods of upswing and downswing correspond very closely to different patterns of industrial relations and that the turning points from one to the other are associated with dramatic changes in a series of industrial relations indicators: union membership and density, union organization, union mergers, strike activity, collective bargaining coverage and employer policies on worker participation. (Kelly 1998: 107)

Kelly's underlying assumption was that 'fluctuating fortunes of national labour movements follow predictable patterns that are closely synchronized with the rhythms of the capitalist economy' (1998: 1). As a consequence, he noticed, unionization and industrial action tend to intensify at the peak of an upswing or at the bottom of a downswing and the period of transition to a new wave. He suggested that several structural factors made such outcomes likely. For example, as the economy approaches the culmination of a period of prolonged growth, employers' profits would start to erode and companies will try to restore them in increasingly authoritarian ways, including union bashing, wage restraint, lay-offs, work intensification, and the undermining of class compromises sustaining full employment policies and the welfare state. Workers would then react to such unilateral changes with increasing grievances, which facilitate unionization. Conversely, as the economy is bottoming out after a long decline, prospects of growth, new employment, and job security would improve and opportunities for workers' organizing and mobilization would concomitantly benefit. To an extent, therefore, Kelly's use of long waves reclaimed, especially against postmodernism, the possibility of identifying general principles in the evolution of capitalism. Kelly's approach was, in this sense, consonant with the inspiration of the early regulation school. At the same time, however, the regulationists highlighted the role of uncertainty, unpredictability, and indeterminacy in their approach to long waves, which is in contrast with Kelly's (and Kondratieff's) concerns with regularity.

Kelly nonetheless wanted to avoid an excessively mechanical analysis of the relations between long waves and trade union activism. His mobilization theory emphasized that the translation of the opportunities provided by upswings and downswings into actual labour organization and mobilization depended on the unions' ability to give a collective expression to workers' grievances and sense of injustice:

> Mobilization theory argues that collective organization and activity ultimately stem from employer actions that generate amongst employees a sense of injustice or illegitimacy. Employees must also acquire a sense of common identity which differentiates them from the employer; they must attribute the perceived injustice to the employer; and they must be willing to engage in some form of collective organization and activity. This whole process of collectivization is heavily dependent on the actions of small numbers of leaders or activists. (Kelly 1998: 44)

Kelly thought that in the late 1990s global capitalism was ending its long downswing and entering a phase of transition. He thus argued that, despite the postmodernists' dismissive attitudes, 'the classical labour movement' was 'likely to be on the threshold of resurgence' (Kelly 1998: 1). But resurgence still depended in the final analysis on the unions' strategies, politics, organizing styles, and the correspondence of all this with the workers' sense of justice. Therefore the concrete modalities of the collectivism to come were ultimately unpredictable. Kelly in fact identified as a dilemma of the transition period during which he wrote the fact that a clear increase in workers' grievances in many capitalist economies did not correspond to an equally visible growth in unionization. For him, however, the decline of some forms of collectivism did not necessarily mean a trend towards the individualization of employment relations. Other collectivisms could rather emerge to counterbalance the perceived ineffectiveness of established union models and turn membership of a workers' organization into an attractive individual choice. Possibilities remained open for alternative types of unions exercising collective power in different ways:

> Unions can also be seen, however, as components of a social movement, whose aims and methods include, but are not coterminous with, collective bargaining and some of whose actions are expressive of the movement's core values and instrumental in reinforcing and winning support for those values. (Kelly 1998: 52)

Kelly's book, and its defence of a study of employment relations grounded in social conflict and historical processes, held a significant appeal, especially among critical scholars concerned that the transformation of the field of industrial relations in the early twenty-first century would lead either to its absorption into human resource management or to its subordination to institutionalist perspectives that stressed corporate stability (Ackers and Wilkinson 2003; Watson 2008: 277).

Beverly Silver (2003) also discussed, in her global analysis of workers' politics influenced by world systems theory, 'labour unrest waves' as shaping recurring patterns of capitalist globalization. In her view, labour struggles at the nation-state level tend to connect during phases of globalization, also thanks to mutually embedded dynamics of global governance, migration, and transnational division of labour. Similarly to Kelly, whom she does not cite, Silver's aim was to counter perceptions of a global decline of labour movements with a historically grounded definition of capitalist relations of production as reflecting cycles of class formation, restructuring, and resistance. Drawing on David Harvey, she questioned the idea of a 'race to the bottom' and argued that capital mobility and relocation as responses to workers' militancy in a Fordist context 'constitute[s] an attempted spatial fix for crises of profitability and control that only succeeds in rescheduling crises in time and space' (Silver 2003: 39). Silver rejected, in particular, the idea that the growing financialization of the global economy in the late twentieth century was a qualitatively new phenomenon implying a decisive and irreversible shift of power relations in favour of the employers. She rather regarded it as a replica of the growth of finance capital in the late nineteenth century under similar conditions of class conflicts. As in that age, she continued, financialization and the related undermining of workers' rights and protections would bring a crisis of legitimacy ultimately heightening the instability of capitalism. The outcomes of the current crisis are for her open-ended, but they do involve at least the possibility of a resumption of labour activism, perhaps in combination with social movements contesting global economic liberalization, as she detected with regard to the Seattle demonstrations against the World Trade Organization in 1999. Informing Silver's analysis is a view of capitalism as ultimately unable to escape the turmoil of its inherent instability, which manifests itself through increasingly dramatic, socially destructive, and politically risky cycles of crisis and restructuring. Workers' struggles would then follow what she terms waves of a 'Marx type', marked by collective organizing, solidarity, and internationalism, and 'Polanyi type' waves, reflected in claims for national and supranational regulations on capital mobility, privatization, and employment flexibility.

In the field of employment relations, as in other disciplines, the intellectual climate at the turn of the twenty-first century was, however, hardly sympathetic to ideas of recurrent capitalist crises or post-capitalist ruptures and transitions. The end of the Soviet Union and the socialist bloc, the emergence of 'communist' China as the fastest growing market economy, the liberalization of global financial flows, and rapid economic growth in the wake of new information and communication technologies had in fact made capitalism appear triumphant, marginalizing ideas of social change and alternatives. The ascent of the 'varieties of capitalism' (VOC) approach encapsulated many of these trends. Its proponents assumed capitalism to be the sole viable socio-economic system in a multipolar globalized world as well as the only possible object for 'macro' empirical social and comparative analysis. The VOC approach then recast the problematic of change into one of 'convergence' or 'divergence' among capitalisms understood as 'social systems of production' embedded in various countries' social, legal, policy, cultural, and technological characteristics. Scholars of VOC regarded the combination of corporate strategies and state interventions, rather than employees' collective initiative, as the cause of economic differentiation and change. They distinguished between national cases according to modes of business coordination: in 'liberal market economies' (LMEs) coordination takes place through liberalized markets and a 'stockholder' mode of financing, while in 'coordinated market economies' (CMEs) political institutions, national or regional social compacts, and 'stakeholder' participation play a prominent role (Hall and Soskice 2001).

The distinction between LME and CME evoked older debates on 'high' and 'low' roads. It aimed to define conditions of comparative advantage and possible scenarios of convergence or divergence based on the institutional interactions of subsystems—employment relations, finance, education, law, public policies—underpinning the respective efficiency of different systems. LMEs thus mostly rely on low production costs—which imply weak unions and an emphasis on easy hiring and firing—and continuous innovation, while CMEs display a greater dependence on value added, training, job security, and workers' participation. In this perspective, even if the CME evokes the 'high road' idea, moving from one type to another is hampered by the stickiness of ingrained cultural and institutional traditions, which in the end determine the nature and persistence of employment relations models (Müller-Jentsch 2004: 18).

Critical appraisals of the 'varieties of capitalism' paradigm rejected its static framework of analysis and its neglect of social conflict and power relations as factors of change. Müller-Jentsch's (2004: 26–9) 'extended (actor-centred) institutional approach' takes aim at the institutionalist bias in the 'varieties of capitalism', which, as a variant of what he terms a 'governance approach', is obsessed with the normative preoccupation of maintaining and reproducing order. For Müller-Jentsch, instead, institutions—which include employment contracts, labour markets, collective bargaining, workplace rules, and human resource management—are not so much the product of rational choices and strategies but the outcome of the exercise of power by conflicting actors. As they become self-reproducing through path dependency in the form of ideologies, norms, traditions, and culture, institutions operate as 'arenas' where conflicts are continuously enacted and mediated. Order crucially depends in the end, according to Müller-Jentsch, on the ability of the state to govern conflicts by fragmenting and decentralizing arenas, for example by separating collective bargaining from macroeconomic policy, so that actors opposed in one arena can cooperate in another, thereby finding some sort of interdependence that does not threaten the system. Order is therefore always the contingent outcome of negotiations among actors—especially employers and workers—with divergent interests and asymmetrical resources. An understanding of employment relations as an essentially conflictual ambit is, conversely, missing from the VOC approach, where employment relations seem to mostly matter according to how they functionally serve different types of capitalism, which denies autonomy and scope to the strategies of actors, especially workers (Hancké et al. 2007).

Attempts to incorporate dimensions of change in the debate on 'varieties of capitalism' have focused on how employment relations adapt to liberalization through institutional replacement, functional accretion, or gradual conversions to new purposes (Streeck and Thelen 2005). Bosch et al. (2009: 17–19), however, conclude that a fixation on national comparative advantage in the VOC approach narrows its understanding of change down to mere country-specific adaptations to the requirements of economic liberalization. Despite imposing on corporate and business models similar pressures and regulatory scenarios, they argue instead that liberalization and globalization also produce radical ruptures, particularly evident in employment relations. They cite in this regard the example of post-unification Germany, where a rapid decline of historically entrenched co-determination schemes, regional social compacts, and job security is allowing a shift from a 'coordinated' to a 'liberal' market economy. More generally, they conclude, the impact of global finance on national employment relations systems involves changes of such magnitude that can hardly be captured by adaptive and gradualist evolutionary models.

The significance of financial capital, especially as it played a crucial role in the global economic crises of the early twenty-first century, does not only test the plausibility and relevance of employment relations paradigms concerned with stability and adaptive change. It also questions more radical analyses premised on structural conflicts, particularly long-wave theories, as the final section of this chapter will highlight.

Employment Relations, Conflict, and Change in an Age of Global Economic Instability

Critical discussions of global economic instability in the early twenty-first century have often emphasized the intimate connection between capitalist crises and the transformations of employment relations during the preceding decades (Harvey 2007; Duménil and Lévy 2011). In particular, the financialization of the world economy, a major factor in the global economic turmoil which began in 2007, reflected and responded to major shifts in the world of work. The breakdown of Keynesian social compacts in older industrial democracies—often underpinned by supranational institutional commitments to fiscal discipline and public spending containment as in the case of the European Union—accompanied the casualization of labour forces and the stagnation or contraction of employees' buying power, which in the United States has hardly increased since the early 1970s. Investment in manufacturing has conversely moved towards low-wage, export-orientated emerging economies in Latin America and Asia, chiefly China, which by 2010 was the world's pre-eminent industrial power and second largest economy. The growing inability of workers' wages to sustain domestic demand has made consumption for globally produced and circulated goods depend on credit card or asset-backed lending, which provided further avenues for financialization in the form of booming real estate markets. The securitization of personal debt underscored financial corporations' escalating rates of return. Soaring profit margins in the financial sector then placed further pressure on manufacturing companies to raise their own profitability through the increased exploitation of insecure and unprotected workforces, especially young people in their first jobs, for which national and supranational legislation relaxed constraints on hiring, firing, benefits, minimum wages, and employment conditions.

In such a scenario, economic crises, 'upswings', and 'downswings' have displayed features that are more and more difficult to analyse in terms of 'long waves'. Rather than witnessing regular phases of expansion and decline, the global economy seems to be susceptible to rapid successions of booms and busts, whose massive and often devastating and enduring social, economic, and policy consequences can hardly be regarded as episodes within 'waves'. The crisis of the late 2000s and early 2010s has not only led to a vast increase in unemployment rates and the near budgetary collapse of various governments, for example in the Mediterranean fringe of the European Union, it has also been met with unprecedented austerity programmes which, in Europe as well as North America, placed social safety nets and employment regulations under enormous strain (Fumagalli and Mezzadra 2010). As a result, it is difficult to imagine how and when an 'upswing' related to a new phase of worker mobilization and economic recovery can take place along Kelly's predictions. Even where timid improvements have occurred, as in the United States, they were conducive to workers' mobilization only to a very limited and uneven extent, largely confined to the public sector.

When Kelly published his work on long waves, in 1998, he temporally located it in a 'transition period', which followed the downswing from the early 1970s to the mid-1990s. Earlier transitions had lasted for him between six and eight years (Kelly 1998: 85). The fact that, at least fifteen years into his latest transition, there is at best questionable evidence of an upswing accompanied by worker mobilization, globally or in individual major economies, casts serious doubts on the continuous relevance of the application of 'long waves' to employment relations. Attempts to find recurring patterns in capitalism remain nonetheless relevant at least because, as Boyer (2011) notices, the increasingly dramatic succession of booms and busts makes the mainstream notion of a static 'market economy' inadequate and encourages us to understand capitalism as a dynamic social process with discernible temporal trends. Such trends probably manifest themselves, Boyer concludes, not so much as regular waves but as 'common qualitative dynamic patterns' around which countries and actors—institutions, firms, and labour—converge through pragmatic experimentations and adaptations. Even a research agenda focused on the 'varieties of capitalism' cannot simply rule out the significance of such patterns.

At the same time, the transformation of global hegemonies and the rise of new economic powers, namely China, India, and Brazil, from what used to be called the 'global South' question many standard features of neo-liberal discourse. Despite those countries' advantages in terms of labour costs, their ascent has been paralleled by modalities of state intervention and social policy-making that depart from the mere fixation with liberalization, privatization, and deregulation, typical of the 'Washington consensus' (Khan and Christiansen 2011). Chinese developmentalism has greatly relied, somehow reflecting and amplifying trends already evident in earlier East Asian industrializing economies, on massive and targeted state investment. India and Brazil have built the legitimacy of their growth experiments on large-scale policies of public employment and cash transfers, respectively 'employment guarantee' schemes and the *Bolsa Família* programme. Albeit focused on making poor and uneducated sectors of the population employable (OECD 2010), they refrain from merely cutting social protections to achieve that end, as 'workfare' approaches of a neo-liberal flavour recommend. Not only do these trajectories challenge the idea of a global ideological convergence around the precepts of neo-liberalism, but they also probably concur in explaining the fact that emerging economies have been more capable than older industrial ones to withstand financial instability and crisis. As a consequence, the nature and regularity of future global economic swings become even more difficult to prognosticate. It may indeed be the case that the rise of Asian or Latin American economies can spur short-term growth cycles even as the global economy remains mired in its long downswing. According to Phillip O'Hara (2006) the persistence of neo-liberalism as the dominant macroeconomic paradigm is indeed responsible for prolonging the downswing and preventing the passage to a new wave. For him, in fact, neo-liberalism cannot become a new global mode of regulation suited to solve the current crisis because it undermines social institutions, mediations, and practices—including social solidarity, trust, cooperation, and collectivism—that tend to favour wage earners and productive investment. State resources are then diverted towards supporting 'unproductive' functions such as financial bailouts and military spending. As these problems particularly plague the United States as the current aspiring global hegemon, O'Hara continues, prospects for a global upswing heralding a new long wave are inextricably linked to the emergence, by now far from evident, of a labour-friendly post-Washington consensus.

Beverly Silver's notion of 'waves of labour unrest' was crucially premised on workers' recurrent ability to exercise their 'associational power'—derived from collective

organization—and 'structural power'—entailing bargaining power in tight labour markets—thanks to their strategic location 'within a key industrial sector' (Silver 2003: 13).
It is plausible to assume, as she argues, that the globalization of production does not
necessarily imply a weakening of workers' structural power as transnational commodity chains and supply networks become more, not less, vulnerable to localized disruptions. One can also imagine how rising industrial employment in emerging economies
can provide new opportunities for workers' organization and mobilization in erst-
while pools of low-wage and casualized jobs. Silver's approach is vulnerable, however,
to a criticism that Wood and Lane (2012: 19–21) have moved to long waves in general.
Theories of long waves, they argue, tend to underestimate complex causal dynamics that
are responsible for diverse trajectories and results at the level of nation-states, regions,
or sectors. As a global phenomenon, the owners of fungible and transferable assets—
chiefly financial rents—have gained prominence over relatively immovable activities,
such as manufacturing plants and their wage earners. But the rise of rentier classes
and their weakening of labour-friendly mediations and regulations cannot be simply
ascribed to global forces such as the liberalization of trade, investment, and finance. It
also crucially depends on changes in state policies and localized technological, energy,
or environmental constraints that have different specific effects on the capacity of workers' organizations to mobilize and connect across national borders. Questions can thus
be cast on the possibilities of Silver's stated *potential* structural power of workers to
manifest itself into actual mobilization.

Scholars working on the notion of 'cognitive capitalism' (Cvijanovic et al. 2010;
Moulier-Boutang 2011) have debated financialization and the growing precariousness of
jobs as aspects of a broader shift in which capitalist accumulation decreasingly relies on
the direct employment of workers and increasingly depends on appropriating knowledge, affects, and relationships across the social spectrum. In this perspective, the precarization, vulnerability, and disposability of workers at the point of production reflects
the turn of financial capital from workplace-based profit making towards the accumulation of rent from everyday life dynamics, such as the informal networks through which
young people acquire cognitive skills that make them employable, the online development of new software during leisure time, or household debt itself. As a result, the very
boundaries between production and consumption are blurred by the rise of the 'pro-
sumer', a combination of producer and consumer for which every aspect of physical,
psychical, and social existence is turned into value. A similar set of questions has been
debated by scholars of employment 'precarity' (Standing 2011), which somehow overlap
with the 'cognitive capitalism' approach in underlying the importance of demands that
are not principally focused on wages and working conditions, but also include forms of
universal basic income not dependent on employment status. In such approaches basic
income would in fact be not only a way of enhancing the economic security of increasingly unstable working populations but also a redistributive intervention to make capital pay for the everyday existence it appropriates outside the workplace (Lucarelli 2008).

As capitalism tries, in sum, to re-establish order out of its increasing instability by
colonizing life outside the workplace, workers' organizations will face the challenge of

exploring new coordinates of conflict beyond the classic sites of production. A more important asset than Silver's 'structural power' would then be the ability of labour movements to build alliances and claims that are meaningful to highly diverse constituencies, often not unionized when not overtly suspicious of the self-centredness of traditional unions. The literature on 'social movement unionism' has started engaging these issues (Dibben 2004), but the relevance of trade unions for changing modalities of conflict is also continuously tested—especially in Europe and the Americas, the very birthplaces of industrial unionism—by recurrent and often radical mobilizations against austerity and precarization.

CONCLUSION

The persistent instability of the global economy and the crises, perhaps even decline, of neo-liberalism have profoundly redefined the problematic, with which this chapter started, of conflict, order, and change in employment relations. Proponents of a renewed social partnership aimed at providing some protection, which some term 'flexicurity' (Regalia 2006), to a vulnerable labour force—for which precarious jobs are no longer to be considered 'atypical'—confront realities in which capital is not only making work insecure but is rendering it actually disposable as its accumulation strategies reach beyond the workplace.

Confronted with the current crisis, explanations for conflict and change that invoke capitalism's recursive, regular, or predictable patterns have been found wanting in several respects. As an alternative, critics of structuralist views of employment relations and the labour process have long reclaimed the significance of workers' subjectivity not only as a terrain where individuals are moulded into active, enterprising, and consenting employees but also as a way for workers to appropriate and resignify norms and discourses of production (Knights and McCabe 2000). It is a promising line of inquiry, which furthermore problematizes the very meanings of work, employment, and working-class identities as they are less and less conducive to security and inclusion.

Much Durkheim-inspired sociology has deprecated the degradation, which would 'corrode' human character, of work as a principle of social order (Sennett 2000). Others, however, have seen a problem not only in the deterioration of employment conditions as such but also in the fact that, despite its deterioration, employment remains in popular and policy discourse the abstractly universalized foundation of responsibility, public virtue, citizenship, and social integration (Offe 1997). The study of employment relations has been especially preoccupied with conflict in order to identify conditions either for its emergence and propagation or for its institutionalization, containment, or avoidance. Despite the transformations of traditional forms of labour politics, conflict remains indeed at the core of inquiries into the world of work. The possibility exists, however, that merely assuming the centrality of organized labour, collective bargaining institutions, or firm-level interactions is no longer adequate to such inquiries.

An alternative could consist in grounding critical analyses of employment relations more firmly in a multidimensional understanding of workers' subjectivity not as merely determined, as in older structuralist paradigms on the left, by the opportunities and constraints arising within production. Rather, the notion of subjectivity also points at workers' autonomous capacity to open up political possibilities in accordance with broader modalities of social imagination and claims, which workers derive from their productive locations as much as from their everyday lives, sociality, and affects (Barchiesi 1998). Similar reflections have played a prominent role in the study of labour struggles by postcolonial theorists (see Chakrabarty 1988) and remain therefore quite useful to counter what Kaufman (2011: 30–1) identifies as a Western-centric bias in employment relations scholarship. Postcolonial studies have in particular criticized the normative universalism of discourses of work and employment. Workers in societies with limited and uneven working-class formation and weak trade union traditions in fact contest capitalist discipline by deploying place-specific cultural practices and repertoires of resistance even when they are keenly aware of their position in globalized production networks. Such complex assemblages hardly fit macro-theorizations of long waves, especially as these see workers' collectivism as a strategy predicated upon the assumed superiority of trade unionism as an organizing method. In postcolonial societies the limitations of union organizations have rather facilitated workers' identifications around other collectivities and movements, often of a spiritual, cultural, or ethnic kind, which traditional approaches to employment relations have neglected.

Similar criticisms to the political centrality of production-based collective identities are raised by feminist refutations of the alleged neutrality of the concept of working class, which is, instead, characterized by internal inequalities and fractures along gender lines. A de-gendered, universalized meaning of work would thus not only reproduce the stereotype of male breadwinning but also contribute to the invisibility of unpaid female household labour, which crucially underpins capital's ability to extract surplus (Weeks 2011). The problem of conceptualizing work outside the workplace becomes, conversely, crucial to understanding transformations of labour that question any clearly defined boundary between production and reproduction. More and more women—especially in the fast-growing economies of the old 'global South', now joined by various African countries—add in fact flexible and informal jobs to their household chores as vital sources of income. Far from being a residual and premodern element, the informality of productions and economies, which is often supported by outsourcing and subcontracting by formal firms and corporations, may well prefigure future dynamics of restructuring of the global division of labour (Lindell 2010). In this regard, Africa, a continent usually excluded from analyses of globalization as a 'convergence narrative' (Ferguson 2006: 25–48) due to the prevalence there of 'informal' economic modalities, acquires instead new significance as a vantage point from which capitalist globalization can be interrogated as a reality of unevenness, exclusion, domination, and inequality. It would thus be an interesting paradox if the renewal of a critical agenda, centred on conflict and radical change, for the study of employment relations drew its inspiration from those regions and histories that have for long stayed at the margins of employment relations scholarship.

REFERENCES

Ackers, P. and Wilkinson, A. (2003). 'Introduction: The British Industrial Relations Tradition. Formation, Breakdown, and Salvage', in Ackers and Wilkinson (eds.), *Understanding Work and Employment: Industrial Relations in Transition*. Oxford and New York: Oxford University Press, 1–31.

Albert, M. (1993). *Capitalism vs. Capitalism: How America's Obsession with Individual Achievement and Short-Term Profit Has Led It to the Brink of Collapse*. New York: Four Walls Eight Windows.

Barbash, J. (1984). *The Elements of Industrial Relations*. Madison, WI: University of Wisconsin Press.

Barchiesi, F. (1998). 'Restructuring, Flexibility, and the Politics of Workplace Subjectivity: A Worker Inquiry in the South African Car Industry', *Rethinking Marxism*, 10(4): 105–33.

Blossfeld, H.-P., Buchholz, S., Bukodi, E., and Kurz, K. (eds.) (2008). *Young Workers, Globalization and the Labour Market: Comparing Early Working Life in Eleven Countries*. Cheltenham: Edward Elgar.

Bosch, G., Lehndorff, S., and Rubery, J. (2009). 'European Employment Models in Flux: Pressures for Change and Prospects for Survival and Revitalization', in Bosch, Lehndorff, and Rubery (eds.), *European Employment Models in Flux: A Comparison of Institutional Change in Nine European Countries*. Basingstoke: Palgrave Macmillan, 1–56.

Boyer, R. (1990). *The Regulation School: A Critical Introduction*. New York: Columbia University Press.

—— (2011). 'Are There Laws of Motion of Capitalism?' *Socio-Economic Review*, 9(1): 59–81.

Braverman, H. (1974). *Labor and Monopoly Capital: The Degradation of Work in the Twentieth Century*. New York: Monthly Review Press.

Burawoy, M. (1985). *The Politics of Production: Factory Regimes Under Capitalism and Socialism*. London: Verso.

Castells, M. (2000). *The Rise of the Network Society: The Information Age: Economy, Society, and Culture, Volume I*, 2nd edn. Oxford: Blackwell.

Chakrabarty, D. (1988). *Rethinking Working Class History: Bengal 1890–1940*. Princeton: Princeton University Press.

Clegg, S. (1994). 'Power Relations and the Constitution of the Resistant Subject', in J. M. Jermier, D. Knights, and W. R. Nord (eds.), *Resistance and Power in Organizations*. London: Routledge, 274–325.

Cvijanovic, V., Fumagalli, A., and Vercellone, C. (eds.) (2010). *Cognitive Capitalism and Its Reflections in South-Eastern Europe*. Bern: Peter Lang.

Deery, S. and Mitchell, R. (eds.) (1999). *Employment Relations: Individualisation and Union Exclusion—An International Study*. Sydney: The Federation Press.

Dibben, P. (2004). 'Social Movement Unionism', in M. Harcourt and G. Wood (eds.), *Trade Unions and Democracy: Strategies and Perspectives*. Manchester: Manchester University Press, 280–302.

Duménil, G. and Lévy, D. (2011). *The Crisis of Neoliberalism*. Cambridge, MA: Harvard University Press.

Dunlop, J. (1958). *Industrial Relations Systems*. New York: Holt.

Edwards, P. (1986). *Conflict at Work: A Materialist Analysis of Workplace Relations*. Oxford: Blackwell.

Esping-Andersen, G. (1990). *The Three Worlds of Welfare Capitalism*. Princeton: Princeton University Press.

Esping-Andersen, G. and Regini, M. (eds.) (2000). *Why Deregulate Labour Markets?* Oxford and New York: Oxford University Press.

Ferguson, J. (2006). *Global Shadows: Africa in the Neoliberal World Order*. Durham, NC: Duke University Press.

Flora, P. and Heidenheimer, A. J. (eds.) (1981). *The Development of Welfare States in Europe and America*. New Brunswick, NJ: Transaction Publishers.

Fox, A. (1974). *Beyond Contract: Work, Power and Trust Relations*. London: Faber & Faber.

Fumagalli, A. and Mezzadra, S. (eds.) (2010). *Crisis in the Global Economy: Financial Markets, Social Struggles, and New Political Scenarios*. New York: Semiotext(e).

Hall, P. A. and Soskice, D. (eds.) (2001). *Varieties of Capitalism: The Institutional Foundations of Comparative Advantage*. Oxford and New York: Oxford University Press.

Hancké, B., Rhodes, M., and Thatcher, M. (eds.) (2007). *Beyond Varieties of Capitalism: Conflict, Contradictions, and Complementarities in the European Economy*. Oxford and New York: Oxford University Press.

Hancock, P. and Tyler, M. (2001). *Work, Postmodernism and Organization: A Critical Introduction*. London: Sage.

Harvey, D. (2007). *A Brief History of Neoliberalism*. Oxford and New York: Oxford University Press.

Hyman, R. (1975). *Industrial Relations: A Marxist Introduction*. Basingstoke: Macmillan.

Jessop, B. (2001). 'Series Preface', in Jessop (ed.), *Regulation Theory and the Crisis of Capitalism. Volume 5: Developments and Extensions*. Cheltenham: Edward Elgar, ix–xxiii.

——— (2002). *The Future of the Capitalist State*. Cambridge: Polity Press.

Kalleberg, A. (2000). 'Nonstandard Employment Relations: Part-Time, Temporary and Contract Work', *Annual Review of Sociology*, 26: 341–65.

Kaufman, B. (2011). 'The Future of Employment Relations: Insights from Theory', in K. Townsend and A. Wilkinson (eds.), *Research Handbook on the Future of Work and Employment Relations*. Cheltenham: Edward Elgar, 13–44.

Kelly, J. (1998). *Rethinking Industrial Relations: Mobilization, Collectivism and Long Waves*. London: Routledge.

Kerr, C., Dunlop, J., Harbison, F., and Myers, C. (1960). *Industrialism and Industrial Man: The Problems of Labor and Management in Economic Growth*. Cambridge, MA: Harvard University Press.

Khan, S. R. and Christiansen, J. (eds.) (2011). *Towards New Developmentalism: Market as Means Rather Than Master*. Abingdon: Routledge.

Knights, D. (1989). 'Power and Subjectivity at Work: From Degradation to Subjugation in Social Relations', *Sociology*, 23(4): 535–58.

Knights, D. and McCabe, D. (2000). ' "Ain't Misbehavin' "? Opportunities for Resistance Under New Forms of "Quality" Management', *Sociology*, 34(3): 421–436.

Kochan, T., Katz, H., and McKersie, R. (1986). *The Transformation of American Industrial Relations*. Ithaca, NY: Cornell University Press.

Korpi, W. (1983). *The Democratic Class Struggle*. London: Routledge & Kegan Paul.

Lindell, I. (ed.) (2010). *Africa's Informal Workers: Collective Agency, Alliances and Transnational Organizing in Urban Africa*. London: Zed Books.

Locke, R., Kochan, T., and Piore, M. (eds.) (1995). *Employment Relations in a Changing World Economy*. Cambridge, MA: MIT Press.

Lombard, K. V. (2001). 'Female Self-Employment and Demand for Flexible, Nonstandard Work Schedules', *Economic Inquiry*, 39(2): 214–37.

Lucarelli, S. (2008). 'Basic Income and Productivity in Cognitive Capitalism', *Review of Social Economy*, 66(1): 71–92.

Moulier-Boutang, Y. (2011). *Cognitive Capitalism*. Cambridge: Polity Press.

Müller-Jentsch, W. (2004). 'Theoretical Approaches to Industrial Relations', in B. Kaufman (ed.), *Theoretical Perspectives on Work and the Employment Relationship*. Champaign, IL: Industrial Relations Research Association, 1–40.

O'Hara, P. A. (2006). *Growth and Development in the Global Political Economy: Social Structures of Accumulation and Modes of Regulation*. Abingdon: Routledge.

OECD (2010). *Tackling Inequalities in Brazil, China, India, and South Africa: The Role of Labour Market and Social Policies*. Paris: OECD Publishing.

Offe, C. (1997). 'Towards a New Equilibrium of Citizens' Rights and Economic Resources?', in W. Michalski, R. Miller, and B. Stevens (eds.), *Societal Cohesion and the Globalising Economy: What Does the Future Hold?* Paris: OECD Publishing, 81–108.

Peck, J. (2001). *Workfare States*. New York: Guilford Press.

Regalia, I. (2006), 'New Forms of Employment and New Problems of Regulation', in Regalia (ed.), *Regulating New Forms of Employment: Local Experiments and Social Innovation in Europe*. Abingdon: Routledge, 4–22.

Ritzer, G. (2000). *The McDonaldization of Society*. Thousand Oaks, CA: Pine Forge Press.

Rothstein, B. (1987). 'Corporatism and Reformism: The Social Democratic Institutionalization of Class Conflict', *Acta Sociologica*, 30(3–4): 295–311.

Sennett, R. (2000). *The Corrosion of Character: The Personal Consequences of Work in the New Capitalism*. New York: Norton.

Silver, B. (2003). *Forces of Labor: Workers' Movements and Globalization since 1870*. Cambridge: Cambridge University Press.

Standing, G. (1997). 'Globalization, Labour Flexibility and Insecurity: The Era of Market Regulation', *European Journal of Industrial Relations*, 3(1): 7–37.

—— (2011). *The Precariat: The New Dangerous Class*. London: Bloomsbury.

Streeck, W. (1987). 'The Uncertainties of Management in the Management of Uncertainty: Employers, Labour Relations and Industrial Adjustment in the 1980s', *Work, Employment and Society*, 1(3): 281–308.

Streeck, W. and Thelen, K. (2005). 'Introduction: Institutional Change in Advanced Political Economies', in Streeck and Thelen (eds.), *Beyond Continuity: Institutional Change in Advanced Political Economies*. Oxford and New York: Oxford University Press, 1–39.

Thompson, P. (1989). *The Nature of Work: An Introduction to Debates on the Labour Process*, 2nd edn. Basingstoke: Macmillan.

Watson, T. J. (2008). *Sociology, Work and Industry*, 5th edn. Abingdon: Routledge.

Weeks, K. (2011). *The Problem with Work: Feminism, Marxism, Antiwork Politics, and Postwork Imaginaries*. Durham, NC: Duke University Press.

Wood, G. and Lane, C. (2012). 'Institutions, Change, and Diversity', in Lane and Wood (eds.), *Capitalist Diversity and Diversity within Capitalism*. Abingdon: Routledge, 1–31.

PART III

COMPARATIVE EVIDENCE

CHAPTER 12

....

EMPLOYMENT RELATIONS IN LIBERAL MARKET ECONOMIES

....

GREGORY JACKSON AND
ANJA KIRSCH

INTRODUCTION

....

IN the field of employment relations, the comparative capitalisms literature is used to classify the employment relations institutions in various countries into distinct categories. While the number of categories identified and the key features of each category differ according to the particular theoretical approach (Amable 2003; Jackson and Deeg 2008, 2012; Thelen 2010; Whitley 1999; Wilkins et al. 2010), the employment relationship in a group of English-speaking countries is widely recognized and labelled as being more liberal and market-based than in other countries. This chapter focuses on the six countries that are classified as liberal market economies (LMEs) in the varieties of capitalism (VOC) approach (Hall and Soskice 2001): the United Kingdom, Ireland, Canada, the United States, Australia, and New Zealand.[1]

According to the VOC approach, employment relations in LMEs are market-based in the sense that institutions facilitate investment by employers and employees in transferable assets, and private ordering at the level of firms and individuals plays a large role. Generally, unions and employer associations are weak, wage setting is decentralized, management has unilateral control of firms with no institutionalized employee voice, and employment protection is weak. As a result, job tenure tends to be low, wage inequality is high, employees seek transferable skills that facilitate their movement between firms, and external labour markets are used widely to match skills to jobs. On closer inspection, however, employment relations in all six countries examined here do not fully correspond to this ideal type, and have done so far less in the past. While institutions and practices in each country have recently converged towards this liberal ideal, the decentralized nature of employment relations with few institutional constraints on managers also contributes to a significant degree of within-country variation between firms and sectors.

In this chapter, we illustrate the *defining features* of employment relations in LMEs and also reveal the *key differences* between countries. First, we describe employment outcomes in LME countries, particularly the short-term nature of employment and the inequality in wages and salaries. Second, we examine the institutional determinants of these outcomes, by discussing the role of the key actors in employment relations, namely the state, unions, and employer associations, and next by examining the employment relations processes of collective bargaining, industrial conflict, and employee voice. In the final section we discuss the importance of recognizing both the similarities and differences among the six LME countries for scholars of comparative employment relations.

EMPLOYMENT OUTCOMES IN LMES

Employment in LMEs tends to be relatively short-term in nature. This characteristic can be measured in various ways, although each is imperfect. While good comparative data across a breadth of countries are lacking, we discuss several indicators in this section that arguably point to a consistent overall picture.

A number of OECD studies from the mid-1990s show substantial differences in average employee tenure and the share of long-term employees with tenures of over 20 years.[2] For example, in 1995, LME countries had average tenures between 6.4 years in Australia and 8.7 years in Ireland, below the levels of Germany (9.8 years) or Japan (11.3 years) (OECD 1997: 140). Looking at the proportion of employees with more than 20 years' tenure at their current employer, LME countries ranged between 6.8% in Australia and 11.9% in Ireland compared to 17% in Germany or 21.4% in Japan. Similarly, OECD data[3] show that these differences persist between 2000 and 2007, prior to the 2008 financial crisis. Here, the proportion of employees with tenures of less than one year was generally high in LME countries—ranging between 23–25% in Australia, 22–23% in Canada, and 23–28% in the USA, but slightly lower at 17–22% in Ireland or 18–21% in the UK. All these ratios were substantially higher than in ideal-typical CME countries, e.g. 9% in Japan or 13–16% in Germany during the same period. These differences can also be seen in average tenures during this later period of 8.6 years in the UK compared to 10.8 years in Germany. This picture is summarized in Table 12.1, based on estimated multi-year averages for a wider range of countries. This snapshot confirms a lower proportion of long-term employees with tenure of ten years or more in LME countries.

The short-term nature of employment can also be captured by looking at the rate of involuntary dismissals across countries. The OECD shows that annual dismissal rates in the UK, Australia, and USA fall in the range of nearly 4–5% of employees, whereas Germany is slightly lower at 3% (OECD 2010). Similarly, a comparative study by Jackson

Table 12.1 Distribution of job tenure, annual averages

Country	Time period	<1 year	1 to 5 years	5 to 10 years	>10 years
Australia	1992–2006	21	36	18	24
Canada	1992–2006	22	31	17	30
Ireland	1992–2004	17	29	17	37
United Kingdom	1992–2004	18	31	19	32
United States	2000–2006	24	30	19	26
LME average		**20.4**	**31.4**	**18**	**29.8**
Belgium	1992–2004	11	24	18	46
Denmark	1992–2004	21	30	17	32
Finland	1995–2004	19	22	18	41
Germany	1992–2004	14	27	19	40
Netherlands	1992–2004	13	31	19	36
Norway	1995–2004	16	30	18	36
Sweden	1995–2004	14	25	18	43
Switzerland	1996–2004	16	29	20	35
CME average		**15.5**	**27.3**	**18.4**	**38.6**

Source: Hobijn and Şahin (2007).

(2005) showed that downsizing rates, measured as a percentage of large listed corporations with a decline in employment by 10% or greater, were significantly higher in the UK and USA during the 1990s, and persisted relative to many CME countries after controlling for firm-level factors, including financial performance. Downsizing is often associated with negative labour market effects. For example, studies of the USA show that job loss and re-employment of people in lower paid jobs is an important driver of the aggregate growth in wage inequality (Mouw and Kalleberg 2010).

Employee turnover is also driven by voluntary changes in employment. Studies based on the Cranet dataset have shown that average staff turnover at the firm level is higher in LME countries than in continental Europe, although similar to levels in certain Nordic countries (Croucher et al. 2012; Kabst et al. 2009). Some job changes are the result of 'push' factors. For example, the high willingness to change jobs in the UK and Canada is driven by poor working conditions and lack of job satisfaction, but driven more by positive job opportunities in the United States and New Zealand (Sousa-Poza and Henneberger 2004). Likewise, high turnover has also resulted from the spread of atypical forms of employment and employer demands for greater flexibility in working hours. Whereas CME countries have often achieved greater flexibility within the context of long-term employment patterns, a strong empirical relationship exists between flexibilization and increasing employee turnover in LMEs (Stavrou and Kilaniotis 2010). Job changes may also result from 'pull' factors, as suggested above. For example, workers with high earnings and skills may leave firms in order to set up new ventures (Campbell et al. 2012) or in the pursuit of 'butterflying' careers based on the accumulation of human capital via experiences with different employers or project teams (McCabe and Savery 2007).

After high labour turnover, a second distinguishing feature of employment outcomes in LMEs is the high level of inequality in wages and salaries. Table 12.2 presents a simple proxy for earnings inequality based on the ratio of earnings in the 90th percentile to those in the 10th percentile. This ratio shows that the gap between the top and bottom 10% of earnings is substantially higher for the group of six LME countries relative to CME countries. One exception is New Zealand, where inequality is relatively low, whereas the United States stands out for having particularly high levels of inequality. Table 12.2 also shows the incidence of low pay, defined as workers earning less than two-thirds of the median wage. As a group, the LME countries have rates of low pay that are consistently around 7 percentage points higher than the CME countries, although data here are admittedly patchy. Low pay is less common in Australia and New Zealand, even relative to some more coordinated economies such as Germany or Japan. As will be discussed later, these two countries benefit from setting a relatively high floor for minimum wage legislation (Colvin and Darbishire 2013), and some supports for earnings in atypical employment contracts (Campbell and Brosnan 2005). But in all of the LME countries, the phenomenon of working poor is a more prevalent issue than in most CME countries. The growth in inequality over time has also led to declines in earnings mobility (Kopczuk et al. 2010).

While the structure and determinants of earnings inequality vary across countries, high inequality reflects the highly decentralized system of wage setting and use of market-based incentives in LME countries. For example, one driver of inequality has been the growing diffusion of performance pay. Performance pay can take on many different complex forms—such as financial participation (e.g. stock options, profit sharing, and employee share ownership) or bonuses based on firm, group, or individual performance. Comparative data on the composition of performance pay are scarce, since meaningful comparisons require careful disaggregation among occupational groups and firm size.[4] Performance pay schemes can also be used in different ways, such as to enhance market-based incentives or to support firm-specific commitments. These effects are often combined. For example, performance pay systems have diffused widely in young, entrepreneurial ventures as an instrument for recruitment of personnel from the external labour market, as well as linking goals to overall enterprise performance (for New Zealand, see Fabling and Grimes 2010). More broadly, performance pay may thus have very different effects on earnings dispersion depending on the wider institutional context of employment relations—such as whether performance schemes are jointly regulated by employers and labour representatives, or set unilaterally as is often the case in LME countries.[5] In the USA, for example, Lemieux et al. (2009) find that performance pay is set unilaterally by management and provides a channel through which underlying changes in returns to skill get translated into higher wage inequality, particularly among workers at the top fifth of the earnings scale. The use of performance pay has also been shown to increase the role of subjective evaluations of supervisors, and therefore magnifies inequalities based on social categories such as race (Heywood and O'Halloran 2005).

Table 12.2 Earnings dispersion and incidence of low pay 1995–2010

Country	Ratio of 9th to 1st earnings deciles				Incidence of low pay			
	1995	2000	2005	2010	1995	2000	2005	2010
Australia	2.91	3.01	3.12	3.33	13.83	14.55	15.86	16.10
Canada	3.53**	3.61	3.74	3.71	21.85**	23.24	21.34	21.11
Ireland	3.93**	3.27	3.73	3.63	20.40**	17.79	20.10	20.10
New Zealand	2.41**	2.63	2.77	2.83	13.20**	11.73	12.36	12.80
United Kingdom	3.49	3.46	3.60	3.58	20.87	20.42	20.73	20.67
United States	4.59	4.49	4.86	5.01	25.17	24.70	23.96	25.29
LME average	**3.48**	**3.41**	**3.64**	**3.68**	**19.22**	**18.74**	**19.06**	**19.35**
Austria			3.26	3.39			15.28	16.47
Belgium		2.37	2.49	2.38			6.70	4.30
Denmark	2.47	2.51	2.64	2.80	8.60*	8.77	11.27	13.44
Finland	2.34	2.41	2.49	2.52		4.60****	6.91	8.12
Germany	2.91	3.04	3.17	3.33	14.12	15.84	17.65	18.78
Japan	3.01	2.98	3.12	2.96	15.36	14.57	16.10	14.48
Netherlands	2.77	2.90	2.91		13.81	14.81***		
Norway	1.94**	2.00	2.12	2.30				
Sweden	2.21	2.35	2.23	2.23				
Switzerland	2.41*	2.56	2.65*****	2.70		9.60	9.00*****	9.20
CME average	**2.51**	**2.57**	**2.71**	**2.73**	**12.97**	**11.37**	**11.84**	**12.11**

Notes: Earnings dispersion is measured by the ratio of 9th to 1st deciles limits of earnings. The incidence of low pay refers to the share of workers earning less than two-thirds of median earnings.
* 1996, ** 1997, ***1999, **** 2001, *****2006
Source: OECD.Stat.

The complex dynamics related to performance pay have been extensively studied in the UK. While British manufacturing traditionally used individual performance pay such as piecework, performance pay has become more complex and focused on organizational outcomes as union control over these systems has declined (Arrowsmith and Marginson 2010). Performance pay systems are often designed with strong reference to external market rates as a mechanism of recruitment and retention (Armstrong and Brown 2005). The diffusion of performance pay practices is thus associated with substantial increases in wage inequality within the enterprise (Belfield and Marsden 2003). Looking at other sectors such as banking, however, new variable and performance-based pay systems have only partially undermined the more centralized and standardized approach to wage setting. Pay systems have given unions new areas of voice concerning performance criteria within firms (Arrowsmith and Marginson 2011).

Nonetheless, performance pay largely matters for those at the top end of the spectrum. In banking, the spread of new bonus awards has fuelled massive growth at the very top of the earnings scale, while ordinary earnings have remained surprisingly flat (Bell and Van Reenen 2010).

Returning to the VOC perspective, employment outcomes in LME countries are widely thought to yield particular comparative institutional advantages for firms. The original VOC argument was that fluid external labour markets and the transferability of skills across firms support more radical forms of innovation. The success story of Silicon Valley in the USA provided much anecdotal support for this view, although more systematic comparative studies on sectoral export performance using patent data or R&D intensity to measure innovation patterns have shown some partial support but also important qualifications to this view (Akkermans et al. 2009; Boyer 2004; Schneider and Paunescu 2012; Schneider et al. 2009; Taylor 2004). For example, while the United States is certainly a leader in radical innovation, this is less clearly true of Australia or New Zealand. Ireland also has a very distinct economic model based on attracting high levels of foreign direct investment (FDI) by multinational firms with technological know-how, while exploiting labour with relatively low cost but strong general skills.

Looking across the competitiveness of different sectors, most LME countries have, in fact, deindustrialized very rapidly. In manufacturing, LME countries have been very vulnerable to globalization, as low wage and cost-sensitive industrial segments have been relocated to emerging economies. While many CME countries perform well based on quality and upgrading of industrial skills, LME economies have been less able to reskill and preserve their manufacturing base (Whitford 2005). Meanwhile, the boom in employment in LME countries has focused on geographically immobile service sectors. At the high end, financial services have been a major driver in employment growth, capitalizing on strong professional skills but also flexible combination of skills across firms and locations (Wójcik 2012). Similarly, the growth of services focused on retail, security, and domestic household work is highly dependent on a large external labour market of persons with relatively general qualifications and low wages. For example, LME institutions support the relatively strong use of non-standard working time in services (Richbell et al. 2011). But much more comparative research needs to be done in order to better understand how the diversity of employment relations translates into comparative advantages for firms in these sectors (for a comparative study of call centres see Batt et al. 2009).

THE INSTITUTIONAL CONTEXT OF EMPLOYMENT RELATIONS IN LMES

The previous section stressed the similarities of employment outcomes among the group of LME countries, which set them apart from coordinated market economies. This section turns to some of the institutional determinants of these outcomes. Specifically, it emphasizes the roles of the state, unions, and employer associations in each country.

Role of the State and Legal Framework

Diverse legal and political factors have shaped employment relations in the six countries. Nonetheless, over the last several decades, these countries have undergone very substantial liberalization and deregulation, and a corresponding weakening of past employment relations frameworks. In short, all six countries have become substantially *more liberal* in their recent history. Still, understanding these diverse institutional origins and pathways is important to understanding the dynamics of employment relations and how they are likely to evolve in the future.

Recent literature has stressed the shared common law traditions of these countries, and argued that the historical legacy of legal systems in these countries set their employment relations on a more liberal trajectory than in civil law countries (Botero et al. 2004). The basic intuition is that common law legal systems placed greater emphasis on contractual modes of economic governance, and have evolved through judge-made law based on cases and a large body of legal precedent rather than state regulation. However, other research has come to question the causal mechanisms related to legal origins. For example, Deakin (2009: 60) argues:

> In the common law, the separation of worker interests from the firm was reflected in a weakly institutionalized notion of the contract of employment. In this respect, British experience reflected the lingering influence of the pre-modern master–servant regime, which was transplanted to other common law systems via colonization.

Indeed, the British approach to the employment contract had much more in common with the exchange of goods, and did not acknowledge (or regulate) the social relationship between employer and employee to a large extent (Biernacki 1995). This approach was a historically contingent product of the timing of industrialization in relation to pre-modern and pre-democratic social order (Jackson 2001).

Going beyond legal origins, Crouch (1993) argues that the liberal and voluntarist nature of employment relations in LME countries is also an outgrowth of wider state traditions and the style in which the state solves conflicts in general. The pluralist approach to industrial relations in the UK arose due to the low level of collective organization by both employers and employees. Institutions became focused on arbitration mechanisms for handling contractual disputes, rather than more encompassing institutions that regulate conflict more generally. As Crouch (1993: 324–5) explains:

> A particularly important moment in the development of United Kingdom industrial-relations institutions was the Trade Union Act of 1871, which made the historically important decision to embody trade-union rights in the negative form

of immunities rather than as positive rights, on the grounds that to grant rights to organizations would impugn the essential individualism of the Common Law. This is significant in demonstrating how alien to English liberalism was the idea of co-opting organizations as components of public order.

Nonetheless, trade unions had a large post-war political influence in the UK through their close relationships with the Labour Party. Indeed, the state intervened in gradual and piecemeal ways to gradually institutionalize substantive collective rights of employees—what came to be dubbed as collective laissez-faire (Gospel and Edwards 2012; Howell 2005). The decline of more institutionalized forms of employment relations was, in fact, a political outcome of the Thatcher era (Marsh 1992), and was reinforced by the declining competitiveness of manufacturing industries relative to CME countries. This trend towards de-collectivization of employment relations continued under the 'Third Way' of New Labour after 1997 (Brown 2011).[6]

Emerging as British colonies and settler societies (Denoon 1983), other LME countries developed modern state structures based on a direct link of citizens and the state less burdened by a history of conflicts requiring corporatist intermediation. These political factors help explain the strong role of individual rights, as opposed to collective or status-like rights and obligations, within labour law in LMEs. Despite similar origins, however, national labour law developed in different ways during the twentieth century. Colvin and Darbishire (2013) distinguish between three pairings at the outset of the Thatcher/Reagan era: the Wagnerite model in the United States and Canada, the voluntarist model in the UK and Ireland, and the Award system in Australia and New Zealand. In the Award system, for example, the state historically played an active role through the system of compulsory arbitration, which gave the state rights to settle disputes and enforce those settlements. This system also supported the institutionalization of trade unions and led to relatively high union membership rates (Cooper and Ellem 2008). By contrast, the role of state-mandated mediation in the USA or conciliation in Canada has remained far more limited.

Beginning in the 1980s, a process of liberalization and deregulation has taken place, with the most extensive shifts in legislation occurring in Australia and New Zealand, in contrast to legislative stability in the USA and Canada. The result has been a convergence of labour law across the six countries, so that private ordering of employment relations at the firm level is now the dominant approach (Colvin and Darbishire 2013). It would nonetheless be easy to overstate the claim that the role of the state has become insignificant or that employment relations are purely laissez-faire in LME countries. The defining feature relates more precisely to the style of state intervention, which emphasizes the legal rights of individuals (both employers and employees), as opposed to collective rights for employees and their representatives, such as unions or works councils. The state also plays an important role by directly intervening to address market failure, such as through minimum wage legislation.

A good example of the liberal approach to regulating employment relations concerns protection against dismissal. Looking at the OECD employment protection index

Table 12.3 Employment protection: regulations on dismissal of employees on regular contracts and collective dismissals 1985–2005

Country	Regular employees					Collective dismissals	
	1985	1990	1995	2000	2005	2000	2005
Australia	1.00	1.00	1.00	1.50	1.50	2.88	2.88
Canada	1.25	1.25	1.25	1.25	1.25	2.63	2.63
Ireland	1.60	1.60	1.60	1.60	1.60	2.38	2.38
New Zealand		1.35	1.35	1.70	1.70	0.38	0.38
United Kingdom	0.95	0.95	0.95	1.12	1.12	2.88	2.88
United States	0.17	0.17	0.17	0.17	0.17	2.88	2.88
LME average	0.99	1.05	1.05	1.22	1.22	2.34	2.34
Austria	2.92	2.92	2.92	2.92	2.37	3.25	3.25
Belgium	1.68	1.68	1.68	1.73	1.73	4.13	4.13
Denmark	1.68	1.68	1.63	1.63	1.63	3.88	3.88
Finland	2.79	2.79	2.45	2.31	2.17	2.63	2.63
Germany	2.58	2.58	2.68	2.68	3.00	3.75	3.75
Japan	1.87	1.87	1.87	1.87	1.87	1.50	1.50
Netherlands	3.08	3.08	3.08	3.05	3.05	3.00	3.00
Norway	2.25	2.25	2.25	2.25	2.25	2.88	2.88
Sweden	2.90	2.90	2.86	2.86	2.86	3.75	3.75
Switzerland	1.16	1.16	1.16	1.16	1.16	3.88	3.88
CME average	2.29	2.29	2.26	2.25	2.21	3.27	3.27

Note: scale from 0 (least restrictions) to 6 (most restrictions) on dismissals.
Source: OECD.Stat.

(see Table 12.3), LME countries have fewer restrictions of the employers' right to dismiss employees, both individually and collectively. The United States is perhaps the archetypal 'hire and fire' regime, supported by a legal doctrine of employment-at-will. Traditionally this doctrine suggests that private sector employers can legally dismiss an employee for a good reason or even no reason at all, provided the dismissal does not violate any specific law, such as the Civil Rights Act (Ballam 2000).[7]

A second example of the liberal approach is the extensive use of minimum wage legislation that characterizes LMEs, whereby state regulation substitutes for other institutions, such as collective bargaining, as a way of binding employers. After the disappointing results of deregulation in New Zealand during the 1990s, the state has sought to address low wages through implanting cumulative increases to the minimum wage of 85%, from $6.50 in 1999 to $12 in April 2008 (McLaughlin 2009). New Zealand has now established a comparative high wage floor (Colvin and Darbishire 2013). While some industries have adjusted successfully, other sectors have sought support through new initiatives focused on building new institutions aiming to coordinate voluntary training by employers in order to increase the productivity for these workers (McLaughlin 2009). Similarly, the introduction of a national minimum wage in the UK during 1999 has had no negative effects on employment levels (Metcalf 2008), but has reduced levels of inequality at the low end of the earnings distribution (Dolton et al. 2012). Recent studies of the United States show similar effects (Addison et al. 2009; Dube et al. 2010). In sum, we see evidence of a politically contingent but positive role of state intervention in LME countries, which shapes employment outcomes as a way of complementing a largely liberal and market-oriented institutional framework.

From a historical perspective, the individual-centred style of state intervention in employment relations is shaped by the particular political characteristics of each country. In the USA, the political economy is shaped by the Federalist structure of the US government, the strong political role of the executive branch, and active role of the courts (Deeg 2012). For example, labour law in many US states protects the individual employee's 'right to work' without being coerced to join a labour union. Another example concerns the role of the courts in promoting equal opportunity for women and minorities in the workplace, particularly the Civil Rights Act of 1964 and resulting litigation. While anchoring strong individual rights in the workplace, the ambiguous nature of the regulation and the fragmented nature of government enforcement created, perhaps paradoxically, a particularly strong normative effect on large corporations— the professionalization of human resource management (HRM), the diffusion of new models of legal compliance, and the recasting of diversity policies in economic terms (Dobbin and Sutton 1998; Sutton and Dobbin 1996). This legalization of employment relations represents a strong restriction to the notion of employment at will, and shows the importance of state regulation in LMEs—even if this is based more strongly on notions of individual rights, rather than collective participation, as in CMEs.

Other LME state traditions had greater scope for collective rights, despite their primary focus on the individual and contractual freedoms. In Australia, compulsory arbitration and the strong role of the Labor Party reflect the important role of the state in regulating employment. Ireland provides a different example where, despite a history of weak state regulation, the state also came to play an important role, particularly through the social partnership of the 'Celtic tiger' era of the 1990s and 2000s (Baccaro and Simoni 2007; Donaghey 2008). Likewise, in New Zealand, the state played a similar role to Australia in facilitating union–management relations through an arbitration system, but changed more radically away from this approach following the 1991 Employment Contracts Act (Barry and Walsh 2007; Latornell 2006; Rasmussen 2010). The state has oscillated back to a more moderate approach since the 2000 Employment Relations Act, albeit with limited impact in terms of training or collective forms of employee representation.

As will be discussed further in later sections, the state has played a central role in changing employment relations. The widespread deregulation and erosion of employment relations should not be understood as a natural progression of market forces, but also in terms of very conscious state policies aimed at withdrawing state support for unions. The neo-liberal intervention in employment relations has, perhaps paradoxically, increased the direct relevance of the state in employment relations (Cooper and Ellem 2008).

Unions and Employer Associations

Unions and employer associations are organizations that seek to regulate employment relations to reflect the interests of their members. In this process, employment relations become based less on short-term market exchanges and more on long-term interaction between these organizations. Relative to many CME countries, unions and employer associations play a lesser role in LMEs. Particularly after the decline of Fordism and growing liberalization of employment over the last three decades, firms have correspondingly sought to build their comparative institutional advantages on the relative flexibility of market exchanges.

Unions

The strength and relevance of unions in an economy can be measured in several ways. Most commonly, union density, defined as union membership as a proportion of wage and salary earners in employment, is compared across countries and over time.

Union density rates between CMEs and LMEs do not show clearly that unions are less relevant in LMEs than in CMEs. In the 1980s, union density was around 50% or above in Australia, Ireland, New Zealand, and the UK, while only 30–35% in some CMEs—Germany, Japan, and the Netherlands. In fact, density in New Zealand was comparable with the Nordic countries. Since this time, a common trend is the prolonged decline in union density since the late 1970s (Visser 2006), affecting all six LME countries but also most CMEs. Density was high and peaked at approximately 69% in New Zealand, 55% in Ireland, and 50% in Australia and the UK, and has dropped most dramatically in Australia and New Zealand, where it is now around 20%. Union density was never high in the USA, peaking at around 30% in 1960 and dropping to 11% today. Canada is something of an exception, where density has remained comparatively stable, shifting from 36% in 1983 to 28% in 2010 (see Table 12.4). While these developments indicate a declining relevance of unions, density has also declined in many CME countries—for example in 2010 density in Germany, Japan, and the Netherlands was approximately 19%, comparable to the levels in Australia and New Zealand, and significantly lower than in Canada, Ireland, and the UK.

In addition, collective bargaining coverage, defined as the share of workers covered by collective agreements negotiated by unions, provides information on the role of unions in regulating employment. Table 12.5 shows adjusted bargaining coverage, defined as the number of employees covered by wage bargaining agreements as a proportion of the number of employees with the right to bargaining. This adjusted rate takes into account that some groups of employees (for example in the public sector) may be excluded from

Table 12.4 Union density (%) and density change in LMEs 1980–2010

Country	1980	1990	2000	2010	Change 1980–2010, % points
Australia	49	40	25	18	−31
Canada	34	34	28	28	−7
Ireland*	54	49	38	34	−21
New Zealand	69	50	22	21	−48
UK	50	38	30	27	−23
USA	22	15	13	11	−11
Mean LMEs	**46**	**38**	**26**	**23**	**−23**

Note: *1980–2009
Source: OECD.Stat.

Table 12.5 Bargaining coverage (%), adjusted, and coverage change in LMEs 1980–2010

Country	1980	1990	2000	2010	Change 1980–2010, % points
Australia	85	80	50**	40***	−45
Canada	37	38	32	32*****	−5
Ireland	64	60	55	44****	−20
New Zealand	70*	61	20	17***	−53
UK	71*	54	36	33*****	−38
USA	26	18	15	13	−13
Mean LMEs	**59**	**52**	**35**	**30**	**−29**

Notes: *1979, **2001, ***2007, ****2008, *****2009
Source: Visser (2011).

collective bargaining. As bargaining coverage shows the extent to which employees are subject to union-negotiated terms and conditions of employment, it is a complementary indicator of union strength and relevance in an economy.

Declining union density has been accompanied by a similarly large decrease in collective bargaining coverage in LMEs since 1980. Canada is the only country in which density and coverage have remained relatively stable. As bargaining is mainly conducted at the company level in LMEs, declining union density is strongly associated with declining coverage. By contrast, when bargaining is more centralized, as in many CME countries, density and coverage are not as so closely aligned. For example, in 2009 union density was 19% and collective bargaining coverage was 62% in Germany.

Various explanations have been offered for the decline in union strength in LME countries (Blanchflower 2007; Bryson et al. 2011; Checchi and Visser 2005; Kleiner 2001). Some factors are internal to unions such as a failure to reform organizing strategies and service provision in order to appeal to new groups of workers in new types of workplaces. Other factors are external to unions, including economic, societal, and political factors. Economic factors associated with union decline are de-industrialization, a shift of employment from the manufacturing to the service sector and from blue-collar to white-collar work, privatization of public services, downsizing, outsourcing, and offshoring. Small workplaces, flexible working hours, and the rise in atypical and precarious employment relationships make it difficult for unions to access and organize workers. Together with changes in technology and modes of production, these factors see employers demanding the decentralization of collective bargaining and increased flexibility and deregulation in employment relations. Societal factors linked to union decline include changes in social values and the erosion of working-class identities. Workers' focus on individualist lifestyles and values as well as managers' disinclination to adopt traditional forms of regulating employment relationships or open anti-unionism create challenges for unions. In addition, employers have used HRM techniques to replace the role of unions at the workplace level. Political factors associated with union decline are hostility to trade unionism from conservative governments and increasingly arm's length relations between unions and labour parties.

The role of legislation has played a prominent role in precipitating union decline. Legislative changes affecting union recognition, access to workplaces, collective bargaining, and industrial action have served to limit unions' organizing and mobilization capacities. Clear examples are the reforms introduced by Conservative governments in the UK from the 1980s onwards, the Work Choices Act 2005 in Australia, and the Employment Contracts Act 1991 in New Zealand, all of which aimed at restricting union activity. US legislation is widely seen to allow employers to suppress unionization in workplaces where employees would like to be represented by a union. Indeed, Freeman et al. (2007) have established that there is a sizeable union representation gap in all six LMEs, with workers desiring greater union representation than currently available.

In the USA, the substantial difference in union density in the public and private sectors (see Table 12.6) also indicates that legislation in the private sector (the National Labor Relations Act) contributes to the low private sector density rates. While legislation in the public sector generally provides fewer opportunities for employers to avoid unionization, significant differences exist in the nature of that legislation across states. For example, some states mandate, others permit, and a third group prohibits collective bargaining for some or all groups of public employees (such as police, fire fighters, teachers, and nurses). Union density varies across states (from 71% in New York to 9% in Georgia in 2008), and this variance is highly associated with the state legal environment for collective bargaining (Kearney 2010). Union density is much lower in states that limit or outlaw collective bargaining in the public sector than in states providing

Table 12.6 Union density in the public and private sectors 2010 (%)

Country	Private sector density (%)	Public sector density (%)
Australia	14	42
Canada	16	71
Ireland*	25	71
New Zealand**	12	62
UK	14	56
USA	7	36

Notes: *2007; **2008
Sources: Achur (2011); Australian Bureau of Statistics (2010); Blumenfeld and Ryall (2010); Bureau of Labor Statistics (2011); Central Statistics Office (2009); Uppal (2011).

full union recognition and collective bargaining rights. The state legal environment is, however, subject to change. Most recently, changes in labour law in Wisconsin have generated much public attention. Wisconsin was the first state to confer collective bargaining rights to public employees in 1959, and most of these rights were revoked by the Republican governor Scott Walker in 2011. This new law limits collective bargaining to basic pay only and limits pay raises to the inflation rate. A similar law eliminating collective bargaining in the public sector was passed in Ohio, but overturned by public referendum before taking effect. Further Republican state governments considered similar measures to curb union power and limit public sector employees' rights to collectively bargain (Maher and Brat 2011; Maher and Nicas 2011; Merrick 2011). It remains to be seen how much such legislative changes depress union density rates in the public sector.

Concurrent with the decline of unionism in LMEs, new research on union revitalization has developed which deals with the union movement's prospects for renewal. Rather than viewing unions' fate as determined by economic, political, and societal factors, unions are conceived as strategic actors who attempt to tackle and reverse their decline (Frege and Kelly 2003). The main revitalization strategies identified include organizing new members, coalition building with social and community groups, political action and campaigns, partnerships with employers and governments, international solidarity with other unions, and organizational restructuring (Frege and Kelly 2004). This research is concerned with how unions develop these strategies, their nature and content, and effects on revitalization of union power and influence (Turner 2005). Some unions in LMEs have been particularly innovative in mobilizing new groups of workers, and addressing the changing composition of the workforce towards more women, ethnic minorities, and service sector workers. While membership gains in these areas have not been large enough to offset the aggregate union decline, revitalization strategies remain an important area of future research and policy development.

Employer Associations

Employer associations represent the labour market interests of employers vis-à-vis unions and the state. In doing so, they engage in collective bargaining as well as lobbying on labour law issues. Increasingly, they also provide services to member companies, such as providing information, legal advice, consultancy, and training (Traxler 2008). Employer associations were initially formed in response to the rise of the union movement and to increasing state regulation of employment. Besides ensuring that business interests are reflected in collective agreements and in legislation, employer associations seek to manage competition among employers and thus have a cartelizing function (Barry and Wilkinson 2011).

In LME countries, employer associations have been weak and remained so in recent years. The decline of unionization has reduced the interest of employers in organizing. In addition, the pronounced role of inter-firm competition reduces the significance of the cartelizing function. As Traxler (2004, 2008) points out, the prevalence of multi-employer bargaining and state regulation regarding extension practices (which make collective agreements applicable to companies that are not members of an employer association and thus not signatory to the agreements) augment employers' propensity to associate—but both multi-employer bargaining and extension practices are rare in LMEs.

Data on employer associations are rare and difficult to compare cross-nationally. Nevertheless, Traxler (2004, 2008) indicates that employer associations have never played a significant role in employment relations in the USA or in Canada. Likewise, their role decreased in the UK and New Zealand when collective bargaining was decentralized in the 1980s and 1990s, respectively. Similarly, the decline of the centralized bargaining system in Australia was accompanied by employer associations focusing less on advocacy and more on fee-based services for members (Lansbury and Wailes 2011). In Ireland, unions and employer associations were involved in economic policy-making within a 'social partnership' from 1987 to 2009 which included the conclusion of centralized wage agreements at the national level (Traxler and Walshe 2007). In addition, employer associations provided advice, assistance, and training to member firms in conducting company-level bargaining (Carley 2010). Thus, employer associations have been important employment relations actors during this period, yet how their role will evolve after the collapse of the social partnership is unclear.

INSTITUTIONAL DYNAMICS OF EMPLOYMENT RELATIONS

The state, unions, and employers interact in different ways across countries, giving rise to different processes of regulating employment relations. This section turns to three key processes: collective bargaining, industrial conflict, and employee voice.

Collective Bargaining

Collective bargaining is an important dimension and indicator of the overall coordination of employment relations. The level at which bargaining takes place and the degree of coordination between negotiations are both relevant. Collective agreements may be concluded on the national level, the sector or industry level, and the local or company level. Bargaining coordination occurs when key negotiations influence other negotiations, effectively setting a pattern that is followed in other, formally independent, bargaining rounds. As a result, decentralized bargaining may include some centralized aspects if pattern bargaining takes place. Conversely, centralized bargaining at the national or industry level may be supplemented by further bargaining at lower levels, rendering it more decentralized than it first appears.

Bargaining is generally considered more centralized and coordinated in CMEs and more decentralized and uncoordinated in LMEs. The reality is more varied and complex. As Table 12.7 indicates, collective bargaining is decentralized to the local level in the USA and Canada. But in the 1980s, Ireland, New Zealand, and Australia had quite centralized collective bargaining, and each changed towards a more decentralized system at different times. While decentralization has been the predominant trend across many developed economies since the 1980s, Traxler (1998) detects a polarization of bargaining structures, with a tendency to single-employer bargaining in English-speaking countries and a continued dominance of multi-employer bargaining in continental Europe. Today, a common feature of all LME countries is the decentralization of collective bargaining to the local level coupled with a low degree of bargaining coordination. According to Katz (1993), the USA has become even more decentralized and uncoordinated when the reach of multi-employer agreements (for example in trucking and coal mining) diminished, and pattern bargaining (prevalent for example in the auto assembly and aerospace industries) weakened in the 1980s.

There are various explanations for the observed decentralization trend. For example, the shift to post-Fordist production systems is argued to require the involvement of local actors in bargaining, and both international competition and industry deregulation may turn centralized wage setting into competitive hindrances. A further explanation regards conflict over the bargaining level as part of the struggle for power and control over the terms of employment, whereby decentralization is a consequence of a shift in power towards employers who expect it to lead to more favourable outcomes for them. Furthermore, legal support for multi-employer bargaining has been found to be an essential determinant of a country's overall bargaining structure. Where legal support is withdrawn, bargaining structures become more decentralized (Flanagan 2008; Katz 1993; Traxler 2003).

Australia and New Zealand are current examples of how legislative reform brings about changes to bargaining structure. Historically, wages and employment conditions in Australia and New Zealand were set centrally by arbitration, where tribunals handed down 'awards' regulating employment conditions at the industry level. Only

Table 12.7 The dominant level at which wage bargaining takes place in LMEs 1980–2010

Country	1980	1990	2000	2010
Australia	3	4	2	2
Canada	1	1	1	1
Ireland	4	5	4	1
New Zealand	4	1	1	1
UK	2	1	1	1
USA	1	1	1	1

Notes: 5 = national or central level; 4 = national or central level, with additional sectoral / local or company bargaining; 3 = sectoral or industry level; 2 = sectoral or industry level, with additional local or company bargaining; 1 = local or company bargaining.
Source: Visser (2011).

after legislative reforms in the 1990s did enterprise bargaining spread and become the norm. In Australia, decentralization began under a Labor government and with union agreement. But it was pushed to the extreme by a neo-liberal government after 1996, which reduced awards to safety nets of minimum standards. This government promoted non-union collective agreements as well as 'employer greenfield agreements' for new businesses, which employers concluded without a bargaining partner of any kind, and introduced individual statutory contracts known as Australian Workplace Agreements (AWAs), thereby providing employers alternatives to any form of collective bargaining (Cooper and Ellem 2008). A moderate re-centralization took place when the Labor government revised industrial relations legislation in 2009. It removed AWAs and introduced multi-employer bargaining in a low pay bargaining stream for previously award-dependent employees (Cooper 2010). A further example of the effect of legislation on bargaining structure is the UK, where deregulation in the early 1980s similarly precipitated bargaining decentralization. Recently, New Zealand also removed requirements for employers to bargain in good faith, and made it possible for firms to opt out of multi-employer agreements (Shuttleworth 2012).

Finally, the Irish case shows how the relative power of the social partners affects the level at which bargaining takes place. As mentioned earlier, from 1987 to 2009, unions and employers were involved in economic policy-making within a 'social partnership'. Centralized wage agreements concluded at the national level were a key component of this social partnership. Previously, collective bargaining oscillated between centralization and decentralization, and was highly decentralized and market-based previous to the era of social partnership (Baccaro and Simoni 2007). The social partnership came about as a deal between a weak minority government facing an economic crisis and the decision by general and public sector unions to exchange wage moderation for involvement in key economic policies. Employer associations initially opposed the social partnership, but changed their stance when it became clear that centralized bargaining effectively ensured wage moderation (Baccaro 2003). The collapse of the social partnership in 2009 came about when the government planned to cut public sector pay and public sector unions opposed. Union leaders believed that the government, together with the major employer association IBEC, favoured public sector wage cuts in order to put downward pressure on pay rates in the private sector (EIRO 2010). Since the collapse of the social partnership, local bargaining may once again become the norm (EIRO 2011).

Industrial Conflict

Strikes and lockouts are overt expressions of industrial conflict. While a general trend towards quiescence has been observed in many industrialized countries, significant cross-national variation in conflict levels remains (Brandl and Traxler 2010; Piazza 2005). Industrial relations institutions play an important role in lessening and in resolving industrial conflict (Korpi and Shalev 1979). Collective bargaining structure, trade union organization, and the involvement of unions in public policy-making are seen to influence the volume of industrial conflict. Each explanation suggests that industrial conflict will be higher in LME countries than in CME countries. First, centralized collective bargaining may reduce strikes because the distribution of information between unions and employers is more symmetrical than in a decentralized system, strikes are more costly due to their larger size, and well-developed centralized collective bargaining processes exercise behavioural constraints on unions and employers (Bean 1994; Brandl and Traxler 2010; Clegg 1976). All this results in greater cooperation, whereas conflict will likely be higher in LMEs with their decentralized bargaining systems. Second, the fragmentation of unions in LME countries leads to competition among unions for members, including competition over bargaining outcomes, increasing unions' propensity to call strikes (Brandl and Traxler 2010). Third, when unions are integrated into corporatist public policy-making and the state is actively involved in redistributing income, peaceful cooperation becomes more likely (Hibbs 1978). The absence of such corporatist arrangements in LMEs also makes them more prone to conflict.

In contrast to the arguments above, three factors may decrease the level of industrial conflict in LMEs. First, the development and implementation of company HR strategies may be particularly widespread in LMEs and serve as a substitute for unionization and the expression of conflict through strikes and lockouts. Second, legal constraints on strike activity that have been introduced by various neo-liberal governments can also have a dampening effect. Third, the decline in union density observed in most LMEs also negatively affects unions' capacity for collective action.

Comparing statistics on industrial conflict internationally is fraught with difficulties. Data collection methods differ across countries—for example, only strikes involving a certain minimum number of workers or minimum duration are counted, and data on political strikes or public sector strikes are not gathered. In addition, such statistics cannot capture forms of collective action such as go-slows, work-to-rule, or overtime bans, nor are individual and covert forms of conflict such as absenteeism and turnover measured. Despite these limitations, these statistics are the one source of data that is readily available for comparative analyses of industrial conflict (Wallace and O'Sullivan 2006).

The data show a decline in annual average working days lost due to work stoppages over recent decades in all six LMEs, in line with broader international trends (see Table 12.8). A comparison of annual average working days lost per 1,000 employees in

Table 12.8 Working days lost (per 1,000 employees), average per year 1970–2007

Country	1970–79	1980–89	1990–99	2000–07
Austria	11	2	4	0
Belgium	275	59	33	89
Denmark	261	178	168	37
Finland	613	408	168	81
Germany	52	27	11	5
Japan	124	10	2	0
Netherlands	40	15	22	8
Norway	45	99	81	57
Sweden	46	182	50	22
Switzerland	2	0	2	4
Mean CMEs	**146.9**	**98**	**54.1**	**30.3**
Australia	634	351	123	36
Canada	882	520	220	164
Ireland	758	380	119	33
New Zealand	373	528	65	13
United Kingdom	569	334	30	30
United States	507	123	40	32
Mean LMEs	**620.5**	**372.7**	**99.5**	**51.3**

Notes: AUS: Excluding work stoppages in which fewer than 10 workdays not worked; BE: Excluding public sector; CAN: Excluding work stoppages in which fewer than 10 workdays not worked; CH: Excluding work stoppages lasting less than one day; DE: Including work stoppages lasting less than one day if more than 100 workdays not worked; IRL: Work stoppages lasting at least one day or with at least 10 days not worked; NZ: Excluding work stoppages in which fewer than 10 workdays not worked. Prior to 1988: Excluding public sector stoppages; UK: Including stoppages involving fewer than 10 workers or lasting less than one day if 100 or more workdays not worked. Excluding political strikes; USA: Excluding work stoppages involving fewer than 1000 workers and lasting less than a full day or shift.
Source: Lesch (2009).

the group of LMEs with the group of CMEs shows that in each decade from the 1970s until today, conflict levels have been higher in LMEs than in CMEs, confirming institutional arguments. But over time the differences have decreased and in the 2000s both groups of countries had similarly low levels of conflict. In fact, in individual LME countries, conflict levels are now lower than in some CME countries. For example, in the 2000s in Australia, Ireland, New Zealand, the UK, and the USA, there were fewer annual average working days lost per 1,000 employees than in Belgium, Denmark, Finland, and Norway.

While there have been some changes to bargaining structures, union mergers have reduced the fragmentation of the union system and Ireland also had corporatist arrangements for many years. Nonetheless, these factors cannot account for the significant decrease in conflict levels in LMEs. Rather, legislative constraints, declining unionization, and the increasing use of HR practices appear to be plausible explanations.

Employee Voice

Employee voice encompasses the myriad ways in which employees are able to have a say regarding their work activities and in organizational decision-making. Many indirect and direct forms of employee voice exist, including works councils, joint consultative committees, self-managed teams, quality circles, suggestion schemes, grievance procedures, employee share ownership plans, and profit-sharing schemes. These forms differ regarding the managerial and worker goals attached to them, in the degree to which they confer power to employees, and whether they can be unilaterally revoked by management or receive legislative backing. Indeed, the amount of employee influence and the types of decisions included vary significantly across organizations (Wilkinson and Fay 2011). National institutions play a role in what voice regimes are adopted in organizations.

Comparing employee voice in the Anglo-American economies, Freeman et al. (2007) establish that a representation gap exists in all six LMEs, with workers desiring both more union and non-union forms of voice at the workplace. Marchington (2007) points out that many factors impede the adoption of voice systems in LMEs, such as a voluntarist approach to worker rights (and the absence of national institutions and employment laws supporting employee voice), the predominance of the shareholder perspective, adversarial management–union relations, and the paucity of long-term careers in organizations. Since fewer statutory provisions for employee voice exist in LMEs than in CMEs, employers have more leeway to adopt voice regimes of their preference, resulting in greater experimentation and variation in voice systems (Bryson et al. 2006; Lansbury and Wailes 2008; Wilkinson and Fay 2011). Employee voice is thus often associated with high performance work systems, including various forms of non-union representation and direct involvement of employees as well as financial participation. As Wilkinson and Fay (2011: 69) note, the benefits of voice tend to be seen in terms of its contribution to shareholder value, profits, product quality, customer service, staff retention, and so on.

In both the UK and Ireland, EU regulations have introduced some elements of employee voice drawn from other European traditions. European works councils provide voice for employees in multinational firms, and create new avenues of European-level representation (Waddington 2011). In terms of national institutions, the Information and Consultation Directive (Directive 2002/14/EC) necessitated the establishment of a statutory framework giving employees the right to be informed and consulted by their employers on a range of business, employment, and restructuring matters. As a result, employee voice institutions and practices in the UK and Ireland now differ from those in the remaining LME countries, where statutory employee voice institutions are non-existent. In the UK, national legislation (Information and Consultation of Employees Regulations 2004) transposing the EU Directive came into effect from April 2005 onwards. For the first time in UK industrial relations, employee voice was thereby given institutional support through legislation. Nonetheless, this legislation included high barriers for any employee-initiated introduction of employee voice at the workplace. The establishment of information and consultation (I&C) arrangements is not mandatory, but must be initiated by either employers or employees. High levels of employee support are required to trigger negotiations, and recognized unions are not able to do so on the employees' behalf (Hall 2010). If employers choose to introduce I&C arrangements, the law gives them considerable leeway in adopting voice mechanisms of their preference. Little information is available on the extent to which I&C bodies have been introduced in UK workplaces as a result of the legislation. Nevertheless, data from a 2009 European survey indicate 24% of UK establishments or 45% of employees were covered by some institutional form of employee representation, which remains below the EU-27 average of 37% and 63%, respectively (Hall and Purcell 2011). These results indicate that great variation in the existence and scope of employee voice systems continues in the UK.

Conclusion

This chapter has shown that employment relations in the six countries examined are liberal and market-based in nature, and have become increasingly so over time. These similarities are reflected in the common trends towards short-term employment and inequality of earnings, documented in the second section. The role of the state is also broadly similar in its focus on the rights of individuals and on providing minimum standards to address market failure. However, this chapter has also documented very important differences in employment relations within the broad category of liberal market economies.

To start with, the trajectory of liberalization has differed significantly. The most extensive shifts in legislation have occurred in Australia and New Zealand, in contrast to stability in the USA and Canada (Colvin and Darbishire 2013). The decline in union strength and influence is a common trend among LME countries, but the extent of decline differs markedly. Again, the most significant changes occurred in Australia and New Zealand, while union density and bargaining coverage have remained comparatively stable in Canada. Employer associations play a lesser role in LME countries than in CME countries, but their significance also varies across countries and over time: while historically less important in the USA and Canada, they played a more prominent role in the UK, Australia, and New Zealand when bargaining was more centralized than it is today. In Ireland, employer association involvement in social partnership provided them with large influence until very recently. Decentralized and uncoordinated collective bargaining is a contemporary feature of all six countries, but Ireland, New Zealand, and Australia moved away from their more centralized wage setting systems at different points in time. Levels of industrial conflict have decreased drastically in all countries, but remain comparatively high in Canada. The widespread absence of statutory provisions on employee voice has contributed to a representation gap, with employees desiring more voice at the workplace in all six countries. However, EU influence and employer-led practices have both contributed to variation in the voice systems that are adopted.

Recognizing both the similarities *and differences* among the six LME countries has important implications for scholars of comparative employment relations. First, relatively few studies exist that examine employment relations in these countries empirically from a broad and historical institutional perspective (for exceptions, see Doellgast 2012; Jacoby 2004). Rather, the LME concept is often invoked as a baseline ideal type in order to study CME countries, but this leads to a variety of misconceptions. Second, employment relations are more variable and internally diverse than often claimed. Rather than coherent national 'models' of employment relations, liberal institutions have tended to support decentralized forms of employment relations, which leads to great variability in how employment relations are organized in practice across sectors, regions, and types of firms. In particular, employment relations allow for a very wide range of HR practices by firms, ranging from very 'calculative' HRM to high performance work systems. But an important research agenda remains to understand how HR practices are enabled, constrained, and achieve fit with these liberal institutional contexts. Third, the complementarities between employment relations and other institutions are likely to be more complex and varied than often assumed in the literature. For example, the success of venture capital in Silicon Valley is not based on short-term market transactions, but uses more relational forms of organization via social networks to bring together committed finance with high-skilled professionally oriented labour (Aoki and Jackson 2008; Ferrary and Granovetter 2009). In fact, liberal institutions may require different, even functionally opposite, sorts of institutional logics in order to be effective—such as decentralized bargaining being complemented by statutory minimum wages. The concept of complementarities must be extended to explore the role of coordination and more relational forms of employment within LME contexts. Finally, although employment relations are often considered to be less regulated than in CMEs, the role of the state is actually crucial in the political construction of liberal markets (Hamann and Kelly 2008). While the political forces have followed similar trajectories over the past decades, this trend is not irreversible. For example, the UK and Ireland will be more influenced by developments in the EU on issues such as worker participation, gender equality, welfare state reform, and taxation policies. In looking to the future, LME countries will all face rising inequality, and the contingent political responses to this challenge will remain an important area of research.

NOTES

1. Following Hall and Soskice (2001), this group of liberal countries is contrasted with the coordinated market economies (CMEs), which include some continental European countries (Austria, Belgium, Netherlands, Germany, and Switzerland), Nordic countries (Denmark, Finland, Norway, Sweden), and Japan. While we use this CME group as a reference point for some comparisons in the text, this is done for illustrative purposes only. The limitations of the VOC approach for comparing Nordic, continental, Mediterranean, and Asian countries has been widely discussed and critiqued elsewhere (Deeg and Jackson 2007; Jackson and Deeg 2012).
2. No comparable data on job tenures are available for New Zealand.
3. Figures taken from the OECD.Stat database.
4. Existing studies show that the use of financial participation schemes is higher in LME countries—specifically, share ownership by employees is higher than in CME countries (Croucher et al. 2010; Pendleton and Poutsma 2012). This fact may reflect complementarities between pay systems and the greater prevalence of shareholder value-oriented corporate governance in these countries (Gospel and Pendleton 2005).
5. For example, performance pay has been implemented very differently across countries, even in the same sector such as banking or metal, depending on the context of collective bargaining (Nergaard et al. 2009; Traxler et al. 2008). Even in LME countries, considerable diversity exists depending on sectoral and firm-level characteristics, as shown by comparisons of Canada and Australia (Long and Shields 2005).
6. While easing union recognition and strengthening arbitration mechanisms, New Labour's approach had modest overall effects. More marked was the direct intervention of the state through the national minimum wage, which regulated low pay but also reflected the fact that wage negotiations had become increasingly individualized.
7. The Tennessee Supreme Court famously wrote in 1884 'men must be left, without interference to buy and sell where they please, and to discharge or retain employees at will for good cause or for no cause, or even for bad cause without thereby being guilty of an unlawful act per se' (*Payne* v. *Western & Atlantic Railroad*, Tennessee 1884) (Autor 2003).

REFERENCES

Achur, J. (2011). *Trade Union Membership 2010*. London: Department for Business Innovation and Skills.

Addison, J. T., Blackburn, M. L., and Cotti, C. D. (2009). 'Do Minimum Wages Raise Employment? Evidence from the U.S. Retail-Trade Sector', *Labour Economics*, 16(4): 397–408.

Akkermans, D., Castaldi, C., and Los, B. (2009). 'Do "Liberal Market Economies" Really Innovate More Radically than "Coordinated Market Economies"? Hall and Soskice Reconsidered', *Research Policy*, 38(1): 181–91.

Amable, B. (2003). *The Diversity of Modern Capitalism*. Oxford and New York: Oxford University Press.

Aoki, M. and Jackson, G. (2008). 'Understanding an Emergent Diversity of Corporate Governance and Organizational Architecture: An Essentiality-Based Analysis', *Industrial and Corporate Change*, 17(1): 1–27.

Armstrong, M. and Brown, D. (2005). 'Reward Strategies and Trends in the United Kingdom: The Land of Diverse and Pragmatic Dreams', *Compensation & Benefits Review*, 37(4): 41–53.

Arrowsmith, J. and Marginson, P. (2010). 'The Decline of Incentive Pay in British Manufacturing', *Industrial Relations Journal*, 41(4): 289–311.

—— (2011). 'Variable Pay and Collective Bargaining in British Retail Banking', *British Journal of Industrial Relations*, 49(1): 54–79.

Australian Bureau of Statistics (2010). *Catalogue No. 6310.0: Employee Earnings, Benefits and Trade Union Membership*. Canberra: Australian Bureau of Statistics.

Autor, D. H. (2003). 'Outsourcing at Will: The Contribution of Unjust Dismissal Doctrine to the Growth of Employment Outsourcing', *Journal of Labor Economics*, 21(1): 1–42.

Baccaro, L. (2003). 'What is Alive and What is Dead in the Theory of Corporatism?', *British Journal of Industrial Relations*, 41(4): 683–706.

Baccaro, L. and Simoni, M. (2007). 'Centralized Wage Bargaining and the "Celtic Tiger" Phenomenon', *Industrial Relations*, 46(3): 426–55.

Ballam, D. A. (2000). 'Employment-at-Will: The Impending Death of a Doctrine', *American Business Law Journal*, 37(4): 653–87.

Barry, M. and Walsh, P. (2007). 'State Intervention and Trade Unions in New Zealand', *Labor Studies Journal*, 31(4): 55–78.

Barry, M. and Wilkinson, A. (2011). 'Reconceptualising employer associations under evolving employment relations', *Work, Employment & Society*, 25(1): 149–62.

Batt, R., Holman, D., and Holtgrewe, U. (2009). 'The Globalization of Service Work: Comparative Institutional Perspectives on Call Centers', *Industrial and Labor Relations Review*, 62(4): 453–88.

Bean, R. (1994). *Comparative Industrial Relations: An Introduction to Cross-National Perspectives*. London: International Thomson Business Press.

Belfield, R. and Marsden, D. (2003). 'Performance Pay, Monitoring Environments, and Establishment Performance', *International Journal of Manpower*, 24(4): 452–71.

Bell, B. and Van Reenen, J. (2010). *Bankers' Pay and Extreme Wage Inequality in the UK*. Centre for Economic Performance CEPSP21. London: London School of Economics and Political Science.

Biernacki, R. (1995). *The Fabrication of Labor: Germany and Britain, 1640–1914*. Berkeley, CA: University of California Press.

Blanchflower, D. G. (2007). 'International Patterns of Union Membership', *British Journal of Industrial Relations*, 45(1): 1–28.

Blumenfeld, S. and Ryall, S. (2010). 'Unions and Union Membership in New Zealand: Annual Review for 2008', *New Zealand Journal of Employment Relations*, 35(3): 84–96.

Botero, J. C., Djankov, S., La Porta, R., Lopez-de-Silanes, F., and Shleifer, A. (2004). 'The Regulation of Labor', *Quarterly Journal of Economics*, 19(4): 1339–82.

Boyer, R. (2004). 'New Growth Regimes, but Still Institutional Diversity', *Socio-Economic Review*, 2(1): 1–32.

Brandl, B. and Traxler, F. (2010). 'Labour Conflicts: A Cross-National Analysis of Economic and Institutional Determinants, 1971–2002', *European Sociological Review*, 26(5): 519–40.

Brown, W. (2011). 'Industrial Relations in Britain under New Labour, 1997–2010: A Post Mortem', *Journal of Industrial Relations*, 53(3): 402–13.

Bryson, A., Ebbinghaus, B., and Visser, J. (2011). 'Introduction: Causes, Consequences and Cures of Union Decline', *European Journal of Industrial Relations*, 17(2): 97–105.

Bryson, A., Gomez, R., and Willman, P. (2006). 'Voice at Work... What Do Employers Want? A Symposium Summary', *Socio-Economic Review*, 4(2): 279–82.

Bureau of Labor Statistics (2011). *News Release: Union Members—2010*. Washington, DC.

Campbell, B. A., Ganco, M., Franco, A. M., and Agarwal, R. (2012). 'Who Leaves, Where To, and Why Worry? Employee Mobility, Entrepreneurship and Effects on Source Firm Performance', *Strategic Management Journal*, 33(1): 65–87.

Campbell, I, and Brosnan, P. (2005). 'Relative Advantages: Casual Employment and Casualisation in Australia and New Zealand', *New Zealand Journal of Employment Relations*, 30(3): 1–14.

Carley, M. (2010). *Developments in Social Partner Organisations—Employer Organisations*. Dublin: European Foundation for the Improvement of Living and Working Conditions.

Central Statistics Office (2009). *National Employment Survey 2007, Supplementary Analysis*. Dublin: Government of Ireland.

Checchi, D. and Visser, J. (2005). 'Pattern Persistence in European Trade Union Density', *European Sociological Review*, 21(1): 1–21.

Clegg, H. A. (1976). *Trade Unionism Under Collective Bargaining: A Theory Based on Comparisons of Six Countries*. Oxford: Blackwell.

Colvin, A. J. S. and Darbishire, O. R. (2013). 'Convergence in Industrial Relations Institutions: The Emerging Anglo-American Model?', *Industrial and Labor Relations Review*, 66(5).

Cooper, R. (2010). 'The "New" Industrial Relations and International Economic Crisis: Australia in 2009', *Journal of Industrial Relations*, 52(3): 261–74.

Cooper, R. and Ellem, B. (2008). 'The Neoliberal State, Trade Unions and Collective Bargaining in Australia', *British Journal of Industrial Relations*, 46(3): 532–54.

Crouch, C. (1993). *Industrial Relations and European State Traditions*. Oxford: Clarendon Press.

Croucher, R., Brookes, M., Wood, G., and Brewster, C. (2010). 'Context, Strategy and Financial Participation: A Comparative Analysis', *Human Relations*, 63(6): 835–55.

Croucher, R., Wood, G., Brewster, C., and Brookes, M. (2012). 'Employee Turnover, HRM and Institutional Contexts', *Economic and Industrial Democracy*, 33(4): 605–20.

Deakin, S. (2009). 'Legal Origin, Juridical Form and Industrialization in Historical Perspective: The Case of the Employment Contract and the Joint-Stock Company', *Socio-Economic Review*, 7(1): 35–65.

Deeg, R. (2012). 'The Limits of Liberalization? American Capitalism at the Crossroads', *Journal of European Public Policy*, 19(8): 1249–68.

Deeg, R. and Jackson, G. (2007). 'Towards a More Dynamic Theory of Capitalist Variety', *Socio-Economic Review*, 5(1): 149–80.

Denoon, D. (1983). *Settler Capitalism: The Dynamics of Dependent Development in the Southern Hemisphere*. Oxford: Clarendon Press.

Dobbin, F. and Sutton, J. R. (1998). 'The Strength of a Weak State: The Rights Revolution and the Rise of Human Resources Management Divisions', *American Journal of Sociology*, 104(2): 441–76.

Doellgast, V. L. (2012). *Disintegrating Democracy at Work: Labor Unions and the Future of Good Jobs in the Service Economy*. Ithaca: ILR Press.

Dolton, P., Bondibene, C. R., and Wadsworth, J. (2012). 'Employment, Inequality and the UK National Minimum Wage over the Medium-Term', *Oxford Bulletin of Economics and Statistics*, 74(1): 78–106.

Donaghey, J. (2008). 'Deliberation, Employment Relations and Social Partnership in the Republic of Ireland', *Economic and Industrial Democracy*, 29(1): 35–63.

Dube, A., Lester, T. W., and Reich, M. (2010). 'Minimum Wage Effects across State Borders: Estimates Using Contiguous Counties', *Review of Economics and Statistics*, 92(4): 945–64.

EIRO (2010). *End of Social Partnership as Public Sector Talks Collapse*. Document ID IE0912019I. Available at <http://www.eurofound.europa.eu/eiro/2009/12/articles/ie0912019i.htm>, accessed 6 February 2012.

—— (2011) *Ireland: EIRO Annual Review 2009*. Document ID IE1004019Q. Available at <http://www.eurofound.europa.eu/eiro/studies/tn1004019s/ie1004019q.htm>, accessed 6 February 2012.

Fabling, R. and Grimes, A. (2010). 'HR Practices and New Zealand Firm Performance: What Matters and Who Does It?', *International Journal of Human Resource Management*, 21(4): 488–508.

Ferrary, M. and Granovetter, M. (2009). 'The Role of Venture Capital Firms in Silicon Valley's Complex Innovation Network', *Economy and Society*, 38(2): 326–59.

Flanagan, R. J. (2008). 'The Changing Structure of Collective Bargaining', in P. Blyton, N. Bacon, J. Fiorito, and E. Heery (eds.), *The Sage Handbook of Industrial Relations*. London: Sage, 406–19.

Freeman, R. B., Boxall, P. and Haynes, P. (eds.) (2007). *What Workers Say: Employee Voice in the Anglo-American Workplace*. Ithaca: ILR Press.

Frege, C. M. and Kelly, J. (2003). 'Union Revitalization Strategies in Comparative Perspective', *European Journal of Industrial Relations*, 9(1): 7–24.

—— (2004). 'Union Strategies in Comparative Context', in Frege and Kelly (eds.), *Varieties of Unionism: Strategies for Union Revitalization in a Globalizing Economy*. Oxford and New York: Oxford University Press, 31–44.

Gospel, H. and Edwards, T. (2012). 'Strategic Transformation and Muddling Through: Industrial Relations and Industrial Training in the UK', *Journal of European Public Policy*, 19(8): 1229–48.

Gospel, H. and Pendleton, A. (eds.) (2005). *Corporate Governance and Labour Management: An International Comparison*. Oxford and New York: Oxford University Press.

Hall, M. (2010). 'EU Regulation and the UK Employee Consultation Framework', *Economic and Industrial Democracy*, 31(4S): 55–69.

Hall, M. and Purcell, J. (2011). *Information and Consultation Practice across Europe Five Years after the EU Directive*. Document ID TN1009029S. Available at <http://www.eurofound.europa.eu/eiro/studies/tn1009029s/tn1009029s_4.htm>, accessed 18 January 2012.

Hall, P. A. and Soskice, D. (eds.) (2001). *Varieties of Capitalism: The Institutional Foundations of Comparative Advantage*. Oxford and New York: Oxford University Press.

Hamann, K. and Kelly, J. (2008). 'Varieties of Capitalism and Industrial Relations', in P. Blyton, N. Bacon, J. Fiorito, and E. Heery (eds.), *The Sage Handbook of Industrial Relations*. London: Sage, 129–48.

Heywood, J. S and O'Halloran, P. L. (2005). 'Racial Earnings Differentials and Performance Pay', *Journal of Human Resources*, 40(2): 435–52.

Hibbs, D. A. (1978). 'On the Political Economy of Long-Run Trends in Strike Activity', *British Journal of Political Science*, 8(2): 153–75.

Hobijn, B. and Şahin, A. (2007). *Job-Finding and Separation Rates in the OECD*. Federal Reserve Bank of New York Staff Report no. 298.

Howell, C. (2005). *Trade Unions and the State: The Construction of Industrial Relations in Britain, 1890–2000*. Princeton: Princeton University Press.

Jackson, G. (2001). 'The Origins of Nonliberal Corporate Governance in Germany and Japan', in W. Streeck and K. Yamamura (eds.), *The Origins of Nonliberal Capitalism: Germany and Japan in Comparison*. Ithaca: Cornell University Press, 121–70.

—— (2005). 'Toward a Comparative Perspective on Corporate and Labour Management: Enterprise Coalitions and National Trajectories', in H. Gospel and A. Pendleton (eds.), *Corporate Governance and Labour Management: An International Comparison*. Oxford and New York: Oxford University Press, 284–309.

Jackson, G. and Deeg, R. (2008). 'From Comparing Capitalisms to the Politics of Institutional Change', *Review of International Political Economy*, 15(4): 680–709.

—— (2012). 'The Long-Term Trajectories of Institutional Change in European Capitalism', *Journal of European Public Policy*, 19(8): 1109–25.

Jacoby, S. M. (2004). *The Embedded Corporation: Corporate Governance and Employment Relations in Japan and the United States*. Princeton: Princeton University Press.

Kabst, R., Giardini, A., and Wehner, M. C. (eds.) (2009). *International komparatives Personalmanagement: Evidenz, Methodik and Klassiker des Cranfield Projects on International Human Resource Management*. München/Mering: Hampp.

Katz, H. C. (1993). 'The Decentralization of Collective Bargaining: A Literature Review and Comparative Analysis', *Industrial and Labor Relations Review*, 47(1): 3–22.

Kearney, R. C. (2010). 'Public Sector Labor–Management Relations: Change or Status Quo?', *Review of Public Personnel Administration*, 30(1): 89–111.

Kleiner, M. M. (2001). 'Intensity of Management Resistance: Understanding the Decline of Unionization in the Private Sector', *Journal of Labor Research*, 22(3): 520–40.

Kopczuk, W., Saez, E., and Jae, S. (2010). 'Earnings Inequality and Mobility in the United States: Evidence from Social Security Data since 1937', *Quarterly Journal of Economics*, 125(1): 91–128.

Korpi, W. and Shalev, M. (1979). 'Strikes, Industrial Relations and Class Conflict in Capitalist Societies', *British Journal of Sociology*, 30(2): 164–87.

Lansbury, R. D. and Wailes, N. (2008). 'Employee Involvement and Direct Participation', in P. Blyton, N. Bacon, J. Fiorito, and E. Heery (eds.), *The Sage Handbook of Industrial Relations*. London: Sage, 434–46.

—— (2011). 'Employment Relations in Australia', in G. J. Bamber, Lansbury, and Wailes (eds.), *International and Comparative Employment Relations: Globalisation and Change*, 5th edn. Sydney: Allen & Unwin, 117–37.

Latornell, J. (2006). 'Uncovering the Origins of New Zealand's Employment Relations Act 2000: A Research Framework', *New Zealand Journal of Employment Relations*, 31(3): 88–100.

Lemieux, T., Macleod, W. B., and Parent, D. (2009). 'Performance Pay and Wage Inequality', *Quarterly Journal of Economics*, 124(1): 1–49.

Lesch, H. (2009). 'Erfassung und Entwicklung von Streiks in OECD-Ländern' [International Comparison of Strike Statistics], *IW-Trends*, 36(1): 1–17.

Long, R. J. and Shields, J. L. (2005). 'Performance Pay in Canadian and Australian Firms: A Comparative Study', *International Journal of Human Resource Management*, 16(10): 1783–1811.

McCabe, V. S. and Savery, L. K. (2007). '"Butterflying" a New Career Pattern for Australia? Empirical Evidence', *Journal of Management Development*, 26(2): 103–16.

McLaughlin, C. (2009). 'The Productivity-Enhancing Impacts of the Minimum Wage: Lessons from Denmark and New Zealand', *British Journal of Industrial Relations*, 47(2): 327–48.

Maher, K. and Brat, I. (2011). 'Wisconsin Curbs Unions', *The Wall Street Journal*, 11 March.

Maher, K. and Nicas, J. (2011). 'Ohio Voters Reject Public-Union Limits', *The Wall Street Journal*, 9 November.

Marchington, M. (2007). 'Employee Voice Systems', in P. Boxall, J. Purcell, and P. Wright (eds.), *The Oxford Handbook of Human Resource Management*. Oxford and New York: Oxford University Press, 231–50.

Marsh, D. (1992). *The New Politics of British Trade Unionism: Union Power and the Thatcher Legacy*. Ithaca: ILR Press.

Merrick, A. (2011). 'Wisconsin Union Law to Take Effect', *The Wall Street Journal*, 15 June.

Metcalf, D. (2008). 'Why has the British National Minimum Wage had Little or No Impact on Employment?', *Journal of Industrial Relations*, 50(3): 489–512.

Mouw, T. and Kalleberg, A. L. (2010). 'Do Changes in Job Mobility Explain the Growth of Wage Inequality among Men in the United States, 1977–2005?', *Social Forces* (University of North Carolina Press), 88(5): 2053–77.

Nergaard, K., Dølvik, J. E., Marginson, P., Díaz, J. A., and Bechter, B. (2009). 'Engaging with Variable Pay: A Comparative Study of the Metal Industry', *European Journal of Industrial Relations*, 15(2): 125–46.

OECD (1997). *OECD Employment Outlook*. Paris: OECD.

—— (2010). *OECD Employment Outlook*. Paris: OECD.

Pendleton, A. and Poutsma, E. (2012). 'Financial Participation', in C. Brewster and W. Mayrhofer (eds.), *Handbook of Research on Comparative Human Resource Management*. Cheltenham: Edward Elgar, 345–68.

Piazza, J. A. (2005). 'Globalizing Quiescence: Globalization, Union Density and Strikes in 15 Industrialized Countries', *Economic and Industrial Democracy*, 26(2): 289–314.

Rasmussen, E. (ed.) (2010). *Employment Relationships: Workers, Unions and Employers in New Zealand*. Auckland: Auckland University Press.

Richbell, S., Brookes, M., Brewster, C., and Wood, G. (2011). 'Non-Standard Working Time: An International and Comparative Analysis', *International Journal of Human Resource Management*, 22(4): 945–62.

Schneider, M. R. and Paunescu, M. (2012). 'Changing Varieties of Capitalism and Revealed Comparative Advantages from 1990 to 2005: A Test of the Hall and Soskice Claims', *Socio-Economic Review*, 10(4): 731–53.

Schneider, M. R., Schulze-Bentrop, C., and Paunescu, M. (2009). ,Mapping the Institutional Capital of High-Tech Firms: A Fuzzy-Set Analysis of Capitalist Variety and Export Performance', *Journal of International Business Studies*, 41(2): 246–66.

Shuttleworth, K. (2012). 'New Industrial Relations Laws Rewrite Labour Rules', *The New Zealand Herald*, 14 May.

Sousa-Poza, A. and Henneberger, F. (2004). 'Analyzing Job Mobility with Job Turnover Intentions: An International Comparative Study', *Journal of Economic Issues*, 38(1): 113–37.

Stavrou, E. and Kilaniotis, C. (2010). 'Flexible Work and Turnover: An Empirical Investigation across Cultures', *British Journal of Management*, 21(2): 541–54.

Sutton, J. R. and Dobbin, F. (1996). 'The Two Faces of Governance: Responses to Legal Uncertainty in U.S. Firms, 1955 to 1985', *American Sociological Review*, 61(5): 794–811.

Taylor, M. Z. (2004). 'Empirical Evidence against Varieties of Capitalism's Theory of Technological Innovation', *International Organization*, 58(3): 601–31.

Thelen, K. (2010). 'Economic Regulation and Social Solidarity: Conceptual and Analytic Innovations in the Study of Advanced Capitalism', *Socio-Economic Review*, 8(1): 187–207.

Traxler, F. (1998). 'Collective Bargaining in the OECD: Developments, Preconditions and Effects', *European Journal of Industrial Relations*, 4(2): 207–26.

—— (2003). 'Bargaining (De)centralization, Macroeconomic Performance and Control over the Employment Relationship', *British Journal of Industrial Relations*, 41(1): 1–27.

—— (2004). 'Employer Associations, Institutions and Economic Change: A Crossnational Comparison', *Industrielle Beziehungen*, 11(1&2): 42–60.

—— (2008). 'Employer Organizations', in P. Blyton, N. Bacon, J. Fiorito, and E. Heery (eds.), *The Sage Handbook of Industrial Relations*. London: Sage, 225–40.

Traxler, F., Arrowsmith, J., Nergaard, K., and Molins López-Rodó, J. M. (2008). 'Variable Pay and Collective Bargaining: A Cross-National Comparison of the Banking Sector', *Economic and Industrial Democracy*, 29(3): 406–31.

Traxler, F. and Walshe, E. (2007). 'Ireland', in F. Traxler and G. Huemer (eds.), *Handbook of Business Interest Associations, Firm Size and Governance: A Comparative Analytical Approach*. London: Routledge, 192–203.

Turner, L. (2005). 'From Transformation to Revitalization: A New Research Agenda for a Contested Global Economy', *Work and Occupations*, 32(4): 383–99.

Uppal, S. (2011). 'Unionization 2011', *Perspectives on Labour and Income* 23(4): Statistics Canada Catalogue no. 75–001-XIE.

Visser, J. (2006). 'Union Membership Statistics in 24 Countries', *Monthly Labor Review*, 129(1): 38–49.

—— (2011). *Database on Institutional Characteristics of Trade Unions, Wage Setting, State Intervention and Social Pacts 1960–2010 (ICTWSS)*, version 3.0, May. Amsterdam Institute for Advanced Labour Studies, University of Amsterdam. Available at <http://www.uva-aias.net/208>.

Waddington, J. (2011). *European Works Councils and Industrial Relations: A Transnational Industrial Relations Institution in the Making*. New York: Routledge.

Wallace, J. and O'Sullivan, M. (2006). 'Contemporary Strike Trends since 1980: Peering through the Wrong End of a Telescope', in M. J. Morley, P. Gunnigle, and D. G. Collings (eds.), *Global Industrial Relations*. London: Routledge, 273–91.

Whitford, J. (2005). *The New Old Economy: Networks, Institutions and the Organizational Transformation of American Manufacturing*. Oxford and New York: Oxford University Press.

Whitley, R. (1999). *Divergent Capitalisms: The Social Structuring and Change of Business Systems*. Oxford and New York: Oxford University Press.

Wilkins, M., Thelen, K., Whitley, R., Miller, R. M., Martin, C. J., Berghahn, V. R., Iversen, M. J., Herrigel, G., and Zeitlin, J. (2010). '"Varieties of Capitalism" Roundtable', *Business History Review*, 84(4): 637–74.

Wilkinson, A. and Fay, C. (2011). 'New Times for Employee Voice?', *Human Resource Management*, 50(1): 65–74.

Wójcik, D. (2012). 'The End of Investment Bank Capitalism? An Economic Geography of Financial Jobs and Power', *Economic Geography*, 88(4): 345–68.

CHAPTER 13

....

SOCIAL DEMOCRATIC CAPITALISM

....

KRISTINE NERGAARD

INTRODUCTION

....

THE concept of 'social democratic capitalism' is associated with the mixed economies that evolved in the Scandinavian countries (Denmark, Sweden, and Norway) and eventually in the broader group of Nordic countries (including Finland and Iceland) in the wake of the Second World War. In these countries, a comprehensive range of welfare services, income transfers, and labour markets characterized by strong collective institutions and regulations were developed in small open market economies. This development occurred during a period when the Scandinavian countries tended to have social democratic governments or coalition governments dominated by social democratic parties.

Although the characteristics of the Nordic labour and welfare systems had been highlighted in previous studies of the individual countries, Gøsta Esping-Andersen's *The Three Worlds of Welfare Capitalism* (1990) is considered a key work on the distinct 'social democratic' model of the institutional features and outcomes that characterize the Scandinavian countries. The book refers to the evolution of universal tax-funded welfare states in a labour market context of high participation, strong trade unions, and employer associations, encompassing coordinated collective bargaining. These countries thus differed from, on the one hand, the insurance-based continental welfare systems, with their emphasis on family-based welfare services and the association of wage labour with a family breadwinner model, and, on the other, Anglo-American deregulated labour markets where public welfare schemes mainly functioned as a safety net.

Studies that focus on industrial relations systems have particularly emphasized the shared characteristics of the Nordic countries (Kjellberg 1992; Traxler et al. 2001; Dølvik 2008; Dølvik et al. 2014). According to these studies, the multi-tiered Nordic systems of industrial relations are distinguished by high rates of organization among workers and employers, centralized bargaining coordination, a strong company tier of negotiations and participation, low wage dispersion, and a culture of trust and cooperation among social partners.

Whereas the debate over the Scandinavian or Nordic model originally emphasized the interests of organized labour—or 'social democracy'—as driving the evolution of the Nordic welfare states (Korpi 1978; Esping-Andersen 1990), recent theories have focused on production regimes and the strategies of enterprises and capital owners in shaping coordinating institutions (Hall and Soskice 2001; Thelen 2001). In the varieties of capitalism (VOC) literature, the Nordic countries are all subsumed under the heading 'coordinated market economies', along with Germany, for example. According to VOC theory, the labour markets in such economies are marked by well-developed systems of vocational education and strong employer investment in enterprise- or industry-specific training and the development of their workforce. As discussed below, however, this only partly describes the Nordic countries.

Another approach to the diversity of capitalist systems (Amable 2003) considers various combinations of five main categories of institutional features, and identifies a need to refine the VOC division in coordinated and liberal market economies. Amable points to a social democratic cluster of countries, namely the Nordic countries, where product markets are marked by the importance of competition for quality (because they are high-cost countries), state involvement, and openness to foreign competition and investment. Unlike continental European capitalist economies, social democratic economies are characterized by moderate employment protection and, unlike market-based economies, public spending on education is high.

The emphasis on coordination of macroeconomic policies, wage setting, and social policies is highlighted in studies of the evolution of the Nordic labour market models. The export dependence of the small, open Nordic economies and their vulnerability to fluctuations in international markets have been viewed—not least by Nordic researchers—as essential for development of the centralized coordination of wage setting, the close collaboration between labour, capital, and the state, and the strong emphasis on restructuring and active labour market policies (Dølvik and Stokke 1998; Dølvik and Vartiainen 2002; Erixon 2010; Dølvik et al. 2014).

The so-called Nordic model should not be seen as a static set of institutions and outcomes. Dølvik et al. (2014) and Pontusson (2011) argue that an important characteristic of the model is its capacity to adapt to changes in circumstances, and they link this capacity to what they see as its success in recent decades. Nevertheless, over the past three to four decades, the Nordic countries and their labour market models have experienced crises as well as recoveries. Furthermore, it should be stressed that although the labour market institutions of the Nordic countries share a number of common factors, they are far from identical. Detailed analyses reveal clear differences between the countries in labour market regulation, collective bargaining systems, and social welfare institutions, and national researchers often refer to a Swedish, Danish, or other model. However, there are important similarities both in institutional frameworks and in outcomes, leading to the concept of a common model.

HISTORICAL BACKGROUND

In the years after the Second World War, Denmark, Sweden, and Norway were characterized by high employment rates, strong trade unions, and a collectively regulated labour market based on centralized wage coordination. Following this period, the countries gradually expanded the 'welfare state', offering generous social benefits and a comprehensive range of services for citizens (Esping-Andersen 1990; Anttonen 2005; Kangas and Palme 2005). The public welfare schemes were sustained by relatively high taxes, which funded both labour-related benefits and a gradual expansion of public services in a number of areas. A key element in the expansion of the welfare state included the emergence of an education system with loans and scholarships that would extend higher education to working-class children. A greater emphasis on gender equality was another element. The expansion of public care services for the elderly and care for children in the form of day-care centres allowed women to work outside the home while also generating new workplaces for women.

The emergence of the Nordic welfare states was associated with long periods of social democratic governance and close cooperation between the two pillars of the Nordic labour movement: the social democratic parties and the trade unions, organized in powerful confederations. The labour movement no longer challenged the market economy, but rather used its influence to fight for reforms, real wage increases, and low unemployment rates.

Furthermore, the Nordic models had their basis in far broader alliances than the traditional labour movement. The early social benefits developed well before the social democratic parties came to power and established rights for all groups in society in case of illness or unemployment. The scope and level of such income security benefits, which generally depended on former income, eventually ensured that wide sections of the population benefited from the schemes, thus generating broad political support for the welfare state (Esping-Andersen 1990).

At that time, the success of the Nordic model was largely attributed to the centralized organizations and wage formation systems. All the Nordic countries had strong, centralized labour organizations, especially in the form of powerful blue-collar confederations. Employers were early to organize, and the multi-employer bargaining system emerged in the early twentieth century. In the 1970s and 1980s, these countries scored high on indexes of bargaining coordination and centralization, and were often described as 'neo-corporatist' when the degree of bargaining centralization was under discussion (Cameron 1984; Calmfors and Driffill 1988; Calmfors 1993; Iversen 1999). The centralized bargaining system also led to a compressed wage structure (Wallerstein 1999), which, together with the welfare arrangements, contributed to low levels of inequality (Barth and Moene 2009).

Mutual recognition, the peace duty, and the employer's governance prerogative are key principles of the Nordic labour market model. These principles have a long tradition in Nordic industrial life, first codified in the Danish Basic Agreement of 1899, and imply a balance of power between social partners. Similar agreements were signed for the other countries during the 1930s (Norway and Sweden) and 1940s (Finland), although the main principles were by then already implemented in other agreements in Sweden and Norway.

Mutual recognition means, in practice, that employers recognize the right of employees to unionize and to choose representatives, although this also gives employers the right to organize. This meant that the employer side never attacked unionism itself, even when tensions ran high (Fahlbeck 2002).

The peace duty implies that collective agreements are legally binding and that disputes arising during the agreement period should be resolved between the parties or by labour courts, not by industrial action (Stokke and Thörnqvist 2001; Fahlbeck 2002). As a rule, this obligation also pertains to local bargaining, with disputes at the company level resolved by involving the parties at the central level or by various conflict resolution mechanisms (Stokke 2008). This obligation is normally honoured, which means that Nordic employers face little risk of 'wildcat' or illegal strikes. The Nordic countries are not exceptional in terms of few working days lost to strikes (Stokke and Thörnqvist 2001; EIRO 2009). However, because strikes are mainly associated with the centralized wage bargaining processes, employers benefit from a certain level of predictability.

The employers' prerogative to lead implies that the trade unions recognize the employers' right to direct, distribute, and control the work, as well as the right to sign and terminate employment contracts (Fahlbeck 2002). This principle is counterbalanced by the obligation for employers to bargain and conclude collective agreements. In practice, the employers' governance prerogative is curtailed by legislation as well as collective agreements; for example, the countries (with the exception of Denmark) follow the generally strict provisions defined in the collective agreements or legislation as to whether collective lay-offs should adhere to the principle of seniority.

Although much of the attention on the Nordic model or models initially focused on characteristics of welfare state institutions and centralized tripartite cooperation, the micro-tier of the Nordic models gradually grew in salience. Workplace participation and 'good workplaces' gradually assumed importance in the development of legislation and collective agreements. Especially in the 1970s, trialled flat work organizational structures and autonomous work groups were praised as the key to democratic workplaces (Gustavsen 2007; see also Sandberg 1995 for an example). All the countries gradually introduced working environment legislation to ensure an appropriate physical working environment and to develop workplaces conducive to personal development and good psychosocial working conditions.

During the 1980s and 1990s, the future viability of the Nordic model was questioned. All the countries experienced economic crises in the early 1990s, which led to increasing unemployment and cutbacks in welfare. Doubts were raised as to whether the thoroughly regulated labour markets were compatible with a full-employment model. The centralized bargaining systems also failed to produce wage growth and a wage structure that could persuade industrial organizations to leave wage formation to the confederations. Swedish employers' rejection of coordinated bargaining constituted the most dramatic challenge to the centralized wage-setting model (Kjellberg 1992; Swenson and Pontusson 2000). In Denmark and Norway also, bargaining at the confederation level no longer played the same role as previously (see, for example, Dølvik and Stokland 1992; Scheuer 1992; Due et al. 1993; Dølvik 2008). The pressure on the centralized bargaining system was driven not only by employers' desire for decentralization; discord within trade unions increased in several countries, reflecting conflicts between private and public sector unions as well as between traditional industrial workers and white-collar unions.

However, during the 2000s, the Nordic countries re-emerged as successful labour market regimes, with rising employment rates and GDP growth (Pontusson 2011; Dølvik et al. 2014). We argue that central elements of the industrial relations and labour market institutional framework are intact, albeit revised and adapted to new circumstances. In the next three sections, we discuss the characteristics of Nordic industrial relations, in the form of employment and collective labour relations in the 2000s. Then we discuss the challenges these countries face in the wake of the recent economic crisis, increased labour migration, and changes in labour market policies and collective partnerships.

Employment Relations and Labour Market Organization

Employment and Unemployment

The Nordic countries have high rates of employment. In 2011, the employment rate in Norway and Sweden was more than ten percentage points above the EU average (Table 13.1). In 2007, Denmark had an employment rate at the same level as Sweden and Norway, but in 2011 high unemployment figures began to affect the employment rate. By 2011, Finland had the lowest employment rate of the Nordic countries, but it remained above the EU average.

One characteristic of the Nordic model has been its high rate of employment among women. The countries have notably high rates of female labour participation, which contribute significantly to the high employment rates. For the 20- to 64-year-old age group, we find a gender gap of 5–7 percentage points in the Nordic countries (2011), compared with 12% in the EU as a whole. Whereas female labour participation overall has increased in the EU, employment rates among Nordic women have remained fairly stable.

Another distinction of the Nordic labour model is the high employment rate among older workers. In Norway and Sweden in particular, a high number of people continue working after the age of 55; the proportion of the 60- to 64-year-old age group who

Table 13.1 Employment rates among those aged 20–64 years: total and by gender, 2000, 2007, and 2011

	2000	2007	2011
Total			
Denmark	77.9	79.0	75.7
Finland	72.3	74.8	73.8
Norway	80.7	80.9	79.6
Sweden	76.3	80.1	80.0
EU-27 average	66.5	69.9	68.6
Men			
Denmark	82.4	83.2	79.0
Finland	75.5	77.2	75.6
Norway	84.9	84.3	82.1
Sweden	78.2	83.1	82.8
EU-27 average	75.8	77.8	75.0
Women			
Denmark	73.3	74.7	72.4
Finland	69.0	72.5	71.9
Norway	76.4	77.5	77.1
Sweden	74.4	77.1	77.2
EU-27 average	57.1	63.0	63.4

Source: Eurostat, Labour Force Surveys.

remain employed is twice as high in Norway and Sweden as that in the EU as a whole (Table 13.2).

As experience during the past three to four decades has shown, the Nordic countries are far from protected against high unemployment caused by external shocks or internal crises. The countries underwent periods of high unemployment in the early 1980s (Denmark) and in the mid-1990s (Finland, Sweden, and to some extent Norway). However, unemployment rates rapidly declined in the 1990s, and in the first half of the 2000s, all the countries—with the exception of Finland—were well below the EU average (Fig. 13.1). Unemployment rates in Finland increased dramatically throughout the 1990–3 crises and never really returned to the 'Nordic' level. Finland nevertheless stood out for its strong reduction in unemployment during 1995–2008. The Nordic countries were affected to varying degrees by the global financial crisis in the late 2000s; Norway was least affected in terms of unemployment, Denmark most profoundly.

Table 13.2 Employment rates among older workers (55–64 years and 60–64 years) 2011

	From 55 to 64 years	From 60 to 64 years
Denmark	59.5	42.9
Finland	57.0	41.8
Norway	69.6	59.7
Sweden	72.3	63.2
EU-27 average	47.4	33.5

Source: Eurostat, Labour Force Surveys.

----- Norway   ——— Denmark   ········ Sweden   ━━━ Finland   — — OECD average

FIGURE 13.1 Unemployment rates 1990–2011: 15- to 64-year-olds

Source: OECD, Labour Force Surveys.

The high employment rate (and high rate of economic activity), rather than stable low rates of unemployment, is the defining characteristic of the employment pattern in the Nordic countries.

With the exception of Finland, the Nordic countries have a sizeable proportion of part-time workers, mainly women. In 2011, one third of all Danish women aged 20–64 worked part-time; this proportion was 37% in Sweden and 40% in Norway. Female part-time work is much higher than the EU average, and has remained stable for a long time (Berglund et al. 2010). In Finland, by contrast, the rate of female part-time employment is very low.

Part-time jobs are often regarded as increasing the flexibility of the labour market, and are considered atypical work, as are temporary jobs and temporary agency work (Kalleberg 2000; Bredgaard et al. 2009a). In the Nordic countries, by contrast, the emergence of part-time positions is regarded as an adaptation to working hour preferences among married women (Ellingsæter 2009). Part-time work has long been described as normalized (Ellingsæter 1989), and women who work part-time have a stable association with the labour market (Berglund et al. 2010).

Whereas access to part-time work has been hailed outside the Nordic region as a useful strategy for increasing (female) labour participation (Berglund et al. 2010; Nicolaisen 2011), it is seen as a challenge to gender equality in the Nordic labour markets, not least in Norway and Sweden, which have the highest proportions of part-time workers.

Gender Equality

All five Nordic countries (including Iceland) are among the six European countries with the highest rates of female labour participation. This is seen as a precondition for, and result of, the Nordic welfare regimes, which include a comprehensive range of services funded by high tax revenues through high employment rates. Equally importantly, the high employment rate among women can be regarded as an element of a comprehensive gender equality project encompassing participation in politics and education, in which labour activity is seen as a precondition for the economic independence of women.

The high employment rate among women is largely associated with arrangements that allow women with children to continue working, such as a well-developed system of day care and generous periods of leave after childbirth. A place in a day-care centre has been a statutory entitlement in most Nordic countries since Finland was the first country in the world to introduce it (Gíslason and Eydal 2011). More than 95% of all children aged 3–5 years are in day care, and the proportion of 1- and 2-year-old children in day care is also high. Nordic parents are entitled to parental leave with wage compensation for approximately one year, including opportunities to combine parental leave and part-time work. The level of wage compensation varies from 70% to 100%. Work life is facilitated for working mothers (and fathers) by schemes allowing for parental leave when children are ill. In recent years, more attention has been devoted to fathers and to schemes to distribute the responsibility for childcare more evenly between parents. In all countries except Denmark—which discontinued this form of arrangement—parts of the parental leave period are reserved for fathers (Ellingsæter and Leira 2006; Gíslason and Eydal 2011).

Despite the high employment rates among Nordic women, certain gender equality challenges persist. In particular, part-time rates are high among women and men remain overrepresented in higher management positions. Another prominent point of contention is the pay discrepancy between men and women, and between male- and female-dominated occupations.

Increased Emphasis on Activation

During the 2000s, all the Nordic countries intensified measures to accelerate the transition from unemployment to work, known as the transition from passive to active labour market policies. Such policies partly involved more stringent requirements for job-seeking activity or participation in training programmes to help the unemployed find work. It has also involved a tightening of entitlements, such as lower levels of compensation or curtailing of benefit periods, or stricter requirements for acceptance of job offers. Measures have included reforms to improve the effectiveness of the assistance apparatus. Norway and Denmark have introduced a service that encompasses both the labour market agency and the authorities responsible for benefits and social assistance. The stated aims of these reforms were to provide more effective assistance to job seekers. Other reforms support these activation policies, including introduction of pension reforms linking higher pension payments to accumulated contributions and number of years in the labour market (Norway, implemented in 2011) and the tightening of arrangements allowing for early retirement (Denmark). Denmark and Sweden have also introduced special tax relief measures for working people, to encourage mobility from social benefits to employment (Finseraas and Pedersen 2013). Another measure was Swedish tax deductions for household renovation and cleaning services. Similar schemes exist in Finland (since the late 1990s) and Denmark (introduced in 2011), based on the rationale that this policy would stimulate demand for such services and thereby create more jobs as well as discourage undeclared work.

The Danish 'Flexicurity' Model

Along with the Netherlands, Denmark has been at the forefront of the so-called 'flexicurity' model, which assumed a key place in the debate on labour market policies in the 2000s. The flexicurity model is characterized by deregulated job protection (flexibility) combined with a high degree of income security and intensive measures to bring redundant employees into other work (Madsen 2006; Bredgaard et al. 2009b). Thus, flexicurity meets both the economic and social demands of firms as well as of workers (Boyer, in this volume).

The advantage of the flexicurity model is that it shifts the emphasis away from job security, that is, the retention of a job, to employment security, which is the opportunity to find other work of similar quality. Although all the Nordic countries have policies to ensure income security in case of unemployment, Denmark stands out as having less job protection and a comprehensive set of active labour market measures. In consequence, Denmark, along with the Netherlands, is regarded as a striking example of successful modernization of the labour market, where restructuring and weak job protection do not occur at the expense of employees' income security and opportunities to find new work (OECD 2004; European Commission 2006).[1]

The other Nordic countries have not adopted the institutional framework linked to the flexicurity model to the same extent. Norway still has strict job protection, without significant deregulation of the opportunity to lay off workers or the requirements for permanent employment. In Sweden and Finland, employers obtained better opportunities for temporary employment contracts during the 1990s, but Sweden in particular, where the principle of seniority is strong, has retained strict job protection with regard to lay-offs.

Is Denmark different from the other Nordic countries in terms of labour market flexibility? The combination of flexibility and security may be seen as a particular example of a more general principle of the Nordic models, namely the need for companies to adapt to increased competition combined with systems that take care of employees who are made redundant (Boyer, in this volume). This principle is perhaps most explicitly formulated through the Swedish Rehn–Meidner model from the 1950s (Erixon 2010). A study of mobility in the labour market in the period 2000–6 used panel data from national labour force surveys and showed that Denmark has larger flows both into and out of employment (Berglund et al. 2010). However, even Norway, with its strict limitations on the use of temporary employment, had a high degree of positive mobility in the sense of transitions from unemployment to employment, and from temporary to permanent employment. The study nevertheless indicates that Denmark is distinct in its particularly high mobility in the labour market as well as high investments in active labour market policy measures.

In the past few years, Denmark has reduced the entitlement period for unemployment benefits from four to two years (a common duration in the other Nordic countries) and has tightened the scheme allowing employees to take early retirement on very favourable terms. At the same time, no other Nordic country has seen a similarly rapid increase in unemployment in the wake of the international crisis. The problems in the Danish economy are partly linked to problems in the housing market as well as in the banking sector, and Denmark saw a sharper fall in GDP than the other Nordic countries (Dølvik et al. 2014). The labour market instruments have been expanded too slowly to assist the rising number of unemployed people into active measures or training. Trade unions have also demanded better job protection to counteract the gradual decline in the level of compensation in the unemployment benefits system, which may result in less flexibility for employers if successful. Although there is little doubt that the Danish flexicurity model is under pressure, there remains some disagreement as to whether Denmark can be said to have abandoned the model (Goul Andersen 2011; Madsen 2011).

Education and Training

Education policy and the development of general skills have been regarded as key instruments for social equality in the Nordic countries. Development of a public support system for young people seeking higher education was an important element in the expansion of the Nordic welfare states in the decades following the Second World War. The important objective of this system—as well as the development of an upper secondary school system—was not only to provide society with a sufficient supply of well-educated workers, but also to allow access to higher education for people of all social strata (Antikainen 2006; Telhaug et al. 2007).

The education systems of the Nordic countries are primarily based on public funding, with a limited number of private schools. One feature of this system is that students in higher education pay only small fees, and the state provides education loans and scholarships to cover living costs during study. The countries have some of the world's highest entry rates to higher education, although the proportion that completes it is not significantly different from that in other Western countries (OECD 2011a).

One key distinction between the countries' education systems is the extent to which training, especially vocational training, takes place directly in the enterprises and within systems that involve labour market actors or industrial organizations. In countries where the development of labour skills is primarily undertaken by enterprises or industries, employers have a greater investment in retaining and developing this labour (Hall and Soskice 2001).

All the Nordic countries have vocational training systems that can be described as universal and partly classroom-based. At the same time, the countries differ in terms of whether vocational training takes place in enterprises in the form of apprenticeships, and in the extent to which the social partners are involved in the design and operation of such systems. Sweden and Denmark are at opposite ends of this spectrum: Sweden has a school-based vocational training system without any significant participation by social partners, whereas Denmark attaches great importance to placing parts of the training directly in enterprises (apprentice systems). Norway in this respect is closer to Denmark than to Sweden and Finland (Olofsson and Panican 2008; OECD 2010).

Lifelong learning—and on-the-job training—is regarded as key for ensuring employability and developing a workforce with necessary, updated skills; Amable (2003) describes it as an important feature of the Nordic education models in his alternative categorization of capitalist systems. Compared with other European countries, a high proportion of employees are provided with further and continuing education. Here Denmark is notable, with further and continuing education closely linked to labour market policies through various types of educational leave, and generous leave arrangements that have been seen as an important pillar of the active labour market policy (Berglund et al. 2010; Bredgaard et al. 2009b).

The education systems of the Nordic countries can be regarded as a hybrid of characteristics associated with coordinated market economies and liberal market economies.

Vocational training is partly based on apprentice systems in which representatives from the relevant industries play an important role, although with substantial variation among the countries, and lifelong learning and on-the-job training are emphasized. However, the general education system is built around standardized systems, and access to higher education is considered imperative for social equality.

PERSISTENCE OF COLLECTIVELY REGULATED LABOUR RELATIONS

The Nordic countries were long characterized by strong trade unions, centralized coordination of bargaining and wage formation across industries, and institutionalized cooperation between social partners at the central and company levels. During the 1980s and 1990s, the centralized bargaining structure in particular came under pressure. What has been the situation since the 2000s?

Trade Unions Remain Strong, Despite Declining Membership

The Nordic rates of employee unionization remain high by international standards, especially in Denmark, Finland, and Sweden. During the first half of the 1990s—when unionization was at its peak in many of the Nordic countries—approximately 80% of all Swedish, Danish, and Finnish employees were members of a trade union. This high unionization rate is particularly associated with institutional arrangements that favour recruitment to the unions, especially unemployment insurance funds, which are administered by the unions (the so-called Ghent model). For a long time, it was uncommon—and in practice difficult—not to be a member of both a union and its associated unemployment insurance scheme (Böckerman and Uusitalo 2006; Due et al. 2010; Kjellberg 2011). The exception is Norway, where these schemes were abolished in the 1930s; however, the Norwegian unionization rate, which in 2012 was slightly over 50%, is nevertheless high by international standards (Nergaard and Stokke 2007b; Nergaard 2010).

The traditionally strong influence of the unions can be explained not only by their large membership, but also by the organization of the labour movement. Nationwide unions dominate, and most are affiliated to confederations. The centralized structure has enabled the unions to exert influence in wage bargaining as well as at the political level through coordination of wage demands and policy proposals and the unions' ability to commit their subordinate organizational levels and ensure compliance (Traxler et al. 2001).

Another feature of the strength of the Nordic trade unions is that their scope extends beyond blue-collar workers. In Denmark, Finland, and Sweden, the majority of white-collar workers in the private sector are unionized and are covered by collective agreements. The usual organizational pattern in the Nordic countries includes separate unions for blue-collar workers and clerical staff, as these groups often have differing priorities, for example with regard to wages and wage systems. Structural changes in the labour market, such as increasing levels of education, have also entailed a shift from organizations associated with the blue-collar confederations to organizations and confederations for clerical staff or academics.

A third characteristic of the Nordic labour movement that adds to its strength is strong local organizational levels within a single-channel system of representation. Co-determination and bargaining at the enterprise level can primarily be undertaken by shop stewards elected from among—and normally by—union members in the individual workplace (Edström 2002). A precondition for this system is that the unions can develop local organizational units. Nordic trade unions therefore devote considerable funds to the training and support of their local representatives.

The Nordic trade unions retained their large membership throughout the 1980s and 1990s, at a time when labour unions in many other Western countries saw their membership dwindle. In recent years, however, Danish, Finnish, and Swedish trade unions have seen a considerable reduction in their membership figures (Table 13.3). This loss of membership has particularly afflicted the traditional blue-collar unions. This trend can be attributed primarily to changes in the organization of unemployment insurance schemes, which raised the cost of premiums or facilitated alternatives outside the traditional labour unions. In addition, compensation rates for social insurance schemes have been reduced, also reducing the 'value' of the voluntary unemployment schemes. As a result, more employees are choosing to remain outside both the unions and the unemployment insurance scheme (Sweden, see Kjellberg 2011) or to choose 'budget unions', which are not party to a collective agreement and do not have a presence in the workplace (Denmark, see Due et al. 2010). In Finland, a growing number of employees have chosen to join the independent unemployment insurance scheme (Böckerman and Uusitalo 2006).

The decline in union membership appears to be especially strong among younger employees, who are overrepresented in the private service industries (Nergaard 2010). Whereas many young workers—new on the labour market—choose not to join a union, older workers have tended to remain unionized even with the recent changes to the institutional framework. Over time, these trends may exacerbate the difficulties faced by Nordic trade unions.

The structural changes in the labour market have also given rise to a growth in membership for unions organizing employees with high levels of education or in typical white-collar professions. This implies a potential shift in the power balance within the trade unions and a decrease in the strength of blue-collar unions, traditionally seen as the main driving force behind the development of a strong welfare state within a market economy.

Table 13.3 Union density rates in the Nordic countries

	Finland	Denmark	Norway	Sweden
1985	69	78	57	78
1990	73	75	57	81
1995	82	73	56	85
2000	76	72	53	81
2005	71	72	53	78
2010	70	67	52	71
2011		67	52	70

Note: Finland: OECD figures for 1985 and 1990, figures from Böckerman and Uusitalo (2006), and updates by Böckerman. Norway: Nergaard and Stokke 2010 (updated). Denmark: Due et al. 2010, Ibsen et al. 2011b. Sweden: Kjellberg 2013.

The Organized Employer Side: Centralized Control and Broad Agenda

Industrial relations in the Nordic countries were for a long time characterized by centralized organizations on both sides of the labour market. The early centralization of the bargaining system—with industry-wide collective agreements—in which Denmark, Norway, and Sweden took part was partly initiated by employers seeking to prevent enterprises from being played off against each other in company-level wage bargaining processes (Jensen 2000). Centralization also allowed the employer side to concentrate coercive power and to employ the lockout strategy.

For a long time, the Nordic employers' organizations preferred to concentrate bargaining power at the central level. Employer confederations were also central in the development of a system based on cooperation between social partners to promote productivity and economic growth, partly on the basis of moderate wage growth. This system also secured full employment and a gradual expansion of the welfare state. However, the employer side also played a significant role in the partial collapse of this centralized bargaining system during the 1980s.

The organized employer side remains powerful in the Nordic countries. The emergence of combined employer and business associations at the industrial and confederate levels implies a stronger coordination of employer and industrial interests, and gives the organizations a broader basis for their relations with their members and the authorities (Vartiainen 2011; Dølvik et al. 2014). By the early 2010s, only employer confederations in Finland and Norway were conducting direct wage bargaining. The Danish and Swedish confederations lost—or relinquished—their direct role in the 1980s and 1990s. At the same time, employers' organizations have reinforced their position at the industry level through mergers that have established larger organizational units.

The majority of enterprises in the Nordic countries remain members of an employer organization, and multi-employer bargaining at the industry level is the dominant mode of negotiations. Actual wage formation in large parts of the private sector has been decentralized, with the introduction of a greater emphasis on enterprise-level negotiations allowing the company actors considerable flexibility in deciding wages and working time arrangements (Dølvik and Nergaard 2012; Ilsøe 2012).

Bargaining Level and the Capacity to Regulate

The Nordic system of collective agreements is dominated by nationwide agreements that encompass an industry or a sector. In Sweden and Denmark, the system of coordinated bargaining at the confederate level broke down in the 1980s, but Norway also had several bargaining rounds that suggested that the Nordic countries were in the process of abandoning centralized and coordination of wage setting. The exception was Finland, where the traditional system of bargaining at the confederate level remained important during the crises of the early 1990s and was not questioned until around 2007 (Vartiainen 2011).

Recent studies of the bargaining systems attach less importance to the formal level of bargaining, focusing instead on other mechanisms of coordination (Traxler et al. 2001). During the 1990s and 2000s, all the Nordic countries witnessed increased coordination of wage formation (Vartiainen 2011; Dølvik et al. 2014). This occurred not in the form of a new bargaining mandate to the confederations, but rather through various mechanisms of sectoral coordination. Examples include the emergence of broad sectoral bargaining cartels on the labour side, and a stronger concentration of employers' organizations. The countries also developed institutions to establish an understanding of the level of wage growth that the economy can 'bear', in the form of tripartite organizations such as the Calculation Committee for Income Settlements (Norway), independent experts (Denmark), or framework agreements (Sweden). In addition, the systems of state/national mediators play a role in enhancing coordination across industries and sectors.

In Norway, this recentralization took the form of moderate peak-level wage settlements periodically bolstered by income-policy cooperation, in which the government assisted with social reforms (Dølvik and Stokke 1998). The so-called 'trend-setting industries model', under which the results of negotiations for the metalworking industry—or export-oriented industries—are used to establish the economic framework, has been widely accepted in principle, although public sector unions challenge the model at irregular intervals. In Sweden, too, the parties reverted to a bargaining model with stronger coordination at the sector level. Through a general agreement (Industriavtalet), parties in the manufacturing industry agreed on the main features of the wage policy. In the important metalworking industry, bargaining is now coordinated across the blue/white-collar divide (Vartiainen 2011).

Decentralization of actual wage formation has taken place in all the countries—with the exception of Finland—in the sense that local wage bargaining plays a more prominent role than previously. As an example, more industries have started to allow local wage formation, the role of new performance-related wage systems has increased, and a considerable proportion of total wage growth is generated at the local level. Local wage growth has also become more important in the public sector, although less so in Norway and Finland than in Sweden and Denmark.

The changes in the Nordic countries are referred to as organized decentralization or centralized decentralization (Traxler et al. 2001; Due and Madsen 2008), a concept that indicates the balance between the bargaining levels in systems with two-tier bargaining. Guidelines for local bargaining over wages and working hours are defined by central-level agreements, and the degree of local autonomy varies between countries and sectors. In the Norwegian private sector, the parties have agreed that company-level wage rises should be based on the enterprise's financial position, productivity, competitiveness, and future prospects (Dølvik and Nergaard 2011; Stokke 2012). In the public sector, local bargaining takes place within a framework defined by central-level bargaining. In Denmark, the parties at the local level may choose to disregard central-level agreements if they concur on this point. In Sweden, there is relatively widespread use of a model whereby the parties bargain locally for local wage increments, but where the central-level organizations have agreed on a default pot that is applied in cases where the local parties fail to agree (Vartiainen 2011).

Wage Distribution and Low-Wage Workers

Compressed wage distribution is a long-standing feature of employment relations in the Nordic countries. This is commonly explained by a long tradition of a solidaristic wage policy reducing the wage differentials across enterprises and employees, obtained by centralized coordination in wage formation. However, favourable welfare arrangements for those in the weakest positions in the labour market mean that they do not need to offer their labour at extremely low wages (the 'reservation wage'). In this context, Nordic economists have argued that the combination of a narrow wage distribution and generous welfare benefits results in an 'equality multiplier', whereby narrow wage differences lend political support to good welfare schemes, and good welfare schemes result in a narrow wage distribution (Barth and Moene 2009). However, figures for the 2000s reveal a recent widening in wage distribution, although the Nordic countries remain in the group with the most equal wage structure (OECD 2011b).

None of the Nordic countries has a statutory minimum wage. Nor, with the exception of Finland, do they have a tradition of extending collective agreements to unorganized enterprises (Eldring and Alsos 2012). The potential for regulation—and equalization—inherent in the collective agreements has thus depended on the ability of the labour market parties to impose the collective agreement on individual enterprises. In Denmark and Sweden, this has largely followed from the high rates of employee unionization.

The overall coverage rates remain very high: 88% in Sweden in 2011 (Kjellberg 2013) and an estimated 83% in Denmark in 2007 (Due et al. 2010). The recent decline in union density rates has apparently not had much influence on the collective agreement coverage rate, although the situation suggests a slightly declining coverage rate, especially in Denmark. In Norway, slightly more than half of all private sector employees are covered by a collective agreement (Nergaard and Stokke 2010); the coverage rates are lowest in parts of the private service sector.

Increased labour migration, and low or declining unionization rates in parts of the private service sector, may weaken the regulatory capacity of collective agreements. Questions have been raised in Norway over how much longer collective agreements may function as an informal minimum standard in industries where only 20–30% of employees are unionized, and where employers face growing competition from enterprises that do not need to adhere to such provisions (Nergaard and Stokke 2007a). In Denmark also, a debate is underway over the effects of the decreasing coverage of collective agreements on the Danish model, which mainly bases regulations on rights in the labour market under collective agreements (Due et al. 2010).

EU Challenges for the Regulatory Systems

The Nordic countries have chosen different forms of affiliation with the EU. Whereas Denmark, Finland, and Sweden are members, Norway and Iceland have remained outside. However, the Agreement on the European Economic Area implies that the two latter countries come under EU regulations in a number of areas, including the entire single market regime and free movement of workers and services. As a consequence of EU enlargement in 2004 and 2007, the Nordic countries received an influx of labour migrants who were willing to work for lower pay and under different conditions than the native workers. This labour immigration was particularly marked in Norway, which after 2004 had a tight labour market and a large demand for workers (Dølvik and Eldring 2008).

This influx of workers has raised questions about how the authorities and social partners can safeguard the wages and labour conditions of these new groups. This is a particular challenge with regard to workers who are not employed directly in Nordic enterprises, but are posted from enterprises in their home country, work for temporary work agencies, or are self-employed. Studies of Polish employees in Norway, Sweden, Denmark, and Iceland have revealed wage levels and labour conditions that deviate considerably from the norm in the Nordic labour markets (Dølvik and Eldring 2008; Friberg et al. 2012).

As these countries have no tradition of either a statutory minimum wage or—with the exception of Finland—extension of collective agreements, work migration creates challenges in those cases where collective agreements cannot be applied in any simple fashion (Eldring and Alsos 2012). Increased labour immigration, especially in the form of posted workers, creates challenges for institutions with regard to wage formation. In

Sweden, the dispute has mainly centred on the legitimacy of unions' use of blockades to enforce 'Swedish conditions'. A verdict by the European Court of Justice (the Laval ruling), together with other rulings, imposed limitations on the possibility of trade unions initiating collective action to force employers to sign collective agreements. This was followed by legislation that permits industrial action against foreign firms only for the purpose of obtaining minimum pay rates as defined in nationwide agreements and for conforming to the amended Swedish law on posted workers (Malmberg 2010).

The particular Norwegian scheme for extension of collective agreements allows for a collective agreement to be extended in industries where foreign workers receive wages that are materially below the general standard in the Norwegian labour market. The large amount of labour immigration from Poland and the Baltic countries spurred several rulings for extensions from 2005 onwards, and gave rise to a new principle in Norwegian wage formation (Alsos and Eldring 2006).

THE MICRO-MODEL OF COOPERATION: PARTICIPATION AND REPRESENTATION

Discussions of the Nordic labour market regimes particularly emphasize workplace democracy and participation. The Nordic model of representation is based on a single-channel model, meaning that the unions constitute the main channel for participation at the workplace level. Consultation and representation remain the main mode of employee participation. Arrangements are based partly on legislation and partly on collective agreements, and employers in all the countries are obliged to inform and consult trade union representatives in a large number of cases that pertain to the enterprise and the employees. In addition, the rights and duties of shop stewards are regulated by central-level agreements that provide trade union representatives with sufficient time and opportunity to fulfil their duties, as well as extra protection against redundancy. Legislative provisions that ensure employee representation on enterprises' boards of directors were introduced in the 1970s (Edström 2002), although employee representatives comprise a minority of board members. In Sweden, the introduction of union-administered wage-earner funds during the 1980s was highly controversial and the arrangement was abolished in the early 1990s.

Participation and influence over individual job situations are initial key elements in the quality of working life. Factors that are often noted in comparative studies of the quality of working life include job autonomy and the potential to influence job content, whether the job provides an opportunity for learning, and whether the employment relationship is perceived as secure (Gallie 2007). This goal of personal development in working life is also embedded in Nordic legislation that emphasizes the organizational working environment. European studies of the working environment show that the Nordic countries are characterized by trust. A large proportion of employees feel that they are included in decision-making processes that have a bearing on their own workplaces, and Nordic employees more frequently than others report that they find their jobs to be personally rewarding (Gallie 2003; Eurofound 2012). With regard to job security, on the other hand, no clear Nordic trend is discernible. However, Denmark is distinguished by lower job security compared to Sweden and Finland (Norway was not included in the study), which must be assumed to reflect the different employment protection regulations in these countries.

The relationship between trade unions and employers in the Nordic countries is regulated not only by collective agreements and legislative acts that specify rights and obligations in situations where the parties have opposing interests. There are also cooperation agreements (framework agreements) that define shared goals for the development of the enterprise as well as good working conditions. The period since the 1960s has been characterized by frequent initiatives by the labour market parties, often in collaboration with research institutions, for various development projects at the enterprise level (Gustavsen 2011). Initially, these projects focused on 'the learning workplace', whereas more recent programmes have tended to emphasize enterprise collaboration and regional development, with less focus on participation and development of the work organization (Gustavsen 2007, 2011). Although the emphasis on such programmes was stronger in earlier decades—and doubts were raised regarding the proliferation effect produced by such projects and programmes—such programmes illustrate the lack of a clear distinction between collective representation and measures intended to improve workplace conditions for individual workers.

Concluding Discussion

Employment relations in Nordic countries have undergone extensive changes since the concept of social democratic capitalism was first introduced. Key features were strong trade unions and employer organizations, coordinated and centralized wage formation, cooperation at both central and company levels, narrow income distribution, high employment rates, universal social benefits, and comprehensive welfare state services. In addition, the fact that all the Nordic economies are small, open, and vulnerable to international competition led to an emphasis on the ability to adapt, and labour market measures have been more important than strong employment protection. More recent analyses have included features of education and financial systems as characteristics of the Nordic—or social democratic—labour market models.

During recent decades, collective bargaining systems have undergone significant changes, trade union density has declined significantly in those countries where it had been highest, and many welfare systems have been modified to increase employment rates and save money. However, it can be argued that the basic elements remain intact. Decentralization of wage formation is followed by central coordination, union density rates remain very high in an international context, and periods of rising unemployment have been followed by smooth recoveries.

Against this backdrop, some current and long-term challenges to the Nordic labour market models may be highlighted. The long-term demographic challenge will require effective measures to ensure that high employment rates continue. Given the overall high employment rates in these countries, measures must primarily be directed towards those who, for various reasons, are at the margins of—or outside—the labour market. This probably means an increased focus on active labour market measures, incentive effects of pension systems, eligibility for social benefits, and compensation rates. To the extent that labour migration will resolve labour shortages, issues related to wages and working conditions for migrant workers will be accentuated.

The Nordic countries are no longer socially democratic in the sense that social democratic governments dominate. The recent centre-right governments of Denmark and Sweden have introduced reforms—not least in their social security systems—that have challenged the union movement. However, also social democratic governments have seen the need for stronger incentives to work.

Increased international competition and integration into the EU has also affected employment models. Whereas these countries could previously resolve dissonance in international wage and price developments through currency devaluations, new monetary regimes have removed this as an option. This is arguably an important driver of what is seen as the renaissance of wage coordination in several Nordic countries. Nevertheless, this mode of bargaining is periodically challenged, as in Sweden in 2010, when the cooperation between blue- and white-collar workers broke down and employers broke from the framework agreement (Ibsen et al. 2011a). Finnish employers have questioned the present model (Vartiainen 2011), and in 2013, the labour market parties in Norway are considering how to achieve increased competitiveness within the present bargaining model.

The international financial crisis has also affected the open economies of the Nordic countries, which have responded with a range of measures, including access to various forms of temporary lay-offs. In Sweden, which does not have this opportunity, labour market parties within the metal sector entered into an agreement permitting reduced working hours and wages, a novelty in Nordic industrial relations. Denmark has special challenges related to banking and housing crises, and has seen the most rapid increase in unemployment rates. The questions that arise therefore are whether the countries can again recover quickly, and for Denmark, what will happen to the flexicurity model, which for a decade was the central feature of the Danish employment model.

In recent years, EU enlargement has led to substantial labour migration, partly in the form of posted workers. Reports of incidents of low wages and substandard working conditions show that national regulatory systems based mainly on collective agreements have limitations when it comes to these types of workers. Norway—with the lowest collective agreement coverage and highest labour migration—has introduced the general application of collective agreements, a measure that had not been implemented previously. However, with reports of incidents of low wages, the efficiency of traditional regulation systems has become the subject of discussion in other Nordic countries. Nonetheless, a statutory minimum wage is so far of little relevance to the Nordic context, although employers have raised it as an option.

ACKNOWLEDGEMENTS

I am grateful to the editors and Jon Erik Dølvik for comments.

NOTE

1. The flexicurity concept covers a combination of existing institutional characteristics that were seen as imperative for the successful recovery of the Danish labour market in the late 1990s and 2000s.

REFERENCES

Alsos, K. and Eldring, L. (2006). 'Extension of Collective Agreements: The Norwegian Case', *CLR News*, 3/2006: 10–22.

Amable, B. (2003). *The Diversity of Modern Capitalism*. Oxford and New York: Oxford University Press.

Antikainen, A. (2006). 'In Search of the Nordic Model in Education', *Scandinavian Journal of Educational Research*, 50(3): 229–43.

Anttonen, A. (2005). 'Empowering Social Policy: The Role of Social Care Services in Modern Welfare States', in O. Kangas and J. Palme (eds.), *Social Policy and Economic Development in the Nordic Countries*. Basingstoke: Palgrave Macmillan, 88–117.

Barth, E. and Moene, K. (2009). 'The Equality Multiplier'. NBER Working Paper No. 15076.

Berglund, T. et al. (2010). *Labour Market Mobility in Nordic Welfare States*. TemaNord 2010:515. Copenhagen: Nordic Council of Ministers.

Böckerman, P. and Uusitalo, R. (2006). 'Erosion of the Ghent System and Union Membership Decline: Lessons from Finland', *British Journal of Industrial Relations*, 44(2): 283–303.

Bredgaard, T., Larsen, F., Madsen, P. K., and Rasmussen, S. (2009a). *Flexicurity and Atypical Employment in Denmark*. Aalborg: CARMA Research Paper.

—— (2009b). *Flexicurity på Dansk*. Aalborg: CARMA Research Paper.

Calmfors, L. (1993). 'Centralisation of Wage Bargaining and Macro-Economic Performance: A Survey', *OECD Economic Studies*, 21. Available at <http://www.oecd.org/eco/growth/33945244.pdf>.

Calmfors, L. and Driffill, J. (1988). *Bargaining Structure, Corporatism and Macroeconomic Performance*. Stockholm: Institute for International Economic Studies, University of Stockholm.

Cameron, D. R. (1984). 'Social Democracy, Corporatism, Labour Quiescence, and the Representation of Economic Interest in Advanced Capitalist Society', in J. Goldthorpe (ed.), *Order and Conflict in Contemporary Capitalism*. Oxford and New York: Oxford University Press, 143–78.

Dølvik, J. E. (2008). 'The Negotiated Nordic Labor Markets: From Bust to Boom'. Center for European Studies Working Paper 162. Cambridge, MA: CES.

Dølvik, J. E., Andersen, J. G., and Vartiainen, J. (2014). 'The Nordic Social Models in Turbulent Times: Consolidation and Renewal', in Dølvik and A. Martin (eds.), *European Social Models Faced with Global Crisis* (Working title, forthcoming from Oxford University Press).

Dølvik, J. E. and Eldring, L. (2008). *Mobility of Labour from New EU States to the Nordic Region.* TemaNord 2008:537. Copenhagen: Nordic Council of Ministers.

Dølvik, J. E. and Nergaard, K. (2012) 'Variable Pay, Collective Bargaining and Trade Unions: A Comparison of Machinery and Banking Companies in Norway', *Economic and Industrial Democracy*, 33: 267–93.

Dølvik, J. E. and Stokke, T. A. (1998). 'Norway: Revival of Centralized Concertation', in A. Ferner and R. Hyman (eds.), *Changing Industrial Relations in Europe.* Oxford: Blackwell, 118–45.

Dølvik, J. E. and Stokland, D. (1992). 'Norway: The "Norwegian Model" in Transition', in A. Ferner and R. Hyman (eds.), *Industrial Relations in the New Europe.* Oxford: Blackwell, 143–67.

Dølvik, J. E. and Vartiainen, J. (2002). *Globalisering og europeisk integrasjon: Utfordringer for lønnsdannelse og kollektivavtaler i de nordiske land.* Report No. 7:2002. Stockholm: Arbets-livsinstitutet.

Due, J. and Madsen, J. S. (2008). 'The Danish Model of Industrial Relations: Erosion or Renewal?', *Journal of Industrial Relations*, 50(3): 513–29.

Due, J., Madsen, J. S., Jensen, C. S., and Petersen, L. K. (1993). *The Survival of the Danish Model.* København: DJØF Publishing.

Due, J., Madsen, J. S., and Pihl, M. D. (2010). *Udviklingen i den faglige organisering: årsager og konsekvenser for den danske modell. A-kassernes og fagforeningernes medlems-udvikling og organisationsgrader siden 1994.* Copenhagen: LO-dokumentation 1/2010.

Edstrom, Ö. (2002). 'Involvement of Employees in Private Enterprises in Four Nordic Countries', *Scandinavian Studies in Law*, 43: 160–88.

EIRO (2009). *Developments in Industrial Action 2005–2009.* Available at <http://www.eurofound.europa.eu/eiro/studies/tn1004049s/tn1004049s.htm>.

Eldring, L. and Alsos, K. (2012). *European Minimum Wage: A Nordic Outlook.* Fafo-report 2012:16.

Ellingsæter, A. L. (1989). *Normalisering av deltidsarbeidet: en analyse av endring i kvinners yrkesaktivitet og arbeidstid i 80-årene.* Oslo: Statistisk sentralbyrå.

—— (2009). *Vår tids moderne tider.* Oslo: Universitetsforlaget.

Ellingsæter, A. L. and Leira, A. (eds.) (2006). *Politicising Parenthood in Scandinavia: Gender Relations in Welfare States.* Bristol: Policy Press.

Erixon, L. (2010). 'The Rehn-Meidner Model in Sweden: Its Rise, Challenges and Survival', *Journal of Economic Issues*, 44(3): 677–715.

Esping-Andersen, G. (1990). *The Three Worlds of Welfare Capitalism.* Cambridge: Polity Press.

Eurofound (2012). *Trends in Job Quality in Europe.* 5th European Working Conditions Survey. Luxembourg: European Union.

European Commission (2006). *Employment in Europe.* Brussels.

Fahlbeck, R. (2002). 'Industrial Relations and Collective Labour Law: Characteristics, Principles and Basic Features', *Stability and Change in Nordic Labour Law, Scandinavian Studies in Law*, 43: 87–134.

Finseraas, H. and Pedersen, A. W. (2013). *Den nye gulroten i arbeidslinja? Arbeidsbetingede stønader—en kunnskapsoppsummering.* Report 2013:002. Oslo: Institutt for samfunnsforskning.

Friberg, J. H. et al. (2012). 'Institutional Differences and Varieties of Social Dumping: A Comparative Study of Wages and Working Conditions among Recent Polish Migrants in Oslo, Copenhagen and Reykjavik', paper presented at the 6th Nordic Working Life Conference, Elsinore, Denmark, 25–27 April.

Gallie, D. (2003). 'The Quality of Working Life: Is Scandinavia Different?', *European Sociological Review*, 19(1): 61–79.

—— (2007). 'The Quality of Work Life in a Comparative Perspective', in D. Gallie (ed.), *Employment Regimes and the Quality of Work.* Oxford and New York: Oxford University Press, 205–32.

Gíslason, I. and Eydal, G. B. (eds.) (2011). *Parental Leave, Childcare and Gender Equality in the Nordic Countries.* TemaNord 2011:562. Copenhagen: Nordic Council of Ministers.

Goul Andersen, J. (2011). 'From the Edge of the Abyss to Bonanza—and Beyond: Danish Economy and Economic Policies 1980–2011', in L. Mjøset (ed.), *The Nordic Varieties of Capitalism.* Comparative Social Research Volume 28. Bingley, UK: Emerald Books, 89–166.

Gustavsen, B. (2007). 'Work Organization and "the Scandinavian Model"', *Economic and Industrial Democracy*, 28(4): 650–71.

—— (2011). 'The Nordic Model of Work', *Journal of the Knowledge Economy*, 2(4): 463–80.

Hall. P. A. and Soskice, D. (2001). 'An Introduction to Varieties of Capitalism', in Hall and Soskice (eds.), *Varieties of Capitalism: The Institutional Foundations of Comparative Advantage.* Oxford and New York: Oxford University Press, 1–68.

Ibsen, C. L., Andersen, S. K., Due, J. J., and Madsen, J. S. (2011a). 'Bargaining in the Crisis: A Comparison of the 2010 Collective Bargaining Round in the Danish and Swedish Manufacturing Sectors', *Transfer: European Review of Labour and Research*, 17(3): 323–39.

Ibsen, C. L., Madsen, J. S., and Due, J. J. (2011b). *Hvem organiserer sig? Forklaringer på medlemskab af fagforeninger og a-kasser.* LO-dokumentation, no. 3. Copenhagen: Landsorganisationen i Danmark.

Ilsøe, A. (2012). 'Safety Nets or Straitjackets? Regulating Working Time in the Danish, German and American Metal Industries', *European Journal of Industrial Relations*, 18: 37–51.

Iversen, T. (1999). *Contested Economic Institutions: The Politics of Macroeconomic and Wage-Bargaining in Organized Capitalism.* Cambridge: Cambridge University Press.

Jensen, C. S. (2000). 'Arbejdsgiverorganisering i Norden—Et komparativt perspektiv: Danmark, Finland, Norge og Sverige', in C. S. Jensen (ed.), *Arbejdsgivere i Norden.* TemaNord 2000:2. Copenhagen: Nordic Council of Ministers, 373–418.

Kalleberg, A. L. (2000). 'Nonstandard Employment Relations: Part-Time, Temporary and Contract Work', *Annual Review of Sociology*, 26: 341–65.

Kangas, O. and Palme, J. (2005). 'Coming Late—Catching Up: The Formation of a "Nordic Model"', in Kangas and Palme (eds.), *Social Policy and Economic Development in the Nordic Countries.* Basingstoke: Palgrave Macmillan, 17–59.

Kjellberg, A. (1992). 'Sweden: Can the Model Survive?', in A. Ferner and R. Hyman (eds.), *Industrial Relations in the New Europe.* Oxford: Blackwell, 88–142.

—— (2011). 'The Decline in Swedish Union Density since 2007', *Nordic Journal of Working Life Studies*, 1(1): 67–93.

—— (2013). *Kollektivavtalens täckningsgrad samt organisationsgraden hos arbetsgivarförbund och fackförbund.* Lund University Studies in Social Policies, Working Life and Mobility. Lund: Department of Sociology, Lund University.

Korpi, W. (1978). *The Working Class in Welfare Capitalism: Work, Unions and Politics in Sweden.* London: Routledge & Kegan Paul.

Madsen, P. K. (2006). 'How Can it Possibly Fly? The Paradox of a Dynamic Labour Market in a Scandinavian Welfare State', in J. L. Campbell, J. A. Hall, and O. K. Pedersen, (eds.), *National Identity and the Varieties of Capitalism: The Danish Experience.* Montreal: McGill-Queen's University Press, 321–55.

—— (2011). 'Flexicurity i modvind—en analyse af den danske flexicurity-model under den økonomiske krise', *Tidsskrift for Arbejdsliv*, 13(4): 7–20.

Malmberg, J. (2010). *Posting Post Laval International and National Responses.* Working Paper 2010:5. Uppsala: Center for Labor Studies, Department of Economics, Uppsala University.

Martin, Andrew (2000). 'The Politics of Macroeconomic Policy and Wage Negotiations in Sweden', in T. Iversen, J. Pontusson, and D. Soskice (eds.), *Unions, Employers, and Central Banks: Macroeconomic Coordination and Institutional Change in Social Market Economies.* Cambridge: Cambridge University Press, 232–64.

Nergaard, K. (2010). *Fagorganisering i Norden. Status og utviklingstrekk.* Fafo-notat 2010:25. Oslo: Fafo.

Nergaard, K. and Stokke, T. A. (2007a). 'Har den norske forhandlingsmodellen overlevd?', in J. E. Dølvik, T. Fløtten, G. Hernes, and J. M. Hippe (eds.), *Hamskifte. Den norske modellen i endring.* Oslo: Gyldendal Akademisk, 39–67.

—— (2007b). 'The Puzzles of Union Density in Norway', *Transfer: European Review of Labour and Research*, 13(4): 653–70.

—— (2010). *Organisasjonsgrader, tariffavtaledekning og tillitsverv. Arbeidslivets organisasjoner 2008/2009.* Fafo-rapport 2010:47. Oslo: Fafo.

Nicolaisen, H. (2011). 'Increasingly Equalized? A Study of Part-Time Work in "Old" and "New" Part-Time Work Regimes', *Nordic Journal of Working Life Studies*, 1(1): 95–115.

OECD (2004). *Employment Outlook 2004.* Paris: OECD.

—— (2010). *Learning for Jobs.* Paris: OECD.

—— (2011a). *Education at a Glance 2011.* Paris: OECD.

—— (2011b). *Divided We Stand: Why Inequality Keeps Rising.* Paris: OECD.

Olofsson, J. and Panican, A. (eds.) (2008). *Ungdomars väg från skola till arbetsliv—nordiska erfarenheter.* TemaNord 2008:584. Copenhagen: Nordic Council of Ministers.

Pontusson, J. (2011). 'Once Again a Model', in J. E. Cronin, G. W. Ross, and J. Shoch (eds.), *What's Left of the Left: Democrats and Social Democrats in Challenging Times.* Durham and London: Duke University Press, 89–115.

Sandberg, Å. (ed.) (1995). *Enriching Production: Perspectives on Volvo's Uddevalla Plant as an Alternative to Lean Production.* MPRA Paper No. 10785. Aldershot: Avebury (digital edition, Stockholm 2007).

Scheuer, S. (1992). 'Denmark: Return to Decentralization', in A. Ferner and R. Hyman (eds.), *Industrial Relations in the New Europe.* Oxford: Blackwell, 168–97.

Stokke, T. A. (2008). 'The Anatomy of Two-Tier Bargaining Models', *European Journal of Industrial Relations*, 14: 7–24.

—— (2012). *Etableringen av kriterier for lokale forhandlinger i privat sektor.* Fafo-notat 2012:01. Oslo: Fafo.

Stokke, T. A. and Thörnqvist, C. (2001). 'Strikes and Collective Bargaining in the Nordic Countries', *European Journal of Industrial Relations*, 7(3): 245–67.

Swenson, P. and Pontusson, J. (2000). 'The Swedish Employer Offensive against Centralized Bargaining', in T. Iversen, J. Pontusson, and D. Soskice (eds.), *Unions, Employers and Central Banks*. Cambridge: Cambridge University Press, 77–106.

Telhaug, A. O., Mediås, O. A., and Aasen, P. (2007). 'The Nordic Model in Education: Education as Part of the Political System in the Last 50 Years', *Scandinavian Journal of Educational Research*, 50: 245–83.

Thelen, K. (2001). 'Varieties of Labor Politics in the Developed Democracies', in P. A. Hall and D. Soskice (eds.), *Varieties of Capitalism: The Institutional Foundations of Comparative Advantage*. Oxford and New York: Oxford University Press, 71–103.

Traxler, F., Kittel, B., and Blaschke, S. (2001). *National Labour Relations in Internationalized Markets*. Oxford and New York: Oxford University Press.

Vartiainen, J. (2011). 'Nordic Collective Agreements: A Continuous Institution in a Changing Economic Environment', in L. Mjøset (ed.), *The Nordic Varieties of Capitalism* (Comparative Social Research, Volume 28). Bingley, UK: Emerald Group Publishing, 331–63.

Wallerstein, M. (1999). 'Wage Setting Institutions and Pay Inequality in Advanced Industrial Societies', *American Journal of Political Science*, 43(3): 649–80.

CHAPTER 14

EMPLOYMENT REGIMES, WAGE SETTING, AND MONETARY UNION IN CONTINENTAL EUROPE

BOB HANCKÉ

INTRODUCTION

IN 1999, the introduction of the euro heralded the crowning achievement of post-war political and economic integration in Europe—at least for those who chose to partake. A single market was complemented by a single currency, which, in turn, formed the basis for a closer alignment of economic policies across the continent, and would ultimately lead to the formation of a pan-European social and political identity—the foundations for the European demos whose absence was decried by many political philosophers sympathetic to the European project. By 2009, less than two years after the first signs of the crisis that enveloped the global financial system, the first cracks in this novel, unique, political-economic edifice began to show. Ireland's prime minister had just mortgaged away the future of the country by underwriting the failure of the country's banks in full, Portugal was facing a slow-motion crisis of confidence from financial markets, and, perhaps most spectacularly of all, Greece was unable to roll over its sovereign debt without paying excessively high interest rates. In the months that followed, Spain, Italy, and, at some point, even France and Belgium, risked being dragged into the turmoil of the sovereign debt crisis, leading many observers to wonder publicly about the survival of the single currency.

A decade after its inception, therefore, the single currency faced an existential crisis, both political and economic. Governments of many—and by early 2014 possibly most—Economic and Monetary Union (EMU) member states had been rejected by their electorates, while most of their successors fared little better, facing massive protests and extremely low popularity ratings very early on in their terms. Populist parties both on the left and the right upset party systems in Italy, Greece, France, the Netherlands, and Belgium. A handful of eurozone member states were forced to go, cap in hand, to the European Central Bank (ECB), the European Commission, and the International Monetary Fund (IMF), begging for financial support. In practically every EMU member state, several banks that faced potential bankruptcy as a result of their exposure to shady private and public debt had to be nationalized by their governments. Defying its own strict mandate, the ECB all but promised unlimited support to the euro's financial system in the summer of 2012 up to the point, it appeared, of effectively bailing out governments who were unable to borrow at reasonable rates in international capital markets. And in early 2013, the logical foundations of a single currency were shaken when Cyprus, an economy accounting for barely 0.2% of eurozone GDP, introduced capital controls to stop a run on its banks: from then on a euro in a bank account in Cyprus was different from a euro in a German or French bank account.

Most observers, especially in policy-making circles in the Brussels–Frankfurt axis, think of the crisis of EMU primarily as a crisis of failed fiscal discipline in a monetary union. Once a country has become a member of EMU, its loose fiscal policy can no longer be checked by national or international institutions: the Stability and Growth Pact, EMU's economic quasi-constitution, has turned out to be the paper tiger that many feared it was, and the result was fiscal incontinence everywhere. While a priori appealing, there is a serious problem with this argument: very few of the member states that have found themselves in fiscal problems after the crisis erupted in 2010 actually ran a primary deficit, and most did not even run a deficit beyond 3% over the first nine years of the euro. Greece, held up as the most visible point of the iceberg, is the exception here, not the rule. Others see it primarily as a crisis of the financial sector that spilled over into the public sphere following the financial crisis of 2007–8, which exposed the weakness of a deregulated international financial system. As banks became weaker, governments were forced to take them over, thus adding to their debt burden. The upshot: banks that held sovereign bonds were weakened even more, thus producing a vicious spiral of weak banks and increasing government debt (De Grauwe 2011). That argument, though, does not help us understand why countries such as the Netherlands and Belgium, with high private (NL) or public debt (BE), appear to be almost immune from the problems and pressures that Southern European and other peripheral countries in EMU have faced since the onset of the crisis.

This chapter makes a very different argument. The crisis of EMU since 2009 has laid bare problematic aspects of the interaction between employment relations, and in particular wage bargaining systems, on the one hand, and central banks on the other. Somewhat schematically, continental (Western) Europe consists of two very different systems of employment and labour relations, roughly along the lines of what Hall and Soskice (2001) call 'coordinated market economies' (CMEs) in the northwest of the continent (including Austria—geography is not the defining characteristic of this group or the others), and, for want of a better term, 'mixed market economies' (MMEs) in the south, in the form of the now infamous GI(I)PS, Greece, Italy, (Ireland), Portugal, and

Spain (Hall and Soskice 2001; Hancké et al. 2007). The main difference between the two lies in the nature of the actors and the configuration of institutions and rules that they face. In CMEs, strong labour unions encounter strong employers' associations, particularly in the export sector; as a result, they negotiate wage settlements which simultaneously safeguard real wages and profitability; and that is done through negotiating wage rates between a floor set by inflation and a wage ceiling set by labour productivity. Labour productivity, in turn, is high as a result of the micro-level arrangements for training and work organization in the northern CMEs. Strong systems of wage coordination then transmit these moderate wage rates to the rest of the economy. In MMEs, the situation is different. First of all, the state regularly has to step in to compensate for the lack of autonomous bargaining capacity among the key actors. Second, cross-industry wage coordination is considerably weaker than in the north of Europe, and as a result inter-sectoral wage drift is endemic. These differences in employment relations and wage-setting systems implied that, against the background of a relatively restrictive one-size-fits-all monetary policy in place since 1999, the northwest of the continent systematically improved its competitiveness, while the south lost competitiveness in parallel. Small differences between the two groups of countries at the start of EMU thus were accentuated and, against the background of low growth and an almost closed economy (the virtual economy known as EMU trades less than 10% outside the EU), the northern CMEs accumulated current account surpluses while the GIIPS ran into severe balance of payments problems in 2010 and 2011. The sovereign debt crises of 2010–11, which threatened the survival of the eurozone itself in November and December 2011, simply reflected these structural imbalances: current account deficits are financed through debt, private and public. The problem with EMU, in other words, is one of current accounts, not fiscal deficits.

This chapter starts with a review of the debate on the political economy of EMU and the crisis that the single currency has faced in the wake of the financial crisis of 2007–8, and develops the argument above in contrast to the prevailing explanations. It then continues to its empirical point of gravity: in three sections the chapter reconstructs the development of wage-setting systems against the background of monetary integration in Europe since the second oil shock—the emergence of the DM-bloc and its effects on wage setting and labour relations, the Maastricht process, and the introduction of the euro. The final section concludes by putting this analysis in the wider context of the debates on EMU.

Understanding the Crisis of EMU

The crisis of EMU is an excellent place to analyse what makes the institutional architecture around the single currency so fragile. Four types of explanations have been offered for why EMU faces the problems it does. The first—labour market rigidities—is an old stalwart of orthodox economics, which harks back to theories of optimal currency areas. In a world in which all other macroeconomic adjustment mechanisms—monetary and fiscal policies as well as exchange rates—are more or less fixed, as they are in EMU, labour markets and therefore wages have to become more flexible. The lack of labour market flexibility in the south thus exacerbated the pre-existing problems in that region. Even though this perspective certainly helps us understand part of the problem, one observation should give pause for thought: the equally inflexible or possibly even less flexible labour markets in countries such as Austria, Belgium, Germany, and the Netherlands have not produced the same adjustment problems. In fact, the highly organized ('rigid') wage-setting systems in the north appear to be at the basis of their strong economic performance in the shape of low inflation (and relatively low unemployment) and international competitiveness.

The other orthodox interpretation of the crisis was fiscal mismanagement, possibly supported by aloof capital markets. During most of the euro's first decade, interest rate differentials between Germany's baseline and Greek and Italian debt were negligible, which was at least as much a reflection of the lack of credibility of the no bailout clause in the Maastricht Treaty as of the massive incompetence of rating agencies who were supposed to report on the relative risk in government debt. Governments in the south thus were able to run up large public debt without paying a penalty in higher interest rates, which created the fiscal imbalances at the heart of the euro crisis in 2010 and after. While this explanation may help us understand the Greek situation, it meets its limits when used to understand the problems of Ireland and especially Spain, two countries that, in fact, ran budget surpluses until the financial crisis of 2008. In addition, during the period between the start of EMU in 1999 and the start of the financial crisis in late 2007, only Greece ran, averaged over that period, a public deficit beyond the 3% limit imposed by both Maastricht and the Stability and Growth Pact—hardly a persuasive indication of widespread fiscal irresponsibility (see Hancké 2013 for detail on this and other empirical points in this chapter).

Spain and Ireland are, not surprisingly, at the basis of a third explanation, which revolves around asset price inflation and bursting bubbles. While headline consumer price inflation has hardly been problematic on the continent, both in the aggregate and in most individual member states, the ultra-low interest rates in some of the member states stoked an asset boom: low interest rates begot cheap mortgages, which begot massively rising housing prices and, on the back of that, a construction boom. Spain and Ireland, indeed, began to resemble, in the words of the Dublin economist Morgan Kelly, a country where one half of the population was building houses for the other half. This dynamic gets us closer to the problem, as I will explain in a moment, but it fails to explain outcomes in countries like Greece, Italy, and Portugal, whose sovereign debt problems could hardly have been fuelled by asset price inflation since that was more or less absent in those countries.

The final possible explanation was poor financial regulation, a host of dangerous mistakes on the back of that and a 'deadly embrace' (De Grauwe 2011) between banks and sovereigns. Ireland is the case in point here: lax regulation attracted risky capital, which maximized profits in the implicit knowledge of a government bailout if and when things were to go wrong. That government bailout implied nothing less than a transfer of debt from the private to the public sector, and, against a backdrop of rapidly collapsing growth, a sovereign debt crisis was born. Financial developments in Ireland without doubt were not as well regulated as they could have been, and the decision in 2010 by then Prime Minister Brian Cowan to guarantee all bank debt will certainly go down as one of history's largest self-inflicted policy mistakes. But the lack of financial acumen in Irish government circles hardly explains most of the other problematic cases. Regulation in Spain, for example, one of the only other countries with a sizeable, active, and open banking sector, was never considered a problematic aspect of the new Spanish model. And most other countries facing fiscal problems in 2010 and 2011 had, in fact, relatively strict regulation or, as in Italy, a relatively closed banking sector.

All four of these explanations help us understand pieces of the puzzle—but, at best, only pieces. One problem that they share is that they consider the problem to be very similar everywhere, thus implicitly also suggesting that the problems (and the solutions) are primarily or even solely found at the national level. Labour market flexibility, fiscal rules, and better regulation remain subject to national policy-making, helped but not steered by European institutions. This assumption is probably incorrect: even granting the arguable point that the problems were the same everywhere, the different organization of domestic economies in Europe means that they probably do not have the same effects in every country. More importantly, there are reasons to believe that the new international political economy associated with EMU is itself part of the problem: some of the dynamics underlying the euro crisis, such as the massive current account divergences, almost perfectly coincide with the 1999 start of EMU. Combining these two insights—one loosely emanating from a 'varieties of capitalism' approach to comparative political economy (Hall 2012), and the other inspired by New Keynesian macroeconomics (Carlin and Soskice 2006)—suggests a more systemic explanation of the crisis.

One key stylized fact that helps us understand the more structural dimension of the crisis of EMU is that since its inception in 1999, EMU has witnessed an increased divergence of inflation and wages, as well as of economic performance more generally in the single currency area. In part this has been a relatively standard, more or less anticipated process of inter-country adjustment, especially since some countries, most notably Germany, entered EMU with an overvalued exchange rate. But it is equally a consequence of Germany's reliance on exports for growth, which imposes a tight wage moderation strategy on its key industrial sectors, diligently followed by unions, both in the export and in the sheltered sectors, including the public sector (note that the 'wage moderation' referred to in this chapter is, unless explicitly stated otherwise, expressed in the evolution of unit labour costs—abbreviated as ULC henceforth—which measure the ratio of wage rates over labour productivity rates). This neo-mercantilist adjustment argument, again, helps us understand part of the problem: it explains why competitiveness rose in the north and fell in the south. But it probably attributes too much to a prevailing consensus among the key political-economic actors in Germany and particularly to their capacity to set relative wage rates. Leading trade unions in Germany, among them the engineering union *IG Metall* and the services union *ver.di* have, in fact, campaigned for higher wages for most of the euro's existence, but failed to gain them. Explaining why these strong labour unions have been unable to set wages in their favour requires a more structural approach: in the EMU set-up, as I will show with a simple model below, there are strong systemic pressures that force a divergence of inflation and wage rates across the eurozone, and thus wage deflation in Germany (see Hancké and Soskice 2003 for a more formal elaboration of the basic idea).

Imagine, for ease of exposition, that EMU consists of two economies of equal size, called DE (i.e. Germany and its immediate neighbours in northwestern Europe including Austria), and RE (for Rest of Europe). At some point after the start of EMU, DE's inflation rate is, because of its more strongly coordinated wage-setting system, slightly below RE's; they average 2%, which is the ECB's inflation target. Since the ECB sets its interest rate for all members to reflect the difference between the target and the actual (i.e. the aggregate/average) inflation rate of DE and RE, the real interest rate (the nominal interest rate that the ECB sets for all minus the country-specific inflation rate) is therefore lower in the country with high inflation (RE) and higher in the low-inflation country (DE). These differences between real interest rates and domestic institutions have several consequences that are poorly understood.

First of all, monetary policy is effectively pro-cyclical. The country with higher inflation faces a more accommodating monetary policy than it should, because the bank's target is lower than its actual inflation rate. The country with a lower inflation rate, on the other hand, will experience an unnecessarily restrictive monetary policy, which will not have a significant effect on price dynamics (since inflation is low already), but only on growth. Note that the opposite would happen if monetary policy were decided for each country individually (Allsopp 2002): if inflation in DE were to remain low or fall, DE's central bank would almost certainly lower the nominal, and therefore in effect the real, interest rate; if inflation rises in RE, its monetary policy would undoubtedly tighten. None of that happens in EMU, however, where rising inflation is implicitly rewarded through a falling real interest rate. In part, of course, this pro-cyclical dynamic is compensated by a lower real exchange rate (RER) in the low-inflation countries: the goods and services they export become less expensive relative to those with a rising RER. However, two caveats are in order here: one, this compensatory effect is limited to the export sector, which makes up at most half of the GDP of small economies in EMU and essentially not more than a quarter of output in large economies; most importantly, perhaps, an RER depreciation in the low-inflation countries is at the root of their stellar competitiveness performance, and thus indirectly at the basis of massive current account deficits in countries with a higher RER. A depreciation of the RER in the low-inflation countries is, in other words, part of the problem, not of the solution.

The second ill-understood effect is that the lower real interest rate that RE has faced during the first ten years of EMU has for most of the southern economies (with the exception of Italy, in fact) fed into a path of higher growth in RE, fuelling (wage) inflation. At the same time, the tighter than necessary monetary policy has imposed further disinflation through wage moderation on DE. The very small differences in inflation that existed at the start of EMU thus have become more pronounced in the second round (rising asset prices fuelled inflation in RE, externally imposed disinflation further reduced export prices in DE) and the perverse pro-cyclical effects gained in strength, pushing inflation rates and competitiveness of DE and RE on sharply diverging paths.

Finally, the differences in wage setting between DE and RE play a crucial role in this process. Not only did different wage-setting systems put DE and RE on different tracks from the start; in addition the ability of DE to counter inflationary pressures through wage coordination around more slowly growing unit labour costs is almost perfectly mirrored by the inability of RE to do so. Since inflation is more of a problem in RE (though hidden under the beneficial effects of very low real interest rates), the lack of capacity to disinflate implies that RE slowly but steadily loses competitiveness relative to RE. In itself that does not have to be deeply problematic: if RE can grow through trade outside EMU, it can compensate its falling competitiveness within EMU through rising competitiveness outside EMU. But EMU is essentially a closed trade area, with only about 10% of GDP leaving the single currency zone, most of which goes to other EU member states. Within such a closed trade bloc which, in addition, has faced a relatively low growth regime since its inception, DE's rising competitiveness *must imply* RE's falling competitiveness. Trade in EMU has, in effect, become a zero-sum game in which one's gains are another one's losses, and DE's improving competitiveness and current account surplus are mirrored in current account deficits in RE.

What follows traces the design and the emergence of this system back to the start of monetary integration in Europe, the construction of the DM-bloc within the European Monetary System (EMS). It then continues with the generalization of the model to the rest of Europe through the Maastricht process in the 1990s. At the start of EMU, the political economy of the prospective eurozone member states was, in effect, a robust disinflationary system, calibrated by the interaction between strong wage setters and central banks. The introduction of the euro changed all that by transferring monetary policy to a single central bank without a parallel centralization of wage setting and fiscal policy. The outcome was a dramatic divergence of inflation rates and competitiveness.

LABOUR MARKETS AND MONETARY INTEGRATION IN EUROPE: A DRAMA IN THREE ACTS

The key point of this chapter is that the crisis of the euro in 2010–11 has to be understood against the longer-term history of monetary integration in Europe, and most importantly, the interaction between that process and the evolution of domestic wage-setting systems. Let us start with giving credit where it is due: older theories of optimal currency areas were probably right in their broad implications that adjustment in a single currency area without fiscal federalism or fiscal discretion takes place through labour markets; they were wrong, however, in the substantive policies that this entailed. Put simply, the first steps of monetary integration—before, it is important to point out, the introduction of a single monetary policy—forced individual member states to reorganize their domestic macroeconomies and their wage-setting systems in particular. Yet, where optimal currency area theories were wrong is that this did not entail more labour market flexibility, but more central coordination (and therefore more organized labour markets, with strong trade unions and employers' associations). Monetary integration, from the DM-bloc in the early 1980s to the institution of EMU, produced its best results in terms of economic performance when labour markets evolved into more rather than less centrally organized arrangements, and relatively weaker results in countries with intermediate levels of wage coordination. (Significantly more decentralized wage setting, as found in the UK, might be another way to achieve successful wage adjustment; however, since the UK is not a member of EMU, I will ignore this mechanism in this analysis. Calmfors and Driffill (1988) is the *locus classicus* for this argument.) In continental Europe, as the balance of this chapter will analyse, this process took place in three stages: the construction of the DM-bloc at the core of the EMS, the Maastricht process and the emergence of social pacts in response to the convergence criteria, and the period after the introduction of the euro in 1999, which installed the ECB at the helm of monetary policy.

Act I: The Construction of the Deutschmark Bloc

In the first half of the 1980s, several countries in northwestern Europe, including France, embarked on deeper monetary integration. Austria, Belgium, Denmark, France, and the Netherlands pegged their currencies to the Deutschmark, thus importing the credibility of the Bundesbank in fighting inflation. This monetary anchoring was not without a cost, however. Aligning inflation and interest rates required disciplining labour unions: wage growth had to become non-inflationary, since upward price/wage pressures forced national central banks to raise interest rates in order to maintain the exchange rate peg. More importantly, it required that wages in the sheltered sector, primarily in the public sector, followed wage developments in the exposed (primarily manufacturing) sector, where external competitiveness was a strong disinflationary anchor.

Governments, supported by conservative central banks, played a critical role in this alignment of wages during this period. Central banks became, in effect, last movers in this set-up, always in a position to punish wage settlements that threaten monetary stability. The exposed sector, consisting mainly of the manufacturing export sector, however, did not require such a back-stop function by the central bank, since it faced a market-imposed competitiveness constraint on wage setting as a result of economic integration. The sheltered sector, and the public sector in particular, by definition do not face such a constraint. The wage restraint policies imposed by central banks and governments thus targeted the sheltered sector, specifically wages in the highly unionized public sector, and forced it to follow wage rates adopted by the exposed sector. Not surprisingly, imposing such constraints against the will of strong labour unions was far from easy.

All countries aspiring to DM-bloc membership in the early 1980s faced a period of protracted social conflict when governments pegged currencies to the DM and thus were forced to contain wage growth and public spending as a result. Both the number of strikes and working days lost to strikes, in the public sector in particular, increased suddenly and significantly in the years leading up to the formal peg between the domestic currency and the DM. Belgium and the Netherlands faced a massive public sector strike in the autumn of 1983, which paralysed large parts of the countries for several weeks. The strikes ultimately ended in defeat for the public sector unions, and led to the institutionalized subordination of wages in the public sector to those in the private exporting sector. In Denmark the number of working days lost through strikes jumped a massive 500% from about 160 strikes on average in 1982, 1983, and 1984 to 820 in 1985, while working days lost to strikes increased from about 100,000 on average before 1985 to over 2 million in that year (ILO labour statistics). In France the high-strike years 1983–5, immediately following the Mitterrand U-turn on economic policy, the Franc–DM peg, and the forced disinflation after 1982 (Taddéi and Coriat 1993), heralded the shift towards a regime where labour was, in effect, sidelined on the political-economic scene. Between 1980 and 1985, Belgium, Denmark, France, and the Netherlands combined passed no fewer than thirteen laws that aimed at containing wage growth in the public sector, with the effect that average annual real wage growth for the 1980s in Belgium was 0%, negative in the Netherlands, and below 2% in Denmark, after a decade in which these were, for the same countries, 7.5% (BE), 5.5% (NL), and 5.4% (DK) (Johnston 2011: 80–1). More, therefore, than keeping the private (exporting) sector under control, government and central bank policies were aimed at reducing the wage margins of the public sector.

The outcome of this period of social conflict was a tightly organized system in which national central banks of the DM-bloc members were hierarchically linked to the Bundesbank, labour unions (and wages) in the exposed sector were hierarchically linked to German wage setting, and public sector wages in each country were hierarchically linked to exposed sector wages. The first of these linkages assured the credibility of the peg: national central banks made clear to domestic audiences that they would defend the currency, even if that entailed raising interest rates to a prohibitively high level. The composition of government in terms of left and right mattered little for this process: after Mitterrand's U-turn in 1983, all EU (and prospective EMU) governments adopted low inflation as the key target as a means of preserving their exchange rate peg on which economic policy credibility now hinged. The second linkage, between the key German trade unions and their counterparts elsewhere, assured that the German set-up with a strong conservative central bank that disciplined excessive wages was transmitted to all other countries in the currency bloc. After some resistance in the early years of the decade, labour unions in the strong export sectors faced strong incentives to keep the public sector under control.

Wages outside Germany thus were kept under control through two mechanisms: one was direct wage shadowing, whereby wages outside Germany grew, adjusting for labour productivity, at a similar rate as German wages; the other was provided by credible conservative monetary policies as the back-stop in case of excessive wage settlements, supported by an implicit coalition of governments and export unions.

Act II: Adjusting to Maastricht

This set-up became the template for future monetary integration. When the Maastricht Treaty in 1991, mapping the road to EMU, was negotiated, average inflation differentials between the DM-bloc and the non-DM bloc (Italy, Spain, Portugal, and Greece) in the EMS were about 9% (all inflation data are taken from the OECD *Employment Outlook 2002*). By the late 1990s, a few months before the introduction of the euro, inflation rates across the prospective eurozone had converged on an average slightly above 1%, with a differential between the DM and non-DM countries of just 1% and, per Maastricht criteria, none more than 1.5% above the best performers.

The importance of inflation in this reasoning is that it is, despite the formal multiple targets in the Maastricht Treaty, the key variable for meeting the convergence criteria: stable domestic prices not only were a target in themselves, but they also stabilized both the currency peg and the interest rate against the key target rates embodied in the Treaty. Long-term interest rates thus fell, both as a result of the exchange rate peg and through imported credibility, which alleviated budgetary pressures in turn. Whatever other conditions may have been necessary, keeping domestic inflation under control was vital for a country's entry into EMU. Put differently, the prospect of EMU forced similar wage adjustments in all aspiring members, particularly those outside the existing DM-bloc.

Governments, assisted by central banks, again played a crucial role in this process. In essence, an implicit deal was proposed everywhere along the following terms: if the social partners agreed to keep wage growth under control and refrained from raising prices, governments would support those disinflationary moves by co-opting labour market parties in major welfare, labour market, and budgetary reforms, while central banks would keep interest rates as low as possible; if social partners failed, however, determined governments and central banks would reduce inflation nonetheless, almost certainly with higher social costs (and possibly higher political costs for governments, but these would have to be weighed against the political costs of non-EMU membership). In a subtler, and definitely more cooperative form, therefore, these post-Maastricht arrangements thus replicated the government policies and institutions of the prospective DM-bloc countries almost a decade earlier (Pochet 2002).

But social partners in these countries were not necessarily able to deliver low wage inflation very easily. Southern Europe has a long history, in fact, of failed attempts at instituting centralized incomes policies and more broadly neo-corporatist decision-making structures to steer the economy, usually associated with competition between ideologically opposed labour union confederations, low union density, or the organizational inability of federations to control lower-level labour unions (see, for example, Regini 1984; Salvati 1982; Molina and Rhodes 2007). In the past, the state stepped in to compensate for this lack of organization on the labour side, with a comparatively heavy hand in labour law and employment relations, and the same happened during the Maastricht adjustment process in the 1990s. The implicit deal sketched above was sanctioned in social pacts: governments offered consultation and negotiation on the means for wage and fiscal restraint if social partners agreed on the broad targets (which themselves followed the Maastricht Treaty: low and stable inflation, a stable exchange rate, a low and stable interest rate, and fiscal consolidation with a deficit level of 3% and a debt level of 60% of GDP). Even the countries where the past caught up with the social partners and government and where a social pact turned out to be impossible to reach, ended up negotiating an incomes policy, either stand-alone or as part of a broader deal, which kept wage inflation in check and engendered all the beneficial effects that follow (Hancké and Rhodes 2005).

One small irony should not go unappreciated here: the highly organized northern economies, often held up as shining examples of tri-partite or bi-partite neo-corporatism, transitioned into the monetarist macroeconomic model underlying the DM-bloc through major social conflicts. The southern EMU member states, on the other hand, often considered 'ungovernable' because of their highly ideological labour unions and adversarial employment relations systems, adopted a considerably more conciliatory approach. With governments and central banks as the drivers of monetary regime change, organized labour in the south appeared to have accepted the new policy regime as a *fait accompli* and worked within the margins that this regime offered.

The effects of these reorganizations of the macroeconomic policy framework everywhere, but especially in the south, have been nothing short of spectacular. All the major Maastricht convergence criteria were easily reached, and all applying EU member states save Greece 'irrevocably' fixed their exchange rate to the new single currency in 1999 (Greece joined in 2001). EMU was born.

Act III: Labour Unions, Wages, and the ECB

The introduction of the euro in 1999 set the stage for the third and final act of the drama. Most citizens of EMU member states associate the euro with ease of travel, companies in the eurozone associate it with exchange rate stability and price transparency, and financial markets with a credible low inflation regime. These aspects of the euro are certainly important; its essence for the purposes of this chapter, however, lies elsewhere. The introduction of the single currency dramatically changed the institutional framework of macroeconomic policy, both within and between countries. First of all, it produced a pro-cyclical monetary regime. The single nominal interest rate, reflecting the ECB's 2% inflation rate target, translated into excessively accommodating real interest rates (the nominal interest rate minus the actual inflation rate) in countries with inflation above the 2%, and excessively tight monetary policy in countries with a low inflation rate. That fed into higher growth and higher inflation in the first group and lower growth in the second group, thus pushing both groups of countries in opposite directions: inflation rose in the high-inflation group in the first period and fell in the low-inflation group—thus fuelling asset price inflation in the first and stifling growth in the second group of countries.

These perverse effects could easily be offset through fiscal policy. But two considerations make that a less appetizing choice than it would seem. Governments are on the whole loath to impose taxes, especially in times of fiscal surplus: fiscal tightening to counter monetary relaxation is thus very hard to implement. The Stability and Growth Pact (SGP), in addition, makes annual deficits above 3% of GDP problematic: that raises the bar for counter-cyclical fiscal policy in a tight monetary regime. (The SGP, in fact, operates in a moderately pro-cyclical fashion as well, by rewarding countries with a surplus and punishing countries with a deficit, thus exacerbating the problems that pro-cyclical monetary policy produces.)

Against the background of this shift in the international regime toward a pro-cyclical monetary policy, domestic wage-setting regimes witnessed an important but underappreciated structural shift. EMU transferred stewardship of the economy from national central banks, with all the power they held over wage setters and governments, to a single ECB. The implicit effect of this upward relocation of sanctioning tools was that the domestic pressure exercised by the central bank on wage setters in each of the EMU member states effectively disappeared. Many observers in the late 1990s predicted a massive inflationary scramble as a result: since the ECB is unable to retaliate against one union in one country—in contrast to how national central banks had increasingly threatened tightening during the previous two decades—excessive wage rates could no longer easily be punished (Iversen and Soskice 1998; Hall and Franzese 1998). To take an example: in the limiting case even the German engineering union *IG Metall*, the leader in most wage settlements in the country and one of the largest and strongest trade unions in the world), saw its weight in the central bank's reaction function diminish from nominally about 30% for the Bundesbank (but in real terms almost certainly much more because of the union's pilot function for wages throughout Germany) to (again nominally) about 10% for the ECB: engineering accounts for roughly one-third of German GDP, and Germany for roughly one-third of eurozone GDP. Since every labour union in every country finds itself in a parallel position, all have an incentive to exploit their new-found freedom: a classic collective action problem that produces wage inflation everywhere—thus the argument.

The first ten years of EMU demonstrate rather convincingly that this is not what happened. While wage inflation rates diverged between member states, EMU's aggregate inflation rate remained low throughout the first decade, usually hovering between 2 and 3%. Wage growth was, on the whole, moderate, and there were very few signs of the inflationary scramble that many observers feared. While inflation rates in the different EMU member states diverged after 1999, from a spread of about 1% in 1998 to a spread of about 6% by the onset of the crisis, and the average inflation rate remained close to the ECB's target range of 2%, the highest inflation rate recorded was hardly excessive: in Slovenia, inflation went up to about 5.5% in 2008.

The introduction of the single currency did reveal, however, that wage setting in the member states were aggregations of two increasingly divergent trajectories: the exposed sector's path, on the one hand, where markets had sufficient power to contain excessive wage demands, and the sheltered sector's, on the other, where international competition (and in the case of the public sector any competition whatsoever) which restrains wage growth was absent. All other things equal, wage inflation was unlikely in the former, lest the export sector began to price itself out of the market and workers therefore out of a job, while it was, for the mirror reason of job stability, almost certain to emerge in the latter. The institution of EMU thus, somewhat perversely, reopened a cleavage within the labour unions that had been closed in the previous decades (Johnston 2012; Hancké 2013).

Yet, things were not wholly equal across EMU's member states: in northwestern Europe, wage coordination across different sectors constrained the public sector in its wage setting—mostly because shadowing wage rates in the leading manufacturing sector possibly secured the best medium-term wage deal for the public sector, but sometimes also because of coercion, as in Austria and Belgium, where institutional and legal constraints, such as labour law, budget rules (Hodson 2011: 78–94), or organizational power within the union confederation, imposed a hard ceiling on public sector wages (Johnston and Hancké 2009; Johnston 2012). In countries where the exporting manufacturing sector was not the leading trade union, however, and/or where public sector unions were capable of extricating themselves from the wage-setting system that revolved around the leading export-sector unions, wages (expressed in ULC) in the public and in the manufacturing export sector diverged rapidly. This was the case in Ireland, Portugal, Spain, Italy, and Greece for much of the first decade of EMU up until the crisis of 2008. Since domestic wage inflation is, in effect, the weighted average of sheltered (including, and possibly dominated by, public) sector wage inflation and exposed (manufacturing and other export) sector wage inflation, inflationary pressures thus started to rise in these countries.

Rising wage inflation in the public sector is, in principle, relatively easy to compensate in the exposed (export) sector, as long as the productivity rate of the latter is high enough—which it is in much of the key manufacturing sectors—and wages grow at a moderate enough rate. But in some cases the export sector may have only a low potential to compensate, because it consists primarily of relatively low value-added sub-sectors, because the export sector is too small compared to the sheltered sector, or the export sector might simply set its own wages above productivity regardless of the consequences, thus exacerbating the inflationary pressures emanating from the sheltered private and public sectors. Under those circumstances, the ability to compensate for high wage inflation in the sheltered (public) sector is drastically limited, aggregate domestic wage inflation rises faster and higher, and the competitiveness of the export sector falls rapidly as a result of what is, in effect, an appreciation of the real exchange rate. That was also exactly what we witnessed in the EMU economies that faced important public debt problems in the 2010–13 period. Before the introduction of the euro in 1999, manufacturing wages and public sector wages roughly followed the same pattern in all prospective member states. From 1999 onwards, however, the evolution of the two diverged sharply: manufacturing wage rates across the eurozone remained tightly controlled (expressed in unit labour cost terms, they were negative, in fact—Johnston 2012), while public sector wages were on an upward trajectory until 2007.

This potentially explosive reconfiguration of relations between the sheltered and the exposed sectors took place against the background of the newly instituted centralized monetary policy in EMU. The ECB's single interest rate, which reflects the distance from the central bank's asymmetric inflation target of 2%, has had very different consequences for different regions within EMU—which is what the member states in the single currency area effectively have become. Somewhat ironically, therefore, by implicitly rewarding high-inflation countries with a lower real interest rate, the ECB ended up *de facto* also sanctioning excessive wage claims by the public sector.

Two inadvertent consequences of EMU thus interacted to produce the dramatic outcomes we saw in the late 2000s and after. One of these is related to the structure of wage bargaining: the introduction of the ECB lifted the restraints by central banks on wage setting in the public sector in each of the member states. If wage coordination remained successful in the absence of a tough reaction by the central bank, wages in the public sector remained contained; if not, a dramatic divergence of wages (expressed in ULC terms) followed, inflation rose, and export competitiveness fell. The second relates to the pro-cyclical effects of a single monetary policy: EMU's single interest rate means that low-inflation countries have a higher real interest rate than high-inflation countries, thus fuelling inflation in the latter and thereby exacerbating the structural competitiveness problems. Fiscal policy appears unable to alleviate these pro-cyclical effects, and even the accompanying counter-cyclical evolution of the real exchange rate (which falls in low-inflation and rises in high-inflation countries, thus improving competitiveness in the first) compensates but far from totally, since it only applies to the export sector. In fact, this divergence of relative competitiveness is actually part of the problem: it feeds in to the dramatic current account imbalances across EMU.

CONCLUSION

Employment relations remain important institutional ingredients of different varieties of contemporary capitalism, even (or perhaps especially) in such complicated macroeconomic arrangements as EMU. They set the basic parameters for adjustment in a tight macroeconomic regime such as EMU. Because of the basic EMU configuration of fixed exchange rates, a single interest rate and a relatively tight fiscal regime, much of the burden of adjustment falls on labour markets, especially on wages. Wage bargaining systems, underpinned by arrangements for skill production and acquisition, were distributed very unevenly across the eurozone. In the northwest of the continent—what I called DE earlier in this chapter—these were highly organized ('coordinated') affairs, which kept unit labour costs under control, and allowed companies to raise productivity by relying on the sophisticated skills of their workforce, especially in the manufacturing export sector. In the south (and to some extent in Ireland) the considerably less organized wage setting and skill systems mirrored the situation in the north of the continent. The outcome of these different types of employment relations in EMU was that, against the background of a one-size-fits-all, essentially pro-cyclical monetary policy, current accounts between the two blocs started to diverge. Germany and the rest of northern Europe gained competitiveness under the EMU regime, while the south's competitiveness fell in tandem. Ironically, even a good pupil like France, where labour productivity more or less followed Germany's, and where unit labour cost growth was not dramatically out of line with Germany's, suffered—not from being unproductive but from being caught in a monetary union that forced the export sector in Germany to deflate by keeping its relative unit labour costs under control and thus undercut French exports. The small differences between France and Germany at the start of EMU were exacerbated over time not by poor economic judgement or dysfunctional employment regimes, but by the logic of EMU itself, which pushed for these divergences.

The crisis of EMU is obviously not just a matter of misaligned wage-setting systems. The global financial crisis after 2007 started the process, and a certain lack of fiscal discipline in some of the EMU member states certainly may have contributed to the crisis. But those two processes cannot easily explain the current account divergences that we have witnessed since the start of EMU. And if, as I started out the analysis in this chapter, current account deficits are at the basis of the crisis of EMU, then the mechanisms that drive these divergences are critical for the long-term adjustment capacity of EMU. That is why wage-setting systems, skill production, and work organization are so important in this analysis: these are key elements in a political economy with a long history that are relatively hard to change, and therefore remain with us even if some of the other elements in the political economy, such as the financial sector and fiscal policy, could be sorted out. Put differently, while it is easy to imagine a solution to the current crisis of EMU—although not necessarily politically feasible—it is far from clear if a solution exists that also sorts out the underlying structural adjustment problems of roughly half of the eurozone.

The demise of the nested arrangement that preceded EMU, in which national central banks held wages in both the exposed and sheltered sectors in check and were themselves subject to Bundesbank-imposed discipline, has turned EMU into a monetary union that invites the imbalances between creditor and debtor states—the former mainly coordinated market economies and the latter mainly mixed market economies (and the liberal market economy Ireland). While austerity policies in the early 2010s will obviously force down the weight of the public sector, it is hard to see how that would redress the structural imbalances. Current account deficits have started to come down dramatically in all southern GIPS and Ireland by mid-2013, but mainly as a result of falling demand for imports. To redress the balance structurally, these countries would also—primarily—have to increase their exports in absolute and relative terms significantly by producing and exporting more high value-added goods and services. At the same time, and as a logical complement, Germany and its neighbours would have to reorient their domestic economies away from exports into private and public consumption. Easy to imagine on paper, perhaps, but nigh impossible in practice.

That said, Italy and Spain, and possibly Ireland once it finds itself on its feet again, could, perhaps, slowly sort out their competitiveness issues—even though that would take at least a decade or more of economic growth in the eurozone, and would involve the not insignificant task of constructing domestic institutional arrangements to underpin these shifts in competitiveness. But it is much harder to imagine Greece and Portugal doing so: neither of these countries have a competitive manufacturing or even modern sector to speak of on which they could build this adjustment strategy. And things may not be quite that easy: all of these countries lack robust domestic institutions such as well-developed training systems, strong trade unions and employers' associations, coordinated wage bargaining institutions, and cooperative workplace labour relations that would allow them to make a move up-market in their export profiles, and it is far from obvious how easily these can be constructed from scratch. If differences in employment relations have been as important in producing the crisis of EMU as this chapter suggests, then their continued diversity will also remain a deep source of tension within the single currency area, probably regardless of the immediate resolutions of the current crisis of EMU. Taking seriously that problem is a necessary first step towards understanding the crisis of the euro and its solution.

Acknowledgements

This chapter builds on joint previous research with Alison Johnston. An earlier version was published in *Transfer*, 19(1): 89–101, which built in part on Hancké (2013). For comments and discussions, my thanks go to Christopher Allsopp, Richard Bronk, Steven Coulter, Richard Deeg, Simon Glendinning, Michel Goyer, Henrike Granzow, Anke Hassel, Dermot Hodson, Richard Jackman, Maria Jepsen, Alison Johnston, Philippe Pochet, Waltraud Schelkle, Marco Simoni, David Soskice, Alessio Terzi, Tim Vlandas, Marco Zappalorto, and participants in seminars at the School of International Studies in Vienna and at the LSE. The usual exculpations apply.

References

Allsopp, C. (2002). *The Future of Macroeconomic Policy in the European Union*. Bank of England: External Monetary Policy Committee Unit Discussion Paper no 7.

Calmfors, L. and Drifill, J. (1988). 'Centralization of Wage Bargaining', *Economic Policy*, 6: 13–61.

Carlin, W. and Soskice, D. (2006). *Macroeconomics: Imperfections, Institutions and Policies*. Oxford and New York: Oxford University Press.

De Grauwe, P. (2011). 'The Governance of a Fragile Eurozone'. CEPS Working Document 346. Brussels: Centre for European Policy Studies.

Hall, P. A. (2012). 'The Economics and Politics of the Euro Crisis', *German Politics*, 21(4): 355–71.

Hall, P. A. and Franzese Jr., R. J. (1998). 'Mixed Signals: Central Bank Independence, Coordinated Wage Bargaining, and European Monetary Union', *International Organization*, 52(3): 505–35.

Hall, P. A. and Soskice, D. (eds.) (2001). *Varieties of Capitalism: The Institutional Foundations of Comparative Advantage*. Oxford and New York: Oxford University Press.

Hancké, B. (2013). *Unions, Central Banks and EMU: Labour Markets and Monetary Integration in Europe*. Oxford and New York: Oxford University Press.

Hancké, B. and Rhodes, M. (2005). 'EMU and Labor Market Institutions in Europe: The Rise and Fall of National Social Pacts', *Work and Occupations*, 32(2): 196–228.

Hancké, B., Rhodes, M., and Thatcher, M. (eds.) (2007). *Beyond Varieties of Capitalism: Conflict, Contradictions, and Complementarities in the European Economy*. Oxford and New York: Oxford University Press.

Hancké, B. and Soskice, D. (2003). 'Wage-Setting and Inflation Targets in EMU', *Oxford Review of Economic Policy*, 19(1): 149–60.

Hodson, D. (2011). *Governing the Euro Area in Good Times and Bad*. Oxford and New York: Oxford University Press.

Iversen, T. and Soskice. D. (1998). 'Multiple Wage Bargaining Systems in the Single European Currency Area', *Oxford Review of Economic Policy*, 14(3): 110–24.

—— (2001). 'Multiple Wage Bargaining Systems in the Single European Currency Area', *Empirica*, 28: 435–56.

Johnston, A. (2011). 'European Monetary Union and Institutional Change: The Perverse Effects of Supranational Macroeconomic Regimes on Wage Inflation'. Ph.D. thesis, London School of Economics and Political Science.

—— (2012). 'European Economic and Monetary Union's Perverse Effects on Sectoral Wage Inflation', *European Union Politics*, 13(3): 345–66.

Johnston, A. and Hancké, B. (2009). 'Wage Inflation and Labour Unions in EMU', *Journal of European Public Policy*, 16(4), Special Issue: 'Ten Years of EMU'.

Molina, O, and Rhodes, M. (2007). 'The Political Economy of Adjustment in Mixed Market Economies: A Study of Spain and Italy', in B. Hancké, Rhodes, and M. Thatcher (eds.), *Beyond Varieties of Capitalism: Conflict, Contradictions, and Complementarities in the European Economy*. Oxford and New York: Oxford University Press, 223–52.

Pochet, P. (ed.). (2002). *Wage Policy in the Eurozone*. Brussels: PIE/Peter Lang.

Regini, M. (1984). 'The Conditions for Political Exchange: How Concertation Emerged and Collapsed in Italy and Great Britain', in J. Goldthorpe (ed.), *Order and Conflict in Contemporary Capitalism*. Oxford: Clarendon Press, 126–42.

Salvati, M. (1981). 'May 1968 and the Hot Autumn of 1969: The Responses of Two Ruling Classes', in S. Berger, *Organizing Interests in Western Europe*. Cambridge: Cambridge University Press, 331–66.

Scharpf, F. W. (1991). *Crisis and Choice in European Social Democracy*. Ithaca: Cornell University Press.

—— (2011). *Monetary Union, Fiscal Crisis and the Preemption of Democracy*. LSE Europe in Question Discussion Paper 36/2011. London: London School of Economics.

Taddéi, D. and Coriat, B. (1993). *Made in France: L'Industrie Française dans la Compétition Mondiale*. Paris: Librairie Générale Française.

Wihlborg, C., Willett, T. D., and Zhang, N. (2011). 'The Euro Crisis: It Isn't Just Fiscal and It Doesn't Just Involve Greece'. Robert Day School Working Paper No. 2011-03. Available at <http://ssrn.com/abstract=1776133>.

CHAPTER 15

CONTINUITY AND CHANGE IN ASIAN EMPLOYMENT SYSTEMS

A Comparison of Japan, South Korea, and Taiwan

HARALD CONRAD

INTRODUCTION

OVER the 1990s, there was a widespread debate in the comparative capitalism literature over the possibility of international convergence of economic institutions (Degg
and Jackson 2007). While one school of thought has suggested an erosion of institutional differences among different national economies and a trend towards more
market-oriented institutions (e.g. Lane 1995), proponents of the varieties of capitalism
(VOC) school have maintained that there exist different types of more or less stable
nationally organized economic systems (liberal market vs. coordinated market economies) built on the foundations of 'institutional complementarities' with strong path
dependent developments (e.g. Hall and Soskice 2001). The VOC school of thought was
subsequently criticized for being overly synthetic and for neglecting issues of institutional change (Degg and Jackson 2007). Over the 2000s, we have witnessed the emergence of a broad consensus in the comparative institutionalist literature that highlights
the uneven and contested manner of institutional changes against the background of an
ecosystemic dominance of neo-liberalism that undermines more coordinated ways of
organization, even if it does not lead to a 'flat' homogenization of practices (Dore 2008;
Streeck 2009; Lane and Wood 2012; Jessop 2012).

It is against the backdrop of this academic debate that this chapter discusses continuity and change in human resource management (HRM) practices and labour relations of the three most developed industrial economies in East Asia: Japan, South Korea

(subsequently referred to as 'Korea'), and Taiwan. Historically, these three countries show a number of similarities in their traditional employment practices which can be explained by institutional and economic factors, Japan's long colonial influence in Korea (1910–45) and Taiwan (1895–1945), and cultural influences such as Confucianism. Common elements of these countries' employment systems have included factors such as group orientation, on-the-job training, stable employment, and seniority-oriented pay. Several of these factors have historically influenced the development of Western, predominantly American, conceptualizations of the human resource management paradigm (Zhu et al. 2007). Increasing cost pressures due to globalization and economic shocks such as the bursting of Japan's bubble economy in the early 1990s and the 1997 Asian economic crisis have had a considerable impact on the employment systems in each country. How these 'Asian' practices have changed since the 1990s is at the centre of analysis in this chapter.

Despite a growing academic literature shedding light on various aspects of the employment practices in Asian countries, there are to date only a few substantial and fully comparative accounts, covering selected human resource management practices (e.g. Huo et al. 2002). Other studies are broader in scope and take a longitudinal perspective, but they do not cover all three countries and have a much weaker empirical cross-sectional data basis (e.g. Bae et al. 2011; Jung and Cheon 2006). Against the backdrop of such data limitations, this chapter can only aim to take account of comparative trends.

As a basis for this comparative account, the next section will introduce typologies of HRM practices and labour unions. These typologies will serve as a reference point to compare the employment practices of the three Asian countries with each other over time. The third section will discuss each country's traditional employment system, evaluating the systems along the lines of the above typologies. This is followed, in the fourth section, by a short discussion of each country's post-war economic performance and the particular pressures they have faced during the last two decades. The fifth section focuses on the analysis of the resulting changes in the three countries, while the concluding section briefly takes account of these changes with reference to the academic debate highlighted above.

A Typology of Human Resource Management Practices and Labour Unions

Referring to a seminal paper by Adler (2001), Bae et al. (2011) have suggested a typology of HRM practices, which serves as useful reference point for the analysis of our three country cases.

Adler (2001) discusses how firms differ in terms of three organizing modes: 'market', 'hierarchy', and 'community'. While these institutional forms are not exclusive, they are three dimensions that characterize a firm's overall profile. Depending on the dominant

Table 15.1 Stylized forms of HRM

	Paternalistic type	Market type	Commitment type
Employment security of core workers	Very high	Very low	High
Extensive training of non-managerial staff	Moderately high	Low	High
Performance-based pay	Low	Very high (mainly individual performance-based)	Moderately high (mainly team or organization performance-based)
Influence of non-managerial staff in decisions on how work is allocated and conducted	Low	High (but various levels possible)	High

Source: adapted with minor changes from Bae et al. (2011: 710).

organizing mode, firms are expected to choose different sets of human resource policies and practices (Adler 2001). Firms with a market-oriented human resource approach are, for example, likely to adopt human resource practices that stress numerical and financial flexibility achieved by a large number of contingent workers, individual performance-based remuneration, and comparatively little investment in employees' training. Firms subscribing to a 'hierarchical' mode are more likely to stress a mechanical vertical division of labour with authority-based coordination in combination with loyalty-based long-term employment. Finally, the 'community' mode stresses team-based approaches with high employee influence, flat hierarchies, remuneration linked to team/organizational performance, and high employment security (Bae et al. 2011).

Table 15.1 illustrates how the different organizing modes correspond to human resource management policies in four dimensions: employment security, extensive training, performance-based pay, and employee influence.

While the predominant organizing mode of a firm's human resources will depend on its business strategy (Boxall 1992)—and any one country is therefore likely to have examples of firms operating in different modes—one can argue that some organizing modes are more prevalent in a country than others. In the sections below we will characterize the nature of HR practices in our three countries with reference to this model.

Besides its HRM practices, the nature of a country's employment system is strongly influenced by the structures and functions of its labour unions. In terms of union structures, one might focus on the level of union organization, membership, peak organizations, and the relationship with the state. For the union roles, one can discuss their insurance, regulation, and bargaining functions (Gospel 2008). While these issues will be addressed in due course in the sections below, we introduce here also briefly a typology of

Table 15.2 Stylized forms of unionism

	Market-oriented unionism	Society-oriented unionism	Class-oriented unionism
Class struggle	Low	Moderate	High
Social integration	Low	High	Low–moderate
Representation of occupational interests	High	Moderate	Low
Demarcation between 'politics' and 'industrial relations'	High	Moderate	No
Collective bargaining	High	High	Moderate

Source: the author based on Hyman (2001).

ideal types of labour unions, based on Hyman's (2001) analysis of European trade union-ism (see Table 15.2): 'Market-oriented' unions are considered as economic actors pur-suing primarily economic goals through collective bargaining. 'Class-oriented' unions promote working-class interests and the transformation of society. 'Society-oriented' unions act as social actors and voice workers' interests in the pursuit of social, moral, and political integration. Within this triangle of market, class, and society, European unions have oriented themselves often to one side of the triangle that is between class and mar-ket, between market and society, or between society and class. Hyman (2001) suggests further that a reorientation can occur, with a third, hitherto neglected, dimension exert-ing greater influence. The sections below will consider whether such a transformation can also be witnessed among the unions in our set of countries.

EMPLOYMENT PRACTICES IN JAPAN, SOUTH KOREA, AND TAIWAN UNTIL THE 1990S

This section discusses 'traditional' employment practices in Japan, Korea, and Taiwan. The account begins with an illustration of Japanese practices, followed by shorter discus-sions of the Korean and Taiwanese cases, highlighting commonalities and differences.

Japan

The Japanese labour market and employment practices have historically been char-acterized by a pronounced dual structure between larger and smaller firms. Almost 50% of Japanese workers are employed in establishments with less than 100 employees

(Ministry of Internal Affairs and Communications 2012). The 'traditional' employment practices discussed in this section are mainly to be found in larger establishments, although certain aspects have gained a normative character to which also small and medium-sized enterprises (SMEs) aspire (Conrad 2010).

The academic literature makes frequent references to the so-called 'three pillars of the traditional Japanese employment system', namely 'seniority-based pay', 'lifetime employment', and 'enterprise labour unions' (e.g. OECD 1977; Debroux 2003). Especially the first two practices have attracted considerable academic attention. While a few authors argue that these practices are a reflection of Confucian values such as the care and concern for other human beings and the significance of seniority and hierarchy (e.g. Zhu et al. 2007), there is a large body of literature that stresses instead economic factors and institutional complementarities. For example, the emergence of seniority-based pay at the end of the nineteenth century in Japan can be linked to labour shortages and high labour mobility at the time. Moreover, the practice was not prevalent in earlier periods when Confucian ideology was more influential (Conrad 2010). Aoki (1988) has demonstrated that particular features of the post-war Japanese production system, such as frequent job-rotations, mutual coordination of operating tasks among workers, team work, and feedback loops require an incentive system like seniority-based pay where remuneration is not tightly linked to a specific job category and which motivates wide-ranging job experiences among employees. What is more, since seniority-based remuneration is considered to be below individual productivity during the early stages of a worker's career, employee commitment can only be achieved by a long-term employment guarantee (Lazear 1979). These two traditional practices are thus closely interrelated.

While most authors would agree that lifetime employment is an important feature of the Japanese employment system, estimates of its prevalence remain difficult. This has to do with the fact that lifetime employment is not based on a permanent and thus observable employment contract, but is better understood as an implicit commitment to employ workers up to a company's retirement age. There are thus various data and measurement problems that make it difficult to assess how prevalent lifetime employment actually is. Ono (2010), applying different measurement methods in one of the most thorough analyses of the phenomenon to date, comes to the conclusion that the practice applies only to roughly 20% of the Japanese labour force. Moreover, the lifetime employment rate varies considerably, depending on firm size, educational level, and gender. Overall, larger firms offer bigger benefits and higher employment security than small and medium-sized firms (Rebick 2005). The lifetime employment rate of male workers with university degrees in large firms is estimated to be 45.5%, while female lifetime employment rates do not exceed 25% in any age group (Ono 2010).

A closer look at pay practices in Japan reveals that the term 'seniority-based pay' is similarly misleading as is the term 'lifetime employment'. In fact, pay systems have been and for the most part remain highly complex and take into account numerous factors. According to the General Survey on Working Conditions, which covers establishments with more than 30 employees, total compensation can be divided into 78.9% monthly cash payments and 21.1% semi-annual bonuses. Base pay makes up the largest portion of total compensation, at 67.6%. Furthermore, various allowances for the family, commuting, housing, etc. make up another 5% of total compensation (Rebick 2005). Base pay closely reflects the position of employees in the rank hierarchy and is a function of ability/skills, age, and performance. However, the latter used to play only a marginal role, whereas ability/skills and age have been the most important determinants.[1] Most companies used to have a pay component which was explicitly and directly linked to age, but ability/skills as criteria for the evaluation in the skill-grading system have in principle been the most important factors for base pay.

Bonuses have traditionally been paid bi-annually. Although they might appear be a kind of profit-sharing scheme, academic opinion on this issue has been divided, with some stressing the profit-sharing aspect (e.g. Freeman and Weitzman 1987), but most others downplaying it (e.g. Ohashi 1989; Brunello 1991; Morishima 2002). Bonus payments have usually been negotiated twice a year between employers and labour unions, and the latter have, at least until recently, considered bonuses as part of regular pay, which should not be linked to company profits.

The third pillar of the traditional Japanese employment system is its in-house company or enterprise unions, which band together in industry- and economy-wide federations. The Japanese labour movement goes back to the pre-Second World War period, but due to the restriction of labour union activities by the Public Peace Law of 1900 and their outlawing in 1938, the rise of an independent and free labour movement was possible only after the Second World War and subsequent democratization (Rebick 2005). There remain different views about why Japanese labour unions developed primarily at the enterprise level. While early labour scholars stressed the impact of migratory wage labourers, later scholars have linked their existence to internal labour market theories (Kawanishi 1992).

Today, some Japanese craft and industrial unions exist, but more than 90% of unions remain enterprise-based. Union density has been decreasing steadily from 35.4% in 1970 to an estimated 18.5% in 2010, with major variations depending on employer size. While the union participation rate of companies with more than 1,000 employees is 46.6% (2010), only 1.1% of workers in companies with less than 99 employees are labour union members. Moreover, roughly 65% of labour unions are organized as union or closed shops (Kōseirōdōshō 2010). Members of enterprise unions are usually only regular white- and blue-colour employees up to and including the level of section chief. The Trade Union Law does not allow participation by managers in any higher management positions.

Collective bargaining is primarily conducted by the enterprise unions, whose bargaining power is perceived to be limited, although Benson (1996) shows that there are important differences in terms of Japanese unions' structural and functional independence. To compensate for the limitations of a decentralized bargaining system at the enterprise level, enterprise unions have created industrial and national confederations and developed in 1955 the so-called Spring Wage Offensive (*shuntō*). The Spring Wage Offensive is a coordinated campaign, primarily focusing on higher wages. It is launched every spring by the industrial and national confederations, which formulate overall targets for wage increases and time schedules for negotiation. Following this, wage settlements are first agreed between the top firms and largest enterprise unions in each major industry. These settlements function subsequently as pattern setters for the demands of enterprise unions in other industries and small- and medium-sized companies, and influence eventually even wage setting in the non-union and public sector (Morito 2006).[2] The lead in *shunto* wage increase negotiations was historically taken by the Japan Council of Metalworkers' Unions (IMF-JC), an industrial confederation of unions in steel, shipbuilding, engineering, electrics, and automobiles.

By international standards, industrial action in connection with collective bargaining is low in Japan. The annual average of lost working days due to labour disputes in the period from 1993 to 2002 was just 1 per 1,000 employees in all industries and services (Carley 2005).

To sum up we assess Japanese traditional HRM practices and labour union characteristics against the typologies presented above. Being mindful of the inherent simplifications of such typologies, we can conclude that the overall nature of Japanese HRM practices has been 'paternalistic', with a clear emphasis on seniority-based pay, high employment security, and extensive on- and off-the-job training. Moreover, Japanese firms have formalized systems of labour–management consultations, but employee involvement and influence on strategic management decisions is low (Fujimura 2007). The Japanese labour union movement of the 1950s and 1960s included several 'class-oriented' radical organizations. However, after the decline of these unions in the 1970s, most Japanese labour unions took on a 'market-oriented' character, focusing primarily on the immediate needs of their members.

Korea

Similar to Japan, Korea has a pronounced dual industrial structure dominated by a few large, diversified conglomerates (*chaebol*) and many SMEs. Almost 60% of employees are employed in establishments with less than 100 workers (*Korea Statistical Yearbook* 2010). While employment conditions in Japanese firms of different sizes have historically been very different, this was not necessarily the case in Korea. For example, wage differentials by firm size were almost non-existent in the mid-1980s. However, differences have widened dramatically since then. Since the mid-2000s the wage level of workers in companies with 10–29 workers has only been 60% of the level of workers in companies with 500 or more employees (Lee et al. 2009).

In contrast to dominant views in the Japan-related literature, academic accounts on Korean (and Taiwanese) employment practices continue to stress the influence of the Confucian value system, emphasizing factors such as seniority, harmony, and hierarchy (e.g. Zhu et al. 2007). Regardless of whether such cultural explanations will be held up by future research, we can maintain that the Korean employment system during the high economic growth periods from the mid-1960s to late 1990s shared many similarities with its Japanese counterpart: strong employee–employer interdependence in highly internalized labour markets with lifetime employment and seniority-oriented pay securing employee commitment and loyalty (Kim and Kim 2003). Moreover, similar to Japan, government and firms were known to invest in long-term employment practices which included mass recruitment at entry level followed by training and development as part of long-term internal career paths. In addition, there was a high degree of functional flexibility with employees being more generalists than specialists in a particular field (Yu and Rowley 2009).

As for seniority-based pay, employees with the same job grade and pay class would receive pay raises based on seniority every year until retirement. The largest part of the compensation package would be made up of a base salary, primarily based on an employee's job grade and years of service. In addition, employees received a number of stable allowances, reflecting, for example, the number of dependants.

The Korean labour movement had historically strong links with the independence movement under the Japanese occupation (1910–45), which was characterized by frequent exploitation and discrimination against Korean workers. After the Second World War hopes for a free labour movement were quelled against the backdrop of the Korean War and the division of the Korean peninsula. In the emerging authoritarian industrial relations regime, only anti-communist labour unions were allowed to take root in South Korea. Prior to the democratization of the country in the late 1980s (Declaration of Democratization in 1987), Korean industrial relations were characterized by strong government-led authoritarian control of the unions for the sake of an export-led economic development strategy based on low wages. Enterprise unions had to affiliate with the government-sponsored Federation of Korean Trade Unions (FKTU), which acted as a junior partner of the state and management (Rowley and Yoo 2008). The democratization in 1987 saw a boom in the organization rate, which jumped from 12.3% (1986) to 18.6% (1989). Strikes also increased to 3,749 in 1987, compared with just 276 strikes a year earlier (Korea International Labour Foundation 2011). Following democratization, unions became more important players in Korea's national politics and the economy, but the unionization rate continued to drop steadily after 1989, reaching 10.5% in 2008 (Korea International Labour Foundation 2011).

The rise of the labour movement during the 1987 democratization strengthened both employment stability and seniority-based wages in larger firms. For example, average monthly turnover rates in firms with 500 and more employees, which had been above 3% during the 1980s, dropped to 1.7% in 1997 (Jung and Cheon 2006). Larger companies subsequently abolished ceilings on wage increases for blue-collar workers and the unions achieved uniform wage increases irrespective of individual ability or performance. Jung and Cheon (2006) claim that the Korean wage structure became thus even more seniority-oriented than its Japanese counterpart, an assessment that is confirmed by recent comparative data presented by Lee et al. (2009).

Collective bargaining in Korea shares several similarities with Japan. The national peak organizations of employers and unions announce desirable pay increase rates based on productivity and living cost increases. However, the actual bargaining is in almost 80% of cases undertaken at the enterprise level, with leading large companies functioning as pattern setters.

In conclusion, very similar to the Japanese case, traditional Korean HRM practices have been characterized by a 'paternalistic' orientation with a strong emphasis on employment security and training, coupled with seniority-oriented wage structures and strong hierarchies with low employee influence. Marked differences exist, however, with regards to the countries' labour movement. The Korean labour union movement played an important role in the country's democratization in the 1980s and the unions have since then influenced national politics to a much greater degree than their Japanese counterparts. Following Hyman's concept (2001), we can conclude that Korean unions, at least since the 1980s, have had both a market- and society-orientation.

Taiwan

Small and medium-sized enterprises are the dominant form of business organization in Taiwan. In 1995, companies with less than 30 employees employed about 65% of workers in the private sector, while firms with more than 500 workers employed only 5.5% of the workforce. Moreover, many SMEs are short-lived and key employees are often members of the owner's immediate or extended family. Large conglomerate-like organizations such as the Japanese *keiretsu* or the Korean *chaebol* are not so significant in Taiwan (Chen et al. 2003).

The development of Taiwanese post-war employment practices can be divided into three periods (Wu 2004). Before the mid-1960s, local Taiwanese firms had very simple and loose human resource management practices, which where characterized by a lack of manpower policies, low spending on staff training and development, seniority-oriented pay, and relatively little employee influence (Negandhi 1973).

After investment of primarily Japanese and American multinational companies between the mid-1960s and mid-1980s, Taiwanese firms started to adopt selected practices from these foreign examples, which led to the development of hybrid HRM styles. Comparing HRM practices in large Taiwanese firms with those in American and Japanese subsidiaries, Yeh (1991) reported the following findings for the mid-1980s: Taiwanese firms had a similar level of horizontal functional specialization as American firms, but were more similar to Japanese firms in terms of vertical specialization. In terms of job security, Taiwanese and Japanese firms were quite similar in that they did not easily lay off workers during a recession, which was far more common in American subsidiaries. Taiwanese and Japanese firms were also quite similar with regards to the importance of seniority, competency, and loyalty factors in promotion, but Taiwanese firms placed even more emphasis on loyalty than their Japanese counterparts. As noted above, the literature on traditional Taiwanese employment practices tends to relate the importance of factors such as loyalty, family, harmony, and hierarchy to the Confucian value system (e.g. Zhu et al. 2000; Wu 2004).[3]

With regards to employees' autonomy in decision-making, Taiwanese firms gave workers more power than their Japanese counterparts but autonomy was not as high as in American firms. Moreover, Taiwanese firms were similar to Japanese firms in their preferences for hiring new graduates, the obtaining of referrals from current employees, and the adoption of quality circles and group-centred activities (Yeh 1991).

The third stage in the development of Taiwanese HRM systems started according to Wu (2004) after the mid-1980s. At this time, the Taiwanese industry became more service-oriented with a focus on IT industries. Over the 1990s, HRM issues were brought into the board room as HRM took on a strategic importance.

The historical development of the Taiwanese labour movement shares similarities with the Korean case. Similar to developments in Korea, the Japanese colonization of Taiwan (1895–1945) prevented the establishment of an organized labour movement until the late 1940s (Minns and Tierney 2003). Since that time, the emerging labour movement has undergone several stages of transformation. The period from the late 1940s to the 1980s was characterized by authoritarian labour policies and a form of state corporatism, with labour organizations being controlled by the Nationalist Party (Kuomintang, KMT) (Chen et al. 2003). During the authoritarian KMT rule, all union branches were controlled by the Chinese Federation of Labour (CFL), with its non-elected executive officers influencing the unions to act in line with KMT policies (Minns and Tierney 2003). Due to massive state support, the CFL was very successful in recruiting union members. This was an important reason for a comparatively high unionization rate, which reached 22.8% by 1984 (Lee 1988). After an amendment to the Trade Union Law in 1975, unions had to be established in workplaces with more than 30 employees in most sectors, but due to a lack of enforcement a large number of enterprises remain in fact without any union organization (Zhu 2003). The law defines two types of unions, namely industrial and craft unions, but the industrial unions are in fact more akin to enterprise unions. Craft unions act mainly as worker beneficial organizations with publicly subsidized labour insurance programmes (Chen 1997; Chen et al. 2003).

Minns and Tierney (2003) identify the late 1970s as the starting point for the emergence of a more independent Taiwanese labour movement. In the 1970s and early 1980s, union activity accelerated with campaigns for new industrial legislation, including minimum wage rates and working conditions. Although the government had long resisted such calls, the economic climate of sustained economic growth, low unemployment, severe labour shortages, and heightened industrial unrest led the KMT to eventually change its position and adopt a pro-labour orientation. Resultant changes to various labour laws led to an overall improvement of working conditions in the 1980s and early 1990s. In particular, the passage of the Labour Standards Act (LSA) in 1984 and the lifting of martial law in 1987 altered industrial relations after the mid-1980s, resulting in a more adversarial climate (Chen et al. 2003). The LSA gave workers the opportunity to join craft unions in order to contribute to and receive various social insurance benefits (Zhu 2008). The high union density in Taiwan can thus be linked to the LSA and issues of access to social insurance benefits and should not be mistaken as a sign of a strong labour movement. In fact, Chen et al. (2003) maintain that collective bargaining is not the major function of Taiwanese trade unions. Chen (2007) reports 2005 data from the Council of Labour Affairs according to which less than 10% of Taiwanese unions engaged in collective bargaining. Moreover, trade unions are to a large extent financed by the companies of their members and firms exert a strong influence on the election of pro-company union leaders (Chen 2007).

An important characteristic feature of trade unionism in Taiwan is its strong link to party politics. While trade unions were a tool for the ruling KMT during the martial law period in the past, newly established independent unions were instrumental in supporting the formation of the new Democratic Progressive Party (DPP) government which won the 2000 presidential elections. Political confrontation among different unions supporting different political parties remains a feature of the Taiwanese labour movement (Zhu 2008).

In conclusion, very similar to the Japanese and Korean cases, 'traditional' Taiwanese HRM practices have been characterized by a 'paternalistic' orientation with a strong emphasis on employment security and training, coupled with seniority-oriented wage structures and strong hierarchies with low employee influence. The Taiwanese labour movement played an important part in the country's democratization process but has been largely enterprise-based, combining aspects of society- and market-oriented unionism.

PRESSURES FOR CHANGE

Among the three countries analysed in this chapter, Japan was the first to enter a sustained period of high economic growth in the post-war period, lasting from the early 1950s to the early 1970s. Over this period, yearly average GDP growth rates were around 10% (Alexander 2008). Following the oil shocks of the early 1970s growth rates declined, but remained on average around 4.5% during the 1970s and 1980s. A watershed in Japan's post-war economic history was the burst of the so-called 'bubble economy' in 1989–90. The burst of this bubble, which was largely based on property speculation induced by a sustained period of low interest rates, led to a balance-sheet recession characterized by massive bad loan problems in the financial sector, a sharp drop in economic demand, and rising unemployment. What followed were two decades of rather sluggish GDP growth, averaging a little over 1% during the 1990s and slightly below 1% during the 2000s (USDA 2012). Confronting stronger competition from other Asian countries since the 1990s, Japanese companies began to restructure their workforces and employment practices at home and shifted significant production capacities to South- and Northeast Asia, a trend which came to be described as the hollowing-out of Japan's manufacturing sector. Unemployment rates rose from the 2% range in the late 1980s to the higher 4% range in the late 1990s and 2000s (ILO 2012).

Korea's rapid economic growth period started in the early 1960s, based on labour-intensive production for the export market. Between 1965 and 1979 real GDP growth averaged over 9% per year (Collins 1990). After a short recession in 1980, high growth rates returned, averaging 8.7% in the 1980s and 6.2% in the 1990s (USDA 2012). The watershed in Korea's modern economic history was the 1997 Asian financial crisis which resulted in a bailout by the International Monetary Fund (IMF). Responding to the bailout conditions, the Korean government undertook major changes in employment laws, legalizing dismissals for managerial reasons and temporary work agencies. Responding to these legal changes, firms started to engage in large-scale restructuring through dismissals and redundancies by means of early retirement plans, employment of more contingent workers, and production relocation overseas (Yu and Rowley 2009). Unemployment rose sharply from very low levels in the 2% range prior to the Asian crisis to 6.5% in 1998. The unemployment rates over the 2000s were in the 3% range (ILO 2012), while GDP growth rates declined to an average of 4.2% over the 2000s (USDA 2012).

Taiwan's economic development since the 1960s until the 1997 Asian financial crisis can be divided into two periods. The period between 1961 and 1980 was characterized by significant export expansion, primarily based on labour-intensive industries with an average GNP growth rate above 8% (Zhu 2003). The 1980s and 1990s saw the expansion of technology-intensive industries and the relocation of manufacturing facilities to China and Southeast Asia, with average yearly GDP growth rates of 7.7% and 6.2% respectively (USDA 2012). Compared to Korea, Taiwan's growth was less affected by the 1997 Asian financial crisis, declining somewhat in 1998 but regaining former levels a year later. However, the crisis accelerated Taiwanese firms' restructuring efforts characterized by hiring freezes, downsizing, plant closures, and plant relocations to China. While the unemployment rate had been relatively low before the Asian crisis, it increased to over 5% in 2002 and was in the high 3% to low 4% range over the 2000s (ILO 2012). Average Taiwanese GDP growth rates over the 2000s were close to Korean levels at 3.9% (USDA 2012).

ADJUSTMENTS TO EMPLOYMENT PRACTICES SINCE THE 1990S

Japan

Between 1985 and 2010 the Japanese labour market underwent significant structural changes. Employment in manufacturing and agriculture dropped to 25.3% and 4% respectively, while the service sector employs today more than 70% of workers (Ministry of Internal Affairs and Communications 2012). Reacting to worsening domestic economic conditions after the burst of the country's bubble economy, Japanese companies reacted first by reductions in overtime, hiring freezes, as well as reassignments and temporary transfers (*shukkō*) to affiliated firms within their production networks. At least in larger companies, involuntary dismissals were largely not part of the adjustment processes. To this day Japan has some of the highest levels of employment protection in the OECD. Employers must meet four stringent conditions before they can dismiss workers: (a) the firm must be in severe financial difficulties; (b) the firm must have exhausted other efforts to avoid redundancies such as hiring freezes, temporary transfers, and voluntary retirements; (c) the firm has to consult with the labour unions and employees; (d) the firm must have a rational selection procedure to decide on redundancy candidates (Rebick 2005). Due to these limits on involuntary dismissals, many companies used voluntary retirement plans sweetened by the provision of attractive lump-sum payments to reduce their headcounts. Moreover, employees found themselves often subject to explicit or implicit pressures to accept such retirement requests (Jung and Cheon 2006).

Unemployment figures thus did not rise quickly and dramatically after the burst of the bubble but over a period of several years. With new hiring remaining limited for some years and older employees leaving through early retirement, the ratio of regular employees in the labour force decreased to 62.2% in 2007, while non-regular forms of employment such as part-time work (22.5%), dispatched work (4.7%), contract-based work (2.8%), and other forms of non-regular employment (6.7%) gained substantially in importance (JILPT 2011). Lifetime employment remains an important practice, but covers thus an ever decreasing ratio of workers.

Seniority-oriented pay practices have undergone considerable changes since the 1990s. Due to the growing diversity of pay systems across and within companies, generic features are nowadays much harder to condense than in the past, when companies often followed similar models. Nevertheless, we might try to summarize the general trend of the pay system reforms as far as they relate to the core labour force (excluding the growing ranks of non-regular workers) as follows (based on Ishida 2006; Nakamura 2006; NRSKKK 2006): the pay systems of managers (section or department managers and above) show the greatest changes, whereas changes for rank-and-file employees remain more limited but are also significant. Generally, the number of pay components is decreasing. More and more companies are eliminating or at least reducing age-based pay (*nenreikyū*) as well as the different allowances. For management positions, ability/skill pay (*shokunōkyū*) is often abolished, whereas it continues to play an important but also diminishing role for rank-and-file employees. Accordingly, the surveys of the Japan Productivity Centre for Socio-Economic Development indicate that between 2000 and 2005 the percentage of companies that claimed to have ability/skill pay declined from 82.4% to 57.5% for managers, and from 87% to 70.1% for non-managers (Shakai Keizai Seisansei Honbu 2006).

For workers in managerial positions, regular pay rises which formed the core of the seniority-based wage system have more or less been abolished. For these workers, ability/skill pay is often replaced with a pay component that reflects a particular job class or hierarchical role that an employee fulfils in an organization (*yakuwarikyū*). There are, however, also companies like Mitsubishi Motors that have introduced *yakuwarikyū* for their manufacturing workers (Mitsubishi Motors 2003). As can be seen in Figure 15.1, in over 30% of

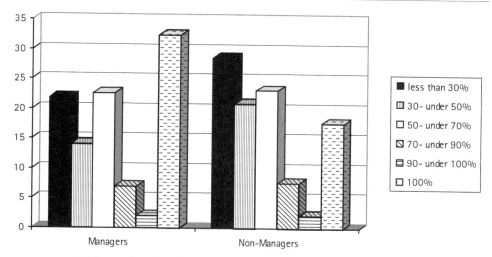

FIGURE 15.1 Weight of the role/job pay component (*yakuwarikyū*) in base pay (%)

Source: Shakai Keizai Seisansei Honbu (2006: 13).

companies, role/job pay for manager-class workers makes up 100% of base pay. Frequently, this job or role pay component consists of a fixed amount and a performance-related part, resulting in a monthly salary range. Managers within each class thus receive different and fluctuating salaries, depending on the assessment of their performance.

Although role/job pay also plays an increasingly important role for non-managerial workers, the overall weight of this component, and consequently the significance of performance for pay determination, remains limited. Table 15.3 indicates how the weight of the different pay components might change over an employee's career course.

What is being evaluated as performance varies among companies is commonly a combination of individual and/or team performance. In regard to the performance appraisals, it is important to note that performance is only rarely assessed in terms of simple quantitative results such as sales, profits, or cost reductions. The new performance systems focus generally on what Nakamura (2006) calls process-oriented performance-based salary systems (*purosesu jūjigata seika shugi*). Here, performance is evaluated not only in terms of the degree of success in achieving quantitative goals, but also in terms of the process of achieving those goals.

Although performance has thus gained in importance as a determining variable for pay, skill factors have not been abolished and skill-grading systems still play a large role, at least for rank-and-file employees. This is confirmed by a survey of the 199 largest employers on the Tokyo Stock Exchange, which found that only 23.9% of employers that use employee performance to determine employee wages plan to discontinue the skill grading system (Morishima 2002). However, whereas companies used to operate with an all-embracing concept of skills, which included personal attributes such as educational background and age (with a focus on 'capable of doing'), the evolving systems focus more on work-related usable skills and performance (with a focus on

Table 15.3 Model of the relative importance of different wage components over the career course

	Non-managerial workers 20s	Lower managers 30s	Section chief 40s	Department chief 50s
Age pay (*nenreikyū*) *Seikatsushugi*	OO	O	–	–
Ability/skill pay (*shokunōkyū*) *Nōryōkushugi*	O	OO	OO	O
Role/job pay (*yakuwarikyū*) *Seikashugi*	–	–	O	OO

Source: Shakai Keizai Seisansei Honbu (2002: 17).

'doing'), with much less emphasis on the age factor. In line with this transformation, the rather vague assessment of skills in the past has been replaced with more objective 'management by objectives' appraisal systems. Despite the continuation of skill-based pay systems for rank-and-file employees, this change in skill assessment has in principle capped age-related wage increases as they were found in the past.[4]

As for Japan's industrial relations since the 1990s, Japanese employers and even some unions started to question the nationally coordinated and cascading *shuntō* approach of wage bargaining (Benson 2008). In 2002, IMF-JC stopped making a unified request for hikes in base pay and industry-wide settlements have since come to an end (JILPT 2006). Moreover, since the 1990s labour–management joint consultation systems at the enterprise level have become important mechanisms for the discussion of working conditions. While wage determination remains in principle part of a collective bargaining process at the enterprise level, a recent Japanese survey indicates that almost half of the responding firms used labour–management joint consultation systems to settle collective bargaining issues too (JILPT 2011). While the difference between collective bargaining and joint consultation might appear somewhat artificial, these issues highlight the decentralization of Japanese industrial relations in recent years (Benson 2008). Overall, with many companies experiencing financially difficult times, unions were often forced to trade off wage increases and benefit cuts in occupational pensions for employment guarantees (Conrad 2011).

Korea

The Korean employment structure has changed markedly over the last two decades. Between 1985 and 2010 the percentage of employees in manufacturing dropped from

30.8% to 24.7%, while employment in the service sector rose from 44.3% to 68.5% during the same period (Statistics Korea 2012). Mirroring such structural changes, Korean HRM practices have transformed considerably, possibly showing the largest changes among the three countries considered in this chapter.

The rise of the labour movement after 1987 led to strong pay increases which exceeded the rate of labour productivity gains and weakened Korea's international competitiveness (Chung 2008). Beginning in the early 1990s, against the backdrop of economic globalization and a gradual decline in economic growth rate, some Korean companies started therefore to experiment with new compensation systems such as Japanese ability-based (Chung 2008) and US-style performance-based systems (Kang and Yanadori 2011). Elements of the traditional HR management system that had been considered to be vital ingredients of Korea's successful economic growth periods became increasingly regarded as problematic. However, only the financial crisis of 1997 triggered more widespread and fundamental changes. Kang and Yanadori (2011) argue that Korea's major business groups (*chaebol*) proactively leveraged the crisis to extensively use performance-based pay practices that they had started to consider in the early 1990s. Data from the Korean Ministry of Labour show that annual salary systems, as one particular kind of performance-based pay plan, existed in only 3.6% of firms employing more than 100 employees back in 1997. In 2007, 52.5% of such companies had introduced those systems. However, it is important to note that not all workers are uniformly affected by the new systems. While the adoption rate for managerial jobs and office jobs is 91% and 72% respectively, the new systems are less frequently used for service/sales staff (33%) and production jobs (22%) (Korea Labour Institute 2007), mirroring largely developments in Japan.

Also similar to the situation in Japan, the new Korean performance-based systems are often complex and reflect both individual and group performance evaluations. Furthermore, most companies tie evaluation ratings only partially to base pay, with other base pay components remaining linked to seniority. In one of the most comprehensive analyses of the adoption of performance-related pay in Korea to date, Kang and Yanadori (2011) found that 81% of the publicly listed companies in their sample reported that less than 30% of employee pay was tied to performance. Only 4% of companies tied more than 50% of pay to performance. Kang and Yanadori's (2011) study also reveals that the adoption of performance-related pay in Korea is significantly and positively correlated with high pay levels prior to their adoption, affiliation with the 30 largest business groups, and the adoption by other firms in the same industry. Coverage by performance-related pay is related to workforce composition and unionization. While blue-collar workers and Korean unions have found it difficult to resist the adoption of performance-related pay as such, they have apparently had some influence on which type of employees have been covered by the new schemes. Firms with a high percentage of manual workers and higher unionization tend to limit coverage by performance-based pay to managerial class workers (Kang and Yanadori 2011).

While the introduction of performance-based pay in Korea is widely considered to have raised employee motivation and productivity, labour cost effects have been relatively weak. Moreover, similar to the situation in Japan (Conrad 2010), not a few companies are reporting side effects such as an obsession with short-term achievement and weakened cooperation among teams and departments (Chung 2008).

The 1997 financial crisis led to a considerable weakening of lifetime employment practices. Legal changes to the Korean labour laws, which legalized dismissals for managerial reasons and temporary work agencies, enabled companies to adopt more numerical flexibility. Involuntary dismissals and early retirement plans increased in numbers, although strong opposition from the labour unions restricted large *chaebol* like Hyundai in making even more significant cuts to its workforces (Rowley and Bae 2002). Similar to the situation in Japan, the number of regular employees in large conglomerates decreased while the ratio of non-regular workers increased significantly from 27.8% in 2002 to 35.5% in 2006 (Bae et al. 2011).

In recruiting, where typical assessment criteria used to be academic performance, educational history, and physical appearance, competency and personality tests have gained in importance. Furthermore, the large *chaebol*, which used to recruit only few female college students in the past, have started to employ more women (Yu and Rowley 2009). Changes to the internal selection process have been slower. While the traditional system relied mostly on seniority or paper-and-pencil tests, assessment centres have become an important selection tool in recent years (Yu and Rowley 2009).

Major characteristics of older HRM practices were intensive training and development efforts which focused on relevant employees according to their positions and jobs and were regarded as a kind of employee benefit. After the 1997 financial crisis companies cut down on employee development costs and focused their training and development efforts on smaller groups of core employees including engineers and top talent for senior management positions. Data presented by Bae and Rowley (2004) shed light on the development of training and development (T&D) and research and development (R&D) expenditures before and after the financial crisis. If measured in per sales expenditure terms, the R&D ratio increased consistently between 1990 and 2002. However, the T&D ratio fell after the financial crisis to the level reached in 1995 and continued to stay at this level thereafter.

Challenging the FKTU as the single national centre of the labour unions after 1987, another more confrontational national centre emerged in 1995 with the establishment of the Korean Confederation of Trade Unions (KCTU). Reacting to higher unemployment and lay-offs in the aftermath of the Asian crisis of 1997, both national centres have aimed to strengthen the labour movement by the formation of more industrial and occupational unions. While FKTU's membership base remains predominantly enterprise-based (61.7% of all members), KCTU's members are mostly non-enterprise unions (77.6%). KCTU represents 39.5% and FKTU 43.5% (2008) of the 1.66 million union members in South Korea (Korea International Labour Foundation 2011).

National level trade unions often support and at times illegally intervene in negotiations at larger companies to achieve overall higher wage increases, but they have not been able to prevent a rising wage gap between larger and smaller companies.

Changes in the reasons for labour disputes give some indication of the changing character of collective bargaining before and after the financial crisis of 1997. While collective bargaining before the financial crisis was dominated by issues like wage rates, participation in personnel and disciplinary committees, and closed shop agreements, employment security became the central focus of negotiations after the crisis (Rowley and Yoo 2008).

Taiwan

Starting in the late 1980s, Taiwan's labour-intensive industries began to relocate their production facilities to mainland China and Southeast Asia to take advantage of lower labour costs. This had a profound impact on the country's employment structure. Employment in the manufacturing sector declined from 32% in 1990 to 27.2% in 2009, while the respective shares in the service sectors rose from 46.3% to 68.9% over the same period (Lee 2010).

Comparing HRM practices in Taiwanese-owned, Western-owned, and Japanese-owned firms in Taiwan in 2002, Wu (2004) found that Taiwanese-owned firms had adopted a number of similar HRM techniques as their foreign counterparts. While no significant differences were found in selection and training and development policies, significant differences continued to exist in communication, feedback, performance-related pay, and performance appraisals. Taiwanese- and Japanese-owned firms offered less performance feedback, conducted less formal appraisals, had less open communication with their employees, and used less performance-related pay. Wu (2004) concluded from these findings that the convergence of Taiwanese HRM practices towards Western practices could be found in more easily quantifiable technologies (planning, staffing, and training), but remained limited in relationship-based technologies such as career development, performance management, work design, and pay and reward systems. These findings were largely confirmed by a study from Bae et al. (2011) investigating HRM changes in Taiwan between the mid-1990s and mid-2000s: extensive training measures became more important, but employment security of regular workers, the prevalence of performance-based pay, and employee influence appeared to have decreased over the same period.[5] Interpreting these findings, the authors conclude that formal performance appraisals and stronger employee influence are mitigated by prevailing Confucian values, which emphasize interpersonal obligation and hierarchical relationships (Bae et al. 2011). The limited importance of individual performance pay is also confirmed by a study from Zhu (2003), who finds that group-oriented performance pay and relatively equal bonus pay were the main remuneration systems.

While Taiwanese firms have sought greater numerical flexibility by using contingent part-time and temporary workers (Chen et al. 2003), it is important to keep in mind that the overall ratio of part-time workers to the total labour force remained less than 5% in 2007 (Council of Labour Affairs 2008 after Bae et al. 2011).

The lifting of the martial law in 1987, which induced groups of labour activists and anti-government leaders to form unofficial enterprise-centred organizations, and the replacement of the long-ruling KMT by the pro-labour Democratic Progressive Party (DPP) in 2000 changed significantly the Taiwanese political landscape and could have invigorated the Taiwanese labour movement. However, the increase in unemployment following manufacturing relocations to China and Southeast Asia and the increasing importance of high-tech industries with high-performance work practices have deterred the development of independent Taiwanese unions (Chen et al. 2003; Chen 2007). The unionization rate of industrial workers dropped from 31% in 1990 to 19.7% in 2005 (Lee 2010) and led to an overall stagnation of the union movement, with the total unionization rate remaining at 36.9% (Zhu 2008). Wu (2004), investigating the impact of labour unions and the labour representative committee on the formulation of HRM practices in the early 2000s, found that employee influence remained very weak. Western companies' subsidiaries showed more willingness to listen to their employees' viewpoints than Taiwanese-owned and Japanese-owned firms. These findings are confirmed by Zhu (2003), who maintains that unions are not part of companies' decision-making processes and lack independence from management. Overall, Zhu (2008) has described the last two decades as a period of stagnation of the Taiwanese labour union movement.

Conclusion

This chapter has demonstrated that HRM practices and industrial relations have undergone some considerable changes in Japan, South Korea, and Taiwan since the 1990s. In particular, long-term employment practices and seniority-oriented wage systems have lost some of their former significance. Overall, our discussion of changes has highlighted the fact that the 'Asian' employment systems appear to move away from paternalistic-type practices towards more market-type practices. Some authors have therefore explicitly subscribed to a convergence thesis. For example, Suda (2007) concluded that Japanese pay systems have converged towards UK market-based practices. Within Suda's theoretical framework about fundamental differences between pay systems, her conclusions about convergent developments are credible. However, her approach and conclusions highlight some important theoretical aspects of the convergence debate that are easily overlooked. First, similar trends are not identical with convergence. Convergence in the strict sense requires that the developments of a variable in different countries point towards a common end point so that we can witness a consistent diminution of variance over time (Wood et al. 2009; Mayrhofer and Brewster 2005). Second, the interpretation of whether a development is convergent depends heavily on the choice, definition, and degree of aggregation of the researched variables. For example, Jacoby (2005) has argued that while employment and pay policies in Japan and the USA are moving towards a market-orientated model, their differences are actually widening since the USA is transforming at a quicker speed than Japan. Furthermore, there is substantial evidence that *within*-country variation in employment practices is growing in many industrialized countries, including Japan, the USA, and the UK (Jacoby 2005; Katz and Darbishire 2000). These issues highlight some inherent difficulties of the convergence/diversity debate and showcase the limitations of the model introduced at the beginning of this chapter. For example, despite the growing importance of performance-based pay and less employment security, extensive training remains a crucial feature of Japanese and Korean employment practices. Taiwanese companies, on the other hand, have adopted more Western-style practices in staffing and training, but continue to value aspects of seniority-oriented pay. Within the presented typology framework, we would therefore need to characterize the respective employment systems as *hybrid* types.

Our discussion of trends in the employment systems of the three countries has highlighted some key issues:

First, as in many other industrialized countries (Jacoby 2005; Katz and Darbishire 2000), we find growing *within-country* variations, both between SMEs and larger firms as well as among larger firms. This underlines the importance of taking internal diversity seriously and not exaggerating the coherence of practices in coordinated market economies (Lane and Wood 2012), such as Japan and Korea.

Second, companies in all three countries have been developing more diversified HR practices to target different types of employees. For example, performance-oriented pay has gained in importance for white-collar workers in all three countries, but blue-collar schemes continue to have a stronger seniority-orientation, highlighting *within-company* variations.

Third, not only do companies combine practices from different ideal types of HRM as mentioned above, they might also combine old and new practices within a certain domain like the wage system. For example, the same Japanese companies that have introduced new performance factors to their wage systems often continue to use a wide range of traditional welfare benefits such as defined benefit pensions. This kind of change might be understood with reference to what Streeck and Thelen (2005) have called 'layering'. This mode of change describes a situation in which 'original institutions are left in place, but new elements are added alongside the old system' (Thelen 2009: 484). The reasons for layering are strong vested interests in the maintenance of the old system. Instead of replacing the old system, reformers will work around those elements of an institution that have become unchangeable and add instead another institutional layer. Over time, differential growth might siphon off support for the older institution.

Fourth, the newly evolving compensation systems have in some cases led to institutional innovations in the sense that new and old practices are combined in ways not found in other countries. For example, while we have witnessed a rapid decline of defined benefit-type occupational pensions in the USA and the UK over the last two decades, Japanese companies appear to have bucked this trend. Instead of simply replacing defined benefit with defined contribution pensions, as it has at best happened in the USA and the UK, Japanese companies have created unique multilayered retirement benefit systems that combine benefits of both schemes and also reflect increasingly employee performance indicators (Conrad 2011).

Fifth, as for industrial relations, we have pointed to some changes in union organization, declining membership rates and bargaining functions, but the overall character of the labour union movements as defined by the Hyman (2001) framework appear not to have changed markedly in the last twenty years, but rather a decade earlier in the case of Korea and Taiwan.

NOTES

1. For a detailed example of a traditional pay system see Shibata (2000).
2. Hara and Kawaguchi (2008) speculate that these spillover effects might explain the absence of a strong union wage premium in the past. The union wage premium concerns the issue of whether unionized firms in Japan pay more to typical workers than non-unionized firms. The results of academic research into this issue indicate that the effects have varied over time. While Kalleberg and Lincoln (1988), Tsuru and Rebitzer (1995), and Tachibanaki and Noda (2000) report a negligible union wage premium for the 1990s, Noda (2007) and Hara and Kawaguchi (2008) find a robust union wage premium during the early 2000s. Noda (2007) reports that the average wage of men in the early 2000s was 11–20% higher at companies with labour unions, while no statistically significant higher wage was found for women. According to Noda (2007: 36) these findings indicate that the 'effects of labour unions appear under conditions when working conditions are apt to deteriorate'.
3. However, Wu (2004) remarks that the respective were carried out in the 1980s and that there is now a need for up-to-date academic studies to explore how Taiwanese value orientations have changed and impacted HRM practices since then.
4. See Conrad (2010) for a detailed analysis of Japanese pay system reforms since the 1990s.
5. The results from this study need to be considered with some care because the underlying sample is of a cross-sectional nature and does not systematically compare the same companies over the entire period.

REFERENCES

Adler, P. S. (2001). 'Market, Hierarchy, and Trust: The Knowledge Economy and the Future of Capitalism', *Organization Science*, 12(2): 215–34.

Alexander, A. (2008). *The Arc of Japan's Economic Development*. London and New York: Routledge.

Aoki, M. (1988). *Information, Incentives and Bargaining in the Japanese Economy*. Cambridge: Cambridge University Press.

Bae, J., Chen, S., and Rowley, C. (2011). 'From a Paternalistic Model Toward What? HRM Trends in Korea and Taiwan', *Personnel Review*, 40(6): 700–22.

Bae, J. and Rowley, C. (2004). 'Macro and Micro Approaches in Human Resource Development: Context and Content in South Korea', *Journal of World Business*, 39(4): 349–61.

Benson, J. (1996). 'A Typology of Japanese Enterprise Unions', *British Journal of Industrial Relations*, 34(3): 371–86.

—— (2008). 'Trade Unions in Japan: Collective Justice or Managerial Compliance', in Benson and Y. Zhu (eds.), *Trade Unions in Asia*. London and New York: Routledge, 24–42.

Boxall, P. F. (1992). 'Strategic Human Resource Management: Beginnings of a New Theoretical Sophistication?', *Human Resource Management Journal*, 2(3): 60–79.

Brunello, G. (1991). 'Bonuses, Wages and Performances in Japan: Evidence from Micro Data', *Ricerche Economiche*, 45(2–3): 377–96.

Carley, M. (2005). *Industrial Relations in the EU, Japan and USA, 2003–4*. European Industrial Relations Observatory Online. Available at <http://www.eurofound.europa.eu/eiro/2005/02/feature/tn0502102f.htm> accessed 2 February 2012.

Chen, S. (1997). 'The Development of HRM Practices in Taiwan', *Asia Pacific Business Review*, 3(4): 152–69.

—— (2007). 'Human Resource Strategy and Unionization: Evidence from Taiwan', *International Journal of Human Resource Management*, 18(6): 1116–31.

Chen, S., Ko, J., and Lawler, J. (2003). 'Changing Patterns of Industrial Relations in Taiwan', *Industrial Relations*, 42(3): 315–40.

Chung, K. (2008). 'Korea's Shift to Pay-for-Performance', *SERI Quarterly*, 1(2): 9–17.

Collins, S. M. (1990). 'Lessons from Korean Economic Growth', *American Economic Review*, 80(2): 104–7.

Conrad, H. (2010). 'From Seniority to Performance Principle: The Evolution of Pay Practices in Japanese Firms since the 1990s', *Social Science Japan Journal*, 13(1): 115–35.

—— (2011). 'Change and Continuity in Japanese Employment Practices: The Case of Occupational Pensions since the Early 2000s', *International Journal of Human Resource Management*, 22(15): 3051–67.

Debroux, P. (2003). *Human Resource Management in Japan: Changes and Uncertainties*. Aldershot: Ashgate.

Degg, R. and Jackson, G. (2007). 'The State of the Art: Towards a More Dynamic Theory of Capitalist Variety', *Socio-Economic Review*, 5(1): 149–79.

Dore, R. (2008). 'Best Practice Winning Out?', *Socio-Economic Review*, 6(4): 779–84.

Freeman, R. B. and Weitzman, M. L. (1987). 'Bonuses and Employment in Japan', *Journal of the Japanese and International Economy*, 1(2): 168–94.

Fujimura, H. (2007). 'Current Situation of and Issues in Labour–Management Communication', *Japan Labour Review*, 4(1): 69–89.

Gospel, H. (2008). 'Trade Unions in Theory and Practice: Perspectives from Advanced Industrial Countries', in J. Benson and Y. Zhu (eds.), *Trade Unions in Asia*. London and New York: Routledge, 11–23.

Hall, P. A. and Soskice, D. (2001). 'An Introduction to Varieties of Capitalism', in Hall and Soskice (eds.), *Varieties of Capitalism: The Institutional Foundations of Comparative Advantage*. Oxford and New York: Oxford University Press, 1–68.

Hara, H. and Kawaguchi, D. (2008). 'The Union Wage Effect in Japan', *Industrial Relations*, 47(4): 569–90.

Huo, Y. P., Huang, H. J., and Napier, N. K. (2002). 'Divergence or Convergence: A Cross-National Comparison of Personnel Selection Practices', *Human Resource Management*, 41(1): 31–44.

Hyman, R. (2001). *Understanding European Trade Unionism: Between Market, Class, and Society*. London: Sage.

International Labour Organization (ILO) (2012). *Laborsta Internet Database.* Available at <http://laborsta.ilo.org/default.html>, accessed 2 February 2012.

Ishida, M. (2006). 'Chingin Seido Kaikaku to Rōshi Kankei' [Wage System Reform and Industrial Relations], in *Chingin Seido to Rōdō Kumiai no Torikumi ni kan suru Chōsa Kenkyū Hōkokusho.* Tokyo: Rengō Sōgō Seikatsu Kaihatsu Kenkyūjo, 11–49.

Jacoby, S. M. (2005). *The Embedded Corporation: Corporate Governance and Employment Relations in Japan and the United States.* Princeton: Princeton University Press.

Jessop, B. (2012). 'Rethinking the Diversity and Variability of Capitalism: On Variegated Capitalism in the World Market', in C. Lane and G. Wood (eds.), *Capitalist Diversity and Diversity within Capitalism.* London: Routledge, 209–37.

JILPT (Japan Institute for Labour Policy and Training) (2006). *Labour Situation in Japan and Analysis: General Overview 2006/2007.* Tokyo: JILPT.

—— (2011). *Labour Situation in Japan and Analysis: General Overview 2011/2012.* Tokyo: JILPT.

Jung, E. and Cheon, B. (2006). 'Economic Crisis and Changes in Employment Relations in Japan and Korea', *Asian Survey,* 46(3): 457–76.

Kalleberg, A. L. and Lincoln, J. R. (1988). 'The Structure of Earnings Inequality in the United States and Japan', *American Journal of Sociology,* 94 (suppl.): 121–53.

Kang, S. and Yanadori, Y. (2011). 'Adoption and Coverage of Performance-Related Pay during Institutional Change: An Integration of Institutional and Agency Theories', *Journal of Management Studies,* 48(8): 1837–65.

Katz, H. C. and Darbishire, O. (2000). *Converging Divergencies: Worldwide Changes in Employment Systems.* Ithaca and New York: Cornell University Press.

Kawanishi, H. (1992). *Enterprise Unionism in Japan.* London and New York: Kegan Paul.

Kim, D.-O. and Kim, S. (2003). 'Globalization, Financial Crisis, and Industrial Relations: The Case of South Korea', *Industrial Relations,* 42(3): 341–67.

Korea International Labour Foundation (2011). Statistics. Available at <http://www.koilaf.org/KFeng/engStatistics/bbs.php?code1=8>, accessed 2 February 2012.

Korea Labour Institute (2007). *2007 Nyŏ ingŭn chedo silt'ae chosa* [2007 Survey of the Wage System]. Seoul: Korea Labour Institute.

Kōseirōdōshō (2010). *Heisei 22-nen Rōdō Kumiai Kiso Chōsa* [2010 Basic Survey on Labour Unions]. Available at <http://www.e-stat.go.jp/SG1/estat/NewList.do?tid=000001015698>, accessed 13 July 2012.

Lane, C. (1995). *Industry and Society in Europe: Stability and Change in Britain, Germany and France.* Aldershot: Edward Elgar.

Lane, C. and Wood, G. (2012). 'Institutions, Internal Diversity and Change', in Lane and Wood (eds.), *Capitalist Diversity and Diversity within Capitalism.* London: Routledge, 1–31.

Lazear, E. P. (1979). 'Why is there Mandatory Retirement?', *Journal of Political Economy,* 81(6): 1261–84.

Lee, B., Kim, H., Jeong, J., and Cho, S. (eds.) (2009). *Labour in Korea 1987–2006: Looking Through the Statistical Lens.* Seoul: Korea Labour Institute.

Lee, J. S. (1988). Labour Relations and Stages of Economic Development: The Case of the Republic of China', Proceedings of the Conference on Labour and Economic Development, held at the Chung Hua Institution for Economic Research, Taipei, Taiwan.

—— (2010). 'Globalization and Changing Industrial Relations in Taiwan's Banking Industry', *Indian Journal of Industrial Relations,* 45(4): 609–21.

Mayrhofer, W. and Brewster, C. (2005). 'European Human Resource Management: Researching Developments over Time', *Management Revue,* 16(1): 36–62.

Ministry of Internal Affairs and Communications (2012). *Japan Statistical Yearbook 2012*. Available at <http://www.stat.go.jp/english/data/nenkan/index.htm>, accessed 26 February 2012.

Minns, J. and Tierney, R. (2003). 'The Labour Movement in Taiwan', *Labour History*, 18: 103–28.

Mitsubishi Motors (2003). *Kumiaiin Shain no Jinji Seido Kaisei Keikaku ni tsuite*. [Reform of the New Human Resource Management System for Union Members]. Tokyo: Mitsubishi Motors.

Morishima M. (2002). 'Pay Practices in Japanese Organizations: Changes and Non-Changes', *Japan Labour Bulletin*, 1 April: 8–13.

Morito, H. (2006). *Decentralizing Decentralized Industrial Relations? The Role of Labour Unions and Employee Representatives in Japan*. Country Report for the JILPT Comparative Labour Law Seminar, Tokyo, February.

Nakamura, K. (2006). *Seika Shugi no Jijitsu* [The Truth about Performance-Based Pay]. Tokyo: Tōyō Keizai Shinpōsha.

Negandhi, A. E. (1973). *Management and Economic Development: The Case of Taiwan*. The Hague: Martinus Nijhoff.

Nihon Rōdō Seisaku Kenkyū Kenshū Kikō (NRSKKK) (2006). 'Gendai Nihon Kigyō no Jinzai Manējimento' [The Contemporary Management of Japanese Companies]. *Rōdō Seisaku Kenkyū Hōkokusho No. 61*.

Noda, T. (2007). 'Effects of Enterprise Labour Unions: Reviewing the Effects on Wages and Employment Adjustment', *Japan Labour Review*, 4(1): 23–40.

Ohashi, I. (1989). 'On the Determinants of Bonuses and Basic Wages in Large Japanese Firms', *Journal of the Japanese and International Economy*, 3(4): 451–79.

Ono, H. (2010). 'Lifetime Employment in Japan: Concepts and Measurements', *Journal of the Japanese and International Economies*, 24(1): 1–27.

Organisation for Economic Co-operation and Development (OECD) (1977). *The Development of Industrial Systems: Some Implications of the Japanese Experience*. Paris: OECD.

Rebick, M. (2005). *The Japanese Employment System: Adapting to a New Economic Environment*. Oxford and New York: Oxford University Press.

Rowley, C. and Bae, J. (2002). 'Globalization and Transformation of Human Resource Management in South Korea', *International Journal of Human Resource Management*, 13(3): 522–49.

Rowley, C. and Yoo, K. (2008). 'Trade Unions in South Korea: Transition Towards Neocorporatism?', in J. Benson and Y. Zhu (eds.), *Trade Unions in Asia*. London and New York: Routledge, 43–62.

Shakai Keizai Seisansei Honbu (2002 and 2006). *Nihonteki Jinji Seido no Genjō to Kadai* [Actual State and Issues of the Japanese Human Resource Management System]. Tokyo: Shakai Keizai Seisansei Honbu Seisansei Rōdō Jōhō Sentâ.

Shibata, H. (2000). 'The Transformation of the Wage and Performance Appraisal System in a Japanese Firm', *International Journal of Human Resource Management*, 11(2): 294–313.

Statistics Korea (2012). National Korean Statistics. Available at <http://kostat.go.kr/portal/english/index.action>, accessed 29 February 2012.

Streeck, W. (2009). *Reforming Capitalism: Institutional Change in the German Political Economy*. Oxford and New York: Oxford University Press.

Streeck, W. and Thelen, K. (2005). 'Introduction: Institutional Change in Advanced Political Economies', in Streeck and Thelen (eds.), *Beyond Continuity: Institutional Change in Advanced Political Economies*. Oxford and New York: Oxford University Press, 1–39.

Suda, T. (2007). 'Converging or Still Diverging? A Comparison of Pay Systems in the UK and Japan', *International Journal of Human Resource Management*, 18(4): 568–601.

Tachibanaki, T. and Noda, T. (2000). *The Economic Effects of Trade Unions in Japan*. New York: Macmillan.

Thelen, K. (2009). 'Institutional Change in Advanced Political Economies', *British Journal of Industrial Relations*, 47(3): 471–98.

Tsuru, T. and Rebitzer, J. (1995). 'The Limits of Enterprise Unionism: Prospects for Continuing Union Decline in Japan', *British Journal of Industrial Relations*, 33(3): 459–92.

USDA (2012). 'Real Historical Gross Domestic Product (GDP) and Growth Rates of GDP'. Available at <http://www.ers.usda.gov/data>, accessed 2 February 2012.

Wood, G., Brewster, C., Johnson, P., and Brookes, M. (2009). 'The Antecedents of Comparative Differences in Collective Bargaining'. Working Paper, School of Management, University of Sheffield.

Wu, P. (2004). 'HRM in Taiwan', in P. Budhwar (ed.), *Managing Human Resources in Asia-Pacific*. London and New York: Routledge, 93–112.

Yeh, R. (1991). 'Management Practices of Taiwanese Firms: As Compared to Those of American and Japanese Subsidiaries in Taiwan', *Asia Pacific Journal of Management*, 8(1): 1–14.

Yu, G. and Rowley, C. (2009). 'The Changing Face of Korean Human Resource Management', in Rowley and Y. Paik (eds.), *The Changing Face of Korean Management*. London and New York: Routledge, 29–51.

Zhu, Y. (2003). 'The Post-Asian Financial Crisis: Changes in HRM in Taiwanese Enterprises', *Asia Pacific Business Review*, 9(4): 147–64.

—— (2008). 'Trade Unions in Taiwan: Confronting the Challenge of Globalization and Economic Restructuring', in J. Benson and Zhu (eds.), *Trade Unions in Asia*. London and New York: Routledge, 63–80.

Zhu, Y., Chen, I., and Warner, M. (2000). 'HRM in Taiwan: An Empirical Case Study', *Human Resource Management Journal*, 10(4): 32–44.

Zhu, Y., Warner, M., and Rowley, C. (2007). 'Human Resource Management with "Asian" Characteristics: A Hybrid People-Management System in East Asia', *International Journal of Human Resource Management*, 18(5): 745–68.

....

CHAPTER 16

ECONOMIES UNDERGOING
LONG TRANSITION

Employment Relations in Central and Eastern Europe

....

MARTIN MYANT

THE economic and political systems of the countries of Eastern Europe and the former Soviet Union underwent dramatic transformations in the years after the collapse of communist power at the end of the 1980s.[1] Employment relations systems, which had previously been very similar, also underwent massive changes, raising questions of whether the countries should be seen as a single group and of how far the emerging system, or systems, fitted with recognized international models.

The argument here is that there are important common features, particularly in the extent of informal practices and in the importance of the legal framework for determining workplace employment relations. However, there are differences among workplaces within each country in how far laws are respected and implemented and how far other actors help to set employment relations. The result is a variety of hybrid, or segmented, systems of employment relations.

The amount of reliable research is not enough to give certainty on common features and divergences between countries. Nevertheless, there are enough areas of corroboration to give reasonable confidence in the existence of broad trends. The state socialist past was important, as reflected in elements of continuity and also in elements of deliberate discontinuity. These have been heavily dependent on the emerging political systems and on the transformations of economic structures. The outcomes in all cases reflect the processes of evolution from the state socialist past. Some still show considerable continuity, while others are closer to familiar Western European models, albeit with less stability in institutional structures—there are more frequent cases of the vagaries of the political process disrupting tendencies towards stabilization—and with very few fitting neatly with recognized varieties of capitalism.

Literature on these changes has followed three main themes that set employment relations in a comparative framework. The first is the degree of convergence towards a model based on 'social partnership', as is prominent in EU thinking. The second is a possible divergence from that trend due to a weaker social influence for labour, leading to greater freedom for employers to impose the system of labour relations judged most favourable to themselves. The third is the degree of continuity from the past, in habits and expectations, employment law, payments systems, and the activities of trade unions.

The chapter starts with a brief summary of the employment relations systems under state socialism followed by a survey of economic changes after 1989. This provides the background for discussion of arguments about the weakness and decline of trade unions, leading into more detail on the kinds of unions that emerged and their ability to influence the formulation of a new framework of employment law. This points to a model of employment relations with a substantial role for rules set by law and governments. However, subsequent sections demonstrate the ability of employers to influence conditions in workplaces, whether unions exist or not and whether there is collective bargaining or not, and also the constraints that they face.

Employment Relations under State Socialism

The state socialist countries before 1989 were one-party states in which no open opposition to the authorities was allowed. The formal systems of employment relations had followed similar paths of evolution across all countries, such that pay was linked to unified, centrally set, scales (Nagy 1990) and trade unions played no significant role in the collective representation of employees, but laws gave protection against excessive work and arbitrary dismissal. The Soviet Union was the first country with a centrally planned economy, but the evolution there was similar to that in its allies in Central Europe from the early 1950s and probably reflected similar pressures (for the Soviet Union, see Nove 1992; Filtzer 1992, 2002). Evolution is summarized under the three themes of payment systems, employee influence, and the role of trade unions.

The initial aim in payment systems was to use individual piece rates to differentiate pay and create incentives for greater work effort. In the late 1950s the emphasis shifted to stable piece rates, or away from piece rates altogether. Instead, basic pay was supplemented with individualized bonuses which were to be set by the immediate line manager. This was associated with some differentiation in earnings, but immediate superiors, seeking good relations with their close workmates, were typically reluctant to differentiate pay on any basis other than seniority. Payments systems were therefore continually criticized from above for failing to achieve pay 'de-levelling' which, it was argued from the start to the finish of central planning, was the key to higher effort and productivity (cf. Myant 1989: 133–43).

In fact, overall earnings differentiation was less than in capitalist economies, but largely because of a different structure of relative earnings between sectors rather than greater equality within workplaces (Myant and Drahokoupil 2011: 28–30). Pay in some core industrial sectors—especially mining—was relatively high for all grades of employee. It was relatively low for all grades in light industry and public services. The result was a substantial degree of overlap between manual and non-manual earnings. However, the view that pay was somehow not differentiated enough formed a large part of the subsequent discourse, expressed in a readiness on all sides to use individualized bonus systems.

The failure of piece rate systems was a general feature across state socialist countries in the 1950s. Available evidence leaves little doubt that it was the direct result of opposition from employees who saw themselves being fooled into making ever greater efforts for no more reward as norms, once achieved, were soon raised to even higher levels. Opposition was usually passive, in the form of absenteeism, high turnover, and non-participation in management initiatives. There were also quite frequent small-scale strikes. Evidence is most systematic from East Germany—the history of worker protests continues to be a theme of some interest in Germany but attracts less attention in Eastern Europe—but compatible accounts come from other countries (Hübner 2001; Heumos 2005). The picture is of strikes usually involving very small numbers of employees over quite specific issues of pay and working conditions. The authorities acted very rapidly to stop publicity from any such protests and to end them as quickly as possible, often accepting the employees' demands. Strike activity subsided in the late 1950s as the authorities learned to leave piece rate norms stable and as employees found alternative means of protesting, notably by developing extremely effective methods for small groups to cut work effort without formally transgressing labour discipline (e.g. Kemény 1986).

There were also some mass protest strikes, typically over living standards and consumer goods shortages, but also often sparked by harsh employment conditions. These were a feature primarily of the early 1950s—well-known cases occurred in East Germany in 1953, Czechoslovakia in 1953, and Poland in 1956—but the effect was general and long-lasting, frightening the authorities across the region. Thus taken together, these two forms of employee protest led to caution from managements and political leaders, to determination to avoid where possible reductions in living standards for workers in large-scale industry—the part of the population initially most sympathetic to the regimes but also with the potential strength to bring them down—and to a willingness to seek compromises over increasing work effort.

The place of trade unions evolved alongside these changes and pressures. In the early days of the Soviet Union it was even doubted whether trade unions were necessary at all in what was said to be a workers' state. Lenin famously resolved the issue in January 1922 with his formulation of trade unions as 'the transmission belt from the Communist Party to the masses' (Lenin 1965: 192). That deprived them of autonomy in determining their role, forcing them to take on tasks assigned from the party leadership. The practical meaning of a transmission belt changed over time partly as the leadership's priorities shifted and partly because to be effective unions had to have credibility with employees. However, rigid control from above was later to leave a heritage of deep opposition to any centralization of authority.

Unions were involved in some forms of bargaining in the Soviet Union, but this had ended by the 1950s (Filtzer 2002). In all cases, commitment to raising piece-rate norms meant a loss of trust in unions as collective representatives. Indeed, protest actions in the 1950s were frequently accompanied by employees criticizing union organizations and by significant numbers resigning their membership. That was evidently seen as undesirable by communist regimes that wanted displays of loyalty from the population. The response was to find activities for unions that could continue to ensure near universal membership from employees (see Ruble 1981; Pravda and Ruble 1986).

Trade unions therefore expanded and took on increasing ranges of welfare functions, providing individual benefits to employees, and organized sporting and recreational activities. That ensured that unions had a firm enough place in employees' lives to maintain near-universal membership: those who did not join lost benefits that were worth more than their membership subscriptions. It also ensured that these diverse activities were under the control of bodies that were in turn controlled from above by the party leadership.

Unions had two further important functions. One was to encourage work effort, justifying this as the means to ensure higher living standards in cooperation with, rather than in conflict with, managements. However, this took increasingly unobtrusive and ritualized forms. One such was 'socialist competition' whereby employees took out collective commitments to work to fulfil their plan targets. It was never mentioned in economics or management textbooks and a reasonable estimate is that it made no difference to productivity. Claims of success in official reports were based on the numbers participating rather than on any estimated economic impact and even the numbers were probably exaggerated (Kaplan 2007: 212–14; Heumos 2005: 57).

The second function was to represent employees with individual grievances, defending them when managements acted too harshly or illegally. This meant protection against dismissal, against excessive overtime, and against unsafe working conditions. The authorities often behaved as if they wanted these jobs done well, as a means to ensure a stable, contented, and healthy workforce and as a means to ensure that unions retained trust and confidence of employees. However, unions were effectively subordinated to the established power structure and were therefore typically reluctant to challenge managements. They did appear to be quite effective in blocking the hardening of piece-rate norms, a power they were given in the late 1950s presumably to pre-empt the small-scale protests referred to above. They may have been less effective in blocking management imposition of excessive overtime, although that might even have been welcomed by some employees as a means to increase earnings. A Soviet legal expert reported that, instead of 120 hours allowed by law per worker annually, in some enterprises 'overtime amounted to 300, 500 and more hours' (Ivanov 1992: 233–4).

Thus state socialism bequeathed a specific heritage of employment relations. Unified pay scales masked a continual attempt to achieve differentiation by forms of individual payment determination. Employee protest was definitely present, but was fragmented and isolated. It left little heritage of collective militancy that could be taken up by later generations and no experience of systematic bargaining. Those involved in protests remained isolated and unknown beyond small groups. Trade unions were assigned the functions of heading off employee discontent and of tying employees in with the system. However, they differed from associations created by employers as part of a paternalistic management system in some capitalist countries partly in the scope of their activities—they were concerned with tying employees into the system as a whole—and partly in their scale. They were mass organizations with substantial apparatuses and that gave them great potential strength should they be able to assert their independence.

Poland represented a partial exception. The Solidarity union emerged out of mass strikes in the summer of 1980 and won recognition as the first independent trade union in a state socialist country. That followed previous waves of worker protest in 1956, 1970, and 1976 which had convinced worker activists and supporting intellectuals of the need for a fully independent trade union. Simply reforming those that existed was not enough. However, Solidarity was as much a political movement as a trade union. It did not bargain over demands with enterprise managements and did not negotiate at the national level in a formally structured way. Its own recognition and status remained precarious and it 'never enjoyed anything other than a *de facto* legitimacy from the government' (Keenoy 1986: 156).

THE ECONOMIC TRANSFORMATION

All former state socialist economies underwent enormous changes from the start of the 1990s (Myant and Drahokoupil 2011), affecting ownership relations, sectoral structures, the organizational structure of economic units, and the differentiation of personal incomes.

The European Bank for Reconstruction and Development (EBRD) provides estimates of the share of GDP from the private sector which was insignificant in most of the countries before 1990. The typical figure in Central and Eastern Europe in 2010 was in the 70–80% range. Russia and Ukraine were lower, at 65% and 60% respectively, and a few countries still had majority state ownership, including Belarus with only 30% of GDP from the private sector (EBRD 2011).

The growing private sectors represented a diverse range of activities. In some cases state-owned enterprises were acquired by domestic private owners. In CIS countries new and powerful groups of domestic capitalists emerged, but this was less common in Central Europe where large business units were increasingly either firms privatized into foreign ownership or newly established branches of foreign multinational companies. Their importance is indicated by ratios of the stock of FDI to GDP, ranging in 2008 from 67.5% in Estonia to 11.2% in Belarus (Myant and Drahokoupil 2011: 343).

Private sectors also grew through the establishment of new, small enterprises which had been heavily restricted, if not completely banned, under state socialism. ILO data show the self-employed and employers making up relatively high percentages of the active labour force, but with wide variations that depended largely on the fate of formerly collectivized agriculture and partly also on institutional support for new entrepreneurs. Russia, where large-scale agriculture continued, appeared with only 7.1% of its labour force recorded as employers plus self-employed. In Poland agriculture had never been fully collectivized and employers plus self-employed were recorded as 19.2% of the active labour force. Other Central European countries also recorded high figures—15.6% in the Czech Republic—even without much private agriculture, reflecting the rapid appearance of a new private sector from the early 1990s (Myant and Drahokoupil 2011: 232).

The implications of these changes for employment relations are two-fold. First, new owners, especially foreign companies, could be expected to bring new practices. Second, the changes pointed towards less rigidity and formalization. Employing units were smaller and there was a greater weight for service activities with greater demands for flexibility in working hours. There was less control over all work and business practices and more scope for casual forms of business activity and it would be reasonable to expect a growth in informal forms of employment relations.

Indeed, self-employment can be a legal form pressed on an employee so that the employer can avoid formal tax and employment law obligations. High reported levels of self-employment may partly reflect employees having to accept contracts that do not give the normal rights of employees. The extent of this practice remains difficult to estimate. In the Czech Republic it acquired the name of the Švarc (the Czech transliteration from the German Schwartz) system, after the appropriately named entrepreneur who used it in the early 1990s but, as it has been illegal, there are no reliable estimates of its extent (Myant 2010b: 56). However, this and other forms of casual employment relations are probably important across Eastern Europe. Among the most widespread is an extra payment on top of wages that is not declared for tax and insurance purposes. Woolfson (2007: 202) quotes widely divergent estimates for Latvia in which up to 45% of employees may receive some such supplement, encouraging OECD suspicion of any official wage statistics.

These transformations in ownership and economic structure were accompanied by a period of falling GDP and living standards, referred to as the 'transformational recession'. Official data show some staggering declines and GDP in a number of countries in 2009 was still below the 1989 level, including Russia, Latvia, and Ukraine. A number of others were little better off, such as Estonia and Hungary where GDP was only 26% and 27% above the 1989 level (Myant and Drahokoupil 2011: 334).

There are serious reservations to these data. The growth in poorly recorded informal economic activities, as indicated above, means that official figures probably exaggerate the falls in the early 1990s, but there are no serious grounds for doubting widespread hardship for parts of the populations. Any pain, it should be added, was not evenly shared. Gini coefficients, where available, demonstrate growing inequality in all countries, irrespective of the extent of transformations in property or economic structures (Myant and Drahokoupil 2011: 349). This is most marked with the new super-rich at one extreme and unemployment and poverty at the other.

TRADE UNION WEAKNESS AND DECLINE

These changes in the economic systems set the framework for changes in employment relations. The most visible actors at first were trade unions, but the extent of their practical influence has been a matter of some controversy. Indeed, there is a powerful argument, backed by a substantial body of literature, that the essential feature of employment relations in post-communist countries is the weakness of labour's influence. In this view, the question is 'Why has labor been so acquiescent in postcommunist Europe?' (Ost and Crowley 2001: 1).

This is so dominant a feature across all these countries, so it is argued, that 'the most compelling task is not explaining how the post-communist cases differ but explaining what they have in common' (Crowley 2004: 419). The argument is built around observation of slightly different indicators of labour's weakness between countries (Crowley 2004: 394–7; Kubicek 2004: 32–7) that include declining membership, although in some cases quite high by international standards, a poor ability to mobilize members or to recruit new members, low levels of strike activity, and very limited influence on policy-making. The trend appears to be downward in all cases and contrasts with expectations that labour might have had a powerful voice in the new societies—not least in view of the decline in living standards and greater job insecurity—or that employment relations would quickly settle into a Western European pattern.

Quantitative data for former state socialist countries are consistently unreliable (cf. Crowley 2004: 401). Unions frequently do not collect precise membership data, do not report accurately to outside bodies—many have a strong desire to exaggerate—and do not separate out pensioners from employed membership: numbers of the former range from zero to about one third among unions within a country, depending on the union. Nevertheless, the available data do point to decline. From levels of over 90%, density in Central and Eastern European countries had fallen by 2009 to levels that were around the reported OECD average of 17%. The OECD figures show density levels of 8% in Estonia (the lowest of any OECD country apart from Turkey), 15% in Poland, 17% in Hungary, Slovakia, and the Czech Republic, 20% in Bulgaria, 25% in Slovenia, and 34% in Romania (OECD 2012).

Careful research on union membership shows a Czech figure of little over 10%, once exaggeration by some unions and pensioner members had been excluded (Myant 2010b: 45). For Poland, where a number of unions also did not wish to provide, or could not provide, membership data, evidence from opinion surveys suggests a 16% density level (Gardawski et al. 2012: 54). Data are even less precise and reliable for CIS countries and that must be a reservation to figures that point to less dramatic declines. Russia and Ukraine still recorded union density levels in the 40–60% range in the early 2000s. The lowest figure was 23% for Georgia (Borisov and Clarke 2006: 609, 627).

There are two obvious explanations for this decline. One focuses on structural changes in the economy unfavourable to union organization (Bohle and Greskovits

2006). This fits well with comparisons between countries. The shifts towards smaller, private firms, towards services and generally away from state ownership could all be expected to lead to lower levels of unionization, as could organizational changes and the closure of established workplaces. These were most marked in Baltic republics where the inherited industrial structure was largely lost. They were less marked in the Czech Republic where there was significant organizational continuity in motor vehicles, heavy industry, and mining: these remained areas of relative union strength. The slowest declines were in those CIS countries that retained most state ownership and supported inherited industries, notably Belarus where union density remained over 60% (Borisov and Clarke 2006: 609).

However, an explanation starting from structural change needs to be combined with an account of what happened in the different sectors. Gardawski and colleagues, writing on Poland, referred to continued union presence in state-owned enterprises and public services, as was the case in other countries, a dual process of 'erosion and marginalization' in privatized enterprises (Gardawski et al. 1999: 248)—meaning disappearance of organizations and reduced influence for those that survived—and practically no presence at all in new private enterprises. Marginalization was often at least in part promoted by employers, in its mildest form by blocking promotion for union members and there is evidence of widespread hostility to unions from some employers.

Russian unions at one time estimated that a quarter of employers would sack an employee for union activity (Ashwin and Clarke 2002: 184). However, even there decline was due more to lack of interest on the part of employees such that 'where the union had disappeared from enterprises it was because people had left the union and nobody had tried to reconstitute it'. Very rarely was it removed by the administration (Ashwin and Clarke 2002: 260). There were also cases in Central Europe of incoming firms fighting lengthy battles to block unionization but, again, unions themselves complained of low levels of interest from potential members and a remarkable willingness to dissolve organizations when asked to by management (Myant 2010b: 49–50). Indeed, a generally low level of commitment to unions is reflected in declining membership also in established organizations, and it proved extraordinarily difficult to create union organizations in new workplaces. This included those, such as motor vehicle assembly plants, that could be considered highly favourable for union activity.

The second explanation for union weakness and decline focuses on the legacy of the communist past, as put most forcefully in Ost's writing on Poland (2001; Crowley 2004). This opens up some complex themes, going beyond the arguments Ost uses, as the past had implications for public perceptions of unions and also for choices made by union organizations at every level.

Organizational changes, influenced by hostility to centralization, left the basic organizations in workplaces with most of the union finances. One consequence of this was to weaken central organizations and hence to limit their ability to develop activities in new workplaces. Concentration of resources at workplace level was also often associated with continuation of some welfare and recreational activities. That tied unions to an outdated image as social clubs for those approaching retirement age, a comment frequently made to explain the unwillingness of young people to join. It also took up activists' time in work that had little to do with defending members' interests. In Russia and Ukraine union organizations were, it has been argued, embroiled in the continuation of paternalistic management, even after privatization, thereby ensuring their reluctance to oppose, or come into conflict with, managements (cf. Kubicek 2004: 179; Varga 2011).

An alternative line of explanation for the impact of the past follows the common view among union officials and activists that they faced an uphill struggle thanks to a very general association with the old system. This is not convincing as a full explanation for union weakness and decline, not least because it does not explain the even weaker position of explicitly anti-communist unions, as indicated below. Nor does it explain the failure to develop any more combative kind of trade unionism. It is therefore reasonable to argue that there was an even more fundamental problem coming from the state socialist past in the absence of traditions of, and belief in, collective action as a means to advancement.

This is an important difference from Western European union movements, the development of which followed a rough historical progression (Crouch 1993) through unregulated conflict in workplaces, followed by more regularized collective bargaining as both sides learned to respect each other's strength and to see the benefits of reaching agreement without unnecessary conflict, and culminating, in some cases, in neo-corporatist forms of bargaining including government as well as employees' and employers' representatives. Sweden was the supreme example, for a time at least, but the will to reach agreement there was predicated on a history of previous conflicts and on the continuing threat of damage from unregulated conflict. That contrasts with the history of unions under state socialism which were not organizers of collective action but rather providers of individual benefits. New unions for the most part emerged out of organizational continuity rather than out of a new upsurge in employee militancy. The membership therefore retained a conception of unions as clubs providing individual benefits in exchange for individual contributions. That left union activity exceptionally dependent on management goodwill.

However, the trade-union-weakness-and-decline thesis requires some qualification. It was much more pronounced in some sectors than others, with unions largely absent from most of the new, private sector. Also, as is argued below, employers were still constrained by inherited traditions and by trade unions' ability to wield influence at the political level. This is taken up after a discussion of the kinds of trade unions that emerged after 1989.

REFORMED, OLD TRADE UNIONS

The new structure of trade unions reflected elements of continuity alongside a conscious rejection of the past. Continuity was most visible in the structure of basic organizations—generally bringing together all grades of employee in a workplace—and in a lasting emphasis on providing individual benefits and services in exchange for a standard membership fee equivalent to 1% of earnings. Discontinuity was most visible in fragmentation, subdivision, and a new diversity as the centralized authority of the past was firmly rejected. Basic organizations and branch unions split off from union centres, which no longer had any real power over their affiliates, and new unions appeared either with distinct political complexions or to represent specific professional and occupational groups.

The result was a proliferation of unions—reportedly 23,995 in Poland in the late 1990s (Gardawski et al. 2012: 33) and probably several hundred in the Czech Republic in 2010 (Myant 2010b: 56)—in many cases with no evidence of much influence in workplaces. Only when affiliated to centres did unions wield any influence on the political stage. These centres took two forms. Either they were reformed versions of those inherited from the past or they were formed as alternative, anti-communist forces as the state socialist system broke down. The first of these proved most resilient, benefiting from inherited memberships and property, although that wealth was itself a source of conflict between unions and with governments.

These unions developed generally similar strategies. Political involvement was restricted, based on avoidance of links to any particular political party and on avoidance of pronouncements beyond a narrow range of issues. Czechoslovak unions adopted this stand immediately in 1990, making no substantial statements on the strategy of economic transformation beyond a hope that the rights of employees would also be respected (Myant 1994). The equivalent Russian federation came with a history of distrusting Gorbachev's perestroika reforms of the late 1980s and tried to mount protest actions against government economic policies in the early 1990s (Ashwin and Clarke 2002: 31–2). They quickly learned that they could mobilize little serious support and that active opposition to governments carried penalties, including threats to their property. The same lessons were learned elsewhere (Makó and Simonyi 1997: 226 for Hungary). There were a few cases in the early years of more successful protest actions against government economic policies: they even contributed to the downfall of governments in Bulgaria in 1990 and 1992 (Thirkell 1994; Petkov and Gradev 1995; Gradev 2001), but opposition to economic reform in general proved to be a recipe for decline.

Some authors have implicitly challenged this view, pointing to the possibly demoralizing effect of the more cautious approaches of unions that emphasized moderation and social dialogue (Pollert 2001). Ashwin and Clarke are more nuanced when characterizing Russian unions' strategy of social partnership as 'double-edged'. It enabled unions, they claim, 'to find a place in the new Russia', but it also 'set up barriers' to becoming effective unions by 'securing the reproduction of inactivity of primary organizations' (Ashwin and Clarke 2002: 263–4).

In practical terms, rejecting social dialogue would have meant rejecting the gains it did bring in the system of employment law. Opposing economic changes would have meant isolation from the political mainstream and from much of the unions' membership. Even taking a tougher stand against social consequences appeared impossible to the leading figure in Czech unions who despairingly declared in 1993, 'in our country trade unionists don't behave like trade unionists'. Instead, 'the great majority of citizens and of trade unionists are content to tolerate the fall in living standards' (R. Falbr, quoted in Myant 1994: 59). A lack of interest in openly opposing governments is broadly confirmed by opinion poll evidence and by voting behaviour of trade union members.

New, Political Unions

Alongside the reformed unions from the state socialist period, completely new organizations emerged in all but a few countries. They were strongest where the breakdown of the state socialist system was the most prolonged and involved the most social and political conflict (Myant and Waller 1994: 180). The most important of these, including Podkrepa in Bulgaria and Liga in Hungary, were allied to political movements with the clear objective of ending the communist system. However, these links proved problematic when the new unions found themselves supporting policies that led to increased hardship for their natural constituencies. In Russia new and independent unions emerged around miners' strikes, but failed in similar ways as they built their hopes on the radical economic reforms that did not benefit their supporters. These unions therefore remained smaller than the reformed versions of unions inherited from the past.

Poland was the only exception. Solidarity enjoyed a special place in Polish society, but even it emerged in 1989 as a shadow of its former self in terms of membership, down from 9 million members in 1981 to 2.25 million in 1991 (Gardawski et al. 2012: 51–3). Reformed official unions, initially formed in the 1980s after Solidarity had been banned, had a slightly lower membership.

Solidarity is the clearest case of a union caught by the dilemmas of support for market-oriented reform. Its political involvement at the national level was deep and lasting and it continued with active participation in elections through the 1990s—even as opinion poll evidence showed that most members were not voting for Solidarity's preferred candidates—and its leadership declared clear preferences even after that. Strident support for market-oriented reform continued even as employees in large state-owned enterprises, the initial core of Solidarity's support, were shifting to a clear preference for staying in state-owned firms: private ownership had not delivered the promised benefits (Gardawski 1996: 117).

A resolution to the conflict between Solidarity's aims, so it has been argued, meant that 'instead of building a strong union, Solidarity set out to build a weak one' (Ost 2001: 82). Indeed, Lech Wałęsa famously declared that a strong representation for labour would block reform towards a free market economy (Gortat 1994: 118) and militant basic organizations in the early 1990s were reported responding to falling living standards by pressing even harder for market-oriented reform (cf. Kloc 1994: 130; Rainnie and Hardy 1995: 278). However, union centres and workplace organizations lived partly separate lives. Detailed evidence on the activities of Solidarity organizations suggests at least as much willingness to seek conflict with managements. Nevertheless, there were costs at the grass-roots level of a strident political identity. The subsequent creation of organizations in new workplaces was greatly eased by dropping political links and references to the union's own history as an anti-communist force in the 1980s: those themes were not of interest to new members in the new millennium (Krzywdzinski 2010; Mrozowicki and van Hootegem 2008).

SOCIAL DIALOGUE AND TRIPARTISM

The claim of limited influence on policy-making is an oversimplification. In no case did trade unions have influence across the full range of policy issues, but they could have some influence over specific areas of social and economic policy, especially employment relations. Influence in that sphere depended on expertise linked to international contacts and skill in developing forms of lobbying (cf. Myant 2010a).

Instead of direct political involvement, the reformed unions from the communist period moved with increasing clarity towards a strategy of 'social dialogue'. The ideal target was collective bargaining at enterprise and sectoral level and overarching national-level negotiations through a tripartite body. Such bodies were formed in almost all countries, with differing degrees of legal status. They have been interpreted both as a new form of governance (Iankova 2002) and as a sham helping to 'secure labor's acceptance of its own marginalization' (Ost 2000: 503). Neither view is accurate. Tripartite councils carried influence only when the government of the day saw a need to listen to the trade union side—employers were never important—and that meant when the government was ideologically sympathetic or when there was a plausible threat of labour unrest.

The second of these was the case in the period around 1990 when fears that falling living standards would lead to social unrest led to acceptance for what Helmut Wiesenthal (1996) described as 'pre-emptive corporatism', meaning that governments listened to the unions' voice so as to pre-empt potential social unrest. This did not mean that trade union influence was positively welcomed in any country. It was rather tolerated or accepted by new governments. Even in Bulgaria, where unions were able to stage big protests, they were never accepted as 'responsible agents of change' (Gradev 2001: 137) and moves towards a form of corporatism remained fragile and easily reversible.

In the early 1990s the levels of unrest triggering nervousness in new elites were remarkably low. A protest by taxi and lorry drivers in Budapest in 1989 was enough to give life to a tripartite council formed shortly beforehand and to warn governments across Central Europe that dangers could lie ahead. Nor did protest need to be coordinated by established unions: they benefited from a general threat of unrest enabling them to pose as a preferable, moderating influence. When not backed by some kind of external threat, tripartite councils could become less important to governments and sink into inactivity, but this was countered by a general trend, over time, towards permanent institutionalization around a limited role as consultative organs on employment and economic issues.

Thus in the Czech Republic a stable organizational form and remit took shape after 1997 and the tripartite council became one part of a mechanism whereby unions influenced politics, which included extra-parliamentary activities, such as demonstrations and petitions, and lobbying of governments and MPs. At best, they could reach agreement with employers' organizations and use that consensus to persuade the government of their position. At worst, they had early warning of government plans and could formulate a response and lobby for alternatives (Myant 2010b). Unions in Russia used similar methods, but with more weight to influencing parliament. Tripartite structures were slower to develop their role in Poland where the two main union centres were closely tied to political parties, and hence governments, making cooperation extremely difficult.

The nearest to a full corporatist system was Slovenia. Unions were fragmented with the reformed 'old' unions accounting for about half of total union membership. Contrary to expectations and evidence from other countries (e.g. Avdagic 2005: 37–40), this was not a major disadvantage. The overall strength of labour was enhanced by strike activity, and not just the threat of strikes, including a warning general strike in 1992. Centre–left coalitions, in power through most of the 1990s, oversaw the development of 'an industrial relations system which secured a "voice" for labour during transition' (Stanojević 2003: 290–1). In contrast to other countries, dialogue 'became a permanent feature' (Stanojević 2003: 290). Union power was important beyond the employment relations sphere, even proving crucial in preventing pension privatization and plans in 2005 to introduce a 'flat tax' (Stanojević 2007: 357–9), although union influence did later come under pressure following accession to the EU (Stanojević 2010).

Employers, it will be argued, were more central to the development of employment relations in individual workplaces but, although included in tripartite councils, employers' organizations were not important as political forces. The first employers' organizations either represented very small businesses, which prioritized ownership and taxation issues rather than employment relations, or top managers in state-owned enterprises. These were generally cautious on employment relations issues: the personnel function was discredited by its political links under the old regime and new managers had little conception of what to change (cf. Soulsby and Clark 1998; Pollert 1999b: 184). In some countries these organizations did have their own agendas, favouring supportive industrial policies, and found common ground with trade unions, as in Russia in the early and mid 1990s, but that became less important after large-scale privatization.

Changing Employment Laws

Following the common heritage of state socialism, all countries came with similar frameworks of employment law and also implemented similar changes. The first were often rapid, for example giving freedom to depart from rigid payment systems. Governments were keen to move quickly to find a consensus, balancing fears from a neo-liberal trend that excessive union power could hamper reform—often backed by claims that socialism had failed from being too soft on social interests—against a fear that failure to agree could lead to social unrest.

Trade unions were potentially strong enough to be feared—in Czechoslovakia they threatened a warning general strike in December 1990 if the changes they had agreed with the government through the tripartite council were rejected by parliament (Myant 1994)—and came with the clearest conception. They looked to international agencies with a voice on employment issues, particularly the ILO and EU, and aimed for what they saw as a Western European model. This was most true for those reformed old unions that quickly gained international recognition, such as those in Czechoslovakia. It was less true of Russia, where affiliation to the Brussels-based International Confederation of Free Trade Unions came only in 2000 and where there was no aim of EU accession. There were therefore some differences in timing, but changes were ultimately quite similar.

The formal process was usually to amend existing Labour Codes, but the changes were very substantial in content (for comparisons between countries, see the contributions in Blanpain and Nagy 1996 and ILO 2009). The firmly liberal position prevailed in no country, thanks to arguments about the continued weakness of employees' position, to the lack of experience in collective bargaining, and to the need to prevent excessive hardship in a difficult period of transition (cf. Nagy 1996: 6). Nevertheless, this was often an area of considerable disagreement in parliamentary debates and there were frequent suggestions that, as collective bargaining came to be better established, so rules could be made more flexible.

The practical compromise was to relax rules, thereby creating scope for free collective bargaining, but to maintain protection through minimum standards. Thus central wage scales were replaced by minimum levels. Set holidays were replaced by a legal minimum and set hours and overtime levels by maximums, allowing for negotiation of more favourable conditions for employees through collective bargaining. Protection against individual dismissal, previously requiring consultation with a trade union organization, was replaced by specification of justifiable grounds which had to be put in writing by the employer, and a right for the employee to appeal to a court. Powers for effectively arbitrary dismissal on grounds of state security were removed as were a number of powers to direct labour of those newly qualified. Employers also lost the legal right to penalties, such as denial of holiday entitlements, which they had been able to impose in the past. Thus in several respects the new labour law gave more protection against authoritarian management. Moreover, trade unions frequently retained some of their powers, notably over health and safety and over overtime conditions.

A logical new feature was a place for trade unions and collective bargaining. In all countries provision was made for trade union pluralism and for protection from victimization of trade union representatives. Strikes, not mentioned in inherited legal frameworks, were allowed, but under conditions that usually ruled out political strikes and included extraordinarily tough requirements for prior consultation, conciliation attempts, and membership support. Collective bargaining was recognized with the proviso that it could not lead to conditions worse than those specified in employment law.

There were some differences between countries. Rules for collective bargaining in Slovenia and Romania effectively required employers to reach an agreement (Trif 2007: 243–4), a legal provision that clearly strengthened the position of unions by making them essential to all employers. Slovenia and Hungary were also unusual in adopting a version of the German system of works councils. In the latter case it helped new union organizations, by giving them a guaranteed voice, but powers were severely limited when compared with German bodies, reflecting fears of excessive employee influence (Makó and Simonyi 1997: 231–2; Nagy 1996: 79–81; Pollert 1999a: 213).

There were some differences in trends after the initial changes. In Central Europe the first, post-1989 changes proved remarkably resilient, but incremental changes were towards liberalization, partly to allow for alternative forms of work organization—such as part-time or complicated shift working—and partly to weaken protections over individual and collective dismissals. These pressures were countered to some extent by the process of EU accession[2] which included a number of requirements for employment law, notably anti-discrimination legislation and limits to working hours. However, by this time the early fears of social unrest had passed and leeway over the precise form of implementation enabled less sympathetic governments—meaning those not dominated by Social Democrats—to delay and to choose the weakest possible forms of implementation. Enforcement was even weaker, characterized by 'dead letters galore', as individuals lacked the means, or courage, to take employers to court (Falkner and Treib 2008: 303, 306).

In CIS countries there was much more variety. They were not under any pressure to follow the EU example and more authoritarian political structures could lead to a minimal voice for trade unions. However, there was also some catching up with changes implemented earlier in Central Europe through the 1990s. In Russia a government proposal in 1999, following agreement with the IMF that a new Labour Code would be introduced, threatened a major reduction in trade union rights and a spread of fixed-term individual contracts (Ashwin and Clarke 2002: 64). Unions mounted some public demonstrations. They were poorly supported, but unions found influence through allies in parliament. There proved to be no strong will for a radical liberalization of employment law and the outcome, coming into effect in 2002, even led to some improvements in minimum holiday entitlements. Overall, the new Labour Code retained 'intact the bulk of the soviet protective labour legislation' (Ashwin and Clarke 2002: 114).

In a few countries there was a very radical liberalization. This occurred in Georgia following the so-called Rose Revolution of November 2003 which led to the election of a strongly pro-Western government with no interest in social dialogue. The tripartite council, formed in the 1990s, by then played no role and a new Labour Code, proclaimed to be 'the most liberal…in Eastern Europe' (Borisov and Clarke 2006: 612), made no mention of trade unions and prohibited strikes over pay and conditions. The new minister in charge of employment matters reportedly did not know what the ILO was or which conventions Georgia had signed (Borisov and Clarke 2006: 621).

A few other countries followed an apparently opposite road, restoring trade unions to their transmission-belt status of the communist period. Such was the conscious policy in Moldova after 2001 and in Belarus after 1999 where unions were to become 'part of the state machine' (Borisov and Clarke 2006: 616). That ensured high membership levels, because unions were associated with other benefits, as in the past, but it was accompanied by the suppression of alternative union organizations and changes to employment law, such that employees could be progressively moved onto fixed-term contracts (Borisov and Clarke 2006: 617).

IMPLEMENTATION OF EMPLOYMENT LAW

The successful negotiation and maintenance of a system of employment law appears across almost all former state socialist countries as a clear area of trade union success. This has important implications for the emerging system of employment relations. Thus Kohl and Platzer (2007) have referred to a 'statist' model, with a bigger role for politics and the law than in Western Europe. Unions, they argue, had most power in influencing laws and the government-determined minimum wage level and this compensated for limited power in workplaces. An obvious possible reservation to this is that laws are of little value unless implemented and that is most likely where unions exist and have some influence in workplaces.

Indeed, studies of trade union activity across countries consistently point to taking up individual cases with reference to employment law as a major element of trade union work. There are claims of high success rates, once cases come to court, and strong representation for professional lawyers among trade union officials, ranging up to one third of all professionals in some unions both in Russia and the Czech Republic (Ashwin and Clarke 2002: 189; Myant 2010b: 20–1). Reference to the law, rather than to collective agreements negotiated with employers, resolved disputes over issues ranging across grounds for dismissal, dress codes, and permissible absence from work. Employees also clearly valued this support and individual workplace issues were cited in major surveys in the Czech Republic and Poland as a principal reason for joining unions, coming comfortably above general support for collective representation of employees (Pollert 1999a: 228; Pollert 2001: 29; Gardawski et al. 1999: 132–4).

Violations have been referred to in all countries for which evidence is available. Russia, and other CIS countries, experienced a period of particularly weak law enforcement in the 1990s with close links between some businesses and clearly criminal activity. Inspection agencies in Russia reported 2 million violations of employment law annually in the 1990s—the usual one was late payment, or even non-payment, of wages which was endemic in Russia at the time—and a legal expert referred to 'unbridled, at times flagrant and cynical, violation of labour legislation and citizens' labour rights'. These efforts 'related to gaining the maximum profit' were seen as 'no less, and even more, numerous than those that occurred in Soviet times when they were justified by the need to fulfil the production plan' (Ivanov 1996: 132).

Similar trends were visible in less extreme form in other countries. Polish entrepreneurs who set up their businesses in what was referred to as the 'Wild West' period around 1990 were quoted in one study referring to widespread cheating, corruption, and failure to pay wages and dismissed some colleagues as unable to 'establish any kind of civilized relationship with anybody' (Skowron 2010: 258). A survey of 486 Polish owners and managers in late 1994 still found 68% claiming that existing legal regulations 'force managers to act illegally' (Czapiński 1996: 88), an opinion that was particularly strong among new entrepreneurs. However, surveys also reveal diversity within the new private sector. Some employees complained bitterly of conditions and expressed their discontent in high turnover, but others appeared reasonably satisfied and settled into a framework of stable and paternalistic employment relations (Gardawski et al. 1999: 102–3).

This gives some support to the Kohl and Platzer thesis for workplaces with union representation, or within easy reach of a state inspection system, but varying degrees of informality dominated elsewhere. The forces for, and likely directions of, change are discussed in the final section.

Collective Bargaining and Workplace Employment Relations

At workplace level employees can have a say in employment relations by ensuring enforcement of the law as it affects individuals or by collective bargaining with employers. This depends on union organizations, but covers employees who are not union members. The extent of collective bargaining coverage is therefore greater than union membership.

Data on collective bargaining coverage are imprecise, with no requirement to report an agreement in many countries. Levels are in most cases low by Western European standards. Data put together from various sources for 2009 (ETUI 2012) showed some Western European countries close to 100% bargaining coverage, joined by Slovenia and Romania, at least when smaller employers are excluded. Other former state socialist countries were below the EU average, falling from 50% in the Czech Republic through 33% for Estonia, 30% for Poland, to 15% in Lithuania. Other research points to substantially lower figures of slightly over 30% for the Czech Republic, about 20% for Poland, and 11% for Estonia. This suggests lower levels of influence than in Western Europe, albeit with the two exceptions of countries in which collective agreements were a legal requirement.

Some form of bargaining took place at three levels: national, sectoral, and enterprise. Pay for much of the public sector depended on state budgets and unions tried to influence these through political processes, leading to a common feature of a relatively high strike rate in education. Genuine bargaining at national levels, through tripartite councils, was very limited. So-called General Agreements were signed between all parties in a number of countries, involving pay restraint in exchange for policy commitments, but typically broke down as governments failed to deliver on promises to limit the extent of austerity. That was the experience of Czechoslovakia in 1991 and Hungary in 1995. Any global agreements after that were at such a general level, with no definite commitments, as to be of no practical significance, as was broadly the case in other countries.

Bargaining at the sectoral level was more widespread in Central Europe, but also of limited significance in terms of content, essentially setting minimum levels and agendas for enterprise level bargaining. The extent depended on employers' organizations and these if anything weakened over time with privatization and as foreign-owned companies dominated. They were likely to opt out, particularly if they brought their own conception of employment relations. In all countries the enterprise level was the most important, but here too there are doubts over the extent of union influence. At least in the early years, agreements often did little more than restate much of existing employment law and any additions often followed management proposals.

Strike activity, as reported to the ILO (laborsta.ilo.org; Crowley 2004: 405), was both low and typically limited to a very few sectors. In Russia in the years up to 2008 there were hardly any strikes outside education and mining. In the Czech Republic and Slovakia there were hardly any at all. Poland saw considerable strike activity in the early 1990s and an increase in 2008, in both cases often over issues of sectoral restructuring and job losses. Where information is available, strike activity was most common in public services, where it amounted to short protest actions to influence government decisions. It was rare in private companies and hardly ever linked in those cases to collective bargaining or pay claims. It was more likely to be defensive, opposing workplace closures or protesting about non-payment of wages.

Low levels of strike activity are not necessarily an indicator of union weakness—unions could be so strong that they can get their way without striking—but plenty of other evidence across several countries confirms a willingness from the union side to avoid conflict and to reach agreements which do not threaten management. Even in Poland, with the appearance of significant levels of protest action, the reputation for union militancy 'is a myth'. Unions used predominantly the least threatening forms of protest, avoided conflict whenever possible, and, in the view of managers, 'were more likely to be guided by the interests of the enterprise than by the hard, uncompromising defence of the workers' (Gardawski et al. 1999: 250).

The weakness of trade unions at the workplace level is further indicated by the limited evidence on the wage mark-up for union members or for workplaces with collective agreements. A careful study of Hungarian pay levels from 1996–9 used sectoral data to compare total earnings in enterprises with and without collective agreements, irrespective of their content, and showed a mark-up of, at the most, 3–5%. It appeared that benefits from union activity in Hungarian-owned enterprises were largely outweighed by higher pay in foreign-owned companies which frequently lacked union representation (Neumann 2002). Data from the Czech engineering industry in 2005 show pay 5% above the sectoral average in enterprises where collective agreements were signed (Myant 2010b: 20). Survey data from Poland show union members better paid in public services, but worse paid in much of industry where 'marginalized' union organizations tended to survive in the least successful enterprises (Gardawski et al. 1999: 89–91). Data from a Russian household survey from 1998 suggested no significant difference between unionized and non-unionized employees, once account was taken of differences due to branch and enterprise size (Ashwin and Clarke 2002: 259). In this context it is hardly surprising that a 2001 survey showed Russian workers to be overwhelmingly sceptical of unions' ability to achieve better pay levels and one third were thinking of resigning their membership (Ashwin and Clarke 2002: 246).

Union organizations did learn over time how to use collective bargaining. At the start they could be taken by surprise by management initiatives. One study from the Czech Republic in the mid-1990s found an employer in a major engineering enterprise sweeping aside old pay scales, leaving line managers to set individuals' pay. There was no union comment, let alone opposition, but the experiment failed as a means to achieve 'de-levelling', still a major theme among domestically owned firms. As in the past, personal ties stood in the way of pay differentiation among those doing the same work on any basis other than seniority (Pollert 1999b: 186–93).

Evidence for later years in the Czech Republic shows the formal continuation of significant bonus elements in pay (MPSV 2010), for top managers and for many kinds of manual work. In some countries of Eastern and Central Europe a significant minority of employees had no fixed element at all (European Foundation for the Improvement of Living and Working Conditions 2007: 87). Bonuses had grown in importance in Czechoslovakia from the late 1950s, as piece rates became less popular, to reach about 20% of total pay in 1985 (Federální statistický úřad 1986: 354). Remarkably, in 2000 they accounted for 18% of pay, a figure that fell slightly in the years of economic crisis from 2008. However, where bargaining was effective, they were typically covered by collective agreements and linked to enterprise, rather than individual, results. Management's formal power to set individual pay levels was therefore substantially reduced.

There are no comprehensive data on the content or outcomes of collective bargaining across the region. The best comes from the Czech Republic where the relevant ministry has published analyses of over 1,000 collective agreements annually (MPSV 2011). Negotiations ranged beyond pay to include overtime and flexibility conditions, additional holidays and reductions in working hours, alongside less central issues of gifts on an employee's fiftieth birthday, supplements for knowledge of foreign languages, and subsidies for meals. The breadth and extensive nature of these agreements leaves little doubt that union organizations had some influence over working conditions.

Incoming multinationals could be expected to bring in new practices from outside, but their impact has been varied, sometimes leading to more systematic managerial power over the organization of work and sometimes leading to a stronger base for collective bargaining. Smaller firms in the service sector often contributed to the trend towards casualization and informal payment methods. Large retailers frequently brought a complete formal system, including flexible working times and payment systems (cf. Pollert 1999a: 211–18), often ignoring legal constraints on working hours. Whether union organizations existed or not, and unionization was very low in this sector, managements were able to sweep aside much of established practice in the country concerned.

Manufacturing companies typically brought completely new technology, but employment relations systems were more decentralized and developed gradually from existing customs, practices, and laws. German manufacturing firms investing in Central Europe have been the most extensively studied. Some seemed to be investing in Central Europe in part to escape from the German model and to apply textbook ideas of human resource management (cf. Meardi 2012). Others made efforts to import parts of the established German system. Many, however, rather than applying a clear conception, were feeling their way. If they came expecting a blank slate with the potential for unlimited flexibility, then they quickly learned that they had to confront the constraints of a legal framework that gave considerable protection to employees. Thus some managements did try to impose radical changes in payment systems, objected to union rights over health and safety, and resented laws that made working hours less flexible than in Germany. Their attempts to ignore rules and practices led to conflict, involving the local and German press and local and German trade unions and this was very uncomfortable for the largest and best-known companies (cf. Bluhm 2007: 241–1; Bluhm 2001; Tholen 2007). These workplaces frequently became areas of relative union strength. This was particularly true for those large companies which, under EU law, established European Works Councils giving trade unions from Central Europe direct and easy contact with their colleagues in the West. Thus, irrespective of initial company intentions, there was a tendency for employment relations in branches of multinational manufacturing companies to follow practices of dialogue and bargaining that were common in Western Europe.

TRENDS AND PROSPECTS

The former state socialist countries do not form a unified group and do not fit into any established model of employment relations, as derived from experience in advanced capitalist countries. It is possible to find analogies with the ideal types used in the varieties of capitalism literature, but those authors who refer to 'diversity within capitalisms' or 'variegated capitalism' and accept the normality of hybridization provide a better starting point (Jessop 2012; Lane and Wood 2012). Not only are the employment relations diverse and internally varied, but they are continually evolving and changing. As they do the weights and forms of different elements—including forms of informalized employment relations, regular bargaining over conditions, and legal protections that may or may not be applied in practice—are continually shifting. This section therefore covers three themes: the forces that have led to diversity among former state socialist countries, the extent to which the outcomes can be compared with recognized models from international experience, and the likely directions of future changes.

Emerging forms are the result of developments in both economic structures and the political systems which create the basis for different social interests to wield influence. There is a strong divergence between the countries that have been CIS members and the other countries of Eastern and Central Europe, but there are also substantial differences within those broad groupings.

Economic developments led to the destruction of inherited industries, a prominent feature in the Baltic republics and smaller CIS countries. These countries have frequently acquired features of liberal market economies, with weak employee representation, more limited formal protection for employees, and often weak enforcement of laws that do exist. In Central European countries destruction of old industries was less complete and incoming multinational companies brought some base for effective employee representation in forms familiar from Western European experience. In several CIS countries, notably Russia, inherited enterprises proved more resilient and that created a base for a degree of continuity in previous forms of employment representation and management practices.

These economic changes created bases for different kinds of employment relations, but the outcome depended on other institutional factors and on changes in the political sphere. The important differences here were in the more secure base for political democracy in the countries outside the CIS, leading in turn to greater scope for interest representation at the political level and to greater respect for the laws once enacted. Characterizations of the kinds of capitalism without reference to political forms, as is the case with the Hall and Soskice firm-centred version, therefore miss features that lead to change and diversity among former state socialist countries.

Nevertheless some approximations can be found to familiar forms. At one extreme, the nearest to a coordinated market economy, with corporatist structures allowing regularized negotiation and bargaining at all levels, has been Slovenia. Closer to a liberal market economy, with less labour market regulation and much weaker interest representation, are the Baltic republics in which there is less protection against informalized employment relations (cf. Buchen 2007). The Central European countries stand somewhere between these two extremes, with laws and regulations that are often enforced, but also often ignored, and with effective representation and bargaining protecting parts of their labour forces. Among CIS countries there are neo-liberal versions, with minimal employee protection provided in legal frameworks. There is less sign of a corporatist version which would depend on institutionalized interest representation which is problematic where formal democracy is less firmly established. Nevertheless, trade unions at the national level differ from their Soviet-era predecessors in that they are fully independent bodies. Cases are cited above of the employee voice proving effective, albeit without stable institutionalization. There were also cases, uniquely among CIS countries, of a conscious restoration of the political role of trade unions from state socialist times, leading to a form of passive incorporation into the power structure that bears a formal, but not real, similarity to forms of corporatism.

Following the logic of what has been argued above, future trends depend to a great extent on economic and political changes. Changes in economic structures were most rapid in the 1990s and the differences between countries were largely set in that period and shortly after. Changes at the political level have been more continuous and less predictable, but with frequent attempts to shift in a neo-liberal direction, even in countries where elements of corporatism had seemed the strongest. This happened in Romania in 2011, previously a country with near universal bargaining coverage, when a right-wing government radically reduced the scope for collective bargaining and union organization. Also in Slovenia a reduction in bargaining coverage followed changes in employer representation after EU accession and governments tried to ignore established forms of social dialogue until threatened by continuing protest actions. In these, as in other countries, institutionalized employee representation was still insecure, so that the nature of the parties in power and the ability of employee representatives to influence them remained crucial in determining the direction of employment relations.

Politics at the macro-level set the broad framework, but a great deal more changes as different actors learn from experience to exploit opportunities that present themselves. This is visible in two areas. Where collective bargaining exists and is firmly established, both sides have learned to evaluate and respect each other's strengths, leading to institutionalization of practices that emerged in the early and mid-1990s. Where direct employee representation is absent, weak, or ineffective, the important issues are the respect for the law or the ability to find means towards informal employment relations even within the law. The first of these can be assumed to have increased with growing distance from the early 'Wild West' period. However, employers have also been learning to shift employment relations by exploiting legal methods, such as conversion of employees into self-employed subcontractors or by offering only commercial contracts to individuals, again avoiding all responsibilities as a regular employer. This leaves the future shape of employment relations unclear, but the outcome will remain a matter of conflict both at the political level and at the level of the individual workplace.

Notes

1. The countries covered here include the Central European group of Poland, Hungary, and Czechoslovakia, dividing into the Czech Republic and Slovakia in 1993, a southeastern European group of Bulgaria and Romania and the former Yugoslav republics, of which only Slovenia is referred to directly in this chapter. Yugoslavia had a slightly different socialist system, but there was also much in common in the background to changes in employment relations. Countries that belonged in the Soviet Union until its dissolution include the three Baltic republics of Estonia, Latvia, and Lithuania and countries that joined or participated in the Commonwealth of Independent States (CIS). Of these Russia, Ukraine, Moldova, and Belarus are referred to in the text as is Georgia which resigned from the CIS in 2008. Collectively these can be referred to for the period up to 1989 as 'communist' or 'state socialist' countries. The latter term is preferred here as a general characterization of

the systems as a whole, while 'communist' is used to refer more narrowly to the system of political power.

2. Eight former state socialist countries joined the EU in 2004, these being the Czech Republic, Estonia, Hungary, Latvia, Lithuania, Poland, Slovakia, and Slovenia. They were joined in 2007 by Bulgaria and Romania. Accession required fulfilling certain conditions on political and economic systems and harmonization of some laws.

References

Ashwin, S. and Clarke, S. (2002). *Russian Trade Unions and Industrial Relations in Transition*. Basingstoke: Palgrave Macmillan.

Avdagic, S. (2005). 'State–Labour Relations in East Central Europe: Explaining Variations in Union Effectiveness', *Socio-Economic Review*, 3(1): 25–53.

Blanpain, R. and Nagy, L. (eds.) (1996). *Labour Law and Industrial Relations in Central and Eastern Europe (From Planned to a Market Economy)*, Bulletin of Comparative Labour Relations, 31. The Hague: Kluwer Law International.

Bluhm, K. (2001). 'Exporting or Abandoning the "German Model"? Labour Policies of German Manufacturing Firms in Central Europe', *European Journal of Industrial Relations*, 7(2): 153–73.

—— (2007). *Experimentierfeld Ostmitteleuropa? Deutsche Unternehmen in Polen und der Tschechischen Republik*. Wiesbaden: Verlag für Sozialwissenschaften.

Bohle, D. and Greskovits, B. (2006). 'Capitalism without Compromise: Strong Business and Weak Labor in Eastern Europe's new Transnational Industries', *Studies in Comparative International Development*, 41 (1): 3–25.

Borisov, V. and Clarke, S. (2006). 'The Rise and Fall of Social Partnership in Postsocialist Europe: The Commonwealth of Independent States', *Industrial Relations Journal*, 37(6): 607–29.

Buchen, C. (2007). 'Estonia and Slovenia as Antipodes', in D. Lane and M. Myant (eds.), *Varieties of Capitalism in Post-Communist Countries*. Basingstoke: Palgrave Macmillan, 65–89.

Crouch, C. (1993). *Industrial Relations and European State Traditions*. Oxford and New York: Oxford University Press.

Crowley, S. (2004). 'Explaining Labor Weakness in Post-Communist Europe: Historical Legacies and Comparative Perspective', *East European Politics and Societies*, 18(3): 394–429.

Czapiński, J. (1996). 'The Polish Manager: A Profile', in R. Rapacki (ed.), *Enterprise Culture in a Transition Economy: Poland 1989–1994*. Warsaw: Warsaw School of Economics, 83–104.

European Bank for Reconstruction and Development (EBRD) (2011). *Structural Change Indicators*. Available at <http://www.ebrd.com/pages/research/economics/data/macro.shtml#macro>, accessed 16 January 2012.

European Foundation for the Improvement of Living and Working Conditions (2007). *Fourth European Working Conditions Survey*. Dublin: European Foundation for the Improvement of Living and Working Conditions.

European Trade Union Institute (ETUI) (2012). *Collective Bargaining*. Available at <http://www.worker-participation.eu/National-Industrial-Relations/Across-Europe/Collective-Bargaining2>, accessed 16 January 2012.

Falkner, G. and Treib, O. (2008). 'Three Worlds of Compliance or Four? The EU-15 Compared to New Member States', *Journal of Common Market Studies*, 46(2): 293–313.

Federální statistický úřad (1986). *Statistická ročenka Československé socialistické republiky 1986.* Prague: SNTL.

Filtzer, D. (1992). *Soviet Workers and de-Stalinization: The Consolidation of the Modern System of Soviet Production Relations, 1953–1964.* Cambridge: Cambridge University Press.

—— (2002). *Soviet Workers and Late Stalinism: Labour and the Restoration of the Stalinist System after World War II.* Cambridge: Cambridge University Press.

Gardawski, J. (1996). 'Workers on Private and State Ownership', in R. Rapacki (ed.), *Enterprise Culture in a Transition Economy: Poland 1989–1994.* Warsaw: Warsaw School of Economics, 105–21.

Gardawski, J., Gąciarz, B., Mokrzyszewski, A., and Pańków, W. (1999). *Rozpad bastionu? Związki zawodowe w gospodarce prywatyzowanej.* Warsaw: Instytut Spraw Publicznych.

Gardawski, J., Mrozowicki, A., and Czarzasty, J. (2012). *Trade Unions in Poland.* Brussels: ETUI.

Gortat, R. (1994). 'The Feud within Solidarity's Offspring', in M. Waller and M. Myant (eds.), *Parties, Trade Unions and Society in East-Central Europe.* Ilford: Frank Cass, 116–24.

Gradev, G. (2001). 'Bulgarian Trade Unions in Transition: The Taming of the Hedgehog', in S. Crowley and D. Ost (eds.), *Workers after Workers' States: Labor and Politics in Postcommunist Eastern Europe.* Lanham, MD: Rowman & Littlefield, 121–40.

Heumos, P. (2005). 'State Socialism, Egalitarianism, Collectivism: On the Social Context of Socialist Work Movements in Czechoslovak Industrial and Mining Enterprises, 1945–1965', *International Labor and Working-Class History*, 68: 47–74.

Hübner, P. (2001). 'Identitätsmuster und Konfliktverhalten der Industriearbeiterschaft der SBZ/DDR', *Bohemia*, 42(2): 220–43.

Iankova, E. (2002). *Eastern European Capitalism in the Making.* Cambridge: Cambridge University Press.

International Labour Organization (ILO) (2009). *National Labour Law Profiles.* Available at <http://www.ilo.org/ifpdial/information-resources/national-labour-law-profiles/lang--en/index.htm>, accessed 16 January 2012.

Ivanov, S. (1992). 'Workers' Participation: Influence on Management Decision-Making by Labour in the Private Sector: The USSR', *Bulletin of Comparative Labour Relations*, 23 (Deventer: Kluwer Law and Taxation Publishers): 221–40.

—— (1996). 'Labour Law of Russia in the Transition from Planned to the Market Economy', in R. Blanpain and L. Nagy (eds.), *Labour Law and Industrial Relations in Central and Eastern Europe (from Planned to Market Economy).* The Hague: Kluwer Law International, 131–8.

Jessop, B. (2012) 'Rethinking the Diversity and Variability of Capitalism: On Variegated Capitalism in the World Market', in C. Lane and G. Wood (eds.), *Capitalist Diversity and Diversity within Capitalism.* London: Routledge, 209–37.

Kaplan, K. (2007). *Proměny české společnosti 1948–1960.* Prague: Ústav pro soudobé dějiny AV ČR.

Keenoy, T. (1986). 'Solidarity: The Anti-Trade Union', in A. Pravda and B. Ruble (eds.), *Trade Unions in Communist States.* Boston: Allen & Unwin, 149–72.

Kemény, I. (1986). 'Trade Unions and Workers' Interests in Hungary', in A. Pravda and B. Ruble (eds.), *Trade Unions in Communist States.* Boston: Allen & Unwin, 173–91.

Kloc, K. (1994). 'Trade Unions and Economic Transformation in Poland', in M. Waller and M. Myant (eds.), *Parties, Trade Unions and Society in East-Central Europe.* Ilford: Frank Cass, 125–32.

Kohl, H. and Platzer, H.-W. (2007). 'The Role of the State in Central and Eastern European Industrial Relations: The Case of Minimum Wages', *Industrial Relations Journal*, 38(6): 614–35.

Krzywdzinski, M. (2010). 'Organizing Employees in Central Eastern Europe: The Approach of Solidarność', *European Journal of Industrial Relations*, 16(3): 277–92.

Kubicek, P. (2004). *Organized Labor in Postcommunist States: From Solidarity to Infirmity.* Pittsburgh, PA: University of Pittsburgh Press.

Lane, C. and Wood, G. (2012). 'Institutions, Change, and Diversity', in Lane and Wood (eds.), *Capitalist Diversity and Diversity within Capitalism.* London: Routledge, 1–31.

Lenin, V. I. (1965). *Collected Works Vol. 33.* London: Lawrence & Wishart.

Makó, C. and Simonyi, Á. (1997). 'Inheritance, Imitation and Genuine Solutions (Institution Building in Hungarian Labour Relations)', *Europe-Asia Studies*, 49(2): 221–43.

Meardi, G. (2012). *Social Failures of EU Enlargement: A Case of Workers Voting with Their Feet.* London: Routledge.

MPSV (Ministerstvo práce a sociálních věcí: Ministry of Labour and Social Affairs) (2010). *Informační systém o průměrném výdělku.* Available at <http://www.mpsv.cz/cs/1928>, accessed 16 January 2012.

—— (2011). *Informační systém o pracovních podmínkách.* Available at <http://www.mpsv.cz/cs/3360>, accessed 28 June 2012.

Mrozowicki, A. and van Hootegem, G. (2008). 'Unionism and Workers' Strategies in Capitalist Transformation: The Polish Case Reconsidered', *European Journal of Industrial Relations*, 14(2): 197–216.

Myant, M. (1989). *The Czechoslovak Economy 1948–1988: The Battle for Economic Reform.* Cambridge: Cambridge University Press.

—— (1994) 'Czech and Slovak Trade Unions', in M. Waller and Myant (eds.), *Parties, Trade Unions and Society in East-Central Europe.* Ilford: Frank Cass, 59–84.

—— (2010a). 'Trade Union Influence in the Czech Republic since 1989', *Czech Sociological Review*, 46(6): 889–911.

—— (2010b). *Trade Unions in the Czech Republic.* Brussels: European Trade Union Institute.

Myant, M. and Drahokoupil, J. (2011). *Transition Economies: Political Economy in Russia, Eastern Europe, and Central Asia.* Hoboken NJ: Wiley-Blackwell.

Myant, M. and Waller, M. (1994). 'Parties and Trade Unions in Eastern Europe: The Shifting Distribution of Political and Economic Power', in Waller and Myant (eds.), *Parties, Trade Unions and Society in East-Central Europe.* Ilford: Frank Cass, 161–81.

Nagy, L. (1990). 'Wages in Socialist Countries', *Bulletin of Comparative Labour Relations*, 19 (Deventer: Kluwer Law and Taxation Publishers): 83–117.

—— (1996). 'Transformation of Labour Law and Industrial Relations in Hungary', in R. Blanpain and L. Nagy (eds.), *Labour Law and Industrial Relations in Central and Eastern Europe (from Planned to Market Economy).* The Hague: Kluwer Law International, 67–84.

Neumann, L. (2002). 'Does Decentralized Collective Bargaining Have an Impact on the Labour Market in Hungary?', *European Journal of Industrial Relations*, 8(1): 11–31.

Nove, A. (1992). *An Economic History of the USSR, 1917–91.* London: Penguin.

Organisation for Economic Co-operation and Development (OECD) (2012). *OECD. StatExtracts.* Available at <http://stats.oecd.org/index.aspx>, accessed 16 January 2012.

Ost, D. (2000). 'Illusory Corporatism in Eastern Europe: Neoliberal Tripartism and Postcommunist Class Identities', *Politics and Society*, 28(4): 503–30.

Ost, D. (2001). 'The Weakness of Symbolic Strength: Labor and Union Identity in Poland, 1989–2000', in S. Crowley and Ost (eds.), *Workers after Workers' States: Labor and Politics in Postcommunist Eastern Europe*. Lanham, MD: Rowman & Littlefield, 79–96.

Ost, D. and Crowley, S. (2001). 'Introduction: The Surprise of Labor Weakness in Postcommunist Society', in Crowley and Ost (eds.), *Workers after Workers' States: Labor and Politics in Postcommunist Eastern Europe*. Lanham, MD: Rowman & Littlefield, 1–12.

Petkov, K. and Gradev, G. (1995). 'Bulgaria', in J. Thirkell, R. Scase, and S. Vickerstaff (eds.), *Labour Relations and Political Change in Eastern Europe*. London: UCL Press, 31–59.

Pollert, A. (1999a). 'Trade Unionism in Transition in Central and Eastern Europe', *European Journal of Industrial Relations*, 5(2): 209–34.

—— (1999b). *Transformation at Work in the New Market Economies of Central Eastern Europe*. London: Sage.

—— (2001). 'Labor and Trade Unions in the Czech Republic', in S. Crowley and D. Ost (eds.), *Workers after Workers' States: Labor and Politics in Postcommunist Eastern Europe*. Lanham, MD: Rowman & Littlefield, 13–36.

Pravda, A. and Ruble, B. (1986). 'Communist Trade Unions: Varieties of Dualism', in Pravda and Ruble (eds.), *Trade Unions in Communist States*. Boston: Allen & Unwin, 1–21.

Rainnie, A. and Hardy, J. (1995). 'Desperately Seeking Capitalism: Solidarity and Polish Industrial Relations in the 1990s', *Industrial Relations Journal*, 26(4): 267–79.

Ruble, B. (1981). *Soviet Trade Unions: Their Development in the 1970s*. Cambridge: Cambridge University Press.

Skowron, I. (2010). 'Contemporary Enterprise Culture in Poland: Attitudes of Entrepreneurs and Society', Ph.D. dissertation, University of the West of Scotland.

Soulsby, A. and Clark, E. (1998). 'Controlling Personnel: Management and Motive in the Transformation of the Czech Enterprise', *International Journal of Human Resource Management*, 9(1): 79–98.

Stanojević, M. (2003). 'Workers' Power in Transition Economies: The Cases of Serbia and Slovenia', *European Journal of Industrial Relations*, 9(3): 283–301.

—— (2007). 'Trade Unions in Slovenia', in C. Phelan (ed.), *Trade Union Revitalisation: Trends and Prospects in 34 Countries*. Oxford: Peter Lang, 347–62.

—— (2010). 'The Europeanisation of Slovenian Corporatism'. Available at <http://www.fafo.no/irec/papers/miroslavStanojevic.pdf>, accessed 23 December 2011.

Thirkell, J. (1994). 'Trade Unions, Political Parties and Governments in Bulgaria, 1989–92', in M. Waller and M. Myant (eds.), *Parties, Trade Unions and Society in East-Central Europe*. Ilford: Frank Cass, 98–115.

Tholen, J. (2007). *Labour Relations in Central Europe: The Implications of Multinationals' Money*. Aldershot: Ashgate.

Trif, A. (2007). 'Collective Bargaining in Eastern Europe: Case Study Evidence from Romania', *European Journal of Industrial Relations*, 13(2): 237–56.

Varga, M. (2011). 'Containing Militancy: Workers, Trade Unions and Factory Regimes in Ukraine', *Debatte: Journal of Contemporary Central and Eastern Europe*, 19(1–2): 397–419.

Wiesenthal, H. (1996). 'Organized Interests in Contemporary East Central Europe: Theoretical Perspectives and Tentative Hypotheses', in A. Ágh and G. Ilonszki (eds.), *Parliaments and Organized Interests: The Second Steps*. Budapest: Hungarian Center for Democracy Studies Foundation.

Woolfson, C. (2007). 'Labour Standards and Migration in the New Europe: Postcommunist Legacies and Perspectives', *European Journal of Industrial Relations*, 13(2): 199–218.

CHAPTER 17

....

EMPLOYMENT RELATIONS IN ANGLOPHONE SUB-SAHARAN AFRICA

....

JOHANN MAREE

INTRODUCTION

....

THE central aim of this chapter is to explore the relationship between the employment relations (ER) system and the extent of democracy in African countries. In addition, it examines how the ER system is influenced by the institutional context in which it is embedded. The chapter does so by examining ER in eight Anglophone countries located in sub-Saharan Africa (SSA). The countries are Ghana, Kenya, Namibia, Nigeria, South Africa, Swaziland, Zambia, and Zimbabwe. The chapter tests the hypothesis that the central requirement for a comprehensive ER system is to have a democratic regime as it enables a strong trade union movement to emerge.

Africa has thus far not achieved a good track record in establishing democratic regimes. A typical phenomenon in SSA has been that liberation movements which led the struggle for independence against former colonial rulers during the 1960s became the ruling parties in the newly independent countries. These countries usually started off with democratic constitutions and institutions. However, in many cases the ruling parties and their presidents undermined and dispensed with the democratic institutions and practices in order to entrench themselves as authoritarian or autocratic regimes.

This has led Michael Bratton, a leading scholar on democracy in Africa, to say:

> It may seem odd to couple the words 'democracy' and 'Africa' in the same sentence. After all, the international news media portray the Sub-Saharan sub-continent as a terrain of autocratic government and failed states. (Bratton 2009: 339)

However, there has been a turnabout in African politics over the past 20 or so years:

> Since 1990 the rate of democratization has been faster in Sub-Saharan Africa than in any other region of the world except the communist bloc... The 1990s were a decade of democratization in Sub-Saharan Africa. (Bratton 2009: 340)

The democratization process in Africa facilitated the upgrading of ER systems in some countries, but not necessarily to the point where they became comprehensive.

The next section provides an outline of the theoretical and empirical context within which ER institutions and practices in SSA are located in this chapter. This is followed by clarification of some of the concepts used in this chapter. They are democracy, democratization, transition to democracy, and consolidation of democracy. Thereupon the chapter examines the extent of democracy existent in Africa. Having prepared the ground, the chapter investigates ER institutions and practices in eight Anglophone SSA countries and draws its final conclusions.

INSTITUTIONAL APPROACHES AND ER INSTITUTIONS AND PRACTICES IN SSA

Wilkinson and Wood (2012) have outlined contemporary institutionalist approaches and their relevance for the study of ER. They provide a bird's-eye view of a range of approaches. A rational choice approach from a neo-classical economics perspective sees institutions as distorting the smooth operation of markets. This approach has broadened to explore the impact of worker rights which are depicted as weakening owner rights and hence bad for firms. The policy implications thereof have been to weaken worker rights by rolling back labour law. This has had considerable impact (Wilkinson and Wood 2012: 375).

Another approach relevant to ER is historical institutionalism. It 'suggests that institutions are structural frames, which are bedded down and entrenched at specific times. In short, a formative event, trauma, or crisis leads to institutions building and then consolidation' (Wilkinson and Wood, 2012: 378). The process of institution building 'meanders and is temporarily specific' as social actors contest and enact frameworks that try to adapt structures to suit their interests and needs (Wilkinson and Wood 2012: 381).

According to DiMaggio and Powell (1983), who fall under the organizational-societal approach to institutions, the structure of frameworks is not only shaped for profit-maximizing reasons, but also for reasons of legitimation. This is because, as Wilkinson and Wood (2012: 376) explain, 'it is desirable for managers and owners to at least have some legitimacy with the eyes of their workforce'. From the side of employees, rules and conventions that are seen as reasonable and fair enable them to enforce the mutually agreed rules more easily.

Business systems theory set out 'to develop a comprehensive framework for comparing systems of economic coordination and control... Whitley (1999) argues that one of the defining features of distinct business systems is employer–employee inter-dependence and delegation' (Wilkinson and Wood, 2012: 380). Wood and Frynas (2006: 239) build on Whitney's business systems theory by drawing on East African observations. They identify a new type based on the experience of East Africa, the segmented business system. 'What sets segmented systems apart are the deep cleavages that exist between export orientated and non-export orientated sectors, and, within the latter, between formal and informal economic activity' (Wood and Frynas 2006: 249).

ER in the segmented business system, as typified by Kenya, Tanzania, and Uganda, are dualistic in nature, reflecting the divide between large transnational corporations (TNCs) and state institutions on the one hand and indigenous private firms, many of which are family owned, on the other hand. Trade unions have very limited social impact with their activities being largely confined to state institutions and the manufacturing sector (Wood and Frynas 2006: 255).

The varieties of capitalism approach, such as work by Whitley (1999) and Hall and Soskice (2001), bases its analysis on developed market economies where the formal sector is dominant. However, as Dibben and Williams (2012: 563, 565) point out, most of the world's workers are in the informal sector. Out of a global working population of some 3 billion, around 60% (1.8 billion) work in the informal sector. In many emerging economies, over 75% of the labour force consists of informal sector enterprises and workers. In SSA one study has found that 76% of non-agricultural employment is in the informal sector (ILO 2002, reference in Dibben and Williams 2012: 565).

Dibben and Williams (2012: 564) thus propose that a new variety of capitalism needs to be recognized, namely informally dominated market economies (IDMEs). Within the IDMEs the role of institutions governing ER would have to be reconsidered in both the formal and informal sectors as well as how they interact with each other in the two sectors. The institutions include: the state; trade unions (particularly their strength), collective bargaining, and participation; training and educational systems; and security of tenure and social security.

Using Mozambique in East Africa as an extreme case study, Dibben and Williams (2012: 564) point out that around 75% of its workforce is in the informal sector, 17% is unemployed, and only 8% is in formal employment. Consequently the largest trade union centre in Mozambique, OTM, has organized only 2.5% of the total workforce. In Mozambique the employment legislation applies only to formal sector workers, excluding the overwhelming majority in the informal sector and peasant production. However, in practice formal regulation is undermined by informal norms and behaviour. Even the unions' legal right to participation and collective bargaining is dominated by informal rules and practices (Dibben and Williams, 2012: 571–5).

In view of these realities Dibben and Williams made use of the following definition of institutions by Douglass North because it draws attention to both formal and informal rules:

> [Institutions are] a set of rules, formal or informal, that actors generally follow, whether for normative, cognitive, or material reasons, and organisations as durable entities with formally recognized members, whose rules also contribute to the institutions of the political economy. (North 1990: 3, as cited by Dibben and Williams 2012: 567)

The theoretical and empirical framework of the countries dealt with in this chapter falls under the IDMEs variety of capitalism. This is because in all the countries with one exception—South Africa where it constitutes only 19% of total non-agricultural employment (Kingdon and Knight 2003: 391–2)—the majority of the workforce is located in the informal sector. It thus has to be borne in mind that informal workers, the majority of workers in seven of the countries examined in this chapter, fall outside the regulatory reach of ER institutions and practices and that the rules prevailing in the informal sector impinge on those in the formal sector.

CLARIFICATION OF CONCEPTS

Comprehensive Employment Relations

In order for an ER system to be regarded as completely comprehensive the following institutions and practices have to be present.

- A comprehensive labour law framework that incorporates the rights and obligations of workers and employees and their representative unions as well as employers and their representative associations.
- Freedom of association for employees and employers with the right to strike, picket, and lockout.
- Collective bargaining institutions at whatever level the parties decide appropriate and negotiated agreements that are implemented and adhered to by the parties with an enforcement mechanism.
- Mediation and arbitration facilities to resolve and settle disputes.
- Employment security, flexible employment with security (flexicurity), and social security.
- The availability and opportunity for staff to receive training and education.
- A tripartite forum with state, labour, and business representatives as the social partners.

Democracy

The literal meaning of democracy is 'rule by the people', but that is not a feasible proposition in any country in the world today. Thus it is necessary to develop a set of criteria to classify a country as democratic or not. First of all it is necessary to bring the state into the concept since it is the way that a country is governed that determines whether it is democratic or not. Two necessary but not sufficient prerequisites for a state to be democratic are the rule of law and free and fair elections. The rule of law ensures that the rulers are held in check by the constitution and courts of law while free and fair elections ensure that the rulers are representative and accountable to the citizenry (Rose 2009: 12–13).

However, these are minimal requirements for a country to be regarded as democratic and more criteria are considered when discussing transition to and consolidation of democracy below.

Democratization

By democratization is meant providing greater space for autonomous working-class and civil society organization, allowing freedom of expression and protest, the process of acquiring legal safeguards for individuals, as well as open contestation to win control of the government by means of free competitive elections (Linz and Stepan 1996: 3). This process is reversible, i.e. countries where democratization has taken place could revert back to authoritarian rule.

Transition to Democracy

Transition to democracy refers to completion of the procedures and election of a government that is the direct result of a free and universal vote and has the authority to generate new policies. In addition, there is a separation of executive, legislative, and judicial powers (Linz and Stepan 1996: 3). As with democratization, this process is reversible, i.e. countries where transition to democracy has taken place could revert back to authoritarian rule.

Consolidation of Democracy

Consolidation of democracy is different from democratization and transition to democracy. Linz (1990) has provided a valuable definition of a consolidated democracy. It is:

> One in which none of the major political actors, parties, or organized interests, forces or institutions consider that there is any alternative to democratic processes to gain power, and that no political institution or group has a claim to veto the action of democratically elected decision makers. This does not mean that there are no minorities ready to challenge and question the legitimacy of the democratic process by non-democratic means. It means, however, that the major actors do not turn to them and that they remain politically isolated. To put it simply, democracy must be seen as the 'only game in town'. (Linz 1990: 158, as cited by de Villiers and Anstey 2000: 35)

Another aspect of consolidation of democracy in the post-colonial African context is that a ruling party and president relinquish power to an opposition party and presidential candidate when they are defeated in a free and fair election.

EXTENT OF DEMOCRACY IN AFRICA

In order to gauge the extent of democracy in Africa, use was made of Diamond's (2002) classification of countries around the world into democratic and authoritarian regimes. He pointed out that many regimes in the world can be classified as neither fully democratic nor as totally authoritarian. He calls these hybrid regimes (Diamond 2002: 21–3); although there has been a surge of democratization in Africa over the past 20 years, it still has a large number of hybrid regimes.

Diamond (2002: 31, Table 2) classified 48 sub-Saharan African countries into six categories ranging from fully democratic to completely authoritarian. The classification applied to the end of 2001. In order to bring the information up to date and demonstrate the progress in democratization and transition to democracy in sub-Saharan Africa the situation at the end of 2011 was derived by the author with the aid of Bratton et al. (2005: 17, Table 1.1) and Freedom House (2012: 14–18).[1]

The classification used by Diamond and Bratton produced the following findings for the African continent. Full democracies are regimes where not only free and fair elections are held regularly, but where civil and political liberties also exist along with a free press even though political leaders do not usually encourage or embrace criticisms (Bratton et al. 2005: 16). There also exist independent and relatively effective legislative and judicial institutions that uphold the rule of law. Only five countries were classified as full democracies in 2001, but the number has increased to eight by 2011.

Flawed democracies are regimes that meet minimal democratic standards by holding elections that are usually deemed free and fair, but where civil and political liberties are not secure, especially between elections. Political minorities are often sidelined and complain of neglect and even repression. 'Most importantly', say Bratton et al. (2005: 16), 'political power remains concentrated in the hands of executive presidents to the point that significant arenas of decision making lie beyond the control of other elected officials.' Nine countries were included in this category in 2001. The number increased to 12 by 2011.

A large majority of countries were classified as authoritarian of one type or another. The competitive authoritarian regimes have multiparty electoral competitions of some sort, but in the hegemonic ones the democratic institutions are largely facades (Diamond 2002: 25–6). Diamond refers to the competitive authoritarian ones as pseudo-democracies in that they use the trappings of formal democratic institutions such as multiparty elections in order to mask the reality of authoritarian domination (Diamond, 2002: 24). Twenty-one regimes fell into either the competitive or hegemonic authoritarian category in 2001, but this decreased to 17 by 2011.

The politically closed authoritarian regimes are ones where the governments do not even make any pretence at being democratic. They either hold sham elections or come to power through heredity, military coups, or armed insurgency (Bratton et al. 2005: 18). The number of completely authoritarian regimes increased from seven to nine between 2001 and 2011, indicating that there has also been political deterioration in a couple of countries.

Table 17.1 Classification of sub-Saharan African regimes in 2001 and 2011

Type of regime	Number of countries	
Year	2001	2011
Full democracy	5	8
Flawed democracy	9	12
Hybrid	6	2
Authoritarian	21	17
Autocratic	7	9

Sources: Diamond (2002: 31, Table 2); Bratton et al. (2005: 17, Table 1.1); Freedom House (2012: 14–18).

The residual countries, six in 2001 and two in 2011, have been classified as hybrid as they could not be placed in either the democratic or the autocratic camp and were truly hybrid regimes.

In summary, out of the 48 regimes in sub-Saharan Africa the number of countries classified as democratic increased from 14 to 20 from 2001 to 2011, while the number of authoritarian countries decreased from 28 to 26.

Table 17.1 summarizes the classification, but the classification has been simplified with a slight change in terminology in order to signify the distinction between different types of regimes more clearly. Competitive and hegemonic authoritarian countries have been classified together under one heading, 'Authoritarian', while politically closed authoritarian regimes have been renamed 'Autocratic' as it is a better description of the true nature of the regimes.

Table 17.2 contains the classification of the regimes of eight sub-Saharan countries that are discussed later in the chapter. The classification is for 2001 and 2011 and shows that some of the regimes became more democratic, others remained the same, while one (Zimbabwe) deteriorated. Although Zimbabwe is classified as authoritarian in both years, it deteriorated according to Bratton and Freedom House from competitive authoritarian to hegemonic authoritarian. Both classifications, in the opinion of the author, are however wrong as Zimbabwe had deteriorated quite soon after it attained independence into a harsh and oppressive autocratic state under President Mugabe with strong support from the military and its leaders. (See the discussion on Zimbabwe below; see also Catholic Commission for Justice and Peace in Zimbabwe 2007; Meredith 2002; Moorcroft 2012; Raftopoulos and Savage 2004; Sachikonye 2011). In the remainder of this chapter the Zimbabwe regime is accordingly referred to as autocratic.

Table 17.2 Classification of regimes of eight countries in 2001 and 2011

Country	Classification of regime	
	2001	2011
Ghana	Flawed democracy	Full democracy
Kenya	Authoritarian	Flawed democracy
Namibia	Flawed democracy	Full democracy
Nigeria	Hybrid	Hybrid
South Africa	Full democracy	Full democracy
Swaziland	Autocratic	Autocratic
Zambia	Hybrid	Flawed democracy
Zimbabwe	Authoritarian	Authoritarian

Sources: Bratton et al. (2005: 17, Table 1.1); Freedom House (2012: 14–18).

ER in Eight Countries in Africa

Countries with Full Democracy, Strong Trade Unions, and Comprehensive ER

Of the eight countries considered, there are three, Ghana, Namibia, and South Africa, which are regarded as full democracies. However, it is only Ghana and South Africa that have strong trade union movements. They are also countries with comprehensive ER institutions and practices. The reasons for this are discussed below.

Ghana

The trade unions were influential politically at the time of independence of Ghana in 1957, but the Trade Union Congress (TUC) had to fight for its independence and worker rights for over 40 years. The trade union movement was in alliance with Kwame Nkrumah's Convention People's Party (CPP) and managed to get the pro-union Industrial Relations Act passed in 1957 which introduced the duty to bargain and check-off system for union dues on the one hand, but made strikes virtually illegal on the other hand. It also granted the TUC a monopoly role. It had the power to certificate unions that had to affiliate to it. By the end of Nkrumah's rule there were tensions between the TUC and CPP with the government controlling the trade union movement.

In 1966 there followed a series of military coups interspersed with brief democratic rules in between. During this time the TUC experienced fluctuating fortunes, falling in and out of favour with regimes (Akwetey and Dorkenoo 2010: 39, 43). The military coup that lasted longest and had the most severe impact on unions was the one in 1981 by Jerry Rawlings and the Provisional National Defence Council (PNDC). It set up Workers' Defence Committees (WDCs) that challenged unions and management in the workplace. Throughout the period that Rawlings and the PNDC ruled, the unions had to fight hard to maintain their leadership role in the workplace and their autonomy and independence as organizations.

Ghanaian trade union leaders learned from this period that trade union independence was very important and that a democratic political regime enabled them to become independent (Kraus 2007: 89–92). They also learned that democracy gave them freedom to pursue their interests and that dictatorships did not (Kraus, 2007: 117).

The Industrial Relations Act of 1965 was the predominant piece of legislation covering industrial relations in Ghana from 1965 to 2003. The Act gave monopoly union status to the TUC in that unions could only gain official status if they were affiliated to the TUC (Frazer 2007: 186–7).

In 1992 there was a return to civilian rule with the passage of a democratic constitution that granted public sector associations the legal right to bargain collectively. The constitution also ensured freedom of association for workers and trade union plurality (Frazer 2007: 195).

In 2003 the Labour Act (Act 651) replaced the IR Act of 1965. The Act ensured freedom of association, thereby releasing unions from registering exclusively through the TUC. As a result new unions were established that joined the rival Ghana Federation of Labour. In addition the Act enabled public service employees to form registered unions for the first time. It also met business' requirement to clarify labour relations laws, and set up the National Labour Commission to resolve labour disputes. The Commission appoints a mediator to resolve the dispute and if that does not work, the dispute moves on to arbitration sooner or later. This is because a strike or lockout is allowed to carry on for only seven days after which it must go to arbitration (Frazer 2007: 188–90).

The 2003 Labour Act also made provision for the setting up of a tripartite committee. The National Tripartite Committee, comprising organized labour, the employers' organization, and government meets from time to time to deal with work-related issues and the fixing of the national minimum wage (Akwetey and Dorkenoo 2010: 49).

As a result of all these developments, trade unions became quite strong. In 2001 union density in the formal sector varied between 45% and 65%, with union density higher in the public sector than in the private sector. However, when the informal sector is included union density among the employed labour force in 2001 was in the vicinity of 5–8%. An indication of union strength in the formal sector is that the wage premium in manufacturing was approximately 28% (Frazer 2007: 192–3).

By 2010 the trade union movement in Ghana, especially the TUC, had several achievements to its credit. First, it had managed to get all the major political actors to accept and recognize its independence. Second, it had become an important player in tripartite negotiations with regards to the labour market and succeeded in pushing the government to place the issue of employment on its agenda. Consequently the government launched the National Youth Employment Programme aimed at creating jobs for the youth. Finally, it has teamed up with civil society movements in engaging the government and international financial institutions with regards to development programmes and poverty reduction (Akwetey and Dorkenoo 2010: 50–3). Trade unions have also engaged with civil society organizations in strategies to provide social protection for informal workers (Croucher 2007: 213–17).

These achievements, along with the employment relations institutions and practices developed since 1992, have created a fairly comprehensive employment relations system in Ghana's formal economy.

South Africa

South Africa came into existence as a colonial but autonomous state in 1910. White political and economic domination was firmly entrenched right from the outset. As a result of diamond and gold mining, White craft and industrial unions existed from early on. After a strike by White goldmine workers that turned into a rebellion in 1922, the Industrial Conciliation Act was passed in 1924. It made provision for the establishment of industrial councils by registered trade unions and employers' associations representing a particular industry in a particular region. The parties of an industrial council could engage in collective bargaining over wages and working conditions of the employees they represented on the council. Once an agreement was reached and gazetted by the Minister it had the force of law (du Toit et al. 2003: 6–8).

A fundamental flaw of the Act was that it excluded Black African workers from membership of registered trade unions and hence representation on industrial councils. Because Black Africans were not allowed to establish or belong to registered trade unions, they struggled to organize themselves. Then, in 1973 extensive strikes in Durban gave an immense impetus to the unionization of Black workers. As a result of the emergence of these unions and international pressure the state conceded the same workplace rights to Black workers as to White, Coloured, and Indian workers by amending the Industrial Conciliation Act in 1979 and 1981, renaming it the Labour Relations Act. As a result, Black unions experienced explosive growth during the 1980s (Friedman 1987). After initial hesitation they joined industrial councils and transformed the power relations within them, becoming the largest and major unions on the councils (Godfrey 1992; Godfrey et al. 2010: 60–6).

The Labour Relations Act also made provision for the establishment of an Industrial Court that was granted an extensive unfair labour practice jurisdiction. The Court was granted wide discretion to interpret the concept 'unfair labour practice'. It managed 'to fashion an extensive, although uneven and sometimes contradictory, jurisprudence on individual employment rights as well as collective labour law' (du Toit et al. 2003: 10–12).

In November 1985 the Congress of South African Trade Unions (COSATU) was established. It was a predominantly Black African trade union centre and was overtly political from the outset. It supported the African National Congress (ANC) and the South African Communist Party (SACP) which were both operating underground at the time. After the unbanning of these liberation movements in 1990, COSATU entered into a

Tripartite Alliance with both of them. Thereupon COSATU as the major Black trade union centre—along with other trade union centres and social movements—played a major role in compelling the apartheid state to reach a negotiated agreement with the liberation movements and other political parties to create the new South Africa. It did so through concerted mass action (Adler and Webster 1995: 93–4). These parties negotiated a new Constitution with a strong Bill of Rights that enshrined equality, political rights, freedom of association, collective bargaining, and the right to strike.

Legislation that enhanced worker and trade union rights through new and existing institutions followed soon after the political transition of 1994. The Nedlac Act of 1994 set up the National Economic Development and Labour Council (Nedlac) with equal representation by the government, organized business, organized labour, and nationally representative community bodies in each of its four chambers. All draft bills relating to labour first have to go to the Labour Market chamber where the parties negotiate over their contents until they reach consensus. This gives organized labour considerable power and input over all legislation relating to employment relations (Webster 1995; Gostner and Joffe 2000).

The redrafted Labour Relations Act (LRA) of 1995 extended the rights of workers and trade unions considerably. It extended the provisions of the Act to almost all public servants as well as to domestic and agricultural workers. It retained the industrial council system, but changed the name to bargaining councils as public servants were explicitly allowed to establish such councils. The outcome has been the rapid growth of large and powerful public service unions and bargaining councils. By 2009 the Public Services Coordinating Bargaining Council, the largest public service bargaining council, represented more than a million civil servants.

The bargaining councils covered 20.3% of the total labour force in 2004, but this figure includes occupational categories that the councils do not normally include. When considering only the occupational categories that generally fall within the bargaining councils' scope and the sectors that have bargaining councils, the proportion rises to 32.6%, or almost one-third of all employees in the relevant occupations and sectors (Godfrey et al. 2010: 114–15).

Collective bargaining also takes place outside the bargaining council system. Centralized bargaining takes place in the gold and coal mining industries as well as the automobile manufacturing industry. The gold mining bargaining forum is highly representative with up to 75% of employees covered in the industry, while all seven employers in the automobile manufacturing industry are represented on its National Bargaining Forum (Godfrey et al. 2010: 204, 213).

In addition, the Minister of Labour may promulgate sectoral determinations that lay down minimum wages and working conditions in sectors not covered by collective bargaining agreements. Over four million employees are covered by sectoral determinations with domestic work and retail constituting the two largest sectors (DPRU 2010: 5).

The LRA of 1995 also instituted the Commission of Conciliation, Mediation and Arbitration (CCMA) as a statutory body, taking over the role that had largely been performed by a non-statutory body, the Independent Mediation Service of South Africa (IMSSA). The CCMA provides its services free of charge and rapidly became the most extensively used dispute settlement institution in South Africa. In only one month, December 2011, it dealt with almost 10,000 cases of which 79% were unfair dismissal disputes. The average settlement rate was around 73% (CCMA 2012).

To summarize, it was not until South Africa became a full democracy that the employment relations system was extended to the whole workforce. Prior to that, Blacks, who constitute the overwhelming majority of the population, were excluded from its institutions and practices. The growth of a powerful Black trade union movement that commenced in the early 1970s played a crucial role in extending workplace rights to all workers and in the peaceful transition to democracy in 1994. Their political influence as a member of the Tripartite Alliance has ensured that a comprehensive set of employment relations practices and institutions have come to exist in South Africa.

Country with Full Democracy, Weak Trade Union Movement, and Incomplete ER

Namibia

Namibia has consistently been classified as a full democracy, but has a weak trade union movement unable to enforce comprehensive ER practices.

Namibia was a German colony until the end of the First World War, but in 1920 the League of Nations put it under South Africa's trusteeship. In 1945 the United Nations appointed South Africa as trustee of Namibia. The Wage and Industrial Conciliation Ordinance of 1952 allowed trade unions to organize in the territory, but excluded Black African workers from the definition of 'employee' and therefore from participation in trade unions (Bauer 1997: 68).

South Africa imposed its apartheid laws on the country. It led to uprisings and resistance by its African citizens and the formation of a liberation movement, the South West Africa People's Organization (SWAPO) in 1960. It soon became the dominant resistance movement in the territory.

In 1989 SWAPO re-established the National Union of Namibian Workers (NUNW) as a federation of trade unions, but completely dominated it at that stage (Bauer 1998: 78–9). SWAPO's Department of Labour and the NUNW were effectively a single body and the trade union federation's constitution stipulated that its main objective was 'the total liberation of Namibia' (Ranchod 2007: 85). The NUNW also affiliated to SWAPO. In 1997 it signed an affiliation accord in which it recognized SWAPO as the senior partner in the relationship (Jauch 2010: 172). It thereby presented itself with a conflict of interests in years to come: whether its main aim was to support SWAPO's political objectives or to represent workers.

In 1987 there was an escalation of strikes in Namibia. In the same year the Wiehahn Commission of Inquiry into Labour Matters was appointed. In 1990 Namibia became independent with SWAPO as the ruling party. According to Bauer, 'at independence in Namibia collective labour relations hardly existed in any coherent and institutionalized fashion' (Bauer 1998: 119). In 1992 the Labour Act was passed. The Wiehahn Commission report, along with the new Constitution and Conventions of the International Labour Organization (ILO) contributed to the new Act (Klerck 2007: 105).

The Labour Act of 1992 is very wide-ranging, including all the usual economic sectors and extending to the agricultural, domestic, and public sectors for the first time. It strengthened the legal protection of trade unions' organizational rights and unfair labour practice in the workplace with a Labour Court to adjudicate over such practices and other related issues. However, collective bargaining still remained voluntary even though the Act provided for an extensive right to strike. It also introduced a soft version of tripartism. A Tripartite Labour Advisory Council was set up in May 1993 which could only advise the Minister (Bauer 1997: 74: Klerck et al. 1998: 87; Klerck 2007: 106).

The unions negotiated on a decentralized company-by-company basis. By May 1996, 29 collective agreements had been registered with the Office of the Labour Commissioner. The highest number of agreements was in manufacturing with nine agreements. In mining there were four agreements (Klerck and Murray 1997: 250). They concentrated on industries where there were mostly Black male employees and neglected ones with more female and casual labour such as retail and construction. These strategies had the effect of preventing the unions from becoming strong and strategic (Klerck 2007: 107–8).

The NUNW's affiliation to SWAPO remained a controversial issue. This was because NUNW was perceived to put SWAPO's interests above the rights of their worker members. For instance, in 1995 the Export Processing Zone Act was passed. After a meeting with SWAPO, the NUNW compromised on workers' rights in Export Processing Zones (EPZs), agreeing to the outlawing of strikes in EPZs for five years (Nakanyane 2000: 89). As a result of many unions' rejection of NUNW's affiliation to SWAPO an alternative trade union federation, the Trade Union Congress of Namibia (TUCNA) was formed in 2002. It consisted of 14 unions with a combined membership of around 45,000 members. At that time the NUNW had some 70,000 members. In addition, rival camps started emerging within the NUNW to the extent that the battle for political control overshadowed worker issues at the federation's 2006 congress (Jauch 2007: 60–1).

Trade unions have been challenged by a dwindling membership base as well due to the increased 'casualization' of labour. This was a result of the emergence of temporary employment agencies in Namibia since the late 1990s. By 2006 over 12,000 workers were contracted out by these agencies. The unions found it difficult to recruit and represent these workers due to the temporary nature of their contracts (Jauch 2007: 59).

Namibia has been able to hold free and fair elections since its independence in 1990. Despite that, the trade union movement has remained weak for the reasons outlined above.

Countries with Flawed Democracies, Weak Trade Unions, and Incomplete ER

Zambia and Kenya are two countries that have flawed democracies and weak trade unions with the result that their ER institutions and practices are not comprehensive.

Zambia

Zambia became independent in 1964 under the leadership of President Kaunda of the United National Independent Party (UNIP). He presided over an economy dominated by the copper mining industry. Copper accounted for about 90% of the country's foreign earnings. In addition, employment in the formal sector constituted only a very small proportion of total employment in the economy. From 1996 to 2000 informal employment remained steady at 88% of total employment (Fashoyin 2008: 392, 394). Since employment relations institutions and practices do not extend into the informal economy it is important to realize that only a small proportion of Zambia's labour force is governed by ER institutions.

The Zambia Congress of Trade Unions (ZCTU) was established in 1964 as the sole trade union centre by law. Trade unions were expected by President Kaunda to play a developmental rather than representative role. That is, the unions were expected to focus on worker productivity and restrain wage demands and industrial action. There were close union–government ties as President Kaunda tried to subordinate the trade union movement with favourable treatment, but according to Fashoyin (2008: 395), this was to no avail as the union movement grew stronger and retained its independence.

The unions' ability to grow strong was facilitated by the Industrial Relations Act of 1964, the core employment relations law passed by the Kaunda regime. The Act provided for the establishment of Joint Industrial Councils (JICs) by trade unions and employers' associations. This centralized collective bargaining and agreements reached could be extended to all workers in the industry covered by the JIC (Fashoyin 2008: 397). Even as early as 1961 both the public and private sectors enjoyed the right to bargain collectively. A group of only 25 workers had 'the right to enter into a recognition agreement and bargain collectively on behalf of the workers' (Fashoyin 2008: 398). Consequently 'collective bargaining gained firm root in key economic sectors, notably transport, mining, manufacturing, financial services, security and agriculture, as well as the public sector'. It is thought that nearly 80% of employees in the formal sector were covered by collective bargaining during the 1970s and 1980s (Fashoyin 2008: 398).

Democracy in Zambia was delivered a blow in 1973 when President Kaunda and UNIP formally declared Zambia a one-party state under a new constitution. The state also nationalized the copper mines, but from 1974 to 1989 the price of copper fell. As it accounted for 90–95% of Zambian exports the economy declined. The International Monetary Fund (IMF) provided loans, but imposed austerity measures and structural adjustment programmes (SAPs).

From then on the UNIP regime imposed a market-oriented economy that was inimical to workers and trade unions. In 1993 it amended the Industrial Relations Act to implement economic liberalization and again in 1997 to remove the mandatory duty of employers to bargain on JICs and allowed them to bargain at enterprise level instead (Fashoyin 2008: 397). Wage freezes were imposed and workers' standard of living dropped. Consequently ZCTU resistance to government policies increased and protest strikes were launched (Gostner 1997: 56).

In 1990 the ZCTU called for the restoration of multiparty democracy and took the initiative to campaign for its restoration (Adler and Buhlungu 1997: 48). The campaign grew into a mass movement with the support of a range of community-based organizations, disaffected UNIP members, university lecturers, businesses, clergy, and traditional rulers. In July 1990 the Movement for Multiparty Democracy (MMD) was launched. The ZCTU provided the mass mobilization while business provided the funds. The MMD defeated UNIP in the general election of October 1991 and Frederick Chiluba, former leader of the ZCTU, immediately took over as president from Kaunda (Kraus 2007: 125–35). This was the first time in African history that a trade union movement had facilitated the formation of a political party that won an election against a former liberation movement and instated multiparty democracy (Kraus 2007: 152).

Chiluba started implementing the austerity measures advocated by the IMF and, as a result, the initial close relationship that existed between the ZCTU and the MMD came to an end after 1991 as the trade union movement took up the cudgels on behalf of their worker members once again (Tshoaedi 2000: 86; Kraus 2007: 135–46). Chiluba was nonetheless elected for a second term of office. The MMD won the elections again in 2002 and in 2006 with the new leader of the MMD, Levy Mwanamasa, as President (Wikipedia 2010).

Since the liberalization of the economy commenced in the early 1990s collective bargaining declined in the private sector. By 2008 it was virtually non-existent in manufacturing and services as new investors preferred individual contracts and the use of temporary labour. Only a few JICs remained in operation, notably in mining and agriculture, but it is doubtful whether they are functioning properly. However, in the public sector collective bargaining remained strong, covering over 90% of eligible members (Fashoyin 2008: 398).

In the 2011 elections there was a second change of political parties in a free election in Zambia. The Patriotic Front received the largest proportion of votes and Michael Sata became president (Bloomberg.com 2011). President Sata dismissed the country's police chief, the central bank governor, and scores of public servants in a relatively short period of time (*Guardian* 2011). He made such rapid changes that procedural requirements were most likely sidestepped.

In the period up to 1991 the trade union movement was able to consolidate its strength and favourable legislation assisted in establishing strong employment relations and collective bargaining institutions in Zambia. However, a badly timed nationalization of copper mines and a World Bank imposed free market economy weakened collective bargaining institutions and practices considerably in the private sector. ER is thus not extensively implemented even in the formal sector of its economy.

Kenya

Kenya achieved its independence from the United Kingdom on 31 December 1963. Jomo Kenyatta became president and ruled for 15 years until his death in 1978. Thereupon Daniel arap Moi became president and ruled with an iron rod for 24 years until he was finally defeated at an election in 2002. Kenya thus experienced 39 years of autocratic rule before democratization could commence in 2002.

In 1964 the Trades Dispute Act was amended. It established arbitration tribunals and an Industrial Court. 'Fine-tuning' legislation was passed in 1965 which set up procedures for settling disputes, limited secondary strikes, lockouts, mandatory binding arbitration by the Industrial Court in 'essential services' disputes, and gave unions mandatory check-off of union dues if agreed to by the Minister for Labour. There was thus voluntary arbitration in non-essential services and compulsory arbitration in essential services (Hagglund 2007: 33).

From the outset the Industrial Court regarded itself as the guardian of the Kenyan economy's competitiveness by means of low wages. In this the Court was aided and abetted by an amendment to the Act in 1971 that enforced the Court to cap wage increases to no higher than the rate of inflation (Hagglund 2007: 33–4).

The Central Organization of Trade Unions (COTU), was formed in 1965 at the insistence of government because of feuding between two trade union centres. Gona (2009: 136) maintains that 'From its inception COTU was obliged to serve the government and not the workers.'

In 1982 Moi made Kenya a *de jure* one-party state by amending the Constitution and banning opposition parties. Four years later he removed the security of tenure of the attorney-general, comptroller, auditor general, and High Court judges, making all these positions personally beholden to the president. In the run-up to the 1987 election he jailed opposition leaders and ruled in 'virtual autocracy' for the 15 years he continued to remain in office (Fitzpatrick et al. 2009: 270).

The Export Processing Zones Act was passed in 1990 enabling foreign investors to set up businesses with substantial protection, including exemption from all the labour laws. The ILO subsequently succeeded in having the policy revised to bring the zones under the effective protection of the labour laws, but at the time of writing by Fashoyin (2007: 41) the government still had to approve it.

The 1990s was a decade in which civil society and political organizations agitated for the democratization of politics and society and a return to multiparty politics. Gona (2009: 136–50) argues that the coercive policies of the state forced COTU into subservience and it consequently played no role among civil society organizations in the democratization process of the 1990s. He concludes, 'The labour movement as part of the organised spheres of civil society did not play a significant role in the democratisation period of the 1990s' (Gona 2009: 151). In addition, non-governmental organizations (NGOs) and civil society organizations (CSOs) 'had entered the terrain traditionally reserved for the labour market actors, and in some way operated in a destabilising manner' (Fashoyin 2007: 45).

In 1994 the labour laws—and hence the trade unions—were emasculated by the Minister of Finance who 'took the extraordinary step' of introducing a Finance Bill to Parliament that amended both the Regulation of Wages and Conditions of Employment Act and the Trade Disputes Act. It moved the issue of redundancy from the latter to the former Act thereby giving a free hand to enterprises to restructure with the obligation only to *inform* but not to *report* the proposed measure to the labour ministry (Fashoyin 2007: 42).

In spite of a deteriorating economy under his presidency and two elections where there were violent ethnic clashes President Moi hung on to power until 2002 (Hagglund, 2007: 36–7). In a rare peaceful and fair election in December, President Mwai Kibaki and the National Rainbow Coalition (Narc) won a landslide two-thirds victory (Fitzpatrick et al. 2009: 271).

With the exception of 2003 when the number of strikes peaked at 160 there was a downward trend in strike incidence between 1996 and 2005, yet another indication of a weakening trade union movement. The high incidence of strikes in 2003 was due to the ending of the Moi era and the 'democratic rapture that accompanied the election of President Kibaki' (Fashoyin 2007: 47). This seems to confirm Gona's statement that, 'From its inception, COTU was to serve government and not the trade union members' (Gona 2009: 136).

On the other hand, Fashoyin maintains that, 'Collective bargaining is an old tradition in Kenya' and over 200 collective bargaining agreements (CBAs), at both the sectoral and enterprise level, are made annually across industries in the country. Furthermore, it is estimated that the agreements cover about 1.5 million 'direct beneficiaries'. Nevertheless, given the large informal sector, the majority of workers remain outside the direct cover of CBAs. The number of CBAs has been falling: in 2000 the number was only half of what it had been in 1998. This was due to declining industrial activity, reluctance of employers to sign agreements, and the absence of trade union activities in the EPZs. Finally, collective bargaining has shifted from industry to enterprise level due to economic difficulties. Employers have a freer hand this way. Industry bargaining has been confined to a few industries such as tea plantations, agriculture, banking, engineering, and mining (Fashoyin 2007: 46–8).

In Kenya the 33 years of autocratic rule severely undermined the trade union movement and compromised collective bargaining institutions and practices through state and political domination. Although the trade unions do have a presence and role in some sectors of the economy, Kenya does not yet have an extensive set of employment relations practices and institutions.

Country with Hybrid Regime, Weak Trade Union Movement, and Incomplete ER

Nigeria

Nigeria still hovers between authoritarianism and democracy with a hybrid regime, but it has a weak trade union movement and incomplete ER system.

Nigeria is the most populous country in Africa with a population of 158 million in 2010. Trade unions emerged during the period of colonialism as politically conscious institutions (Fajana 2007: 147). The Nigerian Labour Congress (NLC) was established in 1950, but factionalism preceded and followed its birth. By the early 1970s no less than four trade union centres and 751 registered trade unions existed with a combined membership of 700,000 (Fajana 2007: 154).

In 1960 Nigeria gained independence from the United Kingdom and experienced civilian rule during its first six years of independence. From 1966 up to 1999, a period of 33 years, Nigeria was under military rule except for a brief interregnum from 1979–83 (Otobe 2007: 164).

Otobe has argued that the intention of the military regime was to control the labour movement by incorporating it into the state (Fajana 2007: 156). The military regime certainly continued to intervene and dominate the trade union movement. The Minister of Employment, Labour and Productivity could intervene in any industrial dispute, essentially in essential services, and prescribe appropriate steps in settling it. In addition, the Minister was empowered to enforce any provisions of a bilateral collective agreement on the parties. The policy became necessary, according to Fajana (2007: 156), due to 'the chaotic industrial relations situation in the country before 1975'.

In 1978 the military regime re-established the Nigeria Labour Congress (NLC) and dissolved other existing labour federations. All existing unions were also dissolved and reorganized into industrial unions with compulsory deductions of union dues by employers (Beckman and Lukman 2010: 60). The number of unions declined from over 1,000 to just 70 (Fajana 2007: 150–1).

The number of unions continued to decline over the next two decades. By 1990 there were only 41 unions and in 1996 the state enabled the amalgamation of overlapping industrial unions, reducing the number from 41 to 29 (Fajana 2007: 152). A decade later less than 3 million (11%) wage earners out of a total 29 million were organized into trade unions and senior staff associations (Otobe 2007: 165).

The regime also consistently limited the right of Nigerian workers to strike. Some of the legislation was contained in the Trades Dispute Acts 1969, 1976, 1996, and 2005. Strikes in essential services were forbidden. The 1976 Act listed the economic sectors falling within essential services as 'the supply of electricity, power, water, and fuel of any kind'. In addition any trade union activities that constituted 'wrongful politically motivated activities' were declared illegal (Fajana 2007: 157). Under these conditions it has been extremely hard for the unions to develop their strength and build an independent platform.

Oil has come to dominate the Nigerian economy. According to Fajana (2007: 160), 'industrial relations in Nigeria since the turn of the (21st) century has been characterized by the politics of petroleum pricing'. In June 2003 the government announced 'yet another plan' to increase oil prices by 50%. In the ensuing general strike 19 trade unionists were killed by police. A further six were arrested and beaten up in prison (Fajana 2007: 158).

The 2004 Trade Union Act granted greater freedom to trade unions and allowed the registration of multiple trade union centres (Fajana 2007: 155). However, in both the public and private sectors there are very inadequate industrial relations practices with employers in both sectors getting away with extremely poor treatment of employees and the trade unions apparently incapable of preventing infringements of human rights (Otobe 2007: 168–72).

The weakness of the trade union movement in Nigeria can be ascribed to the militarization of civil society politics in Nigeria which has 'tended to increase unilateralism, to the detriment of tripartism or social dialogue, in policy-making'. There has thus been 'declining capacity among union leadership' and 'the rapid growth in the number of rival non-governmental organisations (NGOs) many of which concentrate on some traditional concerns of the labour movement (civil liberties, human rights, occupational hazards, inequity and corruption, etc.) to deliberate anti-unionism tactics of both private and public employers, especially sub-contracting of operations and labour' (Otobe 2007: 178, 179).

The 33 years of almost continuous military rule in Nigeria since independence in 1960 took its toll on the trade union movement. The military regimes dominated the unions and curtailed the right of workers to strike. Although the 2004 Trade Union Act granted greater freedom to trade unions, employment relations practices remained inadequate with trade unions incapable of preventing employer infringements and poor treatment of employees.

Countries with Autocratic Regimes, Weak Trade Union Movements, and Incomplete ER

Zimbabwe and Swaziland are two countries with autocratic regimes that have dealt harshly with opposition, especially Zimbabwe. Consequently their trade union movements are weak and ER institutions and practices incomplete.

Zimbabwe

Employment relations in Zimbabwe prior to its establishment in 1980 can be divided into two periods: the colonial era from 1890 to 1950 and the institutionalization of ER from the 1950s to 1980.

During the colonial period the key legislative measure for regulating Black African workers was the Masters and Servants Act of 1901 (Shadur 1994: 57). ER for White employees were regulated by the Industrial Conciliation Act of 1934 which recognized the rights of White employees to form trade unions and bargain collectively on industrial councils, but specifically excluded Black workers.

The institutionalization of ER involved an amendment to the Industrial Conciliation Act in 1959 that extended the definition of 'employee' to Black workers. This allowed Black worker representation on Industrial Councils and Industrial Boards, but 'the weighting of votes according to skill meant substantial influence by Whites in multi-racial unions which dampened Black workers' moves for major changes' (Shadur 1994: 59).

Zimbabwe was founded in 1980 after the overthrow of the White-dominated Rhodesia in which the Zimbabwe African National Union (ZANU) played the leading role. ZANU won the founding election and its leader, Robert Mugabe, became premier and later president of Zimbabwe. Although Mugabe called for reconciliation of all warring factions in his inaugural speech, his party soon demonstrated a complete disregard for it. Instead, it opted for brutal violence against its main opposition party (ZAPU) as divisions, suspicion, and mistrust developed between the cadres of their guerrilla armies. Within the first few weeks of the onslaught—known as Operation Gukurahundi—which commenced in January 1983, Mugabe's 5th Brigade soldiers 'had massacred thousands of civilians and tortured thousands more' (Eppel 2004: 45).

The Labour Relations Act of 1985 was the central labour legislation introduced by the post-independence government. It dealt with the regulation of conditions of employment, negotiation and collective bargaining, employment agencies, and trade unions. A controversial aspect of the Act related to strikes which were prohibited in a large proportion of the economy. The Act was amended in 1992 and then again in 2002 (Sachikonye 2007: 81).

At the time Zimbabwe came into existence the labour movement was weak and divided. It had played no significant role in the negotiation over transition to majority rule. In 1981 the state played a major role in establishing a central labour federation, the Zimbabwe Congress of Trade Unions (ZCTU), which it dominated up to the mid-1980s. In 1987–8 a leadership struggle emerged in the ZCTU. A substantially new leadership emerged and a new secretary-general, Morgan Tsvangirai, was appointed.

The strengthening of the trade union movement resulted in a switch from the situation in the 1980s when state-sanctioned minimum wages were the norm to one in the 1990s where collective bargaining and negotiation became the main instrument determining wages and other conditions of work (Sachikonye 2007: 81).

From the mid-1990s onwards a deepening economic crisis set in due to the politically expedient and rash policies of the Mugabe regime. Economic growth slowed down and from 1999 onwards the economy started shrinking. It shrank by about 30% between 2000 and 2004. At the same time the rate of inflation, already high, started accelerating exponentially. It went up from 18.9% p.a. in 1997 to 55.9% in 2000 and to 600% p.a. in 2003. (Sachinkonye 2007: 78, Table 7.1). The resulting collapse in the real income of workers led to an unprecedented wave of strikes. While there were only two strikes in 1994, there were 62 in 1996 including the largest strike in post-independence Zimbabwe yet by public service workers for economic and political reasons. In 1997 the number of strikes shot up to 232 (Sachikonye 2007: 82).

From this time on industrial relations became politicized. The state viewed the ZCTU as harbouring political ambitions. It banned strikes and stay-aways, and took punitive action against some of ZCTU's leaders. It also aided in the setting up of a rival trade union movement, the Zimbabwe Federation of Trade Unions (ZFTU), in 1998 (Sachinkonye 2007: 82–3).

The ZCTU decided it was time to form a broad political alliance. In February 1999 it stepped up its political campaign and facilitated a National Working People's Convention. It brought together people from urban, peri-urban, and rural areas, representing unions, women's organizations, professional associations, development organization, churches, human right groups, the informal sector, communal farmers, industry, the unemployed, and student organizations. The Convention gave the ZCTU a mandate to facilitate the formation of a political party. As a result, the Movement for Democratic Change (MDC) was launched on 11 September 1999 (Raftopoulos 2001: 14–16). It decided to compete in the general election of June 2000. In the election campaign 30 people, mostly MDC members, were killed. Notwithstanding the pre-election violence, the MDC performed remarkably well for a newly formed party. It won 57 seats against ZANU-PF's 62 (Raftopoulos 2001: 18, 21).

From 2000 to 2003 ruling party violence increased with the aim of crushing the MDC. The violence did have a harmful effect on MDC party structures, but did not destroy the movement. There were human rights violations including assaults, death threats, and interference with the right to campaign and vote freely.

The party, which had by then split into two 'formations', the Tsvangirai and the Mutambara formations, resolved to take part in the March 2008 election. The ZCTU decided shortly before the election that it would mobilize support for the MDC (Chagonda 2008: 2–3, 6–7). The outcome was that the MDC achieved an historic victory at the polls. The two MDC formations combined won 109 seats in the 210-seat parliament whereas ZANU-PF gained only 97 seats. In the presidential election the official outcome gave Tsvangirai 47.8% of the votes cast and Mugabe only 43.2%.

Because neither presidential candidate had won more than 50% of the vote, a run-off election for the president had to be held. Mugabe and his military supporters unleashed a violent and brutal assault on MDC and the ZCTU followers and leaders to the point that Tsvangirai had to withdraw from the race in order to try to secure the safety and security of his followers. Not surprisingly, Mugabe secured 86% of the votes cast in the June 2008 run-off.

Thereupon a long and difficult period of negotiation followed. In September 2008 a power-sharing agreement, the Global Political Agreement, was finally signed with Mugabe remaining president and Tsvangirai becoming prime minister. However, it has become clear that neither Mugabe nor ZANU-PF are committed to power-sharing and are still doing their best to undermine the MDC.

A Commission of Inquiry by the ILO on trade union rights in Zimbabwe reported in 2009 that it 'saw a clear pattern of arrests, detentions, violence and torture of trade union leaders and members by the security forces coinciding with Zimbabwe Congress of Trade Unions (ZCTU) nationwide events, indicating some contralized direction to the security forces to take such action' (ILO 2009: vii). In addition, the Commission found that, 'on occasion, armed police and the army fired upon and killed demonstrators' (ILO 2009: 74).

In such a repressive state and weak economy it is not possible for a trade union movement to function properly and to acquire the power it requires to operate effectively across the whole field of employment relations practices and institutions. ER in Zimbabwe can therefore not be regarded as sound.

Swaziland

Swaziland became independent from Britain in 1968 as a constitutional monarchy under King Sobhuzu II. The monarch had consolidated his support base amongst the Swazi populace through the royalist Imbokodvo National Movement (INM).

During the 1960s there had been a series of strikes spearheaded by the Ngwane National Liberatory Congress (NNLC). In the 1972 elections the opposition NNLC won three seats in the House of Assembly due to strong working-class support. As a reprisal the king issued a royal decree in April 1973 which suspended the Constitution and banned all political parties. He then took over the full legislative and executive capacity of the state.

As regards the regulation of basic working conditions and wages, the Swaziland regime passed Acts from time to time. These included the Wages Act of 1964, Factories Machinery and Construction Works Act of 1972, Employment Act of 1980, Workman's Compensation Act of 1983, and the Occupational Health and Safety Act of 1999. ER was governed by the Industrial Relations Act of 1996 which was amended in 2000.

In 1975 Swaziland became a member of the ILO and in 1978 the government ratified a swathe of ILO Conventions including No. 87—Freedom of Association and Protection of the Right to Organise, and No. 98—Right to Organise and Collective Bargaining (Dodds 1993).

There have been two trade union federations in Swaziland. The older one is the Swaziland Federation of Trade Unions (SFTU). The other, the Swaziland Federation of Labour (SFL), was set up as a rival in 1988. The SFTU is the dominant federation with a wide range of unions, 17 in all, and a claimed total membership of 83,000 in 2000. Although the unions are protected by law, it has not worked out like that in practice. This is because the state has been repressive, arresting and harassing union officials (Motala 2000: 87–8).

The People's United Democratic Movement (PUDEMO) emerged in 1983 with a central objective to 'build and popularise working class consciousness and rally social forces for change behind this revolutionary form of consciousness' (Ranchod 2007: 122). The SFTU was a major constituency of PUDEMO which also included youth groups, student organizations, and other civil society groupings.

In 1993 the SFTU lodged 27 demands with the regime. The demands included the unbanning of the political parties, freedom of the press, freedom of association, the right to strike and organize without state repression, the right to assemble, march, and demonstrate, the introduction of a reinstatement clause to empower the Industrial Court to order the reinstatement of unfairly dismissed workers, and other labour-related demands (Dlamini 1995: 86). Early in 1994 it launched a 'massive national strike' in support of the 27 demands.

The Prime Minister and Minister of Labour were forced to set up a tripartite forum to look at the 27 demands and make recommendations (Dlamini 1995: 87). The forum recommended that the government meet the demands, but the regime responded with only token reform. Consequently, in January 1996 more than 100,000 workers heeded a call by the SFTU to participate in a national strike that lasted nine days. The strikers demanded the unbanning of the political parties and the repeal of the Industrial Relations Act of 1995 which criminalized strike action and mass meetings called by union federations (Dlamini 1995: 67–8).

By the end of 1996 there were still outstanding demands, so in 1997 members of the SFTU once again embarked on a general strike. The Swazi state responded harshly to the strike. It obtained two court orders that ruled the strike illegal and deployed army units in the major towns. In spite of that the strike still went ahead (Dlamini and Levin 1997: 81–2).

South Africa's Tripartite Alliance supported the strike, but it was particularly COSATU that gave overt active support. At the beginning of March 1997 COSATU, joined by Mozambique's trade union federation, OTM, staged a one-day blockade of Swaziland (Dlamini and Levin 1997: 82).

The amendment to the Industrial Relations Act in 2000 extended the jurisdiction of the Industrial Court originally founded in 1980. It also established a new legal entity, the Conciliation, Mediation and Arbitration Commission (CMAC) to resolve disputes (Sweeney 2006: 21–2). In spite of that anti-union discrimination remained common, especially in the garment industry (Sweeney 2006: 31–2).

In 2002 the draconian Internal Security Act was reintroduced. It specified severe penalties for the participation in political activities in addition to restricting trade union activity. As a result the Swaziland trade union movement became more docile and timid on the political front.

In January 2006 a new Constitution became law in Swaziland. The Constitution offered nothing more than the status quo by protecting the monarchy and not allowing the space for other actors to define a democratic future for Swaziland. Hope for a full democracy was still strongly pinned on the trade union movement. When interviewed in November 2005, the president of PUDEMO said:

> I don't see another way of getting democracy without the vehicle of the trade union movement. The trade union movement is at the means of production, they sustain the economy, they are still organised and make the country tick, and I believe, no matter how few there may be, they are still the vehicle for change. (Ranchod 2007: 132)

Under these oppressive conditions trade unions have not been able to function properly. Effective ER practices have thus been severely compromised in Swaziland.

CONCLUSION

The findings for the eight Anglophone sub-Saharan African countries examined in this chapter seem to lend support to the hypothesis that comprehensive ER systems only manage to exist in countries with fully democratic regimes, for it was only the countries with democratic governments where strong trade union movements could emerge and contribute to comprehensive ER systems. There were only two countries with comprehensive ER institutions and practices as well as democratic regimes. They are Ghana and South Africa. The requirement that a democratic regime has to exist for a strong trade union movement to emerge is, however, only a necessary but not sufficient condition. Namibia, for instance, has been democratic for a long time, but does not have a strong trade union movement. Conversely, it was found that the countries with incomplete ER institutions and practices were all countries with weak trade unions and where the political regimes were not fully democratic.

The strength of the trade union movements and the nature of the political regime were not the only factors that influenced the comprehensiveness or otherwise of the countries' ER systems. There were also other influences. In the case of Zambia the shrinking of the economy after the collapse of the copper price, followed by the involuntary implementation of free market principles driven by the World Bank, undermined and weakened the trade union movement. Consequently, even though Zambia experienced a regime change to a party that was founded by the trade union movement in a free and fair election, the trade union movement was not able to grow strong economically and initiate comprehensive ER practices.

On the other hand the study also shows that the trade unions themselves are actors that respond in different ways to the forces ranged against them. Ghana, Nigeria, and Kenya are countries that experienced the imposition of authoritarian regimes straight or soon after the attainment of independence. Ghana experienced intermittent military rule for 26 years, Nigeria almost uninterrupted military rule for 33 years, and Kenya authoritarian rule for its 39 years of independence. In Ghana the trade union movement fought strenuously to retain its independence and to remain the legitimate representative of employees in the workplace. These struggles made the unions strong and independent. On the other hand the trade union movements in Nigeria and Kenya were persistently subordinated by authoritarian regimes and failed to grow strong. Consequently they did not have the ability to drive the implementation of comprehensive ER practices in their countries.

Finally, the regimes in two countries, Swaziland and Zimbabwe, became increasingly authoritarian and autocratic after attaining independence. The trade union movements in both countries took the lead in developing and founding countervailing political and civic movements. These acts brought harsh state repression down on them. Under these circumstances the union movements were not able to grow strong and enforce comprehensive ER practices.

In addition to trade unions and their relative strength, there are thus other forces that also come to bear in determining whether a country manages to initiate comprehensive ER or not. Some of these are under control of the state and are crucial for democracy to exist. Among them are political rights and civil liberties, freedom of the press and media, the rule of law and independence of the judiciary, freedom of association and the right to protest peacefully. Where these have been absent, as in Swaziland and Zimbabwe, the trade unions have neither been able to democratize the regimes nor to ensure comprehensive ER institutions and practices.

However, as democratization is slowly but steadily on the ascent in sub-Saharan Africa, it is reasonable to expect that a greater number of sound and comprehensive ER systems will emerge across the continent as well.

NOTE

1. Bratton et al. (2005) duplicated Diamond's Table 2, but included the Freedom House political rights and civil liberties scores for each country for 2001. Freedom House (2012) was then used to classify countries into Diamond's six categories based on the Freedom House scores allotted to each country with each category still retaining the same meaning.

REFERENCES

Adler, G. and Buhlungu, S. (1997). 'Labour and Liberalisation in Zambia', *South African Labour Bulletin*, 21(3): 48–50.

Adler, G. and Webster, E. (1995). 'Challenging Transition Theory: The Labour Movement, Radical Reform, and Transition to Democracy in South Africa', *Politics & Society* 23(1): 75–106.

Akwetey, E. and Dorkenoo, D. (2010). 'Disengagement from Party Politics: Achievements and Challenges for the Ghana Trades Union Congress', in B. Beckman, S. Buhlungu, and L. Sachikonye (eds.), *Trade Unions and Party Politics: Labour Movements in Africa*. Cape Town: HSRC Press, 39–58.

Bauer, G. (1997). 'Labour Relations in Occupied Namibia', in G. Klerck, A. Murray, and M. Sycholt (eds.), *Continuity and Change: Labour Relations in Independent Namibia*. Windhoek: Gamsberg Macmillan, 55–78.

—— (1998). *Labor and Democracy in Namibia, 1971–1996*. Athens, OH: Ohio University Press.

Beckman, B. and Lukman, S. (2010). 'The Failure of Nigeria's Labour Party', in B. Beckman, S. Buhlungy, and L. Sachikonye (eds.), *Trade Unions and Party Politics: Labour Movements in Africa*. Cape Town: HSRC Press, 59–84.

Bloomberg.com (2011). <http://www.bloomberg.com/news/2011-09-23>, accessed 14 Apr 2012.

Bratton, M. (2009). 'Sub-Saharan Africa', in C. Haerpfer, P. Bernhagen, R. Inglehart, and C. Welzel (eds.), *Democratization*. Oxford and New York: Oxford University Press, 339–55.

Bratton, M., Mattes, R., and Gyimah-Boadi, E. (eds.) (2005). *Public Opinion, Democracy and Market Reform in Africa*. Cambridge: Cambridge University Press.

Catholic Commission for Justice and Peace in Zimbabwe (2007). *Gukurahundi in Zimbabwe: A Report on the Disturbances in Matabeleland and The Midlands 1980–1988*. Auckland Park: Jacana.

CCMA (2012). Commission for Conciliation, Mediation and Arbitration website: <http://www.ccma.org.za/Display.asp?L1=36&L2=21&L3=54>, accessed 25 June 2012.

Chagonda, T. (2008). 'Starving Billionaires: The Case of Zimbabwe's Working Class and the 2008 Elections', paper presented at the South African Sociological Association (SASA) Conference, Stellenbosch.

Croucher, R. (2007). 'Organising the Informal Economy: Results and Prospects—The Case of Ghana in Comparative Perspective', in G. Wood and C. Brewster (eds.), *Industrial Relations in Africa*. Basingstoke: Palgrave Macmillan, 209–18.

de Villiers, D. and Anstey, M. (2000). 'Trade Unions in Transitions to Democracy in South Africa, Spain and Brazil', in G. Adler and E. Webster (eds.), *Trade Unions and Democratization in South Africa, 1985–1997*. Basingstoke: Macmillan, 20–41.

Diamond, L. (2002). 'Elections without Democracy: Thinking about Hybrid Regimes', *Journal of Democracy*, 13(2): 21–35.

Dibben, P. and Williams, C. (2012). 'Varieties of Capitalism and Employment Relations: Informally Dominated Market Economies', *Industrial Relations*, 51(Suppl.): 563–82.

DiMaggio, P. and Powell, W. (1983). 'The Iron Cage Revisited: Institutional Isomorphism and Collective Rationality in Organizational Fields', *American Sociological Review*, 48(2): 147–60.

Dlamini, K. (1995). 'The Old Order is Dying: Worker Militancy in Swaziland, *South African Labour Bulletin*, 19(1): 85–90.

Dlamini, K. and Levin, R. (1997). 'Breaking Tradition: The Struggle for Freedom in Swaziland', *South African Labour Bulletin*, 21(2): 81–6.

Dodds, P. (1993). 'Swaziland's Experience: ILO Conventions and the Revision of Labour Legislation', in E. Kalula (ed.), *Labour Relations in Southern Africa*. Braamfontein: Friedrich Ebert Stiftung, 170–81.

DPRU (2010). 'Addressing the Plight of Vulnerable Workers: The Role of Sectoral Determinations'. Report prepared for the Department of Labour. Development Policy Research Unit, School of Economics, University of Cape Town. Available at <http://www.labour. gov.za/DOL/downloads/documents/useful-documents/basic-conditions-of-employment/ The%20role%20of%20Sectoral%20Determinations.pdf>. Accessed 31 October 2013.

du Toit, D., Bosch, D., Woolfrey, D., Godfrey, S., Rossouw, J., Christie, S., Cooper, C., Giles, G. and Bosch, C. (2003). *Labour Relations Law: A Comprehensive Guide*, 4th edn. Durban: Lexis Nexis Butterworths.

Eppel, S. (2004). '"Gukurahundi": The Need for Truth and Reconciliation', in B. Raftopoulos and T. Savage (eds.), *Zimbabwe: Injustice and Political Reconciliation*. Rondebosch: Institute for Justice and Reconciliation, 43–62.

Fajana, S. (2007). 'The Development of Industrial Relations in Nigeria: 1900–2006', in G. Wood and C. Brewster (eds.), *Industrial Relations in Africa*. Basingstoke: Palgrave Macmillan, 147–61.

Fashoyin, T. (2007). 'Industrial Relations and the Social Partners in Kenya', in G. Wood and C. Brewster (eds.), *Industrial Relations in Africa*. Basingstoke: Palgrave Macmillan, 39–52.

—— (2008). 'Employment Relations in Zambia', *Employee Relations*, 30(4): 391–403.

Fitzpatrick, M., Bewer, T., and Firestone, M. (2009). *East Africa*. Footscray: Lonely Planet.

Frazer, G. (2007). 'Industrial Relations in Ghana', in G. Wood and C. Brewster (eds.), *Industrial Relations in Africa*. Basingstoke: Palgrave Macmillan, 182–97.

Freedom House (2012). *Freedom in the World 2012: The Arab Uprisings and Their Global Repercussions*. Available at <http://www.freedomhouse.org>.

Friedman, S. (1987). *Building Tomorrow Today: African Workers in Trade Unions 1970–1984*. Johannesburg: Ravan Press.

Godfrey, S. (1992). *Industrial Council Digest: Statutory Institutions for Collective Bargaining in South Africa, 1979–1992*. Cape Town: Industrial Relations Project, Department of Sociology, University of Cape Town.

Godfrey, S., Maree, J., du Toit, D., and Theron, J. (2010). *Collective Bargaining in South Africa: Past, Present and Future?* Cape Town: Juta & Co.

Gona, G. (2009). 'The State of the Labour Movement in Kenya and its Effect on the Consolidation of Democracy', in R. Ajulu (ed.), *Two Countries One Dream: The Challenges of Democratic Consolidation in Kenya and South Africa*. Rosebank, Johannesburg: KMM Review Publishing, 133–56.

Gostner, K. (1997). 'Playing Politics: Labour's Political Role in Zambia', *South African Labour Bulletin*, 21(3): 55–60.

Gostner, K. and Joffe, A. (2000). 'Negotiating the Future: Labour's Role in NEDLAC', G. Adler (ed.), *Engaging the State and Business: The Labour Movement and Co-Determination in Contemporary South Africa*. Johannesburg: Witwatersrand University Press, 75–100.

Guardian (2011). 'Has Zambia's "King Cobra" delivered on his 90-day promise?' Available at <http://www.guardian.co.uk/world/2011/dec/21/michael-sata-king-cobra-90-days-zambia>. Accessed 14 April 2012.

Hagglund, G. (2007). 'The Development of Industrial Relations in Kenya', in G. Wood and C. Brewster (eds.), *Industrial Relations in Africa*. Basingstoke: Palgrave Macmillan, 28–38.

Hall, P. A. and Soskice, D. (eds.) (2001). *Varieties of Capitalism: The Institutional Foundations of Comparative Advantage*. Oxford and New York: Oxford University Press.

International Labour Organization (ILO) (2002). *Decent Work and the Informal Economy*. Geneva: ILO.

—— (2009). *Truth, Reconciliation and Justice in Zimbabwe*. Report of the Commission of Inquiry appointed under Art. 28 of the Constitution of the ILO to examine the observance by the Government of Zimbabwe of the Freedom of Association and Protection of the Right to Organise Convention, 1948 (No. 87), and the Right to Organise and Collective Bargaining Convention, 1949 (No. 98). Geneva: ILO.

Jauch, H. (2007). 'Between Politics and the Shop Floor: Which Way for Namibia's Labour Movement?' in H. Melber (ed.), *Transition in Namibia: Which Changes for Whom?* Uppsala: Nordiska Afrikainstitutet, 50–64.

—— (2010). 'Serving Workers or Serving the Party? Trade Unions and Politics in Namibia', in G. Wood and C. Brewster (eds.), *Industrial Relations in Africa*. Basingstoke: Palgrave Macmillan, 167–90.

Kingdon, G. and Knight, J. (2003). 'Unemployment in South Africa: The Nature of the Beast', *World Development*, 32(3): 391–408.

Klerck, G. (2007). 'Labour Regulation in Namibia: From "Colonial Despotism" to "Flexible Taylorism"', in G. Wood and C. Brewster (eds.), *Industrial Relations in Africa*. Basingstoke: Palgrave Macmillan, 98–110.

Klerck, G. and Murray, A. (1997). 'Collective Bargaining: The Joint Regulation of Terms and Conditions of Employment', in G. Klerck, A. Murray, and M. Sycholt (eds.), *Continuity and Change: Labour Relations in Independent Namibia*. Windhoek: Gamsberg Macmillan, 159–99.

Klerck, G., Murray, A., and Sycholt, M (1998). 'Social Partnership? Labour Relations in Namibia', *South African Labour Bulletin*, 22(3): 84–90.

Kraus, J. (2007). 'Trade Unions, Democratization, and Economic Crises in Ghana', in J. Kraus (ed.), *Trade Unions and the Coming of Democracy in Africa*. Basingstoke: Palgrave Macmillan, 83–122.

Linz, J. (1990). 'Transitions to Democracy', *The Washington Quarterly*, 13(3): 143–64.

Linz, J. and Stepan, A. (1996). *Problems of Democratic Transition and Consolidation: Southern Europe, South America, and Post-Communist Europe*. Baltimore: Johns Hopkins University Press.

Mail & Guardian (2011). 'Cosatu meeting to focus on alliance summit', 18 February.

Meredith, M. (2002). *Robert Mugabe: Power, Plunder and Tyranny in Zimbabwe*. Jeppestown: Jonathan Ball.

Moorcroft, P. (2012). *Mugabe's War Machine*. Jeppestown: Jonathan Ball.

Motala, M. (2000). 'Trade Unions in Swaziland', *South African Labour Bulletin*, 24(2): 85–90.

Nakanyane, S. (2000). 'Trade Unions in Namibia', *South African Labour Bulletin*, 24(1): 84–9.

North, D. (1990). *Institutions, Institutional Change and Economic Performance*. Cambridge: Cambridge University Press.

Otobe, D. (2007). 'Contemporary Industrial Relations in Nigeria', in G. Wood and C. Brewster (eds.), *Industrial Relations in Africa*. Basingstoke: Palgrave Macmillan, 162–81.

Raftopoulos, B. (2001). 'The Labour Movement and the Emergence of Opposition Politics in Zimbabwe', in B. Raftopoulos and L. Sachikonye (eds.), *Striking Back: The Labour Movement and the Post-Colonial State in Zimbabwe 1980–2000*. Avondale: Weaver Press, 1–24.

Raftopoulos, B. and Savage, T. (2004). *Zimbabwe: Injustice and Political Reconciliation*. Cape Town: Institute for Justice and Reconciliation.

Ranchod, R. (2007). 'Between Consolidation, Promotion and Restoration: Trade Unions and Democracy in South Africa, Namibia, Zimbabwe and Swaziland', M.Phil. dissertation, University of Cape Town.

Rose, R. (2009). 'Democratic and Undemocratic States', in C. Haerpfer, P. Bernhagen, R. Inglehart, and C. Welzel (eds.), *Democratization*. Oxford and New York: Oxford University Press, 10–23.

Sachikonye, L. (2007). 'Industrial Relations in Conditions of Economic Stress: The Zimbabwe Case', in G. Wood and C. Brewster (eds.), *Industrial Relations in Africa*. Basingstoke: Palgrave Macmillan, 77–86.

—— (2011). *When a State Turns on its Citizens: 60 Years of Violence in Zimbabwe*. Auckland Park: Jacana.

Shadur, M. (1994). *Labour Relations in a Developing Country: A Case Study on Zimbabwe*. Aldershot: Avebury.

Solidarity Center (2006). 'The Struggle for Workers' Rights in Swaziland: A Report by the Solidarity Center'. Washington DC: Solidarity Center.

Sweeney, J. (2006). *Justice for All: The Struggle for Worker Rights in Swaziland*. A Report by the Solidarity Center. Washington DC: Solidarity Center. Available at: http://www.solidaritycenter.org/files/SwazilandFinal.pdf. Accessed 27 Oct. 2013.

Tshoaedi, M. (2000). 'Trade Unions in Zambia', *South African Labour Bulletin*, 24(3): 86–90.

van der Horst, S. (1971 [1942]). *Native Labour in South Africa*. London: Frank Cass.

Webster, E. (1995). NEDLAC—Corporatism of a Special Type?', *South African Labour Bulletin*, 19(2): 25–9.

Whitley, R. (1999). *Divergent Capitalisms: The Social Structuring and Change of Business Systems*. Oxford and New York: Oxford University Press.

Wikipedia (2010). 'Politics of Zambia', accessed 21 February 2010.

Wilkinson, A. and Wood, G. (2012). 'Institutions and Employment Relations: The State of the Art', *Industrial Relations*, 51(S1): 373–88.

Wood, G. and Frynas, J. (2006). 'The Institutional Basis of Economic Failure: Anatomy of the Segmented Business System', *Socio-Economic Review*, 4(2): 239–77.

CHAPTER 18

THE LEFT TURN IN LATIN AMERICA

Consequences for Employment Relations

JOSE ALEMAN

INTRODUCTION

SINCE 1999, left governments have taken power in ten Latin American countries: Venezuela, Chile, Brazil, Argentina, Uruguay, Bolivia, Nicaragua, Ecuador, Paraguay, and El Salvador. By 2009, they governed more than two-thirds of the continent's inhabitants, a state of affairs never before witnessed in the continent's history (Levitsky and Roberts 2011a: 2). This 'left turn' (Castañeda 2006) has sparked considerable interest among scholars, particularly in regards to the effect of these governments on democratic governance and policy-making (Barrett et al. 2008; Cameron and Hershberg 2010; Levitsky and Roberts 2011c; Weyland et al. 2010).

This chapter investigates what effects, if any, progressive governments have had on employment relations in Latin America. Employment relations are sets of rules, policies, and practices that structure interactions among employers (whether private or public) and employees. Of interest to many is how progressive governments have addressed the poverty, unemployment, and abuse that labourers routinely experience in Latin America. When it comes to protecting workers against poverty and unemployment, the canonical literature on employment relations is quite clear in its recommendations. Scholars favour systems of protection that pool risks throughout the economy. This is typically accomplished by universal, taxpayer-funded systems of unemployment, pensions, and sickness benefits. Another way to provide some protection to workers is through employment regulation—also referred to as employment protection legislation (EPL). EPL consists of rules concerning hiring and firing. Taking into account changes in the partisan composition of governments in the region, the chapter examines how left governments have affected the provision of security and protection for the most vulnerable in these countries.

Due to its position in the world economy, its factor endowments, and its history, Latin America developed a model of employment relations known as the hierarchical market economy (HME) (Schneider 2009; Schneider and Soskice 2009). This model is characterized, among other factors, by labour markets with large numbers of informal, low-skilled workers, job tenures with some of the shortest durations in the world, economies with a few but highly diversified business groups, and atomistic labour relations. As Schneider (2009: 557) writes, under HMEs

> employees lack formal grievance procedures and representation and informally lack voice, because most of them are quite temporary. Unions have little influence on hierarchies within the firm, in part because so few workers are unionized, and in part because where unions do exist they are often distant from the shop floor. Finally, industrial relations are further structured by top-down regulations issued by national governments.

Of particular interest then is to what extent Latin America's progressive governments operate within the confines of this model. It is also important to ask to what extent the policies of incumbent leftists differ from those of previous left-leaning governments. Although employment policies have not attracted as much attention as reforms in other areas, rules and policies governing employment can achieve important macroeconomic goals such as income redistribution and employment stability. Therefore, employment relations systems provide an ideal setting to examine changes in economic policy-making resulting from the turn to the left in the region.

This chapter demonstrates that employment relations have significantly changed in Latin America since the progressive turn. Nevertheless, it is important not to exaggerate the extent of these changes. Progressive reforms are to be expected given the ideological leanings of these governments and the perceived need to address some of the continent's long-standing problems, but they do not primarily result from diffusion of a model of employment relations unique to these governments. Indeed, in countries such as Chile where a centre-left coalition governed before the election of President Lagos, the turn to a socialist government has only brought continuity with previous policies. What has changed to some extent is the environment in which progressive governments have come to power and attempted to pursue their respective agendas.

To argue that the nature of these governments is more important than their coming to power simultaneously is not to deny the role they have played in enacting reforms. After all, different governments would probably have maintained existing policies or made employment relations more flexible (Murillo et al. 2011b). Nevertheless, policies enacted in several countries in the last decade can be seen as an extension of changes introduced in the previous decade. This chapter discusses reforms in the region since the inauguration of Hugo Chávez as Venezuela's president on 2 February 1999, and situates these reforms in the context of previous ones and more enduring aspects of the political economy of employment relations in the region. The discussion highlights simultaneously what is unique about these countries in the last decade or so, and what can more properly be seen as a continuation with the past and the policies of other countries. The chapter proceeds as follows.

The first section reviews Latin America's left turn, that is, cataloguing which governments have come to power in which countries, and what makes this historical period unique in light of policy and other trends affecting the region. I am particularly interested in features of Latin American economies and labour markets that have conditioned the nature and scope of these reforms. The following section looks in more detail at different aspects of these reforms. Of particular interest is within-country variation in reforms before and after the left turn, and differences between progressive and non-progressive governments in their approach to employment relations. The chapter concludes with a brief discussion of continuity and change in Latin America in light of changes to employment relations around the world.

THE LEFT TURN IN LATIN AMERICA

The election and inauguration of Hugo Chávez Frías as president in Venezuela is typically seen as marking the beginning of the left turn in Latin America.

> Chávez was followed in quick succession by Socialist candidate Ricardo Lagos in Chile (2000); ex-metalworker and Worker's Party (PT) leader Luiz Inácio Lula da Silva in Brazil (2002); left-of-centre Peronist Néstor Kirchner in Argentina (2003); Tabaré Vázquez of the leftist Broad Front (FA) in Uruguay (2004); and coca grower's union leader Evo Morales of the Movement toward Socialism in Bolivia (2005)...In 2006, ex-revolutionary leader Daniel Ortega and the Sandinista National Liberation Front (FSLN) returned to power in Nicaragua, while independent left-wing economist Rafael Correa won the Ecuadorian presidency. By decade's end, leftist candidates had also scored improbable victories in Paraguay (ex-Catholic bishop Fernando Lugo) and El Salvador...Incumbent leftist presidents or parties were subsequently re-elected in Venezuela (2000, 2006), Chile (2006), Brazil (2006, 2010), Argentina (2007), Ecuador (2009), Bolivia (2009), and Uruguay (2009). (Levitsky and Roberts 2011a: 2)

To the list one also has to add Cristina Fernández de Kirchner's re-election to a second term in 2011 in Argentina. In inaugurating Sebastián Piñera as president on 11 March 2010, however, Chile became the first protagonist of the wave to return a conservative politician and party to power. What sorts of policies and labour market conditions did these politicians inherit upon taking up the reins of power?

The conventional wisdom is that Latin America is, comparatively speaking, generous in its provision of both employment and social insurance considering the presence in this region of many less developed countries (LDCs). There appears to be some truth to these claims, as Botero et al.'s (2004) comprehensive study reveals. The project, the first global study of labour market regulation, includes two indexes that can be used to compare Latin America to the rest of the world for 1997, the year in which the study is based. Specifically, I compare the mean score for thirteen Latin American countries[1] with a global mean for eighty-five countries on two indexes—the employment laws index and the social security laws index.[2] For the employment laws index, the question is to what extent the regulation of the individual employment contract—including advance notice requirements and severance payments due when terminating a redundant worker—makes firms more likely to hire and keep workers. For the social security laws index, the question is to what extent the government requires employers to make contributions to unemployment, sickness, disability, and pension benefits, redistributing money from currently employed workers and employers to those without a job.

Whereas the mean employment laws index is lower for Latin America than the world (0.451 versus 0.488), this is not the case with the social security laws index (0.578 versus 0.569). One caveat is that these measures, which are based on formal legislation, do not take into account the poor or non-existent enforcement of labour regulations in Latin America.[3] The contrast between the government's avowed goals as reflected in labour legislation and actual protection as manifested in legal enforcement, is in part why widespread informality characterizes employment relations in the region (Schneider and Karcher 2010: 624; Schneider and Soskice 2009: 42). Due to the high cost of protective regulations, firms ignore their obligations, leaving many workers without a permanent contract and benefits.[4]

It is also noteworthy that at least on paper, governments in the region have made commitments to worker representation that rank as favourably as those made by governments of other nations. The collective relations laws index, for example, was slightly higher for Latin America than the world in 1997 (0.466 versus 0.445).[5] In her comparison of labour standards in four developing regions in 2006, however, Stallings (2010: 136) found that the difference between *de jure* and *de facto* labour standards is highest in Latin America and the Middle East. *De jure* labour standards are commitments governments have made to workers in the areas of freedom of association, the right to bargain collectively, and the right to strike. *De facto* standards take into account violations of these rules.

I do not disaggregate the data any further (i.e. geographically) because it is difficult to find additional patterns using aggregated indices of regulation. When regulation more accurately reflects the cost employers must bear for adjusting employment levels, however, the employment relationship in Latin America emerges as being considerably more regulated, particularly in regards to industrial countries (Heckman and Pagés-Serra 2000).[6] A comparison, moreover, of Latin America in recent decades to developed countries (DCs) when these countries were at a similar stage in their development—the mid-twentieth century—reveals profound differences. DCs in the early post-war period were characterized by higher levels of union density and lower levels of informality than Latin America in the last decade (Schneider and Karcher 2010: 626–7). Current indices of regulation are also higher for Latin America than other developing regions (Stallings 2010: 136).

If this generosity seems puzzling, it is because it is the legacy of the strongly protectionist development policies centred on import substitution industrialization (ISI) that countries in the region pursued. As Wibbels and Ahlquist (2011) explain, social insurance benefits were a crucial ingredient in the creation of privileged, urban workforces that could consume the goods produced by domestically oriented industries. It is important to emphasize, however, that in LDCs these policies have typically benefited only a small number of workers in the formal sector and data from Botero et al. (2004), as previously mentioned, cannot provide a sense of how many are covered by formal legislation or how strictly rules are enforced. This problem is germane to any attempt to evaluate employment relations using *de jure* rules and regulations unless a *de facto* measure is also computed (e.g. Stallings 2010).[7]

The study by Botero et al. (2004) provides a snapshot of employment relations two years before the onset of the left turn. Beginning with Ecuador's democratic transition in 1979, several countries transited to democracy in the region; at the same time globalization gave politicians the cover to carry out profound economic reforms.[8] Both trends led to a number of changes in employment relations. Governments generally made collective labour laws—which regulate organizing activity, collective bargaining, and strikes—friendlier to the interests of workers, whereas they tended to deregulate individual employment contracts and their associated costs (Murillo 2005: 443).[9] According to Murillo, new democratic regimes, in particular those led by left-wing parties, responded to economic pressures that called for reductions in labour costs, while taking care to provide rewards to their electoral constituency. Murillo (2005) only considered reforms to labour codes that required parliamentary approval, neglecting changes that brought about more flexibility in employment relations enacted by presidential decree (Cook 2007: 55). Most democratic governments in the region, however, did not reform their employment practices to any significant degree (Cook 1998). Overall then, democratization resulted in some changes to employment relations, but not to the extent experienced in other areas of policy-making (Schneider and Karcher 2010: 629). Edwards and Lustig (1997: 2) went so far as to claim that '[i]t is no exaggeration to say that the labor market has been forgotten in Latin America's economic reform'.

Politicians' reluctance to deregulate employment relations to any significant degree is easy to explain in light of the structural constraints they inherited. The countries' HMEs have evolved over many decades and their limitations cannot be easily overcome. This gives democratic politicians no reason to tinker extensively with rules and regulations that provide certain benefits, at least to firms and a core group of workers. Nevertheless, market reforms are widely perceived as having failed to generate economic growth, reduce market inequalities, and create employment opportunities in the region (IBRD 2004: xi).

Progressive governments in recent years have then faced pressures to increase growth, reduce insecurity, and expand opportunities, albeit within the constraints set by the informality, lack of education, high turnover, and atomization that define employment relations in the region (Schneider and Karcher 2010). These conditions, moreover, are more constitutive of employment relations in Latin America than traits that define other models of employment relations such as those present in liberal market economies (LMEs) and coordinated market economies (CMEs) (Schneider 2009: 557; Schneider and Karcher 2010: 627).[10] The pervasiveness of HMEs, however, does not preclude differences between countries that turned left recently and those that did not. It is important then to determine to what extent employment relations differ between participants in the left wave and non-participants. To do so, I take advantage of the World Bank's *Doing Business Project*, a compendium of indicators of employment regulation and their associated costs for 183 countries that builds on Botero et al.'s (2004) study.[11]

The indicators made available measure flexibility (or rigidity) in the regulation of employment, specifically in hiring and firing of workers and working hours. They also provide information on money that firms have to set aside to cover social insurance charges and contributions (non-wage labour costs), and the cost of advance notice requirements, severance payments and penalties due when terminating a redundant worker (firing costs), expressed in weekly wages. Their advantage is that they provide the only measures of regulations and their associated costs that are comparable across time and space. Since the methodology used to calculate these measures has changed over time and data for non-wage labour costs are only available for three years (2006–8), I will only compare the overall measure of employment rigidity, the 'rigidity of employment index', in countries governed by left governments and those that are not. The rigidity of employment index is the average of three sub-indices: the difficulty of hiring index, the rigidity of hours index, and the difficulty of firing index.[12]

By construction, all the employment security variables are given on a 0–100 scale, with higher values indicating more rigid regulation. One drawback of the analysis is that data are only available from 2004 to 2010, missing several years of rule by left governments in some countries.[13] Nevertheless, there are enough observations to attempt to outline some significant patterns.[14] A one-way ANOVA indicates that the mean employment regulation score is similar in country-years under a left government as in country-years under other kinds of government (45.85 versus 40.07), but the difference is statistically significant. It would be interesting if this comparison could be extended back in time as well, especially in light of Latin America's higher than expected levels of employment regulation (IBRD 2004: 86).

I next conduct an exploratory factor analysis of five different indicators of employment regulation and their associated costs: the three sub-indices of employment regulation introduced above—the difficulty of hiring index, the rigidity of hours index, and the difficulty of firing index—and the indicators of non-wage and firing costs. Factor analysis is a statistical technique that looks for dimensionality in data, that is, it reduces multiple indicators of what is thought to be a latent variable to a smaller number of dimensions or factors that can be more easily interpreted conceptually. One can, for example, examine the loading of variables on factors, their sign, the variance that is not shared with other variables (a variable's uniqueness), and to what extent a correlation exists among the factors. In so doing, the analysis provides some idea of how much a particular factor matters, how important individual variables are to a factor, and how these dimensions relate to one another.[15]

Table 18.1 Employment regulation and non-wage labour costs in countries ruled by left governments

Variable	Factor 1	Factor 2	Uniqueness
Rigidity of hiring	0.511	0.492	0.407
Rigidity of hours index	0.476	−0.032	0.594
Rigidity of firing	−0.184	0.698	0.544
Non-wage labour costs	0.803	−0.072	0.335
Firing costs	0.057	0.480	0.660

Note: Columns represent rotated factors. Oblique method used, which allows factors to correlate with one another. High loadings, indicative of belonging to a factor, are highlighted. Positive signs indicate more rigidity/higher costs, negative signs the opposite. Uniqueness is the variability of a variable minus its communality, that is, it is an indicator of how relevant the variable is to the factor model (the more unique, the less relevant).

Table 18.1 presents the rotated factor matrix for twenty-one observations corresponding to left governments. Three factors were extracted from these observations, but since the first two account for most of the cumulative variance in the data, the third factor was dropped from the rotated factor matrix. Because the rigidity of hiring index loads highly on *Factor 1*, the first factor can be construed as identifying a latent dimension of hiring rigidity. The difficulty of hiring index, it should be pointed out, measures the existence and cost of alternatives to the standard employment contract. Its three sub-indices indicate (i) whether fixed-term contracts can be used only for temporary tasks; (ii) the maximum cumulative duration of fixed-term contracts; and (iii) the ratio of the minimum wage for a trainee or first-time employee to the average value added per worker. This factor alone explains nearly 82% of the variance in the data. Since the variables 'rigidity of firing' and 'firing costs' load highly on *Factor 2*, the second factor can be construed as a latent dimension related to firing rigidity.

The most revealing piece of information in this analysis comes from the high loading of 'non-wage labour costs' on the first factor. This indicates that in countries governed by left governments, employers cannot easily cut costs by avoiding the standard employment contract, while being required to contribute to social security benefits for their workers. *Factor 2* indicates that left governments also make it difficult and costly for employers to fire workers. The results reveal then that left governments strive to reduce precarious employment, while decommodifying to some extent the employment relationship for workers.

The contrast between left and non-left governments becomes more evident when we examine the rotated factor matrix for country-years under non-left governments in Table 18.2. Since no particular pattern emerges from this analysis, it is evident that there is something distinctive to the left turn in terms of employment relations. Perhaps not surprisingly, left governments in Latin America have tried to reduce precarious

Table 18.2 Employment regulation and non-wage labour costs in countries ruled by non-left governments

Variable	Factor 1	Factor 2	Uniqueness
Rigidity of hiring	0.381	0.159	0.809
Rigidity of hours index	0.665	0.017	0.554
Rigidity of firing	0.464	−0.022	0.788
Non-wage labour costs	0.324	0.308	0.767
Firing costs	0.282	−0.268	0.874

Note: Columns represent rotated factors. Oblique method used, which allows factors to correlate with one another. High loadings, indicative of belonging to a factor, are highlighted. Positive signs indicate more rigidity/higher costs, negative signs the opposite. Uniqueness is the variability of a variable minus its communality, that is, it is an indicator of how relevant the variable is to the factor model (the more unique, the less relevant).

employment, while providing workers some insurance should they become unable to work.

DCs rely more on unemployment insurance (UI) than on EPL, both because UI requires more economic resources to enact and political capital to implement, and because it is more redistributive while distorting the economy less. By pooling risks within the firm as opposed to society, EPL increases labour costs and undercuts redistribution (Murillo et al. 2011b: 809). Due to their low levels of development, however, LDCs may have to fall back more on employment regulation. The expectation is then that as countries develop, they relax employment regulation in favour of more generous social security benefits. If leftist governments in Latin America were moving in this direction, we would expect our analysis to delineate a dimension for non-wage labour costs separate from that of hiring rigidity, albeit possibly correlated to it. But Latin America may be an outlier in this sense since the region is home to countries like Argentina and Brazil with rigid employment regulations that also require businesses to pay high social security taxes (IBRD 2006: 24).

Having situated the left turn both historically and structurally, we can now examine in some detail which countries have made changes to their employment relations and what reforms left governments have enacted.

EMPLOYMENT RELATIONS AFTER THE LEFT TURN

Students of employment relations in Latin America have observed that the economic reforms of the 1980s and 1990s had deleterious effects on workers and their labour market status: the number of workers in the informal sector increased, labour organizations weakened, and the public sector shrank as a result of extensive privatizations (Cook 2007: 15–33). Incumbent governments could not claim that their reforms 'were having a positive impact on formal-sector employment creation' (Cook 2007: 36). How then did progressive governments address these challenges?

Murillo et al. (2011b: 795) claim that from 2000 to 2010, there were fourteen reforms to EPL in Latin America, of which eight reduced employment flexibility and the rest increased it.[16] They define progressive reforms as the extent to which the regulation of the individual employment contract—and severance payments in particular—makes it more difficult for employers to hire and fire workers (Murillo et al. 2011b: 792). This contrasts with the 1985–99 period, when ten countries reduced employment flexibility, while twelve increased it.

Murillo et al. (2011b) also measure reforms in what they term 'personal compensation', which refers to costs employers have to bear both in terms of increased severance payments and/or expanded unemployment insurance when firing workers. These non-wage labour costs, as we have seen, are determined by employment regulations but are sometimes measured separately in studies of employment relations. The logic of considering these costs separately is that both programmes 'provide employed workers compensation for the risk of job loss, and in so doing affect their propensity to invest in skills that may affect the productivity of their firms' (Murillo et al. 2011b: 792). Comparing the left wave with the period immediately preceding it in terms of these costs, eleven countries experienced reductions and twelve increases from 1985 to 1999, while six experienced reductions and eight increases in 2000–9. At least in the areas of EPL and personal compensation then, the balance of reforms appears to be in favour of progressive governments.

Government partisanship is a very strong predictor of the type of reforms carried out, that is, left governments favoured progressive reforms in this period (particularly after 1999), whereas their conservative counterparts favoured labour maker deregulation (Murillo et al. 2011b: 802). When it comes to EPL, for example, government partisanship 'all but perfectly predicts the direction of reform in the post-1999 period'—more specifically, the progressive reforms of Néstor Kirchner in Argentina, Morales in Bolivia,[17] Lagos in Chile, and Correa in Ecuador. According to these scholars, partisanship also provides a perfect prediction of shifts in personal security in the post-1999 period. Both results corroborate my previous finding that left governments tend to couple rigidity in hiring and firing with more generosity in social insurance.

Turning now to reforms in unemployment insurance, it is true that no countries experienced reductions since 1985. But four countries enacted progressive reforms in 1985–99, whereas only two—Chile and Colombia—did in 2000–9, and Colombia did not take part in the left wave. It is hard to argue then that the left turn has resulted in societies that more consistently pool the risks of income loss and unemployment. As a number of students of UI programmes have argued, only seven countries offer unemployment compensation, and those that do provide meagre benefits for a short duration to a small percentage of the unemployed population (Murillo et al. 2011b: 796). The lack of more comprehensive systems of UI is at once a reflection and a cause of the segmentation and informality that exists in the region (Schneider and Soskice 2009; Schneider and Karcher 2010). It serves as a reminder of how difficult it remains, even for left governments, to break out of the confines of the HME.

It is in the area of UI then where left governments have not lived up to expectations. Students of social policy have argued that societies cannot ignore the pressures to reduce labour costs and increase economic competitiveness that globalization creates. As they do so, however, they also need to provide their workforces with the tools to survive and thrive in an increasingly interdependent world. A particularly successful formula in this regard is the provision of external flexibility and personal security that Denmark pioneered. This model is referred to as 'flexicurity', a combination of flexibility and security (Wilthagen and Tros 2004: 170). Where flexicurity operates, unions exchange strict EPL for more commitment on the part of employers and the government to fund social security benefits. Murillo et al. (2011b: 798) observe that these compromises are absent in Latin America even after 1999, as not a single country has increased the generosity of UI in exchange for reductions in severance payments.

Overall then, progressive governments have significantly affected employment relations in Latin America, but their impact remains limited and, as we have seen, it cannot be said that they clearly delineate a before- and an after-1999 era in employment relations. As Murillo et al. (2011: 793) note, 'cross-country variation in labor market reform is greater within than between time periods', an observation that sheds more light on the environment in which these governments came to power than the distinctiveness of the policy paradigm left governments have instituted. A post-2002 commodities boom (Schneider 2010: 209; Levitsky and Roberts 2011b: 423), improvement in the region's terms of trade, and the corresponding growth of policy autonomy can go some way towards accounting for the successes of progressive governments (Murillo et al. 2011a). It is also important to note that the reforms just reviewed were enacted with parliamentary approval. When less visible changes are considered, it is obvious that left governments may not consistently affect employment relations in a progressive direction. In 2005, for example, the Argentine government reduced the severance payment for a worker with twenty years of seniority from thirty months to twenty. After its unemployment rate fell below 10%, a 2007 decree abolished the 50% increase in severance payments that had been part of the 2002 emergency laws (IBRD 2008: 21).

THE LEFT TURN AND EMPLOYMENT RELATIONS: PLUS ÇA CHANGE?[18]

The previous section has documented in some detail the reforms Latin American governments have undertaken in the area of employment relations. The discussion raises the question of whether these reforms are transforming the HME model in the region or are helping to perpetuate it. In this section, I examine more closely complementarities and continuities in this model and propose that a healthy scepticism should be adopted in assessing the ability of left governments to transform it. The argument made is that it is easier to reproduce the HME model of employment relations because there are important synergies at work involving their individual components (Schneider and Karcher 2010). Scholars have extensively discussed the permanence and viability of different models of capitalist accumulation and exchange despite common pressures to harmonize policies and institutions (e.g. Hall and Soskice 2001; Hall and Gingerich 2009). The synergies involved are usually in the form of one institution generating positive returns for another, as when vocational training in CMEs increases the return to employers of providing generous employment protection to their workers. In the Latin American context, the interaction of different aspects of the HME model usually produces sub-optimal outcomes by preventing those aspects of the model that function properly in other settings from having their intended effect.

Analysts generally agree on a few common characteristics of Latin American political economies: high levels of labour market regulation; unions (in the larger countries) that are too strong to be mere price takers in the labour market but too weak to force governments and particularly employers to partake in a comprehensive social contract;[19] a sizeable informal sector; and workforces with minimal education and skills. The interaction of these characteristics generates pervasive incentives that can blunt or negate the best intentions of social reformers. Let us take as an example the strict regulation of the labour market which, as already explained, dates back to the ISI period when governments sought to create economically secure and politically dependent urban working classes. From the standpoint of both employers and workers, the inclusion of some kind of protection in the employment contract is desirable. Typically, employers and workers cannot anticipate when the next downturn in the business cycle will occur. In this setting, the primary purpose of employment regulations is to give firms the incentive to internalize the risks associated with adverse market shocks while enhancing economic efficiency (see OECD 2004: 91). This reduces the volatility both workers and employers experience as a result of the business cycle.

Employment protection, however, is costly for firms since it can result in a larger workforce than managers would consider optimal, particularly in difficult economic times. This can leave employers saddled with wage and social contributions that they may be unable or unwilling to meet. When this occurs, managers are tempted to dismiss workers. In the presence of strong unions and strict EPL, however, they have to consider practices that redistribute available work opportunities. Japanese firms, for example, have traditionally responded to economic slowdowns by shortening work hours and retraining workers, as German companies also demonstrated in response to the 2008 financial crisis. These policies typically increase firm productivity, albeit in the medium- to long-term. To force employers to accept work-sharing, however, unions have to be strong both nationally and in work councils within the firm, far from the reality in Latin America, where labour groups exert some influence over political parties but lack leverage on the company floor.

Employers in Latin America are better organized, but hardly as organized as their European and Japanese counterparts. Ben Ross Schneider (2010: 313) writes in this regard that 'most of the thousands of business associations in Latin America are voluntary (save Brazil), sectoral, biased towards larger firms, and rarely geared toward bargaining collectively with labor'. Employers' lack of organization explains their inability to recognize EPL for what it is, an opportunity to raise the productivity of the firm. Doing so would result in a relationship between EPL and job tenure that is more in line with the global norm: workers tend to last longer in their jobs the more protected the employment contract is. In Latin America, on the contrary, EPL shortens job tenure (Schneider and Karcher 2010: 638).

The presence of strict EPL, or rather, the gap between *de jure* and *de facto* employment regulation, ensures that labour regulations are neither relaxed nor appropriately enforced. Employers for one have no incentive to reform a system that provides a buffer for managers who are reluctant to hire workers on permanent terms or to keep workers who have become redundant. For unions on the other hand, informality is not a pressing problem since they mostly represent the interests of formal sector workers. In addition, UI minimally protects the unemployed, ensuring workers have nowhere but the informal sector to turn to when they are laid off. A recent study on the effects of employment laws in developing countries finds in this regard that LDCs with rigid employment laws tend to have larger informal sectors and higher unemployment, especially among young workers (Djankov and Ramalho 2009: 3). The authors go on to note that the recent regulatory reforms enacted in several Latin American countries are larger in magnitude than similar reforms carried out in their developed counterparts.

Another perverse set of incentives involves unions and their ability to work with employers and governments to reduce informality and increase investments in education and vocational training. Proponents of the varieties of capitalism (VOC) approach note that the political economies of DCs can be divided into two groups depending on whether employees are in possession of mostly general as opposed to specific skills (Hall and Soskice 2001). Firms that employ workers with general skills, such as those in LMEs, do not favour vocational training programmes since skills are quite portable and workers are thus expected to change jobs frequently. Employers in CMEs, on the other hand, are said to be favourably disposed towards policies of skill upgrading since their workers are quite bound to their firms by virtue of the specific nature of their skills (Iversen 2005).

The distribution of skills in Latin American labour markets is, as we have seen, neither general nor specific. Labour forces are simply not very skilled. That said, labour unions, which have taken the lead in demanding job benefits and investments in skills in CMEs, are not in a position to do the same in Latin America. As students of DCs remind us, investments in skills specific to an industry, firm, or occupation are unlikely if both workers and employers face a risk of losing their investment (Estevez-Abe et al. 2001). Workers and employers, in other words, will not commit to costly investments in skills if skilled positions are not widely available and employers do not expect to keep their employees around for very long.

Were unions to be committed to upgrading the skills of their base, moreover, they would find that they lack the numbers and coordination needed to act as a counterpart to employers. The vast numbers of labourers in the informal sector, who are notoriously difficult to organize, keep a ceiling on how large unions can grow. Even assuming a higher number of unionized workers, it is difficult to imagine a situation in which unions would join employers in pursuit of long-term collective interests as opposed to narrow sectoral ones. In DCs, strong unions that are able to work in the public interest have emerged as coalitions of skilled and unskilled workers, primarily because the former have taken the lead in organizing their less-skilled counterparts (Carbonaro 2006: 1821). In Latin America, not only are the numbers of skilled workers low, but they are concentrated in large firms with limited local presence such as multinational corporations (MNCs).

Societies that continuously adapt to competitive market pressures, optimizing economic performance in the process, feature encompassing interest organizations (Wright 2000). This is particularly the case with workers, since the structural dependence of politicians on business managers sometimes translates into policies that allow substantial capital accumulation without a corresponding reinvestment of profits (Przeworski 1985).[20] Nevertheless, I do not wish to imply that if the will is there to break decisively with the HME, countries cannot undertake the reforms necessary to stop some of its perverse incentives, or at least to begin addressing them. In recent decades, globalization—by creating transnational networks of production and finance—may have had the unintended consequence of empowering workers in the countries where they most lack support (Anner 2011). Workers in these countries have taken advantage of transnational labour networks and campaigns to push for higher wages and better working conditions.

Criticisms of the VOC approach also serve as a reminder that analytical categories should not reify similarities among countries or preclude the possibility of change. In this respect, the HME model blinds us to the intra-regional variation in state structures and institutions affecting labour market actors across Latin America.[21] Many countries in the region, for example, feature corporatist systems of labour representation in which the state subordinates organized labour to its authority in exchange for various subsidies and benefits, but these structures vary from country to country, affecting in turn the ability of labourers to make demands and of governments to address them. Brazil and Argentina, for example, have experienced long histories of state corporatism. Yet in Argentina workers enjoy considerable state support for strong national unions and collective agreements, while Brazil has yet to allow national union centrals and national collective bargaining (Anner 2011: 9–11).

Conclusion

On balance, it is fair to conclude that in employment relations, as in other social and economic policies, 'no comprehensive alternative model' (Levitsky and Roberts

2011b: 413) or 'state guided development strategy' (Madrid et al. 2010: 158) has emerged from countries governed by the left in Latin America. It may be too soon for this, but there are reasons to be hopeful that reforms to employment relations may be setting the stage for solutions to some of the region's most intractable problems. A favourable political and policy climate, however, does not appear sufficient to generate these changes. Ironically, when unions have mobilized effectively, a number of progressive governments have stepped up enforcement and reformed labour laws (Anner 2011: 179). In Chile, for example, a wave of protest that began with the country's first general strike since the return to democracy in 2003 has led to reforms that significantly mitigate the level of informality. With the passage of the Outsourcing and Supply of Labour Act on 16 October 2006, the Chilean government took a decisive step to regularize the status of outsourced workers in one of the region's most flexible and unequal economies (Atzeni et al. 2011: 144–5). Resistance by employers to this Act has not gone unchallenged by workers, who have staged a series of strikes in the industries that most rely on these workers.

In Argentina, labour market deregulation, economic austerity, and neo-liberal restructuring in the 1990s caused a reduction in labour conflict (Atzeni et al. 2011: 143). The economic collapse of 1999–2002, conversely, coincided with an explosion in political protest and factory occupations by unemployed workers and radical grassroots movements just before the turn to the left in that country in 2003. The Kirchner government at first welcomed this activism before turning more repressive. Finally, of all the countries in the region, Uruguay best reflects the employment relations characteristic of social democracy (Lanzaro 2011). Yet even there, unions have used strikes and protests as a means to pressure the Frente Amplio government. By egging sympathetic governments on, grassroots mobilization contributes to the enactment and implementation of much needed reforms.

NOTES

1. The thirteen Latin American countries for which data are available are Argentina, Bolivia, Brazil, Chile, Colombia, Dominican Republic, Ecuador, Jamaica, Mexico, Panama, Peru, Uruguay, and Venezuela.
2. All indexes range from a low of zero to a high of one. The global mean also includes the thirteen Latin American countries.
3. By relying on these indicators, I do not mean to suggest that flexibility is preferable since it lowers the cost of doing business for employers. Thinking of employment relations as a matter of degrees of regulation merely reflects the approach taken in the empirical and theoretical literature, which regards regulations and social charges as a cost employers must bear for adjusting employment levels (Heckman and Pagés-Serra 2000). Another criticism that is often made of Botero et al. (2004) is their leximetric approach, i.e. their attempt to quantify the economic effects of legal rules on businesses. This is somewhat inevitable, however, if the goal is to explain why certain governments create laws and regulations that make workers less dependent on the commodification of their labour. For a summary of criticisms of these measures, see Cooney et al. (2011).

4. Although studies indicate that the percentage of the workforce that is engaged in non-agricultural informal work has averaged 40% for the past several decades in the region, it is also important to note that this does not result in a stark dualism between insiders and outsiders, mostly because workers possess little formal or vocational training and job turnover is very high (Schneider and Karcher 2010: 631).

5. The index '[m]easures the statutory protection and power of unions' (Botero et al. 2004: 1349).

6. Botero et al. (2004) attempt to compute the full cost of employment regulation on labour demand, but this approach may not be ideal for engaging in cross-national, cross-regional comparisons. As studies of labour markets in Latin America make clear, what holds firms back from employing and training more workers is the high cost of regulations that preponderantly affect insiders. In contrast to the measure of firing costs provided by Botero et al. (2004) and included in their employment laws index, Heckman and Pagés-Serra (2000: 114) measure firing costs as 'the marginal costs of dismissing full-time indefinite workers'.

7. Even when both measures are provided, it is difficult to eschew leximetric comparisons because many aspects of the employment relationship refer to expectations about the cost of certain benefits embodied in a nation's legal and administrative codes. The only other available measure of labour market flexibility, for example, similarly uses the World Bank's rule of law (ROL) index to estimate the impact of enforcement on labour market flexibility (Stalling 2010: 148). Its drawback is that it is only available for one year, 2006.

8. The Third Wave in Latin America refers mostly to countries that were once democratic, succumbed to military coups, and then experienced a return to democracy. Some countries in the region—namely Colombia, Costa Rica, and Venezuela—never experienced a democratic collapse.

9. See also Murillo and Schrank (2005). More precisely, from 1984 to 2003, Murillo records twelve instances of regulatory and five of deregulatory reforms in collective laws, whereas in the same period she records six instances of regulatory versus ten of deregulatory reforms in individual labour laws.

10. LMEs refer to Australia, Canada, Ireland, New Zealand, the United Kingdom, and the United States. CMEs include Austria, Belgium, Denmark, Finland, Germany, Japan, Netherlands, Norway, Sweden, and Switzerland. In Hall and Soskice (2001: 21), France and Italy are 'in more ambiguous positions' and are hence categorized as mixed economies (or MIX).

11. <http://www.doingbusiness.org/methodology/employing-workers>, accessed 6 October 2011.

12. For more details of how these indexes are defined, see <http://www.doingbusiness.org/data/exploretopics/~/media/FPDKM/Doing%20Business/Documents/Annual-Reports/English/DB12-Chapters/Employing-Workers.pdf>.

13. Those countries are Venezuela (1999–2003), Chile (2000–3), Brazil (2003), and Argentina (2003).

14. As previously noted, ten countries form part of the left turn. Countries governed by non-left parties for which data are available are Colombia, Costa Rica, Dominican Republic, Guatemala, Haiti, Honduras, Jamaica, Mexico, Panama, Peru, Puerto Rico, and Trinidad and Tobago. Countries with a population of less than half a million inhabitants for which data are not consistently available were excluded from these comparisons.

15. Since 2007, the methodology used to calculate these measures has changed so as to align the measures better with the letter and spirit of ILO conventions. This, however, should not affect the results since the purpose of the analysis is to establish how particular variables relate to one another, not to estimate latent scores for the factors. As long as the methodology was applied consistently across observations, it should not affect the pattern matrix of the variables. See <http://www.doingbusiness.org/data/exploretopics/~/media/FPDKM/Doing%20Business/Documents/Annual-Reports/English/DB12-Chapters/Employing-Workers.pdf>, page 4. The goal of determining rough correlations among the variables also implies that the lack of validity of some of the indicators (Cooney et al. 2011: 85) should not unduly influence our conclusions.

16. To be more precise, they refer to EPL as 'external flexibility'. Two of the progressive reforms took place before the turn to the left in Argentina (2002) and Ecuador (2000).

17. According to the IBRD (2006: 18), Bolivia, which is among the countries with the most rigid labour regulations, made hiring and firing even more difficult in 2006 with a new decree that requires employers to get workers' permission before firing them.

18. This section is largely based on the work of Ben R. Schneider and his collaborators.

19. Union density rates among unionizable workers in Argentina, for example, have averaged 40% in recent years (Atzeni et al. 2011: 142). Even there, however, the decentralization of collective bargaining remains high. In addition, although autonomous national unions, employers, and the government negotiate a minimum wage and wage restraint in exchange for productivity-induced wage gains, the agreements apply only to the formal sector of the working class (Etchemendy and Collier 2007).

20. When profits are effectively reinvested, the result is more jobs and higher wages. Latin America, the region with the second highest level of income inequality in the world, is testament to how little liberal democracy has done in this respect (IBRD 2005: 38).

21. Other models of employment relations such as those analysed in Hall and Soskice (2001) also exhibit considerable intra-group variation that may be greater than the variance between CMEs and LMEs (Hudson 2012: 190).

References

Anner, M. S. (2011). *Solidarity Transformed: Labour Responses to Globalization and Crisis in Latin America*. Ithaca: Cornell University Press.

Atzeni, F., Durán-Palma, F., and Ghigliani, P. (2011). 'Employment Relations in Chile and Argentina', in M. Barry and A. Wilkinson (eds.), *Research Handbook of Comparative Employment Relations*. Cheltenham: Edward Elgar, 129–52.

Barrett, P. S., Chavez, D., and Rodriguez-Garavito, C. (2008). *The New Latin American Left: Utopia Reborn*. London: Pluto Press.

Botero, J., Djankov, S., La Porta, R., Lopez-de-Silanes, F., and Shleifer, A. (2004). 'The Regulation of Labor', *Quarterly Journal of Economics*, 119(4): 1339–82.

Cameron, M. A. and Hershberg, E. (2010). *Latin America's Left Turns: Politics, Policies, and Trajectories of Change*. Boulder, CO: Lynne Rienner Publishers.

Carbonaro, W. (2006). 'Cross-National Differences in the Skills–Earnings Relationship: The Role of Labor Market Institutions', *Social Forces*, 84(3): 1819–42.

Castañeda, J. G. (2006). 'Latin America's Left Turn', *Foreign Affairs*, 85(3): 28–43.

Cook, M. L. (2007). *The Politics of Labor Reform in Latin America: Between Flexibility and Rights.* University Park, PA: Pennsylvania State University Press.

—— (1998). 'Toward Flexible Industrial Relations? Neo-Liberalism, Democracy, and Labor Reform in Latin America', *Industrial Relations,* 37(3): 311–37.

Cooney, S., Gahan, P., and Mitchell, R. (2011). 'Legal Origins, Labour Law and the Regulation of Employment Relations', in M. Barry and A. Wilkinson (eds.), *Research Handbook of Comparative Employment Relations.* Cheltenham: Edward Elgar Publishing, 75–97.

Djankov, S. and Ramalho, R. (2009). 'Employment Laws in Developing Countries', *Journal of Comparative Economics,* 37(1): 3–13.

Edwards, S. and Lustig, N. (1997). *Labor Markets in Latin America.* Washington, DC: Brookings Institution.

Estevez-Abe, M., Iversen, T., and Soskice, D. (2001). 'Social Protection and the Formation of Skills: A Reinterpretation of the Welfare State', in P. A. Hall and Soskice (eds.), *Varieties of Capitalism: The Institutional Foundations of Comparative Advantage.* Oxford and New York: Oxford University Press, 145–83.

Etchemendy, S. and Collier, R. B. (2007). 'Down but Not Out: Union Resurgence and Segmented Neocorporatism in Argentina (2003–2007)', *Politics & Society,* 35(3): 363–401.

Hall, P. A. and Gingerich, D. W. (2009). 'Varieties of Capitalism and Institutional Complementarities in the Political Economy: An Empirical Analysis', *British Journal of Political Science,* 39(3): 449–82.

Hall, P. A. and Soskice, D. (eds.) (2001). *Varieties of Capitalism: The Institutional Foundations of Comparative Advantage.* Oxford and New York: Oxford University Press.

Heckman, J. and Pagés-Serra, C. (2000). 'The Cost of Job Security Regulation: Evidence from Latin American Labor Markets', *Economia,* 1(1): 109–54.

Hudson, R. (2012). 'Regions, Varieties of Capitalism and the Legacies of Neoliberalism', in C. Lane and G. T. Wood (eds.), *Capitalist Diversity and Diversity within Capitalism.* New York: Routledge, 199–208.

International Bank for Reconstruction and Development (IBRD) (2004). *Doing Business in 2004: Understanding Regulation.* Washington, DC: World Bank/Oxford University Press.

—— (2005). *World Development Report 2006: Equity and Development.* Washington, DC: World Bank/Oxford University Press.

—— (2006). *Doing Business in 2006: Creating Jobs.* Washington, DC: World Bank and the International Finance Corporation.

—— (2008). *Doing Business 2009.* Washington, DC: World Bank and the International Finance Corporation.

Iversen, T. (2005). *Capitalism, Democracy and Welfare.* Cambridge: Cambridge University Press.

Lanzaro, J. (2011). 'Uruguay: A Social Democratic Government in Latin America', in S. Levitsky and K. M. Roberts (eds.), *The Resurgence of the Latin American Left.* Baltimore: Johns Hopkins University Press, 348–74.

Levitsky, S. and Roberts, K. M. (2011a). 'Latin America's "Left Turn": A Framework for Analysis', in Levitsky and Roberts (eds.), *The Resurgence of the Latin American Left.* Baltimore: Johns Hopkins University Press, 1–28.

—— (2011b). 'Democracy, Development, and the Left', in Levitsky and Roberts (eds.), *The Resurgence of the Latin American Left.* Baltimore: Johns Hopkins University Press, 399–427.

Levitsky, S. and Roberts, K. M. (eds.) (2011c). *The Resurgence of the Latin American Left*. Baltimore: Johns Hopkins University Press.

Madrid, R. L., Hunter, W., and Weyland, K. (2010). 'The Policies and Performance of the Contestatory and Moderate Left', in Weyland, Madrid, and Hunter (eds.), *Leftist Governments in Latin America: Successes and Shortcomings*. New York: Cambridge University Press, 140–80.

Murillo, M. V. (2005). 'Partisanship amidst Convergence: The Politics of Labor Reform in Latin America', *Comparative Politics*, 37(4): 441–58.

Murillo, M. V., Oliveros, V., and Vaishnav, M. (2011a). 'Economic Constraints and Presidential Agency', in S. Levitsky and K. M. Roberts (eds.), *The Resurgence of the Latin American Left*. Baltimore: Johns Hopkins University Press, 52–70.

Murillo, M. V., Ronconi, L., and Schrank, A. (2011b). 'Latin American Labor Reforms: Evaluating Risk and Security', in J. A. Ocampo and J. Ros (eds.), *The Oxford Handbook of Latin American Economies*. Oxford and New York: Oxford University Press, 790–812.

Murillo, M. V. and Schrank, A. (2005). 'With a Little Help from my Friends: External and Domestic Allies and Labor Rights in Latin America', *Comparative Political Studies*, 38(8): 971–99.

Organisation for Economic Co-operation and Development (OECD) (2004). *OECD Employment Outlook 2004: Reassessing the OECD Jobs Strategy*. Paris: OECD.

Przeworski, A. (1985). *Capitalism and Social Democracy*. Cambridge: Cambridge University Press.

Schneider, B. R. (2009). 'Hierarchical Market Economies and Varieties of Capitalism in Latin America', *Journal of Latin American Studies*, 41(3): 553–75.

—— (2010). 'Business Politics in Latin America: Patterns of Fragmentation and Centralization', in G. Wilson, W. Grant, and D. Coen (eds.), *The Oxford Handbook of Business and Government*. Oxford: Oxford University Press, 307–29.

Schneider, B. R. and Karcher, S. (2010). 'Complementarities and Continuities in the Political Economy of Labour Markets in Latin America', *Socio-Economic Review*, 8(4): 623–51.

Schneider, B. R. and Soskice, D. (2009). 'Inequality in Developed Countries and Latin America: Coordinated, Liberal, and Hierarchical Systems', *Economy and Society*, 38(1): 17–52.

Stallings, B. (2010). 'Globalization and Labor in Four Developing Regions: An Institutional Approach', *Studies in Comparative International Development*, 45(2): 127–50.

Weyland, K., Madrid, R. L., and Hunter, W. (eds.) (2010). *Leftist Governments in Latin America: Successes and Shortcomings*. Cambridge: Cambridge University Press.

Wibbels, E. and Ahlquist, J. (2011). 'Development, Trade, and Social Insurance', *International Studies Quarterly*, 55(1): 125–49.

Wilthagen, T. and Tros, F. (2004). 'The Concept of "Flexicurity": A New Approach to Regulating Employment and Labour Markets', *Transfer: European Review of Labour and Research*, 10(2): 166–86.

Wright, E. O. (2000). 'Working-Class Power, Capitalist-Class Interests, and Class Compromise', *American Journal of Sociology*, 105(4): 957–1002.

CHAPTER 19

DEVELOPING SOCIETIES—ASIA

MICHELE FORD

INTRODUCTION

ASIA is a region of great economic diversity. Japan, the Asian Tigers (Taiwan, South Korea, Hong Kong, and Singapore), and the oil-rich sultanate of Brunei are wealthy but Asia's remaining 20 states have 'developing country' status (World Bank 2012). There is also great economic inequality within developing Asia, which is home not only to a substantial proportion of the world's poor but also to some of the world's richest individuals. Afghanistan is the poorest country in the region, with a 2010 average per capita GDP parity purchasing power of just over US$900, followed by Myanmar (Burma) and Nepal at around US$1,300. The richest is middle-income Malaysia, whose citizens enjoy an average parity purchasing power of almost US$15,000—well ahead of that of the next-richest, Thailand, at just over US$9,000. Among the most populous nations (which collectively account for 40% of the world's people), China is the richest, with around US$7,500 per capita GDP parity purchasing power. India is the poorest of the three, at just under half that amount, while Indonesia sits a little higher at around US$4,300 (International Monetary Fund 2011).

Many countries in developing Asia have attempted to emulate the Asian Tigers' export-oriented production-led rise to economic power-house status. Although some countries have significant natural resource bases, labour-intensive manufacturing has become the cornerstone of economic development in the region since the 1970s. Bangladesh, Cambodia, China, Indonesia, Malaysia, Sri Lanka, Thailand, and Vietnam—and to a lesser extent Laos and the Philippines—are integrated into global production chains, particularly in labour-intensive manufacturing industries such as electronics, garments, and footwear. Consumer electronics and electronic components account for a significant share of low-skilled manufacturing. In the footwear and clothing export sector, leisurewear produced for international brands like Nike and Adidas features heavily. A significant proportion of labour-intensive production takes place in dedicated Export Processing Zones (sometimes known as Free Trade Zones or Bonded Zones), but factories are also scattered around major urban centres and in some cases in more isolated locations, such as Mae Sot on Thailand's western border with Myanmar.

Many of these countries also share other characteristics. They have large informal economies, relatively low levels of formal education and poor job tenure in the private sector. Business is dominated by domestic conglomerates and multinational corporations, which play an important role in the creation of low-level formal sector jobs. As a result of a continuing emphasis on agriculture and the informal sector in the labour market, state-sanctioned employment relations systems have relatively limited reach in most countries in the region. Within the employment relations system itself, there is often a significant gap between policy and practice such that even within the formal sector many firms effectively operate with little reference to a nationwide framework of processes underpinned by black-letter labour law. And although some countries (most notably India) have a long tradition of democracy, most have experienced long periods of authoritarian rule.

What explains the convergence in much of developing Asia around labour-intensive, export-oriented manufacturing and punitive employment relations regimes? Is there such a thing as a variety of capitalism (VOC) that captures the experience of these outward-looking countries? In their seminal discussion of the concept, Hall and Soskice (2001) identified two ideal types of capitalism—liberal market economies (LMEs) and coordinated market economies (CMEs)—each of which is characterized by different 'institutional complementarities' that push firms in different directions, in turn reinforcing the particular institutional structures of the economies in which they operate and ultimately leading to greater economic divergence.[1] Schneider and Soskice (2009: 37–40) later formulated a third model describing the 'hierarchical market economies' (HMEs) of Latin America, which are characterized by much larger informal economies and much lower levels of formal education than LMEs or CMEs.[2] HMEs are dominated by large, highly diversified family-owned domestic business groups and subsidiaries of US-owned multinational corporations (MNCs). In the employment relations arena, they have lower trade union densities than LMEs, but with a level of labour market regulation comparable to CMEs. They also have weak business associations, which Schneider and Soskice attribute to two causes: their lack of influence over either domestic conglomerates or MNCs and the weakness of trade unions in the workplace. As a result of the latter, trade unions operate through the political system to maintain labour market regulation and collective bargaining even in sectors of the economy which are relatively highly unionized.

On the surface, the VOC framework—or, more precisely, its Latin American variant—provides a starting point for analysis of the link between political systems, economic structure, and employment relations in developing Asia.[3] Schneider and Karcher's (2010: 633) concept of negative complementarities, in particular, is a useful way of understanding low-road models that trap countries in a vicious circle of dependence on cheap production for export, in turn making it difficult for governments to up-skill their workforce or acknowledge a possible role for trade unions in promoting 'high-road' production. This chapter examines the possibilities of this model with reference to Indonesia, Vietnam, and Malaysia—three Southeast Asian countries with relatively developed formal sector workforces and a relatively high level of integration in global production chains.[4] On the basis of this analysis, the chapter draws two conclusions. The first is that historical legacies and political context remain the key determinants in the structure and operation of employment relations mechanisms in developing Asia. The second is that Malaysia's attempts to pursue a high-road export manufacturing strategy have not been accompanied by the development of more effective structural mechanisms for the representation of workers' interests. Indeed, as the discussion that follows shows, the Malaysian government has actively sought ways of embracing elements of high-road production while maintaining the kinds of employment relations structures found in the low-road export production-led economies of Indonesia and Vietnam.[5]

EMPLOYMENT RELATIONS IN DEVELOPING ASIA

A multitude of factors can be taken into account when comparing employment relations systems: political context; the extent to which a system covers waged workers; whether that system is predominantly bipartite or tripartite; and the extent and nature of trade unionism (as the primary vehicle for employee collective action) in a particular country. Since employment relations systems focus almost exclusively on formal sector workers, system coverage is determined primarily by the relative size of the formal and informal sectors, but also by the extent to which employment relations policies and mechanisms are actually implemented. The elements most commonly used to assess the extent and nature of trade unionism are sectoral spread, membership density, and some measure of trade union power as expressed through their capacity to determine employment relations policy and/or outcomes. In order to assess the latter, it is necessary to analyse the *nature* of trade unions in a particular national setting through a consideration of factors such as whether they are more politically or economically oriented; the extent to which they can operate free from government or employer control; and the extent to which they are reliant on external support.

In developing Asia, national employment relations systems have to a significant extent been shaped by the experience of colonialism, which ended as late as the 1960s in some countries.[6] The French, British, Portuguese, and Americans colonized all but Bhutan, China, Mongolia, and Thailand—in some cases, for several centuries. Their infiltration of local economies was patchy, but they controlled the modern economy (and thus formal sector employment) and designed the systems through which the employment relationship was regulated. In employment relations terms, the British colonial legacy in South and Southeast Asia has been perhaps the most enduring. With the exception of Myanmar (where trade unions were banned between 1962 and 2011), former British colonies have retained many of the employment relations structures established in the colonial period. Trade unions in Bangladesh, India, Nepal, Sri Lanka, and Malaysia are primarily occupationally based and have little interest in the informal sector or peripheral occupations in the formal sector, reflecting the legacy of the British craft system, with its commitment to the 'labour aristocracy'. Like British trade unions, also, trade unions in Britain's ex-colonies have a tradition of political engagement. And while Malaysia's trade unions are now depoliticized, South Asia's trade unions continue to be strongly political, with many maintaining links to leftist parties.

A second key historical influence in the region was the Cold War. China and Mongolia were, of course, already communist, and South Asia remained largely at the periphery of the struggle between capitalism and communism. However, East and Southeast Asia became a key Cold War battlefield from the 1950s, when the Cold War became hot on the Korean Peninsula and then in Indochina where, ultimately, the communists were victorious. Fearful of the domino effect, Western allies concerned with keeping the rest of East and Southeast Asia out of the hands of the communists gave almost unconditional support to the authoritarian developmentalist regimes of South Korea, Taiwan, and the Association of Southeast Asian Nations (ASEAN), which then consisted of the so-called 'ASEAN five' (Indonesia, Malaysia, Thailand, the Philippines, and Singapore).[7] In the employment relations arena, the geopolitical situation in the 1960s, 1970s, and 1980s meant that governments in capitalist developing Asia were free to implement anti-labour policies without fear of opprobrium. The early successes of Japan and the Asian Tigers has also been a major influence in developing Asia, with countries like Malaysia seeking to 'look East' in political and employment relations terms.

In the employment relations arena, Asia's authoritarian developmentalist regimes found unexpected legitimation in the International Labour Organization's West European-inspired emphasis on national tripartism. Superficially, the models were surprisingly compatible because of their emphasis on peak-level collaboration between the state, unions, and employers' bodies over workplace negotiations. As a consequence of this strange confluence of influences, very similar employment relations systems emerged under communist regimes in China, Vietnam, and Lao PDR, but also at the opposite end of the ideological spectrum in Indonesia and, to a lesser extent, in Malaysia and even wealthy Singapore. These authoritarian corporatist arrangements—in which workers and employers were formally represented by national-level peak bodies but had little opportunity to act independently—proved to be well suited to the demands of foreign investment-driven, labour-intensive, export-oriented production because they provided multinationals not only with a low wage, low production cost environment but also with unparalleled stability in both the political and employment relations arenas.

However, the geopolitical situation—and, along with it, the employment relations climate—changed dramatically with the end of the Cold War. The USA and its Cold War allies no longer had a compelling reason to turn a blind eye to human rights abuses, or to ignore protest movements in the region or the campaigns of the growing global movement against sweated labour in Asia's factories. The situation came to a head with the Asian financial crisis of 1997, when a run on the Thai Baht quickly developed into a regional melt-down. Countries like Singapore and Malaysia weathered the crisis, but much of Southeast Asia (along with countries further afield, like South Korea) experienced a serious economic shock. In Indonesia's case, it provided the final impetus needed to dislodge President Suharto, whose New Order regime had ruled Indonesia for 32 years—the first in a series of dramatic reversals that led to the birth of Timor-Leste, developing Asia's youngest country, and saw Indonesia democratize and decentralize.

The fluidity of state structures in democratizing Indonesia and newly independent Timor-Leste opened up space for foreign influence over institution-building processes on an unprecedented scale. In the employment relations arena, the International Labour Organization has played a major role, advising on labour law and bank-rolling the establishment of new peak union bodies. As had been the case in post-Soviet Eastern Europe, international labour movement organizations like the International Trade Union Confederation, the Global Union Federations, and the Solidarity Support Organizations associated with the national trade union movements of Western Europe and the United States also invested heavily in the post-Suharto period. In Indonesia, this international intervention underwrote the substantive restructuring of employment relations mechanisms as well as an explosion in trade union numbers. In Timor-Leste, it saw the fashioning of an entire employment relations system. With the possible exception of Cambodia, opportunities for interventions have been more limited elsewhere in developing Asia. Global Union Federation and Solidarity Support Organization programmes are nevertheless significant in many countries in the region.

These historical legacies and international norms—as well as economic strategy and degree of foreign investment—have clearly influenced the structures and practices of employment relations. The relative strength of centralization, colonial legacies, and foreign influence vary between, in some cases even within, national contexts. But while there are great differences between economic structures and employment relations systems of developing Asia, there are also many similarities, as illustrated by a comparison of Indonesia, Malaysia, and Vietnam.

Southeast Asia's Export Manufacturing-led Economies

Vietnam, Indonesia, and Malaysia have very different histories and political, economic, and employment relations systems. At the same time, though, they share perhaps more similarities than differences. All three were colonized (by different European powers), and all were key sites of ideological (in Vietnam's case, physical) struggle between the USA and its allies and the communists during the Cold War. Although Vietnam's socialist market economy is not strictly capitalist, all have to a significant extent engaged in foreign capital-driven, labour-intensive, export-oriented manufacturing over a sustained period of time.

Vietnam and Indonesia have continued to pursue this low-cost, low-skill labour strategy, a decision that led to similar pressures in worker communities and similar employment relations strategies, until such time as broader political events in Indonesia created space for independent trade unionism in that country. By contrast, Malaysia sought to adopt a 'high-road' strategy aimed at developing a new comparative advantage as it moved into middle-income country status and could no longer compete on cost alone. Yet despite these significant differences, all three continue to engage in a form of employment relations that privileges the interests of local and foreign investors over those of workers and their organizational representatives.

Indonesia

Indonesia provides the classic example of how colonial legacies and Cold War struggles have played out in the employment relations arena.[8] Indonesian trade unionists look back to the late colonial period as the golden era of the Indonesian labour movement. In the 1920s and 1930s, trade unions had a membership of around 100,000—some five times the total membership of political parties at that time (Ingleson 2000: 471–7). The labour movement was closely tied to the nationalist movement, and maintained prominence in the revolutionary struggle against the Dutch (1945–9). Trade unionists had significant influence on social policy in the first decade of the new Republic, the period in which much of Indonesia's progressive employment relations framework was established.

Leftist trade unions were crushed, along with other leftist groups, when General Suharto seized power in 1965–6. The Social Democratic, Christian, and Muslim trade unionists who remained initially believed they could leverage the situation to establish a middle-of-the-road trade union movement, positioned within a consensus model of employment relations based on the Western European model (Hadiz 1997). What happened, instead, was that trade unions were forced to amalgamate and join a single federation that focused entirely on the private sector. Labour repression reached another peak in the mid-1980s after Indonesia adopted an export-oriented industrialization strategy heavily dependent on foreign investment in light manufacturing (Hadiz 1997). In order to ensure that the investment climate remained 'conducive', trade unions' independence was further undermined. In 1985, the industrial unions that belonged to the state-approved federation were forced to give up their status as independent organizations and become mere departments within a single state union with even less influence over employment relations outcomes (Ford 1999).

The restructuring of the trade union movement was part of the broader restructuring process, which led to the incorporation of a grab-bag of tripartite, bipartite, and unitarist elements into Indonesia's employment relations system. On the one hand, Pancasila Industrial Relations was based on the unitarist premise that employers and workers should coexist in harmony in line with the 'family' principle said to underpin the Indonesian way of life. On the other, it incorporated elements of the pro-worker employment relations system established in the 1940s and 1950s, and thus included firm-level bipartite collective bargaining mechanisms and regional and national tripartite mechanisms to manage industrial dispute resolution, wage fixing, and a range of other employment relations functions (Ford 1999). These tripartite bodies were unquestionably subordinated to the state—and therefore, to the interests of capital—but they preserved some semblance of conformity with international norms. It was this gesture towards tripartism that made it possible for the International Labour Organization and Indonesia's political allies to turn a blind eye to the regime's gross and repeated violations of the principle of freedom of association in the last four decades of the twentieth century.

Equally, however, Indonesia offers a valuable example of the extent to which employment relations mechanisms can be transformed when an authoritarian corporatist system is weakened and finally collapses. With the end of the Cold War and increases in foreign investment, international criticisms of labour conditions in Indonesia became more widespread and more strident. At the same time, the rapid expansion of light manufacturing was attracting large numbers of workers to the neighbourhoods around the factories that were being built on the fringes of Indonesia's major cities (Warouw 2008). This combination of foreign interest, worker discontent, and democracy activists' growing interest in labour as a core element of regime change saw a series of labour non-governmental organizations (NGOs) and unofficial trade unions emerge in the late 1980s and early 1990s (Ford 2009). Together, these organizations worked to harness and systemize spontaneous labour protests within an alternative labour movement, which had no official standing but nevertheless represented a significant threat to the New Order's attempts to control all aspects of employment relations.

Although it failed to gain formal recognition, this alternative labour movement, with its strong international links, managed to force some concessions from the regime, including recognition of factory-level enterprise unions independent of the state-sanctioned union. It also educated workers about alternative modes of organizing, preparing the ground for the time when it again became possible for independent trade unions to participate in the formal mechanisms of the employment relations system. That time finally came not because of the growing strength of the labour movement, but as a result of the Asian financial crisis, the aftermath of which ultimately forced Suharto to resign. Responding to international pressure, one of the first acts of his immediate successor was to liberalize the employment relations system. By 2004, a comprehensive Labour Law Reform Package had been implemented, which revolutionized many aspects of employment relations. The package included a new Trade Union Law, under which as few as ten workers could form a trade union and multiple unions were permitted to operate in a single workplace. Employees of state-owned enterprises were now able to establish and join independent trade unions. The trade union movement also experienced a small but significant shift in union activity away from the labour-intensive, export-oriented manufacturing sector and towards white-collar private sector occupations, such as finance and journalism.

A key driver of the rapid expansion of the Indonesian trade union movement has been international support. Under Suharto, international trade unions were formally restricted to working with the official union, though bilateral Solidarity Support Organizations like the American Center for International Labor Solidarity (formerly the Asian American Free Labor Institute) found ways to work with alternative trade unions and labour NGOs. With the advent of democracy, however, international labour movement organizations flooded into the country, bringing with them deep pockets and a determination to demonstrate that trade unionism had a future in the developing world. New confederations were supported (and, in one case, brought into being) by the international labour movement, while key new sectoral unions were fostered and funded by the Global Union Federations.

These new trade unions have gone a considerable way to reasserting organized labour's role in the employment relations arena. Yet, notwithstanding its rapid transformation in the first decade of the twenty-first century, the Indonesian labour movement continues to struggle on a number of fronts. Union density has actually decreased despite the massive increase in the number of trade unions and the expansion in trade union activities. At approximately 11%, density is low even in the formal sector, which accounts for just 34% of employment opportunities in Indonesia (Badan Pusat Statistik 2011). Moreover, although many employers recognized that they could no longer ignore trade unions in the workplace or in higher-level negotiations, others continued to resist trade union attempts to negotiate at the shop-floor and at the national level, or to seek to reduce trade union power through large-scale labour outsourcing (Ford 2013).

Vietnam

Like trade unions in many other countries in the region, Vietnam's first trade unions were heavily involved with the revolutionary struggle in the colonial period. Although trade unions were illegal in Vietnam under French rule, the country's first union federation, the Red Federation of Trade Unions, was established in 1929 by Vietnamese who had come into contact with communist trade unionists while working in France (Pringle and Clarke 2011). The Vietnam General Confederation of Labour (VGCL) was subsequently established by Ho Chi Minh in 1946, using the model of the Confédération générale du travail.

As in Indonesia and Malaysia, attempts were made by the colonial power to shift the ideological balance within the trade union movement by encouraging non-communist unions—in Vietnam' case, a Christian union established in 1948. Although the Vietnamese Confederation of Christian Workers was legalized four years later, it failed to dislodge the communists, and was destroyed in the north when Vietnam was partitioned in 1954, and then altogether with the fall of the south in 1974 (Pringle and Clarke 2011: 65–6). In modern Vietnam, the VGCL has extremely close links to the Communist Party, and has remained closely integrated into the state structure. High-level officials must be members of the Communist Party, and its chairperson a member of the Party's Central Committee (Clarke et al. 2007).

In many ways, the contemporary Vietnamese employment relations system is a mirror image of Pancasila Industrial Relations. The architects of Indonesia's New Order regime argued that interest groups (and particularly workers) were inseparable parts of an organic whole, whose interests were indivisible from those of the state, and thus the primary function of the state union was to prioritize national development over the individual or collective interests of its members. Similarly, in Vietnam (as in China), trade unions are expected to subordinate the immediate interests of their members to the 'wider social, economic and political goals of the Party' (Clarke et al. 2007: 553). The primary difference between Pancasila Industrial Relations and the employment relations system in post-independence Vietnam lies in the fact that until recently the state was also the sole institutional employer in the latter, and thus there was no place for even a token commitment to tripartism.

Although the transformation of Vietnam's employment relations system has been not nearly as dramatic as that of Indonesia's, there, too, the structures of employment relations have undergone significant change since the introduction of *doi moi* (renovation) in December 1986. Since opening up to foreign investment, the Vietnamese economy has grown rapidly, achieving an average of 7.2% growth in GDP (Clarke et al. 2007: 548). Export-oriented manufacturing has not only played a central role in Vietnam's industrialization, but the manufacturing industries most open to foreign investment have generated the greatest number of challenges to the country's employment relations system (Quynh 2008).[9]

A new legal and institutional framework was put in place to support the transition to the market economy and to accommodate pressure from the international community, including the International Labour Organization. Collective bargaining was introduced on matters such as working hours and rest breaks, allowances, occupational safety, and social insurance under the 1994 Labour Code. Strikes were also legalized subject to prior engagement in mediation and arbitration (Pringle and Clarke 2011). All enterprises that have a trade union are required to have a conciliation council staffed by an equal number of representatives of management and employees, which represents a significant change from the previous situation, as foreign firms had been exempted from this requirement under the 1994 law (Pringle and Clarke 2011: 123). If agreement is not achieved, or if there is no conciliation council in the workplace, collective disputes are referred to the regional Arbitration Council. If the trade union is not satisfied with the result, it can refer the case to court or call a strike, on the condition that it have the support of the majority of the workforce (Clarke et al. 2007: 559).[10]

The VGCL has also undergone dramatic changes since the economy was liberalized, most notably through its expansion into the private sector (Edwards and Phan 2008). As of 2003, it claimed to have 4.3 million members (around 40% of those in employment). Union density sat at around 95% in the public sector, 90% in state enterprises, 30% in domestic private enterprises, and around 50% in foreign firms (Clarke et al. 2007: 550).[11] However, it was not until the revision of the Labour Code in 2002 that responsibility for employment relations in Vietnam began to focus primarily on employers and employ-ees (Clarke et al. 2007: 548). And it was only in 2004 that national tripartite mecha-nisms were formalized, creating a mechanism though which the government could consult the VGCL, the Vietnam Chamber of Commerce and Industry, and the Vietnam Cooperative Alliance on the formulation of labour policy and legislation (Pringle and Clarke 2011: 105). According to research carried out by the Ministry of Labour, Invalids and Social Affairs (MOLISA), as of 2006, 73% of state-owned enterprises, 21% of foreign firms, and just 5% of Vietnamese private companies had collective agreements (Pringle and Clarke 2011: 96–7)—although questions have been raised about the quality of the collective bargaining process, with most observers noting that agreements simply fol-low a set template.

Ultimately, though, this complex new system of employment relations mechanisms has failed to accommodate the changes brought by the rapid increase in labour-intensive export-oriented manufacturing. As a consequence, the primary mechanism for resolv-ing industrial disputes has remained highly organized wildcat strikes, particularly in foreign-owned companies located in the country's Export Processing Zones. Almost 70% of strikes between 1997 and 2007 occurred in foreign-owned companies (Quynh 2008). In absolute numbers, strikes in foreign-owned companies gradually increased from 28 in 1995 to 66 in 2002, then grew more rapidly, reaching several hundred annu-ally (Pringle and Clarke 2011: 67).[12] The labour movement subsequently reached a major turning-point in late 2005, when employees in foreign-owned enterprises engaged in a series of massive strikes in protest against the fact that the minimum wage had not risen since 1999. Such was the effect of those strikes that many employers chose to raise wages unilaterally, a decision followed rapidly by the government, which increased the mini-mum wage in foreign-owned firms by around 40% in early 2006 (Pringle and Clarke 2011: 107–8).

As Quynh (2008) has noted, in Vietnam, attempts to balance the desire for eco-nomic growth and the need to maintain political stability are complicated by the party's status as the vanguard of the working class. Research suggests that labour department functionaries (who are more often than not also senior trade union lead-ers) recognize worker grievances, and have responded to the challenges posed by wildcat strikes through a series of measures, which have included seeking to increase local trade union officials' capacity to respond to worker demands; the provision of training to improve the skills of union officers; setting up legal aid centres within the provincial and sectoral levels of the union; and promoting collective bargain-ing to achieve better than minimum benefits for workers. Indeed, on the basis of a detailed analysis of the outcomes of 50 wildcat strikes, Lee (2005) found that work-ers' key demands were met in 48 of those cases, often with the encouragement of local labour officials. District-level unionists have also collaborated with provincial labour inspectorates to investigate suspected violations of the labour legislation in the EPZs (Quynh 2008). Quynh (2008) concludes, however, that the VGCL is yet to tackle its 'core problem' of unionists' structural subordination to management in the workplace.

Malaysia

The third case, Malaysia, represents a hybrid between the British system, the legacy of which remains strong also in Singapore and South Asia, and a commitment to the East Asian 'strong state', which became increasingly important during the 22-year prime ministership of Mahathir Mohamad, a modernizer inspired by the successes of the Asian Tigers. Malaysia is formally a multi-party constitutional monarchy broadly modelled on Britain's Westminster system. However, the ruling coalition has held power for more than 40 years, a great number of them under Mahathir. Thus, although Malaysia has never formally adopted a corporatist model, influential political scientists point to a shift towards bureaucratic state authoritarianism in the 1980s (Crouch 1992; Khoo Boo Teik 1995), which had much in common with the systems in place in Singapore and Indonesia at that time.

The colonial legacy has remained an important influence on the institutional structures of contemporary employment relations, both in terms of the particular combination of bipartite and tripartite mechanisms that characterize the system, and in the ethnic and industrial contours of the trade union movement. Malayan trade unionism had its origins in the late nineteenth century among the Malay working class, as immigrant workers from China and India were reluctant to unionize (Jomo and Todd 1994). By the 1940s, however, Chinese and Indians comprised the majority in a trade union movement that, like the labour movement of neighbouring Indonesia, was highly politicized. At that time, the movement was dominated by Chinese-led unions, many of which had communist sympathies. When almost half of all trade unions were outlawed under amendments to the Trade Union Ordinance in 1948, union leadership shifted from the Chinese to the Indians with encouragement from the British, who supported anti-communist Indian-dominated unions over their Chinese rivals (Bhopal and Rowley 2005). It was not, however, until after the implementation of the New Economic Plan in the early 1970s that Malay participation in the workforce, and subsequently the trade union movement, again grew (Jomo and Todd 1994). Malays have since increased their presence in the trade union leadership, although Indian Malaysians continue to be strongly represented in the upper levels of many unions.

Politics and ethnic tensions continued to spill over into employment relations after Malaysia achieved its independence from Britain. Prime Minister Tun Razak warned after the race riots of 1969 that Malaysia 'must have a loyal, disciplined and dedicated labour force' and that the role of government 'is to ensure that the trade unions are run in the interest of the country' (cited in Jomo and Todd 1994: 129). Continuing in this tradition, Mahathir argued that Malaysians should, as Asian workers, be disciplined and loyal, and that trade unions should be closely controlled, because they alienate foreign investors and threaten national development (Crinis 2003). These statements were made at a time when the government was preparing to actively pursue a policy of foreign investment-driven export-oriented industrialization, which they hoped would provide a foil for Chinese-owned businesses and create employment opportunities for Malays (Elias 2005).

The state has since had a crucial role in determining the extent to which trade unions are capable of representing worker interests in the employment relations system

(Arudsothy and Littler 1993). The Trade Unions Act of 1959 cemented the requirement for unions to register in order to gain legal status, while the Pioneer Industries Ordinance of the previous year included provisions that limited trade union activity in an attempt to attract foreign investors. Repression of trade unions increased in response to widespread strike action in the early to mid-1960s, including the introduction of compulsory arbitration and limitations on the right to strike in essential industries.[13] Further amendments were subsequently made to both the Industrial Relations Act and the Trades Union Ordinance in 1980, which made it easier for the state to suspend strike action and dissolve unions.

Perhaps the most radical attempt to undercut existing trade unions was Mahathir's in-house union policy, which he promoted as part of a 'Look East' strategy launched in 1982 (Wad 1997). Although some enterprise unions had existed before that time, the state increasingly 'encouraged' the formation of enterprise unions rather than national unions, particularly in sensitive industries such as electronics. A discussion of the electronics industry in Malaysia cannot be divorced from a discussion of Export Processing Zones, which were first introduced through the 1971 Free Trade Zone Act. For the first 15 years of their existence, electronics factories in Free Trade Zones were effectively excised from Malaysia's employment relations system, and Free Trade Zone workers were denied the right to form trade unions (Caspersz 1998: 265–72). Enterprise unions have been permitted in the sector for some years, and in 2009 the federal government gave permission to establish industrial unions for electronics at the regional level. However, authorities have continued to obstruct attempts to form a national electronics union (interview with Electrical Industrial Workers Union official, Penang, May 2010).[14]

Yet while successive Malaysian governments have gradually extended the state's influence over employment relations, there has been no effort to explicitly co-opt trade unions as organs of the state. And, unlike New Order Indonesia, where only private sector workers could legally organize, most Malaysian formal sector workers have maintained the right to engage in trade union activity. Nor has the state attempted to fully centralize trade unions, although the predominantly private-sector Malaysian Trades Union Congress (MTUC) and the public-sector Congress of Unions of Employees of Public and Civil Services (CUEPACS) were established under government auspices (Jomo and Todd 1994; Ariffin 1997).[15] Nonetheless, Malaysia's bureaucratic authoritarian tendencies remain evident in its employment relations system and, in particular, in its attempts to limit the power of trade unions and harness them in the national interest.

Conclusion

Malaysia differs significantly from Vietnam and Indonesia in a number of respects. Among other things, it is considerably more wealthy and its labour costs are much higher. These and other factors, including its historic rivalry and desire to compete with neighbouring Singapore, have driven Malaysia to adopt a high-road strategy in key industries including electronics and segments of the garment and textiles industry.[16] This emphasis on higher production values requires tighter control over supply chains, which, according to the literature on global production chains, should prompt buyers to favour large subcontractors with a higher level of professionalization of human resource management and a greater concentration of trade unions (Crinis 2010). Or, as Kuruvilla (1995) puts it, whereas low-wage export-oriented industrialization strategies focus on cost containment and repressive policies on trade unionism, as countries move up the production ladder, their competitive edge relies on niche production and higher skills.

But does the 'high road' necessarily lead to better opportunities for workers to engage collectively in the formal employment relations system? In Malaysia, this has not been the case, as is nowhere clearer than in the garment and textile industries. Prompted by the threat posed to Malaysian competitiveness by the Multi-Fibre Arrangement, the Malaysian government encouraged garment and textile manufacturers to move up the production chain, offering special incentives for investment in technology and training (Crinis 2010). However, Malaysia's foray into high-end garment production has been balanced strategically by a range of cost-cutting strategies at the lower end of the market and strategies to maintain control over trade unions. With government support, Malaysian garment and textile firms have employed three strategies to maintain a large, low-end production base to complement high-end production: the relocation of factories to rural areas in less-developed states such as Johor and Kedah; increasing reliance on subcontractors and home-workers in traditional garment and textile-producing regions; and the large-scale employment of foreign workers (Crinis 2003). Moreover, not only have firms involved in high-end production refused to engage with trade unions at the firm level, but the federal government has neither encouraged them to do so, nor empowered national-level trade unions to demand a seat at the bargaining table (Crinis 2010). Instead, the Malaysian government continues to repress independent trade unionism to a far greater extent than does the government of neighbouring Indonesia, where high-road production strategies have not been embraced.

So what does this mean for a so-called Asian variety of capitalism? Adopting Schneider and Karcher's (2010: 633) concept of negative complementarities, it is clear that the historical nexus between Malaysia's semi-authoritarian political system, its aggressive development strategy, and its repression of trade unionism is stronger than any structural imperative associated with high-road export production. Thus, while high-road strategies have indeed provided access to skills development—and, through the creation of value-added production niches, better wages and conditions—they have not guaranteed better access to collective representation.

Conversely, in the Indonesian case, it is evident that the serious disruption in the historical nexus between authoritarian rule, export-led industrialization, and repression of the labour movement has opened up room for trade unions, but not to such an extent that the imperatives of low-road export-oriented production have been overcome. Similarly, in Vietnam, while large-scale private investment has given rise to worker protest (the causes of which state officials have recognized and to some extent addressed), it has yet to pose a real threat to authoritarian rule or to disrupt the subordinate position of trade unions to the party.

In other words, the legacies of colonial rule and Cold War politics, and compacts made with capital in the establishment of low-road export-oriented production strategies, continue to drive employment relations in all three countries. While not necessarily constituting a discrete 'variety of capitalism', these shared characteristics continue to be dominant despite the changing political context of Indonesia, Malaysia's experiments with the high road, and the contradictions between socialist discourse and market capitalism in Vietnam.

Notes

1. Although they focused firmly on Western Europe and the advanced democracies of the Anglophone settler world, Hall and Soskice (2001: 2) asserted that the model has relevance in the South. They also made passing reference in their 2001 account of varieties of capitalism to a 'Mediterranean economy', but did not develop this model.
2. This article was one of a number co-authored by one of the framework's architects which seek to address criticisms of the limitations, and in particular, its inability to explain economic and political change. See also Iversen and Soskice (2009) and Hall and Thelen (2009).
3. A number of scholars have adopted elements of the VOC framework (e.g. Andriesse and van Westen 2009; Carney and Loh 2009; Kong 2006). Others have proposed that the scope of the VOC model be expanded to better account for the Asian experience (e.g. Ritchie 2009; Tipton 2009). Others still have emphasized the poor 'fit' of the original model (e.g. Nottage 2002; Ahrens and Junemann 2007).
4. For a discussion of employment relations in China and India, see the following chapter in this volume on the BRICS.
5. This chapter is based on research funded by Australian Research Council grants DP120100654 and FT120100778. I would like to thank my research assistant Nicola Edwards for her help with an initial review of the literature on varieties of capitalism.
6. When the Portuguese left Timor-Leste, the territory was occupied by Indonesia, only achieving independence in 1999.
7. ASEAN has since grown to include all of Southeast Asia, with the exception of Timor-Leste, which at the time of writing was pursuing membership.
8. The discussion that follows draws on sections of Ford (2009).
9. Lee (2006) and others have observed that the approaches to economic and political reform in China and Vietnam share many common features. Most analysts argue, however, that Vietnam's system is more liberal than China's.
10. Strikes are prohibited in 54 sectors considered to provide essential public services or be of importance to national security. The government also has the power to terminate any strike deemed to be a threat to the national economy (HRW 2009: 16).
11. In the Vietnamese context, what I am here calling 'foreign firms' are officially known as Foreign Invested Enterprises, a category that includes joint ventures as well as wholly foreign-owned concerns.
12. A record 2,150 strikes occurred in 2009 (Pringle and Clarke 2011: 108).

13. Under the 1969 Industrial Relations Act, a range of tripartite bodies were established, including regional labour courts and the central Industrial Court. Wage councils, similar to those found in Sri Lanka, were established under a 1947 ordinance (Dunkley 1982).

14. For case studies of migrant workers' experiences in the electronics industry, see Bormann et al. (2010).

15. In 1989, a third umbrella organization called the Malaysian Labour Organization (MLO) was formed with government encouragement to rival MTUC. However, it was dissolved in 1996. As of 2011, there were 697 trade unions with a total of 800,000 members registered in Malaysia. Of these, 441 were located in the private sector, while the remainder operated in the public sector or in statutory bodies and local authorities. Just under half the total number were located in services, and a further quarter in manufacturing (Department of Trade Union Affairs 2012).

16. For details of Malaysia's high-road strategy, see Elias (2011).

REFERENCES

Ahrens, J. and Junemann, P. (2007). 'Transitional Institutions, Institutional Complementarities and Economic Performance in China: A "Varieties of Capitalism" Approach'. Workshop Series on the Role of Institutions in East Asian Development: Institutional Foundations of Innovation and Competitiveness in East Asia. Duisburg: Institute of East Asian Studies, Universität Duisburg-Essen.

Andriesse, E. and van Westen, G. (2009). 'Unsustainable Varieties of Capitalism along the Thailand–Malaysia Border? The Role of Institutional Complementarities in Regional Development', *Asia Pacific Journal of Management*, 26(3): 459–79.

Ariffin, R. (1997). *Women and Trade Unions in Peninsular Malaysia with Special Reference to MTUC and CUEPACS*. Pulau Penang: Universiti Sains Malaysia.

Arudsothy, P. and Littler, C. (1993). 'State Regulation and Union Fragmentation in Malaysia', in S. Frenkel (ed.), *Organized Labor in the Asia-Pacific Region*. Ithaca: International Labor Relations Press, 107–30.

Badan Pusat Statistik (2011). 'Penduduk 15 Tahun Ke Atas Menurut Status Pekerjaan Utama 2004, 2005, 2006, 2007, 2008, 2009, 2010, dan 2011'. Available at <http://www.bps.go.id/tab_sub/view.php?tabel=1&daftar=1&id_subyek=06&notab=3>, accessed 31 January 2012.

Bhopal, M. and Rowley, C. (2005). 'Ethnicity as a Management Issue and Resource: Examples from Malaysia', *Asia Pacific Business Review*, 11(4): 553–74.

Bormann, S., Krishnan, P., and Neuner, M. (2010). *Migrant Workers in the Malaysian Electronics Industry: Case Studies on Jabil Circuit and Flextronics*. Berlin: World Economy, Ecology and Development.

Carney, R. and Loh Yi Zheng (2009). 'Institutional (Dis)Incentives to Innovate: An Explanation for Singapore's Innovation Gap', *Journal of East Asian Studies*, 9(2): 291–319.

Caspersz, D. (1998). 'Globalisation and Labour: A Case Study of EPZ Workers in Malaysia', *Economic and Industrial Democracy*, 19(2): 253–85.

Clarke, S., Lee, C. H., and Chi, D. Q. (2007). 'From Rights to Interests: The Challenge of Industrial Relations in Vietnam', *Journal of Industrial Relations*, 49(4): 545–68.

Crinis, V. (2003). 'Innovations in Trade Union Approaches in Malaysia's Garment Industry', *Economic and Labour Relations Review*, 14(1): 81–91.

Crinis, V. (2010). 'Sweat or No Sweat: Foreign Workers in the Garment Industry in Malaysia', *Journal of Contemporary Asia*, 40(4): 589–611.

Crouch, H. (1992). 'Authoritarian Trends, the UMNO Split and the Limits to State Power', in J. Kahn and Loh Kok Wah (eds.), *Fragmented Vision: Culture and Politics in Contemporary Malaysia*. St Leonards: Allen & Unwin, 21–43.

Department of Trade Union Affairs (2012). Statistics. Available at <http://jheks.mohr.gov.my/index.php?option=com_content&view=article&id=145&Itemid=101&lang=en>, accessed 19 January 2012.

Dunkley, G. (1982). 'Industrial Relations and Labour in Malaysia', *Journal of Industrial Relations*, 24(3): 24–42.

Edwards, V. and Phan, A. (2008). 'Trade Unions in Vietnam: From Socialism to Market Socialism', in J. Zhu (ed.), *Trade Unions in Asia: An Economic and Sociological Analysis*. Oxford: Routledge, 199–215.

Elias, J. (2005). 'The Gendered Political Economy of Control and Resistance on the Shop Floor of the Multinational Firm: A Case Study from Malaysia', *New Political Economy*, 10(2): 203–22.

—— (2011). 'The Gender Politics of Economic Competitiveness in Malaysia's Transition to a Knowledge-Economy', *Pacific Review*, 24(5): 529–52.

Ford, M. (1999). 'Testing the Limits of Corporatism: Reflections on Industrial Relations Institutions and Practice in Suharto's Indonesia', *Journal of Industrial Relations*, 41(3): 371–92.

—— (2009). *Workers and Intellectuals: NGOs, Trade Unions and the Indonesian Labour Movement*. Singapore: NUS/KITLV/Hawaii.

—— (2013). 'Employer Anti-Unionism in Democratic Indonesia', in G. Gall and T. Dundon (eds.), *Global Anti-Unionism: Nature, Dynamics, Trajectories and Outcomes*. Basingstoke: Palgrave Macmillan, 224–43.

Hadiz, V. (1997). *Workers and the State in New Order Indonesia*. London and New York: Routledge.

Hall, P. A. and Soskice, D. (eds.) (2001). *Varieties of Capitalism: The Institutional Foundations of Comparative Advantage*. Oxford and New York: Oxford University Press.

Hall, P. A. and Thelen, K. (2009). 'Institutional Change in Varieties of Capitalism', in B. Hancké (ed.), *Debating Varieties of Capitalism: A Reader*. Oxford and New York: Oxford University Press, 251–72.

Human Rights Watch (HRW) (2009). *Not Yet a Workers' Paradise: Vietnam's Suppression of the Independent Workers' Movement*. New York: HRW.

Ingleson, J. (2000). 'Labour Unions and the Provision of Social Security in Colonial Java', *Asian Studies Review*, 24(4): 471–500.

International Monetary Fund (2011). 'World Economic Outlook Database'. Available at <http://www.imf.org/external/pubs/ft/weo/2011/02/weodata/download.aspx>, accessed 18 January 2012.

Iversen, T. and Soskice, D. (2009). 'Distribution and Redistribution: The Shadow of the Nineteenth Century', *World Politics*, 61(3): 438–86.

Jomo, K. S. and Todd, P. (1994). *Trade Unions and the State in Peninsular Malaysia*. Kuala Lumpur: Oxford University Press.

Khoo Boo Teik (1995). *The Paradoxes of Mahathirism: An Intellectual Biography of Mahathir Mohammad*. Kuala Lumpur: Oxford University Press.

Kong, Tat Yan (2006). 'Globalization and Labour Market Reform: Patterns of Response in Northeast Asia', *British Journal of Political Science*, 36(2): 359–83.

Kuruvilla, S. (1995). 'Economic Development Strategies, Industrial Relations Policies and Workplace IR/HR Practices in Southeast Asia', in K. Wever and L. Turner (eds.), *The*

Comparative Political Economy of Industrial Relations. Madison, WI: Industrial Relations Research Association, 115–50.

Lee Chang-Hee (2005). 'Strikes and Industrial Relations in Viet Nam'. Unpublished ILO discussion paper, Bangkok: ILO.

—— (2006). 'Recent Industrial Relations Developments in China and Viet Nam: The Transformation of Industrial Relations in East Asian Transition Economies', *Journal of Industrial Relations*, 48(3): 415–29.

Nottage, L. (2002) 'Japanese Corporate Governance at a Crossroads: Variation in "Varieties of Capitalism"?', *North Carolina Journal of International Law and Commercial Regulation*, 27(2): 255–99.

Pringle, T. and Clarke, S. (2011). *The Challenge of Transition: Trade Unions in Russia, China and Vietnam*. Basingstoke: Palgrave Macmillan.

Quynh Chi Do (2008). 'The Challenge from Below: Wildcat Strikes and the Pressure for Union Reform in Vietnam', paper presented at the 2008 Vietnam Update, The Australian National University, Canberra, 6–7 November.

Ritchie, B. (2009). 'Economic Upgrading in a State-Coordinated, Liberal Market Economy', *Asia Pacific Journal of Management*, 26(3): 435–57.

Schneider, B. R. and Karcher, S. (2010). 'Complementarities and Continuities in the Political Economy of Labour Markets in Latin America', *Socio-Economic Review*, 8(4): 623–51.

Schneider, B. R. and Soskice, D. (2009). 'Inequality in Developed Countries and Latin America: Coordinated, Liberal and Hierarchical Systems', *Economy and Society*, 38(1): 17–52.

Tipton, F. (2009). 'Southeast Asian Capitalism: History, Institutions, States, and Firms', *Asia Pacific Journal of Management*, 26(3): 401–33.

Wad, P. (1997). 'Enterprise Unions: Panacea for Industrial Harmony in Malaysia?', *Copenhagen Journal of Asian Studies*, 12: 89–125.

Warouw, N. (2008). 'Industrial Workers in Transition: Women's Experiences of Factory Work in Tangerang', in M. Ford and L. Parker (eds.), *Women and Work in Indonesia*. Abingdon and New York: Routledge, 104–19.

World Bank (2012). 'Country and Lending Groups'. Available at <http://data.worldbank.org/about/country-classifications/country-and-lending-groups#East_Asia_and_Pacific>, accessed 18 January 2012.

CHAPTER 20

EMPLOYMENT RELATIONS IN THE BRICS COUNTRIES

FRANK HORWITZ

INTRODUCTION

THE cultural, labour market, and institutional complexity of emerging markets precludes over-simplified analysis. Brazil, Russia, India, China, and South Africa (BRICS) are an economic grouping of increasingly powerful emerging market countries from different continents. The BRICS countries foster trade and investment and economic development cooperation with each other. They also transfer labour, skills, and capital to one another: for example, there are extensive Chinese infrastructural projects and business operations in Africa and Brazil, while Indian information technology (IT) skills are utilized in Russia and Africa.

BRICS countries themselves are complex transitional societies with diverse demographic, ethnic, and employment relations systems and face difficult challenges of human development. But for economic development and continued high GDP growth to be sustainable in the long term, there are large human resource and infrastructural development challenges. The analytical framework adopted for this chapter applies institutional and labour market analysis approaches. There is an emerging body of work on transitional labour markets focusing on human resource development issues (Judge et al. 2009; Horwitz and Mellahi 2009; Horwitz 2006). Using secondary data, the institutional and labour market analysis approach is used to understand the nexus of public policy, institutional interventions, and factors influencing demand and supply in these diverse labour markets. This analysis then seeks to evaluate the further relationship between these policy, regulatory, and institutional mechanisms in the labour markets of the BRICS countries. The employment relations systems of each are described and evaluated and conclusions drawn.

Nearly a quarter of the Fortune Global 500 firms, the world's biggest by revenue come from emerging markets. In 1995 it was 4%. Emerging markets' share of world stock market capitalization surged to 35% in 2011, and emerging markets' exports edged over 50% of the world total, up from 27% in 1990 (*The Economist* 2011a). In 2011, South Africa was invited to join the BRIC group—Brazil, Russia, India, and China, a group of leading cross-continental emerging market countries. The BRICS (a term coined by Goldman Sachs) countries' combined share of market capitalization at the beginning of 2010 was US$8,922 billion with only the USA ahead of this and China in second position (*The Economist* 2011b: 68). As a combined group the BRICS have contributed 36% of world GDP growth in purchasing power parity during the first decade of the twenty-first century. By 2020, this figure is forecasted to reach 49% (Peters et al. 2011).

The combined GDP of the BRICS countries in 2008 was US$9,093 billion, second to the USA, but combined purchasing power of the BRICS populations was US$16,000 billion, more than the USA and China (*The Economist* 2011b). A recent estimate of the expansion and deepening of economic, trade, and investment ties between BRICS countries gives a combined net worth of US$12 trillion (Dlamini 2011).

In terms of global export contribution the combined BRICS percentage of world exports was 12.6%, second only to the euro area (15 countries). China itself is the world's biggest trader at 9.6% of goods traded and combined with the other four BRICS countries constitutes 14.4% of goods traded globally (*The Economist* 2011b: 32–3). China has the largest surplus on balance of payments current account with Russia fifth in the world (*The Economist* 2011b: 34). The total external assets held by the BRICS countries are more than US$4.7 billion (Poshakwale 2011).

Further, the combined industrial output of the BRICS countries—US$3,597 billion—is the highest of any geo-political grouping (*The Economist* 2011b: 46). China is today the largest economy in terms of manufacturing output, and again the combined total of US$2,679 billion of BRICS countries is higher than that of the USA, Germany, and Japan. The USA remains ahead of the BRICS countries with regard to services output, but this could well change within the next five to ten years. Quite significantly, the combined BRICS share of consumer spending of US$3,593 billion puts these countries ahead of Europe and the USA.

The above discussion indicates that there has been a shift in the global balance of economic power over the past five years. These trends underline the importance of understanding labour markets and employment relations within and between developed and emerging markets in general and specifically for BRICS countries.

Labour Markets in BRICS Countries

Within the BRICS group, China has a population of over 1.2 billion, but as a result of its controversial one-child family policy is experiencing a slowdown in population growth and a shifting generational balance in terms of a rapidly ageing population. India, Brazil, and South Africa in contrast are experiencing population growth. Inward migration from regional neighbours rather than increasing fertility rates is the reason for population growth in these countries. On the assumption that the purchasing power of these young populations will increase, India's economy could be as large as China in 10–15 years (*The Economist* 2011a: 51–2).

India's economy, with its population of over 1.1 billion, has almost quadrupled in size over the past two decades, growing at around 7% annually. Its labour market demography could underpin its future growth according to *The Economist* (2011e: 8). Most recently, however, inflation is rising and there is a slight slowdown in growth. Each year over 25 million Indians are born and 10 million enter the labour market. India's liberalization began in 1991 and it is a relatively resilient economy. Relatively flexible labour market policies over this period have seen more recent regulatory interventions seeking to stabilize employment by making dismissal procedures more stringent and measures 'inimical to employment creation' (*The Economist* 2011a: 57).

There is a nexus in employment practices between certain BRICS countries. China, for example, is Africa's biggest trading partner and buys more than a third of its oil from the continent through its large Chinese firms such as Sinopec or China Sonangol. It has also become a major investor in countries such as Angola and South Africa. Its employment practices have been criticized in African countries such as South Africa where the wages and conditions of employment in the textiles and clothing industries are below minimum legal requirements. This has attracted trade union protests in towns such as Newcastle in South Africa.

However, it might be said that in certain situations a poorly paid job might be better than none at all. Of the BRICS group, South Africa's population of some 47 million is the smallest. Like China and India it has large formal–informal sector disparities in employment and earnings. China arguably has boosted employment in Africa and made basic goods such as shoes and radios more affordable. Critics, however, argue that China's often below minimum wage employment standards have resulted in the collapse of local companies in sectors such as clothing and textile manufacturing. Nonetheless trade with Africa surpassed US$120 billion in 2010 (*The Economist* 2011c). The China–African nexus therefore also has its proponents who argue that it has enhanced trade, increased building and construction and infrastructural development, and has involved investment in large local companies—for example, the Industrial and Commercial Bank of China's 20% investment stake in South Africa's Standard Bank. China has brought in a new entrepreneurial class and on aggregate is said to have created employment. Critics argue that this is a form of 'neo-colonialist economic exploitation' which has adversely affected certain local industries and offers below living wage employment conditions. An India–Africa nexus is expanding too with major investments in Africa by companies such as the Tata Group.

A China–Africa or Afro–Asian nexus has been a prospect for a long time. Similarly, China became the largest foreign investor in Brazil in 2010 with US$19 billion in FDI from the US$500 million before 2009. Total trade between China and Brazil has risen 17-fold since 2002 (*The Economist* 2012). However, there are accusations of dumping of Chinese imports having an adverse effect on local manufacturing. Short-term protectionist measures including high import duties have been introduced. However, longer-term policy changes are aimed at encouraging particularly auto manufacturers to build plants thereby increasing employment in Brazil for automobile manufacturers such as Tata Motors, Jaguar Land Rover, and BMW.

Like most emerging markets the BRICS are complex transitional societies often with diverse demographic and ethnic mixes and difficult challenges of human development. This complexity and diversity is important in understanding the employment relations systems of these countries. They are not homogeneous and even within BRICS countries such as China and India there is considerable labour market and socio-cultural variation in employment practices. This diversity may arguably provide a measure of adaptability and resilience which positions BRICS strongly and adroitly in international markets. But for economic development and growth to be sustainable in the long term, there are still massive human resource, employment relations, and infrastructural development challenges (Kamoche et al. 2004: xvi).

The next sections provide an analysis of employment relations developments in each of the BRICS countries.

Brazil

An increased globalized economy over the past two decades has seen Brazil experience significant economic restructuring and privatization. This has brought challenges for trade unions as the labour market has experienced increased outsourcing and subcontracting following privatization. In the Brazilian telecommunications industries, for example, trade unions have been attempting to organize more globally in order to gain influence in protecting employment rights and standards (Guimaraes 2007).

Latin American countries including Brazil 'have in the last quarter of a century abandoned an economic model based on import substitution adopting more open neo-liberal economic policies' (Lucena and Covarrubias 2006: 61). 'Foreign owned investments have become very important in economic modernization' (Lucena and Covarrubias 2006: 61). A significant transition in employment relations has taken place moving from a centralized state-directed and controlled corporatist system to a more decentralized model. Trade union membership as in most Latin American countries declined from 24.9% to under 23% in the period 1990–2000 with further declines since (Lucena and Covarrubias 2006: 59). Strike action figures have also seen a downward trend, though this is not as pronounced in Brazil as in other Latin American countries (Lucena and Covarrubias 2006: 64).

Following economic crises with soaring inflation of up to 80% in the 1980s the government of Fernando Collor introduced a new National Privatization Plan in 1990 affecting several sectors including telecommunications. These remained in place through the 1990s. This in part helped to stabilize the economy. In the 1990s market liberalization enhanced competition within the economy. The privatization programme generated US$82.1 billion in revenue and shifted US$18.1 billion public debt to the private sector

(Guimaraes 2007: 44). Economic growth increased to an annual real GDP growth of 4.8% from 2003–8 and is predicted to continue at around 4–5% to 2012 (The Economist Intelligence Unit 2008: 37). Because of positive capital flows the Brazilian currency has risen nearly 40% (Poshakwale 2011). The restructuring of the economy involved political controversy over the scale of transfer of state ownership to the private sector. Part of the national debate was on the question of the national strategic importance of certain sectors like telecommunications and state monopoly firms such as Telebras.

With the restructuring of state enterprises came similar practices as seen in developed and rapidly growing BRICS countries. These were flexible work practices, 'lean production' methods, increased casualization of work including part-time work, and precarious employment conditions associated with casual and subcontracted work, given the increased prevalence of outsourcing. These developments had significant implications for labour market participants especially trade unions, who were placed on the defensive trying to protect the employment standards and security of their members. Public protests by trade unions were not successful as privatization and new flexible, non-standard employment gained pace. A case example was Telebras, the state holding company established in 1972 with some 27 regionally based subsidiary companies. The case for privatization was based on low productivity and poor service quality. The organization required high skills but was not responsive to market needs and consumer pressures (Guimaraes 2007: 47). Renewed growth occurred after its privatization, including investment in new infrastructure begun in 2004. Wireless networks and bandwidth expansion occurred, as did the 'teledensity' of landline phones, thus enhancing the industry's overall productivity and performance.

The employment relations implications of this new economic model were significant. Certain business practices are associated with market restructuring measures such as privatization. These include downsizing, flexible work practices, increased part-time work, and subcontracting. The labour market also saw changes in the age profile of workers. Workers over the age of 50 declined and the overall workforce became younger. This had potentially adverse impacts on trade union strategies with unions traditionally having older workers as members and a younger workforce with a lower propensity to join trade unions. This is not unique to Brazil though, as global restructuring of labour markets has occurred over the past two decades. But it raises significant challenges for unions. Unions began to develop strategies for organizing workers in fragmented outsourced supplier firms. Gender changes also occurred in the Brazilian workforce: 'between 1995 and 2002, women increased from 34 to 41% of the workforce' (Guimaraes 2007: 49). Some 62% of university graduates are women, though more education has not meant better opportunities or salaries for women (Olivas-Lujan et al. 2009). They occupy only 21% of managerial positions in the private sector and work largely in specific industries. For example, women are prominent in social and community services (50.2%), followed by other support and health services sectors such as cultural (47.3%), clinical, and hospital services (30.5%) (Santos 2006).

The nature of subcontracting in Brazil especially in industries such as IT and telecommunications changed over the 1990s and 2000s. Traditionally single firm subcontractors assumed more aspects of core or lead firm responsibilities including production, technological innovation, and maintenance. This increasingly required subcontractors to invest in new equipment and technology themselves in order to provide the level of service quality required by the core firm.

The employment relations context had changed from a previously state-regulated economy in a number of spheres and a corporatist system institutionalized in the 1930s. Trade unions, as in other BRICS countries such as China, India, and South Africa registered with the state Ministry of Labour. Unions became important social actors in collective bargaining and dispute resolution in Brazil with the latter addressed by labour courts as in South Africa. In Brazil strong unions were major players in the auto and metal industries. Collective bargaining was centralized and management–union relations were relatively cooperative if not paternalistic (Guimaraes 2007: 52–3). Trade union coordinating bodies such as the Central Unica dos Trabalhadores (CUT) was established in 1983 representing unions taking a position more independent of the state. The second important labour federation is the Forca Sindical (FS) formed in 1991 which adopts a more pragmatic and less adversarial position according to Guimaraes (2007: 52). One significant effect of privatization as in other BRICS countries is the fragmentation of the enterprise and its workforce into smaller outsourced supplier forms. This has made union organization more difficult. New forms of work organization associated with the changing skills required for rapidly changing technology, differences in remuneration, and career perspectives among the fragmented workforce tend to reduce the ability for effective collective organization. A proliferation of subcontractor suppliers who are smaller and more fragmented than the core/lead firm also creates more autonomy to adopt 'less progressive' employment practices.

Trade unions in Brazil appear to have responded to these challenges in several ways. These include more pragmatic negotiating stances, broadening the scope of employees they seek to organize to include subcontracting employees, and acceptance of the need to agree on profit sharing and productivity arrangements. Negotiations have become more decentralized which also makes for negotiation of performance-based pay schemes. Nonetheless certain previously held benefits had to be traded off in these new collective agreements, for example seniority- and inflation-linked remuneration. The outcome of this more decentralized collective bargaining system is greater diversity in the content of collective agreements, for example disparity in wage agreements, varying provision of training and development programmes, and different work hours and work weeks between parts of the same industry.

More recently, however, the growth of subcontracted firms has seen a reduction of the employment conditions gap between them and lead/core firms. This development is more likely to occur in rapidly growing emerging market countries like Brazil. Unions have also begun to make substantive gains and improvements in labour standards in the subcontracting sector. While union influence and revised strategies may be a factor, it appears that the changing nature of the labour market with increasing numbers of younger workers, who are better educated, more technologically literate, and who seek training and development and upward mobility, are important factors. Union density may not necessarily have increased but improvements have nonetheless occurred due to changing labour force demographics and different generational expectations.

Trade unions in this context have therefore learned to operate in a more complex environment in more flexible, pragmatic ways, and have learned more about organizational and sector differences and the cultural variation between firms (Guimaraes 2007: 54–6). Importantly the new ownership structure of the increasingly globalized economy has meant increasing multinational ownership of what were locally owned firms. Trade union federations have therefore also had to develop globalized strategies. Hence, new transnational trade union groupings have emerged, such as the Union Network International (UNI). The aims of UNI include seeking consistency in labour standards and workers' rights access to information and policies across countries in which a multinational firm operates. There is some evidence in Brazil that this transnational and regional dialogue has contributed to better employment relations, for example the negotiation of collective agreements in some subcontracting firms (Guimaraes 2007; Croucher and Cotton 2009: 77). An example of this is Telefonica. But this cannot be said to be the case more widely where subcontracting and non-standard numerical and functional flexibility still present serious difficulties for trade unions. This and contingency approaches to work have meant a profound socio-political, cultural, and institutional shift in Brazilian employment relations—from a more traditional centralized, corporatist, and collective system to a devolved, flexible, and culturally individualistic system, a workplace regime of differentiation, and working condition segmentation and diversity, rather than standardization and homogeneity. Nonetheless unions in Brazil still exert influence through a measure of political authority (Croucher and Cotton 2009: 49).

Russia

In Russia, the transition from a centrally planned Soviet economy to a market economy has involved a formal institutional regulatory system of codes and rules coexisting with a large informal labour market which has circumvented or ignored formal institutions. This is evidenced by a plethora of non-standard work practices such as flexible working time and flexible pay (Kapelyushnikov et al. 2011; Bjorkman et al. 2007). This fundamental shift underpins the emergence of market-driven rather than centrally planned economic growth of these economies, with important socio-political, institutional, and regulatory shifts as more state-run enterprises adopt market-driven business models, with Central and Eastern European (CEE) economies attracting more foreign direct investment. The transitional markets of CEE countries reflect a post-socialist legacy, aspects of which endure with counter-influences occurring in post-socialist ideology (e.g. notions of 'new Europe' and 'old Europe'). After a decade-long boom with rising GDP averaging some 7% until 2008, Russia experienced rising unemployment in the ensuing recession, with GDP falling nearly 8% and the rouble losing one-third of its value versus the dollar (A.T. Kearney 2011). However, real GDP growth is forecasted to be between 4 and 5% from 2011 (The Economist Intelligence Unit 2008: 53). The country has proved quite resilient, but like other BRICS countries has a major challenge of appropriate skills development and being competitive in the so-called 'war for talent'. The global recession has also caused a systematic 'brain drain' as more young people study and work abroad (A.T. Kearney 2011: 13).

Adopting an institutional framework of analysis, Kapelyushnikov et al. (2011: 395–405) evaluate the coexistence of institutional Labour Codes adopted in 2002 aimed at amendments to the earlier Soviet Labour Code of 1971, and a plethora of over 100 laws and regulations alongside an extensive 'shadow system' of informal arrangements between employers and employees.

The role of trade unions changed with the new constitution of the Russian federation in 1993. Trade unions were separated from the state in a move away from a state-controlled labour representation system. Previously their relationship with the state was a form of 'social partnership' with unions upholding social stability in exchange for a part in running social policy (Kapelyushnikov 2011: 405). This changed, however, with the post-Soviet transition to a more flexible dual, mixed market of formal (often ignored) and 'informal grey' labour market, with unions losing their central influence and characterized by a fundamental increase in flexible non-standard work agreed informally and directly with employees. In the Soviet era union membership had been as high as 80% which has since declined as in most of the BRICS and other countries. Ostensibly unions retain certain rights as in the Soviet system but the devolvement of the labour market to enterprise level has seen a significant rise of employment practices which may not have been agreed with unions. However, Russian unions remain relatively politically influential (Croucher and Cotton 2009: 49). Kapelyushnikov et al. (2011) argue that a relatively unique feature of the new transitional labour market is the duality of this formal and informal institutional regime, existing more extensively than in other CEE transitional economies.

The Russian labour market ostensibly remains highly regulated but in practice is overshadowed by the 'ubiquity of the shadow labour market' with its emphasis on non-standard work and 'blurring the distinction between formal and informal sectors' (Kapelyushnikov et al. 2011: 408), as well as a lack of regulatory transparency (A.T. Kearney 2011: 10). The lack of rule enforcement has evidently had a positive outcome in that the labour market has retained a high degree of stability and resilience against major economic shocks. This is attributable to a preference in enterprises (many of them formerly state-owned and others still so) to retain employment rather than retrenching, by adopting variable pay or wage flexibility and temporal flexibility in working hours, reducing costs rather than large-scale employee dismissals. This is confirmed by relatively stable employment levels, though the recent recession has seen unemployment rise. Other research has found a 'de-institutionalization' of the human resource practices of former socialist planned economies with new practices emerging, particularly performance appraisal, performance-based pay, and promotion and training (Bjorkman et al. 2007: 443; Fey et al. 2004; May et al. 2005). In Russia firms that have employee empowerment practices also put stronger emphasis on these practices together with work/family balance issues (Dirani and Ardichvili 2008).

In evaluating these factors, Judge et al. (2009) argue that firm-level strategic performance in transitional economies is a function of 'organizational capacity for change'. Judge et al.'s research in Russian firms found that this capacity is positively associated with firm performance. These authors contend that institutional turbulence associated with transformational change in transitional economies makes public policy and firm strategic choices different than in developed economies. These developments follow privatization and other transitional economic policy reforms in various CEEs. While some practices persist in state-run enterprises, Russian firms vary in their employment practices such as the payment of bonuses (Russell and Callanan 2001). The Russian labour market and industrial relations system therefore has particular idiosyncrasies not dissimilar to another BRICS country, South Africa—the dualistic formal and informal/shadow system and the persistence and pervasiveness of non-standard flexible work practices (Kapelyushnikov 2011: 402). These occur in the context of similar trends in other BRICS and CEE countries in terms of privatization, new technology, and a loosening up of state-directed employment relations. These practices tend to reflect lower employment standards with as much as a quarter of Russian workers working part-time, often on lower pay, with a fall in real wages.

In addition, skills mismatches and uneven shortages and over-staffing occur in various sectors with adverse effects on output and chronic labour market disequilibrium (Gimpelson et al. 2010; Bjorkman et al. 2007: 434–5). Flexible wages might often mean uncompetitive wages and less skills training with a negative effect on skills attraction and economic performance. Compared to other BRICS countries, Russia trails behind China and Brazil although it is ahead of India in training incidence (Gimpelson et al. 2010: 323). Gimpelson et al. argue that (not unlike the employment relations system) the institutional environment fails to enable an optimal employment mix in the labour market (Gimpelson et al. 2010: 329).

India

As in Brazil, India has since the early 1990s post-reform era moved from an economic model of import substitution to export orientation. India had high GDP growth of 8.7% over the period 2003–8, with a slight drop was forecasted to be above 7% for 2011–12 (The Economist Intelligence Unit 2008: 45), and dropped to 4.4% in September 2013. This liberalization transition in macroeconomic policy has also resulted in changes in labour market policy and the industrial relations framework. The employment relations system in the earlier phase of industrialization in India was a state-driven system or 'state pluralism' (Bhattacherjee and Ackers 2010).

A seminal point in the transition from colonialism to democracy was the 1991–2 balance of payments crisis, which with globalization and technological change (including the rapidly growing IT sector in India), gave impetus to market reforms. India has in the past decade seen the emergence of major Indian multinational firms who today are leading global competitors in their sectors, for example the Tata Group. The reasons why the Indian economy has been quite resilient during the credit crisis are varied. Arguably one reason is the strategy of its multinational corporations (MNCs) adopting diversification rather than single sector business models. This has increased their agility and reduced their exposure to risk, indeed diversifying their risk.

Though low in density, representing less than 23% of the organized formal sector and less than 2% in both formal and expanding informal sectors, the trade union movement is well established in India with 'positional power' (Bhattacherjee and Ackers 2010: 114; Lansbury et al. 2006). Collective bargaining coverage in India is as low as 3% (Shyam Sundar 2010: 591). The All India Trade Union Congress (AITUC) is affiliated to the Communist Party. The Centre of Indian Trade Unions (CITU) is also affiliated to the Party. The Indian National Trade Union Congress (INTUC) is affiliated to the Congress Party and the largest union federation Bhartiya Mazdoor Sangh (BMS) to the Bhartiya Janata Party (BJP) (Badigannavar 2006: 201–2). Unions have therefore come to be seen as an 'electoral asset' (hence, the notion of 'positional power'), similar to the Congress of South African Trade Unions (COSATU) in its relationship with the ruling African National Congress (ANC). Some argue that the union movement in India remains relatively strong as a result of this political influence and patronage rather than actual membership strength, though this is weakening with the growth of independent enterprise unions.

The labour market is differentiated between a very large informal unorganized sector and the formal sector which has trade union coverage including a large civil service which is highly unionized as in countries like South Africa. Labour laws provide a regulated framework for employment relations for the organized sector, with centralized collective bargaining in some sectors such as insurance. However, an increasingly devolved labour relations system has been a consequence of market reforms with moves towards increased enterprise bargaining with enterprise unions. This has seen a proliferation and fragmentation of trade unions in the past 15 years to some 65,286 unions (Badigannavar 2006: 203). Enterprise unions have become more prevalent given the failure in the 'political unionism' model and subordination to party and organizational politics (Shyam Sundar 2010). Mainstream unions have, however, neglected the informal economy but appear to be reviving their efforts in this area (Shyam Sundar 2010: 589) as in Brazil.

India appointed a second National Labour Commission (NCL) in 1999 to further labour market reforms. Part of its brief was to develop more cooperative rather than adversarial employment relations. However, with increased globalization, market liberalization, and technological shifts, employers have taken the initiative through an enhanced propensity for militant action, for example, the tactical use of lockouts (rather than closures) to downsize, varying terms and conditions of employment, usually downwards to secure subcontracted non-standard employment with a lower cost, and more flexible wage regimes. This is consistent with trends in other BRICS countries.

Interestingly the incidence of strike action has declined in India over the past decade while lockouts have increased, although intensified inter-union competition is also associated with union militancy. Some argue that employers do not often adopt progressive practices such as functional flexibility and training, rather using numerical flexibility (Badigannavar 2006: 214–15). Budhwar (2003), however, notes that there has indeed been increasing money spent on training and development of the organized workforce in India with a focus on skills training for changing technologies and in workforce attitudes.

The Indian Industrial Relations Act provides a range of rights for workers and unions, such as freedom of association, collective bargaining, and multiple unions in workplaces. It provides dispute resolution including third-party mediation and adjudication to resolve labour disputes. Collective bargaining remains quite embedded in an array of labour laws and institutions with a high level of state intervention, a legacy of India's colonial past. The three important laws are the Trade Unions Act (1926), the Industrial Employment Standing Orders Act (IEA) (1946), and the Industrial Disputes Act (IDA) (1947). These form the pillars of the collective bargaining system, with incremental reforms made since 1991. Decentralized bargaining has been increasingly accommodated through devolving central labour relations legislative powers to state governments. India has a system of labour courts and industrial tribunals to resolve labour disputes. Legislation also regulates minimum wages through the Minimum Wages Act (1948), though unions seek agreements above these levels in the organized sectors.

Except in some sectors such as insurance and banking, in most other sectors bargaining occurs at enterprise and workplace levels (Badigannavar 2006: 205). However, some foreign multinational firms such as Hyundai have succeeded in union-avoidance policies in spite of the motor industry being highly organized, and there are collective agreements with most local auto manufacturers. The works committees, direct representation, and human resource practices leave employees with little bargaining power in this company (Lansbury et al. 2006: 143–6). Research shows a convergence of Indian business culture and technology levels with practices of foreign multinational firms (Mathew and Jain 2008). Technological change also has had a significant effect on the changing nature of work and occupations and hence the work profile of employees given the growth of the services and ITC sectors in India (Krishnan 2010). Unions no longer resist changes in work practices resulting from modernization or computerization except in the case of alternative use of subcontracting and casualization (Ratnam 1991; Krishan 2010: 375).

Though the labour market is highly regulated, organizations seek to circumnavigate 'artificial inflexibilities' in the labour market (Badigannavar 2006: 206–7). As in other BRICS countries such as Brazil, Russia, and South Africa, employers have increasingly outsourced both functions and actual operations. As in South Africa, employers of a certain size may fall outside the jurisdiction of certain labour laws. In India an employer with less than 100 employees is not bound by the same standard in respect of employment conditions. Employers may re-designate or restructure jobs or change the nature of work processes. Managerial strategies include lockouts which are quite frequently used as a tactic to change employment conditions and work practices effecting casualization. Negotiating performance-based pay where enterprise unions are recognized has become more common as certain unions seek a more cooperative relationship at plant level. Only about 13–14% of employees nationally are employed in longer-term regular employment (Bhaumik 2003). There is an intense debate as to whether the laws should be made more stringent to prevent avoidance strategies or eased further to recognize the new realities (Popola 2004).

China

Prior to 1979, the employment relations framework under China's centrally planned command economy was characterized by lifetime employment, 'cradle-to grave' welfare provided by the state, centrally set wages, and state-controlled managerial appointments and promotions (Zou and Lansbury 2009). However, 'the landscape of industrial relations in China has changed significantly over the last two decades mainly due to diversification of ownership forms which has given rise to a proliferation of categories of workers with different needs and expectations' (Cooke 2008: 111). The changing patterns of ownership with privatization of state-owned enterprises (SOEs) has seen large-scale restructuring, downsizing, and shifts to subcontracting, casual, and other flexible forms of employment. This has adversely impacted on job security and employment conditions. Labour disputes have increased as result (Cooke 2008: 112–13). Today, China still has a very large rural and migrant workforce of millions in informal employment and who remain largely unprotected by labour law.

With economic growth consistently over 8%, over the past two decades, China has had significant growth in foreign direct investment and MNCs. It is one of the largest three manufacturers globally. In 2007 foreign-invested firms in China generated 27% of value-added production and 58% of foreign trade, and employed more than 24 million Chinese workers in urban areas (Zou and Lansbury 2009: 2349). Wages and employment conditions tend to be better in MNCs than in other firm types. These firms and joint ventures (JVs) are required to pay wages no lower than the average of their sector in the area (Cooke 2008: 115). Contrary to the trend towards privatization and a market system over the past two decades, more employment regulations have been introduced ostensibly to provide minimum protections and institutionalize conflict though dispute resolution. Employment relations have become more regulated though product and service markets may have liberalized. These laws include the Labour Law of China (1995) and the subsequent Labour Contract Law (2008), which provides the framework for employment relations including contract provisions, rights and obligations of the parties, written contracts and conditions of employment such as for probationary periods and termination protection provisions, and regulation of temporary work agencies. There are also recent regulations aimed at improving gender equality in employment as well as minimum wages regulations. The law provides minimum protections and labour standards and a legal framework for dispute resolution. The latter includes provision for mediation, arbitration, and Peoples' Courts. Similar to employers in other BRICS countries, many employers in China subscribe to the 'burden theory'—that this increased regulatory protection of employee rights will raise labour costs which employers will find ways of avoiding (Fashoyin 2010).

Not all sectors are equally covered and some not at all. Small enterprise employees have weak protections as do rural and migrant workers who are most vulnerable to unfair treatment, poor working and living conditions, and dismissal. However, there is some evidence of employees in small (clothing) firms successfully negotiating relatively high wages but in return for significantly increased work hours (Li and Edwards 2008). In China ownership type rather than size, location, or sector, is the dominant factor in determining the type and extent of employee protections (Cooke 2008: 118). Informal employment makes up more than a quarter of the urban workforce with more than 70 million urban workers in informal work in the early 2000s (Cooke 2006). The All-China Federation of Trade Unions (ACFTU) notes that 80–90% of laid-off workers who regained employment were in informal work (Jiang 2003). Informal employment has been advocated by policy-makers as a way of job creation and absorbing the unemployed. However, most employees in informal employment remain under-protected by social security, and there is a lack of enforcement of employment-related regulations and inadequate functioning of employment agencies (Cooke 2011). These jobs tend to have low wages and suffer from job insecurity and poor working conditions, and trade unions are relatively ineffective in organizing in the informal and private sectors (Cooke 2011: 103, 109).

The term 'negotiation' rather than 'collective bargaining' is preferred in employment relations seeking to reinforce the notion of 'workplace harmony' rather than Western-style adversarial employment relations. Such negotiation occurs largely at the enterprise level. However, the regulatory system is perceived as ineffective with arbitration disputes rising some 32 times from 8,150 to 260,471 cases between 1992 and 2004 up to 500,000 in 2007 (*China Statistical Yearbook* 1993, 1995–7) and continuing to rise, while mediation has declined relatively. Labour arbitration has become the most important mechanism for dispute resolution since the middle 1990s (Shen 2007b). In 2004 only 32% of cases were settled through mediation and 43% through arbitration (*China Statistical Yearbook* 1998–2004; Cooke 2008: 123). Causes of disputes are not dissimilar to those in other BRICS countries. These disputes include pay, changes to employment contracts, social insurance and welfare, living conditions, delays or non-payment of wages, termination of employment, and increased casualization due to restructuring and downsizing following privatization of former SOEs. SOEs, collectively owned and foreign-funded private enterprises from Hong Kong, Macao, and Taiwan, and private enterprises all have a relatively high proportion of labour dispute cases, more so than public sector organizations which still have a relatively high share of employment. This may be because pay and employment conditions in the public sector are relatively better than in most other sectors and the state as an employer intervenes to seek resolution.

Although the intent of employment law is to seek better workplace harmony and cooperation, the rise of adversarial disputes is evidenced by both the preference to have disputes arbitrated rather than mediated, and a rise in unofficial and illegal 'street protest' action and demonstrations where formal dispute resolution procedures are ignored or perceived to be ineffectual. In 2003–4 over 1.44 million workers participated in these kinds of collective actions (Qiao and Jiang 2004: 300). Analysing causes of rising levels of labour disputes Cooke (2008: 111–38) gives the following reasons: growth of non-state sector employment with weaker levels of state intervention and regulations not actively enforced; employer violations either deliberately to circumvent regulations or out of ignorance of these; reactions to state enterprise reform with increased enterprise autonomy; and increased statutory rights for employees in recent years.

Arguably although labour regulations put more emphasis on the individual relationship than the collective relationship, with some exceptions such as the Beijing Hyundai Motor Company (Zou and Lansbury 2009: 2361), trade unions have not been strong and organizationally active at enterprise level other than in worker supporting or advisory roles. It is estimated that some 30% of private firms have unions, but unions do not often have active workplace representation. However, there are important changes underway in employment relations in China and one should avoid short-term, snap assessments. For example, where unions have workplace recognition, there appears to be a positive association with labour productivity, contract adherence, and employee benefits (Yi et al. 2010). The development of both individual and collective contracts introduced in 1992 has according to Shen (2007a: 126) become one of the most important features of China's reforms, replacing lifetime employment guarantees and the old social contract. The collective labour contract system replaced political and state administrative management of employment relations by legalizing responsibilities and obligations of employers and employees, moving to what has been described as 'marketized employment relations' (Friedman and Lee 2010).

The Chinese employment system is an evolving one and there has been recent exploration of the notion of a transition from a command to a regulatory system through the development of an emergent tripartite consultation system (Chang and Bain 2006; Shao et al. 2011). In 2001 tripartite consultation conferences (TCCs) were established at various levels and jurisdictions, the main parties being the Chinese Ministry of Labour and Social Security (MOLSS), the ACFTU, and the employers' organization the China Enterprise Confederation (CEC). The outcomes of this largely consultative rather than judicial process have been a more formal consultation of the main employment relations actors in respect of changes to employment law. The development of tripartism in China may reflect some convergence with the International Labour Organization (ILO) and Western understandings of this construct. However, it is underpinned by a strong party- and state-driven approach consistent with China's approach to gradualism and social harmony. The union role of promoting employees' interests may not require an abandonment of their traditional role of harmonizing employment relations (Yi et al. 2010: 202). Employment relations practices in China appear therefore to be a blend of new foreign-influenced practices and remnants of the former centrally planned system (Zou and Lansbury 2009: 2355).

SOUTH AFRICA

Employment relations in post-apartheid South Africa have undergone major changes over the past two decades (Horwitz et al. 2004). An adversarial race-based dualistic system evolved following labour legislation in 1924 which led to trade union rights excluding Black Africans. In 1980 unions representing African workers were legitimized. Inclusive bargaining councils were established through the Labour Relations Act (1995). African unions grew to over 3 million members from 2001 from less than 10% of the formal sector workforce in the late 1970s. Formal sector coverage by collective agreements is around 36%, with 22% overall labour force density. However, the development of non-standard employment including casualization and informalization of work as in other BRICS countries has had an adverse effect on union density over the past eight years. In the mining industry, for example, collective bargaining agreements have dropped to below 50% from 58% in 1997. Large-scale absorption into a shrinking formal sector labour market is problematic with economic growth at around 5% over the past decade and lower in the past two years (Horwitz and Jain 2008). The largest unions are affiliated to union federations such as COSATU and the National Council of Unions (NACTU). Unemployment at around 23% is high with a paradox of a skills shortage and an oversupply of unskilled workers, not dissimilar to China and Brazil. The largest proportion of union members is in the public sector not unlike Russia and China.

The post-apartheid Labour Relations Act (1995) established a labour and labour appeal courts, and a statutory dispute resolution body, the Commission for Conciliation, Mediation and Arbitration (CCMA). The CCMA handles both procedural and distributive or substantive justice in considering the fairness of a matter such as dismissal. This Act brought employment law in line with the constitution and ratified Conventions of the ILO. It aims to give effect to constitutional rights permitting employees to form unions, to strike for collective bargaining purposes, and the right to fair labour practices. Employers have the right to form and join employers' organizations and recourse to lockout for the purpose of collective bargaining. Strike action is protected only if a specified dispute procedure is followed. Collective agreements are negotiated at either industry (though industry Bargaining Councils) or enterprise levels where a union has significant representation. The CCMA or Bargaining Councils deal with unfair dismissal (disputes of rights) and mutual interest wage disputes. This helps to institutionalize conflict, though the ready accessibility of the CCMA does involve managers sometimes having to spend considerable time and effort in conflict resolution, with no administration cost to an employee who wishes to lodge a dispute. The statutory dispute resolution is widely used with conciliation and arbitration through either the CCMA or Labour Court both increasing over the past fifteen years.

While both centralized industry level and decentralized enterprise or plant bargaining may occur, increased devolution and fragmentation of bargaining have occurred in the past decade. The number of bargaining councils has declined to less than 80 as employers withdraw from them, favouring plant or enterprise bargaining and increased employment flexibility. This has occurred, for example, in the building and construction industries, with new forms of employment emphasizing flexibility using independent subcontractors, outsourcing, part-time and temporary work, and increased casualization and informalization of work. Changes in labour market policy and structures have occurred, with both the state and employers in BRICS countries either promoting or turning a blind eye to ineffective monitoring of legislative protections and collective agreements; as increased cost reduction and flexibility are sought there has been a consequent deterioration in employment standards, social protection, and rising casualization in the labour market. Examples include the decline of regional centralized bargaining structures in the building and construction industry in South Africa. Over 50,000 retrenchments have occurred in the clothing industry, largely due to cheap imports from lower cost producers in Asia and Chinese and Taiwanese manufacturers in Southern Africa paying below the legal minimum. The South African Clothing and Textile Workers Union (SACTWU) has struggled to fight this trend but has recently persuaded government to successfully negotiate some import restrictions on Chinese clothing to try and preserve jobs. These industry examples reflect the increasingly precarious nature of employment and the flexible labour market.

Even with a strongly protective Labour Relations Act (1995) institutionalized Labour Court, and CCMA, as well as minimum standards legislation in the form of the Basic Conditions of Employment Act (1997), and arguably the strongest union movement on the continent, precarious, non-standard work has increased while formal standard work has declined. As in China, the government has sought to limit the scope of employment agencies and provide increased protections for part-time workers.

These practices are associated with a recent decline in private sector union density of some 20% and some evidence of deterioration in employment standards in certain sectors. The Basic Conditions of Employment Act (1998), however, provides for establishing minimum standards of employment. These conditions cover areas from the designation of working hours to termination regulations and have been extended to farm and domestic workers. Work days lost through strike action have also declined since 1994. While under apartheid African unions fought for fair labour practices, worker rights and better pay and conditions of employment, they also were at the forefront of the struggle for political rights. Once political and labour rights complemented each other in the first democratic elections in 1994, this labour paradox was resolved. This resulted in an intense policy debate within the union movement as to its repositioning in the new South Africa. The workplace as an arena for political struggle has largely been replaced with an emphasis on measures to preserve and promote good employment conditions and human resource management (HRM) through training and development and employment equity (Horwitz et al. 2004). The Labour Relations Act seeks to promote employee participation in decision-making through workplace forums and employee consultation and joint decision-making on certain issues. New forms of dispute resolution were developed in the mid-2000s to include pre-dismissal arbitration and one-stop dispute resolution known as CON-ARB. Both unions and management have the power to request the CCMA to facilitate retrenchment negotiations to achieve constructive outcomes.

In post-apartheid South Africa, legislative prohibitions against unfair discrimination are intrinsic to its Constitution (1996). Chapter 2 (the Bill of Rights) contains an equality clause, which specifies a number of grounds which constitute unfair discrimination. Additionally, Schedule 7 of the Labour Relations Act (1995) considers unfair discrimination either directly or indirectly as a residual unfair labour practice. Grounds include race, gender, ethnic origin, sexual orientation, religion, disability, conscience, belief, language, and culture. The Employment Equity Act (1998) focuses on unfair discrimination in employment and HR practices. Employers are required to take steps to end unfair discrimination in employment policies and practices. It prohibits unfair discrimination against employees including job seekers on any arbitrary grounds including race, gender, pregnancy, marital status, sexual orientation, disability, language, and religion. All designated employers (these who employ 50 or more people) have to prepare and submit to the Department of Labour an employment equity plan setting out goals, targets, timetables, and measures to be taken to remove discriminatory employment practices and achieve greater workforce representation, especially at managerial and skilled category levels. The Employment Equity Act does not set quotas, but rather enables individual employers to develop their own HR and equity plans. Criteria regarding enhanced representation include national and regional demographic information and special skills supply/availability. Additionally, the Broad Based Black Economic Empowerment Power Act (BBBEEA, 2004) promotes Black equity ownership in firms with a points scorecard system for achieving targets which include procurement, employment equity, enterprise development, and training and development (Horwitz and Jain 2011). Though enhancing the Black stake in the economy through share ownership of large organizations, BBBEE has been controversial in that it has not always had a 'trickle-down' benefit. The Employment Equity Act includes provisions against unfair discrimination in selection and recruitment, aptitude testing, HIV/AIDS testing, promotions, and access to training and development opportunities.

South African labour law allows discrimination on the basis of inherent job requirements. But the object of an employer's conduct must be fair, and the means rational. It is in these areas, as well as in the provision of substantive benefits and conditions of employment, where unfair discrimination is most likely. The notions of disproportionate effect and adverse impact are considered in this regard. Once an employee claims discrimination, the evidentiary burden shifts to the employer to show that the discrimination is not unfair. An employer may submit that pay and skill differences were not the result of unfair discrimination, but due to factors such as differences in performance, experience, competence, and service. Both the policy and organizational context in which the dispute arises is pertinent. Change management and 'soft' HR strategies focusing on relationship building and cultural transformation to integrate diversity as a value in itself for effective work group relations, have been found to be more effective than reliance on procedural justice approaches alone (Horwitz et al. 2004).

Given the diverse ethnic demography of SA society, most of the underclass is African. South Africa faces a double transitional challenge—to redress the historical inequalities by building a democracy based on human rights and tolerance, and to simultaneously and speedily develop its human capital capacity to compete in a harsh global economy. Arguably this is a bigger policy and practical challenge than managerial and executive employment equity, where the focus seems to lie at present. Skills formation and entrepreneurial development are vital, especially in a country with huge transitional challenges (Horwitz et al. 2004). National skills policies have introduced mechanisms such as a 1% of payroll levy to finance human resource development in order to meet national, sector, and organizational development objectives. Particular sector skills formation through sector training authorities (SETAS) and a national qualifications framework (NQF) are encouraged by law. Economic empowerment and employment equity are not possible without human resource development and education as a fundamental national priority. Large-scale labour absorption into a shrinking formal labour market is unlikely, given the shift of employment to service and informal, non-core work mainly outside the ambit of employment equity legislation.

Though declining, HIV/AIDS has had an adverse impact on employment, employment and health care costs, and union membership. HIV/AIDS also has a deleterious effect on absenteeism, training, career and succession planning, and adverse effects on state and union negotiated medical schemes. The priority of practical policy initiatives by government, private sector firms, and labour market institutions such as sector training authorities and bargaining councils, must be large-scale initiatives to train and retrain for enhancing employability in the changing labour market. A key challenge in employment relations is the need to shift from a legacy of adversarial relationships to workplace cooperation to successfully compete in the marketplace (Horwitz 2009). There is evidence in some sectors such as auto assembly that this is understood by both parties. The employment relations agenda will need to focus beyond the traditional collective bargaining items and adversarial dismissal disputes, to organizational transformation, performance improvement, human resource development, and employee benefits. Traditional trade union contestation and power/conflict models may be inappropriate as are traditional distributive forms of collective bargaining based on an adversarial tradition. In BRICS countries union and employer strategies will need to increasingly focus on human resource development. Joint collaboration in the workplace will be vital for effective competition in the marketplace.

Conclusions

It is debatable how long the paradigm of emerging markets and the developed/developing market construct will be able to explain the fundamental shift of global economic power underway. The economic primacy of the once-called West—now called the industrialized North—is no longer a given and these nations are no longer able to take unilateral decisions affecting emerging economies. Managing employment relations strategically has become more important given the increased globalization of markets, including labour markets, high economic growth of BRICS countries (although there are indications this is slowing with the global economic downturn), and increased foreign direct investment between BRICS themselves and other countries, especially from China and India in other emerging markets such as Africa. While there is some evidence of a rise in employment relations institutions such as collective bargaining and dispute resolution, independent trade unions not linked to the state or employers are emerging gradually in some BRICS countries and positively, tripartite corporatist engagement is not uncommon albeit in quite different ways, for example in South Africa and China.

With diverse labour markets between and within BRICS, variation in institutional and regulatory systems and employment practices as well as cultural diversity, BRICS countries with large underclass populations face a double transitional challenge—to redress workplace inequalities and to simultaneously and speedily develop the institutional skills capacity to sustain high growth and competitiveness in a harsh global economy (Horwitz and Mellahi 2009).

An area of particular importance for further investigation is the performance of BRICS MNCs in other emerging markets. There is little research on this theme, but as BRICS MNCs such as Haier, Tata Corporation, Infosys, and SAB Miller have become global players, their employment relations and HRM policies and practices have increasing influence on their global operations. Hence the diffusion of emerging market MNC practices is an increasingly important area of study, particularly the extent to which these exert positive or negative influence on the labour markets in which they operate. Research indicates that the diffusion of employment practices by Chinese and Indian medium-sized firms operating in African countries such as Ghana is mediated by weak national institutional and regulatory systems often resulting in a reluctance to voluntarily adopt high-level labour standards and little enforcement of compliance to minimum employment standards (Akorsu and Cooke 2011).

An allied area for further research is a deepened analysis of the interrelationship or nexus of political economy networks particularly trade and investment policies and employment relations practices between (1) BRICS countries themselves (2) supranational global economic players between BRICS countries and MNCs from mature economies, and (3) the changing role of international financial institutions including development finance institutions. The latter's engagement with BRICS varies. Arguably the BRICS countries have differing but relatively modest (and some not at all) levels of involvement or intervention by organizations such as the International Monetary Fund (IMF) and the World Bank. Other emerging markets particularly those in Africa and Southeast Asia, have had structural adjustment programmes required by the IMF in order to secure international loans. The socio-economic effects of this have been mixed with restructuring and increased job losses during the 1970–2000 period.

On the other hand, with the more recent ascendancy of emerging market countries, and significant trade and investment (rather than loan finance only) of countries such as China, including its banks in Africa, has arguably boosted these economies more, given the GDP growth of over 5% in Africa over the past five years. This might also contrast to Gourevitch's (1978) postulation of a 'Second Image Reversed theory' where, for example, the BRICS to varying degrees have been able to selectively reshape or assume a much stronger position against transnational actors. Mature market players are less able today to exert the same level of influence they had previously on local organizations and domestic structures of so-called host countries as suggested by Gourevitch.

As discussed earlier, this reflects a fundamental shift in power relations towards large rapidly growing emerging markets in the past decade. This is further evidenced by the unprecedented increase of foreign direct investment from MNCs and institutional investors leading to real shifts in bargaining power towards large, high growth emerging markets and a weakening of the exigencies of the international system on local context, which Gourevitch had posited derived from effects of the international system. In the international HRM discourse these issues are located in the ongoing debate about convergence, divergence (Brewster and Mayrhofer 2012), and even 'cross-vergence'.

A further example is China's large retained foreign exchange reserves which means it can deal with international financial institutions and firms on a different basis than before. The construct of unidirectional diffusion of relatively unchanged human resources and employment relations practices from Western mature-economy MNCs to their emerging market operations is less valid and indeed over-simplistic today. This notion of singular unidirectionality and influence is now mitigated as the latter countries' own MNCs and state-run enterprises (e.g. from China and Russia) exert increasing, though not always progressive influence on their transnational operations abroad. But there are also instances of socially positive outcomes such as infrastructural development in other countries where they now operate. Another example is the impact of emerging market MNCs who have acquired Western MNCs, such as Tata's ownership of Jaguar Land Rover, where new investment in the UK from India has enhanced employment in this sector. The notion of reverse diffusion of emerging market MNC practices is therefore becoming an increasingly pertinent theme (Horwitz et al. 2002).

In conclusion, notwithstanding the diversity of employment conditions, a number of common themes emerge from an analysis of BRICS employment relations systems. These include increasing decentralization of collective bargaining to enterprise levels, employer adoption of flexible or non-standard work practices, and subcontracting and informalization of work. These result in fragmented bargaining with increased use of outsourcing and subcontracting, part-time, and casual work—often with fewer protections and attendant employment insecurity. Promoting fair employment practices, skills, and entrepreneurial development are important challenges given the BRICS' shift towards open transitional market economies.

References

Akorsu, A. D. and Cooke, F. L. (2011). 'Labour Standards among Chinese and Indian Firms in Ghana: Typical or Atypical?', *International Journal of Human Resource Management*, 22(13): 2730–48.

Badigannavar, V. (2006). 'Industrial Relations in India', M. Morley, P. Gunnigle, and D. Collings (eds.), *Global Industrial Relations*. London: Routledge, 198–218.

Bhattacherjee, D. and Ackers, P. (2010). 'Introduction: Employment Relations in India—Old Narratives and New Perspectives', *Industrial Relations Journal*, 41(2): 106–21.

Bhaumik, S. (2003). 'Casualisation of the Workforce in India', *Indian Journal of Labour Economics*, 46(4): 907–26.

Bjorkman, I., Fey, C., and Park, H. J. (2007). 'Institutional Theory and MNC Subsidiary HRM Practices: Evidence from a Three-Country Study', *Journal of International Business Studies*, 38: 430–46.

Brewster, C. and Mayrhofer, W (2012). 'Comparative Human Resource Management: An Introduction', in Brewster and Mayrhofer (eds.), *Handbook of Research on Comparative Human Resource Management*. Cheltenham: Edward Elgar, 1–26.

Budhwar, P. S. (2003). 'Employment Relations in India', *Employee Relations*, 25(2): 132–48.

Chang, C. and Bain, T. (2006). 'Employment Relations across the Taiwan Strait: Globalization and State Corporatism', *Journal of Industrial Relations*, 48(1): 99–115.

China Statistical Yearbook (various years). Beijing: National Bureau of Statistics of China.

Cooke, Fang Lee (2006). 'Informal Employment and Gender Implications in China: The Nature of Work and Employment Relations in the Community Services Sector', *International Journal of Human Resource Management*, 17(8): 1471–87.

—— (2008). 'The Changing Dynamics of Employment Relations in China: An Evaluation of the Rising Level of Labour Disputes', *Journal of Industrial Relations*, 50(1): 111–38.

—— (2011). 'Labour Market Regulations and Informal Employment in China', *Journal of Chinese Human Resource Management*, 2(2): 100–16.

Croucher, R. and Cotton, E. (2009). *Global Unions, Global Business: Global Union Federations and International Business*. London: Middlesex University Press.

Dirani, K. K. and Ardichvili, A. (2008). 'Human Capital Theory and Practice in Russian Enterprises', *Advances in International Management*, 21: 125–44.

Dlamini, A. (2011). 'Exploiting BRICS Status'. Available at <http://www.businesslive.co.za>.

The Economist (2011a). 'The Other Asian Giant', 6 August: 51–7.

—— (2011b). *Pocket World in Figures*. London: Profile Books.

—— (2011c). 'Trying to Pull Together', 23 April: 74–6.

—— (2011d). 'Why the Tail Wags the Dog', 6 August: 63.

—— (2011e). 'India's Economy: The Half-Finished Revolution', 23 July: 8.

—— (2012). 'Brazil's Trade Policy: Seeking Protection', 14 January: 44–5.

The Economist Intelligence Unit (2008). *White Paper Report on Emerging Markets*.

Fashoyin, T. (2010). 'Changing International Industrial Relations: A Summary', *Indian Journal of Industrial Relations*, 45(4): 513–22.

Fey, C. F., Pavlovskaya, A., and Tang, N. (2004). 'A Comparison of Human Resource Management in Russia, China and Finland', *Organizational Dynamics*, 33(1): 79–97.

Friedman, E. and Lee, C. K. (2010). 'Remaking the World of Chinese Labour: A 30-Year Retrospective', *British Journal of Industrial Relations*, 48(3): 507–33.

Gimpelson, V., Kapeliushnikov, R., and Lukiyanova, A. (2010). 'Stuck between Surplus and Shortage: Demand for Skills in Russian Industry', *Labour*, 24(3): 311–32.

Gourevitch, P. (1978). 'The Second Image Reversed: The International Sources of Domestic Politics', *International Organization*, 32(4): 881–912.

Guimaraes, S. M. K. (2007). 'Brazil's Telecom Unions Confront the Future: Privatization, Technological Change and Globalisation', *International Labor and Working-Class History*, 72: 42–62.

Horwitz, F. M. (2006). 'Industrial Relations in Africa', in M. Morley, P. Gunnigle, and D. Collings (eds.), *Global Industrial Relations*. London: Routledge, 178–98.

—— (2009). 'Managing Human Resources in Africa: Emerging Market Challenges', in J. Storey, P. M. Wright, and D. Ulrich (eds.), *The Routledge Companion to Strategic Human Resource Management*. New York: Routledge, 462–75.

Horwitz, F. M. and Jain, H. (2008). 'Managing Human Resources in South Africa: A Multinational Firm Focus', in J. Lawler and G. Hundley (eds.), *The Global Diffusion of Human Resource Practices: Institutional and Cultural Limits*. Bingley, UK: Emerald Publishing, 89–123.

—— (2011). 'An Assessment of Employment Equity and Broad Based Black Economic Empowerment Developments in South Africa', *Equality, Diversity and Inclusion: An International Journal*, 30(4): 297–317.

Horwitz, F. M., Kamoche, K., and Chew, I. (2002). 'Looking East: Diffusing High Performance Work Practices in the Southern Afro-Asia Context', *International Journal of Human Resource Management*, 13(7): 1019–41.

Horwitz, F. M. and Mellahi, K. (2009). 'Human Resource Management in Emerging Markets', in D. G. Collings and G. Wood (eds.), *Human Resource Management: A Critical Approach*. London: Routledge, 263–95.

Horwitz, F. M., Nkomo, S. M., and Rajah, M. (2004). 'HRM in South Africa', in K. Kamoche, Y. Debrah, Horwitz, and G. Muuka (eds.), *Managing Human Resources in Africa*. London: Routledge, 1–18.

Jiang, Y. P. (2003). 'Gender Equality in the Labour Market: Attention is Needed', *Collection of Women's Studies*, 2: 51–8.

Judge, W. Q., Naoumova, I., and Douglas, T. (2009). 'Organisational Capacity for Change and Firm Performance in a Transition Economy', *International Journal of Human Resource Management*, 20(8): 1737–52.

Kamoche, K., Debrah, Y., Horwitz, F. M., and Muuka, G. (eds.) (2004). *Managing Human Resources in Africa*. London: Routledge.

Kapelyushnikov, R., Kuznetsov, A., and Kuznetsova, O. (2011). 'Diversity within Capitalism: The Russian Labour Market Model', *Employee Relations*, 33(4): 395–412.

Kearney, A. T. (2011). 'Riding Russia's Consumer Boom', *Executive Agenda*, 14(1). Available at <http://www.atkearney.com/en_GB/executive-agenda/full-article/-/asset_publisher/oHoTuo1PO8ov/content/riding-russia-s-consumer-boom/1019>.

Krishnan, T. N. (2010). 'Technological Change and Employment Relations in India', *Indian Journal of Industrial Relations*, 45(3): 367–80.

Lansbury, R. D., Kwon, S. K., and Suh, C.-S. (2006). 'Globalization and Employment Relations in the Korean Auto Industry: The Case of Hyundai Motor Company in Korea, Canada and India', *Asia Pacific Business Review*, 12(2): 131–47.

Li, M. and Edwards, P. (2008). 'Work and Pay in Small Chinese Clothing Firms: A Constrained Negotiating Order', *Industrial Relations Journal*, 39(4): 296–313.

Lucena, H. and Covarrubias, A. (2006). 'Industrial Relations in Latin America', in M. Morley, P. Gunnigle, and D. Collings (eds.), *Global Industrial Relations*. London: Routledge, 53–65.

Mathew, M. and Jain, H. (2008). 'International Human Resource Management in the Indian Information Technology Sector: A Comparison of Indian MNCs and Affiliates of Foreign MNCs in India', in J. Lawler and G. Hundley (eds.), *The Global Diffusion of Human Resource Practices: Institutional and Cultural Limits* Bingley, UK: Emerald Publishing, 269–300.

May, R., Puffer, S. M., and McCarthy, D. J. (2005). 'Transferring Management Knowledge to Russia', *Academy of Management Executive*, 19(2): 24–35.

Olivas-Lujan, M. R., Monsarrat, S. I., Ruiz-Gutierrez, J. A., Greenwood, R. A., Gomez, S. M., Murphy, E. F., and Santos, N. M. (2009). 'Values and Attitudes towards Women in Argentina, Brazil, Colombia and Mexico', *Employee Relations*, 31(3): 227–44.

Peters, S., Miller, M., and Kusyk, S. (2011). 'How Relevant is Corporate Governance and Corporate Social Responsibility in Emerging Markets?', *Corporate Governance: The International Journal of Business in Society*, 11(4): 429–45.

Popola, T. S. (2004). 'Globalisation, Employment and Social Protection: Emerging Perspectives for Indian Workers', *Indian Journal of Labour Economics*, 47(3): 541–50.

Poshakwale, S. (2011). 'BRICS Economies and Global Growth'. Cranfield Knowledge Interchange, University of Cranfield. Available at <http://www.cranfield.ac.uk/som>.

Qiao, J. and Jiang, Y. (2004). 'An Analysis of Labour Demonstrations', in X. Yu, X. Y. Lu, P. Li, P. Huang, and J. H. Lu (eds.), *Analysis and Forecast on China's Social Development*. Beijing: Social Sciences Academic Press, 296–314.

Ratnam, V. (1991). *Unusual Collective Agreements*. New Delhi: Global Business Press.

Russell, R. and Callanan, V. (2001). 'Firm-Level Influences on Forms of Employment and Pay in Russia', *Industrial Relations*, 40(4): 627–34.

Santos, N. M. (2006). 'Successful Women: A Vision of Brazil', in B. J. Punnett, J. A. Duffy, S. Fox, A. Gregory, T. R. Lituchy, S. I. Monserrat, M. R. Olivas-Lujan, and Santos (eds.), *Successful Professional Women of the Americas: From Polar Winds to Tropical Breezes*. Cheltenham: Edward Elgar, 183–94.

Shao, S., Nyland, C., and Zhu, C. J. (2011). 'Tripartite Consultation: An Emergent Form of Governance Shaping Employment Relations in China', *Industrial Relations Journal*, 42(4): 358–74.

Shen, J. (2007a). 'Labour Contracts in China: Do They Protect Worker Rights?', *Journal of Organisational Transformation and Social Change*, 4(2): 111–29.

—— (2007b). 'The Labour Dispute Arbitration System in China', *Employee Relations*, 29(5): 520–39.

Shyam Sundar, K. R. (2010). 'Emerging Trends in Employment Relations in India'. *Indian Journal of Industrial Relations*, 45(4): 585–95.

Yi Lu, Zhigang Tao, and Yijiang Wang (2010) 'Union Effects on Performance and Employment Relations: Evidence from China', *China Economic Review*, 21: 202–10.

Zou, M. and Lansbury, R. D. (2009). 'Multinational Corporations and Employment Relations in the People's Republic of China: The Case of Beijing Hyundai Motor Company', *International Journal of Human Resource Management*, 20(11): 2349–69.

PART IV

....

SUBSTANTIVE THEMES

....

CHAPTER 21

GLOBALIZATION AND LABOUR MARKET GOVERNANCE

MICHEL GOYER,
JULIANE REINECKE, AND
JIMMY DONAGHEY

INTRODUCTION

MUCH has been written about the effects that globalization has had on employment relations, particularly in developed economies. At the level of the state, national economies have developed distinctive labour regimes, which to use the terminology from the varieties of capitalism (VOC) literature bring 'comparative institutional advantage' (Hall and Soskice 2001; Morgan 2012). However, international competitive pressures threaten distinct labour regimes. An important development associated with the globalization of economic activities is the increased mobility of capital across borders and its associated pressures on employment relations. The ability of actors to shift capital in an unimpeded manner across borders comes in two forms. The first feature of the globalization of finance refers to constraints on policy-making associated with capital mobility and its ensuing consequences for employment relations including the ability of policy-makers to pursue macroeconomic policies that are favourable to the interests of organized labour (Garrett 1998; Scharpf 1991). The second feature of the globalization of finance is the process of capital mobility in the form of flows of funds from shareholder value oriented institutional investors into equities of listed companies in systems of corporate governance traditionally not focused on financial returns to shareholders (Goyer 2011). Cross-border portfolio investments from UK/US-based institutional investors constitute a challenge for the mode of governance of companies and the distribution of value creation among the different stakeholders of the firm (Gourevitch and Shinn 2005; Roe 2000).

Another important development that threatens regulatory labour regimes has been corporations and states pursuing policies which place downward pressure on labour standards. In this context downward pressures have been placed on labour standards, so-called 'social dumping' which takes two forms that often work in conjunction with each other. First, firms seek to de-invest in economies with high labour standards and relocate to cheaper production regimes. Second, the state often plays its role of 'competition state' (Cerny 1995). With multinational corporations (MNCs) seeking to offshore production, states actively engage in regime building aimed at attracting inward investment and enhancing the comparative advantage of their system vis-à-vis other countries competing for foreign direct investment (FDI).

MNCs have greater ability to 'regime shop' by choosing to locate production where there are lower levels of constraining rules. Evidence surrounding the degree of actual impact of this is contested, though the threat of such practice is widely accepted (Christopherson and Lillie 2005; Traxler and Woitech 2000). With such wide diversity in terms of both substantive terms and conditions of employment as well as different procedural rules, MNCs are either in a position to bargain downwards the terms of these rules, the so-called 'race to the bottom', or to maintain rates of pay and conditions while increasing productivity significantly (Hauptmeier and Greer 2012). A series of new mechanisms have emerged to formulate and implement international labour standards across MNCs and their suppliers. While some of these bear close resemblance to traditional national labour governance, for example collective bargaining, other forms entail inclusion of actors such as non-governmental organizations (NGOs) who previously had little role in national systems.

This chapter analyses these two fundamental aspects of globalization in regard to its impact on employment relations. An analytical overview of these two issue areas provides interesting and common insights for the study of globalization. We highlight the theoretical importance of two sets of causal arguments: institutions and society/interest group centred approaches.

The presence of institutional diversity across national systems of employment relations matters for the evolution of different economies by structuring power relations and, as a result, reducing the range of strategic options (Hall and Soskice 2001; Soskice 1999). Institutional frameworks preclude certain adjustment paths that rely on the presence of other elements in an institutional framework. In other words, different sets of institutional arrangements enable different groups in society to mobilize and push for their preferences (Hall 1986). The translation of globalization pressures on systems of employment relations may be subject to different institutional constraints across national settings.

The constraining character of local institutions does not eliminate the capacities for strategic selection by actors in response to globalization pressures. At the macro-national level, society/interest group centred approaches highlight how policy outcomes reflect the struggle that takes place among various groups (Gourevitch 1986). The adjustment paths of different national systems of employment relations to the pressures of globalization are characterized by the mobilization of different groups of actors pushing for their preferred outcomes (Johnson and Kwak 2010; Milner 1989). The implication is that the erosion of important aspects of national systems of employment relations does not constitute the ineluctable consequences of the globalization of economic activities, but reflects the ability of different groups to secure their preferences with policymakers (Pontusson and Raesss 2012). At the micro-level, society/interest group centred approaches highlight that strategic choices by actors remain compatible with the presence of institutional constraints under the pressures of globalization since different categories of actors are governed by different internally defined rules that influence their behaviour in an institutional framework (Aguilera and Jackson 2003). Institutional frameworks do preclude certain trajectories of change but do not specify how actors operate within an institutional framework (Hancké and Goyer 2005): similar, and equally constraining, institutions can lead to different outcomes. The implication is that the translation of imported practices into local institutional contexts interacts with domestic actors characterized by different capabilities for actions, thereby highlighting the potential for selective globalization pressures (see Djelic 1998). As Jessop (2012) argues, at the meta-level neo-liberal globalization may dominate but significant differences are discernible across economies operating within this wider ecosystem. The remainder of the chapter details how two contrasting areas are demonstrative of this phenomenon.

Financial Globalization and Labour

The Globalization of Finance (I): Its Impact on Policy-Making

While there is widespread agreement that globalization is profoundly disequilibrating to national economies, the mechanisms by which globalization induces discontinuous changes is subject to intense debate. Trade in goods and services, the multinationalization of production, and financial capital mobility (Berger 2000; Garrett 2000) have been presented as sources of constraints on government policies: increasing trade and associated rules have deprived national governments of protectionist tools; the multinationalization of production enhances the credibility of firms to threaten capital flight; and the ability of actors to move reduces the ability of governments to pursue autonomous monetary policies. The implications for employment relations are that processes of globalization in trade, production, and finance potentially undermine the capacities for policy-makers to implement policies that serve the interests of organized labour (Garrett and Lange 1991; Scharpf 1991). Among these components of globalization, the integration of financial markets has been singled out as being both more constraining on the policy repertoires of national governments and as entailing far deeper consequences for organized labour (Garrett 1998). Several factors account for the special character of the globalization of finance.

First, increased capital mobility reduces the range of policies of national governments through its impact on the parameters of the Mundell–Fleming theorem in open macroeconomics (Frieden 1991). Only two of the following policy options can be obtained at once in the case of open economies: a fixed exchange rate, autonomous monetary policy, and free mobility of capital across borders. Technological developments have sharply increased the ability of actors to move funds across borders and the removal of capital controls by national governments in the face of domestic pressures and decreased ability to control capital exits entail that policy-makers are forced to choose between autonomous monetary policies and fixed exchange rates (Goodman and Pauly 1993). This choice is seen as being less favourable to labour than it was under the Bretton Woods regime with embedded liberalism standing at the heart of class comprise policies (fixed exchange rates, capital controls, and autonomous monetary policy in the form expansionist Keynesian policies) (Ruggie 1982). Moreover, the decision of EU member states to opt for fixed exchange rates, first via the exchange rate mechanism (ERM) and currently with the euro, has meant that the mobility of capital across borders has reduced the ability of national governments to pursue autonomous monetary policies.

Second, studies on the partisan composition of governments highlight how exposure to trade and FDI flows have not affected the size of government expenditures in the presence of social democratic governments (Garret 1998; Iversen 1999). Strong left-labour governments have implemented supply-side policies that shape innovation and labour market adjustments according to their partisan preferences—although spending on traditional demand-side Keynesian policies has been less prominent (Garrett and Lange 1991; Scharpf 1991). However, the mediating role of left-leaning governments has been reduced under conditions of high degrees of capital mobility (Garrett 1998). While higher budget deficits do not necessarily cause capital flight to other countries, governments that persistently run higher deficits are punished by financial markets via higher interest rates: capital mobility increases the costs of pursuing budget deficits because of the interest rate premiums demanded by lenders. Two implications follow. First, systems of employment relations characterized by the reliance on state policies, such as France, left organized labour ill-prepared for globalization, compared to economies such as Germany where the strength of organized labour was shaped by the presence of entrenched firm-level works councils with substantial legal rights and capacities to engage in strategic interaction with management (Goyer 2011). Second, the mode of tax collection matters for policy-makers seeking to maintain high levels of spending. Social democratic governments—Denmark, Finland, and Sweden—have been able to pursue more expansionary fiscal policies, despite high levels of government expenditures, since they have been able to run substantial budget surpluses in good times (Cameron 2012). These economies rely heavily on personal income taxes as the main source of revenues that have proven highly elastic in periods of economic expansion.

Third, financial crises in the last 30 years highlight that the volume and speed of global financial flows have rendered national governments vulnerable to switches in assessments by financial investors that are not always predictable and that could also be unrelated to underlying economic conditions (Roubini and Mihm 2010). The transmission of economic crises across borders is more intense under conditions of high capital mobility than under trade integration. Unfettered capital mobility is characterized by significant problems of asymmetric and incomplete information that nurture rapid belief shifts (Shiller 2000), meaning that policy constraints associated with globalization differ across mechanisms (Garrett 1998). The globalization of financial markets constrains the actions of policy-makers in large part based on how participants in financial markets assess how policy outputs shape the value of financial instruments. The relationship between public policy and the two other mechanisms of globalization (trade integration and the multinationalization of production), in contrast, reflects to a greater extent indicators of the 'real economy', such as productivity.

While the increased importance of globalization as a source of constraints on policy-making is widely acknowledged, it is a harder case to make that globalization constraints are so pervasive that interventionist government policies are virtually impossible. The opening of borders creates demands for compensation by the negatively affected parties (Cameron 1978; Rodrick 1997) and the presence of institutional diversity matters for the process by which the preferences of actors benefiting from globalization are translated into policies (Garrett and Lange 1995). The financial crisis of 2007–9 constitutes an interesting setting to investigate the constraints induced by globalization on national economies and its impact on employment relations. The crisis was initially characterized by a mix of government autonomy and policy convergence. First, governments across advanced capitalist economies intervened to rescue financially troubled banks in the form of credit guarantees (Weber and Schmitz 2011). The reactions of national governments were also characterized by the extensive use of 'liberal' Keynesian economic policies, namely a mixture of spending increases, tax cuts, and some monetary easing to stimulate the economy (Hall 2009; Pontusson and Raess 2012).

Second, the institutional arrangements of labour organization across different advanced capitalist economies shaped the content of the adjustment process to the financial crisis where the responses of national governments varied considerably. In mixed market economies characterized by general skills and high level of labour market protection, such as France and Spain, adjustments were characterized by increased reliance on atypical jobs, namely fixed-term contracts and part-time work (Lallement 2011). In Germany, the quintessential coordinated market economy, the initial demand package stimulus emphasized the preservation of existing, highly skilled jobs through the award of subsidies and reductions in payroll taxes for companies who were retaining employees via part-time work (Hall 2009). Preventing job losses for skilled employees was important in the context of firm-specific skills, vocational training, and labour market rigidities regarding dismissals (Estevez-Abe et al. 2001). In liberal market economies, in contrast, reliance on flexible labour market regulations governing redundancies proved important in the adjustment process of companies (Lallement 2011).

Third, the menu of policy options deployed by governments during the 2007–9 financial crisis were relatively narrow, especially compared to the economic downturn of

1974–82, with important implications for the adjustment processes of national systems of employment relations (Pontusson and Raess 2012). More specifically, measures to compensate the unemployed and efforts to protect employees against rising unemployment have been conspicuously absent in this current recession. In contrast to the 1970s, policies have not been undertaken to limit the ability of companies to shed workers during economic downturns since 2007. In fact, relaxation on rules regarding atypical work have been liberalized (Palier and Thelen 2010), spending on unemployment compensation has been curtailed, and eligibility criteria for welfare recipients have become more restrictive in the EU (Gingrich 2011).

Fourth, the decline of active Keynesian management policies after 2009 and the implementation of austerity policies reveals systematic differences across institutionally based varieties of capitalist economies. The absence of a nationally based lender of last resort increases the vulnerabilities of eurozone members to the pressures of the bond markets in the form of a solvency crisis (De Grauwe 2013; Hall 2012). Eurozone members, who by definition do not have their own currency and whose government debt is denominated in euros, do not possess legal means to force the European Central Bank to provide the needed liquidity when hit by economic shocks. Investors could become uncertain about the ability of eurozone member states to raise enough revenues, or to implement sufficient budget cuts, thereby reflecting the inability of national governments to print euros. The implementation of austerity policies in this context is designed to reassure bondholders about the solvency of state finances.

Nonetheless, the role of finance in the changing character of the Keynesian state remains an open issue since the debate is not about the ability of governments to stimulate the economy, but about the content of state intervention and the role of interest groups. First, countries with budget surpluses accumulated during the good times have been able to maintain active demand Keynesian policies after 2009—in contrast to countries with budget deficits even during years of economic expansion (Cameron 2012). Second, Pontusson and Raess (2012) suggest the political importance of the preferences of interest groups to understand the shift in the content of Keynesian policies with an emphasis on the decline of unions and the rise of actors in the financial sector. The decline of redistributive Keynesianism across a range of diverse contexts in which policies are implemented constitutes strong evidence of the insights of society/interest group centred approaches. The internationalization of global value chains and the mobilization of export-oriented firms constitute important factors that provide insights on why the current recession is not associated with a return to protectionist policies (Berger 2006, 2009). Moreover, the ability of actors in the financial sphere to convince policy-makers to implement their preferred sets of policies is remarkable (Johnson and Kwak 2010). The implication is that the decline of redistributive Keynesianism is not the ineluctable consequence of financial globalization. An important issue concerns the shortcomings in the ability of organized labour to influence the content of Keynesian policies in the political sphere. This issue is particularly pressing in systems of employment relations characterized by increased flexibility of labour market regulations as a means of adjustment.

The Globalization of Finance (II): Its Impact on Firm-Level Corporate Governance

The second aspect of the globalization of finance deals with capital mobility across borders in the form of flows of funds from shareholder value oriented institutional investors into equities of listed companies in countries traditionally not exposed to shareholder value pressures (Goyer 2006, 2011). The political implications resulting from impressive cross-border flows have been analysed most notably, but not exclusively, in regard to their effects on government macroeconomic and monetary policies (Cohen 1996), political preferences of actors (Frieden 1991), and on the development of legal rules and norms in international finance (Abdelal 2007). While studies of international finance are not new, the analysis of cross-border investments via equity purchases has not been extensively covered, reflecting the prior lack of capital mobility across borders for national stock markets which had previously been far less integrated than other forms of cross-border capital flows such as bank lending and the trading of currencies (Cohen 1996; Frieden 1991). However, the greater international integration of stock markets since the early 1990s has made it imperative to investigate the consequences of cross-border portfolio investments—especially from shareholder value oriented investors.

The first rise of shareholder value investors in corporate governance originated in the late 1970s with the advent of shareholder activism in the USA. Increased ownership by institutional investors over the last three decades has transformed the nature of corporate governance in the USA: creating shareholder value at the expense of other stakeholders, especially employees, is increasingly seen as the fundamental purpose of corporations (Davis 2009). Drastic corporate restructuring activities, such as employee lay-offs and asset divestitures, have been prevalent since institutional investors believe that these measures are some of the most effective means to maximize shareholder value (Useem 1996). The incidence of corporate restructuring in the USA in the last three decades is different from those in previous years not only in terms of its extent but also in its nature. Historically, lay-offs were seen as temporary labour force reductions caused by decreased product demand. However, American companies increasingly cut jobs to improve financial performance rather than to respond to a shortage of demand, i.e. 'offensive' lay-offs (Budros 2002; Jacoby 2005).

The consequences associated with the globalization of finance in the form of cross-border portfolio investments reflect the mediating role of institutions (Hall and Soskice 2001; Soskice 1999) and the strategic choices of actors (Aguilera and Jackson 2003; Whittington 1988) as important factors that have influenced the translation of Anglo-Saxon inspired shareholder value in different contexts. We survey two issues: flows of funds from shareholder value oriented investors, and the market for corporate control (takeovers).

First, capital mobility in the form of flows of funds from UK/US-based shareholder value oriented institutional investors is shaped by the institutional characteristics, including firm-level institutions of employment relations, of recipient countries (Goyer 2006, 2011). An influential literature in the field of law and economics emphasizes the importance of the extent to which minority shareholders are legally protected from the actions of corporate insiders before acquiring equity stakes in listed companies outside their home country. The critical precondition for the development of deep and liquid securities markets requires the presence of corporate law that is protective of the rights of dispersed shareholders (La Porta et al. 2000). The legal thesis on the protection of minority shareholders, however, has been criticized for two reasons: the presence of legal protection for minority shareholders does not constitute a sufficient condition for investment as witnessed by the diversity of ownership structures despite the presence of adequate legal protection in many developed capitalist economies, most notably in Germany and Sweden (Roe 2000); and the legal arrangements of corporate law in common law economies do not cover all instances of shareholder (Roe 2002).

This reiterates the firm as a politically contested entity characterized by the presence of different preferences by the various stakeholders (Gourevitch and Shinn 2005). Different sets of institutional arrangements, including institutions of employment relations, enable different categories of firm stakeholders to push for their preferred outcome (Schneper and Guillén 2004). Thus, investment decisions of shareholder value-driven Anglo-Saxon institutional investors pursuing a bottom-up strategy are also driven by judgements made about the nature and likely speed of corporate restructuring—highlighting the adaptiveness of internal stakeholders—such as unions and management (Clark and Wójcik 2007). For instance, Goyer (2011) reports that UK/US-based institutional investors with a short-term horizon are more likely to target France over Germany in acquiring equity stakes, as the French market is attractive to short-term investors given the concentration of power at the top of the managerial hierarchy and the absence of many stakeholders from the decision-making process while German firms, in contrast, are characterized by the imposition of greater institutional constraints on managerial autonomy as well as by the participation of the workforce in important aspects of the decision-making process.

However, an exclusive focus on the constraining character of institutions understates the importance of the strategic choices of actors. For instance, shareholder value oriented institutional investors are characterized by the presence of subgroups with different interests, and governed by different internally defined rules (Aguilera and Jackson 2003; see also Whittington 1988). Institutional investors can be divided along their investment strategies, size of their equity stake, time horizon, prominence of commitment versus liquidity concerns, and the degree of their embedded position in national corporate networks (Klein and Zur 2009). Variations in the interests of different categories of institutional investors, building from the presence of differences in internally defined governance rules, matter for how they operate in specific institutional frameworks. The implication for employment relations is that the globalization of finance exhibits important variations in regard to its effects. The international investment strategy of some categories of investors, such as hedge funds which favour short-term returns, is potentially more challenging to the governance of companies as compared to other investors, such as pension funds, which emphasize risk reduction, and whose goals are compatible with the longer-term orientation of companies in coordinated market economies. From the perspective of foreign investors, the presence of constraints on the ability of German companies to implement strategies of shareholder value in a relatively quick fashion constitutes an important concern for short-term investors, but nowhere to the same extent for funds with a long-term horizon (Goyer 2011).

Second, institutional arrangements of employment relations are influential in shaping the investment allocation of institutional investors regarding takeovers. The market for corporate control constitutes an important form of financial globalization, namely the ability of companies to enter new markets in the presence of barriers to entry. From the perspective of shareholders primarily interested in financial returns, the presence of substantial financial premiums associated with the market for corporate control provides significant incentives for activist institutional investors, such as hedge funds, to identify undervalued firms that are likely to constitute the target of a takeover bid (Klein and Zur 2009). Nonetheless, the market for corporate control exhibits extensively documented cross-national differences in terms of prominence across national systems of corporate governance (Culpepper 2011; Rossi and Volpin 2004). Institutional arrangements of employment relations contribute to the diversity of takeover outcomes. The extent of post-acquisition schemes is shaped by the degree of legal protection of shareholders of acquiring companies and the extent to which national employment laws protect employees of target companies (Atanassov and Kim 2009; Capron and Guillen 2009). While the degree of legal protection of minority shareholders influences the incentives of the managerial team of the acquiring company to deliver greater shareholder value in the post-acquisition process, the presence of strong employment relation protections deters takeovers based on the ability of the acquiring company to restructure the target's assets via employee lay-offs. In other words, takeovers based on the restructuring target firms and/or recombining resources of the two newly combined entities are unlikely to succeed in the presence of strong employment rights. The implication is that while takeovers can be associated with extensive restructuring schemes and constitute a source of disruption to national systems of employment relations, the presence of institutional diversity, including institutions of employment relations, shapes the prominence of takeovers across economies.

THE EMERGING REGIME OF GLOBALIZED LABOUR GOVERNANCE[1]

Employment relations have generally followed a model which emphasized governance being provided through two modes: state regulation and collective bargaining. Yet, under globalization, both state regulation and collective bargaining are significantly diminished in effectiveness. Nevertheless, a growing web of new forms of institutional regimes is emerging across borders around the issue of labour standards. Thus, this section focuses on the emergence of international labour standards, arguing that labour standards are emerging from social movements, industry-led collaborations, and individual corporations to operate alongside more traditional collective bargaining driven mechanisms. These are effectively 'private labour governance' regimes, which operate across borders. This shift, driven by increasingly weak public regulation, has initiated new patterns of labour governance that require new forms of interaction between wider socio-economic forces.

Globalization has posed many issues for the future of collective bargaining (Thelen and Kume 2003; Standing 1997). Wide-scale collective bargaining and joint regulation were primarily West European phenomena. As such, the industrialization of many developing countries is occurring in systems where state and/or managerial determinism dominate, evidenced by weak collective bargaining systems. The International Labour Organization (ILO) estimates that in about 60% of countries, less than 20% of wage earners are covered by collective bargaining agreements and that less than 50% of workers in the world live in a country that has ratified ILO collective bargaining conventions (ILO 2012). Alongside this, a shift has occurred towards post-production pressure being exerted on multinational corporations which holds them responsible for labour standard breaches within their suppliers.

The lack of a legal framework of global regulation and enforceability has led to the emergence of a global private regime of labour governance which has increasingly migrated from governmental institutions to private and non-governmental actors, in which no single actor is dominant (Bernstein and Cashore 2007; Hassel 2008). What scholars have labelled 'soft' or 'civil regulation' (Vogel 2008) or private, transnational governance (Djelic and Sahlin-Andersson 2006; Wood and Demirbag 2012) can be defined as 'a process in which non-state actors from more than one country generate behavioural prescriptions that are intended to apply across national borders' (Dingwerth and Pattberg 2009: 711), thereby filling the regulatory gap left by weak states (Djelic and Sahlin-Andersson 2006; Tamm-Hallström and Boström 2010). Governance is 'non-state driven' in the sense that collective decisions about transnational problems are reached without government participation, although states may stimulate and support their development and promulgation (Haufler 2001). Rather than deriving policy-making ability from states' sovereign authority, private governance uses the pressure of public opinion and consumer choice to move MNCs to take responsibility (Matten and Crane 2005). Private governance can thereby sidestep conflicts about state sovereignty, which have restricted Western governments from using trade policies to promote domestic labour regulation in developing countries (Vogel 2008).

The changing strategy of the ILO exemplifies the shift from governmental regulation to private governance (Hassel 2008). Rather than seeking ratification of each of the 188 ILO conventions by its member states, in 1998 the 'ILO Declaration on Fundamental Principles and Rights at Work' defined fundamental rights. These form the basis of eight 'core labour standards' which all member states should respect and promote, irrespective of whether they have formally ratified them. Yet their implementation has shifted to private and more decentralized enforcement mechanisms that rely on consumer and civil society pressure rather than governmental ratification.

International Framework Agreements

International Framework Agreements (IFAs) have emerged as the main mechanism for regulating labour through negotiated, collective bargaining agreements. Hammer (2005: 512) describes IFAs as 'agreements [negotiated by Global Union Federations] on fundamental labour rights with MNCs', and as such are mechanisms to democratize the labour standards setting process (Stevis 2010). IFAs have been a long time in gestation, with their roots going back over 30 years, yet it is only since the mid-1990s that their proliferation has occurred due to the intensification of processes of globalization. As of 2012, only 70 IFAs are in place whose emergence has been attributed to the strength of trade unions across all units.

For Global Union Federations, they mark a mechanism to be recognized in MNCs across borders and through their supply chains. Agreements can either take the form of 'bargaining', where substantive agreements are made, or 'rights', where initial basic procedural agreements are set (Hammer 2005). Freedom of association and the right to collective bargaining are generally basic minima.

Implementation in both company-owned and suppliers' sites is critical for the sustainability of IFAs. Key issues identified so far relate to whether dissemination is a unilateral or bilateral initiative, whether it is restricted to trade union affiliates (Riisgaard 2005; Niforou 2012), and also the extent to which the IFA is communicated to the MNC suppliers (Fichter et al. 2008; Stevis 2010). Paradoxically, unionization seems to be a prerequisite for successful implementation and, most importantly, enforcement of compliance (Wills 2002; Niforou 2012). Although IFAs may trigger union organizing in MNC subsidiaries or support ongoing national and international campaigns, the absence of active local unions that would integrate IFAs into their organizing activities renders IFAs largely cosmetic. Finally, implementation in suppliers' sites is a difficult task for organized labour. The IKEA agreement was perceived as a 'foreign' instrument in the Russian plant and representatives expressed doubts about its potential to encourage workplace organization (Fichter et al. 2011). In the Chiquita case, although the IFA led to improvements in terms of employment in company-owned plants, it nonetheless made no difference to or even deteriorated working conditions on supplier sites (Riisgaard 2005). There is also the question of the nature of the sanctions a company would be willing to incorporate in an IFA. It is not always a viable solution to foresee the termination of the commercial relationship with the suppliers since that may result in plant closures and subsequently in job losses (Fichter et al. 2011). Stevis (2010) attributes successful IFAs to the combination of three factors: strong national unions, international networks, and a process in place to bring disputes to the attention of central management in a timely manner.

Voluntary Standards as Means of Private, Market-Based Labour Governance

As outlined in the previous section, while IFAs may have the greatest democratic legitimacy and be modelled on collective bargaining principles, their impact is questionable. However, as public pressure has become a key point of influence on MNCs, consumers, rather than governments, have become a critical third party influencing the dynamics of labour governance. Voluntary standards emerge due to pressure from outsiders to the organization expressing concerns over how MNCs police the treatment of labour across sites of the MNCs, their subsidiaries, and even suppliers (Conroy 2007). Even if initially MNCs did not feel responsible for violations of labour standards and human rights within their supply chains, labour rights campaigns have established that a custodial duty of care is owed to ensure that products reaching the consumer are free from human rights' abuses and labour violations (Bartley 2007). Voluntary labour standards and monitoring systems are sponsored by a variety of private actors from business and civil society actors who are often located in foreign target markets, where labour issues are perceived as important (Glasbergen 2011). While they enable firms to express their social responsibility and protect their reputations, scholars have debated whether private labour standards are a supplement to state regulation (O'Rourke 2006) or avoid stricter governmental regulation (Bartley 2007). Despite lacking a central enforcement authority, private standards can have law-like effects (Terlaak 2007), becoming binding and enforceable rules through independent, third-party certification systems and may diffuse globally through institutional pressures (Lim and Tsutsui 2012).

While IFAs are the outcome of political negotiations between international labour representatives and employers, the authority for market-based standards emanates from the market's supply chain (Bernstein and Cashore 2007), as market actors voluntarily sign up to them with little input from rank and file workers: private labour standards typically lack the voice of workers from production sites, or include it more or less symbolically (Elliot and Freeman 2003). Market-based voluntary standards also do not focus exclusively on labour practices, comprising other criteria that are useful for companies, such as product traceability or quality control (Higgins and Tamm Hallström 2007). They also vary in whether, and how, compliance is verified, ranging from self-audited verification to independent, third-party certification. Certification standards are seen as most stringent as they reduce information asymmetries with supply chain partners and provide buyers with information about suppliers' performance (King et al. 2005). We distinguish types of private labour governance according to representation and control of various interest groups, which has been found to shape their content and implementation (Fransen 2011).

Unilateral Standards: Codes of Conduct

Corporations have developed codes of conduct unilaterally to promote good labour conditions in their own internal units and those of their suppliers. Codes of conduct are single-firm-dominated modes of voluntary regulation, and often part of Corporate Social Responsibility (CSR) agendas. With strong unitarist undertones, this internal CSR agenda is viewed as a mechanism through which organizations can both protect their brand reputations from attacks by civil society activists, enhance product quality through improved supplier relations, as well as being seen to benefit wider society (Hassel 2008). At the centre are for-profit organizations that voluntarily assume a political role in global society, filling gaps in global regulation and thereby substituting for the declining governance capability of nation-states (Matten and Crane 2005; Scherer and Palazzo 2011). In terms of their implementation, codes of conduct are based around the ability of organizations to control their subsidiary plants in their internal value chains and to bind contractually independent suppliers into achieving the requisite standards (O'Rourke 2006; Locke et al. 2009). While developing countries may fail to enforce labour regulation, local suppliers have incentives to ensure compliance with the code of conduct given the threat of losing the contract with MNCs due to non-compliance.

However, codes of conduct have been considered the 'lightest' form of private regulation, as they entail a voluntary commitment whose performance is rarely externally verified or certified by independent, third parties (Turcotte et al. 2007). Therefore, a mere compliance-based approach has been associated with symbolic and surface-level implementation (Boiral 2007). Locke and colleagues (2009) found that companies and factories that embrace a commitment-oriented approach to improving labour standards are more effective in improving labour conditions as they build relationships of mutual respect, trust, and even reciprocity between auditors and factory managers/owners.

Civil Society-Led Multi-Stakeholder Standards

Multi-stakeholder initiatives are a collaborative form of governance that attempt to define, implement, and/or enforce rules for the behaviour of corporations (Rasche 2010). Rather than fighting social movement activists and NGOs, MNCs have increasingly aligned themselves with civil society actors, resulting in a range of multi-stakeholder partnership initiatives (O'Rourke 2006; Geppert et al. 2006). Given the absence of a democratic mandate for rule-making, representation of societal interest groups in standards governance has become a key indicator of their legitimacy (Mena and Palazzo 2012). However, multi-stakeholder initiatives differ in whether they are primarily controlled by societal interests, agendas of transnational institutions, or industry actors.

Civil society-led, multi-stakeholder standards have often been pioneered by social movement-based NGOs (Bartley 2007; Boström and Hallström 2010; Fransen 2011). Social movements have shifted in focus from targeting the state to campaigns targeting private sector organizations as arenas for political struggles (McAdam and Scott 2005). These civil society organizations have built a regulatory infrastructure and committed resources from the private sector to address issues of transnational scope (Cashore et al. 2007). Most are 'certification standards' (Gilbert et al. 2011) certifying particular products and sectors, such as the SA8000 standard. Developed by Social Accountability International in 1998, the standard was the first global, auditable social standard focusing on reducing sweatshop labour practices, certifying companies according to specified labour governance criteria based on ILO conventions, the Universal Declaration of Human Rights, and the UN Convention on the Rights of the Child. It is regarded as one of the most stringent management systems certification standards in the area of labour standards (O'Rourke 2006).

Certification standards may communicate with and mobilize consumers through the use of ethical product labels, driving standards adoption by branded companies. Ethical labelling has been portrayed as a powerful mode of governance, allowing firms to use accreditation on their branding once the requisite level of adherence to standards has been met. Conroy (2007) speaks of the 'certification revolution', where civil society groups, NGOs, and social movements become the drivers of market change that might be producing a 'revolutionary' transformation of corporate behaviour. However, because certification standards are demanding and civil society groups dominate their governance, their diffusion has been limited to a few industries, and corporations have been quick in responding by developing their own multi-stakeholder standards (see below).

Transnational Institution-Led Multi-Stakeholder Standards

Transnational institution-led multi-stakeholder initiatives are generally sector-crossing and involve a broad stakeholder base by creating ties between intergovernmental organizations, the business community, labour organizations, NGOs, and academia. Because of this broad scope and base, they are 'principle-based standards' providing broadly defined guidelines for responsible behaviour (Gilbert et al. 2011) that put less emphasis on monitoring and certification and more on integrating private actors. They typically integrate ILO core labour standards within broader guidelines for responsible governance to be adopted by individual companies and adapted more flexibly to individual industry settings.

While transnational institution-led initiatives have achieved widespread corporate uptake, this often remains at signatory level commitment due to a lack of meaningful enforcement mechanisms, as the United Nations Global Compact illustrates. With over 6,000 business participants in 135 countries in 2012, the Global Compact, launched by UN Secretary-General Kofi Annan in 2000, is the world's largest voluntary corporate citizenship initiative (Rasche and Kell 2010). It was purposefully designed to enlist businesses to follow ten universal principles in the areas of human rights, labour standards, the environment, and anti-corruption, yet it deliberately refrains from monitoring its participants. Similarly, signatories to the UN's Principles for Responsible Investment (PRI), a count of more than 1,100, financial market participants, including some of the world's largest institutional investors, pledge to report on the ethics of their investment practices, yet do not yield monitoring authority to third parties.

Industry-Led Multi-Stakeholder Standards

Industry-led, multi-stakeholder standards represent industry-wide self-regulation programs (Christmann and Taylor 2006). They usually represent the second or third generation of standards within a sector established as an industry's reaction to the growing influence and perceived legitimacy of civil society standards (cf. Fransen 2011). Key actors are business associations, mainly from industrialized countries, who focus on promoting better labour conditions in certain, identified 'risk countries', defined as those where violations of workers' rights occur frequently. Some industry-led standards focus on a range of CSR issues within a specific sector, such as the Responsible Jewellery Council or the Roundtable for Sustainable Palm Oil. The International Standardization Organization (ISO), having moved away from standardizing 'nuts and bolts' towards social issues, in 2010 released ISO 26000 defining methods and processes to guide corporations towards global principles of corporate social responsibility (Tamm-Hallström 2008). Others focus more explicitly on improving the working conditions in the global supply chain, such as the BSCI for labour-intensive goods in typical offshoring destinations. These 'business-driven programs looking like stakeholder initiatives' often invite civil society actors and producers to take part in their governance processes to gain legitimacy (Fransen 2012: 172). Their governance, content, and communication may strongly resemble societal-led standards, though they may differ in important aspects. Notably, they usually do not require certification, but focus on gradual implementation and a step up to other, more stringent certification systems.

However, even if designed to be representative of multiple stakeholder groups, the agendas were often driven by a few, powerful stakeholder groups with MNCs often exerting significant influence (Gilbert and Rasche 2007). Tamm-Hallström (2008: 58) reports great differences in stakeholder representation in the context of the ISO 26000 standard, 'as some stakeholders had more financial and other resources to influence not only the content of the standard but also the shaping of the agenda, organization and procedures of the standard-setting work'.

Comparing Mechanisms

The case of global labour standards is demonstrative of the emerging response to the disruptive effects of globalization on employment relations: on the one hand, new institutions are emerging in regulatory regimes; on the other hand, these institutions are far from being a new emerging panacea for industrial relations. For example, the majority of labour standards were developed in a Northern context, yet intended to be applied in the Global South (Stevis and Boswell 2007; Wells 2009) and thus may fail to bring the intended effects for local communities, while being open to accusations of cultural imperialism (Khan et al. 2007). Nevertheless, rather than there simply existing a governance gap in globalized employment relations, what is occurring is the adaptation of established institutions, as in the case of collective bargaining and IFAs, alongside consumer activism which has led to the emergence of a multiplicity of institutions which look similar but function differently in the establishment and implementation of labour standards.

CONCLUSION

Globalization clearly has not meant the end of important institutional arrangements that stand prominently in the regulation of national systems of employment relations. What globalization has been, however, is a process where actors and strategies from other economies may have disequilibrating effects on national patterns of labour governance, thereby highlighting the importance of how national actors operate in particular institutional frameworks in response to these developments. In the area of finance, globalization has been associated at the micro/firm-level with the emergence of a whole range of pressures from actors located in liberal market economies on the governance of employment relations in economies not previously exposed to the shareholder value mantra. Nevertheless, the outcomes of these external sets of pressures reflect both the characteristics of the institutions of the recipient countries and the strategies of actors that are derived from the internally generated sets of preferences. At the macro-level, the globalization of finance has contributed to the narrowing of policy choices for governments. Nonetheless, while macroeconomic adjustment to the crisis has been precipitated by financial institutions, the shape of the responses clearly is influenced by and responsive to national institutional constraints. In the area of labour standards, governance gaps did emerge as MNCs sought to exploit permissive regimes to drive down labour costs. Nevertheless, unions and social movements are mobilizing to generate new institutional configurations. While these responses are far from being optimal and comprehensive, actor strategies emphasize that lessons drawn from national scenarios are being used to inform the strategies being employed at the supranational level.

Thus, in summary, neo-liberal globalization is having a destabilizing effect on global employment relations institutions, but institutions remain important and the response of actors has been to act within the constraints of existing institutions rather than seeking to formulate new institutional configurations. The theoretical insight of our two case studies is that institutions are not only constraining on the strategies of actors, but also offer alternative adjustment paths for employment relations actors that cannot be predicted in advance. How actors operate in (constraining) institutional frameworks matters for their effects, thereby highlighting that two apparently similar institutions from a structural perspective can lead to different outcomes as these 'constraining' institutions offer actors more than one pattern of adjustment (Hancké and Goyer 2005).

NOTE

1. This section draws on Donaghey et al. (2014).

REFERENCES

Abdelal, R. (2007). *Capital Rules: The Construction of Global Finance*. Cambridge, MA: Harvard University Press.

Aguilera, R. V. and Jackson, G. (2013). 'The Cross-National Diversity of Corporate Governance', *Academy of Management Review*, 28: 447–65.

Atanassov, J. and Kim, E. H. (2009). 'Labor and Corporate Governance: International Evidence from Restructuring Decisions', *Journal of Finance*, 64(1): 341–74.

Bartley, T. (2007). 'Institutional Emergence in an Era of Globalization: The Rise of Transnational Private Regulation of Labor and Environmental Conditions', *American Journal of Sociology*, 113: 297–351.

Berger, S. (2000). 'Globalization and Politics', *Annual Review of Political Science*, 3: 43–62.

—— (2006). *How We Compete: What Companies around the World are Doing to Make it in Today's Global Economy*. New York: Doubleday.

—— (2009). 'Troubleshooting Economic Narratives', in A. Hemerijck, B. Knapen, and E. van Doorne (eds.), *Aftershocks: Economic Crisis and Institutional Choice*. Amsterdam: Amsterdam University Press, 103–9.

Bernstein, S. and Cashore, B. (2007). 'Can Non-State Global Governance Be Legitimate? An Analytical Framework', *Regulation and Governance*, 1(4): 347–71.

Boiral, O. (2007). 'Corporate Greening Through ISO 14001: A Rational Myth?', *Organization Science*, 18(1): 127–46.

Boström, M. and Hallström, K. (2010). 'NGO Power in Global Social and Environmental Standard-Setting', *Global Environmental Politics*, 10: 36–59.

Budros, A. (2002). 'The Mean and Lean Firm and Downsizing: Causes of Involuntary and Voluntary Downsizing Strategies', *Sociological Forum*, 17(2): 307–42.

Cameron, D. (1978). 'The Expansion of the Public Economy', *American Political Science Review*, 72(4): 1243–61.

—— (2012). 'European Fiscal Responses to the Great Recession', in N. Bermeo and J. Pontusson (eds.), *Coping with Crisis: Government Reactions to the Great Recession*. New York: Russell Sage Foundation, 91–129.

Capron, L. and Guillen, M. (2009). 'National Corporate Governance Institutions and Post-Acquisition Target Reorganization', *Strategic Management Journal*, 30(8): 803–33.

Cashore, B., Auld, G., Bernstein, S., and McDermott, C. (2007). 'Can Non-state Governance "Ratchet Up" Global Environmental Standards?', *Review of European Community & International Environmental Law*, 16(2): 158–72.

Cerny, P. (1995). 'Globalization and the Changing Logic of Collective Action', *International Organization*, 49: 595–625.

Christmann, P. and Taylor, G. (2006). 'Firm Self-Regulation through International Certifiable Standards: Determinants of Symbolic versus Substantive Implementation', *Journal of International Business Studies*, 37: 863–78.

Christopherson, S. and Lillie, N. (2005). 'Neither Global nor Standard: Corporate Strategies in the New Era of Labor Standards', *Environment and Planning A*, 37: 1919–38.

Clark, G. and Wójcik, D. (2007). *The Geography of Finance: Corporate Governance in a Global Marketplace*. Oxford and New York: Oxford University Press.

Cohen, B. (1996). 'Phoenix Risen: The Resurrection of Global Finance', *World Politics*, 48(2): 268–96.

Conroy, M. E. (2007). *Branded! How the 'Certification Revolution' is Transforming Global Corporations*. Gabriola Islands, Canada: New Society Publishers

Culpepper, P. (2011). *Quiet Politics and Business Power: Corporate Control in Europe and Japan*. New York: Cambridge University Press.

Davis, G. F. (2009). *Managed by the Markets: How Finance Reshaped America*. Oxford and New York: Oxford University Press.

DeGrauwe, P. (2013). 'The Political Economy of the Euro', *Annual Review of Political Science*, 16: 153–70.

Dingwerth, K. and Pattberg, P. (2009). 'World Politics and Organizational Fields: The Case of Transnational Sustainability Governance', *European Journal of International Relations*, 15(4): 707–43.

Djelic, M.-L. (1998). *Exporting the American Model: The Post-War Transformation of European Business*. Oxford and New York: Oxford University Press.

Djelic, M.-L. and Sahlin-Andersson, K. (eds.) (2006). *Transnational Governance: Institutional Dynamics of Regulation*. Cambridge: Cambridge University Press.

Donaghey, J., Reinecke, J., Niforou, C., and Lawson, B. (2014). 'From Employment Relations to Consumption Relations: Balancing Labor Governance in Global Supply Chains'. Forthcoming in *Human Resource Management*.

Elliott, K. A. and Freeman, R. (2003). *Can Labor Standards Improve Under Globalization?* Washington, DC: Peterson Institute.

Estevez-Abe, M., Iversen, T., and Soskice, D. (2001). 'Social Protection and the Formation of Skills: A Reinterpretation of the Welfare State', in P. A. Hall and Soskice (eds.), Varieties of Capitalism: The Institutional Foundations of Comparative Advantage. New York and Oxford: Oxford University Press, 145–83.

Fichter, M., Helfen, M., and Sydow, J. (2011). 'Employment Relations in Global Production Networks Initiating Transfer of Practices via Union Involvement', *Human Relations*, 64(4): 599–624.

Fichter, M., Sydow, J., and Volynets, L. (2008). 'Organization and Regulation of Employment Relations in Transnational Production and Supply Networks: Ensuring Core Labor Standards through International Framework Agreements'. Freie Universität Berlin, Germany.

Fransen, L. W. (2011). 'Why Do Private Governance Organizations Not Converge? A Political–Institutional Analysis of Transnational Labor Standards Regulation', *Governance*, 24: 359–87.

—— (2012). 'Multi-Stakeholder Governance and Voluntary Programme Interactions: Legitimation Politics in the Institutional Design of Corporate Social Responsibility', *Socio-Economic Review*, 10(1): 163–92.

Frieden, J. (1991). 'Invested Interests: The Politics of National Economic Policies in a World of Global Finance', *International Organization*, 45(4): 425–51.

Garrett, G. (1998), 'Global Markets and National Politics: Collision Course or Virtuous Circle?', *International Organization*, 52: 149–76.

—— (2000). 'The Causes of Globalization', *Comparative Political Studies*, 33(6/7): 941–91.

Garrett, G. and Lange, P. (1991). 'Political Responses to Interdependence: What's Left for the "Left"?', *International Organization*, 45(4): 539–64.

—— (1995). 'Internationalization, Institutions, and Political Change', *International Organization*, 49(4): 627–55.

Geppert, M., Matten, D., and Walgenbach, P. (2006). 'Transnational Institution Building and the Multinational Corporation: An Emerging Field of Research', *Human Relations*, 59(11): 1451–65.

Gilbert, D. and Rasche, A. (2007). 'Discourse Ethics and Social Accountability: The Ethics of SA 8000', *Business Ethics Quarterly*, 17(2): 187–216.

Gilbert, D. U., Rasche, A., and Waddock, S. (2011). 'Accountability in a Global Economy: The Emergence of International Accountability Standards', *Business Ethics Quarterly*, 21: 23–44.

Gingrich, J. (2011). *Making Markets in the Welfare State*. New York: Cambridge University Press.

Glasbergen, P. (2011). 'Mechanisms of Private Meta-Governance: An Analysis of Global Private Governance for Sustainable Development', *International Journal of Strategic Business Alliances*, 2(3): 189–206.

Goodman, J. and Pauly, L. (1993). 'The Obsolescence of Capital Controls? Economic Management in an Age of Global Markets', *World Politics*, 46: 50–82.

Gourevitch, P. (1986). *Politics in Hard Times: Comparative Responses to International Economic Crises*. Ithaca: Cornell University Press.

Gourevitch, P. A. and Shinn, J. (2005). *Political Power and Corporate Control: The New Global Politics of Corporate Governance*. Princeton: Princeton University Press.

Goyer, M. (2006). 'Varieties of Institutional Investors and National Models of Capitalism: The Transformation of Corporate Governance in France and Germany', *Politics & Society*, 34(3): 399–430.

—— (2011). *Contingent Capital: Short-Term Investors and the Evolution of Corporate Governance in France and Germany*. Oxford and New York: Oxford University Press.

Hall, P. A. (1986). *Governing the Economy: The Politics of State Intervention in Britain and France*. Oxford and New York: Oxford University Press.

—— (2009). 'The Significance of Politics', in A. Hemerijck, B. Knapen, and E. van Doorne (eds.), *Aftershocks: Economic Crisis and Institutional Choice*. Amsterdam: Amsterdam University Press, 93–102.

—— (2012). 'The Economics and Politics of the Euro Crisis', *German Politics*, 21(4): 355–71.

Hall, P. A. and Soskice, D. (eds.) (2001). *Varieties of Capitalism: The Institutional Foundations of Comparative Advantage*. Oxford and New York: Oxford University Press.

Hammer, N. (2005). 'International Framework Agreements: Global Industrial Relations between Rights and Bargaining', *Transfer*, 11: 511–30.

Hancké, B. and Goyer, M. (2005). 'Degrees of Freedom: Rethinking the Institutional Analysis for Economic Change', in G. Morgan, R. Whitley, and E. Moen (eds.), *Changing Capitalisms?: Internationalization, Institutional Change, and Systems of Economic Organization*. Oxford and New York: Oxford University Press, 53–77.

Hassel, A. (2008). 'The Evolution of a Global Labor Governance Regime', *Governance*, 21(2): 231–51.

Haufler, V. (2001). *A Public Role for the Private Sector: Industry Self-Regulation in a Global Economy*. Washington, DC: Carnegie Endowment for International Peace.

Hauptmeier, M. and Greer, I. (2012). 'Whipsawing: Organizing Labor Competition in Multinational Auto Companies'. Proceedings of the International Employment Relations Association World Congress, Philadelphia, July.

Higgins, W. and Hallström, K. T. (2007). 'Standardization, Globalization and Rationalities of Government', *Organization*, 14(5): 685–704.

International Labour Organization (ILO) (2012). 'The ILO at Work. Development Results 2010–2011'. Available at <http://www.ilo.org/legacy/english/pardev/development-results/2010-2011/index.html>, accessed 25 September 2012.

Iversen, T. (1999). *Contested Economic Institutions: The Politics of Macroeconomics and Wage Bargaining in Advanced Democracies*. New York: Cambridge University Press.

Jacoby, S. (2005). *The Embedded Corporation: Corporate Governance and Employment Relations in Japan and the United States*. Princeton: Princeton University Press.

Jessop, B. (2012). 'The World Market, Variegated Capitalism, and the Crisis of European Integration', in P. Nousios, N. Overbeek, and H. Tsolakis (eds.), *Globalisation and European Integration: Critical Approaches to Regional Order and International Relations*. London: Routledge, 91–111.

Johnson, S. and Kwak, J. (2010). *13 Bankers: The Wall Street Takeover and the Next Financial Meltdown*. New York: Random House.

Khan, F. R., Munir, K. A., and Willmott, H. (2007). 'A Dark Side of Institutional Entrepreneurship: Soccer Balls, Child Labour and Postcolonial Impoverishment', *Organization Studies*, 28: 1055–77.

King, A., Lenox, M., and Terlaak, A. (2005). 'The Strategic Use of Decentralized Institutions: Exploring Certification with the ISO 14001 Management Standard', *Academy of Management Journal*, 48(6): 1091–1106.

Klein, A. and Zur, E. (2009). 'Entrepreneurial Shareholder Activism: Hedge Funds and Other Private Investors', *Journal of Finance*, 64(1): 187–229.

Lallement, M. (2011). 'Europe and the Economic Crisis', *Work, Employment and Society*, 25(4): 627–41.

La Porta, R., López-de-Silanes, F., Shleifer, A., and Vishny, R. (2000). 'Investor Protection and Corporate Governance', *Journal of Financial Economics*, 58: 3–27.

Lim, A. and Tsutsui, K. (2012). 'Globalization and Commitment in Corporate Social Responsibility: Cross-National Analyses of Institutional and Political-Economy Effects', *American Sociological Review*, 77(1): 69–98.

Locke, R., Amengual, M., and Mangla, A. (2009). 'Virtue out of Necessity? Compliance, Commitment, and the Improvement of Labor Conditions in Global Supply Chains', *Politics & Society*, 37(3): 319–51.

McAdam, D. and Scott, R. (2005). 'Organizations and Movements', in G. F. Davis, S. McAdam, and M. N. Zald (eds.), *Social Movements and Organization Theory*. New York: Cambridge University Press, 4–40.

Matten, D. and Crane, A. (2005). 'Corporate Citizenship: Towards an Extended Theoretical Conceptualization', *Academy of Management Review*, 30: 166–179.

Mena, S. and Palazzo, G. (2012). 'Input and Output Legitimacy of Multi-Stakeholder Initiatives', *Business Ethics Quarterly*, 22(3): 527–66.

Milner, H. (1989). *Resisting Protectionism: Global Industries and the Politics of International Trade*. Princeton: Princeton University Press.

Morgan, G. (2012). 'International Business, Multinationals and National Business Systems', in G. Wood and M. Demirbag (eds.), *Handbook of Institutional Approaches to International Business*. Cheltenham: Edward Elgar, 18–40.

Niforou, C. (2012). 'International Framework Agreements and Industrial Relations Governance: Global Rhetoric versus Local Realities', *British Journal of Industrial Relations*, 50: 352–73.

O'Rourke, D. (2006). 'Multi-Stakeholder Regulation: Privatizing or Socializing Global Labor Standards?', *World Development*, 34(5): 899–918.

Palier, B. and Thelen, K. (2010). 'Institutionalizing Dualism: Complementarities and Change in France and Germany', *Politics & Society*, 38: 119–48.

Pontusson, J. and Raess, D. (2012). 'How (and Why) is This Time Different? The Politics of Economic Crisis in Western Europe and the United States', *Annual Review of Political Science*, 15: 13–33.

Rasche, A. (2010). 'The Limits of Corporate Responsibility Standards', *Business Ethics: A European Review*, 19(3): 280–91.

Rasche, A. and Kell, G. (2010). *The United Nations Global Compact: Achievements, Trends and Challenges*. Cambridge: Cambridge University Press.

Riisgaard, L. (2005). 'International Framework Agreements: A New Model for Securing Workers Rights?', *Industrial Relations: A Journal of Economy and Society*, 44: 707–37.

Rodrick, D. (1997). *Has Globalization Gone Too Far?* Washington, DC: Institute for International Economics.

Roe, M. (2000). 'Political Preconditions to Separating Ownership from Corporate Control', *Stanford Law Review*, 53: 539–606.

—— (2002). 'Corporate Law's Limits', *Journal of Legal Studies*, 31: 233–71.

Rossi, S. and Volpin, P. (2004). 'Cross-Country Determinants of Mergers and Acquisitions', *Journal of Financial Economics*, 74(2): 277–304.

Roubini, N. and Mihm, S. (2010). *Crisis Economics: A Crash Course in the Future of Finance*. New York: Penguin Books.

Ruggie, J. G. (1982). 'International Regimes, Transactions, and Change: Embedded Liberalism in the Postwar Economic Order', *International Organization*, 36: 379–415.

Scharpf, F. (1991). *Crisis and Choice in European Social Democracy*. Ithaca: Cornell University Press.

Scherer, A. G. and Palazzo, G. (2011). 'The New Political Role of Business in a Globalized World: A Review of a New Perspective on CSR and its Implications for the Firm, Governance, and Democracy', *Journal of Management Studies*, 48: 899–931.

Schneper, W. D. and Guillén, M. (2004). 'Stakeholder Rights and Corporate Governance: A Cross-National Study of Hostile Takeovers', *Administrative Science Quarterly*, 49(2): 263–95.

Shiller, R. (2000). *Irrational Exuberance*. Princeton: Princeton University Press.

Soskice, D. (1999). 'Divergent Production Regimes: Coordinated and Uncoordinated Market Economies in the 1980s and 1990s', in H. Kitschelt, P. Lange, G. Marks, and J. Stephens (eds.), *Continuity and Change in Contemporary Capitalism*. New York: Cambridge University Press, 101–34.

Standing, G. (1997). 'Globalization, Labour Flexibility and Insecurity: The Era of Market Regulation', *European Journal of Industrial Relations*, 3: 7–37.

Stevis, D. (2010). *International Framework Agreements and Global Social Dialogue: Parameters and Prospects*. Geneva: International Labour Office.

Stevis, D. and Boswell, T. (2007). 'International Framework Agreements: Opportunities and Challenges for Global Unionism', in K. Bronfenbrenner (ed.), *Global Unions: Challenging Transnational Capital through Cross-Border Campaigns*. Ithaca and London: Cornell University Press/ILR Press, 175–94.

Tamm-Hallström, K. (2008). 'ISO Expands Its Business into Social Responsibility', in C. Garsten and M. Boström (eds.), *Organizing Transnational Accountability*. Cheltenham: Edward Elgar Publishing, 46–60.

Tamm-Hallström, K. and Boström, M. (2010). *Transnational Multi-Stakeholder Standardization. Organizing Fragile Non-State Authority*. Cheltenham: Edward Elgar.

Terlaak, A. (2007). 'Order Without Law? The Role of Certified Management Standards in Shaping Socially Desired Firm Behaviors', *Academy of Management Review*, 32: 968–85.

Thelen, K. and Kume, I. (2003). 'The Future of Nationally Embedded Capitalism: Industrial Relations in Germany and Japan', in W. Streeck and K. Yamamura (eds.), *The End of*

Diversity? Prospects for German and Japanese Capitalism. Ithaca: Cornell University Press, 183–211.

Traxler, F. and Woitech, B. (2000). 'Transnational Investment and National Labour Market Regimes: A Case of "Regime Shopping"?', *European Journal of Industrial Relations* 6(2): 141–59.

Turcotte, M.-F., de Bellefeuille, S., and den Hond, F. (2007). 'Gildan Inc.: Influencing Corporate Governance in the Textile Sector', *Journal of Corporate Citizenship*, 27: 23–36.

Useem, M. (1996). *Investor Capitalism: How Money Managers are Changing the Face of Corporate America.* New York: Basic Books.

Vogel, D. (2008). 'Private Global Business Regulation', *Annual Review of Political Science*, 11(1): 261–82.

Weber, B. and Schmitz, S. (2011). 'Varieties of Helping Capitalism: Politico-Economic Determinants of Bank Rescue Packages in the EU during the Recent Crisis', *Socio-Economic Review*, 9(4): 639–69.

Wells, D. (2009). 'Local Worker Struggles in the Global South: Reconsidering Northern Impacts on International Labour Standards', *Third World Quarterly*, 30: 567–79.

Whittington, R. (1988). 'Environmental Structure and Theories of Strategic Choice', *Journal of Management Studies*, 25: 521–36.

Wills, J. (2002). 'Bargaining for the Space to Organise in the Global Economy: A Review of the Accor–IUF Trade Union Rights Agreement', *Review of International Political Economy*, 9: 675–700.

Wood, G. and Demirbag, M. (2012). Institutions and Comparative Business Studies? Supranational and National Regulation. Wood and Demirbag (eds.), *Handbook of Institutional Approaches to International Business.* Cheltenham: Edward Elgar, 3–17.

CHAPTER 22

··

WORK, BODIES, CARE
Gender and Employment in a Global World

··

BARBARA POCOCK

A photograph taken before 1906 at the Steveston fish cannery in the Gulf of Georgia, just south of Vancouver, Canada, shows a line of Japanese women packing salmon into cans (Yesali et al. 1998: 57; see Fig. 22.1). Large, dark, and cold inside, the factory—still standing, now a museum—is built of thick beams, extending out over the water. In the photo, two of the women working on the line have babies tied to their backs with shawls and a third toddler sits in her pram alongside the workers. According to the museum's guide, empty cans were fed down a chute from above these women by their older children—allowed to do this job once they reached the age of eleven or twelve. The salmon the women are packing were caught, heaved from boats, cleaned and cut up by immigrant Japanese, white European, and First Nations men, who fished the Pacific in small, low-lying boats.[1] These workers—men, women, and children—lived near their workplace in communities that mushroomed in 'cannery rows' around their jobs. At one point, Steveston was the site of the largest fishing canneries in the British Empire, with 15 canneries in 1901 (Yesali et al. 1998: 5).

Before the Steveston cannery and factories like it, salmon were first provided to colonial buyers like the Hudson Bay Company—one of the first and certainly the largest such trader in Canadian history—by First Nations fisher people who swapped salmon—caught in the then usually bountiful fishing waters off western Canada—for Hudson Bay blankets.[2] These blankets replaced those woven by Salish (First Nations) women from goat hair and other materials harvested from prickly bushes on hills and mountains; many of these blankets—like that in Figure 22.2—played an important role in ceremonial occasions. Swapping several fish for a Hudson Bay blanket was not uncommon among those living on Canada's western shores at the turn of the twentieth century. British Columbia's Museum of Anthropology exhibits a number of such blankets woven by Salish women in the past and present, illustrating the art of traditional blanket making and celebrating traditions before Hudson Bay blankets and salmon canning factories like that at Steveston.

FIGURE 22.1 Women packing salmon, c.1906, Steveston, Vancouver, Canada

Source: Special Collections, Vancouver Public Library, Image Number 2071. Thanks to Heidi Rampfl, Collections Manager at the Gulf of Georgia Cannery Society, and tour guides at the cannery museum.

I begin a discussion about gender and employment with these two artefacts—the 1906 photo and the Salish blanket—from the millions we might choose from across time and space, as a way in to discussing gender and employment relations in our world.

Together these two artefacts embody complex historical trajectories—with more modern echoes. They suggest the consistency of gendered bodies in gendered hierarchies at work across diverse economic regimes, bringing together the activities of working for a living and reproduction. They reveal something of the theory and practice of gender and employment. While this handbook focuses upon employment relations since 1970, such historical artefacts—and the processes and relations that produced them—illuminate concepts and approaches that are essential to understanding employment relations today—not least the consistent differences between women and men at work across cultures and time, and the perennial challenge of combining work with reproduction—of combining the public domain of work with the private realm. Work involves the body, the body is gendered and culturally inscribed, and the body always does *more* than paid work—with this 'more' circling back and around to shape what is done 'at work'.

The Steveston factories ran for 70 years and employed thousands of workers. This relatively short historical trajectory saw the transformation of fishing employment that began with First Nations people in canoes with their sustenance through work and trade—men fishing, women weaving—to the onset of factory production and fishing on

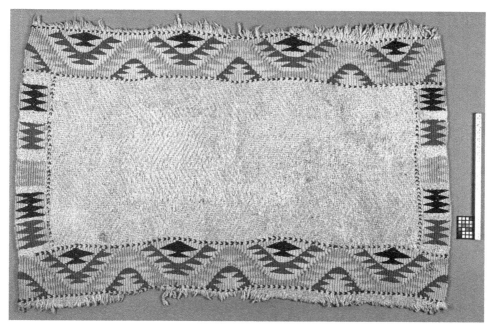

FIGURE 22.2 Swoqw''elh blanket (chief's blanket) made by Sp!aq!elthinoth before 1906, Vancouver

Source: Image courtesy of the UBC Museum of Anthropology, Vancouver, Canada, object number A17200. Photographed by Kyla Bailey. Thanks to Karen Duffek, curator of Contemporary Visual Arts & Pacific Northwest at the Museum of Anthropology, for her advice and assistance.

a massive (and now barely sustainable) scale. Inside the Steveston factories, labour was segmented by both gender and ethnic origin. Japanese men caught fish, which Chinese workers butchered and 'native' women cleaned, washed, and packed. Caucasian men supervised Chinese men, while Chinese men supervised 'native' women (Yesali et al. 1998: 21–2). When new machines replaced their functions, jobs disappeared. Chinese, Japanese, First Nations, and European workers and their families lived and worked in the same factories, often doing distinctive tasks. Workers saw perpetual innovation in the pay systems and technological practices within the factories, which changed rewards, profit, and employment. The Gulf of Georgia Cannery museum records all of this, celebrating the multinational communities, technical innovation, and social pleasures that the Steveston factories saw over their short century—as well as the horrors of fishing in small craft in high seas, the time pressures imposed by piece-rate factory pay systems, and the sweat, speed, and injuries involved in canning fish.

After colonization, workers reproduced their families—through sex-segmented care practices in the factory and beyond, in their adjacent communities—sustained by both their wages, their communities, and slowly emergent state-based forms of social 'wages'—like schools and hospitals. Immigrant workers like the Japanese built their own schools when children of 'non-propertied' workers like them were excluded from local public schools (Yesali et al. 1998: 50). First Nations tribes were repressed: their language and culture was denied, their traditional lands, fisheries, and forms of sustenance privatized by colonization and corporations. Their children were removed from their communities and institutionalized and this continued until well into the 1960s. Lines of ethnicity, class, and gender run together through these complex histories, right up to the present.

CONCEPTUALIZING GENDER AND WORK (NOT EMPLOYMENT)

What concepts and approaches relevant to understanding gender and employment relations—the focus of this chapter—can we draw from these examples to help make sense of gender at work today? Several are pivotal.

First, it is useful to adopt the broader term of 'work' rather than 'employment' to make sense of labour in these scenarios. Employment implies a form of paid labour that takes place in a public workplace: whether through acts of self-employment or by working as an employee. Many people work, both in pre- and post-capitalist societies, without being in employment: they work at home, in voluntary community activities, or in informal 'employment'. The gendered contours of this broader definition of public and private 'work' are marked: men doing more public work, women doing more private. While much of the focus of the field of 'employment relations' over the past several decades has been on the narrower sphere of employment relations—its terms (wages, conditions, bargaining, strikes), actors (employers, unions, labour regulators) and their conflicts—a thorough analysis of gender and labour requires a wider lens.

Second, in making sense of employment relations, analysing gender and the relations between men and women (with men usually exercising more power than, and frequently over, women) is essential in any specific example of working life regardless of time or place. Even in female-only or male-only workplaces, the ghost of gender appears in the sexualized practices and cultures of the workplace and its larger social context.

Third, this gender analysis needs to extend to both the workplace—and the narrower sphere of employment relations within it—but reach beyond it to the sphere of social reproduction and gender relations in the household and surrounding community. The ways and means of social reproduction—who supports the worker by cooking, cleaning, and caring for them and their home, and who cares for children and other dependants—shapes basic patterns of employment. Patterns of social reproduction, and the relative contributions of the state, employers, families, and communities to that reproduction, affect rates of employment participation by men and women, their occupation, their wages, conditions, and hours of work, their health and physical and mental capacities, future labour supply, and the balance of power between working men and women and those who manage or employ them.

Fourth, the example of salmon fishing in western Canada shows us how gendered patterns of work constantly change over time. Women and men come into particular jobs, and then move out of them: the gendered nature of work changes along with the terms of pay and conditions. However, these working lives occur in institutions where dense fabrics of gendered practices construct and reconstruct gendered hierarchies. Based on her close observation of institutions in another North American place, institution, and century (Oregon's state public sector and its pay system in the 1980s), Joan Acker argues that the fundamental definition of a 'job'—made in man's image, free of reproductive capacity—is gendered, and that the organization of jobs and workers into gendered hierarchies in workplaces arises from dense, complex, sexualized practices and processes that reflect the fact that the bodies of women and men are different. Acker describes how gender relations construct organizations and how organizations, in turn, reciprocally construct gender. To say that employment relations and organizations are gendered 'means that advantage and disadvantage, exploitation and control, action and emotion, meaning and identity, are patterns through and in terms of a distinction between male and female, masculine and feminine' (Acker 1990: 146).

Finally these bodies are marked by more than gender: they are also ethnically inscribed and these differences *determine* job allocation, pay and conditions, supervision, treatment by the state, and power—but usually differently for men and women.

WORKERS HAVE BODIES

The fact that women in this 1906 photo work with their babies on their backs or at their sides and with their older children working at the chutes above their heads, shapes the jobs they are in, their patterns of employment, their pay and conditions, their work 'life-cycle'—and help 'make' gendered practices at work. Workers have bodies, and these bodies have a gender, which is relevant to many aspects of work.

Further, the persistence of these gendered practices and habits and in particular the gendered practices of social reproduction—with women responsible in the main for the private sphere of care—are much less open to change than some of the patterns of gendered relations in workplaces and the labour market. They appear more strongly socially embedded: they are 'sticky' practices. How else can we explain the persistence of women's responsibility for care work around the world, despite participation rates in paid work that now parallel men's in many countries? In modern industrialized societies, women have increasingly entered paid work with very little change, on average, in the allocation of unpaid work and care with women continuing to do at least twice as much—and often much more—than men. Capitalism readily shares paid work between women and men, drawing women into jobs, while the private social sphere of care and domestic work remains woodenly resistant to such sharing.

The Gendered Body Works in a Time, Place, and Culture

However, while gender *always* matters in these work-related processes of historical flux, gendered relations are never enacted alone, regardless of time or place: work relations bear the imprint not only of gender, but also age, ethnic origin and status, class, and the power that arises from (or is denied by) immigration and the citizenship rights of workers. Understanding how gender works, and what it does to people, depends on admitting this complexity to analysis. The intricate work and social relations of Japanese, Chinese, Caucasian, and First Nations people are obvious in the photographs at Steveston, with differences between the men and women in each group obvious in terms of who does what work, and on what terms.

While feminist theorists of the 1970s and 1980s sometimes hoped for a settled analytical hierarchy of oppressions (gender trumps race trumps class?), this has proved a useless project in the face of messy reality. The best we can say is that factors like gender, ethnic origin, and socio-economic status all shape power and outcomes—including at work—often in overlapping and changing ways. All (and sometimes more) must be held in view analytically at the same time.

For Indigenous people, colonialism and the commodification of their lives through the introduction of institutions like labour markets, schools, prisons, and rules around the use of language and culture and where and how children are raised and live, create unique losses and disadvantage. While these are often gendered, the scale of fundamental transformation—like the loss of land and children—often makes gender a more minor fault line for analysis in the larger earthquake. In other cases, gender is a more dominant aspect of outcomes.

Colonial Ruptures: Gender at Work

It is important to note the historical rupture to the nature of work that is created by colonialism in the countries affected by it. The western Canadian example illustrates how First Nations peoples were drawn into the commodification of their time, as the privatization of land and sea and the sale of labour time and the onset of labour markets overtook 'making a living' from land and sea outside an employment relationship. Men and women began selling their labour, first as embodied in the fish they caught or the blankets they wove, then in the direct sale of their labour time to factories like that at Steveston (Yesali et al. 1998: 9–12). The care of children is shaped by the actions of the state—for example by the removal of children from their homes, the exclusion of the children of the 'unpropertied' from schooling, or by the actions of employers who employ their parents and thus draw them into the workplace, as in the case of the eleven-year-olds at Steveston.

THE POLITICAL ECONOMY CONTEXT MATTERS

Employment relations—and their gendered experiences and management—occur within a larger political economy. When companies import workers who lack citizenship, exclude unions, and act without restraint from state regulation or social norms—and each of these is potentially gendered in effects—then employment relations unfold in particular ways with different consequences for women and men. When companies instead negotiate with collectives of male and female workers, adhere to effective and comprehensive legislation that protects workers' rights and permit collective organization, including rights to time for care and reproduction, and meet fair and reasonable social norms, then work relations and their gendered characteristics evolve differently. Where unions exclude women from their organization as competitive 'outsiders' (as has often happened in their history: see Wertheimer 1975; Kessler-Harris 1975), then women's access to paid work, decent pay, and good conditions lags behind men's. When male employers and unions prioritize bargaining over, for example, long service leave ahead of paid parental leave, they reflect gendered power and a gendered political context.

Key actors in this larger, gendered political economy context of employment relations are the state (governments of all levels, tribunals and enforcement bodies), employers (owners, managers, and supervisors), unions, workers, households, and communities. Sometimes international agencies (like the International Labour Organization (ILO)) are also relevant, though their capacity to regulate the conditions of work is generally limited, reflecting the weak powers of international governance more generally.

BEYOND THE WORKPLACE: THE CRITICAL ROLE OF HOUSEHOLDS AND COMMUNITY

As the above two artefacts and their contexts suggest, work occurs out of households and in communities made by men and women, and these are affected by, and affect, work relations in many places. In the case of the factories at Steveston, their location created a new community—and the closure of the factories in the 1980s threatened its continuity. The ways in which that community reproduced and enabled social life—care of adults, children, the injured, sick, and aged—and the households within it, affected the condition in which workers went to work, existed over the life-cycle, and shaped local labour supply. The nature of these households and communities also affected the capacity of workers to withdraw their labour from factories like those at Steveston and take strike action to defend and improve their working conditions. Unionism and its power and capacities is critically affected by the social location of workers and their sources of non-wage support, and these can be very differently supplied and utilized by women and men.

Thus work is not an incidental part of community life: it creates activities and social relations at work and beyond it, in the form of larger community fabric, facilities, and sustainability—and vice versa: community and household also shape what occurs at work. For example, community capacity can enable or prevent employment: communities that provide ways of caring for workers' children, for supporting sick or injured workers, and for housing workers, enable employment to occur. One way of looking at this is provided in Figure 22.3, which suggests that work sits within a socio-ecological system, which has gendered effects (see Pocock et al. 2012b for a fuller explication of this model).

In this model work, family (or household), and community are not 'separate worlds' (Kanter 1989; Voydanoff 2007; Bronfenbrenner 1979; Eikhof et al. 2007) but interlocking spheres. The nature of gendered relationships in each microsystem of work, household, and community—and their interaction with each other in their overlapping mesosystems—constructs overall gendered outcomes, in the context of a larger political economy macrosystem. Understanding gender at work, in this context, requires analysis of how households and community life interact with work. A complex socio-ecosystem constructs outcomes for individuals, workplaces, labour markets, families, and

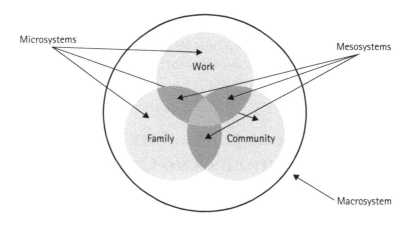

Each domain, and each intersection, creates demands and resources

Note: based on Voydanoff's (2007) adaption of
Bronfenbrenner's (1979) ecological systems model.

FIGURE 22.3 Work, households, and community: a gendered socio-ecological system

Source: Pocock et al. (2012b: 8).

communities, and that analysis of domains, their intersections and larger context, matters to outcomes. It also affects the power and strategies of collective organizations like trade unions (Pocock 2011).

Analysis of the character and evolution of capitalist states across the contemporary world, for example the debate around varieties of capitalism (VOC) (Hall and Soskice 2001), has paid too little attention to the complex interactions of the public/private spheres and the gendered relations which permeate labour markets and households, and their intersections, in all 'types' of capitalisms whether 'liberal' or 'coordinated' (assuming these types can be distinguished: see Brenner et al. 2010, for example, who contest these categories; see also Rubery 2009 for a feminist critique of the narrow lens used in some 'VOC' research analysing gender). Gendered hierarchies persist in both ideal VOC types so that whatever form of socio-economic system prevails—pre-colonial/pre-industrial, socialist, or (most commonly today) a variety of neo-liberalizing capitalism—analysis of gender is important in understanding the way in which socio-ecological systems of work unfold, and their effects. And this analysis is usefully undertaken in a way that simultaneously considers how the spheres of work, household, and community separately and together, construct work outcomes.

MAKING THEORY ABOUT GENDER AT WORK: THE IMPORTANCE OF A VIEW FROM 'THE SOUTH'

While the above discussion builds out from examples of work in the Pacific Northwest of North America, it attempts to bring into view both ancient and modern work, and Indigenous and immigrant workers in pre- and post-colonial worlds. However, for the most part theorizing about employment relations has taken place out of a small number of industrialized cities in the global 'North' (with much work concentrated in the post-Second World War era). It shares these geographic origins with most social science disciplines: the key concepts of sociology and neo-classical economics, for example, have arisen in these locations.

Here I am utilizing Raewyn Connell's (2007) terminology of 'the North' (implying the rich industrialized countries—perhaps best approximated by members of the OECD) with 'the South' referring to the poorer industrializing or pre-industrial countries of Asia (excluding Japan), Africa, and parts of the Pacific. While this terminology is not geographically precise (for example while China is in the northern hemisphere it is in the rapidly industrializing 'South' category, while Australia is a rich industrialized country located in the southern hemisphere), it is suggestive of large, geographically located differences. These North/South categories are preferable to the binaries 'industrialized/pre-industrial' or 'developed/underdeveloped' (often used by the ILO), with their implicit hierarchies of advanced versus backward.

Among social science thinkers, feminists have been more alert to the potentially distorting effects of this 'northern' conceptual standpoint than others in the social sciences (see Boserup 1970 for an early example, and Acker 2003 for an overview of more recent feminist literature engaging with issues of global capitalism and gender). This literature took an early international turn and—while dominated by writing from women of the North—it has maintained a steady stream of research and writing which problematizes rich, northern perspectives and is attentive to the places, bodies, and diversity of women and men living and working around the world (see also Harcourt and Escobar 2005).

However, much analysis of employment relations, including its gendered character, is open to a critique about the distorting effects of a dominating view from 'the North'. Accounting for only about 10% of total world population, the social science theorizing metropolises of Western Europe and North America have crafted concepts that are then applied to the other 90% of the world's population in the global 'South' (Connell 2007). Many of the latter have been colonized by the North and experienced painful, violent historical ruptures. These unacknowledged distortions create a case for social science theorizing which takes a view from the South, 'to learn from, not just about' (Connell 2007: viii).

Taking a global perspective, countries like the United States (with 5% of the world's population) and Australia (with only 22 million people) are minor players. Indeed, the total 2010 population of the entire 34 OECD countries (18%) is close to the population of China (19%) and India (17%) alone, suggesting that a social science theory relevant to today's world needs to shift from the rich North, to take account of the global poor.

Connell argues that several problems arise from social science's domination by a view from the 'North'. These include the erasure of the experience of the majority 'South' and their exclusion from analysis or from the processes of conducting their own analysis. A further problem arises from false claims of universality arising from the 'extreme abstraction of general theory' rather than social thought and theory which is grounded in time and place (Connell 2007: 212–20). Finally, Connell points to the practice of 'reading from the centre' so that the concepts developed in the 'centre' are simply 'laid over' other places—because only its ways of thinking and concepts have legitimacy, a literature and currency. Like many others the study of gender and work is marked by these limitations.

Of course, 'doing theory' about issues like gender and employment in a globally inclusive way does not mean discarding all the ideas that have emerged from the North—where they illuminate and help our understandings globally. But they must be modified and replaced by analysis of the majority South, including through analysis *by* the women and men of the South. Like the larger field of political economy with its narrow 'short list' of global actors—the bourgeoisie, workers, state elites—employment relations need to consider a wider and sometimes different set of actors, contexts, and power sources. However, some established theoretical fields have trouble dealing with gender and race which are particularly salient elements of colonialism (Connell 2007).

An example of this might be provided by an approach to 'work and family' that takes the notion of conflict between paid work and family life—as developed in the northern metropolis—and 'lays it over' the global South—in contexts where informal rather than formal work is dominant, children are often at work with their mothers, intergenerational family structures are dense or different from the northern metropolis, trade unions are non-existent or captives of the state or male political elites, and the state's capacity to adopt the instruments of the North (like paid parental leave) are weak and unenforceable. The problems of women's and carers' employment need to start from another place, look to other instruments, and take account of very different contexts.

Similarly, the nature of key employment actors can also vary widely. For example, a labour 'union' in China is very different from that in the established employment literature, functioning more as a transmission belt of state policy than as an independent instrument of worker organization. In Connell's account, the theorist's boots need to touch the ground conceptually and empirically, with important implications for theorizing work and gender (Connell 2007: 206).

Thinking about Gender and Work, Now, from a Global Perspective

What would it mean to analyse today's patterns of gender and work using concepts produced not in the dominating North but also relevant to the global South? Some hints are provided by the discussion of the two artefacts above: the relevance of the concept 'work' not employment; the need for a gendered analysis that takes account of ethnicity and other fault lines of power, and of time and place; and the relevance of domains beyond work including household and community.

In a world where capitalism now dominates, and labour markets and the commodification of citizen's lives and time is pervasive, some established employment concepts have limited traction. This is especially true with regard to women. Take the category of 'employment': most workers in the world are not in a formal employment relationship of the kind that is at the heart of much analysis of employment relations—and indeed a steady, formal employment relationship, regulated by the state is in decline in many countries.

In the global South, 60% of workers are employed informally. They are disproportionately women, whose jobs are characterized by 'less job security, lower incomes, an absence of access to a range of social benefits and fewer possibilities to participate in formal education and training programmes—in short, the absence of key ingredients of decent work opportunities' (Bacchetta et al. 2010: 9). Further, informal employment is persistent, 'responding only weakly to accelerations in economic growth or trade openness' (Bacchetta et al. 2010: 11). While the scale of informality varies across the global South (from over 90% in India to around 30% in Chile), the region's overall share of the world's population makes informal work the dominant form internationally.

Non-standard and informal work is also increasingly relevant in OECD countries where precarious, limited term, and bogus 'self-employment' are growing—and now make up around a third of jobs in countries like Australia and Canada (Vosko et al.

2009). Women are disproportionately concentrated in these forms of employment in both the North and South.

The nature of labour regulation and enforcement is critical to this persistent informality and its gendered nature. The optimistic hope that more growth in international trade leads to more formal, higher quality employment and fair gender outcomes has been disappointed in many countries in the global South (as well as the North), as key international agencies now recognize. Without effective labour standards, civic institutions, and social norms that enable their enforcement, poor quality feminized informal labour markets accompany growth in global trade.

THE COLONIAL LEGACY: GENDER AND WORK

A view from the South also needs to take account of the ruptures and dislocation arising from colonial relations which have left long legacies of racialized and gendered violence and dispossession, and have inhibited the growth of civic institutions, including labour laws and courts and the civic machinery of labour standard enforcement. In many places, colonization carried with it the imprint of the colonizing powers' gender relations—not least in relation to employment and its management and regulation. This has implications not only for gendered hierarchies but also for the form of colonized femininities and masculinities: the institutions of colonialism—schools, corporations, armies—reconstituted masculinities, positioning colonized men as effeminate and colonizing men as aggressive and violent (Connell 2007: 184–5). A view from the South needs to take account of the ways in which the shadow of colonialism helps construct today's gendered (and often racialized) relations at work.

In most countries, dispossession of Indigenous people has preceded the onset of a market economy, including in some of the world's largest economies like the United States, as well as in peripheral states like Canada and Australia. This means that the average employment fortunes of Indigenous peoples are universally inferior to those of the colonizing population, or to immigrant white Europeans, with women to be found below men in most employment hierarchies regardless of pre- or post-colonial stage—in terms of pay, access to secure work and good conditions, and the exercise of power, management, and leadership at work.

The onset of industrialization is often associated with mass migration both between and within countries. The largest current example exists within China where internal immigration currently exceeds total external immigration across the world (Fan 2008). In China, established patterns of work and care are being transformed by these labour flows, with many communities affected by the disruption of familial patterns of care and social reproduction, as young men and women leave non-metropolitan centres for gendered labour markets in rapidly expanding eastern Chinese cities.

Across the world, low wages and poor conditions in many global South countries make them the recipients of capital from wealthier nations, but result in global divisions of labour which are gendered, and place low-wage, labour-intensive jobs in poorly regulated countries.

Women's Increasing Role in Paid Employment

The World Bank estimates that women now make up 40% of the world's paid workforce. Around the globe, labour markets are hungry for women's participation as labour demand expands and men's labour force participation falls (from 82% across the world in 1980 to 78% in 2009) (World Bank 2012: 200).

The demand for labour also reflects growth in the services sector in particular—which now makes up 75% of employment in many industrialized nations—with its feminized occupations in the domestic, retail, hospitality, health, and education sectors. Women have eagerly entered paid work in pursuit of economic independence, skill, and participation in public life; however, they have not found equality by this route. Women remain concentrated in lower-paid and lower-skilled jobs, in labour markets that are universally sex-segmented by occupation (although not always in the same way). In addition, women remain responsible for the unchanging work of social reproduction which is also strongly sex-segmented, with women mostly responsible for indoor cleaning, cooking, and care, and men undertaking more outdoor household tasks.

This has led to a 'double day' for many women workers and to a rapid expansion in domestic work employment to meet the 'care deficit' created by women's exit from the household and entry to the public world of work. As the ILO describes it:

> In the past two decades demand for care work has been on the rise everywhere. The massive incorporation of women in the labour force, the ageing of societies, the intensification of work and the frequent lack or inadequacy of policy measures to facilitate the reconciliation of family life and work underpin this trend. Today, domestic workers make up a large portion of the workforce especially in developing countries, and their number has been increasing—even in the industrialized world. (ILO 2010: 1)

Production's Dependence upon Gendered Social Reproduction

All forms of public work and employment—regardless of the nature of capitalist, socialist, or post-socialist regime—rest with complete dependence upon *social reproduction*—of oneself, households, families, dependants, and communities. Without the production of workers, economies are impossible to sustain. Social reproductive labour includes both physical and emotional care work (of self and others), and much more: cooking, cleaning, gardening, laundry, home maintenance, and shopping work, for example. The essential nature of this social reproductive labour to public economic life is obvious, but occluded in the measurement and regulation of employment and economic outputs. This occlusion has powerful gendered consequences, given that women do most such work. This fundamental point has been made by feminist economists for 40 years (Waring 1988) but without much practical effect: unpaid domestic work and care remains stubbornly resistant to significant reallocation.

Although women have joined the paid workforce in increasing numbers around the world in recent decades, they have not enjoyed much relief on the home front through the redistribution of unpaid work and care to men. As a result, based on data from 23 countries, women work longer total hours than men, irrespective of income or country (World Bank 2012: 219). This is a significant issue given the size of the unpaid economy: 'time use' experts have drawn attention to the fact that the value of unpaid domestic work and care is equivalent to a large proportion of national gross domestic product (GDP) in many countries (in Australia it is equivalent to more than half of total GDP for example (ABS 1997)).

The labour of social reproduction is either unpaid in the home (by partners and mothers for example), or undertaken for wages either in the home (by nannies or cleaners for example) or in the public sphere (in childcare centres or nursing homes), which we consider below in turn.

Unpaid Domestic Work

According to data assembled by the World Bank (2012: 217–19) women in industrialized countries generally do around twice the level of unpaid work and care compared to men. In countries with very traditional gender roles—such as Italy—women do three times or more, while in most non-industrialized countries the multiplier is larger: for example, it is estimated that in Iraq and much of Africa women do six times the unpaid work of men.

Across the OECD, women generally do one to three times more housework then men, two to ten times more hours on care, and one to four hours less paid work. The gender gap is wider after marriage and childbearing and persists regardless of the relative hours or earnings of men and women. For example, in France even where a woman brings in all the household income she provides 50% of care at home (World Bank 2012: 219–20).

As the World Bank notes, 'allocating more time to market work generally comes at the price of higher total workloads for women' (2012: 218). While there is evidence of convergence in working time and participation patterns among women and men, this is more marked for paid work than for the hours spent in unpaid work and care (World Bank 2012: 220). These patterns of overload for many women help explain the high incidence of time pressures they experience: for example 70% of working mothers in Australia say they are often or almost always rushed and pressed for time (Skinner et al. 2010).

Paid Domestic Work Undertaken in the Home

The work of social reproduction is also increasingly commodified and undertaken through diverse forms of employment in the home. Domestic employment of this type (defined by the ILO as work performed in or for a household by workers in an employment relationship)—most of it in care jobs of one form or another—is expanding rapidly around the world. These jobs account for 52.6 million workers internationally, or 3.6% of global employment (ILO 2011: 1). Most of these workers are women (94.1% in Israel, 90.9% in Spain, and 92.4% in Argentina for example), and almost half have no entitlement to a minimum wage or to any minimum period of weekly rest, while more than half are not subject to any limit on their weekly hours (ILO 2011). Their poor conditions, lack of job security, vulnerability to exploitation, and weak citizenship rights led the ILO to adopt a new Domestic Worker Convention and Recommendation in 2011, which aims to encourage nations to extend to domestic workers the same rights and protections available to other workers (ILO 2011).

Gender and ethnicity intersect in this growing area of domestic employment, creating new international patterns of work and care that leave immigrant women particularly vulnerable. These circuits are the site of a growing body of theoretical and empirical analysis.

Transnational Circuits of Work and Care: Gendered and Racialized

One of the most important developments in the research of work and gender over the past 20 years has focused upon the international division of reproductive labour. Increasing rates of female participation in paid work in the global North have given rise to a 'care deficit', which has pulled immigrant women from the South to provide various forms of paid reproductive labour to households in the global North. Parreñas (2001) formulated the notion of 'the international division of reproductive labour' to describe these 'care chains' (a term coined by Hochschild 2000) as household work is commodified and wealthy women in the North pay migrant women to perform housework and care, while immigrant women in turn often pass on their own housework and care to women in their country of origin. The quality of care and terms available to support it generally deteriorate down this chain.

This reproductive work involves both direct care in-home such as for childcare and aged care, plus a range of other cleaning, maintenance, laundry, and shopping activities. Further, such 'care chains' exist both within the private household sphere and in public institutions: for example health systems in the USA, UK, France, and Australia increasingly rely upon immigrant nurses and doctors. In 2005, 30% of doctors and 10% of nurses in the UK National Health Service had received their initial training overseas and in France a quarter of all hospital doctors were foreign or naturalized immigrants (Williams 2010: 396).

A growing body of studies document the gendered and racialized nature of these chains, (see for example, the 2012 special issue of *Global Networks* (Vol. 12: No. 2)), their local and international consequences, and the role of the state in shaping their outcomes (especially in relation to immigration and citizenship rights, and their intersection with labour law). These chains often result in weak citizenship rights and poor working conditions for immigrant carers, most of them women, especially when they provide informal in-home care. They can also often result in poor care for the children in families of those who remain in the country of immigrant origin (Parreñas 2001).

Rapid Industrialization and its Gendered Effects

Beyond the home and the world of domestic labour, the rapid pace of 'compressed' industrialization has particular effects on women in many newly industrializing countries, especially where welfare supports and labour and social regulation lag. In countries like South Korea, the Philippines, and Mexico, women have been rapidly pulled into manufacturing and services sector employment in compressed industrial revolutions.

Take the case of South Korea where the rapid onset of industrialization in the presence of traditional Confucian values has meant that many women have become overloaded. They continue to be seen in traditional ways—as the 'masterminding servant' of the household in bondage to the family, as Kyung-Sup and Song Min-Young (2010) have put it—but now also work in demanding paid jobs.

South Korean women's response to the harsh effects of rapid industrialization and its effects is to delay marriage, or not marry, or postpone motherhood, and to have very small families—well below the population replacement rate (South Korea's total fertility rate in 2010 was 1.14 and falling and the lowest in the world). In this context, the persistent preference for sons in families where only one child is born has resulted in the disproportionate aborting of female children. Such abortions are illegal and often endanger the lives and health of pregnant women. They also result in the loss of female children (Kyung-Sup and Song Min-Young 2010: 560). The reproductive costs and loss of female children are the unmeasured consequences of rapid industrialization amidst traditional gendered cultures.

For many women in countries that are rapidly industrializing, paid work is a double-edged sword, bringing the possibilities of economic independence, new skills, and social possibilities and geographic mobility. However, in the presence of unchanging cultural expectations and weak labour regulation (e.g. of wages, working time, or maternity leave) and social infrastructure (like childcare), these gains can be accompanied by harsh, gendered penalties.

GENDERED OUTCOMES IN POST-SOCIALIST COUNTRIES

In other parts of the globe, as post-socialist countries have become capitalist, 'public maternalism' policies have come under pressure. New risks emerge for women workers in these contexts where maternal protections (like extended maternity leave) are wound back or employers discriminate against women who use them in the context of weak, or poorly enforced, anti-discrimination laws.

In the post-Soviet bloc, policy-makers talk about the 'maternal walls' which have increased in size and effect with the recent onset of capitalism where the coincidence of weak enforcement of anti-discrimination law, and the state's pursuit of international investment capital, has seen employers discriminate against mothers, increasing the disadvantages in pay and careers that affect women in post-communist Hungary, for example (Glass and Fodor 2011).

Of course it is not only rapidly industrializing countries or post-communist countries that experience persistent or new risks for women in employment. In the United States, for example, working women are yet to enjoy the benefits and protection of a comprehensive paid parental/maternity leave scheme, making them the last OECD country to adopt this basic policy measure, following Australia's 2011 adoption of a national scheme of 18 weeks' state-funded maternity leave, paid at the minimum wage level.

THE REGULATION OF WORK: MADE IN MEN'S IMAGE

All forms of economic regime are engaged—to a greater or lesser degree—in placing limits and minima around the 'wage effort' bargain, and providing public goods that enable the operation of an employment system. Most obviously, states provide at least basic education (and often considerable investment in vocational education), health systems (though these vary widely), and essential infrastructure like the operation of a legal system, law enforcement, transport, and various forms of social support. For the most part these state-provided 'public goods' critically underpin the employment of both women and men—given that it makes little economic sense for employers to individually provide this in light of the mobility of workers and the shared social and economic benefits of such goods. Where such goods—like access to healthcare—are not publicly provided for all, then the nature of bargaining and the regulation of employment can be significantly affected. For example, US workers' access to healthcare and pensions through enterprise-based collective bargaining from the 1950s (rather than more universal systems) has had two important long-term consequences: many of those not covered by such agreements lack access to good pensions and healthcare (50 million citizens in 2011: Christie 2011: 1), and in difficult economic times they tie unions up in defensive collective contract negotiations as they attempt to retain health and pension benefits. These affect women and men differently in different economic sectors.

More specific to the immediate employment relationship, and directly affected by the individual employer and labour regulation specifically, are health and safety, wages, working time, and leave and other employment conditions. In most industrialized countries the shape of these conditions has evolved around male norms: a male body that is expected to work full-time, to be supported by a functioning household (partner or mother), to be available for overtime at short notice, to be capable of sustaining a particular physical and mental capacity over the life-course, to require regeneration through sick and holiday leave—but not maternity leave, for example.

The effects of employment conditions vary according to the gender of the worker. For example, given the limited bargaining power of women and their lower rates of unionization historically, states with strong minimum wage regimes are generally associated with narrower gender pay gaps than those where bargaining is more individualized. The prevailing regime of labour regulation has particular gendered outcomes (Rubery 2011). The male standard and regulation built around it casts a long shadow in labour bargaining and regulation in many times and places, locating the female body as an exception, as non-standard—with its different care responsibilities, sexuality, and life-cycle needs and patterns.

Both Joan Acker (1990) and Joan Williams (2000) have pointed out that the fundamental tenets of work regulation relate to an imagined male body and a male life-cycle— and an 'ideal' male worker, free of care, supported by a wife. This imagined worker does not characterize many workers for most of the world's history. It certainly did not apply in the circumstances of either of the artefacts with which this piece began: the pre-colonial Salish people or the multi-sex, multicultural workforce of the Steveston factory. But the legacy of male worker standards made in men's image continues to characterize the conceptualization and regulation of employment and misses the challenge of understanding and appropriately protecting workers more broadly, whether male or female.

Bodies are also sexual and workplaces are domains in which sexual identities are made and played out. The sexualization of working bodies presents particular risks for women when their looks and sexual behaviours are rewarded or punished, and/or they experience sexual harassment. Issues of sexuality at work are an important aspect of gender at work. In some settings practices of sexualization and sexual harassment are used by men to patrol and police gender-based segmentation of occupations, industries, and specific workplaces, often alongside hetero-normative practices that disadvantage non-heterosexuals. The physical, emotional, and behavioural performance of sexuality and gender at work, and its gendered differences, is an important aspect of the operation of sexuality and gender and work. Practices of male domination, of male bonding and power are also sometimes reproduced to exclude women and create and reinforce male domination and male advantage—in management, board rooms, and unions (Eveline 1994). Some of their most extreme expressions occur in the context of the military where powerful forms of masculinity are dominant and men actively harass and exclude women or men who do not fit dominant masculine or hetero-normative types, and organizations fail to recognize sex-based harassment or deal with it (DLA Piper 2012).

By and large, over the past 30 years women have increasingly entered paid work; however, in many places the labour market's adaptation of its male norms has been partial. Where systems have not adapted to the non-male worker and her body and circumstances, then women have been forced to adjust to its terms: for example, being paid less than men, coping with particular health and safety risks associated with feminized work, dealing with sex-based harassment, reducing family size, going back to work before they want to after giving birth, or overworking. Neo-liberal discourse calls some of these outcomes 'choice'. In fact women have made creative efforts to come to terms with the labour market circumstances and the options available to them—and these options are created by institutional practices and the discourses, habits, and practices of social systems.

Uneven institutional support results in persistent gender inequities, including in pay, women's access to money, land, and credit, and in job segregation, with women concentrated in poorer quality jobs and informal, unregulated work

Gender, Work, Time, and the Clash of 'Clock' and 'Natural' Time Regimes

One of the main ways in which men's and women's work experiences differ is in relation to time, and this is a particularly potent site of difference in the world of work. Most women over their life-cycle will spend some of their time—and much more than most men—putting together two kinds of time: 'clock' time and 'natural' or 'body' time. Most workers internalize a form of clock time which becomes second nature, naturalized through the clock of work (and school) time with regular start and finish times and total hours of work.

'Natural' time refers to the structuring of activities around natural phenomena such as day/night, the seasons, the weather, and the body (Pocock et al. 2012a). It is imprecise, variable, and often related to processes or tasks. 'Natural' time includes 'body' time: that is the time that the body takes to grow and be healthy, heal, reproduce, and live. It is time that, in pre-industrial times, guided the seasonal practices of agricultural life (when to get up, when to go to sleep; when to stay inside or go out; when to reap or sow or hold cultural festivals and celebrations). These forms of 'natural' time are very different from clock time, which is standardized, regular, linear, predictable, universal, and measured at work in seconds, minutes, and hours—and now in nanoseconds (Pocock et al. 2012a: 6).

These two types of times (natural and clock) are not mutually exclusive; they can operate simultaneously. However, in the world of work, clock time dominates natural or body time (Pocock et al. 2012a: 7). When women are carers, their experience of time is outside the clock. And when they attempt—in growing numbers—to reconcile the demands of clock time at work with the unpredictable and often unbounded demands of care or natural time, they experience a clash of time regimes. They need a different working time regime from that of the 'careless'. For example, having flexible start and finish times in a job, control over total working hours, the chance to deal with unexpected care events, opportunities for extended time away from paid work all become important in reconciling the clocks of care and work.

A growing proportion of the world's workers—women—live simultaneously in the worlds of clock and natural time and must deal with their vigorous contest. As Barbara Adam points out, most workers do not live in clock time alone:

> While clock time dominates the world of work and the global economy, the great majority of the world's people function in the shadows of the time economy of money. Children and the elderly, the unemployed, carers the world over and subsistence farmers of the majority world inhabit the shadowlands of un- and undervalued time. Women dwell there in unequal numbers. Their time does not register on the radar of commodified time. (Adam 2006: 124)

When women—living and caring in natural time—enter paid work ruled by clock time, they must reconcile two time regimes. When half the workforce is made up of people who live in a time of bodies and nature, but who must also respond to the discipline of the clock, new forms of working time regulation—over the day, week, year, and lifecycle are required. This needs to include relief from the intensive work of reconciling two forms of time and carrying out both paid work and care work at once, and around each other, on the same day. All over the world, as women's participation in paid work increases, a growing proportion of workers are governed by the workplace clock, without having given up the natural clock. Their times are busy and demanding.

These temporal aspects of working life, and their gendered character and consequences, are of increasing importance in the study of employment. This study needs to extend beyond analysis of formal employment regulation and its adaptation to gendered differences, to analysis of the dense cultures and discourses that shape experiences of time at work. Take for example, the issue of established norms of working time which have powerful effects that are difficult to contest, regardless of regulatory standards, even by powerful workers. In 2012 Sheryl Sandberg, Chief Operating Officer of Facebook, made a public confession that ricocheted around the globe: she regularly left work at 5.30 p.m. to be home to have dinner with her children (CNN 2012). While she had been doing this ever since she became a mother, it was only in 2012 that she felt brave enough 'to talk about it publicly'. For years she had sent emails late at night and early in the morning to maintain the appearance of working long and hard, to meet the time performance norms of her workplace, and 'acting like a man' who works long hours.

Sandberg's story illustrates the demanding power of workplace cultures. Despite being one of the world's most senior and well-paid managers in one of its most successful and profitable companies, Sandberg was reluctant to admit to the priority she placed on the care of her children and the ways she behaved to put together her job and care. When even the most powerful workers conceal this conflict and their responses, less powerful workers—most of them women—have little chance of contesting dominant working time regimes. The gendered character of long hours—mostly carried out by working men—makes this an issue of importance to many men, especially fathers, who struggle to legitimately refuse long hours.

A growing body of research suggests that workplace cultures around time are resistant to the demands on mothers, fathers, and carers, and the conflicting clocks that affect their lives. As long as this is true, mothers and carers will be time-stressed and carers will be under-represented in public institutions that remain made in the image of the 'carefree'.

POWER AND VOICE

In this light it is no surprise that men consistently dominate all the institutions of work—unions, management, board rooms, industrial courts, and tribunals. The under-representation of women in the institutions of governance around the world makes the narrowing of gender inequalities at work a slow and sometimes unreliable project. In 2009, women made up only 17% of the world parliamentarians who pass labour law. This is a positive improvement from only 10% in 1997, but remains far from equality and illustrates the slow rate of progress. Women make up less than a fifth of cabinet positions worldwide and less than one in ten of board positions in listed companies—ranging from 40% in Norway (where female quotas exist) to only 2% in Japan and Korea. Even in countries with decades of experience with equal opportunity and anti-discrimination policies, women make up small numbers of those who exercise public power: only 17% of the 2012 US Congress were women, for example, and 16% of US Fortune 500 company boards, with little change evident in recent years.

Women Got the Job....

Around the world women are increasingly involved in work—paid and unpaid—with more and more working for a wage. But they have not experienced the reallocation of unpaid domestic work and for many, support for the normal life-cycle events of care and reproduction that most women experience (pregnancy, birth, care of children and the aged or infirm) remains weak or meagre.

Narrowing the gender inequalities that are evident in the world of work requires regulation of work that recognizes and responds to women's differences from 'ideal male norms' over the life-cycle. Increasing female participation in paid work, without this renovation of labour and social institutions, results in female adaptation to the existing terms and institutions of work, which are made in men's image. Adaptation is very different to 'choice'. In many countries 'proper citizens' are increasingly required to participate in paid work and access to rights like healthcare, social security, and income support is dependent upon participation in paid work—rather than the work of social reproduction. In this world, work is a pivotal source of citizenship. It is also fetishized—but only a particular form of work. Standing (1999) has described the short parabola of progression from an emphasis in the nineteenth century upon the *rights of* labour (to organize, to improve pay and conditions), to the *right to* labour (in the face of the 1930s depression), to the more recent *requirement to* labour (in exchange for social support and citizenship)—even in parties of labour. A recent example is provided by Australia's Prime Minister who in 2011 set out her Labor Party views about the weight and worth of paid labour:

> To work hard, to set your alarm clocks early, to ensure your children are in school. We are the party of work not welfare, that's why we respect the efforts of the brickie and look with a jaundiced eye at the lifestyle of the socialite. (Gillard 2011)

In this world the good citizen is a paid worker—a brickie, an archetypical male construction worker—and the alternative is the unworthy socialite—archetypically female. There is no recognition in this valorization of the bricklayer for the worker who undertakes care alongside paid labour over the life-cycle. This 'good' worker is made in the image of the male, in standard employment. This vision does not allow the worker a body, a sex, or a reproductive life—one which is as likely to be female as male in many contemporary labour markets.

Once the female body is admitted to this world of labour, the key negotiated and regulated terms of labour change; the reproductive life-cycle becomes more important as does the work undertaken beyond the paid labour market. The key terms of the famous 'wage–effort bargain'—which sits at the centre of employment relations texts—change: they must extend to the redefinition of employment, the regulation of domestic and informal work, and the provision of leave and working time that anticipate care and domestic duties, and the 'putting together' of different types of time.

At present, labour market policy assumes that there is an unlimited supply of unpaid female labour (Elson 1994) and that women can be loaded up without limit. Joan Acker has pointed to capital's energetic 'non-responsibility' (2003) for social reproduction (except where it offers opportunities for profit, as in the case of commercial childcare provision, for example), leaving the costs and labour of care to women, hidden in the private sphere or in informal domestic employment. Neo-liberal employment policies reassert 'non-responsibility', pushing back social reproductive provisions like state support for elder care and childcare in some countries—often on to women and the family.

At national level, regardless of the stage of industrialization or the nature of socialist or capitalist regimes, gender remains a fault line around the world. While local effects vary, women are usually to be found at the bottom of workplace, industry, and labour market hierarchies. There is no sign of a 'natural' evolutionary pathway to reduced gender inequalities at work, as the World Bank has recently recognized:

> [I]n the absence of public policy, globalization alone cannot and will not reduce gender inequality. Despite significant increases in agency and in access to economic opportunities for many women in many countries, the rising tide has not lifted everybody. Those often left behind are women for whom the existing constraints are most binding. That is why *public action aimed at closing existing gender gaps in endowments, agency, and access to economic opportunities is necessary* for countries to fully capitalize on the potential of globalization as a force for development and greater gender equality. (World Bank 2012: 254, my emphasis)

Strong growth in world trade and globalization has not reduced gender inequality, especially when the experiences in the South are considered alongside those in the North. Further, the World Bank conceded that a strong 'intrinsic ethical argument' exists for interventions that work directly to reduce inequality in the labour market (2012: 254). If the world is going to rely—as it increasingly does—on the equal contribution of women to paid work, then there is a strong case for policy action that redresses inequalities between women and men in the world of work—whether that work is paid or unpaid.

What Will Make a Difference?

The analysis of effective policy and action to redress gender inequities at work is an important area of labour reform. This reform needs to deal with direct regulation of labour standards and their enforcement, but also to go well beyond them to a thorough renovation of the 'ideal working man' imaginary that squats at the centre of labour markets and workplaces around the planet. These dense, gendered practices of labour—which have arisen for the most part in the metropolises of the global North—need a thorough renovation, one that reduces gender-based pay gaps and the underpayment of feminized work, as well as establishing appropriate leave, working time, and flexibility arrangements that recognize the gendered character of care responsibilities over the life-cycle. This renovation needs to be particularly attentive to the regulation and appropriate remuneration of domestic work and care jobs—including their associated rights of citizenship and immigration. Institutional protections against discrimination, sexualized work, and sexual harassment are also essential, along with the public provision of quality, accessible, and affordable care options that ensure that the children of workers—and other dependants such as the aged—across the socio-economic spectrum are appropriately cared for, educated, and kept healthy.

Perhaps hardest of all, the redistribution of domestic work is also an important issue if women are not to be burdened unfairly with a double workload of paid and unpaid work; this is a pressing issue in both the North and South. It also seems that quotas on women's leadership in a range of institutions are necessary if the gender power gap in the institutions of work (and beyond) is to be narrowed significantly. For many women whose power at work is weak, state regulation *and* enforcement of core labour standards such as minimum wage, leave, and working time conditions are also vital. The enactment of 'decent work'—including domestic work—requires an international effort, as the ILO has recognized. However, this will remain a forlorn aspiration unless the coordinated efforts of national and international bodies can be made effective.

In all of this, the appropriate conceptualization of gender and work, and the conduct of theoretical and empirical research that frames problems effectively, in international context—remain critical tasks for employment researchers and analysts.

Conclusion

While is sometimes tempting to see the world of work as constantly changing and disrupting old patterns, a longer historical and more international lens suggests that as much as things change, they reinvent ways of staying the same. Gender differences are constant even as their localized patterns and costs change over time. The challenges of rearing children while holding down a job and sustaining a household and community, and of being treated fairly at work, were as real for Caucasian, Japanese, and First Nations women cannery workers in Steveston in the early twentieth century as they remain today.

While the terms of trade, the technologies of work, and labour laws change—and communities swap blankets woven by women from hand-gathered goat hair for those manufactured in distant factories, and commodify their labour to pay for them—gendered hierarchies of work persist, both in the home and in the workplace. And with more than half of all labour time around the planet undertaken by women—and essential to the operation of social and economic life and the production of the bodies who labour—the study of the women and men who populate these hierarchies is an essential aspect of any analysis of employment—both now, in the past, and in the future.

Any easy assumption that gender inequalities melt away is contradicted by contemporary experience. What is more, it is important to avoid what E. P. Thompson called 'the enormous condescension of posterity' (1963: 13)[3] when we analyse women and men at work in the past—or from the northern metropolis—where a similar 'enormous condescension' about the majority labour of the South is also possible. Navigation of working life and its gendered fault lines was and remains hazardous for workers of both the North and the South—and many problems remain unresolved today in varied guises, with long chains that link the gendered fortunes in the North and South in a tight global embrace. Finding solutions for work, bodies, and care around the world is likely to rely on international action and lessons learned from diverse places and times. To paraphrase E. P. Thompson again: causes which are not yet won in England or the United States or Australia 'might, in Asia or Africa, yet be won'—and certainly will require concerted resolve and action across the globe to realize justice for women and gender equality.

ACKNOWLEDGEMENTS

The author would like to thank the Wayne Morse Centre for Law and Politics at the University of Oregon (and especially its Director Professor Margaret Hallock) for hosting my 2012 research visit when this was written. The Australian Research Council supported this research with a grant to research the changing terms, times, and technologies of work (DP110102007). I would also like to thank staff at the museums at the Gulf of Georgia Cannery National Historic Site Steveston, the Vancouver Public Library and the Museum of Anthropology at University of British Columbia (UBC).

NOTES

1. Personal communication, guide, tour of Gulf of Georgia Cannery, National Historic Site Steveston, 5 April 2012.
2. Personal communication, guide, Museum of Anthropology, UBC, 4 April 2012.
3. Thompson was writing of workers at the time of the industrial revolution in England: 'I am seeking to rescue the poor stockinger, the Luddite cropper, the "obsolete" hand-loom weaver, the "Utopian" artisan, and even the deluded follower of Joanna Southcott, from the enormous condescension of posterity.' He continued: 'the greater part of the world today is still undergoing problems of industrialization, and of the formation of democratic institutions, analogous in many ways to our own experience during the Industrial Revolution. Causes which were lost in England might, in Asia or Africa, yet be won' (1963: 13).

References

Acker, J. (1990). 'Hierarchies, Jobs, Bodies: A Theory of Gendered Organizations', *Gender and Society*, 4(2): 139–58.

—— (2003). *Feminism and Sociology*. Cambridge: Polity Press.

Adam, B. (2006). 'Time', *Theory, Culture & Society. Special Issue on Problematising Global Knowledge*, 23: 123.

Australian Bureau of Statistics (ABS) (1997). *Unpaid Work and the Australian Economy, 1997.* Cat. No. 5240.0. Canberra: Australian Bureau of Statistics.

Bacchetta, M., Ernst, E., and Bustamante, J. P. (2010). *Globalisation and Informal Jobs in Developing Countries*. Geneva: World Trade Organization and International Labour Organisation.

Boserup, E. (1970). *Woman's Role in Economic Development*. London: Earthscan.

Brenner, N., Peck, J., and Theodore, N. (2010). 'Variegated Neoliberalization: Geographies, Modalities, Pathways', *Global Networks*, 10(2): 182–222.

Bronfenbrenner, U. (1979). *The Ecology of Human Development*. Cambridge, MA: Harvard University Press.

Christie, L. (2011). 'Number of People without Health Insurance Climbs', *CNN Money*, 13 September. Available at <http://money.cnn.com/2011/09/13/news/economy/census_bureau_health_insurance/index.htm>, accessed 16 July 2012.

CNN (2012). 'Why it's OK to leave a tech job at 5 p.m.', CNN, 16 April. Available at <http://edition.cnn.com/2012/04/16/tech/web/cashmore-facebook-sandberg/index.html> accessed 30 May 2012.

Connell, R. W. (2007). *Southern Theory: The Global Dynamics of Knowledge in Social Science*. Sydney Allen & Unwin.

DLA Piper (2012). *Executive Summary: Report of the Review of Allegations of Sexual and other Abuse in Defence*. Melbourne: DLA Piper.

Eikhof, D. R., Warhurst, C., and Haunschild, A. (2007). 'Introduction: What work? What Life? What Balance? Critical Reflections on the Work–Life Balance Debate', *Employee Relations*, 29(4): 325–33.

Elson, D. (1994). 'Micro. Meso. Macro: Gender and Economic Analysis in the Context of Policy Reforms', in I. Bakker (ed.), *The Strategic Silence: Gender and Economic Policy*. London: Zed Books, 33–45.

Eveline, J. (1994). 'The Politics of Advantage', *Australian Feminist Studies*, 9(19): 129–54.

Fan, C. (2008). *China on the Move: Migration, the State, and the Household*. London and New York.

Gillard, J. (2011). 'The 2011 Whitlam Oration', Sydney. Available at <http://www.pm.gov.au/press-office/speech-inaugural-whitlam-institute-gough-whitlam-oration-sydney>, accessed 30 May 2011.

Glass, M. and Fodor, E. (2011). 'Public Maternalism Goes to Market', *Gender & Society*, 25: 5–26.

Hall, P. A. and Soskice, D. (2001). 'Varieties of Capitalism: An Introduction' in Hall and Soskice (eds.), *Varieties of Capitalism: The Institutional Foundations of Comparative Advantage*. Oxford and New York: Oxford University Press, 1–68.

Harcourt, W. and Escobar, A. (2005). *Women and the Politics of Place*. Bloomfield, CT: Kumarian Press.

Hochschild, A. (2000). 'Global Care Chains and Emotional Surplus Value', in W. Hutton and A. Giddens (eds.), *On the Edge: Living with Global Capitalism*. London: Jonathan Cape, 130–46.

ILO (2010). *Decent Work for Domestic Workers*. Geneva: ILO.

—— (2011). *Coverage of Domestic Workers by Key Working Conditions Laws*. Domestic Work Policy Brief No. 5. Geneva: ILO. Available at <http://www.ilo.org/travail/whatwedo/publications/WCMS_157509/lang--en/index.htm>.

Kanter, R. M. (1989). 'Work and Family in the United States: A Critical Review and Agenda for Research and Policy', *Family Business Review*, 2(1): 77–114.

Kessler-Harris, A. (1975). 'Where are the Organized Women Workers?', *Feminist Studies*, 3: 92–110.

Kyung-Sup, C. and Min-Young, S. (2010). 'The Stranded Individualizer under Compressed Modernity: South Korean Women in Individualization without Individualism', *British Journal of Sociology*, 61(3): 539–64.

Parreñas, R. S. (2001). *Servants of Globalization*. Stanford, CA: Stanford University Press.

Pocock, B. (2011). 'Rethinking Unionism in a Changing World of Work, Family and Community Life', *Relations Industrielles/Industrial Relations*, 66(4): 562–84.

Pocock, B., Skinner, N., and Williams, P. (2012a). *Time Bomb: Work, Rest and Play in Australia Today*. Sydney: New South Publishing.

Pocock, B., Williams, P., and Skinner, N. (2012b). 'Conceptualizing Work, Family and Community: A Socio-Ecological Systems Model, Taking Account of Power, Time, Space and Life Stage', *British Journal of Industrial Relations*, 50(3): 391–411.

Rubery, J. (2009). 'How Gendering the Varieties of Capitalism Requires a Wider Lens', *Social Politics*, 16(2): 192–203.

—— (2011). 'Towards a Gendering of the Labour Market Regulation Debate', *Cambridge Journal of Economics*, 35(6), 1103–26.

Skinner, N., Pocock, B., and Pisaniello, S. (2010). *How Much Should We Work? Working Hours, Holidays and Working Life. The Participation Challenge*. Adelaide: Centre for Work + Life, University of South Australia.

Standing, G. (1999). *Global Labour Flexibility: Seeking Distributive Justice*. Basingstoke: Macmillan.

Thompson, E. P. (1963). *The Making of the English Working Class*. London: Victor Gollancz.

Vosko, L. F., MacDonald, M., and Campbell, I. (eds.) (2009). *Gender and the Contours of Precarious Employment*. Abingdon: Routledge.

Voydanoff, P. (2007). *Work, Family, and Community: Exploring Interconnections*. New York: Psychology Press.

Waring, M. (1988). *If Women Counted: A New Feminist Economics*. New York: Harper & Row.

Wertheimer, B. (1975). *We Were There: The Story of Working Women in America*. New York: Praeger.

Williams, F. (2010). 'Migration and Care: Themes, Concepts and Challenges', *Social Policy and Society*, 212(9): 385–96.

Williams, J. (2000). *Unbending Gender: Why Family and Work Conflict and What to Do About It*. Oxford and New York: Oxford University Press.

World Bank (2012). *World Development Report: Gender Equality and Development*. Washington, DC: World Bank.

Yesali, M., Steves, H., and Steves, K. (1998). *Steveston Cannery Row: An Illustrated History*. Vancouver: Peninsula Publishing Company.

CHAPTER 23

WHERE ARE THE VOICES? NEW DIRECTIONS IN VOICE AND ENGAGEMENT ACROSS THE GLOBE

MICHAEL BARRY, ADRIAN WILKINSON,
PAUL J. GOLLAN, AND SENIA KALFA

INTRODUCTION

IN this chapter we discuss employee voice from two separate yet related conceptual lenses: industrial or employment relations and varieties of capitalism. Our purpose is to explain how and why interest in employee voice emerged and has increasingly become the focus of attention in the employment relations field in recent years. The varieties of capitalism (VOC) literature allows us to examine voice schemes in different national and regional contexts, and, where possible, to show emerging patterns. These two research areas are intrinsically connected through the role of employment relations institutions, such as trade unions or labour regulations, which are contextually specific and shape the practice of voice on an organizational level. The chapter aims to explore the nature, depth, and breadth of voice schemes and highlight the factors that promote or inhibit their development in different places.

The term 'voice' refers to how employees are able to have a say over work activities and organizational decision-making issues, although we note that practitioners and academics use other terms for employee voice such as participation, engagement, involvement or empowerment, and industrial democracy. Voice is then one of a number of terms that denote how employees express themselves in their workplaces. While these terms are sometimes used interchangeably, it is important to note that they have multiple theoretical roots and can be interpreted in different ways across disciplinary boundaries. For example, while the notion of industrial democracy clearly draws on the traditions of political science, and representative participation and collective bargaining emerge from the industrial relations and law literatures, employee involvement and empowerment are more likely to have their roots in human resource management where the focus tends to be on the role of workers as individuals and their relationships with line managers (Wilkinson and Fay 2011).

There are also differences as to the efficacy of voice compared to some of these other terms used to describe worker involvement. Strauss (2006), for example, argues that voice is a weaker term than participation as it does not denote influence and may be no more than spitting-in-the-wind. Thus, while voice is a necessary precursor for participation, it may not in itself lead to participation. For some, voice can be seen as a countervailing source of power on management action while for others voice is part of a mutual gains process (Dundon et al. 2004). In current discourse, organizations are expected to take the high road with high value-added operations or be dragged down into competing for low value-added jobs that are in danger of moving abroad (Handel and Levine 2004). Within this discourse, Strauss (2006: 778) observes, voice has a clear role to provide 'a win-win solution to a central organisational problem—how to satisfy workers' needs while simultaneously achieving organisational objectives'. However, if voice fits neatly into a mutual gains narrative it is also possible that theory and practice can diverge, with strong rhetoric masking weak outcomes (Wilkinson and Fay 2011).

Despite assertions that voice might open a path towards mutual gains, concerns persist about the underlying motivation for voice, particularly where it arises as an employer-inspired initiative. Employers might see benefits of voice in lower turnover (Spencer 1986), improved workplace productivity and organizational performance (Wood 2010), as well as the establishment of effective systems of employee representation and consultation (Befort and Budd 2009; Dundon et al. 2004; Gollan 2007). Notwithstanding these benefits, employees with voice opportunities may be less motivated to support union organizing drives, hence reducing prospects for voice mechanisms that are independent of management (Lewin and Mitchell 1992). For some time this has led sceptics to question whether employer-initiated voice schemes are effective substitutes for employee representation or whether they are more accurately effective schemes to avoid employee representation. What we can say at the outset is that an employer-sponsored perspective is typically less concerned with voice per se, and the related issues of social justice and organizational democracy, and is more likely to be focused on the possible business benefits of voice (Wilkinson et al. 2004).

Looking at voice through the VOC literature provides a valuable lens through which to examine how employee voice is influenced by a country's regulatory framework as well as the local labour and product markets. The importance of the VOC framework as an analytical device is that it helps us understand how governance and representation structures of participation are embedded in particular institutional contexts that have deep historical and cultural roots. As such, efforts to introduce voice mechanisms that are not sensitive to the contextual environment are likely to founder (Block and Berg 2010; Frege and Godard 2010). For example Whitley (1999) as well as Brewster et al. (2007) have argued that the type of capitalism impacts employee voice via the nature and degree of employer–employee interdependence. High interdependence promotes the view that problems could be resolved within the firm thus promoting strong voice mechanisms and discouraging employee exit. On the other hand, low interdependence encourages high turnover rates as employees do not have an ability to impact organizational decision-making (Harcourt and Wood 2007; Storey 2007).

The following sections of this chapter seek to tease out these issues and contradictions. We will examine both traditional voice mechanisms, established primarily through union representation, and emerging models that are increasingly non-union and informal. We also seek to place the concept of voice in an international context so that we can provide examples of the extent to which voice has been realized in practice, and how voice schemes are shaped by not only the actions and interests of the direct parties, but also the important role played by the regulatory environment in either fostering or constraining voice.

WHERE DOES THE VOICE CONCEPT COME FROM AND WHAT DOES IT MEAN IN PRACTICE?

Within the employment relations (ER) literature, employee voice was traditionally equated with union representation. However, we are now seeing non-union voice becoming important in its own right and an acceptance that researchers should look for multiple channels of voice to explore the extent of worker involvement.

So a central issue is that employee voice is a very broad term with considerable scope in the range of definitions given by authors (see, for example, Budd et al. 2010; Dietz et al. 2009; Poole 1986; Sashkin 1976; Strauss 2006). This scope is particularly evident across different disciplinary traditions—from human resource management (HRM), political science, psychology, law, and industrial relations—that have distinct perspectives on voice, as well as the other overlapping and related terms (Wilkinson et al. 2010). It appears that scholars from diverse traditions often know relatively little of the research that has been done in other areas. Equally, each term can carry different connotations or have associated ideological baggage.

Perhaps the best exposition of the term voice goes back to Hirschman's (1970) classic work, although the notion of employee voice could be dated to the ideas of the Human Relations school. Hirschman conceptualized 'voice' in a very specific way, and in the context of how organizations respond to decline. However, the term has been applied in rather different contexts since. Hirschman's (1970: 30) own definition of voice is described as 'any attempt at all to change rather than to escape from an objectionable state of affairs'. The point about voice is that its provision may secure general improvements, although if exit is reduced as a consequence it may force the discontented to take action within the organization, and hence make voice a more powerful tool for change.

Yet, rather than searching for an agreed term or a precise definition of voice, we feel research should focus on what specific practices actually mean to the actors, whether such schemes can improve organizational effectiveness and employee well-being, and the extent to which various practices allow workers to have a say in organizational decisions. Here, much will depend on whether voice initiatives are perceived as faddish, or are embedded within an organization's culture (Cox et al. 2006). Clearly, forms of employee voice through participation can differ in the scope of decisions, the amount of influence workers can exercise over management, and the organizational level at which the decisions are made. Some forms are purposely designed to give workers a voice but not more than a very modest role in decision-making, while others are intended to give the workforce a more significant say in organizational governance.

Following Hirschman, the academic concept of 'voice' used in the employment relations literature was popularized by Freeman and Medoff (1984) who argued that it made good sense for both company and workforce to have a 'voice' mechanism. This had both a consensual and a conflictual image: on the one hand, employee voice could lead to a beneficial impact on quality and productivity, while on the other, it could identify areas of divergence between the interests of employees and employers (Gollan and Wilkinson 2007). Trade unions were seen, at this point in time, as the best or indeed only agents to provide voice as they were an independent vehicle of employee representation.

More recently, research has also looked at representative voice taking into account non-union forms as the literature needed to move past a singular focus on union voice and keep pace with developments that reflect a decline in unionization across most countries and the dwindling share of union-only voice. Indeed, in Britain the union-only form of voice has all but disappeared, with only 5% of British workplaces relying on union-only participation (Willman et al. 2009: 102). Similar trends are evident across much of the rest of Europe, America, and Australia (Gomez et al. 2010; Lewin 2010). Thus, there has been considerable literature on non-union employee representation and the efficacy of such structures (Kaufman and Taras 2010).

While interest in non-union channels has increased, the employment relations literature persists on focusing on unions, which reflects the enduring preoccupation of the field with formal institutions of unions and collective bargaining. What is paradoxical here is that this tends to marginalize analysis of voice in places where it is arguably most imperative; that is in workplaces that do not have access to formal mechanisms of joint decision-making and employee involvement. Moreover, the focus on the unionized sector reveals two other related limitations. First, unions are generally concentrated in larger workplaces, meaning that small and medium-size enterprises (SMEs), which we know are growing in number and share of employment, feature less frequently in studies of formal voice. Second, SMEs are also less likely than larger firms to have 'in-house' HRM specialization, meaning that employer-sponsored (as well as employee representative) schemes are less likely to be introduced. While authors such as Freeman and Rogers (1999) talk about a 'representation gap' which describes the difference between actual and desired employee representation, a possible further gap is revealed here for employees who lack access not only to direct representation, but also indirect voice, and even to basic (let alone sophisticated) HRM policy and practice.

The notion of a 'representation gap' was originally premised on union decline. However, declining union density does not mean employees have a reduced appetite for voice whether it be met through unionization or another means. In many European countries employee voice is buttressed by the role the state plays in providing voice on top of voluntary collective bargaining. Thus, France has statutory elected workers councils while Germany has an elaborate system of Works Councils and Work Directors known as co-determination. Nevertheless, as Gumbrell-McCormick and Hyman (2010) point out, continental countries that have dual or overlapping structures of representation reveal tensions between the role of works councils as a form of participation and the formal bargaining processes that otherwise occur between workers, unions, and management.

A recent extension of the voice literature also highlights the importance of silence which is understood as the antithesis of voice. Silence is an employee's 'motivation to withhold or express ideas, information and opinions about work-related improvements' (Van Dyne et al. 2003: 1361). This literature investigates when and how employees in organizational settings exercise voice and when and how they opt for silence (Milliken et al. 2003). Silence, here, can be seen as closely related to an employee's capacity to withhold discretionary effort as an expression of conflict and a form of resistance. But equally, management might seek to perpetuate voice on a range of issues (Donaghey et al. 2011). While it is possible that regulatory rules and laws force management to do things that they would otherwise neglect (Marchington et al. 2001), management are likely to retain some choice, at least in determining the robustness of voice at workplace level (Willman et al. 2006). Therefore notwithstanding the possibility of employee reluctance to utilize voice, it is management behaviour that lies at the heart of the debate on the operation of voice structures.

DOES VOICE EVOKE GENUINE PARTICIPATION, AND EVEN INDUSTRIAL DEMOCRACY?

The concept of employee participation is common to many different discipline areas in the social sciences. In terms of the classic texts on the topic, there are books that: relate participation to politics and question the real form of that involvement (e.g. Pateman 1970); examine the relationship between participation and satisfaction (e.g. Blumberg 1968); and link participation to notions of industrial citizenship (e.g. Clegg 1960; Webb and Webb 1902). The pioneering work of the Tavistock Institute (Heller et al. 1998) or the Swedish experiments in work design (Berggren 1993) constitute yet more perspectives on the subject. Despite often using the same terminology, it is also clear that the meaning and form that participation can take vary considerably depending on the discipline. On the one hand, it could relate to trade union representation through joint consultative committees and collective bargaining, to worker cooperatives, or to legislation designed to provide channels for employee representatives to engage in some form of joint decision-making with employers. On the other hand, and at a different level, it could encompass myriad mechanisms that employers introduce in order to provide information to their staff, or to offer them the chance to engage in joint problem-solving groups or use their skills/discretion at work via job enrichment programmes.

Participation can be seen as a fundamental democratic right for workers to extend a degree of control over managerial decision-making within an organization. This also brings in notions of free speech and human dignity (Budd 2004). Indeed the argument is that workplace democracy allows for the development of skills and values which then have positive flow on effects outside the workplace, in families and communities (Foley and Polyani 2006; Budd and Zagelmeyer 2010). Unlike notions of industrial democracy, however, which are rooted in employee rights, an economic efficiency argument underlies the mainstream conceptualization of voice. Thus, it is seen to make business sense to involve employees in workplace decisions, as a committed workforce is likely to understand better what the organization is trying to do and be more prepared to contribute to its efficient operation. Yet, in this schema, management decides whether or not employees are to be involved and how they will be involved. Employee participation in its most limited forms could then be characterized as a move away from 'you will do this' to 'this is why you will do this' (Wilkinson et al. 1993: 28). Traditions of participation vary across countries and over time.

Another concern is that involvement programmes are viewed solely in a positive manner, ignoring the contested and mundane nature of much participation. For example, rather than leading to autonomy and self-management, participation may merely produce greater work intensification, increased stress levels, and redundancies (Martinez-Lucio 2010; Wilkinson 2002). There is also a concern that employers are exchanging strong union-centred forms of participation for initiatives that are 'weak on power'.

Within practitioner circles the term 'employee engagement' has replaced participation despite their similarities. The term 'employee engagement' was coined by the Gallup Research Group in the 1990s based on research they conducted with clients over 25 years. Thus, engagement is underpinned by the same economic efficiency basis that seems to underlie normative conceptions of voice and has been argued to increase productivity, profitability, retention, organizational health and safety, and customer satisfaction (Little and Little 2006).

The popularity of the concept with practitioners notwithstanding, academic research on engagement faces numerous challenges. First, there is very little academic empirical research on the topic. What has been written on engagement can be found primarily on practitioner publications where preoccupation with rigour is not paramount. Second, the majority of the existing research draws on data collected by the Gallup Workplace Audit (GWA) which has been designed based on a 'positive psychology approach... the study of the characteristics of successful employees and managers and productive work groups' (Harter et al. 2002: 269). The problem is that research based on such an approach is very likely to suffer from outcome bias: errors made in evaluating the quality of decisions when the outcome of those decisions is already known. In other words, it is natural to portray successful companies in a positive light, since their success is already known.

Third, there is very little agreement as to what engagement actually is. For example Kahn (1990: 700), in the first academic article that appears on the topic, defines engagement as 'the simultaneous employment and expression of a person's preferred self in task behaviors (sic) that promote connection to work and to others, personal presence (physical, cognitive and emotional) and active, full role performances'. In that respect, engagement has a performative character which comes alive when practitioners perform their work roles in a way that allows them to display their true identities. Through qualitative research, Kahn (1990) maintained that three psychological conditions are necessary for engagement: meaningfulness, safety, and availability. It was only in 2001 that another academic definition appeared with the work of Maslach, Shaufeli, and Leiter (2001: 417): 'a persistent positive affective state...characterised by high levels of activation and pleasure'. Finally, Saks (2006) uses Social Exchange Theory to argue that engagement is a means for individuals to repay their employing organization when they receive the resources required to successfully fulfil their role. So far, Saks's (2006) conceptual study is the only one that examines antecedents and consequences of employee engagement.

Given the ambiguity that surrounds the concept of engagement, it is unsurprising that its relationship with employee voice has not yet been explored. However, it could be argued that employee voice, whether direct, indirect, formal, or informal is a prerequisite for employee engagement. Kahn (1990) alludes to this relationship when he claims that the level of openness and supportiveness in relationships with co-workers and management affects individuals' feelings of psychological safety which in turn affect employee engagement. Further, drawing on Saks's (2006) model that defines perceptions of justice as antecedents of engagement, we could argue that employee voice influences engagement through that mechanism, as procedural justice 'includes the extent to which representatives of the organisation ask and use employee input, engage in two-way communication and give employees the opportunity to challenge decisions' (Fields et al. 2000: 548). The importance of giving employees voice has been documented in the literature especially with regards to performance appraisal systems (e.g. Folger 1987; McFarlin and Sweeney 1996).

The rise of interest in voice and engagement has coincided with the decline of indirect, representative participation such as joint consultative committees (JCCs). Unlike the methods of direct voice, JCCs are built upon the notion of indirect participation and worker representation in joint management–employee meetings. The scope of joint consultation is typically wider than collective bargaining—and may, for instance, include financial matters—although the issues discussed are not formally negotiated. For some, they represent a diluted form of collective bargaining, and the shift in interest towards consultation reflects a decline in collectivism. However, JCCs can take a number of forms, often contrasting sharply with each other in terms of their objectives, structures, and processes. Some researchers (e.g. Marchington 1992) suggest that joint consultation has been revitalized in order to cover issues traditionally dealt with through collective bargaining, and involve stewards/delegates more closely with management issues in order to convince them of the 'logic' of their decisions. Others (e.g. Gollan 2007) have argued that the committees have largely been concerned with trivia and are thus marginal to the employment relations processes of the organization. In some organizations, JCCs can act as a safety valve (i.e. an alternative to industrial action) through which deep-seated employee grievances are addressed, while in others they are used to hinder the recognition of trade unions or undermine their activities in highly unionized workplaces. Equally, the relationship between collective bargaining and joint consultation in unionized workplaces can be a source of tension, particularly if management is trying to 'edge out' the unions and there has been a failure to engage in meaningful consultations.

Much of the extant research on these important questions is about how voice structures are established, the motivation for them, and how they operate in practice. Other research takes a largely institutional view—that is, failure is the decline or collapse of the structure. The assumption is that setting up a structure itself sorts the problem (Dietz et al. 2009). But many voice systems have 'deaf ears' and frustration can be evident (Harlos 2001). External influences also shape management choice, and this is evident across large and small as well as single and multi-site organizations. Legislation for trade union recognition or the requirement to establish a European Works Council (EWC; see below) means that choices are made to comply with legislation rather than reflecting a real interest in creating voice structures. However, in a broader context, the research findings indicate that external influences open up new options, and regulation can encourage more creative thinking about the choices available.

Research by Dundon et al. (2004) found that employee voice could impact positively in three general ways. First, employee voice is a means of valuing employee contributions. This might lead to improved employee attitudes and behaviours, loyalty, commitment, and cooperative relations. The second impact relates to improved performance, including productivity and individual performance, lower absenteeism, and (in a few cases) new business arising from employee voice. The final impact relates to improved managerial systems. This incorporates the managerial benefits from tapping into employee ideas, the informative and educational role of voice, along with improved relations with recognized trade unions (Kaufman and Taras 2010; Wilkinson et al. 2013).

In discussions of participation, a key question is who gains what from being involved, and given that in most developed countries management are the key drivers of participation schemes, it is likely they will expect to see some advantage from investing in what some might see as an expensive waste of time. Evidence suggests that senior managers are not likely to persevere with participation if it does not meet their goals, either in the short or the long term, and that the benefits must be seen to outweigh the costs for it to survive. Yet, as versions of high commitment HRM have some form of participation as a centre-piece of their models, it seems to be accepted that rather than being seen as a zero-sum concept where one party's gains come at the expense of the other, participation might lead to a larger cake to be shared among workers and employers. On the other hand, some critics of participation would argue that it is only a fig leaf, behind which the worse excesses of capitalism can hide. Under this scenario, the real purpose of participation schemes, especially those aimed at individual workers, is to increase work intensification and con employees into accepting management ideas that may not necessarily be in their best interests. This might be supplemented by a drive to engage in non-union forms of participation as well.

The Dynamics of Employee Voice in Context

Depending on the societal regime within which employee voice is introduced, the benefits might be seen in different ways. Here we can draw on the VOC literature and in so doing see voice as conditional on, or at least shaped and constrained by national institutions such as a country's overarching regulatory framework. This analysis echoes the type of neo-institutionalist perspective that is prevalent in comparative employment relations and comparative politics in which institutions and history are seen to matter, and where the forces that create employment relations diversity on a national or regional basis are seen to persist, at least to some degree, despite the influence of globalization (see Kaufman 2011 for a review of the institutional perspective on comparative ER).

Within the VOC literature, the most popular and often used typology is by Hall and Soskice (2001). The authors differentiate between liberal market economies (LMEs) and coordinated market economies (CMEs). In an LME shareholder rights dominate decision-making, investor behaviour is less patient, competition among firms is adversarial, relationships are based on contracting with low levels of trust, and there is a focus on short-term immediate competitive advantages (Croucher et al. 2010; Wood et al. 2009). The patterns associated with the employment system in LMEs will feature labour market volatility, weaker unions and low union density, weak employment protection legislation, and decentralized collective bargaining. Thus participation is likely to be measured in terms of generated profit and shareholder value at the organizational level and in customer service, product quality, and staff retention at the workplace level. Issues to do with worker commitment, job satisfaction, and alignment with organizational goals are often the proxies used to measure the success of participation but in themselves these may tell us little about the impact of particular schemes on bottom-line success.

In CMEs, non-market relations are more important than in liberal economies, returns are expected in longer time-frames and are more widely defined in the sense that they incorporate the interests of more stakeholders, such as the government, trade unions, and workers. Firms are not as dependent, as their liberal market counterparts are, on profitability and therefore they are less likely to develop sharp responses to cyclical downturns, such as lay-offs. This promotes greater acceptance in CMEs of employment security and creates incentives for employers to invest in training and development, and structures of employee involvement. In coordinated economies, as the VOC proposition goes, the employment system is expected to demonstrate forms of participation that are representative in nature, high union density, and centralized collective bargaining (Kaufman 2011; Croucher et al. 2010). As such, CMEs might generally be more likely to have the right bundle of HR practices to give voice a chance to succeed, and the expectation is more likely to be of mutual gains, either at the level of the individual employing organization or more broadly in terms of citizenship and long-term social cohesion (Wilkinson et al. 2010).

Despite its analytical value, this deductive model has been criticized for being deterministic and static and for imposing arbitrary labels on countries (Kaufman 2011). A further limitation is the lack of empirical evidence, a lack of attention to Mediterranean and Far Eastern economies (Croucher et al. 2012), and the lack of examination of differences between sectors within the same economy (Lane and Wood 2009). In contrast, Amable (2003), using an inductive approach, identified five different types of capitalism by examining 21 OECD economies. He calls these: market-based, social democratic, Asian, Mediterranean, and Continental European. In a European context, collective participation remains significant in certain countries, notably Germany and the Scandinavian, social democratic economies. However, it is important to mention here that recent research by Croucher et al. (2012) highlights that while social democratic economies—Denmark, Norway, and Sweden—share a similar strong union presence with continental European economies such as Germany, they are simultaneously characterized by weaker employment protection legislation, and less job security.

Through the VOC literature we can also examine the extent to which product and labour markets can determine the forms that voice takes in practice. We know from the studies that have been published over time that voice structures can take diverse forms in different countries given the role of the state and institutional frameworks in shaping the environment in which it operates. If legislation is extensive, then participation will be present—at least in structural terms—in all organizations above a certain size within that country. It could be argued that this therefore provides a safety net and a structure around which other forms of participation can develop, and in most cases that has been assumed to happen. However, there is also the possibility that the presence of formal structures could also hamper the growth, sustainability, and contribution of more informal voice practices, and it is also likely that at least some employers might try to find ways around the requirement to involve their employees. For example, given the growth in subcontracting, employers might seek to avoid some of their responsibilities by shifting work to other organizations, either in the same country or even overseas where the same level of regulations do not exist.

In Anglo-Saxon economies, where the amount of legislation governing participation is limited and employers have a fair degree of choice in what practices to implement, it is easy to assume that markets are very important. The financial turmoil that commenced in 2008–9 shows how influential they can be. However, in countries where legislation is more extensive and there is a stronger state commitment to long-term financial stability, the power of product markets is likely to be constrained and there is a greater chance that higher-level forms of participation will survive. Similarly, in developing countries, labour market expectations may shape participation depending on education and training opportunities for the population as a whole or on the way in which cultural traditions promote acceptance of or challenge to management decisions (Wood 2010).

Empirical literature that examines such claims is slowly emerging, due to the abundance of data from the Cranet survey, which is an international organizational-level survey of the most senior HR manager of an organization, which focuses on a wide variety of key areas of management practice. Further, the Cranet dataset provides the possibility for international comparative work as it is conducted across 39 countries (Wood et al. 2009). Croucher et al. (2012) used the Cranet dataset to examine the relative propensity to exit and found that it still remains higher in market-based economies as opposed to European continental countries. Drawing on Hirschman's (1970) framework which places exit as the opposite of voice, their research seems to support the view that in LMEs voice arrangements are weaker. In an earlier paper, Croucher et al. (2010) found that financial participation is more commonly encountered in LMEs and in firms where employee power is weak whether or not collective bargaining is present.

Finally, in setting the context for voice, it also important to note how forms of participation vary over time, and how they interact with each other. It is clear that new forms of employee participation have emerged during different periods, sometimes replacing and at other times coexisting with prior forms of participation. The political and economic environment has been a key influence on the emergence and spread of particular forms of employee participation, especially in developed economies. During the 1970s, for example, following events like the 'hot autumn' in Europe, the idea of power sharing through broad industrial democracy and narrower representative participation through trade unions took hold. The subsequent decline in union membership, economic austerity following the OPEC oil shocks, and changes in public policy during the 1980s and 1990s combined to move industrial democracy off the domestic agenda of most advanced economies. In its place came a more managerially oriented set of practices where the focus was at the workplace level and the outcomes were more explicitly measured in terms of what employers might gain from these arrangements (Marchington et al. 1992). These initiatives reflect management's dominant concerns about employee motivation and commitment to organizational objectives. For whatever else can be said about it, such direct employee participation in workplace level decision-making is fundamentally different from earlier notions of industrial democracy and representative participation (Marchington and Wilkinson 2005).

Also taking a longer view, Lane and Wood (2013) note that an energy transition is occurring in which there is a decline in the proportion that oil holds as part of the global energy mix. They liken this energy transition to the one that occurred in the first half of the twentieth century when oil replaced coal. Lane and Wood (2013: 12) use these examples to argue that such transitions increase labour market volatility and employment insecurity, leading to the creation of a 'precariat' whose employability depends on their willingness to change occupations and accept inferior roles. 'In short, systemic crises may reinforce—and intensify labour market segmentation and diversity in work and employment relations practice within and across settings' (Lane and Wood 2013: 16). The implications of such bleak predictions for employee voice and participation make the achievement of 'rights-based' employee participation more remote while encouraging the development of employee involvement (EI) as a route to better 'market performance' (Poole et al. 2000: 497).

Before moving on, it is important to highlight that the taxonomies offered in this research area largely reflect 'stylised ideal types, broad macroeconomic data and/or case-study based evidence of firm practices' (Goergen et al. 2012: 506). There is an emerging body of literature that highlights the need to adopt a more empirically based and at the same time flexible approach that brings to the fore the diversity *within* types of capitalism (Goergen et al. 2012; Lane and Wood 2011). Incorporating this research, however, remains outside the scope of this chapter.

Voices in Harmony?

While we have noted above that it is important to highlight the contribution of indirect and informal mechanisms to employee voice (broadly defined), it is also important to understand where these mechanisms intersect with formal and direct schemes in practice. The context for voice has changed with union decline. As Boxall et al. (2007: 215) note:

> Quality circles and other forms of small group problem solving have become commonplace in the Anglo-American world. These management driven forms of involvement are signed to serve employer goals of improved productivity and flexibility. However, our data suggests they increasingly meet the desire of workers to be involved in the things that relate most directly to them.

Thus, some forms of direct voice coexist and overlap with other techniques, such as suggestion schemes, quality circles, or consultative forums. A key issue is the nature of the relationship of these schemes and the extent to which they complement or conflict with each other (Purcell and Georgiadis 2007). For example, Brewster et al. (2007) examined claims of a convergence internationally towards individual forms of employee voice. While they found that to be untrue, they did highlight the increasing diversity of voice mechanisms that go beyond unions and works councils, such as workforce meetings, team briefings, suggestions schemes, and attitude surveys. Similarly, Wood et al. (2009) compared key voice mechanisms in the UK—as an example of an LME—with the following CMEs: Germany, Sweden, Netherlands, Norway, and Austria. They found that different forms of direct voice are likely to be correlated with each other but not with representative forms of voice. In the CMEs examined as well as in the UK the authors found either traditional collective voice mechanisms or what they name 'advanced cooperative paradigms' which combined 'collective voice mechanisms with some form of direct voice and/or training' (Wood et al. 2009: 250). Examples of direct voice include team briefings, communication with management, surveys, or suggestion boxes. For the authors their findings show that a range of individual voice practices can coexist with traditional forms of collective voice, but are unlikely to be correlated.

While formal voice relates to codified or prearranged structures, and is captured in most studies and surveys, informal interaction and dialogue can permeate all voice schemes (Boxall et al. 2007; Mohr and Zoghi 2007; Townsend et al. 2011). To this end, informal voice refers to ad hoc or non-programmed interactions between managers and their staff which provide opportunities for information-passing, consultation, and the seeking of ideas. Most definitions refer to methods, mechanisms, and structures rather than processes and face-to-face dialogue (Dundon and Rollinson 2004; Wilkinson et al. 2010; Wilkinson and Fay 2011). Strauss (1998: 15) specifically defines informal involvement as 'the day-to-day relations between supervisors and subordinates in which the latter are allowed substantial input into decisions… a process which allows workers to exert some influence over their work and the conditions under which they work'. Perhaps 'substantial' input accords too great a degree of influence to informal voice, although at least this directs us away from focusing solely on formal practices. The importance of informal dialogue is similarly noted by Purcell and Georgiadis (2007: 197) who counsel that 'employers who want to gain the maximum value from voice systems would do well to note that all the evidence points to the need for direct face-to-face exchange with employees at their work stations and in groups'.

Finally, several studies have found that many new employee participation initiatives lack sufficient structure and scope (Gollan 2007; Gollan and Markey 2001; Kessler et al. 2000). This research also concludes that an integrated approach to employee participation in which such participation is accompanied by related initiatives in employment security, selective employee hiring, variable compensation, extensive training, and information sharing with employees is most likely to lead to higher levels of organizational performance (Dundon and Gollan 2007; EPOC Research Group 1997; Gibbons and Woock 2007; Guest and Peccei 1998). In other words, a 'bundled' or 'packaged' approach to employee participation (and HRM more broadly) is preferable to narrow, one-dimensional employee participation initiatives (Ichniowski et al. 1997; MacDuffie 1995; Marchington and Wilkinson 2008; Wood and De Menezes 1998).

CONCLUSION

By necessity this review on voice has covered a wide terrain. We have surveyed the voice literature to examine the type, extent, and efficacy of voice in a variety of settings. The chapter has attempted to explain differences in voice by highlighting the preferences of the direct parties, but also situating these preferences within broader regulatory contexts, which in some places facilitate a wide range of structures and practices, and in other places do not.

The review was also wide in its scope because we have sought to highlight the relationship between voice and other important and overlapping concepts that are used in different fields of research. In the employment relations field, voice has become an increasingly popular term because it encompasses forms of employee involvement that are both union and non-union and that occur through both formal structures and informal channels. We explain differences in the balance between union and non-union/formal and informal in different countries and highlight the important of national tradition and culture, the role of the state, and the nature of bargaining between the parties. We also note that the relative mix of voice is changing, and that there is a trend towards non-union and informal mechanisms. As the field comes to grips with the declining role of unions and collective employment relations, it is important that it has concepts such as voice that are relevant to contemporary issues and developments.

The value of voice is then that it encompasses a wide range of practices, but it also points to a broader issue which is what role workers play in contemporary organizations and what rights they have to participate in decisions which affect them. To be sure these are matters that have been of vital concern to labour unions and the employment relations field since its inception, but they are also of importance to researchers in other fields who are interested in matters such as industrial democracy and citizenship, corporate governance, the relationship between shareholder and stakeholder value, and also emerging issues of importance such as corporate social responsibility. In each of these areas we predict a growing number of organizations will develop a fundamental interest in how they involve and give voice to their employees to achieve corporate objectives that include these issues.

REFERENCES

Amable, B. (2003). *The Diversity of Modern Capitalism*. Oxford and New York: Oxford University Press.

Befort, S. F. and Budd, J. W. (2009). *Invisible Hands, Invisible Objectives: Bringing Workplace Law and Public Policy into Focus*. Stanford, CA: Stanford University Press.

Berggren, C. (1993). *The Volvo Experience: Alternatives to Lean Production in the Swedish Auto Industry*. Basingstoke: Macmillan.

Block, R. N. and Berg, P. (2010). 'Collective Bargaining as a Form of Employee Participation: Observations on the United States and Europe', in A. Wilkinson, P. Gollan, M. Marchington, and D. Lewin (eds.), *The Oxford Handbook of Participation in Organizations*. Oxford and New York: Oxford University Press, 186–211.

Blumberg P. (1968). *Industrial Democracy: The Sociology of Participation*. London: Constable.

Boxall, P., Freeman, R. B. and Haynes, P. (2007). *What Workers Say: Employee Voice in the Anglo-American Workplace*. Ithaca: Cornell University Press.

Brewster, C., Croucher, R., Wood, G., and Brookes, M. (2007). 'Collective and Individual Voice: Convergence in Europe?', *International Journal of Human Resource Management*, 18(7): 1246–62.

Budd, J. W. (2004). *Employment with a Human Face: Balancing Efficiency, Equity, and Voice*. Ithaca: Cornell University Press.

Budd, J. W., Gollan, P., and Wilkinson, A. (2010). 'New Approaches to Employee Voice and Participation in Organizations', *Human Relations*, 63(3): 303–10.

Budd, J. and Zagelmeyer, S. (2010). 'Public Policy and Employee Participation', in A. Wilkinson, P. Gollan, M. Marchington, and D. Lewin (eds.), *The Oxford Handbook of Participation in Organizations*. Oxford and New York: Oxford University Press, 476–503.

Clegg, H. (1960). *A New Approach to Industrial Democracy*. Oxford: Blackwell.

Cox, A., Zagelmeyer, S., and Marchington, M. (2006). 'Embedding Employee Involvement and Participation at Work', *Human Resource Management Journal*, 16(3): 250–67.

Croucher, R., Brookes, M., Wood, G., and Brewster, C. (2010). 'Context, Strategy and Financial Participation: A Comparative Analysis', *Human Relations*, 63(6): 835–55.

Croucher, R., Wood, G., Brewster, C., and Brookes, M. (2012). 'Employee Turnover, HRM and Institutional Contexts', *Economic and Industrial Democracy*, 33(4): 605–20.

Dietz, G., Wilkinson, A., and Redman, T. (2009). 'Involvement and Participation', in A. Wilkinson, N. Bacon, T. Redman, and S. Snell (eds.), *The Sage Handbook of Human Resource Management*. London: Sage, 243–66.

Donaghey, J., Cullinane, N., Dundon, T., and Wilkinson, A. (2011). 'Re-conceptualising Employee Silence: Problems and Prognosis', *Work, Employment & Society*, 25(1): 51–67.

Dundon, T. and Gollan, P. J. (2007). 'Re-conceptualizing Voice in the Non-Union Workplace', *International Journal of Human Resource Management*, 18(7): 1182–98.

Dundon, T. and Rollinson, D. (2004). *Employment Relations in Non-Union Firms*. London: Routledge.

Dundon, T., Wilkinson, A., Marchington, M., and Ackers, P. (2004). 'The Meanings and Purpose of Employee Voice', *International Journal of Human Resource Management*, 15(6): 1150–71.

EPOC Research Group (1997). *New Forms of Work Organisation: Can Europe Realise its Potential?* Dublin: European Foundation for the Improvement of Living and Working Conditions.

Fields, D., Pang, M., and Chiu, C. (2000). 'Distributive and Procedural Justice as Predictors of Employee Outcomes in Hong Kong', *Journal of Organizational Behavior*, 21(5): 547–62.

Foley, J. and Polanyi, M. (2006). 'Workplace Democracy: Why Bother?', *Economic and Industrial Democracy*, 27(1): 173–91.

Folger, R. (1987). 'Distributive and Procedural Justice in the Workplace', *Social Justice Research*, 1(2): 143–59.

Freeman, R. B. and Medoff, J. L. (1984). *What Do Unions Do?* New York: Basic Books.

Freeman, R. B. and Rogers, J. (1999). *What Workers Want*. Ithaca: Cornell University Press.

Frege, C. and Godard, J. (2010). 'Cross-National Variation in Representation Rights and Governance at Work', in A. Wilkinson, P. Gollan, M. Marchington, and D. Lewin (eds.), *The Oxford Handbook of Participation in Organizations*. Oxford and New York: Oxford University Press, 526–51.

Gibbons, J. and Woock, C. (2007). *Evidence-Based Human Resources: A Primer and Summary of Current Literature*. New York: The Conference Board.

Goergen, M., Brewster, C., Wood, G., and Wilkinson, A. (2012). 'Varieties of Capitalism and Investments in Human Capital', *Industrial Relations: A Journal of Economy and Society*, 51(s1): 501–27.

Gollan, P. J. (2007). *Employee Representation in Non-Union Firms*. London: Sage.

Gollan, P. J. and Markey, R. (2001). 'Conclusions: Models of Diversity and Interaction', in Markey, Gollan, A. Chouraqui, A. Hodgkinson, and V. Veersma (eds.), *Models of*

Employee Participation in a Changing Global Environment: Diversity and Interaction. Aldershot: Ashgate, 322–43.

Gollan, P. J. and Wilkinson, A. (2007). 'Contemporary Developments in Information and Consultation', *International Journal of Human Resource Management*, 18(7): 1133–44.

Gomez, R., Bryson, A., and Willman, P. (2010). 'Voice in the Wilderness? The Shift from Union to Non-Union Voice in Britain', in A. Wilkinson, P. J. Gollan, M. Marchington, and D. Lewin (eds.), *The Oxford Handbook of Participation in Organizations*. Oxford and New York: Oxford University Press, 383–406.

Guest, D. and Peccei, R. (1998). *The Partnership Company: Benchmarks for the Future.* London: Involvement and Participation Association.

Gumbrell-McCormick, R. and Hyman, R. (2010). 'Works Councils: The European Model of Industrial Democracy?' in A. Wilkinson, P. Gollan, M. Marchington, and D. Lewin (eds.), *The Oxford Handbook of Participation in Organizations*. Oxford and New York: Oxford University Press, 286–314.

Hall, P. A. and Soskice, P. (2001). *Varieties of Capitalism: The Institutional Foundations of Comparative Advantage*. Oxford and New York: Oxford University Press.

Handel, M. and Levine, D. (2004). 'The Effects of New Work Practices on Workers', *Industrial Relations*, 43(1): 1–43.

Harcourt, M. and Wood, G. (2007). 'The Importance of Employment Protection for Skill Development in Coordinated Market Economies', *European Journal of Industrial Relations*, 13(2): 141–59.

Harlos, K. (2001). 'When Organizational Voice Systems Fail: More on the Deaf-Ear Syndrome and Frustration Effects', *Journal of Applied Behavioural Science*, 31(3): 324–42.

Harter, J. K., Schmidt, F. L., Killham, E. A. and Asplund, J. W. (2006). *Q12 Meta-Analysis*. Omaha, NE: Gallup.

Heller, F., Pusić, E., Strauss, G., and Wilpert, B. (1998). *Organizational Participation: Myth and Reality*. Oxford and New York: Oxford University Press.

Hirschman, A. (1970). *Exit, Voice and Loyalty: Responses to Decline in Firms, Organizations and States*. Cambridge, MA: Harvard University Press.

Ichniowski, C., Shaw, K., and Prennushi, G. (1997). 'The Effects of Human Resource Management Practices on Productivity: A Study of Steel Finishing Lines', *American Economic Review*, 87(3): 291–313.

Kahn, W. A. (1990). 'Psychological Conditions of Personal Engagement and Disengagement at Work', *Academy of Management Journal*, 33(4): 692–724.

Kaufman, B. (2011). 'Comparative Employment Relations: Institutional and Neo-Institutional Theories', in M. Barry and A. Wilkinson (eds.), *Handbook of Comparative Employment Relations*. Cheltenham: Edward Elgar, 25–55.

Kaufman, B. and Taras, D. (2010). 'Employee Participation through Non-Union Forms of Employee Representation', in A. Wilkinson, P. Gollan, M. Marchington, and D. Lewin (eds.), *The Oxford Handbook of Participation in Organizations*. Oxford and New York: Oxford University Press, 258–85.

Kessler, I., Jennings, R., and Undy, R. (2000). *A Comparative Study of Employee Communication and Consultation in Private Sector Companies: Final Report*. Oxford: Templeton College, University of Oxford.

Lane, C. and Wood, G. (2009). 'Capitalist Diversity and Diversity within Capitalism', *Economy and Society*, 38(4): 531–51.

Lane, C. and Wood, G. (eds.) (2011). *Capitalist Diversity and Diversity within Capitalism.* London: Routledge.

—— (2013). 'Capitalist Diversity, Work and Employment'. Available at <http://speri.dept.shef.ac.uk/research-areas/capitalist-diversity-work-employment/>.

Lewin, D. (2010). 'Employee Voice and Mutual Gains', in A. Wilkinson, P. Gollan, M. Marchington, and D. Lewin (eds.), *The Oxford Handbook of Participation in Organizations.* Oxford and New York: Oxford University Press, 427–52.

Lewin, D. and Mitchell, D. (1992). 'Systems Of Employee Voice: Theoretical and Empirical Perspectives', *California Management Review*, 34(3): 95–111.

Little, B. and Little, P. (2006). 'Employee Engagement: Conceptual Issues', *Journal of Organizational Culture, Communication and Conflict*, 10(1), 111–20.

MacDuffie, J. P. (1995). 'Human Resource Bundles and Manufacturing Performance: Organizational Logic and Flexible Production Systems in the World Auto Industry', *Industrial and Labor Relations Review*, 48(2): 197–221.

McFarlin, D. B. and Sweeney, P. D. (1996). 'Does Having a Say Matter only if You Get Your Way? Instrumental and Value-Expressive Effects of Employee Voice', *Basic and Applied Social Psychology*, 18(3): 289–303.

Marchington, M. (1992). *Managing the Team: A Guide to Successful Employee Involvement.* Oxford: Blackwell Business.

Marchington, M., Goodman, J., Wilkinson, A., and Ackers, P. (1992). 'New Developments in Employee Involvement', Research Paper No. 2, London: Employment Department.

Marchington, M. and Wilkinson, A. (2005). 'Direct Participation and Involvement', in S. Bach (ed.), *Managing Human Resources*, 4th edn. Oxford: Blackwell, 398–423.

—— (2008). *Human Resource Management at Work*, 4th edn. London: Chartered Institute of Personnel and Development.

Marchington, M., Wilkinson, A., Ackers, P., and Dundon, T. (2001). *Management Choice and Employee Voice.* London: Chartered Institute of Personnel and Development.

Martinez-Lucio, M. (2010). 'Labour Process and Marxist Perspectives on Employee Representation', in A. Wilkinson, P. J. Gollan, M. Marchington, and D. Lewin (eds.), *The Oxford Handbook of Participation in Organizations.* Oxford and New York: Oxford University Press, 105–30.

Maslach, C., Shaufeli, W. B., and Leiter, M. P. (2001). 'Job Burnout', *Annual Review of Psychology*, 52: 397–422.

Milliken, F. J., Morrison, E. W., and Hewlin, P. F. (2003). 'An Exploratory Study of Employee Silence: Issues that Employees Don't Communicate Upward and Why', *Journal of Management Studies*, 40(6): 1453–76.

Mohr, R. D. and Zoghi, C. (2007). 'High-Involvement Work Design and Job Satisfaction', *Industry and Labour Relations Review*, 61(3): 275–96.

Pateman, C. (1970). *Participation and Democratic Theory.* Cambridge: Cambridge University Press.

Poole, M. (1986). *Towards a New Industrial Democracy: Workers' Participation in Industry.* London: Routledge & Kegan Paul.

Poole, M., Lansbury, R., and Wailes, N. (2000). 'A Comparative Analysis of Developments in Industrial Democracy', *Industrial Relations*, 40(3), 490–525.

Purcell, J. and Georgiadis, N. (2007). 'Why Should Employers Bother with Employee Voice?', in R. Freeman, P. Boxall, and P. Haynes (eds.), *What Workers Say: Employee Voice in the Anglo-American Workplace*. Ithaca: Cornell University Press, 181–97.

Saks, A. M. (2006). 'Antecedents and Consequences of Employee Engagement', *Journal of Managerial Psychology*, 21(7): 600–19.

Sashkin, M. (1976). 'Changing toward Participative Management Approaches: A Model and Methods', *Academy of Management Review*, 1: 75–86.

Spencer, D. G. (1986). 'Employee Voice and Employee Retention', *Academy of Management Journal*, 29(3): 488–502.

Storey, J. (2007). 'Human Resource Management Today: An Assessment', in Storey (ed.), *Human Resource Management: A Critical Text*. London: Thomson Learning, 3–21.

Strauss, G. (1998). 'An Overview', in F. Heller, E. Pusic, Strauss, and B. Wilpert (eds.), *Organizational Participation: Myth and Reality*. Oxford and New York: Oxford University Press, 8–39.

—— (2006). 'Worker Participation: Some Under-Considered Issues', *Industrial Relations*, 5(4): 778–803.

Townsend, K., Wilkinson, A., and Burgess, J. (2011). 'Filling the Gaps: Patterns of Formal and Informal Voice'. Working Paper Series. Brisbane: Centre for Work, Organisation and Wellbeing, Griffith University.

Van Dyne, L., Ang, S., and Botero, I. C. (2003). 'Conceptualizing Employee Silence and Employee Voice as Multi-Dimensional Constructs', *Journal of Management Studies*, 40(6): 1359–92.

Webb, S. and Webb, B. (1902). *Industrial Democracy*. London: Longmans Green.

Whitley, R. (1999). *Divergent Capitalisms*. Oxford and New York: Oxford University Press.

Wilkinson, A. (2002). 'Empowerment', in M. Poole and M. Warner (eds.), *International Encyclopaedia of Business and Management Handbook of Human Resource Management*. London: ITB Press, 1720–30.

Wilkinson, A., Ackers P., Marchington, M., and Goodman, J. (1993). 'Refashioning Industrial Relations: The Experience of a Chemical Company over the Last Decade', *Personnel Review*, 22(2): 22–38.

Wilkinson, A., Dundon, T., and Marchington, M. (2013). 'Employee Involvement and Voice', in S. Bach and M. Edwards (eds.), *Managing Human Resources*. Oxford: Blackwell, 268–88.

Wilkinson, A., Dundon, T., Marchington, M., and Ackers, P. (2004). 'Changing Patterns of Employee Voice', *Journal of Industrial Relations*, 46(3): 298–322.

Wilkinson, A. and Fay, C. (2011). 'New Times for Employee Voice?', *Human Resource Management*, 50(1): 65–74.

Wilkinson, A., Gollan, P., Marchington, M., and Lewin, D. (2010). 'Conceptualizing Employee Participation in Organizations', in A. Wilkinson, P. Gollan, M. Marchington, and D. Lewin (eds.), *The Oxford Handbook of Participation in Organizations*. Oxford and New York: Oxford University Press, 1–26.

Willman, P., Bryson, A., and Gomez, R. (2006). 'The Sound of Silence: Which Employers Choose "No Voice" and Why?', *Socio-Economic Review*, 4(2): 283–99.

Willman, P., Gomez, R., and Bryson, A. (2009). 'Voice at the Workplace: Where do we Find it, Why is it There and Where is it Going?', in W. Brown, A. Bryson, J. Forth, and K. Whitfield (eds.), *The Evolution of the Modern Workplace*. Cambridge: Cambridge University Press, 151–75.

Wood, G., Croucher, R., Brewster, C., Collings, D. G., and Brookes, M. (2009). 'Varieties of Firm: Complementarity and Bounded Diversity', *Journal of Economic Issues*, 43(1): 239–58.

Wood, S. (2010). 'High Involvement Management and Performance', in A. Wilkinson, P. Gollan, M. Marchington, and D. Lewin (eds.), *The Oxford Handbook of Participation in Organizations*. Oxford and New York: Oxford University Press, 407–26.

Wood, S. and De Menezes, L. (1998). 'High Commitment in the UK: Evidence from the Workplace Industrial Relations Survey, and Employees' Manpower and Skills Practices Survey', *Human Relations*, 512(4): 485–515.

CHAPTER 24

INSECURE EMPLOYMENT

Diversity and Change

HEIDI GOTTFRIED

INTRODUCTION

THIS chapter explores the employment relations implications of increasing insecurity associated with non-standard employment. Though not new, non-standard employment has become a prominent feature of economies worldwide, absorbing the majority of the working population in developing countries such as China and India, accounting for nearly one-third of the labour force in Korea and Spain, and almost one-quarter in North America, Europe, and Japan. Since the 1990s, non-standard employment has spread across a wider spectrum of occupational types, from more traditional clerical and administrative occupations, labour operatives, and food and janitorial services, to professional positions (accountants, managers) and technical jobs (web designers, engineers). One of the fastest growing sectors of the US economy, healthcare, employs an increasing number of agency temporary workers both to address the needs of ageing baby-boomers, and to manage spiralling healthcare costs. Significantly, non-standard employment destabilizes ways of working and conditions of work, altering contractual relationships, rights, and risks. New risks pose a challenge to old forms of governance no longer able to ensure economic security for an increasing number of workers. As a result, there is a widening gulf between good jobs that once generated middle-class incomes and provided social protections, and bad jobs characterized by insecurity and uncertainty (Kalleberg 2011). Any analysis of the future of work and employment relationships must examine the means and capacities of political actors and institutions to address increasing disparities due to the polarization of work into these good and bad jobs.

The reference point for analysing employment relationships is a historically established standard based on a full-time employment contract, which usually confers a set of benefits and social protections negotiated through collective bargaining and/or through statutory rule, in the welfare states of the West. It is the deviation from this standard that defines non-standard employment. Non-standard employment is any employment arrangement of limited duration or over a finite period. Under non-standard employment relations, firms or individuals may hire a non-regular worker directly or indirectly through third-party companies (e.g. contract worker on a user's payroll, agency worker on the employer's payroll, and on-call worker or a daily worker). Even further, a definition of non-standard employment can integrate the 'social processes that go into daily and intergenerational maintenance of the working population' (Vosko 2006: 17).[1] In this definition, a non-standard employment contract diminishes rights and generates new risks and responsibilities borne by workers and their families with regard to social reproduction. Often, few or minimal benefits (healthcare, education, housing allowances) accrue to those in non-standard employment. What makes non-standard employment insecure then is the lack of implicit (derived from past practices) and explicit (arising out of contractual rights) guarantees for long-term employment (Kalleberg 2011) that reduces worker's ability to secure both their own livelihood and that of their families. This distinction between standard and non-standard employment contracts implies a quantitative and qualitative shift in modes of governance that vary both in time and across countries.

The literature commenting on the causes and consequences of rising non-standard employment emphasizes different aspects of this phenomenon, attributing the trend either to globalization processes or to national-specific factors. A review of theories in this chapter characterizes the nature of change in terms of modes of governance. One set of theories seeks to document the economic and political tendencies informing the transformation of employment relations. For these theories, insecurity is a generalized condition of the global era and the emergent risk society. At such an abstract level, theories of globalization and risk society cannot explain the uneven growth and distribution of insecure employment across advanced capitalist countries. Alternatively, comparative institutional theories differentiate modes of governance by identifying the varieties of capitalism and the three worlds of welfare capitalism in order to distinguish between employment relations systems. These theories focus on labour market regulations and class-based employment regimes in which standard employment is the dominant form. As a result, existing typologies do not adequately explain the patterns of non-standard employment in general, and its gendered distribution in particular. Deciphering patterns of non-standard employment and their consequences requires going beyond theories of varieties of capitalism and welfare states by gendering institutional architectures of capitalism. To do so, the framework for analysing modes of governance must incorporate social reproduction in determining the quality and quantity of different employment forms.

Following the critical review of theories, the chapter outlines a framework for interpreting comparative patterns of employment relations that incorporates welfare states, varieties of capitalism, and social reproduction. A variety of regulations mediates employment relations, so the final section of the chapter chronicles how varying subjects of labour and gender regulations shape the contours of employment relations by comparing four countries. Throughout, a contextualized comparison of employment relations systems in two coordinated economies (Germany and Japan) and two liberal market economies (the US and UK) '... highlight unexpected parallels across cases that the conventional literatures see as very different and, conversely by underscoring significant differences between cases typically seen as "most similar"' (Locke and Thelen 1995: 228). Finally, the chapter concludes with a discussion of the implications of insecure employment on nationally based systems of employment relations.

Theories of Insecurity and the Rise of Non-standard Employment

From Social Contracts to Risk Society

From the 1980s onward, a more knowledge-intensive, flexible accumulation regime began to transform Fordism. With the turn away from mass production to a more flexible labour process, companies have sought a new quality of flexible non-standard labour. The literature scrutinizes growing trends and tendencies towards increasing non-standard employment and insecurity, each using a different lens of social contract, risk society, and globalization theories.

The post-Second World War social contract came to define a negotiated social 'compact' of expanded workers' rights, extended restrictions on the freedom of contract, recognized collective rights and obligations of labour unions to represent workers' interests, and established welfare state protections against market risks experienced by workers in standard employment arrangements. As a doctrine, the social contract inscribes distributive principles undergirding political consent as necessary scaffolding to support the design of institutional architectures and ensure social cohesion in a capitalist society (Zunz et al. 2002). Social contracts vary in accordance with dominant political principles operating across different types of welfare states and varieties of capitalism. On the one hand, access to the market was the primary means of the 'democratization of wealth' advocated by liberal US policy-makers. On the other, 'institutionalized social protection' was pursued by most European states (Zunz et al. 2002: 2). Combining elements from both models, Japan fashioned a hybrid social contract and regulatory regime, anchoring social protection in large corporate structures in support of a strong male-breadwinner. East Asian welfare systems' state-led development balanced national interests against newly gained individual rights (Esping-Andersen 1999). In different ways, changing employment relations shift the burden of risks to individual workers, their families, and communities.

On a broader canvas, the theory of risk society defines the social and political processes and forces that undermine forms of security and governance 'based on hierarchal authority, centralized-bureaucratic administration and formalistic democracy' (Shire

2012: 1). Risk in this sense encompasses the rationality of 'organized irresponsibility' governing social norms and (in)action (Beck 1999). While environmental degradation is the most obvious outcome of risk, financial risk-taking and economic uncertainties are other manifestations. At the same time, risk-taking opens up new opportunities for social transformation through increasing ' "reflexive" capacities of new sets of political actors [who] develop new forms of governance based simultaneously in local and decentralized forms of expertise and transnational networks' (Shire 2012: 2). For Beck, the conditions of uncertainty and 'fragile' work are becoming the norm. The growth of precarious employment undermines the basis of the welfare state and the 'normal' work biography, resulting in a redistribution of risks from state and economy to individuals. To make his case, Beck juxtaposes the semblance of 'ontological security' characterizing the traditional social order with the 'turbulence of the risk society... that is not open to calculation by individual or by politics' (Beck 1999: 11, 12). As captured by this contrast, the theory of risk society emphasizes the organizational tendency towards rationalization and individualization, and the transition to a new ethos of self-responsibility for one's own livelihood (Beck 1999).

Another set of theories posits that globalization, either spurred by increasing interconnectivity through the application of new technologies, especially Information and Computer Technologies (ICTs), by the intensification of world economic competition, and/or by the growing strength of transnational corporations, drives the erosion of the standard employment relationship and the unravelling of the post-war social contract (Standing 1999a, 1999b; Visser 2000). Others stress the global ascendance of neo-liberalism as a potent political rhetoric pushing countries to deregulate even in the most regulated national countries like Germany and Japan. Deregulation contributes to the deterioration of employment conditions in general and the informalization of labour in particular. One of the most compelling arguments by Guy Standing (1999a) identifies sources of insecurity as an attribute of increasing global labour flexibility through the process of informalization which changes the rules and regulations governing employment rights and protections, and extends 'feminized' qualities of work to men on a global basis. In an equally impressive tome on the new economy, Castells (2000: 11) draws similar conclusions that the most important transformation of work and employment, induced by globalization and the network enterprise, 'concerns the development of flexible work, as the predominant form of working arrangements'.

These theories point either to technological or to economic forces impelling the decline of security. In the first instance, the application of new technologies implies a technological determinism, replacing people with machines, undermining future employment prospects through a digital divide. A bleak picture emerges in a scenario whereby computer technologies not only eliminate jobs, but also create winners and losers by rewarding only those with the requisite skills. Turning to the economic sphere, the intensification of competition, especially from low-wage economies, contributes to a downward spiral of wages and a deterioration of working conditions on a world scale. Acknowledging these forces, the impulse for increasing informalization occurs in the context of changing power dynamics between labour and capital, reflected in the erosion of employment regulations and the growth of non-standard employment. In all, insecurity becomes a widespread condition of work and employment relations.

Background conditions, such as deindustrialization, technological change, and the ascendance of neo-liberal policies no doubt drive economic transformation and affect the unravelling of institutionalized employment protections central to the post-war social contract. None of these theories, however, provide an adequate account of the structural features of capitalism that relate to increasing insecurity in the labour market. The unravelling of the social contract is an apt description of this historical shift rather than a theory explaining by what mechanisms and by which actors the transition unfolds over time and across countries. In *World Risk Society* Beck argues, contra both Weber and Marx, that a loss of calculability threatens the social order. It is not so much that the world is becoming more uncertain, though it is, but rather that the reallocation of risk downward among workers and the further concentration of resources upward among elites—under the banner of neo-liberalism[2]—require individual workers and their families to increasingly bear risks and responsibilities for their own welfare and well-being. Critically, the theory of risk society underestimates class conflict, and misrepresents the transformative potential of neo-liberalism to empower subjects to change their work and living realities. From a different point of view, political neo-liberalism refers to the rhetorical justification for dismantling social protections and for deregulation in the name of individual responsibility and austerity. Without a proper understanding of political economy, those theories concerned with technological innovation and economic competition fail to explain relative quality and quantity of non-standard employment in different parts of the world. Each renders institutional contexts of capitalist production and social reproduction out of the picture, and thus cannot adequately account for the numbers and the groups ensnared in non-standard employment. The literature on comparative capitalism offers a more useful conceptualization of the common pressures associated with flexible accumulation as a global economic phenomenon and the political factors that shape diverse labour market outcomes.

Comparative Institutional Theories

Cross-fertilization between once separate theoretical fields has cultivated theoretical approaches integrating welfare states and industrial relations to chart the topography of post-Fordist flexible accumulation regimes (Crouch and Streeck 1997; Soskice 2005; Hall and Soskice 2001; Ebbinghaus and Manow 2001). Despite an otherwise sophisticated development of theories and data on post-Fordism and 'patterns of interaction' and coordination among institutions (Huber and Stephens 2001: 108), an industrialism bias tends to miss sources of insecurity related to gendered patterns of work. In their summary, Ebbinghaus and Manow (2001: 11) diagnose the poor state of debate over the precise specification of the linkages between welfare states and employment regimes: some defer analysis of the 'work–welfare interplay' for another time, while others 'identify patterns of systematic correlations between spheres of production and social reproduction'. An attempt to synthesize welfare state and varieties of capitalism to explain the quantity and quality of non-standard employment requires going beyond existing comparative typologies.

Varieties of capitalism (VOC) theorists differentiate the logic under-girding two primary types of 'institutional architectures' (Boyer 2004: 2), which are consequential for determining the economic well-being of a nation. Liberal and non-liberal designate 'regimes of economic governance', either allowing for more play of the free market or relying on forms of 'hierarchical organizational coordination' to realize non-economic transactions (Streeck 2001: 3–6).[3] A second generation of scholars calls for a view that takes into account 'the intricate "institutional complementarities" between the particular welfare states, production regimes and industrial relations systems that structure the incentives under which actors make decisions on work...' (Ebbinghaus 2001: 97). Implicitly, the perspective refers to work and social regulations designed for standard industrial work and a corresponding form of standard family life.

Core assumptions come under scrutiny even by critics sympathetic to the varieties of capitalism approach. Colin Crouch (2001) argues against the strong claim of path-dependency and the assumption of institutional complementarities that imply a simple or a fixed correspondence between particular types of industrial relations (contestative, pluralist, neo-corporatist) and specific welfare regimes (liberal, social conservative, social democratic). Not only are hybrids ruled out or minimized in the stronger versions, but also little attention is paid to differences within as well as between polar types. Adopting the statistical language of 'institutional probabilism' to chart 'trajectories of change and continuity', Crouch challenges the expectation that the ensemble of institutions necessarily co-evolves over time. Instead, institutional complementarity is never assured, but rather 'represents the outcome of social and political struggle between groups in a society' (Morgan and Kubo 2005: 57).

In general, VOC analyses are aimed at typifying national models of economic governance. Using the metaphor of the nation as a container of social action, as implied by typologizing capitalism into liberal and non-liberal types, does not capture the global pressures on national systems and the increasing porosity of national borders. This liberal/non-liberal demarcation fails to fully take into account the ascendance of neo-liberalization globally. Proponents of varieties of capitalism recognize, for example, that the 'patience of capitalism' may erode in the 'face of opportunities for [transnational capital] migrating out of the ambit of national regulation' (Streeck 2001: 4). Nonetheless, the rationale for studying national models of capitalism is based on solid ground that 'regulating behavior of economic agents requires institutions with the capacity to impose enforceable sanctions... and recourse can be made to legitimate coercion, in the form of legally binding rules and decisions...' (Streeck 2001: 7). Nation-states do occupy *a*, if not *the*, primary political-economic space for the formulation and the implementation of regulation. Failing to adequately examine the work and welfare nexus, the grouping of country types along a liberal/non-liberal axis does not align with working time patterns and the consequences of non-standard employment.

More recently, the 2008 financial crisis and its aftermath unleashed a proliferation of articles, not unlike the Furies, intent on wreaking vengeance for the crime of omission in some theories of capitalism. Lulled into complacency during a period of relative stability, VOC literature was more inclined 'to treat each variety, ideal-type, or clusters separating rather than exploring interdependencies, complementarities, contradictions and co-evolution' (Jessop 2011: 2). Leading up to the crisis, though not necessarily anticipating the meltdown, books such as *Capitalizing on Crisis* (Krippner 2011) turned attention to the process of financialization,[4] the hegemony of the finance sector in the economy. A later intervention noted how 'ecological dominance of neo-liberalism reflects the politically-engineered predominance of financed-dominated accumulation regimes in the world market plus the ecological dominance of financial capital more generally in global capitalist circuits' (Jessop 2011: 13). Subsequently, a number of commentators have returned to an analysis of capitalist crisis (Jessop 2011) and the crisis of democratic capitalism (Streeck 2011), reminding us that instability and conflict are inherent to capitalism when viewed in the *longue durée*. An understanding of crisis, then, is necessary for explaining the patterns of non-standard employment in terms of both time and space across capitalist regimes.

Arguing against methodological nationalism privileging the nation-state, Jessop builds a logical-historical approach and critical institutionalism to understand the dynamic of capitalism and diversity of capitalist regimes operating in the world market. Rather than an ideal type, a complementary set of institutions are 'spatio-temporal fixes'; the relative stability in some places depends on displacing problems into zones of instability elsewhere and/or on postponing the eventual onset of crisis. For Jessop, the VOC is a 'one-sided approach largely silent on how labor power is exploited in the labor process and neglects capital's market-mediated appropriation of surplus value, the multi-layered complexity of competition, cooperation, and conflict within and between capital and labor as economic forces, and the sometimes violent antagonisms of the capital–labor relation' (Jessop 2011: 9–10). In this light, consensus bargaining can be seen as an historical 'institutional fix' aimed at deferring crisis tendencies. One notable exemplar is Japan, where such institutional fixes turn into stylized features. Consensus bargaining appears to be a logical extension of a cultural proclivity for collectivism in the East rather than an historical artefact of what Jessop calls 'instituted processes' by which class conflict was channelled into a specific set of corporate-centred employment relations. This historical narrative moves from the general operation of capitalism, showing parallel trends across countries, to the ecological dominance of neo-liberal policy and the spatio-temporal fixes in specific capitalist regimes.

Taken together, this renewed attention lays bare the dynamics of capitalism, and shows that stability, or what one might call institutional equilibriums, are in fact temporary resolutions to crisis tendencies. By extension, we can use this analysis of the structural features of capitalism to understand insecurity in a comparative perspective of labour markets and welfare states.

Extending Esping-Andersen's model (1999) and ending up with the same conceptual mapping of country types, Burgoon and Baxandall (2004: 439) examine 'partisan-driven work-time policies and welfare-regime institutions giving rise to Social Democratic, Liberal, and Christian Democratic "worlds" of work time'. They argue against the simple equation that union density and union centralization reduces working hours, and instead they consider a broad range of policies shaping the politics of working time practices. The shift of analysis from the usual subject of pensions to a focus on working time is a welcome addition to and expansion of the literature on welfare states. However, the authors readily admit that other conditions such as employers' and unions' behaviour and other unspecified trade-offs contribute to work time patterns. Their case would prove even more convincing if the authors moved further beyond the original three worlds of welfare capitalism theory to consider the ways in which gender structures production regimes, and the impact that the varieties of regulations have on gendering working time practices.

Building on comparative institutional approaches, a new perspective turns attention to the processes of 'dualization' increasing social divides in society. Dualization describes the process by which policies treat unequally different categories of recipients, creating, expanding, and deepening institutional dualism (Emmenegger et al. 2012). Though dualization has been a feature of economic (dual labour markets) and political (two-tracks of welfare and worker rights) institutions, scholars detect a widening gap between insiders and outsiders across all countries. Importantly, the perspective under the rubric of dualization considers how political and economic *processes* shape the variation of inequalities in contrast to polarization, segmentation, and marginalization that more narrowly refer to economic *outcomes* borne by individuals (Emmennegger et al. 2012: 10–11). By showing how politics matters, this perspective synthesizes insights from the VOC (industrial relations and labour market policies) and the three-worlds of welfare capitalism (welfare reforms). Significantly, it analyses the spectrum of policy domains rather than examining social protection regulations in isolation from labour market regulations. To its credit, the perspective also integrates immigration policies and related migration flows to explain patterns of inequality. Comparative studies of France and Germany, for example, find that this coordinated capitalist model shelters 'insiders' in core economic sectors and large companies, and allows for greater diversity among 'outsiders' under different contractual relationships and social protections (Palier and Thelen 2012: 218–19). In the public sector, more specifically, France's strong state support of social services integrates more women into full-time employment than does Germany's 'low road' model of insecure part-time employment (Kroos and Gottschall 2012). At the same time, economic pressure on public sector coffers leads even statist France to seek savings through employment of non-standard workers in expanding social services, especially elder care, challenging the role of the welfare state as a model employer and as a means of closing economic disparities in both countries. While this perspective overcomes some of the weaknesses identified in the comparative literature, the process of dualization and its cross-national variation, and its role in generating insecure employment, cannot be fully understood unless gender, in the context of social reproduction, is mainstreamed into the analysis.

The comparative example of public sector employment in France and Germany hints at the answer of what we gain from an analysis integrating gender and gender-related concepts. Empirically, part-time employment in France resembles the trends in social democratic Sweden more than in Germany; this is the case despite the fact that part-time employment began at the same level of 14.2% in 1995, then diverged, declining to 13.4% (22.7% for women) in France and rising to 22.1% (38.6% for women) in Germany by 2008. The relative employment security among women in France is supported by a social infrastructure of care, especially publicly funded, long-hour childcare (De Henau et al. 2010: 77). In this comparative example, the state's role in social reproduction illuminates why there are differences in terms of the extent and the pattern of non-standard employment.

Gendering Institutional Theories

To truly mainstream gender requires rethinking categories used in deriving institutional architectures of varieties of capitalism. As I have argued elsewhere, models of capitalism embed a reproductive bargain based on the strength or weakness of the male-breadwinner model (Gottfried 2012; Gottfried and O'Reilly 2002). A reproductive bargain structures how women and men are included in and excluded from public arenas of work and politics, and embodies tacit negotiations over working-time practices in a variety of domains. More specifically, the type of welfare state and its reproductive bargain shapes gender relations either by socializing costs of reproduction or by ceding the delivery of care and social services to the family, to non-profits, or to the marketplace. In this way, the state's role varies from minimal support of care to delivering care primarily through direct services, via third-party arrangements (public subsidies) or through transfer payments (taxes and welfare benefits). The extent of state support for care bears on both the quality and quantity of services, and on the quality of employment. The welfare state consists of more than a set of policy prescriptions and income transfers by playing a significant role as an employer in the new economy (Kroos and Gottschall 2012). How, and if, the welfare system intervenes affects whether or not care work and social reproduction remain in the purview of private households or shifts these services to either the market or to the state. Through support of childcare services, for example, the welfare state provides a bridge for reconciling maternal responsibilities and employment. Support of childcare either from fathers doing more of the work or from public financing of affordable and extended childcare hours mitigates the negative effect of children on women's labour force participation. Insecurity is not only a function of the employment contract; it also reflects the ability to sustain oneself and family over time (social reproduction).

The four countries investigated here exhibit different and changing reproductive bargains and modernizing gender relations: the USA is the furthest along the continuum towards a public gender regime with a workfare/welfare state, Germany and Japan have a semi-public gender regime with a male-breadwinner welfare state, and the UK falls in between. The type of welfare state regime, reproductive bargain, and variety of capitalism are consequential for determining the relative 'inclusion and exclusion' of different groups in non-standard employment.

Patterns of Non-standard Employment: Cross-National Comparison

An examination of non-standard employment reveals unexpected patterns within and across countries. Table 24.1 presents data on part-time employment as a proportion of total employment, broken down by gender, and over five-year increments from 1995 to 2008. Somewhat surprisingly, the percentage of part-time employment remained relatively constant and at a low rate in the USA. By 2008 part-time employment had fallen to 12.2% from 14% more than a decade earlier.[5] Conversely, both Japan and Germany saw part-time employment increase during that same period. This pattern contrasts with

Table 24.1 Part-time employment as a share of total employment by country (%)

Country	1995	2000	2005	2008
Japan				
Total	N/A	16.3	18.3	19.6
Male	N/A	7.4	8.8	9.9
Female	N/A	29.1	31.7	33.2
Female share		73.1	71.8	70.4
USA				
Total	14.0	12.6	12.8	12.2
Male	8.3	7.7	7.8	7.0
Female	20.2	18.0	18.3	17.0
Female share	68.7	68.1	68.4	68.1
United Kingdom				
Total	22.3	23.0	23.4	22.9
Male	7.4	8.6	9.8	10.2
Female	40.8	40.8	39.1	37.7
Female share	81.7	79.4	77.4	76.1
Germany				
Total	14.2	17.6	21.8	22.1
Male	3.4	4.8	7.4	8.2
Female	29.1	33.9	39.4	38.6
Female share	86.3	84.5	81.4	79.9

Source: Part-time employment from Table 3-8, *Datebook of International Labour Statistics 2010*, The Japan Institute for Labor Policy and Training, 117–118; women's share in part-time employment, Table 3-9, 119 <http://www.jil.go.jp/english/estatis/databook/2010/03.htm>, accessed 6 September 2010). Based on OECD database, 'Incidence of FTPT employment': <http://stats.oecd.org/>, 2009.

Table 24.2 Employment by gender

	United States	United Kingdom	Germany	Japan
Gender earnings dispersion[a]				
1995	75	73	77	63
2005	81	79	76	69
Gender composition				
Male	45.4	41.7	38.9	25.8
Female	54.6	58.3	61.1	74.2
% Low wage work overall				
2001[b]	25.0	19.6	13.0	15.7
2005[c]	24.0	20.7	15.8	16.1
Male	19.6	12.8	7.6	5.9
Female	32.5	31.2	25.4	37.2
Married/cohabiting mothers 2000[d]				
% Working full-time	62	31	31	
% Working part-time	14	33	31	n/a
% Non-employed	24	35	39	

Source: OECD Employment Outlook (1996: Table 3.2, 73).

[a] OECD (2007: 268) cited in Clement et al. (2009: 246).

[b] Low-paid work is defined as less than two-thirds of median earnings for all full-time employees (OECD 1996: Table 3.2, 72).

[c] OECD (2007: 268) cited in Clement et al. (2009: 246).

[d] Clement et al. (2009: 249).

the UK where part-time employment began at a higher proportion of the total. In 2008, part-time employment accounted for nearly one-quarter of the labour force in the UK, Germany, and Japan. Cross-nationally, the UK and Germany look more alike than the US and the UK.

Comparing men and women's part-time employment shows a highly skewed gendered pattern for all countries, but particularly pronounced in Germany and in the UK. Approximately, 38% of women work part-time in both Germany and the UK. Similarly, women make up the vast majority of part-time workers; the female share of part-time employment exceeds three-quarters of the total. While still gender-dominated, men account for slightly less than one-third of the relative share of part-time employment in Japan and in the USA. From a life-course perspective, we can see different age and gender patterns. The part-time workforce is composed of younger and older workers using the arrangement during education and before and after retirement in the USA, whereas women are more likely to work part-time when they have dependent children in the three other countries (see Table 24.2). Mothers in the USA are more likely to work full-time than part-time whereas the reverse holds true for mothers in the UK. German and Japanese mothers are more likely to drop out of the labour force than their counterparts either in the USA or in the UK.

At first glance, the relatively high percentage of part-time employment confirms the existence of greater diversification of employment relations. Upon closer investigation, the differential growth and the gender distribution of part-time employment do not align with typologies of either varieties of capitalism or three worlds of welfare state. Increasing part-time employment in Japan and Germany suggests that escaping regulation may be one important motivation for employers to use insecure non-standard employment. However, the similar part-time employment rate in Japan, Germany, and the UK doesn't fit expectations. To understand these patterns we must look at the type of regulation and not only the strength (amount) of regulation.

SUBJECTS OF LABOUR AND GENDER REGULATIONS: PATTERNS OF EMPLOYMENT INSECURITY

Scholars have commented on the notable shift away from the rights and obligations once enshrined in the Fordist regulatory mode. In the golden age of Fordism, labour regulation evolved through successive waves of collective bargaining and the institutionalization of bargaining relationships ranging from tightly coordinated and institutionalized relations of corporatism as developed in Germany and in Japan to more decentralized forms of bilateralism and pluralism in the United States and in the United Kingdom respectively. While the histories of institutionalization of bargaining relationships cannot be chronicled here (see Gottfried 2000), generally, but to different extents, labour regulations expanded workers' rights, extended restrictions on the freedom of contract, and recognized collective rights and obligations of peak labour organizations to negotiate benefits and check the excesses of corporate power. The resulting social contract negotiated by trade unions and employers established a standard employment relationship for a male worker in a company structure. Benefits and entitlements were tied to a full-time, full-year working pattern that assumed and reinforced a male-breadwinner family model. Decommodification[6] of risks through access to welfare and income maintenance was a key to the institutional form of this male 'standard'. Labour regulations fashioned a prototypical male industrial citizen as the implicit norm for and the basis of explicit rights to employment protections and entitlements.

A variety of regulations mediates employment relations, affecting contractual adjustments, both implicit and explicit rights and obligations, that are both class- and gender-based. Patterns of employment security vary in ways not predictable from analysis of labour regulations alone. By analytically differentiating labour from gender regulations the next section delves into the contradictory impulses towards, and implications of, deregulation and re-regulation, and the effects these have on shaping the contours of employment relations within and across countries.

In principle, labour regulations delimit a sphere of influence over employment contracts, labour market structures, and institutions that derive from legal statute. These include traditional labour legislation, legally enforceable rules governing trade unions or employer activities and domains of control, obligatory patterns of collective organization, and negotiation or implementation of labour agreements, as well as cus-tomary, habitual, and normative patterns of behaviour and cultural practices in the workplace (Rodgers and Rodgers 1989). In general, labour regulations constrain an unfettered capitalist marketplace, imposing rules on 'the exercise of discretion by those with market or institutional power' (Dyson 1992: 1), which can significantly modify both employer and union behaviour (Pierson 2001a: 5). Yet employers' prerogatives render some subjects out-of-bounds from regulation.

Labour regulation designed around the standard employment relationship has created a legal limbo for many non-standard employees. On the temporal dimen-sion, time thresholds imposed as a basis of qualification for benefits exclude, by defi-nition, non-standard employment from regulation or subject them to different and often inferior protection. For example, on-call workers, waiting for an assignment, may be ineligible for unemployment insurance since they are neither employed nor unemployed. Similarly, fair labour standards regulation basing eligibility against a historically negotiated standard work schedule withholds overtime pay from many non-standard workers when calculating their overall working time. Contractually, new 'multi-employer' arrangements (i.e. triangular relationship with a labour-market intermediary between an employee and client firm) and 'dependent self-employment' or 'pseudo-self-employment' (i.e. an 'employee-like' worker with 'regular' employment for a single employer) represent new forms of employment relationships that blur the distinction between employee and employer and exceed the standard legal definition of 'who is an "employee"...and who is the employer' (Dickens 2004: 605). Labour regula-tions based on the standard employment relationship thus fail to clearly articulate or parcel out responsibilities for protecting workers in non-standard employment rela-tionships. As a result, non-standard employment forms do not neatly fit, and often fall outside the social field of Fordist labour regulations.

These Fordist labour regulations standardized benefits around an implicit male work biography of continuous employment over the life-course and concomitantly appor-tioned rights and responsibilities in terms of a relatively stable employment relation-ship, contractually, temporally, and often spatially. The male-breadwinner model was the basis for the reproductive bargain normalizing standard employment around a gen-der division of working time. Importantly, decommodification of risk was a key to the institutional form of the standard employment relationship, whereby access to welfare and income transfers reduced risk for the core male workforce. As such, labour regula-tions have embodied and reinforced the tacit bargain over the gender division of work-ing time by treating non-standard employment as an inferior employment status.

Gender increasingly has appeared as an explicit category in regulations, opening up previously 'private' subjects to public intervention. Gender regulation delimits a sphere of influence over the relationship between production and reproduction, and over norms about the sexual divisions of labour in domestic and paid employment. Regulation *of* gender regulates gender as a norm: 'A norm operates within social prac-tices as the implicit standard of normalization' (Butler 2004: 41). Regulation *for* gender equality establishes legally enforceable rules targeting unequal employment conditions and work/life balance, including: affirmative action, equal employment opportunity, sexual harassment, comparable worth, and maternity and parental leave (temporality). As specifically aimed at gender relations, gender regulations have implications for labour markets in the treatment of reproductive work and women's role in public production.

The articulation of the varieties of labour and gender regulations influences the quality and the quantity of non-standard employment and the gendering of employment forms. Labour and gender regulations can contradict or complement each other, and deregulation can coexist with re-regulation. Whether or not labour laws extend the principle of equal treatment to non-standard employees can change the calculus for hiring non-standard employees and can affect the quality of non-standard employment. Different principles informing subjects of regulation can create contradictory and unintended consequences; for example, the persistence of the male-breadwinner model framing benefits and entitlements may undermine equal employment regulations. Furthermore, labour regulations and social policies addressing women either as dependants or as individuals, principally as mothers, as wives, as workers, and/or as citizens (Rubery and Grimshaw 2003: 100) can either ease or constrain entry into and the exit out of the labour force, can either increase or lower the penalties for interrupting labour force participation, and can either encourage or discourage the supply of and demand for non-standard employment. Mari Osawa (2007) more thoroughly explores the degree of adherence to a male-breadwinner principle of household organization in welfare policies, tax policies, and equal employment policies and their cumulative impact on the quality and quantity of new employment forms/contracts. Comparative similarities and differences of employment relations come into view through a detailed historical overview of both deregulation and re-regulation.

LABOUR AND GENDER REGULATIONS: TRACKING DEREGULATION AND RE-REGULATION

While insecurity is both a factor and a feature of capitalist economies, the types of regulation and social policies are important to discerning the patterns of non-standard employment among segments of the labour market. An examination of regulatory reforms, chronicling the period from the mid-1970s to the late 1990s, reveals diverse impulses informing deregulation and re-regulation of standard and non-standard employment within and between the four countries. It is shown that deregulation erodes social protections increasing employment insecurity, but that the process unfolds at a different pace, covers different subjects, and thus does not have the same impact in every country. More specifically, by reviewing the design and the impact of regulation overall, and the specific language in regulations over part-time and agency temporary employment in Japan and Germany as coordinated economies, then in the United States and the United Kingdom as liberal market economies, we can better understand the patterns of non-standard employment and its implications for employment relations cross-nationally.

Japan and Germany

In Japan, the first legislative foray to bring non-standard employment under regulation occurred in the mid-1980s after the economy recovered from a series of oil shocks. The Worker Dispatching Law of 1985 signified a departure by making agency temporary employment an explicit subject of labour regulation and addressing women as an implicit referent in the provision limiting agency work to a list of sex-typed jobs (Araki 1994, 1997). From the inception of the law until the mid-1990s, women accounted for nearly 95% of agency temporary employees. In Germany, the Labour Placement Act of 1972, alternatively translated as the Temporary Employment Law (*Arbeitnehmerüberlassungsgesetz*), dealt with the duration and the renewal of contracts, although it did not ensure parity between temporary agency workers and similar permanent workers in the client companies (Garhammar 2001: 8). Germany's stricter regulation assigned full risks to the temporary agency, including a unique provision that required a regular employment contract that guaranteed full-time work of approximately 37 hours to the temporary employee. German men's higher share of temporary employment in contrast to other countries is in part a consequence of this explicit contractual requirement.

While in both countries part-time work is a distinct employment status, Japanese women suffer higher penalties for working part time and experience greater disadvantages in terms of compensation and promotion (Gottfried 2009). In Japan, the Part-Time Labour Law of 1993 represented a major state-led initiative to bring the largest segment of non-standard employment under regulation, but under conditions inferior to full-time employment (Osawa 2001; Gottfried 2009). In principle, all Japanese labour laws cover non-standard employees except in those matters governed by special regulations (Araki 2002: 37). In practice, however, thresholds and exemptions deny equal access to the same protections. In contrast to Germany, Japanese labour regulations do not require equal treatment between full-time and part-time employees, and so equal opportunity, equal pay, and minimum wages are not extended to temporary employees. The language of Japanese labour reforms effectively permits unequal treatment between male regular workers and female non-standard workers.

In the face of anaemic economic growth during the 1990s both Japan and Germany 'began to reform their employment systems in order to expand flexible employment on the basis of temporary work contracts' (Shire 2007: 72). At this time, the Japanese state sought a remedy for activating the external labour market and intervened to promote temporary employment as a flexible 'working style' directed at those deemed to have a loose attachment to the labour market (e.g. students, women, and retirees). Successive legislative rounds gradually lifted restrictions on temporary employment, widening the industrial reach of—and opening new occupational groups to—agency temporary employment, granting agency temporary firms the right to compete with public employment offices (Weathers 2001), and stipulating new rules on individual labour contracts that extended the contract period to three years for newly employed skilled or professional workers engaged in product development, new technologies, and new business.

The impulse for deregulation became evident as the recession dragged on throughout the 1990s and into the twenty-first century. Like Japan in the midst of the recession, the German state deregulated the Employment Protection Act in 1996 by extending terms of the contract from 18 months to two years and allowing contracts with employees over 60 years of age. These reforms gave both employers and employees more flexibility to enter into and maintain longer-term non-standard employment contracts. Re-regulation of the same law acknowledged the possible abuse of 'chain contracts' and outlawed consecutive renewal of two-year temporary contracts over a six-year period in Germany.

With growing business community pressures for flexible labour contracts, the impulse to deregulate has been met with incremental reforms. Rubery and Grimshaw (2003) call the process 'regulated decentralization' in Germany, whereby employers retain social peace even as decentralization of bargaining and the employers demand changes in benefits and hours worked. Regulated decentralization occurs when employers do not seek to opt out of historical obligations and the social contract, but rather try to gain an advantage over unions in negotiating future terms and conditions. After the economy stalled, and faced with increasing unemployment, the German social partners innovated flexible work-time practices for the core male workforce and supported less secure and low wage non-standard employment (e.g. mini-jobs) for youth and a large number of women. In Japan, 'asymmetrical deregulation' (Miura 2001) reflects the differential impact of deregulation on female workers in non-standard employment. Unable to overcome the drive for deregulation, unions supported an amendment preserving limits on the occupational/industrial placement of temporary employment, which slowed down the encroachment of neo-liberal reforms. The proxy of occupational categories used in the language of labour regulation over temporary employment continued to shelter male-type jobs in industries and occupations where worker associations were relatively strong enough to resist full-scale deregulation.

The differences between Germany and Japan are in part attributed to the locus and type of working time regulation, rooted in different coordination mechanisms of corporatism. Lenz (2003) shows that corporatism in Germany (solidarism) was more open to the integration of women's movements and machineries in the form of trade union departments and equal opportunities departments than in Japan (segmentalism) where there was little integration of gender issues into mainstream enterprise-based unions. Japanese unions negotiated welfare through work for men in large corporate enterprises, while the state intervened to 'balance' demographic and economic concerns by tinkering with labour and gender regulations that would spur women to seek part-time and temporary employment without interrupting their fertility decisions and care responsibilities. The Japanese male-breadwinner model featured 'women as atypical workers constituting a low wage sector sustain[ing] the co-existence of highly regulated labor market and high employment rates' (Miura 2001: 1). By contrast, the social partners (the state, labour federations, and employers' associations) in Germany fashioned stronger labour regulations and collective norms in its industrial relations system, but the employment system too was geared towards the family wage. The social partners engaged in highly formalized collective bargaining at the dual plant and branch levels of the industrial relations system.[7] Whereas the highly 'juridified' (*Verrechtlichtung*) German industrial relations system subjects to legal rule collective bargaining and contractual arrangements as compared to corporate-centred rights in Japan for male workers, the Japanese state provided greater support of childcare (Peng 2002)—it was seen as a means of integrating mothers into part-time employment—than in Germany. Nevertheless, the German system of industrial relations experienced the devolution of bargaining in the late 1990s and early 2000s. A wave of firm-level pacts between works councils and management ended with workers agreeing to stronger job guarantees in exchange for wage concessions and workplace flexibility. Though formal institutions may look much the same, the new bargain represents a change in the conditions of standard employment in the sense that employers have more leeway and flexibility in making decisions about workplace practices and unions have less power in negotiations over employment conditions. In the long run, the conditions of standard employment erode and the growth of non-standard employment crowds out standard employment for an increasing proportion of men and women in the labour market (see Table 24.1).[8]

The United States and the United Kingdom

Standard and non-standard employment exhibits a less stark distinction under weaker statutory labour regulations in liberal market economies. In the USA, minimal working time regulations and decentralized industrial relations give employers more freedom to determine pay scales and benefit packages for full-time and part-time employees, both male and female. Importantly, the enduring principle of 'at-will' contracts, which makes it easier for employers to terminate full-time employees, remains at the heart of the US approach to labour regulation. Underdeveloped social rights mean that full-time employment does not necessarily confer eligibility for either firm-specific benefits or statutory entitlements. As a result, employers have less incentive to substitute non-standard employees for regular employees, though non-standard workers suffer wage penalties and forgo benefits to a large extent in the USA.[9]

A strong civil rights movement pioneering equality regulations extended policies aimed at improving women's employment opportunities in the labour market. US equal employment opportunity and affirmative action laws have boosted educated women's entry into professional and managerial ranks.[10] Still, women are more likely to occupy low-wage positions and predominate in non-standard employment without benefits when compared to men, all things being equal (Houseman and Osawa 2003). The courts have been the chief mechanism for enforcing equal opportunities regulations and other civil rights provisions, and limiting government regulation and 'making' labour law in the USA.[11] The recourse to legal remedies in the USA has been attributed to 'the decentralized American system [which] forces Americans to take their problems to court', as compared to Britain's and Germany's 'centralized systems with [more] powerful regulatory agencies to provide safeguards and with generous social welfare benefits to cushion life's blow' (Burke cited in Eviatar 2002: 21).

As in the USA, the UK's 'pluralist model of industrial relations' relies on a strong tra-dition of 'voluntarism', whereby the state remains 'aloof from process of collective bar-gaining in private industry' (Rubery and Grimshaw 2003: 149–50). During the late 1990s and early 2000s, the New Labour government tempered the neo-liberal political pro-ject associated with Thatcherism. Though weakened by Thatcher, the union movement, with the growing presence of women in the rank-and-file, backed new legislation in areas of pay and working time. The Labour Party enacted legislation extending employ-ment protection to part-time workers in order to comply with the European Directives on pay, pro rata benefits, and training; and the European Court ruling that the exclusion of short-term part-timers from equal treatment on pay and benefits constituted a form of indirect discrimination (Rubery and Grimshaw 2003: 168).

The market orientation of liberal economies informs the 'model of voluntarist deregu-lation' and 'strong employer-led' flexibility in the UK and the USA respectively (Rubery and Grimshaw 2003: 171). Both countries lack a social infrastructure for care, but the USA has a longer history of equal employment. Weaker US labour regulations make individual capacities more important to determining outcomes on the labour market, translating into more unequal earnings distribution and higher risks across increasingly diverse employment relations. But the UK, in contrast to the USA, has revised working time regulations, most significantly by extending equal treatment between full-time and part-time employment in response to pressures from the regional level of the EU.

COMPARATIVE EMPLOYMENT RELATIONS

In all four countries, Fordist labour regulations have imposed time and/or earnings thresholds as the basis for eligibility and distribution of entitlements and benefits, effec-tively excluding or disadvantaging many in non-standard employment arrangements. Generally, the types of employment regulations loosely align with liberal and non-liberal varieties of capitalism. As expected, coordinated bargaining structures contribute to rel-atively strict employment regulations over unfair dismissal from work and over tempo-rary employment, protecting core male workers from the vagaries of the market. Japan and Germany represent highly regulated coordinated capitalist economies supporting the standard employment relationship for men in export manufacturing sectors of the econ-omy. Conversely, the USA has the weakest regulation over unfair dismissal. Cross-national variation in regulations over agency temporary employment reflects different approaches to contractual rights and protections. Germany and Japan both regulate agency temporary employment in contrast to minimal regulation in both the USA and in the UK.

The case studies also indicate the existence of diversity that challenges the notion of 'institutionally coherent' (Deeg and Jackson 2007: 157) welfare regimes and varieties of capitalism. The paired comparison between two coordinated economies underscores the importance of paying attention to the principles articulated in and the relationship between varieties of gender and labour regulations (see Tables 24.3 and 24.4). Japan

Table 24.3 Working time employment regulations/employment protection for non-standard workers

	United States	United Kingdom	Germany	Japan[a]
Part-time				
Equal treatment full- & part-time	Unregulated	EU Directive on PT work	EU Directive on PT work	Weak Regulation
Right to change full- to part-time	No	Yes	Yes	No
	No	No		No
Agency temporary				
Collective agreements apply automatically	No	No	Yes to union members	Yes to union members
Equal opportunity	Yes	Yes	Yes	Not explicitly
Equal pay to regular	No	No	Yes	No
Statutory entitlements				
Paid holiday	No	Pro rata with threshold	Pro rata	No[b]
Sick leave	No		Yes	No
Unfair dismissal				
Standard	Weak	Moderate	Strong	Strong
Non-standard	Weak	Moderate	Strong	Moderate to weak
Low wage regulation mechanism	Low statutory minimum wage	Medium statutory minimum wage	High collective bargaining	Medium statutory minimum wage

Source: OECD (1996: Table 3.5, 142).

[a] The initial regulation used a positive list of occupations permitting dispatched temporary employment (Gottfried and O'Reilly 2002).

[b] The statutory right to paid holidays covers employees working at least six months and 80% full-time equivalent.

Table 24.4 Gender regulations

	United States	United Kingdom	Germany	Japan
Equal treatment				
– same work	Yes	Yes	Yes	Yes
– part time	No	Yes	Yes	No
Sexual harassment	Yes	Yes	Yes	Yes, but soft law
Maternity leave	12 weeks	52 weeks	14 weeks	14 weeks
Parental leave	12 weeks	18 weeks	3 years shared	52 weeks

and Germany are similarly situated, indicating relatively weak gender regulations, but occupy different locations in terms of labour regulations. Germany has enacted strong labour protections and Japan resembles the USA in terms of weak national labour standards.[12] The Japanese case is an example of state-led restructuring of labour and gender regulations that have modified the reproductive bargain, contributing to the skewed gender distribution and the rapid growth and diversification of non-standard employment forms. The legacy of the large corporate-centred male-breadwinner model continues to inform and frame the subjects of regulation, although the state pragmatically grafts on new regulations in response to economic, demographic, and social pressures. Many Japanese labour laws fail to extend the principle of equal treatment to non-standard employees, and this failure stems from the assumption that non-standard employees are marginal workers dependent on a male breadwinner for income security and welfare through work. Japan's welfare through work narrowed coverage of employment-based benefits to the core male workforce and excluded female non-standard workers from the corporatist bargain. The United Kingdom belongs in the same regulatory space as the United States, but shares some characteristics with, and is moving closer to Germany as a result of EU directives on working time and equal treatment.

It is also the case that Japan resembles liberal market economies offering a weaker set of labour regulations. Both the USA and Japan share a common history of weak institutionalized labour at the national level and decentralized bargaining structures. As in the USA, high thresholds deny many non-standard workers from receiving social benefits in Japan. Neither Japan nor the USA provides statutory entitlements for paid holidays and sick leave, and such benefits are tied to employment status at the enterprise level in Japan. Here again the standard employment relationship is associated with significantly different expectations and guarantees for continuous employment and benefits in Japan versus the USA. More than Germany or the USA, Japan has sought to activate maternal employment, especially in non-standard work, by including childcare in regulatory reform.

The liberal/non-liberal designation coincides with economic distress measured by the percentage of low-wage work in the overall economy, but the gender composition of low-wage work corresponds to different reproductive bargains. Most consistently, non-liberal economies exhibit less overall low wage work than do liberal economies (see Table 24.2). Germany, as the country with the strongest labour regulations lifts more of the working population out of the low-wage workforce. Low-wage work skews towards women, especially in strong male-breadwinner, semi-public reproductive bargains. Similarly, gender earnings dispersion is less equal in Germany and Japan than in the USA and the UK—Germany has seen little progress on improving earnings equality between men and women in the years from 1995 to 2005. While US and UK women have narrowed the gender earnings gap, this progress reflects in part the decline in men's wages, which have been under stress because of weaker institutionalization of employment relations, and the relatively high levels of low-wage work overall in these liberal market economies.

Finally, diversity exists not only between capitalist regimes but also within a national political economy. Recent comparative analyses of firms and industrial sectors have begun to identify the specific mechanisms and the social forces contributing to diverse employment relations and employment practices within capitalist regimes (Land and Wood 2009). For example, the USA consists of two newer production paradigms alongside the remnants of the Fordist model. As mass production manufacturing declines, a high value-added high technology sector coexists with a low value-added service sector, each with specific work and employment relations (Lane and Wood 2009: 544). In the latter, there is an increasing concentration of insecure employment, especially among women. Alternatively, different employment practices may be employed at the firm level, ranging from retaining standard employment to experimenting with 'more liberal market-type employment practices', as in the case of Japan (Lane and Wood 2009: 546). Further research is needed to understand how changes in capitalist production at both the economy and firm levels have transformed the nature of employment security.

CONCLUSION: CHANGING EMPLOYMENT RELATIONS AND INSECURITY

Contractual adjustments are altering the male standard employment relation and employment protections against market risks that were at the centre of the Fordist manufacturing model. Whether or not non-standard work constitutes a fundamental transformation of work organization and working time practices and life patterns cannot be settled easily by a comparison of only four countries. Comparative analyses of four countries typically paired in typologies test some assumptions behind globalization as well as varieties of capitalism theories. Deregulation figures centrally in both accounts to explain the erosion of labour standards. The impulse towards deregulation certainly is apparent with the ascendance of neo-liberalism from the United States to other regions of the world. As evidence of this trend, globalization does seem to promote deregulation

of temporary employment even in the most regulated economies of Germany and
Japan. However, the quality and quantity of non-standard employment cannot solely be
attributed to the neo-liberal drive for deregulation. When deregulation occurs it does
so in national-specific and, to a certain extent, in path-dependent ways. There has not
been a full-scale dismantling of employment protections as a result of deregulation, and
the tempo of deregulation is modulated by institutionalized relationships within countries. While transnational agents (corporations, NGOs, international organizations and
institutions) diffuse regulatory norms from one place to another, the national context
remains an important arena for regulating labour standards and working time practices.
Moreover, deregulation has occurred alongside re-regulation with the state more or less
facilitating labour flexibility in all four countries. National regulation does not necessarily recede and in fact may increase with globalization.

Clearly there is a general tendency towards path dependency, indicating the resilience
of the nation-state and national social values in shaping the policy process. The attention to historically specific contexts helps gauge why some policies are more resistant or
open to negotiation, compromise, and change. But there is also more internal diversity
between regime types, based on policies and politics. Comparative analysis shows that
national institutional capacities and structures still condition receptivity to the adoption of regulations and how these are translated into action. Faced with similar challenges and global pressures, countries develop different responses, 'often with regionally
specific manifestations' (Jessop 2002: 71), and at different speeds of adjustment. Thus,
we can expect the persistence of national differences rather than simple convergence
towards a single European model. There is also evidence that countries experience
convergence as well as divergence as in the case of the worldwide trend toward labour
informalization at the same time that countries exhibit different national patterns of
non-standard employment.

Categorizing societies as either liberal or non-liberal often becomes an exercise in
inventorying institutional complementarities and functional equivalents as the met-
ric to measure one country type against another. The introduction of path dependency
that was meant to provide a more dynamic account of social change actually ends up
at the same place with a comparison of static institutional architectures. It is necessary
but not sufficient to specify the organizing logic behind the institutional architecture of
capitalism in order to decipher the patterns of new employment forms cross-nationally.
Indeed, non-standard employment tends to be less regulated and less secure than standard employment in all four countries, and non-standard employment reaches higher
levels in non-liberal, coordinated than in liberal market economies. But the liberal/
non-liberal division of governance does not uniquely account for the quality or quantity
of non-standard employment. The least regulated labour market, as in the USA, exhibits
the lowest levels of non-standard employment in the overall economy. The nature and
distribution of risks and chances associated with non-standard employment elude easy
explanation when viewing institutions and regulations without a gender-specific lens.

As derived from class-based structures, the varieties of capitalism approach too
narrowly confines the analysis to institutions regulating industrial relations typical of

core manufacturing sectors. Because gender and social reproduction are absent from conceptualizations of varieties of capitalism, they miss the contradictions and tensions that can arise between modernizing gender relations and the new economy. The legacy of the strong male-breadwinner model has created particular pressures on socially conservative welfare states, such as Germany and Japan, in a period of economic restructuring. Increasing differentiation and individualization have eroded the traditional bases of male authority, yet the legacy of the male-breadwinner model in these coordinated economies continues to bias the design of entitlements to fit with a male standard employment biography even as the family form has lost its saliency. While Fordist labour regulations may have heightened differences between men and women, the changing variety of regulations may alter the fault lines of social inequalities based on variable rights, risks, and responsibilities. As Shire (2007: 72) suggests, 'with forms of direct discrimination outlawed in most advanced economies, the regulation and demand for flexible work contracts has become a major factor in the gendering of employment'. Insecurity is now more widespread for both men and women, as 'feminized' jobs become a reality for larger swathes of the labour force. Still, the growth and distribution of non-standard employment vary depending on the varieties of capitalism, welfare state, and reproductive bargain.

The changing reproductive bargain reflects the transformation of gender relations and women's increasing participation in the waged labour force (Gottfried 2012). Reference to the reproductive bargain clarifies the institutional and regulatory framework for interpreting gendered patterns of labour market outcomes. On the one hand, a public gender regime in a liberal market economy offers limited protections and bases rights on the commodified worker, resulting in less differentiation between standard and non-standard employment in terms of security. On the other, a semi-public gender regime predicated on the male-breadwinner employment model treats women either as mothers or as wives, which privileges the male work biography in standard employment and creates incentives for married women and mothers to work in non-standard employment or to drop out of the labour force. As a result, regulations designed around strong male breadwinner reproductive bargains support and shield insiders in the labour market, contributing to a stark distinction between secure standard and insecure non-standard employment. In this way, insecure non-standard employment among women, particularly for mothers, reflects the legacy of the strong male-breadwinner reproductive bargain. Liberal market economies provide less social protection and weak employment regulations for the overall labour force, with more dual-earner households; for example, in the case of the USA, men and women work full time, when possible, in order to secure their livelihood. This intensification of labour occurs in the context of relative insecurity associated with both standard and non-standard employment.

To explain patterns of insecure employment in the context of social reproduction, then, analyses must consider how the reproductive bargain influences the extension of rights, risks, and responsibilities among different groups in society and consider the relationship between relevant institutions within countries. The role of the state is particularly salient for understanding insecurity in its broadest sense; social reproduction that is left to the market tends to fuel the growth of a low-wage service sector swelling with insecure employment. In contrast, strong state support is more in line with secure employment for those who provide social services in the public sector, and in turn for all workers receiving the benefits of a system of social supports. Consequently, how the state, the market, the family, and civil society organize responsibility for social reproduction affect the nature of insecurity, and the quality and quantity of non-standard employment.

Both welfare state provision and women's unpaid reproductive labour in the family had buffered old sources of insecurity, forestalling crisis and stabilizing capitalist social relations. The conditions underwriting the former reproductive bargain are no longer sustainable at the level of the nation-state. Using neo-liberal rhetoric, debt-strapped national governments justify retreating from the provision of social reproduction. As a result, needs are being met by some combination of the market and by paid and unpaid labour in private households. This type of work is place-bound, is performed by low-wage and marginalized workers (women and migrants) in insecure employment relations, and is mostly through face-to-face interaction at the local level. Reproductive labour, while typically undervalued, creates even greater insecurity when privatized. The marketization and privatization of reproduction will necessarily increase the numbers of workers in insecure employment relations.

Capitalism now operates at multiple scales so that continuing accumulation exceeds the boundaries of a specific economic space. If, indeed, the Fordist spatio-temporal fixes are coming undone, then the employment relations system cannot easily deliver on the promises of the social contract and the reproductive bargain that was negotiated by labour and capital during the economic expansion of capitalist regimes in the West. It also means that traditional trade unions are in a weaker position to resist an emboldened capital's increasing demand for deregulation and flexibility in the overall economy. What Beverly Silver calls 'organizational residue'[13] of unions born in the big bang of capitalist consolidation and subsequent institutionalization of industrial relations has bound trade unions to the modern nation-state as the principal arena for collective bargaining and for the establishment of labour regulations. The realities of 'territorially fixed political actors (government, parliament, unions) and non-territorial economic actors (representatives of capital, finance and trade)' (Beck 1999: 11), global capital and local work (Beck 1999: 11), between 'conflicting principles of resource allocation of the capitalist market (according to marginal productivity [and the imperative for profit maximization realized globally]) and democratic politics (based on social need or entitlement [still largely bound to the nation-state])' (Streeck 2011: 6, 7), leaves unions on the defensive yet more defenceless. Without political left parties, with a weakened trade union movement, and with mounds of public and private debt in the USA, Streeck (2011: 413) expects a time of deeply entrenched politics of austerity, and little mobilization of the public on the horizon. Still, into this void have emerged new subjects, sites, and even modes of organizing.

Importantly, though not discussed in this chapter, civil society actors are contesting and shaping responses from below (Suzuki 2010). For the most part, those in non-standard employment lack representation in traditional unions. Non-standard workers' vulnerability would seem to preclude their ability to form workers' associations and to engage in resistance. Although not yet widespread, such strikes and other worker actions challenge the sustainability of current employment systems and regulatory regimes (Hewison and Kalleberg 2008). New unions advance alternative strategies for regulation of employment relations and forms of representation, ranging from a model of 'new governance' centring on employer codes of conduct and workers' bills of rights, to creating a new model of negotiation between community-unions and employers (Shire 2012). The nature of risk faced by those in non-standard employment relations forces them to fashion innovative organizational strategies beyond the narrowly defined workplace and to secure their livelihood through the building of new organizations in civil society. In this sense, the emergence of civil society actors in response to new risks presents a viable social alternative. How civil society and political actors respond to new risks will shape the terms of social contracts in transition.

APPENDIX

Table 24A.1 Types and conditions of employment contracts

Criteria	Standard employment	Non-standard employment
Term of contract	Permanent	Non-permanent
		– agency worker – fixed-term worker: finite period – casual: for particular cause or condition
Work schedule	Full-time	Part-time
		– permanent part-time worker – temporary part-time worker
User firm & employer firm	Identical	Different
		– contractor worker: user's payroll – agency worker: employer's payroll – on-call worker: daily worker
Type of contract	Standard employment	Non-standard or none
		– pseudo independent contract worker: economically dependent on employer – home worker: work from home

Source: Adapted from Don Moon Cho, Slide 3, 2010

NOTES

1. See Table 24A.1 outlining types and conditions of employment contracts in the appendix.
2. I am indebted to Geoffrey Wood for his comments on an earlier draft.
3. Streeck (2001: 6–7) makes an important caveat that liberal economies are neither unregulated nor devoid of institutions.
4. Financialization denotes 'the tendency for profit making in the economy to occur increasingly through financial channels rather than through productive activities' (Krippner 2011: 4).
5. In defence of Richard Sennett's theory of new capitalism, Tweedie (2012) argues that his critics misinterpret its core tenets and draw misleading conclusions from aggregate data. The age of insecurity characterizes the degradation of work 'experiences', which should not be mistaken either with a nostalgic call for a return to some imagined golden age of the male industrial worker or with a simple quantitative trend. A review of OECD countries' aggregate data on temporary employment indicates a modest 12% of total employment during the period between 2007 and 2010 (cited in Tweedie 2012: 96). The social meaning and qualitative significance cannot be discerned directly from interpretations of aggregate statistics alone; in the UK, for example, temporary employment is concentrated among marginalized groups such as women, racial-ethnic groups and migrant labor (Tweedie 2012: 96).
6. Decommodification refers to the process by which welfare state protections against market risks reduce a worker's dependency on an employer and on the labour market.
7. This dual structure consists of the collective bargaining agreements and co-determination based on labour law (Pries 2001). In the German Constitution the principle of free collective bargaining (*Tarifautonomie*) allocates to the state the role of guarantor and referee (Visser and van Ruysseveldt 1996: 127–8).
8. I want to thank Richard Deeg for reminding me of the decentralization of bargaining in Germany, and pushing me to think about the consequences of firm-level pacts on insecure employment.
9. Women in agency temporary jobs earn a higher wage on average than part-time workers in Japan and their counterparts in the USA. Agency temporary workers also stay longer at a placement in Japan (more than two-thirds remain longer than a year at the same client) than in the USA (most remain less than a year), but exhibit shorter tenure than part-timers in Japan (Kojima and Fujikawa 2000).
10. See Gelb (2003) for a discussion of declining enforcement of these equality measures.
11. Daniel Foote's history of US labour law reform dates the classic liberal impulse: 'From the late nineteenth century through nearly the first four decades of the twentieth century, courts at both the federal and state levels repeatedly struck down attempts by the states and the federal government to establish laws regulating working hours, workers' compensation, and even workplace health and safety. The most common ground for these decisions was that the laws interfered with freedom of contracts...' (2000: 148).
12. In this context, Right to Work Laws passed by the legislature in the State of Michigan, restrictions on collective bargaining rights legislated in Wisconsin, and the repeal of a similar initiative in Ohio, exemplify the contested politics of neo-liberalism.
13. Beverly Silver coined this term in an author-meets-critic session at the Society for the Study of Social Problems in 2001 (see the special issue of *Critical Sociology*, 31(3), 2005 for the complete set of papers from that session).

REFERENCES

Araki, T. (1994). 'Characteristics of Regulation on Dispatched Work in Japan', *Japan Labor Bulletin* (1 August): 5–8.

—— (1997). 'Changing Japanese Labor Law in Light of Deregulation Drives: A Comparative Perspective', *Japan Labor Bulletin* (1 May): 5–10.

—— (2002). *Labor and Employment Law in Japan*. Tokyo: Japan Institute of Labor.

Beck, U. (1999). *World Risk Society*. New York: John Wiley.

Boyer, R. (2004). 'New Growth Regimes, But Still Institutional Diversity'. *Socio-Economic Review*, 2(1): 1–32.

Burgoon, B. and Baxandall, P. (2004). 'Three Worlds of Working Time: The Partisan and Welfare Politics of Work Hours in Industrialized Countries', *Politics & Society*, 32(4): 439–73.

Butler, J. (2004). *Undoing Gender*. London and New York: Routledge.

Castells, M. (2000). 'Materials for an Exploratory Theory of the network Society', *British Journal of Sociology*, 51(1): 5–24.

Cho, D. (2010). 'Making Sense of Non-Regular Workers' Struggles in Korea', paper presented at Political and Social Consequences of Nonstandard Employment Expansion Conference, Sophia University, Tokyo, 27–28 Nov.

Clement, W, Mathieu, S., Prus, S., and Uckardesler, E. (2009). 'Precarious Lives in the New Economy: Comparative Intersectional Analysis', in L. Vosko, I. Campbell, and M. MacDonald (eds.), *Gender and the Contours of Precarious Employment*. London: Routledge, 256–70.

Crouch, C. (2001). 'Welfare State Regimes and Industrial Relations Systems: The Questionable Role of Path Dependency Theory', in B. Ebbinghaus and P. Manow (eds.), *Comparing Welfare Capitalism: Social Policy and Political Economy in Europe, Japan and the United States*. London: Routledge, 105–24.

Crouch, C. and Streeck, W. (eds.) (1997). *Political Economy of Modern Capitalism*. London: Sage.

Datebook of International Labour Statistics 2010, Japan Institute for Labor Policy and Training. Available at <http://www.jil.go.jp/english/estatis/databook/2010/03.htm>, accessed 6 September 2010, <http://stats.oecd.org/>.

Deeg, R. and Jackson, G. (2007). 'Towards a More Dynamic Theory of Capitalist Diversity', *Socio-Economic Review*, 5(1): 149–80.

De Henau, J., Meulders, D. and O'Dorchai, S. (2010). 'Maybe Baby: Comparing Partnered Women's Employment and Child Policies in the EU-15', *Feminist Economics*, 16(1): 43–77.

Dickens, L. (2004). 'Problems of Fit: Changing Employment and Labour Regulation', *British Journal of Industrial Relations*, 42(4): 595–616.

Dyson, K. (1992). 'Theories of Regulation and the Case of Germany: A Model of Regulatory Change', in Dyson (ed.), *The Politics of German Regulation*. Aldershot: Dartmouth Publishing, 1–28.

Ebbinghaus, B. (2001). 'When Labour and Capital Collude: The Political Economy of Early Retirement in Europe, Japan and the USA', in Ebbinghaus and P. Manow (eds.), *Comparing Welfare Capitalism: Social Policy and Political Economy in Europe, Japan and the United States*. London: Routledge, 76–101.

Ebbinghaus, B. and Manow, P. (eds.) (2001). *Comparing Welfare Capitalism: Social Policy and Political Economy in Europe, Japan and the United States*. London: Routledge.

Emmenegger, P., Hausermann, S., Palier, B., and Seeleib-Kaiser, M. (2012). 'How We Grow Unequal', in Emmenegger, Hausermann, Palier, and Seeleib-Kaiser (eds.), *The Age of*

Dualization: The Changing Face of Inequality in Deindustrializing Societies. Oxford and New York: Oxford University Press, 3–26.

Esping-Andersen, G. (1999). *Social Foundations of Postindustrial Economies.* Oxford and New York: Oxford University Press.

Eviatar, D. (2002). 'Is Litigation a Blight, or Built In?' *The New York Times* (23 Nov.): 21.

Foote, D. (2000). 'Deregulation and Labour Law: The United States', *Bulletin of Comparative Labor Relations,* 38: 147–68.

Garhammer, M. (2001). 'Final Report on Temporary Agency Work in Germany'. Project no. 0203. Jena: Institute for Sociology, Friedrich-Schiller-Universitaet.

Gelb, J. (2003). *Gender and Politics: Comparing Women's Movements Rights and Policies in Japan and the United States* New York: Palgrave Macmillan.

Gottfried, H. (2000). 'Compromising Positions: Emergent Neo-Fordisms and Embedded Gender Contracts', *British Journal of Sociology,* 52(2): 235–59.

—— (2009). 'Japan: The Reproductive Bargain and the Making of Precarious Employment', in L. Vosko, I. Campbell, and M. MacDonald (eds.), *Gender and the Contours of Precarious Employment.* London: Routledge, 76–91.

—— (2012). *Gender, Work, and Economy: Unpacking the Global Economy.* Oxford: Polity Press.

Gottfried, H. and O'Reilly, J. (2002). 'Re-regulating Breadwinner Models in Socially Conservative Welfare Regimes: Comparing Germany and Japan', *Social Politics,* 9(1): 29–59.

Hall, P. A. and Soskice, D. (eds.) (2001). *Varieties of Capitalism: The Institutional Foundations of Comparative Advantage.* Oxford and New York: Oxford University Press.

Hewison, K. and Kalleberg, A. (2008). 'Multiple Flexibilities: Nation-States, Global Business and Precarious Labor'. Unpublished paper for SSRC, Dubai.

Houseman, S. and Osawa, M. (2003). *Nonstandard Work in Developed Economies: Causes and Consequences.* Kalamazoo, MI: W. E. Upjohn Institute for Employment Research.

Huber, E. and Stephens, J. (2001). 'Welfare State and Production Regimes in the Era of Retrenchment', in P. Pierson (ed.), *The New Politics of the Welfare State.* Oxford and New York: Oxford University Press.

Jessop, B. (2002). *The Future of the Capitalist State.* Cambridge: Polity Press.

—— (2011). 'Capitalist Diversity and Variety: Variegation, the World Market, Compossibility and Ecological Dominance'. Unpublished paper.

Kalleberg, A. (2011). *Good Jobs, Bad Jobs.* New York: Russell Sage Foundation.

Kojima, N. and Fujikawa, K. (2000). 'Non-Standard Work Arrangements in the U.S. and Japan from a Legal Perspective', paper presented at the Non-Standard Work Arrangements in Japan, Europe, and the United States, sponsored by W. E. Upjohn Institute, The Japan Foundation, and Japan Women's University.

Krippner, G. R. (2011). *Capitalizing on Crisis: The Political Origins of the Rise of Finance.* Cambridge, MA: Harvard University Press.

Kroos, D. and Gottschall, K. (2012). 'Dualization and Gender in Social Services: The Role of the State in Germany and France', in P. Emmenegger, S. Hausermann, B. Palier, and M. Seeleib-Kaiser (eds.), *The Age of Dualization: The Changing Face of Inequality in Deindustrializing Societies.* Oxford and New York: Oxford University Press, 100–23.

Lane, C. and Wood, G. (2009). 'Capitalist Diversity and Diversity within Capitalism', *Economy and Society* 38(4): 531–57.

Lenz, I. (2003). 'Globalization, Gender, and Work: Perspectives on Global Regulation', *Review of Policy Research,* 20(1): 21–44.

Locke, R. and Thelen, K. (1995). 'Apples and Oranges Revisited: Contexualized Comparisons and the Study of Comparative Labor Politics', *Politics & Society*, 23(3): 337–67.

Miura, M. (2001). 'Globalization and Reforms of Labor Market Institutions: Japan and Major OECD Countries'. Discussion Paper F-94. Institute of Social Science, University of Tokyo.

Morgan, G. and Kubo, I. (2005). 'Beyond Path Dependency? Constructing New Models for Institutional Change: The Case of Capital Markets in Japan', *Socio-Economic Review* 3(1): 55–82.

Organisation for Economic Co-operation and Development (1991). *Employment Outlook 1991*. Paris: OECD.

—— (1994a). *Women and Structural Change: New Perspectives*. Paris: OECD.

—— (1994b). *The OECD Jobs Study: Taxation, Employment and Unemployment*. Paris: OECD.

—— (1996). *Employment Outlook*. Paris: OECD.

—— (1997). *Family, Market and Community: Equity and Efficiency in Social Policy*. Paris: OECD.

—— (1998a). *OECD Employment Outlook*. Paris: OECD.

—— (1998b). *Labour Force Statistics 1977–1997*. Paris: OECD.

—— (2002). *OECD Employment Outlook*. Paris: OECD.

Osawa, M. (2001). 'People in Irregular Modes of Employment: Are they Really Subject to Discrimination?', *Social Science Japan Journal*, 4(2): 183–99.

—— (2007). 'Comparative Livelihood Security Systems from a Gender Perspective, with a focus on Japan', in S. Walby, H. Gottfried, K. Gottschall, and M. Osawa (eds.), *Gendering the Knowledge Economy: Comparative Perspectives*. Basingstoke: Palgrave Macmillan, 81–108.

Palier, B. and Thelen, K. (2012). 'Dualization and Institutional Complementarities: Industrial Relations, Labor Market and Welfare State Changes in France and Germany', in P. Emmenegger, S. Hausermann, B. Palier, and M. Seeleib-Kaiser (eds.), *The Age of Dualization: The Changing Face of Inequality in Deindustrializing Societies*. Oxford and New York: Oxford University Press, 201–25.

Peng, I. (2002). 'Social Care in Crisis: Gender, Demography, and Welfare State Restructuring in Japan', *Social Politics*, 9(3): 411–43.

Pierson, P. (2001a). 'Introduction: Investigating the Welfare State at Century's End', in Pierson (ed.), *The New Politics of the Welfare State*. Oxford and New York: Oxford University Press, 1–16.

—— (2001b). 'Post-Industrial Pressures on the Mature Welfare States', in Pierson (ed.), *The New Politics of the Welfare State*. Oxford and New York: Oxford University Press, 80–106.

Pries, L. (2001). 'Change of Employment Interests Regulation Forms?', in Limits of the Disintegration of Work Boundaries—The Necessity of a New Form of Labour. Research proposal for the Federal Ministry for Education and Research.

Review Symposium on Greta R. Krippner, *Capitalizing on Crisis: The Political Origins of the Rise of Finance* (2012). Cambridge, MA: Harvard University Press, 2011. *Socio-Economic Review*, 10(2): 403–18.

Rodgers, J. and Rodgers, G. (1989). *Precarious Jobs in Labour Market Regulation: The Growth of Atypical Employment in Western Europe*. Geneva: ILO.

Rubery, J. and Grimshaw, D. (2003). *Organization of Employment: An International Perspective*. Basingstoke: Palgrave Macmillan.

Shire, K. (2007). 'Gender and the Conceptualization of the Knowledge Economy in Comparison', in S. Walby, H. Gottfried, K. Gottschall, and M. Osawa (eds.), *Gendering the Knowledge Economy: Comparative Perspectives*. Basingstoke: Palgrave Macmillan, 51–77.

—— (2012). 'The Work–Welfare Nexus in Post-Disaster Japan: Deepening Social Risks or New Opportunities for a Better Work–Life Balance?' Paper presented at the DFG Research Training Group 1613.

Soskice, D. (2005). 'Varieties of Capitalism and Cross-National Gender Differences', *Social Politics*, 12: 170–9.

Standing, G. (1999a). *Global Labour Flexibility*. New York: St. Martin's Press.

—— (1999b). 'Global Feminization through Flexible Labor: A Theme Revisited', *World Development* 27(3): 583–602.

Streeck, W. (1992). *Social Institutions and Economic Performance: Studies of Industrial Relations in Advanced Capitalist Economies*. Newbury Park, CA: Sage.

—— (1998). 'The Internationalization of Industrial Relations in Europe: Prospects and Problems', *Politics & Society*, 26(4): 429–59.

—— (2011). 'The Crisis of Democratic Capitalism'. *New Left Review*, 71: 5–29.

Streeck, W. and Yamamura, K. (eds.) (2001). *The Origins of Non-Liberal Capitalism: Germany and Japan in Comparison*. Ithaca: Cornell University Press.

Suzuki, A. (2010). 'The Possibilities and the Limits of Social Movement Unionism in Japan', paper presented at the Conference on Cross-National Comparison of Labor Movement Revitalization. December.

Tweedie, D. (2012). 'Making Sense of Insecurity: A Defense of Richard Sennett's Sociology of Work', *Work, Employment & Society*, 27(1): 94–104.

Visser, J. (2000). 'From Keynesianism to the Third Way: Labour Relations and Social Policy in Post-War Western Europe', *Economic & Industrial Democracy*, 21(4): 421–56.

Visser, J. and van Ruysseveldt, J. (1996). 'From Pluralism to... Where? Industrial Relations in Great Britain', in van Ruysseveldt and Visser (eds.), *Industrial Relations in Europe: Traditions and Transitions*. London: Sage, 42–81.

Vosko, L. (2006). 'Precarious Employment: Towards an Improved Understanding of Labour Market Insecurity', in Vosko (ed.), *Precarious Employment: Understanding Labour Market Insecurity in Canada*. Montreal and Kingston: McGill-Queen's University Press, 3–41.

Walby, S. (2009). *Globalization and Inequalities: Complexity and Contested Modernities*. Los Angeles: Sage.

Weathers, C. (2001). 'Changing White-Collar Workplaces and Female Temporary Workers in Japan', *Social Science Japan Journal*, 4(2): 201–18.

Zunz, O., Schoppa, L., and Hiwatari, N. (2002). 'Introduction: Social Contracts Under Stress', in Zunz, Schoppa, and Hiwatari (eds.), *Social Contracts Under Stress: The Middle Classes of America, Europe and Japan at the turn of the Century*. New York: Russell Sage Foundation, 1–20.

CHAPTER 25

THE MIGRATION–DEVELOPMENT NEXUS, WOMEN WORKERS, AND TRANSNATIONAL EMPLOYMENT RELATIONS

SAMANTHI J. GUNAWARDANA AND LINDAH MHANDO

INTRODUCTION

SOCIOLOGIST and demographer Kingsley Davis's (1974: 96) astute observation that migration 'mirrors the world as it is at the time' regardless of contemporary geopolitical configurations has never been more relevant in understanding employment relations in the twenty-first century, when cross-border circuits of human movement are identified as a constituent element of globalization (Castles 2007; Sassen 1998; Stalker 2000). In 2011, there were 105 million people documented as working in a country other than their country of birth (International Organization of Migration 2012). Approximately half were women (IOM 2012, 2013), as a historically unprecedented number of households have become increasingly dependent on women for their survival (Sassen 2000; Parreñas 2001; Yeates 2009). Writing in the early 1970s, Davis (1974) missed the exponential feminization of international migration for the purpose of employment, particularly of unskilled women from low to middle income regions in South and Southeast Asia. Today, labour migration patterns reflect historically informed local, regional, and global configurations of gender, along with ethnicity and class, within broader evolving social, economic, and political structures in the world economy (ILO 2010).

Although several labour-sending countries such Nepal, Bangladesh, Sri Lanka, and Indonesia have recently restricted women's labour migration (Rosewarne 2012; Bohra and Massey 2009; Oishi 2005), the respective country's economic development policies emphasize migration as a viable, sustainable livelihood strategy for development objectives. Migrant workers have faced precarious and at times, deadly, working conditions in labour-receiving countries (Human Rights Watch 2008; Kitiarsa 2005), compelling states to respond. However, the volume of relatively stable migrant worker remittances has proved to be second only to more volatile flows of foreign direct investment (FDI) (Ratha 2005: 157; Faist 2007). By 2011, migrant remittances amounted to US$350 billion; at the time of writing, the World Bank projected that remittances into developing countries would increase by 6.5% in 2012, despite the global financial crisis (Migration and Remittances Unit 2012). Thus, notwithstanding the myriad forms of migration in the global economy (seasonal, forced, environmental, and kinship migration including marriage), the 'migration–development nexus' is emphasized in policy, and the individual migrant is lauded as an 'agent of development' (Faist 2007).

This contradiction between the pursuit of development objectives via migration and the ban on some categories of women workers highlights the complex interplay between migration and development. This interplay has been shaped by multiple factors, including local and global development policy, migration policy, global restructuring, and the emergence of employment embedded within the intertwined realms of global reproduction and production in both formal and informal economic sectors.

For employment relations scholars, international labour migration has reconstituted the landscape of transnational and local employment relations, and continues to challenge the previously closed nature of what was considered to be within the realm of study, particularly with regards to work traditionally classified as outside of market relations such as domestic work (Wajcman 2000). Migration's importance is framed best as an internal logic of employment relations systems, where the interplay between globalization, mobility, and migration dynamics have 'influenced the way employment relations are structured, articulated and experienced in local and global workplaces' (Rodriguez and Mearns 2012: 1). Yet, studies that incorporate the global South and the imperatives of development policy into employment relations and comparative employment relations are few in number.

This chapter explores the interplay of structural factors of the migration–development nexus, unskilled women's migration patterns, and the transitions taking place in and around global and local economies of labour markets and employment relations. The ways in which states attempt to deal with policy and strategies of inclusion of these women in the global economy, we argue, is not simply an economic process, but rather a by-product of complex relations between socio-cultural embeddedness and the increasing incapacity of nation-states to respond with vision and imagination to the challenges posed by migration and labour market structures that affect the lives of migrants. Examining the gendered political economy of migration, we assess the connections between the state and its relation to non-state actors within a shared global socio-economic space. Globalization and international labour migration have exposed the limitations of extant paradigms that take nation-states as a unit of analysis for development and employment relations.

This chapter is based on a review of a diverse range of literature, including development studies, economics, employment relations, sociology, and anthropology, while incorporating content analyses of key policy documents from various international organizations such as the International Labour Organization (ILO) and International Organization for Migration (IOM). It is structured as follows. The link between migration and development, highlighting the policies pursued by states is introduced first, followed by literature on the treatment of migrations within contemporary employment relations. Then there is an examination of the broad ways in which women workers have been incorporated into global care work through the socially embedded process of migration and the construction of care work. Finally, the chapter concludes with a discussion of the gendered political economy dimensions of migration and employment relations.

MIGRATION AND DEVELOPMENT

The significance of migration to human history in shaping the contours of all societies raises diverse questions and levels of analysis, including the impact on communities left behind, integration into the labour-receiving country, and economic outcomes (Brettell and Hollifield 2007; Kaur and Metcalf 2007; Chang 2000; Graham 1991; Radcliffe 1999; Cock 1984). One of the prominent themes that cut across disciplines is the relationship between migration, development, and poverty. Since the end of the Second World War, the field of Development Studies emerged as a discipline and practice examining institutionalized relations between local and international elements such as capital formation, population, industrialization, monetary and fiscal policies, cultural values and education, and how these relationships helped to shape societies towards modernity (Escobar 1995: 41), modelled on paths observed in Western Europe and North America. Within this context, migration was treated as an outcome of regional economic under-development (Raghuram 2009). Notable development theories focusing on rural–urban migration, societal transformation from agrarian societies to industrialized ones were underpinned by modernist understandings of development as a linear progression (Lewis 1954; Harris and Todaro 1970).

De Hass (2012) notes that views about the potential of migration to aid development have swung like a pendulum between optimism and pessimism. In the 1950s and 1960s, migration was viewed optimistically as a means of aiding reconstruction in post-war Europe and industrialization 'take-off' in developing countries. With the state playing an active role in shaping migration policies, these optimistic studies were underpinned by neo-classical economic accounts of why people migrate and the effects of this migration on sending and receiving countries, often by focusing on wage differentials, labour supply and demand, and rational choice of individual migrations. Following the 1970s oil shocks, migration was viewed more pessimistically as a form of 'brain drain' and remittance dependency that, rather than promote development, would promote under-development. This debate was informed by neo-Marxist frameworks such as dependency theory and world systems theory, and persisted well into the 1990s. These bifurcated views are explored in depth by de Haas (2010, 2012).

Since the late 1990s attention has been given to the economic link between migration and economic development, commonly known as the 'migration–development nexus'. This nexus refers to the flow-on effects of migration on economic well-being for the migrant, the families, communities, and the country, and is noted at other historical points in Europe during the industrial revolution (Massey 1988).

During the same period, 'transnationalism' became a buzzword among social scientists for the study of migration. The term was coined by a group of anthropologists— Glick Schiller, Basch and Szanton-Blanc (1992). They called for a new conceptualization, repositioning contemporary migrant experiences and consciousness in the global capitalist system, and argued that instead of the old images of rupture, uprootedness, and painstakingly difficult immigrant adaptation, immigrants now actively develop and maintain multiple relations across borders. Hence, they define 'transnationalism' as 'the process by which immigrants build social fields that link together their country of origin and their country of settlement' (Glick Schiller et al. 1992: 1). In essence, the transnational approach challenges the unidirectional tendency to treat immigrants as passive subjects against hegemonic power at various scales, such as global capitalism and nationalism, and puts emphasis on human agency. These insights underpin the inquiry into the migration–development nexus.

By the early 2000s, internal and international migration was noted as a constitutive element in global economic integration and restructuring (Castles 2003; DeWind and Holdaway 2005). Greater emphasis, however, came to be placed on temporary labour migration, rather than settlement. Much of the research that comes from this era solidified findings about the exploitative nature of working conditions, particularly for unskilled women, reinforced by the lack of citizenship rights and temporary status (Oishi 2005; Lan 2006; Constable 2007; Lazaridis 2000; Chan 2001; ILO 2010). While much research has been preoccupied with South–North migration, more recent research has examined or advocated examining South–South flows (Hujo and Piper 2007; Lindquist et al. 2012). Kofman and Raghuram (2012), citing figures from the Development Research Centre on Migration, Globalization and Poverty, point out that almost half of all international migration is South–South, and overwhelmingly interregional. Sri Lankan workers, for instance, have predominantly migrated to the Gulf States, Thailand, Malaysia, Singapore, Korea, Hong Kong, Japan, China, India, Pakistan, and the Maldives (Hamada 2012: 51).

It was within this context that transnational bodies such as the World Bank 'discovered' the migration–development nexus, which refers to the way migrant worker remittances trickle down to their households, community networks, and social structures, to aid development (Basch et al. 1994; de Haas 2010; Nyberg-Sørensen et al. 2002; Vertovec

1999). Ideologically, the decentralization of development from states to the individual migrant fits with prevailing global economic ideology, both in terms of the neo-liberal economic reforms that have been pursued by major labour-sending countries such as Indonesia, the Philippines, Sri Lanka, and Mexico (Castells 2007), as well as the 'third way' self-reliance ethos pursued by numerous labour-receiving countries, such as those in the European Union (Kapour 2003, cited in de Haas 2012).

The key concern in international migration policy is now focused on 'managed migration'. It entails an increasing formalization and centralization of migration processes to both protect and regulate migrant workers (Gammeltoft-Hansen and Sørensen 2012; Lindquist et al. 2012: 11) and pertains to formal channels of migration. Indeed, one of the aims of 'managing migration' is to reduce informality and give greater control to both labour-receiving and -sending countries, as well as proactively selecting skills profile of potential migrants (Menz 2008; Basok and Piper 2012). Managing migration therefore, involves bureaucratic target setting, visas, and controlling and monitoring flows (Bakewell 2007). In particular, managed programmes of circular migration—repeated movements involving emigration and return (Wickramasekara 2011: 8), often involving guest worker programmes—have been promoted as a means of generating 'triple wins' to host and home countries as well as the migrant themselves (Vertovec 2007).

MIGRATION AND EMPLOYMENT RELATIONS: GAPS IN THE LITERATURE

It has been noted that migration is 'strangely neglected' by industrial relations scholars (McGovern 2007: 218). In the emerging field of industrial relations in America in the 1950s, Kerr et al. (1964, 1971)—best noted for their comparative work on economies outside of the United States and the United Kingdom and advancing the convergence theory of industrial relations systems (Kaufman 2004)—treated migration in developing countries within the global South as a problem of labour surplus, whereby workers migrated primarily from rural to urban centres in search of employment opportunities in newly created factories and other industrial sites.

Today, there is an emerging recognition that migration is of vital importance in understanding employment relations; migration brings '. . . the institutional nature of labour markets into sharp relief as it exposes, among other things, the influence of the nation state processes of labour market segmentation, and the role of trade union policy and practice' (McGovern 2007: 219). Rodriguez and Mearns (2012: 2), drawing on other studies, assert that 'globalization has destabilized the status quo between capital and labour. . . and in both cases, migration (of capital and labour) has been central to re-shaping employment relations'. Yet, a brief literature review of top industrial relations and employment relations journals between 2000 and July 2012 revealed relatively few studies.

Common themes explored in the contemporary employment relations literature on migration can be summarized as follows. First is the impact that migrants have on local labour markets, labour market institutions, and actors in the global North. As a number of scholars rightly observed (Anderson 2010; Dundon et al. 2007; Donaghey and Teague 2006; Meardi et al. 2012; Barrett et al. 2012), there are numerous studies that examine labour migration into European Union (EU) countries. A prominent theme within this work is the way in which unions have responded to migrant workers (Holgate 2005; Lucio and Perrett 2009; Fitzgerald and Hardy 2010; Meardi et al. 2012). Second, the opening up of markets in globalized industries such as construction has led researchers to examine policy in terms of the migration–labour–citizenship nexus (McGrath-Champ et al. 2011).

In the above studies, the issue of migration is approached from the perspective of the global north, Often overlooking colonialism that reconstituted labour and shaped new employment relationships in many parts of the global South; even today, capital and labour from the global South are embedded in reconstituting new forms of employment relationships. Most importantly, there is little analysis of development policy, so that the literature advocates an examination of the impact of migration *on* employment regimes rather than acknowledging that the relationship is mutually constitutive and migration is a crucial element of employment systems.

Employment relations research has a burgeoning body of work which examines emerging regulatory institutions which formulate, monitor, apply, and enforce working conditions and rights in the global economy (Locke et al. 2007; Thomas 2011; Pries and Seelinger 2013). These studies demonstrate that a complex institutional infrastructure has emerged to regulate employment relations, involving multiple state and non-state actors. There are a few promising studies emerging in the arena of migration (Bach 2007; Thomas 2011; Woolfson 2007), but further research is needed. Regulation encompasses not only labour laws and institutions, but migration policies, household regulation, and different visa regimes (Mishra et al. 2006).

For example, study of the Chinese registration system, *hukou*, demonstrates how the state is able to step back from providing housing and social security for domestic migrant workers, driving workers into factory dormitory systems which increase management control (Ngai 2005). In Saudi Arabia, labour permits (*iqama*) for international workers also double as residence permits and are obtained through an employer. This sponsorship system (*kafala*) grants power to the employer, who is able to transfer sponsorship or terminate the relationship unilaterally, meaning that labour status is equated to residential status, affording workers little recourse to appeal decisions.

Another realm of regulation that requires further study is bilateral agreements between states, or what Rodriguez (2010) terms 'labour diplomacy'. These bilateral agreements are often used in the absence of formal labour laws in labour-receiving countries. For example, South Korea has entered into a Memorandum of Understanding with the Philippines, Thailand, Vietnam, Indonesia, Mongolia, and Sri Lanka for the hiring of workers under its permit system. Negotiation over terms can often lead to a suspension of migration flows between countries as in the case of Indonesia and Kuwait, and

Jordan and Malaysia. As Elias (2013) points out in the case of Malaysia and Indonesia, the market for cheap migrant domestic work is now a major foreign policy concern in the relationship between the two states.

While employment relations scholars have begun to examine the role of new actors in the employment relationship (Heery and Frege 2006), further work is needed in the area of migrant brokerage. Brokers play an active role in transnational marriage and student and unskilled labour migration across Asia. Defined as the agent who mediates between the individual migrant and the employer (Lindquist et al. 2012: 8), labour brokers or middlemen are vital to the recruitment process, and belie the seemingly natural forces of push and pull supply/demand factors inherent to rationalist models of migration. Although they have some resemblance to employment agencies in the global North (Forde 2001), their ties to the informal sector highlight the complexity of implementing managed migrant processes. For example, there has been a large rise in the number of private recruitment agencies in Asia (Lindquist 2010; Rodriguez 2010); however, these often have ties to unregistered individual agents with access to informal social networks (Lindquist et al. 2012). In Sri Lanka, although the state encourages the registration of employment agencies, sub-agents remain an unregistered informal link between workers and formal institutions. Research indicates women in particular have been found to prefer informal channels because of the cost of using official agents (Ukwatta 2010, cited in Institute of Policy Studies 2012: 144). The place of the broker in the employment relationship highlights the 'uneasy distinctions between state and market, formal and informal, regular and irregular', their identity considered in relation to location, time, and power (Lindquist 2010). In other words, the emergence of labour brokers is correlated to the emergence of government regulation of managed migration, and often intertwined with state power and governmentality, as in the case of China (Lindquist et al. 2012).

Another gap in the employment relations literature entails a closer examination of the role of the state in facilitating a 'migration industry' (Lusis and Bauder 2011). Hamada (2012) outlines how in promoting overseas employment, states have sought to cultivate opportunities, establish diplomatic relations, and strengthen placement services. In the labour-sending countries themselves, states have created registries for leaving migrants (Hamada 2012: 58). States have attempted to address the informality of labour brokers (see below) by requiring licensing and placing limits on attributes such as recruitment fees. States have also attempted to provide as much pre-departure assistance as possible for migrant workers. This includes information on legal rights, counselling, providing social insurance, and providing training in host country cultural norms and language (Hamada 2012: 58). Other actions include providing remittance policies and services, providing special financial tools for savings, housing programmes for migrants, and returnee placement and training programmes. Intricate local networks of small-scale bureaucracy have emerged to help deal with increased paperwork associated with these policies (Lindquist et al. 2012: 15).

However, we argue that it is not enough to examine such structures. Rather, as Troung (2012: 77) advocates, migration should be analysed as 'something that profoundly influences overlapping social worlds (sexuality, work, home maintenance, childcare) and re/shapes institutional rules'. In other words, the relationship between migration, development, and employment relations is profoundly socially embedded. Troung (2012: 73) points out that often it is 'the interpretation of migrant realities and how the subject/object of abuse is defined and validated' that decides who is slated for protection and who is not. Often these interpretations are socially embedded, mediated through local structures of power in labour-sending and receiving countries (Portes and Sensenbrenner 1993). Oishi (2005: 49), for example, found that in labour-receiving countries such as Kuwait, low wages are correlated to factors such as language, religion, and national stereotypes.

The Feminization of Migration, Global Care Chains, and the Employment Relations of Domestic Work

Domestic work is now a global industry. In 2010, some 53.6 million people were employed in the sector, an increase from 19 million in the mid-1990s (ILO 2013: 2), of which, 75% are in Asia and the Pacific (ILO 2013: 24). Domestic work, defined as being in an employment relationship within a private household, includes activities such as maids, cooks, nannies, looking after elders, laundresses, gardeners, drivers, babysitters, or tutors (ILO 2013: 8). This highly feminized sector, with more than 83% of all domestic workers being women (ILO 2013: 19), is dependent on international labour migration.

The 'feminization of migration' is used to refer to the way in which more and more women have entered into global labour migration flows over the past 40 years. Beneria et al. (2012) observed that the feminization of international migration since the 1990s has given rise to new debates on migration, gender, and development; a gendered analysis of migration reveals an international division of labour that is configured through interlocking and interlinked forms of power and inequality, often leading to precariousness and abuse (Troung 2012).

Classified as a form of unskilled work (Kofman 2007), women have migrated for care work owing to a number of converging factors. The lack of employment opportunities is one such factor that pushes women to migrate; poverty is increasingly a feminized phenomenon and women face increasing pressures to secure economic survival for their families (Chant 2008; Sassen 1998). 'Pull' factors represent demand in labour-receiving countries, and the conditions within them. Schierup and Castles (2011: 19) point out that the retreat of the welfare state in Europe in the 1980s and the rise of neo-liberal economic policy led to re-commodification, with migrants and ethnic minorities being 'among the chief victims' of these policies in already segmented (by ethnicity, gender, and national origins) labour markets. The retreat of the welfare state was also matched by the rising levels of education and employment of women in labour-receiving countries. In Europe and parts of Asia, such as Malaysia and Singapore, as more educated women entered the labour force, demand for care labouring grew, as the state did not provide welfare resources to support families or women (Teo 2010). In the Gulf countries where women did not participate in the labour market to the same levels, trends in conspicuous consumption led to the rapid growth in the demand for domestic labour (Oishi 2005).

Hochschild (2000: 131) defined global care chains (GCC), as 'a series of personal links between people across the globe based on the paid or unpaid work of caring'. In this pioneering work, Hochschild draws from Parreñas's (2000) research into Filipina migrant domestic workers, articulating what the global care chain involves:

> An older daughter from a poor family who cares for her siblings while her mother works as a nanny caring for the children of a migrating nanny who, in turn, cares for the child of a family in a rich country. (Hochschild 2000: 131)

These networks are not confined to adults only; they also constitute 'global links between the children of service-providers and those of service-recipients' (Hochschild 2000: 132; Yeates 2012). As we go 'down' the chain, the value ascribed to the labour decreases and often becomes unpaid at the end of the chain. Thus, at the end of the chain an older daughter often substitutes for her mother in providing unpaid care for her younger siblings.

Literature on the global care industry and attendant division of labour invariably not only reveals complex and varied migratory patterns, including 'South–South' migration alongside South–North and North–South migration (Mishra et al. 2006), but also these chains tend to elicit embodiment of feminized and precarious employment conditions. Reproductive labour such as domestic and care work are often socially inscribed as 'naturally women's work' and devalued (Hondagneu-Sotelo and Avila 1997; Parreñas 2005). This work is also classified as devalued, 'dirty' jobs, matched to the insecurity of domestic worker's residential status (Hochschild 2000; Rodriguez 2010; Mishra et al. 2006).

In addition, socio-cultural variables such as gender not only shape the contours of opportunity for livelihoods that push women to take the decision to migrate, but also highlight the way in which both migration and employment relations are socially embedded (Mhando and Thomas 2011). Michelle Gamburd's work on Sri Lankan women migrants from the Southern Sinhalese Buddhist village of Naeaegama examined the symbiotic relationship between migration, gender roles, kinship relations, and anxieties around motherhood amidst a contextualized account of the social cost of migration (Gamburd 2000, 2008). Recent work by Molland (2012) demonstrates how in the case of labour brokerage, women are recruited specifically into marriage migration, domestic service, and sex work, and often 'structures the forms brokerage takes, as migrant debt, labour rights and visa processes vary between men and women' with the emergence of the managed migration agenda (Lindquist et al. 2012: 16).

THE GENDERED POLITICAL ECONOMY OF MIGRATION

The regulation of care work remains weak in both labour-sending and labour-receiving countries as well as transnational regulation, which is often wholly or partially omitted from labour legislation coverage. Given the paucity of regulation, it is hardly surprising that reported working conditions include temporary contracts, limited access to rights enforcement mechanisms, social and welfare services, unpaid overtime, unpaid trial periods of work, no time off, unlawful wage deductions, poor accommodation, isolation, and most importantly, the lack of recognition of caring work as work (Piper 2004). These conditions are compounded by social isolation owing to the nature of the work, and restrictions on human rights. By virtue of their outsider status as temporary workers, these workers are denied worker status and have no citizenship rights (Piper 2009; Beneria et al. 2012).

Responding to local pressure, labour-sending countries have developed (often in conjunction with institutions like the ILO), national labour policies which set out minimum standards and conditions for migrating workers such as age limits (Wickramasekara 2011; Piper 2004; Parreñas 2000). Administrative structures have been set up as autonomous agencies but closely aligned to the state also help regulate conditions *and* promote migration (Wickramasekara 2011). Some countries have adopted model contracts setting out conditions such as minimum wages. For instance, following the example of the Philippines, Sri Lanka adopted a model employment contract in 1990, but omitted domestic workers. Bilateral agreements in the form of Memoradums of Understanding (MoU) have been a primary way in which the state has sought to exert influence over other country systems. Yet these agreements have been critiqued for lacking transparency and enforceability, as well as contravening the Migrant Workers Convention (Gunasinghe 2011: 45).

Interestingly, some trade unions from labour-sending countries have pursued bilateral agreements with trade unions in labour-receiving countries. In 2009, bilateral agreements were signed between three Sri Lankan trade unions and their counterpart unions from Bahrain, Jordan, and Kuwait. The agreements represent a pledge by these trade unions to protect Sri Lankan migrant workers in their respective countries (Wickramasekara 2011: 7).

Labour-sending countries have also ratified international conventions such as the 1996 International Convention on the Protection of All Migrant Workers and their Families, the Convention on the Elimination of All Forms of Discrimination Against Women (CEDAW), Core ILO Conventions such as the Convention 97 Migration for Employment Convention (Revised) (1949), 143 Migrant Workers (Supplementary Provisions) Convention (1975), and 181 Private Employment Agencies Convention (1997). Whereas the limitation of such legislation has been discussed elsewhere (Elias 2007), it is important to point out that lapses in labour protection are found not only in the uneven application or inadequacy of the laws above, but also as Troung (2012: 73) highlights, such rights-based regulation is designed to address 'a single cause of discrimination to which other causes can be added… [but] cannot deal with multiple inequalities and multi-causal discrimination occurring simultaneously or sequentially particularly in the stages of migration'. As such, the passing of ILO Convention 189 in 2011 is promising as it attempts to address gendered tropes leading to discrimination, by classifying domestic work as work akin to other forms of work. However, to date, this convention has only been ratified by four countries at the time of writing, with Italy being the only labour-receiving country which has done so.

Examining countries which employ a large percentage of domestic workers, labour-receiving countries have been slow to respond to concerns. While they have participated in several international forums such as the ILO's 2008 Gulf Forum on Temporary Contractual Labour in the UAE, and the IOM Colombo Process, a regional consultative process on managing migration and contract labour, concrete changes have been slow, as host countries respond to local conditions and concerns (McGovern 2007).

There have been some positive developments, such as the UAE introducing a standardized contract for domestic workers, spelling out rights and entitlements in 2007. Jordan soon followed suit and also recognized domestic workers in labour laws, including the right for migrant workers to join unions in 2010 (Kalan 2012). Although Saudi Arabia voted in favour of the ILO Convention 189 on Decent Work for Domestic Workers, reforms to labour laws to include domestic workers in protections such as mandatory time off or limits to working hours, stalled in 2009 (Human Rights Watch 2012). While Kuwait considered abolishing the *kafala* system in 2009–10, it did not come to fruition. In the case of Saudi Arabia, it acted adversely towards the Philippines and Indonesia in 2011 for raising labour standards for their workers, by announcing they would no longer hire Indonesians and Filipinos. More recently the highest court of appeal in Hong Kong ruled against allowing long-term domestic migrant workers access to permanent residency status after seven years—the standard applied to other foreigners (Pak 2013).

Thus with protections remaining weak in labour-receiving countries, labour-sending countries have moved to protect workers by banning migration for some categories of women. In doing so, states often mobilize local feminized tropes around motherhood, femininity, and vulnerability (Badam 2011). Such policy decisions are foregrounded by imaging, planning, and strategizing around local socio-cultural anxiety such as a husband's extra-marital affairs while the wife is working overseas, the neglect of children, or the squandering of the remittances the wife sends. Such discourse holds her accountable for her husband's actions (Mhando 2012). Thus, when state officials, scholars, non-government organizations (NGOs), and labour brokers discuss the implication of overseas employment on the family unit, women migrant workers (especially mothers and wives) often become the focus of their 'disciplinary gaze' (Foucault 1978). On the other hand, husbands, fathers, or even employers typically escape such scrutiny. By blaming women, and placing the primary responsibility for care-giving, marriage, and household maintenance on them, the state escapes responsibility and accountability.

One of the troubling aspects of such policy restricting the migration choices of women is that in precluding women from access to migration opportunities, government officials seldom explicitly reference alternative livelihoods. This highlights policy deficiencies within labour-sending countries. Effectively, the development–migration nexus allows issues of development, livelihood generation, and employment to be exported; remittances allow for sustained consumption and growth without comparative local employment generation.

Moreover, the bans are underscored by a troubling assumption that older, male, or skilled professionals are better able to assert themselves, make informed decisions, and know how to protect themselves in their work; this strategy does not address the gaps in international or labour-receiving country regulation. As Standing (2011) points out, those most likely to fall into the vulnerable precariat class are migrant workers, particularly those lacking citizenship status. Indeed, for labour-importing nations, the managed migration process can help create new pockets of precarity not only in the realm of domestic work, but also for workers in service sectors, agribusiness, and some professions.

Conclusion

This chapter highlighted the continuing importance of the state in pursuing the migration–remittance–development nexus. States have sought to both facilitate migration into precarious employment positions and to step in to protect workers. The state acts upon the employment relationship and social protection in various ways—be it in terms of making agreements with other states, devising development policies, delimiting the types of welfare policies migrant workers are eligible for vis-à-vis their citizenship rights, or balancing populist interests with labour demands. Internal contradictions between pursuing development and acknowledging potential insecurity for workers, and intervention in the employment relationship, is embedded within and reinforced by institutions set up to oversee labour migration, simultaneously protecting workers and promoting migration for its own survival. Thus, the state's role is underscored by the existence of a complex and textured field of institutions, governance mechanisms, and institutions. These are, in turn, found at different levels of the employment relationship (pre-departure, departure, tenure of contract, return). In examining the case of care work jobs, the very core is the unwavering construction of care work as naturally 'women's work', beyond formal market forces and labour legislation. This form of work, particularly domestic maid work and, at times, childcare, is highly deregulated the world over. The core of the GCC is that the problems produced by the gendered division of labour in industrialized countries are not solved, but passed on to other women. Migrant domestic workers can be characterized as dependent largely on voluntary or 'soft' mechanisms such as MoUs between states, minimal standards in labour-receiving countries, and an extensive, multilayered, regulatory, and training-driven approach in labour-sending countries. The focus is often on workers' attributes—be they skills, attitudes, or psychological mindset—rather than the underlying fields of inequality in international labour migration. The solution put forth by states is often to manage the migrant, rather than migration per se. However, because of livelihood pressures, it is unlikely that this approach will stem migration; rather, informal migration is more likely to increase. This policy direction, in the case of domestic workers, further entrenches women workers' disadvantage. Historical degradation of domestic work, coupled with lack of citizenship rights and lack of focus on the socially embedded dimensions of migration including gender-based discrimination, serves to reinforce this disadvantage.

Nonetheless, encouraging developments such as the historical ILO Convention 189, as well as the willingness of some labour-receiving countries to modify labour laws should be monitored for their impact on migrant workers. It is our hope that this chapter will enhance a dialogue and encourage more case studies to trace both narrative and empirical situated-ness of the development–migration nexus, transnational migration of domestic workers, and employment relations.

References

Anderson, B. (2010). 'Migration, Immigration Controls and the Fashioning of Precarious Workers', *Work, Employment & Society*, 24(2): 300–17.

Bach, S. (2007). 'Going Global? The Regulation of Nurse Migration in the UK', *British Journal of Industrial Relations*, 45(2): 383–403.

Badam, R. T. (2011). 'Sri Lanka to discourage its women from working as housemaids'. Available at <http://www.thenational.ae/news/uae-news/sri-lanka-to-discourage-its-women-from-working-as-housemaids#ixzz2GVjhW8IU>, accessed 23 July 2012.

Bakewell, O. (2007). 'The Meaning and Use of Identity Papers: Handheld and Heartfelt Nationality in the Borderlands of North-West Zambia'. International Migration Institute, University of Oxford.

Barrett, A., McGuinness, S., and O'Brien, M. (2012). 'The Immigrant Earnings Disadvantage Across the Earnings and Skills Distributions: The Case of Immigrants from the EU's New Member States', *British Journal of Industrial Relations*, 50(3): 457–81.

Basch, L., Glick-Schiller, N., and Szanton Blanc, D. (1994). *Nations Unbound: Transnational Projects, Postcolonial Predicaments and Deterritorialized Nation-States*. Langhorne: Gordon and Breach.

Basok, T. and Piper, N. (2012). 'Management Versus Rights: Women's Migration and Global Governance in Latin America and the Caribbean', *Feminist Economics*, 18(2): 35–61.

Beneria, L., Deere, C. D., and Kabeer, N. (2012). 'Gender and International Migration: Globalization, Development and Governance', *Feminist Economics*, 18(2): 1–33.

Bohra, P. and Massey, D. S. (2009). 'Processes of Internal and International Migration from Chitwan, Nepal', *International Migration Review*, 43: 621–51.

Brettell, C. and Hollifield, J. (2007). *Migration Theory: Talking across Disciplines*, 2nd edn. New York: Routledge.

Castles, S. (2003). 'Towards a Sociology of Forced Migration and Social Transformation', *Sociology*, 37(1): 13–34.

Castles, S. (2007). 'Twenty-First Century Migration as a Challenge to Sociology', *Journal of Ethnic and Migration Studies*, 33(3): 351–71.

Castles, S. and Schierup, C.-U. (2010). 'Migration and Ethnic Minorities', in F. G. Castles, S. Leibfried, J. Lewis, and C. Pierson (eds.), *The Oxford Handbook of the Welfare State*. Oxford and New York: Oxford University Press, 278–91.

Chan, A. (2001). *China's Workers Under Assault: The Exploitation of Labor in a Globalizing Economy*. New York: M. E. Sharpe.

Chang, G. (2000). *Disposable Domestics: Immigrant Women Workers in the Global Economy*. Cambridge, MA: South End Press.

Chant, S. (2008). 'The "Feminisation of Poverty" and the "Feminisation" of Anti-Poverty Programmes: Room for Revision?', *Journal of Development Studies*, 44(2): 165–97.

Cock, J. (1984). *Maids and Madams: A Study in the Politics of Exploitation*. Johannesburg: Ravan Press.

Constable, N. (2007). *Maid to Order in Hong Kong: Stories of Migrant Workers*. Ithaca: Cornell University Press.

Davis, K. (1974). 'The Migration of Human Populations', *Scientific American*, 231(3): 93–105.

de Haas, H. (2010). 'Migration and Development: A Theoretical Perspective', *International Migration Review*, 44(1): 227–64.

—— (2012). 'The Migration and Development Pendulum: A Critical View on Research and Policy', *International Migration*, 50(3): 8–25.

DeWind, J. and Holdaway, J. (2005). 'Internal and International Migration in Economic Development', paper presented at the Fourth Coordination Meeting on International Migration, United Nations, New York.

Donaghey, J. and Teague, P. (2006). 'The Free Movement of Workers and Social Europe: Maintaining the European Ideal', *Industrial Relations Journal*, 37(6): 652–66.

Dundon, T., González-Pérez, M. A., and McDonough, T. (2007). 'Bitten by the Celtic Tiger: Immigrant Workers and Industrial Relations in the New Globalized Ireland', *Economic and Industrial Democracy*, 28(4): 501–22.

Elias, J. (2007). 'Women Workers and Labour Standards: The Problem of Human Rights', *Review of International Studies*, 33(1): 45–57.

—— (2013). 'The State and the Foreign Relations of Households: The Malaysia-Indonesia Domestic Worker Dispute', in J. Elias and S. J. Gunawardana (eds), *The Global Political Economy of the Household in Asia*. Basingstoke: Palgrave Macmillan.

Escobar, A. (1995). *Encountering Development: The Making and Unmaking of the Third World*. Princeton: Princeton University Press.

Faist, T. (2007). 'Migrants as Transnational Development Agents: An Inquiry into the Newest Round of the Migration–Development Nexus', *Population, Space and Place*, 14(1): 21–42.

Fitzgerald, I. and Hardy, J. (2010). 'Thinking Outside the Box? Trade Union Organizing Strategies and Polish Migrant Workers in the United Kingdom', *British Journal of Industrial Relations*, 48(1): 131–50.

Forde, C. (2001). 'Temporary Arrangements: The Activities of Employment Agencies in the UK', *Work, Employment & Society*, 15(3): 631–44.

Foucault, M. (1978). *History of Sexuality*. New York: Random House.

Gamburd, M. R. (2000). *The Kitchen Spoon's Handle: Transnationalism and Sri Lanka's Migrant Housemaids*. Ithaca: Cornell University Press.

—— (2008). 'Milk Teeth and Jet Planes: Kin Relations in Families of Sri Lanka's Transnational Domestic Servants', *City & Society*, 20(1): 5–31.

Gammeltoft-Hansen, T. and Sørensen, N. N. (eds.) (2012). *The Migration Industry and the Commercialization of International Migration*. London and New York: Routledge.

Glick Schiller, N., Basch, L., and Szanton Blanc, C. (1992). 'Transnationalism: A New Analytic Framework for Understanding Migration', in Glick Schiller, Basch, and Szanton Blanc (eds.), *Toward a Transnational Perspective on Migration: Race, Class, Ethnicity, and Nationalism Reconsidered*. New York: New York Academy of Sciences, 1–24.

Government of Sri Lanka (2008). *National Labour Migration Policy*. Available at <http://www.ilo.org/public/english/protection/migrant/download/mpolicy_srilanka_en.pdf>, accessed 23 October 2010.

Graham, H. (1991). 'The Concept of Caring in Feminist Research: The Case of Domestic Service', *Sociology*, 25: 61–78.

Gunasinghe, M. (2011). '"Discriminated Abroad and at Home": Sri Lankan Women Migrant Workers', in B. Santhakumar (ed.), *Rights, Remittances and Reintegration: Women Migrant Workers and Returnees in Sri Lanka*. Colombo, Sri Lanka: Law and Society Trust, 1–67.

Hamada, Y. (2012). 'National Governance in International Labour Migration', *Migration and Development*, 1(1): 50–71.

Harris, J. R. and Todaro, M. P. (1970). 'Migration, Unemployment and Development: A Two-Sector Analysis', *American Economic Review*, 60(1): 126–42.

Heery, E. and Frege, C. (2006). 'New Actors in Industrial Relations', *British Journal of Industrial Relations*, 44(4): 601–4.

Hochschild, A. (2000). 'Global Care Chains and Emotional Surplus Value', in W. Hutton and A. Giddens (eds.), *On the Edge: Living with Global Capitalism*. London: Jonathan Cape, 130–46.

Holgate, J. (2005). 'Organizing Migrant Workers: A Case Study of Working Conditions and Unionization in a London Sandwich Factory', *Work, Employment & Society*, 19(3): 463–80.

Hondagneu-Sotelo, P. and Avila, E. (1997). '"I'm Here, but I'm There": The Meanings of Latina Transnational Motherhood', *Gender & Society*, 11(5): 548–71.

Hujo, K. and Piper, P. (2007). 'South–South Migration: Challenges for Development and Social Policy', *Development*, 50(4): 19–25.

Human Rights Watch (2008). '"As if I am not human": Abuses against Asian Domestic Workers in Saudi Arabia'. Available at <http://www.hrw.org/sites/default/files/reports/saudiarabia0708_1.pdf>, accessed 4 December 2008.

—— (2012). 'Saudi Arabia: A Step to Aid Migrant Workers'. Available at <http://www.hrw.org/news/2012/04/10/saudi-arabia-step-aid-migrant-workers>, accessed 27 April 2012.

Institute of Policy Studies (2012). *Sri Lanka State of the Economy 2012: Keeping Sri Lankan on the Growth Expressway*. Colombo, Sri Lanka: IPS.

International Labour Organization (ILO) (2010). *International Labour Migration. A Rights-Based Approach*. Geneva: ILO.

—— (2013). *Domestic Workers Across the World: Global and Regional Statistics and the Extent of Legal Protection*. Available at <http://www.ilo.org/wcmsp5/groups/public/---dgreports/---dcomm/---publ/documents/publication/wcms_173363.pdf>, accessed 9 January 2013.

International Organization for Migration (IOM) (2012). *Labour Migration*. Available at <http://www.iom.int/cms/en/sites/iom/home/what-we-do/labour-migration.html>, accessed 25 September 2012.

Kalan, J. (2012). 'Migrant Workers in Jordan are Making Their Voices Heard'. Available at <http://www.ilo.org/global/about-the-ilo/newsroom/features/WCMS_195584/lang--en/index.htm>, accessed 2 December 2012.

Kaufman, B. E. (2004). *The Global Evolution of Industrial Relations: Events, Ideas and the IIRA*. Geneva: ILO.

Kaur, A. and Metcalfe, I. (2007). 'Thematic Introduction: Migration Challenges in the Asia Pacific Region in the Twenty-First Century', *International Journal on Multicultural Societies*, 9(2): 135–57.

Kerr, C., Dunlop, J. T., Harbison, F. H., and Meyers, C. A. (1964). *Industrialism and Industrial Man*. London: Oxford University Press.

—— (1971). 'Postscript to *Industrialism and Industrial Man*', *International Labor Review*, 103: 519.

Kitiarsa, P. (2005). 'The "Ghosts" of Transnational Labour Migration: Death and Other Tragedies of Thai Migrant Workers in Singapore', in N. Piper, B. P. Lorente, S. Hsui-Hua, and B. A. Yeoh (eds.), *Asian Migrations: Sojourning, Displacement, Homecoming and Other Travels*. Singapore: NUS Press, 194–222.

Kofman, E. (2007). 'The Knowledge Economy, Gender and Stratified Migrations', *Studies in Social Justice*, 1(2): 122–35.

Kofman, E. and Raghuram, P. (2012). 'Women, Migration, and Care: Explorations of Diversity and Dynamism in the Global South', *Social Politics: International Studies in Gender, State & Society*, 19(3): 408–32.

Lan, P. (2006). *Global Cinderellas: Migrant Domestics and Newly Rich Employers in Taiwan*. Durham and London: Duke University Press.

Lazaridis, G. (2000). 'Filipino and Albanian Women Migrant Workers in Greece: Multiple Layers of Oppression', in A. Floya and G. Lazaridis (eds.), *Gender and Migration in Southern Europe: Women on the Move*. Oxford: Berg Publishers, 49–79.

Lewis, W. A. (1954). 'Economic Development with Unlimited Supplies of Labour', *The Manchester School*, 22(2): 139–91.

Lindquist, J. (2010). 'Labour Recruitment, Circuits of Capital and Gendered Mobility: Reconceptualizing the Indonesian Migration Industry', *Pacific Affairs*, 83(1): 115–32.

Lindquist, J., Xiang, B., and Yeo, B. S. A. (2012). 'Opening the Black Box of Migration: Brokers, the Organization of Transnational Mobility and the Changing Political Economy of Asia', *Public Affairs*, 85(1): 7–19.

Locke, R. M., Qin, F., and Brause, A. (2007). 'Does Monitoring Improve Labour Standards? Lessons from Nike', *Industrial and Labor Relations Review*, 62(3): 3–31.

Lucio, M. M. and Perrett, R. (2009). 'The Diversity and Politics of Trade Unions' Responses to Minority Ethnic and Migrant Workers: The Context of the UK', *Economic and Industrial Democracy*, 30(3): 324–47.

Lusis, T. and Bauder, H. (2011). 'Migration and Labour Markets: An Interpretation of the Literature', in K. Townsend and A. Wilkinson (eds.), *Research Handbook on the Future of Work and Employment Relations*. Cheltenham: Edward Elgar, 212–29.

McGovern, P. (2007). 'Immigration, Labour Markets and Employment Relations: Problems and Prospects', *British Journal of Industrial Relations*, 45(2): 217–35.

McGrath-Champ, S., Rosewarne, S., and Rittau, Y. (2011). 'From One Skill Shortage to the Next: The Australian Construction Industry and Geographies of a Global Labour Market', *Journal of Industrial Relations*, 53(4): 467–85.

Massey, D. S. (1988). 'Economic Development and International Migration in Comparative Perspective', *Population and Development Review*, 14(3): 383–413.

Meardi, G., Martín, A., and Riera, M. L. (2012). 'Constructing Uncertainty: Unions and Migrant Labour in Construction in Spain and the UK', *Journal of Industrial Relations*, 54(1): 5–21.

Menz, G. (2008). *The Political Economy of Managed Migration: Nonstate Actors, Europeanization, and the Politics of Designing Migration Policies*. Oxford and New York: Oxford University Press.

Mhando, L. (2012). 'Spaces In and Beyond Traffic of Women in Commercial Sex'. Unpublished paper.

Mhando, L. and Thomas, D. (2011). 'Delicate Transaction of Neo-Liberal Policies to Irregular Migration Streams in the CIS Regions 1990s', *Journal of African and Asian Studies*, 11(1–2): 30–65.

Migration and Remittances Unit (2012). 'The Migration and Development Brief'. Washington, DC: World Bank. Available at <http://siteresources.worldbank.org/INTPROSPECTS/Resources/334934-1288990760745/MigrationDevelopmentBrief19.pdf>, accessed 12 December 2012.

Misra, J., Woodring, J., and Merz, S. N. (2006). 'The Globalization of Care Work: Neoliberal Economic Restructuring and Migration Policy', *Globalizations*, 3(3): 317–32.

Molland, S. (2012). 'Safe Migration, Dilettante Brokers and the Appropriation of Legality: Lao–Thai Trafficking in the Context of Regulating Labour Migration', *Pacific Affairs*, 85(1): 117–36.

Munck, R., Schierup, C. U., and Wise, R. D. (2011). 'Migration, Work, and Citizenship in the New World Order', *Globalizations*, 8(3): 249–60.

Ngai, P. (2005). *Made in China: Women Factory Workers in a Global Workplace*. Durham, NC: Duke University Press.

Nyberg-Sørensen, N., Hear, N. V., and Engberg-Pedersen, P. (2002). 'The Migration–Development Nexus: Evidence and Policy Options', *International Migration*, 40(5): 49–73.

Oishi, N. (2005). *Women in Motion: Globalization, State Policies and Labor Migration in Asia*. Palo Alto, CA: Stanford University Press.

Pak, J. (2013). 'Hong Kong Court Denies Domestic Workers Residency'. Available at <http://www.bbc.co.uk/news/world-asia-china-21920811>, accessed 25 March 2013.

Parreñas, R. S. (2000). 'Migrant Filipina Domestic Workers and the International Division of Reproductive Labor', *Gender & Society*, 14(4): 560–80.

—— (2001). *Servants of Globalization: Women, Migration and Domestic Work*. Palo Alto, CA: Stanford University Press.

—— (2005). 'Long Distance Intimacy: Class, Gender and Intergenerational Relations Between Mothers and Children in Filipino Transnational Families', *Global Networks*, 5(4): 317–36.

Piper, N. (2004). 'Rights of Foreign Workers and the Politics of Migration in South-East and East Asia', *International Migration*, 42(5): 71–97.

—— (2009). 'Guest Editorial. The Complex Interconnections of the Migration–Development Nexus: A Social Perspective', *Population, Space and Place*, 15: 93–101.

Portes, A. and Rumbaut, R. G. (2006). *Immigrant America: A Portrait*. Berkley and Los Angeles: University of California Press.

Portes, A. and Sensenbrenner, J. (1993). 'Embeddedness and Immigration: Notes on the Social Determinants of Economic Action', *American Journal of Sociology*, 98(6): 1320–50.

Pries, L. and Seelinger, M. (2013). 'Work and Employment Relations in a Globalized World: The Emerging Texture of Transnational Labour Regulation', *Global Labour Journal*, 4(1): 26–47.

Radcliffe, S. (1999). 'Race and Domestic Service: Migration and Identity in Ecuador', in J. Henshall Momsen (ed.), *Gender, Migration and Domestic Service*. London: Routledge, 83–97.

Raghuram, P. (2009). 'Which Migration, What Development? Unsettling the Edifice of Migration and Development', *Population, Space, Place*, 15(2): 103–17.

Ratha, D. (2005). 'Workers' Remittances: An Important and Stable Source of External Development Finance'. Economics Seminar Series, Paper 9. Available at <http://repository.stcloudstate.edu/econ_seminars/9>, accessed 15 July 2011.

Rodriguez, J. K. and Mearns, L. (2012). 'Problematising the Interplay Between Employment Relations, Migration and Mobility', *Employee Relations*, 34(6): 580–93.

Rodriguez, R. M. (2010). *Migrants for Export: How the Philippine State Brokers Labor to the World*. Minneapolis: University of Minnesota Press.

Rosewarne, S. (2012). 'Trading on Gender: The Perversity of Asian Labour Exports as an Economic Development Strategy', *Work Organisation, Labour and Globalisation*, 6(1): 81–102.

Sassen, S. (1998). *Globalization and Its Discontents: Essays on the New Mobility of People and Money*. New York: New Press.

—— (2000). 'Women's Burden: Counter Geographies of Globalization and the Feminization of Survival', *Journal of International Affairs*, 53/(2): 503–24.

Schierup, C.-U. and Castles, S. (2011). 'Migration, Minorities and Welfare States', *International Political Economy Yearbook*. Boulder, CO: Lynne Rienner.

Stalker, P. (2000). *Workers Without Frontiers: The Impact of Globalization on International Migration*. Geneva: ILO.

Standing, G. (2011). *The Precariat: The New Dangerous Class*. London and New York: Bloomsbury Academic.

Teo, Y. (2010). 'Shaping the Singapore Family, Producing the State and Society', *Economy and Society*, 39(3): 337–59.

Thomas, M. P. (2011). 'Global Industrial Relations? Framework Agreements and the Regulation of International Labor Standards', *Labor Studies Journal*, 36(2): 269–87.

Troung, T. D. (2012). 'Gender in Transnational Migration: Re-Thinking the Human Rights Framework', *Migration and Development*, 1(1): 72–86.

Vertovec, S. (1999). 'Conceiving and Researching Transnationalism', *Ethnic and Racial Studies*, 22(2): 445–62.

Wajcman, J (2000). 'Feminism Facing Industrial Relations in Britain', *British Journal of Industrial Relations*, 38(2): 183–201.

Wickramasekara, P. (2011). 'Circular Migration: A Triple Win or a Dead End', Global Union Research Network Discussion Paper 15.

Wong, T. C. and Rigg, J. (2010). *Migration, Labour and Contested Spaces*. New York: Routledge.

Woolfson, C. (2007). 'Labour Standards and Migration in the New Europe: Post-Communist Legacies and Perspectives', *European Journal of Industrial Relations*, 13(2): 199–218.

Yeates, N. (2009). *Globalizing Care Economies and Migrant Workers: Explorations in Global Care Chains*. Basingstoke: Palgrave Macmillan.

—— (2012). 'Global Care Chains: A State-of-the-Art Review and Future Directions in Care Transnationalization Research', *Global Networks*, 12(2): 135–54.

CHAPTER 26

THE NEO-LIBERAL TURN AND THE IMPLICATIONS FOR LABOUR

COLIN CROUCH

ACCORDING to the stylized facts that social scientists frequently use to impose some order on complex situations and histories, the role of the state in employment relations over the decades since the end of the Second World War can be divided into two periods: a social-democratic one and a neo-liberal one. The former dates roughly from 1945 until the late 1970s; the latter starts around that time and continues today. That stylization will be used here as the basis of hypotheses to test. In the process we should learn how accurate it is, and to the extent that it is not, whether we can define further or alternative concepts. Attention will be limited to the industrialized democracies; broadly, Europe, the Anglophone world in Australasia and North America, and Japan. Other parts of the world are still in the process of industrialization. To include them increases too far the range of variables that need to be considered in a chapter of this length.

A further constant that defines the cases selected for study is that they have all maintained capitalist economies based on private ownership of the means of production, distribution, and exchange, though there is a major exception until 1990 for the countries of Central and Eastern Europe (CEE). From this derives an important constant in the role of the state in employment relations across the whole period. Governments, police forces, and law courts have maintained the right of owners to dispose of their property and to employ labour on terms that subordinate those employed to direction and control by a management. This can be forgotten when, especially in considering the terms of the social-democratic model, attention is often (rightly) focused on the role of state and law in supporting countervailing rights of employees against employers. These rights exist within the context of the state's basic support for the rights of employers, and impart some ambiguities to the social-democratic model. The neo-liberal model is more straightforward in its uncompromised support of employers' rights.

Within this context, Table 26.1 sets out the basic terms of the two models, focusing on just three components: overall macroeconomic policy as it impacts on the labour

Table 26.1 Role of the state in employment relations in social–democratic and neo–liberal models

Element	Social democratic	Neo-liberal
Overall macroeconomic stance	Maintain male full (but not over-full) employment	Maintain price stability
Collective relations	Support	Weaken
Individual workers' rights	Sustain as countervailing power to employers	Replace with market incentives

market; relations to the role of collective actors in that market; and relation to employees' individual rights. Other elements could be added, but these are the most important.

A central aim of social-democratic macroeconomic policy was the use of Keynesian strategies to sustain stable demand in the economy by using the state's own spending and taxation to offset the likelihood of recessions (by expanding spending or cutting taxes) and of inflation (by reducing spending or increasing taxes). The aim was to maintain what was known as full employment, which in the decades concerned was seen as applying to male workers only. However, the need to avoid inflation meant that Keynesian economists accepted that employment could become 'over-full'. The Keynesian approach was not one of constant increases in public spending. According to neo-liberals, however, Keynesian policies will in effect become inflationary. To avoid this, they argued, the prime task of governments and central banks was to maintain price stability, mainly by controlling the supply of money, meaning that if wage rises led to price inflation, demand would decline and unemployment would be created, which would in turn bring prices down again.

Under social democracy trade unions are strong, and employers accept their existence and bargain with them. The fact that Keynesian policies sustained full employment also helped maintain union strength. The state supported these collective bargaining arrangements as contributing to industrial peace. Neo-liberalism has a far more explicit stance on collective employment relations: they are seen as impeding the freedom of market contracts between employers and individual workers, and are likely to lead to inefficient wage-setting, producing wages that will be maintained only at the expense of rising unemployment.

Similar arguments apply to individual labour rights. The central stance of social-democratic labour law is that employment contracts differ from normal contracts, which assume a formal equality of the contracting parties, as property law necessarily supports the subordination of employee to employer. Therefore the employee must be protected from exploitation in the relationship (Davies and Friedland 1993; Knegt and Verhulp 2008; Sinzheimer 1921). Neo-liberalism sees such protection as interfering with management's right to maximize efficiency by disposing of labour as it sees fit. The only role seen for labour law is to support the market in giving people incentives to work.

The neo-liberal turn in general economic and social policy that is considered to have taken place during the time period considered here should be visible in governments' policies in these three areas. The central hypothesis must be that there has been a shift from policies in the social-democratic column of Table 26.1 towards those in the neo-liberal one. In the following discussion we shall develop indicators to test this hypothesis.

There is, however, also the likelihood that individual nation-states adopted neo-liberalism at different times and with different degrees of enthusiasm, depending on their internal political balance. In particular, where trade unions and social-democratic parties have been strong, there should have been greater reluctance in adopting neo-liberal approaches. This hypothesis needs to be tested alongside that based on time periods.

The conventional approach to measuring the political strength of social-democratic or labour-friendly forces is to produce a list of parties considered to come in this category, and then to measure the share of cabinet seats enjoyed by such parties during the period being considered. This is a flawed measure, as it ignores the trade union links of Christian democratic parties (for example, in Belgium, Germany, and (until the 1990s) Italy). It also ignores the possibility that formally social-democratic parties might reduce their commitment to supporting organized labour, or might introduce labour market reforms viewed by many as 'unfriendly' to labour (as happened in the UK in the 1990s, and in Germany in the 2000s). This is therefore an issue that will need to be discussed below, rather than taken for granted. Given that the data being used in this chapter are not appropriate for sophisticated statistical manipulation, mainly because of the small number of cases, there is little point in establishing precise proportions of cabinet seats. Instead the potential 'labour friendliness' of a country's governments will be assessed according to the following scale (based on data provided in Döring and Manow 2011), depending on whether social-democratic, socialist, and/or communist parties are participating in free elections:

5 monopolized government or dominated coalitions throughout the period;
4 monopolized government or dominated coalitions for most of the period;
3 monopolized government or dominated coalitions for a minor part of the period;
2 were junior coalition partners for all or most of the period;
1 were junior coalition partners for a minor part of the period;
0 were never in government.

The results are shown in Table 26.2 for the endpoints of our analysis (the latest data available are for 2008), and for two interim points at 1985 and 1995.

A completely different approach to analysing political differences in approaches to different economic interests emphasizes differences between majoritarian and proportional electoral systems (Gourevitch and Shinn 2005; Roe 2003; Pagano and Volpin 2005). While much of this literature is concerned with corporate governance and relations between external shareholders, managers, and entrepreneurs, Pagano and Volpin

Table 26.2 Political and industrial strength of organized labour

	Party government strength				Union density			
	66–75	76–85	86–95	96–08	66–75	76–85	86–95	96–08
Australia (AU)	3	3	3	4	50.1	45.9	32.4	19.0
Austria (AT)	3	5	5	4	59.0	51.6	41.4	28.1
Belgium (BE)	2	2	2	1	51.9	52.4	55.7	52.0
Bulgaria (BG)	0	0	0	2	Y	Y		66.4
Canada (CN)	0	0	0	0	34.3	35.3	33.7	30.3
Czech R. (CZ)*	0	0	0	4	Y	Y	60.2	17.3
Denmark (DK)	4	4	0	2	68.9	78.2	77.0	67.4
Estonia (EE)	X	X	0	1	Y	Y	32.2	6.7
Finland (FI)	4	4	4	4	65.3	69.1	80.4	70.0
France (FR)**	0	3	4	4	22.2	13.6	9.1	7.6
Germany (DE)***	3	4	0	3	34.6	34.7	29.2	18.6
Greece (EL)	0	3	4	4	Y	37.5	33.6	24.0
Hungary (HU)	0	0	0	4	Y	Y	44.7	16.8
Ireland (IE)	1	1	2	1	61.5	60.2	52.3	33.7
Italy (IT)	1	1	2	3	48.0	42.5	38.1	35.1
Japan (JA)	0	0	1	1	34.5	28.8	24.4	18.5
Latvia (LV)	X	X	0	0	Y	Y	28.3	14.8
Lithuania (LT)	X	X	3	3	Y	Y	32.7	9.5
Luxembourg (LX)	1	1	2	2	45.7	52.1	43.5	37.3
Netherlands (NL)	3	1	1	3	37.8	28.0	25.7	19.0
New Zealand (NZ)	3	0	3	4	60.9	56.0	27.2	21.4
Norway (NO)	3	4	4	4	53.8	57.5	57.3	54.4
Poland (PL)	0	0	3	3	Y	Y	30.8	15.0
Portugal (PT)	0	3	0	4	Y	44.6	25.4	19.3
Romania (RO)	0	0	1	3	Y	Y	45.1	32.8
Slovakia (SK)	X	X	0	3	Y	Y	56.1	17.2
Slovenia (SI)	X	X	1	3	Y	Y	47.7	29.7
Spain (ES)	0	2	5	4	Y	10.2	16.3	15.9
Sweden (SE)	5	3	4	4	74.5	81.3	86.6	68.9
Switzerland (CH)	2	2	2	2	32.3	24.9	22.7	17.8
UK	4	3	0	4	48.3	46.2	33.4	27.5
US	0	0	0	0	21.6	18.0	14.9	11.4

X Country not in existence as separate polity
Y No free trade unions in existence
* Until 1990 Czechoslovakia
** Based on parliamentary government, not party of president
*** Until 1990 West Germany only
Sources: Party strength: Döring and Manow (2011); union density: Visser (2011).

also address an important aspect of employment relations: the strength of employment protection law (EPL). They find a strong positive relationship during the 1990s between the strength of EPL and the existence of proportionality in voting systems. There are, however, some questionable assumptions in their reasoning. First, they take it as axiomatic that rentiers (external shareholders) have more heterogeneous political interests than entrepreneurs or employees. Given the enormous diversity of socio-economic interests represented by the category of 'employee', this is doubtful. For example, they give as the main explanation for stronger EPL in countries with proportional voting systems the fact that 'strong worker protection enables low-productivity workers to retain well-paid jobs' (Pagano and Volpin 2005: 1027). But 'low-productivity workers' constitute only a minority of employees; their interests are not necessarily widely shared. Also, helping such workers retain their jobs will also prevent persons who are unemployed or in temporary posts from obtaining jobs. Furthermore, in a globalized economy external shareholders are often external to the country concerned, and their power cannot be explained in electoral terms. The causal links at work here are more complex than Pagano and Volpin's model provides, which suggests that differences between voting systems are not the right variable. Majoritarian voting systems are, as the authors' evidence shows, mainly a characteristic of Anglophone countries. They dispose well of the familiar argument that somehow the common law tradition that these countries share explains the frequent singularity of their employment relations institutions, but it is not clear that they have yet identified the crucial explanatory variables. Their approach will therefore not be followed here.

A second variable relevant to the power of labour within a political economy is the strength of trade unions. This is normally estimated by the proportion of the employed workforce in membership of unions (union density). Table 26.2 also presents these data. The source for these statistics is the ICTWSS database supervised by Jelle Visser at the University of Amsterdam (Visser 2011).

Restricting analysis to those countries with democratically elected governments at the time, in 1975 there was a close relationship between the level of union density and the presence in power of labour-related parties during the previous decade; the r^2 is 0.5157. There are not enough cases here for advanced statistical analysis, and attention is better focused on broad categories into which countries might be grouped. Table 26.3 divides countries into four quartiles, depending on their values on the scale in question between zero and whatever constitutes 100 per cent. Generalizing broadly, labour can be considered to have been politically and economically strong in Denmark, Finland, and Sweden, slightly less so in Australia, Austria, Belgium, New Zealand, and Norway. In other words, labour was strongest and likely to be best placed to resist neo-liberal labour policies in the Nordics, the Antipodes, and Austria. Outside this group in terms of party strength came Belgium and Ireland. These are both cases where non-labour parties (Christian Socials in Belgium, Fianna Fail in Ireland) had strong labour connections. Labour was weakest in France and the USA, slightly less weak in Canada and Japan, and less still in Italy, Luxembourg, and Switzerland. These are the countries where labour might be expected to resist neo-liberalism least. Finally, Germany, the Netherlands, and

Table 26.3 Political and industrial strength of organized labour (grouped data)

		Union membership density (%)		
		0–25	26–50	51–75	76–100
1975					
Party strength	5, 4		UK	DK FI SE	
	3		DE NL	AU AT NZ NO	
	2, 1		IT LX CH	BE IE	
	0	FR US	CN JA		
1985					
Party strength	5, 4		DE	AT FI NO	DK
	3	FR	AU EL PT UK		SE
	2, 1	ES CH	IT LX NL	BE IE	
	0	US	CN JA	NZ	
1995					
Party strength	5, 4	FR ES	AT EL	NO	FI SE
	3		AU NZ PL		
	2, 1	JA CH	IT LX NL RO SI	BE IE	
	0	US	CN EE DE HU LV LT PT UK	BG CZ SK	DK
2008					
Party strength	5, 4	AU CZ FR EL HU NZ PT ES	AT UK	FI NO SE	
	3	DE LT NL PL SK	IT RO SI		
	2, 1	BG EE JA CH	LX	DK	
	0	LV US	CN IE	BE	

the UK had relatively strong labour-associated parties but relatively weak unions. These form a clear intermediate group.

By the early twenty-first century union density had weakened in nearly every country that had free trade unions in 1975, in some cases very markedly indeed; at the same time, labour-associated parties had experienced very considerable political success. There is by this date an almost complete dissociation between labour's political and industrial strength, the correlation between the two variables being only $r^2 = 0.0214$. The countries which at the earlier period had still been under fascist or state socialist government often shared in this political success, but apart from Romania and Slovenia had very low union densities. Overall, only Finland, Norway, and Sweden (three of the four Nordic countries) can be considered to have all-round powerful labour movements. Labour was weakest of all in Latvia and the

USA, but also in Bulgaria, Switzerland, Estonia, Japan, Canada, Ireland, and Luxembourg. It had considerable union but less political strength in Belgium and Denmark. In all other countries it can be considered to have been politically strong but with weak unions.

The crude comparison between 1975 and around 2010 conceals some interim rises and subsequent declines, as inspection of Tables 26.2 and 26.3 reveals. Those in party strength fluctuate strongly, but more gradual changes affect union density. Between 1975 and 1985 there were increases in density in nine countries (with a further three emerging from dictatorship during the period), and declines in 13. In the subsequent decade there were increases in four (with a further 11 emerging from dictatorship), and declines in 20 (two of which were countries that had emerged from dictatorship during the 1975–85 decade). Between 1995 and 2010 there were no increases in union density at all, but declines in all 35 covered by the statistics. Decline was particularly strong in CEE, where in 1995 unions were still benefiting from the more or less compulsory membership of state-controlled unions that had characterized state socialism. Between 1975 and 1995 union decline was not universal, some countries experiencing increases in the earlier decade. But from around 1995 it became general, suggesting the hypothesis that neo-liberal attacks on collective labour institutions should have been most effective during this last period rather than starting from the point in the late 1970s from which the neo-liberal turn is often dated.

THE GOVERNMENT IN THE ECONOMY

A number of indicators might be taken to estimate the extent that government might be intervening in the economy in a way that would support labour's position. Since, of the variables we shall be examining here, it is the least directly related to collective industrial relations, we shall keep the account simple. One might consider government spending as the most obvious indicator, but that raises the problem of including long-term deficit spending that cannot be sustained. We shall instead take the measure of government's capacity to tax. Although in the short term this might measure government action to deflate the economy and therefore to weaken labour's position, in the long run government can only sustain a capacity to intervene to affect demand if it is able to tax effectively. Low taxes are certainly also a major objective of neo-liberal policies. Table 26.4 presents data on taxation as a proportion of GDP for all countries for which the OECD has data for at least part of the period between 1975 and 2009 (the latest year for which statistics were available for this datum at the time of writing). Unfortunately this involves excluding those CEE countries not in membership of OECD. Figure 26.1, which shows changes between 1975 and 2010, enables us to identify the high and low interveners at each period, as well as any hypothesized swing towards neo-liberalism.

Only a small number of cases (the Netherlands, USA, Ireland, UK) show the overall decline that would be expected if there had been a large swing towards neo-liberal policies since the 1970s. These countries do not fall into any patterns of change based on the measures of labour strength discussed above. It is, however, notable that the

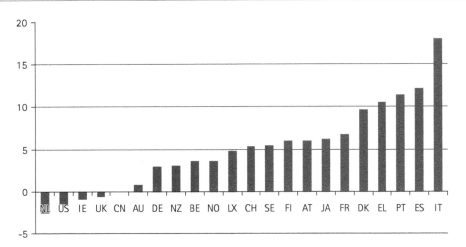

FIGURE 26.1 Changes in taxation levels, 1975–2009

Netherlands declines from an initially very high level, and that the other three countries are Anglophone. The Anglophone countries are often considered to have participated in the neo-liberal turn more readily than others, which is not surprising given that this ideology originated very much in the epistemic community of Anglophone economics. Concentrating initially on 1975 alone, it is notable that the three countries that had the highest combined labour strength scores in Table 26.3 are among the six highest taxers. Eight of the countries with high or very high labour political strength featured in the top nine taxers. The exceptions were on the one hand the two Antipodean countries and, with high taxes but low labour strength, France.

In 2009 the patterns were clearer. Of the nine countries with the highest taxation levels, eight were also among those with the highest levels of either political or economic labour strength. Finland, Norway, and Sweden (all Nordics) had scored highest on both labour variables. The other countries with highest political strength were Austria, France, and Hungary; with highest union strength, Belgium and Denmark. The exception was Italy. No country with the highest levels of union strength falls outside this top ten taxers group, but some with the strongest labour party performances do: Australia, Ireland, and the UK; Greece, Portugal, and Spain; and the Czech Republic. With the exception of this last, there are two clear groups here: all Anglophone countries except those that have no labour party (Canada and the USA, and which therefore cannot be analysed on this variable); and all three southern European countries that had emerged from dictatorship during the 1970s. At the other end of the scale, of the two countries that had the lowest scores on both political and economic labour strength, the USA has predictably the lowest taxation take of all countries under review; unfortunately we do not have OECD data on Latvia's taxation.

Looking at the overall 1975 to 2009 period, countries with consistently low taxation fell into two clear groups: first, those emerging from lengthy periods of dictatorship around 1975 and then increasing taxation very considerably, though still keeping it at low levels; and all Anglophone countries except Canada and the UK. In contrast with the ex-dictator group, the majority of Anglophone countries experienced low or negative taxation growth over the period. It is interesting to note that the strong states of dictatorships do not tax heavily, strengthening the argument for seeing high taxation as an indicator related to social democracy. The remaining consistently low taxers, Japan and Switzerland, cannot be easily grouped. High taxers at both points comprise solely northwestern European countries, and include all such countries except Ireland and Switzerland. (It is interesting to note in passing that 'Germany' is two different countries at the two time points: the western federal republic in 1975, unified east and west Germany in 2009. However, this was not associated with any great change in taxation, the rise being very similar to that in several other northwest European countries.)

Table 26.4 also enables us to determine whether a neo-liberal turn might have set in later than 1975. There was a slight shift in that direction in Belgium and Norway after 1985, though in the latter case this was reversed after 1995. However, between 1995 and 2009 taxation revenues fell in a larger number of countries (see Fig. 26.2): among the countries forming part of the initial data set, rather strongly in Finland and New Zealand, marginally in Canada, Denmark, France, Luxembourg, Spain, and Sweden. Inspection of the full OECD data set shows that in most countries the fall happens between 2005 and 2008 and was not therefore a result of the financial crisis. This is consistent with the finding in our earlier discussion that the decline in union density gathers pace after 1995. If this final point is valid, it is remarkable that labour party governmental strength would seem to be less linked to fiscal resistance to neo-liberalism than union membership. Here our data point to additional variables that go beyond the values that can be captured by statistics alone:

- as already noted, the Anglophone countries, which seemed to participate in the neo-liberal turn more readily than others;
- and the former dictatorships of southern Europe, which are coming from very low historical levels of spending.

The CEE countries are occupying various positions on all variables, though all saw declines between 1995 and 2009, suggesting that we are not yet able to account for variation among them.

COLLECTIVE LABOUR RIGHTS

According to our central hypothesis, the state was supportive of collective labour rights (meaning, largely, the rights of trade unions) in the stylized social-democratic period, but became hostile to them under neo-liberalism. As already noted when discussing statistics on union density, the main source that summarizes in a more or less comparable way the state of collective labour rights and relationships in many parts of the world and over a lengthy range of years is the ICTWSS database (Visser 2011). The price paid for this

Table 26.4 Taxation as % of GDP

	1975	1985	1995	2010
Australia (AU)	25.1	27.5	28.1	25.9
Austria (AT)	36.6	40.8	41.4	42.7
Belgium (BE)	39.5	44.3	43.5	43.2
Canada (CN)	32.0	32.5	35.6	32.0
Czech R. (CZ)*	..	..	37.6	34.7
Denmark (DK)	38.4	46.1	48.8	48.1
Estonia (EE)	X	X	36.3	35.9
Finland (FI)	36.6	39.8	45.7	42.6
France (FR)**	35.5	42.8	42.9	42.4
Germany (DE)***	34.3	36.1	37.2	37.3
Greece (EL)	19.4	25.5	28.9	30.0
Hungary (HU)	..	..	41.5	39.9
Ireland (IE)	28.7	34.6	32.5	27.8
Italy (IT)	25.4	33.6	40.1	43.4
Japan (JA)	20.7	27.1	26.8	26.9
Luxembourg (LX)	32.8	39.5	37.1	37.6
Netherlands (NL)	40.7	42.4	41.5	38.2
New Zealand (NZ)	28.4	30.9	36.2	31.5
Norway (NO)	39.2	42.6	40.9	42.9
Poland (PL)	..	..	36.2	31.8
Portugal (PT)	19.1	24.5	29.3	30.6
Slovakia (SK)	..	..	40.3	29.0
Slovenia (SI)	..	..	39.0	37.4
Spain (ES)	18.4	27.6	32.1	30.6
Sweden (SE)	41.3	47.4	47.5	46.7
Switzerland (CH)	24.4	25.8	27.7	29.7
UK	34.9	37.0	34.0	34.3
US	25.6	25.6	27.8	24.1

For notes see Table 26.2.
Source: OECD annual.

comprehensive coverage is a simplification of information that may conceal some important minor variations. When using the database we must keep this inevitable defect in mind and draw only those conclusions that are very strongly indicated by the statistics.

The most basic way in which states may support or oppose labour's collective organization is through a series of three key legal rights: to associate; to bargain collectively;

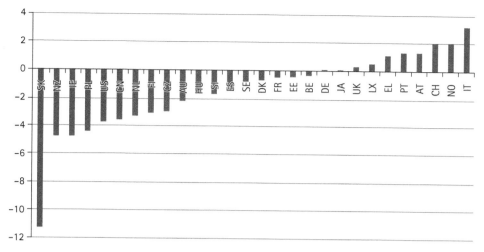

FIGURE 26.2 Changes in taxation levels, 1995–2009

to strike. These often differ between public and private employees, giving six different measures in all. The Visser index grades countries on these variables according to a four-point scale: complete absence of rights (0), rights with major restrictions (1), rights with minor restrictions (2), and unimpeded rights (3)—making a maximum score of 18. Column I in Table 26.5 presents the aggregate scores for each country at four points in time: 1975, 1985, 1995, and around 2010 (in some cases the most recent data are for 2008 or 2009).

If the simple neo-liberalism hypothesis is correct, we should see a decline in these rights between 1975 and 2010, but this can be observed in only two cases: Australia and Italy. (The Visser index seems to miss important reductions in strike rights in the UK during the 1980s.) Some countries saw overall minor improvements in rights (the Netherlands, New Zealand, Portugal), but the most remarkable changes over the period are of course the major extensions in rights among countries moving from various kinds of dictatorship to political democracy. (Portugal's own move in that direction occurs immediately before 1975.) As can be seen from Table 26.5, there are no patterns in the timing of the various minor declines or improvements in rights, but the big changes in CEE countries obviously come between 1985 and 1995, with, in several cases, further improvements some time after 1995. The overall distribution of rights today presents an odd pattern of countries: for example, they are higher in Lithuania than in Austria or Germany; apart from a clustering of the Nordic countries near the top of the range, the members of other familiar geo-cultural groupings of countries (southern Europe, western Europe, CEE, Anglophone countries) are scattered throughout. There is simi-larly little connection to our rankings of labour's political and economic strength. All we can conclude in general is that formal union rights have little relationship to substantive industrial relations phenomena, once the initial hurdle of moving out of dictatorship has been passed. At first sight this is surprising, as one would expect a decline in the political strength of organized labour to be reflected in legal changes. On the other hand,

Table 26.5 Government formal and substantive acceptance of trade unions

	(1) Trade union legal rights				(2) Government substantive recognition of unions				(3) Statutory works councils				(4) Government intervention in bargaining			
	75	85	95	10	75	85	95	10	75	85	95	10	75	85	95	10
AU	14	14	14	12	3	5	3	3	0	0	0	0	3	4	4	3
AT	12	12	12	12	5	5	7	6	5	5	5	4	2	2	2	2
BE	13	13	13	13	7	6	6	6	4	4	4	4	2	5	4	4
BG	2	2	12	12	0	0	2	3	0	0	0	2	5	5	3	3
CN	13	13	13	13	0	0	0	0	0	0	0	0	1	1	1	1
CZ*	2	2	13	14	0	0	3	4	0	0	0	0	5	5	3	3
DK	15	15	15	15	2	2	2	2	4	4	4	4	5	5	2	2
EE	X	X	9	12	X	X	0	1	X	X	0	0	X	X	3	2
FI	17	17	17	17	5	5	6	5	4	4	4	4	4	4	3	3
FR	15	15	15	15	3	3	4	3	4	4	4	4	3	3	3	3
DE***	12	12	12	12	3	2	2	2	5	5	5	5	2	2	2	2
EL	16	16	16	16	2	2	4	4	1	1	1	1	4	4	3	5
HU	2	2	15	15	0	0	3	4	0	0	4	4	..	..	3	3
IE	16	16	16	16	2	2	3	3	0	0	0	2	1	3	4	3
IT	16	16	15	15	1	1	3	3	3	3	3	3	2	3	2	2
JA	12	12	12	12	0	0	0	0	2	2	2	2	1	1	1	1
LV	X	X	11	11	X	X	3	4	X	X	0	2	X	X	3	2
LT	X	X	15	17	X	X	5	4	X	X	0	2	X	X	4	3
LX	12	12	12	12	5	6	6	7	2	4	4	4	3	3	3	3
NL	12	14	17	17	5	5	5	5	4	5	5	5	4	3	2	3
NZ	13	16	15	15	3	2	1	2	0	0	0	0	5	3	2	2
NO	15	15	15	15	4	3	3	3	2	4	4	4	4	3	4	3
PL	2	2	12	11	0	0	4	4	0	0	1	3	5	3	3	2
PT	10	12	12	12	0	4	4	4	0	1	1	1	5	3	3	3
RO	2	2	14	15	0	0	1	4	0	0	0	2	..	5	5	3
SK	X	X	13	14	X	X	4	3	0	0	0	4	X	X	3	3
SI	X	X	14	14	X	X	6	6	X	X	4	4	X	X	4	3
ES	0	17	17	17	0	2	4	5	0	3	3	3	..	4	3	3
SE	17	17	17	17	3	3	2	1	3	4	4	4	2	4	2	2
CH	14	14	14	14	2	2	2	2	2	2	2	2	1	1	1	1
UK	18	18	18	18	3	1	0	0	1	1	1	2	4	1	1	1.5
US	13	13	13	13	0	0	0	0	0	0	0	0	2	1	1	1

For notes see Table 26.2.
Source: Visser (2011).

on other assumptions this is what one might expect to be the case in democracies where labour's power in the market is declining. This decline means that labour will be less able to use its formal strength, while a frontal attack on formal rights might rally opposition. It is compatible with this assumption that, as we shall see immediately below, states have tended to withdraw support from labour in more subtle and less obvious ways than to remove its formal legal rights,

A further potential indicator of the stances of governments in relation to collective labour rights can be found in the extent to which governments in their day-to-day actions support and recognize, or in contrast abstain from engagement with, the activities of trade unions. The Visser index contains several items relevant to this:

> the potential mandatory extension of collective agreements to firms within the sector covered but not themselves parties to the agreement (scale of 0 to 2);
> participation in formal tripartite pacts (the Visser index permits multiple examples during a single year; here we restrict scoring to 0 or 1 for the year concerned);
> the existence of official tripartite councils (scale of 0 to 2 depending on importance);
> whether or not unions and employers' associations are routinely involved in government social and economic policy (scale of 0 to 2).

Combining these variables into a composite scale gives scores ranging from 0 to 7. We should expect the social democratic period to carry high scores, declining as we move into the neo-liberal one. Column II in Table 26.5 provides the scores for a range of countries. Again, the most impressive changes are the increases in formal support for unions and collective labour activity among former dictatorships. If we exclude these from consideration, however, and concentrate on countries that have consistently been political democracies through the period, we find some evidence of downward changes consistent with the neo-liberal hypothesis: in Belgium, Norway, Australia, Germany, New Zealand, Sweden, and most strongly of all the UK. No change was possible in three countries already at zero: Canada, Japan, USA. Some others saw no change at all, while there were improvements in labour's position in Austria, Luxembourg and Italy. Closer inspection of Table 26.5 shows that changes took place at various times and in some countries there are fluctuations up and down. Excluding countries emerging from dictatorship there are moves either way (four up and six down between 1975 and 1985; six up and five down after 1985). Only two countries outside CEE saw further upward moves after 1995 against four downward, and there were then three downward moves in CEE countries. There is therefore some evidence, though small, that any shift towards a neo-liberal approach mainly took place after this date.

It is notable that today the highest levels of government support for collective labour are not to be found in those with the highest scores for labour strength but in certain middle-range Western European countries (Luxembourg, Austria, Belgium) and Slovenia, not in the Nordic countries that scored highest for labour strength—and especially not in Sweden. Moderately high levels are now found in several (but not all) CEE countries. It is today at zero only in some Anglophone countries (Canada, UK, USA) and Japan.

A further dimension of government support for collective labour action concerns the existence and powers of works councils. The Visser index enables us to consider two variables:

> Do works councils exist? (scale of 0 for non-existent. 1 for existing but voluntary; 2 for mandatory);
> What levels of rights do they have? (scale of 0 to 3).

This gives a maximum possible score of 5. As before, the basic data are given in Table 26.5 (Column III).

With the exception of a small decline in works council powers in Austria (formerly one of the few countries with an initial maximum score of five), no countries see a decline. There are important rises, again in CEE, but also in several Western European countries. After 1995 we see here the impact of the European Union's 1994 works council directive, mandating councils in large, trans-European corporations (Marginson et al. 2004; Schulten 1996). It is also notable that, with the exception of Japan, no non-European country has works councils at all; while only two European countries (Czech Republic and Estonia) have none. The temporal pattern is very clear. Six Western European countries saw increases in works council rights after 1975 (a period of exceptional industrial relations activity). After then the only countries outside CEE seeing increases are the two Anglophone EU member states (Ireland and the UK) responding to the European directive after 1995. Works councils arrive in CEE in two bursts, after 1985 and after 1995. Today geo-cultural factors are again more helpful in understanding the spread of countries than simple indicators of labour strength. With the exception of Hungary, Slovakia, and Slovenia, all countries scoring four or five are located in northwest Europe; and the only two countries in that region with lower scores are the two Anglophones, Ireland and the UK. All other Anglophone countries have zero scores. Scores in Southern Europe are relatively low; CEE countries are scattered across the range.

A final means of estimating government activity in relation to collective labour relations concerns involvement (or not) in collective bargaining. The Visser index here uses a five-point scale:

> 5 = government imposes a ceiling on wage increases;
> 4 = government participates directly in bargaining, for a variety of reasons;
> 3 = government influences bargaining outcomes, for a variety of reasons;
> 2 = government provides institutional framework for bargaining;
> 1 = government plays no part in bargaining.

Scores are again given in Table 26.5 (Column IV) for the countries under consideration. This scale cannot be immediately translated into straightforward differences between social democracy and neo-liberalism. The score of 1 can be seen as equivalent to a neo-liberal position, because under neo-liberalism wages are determined by the market alone, by neither government nor collective bargaining. Score 2 is compatible with social democracy, because it assumes that there should be collective labour institutions. Both 3 and 4 are unfortunately ambiguous, as they include interventions to restrict wage increases as well as measures to support the position of some workers in bargaining. Score 5 is hostile to both neo-liberalism and social democracy. Table 26.6 reorganizes the data in this way, calling position 1 'neo-liberal', position 2 'social democratic', positions 3 and 4 'ambiguous', and position 5 'statist'.

Overall there is no shift towards the neo-liberal position. Four countries were found here in 1975 (Canada, Ireland, Japan, Switzerland)—all usual occupants of positions relatively close to neo-liberalism in our other variables. By 1985 the UK and USA had shifted to this position, the UK from an ambiguous, the US from a social-democratic one. This is consistent with the general assumption that these two countries were early movers towards neo-liberalism. But another Anglophone country, Ireland, left the neo-liberal group. There were no further moves towards neo-liberalism by either 1995 or 2010, and the UK moved to a position 1.5, implying part-way between 1 and 2—a score that the Visser index uses only on this occasion. It is particularly notable that none of the CEE countries has moved towards

Table 26.6 Role of government in collective bargaining

1975			
'Neo-liberal'	'Social democratic'	Ambiguous	'Statist'
CN IE JA CH	AT BE DE IT SE US	AU FI FR EL LX NL NO UK	BG CZ DK NZ PL PT

1985			
'Neo-liberal'	'Social democratic'	Ambiguous	'Statist'
CN JA CH UK US	AT DE	AU FI FR EL IE IT LX NL NZ NO PL PT ES SE	BE BG CZ DK RO

1995			
'Neo-liberal'	'Social democratic'	Ambiguous	'Statist'
CN JA CH UK US	AT DK DE NL NZ SE	AU BE BG CZ EE FI FR EL HU IE IT LV LT LX NO PL PT SK SI ES	RO

2010			
'Neo-liberal'	'Social democratic'	Ambiguous	'Statist'
CN JA CH (UK) US	AT DK EE DE LV NZ PL SE (UK)	AU BE BG CZ FI FR HU IE IT LT LX NL NO PT RO SK SI ES	EL

neo-liberalism as it left authoritarianism. In contrast the social-democratic position has grown slightly over time. Its original members were Austria, Belgium, Germany, Italy, Sweden, and the USA. Only Austria and Germany remained there in 1985, Belgium having temporarily became statist, Italy and Sweden ambiguous, and the USA leaving permanently for the neo-liberal group. By 1995, however, the group had grown, being joined by Denmark (from the statist group), the Netherlands, New Zealand, and Sweden (from ambiguous positions), with Italy returning. By 2010 Poland had also arrived there, and both Estonia and Latvia had established this position. By 2010 also the only country with a statist pattern was Greece. All others were in various ambiguous positions.

Conclusions

Examining these various indicators of the relationship of governments to collective labour rights, we can draw only limited conclusions:

First, formal legal union and bargaining rights tell us very little. Only authoritarian (both fascist and state socialist) regimes refuse to grant many rights of this kind. If neo-liberals intend to weaken unions, they do not primarily choose this path. In the USA, and more recently and very strongly in the European Court of Justice (ECJ), the attack on labour's legal rights comes through changes in judges' interpretation of existing labour law. There are interesting issues here for the sociology of law and the circumstances in which judicial opinion follows wider trends in elite opinion. Alternatively, changes in the composition of courts may reflect, more subtly than in the case of actual changes in the law, political influence. This has long been the case in the USA, and recently it has been argued that the ECJ has become more hostile to collective labour rights following the appointment of judges from former state-socialist countries. ECJ decisions have also been affected by the extension of competition law to ever more areas, including public services, though there was still scope for judicial discretion in deciding how to apply that law (Deakin and Rogowski 2011; Höpner 2008). Second, the history of works councils shows an opposite trend from any move to neo-liberalism. Probably as a result of the European works council directive, there has been a growth of such councils throughout Western Europe and several countries in CEE. This affects, though not strongly, even the two Anglophone countries within the EU. Third, examination of the history of government intervention in collective bargaining also fails to reveal any trend to neo-liberal positions. If anything the collapse of statist intervention has benefited broadly social-democratic approaches. Finally, however, there is more evidence of neo-liberalism at work in the more substantive issues concerning various forms of government use, encouragement, endorsement of union actions and participation. There has been a decline over time, and especially in recent years; and strongly neo-liberal countries (the Anglophone group standing mainly as a proxy for this) have generally lower levels on these variables than other kinds of regime other than the dictatorships. On the other hand, social-democratic countries—those in which labour is politically and in particular economically most powerful (here the Nordics are a proxy)—are not the countries in which this government support is most important.

INDIVIDUAL LABOUR RIGHTS

Although our focus is on the role of the state in collective labour relations, this issue cannot be entirely dissociated from the legal rights of individual workers. Neo-liberalism has a strong position on this question, requiring a dismantling of workers' job protection on the grounds that this imposes rigidities on the labour market. Thus this has been the official stance of the European Union (1993) and the OECD (1994) since the mid-1990s. Social democracy on the other hand should be expected to advocate strong individual rights, as the individuals concerned are important to its core constituency. A second issue that can be considered is the role of government in supporting a minimum wage. Here again the position of neo-liberalism should be unequivocally hostile to artificially maintaining the level of wages in this way, while social democracy might be predicted to be concerned for the level of living of its constituents.

Comparative data have been collected by the OECD for its member states on labour protection laws only since the mid-1980s. We cannot therefore reach back to 1975, but have a spread of data for those countries considered here that are OECD members since 1985. Column (1) of Table 26.7 presents these for workers on open-ended contracts for the three years 1985, 1995, and 2008.

Since 1985 there has clearly been a decline in labour protection, affecting 13 of the countries under review for the whole period, with rises only in Australia, France, Ireland, and the UK. With the exception of France, these are all Anglophone countries where the starting levels were very low. This overall decline is in line with the neo-liberal hypothesis. Some countries saw declines in protection between both 1986 and 1995 and 1996 and 2008: Germany, Greece, Portugal, Spain, and Sweden. In others it was concentrated in the latter period: Austria, Belgium, Finland, Italy, and Japan. Only Norway reduced protection only in the earlier period. But the countries registering increases in protection also did this during the more recent period: those already mentioned, plus Czech Republic, Hungary, New Zealand, and Poland. Only France had increases in both periods. Therefore, although it is after 1995 that changes consistent with neo-liberalism are concentrated, this was also a period of general changes in EPL activity.

The pattern across countries with different kinds of regime is interesting. Around 1985, as Table 26.8 shows, the weakest labour protection was not so much found in those countries with the weakest labour movements as in the Anglophone group in general. Also, the strongest labour protection laws were found in Southern European countries, even where labour movements were weak. The countries of Northern and Western Europe, including all those where labour was particularly strong, occupied intermediate positions. By 2008 the picture was more complex, the Southern European countries having undergone the most

Table 26.7 Individual employee protection

	Strength of employment protection laws (1)			(1) deflated by self- employment (2)			(2) deflated by temporary employment (3)			(3) deflated by shadow empl. (4)	(4) as % of (1)
	85	95	08	85	95	08	85	95	08	08	08
AU	0.94	0.94	1.15	0.83	0.83	0.97	..	..		..	..
AT	2.21	2.21	1.93	2.03	2.06	1.75	..	1.93	1.58	1.43	74.29
BE	3.15	3.15	2.18	2.76	2.71	1.88	2.57	2.56	1.72	1.42	64.96
CN	0.75	0.75	0.75	0.66	0.64	0.63	0.61	..	0.55	..	..
CZ*	..	1.90	1.96	..	1.68	1.65	..	1.52	1.50	1.23	62.59
DK	2.40	1.50	1.50	2.20	1.39	1.38	1.93	1.22	1.26	1.05	70.29
FI	2.33	2.16	1.96	2.17	1.94	1.75	..	..	1.47	1.24	63.32
FR	2.79	2.98	3.05	2.50	2.73	2.79	2.38	2.39	2.37	2.05	67.36
DE***	3.17	3.09	2.12	2.94	2.81	1.88	2.64	2.52	1.60	1.36	64.01
EL	3.56	3.50	2.73	2.57	2.54	1.95	2.03	2.28	1.71	1.36	49.91
HU	..	1.27	1.65	..	1.09	1.46	..	..	1.32	1.00	60.50
IE	0.93	0.93	1.11	0.83	0.81	0.97	0.77	0.73	0.88	0.75	67.78
IT	3.57	3.57	1.89	2.83	2.75	1.42	2.70	2.55	1.23	0.95	50.23
JA	1.84	1.84	1.43	1.60	1.66	1.27	1.43	1.49	1.09	1.00	69.73
LX	..	..	3.25	..	..	3.25	..	..	3.02	2.74	84.17
NL	2.73	2.73	1.95	2.50	2.46	1.73	2.30	2.19	1.41	1.25	64.19
NZ	..	0.86	1.40	..	0.72	1.18	..	..		..	..
NO	2.90	2.69	2.69	2.70	2.54	2.51	..	..	2.30	1.92	71.35
PL	..	1.40	1.90	..	1.24	1.65	..	..	1.61	..	..
PT	4.19	3.85	3.15	3.48	3.09	2.63	..	2.78	2.03	1.62	51.30
RO	..	..	1.92	..	..	1.84	..	..	1.58	..	..
SK	X	1.80	1.44	X	1.71	1.25	X	1.65	1.18	0.96	66.96
SI	X	..	2.51	X	..	2.17	X	..	1.80	1.31	52.14
ES	3.82	3.01	2.33	3.17	2.45	1.88	..	1.59	1.41	1.04	44.85
SE	3.49	2.47	1.87	3.32	2.25	1.70	..	..	1.43	1.20	63.99
CH	1.14	1.14	1.14	1.14	1.14	1.14	..	..	0.99	0.91	79.60
UK	0.60	0.60	0.75	0.55	0.53	0.65	0.51	0.49	0.61	0.55	73.04
US	0.21	0.21	0.21	0.19	0.19	0.19	0.18	0.18	0.18	0.17	78.63

For notes see Table 26.2.

Sources: Employment protection laws, self- and temporary employment: OECD annual; shadow economy: Schneider and Böhn (2009).

radical reductions in labour protection laws even though these levels remained relatively high. However, the Anglophone countries remain those with the lowest protection levels.

But the strength of labour protection laws for workers with open-ended contracts gives us only a partial picture of the overall position of workers' security in the labour market. Workers on temporary contracts, in self-employment, and in the black economy will not benefit from such protection and will be more exposed to market forces in line with neo-liberal ideas. For example, assume country A has labour protection laws half as tough again as those of country B, but has only 25 per cent of its labour force in normal open-ended employment contracts while country B has 100 per cent. It would not be accurate to conclude that country A comes closer to a social-democratic labour market while country B has a more neo-liberal one. Rather, country A protects a small proportion of its workforce, at least partly at the expense of large numbers of other workers.

Table 26.7 shows the effect of these issues by deflating the labour protection index score for those employed under open-ended contracts by, successively, the proportions working as self-employed, with temporary contracts, and in the shadow economy (columns (2), (3), and (4)). The last statistic is necessarily less reliable than the others, as it is by definition not easy to calculate precisely the numbers of those working illegally. Unfortunately we lose countries as we add these additional variables, as data are not available for various items for some countries, especially in the earlier periods; and for the shadow economy figures we have data only for the mid-2000s. Figure 26.3 presents the most useful conclusion of the analysis. It plots, for 2008 only, the original scores for EPL in that year against the percentage of that figure represented by the full deflation. The latter is a measure of labour market exclusion: the smaller the deflated score as a percentage of the original one, the smaller the proportion of the workforce benefiting from whatever protection is afforded, and the larger the number of excluded. As we move to the top right-hand corner of the graph we move to positions that offer high levels of protection with low levels of exclusion; what we might call the social-democratic preferred position. Towards the bottom right corner we find low levels of both protection and exclusion: the preferred neo-liberal position. The top left corner provides high security, but to a small proportion of the workforce. This is a minority protection situation, rejected by both social democracy and neo-liberalism. The final corner (bottom left) would provide little protection to anyone and exclude many even from that. It is a theoretically possible position, but unlikely to be found, and it is an empty area here.

The puzzle of high protection in countries with weak labour movements is partly resolved as a protection enjoyed by minorities of the labour force (the top left corner). With the perhaps surprising exception of Slovenia, it is populated solely by south-western European countries, including Italy; and no southern country is found outside that space. The social-democratic area is occupied by the mix of Nordic and West European countries that might be expected on the basis of earlier discussions, though the high positions of France, the Netherlands, and the Czech Republic are surprising. Notably and surprisingly absent from this group is Denmark, which is now found in the neo-liberal space (among the mainly countries Anglophone). Two further CEE

Table 26.8 Minimum wage arrangements

	Statutory minimum wage				Form of minimum wage determination			
	75	85	95	10	75	85	95	10
AU	2	2	2	2	G	T	T	G
AT	0	0	0	0	B	B	B	B
BE	2	2	2	2	B	T	B	B
BG	..	..	2	2	..	..	G	T
CN	2	2	2	2	G	G	G	G
CZ*	..	..	2	2	..	..	G	G
DK	0	0	0	0	B	B	B	B
EE	X	X	2	2	X	X	T	B
FI	0	0	0	0	B	B	B	B
FR	2	2	2	2	G	G	G	G
DE***	0	0	0	1	B	B	B	B
EL	2	2	2	2	B	B	B	G
HU	..	..	2	2	..	..	T	T
IE	0	0	0	2	M	M	M	G
IT	0	0	0	0	B	B	B	B
JA	1	1	1	1	G	G	G	G
LV	X	X	1	1	X	X	G	G
LT	X	X	2	2	X	X	G	T
LX	2	2	2	2	T	G	G	G
NL	2	2	2	2	G	G	G	G
NZ	1	2	2	2	G	G	G	G
NO	0	0	0	0	B	B	B	B
PL	..	..	2	2	..	..	T	T
PT	2	2	2	2	G	G	G	G
RO	..	..	2	2	..	..	G	T
SK	X	X	2	2	X	X	T	G
SI	X	X	1	2	X	X	T	G
ES	..	2	2	2	..	T	T	T
SE	0	0	0	0	B	B	B	B
CH	0	0	0	0	B	B	B	B
UK	1	1	0	2	T	T	M	G
US	2	2	2	2	G	G	G	G

For notes see Table 26.2.
Source: Visser (2011).

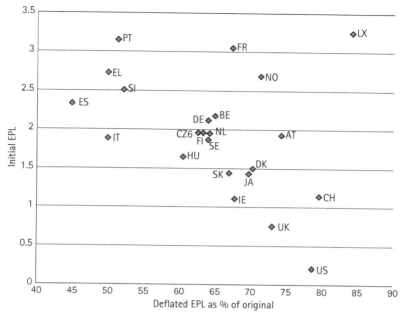

FIGURE 26.3 Deflated EPL as % of initial EPL

countries (Hungary and Slovakia) also appear here. This is consistent with the literature that argues that Denmark has in recent years found a distinctive labour-market position known as 'flexicurity' (Bredgaard et al. 2007; Wilthagen and Tros 2004). This is claimed to balance low levels of legal employment protection with other components of active labour market policy, which are beyond the scope of our analysis here.

Finally, a different form of state assistance to individual workers is the maintenance of minimum wages. Here the Visser index has two kinds of data. First there is a quantitative scale of extent of minimum wages:

2 = statutory minimum across the economy;
1 = statutory minimum in certain sectors;
0 = no statutory minimum wage.

Second, there is a qualitative assessment of forms of minimum wage determination, which, like the assessments discussed above of government involvement in bargaining in general, cannot be reduced to a quantitative scale. The Visser index identifies nine different forms of minimum wage assessment. For our purposes, as with wage determination in general, the relevant information is whether minimum wages are left to the market (neo-liberal), left to the bargaining parties (social-democratic), or determined by government (authoritarian). There is also a position intermediate between these two last of tripartite determination, which we shall also count as social democratic. In Table 26.8 the Visser index is translated into these grades as follows:

o   = market determination (M);
1–3 = bipartite determination (B);
4, 5 = tripartite determination (T);
6–8 = various forms of government or expert determination (G).

Table 26.9 allocates countries to their appropriate boxes at the different time periods. In the mid-1970s countries were concentrated in two positions: minimum wages set by collective bargaining without statutory support; and government-determined general minima. Only a few countries had systems differing from these two. Those that we have identified as having labour politically and economically strong concentrate at the former; social democracy was therefore characterized by strong bargaining, not by a strong state role. In fact, it is—with some exceptions—the more neo-liberal Anglophone countries that have a strong government role in setting minimum wages. The only country following the expected neo-liberal path was Ireland. By 1985 little had changed; some countries changed their systems, but with no overall trend apart from some growth in tripartite determination. By 1995 we have data for many of the CEE countries. The effect of this is to increase numbers in both the government-determined and tripartite boxes; none of these countries adopted either a pure bargaining or a market approach. A notable move among the existing group of countries was the UK joining Ireland in the market box, implying some growth of an Anglophone neo-liberal grouping—but notably without the USA. By 2010, however, both these countries had adopted full government-determined minimum wages, meaning that the often neo-liberal Anglophone area is now fully concentrated at this point. Another notable change is the adoption of limited statutory support for bargaining outcomes in Germany. There is considerable turbulence among the CEE countries between the government-determined and tripartite alternatives, with no overall trend. Only Estonia among these joins the bargaining group, with bargaining outcomes supported by law. On the basis of an exhaustive study of several aspects of economic policy and structure, Bohle and Greskcovits (2012) make a three-fold division among CEE countries, with all three Baltic states standing near the neo-liberal pole, Slovenia resembling the social-democratic model, and the majority of countries coming in between. Other research confirms this general analysis of their employment relations systems, though it does not always appear clearly in the account of government policy. This point suggests that, to be fully understood, public policy actions need to be set in a wider context of economic power variables. This point will be considered further below.

By the present time we can therefore conclude that countries where labour is strong continue to prefer minimum wages determined by bargaining. It is difficult to tell whether it is significant that Germany has acquired some statutory support for its bargaining outcomes following the strong decline of union density. Paradoxically, after years of the neo-liberal turn, the preference of countries normally associated with neo-liberal policies is now unambiguously for state-supported minimum wages, and no country adopts a market position. It is notable that the conditions of the European Union's bailout for Greece, which in general imposed strict neo-liberal labour market rules, required

Table 26.9 Minimum wage arrangements (grouped data)

Market	Bargaining	Tripartite	Government
1975			
IE	2. BE, EL	2. LX	2. AU, CN, FR, NL, PT, US
		1. UK	1. JA, NZ
	0. AT, DK, FI, DE, IT, NO, SE, CH		
1985			
IE	2. EL	2. AU, BE, ES	2. CN, FR, LX, NL, PT, US
		1. UK	1. JA
	0. AT, DK, FI, DE, IT, NO, SE, CH		
1995			
IE, UK	2. BE, EL	2. AU, EE, HU, PL, SK, ES	2. BG, CN, CZ, FR, LT, LX, NL, NZ, PT, RO, US
		1. SI	1. JA, LV
	0. AT, DK, FI, DE, IT, NO, SE, CH		
2010			
IE, UK	2. BE, EE	2. BG, HU, LT, PL, RO, ES	2. AU, CN, CZ, FR, EL, IE, LX, NL, NZ, PT, SK, SI, UK, US
	1. DE		1. JA, LV
	0. AT, DK, FI, IT, NO, SE, CH		

replacement of the role of collective bargaining in fixing the minimum wage by direct government determination. The main overall change over the decades has been a considerable increase in the use of tripartite, statutorily enforced minimum wages. However, with the exception of Spain this trend has been confined to CEE countries.

Taken together with the general avoidance by governments of frontal attacks on formal union rights, this tendency towards acceptance of minimum wages indicates certain limits to any neo-liberal onslaught on labour rights. Concerns for social peace and the avoidance of extreme conditions remain very important in most democracies. Neo-liberalism and democracy have to operate within a framework set by each other. This does not produce a convergence of systems, but it does imply an avoidance of extreme positions on labour issues, which has something of the appearance of convergence.

Conclusions

Although the final discussion above has been primarily concerned with individual rather than collective labour issues, it enables us to draw important conclusions about the latter, consistent with the findings of the earlier sections. Most evidence of the neo-liberal turn has been found in the weakening of employment protection laws, a prime target of neo-liberal labour market reforms. There was also mixed evidence of a decline in governments' substantive use of unions as public policy partners. These changes have not, however, been accompanied by a frontal attack on all aspects of collective or individual labour rights. Instead we see three relatively clear patterns, and some more obscure movements.

First, in countries where labour has retained industrial (not so much political) strength, or where there have been traditions of a public role for unions, governments have preferred to leave existing institutions in place, even strengthening them, avoiding conflict over institutional issues, while pursuing a neo-liberal agenda on substantive ones. We should need more scrutiny of individual cases to determine whether this means that they work with unions on a compromise neo-liberal agenda, or ignore them. In either case the universal decline in labour's industrial strength facilitates such a strategy. This approach characterizes the Nordic countries, some other Western European states, and to some extent the European Union itself, where strongly neo-liberal substantive policies are combined with institutional support for social partnership. This is seen most clearly in the question of works councils, and more generally in the fact that, by its nature as an international collaborative body, the EU can never exclude a major social interest for partisan reasons in the way that a national government can. But the central thrust of EU policies is towards marketization, which necessarily undermines approaches that check market forces—as do most industrial relation institutions. This has been strongly reinforced by the extension of the single market programme to social policy (Barbier 2013; Barbier et al. 2014). It imparts a distinctive quality to the form taken by neo-liberalism in this world region. In a further complication, where labour is industrially strong (mainly the Nordic countries), it prefers to rely on its own bargaining strength rather than statist measures.

More generally, this development alerts us to the complex relationship between political and economic power in democracies already signalled in the above discussion of CEE countries. If an interest to which political authorities are becoming hostile loses economic power, the latter have a choice: to take advantage of declining economic power by weakening the interest even further through political means; or to leave political institutions in place and rely on their losing effectiveness through the economic weakening. Where the interest concerned is generally unpopular with a wider public, one might expect to find their first being used; where it is popular, or at least not unpopular, governments may prefer to save political energy and allow the interest concerned to 'wither on the vine'. Given a general neo-liberal political consensus, one should expect governments to be hostile to trade unions and the industrial relations institutions on which they depend. When, as in the UK at the time of Margaret Thatcher's governments, unions have also become unpopular with a wider public, one will find very public measures being taken to weaken them. If this is not the case, as in most of Western Europe today, the politics becomes more complex. The most important conclusion to be drawn from this is that one needs both political and economic analysis to understand policy developments and changing balances of interests.

Second, in countries where labour has become industrially weak, where there have been only weak traditions of a public role for unions, and where neo-liberal ideology has been strongest, governments have paid less attention to sustaining social partnership institutions. They have also put a basic support for low incomes in place without involvement of social partners. It is beyond our scope here, but there is a tendency for this kind of minimum wage to stagnate. However, it remains the case that no governments have sought the extreme neo-liberal path of removing such protection entirely; though they avoid the engagement of unions in determining it. This approach characterizes the Anglophone countries and a small number of other states, including Japan. The two Anglophone EU members often stand between these two groupings.

Third, there continues to be a separate path in southwestern Europe. This involves some state support for relatively weak labour institutions. Under the impact of neo-liberal reforms this produces a new social compromise whereby parts of the labour market enjoy high protection while a further part is subject to market pressures and the phenomenon of labour exclusion.

Finally, it is difficult to draw conclusions about the CEE group. It might have been predicted that, given the strength of neo-liberal ideology in post-communist polities, they would have clustered around the neo-liberal pole at most points. They have not done so. There are probably two explanations for this. First, they have inherited the mixed package that constitutes the European Union's *acquis communautaire*. Second, the internal politics of most CEE countries has seen frequent changes of government between various forms of neo-liberalism, nationalistic conservatism, and social democracy. This accounts for both the frequent changes in the positions of these states and the lack of any clear overall profile for virtually all of them.

References

Barbier, J.-C. (2013). *Europe sociale: l'état d'alerte*. OSE Paper series 13/4. Brussels: Observatoire Social Européen.

Barbier, J.-C., Colomb, F., and Rogowski, R. (eds.) (2014). *The Sustainability of the European Social Model: EU Governance, Social Protection and Social Rights in Europe*. Cheltenham: Edward Elgar.

Bohle, D. and Greskovits, B. (2012). *Capitalist Diversity on Europe's Periphery*. Ithaca: Cornell University Press.

Bredgaard,. T., Larsen, F., and Madsen, P. K. (2007). 'The Challenges of Identifying Flexicurity in Action: A Case Study on Denmark', in H. Jørgensen and P. K. Madsen (eds.), *Flexicurity and Beyond: Finding a New Agenda for the European Social Model*. Copenhagen: DJØF Publishing, 365–91.

Davies, P. and Friedland, M. (1993). *Labour Legislation and Public Policy*. Oxford: Clarendon Press.

Deakin, S. and Rogowski, R. (2011). 'Reflexive Labour Law, Capabilities and the Future of Social Europe', in R. Rogowski, R. Salais, and N. Whiteside (eds.), *Transforming European Employment Policy*. Cheltenham: Edward Elgar, 229–54.

Döring, H, and Manow, P. (2011) *ParlGov database*. University of Bremen. Available at <http://www.parlgov.org>.

European Commission (1993). *Growth, Competitiveness and Employment*. Luxembourg: Office for Official Publication of the European Communities.

Gourevitch, P. and Shinn, J. (2005). *Political Power and Corporate Control*. Princeton: Princeton Univerrsity Press.

Höpner, M. (2008). 'Usurpation statt Delegation: Wie der EuGH die Binnenmarktintegration radikalisiert und warum er politische Kontrolle bedarf', MPIfG Discussion Paper 08/12. Cologne: Max Planck Institute for the Study of Societies.

Knegt, R. and Verhulp, E. (eds.) (2008). *The Employment Contract as an Exclusionary Device: An Analysis on the Basis of 25 Years of Developments in The Netherlands*. Antwerp: Intersentia.

Marginson, P., Hall, M., Hoffmann, A., and Müller, T. (2004). 'The Impact of European Works Councils on Management Decision-Making in UK- and US-based Multinationals', *British Journal of Industrial Relations*, 42(2): 209–33.

OECD (1994). *The Jobs Study*. Paris: OECD.

—— (annual). *Statistical Database*. Paris: OECD.

Pagano, M. and Volpin, P. (2005). 'The Political Economy of Corporate Governance', *American Economic Review*, 95: 1005–30.

Roe, M. (2003). *Political Determinants of Corporate Governance*. Oxford and New York: Oxford University Press.

Schneider, F. and Böhn, A. (2009). 'Shadow Economy and Corruption all over the World: Revised Estimates for 120 Countries', *Economics*, 1. Available at <http://www.economics-ejournal.org/economics/journalarticles/2007-9>.

Schulten, T. (1996). 'European Works Councils: Prospects for a New System of European Industrial Relations', *European Journal of Industrial Relations*, 2(3): 303–24.

Sinzheimer, H. (1921). *Grundzüge des Arbeitsrechts*. Berlin: Fischer.

Visser, J. (2011). *Data Base on Institutional Characteristics of Trade Unions, Wage Setting, State Intervention and Social Pacts, 1960–2010 (ICTWSS)* Version 3.0. Amsterdam: Amsterdam Institute for Advanced Labour Studies.

Wilthagen, T. and F. Tros (2004). 'The Concept of "Flexicurity": A New Approach to Regulating Employment and Labour Markets', in 'Flexicurity: Conceptual Issues and Political Implementation in Europe' *Transfer*, 10: 2.

PART V

REFLECTIONS

CHAPTER 27

THE STATE AND EMPLOYMENT RELATIONS

GUGLIELMO MEARDI

INTRODUCTION

THE chapter deals with the most political of institutions, the state, and describes its roles in employment relations in a comparative perspective. Economic and political accounts of differences are compared, with particular attention to historical institutionalism and to corporatist theory, which addresses the sharing of power and responsibilities between state and interest associations.

The chapter then addresses the shifting role of the state in the framework of globalization and, more recently, the Western economic crisis: both, rather than undermining the state, have shown its enduring importance.

STATE DEFINITIONS

Unlike other actors and institutions of employment relations, which are largely 'tangible', the state is an inherently theoretical concept that requires a theoretical definition. Conceptual confusion lies behind numerous misunderstandings in debates such as between 'strong' and 'weak', 'interventionist' and 'laissez-faire' states. The characterization of 'strong' or 'interventionist' depends on what is included in the definition of the state. Germany has long been defined as a 'weak state' that delegates authority to associations (Katzenstein 1987; Streeck 2005), but some actually characterize it as a strong one, due to its philosophical tradition and its near-hegemonic role in the EU. The UK of the 1980s, conversely, has been defined at the same time as 'laissez-faire' and as iron-fist interventionist, and the USA is seen, alternatively, as an example of minimal state and, at the other extreme, as an 'Empire', or as the centre of one (Hardt and Negri 2000).

Three different historical traditions of conceptualizing the state involve very different can be identified and contrasted as follows.

(1) Anglo-Saxon *laissez-faire* tradition (dominant in UK and USA): the state is clearly distinct from the society, and embraces only institutions directly responsible for the exertion of political power (government, civil service, courts, police, military, etc.). In society, the emphasis is here on *freedom from the state*, and the concept of state is close to that of government.

(2) Statist traditions (important in France and communist countries): the state *is* the society, it constitutes it, as exemplified by the unity between Revolution and Republic, and it has the direct responsibility of maintaining its cohesion. It includes an important role for public services, and involves a stronger positive relationship between state and citizen.

(3) Corporatist traditions (Germany, Scandinavia, Austria): the state is more than the sum of its institutional parts and overlaps with associations, which may be included in state policies and perform a public role. The boundaries of the state are therefore more blurred.

These three general traditions are reflected in different models of intervention in industrial relations, but they are all inherently disputed and changing, rather than fixed conceptions. Most countries—especially those with less historical state continuity—involve hybrids between more forms, rather than precise models. Traditions of industrial relations research are themselves embedded in different state traditions (Frege 2007), and therefore researchers from different countries tend to use different concepts. Anglo-Saxon research is the one that most frequently confuses 'state' with 'government': in the USA in particular, by 'big government' what is meant is not a big White House, but a large public sector and a high degree of legal regulation. Employment relations studies have therefore tended to pay less attention to the state. Statist traditions are those where the direct bond between citizens and state is the strongest, with specific responsibilities on both sides. In France, the early universal right to vote gave prominent political relevance to social issues, and the *modèle républicain* refers not simply to a form of government, but to a form of social organization. In corporatist traditions, employment relations are inherently political, as demonstrated by the prominence of terms such as 'workplace constitution' and 'industrial *democracy*', and therefore they interact with the state, but exactly because of the blurred description, the latter is not so often considered on its own, unless in the role of public employer.[1]

The conception of the state is not simply a matter of traditions, but also of theoretical debate. With regard specifically to employment relations, three main 'classical' theoretical approaches have addressed states' role in industrial relations, which only in part overlap with the three traditions mentioned before.

(1) Pluralist: the employment relations' parties are employers and trade unions only; the state is external and neutral: if it tries to intervene, this will have negative distorting effects (e.g. politicization, bureaucracy, rigidity).

(2) Corporatist: employment relations *are* about politics, as they affect so many political outputs (order, growth, equality...), and therefore they are regulated according to different principles: state, markets, and, crucially, associations, which can share public responsibilities cooperatively.

(3) Marxist: employment relations are not simply a political matter: they are *the* political issue, i.e. a general conflict between labour and capital; therefore, the state cannot be external, neutral or cooperative: it either supports capital, or labour, and even when it does not interfere, it is not neutral, as in the saying 'if you don't intervene between the lion and the ox, you're not being neutral'.

These three broad approaches have been contested, evolving, and diversifying. A variety of institutionalist theories, including historical institutionalism and the varieties of capitalism (VOC) approach (Hall and Soskice 2001), share some assumptions with the corporatist school, but either downgrade the importance of cooperation, or bring to the fore relations between firms rather than between associations. Debates have been particularly lively in the Marxist field, which has gradually combined with approaches previously defined as 'radical'. The original, economically deterministic Marxist conception of the state as instrument of class dominance has been in different ways nuanced and altered. Clearly, the state does not always defend the immediate interests of the dominant class: quite often, it constrains them to defend the existing social order (Poulantzas 1968). If this is the case, it must have a degree of autonomy, and social democrats have inferred that it may be a contested terrain between classes, especially in the sphere of distribution (Esping-Andersen 1985). On the other side, critical theorists, in particular the Frankfurt School, have underlined the 'control' (rather than simply coercion) of the state, in particular through the legitimation of social order and the incorporation of the working class. The French regulation school makes a similar point when seeing the Fordist state's role in absorbing class struggle through a combination of domination and socialization. The idea of a distinction, rather than autonomy, between political and economic power, has been further elaborated by neo-Marxists in the 'new class struggles' approach (Clarke 1991).

Following Weber, social scientists, while disagreeing on the functions of the state, have converged towards a definition of it as a 'political *apparatus* ruling over a given territory, whose authority is backed by a legal system and by the capacity to use force and the monopoly over it'. This is at the same time broad (open-ended on the functions) and narrow (focused on the political and the apparatus or organization), but allows us to distinguish the object from 'government' as the *process* of making and enforcing political decisions.

Roles in Employment Relations

The analysis of the state is made complicated by the variety of ways in which it may affect employment relations (Bordogna and Cella 1999; Traxler 1999, 2003). Hence, the paradox of periods of supposedly 'laissez-faire' free market policies (such as in the 1980s, especially in the UK and USA) coinciding with the strongest state interventions in industrial relations (through anti-strike interventions, anti-union laws, strict monetarist policies...).

The main categories of government intervention can be listed as follows:

(1) *Substantive binding rules dictating terms of employment and working conditions.* The state can make sure that certain aspects of the employment relations should not be left to the 'free will' of the parts to regulate. The first historical example in the nineteenth century was the working time of children and women, but since then the same argument—that certain employment conditions are politically intolerable even if accepted by the parts—has been applied to a growing variety of issues, from occupational health and safety to the minimum wage.

(2) *Setting the rules-of-the-game for industrial relations.* The state may decide that setting substantial employment conditions should be left to the autonomy of the parts, but at the condition that the parts follow rules that guarantee balanced negotiations. The aim of the state is to avoid specific problems: excessive employer power over individual employees (the 'monopsony' on specific labour markets, to be reduced through the right of association and collective bargaining), information asymmetries (hence legal requirements on the form of the employment contract), and excessive use of force (hence the regulation of strikes and lock-outs). Besides collective employment relations (trade union recognition, information and consultation, collective bargaining rules, etc.), a prominent aspect of this is employment protection legislation insofar as it determines how the parts can modify or rescind the employment contract: strict employment protection tends to foster the bargaining power of employees.

(3) *Indirect support to interest groups.* Besides setting the rules of the game, the state may interfere with the game itself by providing indirect support to the players (or, conversely, withdrawing previous support). The general aim here is to ensure that the bargaining sides have the capacities to perform their role, especially in terms of organization, representativeness, and public responsibility. Forms of indirect support include access to government bodies, involvement in administration of public functions, the indirect granting of organizational monopoly through links with compulsory associations (such as the chambers of commerce and chambers of labour), subsidies, funding of projects, and inclusion in policy-making. A form of indirect support that has been the object of extensive analysis in trade union research is the so-called 'Ghent system' through which countries like Belgium, Sweden, and Denmark involve trade unions in the provision of public unemployment insurance, thereby boosting their membership. The forms of indirect support are often, however, less than transparent and are the object of charges of clientelism and even corruption.

(4) *Provisions of collective goods.* The state may affect to great extents the exchange between employers and employees by providing collective goods. The logic

behind it is that the market may have inherent limitations in the provision of certain goods, either because of the shortage of information and rationality (e.g. on social security) or because of opportunistic behaviour (e.g. on skills). The study of employment relations has long treated the welfare state as something separate and external, but there are three very important reasons why this state function should be integrated. First, the provision of collective goods removes items from the bargaining agenda between employers and trade unions: for instance, pensions and health insurance are prominent collective bargaining topics in the USA but not in most countries of Western Europe, where they are left to the political realm. Second, as argued by Esping-Andersen (1990), the welfare state has a crucial role in the partial 'decommodification' of labour (by providing living resources independently from the market), and therefore alters the nature of the employment relationship itself; most directly, it provides a 'social wage' and a lower floor to employment conditions. Finally, the nature of the welfare state has major gender effects, through the reallocation of care work and therefore the promotion of female employment: industrial relations, household gender relations, and the welfare state are interdependent arenas of exchanges, operating like communicating vessels in the regulation of gendered employment systems (O'Reilly and Spee 1998; O'Reilly 2006).

(5) *Direct behaviour as employer in public sector.* In all industrialized countries, the state is the largest single employer. Precise measurement is difficult because the definition of public sector employee varies country by country, and the practices of outsourcing and public–private partnerships in recent decades have made the boundaries between public and private sectors more blurred. According to the OECD, in 2008, 15% of the labour force in OECD countries was employed in general government (unchanged since 2000) and 4% in public corporations (−0.6 since 2000); the average hides variation from a total of 34.5% for Norway to 8.1% for Japan. In any case, such a number of employees means that the behaviour of the state as an employer necessarily has a macroeconomic and social impact on the labour market as a whole, even if many public sector jobs do not have direct equivalents in the private sector. For most of the twentieth century, industrialized states have tended to behave as 'model employers' with specific policies, although this distinctiveness has been eroded since the 1980s by ideas such as 'New Public Management' (Bordogna 2008), and subsequently, with the economic crisis, there has been a shift towards unilateralism and centralization (EC 2013).

(6) *Macroeconomic management.* This is a much broader role, whose analysis requires going beyond employment relations studies, but which cannot be neglected. Not only areas such as fiscal, industrial, and monetary policy directly affect the labour market (restrictive monetary policies are deemed to 'discipline' labour), but they are in fact connected with developments in collective bargaining. The macroeconomic role of the state, after a period when it was deemed to have declined, has re-emerged strongly during the Western economic crisis that

started in 2008, and in connection with the rise of so-called state capitalism in China. It is important to notice that the state's macroeconomic role is as significant in so-called liberal market economies as in the coordinated and state-led ones, only it is, under normal circumstances, less visible. During 2008/9, the governments' stimulus packages in liberal countries such as UK and USA amounted to around 80% of GDP, as against only around 20% in supposedly less liberal countries like France and Germany (data: IMF), which, with a stronger welfare state, required less emergency intervention.

Explaining Differences: State Political Traditions

A variety of approaches has been used to explain differences in the state role in employment relations. The main distinction is between economy- and politics-focused approaches.

An example of an economistic approach is the analysis of modes of industrialization (Kassalow 1969). In countries where industrialization occurred early and largely spontaneously, through private enterprise and within free trade, the state remained relatively external to the employment relations, that is, affecting it only indirectly. The main example is that of the UK, where not only employers, but also employee organizations developed a characteristic mistrust towards state intervention, which would only diminish in the late twentieth century. By contrast, in countries where industrialization occurred later, it generally needed support from the state, especially through protectionist tariffs for the time required before international competitiveness could be reached. In such situations, employers and employees looked at the state as primary decision-maker and employment relations became politicized or tied to administrative decisions.

From a more political perspective, the evolution of state traditions and their implications for employment relations have been analysed by Crouch (1993), who, in line with corporatist theory, focused on power-sharing between state and associations. Crouch argues that where pre-industrialization traditions of guilds' adopting a regulatory role has not been interrupted (mostly in Central Europe), corporatism still prevails. By contrast, in countries where guilds never existed (USA) or were disrupted by free trade (UK), reciprocal indifference between associations and state prevails, while where they were repressed by the state (as in France), reciprocal aversion emerged. In addition, Crouch identifies an explanatory role in the relations between state and the church. Where relations were competitive (typically, in Catholic countries, because of the tensions between the state as national power and the Catholic Church as supranational source of power), deep ideological divisions and pluralism of competing trade union organizations emerged in the labour movement, unlike in Protestant countries where state and church were more peacefully integrated. Some accounts of the labour movements focus even more than Crouch on politics. Lipset's for instance, focuses on the effects of political and social citizenship on the kind of labour movement that emerges: where social citizenship rights are conceded early, trade unions became less radical and more pragmatic, as in Germany (Lipset 1981).

It should be added that Marxist and post-Marxist approaches in employment relations, although very influential, have tended to neglect the state and the national level of comparison. For instance, in labour process theory the focus is on capitalism as one system, and on the dynamics of employer strategies and labour resistance. In such a framework, national institutions are of secondary importance, as put by Thompson: 'national models [...] spend too much time on the variety and not enough on the capitalism' (Thompson 2010: 12). This contrasts with Marxist extensive elaboration on the state in history and political economy.

The relevance of these theoretical approaches can be illustrated by contrasting four European countries known as representative of different 'industrial relations types', even though national typologies have a number of shortcomings (Bechter et al. 2012) and national models, as we will discuss, change significantly over time (see Table 27.1).

In the UK, the state provides a framework for the functioning of the market (common law), whereas industrial relations are independently and voluntarily (*voluntarism*) regulated by employers and employees through collective agreements (which are not legally enforceable). According to Kassalow, this is due to early industrialization, which paved the road to the emergence of trade unions as craft organizations based on skills and market power, sceptical about ideology and state intervention. According to Crouch, without dismissing economic factors, the explanation is rather to be searched in political and ideological developments that took place before and alongside industrialization: the decline of the guilds since 1750, their abolition in 1835, the Combination Acts of 1799 that forbade trade unions, and finally the Trade Union Act of 1871 that defined trade union freedoms as 'negative' exceptions to common laws, rather than as positive rights.

More recent developments in the UK can also be looked at through a different lens. Economically, the shift to the service economy in the 1980s was more marked than elsewhere, and resulted in a more dramatic decline of union density and collective bargaining coverage. But politically, British industrial relations are deeply marked by political shifts, starting from the creation of the National Health Service and the Beveridgean welfare state in the aftermath of the Second World War, and including attempts at state-sponsored coordinated wage determination in the 1960–70s, before Margaret Thatcher's use of state power to bring union power under control (Howell 2007). Under the New Labour government, a broader set of regulations were introduced, such as the Employment Relations Act of 1999 and the introduction of the minimum wage. Still, the political system concentrates power into the executive, leaving it clearly separate from the society, and the degree of consultation with organized interests is limited.

The political role of the state is even clearer in the case of France, which would be difficult to understand on mere economic and employment relations accounts. Since the French Revolution and Napoleonic reforms, which abolished the *ancien régime* based on feudal hierarchies, the state has been suspicious of any cultural or economic groups

Table 27.1 State roles in selected European countries

Type of state intervention	UK (pluralism)	France (statism)	Germany (soft corporatism)	Sweden (social-democracy)	Italy (micro-corporatism)
Statutory regulation of working conditions	Low—increasing Health and safety; no working time regulation until 1998; Wages Councils in the 1970s, later abolished; minimum wage since 1999	Very high Health and safety; working time; minimum wage	Medium Juridification (*Verrechtligung*) Proposals of minimum wages	Medium Rarely necessary given the strength and high coverage of collective bargaining	Medium-low No minimum wage; little working time regulations until 1998
Rules-of-the-game setting	Low Thatcher limited strike freedom and introduced negative union freedom; soft union recognition regulations; voluntary mediation	High Statutory union recognition and attribution of representative status*; enforcement *erga omnes* of collective agreements; obligatory mediation; few strike restrictions [*reformed in 2008]	Medium Juridification (*Verrechtligung*) 'Workplace constitution' (*Betriebsverfassungsgesetz*) strike restrictions; but non-intervention in collective bargaining (*Tarifautonomie*)	Medium Official union recognition; strike restrictions; voluntary mediation	Medium Workplace trade union rights (*Statuto dei Lavoratori*); no strike restrictions; court-based enforcement *erga omnes* of collective agreements Strict employment contract regulation
Support to associations	Very low Corporatism dismissed as 'beer and sandwiches at Downing Street'; some indirect funding	Medium Involvement in some welfare-state administrative bodies	High Important official public role (e.g. *Berufsgenossenschaften*)	High Ghent system Involvement in central concertation until 1990	Medium Involvement in some welfare-state administrative bodies and in political concertation
Provision of collective goods	Low NHS	High State-led vocational training, inclusive health care and pension system	High Vocational training co-managed with employer associations and trade unions	High Welfare state, investment in R&D, support to female employment	Low Some local-level initiatives
Distinctive role as public employer	Low Specific social model in the 1960–70s; Thatcher used public companies in the fight against unions; broad-scale privatization; public–private partnerships	High Specific responsibility as 'model employer'	High Clear status distinction of *Beamte*	High	High In the 1980s, distinctive 'Prodi' approach to industrial relations; later distinctive regulations progressively reduced

which could promote particular interests and undermine equality among citizens, as with the *lois Chapelier* of 1791 banning any sort of craft association. The importance of the state and politics and late industrialization meant that the labour movement—unlike in Britain and North America—organized first politically, and only later in the form of trade unions. The contrast with Britain is apparently ideological, but the ideologies reflect institutional forces, such as elitist management education in meritocratic *grandes écoles* of Napoleonic origin (Gallie 1983). The tradition of mistrust by the state towards interest associations still endures. In the inaugural speech of his 2012 election campaign, President Nicolas Sarkozy directly attacked the 'intermediary bodies' such as trade unions that stand in the way of the direct relationship between president and citizens.

The resulting role of the French state in employment relations is distinctively direct, not only in the regulation of employment conditions (e.g. working time), but also as interference in collective bargaining. First, the state decides which organizations are 'representative': from 1966 until 2013, this meant a 'presumption of representativeness' for five specific confederations, on merely political grounds (opposition to German occupation during the war) and regardless of membership.[2] Second, it supervises and mediates the signing of sector-level agreements, and obligates employers to bargain at the company level (*Auroux laws* of 1982), determining even some of the bargaining agenda, as with the obligation, since 2001, to negotiate regularly on gender equality. Third, it imposes the content of sectoral collective agreements on all companies and employees in the sector, whether they are members of the signing associations or not. Fourth, the state may even 'enlarge' sector agreements to other sectors.

In Germany, industrialization occurred late and was strongly defended and supported by the state, which was not, however, acting alone. In Germanic Central Europe, trade and craft associations have a longer and more continuous history: they have played an important public role in regulating the economy since the Middle Ages. In addition, after the Second World War the West German state was rebuilt in such a way that would make arduous the re-emergence of totalitarianism: a complex balance of power among different institutions (balance central/regional governments, two chambers of parliament with equal powers, proportional representation, an influential constitutional court, strong institutions like the Bundesbank and the Chambers of Commerce) was created. Within this 'dispersal' of power, economic associations are very important: they are involved in negotiating public policies and may play public roles, for instance in the organization of the important vocational education system.

The German state regulates employment relations through an extensive use of legislative measures (*Verrechtligung*—juridification), but does not interfere in collective bargaining (*Tarifautonomie*—bargaining autonomy). Recent debates and proposals for a minimum wage (introduced in some marginal sectors not effectively covered by collective bargaining, and proposed for the whole economy) indicate a possible shift in regulatory model.

In Sweden, industrialization occurred late and was led by few large companies protected by the state. The concentration of capital produced centralization of labour and eventually a centralized employment relations system, but only after an important political founding event, the Basic Agreement of 1938 defining the collaboration between a Social Democratic-led state and the industrial relations actors, which was then extended in the 1950s. That agreement came after decades of class struggles, and was forced upon employers by the threat of direct legislation by the newly elected Social Democratic government (Fulcher 1991; Therborn 1987). The compromise evolved to include macroeconomic centralized concertation and a large welfare state, reducing employee insecurity and in particular promoting female employment. Given the strength of self-regulation through collective bargaining, the direct role of the state in employment relations remained limited, although important social legislation was introduced in the 1970s. While economic factors are clear in the Swedish case, the strength of organization, according to Crouch, is also due to the fact that guilds, when abolished in the mid-nineteenth century, were immediately replaced by new legally recognized craft associations, showing an enduring state preference for organized capitalism.

Tensions in the Swedish system emerged in 1975–91, with the abandonment of macro-level concertation. After attempts at restoring it in the 1990s, the election of a right-wing government in 2006 started a process of gradual retrenchment of the welfare state. Internationalization, through offshoring and immigration started requiring regulatory changes, for instance to deal with the problem of 'posted workers' from Eastern Europe (Woolfson et al. 2010).

This short overview of the best-known European national systems points at the importance of political traditions, but also at their evolution and possibility of change. If state traditions were at the centre of Crouch's analysis in 1993, by the 2000s the attention of institutional analysis had shifted to the problem of change, something the VOC theory had particular problems accounting for. Crouch's response was to point at the role of 'institutional entrepreneurs' in 'recombining governance' and reshaping state institutions, as in the case of Thatcher in the UK in the 1980s and of foreign investors in Hungary in the 1990s (Crouch 2005).

The Shared Space between State and Associations

The evolution of corporatism is a particularly interesting test of the role of the state in employment relations and its change over time. Corporatism has been defined as a system of regulation in which the state actively promotes the association strength of trade unions and employers, and shares public responsibilities with them (Schmitter 1974). Within corporatism, associations are given a quasi-legal political status and a prescriptive right to speak for their segments of the population, influencing the process of government directly and bypassing the parliament. The corporatist state shares the public space with the organized groups of civil society, who become *Ordnungsfaktoren* (factors of order) and *staatstragende Kräfte* (state-supporting powers) (Crouch 1993: 6). In the 1970s and 1980s a stream of research engaged in measurements of degrees of corporatism, usually putting Austria at the top, followed by Scandinavian countries and Germany. Interestingly, corporatism appeared associated with small, ethnically homogeneous states, where associations can more easily achieve encompassing representation than in large, heterogeneous ones (most typically, the USA).

From the 1990s, in Europe a new wave of apparent corporatist practice emerged in Europe in countries that were not on those previous lists. Southern European countries started signing tripartite 'social pacts', often driven by the necessity to pass swift reforms to meet the requirements of the Economic and Monetary Union (EMU). At the same time, post-communist countries of Central and Eastern Europe introduced tripartite institutions under the influence of the ILO and, to a lesser extent, the EU. Initially, this development was greeted as a new long wave of corporatism (Schmitter and Grote 1997) and as a sign that new forms of corporatism, without traditional prerequisites such as unitary trade unions, were possible (Regini 1997). However, later analysis revealed that the kind of governance provided by social pacts and by new tripartite institutions fell too short of corporatist standards to be placed in the same category: in particular, they were not sufficiently institutionalized and therefore lacked continuity and stability (Advagic et al. 2011). According to Kelly and Hamann (2010), social pacts were mostly driven by contingent political factors and notably weak parliamentary majorities and strong electoral competition. Tripartism in Central Eastern Europe was even feebler, and attracted the label of 'illusory corporatism' (Ost 2000). Table 27.2 indicates the functional and institutional conditions met by countries that signed social pacts: political factors were more frequently associated with social pacts than economic functional imperatives, and institutionally, the most important condition was the pre-existence of multi-employer collective bargaining, although in Central Eastern Europe there have been some weak pacts without it (Poland 1993 and Hungary 2004 in particular).

THE NON-RETREAT OF THE STATE: TRANSNATIONAL CHALLENGES

In the 1990s, the globalization discourse was often associated with the thesis of a 'retreat of the state' (Strange 1996). This appeared to be premature: what was happening was rather a shifting, but by no means less important, form of activity of the state, involving more actors and more international links, and actively contributing to globalization rather than being undermined by it (Jessop 2002; Levy 2006; Le Galès 2012).

The Western economic crisis that started in 2008, following increased concerns with security in the aftermath of the 9/11 terrorist attacks, has restored the visibility of the state. The *amount* of impact was nearly unprecedented in terms of public intervention, with stimulus packages, monetary interventions, and the nationalization of banks. At

Table 27.2 Factors associated with social pacts in Europe, 1990–2010

Feature	Old EU member states	New EU member states
Functional		
Need to control inflation (especially wage inflation)	Italy, Ireland, Finland	
Need to control public deficit	Italy, Spain, Portugal, Greece	
Need to reform the pension system reforms	Italy, Spain, Greece	Slovenia
Privatizations	Italy, Greece	Poland
Labour market reforms	Italy, Spain, Greece, Finland	
Institutional		
Multi-employer collective bargaining	Italy, Finland, Spain, Portugal, Greece, Ireland	Slovenia
Politically divided unions	Italy, Portugal, Greece, Spain	Poland, Slovenia, Hungary
Previous experiences of tripartite negotiations	Italy, Finland, Spain, Portugal, Greece	
Political		
Risk of social unrest, strikes	Italy, Ireland, Spain, Portugal, Greece	Poland
National consensus on need to introduce the euro	Italy, Ireland, Spain, Portugal, Greece	Slovenia
Weak government coalitions	Italy, Ireland, Spain, Portugal, Greece	Hungary
Democratic processes (e.g. union referenda)	Italy, Ireland	

the same time, the process of deregulation that had led to the crisis, the rising public debt crisis, and the patchy attempts at reforms and re-politicization afterwards, raised new questions as to the capacity of modern states to regulate the economy, as well as to their democratic nature (Engelen et al. 2011; Crouch 2011; Schäfer and Streeck 2013).

Also the *forms* of activity indicated the renewed importance of state traditions. While before 2008 some had argued that the German 'model' had long disappeared under the pressure of capitalist logic (Streeck 2009), the immediate reaction to the crisis on the labour market recurred to some traditional corporatist practices, in particular through the rapid negotiation of shorter working hours, financially supported by the state. These practices were not a pure repetition of former corporatism: the content of exchanges was different and probably less sustainable, and attracted the label of 'crisis corporatism' (Lehndorff 2011). Still, it was markedly different from the reaction of countries without that tradition. Although in the UK working time was shortened as well, and some observed that British employers behaved as if a short working hour scheme existed, in fact the different contribution of the state produced different effects and is telling of how states are marked by their traditions. In Germany, the state compensated financially for collectively agreed working time reduction, resulting in more consensual change and in a lesser impact on earnings and therefore on internal demand. In Britain, the cost of shorter working hours fell nearly entirely on the shoulders of employees, and was accompanied by a fall of earnings, internal demand, and even productivity. Tellingly, the Brown government did consider passing legislation to introduce a short working time system similar to the German one. However, the plan was quickly dismissed because of the fear that employers would abuse the system by reducing working hours on paper and paying employees cash in hand for the extra hours: while this risk exists in Germany as well, the risk is considered limited there because of the strength of corporatist governance and associational control, something missing in Britain.[3] The case of Central Eastern Europe is also telling. Poland, under direct influence of German investors, introduced short working hours laws similar to the German one. Their implementation was, however, mostly limited to foreign-controlled manufacturing, because in other companies there were no representative structures, nor social dialogue traditions, for the employers to negotiate the necessary working time changes. In other words, corporatist solutions require traditions and cannot be reproduced overnight in countries with different political histories, as seen in the case of 'social pacts'.

In relation to globalization, the supposed retreat of the state can be analysed in relation to the influence of transnational forces, such as multinational companies, migration, and supranational institutions (Meardi 2012a).

The fast rise of foreign direct investment (FDI) following financial liberalization and the fall of capitalism (sevenfold between 1990 and 2011) led to the perception of multinational capital as 'footloose', forcing states to engage in a 'race to the bottom' and 'regime shopping'. In 2010, for the first time ever, FDI inflows in developing countries, which 20 years previously were a marginal amount, exceeded those into developed economies (UNCTAD). Some quantitative studies did identify a preference for lower labour standards among investors (Cooke 2001). However, more recent studies indicated that within a macromarket like the EU, the availability of lower labour standards in countries with market access to richer neighbours has not become a significant factor in FDI flows (Brandl et al. 2010).

Qualitative research has identified a number of occurrences where multinationals attempt to impact national employment relations systems. This is particularly visible in countries more dependent on foreign sources for capital investment, such as the post-communist ones: in Central Eastern Europe, large investors have often let local authorities know their preferences for lower labour costs and deregulated labour markets. Even in Western Europe they have been vocal sometimes, but with rather limited effects. The American Chamber of Commerce in Germany criticized the works council reform of 2001, to no avail. Volkswagen and Ford in Spain had a centrally driven strategy of changing traditional employment relations, which was largely successful but only because concomitant with a generational change in Spanish trade unions (Hauptmeier 2012): foreign capital and state path dependency interacted, rather than counteracting each other. When the American retailer Toys4You invested in Sweden in the 1990s, it tried to bypass collective bargaining, but union boycotts soon forced it to backtrack. Also in France, occasionally, US investors become vocal in their demands but, in a rather anti-American political environment, this generally backfires. In February 2013, for instance, the CEO of Titan International wrote a letter to French industry minister Montebourg to complain that 'the French so-called workers... don't work longer than 3 hours a day' and that the 'crazy French unions own the French government', (*Les Echos*, 19 February 2013) but attracted universal contempt. A more disruptive case of a multinational's impact on industrial relations is that of Fiat withdrawing, after threatening relocation, from sectoral collective bargaining and from the union representation system in Italy in 2010–12, when its CEO defined national regulations as 'folklore'; but even in this case, it appears that few Italian companies followed.

A review of multinationals and collective bargaining in the late 2000s in Europe revealed that in general, collective bargaining coverage of multinationals is at least as high as for national companies, and that generally foreign investors comply with the existing national system (Marginson and Meardi 2009). On a broader scale, the emerging evidence is that within globalization it is not FDI, but rather trade, that is responsible for worsening labour rights (Mosley 2011).

Labour mobility in the modern economy is inherently lower than capital mobility, and it has been more neglected in employment relations studies. Yet migration challenges in many ways the idea itself of the state's control over a territory and therefore the idea of national models (Ferrera 2005). For sociological theory, the 'stranger' offers a revealing perspective on host societies and actively defines its identity (Simmel 1917). With regard to social issues, the most debated impact is on the welfare state, but that impact is actually largely linked to other forms of migration than labour (e.g. refugees). Until now, the most generous welfare states, i.e. the Scandinavian, have coexisted with higher than average rates of immigration, suggesting that foreigners do not necessarily undermine social solidarity. Social rights remain rooted in national concepts of social citizenship (Evers and Guillemard 2013) and most industrialized countries have tended to extend labour rights to foreign nationals in order to prevent competition between two classes of workers. Nonetheless, in many countries migrants are concentrated in flexible working conditions and according to Standing (2011) have become a core component of new social class, the 'precariat', distinct from the established 'salariat'.

In terms of employment relations, immigrants have historically integrated into national structures, but also contributed to their change, as in the case of ideologically motivated labour militants from Europe to North and South America in the early twentieth century. Today, trade union membership amongst immigrants is broadly in line with that of nationals, with the exception of countries of very recent immigration like Spain (European Social Survey). Moreover, European trade unions have largely avoided exclusionary policies towards immigrants, and integrated them according to their national traditions. For instance, in recent years French unions have mobilized foreign undocumented workers in spectacular occupation strikes, to gain their regularization. Spanish and Italian trade unions have instead acted at the national level, through political pressure for generalized regularization, and at the local level through state-sponsored services for foreigners. German trade unions have stepped up their efforts to increase the share of foreigners in workplace representation, and to defend them better in collective bargaining and in access to apprenticeships; but after increasing labour market dualization and concomitant with the German labour market's opening to workers from the new EU member states, they also broke away from their traditional corporatist approach to wage setting and started campaigning for sectoral and national minimum wages. In the UK, unions' attitudes to migrants is shaped by the influence of racial equality and diversity management discourses, and campaigns have focused on community organizing and on wages, rather than on politics and on regularization.

The role of state traditions on migration is visible in the corporatist involvement of German unions in German migration policy (as in the Süssmuth commission of the early 2000s), their political pressure in France and especially Italy, and their exclusion in the UK. Interestingly, liberal traditions did not prevent a major unions–employers agreement on immigration policy in the USA in 2013. This anomalous case indicates the importance of citizenship issues in the USA, in this sense similarly to France. State traditions do not matter merely with regard to employment relations (as defined by Crouch), but also with regard to citizenship and diversity.

In terms of immigration and citizenship regimes, different national models have been identified (Brubaker 1992; Schnapper 1992). Germany is a case of states based on the idea of community, in particular blood and language bonds, while France is based on the idea of an individual contract between citizen and state, rooted in the ideals of equality and freedom and excluding any role for cultural differences in the public space, and the UK has a community basis for citizenship, but as a multiple rather than unitary construct, given the four constituting nations (England, Scotland, Wales, and Ireland) and the colonial past that included 'home rule' for the colonies. Elective affinities appear to exist, therefore, between corporatism and communitarianism (Germany), between 'dirigiste' state and *laicité* in France, and between pluralism and multiculturalism in the UK: immigration is integrated into the same political traditions that have affected employment relations. There has been a degree of convergence in debates on multiculturalism in recent years, but different state frames are still relevant. In 2013, France is considering banning the use of religious symbols (such as the Islamic headscarf) in private companies, after having banned it in the public sector, something that is hardly conceivable in the UK, and corresponds to a stronger conception of the public realm (including employment) and scepticism towards any group distinctiveness, whether social or cultural.

More recently, a more sensitive form of labour movement than traditional migration has occurred through the movement of services within the EU, leading to conflicts in the construction and transport sectors. In four high-profile rulings (Laval, Viking, Rüffert, and Luxembourg cases in 2007 and 2008) the European Court of Justice established that the freedom of movement of enterprises may take priority over national regulations such as collective bargaining and the right to strike (Dølvik and Visser 2011). Cases of severe abuse of posted workers' rights have been reported across the EU (Cremers 2011).

Responses have been quite different country by country, with the negotiation of sectoral minimum wages in Germany, and stricter legal regulations and inspections in Spain, but overall this is one of the transnational phenomena that national regulations struggle the most to control.

Despite pervasive debates around globalization, the impact of international organizations on labour relations has received little attention in employment relations. Institutional scholars have long highlighted that international organizations can have a 'negative' and 'market-making' effect on industrial relations, but hardly a 'positive' and 'market-correcting' one (Streeck 1995). In the case of the EU, arguably the international organization with the strongest 'social dimension', confirmation comes from the very humble transfer of social regulations to the new member states after 2004 (Meardi 2012b). To critics, intergovernmental economic organizations are essentially ways to, in line with Hayek's thought, remove economic governance from the national democratic level to ring-fence it in international treaties and technocratic governance (Höpner and Schäfer 2007).

While traditional EU policies in the area of employment (whether 'hard' in the form of Directives, or 'soft' in terms of coordination) may have had little effect, the sovereign debt crisis that started in 2010 has increased the interference of supranational institutions over national industrial relations on the countries that needed either bailouts, or European Central Bank intervention on sovereign bonds' secondary market. Following the sovereign debt crisis, the EU, and more specifically the eurozone, have introduced stronger economic governance tools since the beginning of the crisis: a 'European semester' of scrutiny over national budgets, the so-called 'Six-Pack' regulations on preventing macroeconomic imbalances, which include a reference to unit labour costs, and a European Fiscal Pact enforcing tougher budget discipline (Erne 2012). Two rather radical policy proposals have been particularly important for the European institutions since 2010 within the 'Europe 2020 Agenda'. First, under wage setting policies, the promotion of 'new wage setting frameworks in order to contribute to the alignment of wage and productivity growth at sector/company level' (European Commission 2012), i.e. the decentralization of collective bargaining. Second, the liberalization of employment protection through a flexible 'single open-ended contract' that would overcome labour market segmentation, which was proposed in the 'Agenda for New Skills and Jobs' (European Commission 2010). As a result, Italy and Spain passed deeper reforms in a few months of 2011–12 under pressure from the European Central Bank, than over the previous 20 years. If fully enforced (which is still far from certain), by decentralizing collective bargaining, liberalizing employment protection, and raising the retirement age, the reforms would produce a systemic change in the so-called 'Mediterranean' employment and social model (Meardi 2014). The fact that reforms were driven by external pressure also wrong-footed the trade unions, which found their traditional industrial action weapons ineffective and their national political compromises precarious.

CONCLUSION

The state has come back as a particularly complicated, and eminently political, institution in employment relations. In theoretical terms, this requires a reshifting both from pluralist employment relations approaches, and from certain institutionalist approaches like the 'varieties of capitalisms' one, that had not paid much attention to it. Historical institutionalism, as a broad stream with linkages to political economy and political sociology, has been so far the approach with more systematic consideration of the state, and of how it is conditioned by its traditions but also keeps changing. Studies of national business systems are also giving increased attention to states (Morgan and Whitley 2012).

After 20 years of globalization, it is increasingly clear that states are co-authors of it rather than victims. While there have been numerous alarmed accounts of the effects of multinationals, migration, and international organizations, in reality these forces have actually combined with national institutional developments. In short, states affect employment relations in increasingly numerous, and no less important, ways than in the past. Some recent tensions, on movement of services, on international supervision of indebted countries, and on some multinationals' strategies, however, are still unresolved and might contribute to significant change.

The link between state and employment relations is not in one direction only. The inherently political nature of employment relations makes it an important (some Marxists would say *the most* important) source of change for states themselves. Recently, Palier and Thelen (2010) have provided an innovative account of labour market dualization in France and Germany, a process itself linked to the globalization pressures discussed in this chapter. Against neo-classical arguments that trade unions and institutions, by protecting insiders, foster dualization, they argue that the opposite is true. Trade union decline and collective bargaining reforms were the conditions for labour market reforms that entrenched dualization, and later on welfare state reforms that increased inequality. The original driver, therefore, was the sphere of employment relations, whose change affects subsequently the sphere of state policy.

Recent developments call for more analyses of this kind, at the interconnection between employment relations and state policies, and just as employment relations require a deeper attention to the state, policy and politics require a deeper attention to employment relations.

NOTES

1. When in 2010, the German Industrial Relations Association and the journal *Industrielle Beziehungen* organized a congress and a special issue around the topic of 'The state and employment', the predominant topic of submissions was on the public sector (Alewell 2011).

2. In 2013, a new system based on works council elections votes was introduced, which eventually only confirmed the representativeness of the same five organizations.
3. Public funding for working time reduction was introduced in Wales, whose industrial structure and associational landscape are somehow closer to the German.

References

Advagic, S., Rhodes, M., and Visser, J. (eds.) (2011). *Social Pacts in Europe: Emergence, Evolution, and Institutionalization.* Oxford and New York: Oxford University Press.

Alewell, D. (2011). 'Einleitung zum Themenheft "Staat und Erwerbsarbeit"', *Industrielle Beziehungen*, 18(1–2): 7–10.

Bechter, B., Brandl, B., and Meardi, G. (2012). 'Sectors or Countries? Typologies and Levels of Analysis in Comparative Industrial Relations', *European Journal of Industrial Relations*, 18(3): 185–202.

Bordogna, L. (2008). 'Moral Hazard, Transaction Costs and the Reform of Public Service Employment Relations', *European Journal of Industrial Relations*, 14(4): 381–400.

Bordogna, L. and Cella, G. (1999). 'Admission, Exclusion, Correction: The Changing Role of the State in Industrial Relations', *Transfer*, 5(1–2): 14–33.

Brandl, B., Strohmer, S., and Traxler, F. (2010). 'US Foreign Direct Investment, Macro Markets and Labour Relations', *Industrial Relations Journal*, 41(6): 622–38.

Brubaker, R. (1992). *Citizenship and Nationhood in France and Germany.* Cambridge, MA: Harvard University Press.

Clarke, S. (ed.) (1991). *The State Debate.* Basingstoke: Macmillan.

Cooke, W. (2001). 'The Effects of Labour Costs and Workplace Constraints on Foreign Direct Investment amongst Highly Industrialised Countries', *International Journal of Human Resource Management*, 12(5): 697–716.

Cremers, J. (2011). *In Search of Cheap Labour in Europe.* Brussels: International Books.

Crouch, C. (1993). *Industrial Relations and European State Traditions.* Oxford and New York: Oxford University Press.

—— (2005). *Capitalist Diversity and Change: Recombinant Governance and Institutional Entrepreneurs.* Oxford and New York: Oxford University Press.

—— (2011). *The Strange Non-Death of Neo-Liberalism.* Cambridge: Polity Press.

Dølvik, E. and Visser, J. (2011). 'Free Movement, Equal Treatment and Workers' Rights: Can the European Union Solve its Trilemma of Fundamental Principles?', *Industrial Relations Journal*, 40(6): 491–509.

Engelen, E. et al. (2011). *After the Great Complacence: Financial Crisis and the Politics of Reform.* Oxford and New York: Oxford University Press.

Erne, R. (2012). *European Unions: Labor's Quest for a Transnational Democracy.* Ithaca: ILR Press.

Esping-Andersen, G. (1985). *Politics against Markets.* Princeton: Princeton University Press.

—— (1990). *The Three Worlds of Welfare Capitalism.* Cambridge: Polity Press.

European Commission (EC) (2010). *An Agenda for New Skills and Jobs.* Strasbourg: Communication of the European Commission.

—— (2012). *Wage Setting Systems and Wage Developments.* Brussels: European Commission. Available at <http://ec.europa.eu/europe2020/pdf/themes/wage_settings.pdf>.

—— (2013). *Industrial Relations in Europe 2012.* Brussels: European Commission.

Evers, A. and Guillemard, A. (eds.) (2013). *Social Policy and Citizenship: The Changing Landscape*. Oxford and New York: Oxford University Press.

Ferrera, M. (2005). *The Boundaries of Welfare*. Oxford and New York: Oxford University Press.

Frege, C. (2007). *Employment Research and State Traditions: A Comparative History of Britain, Germany, and the United States*. Oxford and New York: Oxford University Press.

Fulcher, J. (1991). *Labour Movements, Conflict and State: Conflict and Cooperation in Britain and Sweden*. Oxford and New York: Oxford University Press.

Gallie, D. (1983). *Social Inequality and Class Radicalism in France and Britain*. Cambridge: Cambridge University Press.

Hall, P. A. and Soskice, D. (eds.) (2001). *Varieties of Capitalism: The Institutional Foundations of Comparative Advantage*. Oxford and New York: Oxford University Press.

Hardt, N. and Negri, A. (2000). *Empire*. Cambridge, MA: Harvard University Press.

Hauptmeier, M. (2012). 'Institutions are What Actors Make of Them: The Varying Construction of Firm-Level Employment Relations in Spain', *British Journal of Industrial Relations*, 50(4): 737–59.

Höpner, M. and Schäfer, A. (2007). 'A New Phase of European Integration: Organized Capitalisms in Post-Ricardian Europe'. MPIfG Discussion Paper 07/4. Cologne: Max Planck Institute for the Study of Societies.

Howell, C. (2007). 'The British Variety of Capitalism: Institutional Change, Industrial Relations and British Politics', *British Politics*, 2: 239–63.

Jessop, B. (2002). *The Future of the Capitalist State*. Cambridge: Polity Press.

Kassalow, E. M. (1969). *Trade Unions and Industrial Relations: An International Comparison*. New York: Random House.

Katzenstein, P. (1987). *Policy and Politics in West Germany: The Growth of a Semi-Sovereign State*. Philadelphia: Temple University Press.

Kelly, J. and Hamann, K. (2010). *Parties, Elections and Policy Reforms in Western Europe: Voting for Social Pacts*. London: Routledge.

Le Galès, P. (2012). 'States in Transition: Research about the State in Flux', in L. Burroni, M. Keune, and G. Meardi (eds.), *Economy and Society in Europe: A Relationship in Crisis*. Cheltenham: Edward Elgar, 100–23.

Lehndorff, S. (2011). 'Before the Crisis, in the Crisis, and Beyond: The Upheaval of Collective Bargaining in Germany', *Transfer*, 17(3): 341–54.

Levy, J. (ed.) (2006). *The State After Statism: New State Activities in the Age of Globalization and Liberalization*. Cambridge, MA: Harvard University Press.

Lipset, S. M. (1981). 'Radicalism or Reformism: The Sources of Working-Class Politics', *American Political Science Review* 77: 1–18.

Marginson P. and Meardi G. (2009), 'Multinational Companies and Collective Bargaining', Dublin: European Industrial Relations Observatory. Available at <http://www.eurofound.europa.eu/eiro/studies/tn0904049s/>.

Meardi, G. (2012a). 'Industrial Relations *after* European State Traditions?', in L. Burroni, M. Keune, and G. Meardi (eds.), *Economy and Society in Europe*. Cheltenham: Edward Elgar, 100–23.

—— (2012b). *Social Failures of EU Enlargement: A Case of Workers Voting with Their Feet*. London: Routledge.

—— (2014). 'Employment Relations under External Pressure: Italian and Spanish Reforms during the Great Recession', in M. Hauptmeier and M. Vidal (eds.), *The Comparative Political Economy of Work and Employment Relations*. Basingstoke: Palgrave Macmillan.

Morgan, G. and Whitley, R. (eds.) (2012). *Capitalisms and Capitalism in the Twenty-First Century*. Oxford and New York: Oxford University Press.

Mosley, L. (2011). *Labor Rights and Multinational Production*. Cambridge: Cambridge University Press.

O'Reilly, J. (2006). 'Framing Comparisons: Gendering Perspectives on Cross-National Comparisons of Welfare and Work', *Work, Employment & Society*, 20(4): 731–50.

O'Reilly, J. and Spee, C. (1998). 'The Future of Regulation of Work and Welfare: Time for a Revised Social and Gender Contract?', *European Journal of Industrial Relations*, 4(3): 259–81.

Ost, D. (2000). 'Illusory Corporatism in Eastern Europe: Neoliberal Tripartism and Postcommunist Class Identities', *Politics & Society*, 28(4): 503–30.

Palier, B. and Thelen, K. (2010). 'Institutionalizing Dualism: Complementarities and Change in France and Germany', *Politics & Society*, 38(1): 119–48.

Poulantzas, N. (1968). *Pouvoir politique et classes sociales de l'état capitaliste*. Paris: Maspéro.

Regini, M. (1997). 'Still Engaging in Corporatism? Recent Italian Experience in Comparative Perspective', *European Journal of Industrial Relations*, 3(3): 259–78.

Schäfer, A. and Streeck, W. (eds.) (2013). *Politics in the Age of Austerity*. Cambridge: Polity Press.

Schmitter, P. (1974). 'Still the Century of Corporatism?', *Review of Politics*, 36(1): 85–131.

Schmitter, P. and Grote, J. (1997). 'The Corporatist Sisyphus: Past, Present and Future', EUI SPS Working Paper 97/4.

Schnapper, D. (1992). *L'Europe des immigrés, essai sur les politiques d'immigration*. Paris: François Bourin.

Simmel, G. (1917). *Grundfragen der Soziologie*. Berlin: G. J. Göschen.

Standing, G. (2011). *The Precariat: The New Dangerous Class*. London: Bloomsbury.

Strange, S. (1996). *The Retreat of the State: The Diffusion of Power in the World Economy*. Cambridge: Cambridge University Press.

Streeck, W. (1995). 'Neo-Voluntarism: A New European Policy Regime', *European Law Journal*, 1(1): 31–59.

—— (2005). 'Industrial Relations: From State Weakness as Strength to State Weakness as Weakness. Welfare Corporatism and the Private Use of the Public Interest', in S. Green (ed.), *Governance in Contemporary Germany: The Semisovereign State Revisited*. Cambridge: Cambridge University Press, 138–64.

—— (2009). *Re-Forming Capitalism: Institutional Change in the German Political Economy*. Oxford and New York: Oxford University Press.

Therborn, G. (1987). 'Does Corporatism Really Matter?', *Journal of Public Policy*, 7(3): 259–84.

Thompson, P. (2010). 'The Capitalist Labour Process: Concepts and Connections', *Capital & Class*, 34(1): 7–14.

Traxler, F. (1999). 'The State in Industrial Relations: A Cross-National Analysis of Developments and Socioeconomic Effects', *European Journal of Political Research*, 36(1): 55–85.

—— (2003). 'Bargaining, State Regulation and the Trajectories of Industrial Relations', *European Journal of Industrial Relations*, 9(2): 141–61.

Woolfson, C., Thornqvist, C., and Sommers, J. (2010). 'The Swedish Model and the Future of Labour Standards after *Laval*', *Industrial Relations Journal*, 41(4): 333–50.

CHAPTER 28

....

UNIONS

Practices and Prospects

....

PETER FAIRBROTHER

INTRODUCTION—UNIONS: PURPOSES AND POSSIBILITIES

SINCE the late 1970s, the future of trade unions has been unclear. Unions have experienced the fallout from widespread restructuring and state reorganization. These measures included the refocusing of economies away from traditional, often mass-based industries to new industries, with dispersed workforces, casual employees, and so on; the persistence and expansion of informal economies in some parts of the world; and shifts in the balance of power towards employers in many industries. In the major liberal democracies, unions continue to face the challenges that derive from government embrace of a neo-liberal agenda, as occurred initially in the United States and the United Kingdom. Such an agenda has been promoted to other parts of the world by the principal international agencies, such as the World Bank and the International Monetary Fund (IMF). For unions, this has constituted a major challenge. In the advanced capitalist economies, union membership levels have declined dramatically, and there has been a narrowing of union interest and purpose (e.g. Fairbrother and Yates 2003). While there has been less comment and consideration of the challenges faced by unions in the former state-socialist societies and the changing societies of Africa, Asia, and South America, structural adjustment and transition are no less challenging for unions (see Pringle and Clarke 2011 on Russia, China, and Vietnam, and Hensman 2011 on India).

There are three aspects to these developments. First, there have been dramatic changes in the composition and organization of labour markets, with the introduction of flexible working arrangements, the reorganization of labour processes, and sectoral shifts particularly from manufacturing to the services. Second, unions have often failed to adapt to the recomposition and increased diversity of workforces, in terms of class, gender, ethnicity, and socio-cultural aspects. Third, the balance of power between employers and unions has shifted, towards employers. These developments have often been reinforced by the policies advocated and pursued by successive governments over the last 20 years.

In the changed circumstances of the 1980s in several advanced capitalist societies, many unions narrowed their interests and purpose, focusing on adaptation rather than alternatives (Freeman and Medoff 1984; MacInnes 1987). Nevertheless, the question remains whether and how unions can refocus their role and shape their purpose in a changing political economy (e.g. Kelly 1998; Hyman 2007). Recent debates about union futures have emphasized the question of union innovation (see, for example, Lévesque and Murray 2002, 2010, 2012). These analyses centre on the development of the capabilities and organizational forms that enable unions to address the challenges they face. Recently, the debate about union building has taken a further shift, from a focus on the definition and importance of capacity to union resources and their capabilities to build their capacity. Another way of furthering the debate is to consider the question of union purpose. The claim is that for unions to renew themselves they also have to address the question of purpose, not a straightforward process (Flanders 1970).

The first question to consider is that of union organization. For much of the recent history of trade unionism, organization has been the focus of debate within and about trade unions. These debates have taken place in many different settings and contexts. Although not always explicitly acknowledged, the foundation for union organization is the workplace, where members work and are employed. The second question concerns union capacities, the resources and their utilization by members in many different unions. These are not straightforward processes and work out in different ways in the workplace, at a national level, and transnationally. Finally the third question relates to union purpose, how unions frame and understand their goals and objectives. These three conceptual questions focus the analysis.

The argument in this chapter is that union innovation, particularly in relation to union renewal, can be examined through a three-part framework, with unions at the core. First, the foundation of trade unionism involves building a practice of collectivity. Over time, unions have forged ways of organizing and operating, shaped by and shaping the political, economic, and social context in which unions act. Second, while there is often a tension between the established ways that unions organize and operate, it is also the case that 'new' or distinctive forms of solidarity may be necessary to develop awareness and construct strategies to address economic and social change. Third, unions face tensions between the pursuit of goals related to 'vested interests' and/or 'social justice'. Such goals are defined by and formed in relation to the specific circumstances and contexts in which unions organize and operate.

THEORETICAL PREMISE

Trade unions are institutionally embedded within the social relations of production. How they organize and operate is shaped in relation to the complex of relations at the workplace level, where unions are embedded. Trade unions carry with them their histories and traditions and face particular sets of relations in different sectors and regions, according to the occupational composition of their memberships. With restructuring and the shifting relations between labour and capital there are no fixed patterns of organization and activity. On occasion, trade union memberships dissipate and the organizations wither in the face of the uncertainties of work and employment, as happened in New Zealand in the early 1990s, with the collapse of the New Zealand Clerical Workers' Union in 1991 and 1992 (Boxall and Haynes 1997; Easton 1997: 125–6). Others will reconstitute themselves and begin to organize in the light of such changing circumstances and conditions.

It is at the workplace that the coercive social relations of the capitalist labour process provide the crucial terrain of collective organization and class struggle, organized as a labour process at the immediate point of production (Braverman 1974; Brighton Labour Process Group 1977; Elger 1979). The collective character of the labour process, involving both cooperation between workers and coordination of the tasks of labour, provide the material basis for both collective organization, in the form of trade unions, as well as resistance, through trade union activity. But, this is also a dynamic relationship in that the way trade unions organize and operate is not only shaped by the labour process, but in turn moulds and fashions the particular configuration of the labour process. It is this struggle, between workers and managers, over employment conditions, the circumstances of work, the relations between manager and worker, individually and collectively, that constitute the social relations of the labour process.

Unions are organizations where representatives negotiate on behalf of the membership and where leaders represent this membership in a variety of fora, including political ones. They are independent organizations, collective bodies giving voice to workers within the employment relationship, as well as politically (cf. Müller-Jentsch 1988). This assumes that trade unions are organizational entities, which theoretically, at least, are distinct and separate from employers, including the state as employer (Fairbrother 1994). Of course, union leaderships may enter into alliances with state representatives as well as employers or be drawn into cooperative relationships at both employer and state level. Nonetheless, as wage labourers, subject to coercive and exploitative relations, workers have common class interests, although in practice the expression of such interests may be uneven and occur in diverse circumstances (Marx and Engels 1950 [1848]: 42). Workers are divided from each other and such differences make for very varied experiences and in some cases tenuous unionism (e.g. Braverman 1974; see also Grusky and Weeden 2001). This means that workers may join and participate in unions for a variety of motives, ranging from security of employment to solidaristic action with other workers.

In a recent study, McIlroy and Daniels (2009) address these themes in relation to the emergence of neo-liberal forms of governance. Their aim is to locate the way unions are shaped by and within the neo-liberal paradigm promoted by governments; for them the focus is on British trade unions under Conservative governments in the 1980s and 1990s and subsequent Labour governments. In a sustained analysis of this period, they (and their fellow contributors) locate unions in relation to the 'long Keynesian boom of capitalism' from 1945 onwards (McIlroy and Daniels 2009: 1). With the shift from the post-war social democratic period to the neo-liberal period, McIlroy and Daniels (2009) argue that the function and purpose of unions has been shaped to emphasize labour market openness, supply-side capacities (particularly via education and learning), and to promote one-sided sets of 'partnership' arrangements (McIlroy and Daniels 2009: 4). While collective organization has not been threatened it has been pushed in particular directions; the result is a compliant union movement. These authors conclude that unions face ongoing pressures between strategies for renewal, in relation to partnerships with employers (and governments). and taking steps towards promoting organizing campaigns and pursuing the goals of social justice.

Union Struggles

Trade unions organize, act, and respond to particular sets of relations in different sectors and regions. To illustrate, as the balance of power over the last three decades in many workplaces worldwide has shifted towards management, it has become difficult for union leaderships to represent their memberships in ongoing and regular ways. With restructuring and the shifting relations between labour and capital there can be no one fixed pattern of organization and activity. In these circumstances, unions have sought to renew themselves, to revitalize the way they organize and operate and re-evaluate their purpose in this changing environment (e.g. Lévesque and Murray 2002, 2010).

Challenges

During the 1980s and 1990s, trade unions in the Anglo-American states addressed major economic restructuring involving deindustrialization and state recomposition, reviewing both their representational and organizational bases. In the main, debates both within unions and about them centred on a distinction between organization and service. For many unions, 'organizing' and 'servicing' as the defining attributes of the way unions organize and operate, especially in relation to the connections between leaders and members, or union staff and the membership, became the reference for renewal (for more elaboration on this aspect, see Bronfenbrenner et al. 1998 on the USA; Carter 2004 on the UK; Oxenbridge 1997 on New Zealand; and Pocock 1998 on Australia).

More recently, after several decades of growth and economic militancy, unions across Western Europe suffered major defeats while, aided by neo-liberal deregulation, employers became increasingly assertive if not hostile. In Western Europe, this meant deteriorating terms and conditions of work and a growth of precarious employment. In the East, workers experienced a savage rupture in their work conditions, living standards, and futures. In most countries, trade union membership plummeted and workplace organization weakened.

Across Europe, economies have been liberalized, public sector companies privatized, others deregulated, and work conditions undermined. In the electricity and steel industries, for example, one-time national and generally publicly owned industries are now internationally competitive, mainly private companies, seeking to exploit the low waged industries in Eastern Europe. European Union (EU) directives stimulated the replacement of the economics of the provision of public goods (however distorted) with market-driven economics, reinforcing existing trends towards privatization and deteriorating pension and other rights across Europe.

While employers' strategies vary, generally they seek competitive advantage by imposing 'flexibility' on their workforces. At the same time, unions argue for and demand security of employment. In this context, the thrust of EU policy underwrites a primarily neo-liberal economic strategy, with unions left on the margins arguing for better jobs and greater social cohesion. Complementing these developments is an increasing tendency across all sectors towards outsourcing and offshore production and service delivery.

The composition of workforces in Europe and elsewhere is also changing, perhaps most sharply exemplified by economic migration. In many parts to the world, unions face specific challenges over migration, especially in its unprotected forms of asylum-seeking and people trafficking. Many large employers exploit labour migration, and the poverty and desperation that lie behind it, by using subcontractors. They employ migrants at low wages and make it difficult for unions to represent workers. Migration is leading to a reshaping of the workforce, and in much of Europe and North America this is exploited by the politics of xenophobia. Unions have often failed to challenge these politics in clear-cut and unambiguous ways.

Tensions

The ongoing tension faced by most unions is between forms of 'responsible' unionism and social movement unionism. Responsible unionism is a union form that can be characterized as 'business' unionism (in the case of liberal democracies), 'official unions' (in state-socialist societies), and versions of 'political unionism' (party-affiliated unions tied to political parties (in India and elsewhere). In this respect, unions operate within and adapt to state-sanctioned structures and modes of organization, where the focus is on the regulation of the labour markets via hours, wages, and conditions of work (e.g. Lind 2007 and Atzeni and Ghigliano 2007). Such unions are organized from the top-down, with an emphasis on 'responsible' leadership. At their most progressive, they provide a regulated voice in the workplace and a rising standard of living and ensure a moderate voice in national politics.

Social movement unionism, in contrast, is a union form that has the capacity to both recruit and mobilize workers. These unions challenge past legacies and in particular 'business unionism', 'official' unionism and the like, although these measures may be tentative and are often compromised. In these cases, leaders are likely to be more accountable and engaged than is often the case with responsible forms of unionism. The emphasis here is on bottom-up membership involvement, an ability to exercise their collective capacities and a willingness to question established routines and engage in direct forms of action, at least occasionally. The way such unions frame their narrative can be more confrontational and may be deemed by others as 'irresponsible'.

The question is how and under what circumstances can trade unions challenge and question the labour–capital relation. On the one hand, union strategies are shaped by economic and social change, institutional arrangements, and the 'immediate bargaining situation' in which they find themselves (on this type of analysis, see Botwinick 1993: 198–210). On the other hand, unions have agency and can begin to open up new agenda, framing challenges in distinctive ways that constitute a challenge to prevailing relations, as some of the recent actions by unions and their confederations have done in relation to 'green' jobs (Snell and Fairbrother 2010). Thus, while unions become institutionally embedded, indicated by characterizations of 'responsible/official' unionism, they also face pressures to open up new policy objectives or pursue old goals in new ways. Such trajectories are often contested both within and between unions.

The Importance of the Workplace

The capacities of union leaders and activists to organize and represent members are shaped by the conditions for union organization and action. Central to this is the relationship between local organization and activity and the broader purpose of labour unions as agents of change. In the 1970s, for example, working-class struggle rooted in the workplace seemingly had potential to facilitate social and political change. There appeared to be a moment when these struggles would open perspectives on capitalist relations in the advanced capitalist states that might enable challenges to the oppression and exploitation of these relations. Time and again, struggles took place in the advanced capitalist states, steelworkers (USA), dockers (UK), the first wave of modern miners' struggles in Britain, postal workers campaigns (USA), autoworkers (USA), transport workers (USA), shipyard workers (UK), and so on. This upsurge was followed by two decades of deindustrialization and the embrace of neo-liberal government policies in the context of globalization.

Such events draw attention to the importance of the local in the context of globalization. Cohen (2006) has argued that the workplace is the site of and the wellspring for resistance in capitalist society; it is 'a central source of trade union renewal and class struggle' (Cohen 2006: 2). Citing Marx's celebration of the union form: 'Permanent combinations…which serve as ramparts for the workers in their struggles' (Cohen 2006: 209), she proposes that trade unions in capitalist society remain the ramparts of resistance, via activism and organization and through workplace leadership. Through a rich historical scrutiny of trade union struggles in two advanced capitalist countries, Britain and the United States, Cohen draws on a valuable and oft-forgotten distinction between union as 'institution' and union as 'movement'. Of note, 'movement' does not simply refer to the larger and the notable struggles, but also involves the smaller, the routine, the often unrecognized events, such as piecework and related payment campaigns, or the recomposition of work tasks and arrangements.

Alongside such analyses, it is also important to consider the state-socialist societies. With the collapse of the Soviet bloc in the late 1980s and early 1990s, the state-sponsored unions, the 'official' unions, were challenged. These unions emerged out of the revolutionary struggles in the early twentieth century, but subsequently became arms of the state, part of the 'Party-state apparatus' (Pringle and Clarke 2011: 1). Their role was that of representing the interests of the working class as a whole, usually as expressed and articulated by the Communist Party. In this respect, these unions became vehicles of control, within and between workplaces.

Nonetheless, trade unions have the potential to play a positive role in the construction of civil society in transition countries, from colonial to sovereign states or from state-socialist societies to post-socialist societies. Further, unions as collective organizations and voluntary organizations can play a critical role in democratization processes in these societies as well as in more established liberal democracies. The transitions taking place in Russia, China, and Vietnam, for example, do not necessarily mean the end of traditional or official unions; nor do they mean that alternative and independent unions will replace such forms of trade unionism (Pringle and Clarke 2011). Trade union reform in these three countries has been driven by worker activism (Pringle and Clarke 2011: 202). While national leaders are often pressured to constrain and encourage reform within the prevailing political arrangements, the conditions for activism are: (1) whether workers are controlled and subordinated and dependent on employers and (2) whether union leaderships are accountable and responsive to memberships. In situations where workers develop a degree of independence and where their leaders are accountable, then the workplace can re-emerge as a wellspring of collective organization and activity.

National and Transnational Unionism

In the 1960s/70s, unions began to address the implications of the internationalization of trade and the rise of multinationals as a form of corporate organization. At this stage, however, the international trade union movement remained relatively disconnected with the international level of organization effectively separated from the national and particularly at the workplace level. In the 1990s, many individual unions began to review the ways they organize, use their capacities, and focus their activities. This reassessment took place in the changing and evolving international order. It led to a rearticulation of relations between global unions and the international agencies and economic organizations.

Trade unions organize and operate in an increasingly deterritorialized context. Production, movement, and consumption of goods and services are no longer confined to the nation-state. Rather governments and supranational organizations (e.g. World Bank) shape an emergent set of economic relations at an international level (see Held et al. 1999). Multinational corporations have become the defining institutions of the international economy. These developments shifted the terrain for trade unionism. International unions, such as the former International Confederation of Free Trade Unions (ICFTU—now the International Trade Union Confederation—ITUC) and the then International Trade Secretariats (designated Global Union Federations (GUFs) in 2000) began to address the emergent international order. These bodies, and particularly the GUFs, have begun to refine their negotiating capacities and capabilities at corporate levels. In these ways, trade unions and their international counterparts are developing their capacities to address the changing architecture of international capital. They have begun to refine their organizational capacities so that they engage in solidarity actions, build alliances, and promote like activity.

Unions have begun to recompose and focus their relations with each other and with international union bodies. The GUFs and the international trade union confederations have transformed themselves, from remote and seemingly irrelevant organizations to ones that have a salience in the global world (see Fairbrother and Hammer 2005). Further, there is a small and growing set of evidence that cross-border alliances are becoming more common; cross-border unions have been set up in a few cases (e.g. the creation of Nautilus from Nautilus UK and Nautilus NL). Of importance, locally based unions often face challenges from global capital and are beginning to organize accordingly, albeit in uneven ways (see Turnbull 2007 on the European waterfront, and Lopez 2004 on care work in the United States).

Many unions have developed and promoted a range of different organizational and representational tools, involving international trade union networks, European Works Councils, World Works Councils, and international framework agreements. These developments form part of a coherent and relatively integrated repertoire of international industrial relations. Additionally, these initiatives focus trade union activity on multinational corporations and governments. This activity is increasingly focused on the emergent international forms of governance, providing a foundation for unions addressing the challenges provided by the complex interrelationship between the local and the global, increasingly in the form of international framework agreements. Although the origins of these agreements lie with the tentative incremental agreements in the mid-1980s, it was not until the early 2000s that the GUFs began to secure these agreements in reasonable numbers, over 90 by 2010.

Thus, there is an evolving set of relations between locally based and internationally based unions. In a number of cases, GUFs have worked with both national unions and more locally based union groups to promote and encourage institution building via training, education, and research (e.g. Barton and Fairbrother 2009). Such developments have also been evident in the post-state-socialist societies, where training programmes on health and safety and collective bargaining have been initiated (see Pringle and Clarke 2011; Croucher and Cotton 2009). Moreover, some evidence suggests that when such programmes are cast in terms of global relations, and in particular the role and place of multinational corporations in this process, workplace and locally based unions can begin to transform themselves (Croucher and Cotton 2009). It is reasonable to conclude that such involvements are the conditions for local trade unions to begin operating and organizing as globally engaged forms of trade unionism.

Unions are no longer limited by nation-state boundaries: increasingly trade union concerns have cross-border reference and implications. Organizationally, these developments have given rise to a multi-faceted form of trade unionism, involving the global unions, national unions, and locally based forms of trade unionism (see Fairbrother and Hammer 2005). This layered form of union organization is signified by a more or less coherent division of labour between the ITUC and the GUFs, as well as with the other components of the international trade union movement. In a more complicated way complex relations define the relations between GUFs and nationally based unions. In the main, the federations are under-resourced, with limited capacities, often leading to a range of formal and informal relations between them and their union constituencies. While increasingly union groups see the GUFs as important players, many still do not make this connection. In such a complex and often opaque world, it often takes time for union groups, particularly at the local level, to exercise power in this context.

Union Renewal

The current challenges facing unions have their roots in the economic and political conditions of capitalist societies. One important observation of such arrangements is that the inequalities that define capitalism also constitute the conditions for collective politics (Wallerstein 1983: 137). In other words, the inequalities and the exclusions associated with them (the privileged and non-privileged) provide the foundation for social movements (such as trade unions) opposed to inequalities. More recent analyses point to complex changes taking place as capitalist societies deal with the economic crisis of 2008 and its fall-out. These analyses focus on the established ways of managing both national and international economic relations, as well as the more specific regional and national variations in capitalist social relations. Various accommodations have been made between labour and capital, complemented and shaped by the specific forms of governance and economic management promoted by a range of governments and policy-makers (Wood and Lane 2011). More specific analyses address relations between the shifts in the financial sector and the implications for policy and resistance (Engelen et al. 2011; see also Erturk et al. 2007), the specific forms of public service modernization and reform that have occurred (e.g. Bach and Kessler 2012), and the changing relations within households as they deal with the fall-out of neo-liberal policies (LeBaron 2010). Such structural tensions also raise questions about social and political stability in many capitalist states (see Streeck 2011).

A number of recent analyses focus on the challenges facing unions in the advanced capitalist societies in the current period (Bronfenbrenner 2007; Freeman et al. 2007; see also Lafferty 2010). The general conclusion that can be drawn is that many unions have diminishing capacities, face a shrinking membership in many of these countries, and have an increasingly blurred focus, resulting in defensive accommodations with governments and employers (e.g. on the Asia-Pacific region, see Lee and Eyraud 2008). In a noteworthy contribution, Peters (2012) focuses on public services, remarking how unions are caught in a double bind that may undermine militant responses to the neo-liberal changes underway. On the one hand, unions cannot avoid the political implications of deficit economics, tax cuts, and pressures from governments to make concessions and show restraint. On the other hand, in dealing with these circumstances, unions have adopted defensive strategies and moved away from more militant and active responses evident in the past (see Fichter and Greer 2003; Upchurch et al. 2009; Bach and Kessler 2012). As Peters notes, such stances are evident in Canada, the United States, the United Kingdom, Germany, and Finland. But he also misses one important point, namely that unions in the public services, unlike other sections of the labour movement, have taken steps to address organization, capacity, and purpose. While there is evidence of defensive responses there is also evidence of attempts to address this situation in active and progressive ways; albeit in uneven and hesitant ways.

Unions thus face complex challenges. One focus in relation to trade unionism in the advanced capitalist states in recent decades has been to consider how unions might renew and revitalize themselves (e.g. Lévesque and Murray 2010). With the collapse of the Soviet Union and the economic transformation of China, a second line of enquiry has been on the position and place of unions in transition societies (e.g. Pringle and Clarke 2011). While the challenges are varied, unions in these different contexts do face similar questions and ways they might develop their capacities to address these challenges (e.g. Phelan 2007). One illustration comes from the increasing moves across the world to begin to transition to a low carbon economy, where unions are caught in a tension between defending current jobs and arrangements and seeking to make jobs and work conditions more environmentally responsible (Snell and Fairbrother 2010).

These challenges and the failure of the unions to, as yet, effectively defend workers and their communities, has led to a significant decline in members and/or active organization. Many union movements, in Europe for example, have union densities of less than 30% (Greece, Hungary, Italy, Poland, Portugal, Spain, and the United Kingdom). In contrast, where unions continue to have some role in relation to state policy, for example playing a part in the administration of some aspects of welfare provision as in Sweden, Norway, and Denmark, unionization is above 70%, though somewhat passive.

To address these challenges more positively, unions have begun to renew themselves and to extend their boundaries of action. In the past, the key union dynamic was based on the assumption that union leaders (at all levels) have the capacity to shape union objectives to meet every, often contradictory, need. But renewal also requires a shift in emphasis from leaders servicing members to mutually involved and accountable forms of organizing.

Unions have begun to re-establish themselves through innovative struggles against the consequences of corporate policy, state restructuring, and the transition of economies in a variety of contexts; for example, the steel unions in Terni in Italy 2004/5, where young workers, supported by local community leaders, played a leading part in challenging corporate decisions (Stroud and Fairbrother 2011) as well as in London, where trade unions have resisted low wages policies (see Holgate 2009). Elsewhere practical international cooperation has been promoted by unions such as ver.di (Germany), Unison (UK), and CGIL (Italy) in the European Social Forum and the maritime unions in Australia and elsewhere.

Trade unions in many states seem to be on the sidelines of some of the mass struggles that have occurred from 2008 onwards. Going back in recent time to the late 1960s, there has been an upsurge of resistance and campaigning, which is both a challenge to trade unionism and involves trade unionists. Across Southern Europe, new mass movements have begun to emerge. Beginning in 2010, there have been a series of strikes and protests in Greece in relation to the ongoing debt crisis and government measures to address these problems. Under the 'Indignant Citizens Movement' in 2011 and 2012, in the context of a deepening economic crisis, a series of dramatic events took place in Spain. For example, under the 15-M movement (15 May 2011) demonstrators protested against high unemployment, government policies on the economic crisis, and established politics. While not led by trade unionists, and often comprising young people, these developments have implications for trade unionism, as do the developments in the Middle East and North Africa as well as in Quebec province in Canada in 2012 (with student strikes against education fees). As in other moments of history such events are a challenge to the established and orderly routines of trade unionism, and suggest that unless unions are flexible such upsurges are likely to by-pass them. Of note, some trade unionists are now involved in these activities and developments which are both new and very old (Kuper 2011).

Renewal involves promoting unions as campaigning organizations, recruiting beyond familiar membership bases, creating mutually supportive relations between different levels of the unions (on the challenges facing unions, in relation to work, household and community, see Pocock 2011). It also, crucially, involves looking beyond the union, creating ways of organizing appropriate to the workplace, the community, and the dispossessed, and to combining local campaigning with organizing internationally. Underpinning these moves is an alternative view of society, where the emphasis is on participation, accountability, and public involvement, framing demands socially and politically rather than just economically. The key to this step is a radically democratic form of unionism in which processes of union mobilization are participative. Only then do unions begin to lay the foundations for genuine alliances with other social movements, addressing and campaigning against the degradations of the present form of European capitalism.

These processes of involvement and engagement are potentially transformative; the promise of trade union renewal requires a consideration of union capacity, the 'power resources' available to unions (Lévesque and Murray 2002; on 'strategic capacity', see Ganz 2000). These processes include the development and implementation of union agenda, internal solidarity (exemplified by forms of union democracy), and external solidarity (the embeddedness of unions within their localities and as part of national and global union movements). However, what are often overlooked in these analyses are the social and political conditions for participative forms of union representation, organization and activity (Fairbrother 2000, 2005; Fairbrother and Webster 2008). Developing union capacity and promoting the conditions for particular forms of participation are the key ingredients of an active trade unionism. Without democracy unions are hollow organizations with limited capacity to engage in collective practices.

New Forms of Unionism?

With increasing concern in the advanced capitalist economies about the current position of trade unions and future prospects, it has become common to promote the idea of social movement unions, based on a critique of prevailing forms of unionism (e.g. Moody 1997a, 1997b, 1997c). Concurrently, parallel debates argue for a distinct form of unionism that addresses the specificities of the emerging capitalist societies of the 'South', while also presenting a critique of the northern forms of unionism just mentioned (e.g. Waterman 2001). Such unions are often characterized as economistic, with narrowly focused and limited views of emancipatory politics. Such unions are usually organized in top-down ways, with low membership participation rates, and a commitment to policies associated with economic instrumentalism and compromise. Nonetheless, in the advanced capitalist states, these unions have not been without some degree of success, having provided:

> workers a voice on the shopfloor, delivered a steadily rising standard of living, and served the purposes of these liberal democratic states by helping give workers an organized (though moderate) voice in national politics. (Lopez 2004: 1)

However, such unionism is limited.

Social movement unionism in contrast can provide a hopeful challenge to the dominance of business unionism, 'official' unions, and party-affiliated or 'political' unions. These unions have been able to exercise forms of social power that periodically have been able to challenge the seemingly overwhelming power of corporations and governments, for example, 'in Britain in the 1890s, Germany in 1918–1920, the United States in the 1930s, and Italy after 1969' (Turner 2003: 50). Such forms of unionism arise periodically, often in more localized settings and at times when there is an 'upsurge' in the conditions for such struggle (see Clawson 2003; Fantasia and Voss 2004; Clarke and Pringle 2011; Hensman 2011).

But, such 'irruptions' are not confined to the advanced capitalist states; they include unions in the emerging capitalist societies, Brazil, Korea, China, and South Africa. Often designated social movement unionism, such unions can provide the opportunity and occasion to question the depredations of capitalist relations, unlike business unions, official unions, or political unionism (Fairbrother and Webster 2008).

The conditions for this type of unionism have been noted by Webster:

> Social movement unionism emerges in authoritarian countries such as the Philippines, Brazil and South Africa, where workers are excluded from the central decision-making processes. It differs from conventional trade unionism in that it is concerned with labour as a social and political force, not simply as a commodity to be bargained over. As a result, its concerns go beyond the workplace to include the sphere of reproduction. Furthermore, it places a strong emphasis on democracy and workers' control. (Webster 1988: 194–5)

Webster argues that the 'essence' of social movement unionism in these political and economic circumstances is 'an appeal to workers that goes beyond the employment relationship to the totality of their lives, as consumers, citizens, family members and women' (Webster 2006: 195). It is an independent, locally based and participative trade unionism, characterized by democratic practices, accountable leaderships, a commitment to build alliances, and potentially transformative in form and object.

Such conditions have become much more widespread. Increasingly, there is an ongoing exclusion of workers from decision-making processes in the advanced capitalist states, with the subversion of liberal democracy by the authoritarian populism that has come to dominate electoral politics in most states. As noted by some, there is a 'drift to social engineering' (Standing 2012: 1), where the social structure of liberal democratic states is marked by a recomposition of class relations, towards a plutocratic elite, a fragmented and recomposed middle and working class, with limited collective and political power (Standing 2012). The outcome according to Standing is 'a class-in-the-making' (Standing 2012: 2), a so-called 'precariat', distinguished in three ways:

> The first variety consists of those drifting from working-class backgrounds into precariousness, the second consists of those emerging from a schooling system over-credentialised for the flexi-job life on offer, and the third are migrants and others, such as the criminalised, in a status denying them the full rights of citizens. (Standing 2012: 2)

Such a class is outside the classic circuits of capital accumulation and outside the logic of collective bargaining.

Further, such social groups (a class-in-the-making or not) are the excluded and marginalized in a world of inequality and privilege (on citizenship, see Wallerstein 2002).

These populations, it can be argued, are susceptible to authoritarian sirens. There has been a recent emergence of authoritarian populist movements in the USA, Australia, and other countries, anti-immigrant and scapegoating politics in France and the Netherlands, and fundamentalist politics of political Islam in northern Africa and the Middle East (Davis 2011). As argued, these political movements and eruptions occur in the context of the wide-ranging tensions and contradictions of modern capitalism.

Given such developments, trade unions as materially based collective moments offer a positive possibility for the future and, in particular, that of social movement unionism. In such conditions, social movement unionism is predicated on an understanding of the transformative features of working-class struggle, that workers' struggles are one of a number of struggles that question prevailing social formations and that this involves alliances between workers and others (for different versions see Scipes 2003 and Waterman 1998, 2001).

Thus, the very definition of unions as collective organizations provides the opportunity for renewal. The choices facing unions are both stark and ongoing; such opportunities have always faced unions in whatever context they organize and operate. It is a choice between responsible, official, or political forms of unionism on the one hand, and social movement unionism, on the other. Today, unions find themselves in a difficult place. The balance between the market and state regulation has shifted towards an acceptance of the market by governments and by default by many unions in practice.

Unions face difficult decisions in reconciling the ongoing tensions in relation to unions in a capitalist society between 'vested interest' and 'social justice'. This tension often takes the form of job protection and security alongside more altruistic concerns, such as the recognition of labour rights. Nonetheless, the immediacy of material concerns often prevails. After all, the union movement is a materialist movement representing those involved in production and related activity. The challenge for unions is to express themselves as social movements, rather than 'vested interests', in the process promoting active forms of renewal and thereby challenging the dominance of capital, and state control. In these respects, unions have a unique role as collective actors in an internationalized capitalist world.

Conclusion

Trade unions are caught in a tension between pressures towards economism and those towards more altruistic goals around rights and justice. Unions increasingly face tensions between attempts by employers, often reinforced by state policy and practice, to weaken the leverage that workers have in relation to management (whether locally based or international). There is an ongoing pressure on workers and their unions from the restructuring of employment relations and relocating work sites, on the one hand, and the disquiet of workers with work intensification and insecurity of employment on the other.

The impact on locally based workforces is often brutal and marked. At the same time, states attempt to satisfy the interests of international capital but are wary of political and labour unrest. The question of union democracy is thus raised in a rather acute way. Clearly one of the key features of democratic relations and forms of organization is the capacity for workers to organize at a local level and to play an active part in formulating and determining union policy and activity. With the consolidation of local forms of organization or the reconstitution of the union form of organization at a local level the opportunity for membership participation becomes more likely. In these circumstances, it is likely that the self-organization of workers will be linked to the emergence of new leaders or leaderships who are able to recast their past practices so as to enable a broader based range of activity to be undertaken by union members.

Unions, as always, look to the material world and to their futures within it. By defining themselves in relation to and demonstrating their capacity to connect with life experiences under capitalism, unions will be in a position to renew and move beyond a narrow economistic and defensive focus. They are and will remain a core dimension of the challenge to the state and capital. However, because of their location within the labour–capital relation, there is an ever-present danger of co-optation and compromise. This is the ongoing struggle at the heart of the future of trade unionism.

References

Atzeni, M. and Ghigliani, P. (2007). 'The Resilience of Traditional Trade Union Practices in the Revitalisation of the Argentine Labour Movement', in C. Phelan (ed.), *Trade Union Revitalisation: Trends and Prospects in 34 Countries*. Oxford: Peter Lang, 105–19.

Bach, S. and Kessler, I (2012). *The Modernisation of the Public Services and Employee Relations: Targeted Change*. Basingstoke: Palgrave Macmillan.

Barton, R. and Fairbrother, P. (2009). 'The Local is Now Global: Trade Unions Organising Globally', *Relations Industrielles/Industrial Relations*, 64(4): 685–793.

Botwinick, H. (1993). *Persistent Inequalities: Wage Disparity under Capitalist Competition*. Princeton: Princeton University Press.

Boxall, P. and Haynes, P. (1997). 'Strategy and Trade Union Effectiveness in a Neo-Liberal Environment', *British Journal of Industrial Relations*, 35(4): 567–91.

Braverman, H. (1974). *Labor and Monopoly Capital: The Degradation of Work in the Twentieth Century*. New York: Monthly Review Press.

Brighton Labour Process Group (1977). 'The Capitalist Labour Process', *Capital & Class*, 1: 3–26.

Bronfenbrenner, K. (ed.) (2007). *Global Unions: Challenging Transnational Capital through Cross-Border Campaigns*. Ithaca and London: ILR Press.

Bronfenbrenner, K., Friedman, S., Hurd, R. W., Oswald, R. A., and Seeber, R. L. (eds.) (1998). *Organizing to Win: New Research on Union Strategies*. Ithaca: ILR Press.

Carter, B. (2004). 'State Restructuring and Union Renewal: The Case of the National Union of Teachers', *Work, Employment & Society*, 18(1): 137–56.

Clawson, D. (2003). *The Next Upsurge: Labor and the New Social Movements*. Ithaca and London: ILR Press.

Cohen, S. (2006). *Ramparts of Resistance: Why Workers Lost Their Power and How to Get it Back.* London: Pluto Press.

Croucher, R. and Cotton, E. (2009). *Global Unions, Global Business: Global Union Federations and International Business.* London: Middlesex University Press.

Daniels, G. and McIlroy, J. (eds.) (2009). *Trade Unions in a Neoliberal World.* London and New York: Routledge.

Davis. M. (2011). 'Spring Confronts Winter', *New Left Review*, 72: 5–15.

Easton, B. (1997). *The Commercialisation of New Zealand.* Auckland: Auckland University Press.

Elger, T. (1979). 'Valorisation and Deskilling: A Critique of Braverman', *Capital & Class*, 7: 58–99.

Engelen, E., Erturk, I., Froud, J., Leaver, A., Johal, S., Moran, M., Nilsson, A., and Williams, K. (2011). *After the Great Complacence: Financial Crisis and the Politics of Reform.* Oxford and New York: Oxford University Press.

Erturk, I., Froud, J., Johal, S., Leaver, A., and Williams, K. (2007). 'The Democratization of Finance? Promises, Outcomes and Conditions', *Review of International Political Economy*, 14(4): 553–75.

Fairbrother, P. (1994). *Politics and the State as Employer.* London: Mansell.

—— (2000). *Unions at the Crossroads.* London: Continuum.

—— (2005). Rediscovering Union Democracy: Processes of Union Revitalization and Renewal', *Labor History*, 46: 368–76.

Fairbrother, P. and Hammer, N. (2005). 'Global Unions: Past Efforts and Future Prospects', *Relations Industrielles/Industrial Relations*, 60(3): 405–31.

Fairbrother, P. and Webster, E. (2008). 'Social Movement Unionism: Questions and Possibilities', *Employee Responsibilities and Rights Journal*, 20(3): 309–13.

Fairbrother, P. and Yates, C. (eds.) (2003). *Trade Unions in Renewal: A Comparative Study.* London: Routledge.

Fantasia, R. and Voss, K. (2004). *Hard Work: Remaking the American Labor Movement.* Berkeley, CA: California University Press.

Fichter, M. and Greer, I. (2003). 'Analysing Social Partnership: A Tool of Union Revitalization', in C. Frege and J. Kelly (eds.), *Varieties of Unionism: Strategies for Union Revitalization in a Globalizing Economy.* Oxford and New York: Oxford University Press, 71–92.

Flanders, A. (1970). *Management and Unions: The Theory and Reform of Industrial Relations*, 2nd edn. London: Faber and Faber.

Freeman, R., Boxall, P., and Haynes, P. (eds.) (2007). *What Workers Say: Employee Voice in the Anglo-American Workplace.* Ithaca and London: ILR Press.

Freeman, R. and Medoff, J. (1984). *What Do Unions Do?* New York: Basic Books.

Ganz, M. (2000). 'Resources and Resourcefulness: Strategic Capacity in the Unionization of California Agriculture, 1959–1966', *American Journal of Sociology*, 105: 1003–62.

Grusky, D. and Weeden, K. (2001). 'Decomposition Without Death: A Research Agenda for a New Class Analysis', *Acta Sociologica*, 44(3): 203–18.

Held, D., McGrew, A., Goldblatt, D., and Parraton, J. (1999). *Global Transformations: Politics, Economics and Culture.* Cambridge: Polity Press.

Hensman, R. (2011). *Workers, Unions and Global Capitalism.* New York: Columbia University Press.

Holgate, J. (2009). *Unionising the Low Paid in London: The Justice for Cleaners Campaign.* Labor Unions and Civic Integration of Immigrant Workers research project.

Hyman, R. (2007). 'How Can Trade Unions Act Strategically?', *Transfer*, 13: 193–210.

Kelly, J. (1998). *Rethinking Industrial Relations: Mobilization, Collectivism and Long Waves*. London: Routledge.

Kuper, S. (2011). 'Indignant? We Should Be?', *Financial Times*, 7 January.

Lafferty, G. (2010). 'In the Wake of Neo-Liberalism: Deregulation, Unionism and Labour Rights', *Review of International Political Economy*, 17(3): 589–608.

LeBaron, G. (2010). 'The Political Economy of the Household: Neoliberal Restructuring, Enclosures, and Daily Life', *Review of International Political Economy*, 17(5): 889–912.

Lee, S. and Eyraud, F. (eds.) (2008). *Globalization, Flexibilization and Working Conditions in Asia and the Pacific*. Geneva: International Labour Office, and Oxford: Chandos Publishing.

Lévesque, C. and Murray, G. (2002). 'Local versus Global: Activating Local Union Power in the Global Economy', *Labor Studies Journal*, 27(3): 39–65.

—— (2010). 'Understanding Union Power: Resources and Capabilities for Renewing Union Capacity', *Transfer*, 16(3): 333–50.

—— (2012). 'Renewing Union Narrative Resources: How Union Capabilities Make a Difference', *British Journal of Industrial Relations*. Available at <http://onlinelibrary.wiley.com/doi/10.1111/bjir.12002/full>.

Lind, J. (2007). 'Trade Unions in Denmark: Still Victorious?', in C. Phelan (ed.), *Trade Union Revitalisation: Trends and Prospects in 34 Countries*. Oxford: Peter Lang, 287–301.

Lopez, S. (2004). *Reorganizing the Rust Belt: An Inside Story of the American Labor Movement*. Berkeley, CA: University of California Press.

McIlroy, J. and Daniels, G. (2009). 'Introduction: Trade Unions in a Neoliberal World', in Daniels and McIlroy (eds.), *Trade Unions in a Neoliberal World*. London and New York: Routledge, 1–18.

MacInnes, J. (1987). *Thatcherism at Work: Industrial Relations and Economic Change*. Milton Keynes: Open University Press.

Marx, K. and Engels, F. (1950 [1848]). 'Manifesto of the Communist Party', in Marx and Engels, *Selected Works*, Vol. 1. Moscow: Foreign Languages Publishing House, 21–61.

Moody, K. (1997a). 'Towards an International Social-Movement Unionism', *New Left Review*, 225: 52–72.

—— (1997b). *Workers in a Lean World: Unions in the International Economy*. London: Verso.

—— (1997c). 'American Labor: A Movement Again?', *Monthly Review*, 49: 63–80.

Müller-Jentsch, W. (1988). 'Industrial Relations Theory and Trade Union Strategy', *International Journal of Comparative Labour Law and Industrial Relations*, 4(3): 177–90.

Oxenbridge, S. (1997). 'Organizing Strategies and Organizing Reform in New Zealand Service Sector Unions', *Labor Studies Journal*, 22(3): 3–27.

Peters, J. (2012). 'Neoliberal Convergence in North America and Western Europe: Fiscal Austerity, Privatization, and Public Sector Reform', *Review of International Political Economy*, 19(2): 208–35.

Phelan, C. (ed.) (2007). *Trade Union Revitalisation: Trends and Prospects in 34 Countries*. Oxford: Peter Lang.

Pocock, B. (1998). 'Institutional Sclerosis: Prospects for Trade Union Transformation', *Labor and Industry*, 9(1): 17–36.

—— (2011). 'Rethinking Unionism in a Changing World of Work, Family and Community Life', *Relations Industrielles/Industrial Relations*, 66(4): 562–84.

Pringle, T. and Clarke, S. (2011). *The Challenge of Transition: Trade Unions in Russia, China and Vietnam*. Basingstoke: Palgrave Macmillan.

Scipes, K. (2003). 'Understanding the New Labor Movements in the "Third World": The Emergence of Social Movement Unionism, a New Type of Trade Unionism'. Available at <http://www.labournet.de/diskussion/gewerkschaft/ smu/The_New_Unions_Crit_Soc. htm#_edn1>.

Snell, D. and Fairbrother, P. (2010). 'Unions as Environmental Actors', *Transfer*, 16(3): 411–24.

Standing, G. (2012). 'The Precariat: Why It Needs Deliberative Democracy', openDemocracy, 27 January. Available at <http://www.opendemocracy.net/guy-standing/precariat-why-it-needs-deliberative-democracy>.

Streeck, W. (2011). 'The Crises of Democratic Capitalism', *New Left Review*, 71: 5–29.

Stroud, D. and Fairbrother, P. (2011). 'The Limits and Prospects of Union Power: Addressing Mass Redundancy in the Steel Industry', *Economic and Industrial Democracy*, 33(4): 649–68.

Turnbull, P. (2007). 'Dockers versus the Directives: Battling Port Policy on the European Waterfront', in K. Bronfenbrenner (ed.), *Global Unions: Challenging Transnational Capital Through Cross-Border Campaigns*. Ithaca and London: ILR Press, 116–36.

Turner, L. (2003). 'Reviving the Labor Movement: A Comparative Perspective', *Research in the Sociology of Work*, 11: 23–58.

Upchurch, M., Taylor, G., and Mathers, A. (2009). *The Crisis of Social Democratic Trade Unionism in Western Europe*. Burlington, VT: Ashgate.

Wallerstein, I. (1983). *Historical Capitalism and Capitalist Civilization*. London: Verso.

—— (2002). 'Citizens All? Citizens Some! The Making of the Citizen', E. P. Thompson Memorial Lecture, University of Pittsburgh, 18 April. Available at <http://www2.binghamton.edu/fbc/archive/iwepthomp.htm>.

Waterman, P. (1998). *Social Movements, Globalisation and the New Internationalisms*. London and Washington: Mansell/Cassell.

—— (2001). 'Trade Union Internationalism in the Age of Seattle', in Waterman and J. Wills (eds.), *Place, Space and the New Labour Internationalisms*. Oxford: Blackwell, 8–32.

Webster, E. (1988). 'The Rise of Social Movement Unionism: The Two Faces of Black Trade Union Movements in South Africa', in P. Frankel, N. Pines, and M. Swilling (eds.), *State, Resistance and Change in South Africa*. London: Croom Helm, 174–96.

—— (2006). Author meets Critics Session: Reorganising the Rust Belt: An Inside Study of the American Labor Movement by Steve Lopez, Monday, 14 August, Recasting Labor Studies in the 21st Century, American Sociological Association, Montreal.

Wood, G. and Lane, C. (eds) (2011). *Capitalist Diversity and Diversity within Capitalism*. London and New York: Routledge.

CHAPTER 29

INSTITUTIONS, MANAGEMENT STRATEGIES, AND HRM

GILTON KLERCK

INTRODUCTION

DRAWING together some of the themes in earlier chapters, this chapter seeks to critique dichotomous understandings of managerial practice; highlight the extent to which firms combine different forms of employee representation, control, and tenure; and explore the institutional underpinnings of this 'hybridization'. The broad goal is to link institutional theory to a deeper understanding of diversity in industrial relations (IR) and human resource management (HRM) practices. Much of the literature on the variations in managerial practice is characterized by inadequately articulated scalar analysis, a failure to take uneven development seriously and a disregard for broader question of meta-theory (Edwards 2005; Fleetwood and Hesketh 2008; James 2009; Thompson and Vincent 2010). The latter is particularly prevalent in the HRM literature and lies at the root of many of its limitations and oversights. As Keegan and Boselie (2006: 1506) note, 'debates on meta theory, the linguistic turn, and reflexivity have not taken root or changed the way most research is undertaken and published in the field of HRM'. Consequently, they argue, debates in HRM tend to be narrow, technocratic, managerialist, exclude consideration of broader moral, social, and political questions on HRM practice and policy, and are lagging behind leading edge theoretical developments in social scientific analysis evident in other fields of management and organization theory.

As social scientists were searching for alternatives to positivism, they often sided with some postmodernist or subjectivist view, which erroneously attempts to dissolve the intransitivity of social life altogether. This is mirrored, in part, by the shift in IR from the empiricism and determinism of 'systems' approaches to the constructivism and indeterminacy associated with models of 'strategic choice'. There is a pressing need to overcome both a voluntaristic idealism whereby individuals create the social structure and a mechanical determinism whereby people are essentially the product of their situation. In other words, the choice is not simply between a deterministic world of regularities or one of endless differences. Bhaskar's (1998) model of transformative social activity sustains the insight that structure and agency are distinct, yet highly interdependent, things. This model is capable of

> accommodating the usual individualist stipulation that agency be given a non-trivial role without reducing social structure to some inadequate notion of context. Additionally the transformational conception of the mode of existence of social structures should, in principle, be acceptable to new institutionalists in that social structure is not viewed as existing 'apart from' individuals... [We] are not presented with a stark choice between viewing the individual as prime-mover or as passive rule-follower. Society is the skilled accomplishment of agents. But the social world may be opaque to social agents in several respects, in that [their] activities may depend upon or involve unacknowledged conditions; unintended consequences; the exercise of tacit skills; unconscious motivations. (Lawson et al. 1996: 148)

These meta-theoretical issues are especially pertinent in the growing concern with international and intra-national variations in work and employment relations in the contemporary literature on HRM and IR. This concern is intimately connected to the range of frameworks, which draw heavily on institutional analysis, that have been developed to account for the diversity across (and, less frequently, within) national forms of capitalism (Almond 2011; Brewster et al. 2006; Ferner et al. 2005; Hyman 2003; Lane and Wood 2009; Rees and Edwards 2009; Wood and Lane 2011). This increasingly influential body of work seeks not only to embed the economy in its institutional context, but also takes as a starting point the functioning of economic institutions and processes of social regulation to account for the diversity of capitalist societies. Key among these are rational choice approaches, organizational-societal approaches, varieties of capitalism approaches, historical institutionalism, business systems theory, production systems theory, regulation theory, and employment systems theory (see Amable 2003; Ebner and Beck 2008; Hall and Soskice 2001; Hollingsworth and Boyer 1997; Marsden 1999; Rubery and Grimshaw 2003; Streeck and Thelen 2005; Thatcher 2007; Whitley et al. 2005). However, as Wood and Lane (2011) point out, much of the comparative institutional literature fails to articulate closely the linkages between particular work and employment relations practices and wider institutional realities. Even some of the institutional approaches that are ostensibly concerned with these linkages tend to prioritize one dimension or aspect at the expense of the other. In other words, insights into the concrete dynamics of employment relations practices are invariably attained at the expense of a deeper understanding of the wider institutional context and vice versa. This is reflected in Hyman's (1989: 135) claim that many of the difficulties that beset the development of theory in employment relations are, in part, 'problems of integrating different levels of generality'.

THE 'INSTITUTIONAL TURN' AND VARIETIES OF CAPITALISM

The 'institutional turn' exemplified by the expanding body of literature on the varieties of capitalism (VOC) emerged in the 1990s in response to the claims, inspired by orthodox economics, that the intensification of globalization in the post-communist era signalled the victory of a single form of (neo-liberal) capitalism. In orthodox economic theory, markets are depicted as areas of unrestricted, spontaneous conduct, abstracted from technical and organizational change, unless obstructed in some way. On this view, responsiveness to price signals is the sole mechanism governing economic behaviour and the social or institutional context is of no consequence. This means that governments are compelled to move towards greater openness in matters of trade, investment, and finance if they wish to achieve sustained economic growth and attract increasingly mobile multinational corporations (MNCs). As a result, orthodox economists argue, governments are compelled to adopt the same neo-liberal and market-based policies with similar fiscal, economic, and social policy implications. The implication is that there is a universal formula for economic success, which includes dismantling the welfare state, deregulating the economy, revitalizing market forces, unravelling the institutional framework of the labour market, minimizing or eliminating the influence of trade unions, reducing wage claims, and increasing flexibility in work and employment.

While the social and political institutions of all countries increasingly bear the mark of the growing internationalization of economic activity, it does not follow that national economies are becoming progressively homogeneous in the face of global economic forces. Since markets are always embedded to some degree and since there are always other modes of regulation present even in the most marketized society, the actual behaviour of agents in concrete markets cannot be read off simply from market structure (though it is constrained and enabled by markets) and hence cannot be predicted and judged purely a priori (Sayer 1995: 144). Persistent divergence in national experiences of and responses to globalization suggests that global trends are reinforced, deflected, obstructed, and diffused differently according to established institutional practices (Brenner et al. 2009, 2010). The VOC approach has made a significant contribution in this regard:

> It has established a plausible analytical counter-narrative to one-world visions of globalization; it has called attention to the institutional embeddedness of economic systems and transformations, in the face of a prevalent free-market discourse; and it has reminded heterodox economists 'that there are particular geographies of production and consumption'... The varieties rubric has been useful in problematizing the systemic institutional logics of a range of national capitalisms, indeed in spawning the concept of national capitalism itself. And it has been successful in inserting geographical questions, of a certain kind, into circulation within mainstream heterodox economics, while breathing new life into the field of comparative political economy. (Peck and Theodore 2007: 766)

In general, institutional approaches reject the notion of general laws based on an abstract price mechanism in favour of a view of the economic process as dependent on an institutional framework (Boyer 2011). Contemporary institutional approaches rely on a taxonomic framework that distinguishes between 'liberal market economies' and 'coordinated market economies'. The latter are exemplified by the 'organized' style of capitalism in Western Europe, which is heavily mediated by state action, extensive welfare provisions, long-term planning, and corporatist forms of interest representation. The former are represented by the 'disorganized' style of capitalism in America, which relies on a smaller, less interventionist state, short-term planning, and deregulated markets. This binary divide, which informs much of the comparative institutional literature, turns on a contrast in the degree of institutional and (to a lesser extent) cultural embedding of the economy. The literature on the VOC catalogues the institutional features of these two ideal-typical forms of capitalism and then attributes the variation in economic features and performance to institutional differences. The tendencies towards static analysis, latent institutional functionalism, and methodological nationalism in the VOC approach, according to Peck and Theodore (2007), are compounded by an inability adequately to balance national specificity and path-dependency with common underlying tendencies in capitalist restructuring.

The distinction between liberal market economies and coordinated market economies incorrectly portrays American capitalism as an exemplar of neo-liberal economics, underestimates the variety of different state–economy–society articulations in the developed world, and has limited traction in the developing world and transitional economies in Eastern Europe. The idea that the United States is a textbook case of a 'free market' economy is contradicted by (among others) extensive state protection of and intervention in the defence industry as well as targeted public investment in research and development. So-called 'liberal' markets are internally diverse and characterized by extensive formal and informal regulation (Wood and Lane 2011). Likewise, coordinated market economies may be differentiated in terms of those forms that are characterized by a strong and inclusively organized labour movement and those forms that are characterized by a weaker and more fragmented labour movement (Elger and Edwards 2002). Furthermore, the economic ascent of China, India, South Korea, and other developing economies underscores the need for a wider range of institutionally based models of capitalism (Jessop and Sum 2006). Finally, the literature on the VOC is largely silent on regional diversity, dysfunctionalities in institutional frameworks, and the connections between the two archetypal forms of capitalism (Peck and Theodore 2007).

Although markets and economic exchanges are always institutionally embedded, such embedding assumes a variety of different forms and degrees (Sayer 1995: 88). However, the variation is not entirely random or arbitrary in the sense that anything is possible. Under competitive conditions, embedding succeeds or fails depending on how well it supports profits. As such, the behaviour of social agents is patterned by economic pressures of competition, budgetary constraints, availability of resources, and the like. The dualistic taxonomies that pervade comparative institutionalism do not provide an adequate basis for a detailed understanding of the dynamic, variegated, and uneven development of capitalism. By drawing on the insights of the various institutional approaches, it can be argued that a comparative model should

> link employment relations to the wider political, economic, and social environments. It should be dynamic, incorporating endogenous and exogenous change. It should be capable of handling the diversity of international, national, and subnational institutions. It should recognize the plurality of interests, the duality of cooperation and conflict within the enterprise, and the dialectic between interests and institutions. (Martin and Bamber 2004: 308)

Distinct national strategies of competitiveness are forged in the context of various organized interests, with particular organizational and institutional resources that struggle to assert discrete paths of restructuring (Boyer 1993; Frenkel 1994; Whitley and Kristensen 1997; Esping-Andersen and Regini 2000). That is, processes of economic development are mediated through a diverse range of cultural and institutional frameworks. The significance of distinctive institutional matrices in generating variant forms of capitalism is reflected in the emphasis on the path-dependent trajectories of change generated by specific national social formations. Variation in the national forms of capitalism is rooted in different configurations of regulatory mechanisms, diverse dynamics and trajectories, and specific institutional arrangements. While broad historical abstractions such as 'Fordism' sacrifice some of the rich detail that typifies a national model of growth in a particular conjuncture, it is argued that the various forms assumed by Fordism across a range of economies in the post-war period were the contingent outcome of a multitude of different conditions and processes that combined in specific ways in different countries (Aglietta 1998; Jessop 1994; Lipietz 1988). Most regulationists, for instance, readily concede that Fordism in different national contexts is not a clone of the American ideal-type, but rather 'different combinations of Fordist and non-Fordist features' (Nielsen 1991: 23). This implies not only different types of Fordism, but also different paths beyond Fordism. Consequently, it is necessary to conceptualize general taxonomic categories not only in terms of successive phases of development, but also in terms of 'historically *coexistent and competing* local alternatives' (Peck 1996: 120). We are therefore more likely to witness the development of composite models, including neo- and post-Fordist developments in some industries or regions and a continued reliance on Fordist and Taylorist techniques in others.

One of the most influential institutionalist approaches—namely, regulation theory—proceeds from the premise that market mechanisms must be supplemented or supplanted by collective action, expressed in institutional forms as social mediation (Boyer and Saillard 2002; Elger and Edwards 2002; Wood and Lane 2011). To this end, regulationists have attempted to specify the institutional forms and modes of struggle within a given stage of capitalist development. The central insight of this approach— that a discernible coherence in capitalist economic development is not simply the outcome of self-equilibrating market mechanisms but the product of a specific mode of social regulation—highlights the recurring instabilities in the processes of valorization, rooted in antagonistic features of the employment relationship and expressed in imbalances between investment, production, and consumption. The *relative* stability of specific cycles of capitalist accumulation is only secured through the interplay of a whole series of regulatory mechanisms (such as government policies, management strategies, bargaining processes, and consumption norms), which yields a variety of different propensities and causal liabilities. The institutional and normative frameworks that give a particular mode of regulation its coherence are exceedingly complex, precarious, and conditional, characterized by discontinuities and tensions between the 'regulatory articulations' that link its constituent institutions, and invariably associated with unpredictable and variable outcomes. The emergence of a stable efficiency–equity coupling is the outcome of 'the history of human struggles... that have succeeded because they ensured some regularity and permanence in social reproduction' (Lipietz 1986: 19) and is therefore best conceived as a chance discovery.

Regulation theory works mostly at the macroeconomic scale and posits a strong link between the employment relationship and the overall pattern of regulation. Although regulation theory is most clearly associated with wide-ranging historical analyses of generic or archetypal patterns of regulation, in principle it is sensitive to institutional variability at more concrete levels of analysis. Regulationists strive to give a determinate social content to the general tendencies of capital accumulation that can explain its dynamic and directionality over time and space. This involves (among others) an exploration of the wide variety of institutional forms existing within the domain of a particular archetypal form. The tendency in some regulationist analyses to reduce intra-national variability to a contingent variability around dominant historical-national models reflected underlying doubts about the value of sub-national scales of analysis and a corresponding commitment to the integrity of the archetypal model and its national variants. By contrast, some institutionalist theories are adept at plant, industry, and even regional level analysis, but remain sceptical about what they view as over-generalized national models. However, as Peck (1996: 99) points out, some regulationists increasingly acknowledge the need 'to bring subnational regulation out of the shadows, not in ritual celebration of diversity and difference but in order to understand *of what* national systems are constituted'. Although regulation theory is a diverse and evolving analytical framework, there is much to be gained by applying some of its key insights to work and employment relations. In fact, Michon's (1992: 227–8) analysis implies that 'the tools proposed by regulation theory [may] be more useful in analysis of the firm than in that of national economies'.

THE INSTITUTIONAL LANDSCAPES OF HUMAN RESOURCE MANAGEMENT

The idea that 'institutions matter' has always been a defining characteristic of the field of IR. In direct contrast to the canons of neo-classical economics, the pioneers of IR theory accentuated the importance of rules and the institutions that underpin them in maintaining order in the employment relationship (Ackers and Wilkinson 2005; Kaufman 2008). However, IR scholars differ significantly in their assessment of the ways in which institutions matter. This is particularly evident in studies of the impact of the diverse contexts in which managers have to perform their functions. Important theoretical developments in recent years have gone some way in dealing with a central weakness of prevailing models, namely their difficulty in explaining the systemic diversity of management behaviour (see Brewster et al. 2008; Ferner et al. 2005; Lane and Wood 2009; Paauwe and Boselie 2003; Rees and Edwards 2009; Schuler and Jackson 2007). Institutional approaches are a key component of these developments. Institutionalists recognize that the IR arrangements, which neo-classical economists regard as obstacles to the 'proper' functioning of the labour market, can generate meaningful benefits in terms of economic efficiency. These approaches assert that institutions can be efficient, rational and provide the incentives necessary to make optimal choices; social actors are prompted to follow institutional rules to secure their legitimacy in the eyes of others; specific institutional frameworks encourage cooperative IR and competitive advantage; institutions reflect historical compromises and obey different logics and rationalities at different times; institutional coordination is a political process that is incomplete, contested, and ongoing; contractual relations depend on embedded formal and informal rules; and that national institutional frameworks consist of competing organizing principles, develop in a non-linear manner, reflect the choices of social actors, and adjust in ways that assume regional and sectoral dimensions (Lane and Wood 2009; Wood and Lane 2011).

Given the interdependence between firms' choices and the support and stability provided by intra- and inter-firm institutions, the employment relationship must be treated as part of a more widely embracing 'employment system' (Boyer 1994; Cappelli 1995; Marsden 2004; Rubery and Grimshaw 2003; Whitley 1999). Such regulatory systems—involving both the basic rules limiting management's authority and the supporting institutions that assist in their enforcement—are differentiated in terms of the manner in which the limits of managerial authority are established (Marsden 1999). While a particular type of employment relationship may not be the ideal form of contracting for a particular type of firm or service, the more widely it is adopted, the more effective it becomes both to constrain and to enable, and so the more likely it is to be chosen by others (Marsden 1999: 5). It is adopted because everyone knows how it works, and is confident it will provide a stable framework for collaboration in the workplace. This level of institutionalization is often used as evidence for the relative uniformity of organizations within particular societies. A second level is provided by the integration of the employment relationship into national employment systems that vary with regard to the extent and reach of institutionalization. These institutional patterns or degrees of embeddedness are widely regarded as providing the key to explaining the significant international variations in the way the employment relationship is organized. Shifts in managerial strategies are often more strongly associated with institutional features of the economy and the local labour market than with any particular policy innovation on the part of employers. Understanding the conditioning effects of institutional constraints on managerial behaviour, however, has not been greatly assisted by the models of strategic choice that have historically informed much of the literature on HRM.

'HRM' is widely regarded as an equivocal and elusive concept (Boselie et al. 2005; Kaufman 2004; Keenoy 1997; Legge 1995). This constitutes a significant obstacle in the way of providing a coherent assessment of HRM. Comparing different typologies of HRM is complicated by the fact that they proceed from different conceptions of its key features and basic assumptions. This problem is compounded by the fact that, in much of the HRM literature, normative prescription elides with empirical description. The prescriptive aspect is, by definition, open to the challenge that it has no bearing on reality. To be sure, HRM's key prescriptions of integrating human resource policies with each other and the organization's business strategy and pursuing 'high commitment' and 'employee involvement' are prone to 'stilted generalizations that neglect both the complexities and dynamism of real organizations' (Legge 1978: 16). The rationalistic, unitary view of the firm, which informs much of the HRM literature, implies that employers have unique insights into the implications of their decisions, largely rules out the possibility of unintended and unanticipated consequences, disconnects managerial practices from the wider institutional context, and overlooks the often-competing interests and objectives guiding the behaviour of actors at various levels within the firm.

An important feature of debates about the value of HRM relates to the opposition between universalistic claims of 'best-practice' and contextualized accounts of 'best-fit' (see Almond 2011; Brewster et al. 2008; Kim and Wright 2010; Paauwe and Boselie 2003). The idea that organizations are embedded in wider institutional environments and that their behaviour is a response to market pressures as well as formal and informal institutional pressures is juxtaposed to the idea that certain human resource practices are universally successful. Besides the significant methodological weaknesses in universalistic accounts of HRM 'bundles' (Hesketh and Fleetwood 2006; Kaufman 2010; Keegan and Boselie 2006; Paauwe 2009), the implication is that employers are largely unconstrained in their ability to manage employees and to construct control mechanisms in the workplace. Since it fails to take seriously the institutional nature of the employment relationship, this conception is fundamentally flawed (Marsden 2004). While the decline in collective representation in many industrialized countries has led some to cast doubt on the continuing relevance and traction of many traditional IR concepts, the idea that non-union firms are arenas of free managerial choice, blind obedience, and unquestioning employee commitment is misleading in the extreme. Several studies have shown that the negotiation of order and the institutionalization of the wage–effort bargain— even in workplaces that lack formal and collective procedures—are far more complex and contradictory than is often assumed (Edwards 1986; Moule 1998; Ram et al. 2001).

The distinction between liberal market economies and coordinated market economies is implicated in the two contrasting versions or forms of HRM: a 'hard' version stresses the idea of 'resource' and proposes that the services of employees should be used dispassionately and in a formally rational manner, whereas a 'soft' version emphasizes the term 'human' and suggests that the potential of employees should be released through communication, motivation, and leadership (Adeleye 2011; Gill 1999; Pudelko 2006; Truss et al. 1997; Storey 1992). According to Keenoy (1997: 825), the differentiation between hard and soft HRM constitutes 'the dominant conceptual-analytical interpretative scheme within the field'. Hard and soft versions of HRM are diametrically opposed along a number of dimensions, and they have been used by many commentators as expedients to classify approaches to managing employees according to utilitarian-instrumentalist or developmental-humanist principles (Legge 1995). To be sure, such binary contrasts are a recurring theme in the work and employment relations literature and not unique to HRM. For instance, McGregor's (1960) influential Theory X and Theory Y managerial approaches are a notable precursor to the basic dichotomy between hard and soft approaches to HRM.

The hard version of HRM amounts to an instrumental approach that regards employees simply as a factor of production, which the enterprise may hire, deploy, and dispose at will. In the processes of planning, the workforce is usually considered rationally in the same way as the other factors of production and their individual needs are seldom taken into account. This version of HRM also emphasizes the development of measurable criteria to select the right candidate for the job and to assess and monitor the performance of existing employees. Key aspects of the hard approach to HRM include the following: the effective management of human resources is incompatible with trade unions and extensive state intervention in the labour market; control of the enterprise must remain firmly in the hands of management to the exclusion of all other stakeholders; the organization is characterized by a formal structure, a clearly defined chain of command, and management-driven policies and goals; cost-control is emphasized by maintaining the lowest possible headcount and matching labour supply closely to product market demand; unitarist assumptions of a coincidence in the interests of employers and employees legitimize management's unilateral decision-making powers and discredit employee opposition to managerial actions; emphasis is placed on individual employee attributes and motivation; and the value of an employee is derived from the match between his or her skills and the requirements of the enterprise.

This model is also known as the 'matching' or 'best-fit' approach to HRM: it requires that human resource strategies are closely integrated into the overall strategies of the business. As such, it limits the role of HRM to a reactive function, which is driven by and derived directly from organizational strategies and is aimed primarily at increasing the firm's competitive advantage. The hard approach to HRM may deliver a more cost-effective workforce where decision-making is quicker and focused on senior managers. Since organizational interests must prevail over those of the employees, hard HRM may necessitate confrontation with the workforce to implement its concepts. The emphasis on rigorous monitoring of employee performance, the maintenance of extensive managerial prerogatives, strict discipline, and a general disregard of the interests and concerns of employees provide fertile soil for employee discontent, resentment, absenteeism, turnover, and instrumental compliance. In an increasingly competitive context, firms that adopt hard practices focused on resource exploitation to the exclusion of soft practices focused on human resource development are likely to gain efficiency in the short term at the cost of long-term decline. Moreover, a labour process can rarely, if ever, be designed to eliminate the need for consent, initiative, and cooperation from employees.

The 'soft' version of HRM regards employees as a vital asset to any business organization and emphasizes the need to support, develop, motivate, and involve the workforce. In contrast to the hard version of HRM, the orientation of the soft approach to HRM is strategic and less functional, authoritarian, and rigid. On this view, employees are not intrinsically lazy, disinclined to work, lacking in responsibility, or motivated exclusively by financial gain. Under the right conditions, employees will accept greater responsibility, be creative and proactive, seek self-fulfilment through their work, and tie the satisfaction of their aspirations and interests to those of the organization. Soft HRM is therefore concerned with the values that the organization must nurture to ensure the commitment, trust, and collaboration of its employees. Key aspects of this version of HRM include the following: a willingness to invest in skills and organizational development; a management style that seeks to elicit trust and partnership; profit-sharing and reciprocal relations in the workplace; communication and conflict management; an organizational culture that values long-term relationships, employee commitment to the goals of the organization, and collaboration between the parties; and an appreciation of the personal and social needs of employees. While this approach also endorses the unitarist assumption that the workplace is a cohesive and harmonious entity, it does allow space for some collective forms of employee representation. The basic assumption that informs soft HRM is that an organization's competitive advantage can best be maintained through its employees rather than at their expense.

By acknowledging and valuing the needs and interests of employees, human resource managers are able to secure higher levels of commitment, motivation, and responsiveness among staff members. A central component of this regime is delegated levels of authority, responsibility, and power. With greater employee commitment to the goals of the organization comes a greater willingness to accept management's control over the organization of work, a more positive attitude towards learning and development, higher levels of job satisfaction, an enhanced adaptability, and a greater inclination to take on additional responsibilities. A soft approach to HRM also raises the productivity of the workforce and reduces any potential human resource costs, which may arise from strikes, turnover, and absenteeism due to adversarial relationships between the parties. By constructing the long-term competitive advantage of an organization on a multi-skilled, flexible, and committed workforce, the soft version of HRM underscores the positive employee responses to inclusive communication channels, comprehensive motivational techniques, cooperative leadership style, increased employee involvement, and an improved quality of working life. The basic features necessary to sustain these aspects of soft HRM include the active promotion of teamwork; extensive and ongoing managerial support for cohesive relations among employees as well as between employees and management; consistent efforts aimed at creating a working environment that is conducive to high-quality performance; and maintaining channels of communication that relate directly to the tasks assigned to individual employees. While the soft approach may address the deficit in employee motivation and commitment associated with the hard approach, an inherent danger of the soft approach is that the costs associated with securing employee commitment may leave the business at a competitive disadvantage. There is also no compelling empirical evidence that committed workers are more productive than closely controlled ones.

Hard and soft versions of HRM have gained widespread currency despite the fact that available empirical evidence seems to suggest that neither model accurately represents what is happening within organizations (Almond 2011; Boselie et al. 2005; Brewster et al. 2006; Gamble 2010; Rees and Edwards 2009). While many organizations claim employees are their most valuable asset, in reality the interests of the organization always take priority over those of the individual employee. Management practice seems to waver between resource-orientated and human-orientated approaches. As Keenoy (1997: 838) points out, hard and soft versions of HRM are mutually implicated tendencies that are complementary and dependent on each other rather than a linear dimension of distinctive, concrete, and separate forms, and that, once separated, become 'deeply deceptive re-presentations'. While this may suggest a combination of both approaches is a more accurate reflection of reality, it does not address the fact that management's actions are caught on the horns of a dilemma: 'solving' problems of commitment and legitimacy raises problems of control and authority (and vice versa). Given a context of increasingly competitive markets, firms face the difficult task of balancing the conflicting requirements of efficiency (cost cutting, innovation, flexibility) and equity (benefits, training, involvement). Achieving and maintaining a balance between efficiency and equity in the workplace depends on the endlessly demanding task of 'creating and maintaining the institutional forms that will maximise [the employees'] willingness to work efficiently' (Brown and Nolan 1988: 353). The broad managerial objectives of minimizing unit labour costs, ensuring internal certainty, and retaining the widest possible degree of control over the decision-making processes are not necessarily consistent and priorities will differ in terms of the demands of a particular situation. In practice, therefore, managers often have to reach compromises between these objectives. As Legge (1995: 14) puts it: the fact that 'personnel specialists oscillate between the "personnel" and "management", between "caring" and "control" aspects of the function, can be attributed to their role in mediating a major contradiction embedded in capitalist systems: the need to achieve both the control *and* consent of employees'.

Despite rhetoric to the contrary, most businesses are said to prioritize hard shareholder goals over soft stakeholder goals. The enduring divide between rhetoric and reality—a central theme in the critical analyses of HRM (Kaufman 2010; Legge 1995; Thompson 2011; Watson 2004)—is reflected in the contrast between the pervasive rhetoric of soft HRM, which insists that employees are a firm's most vital asset and the sole, sustainable basis of competitive advantage, and the hard reality of a slow diffusion of human-centred HRM practices and the primacy of shareholder value. While these criticisms may be valid in some sectors, firms, and/or occupations, the importance of labour costs and allocational efficiencies should not be emphasized at the expense of labour quality and dynamic efficiencies. Given differing socio-institutional contexts and the contesting forces involved in the formulation and implementation of managerial strategies, some trade-offs between hard and soft approaches are to be expected. The particular blend of approaches that is likely to prevail depends in large measure on the constraints and opportunities, as well as the distribution of risks and rewards, associated with the prevailing system of labour regulation.

The hard versus soft HRM dichotomy fails to do justice to the variety of possible combinations of regulatory forms, thereby underestimating the range of organizational types and behaviours that are possible or feasible in different contexts. The implicit notion that there exists 'one best way' to manage the workplace is incompatible with the complex and contingent ways in which order is actually negotiated under specific conditions. Current industrial and employment restructuring proceeds from radically different patterns of work organization and governance. Changes in the workplace are complex and depend on a range of contingencies such as the prevailing systems of labour market regulation, the exposure of the business to the vagaries of international competition, and so on. A system of regulation takes on the character of a trial-and-error process in which each trial changes the environment for the next, so that 'successful' strategies depend not only on their intrinsic qualities, but also on when and where they are implemented. Labour management issues, according to Spencer (2000: 555),

> are dealt with under conditions of deep uncertainty, creating an important gap between intent and outcome in actual managerial practice. In this sense, labour management is an ongoing process, involving frequent surprise and disappointment. Thus, it cannot always be assumed that the actions taken by capitalist employers are in any meaningful sense the 'best' ones, or more importantly, will yield the same results, regardless of when and where they are taken.

While soft HRM is increasingly substituted by 'high commitment' HRM and hard HRM by 'strategic' HRM (Brooks et al. 2011; Kaufman 2010; Kim and Wright 2010), these categories often fail to provide definitive criteria to distinguish between the actual forms that HRM assumes in practice. This disjuncture between theory and practice—as reflected in variations in the actual recruitment, selection, deployment, and control of human resources—has led some to suggest that employers adopt 'hybrid' models of HRM (Meardi and Tóth 2006; Pache 2010; Rees and Edwards 2009; Tregaskis et al. 2001). Broadly defined, 'hybridization' refers to 'the creation of new management practices out of selective adaptation, innovation and change' (Morgan, cited in Gamble 2010: 706). The notion of hybridization is particularly prominent in the comparative HRM literature on the diffusion and adaptation of organizational practices (Almond 2011; Boselie et al. 2005; Boyer et al. 1998; Brewster et al. 2006; Ferner et al. 2005; Kahancova 2007). Far from being a residual possibility, the impact of local institutional conditions on enterprise HRM policies invariably leads to a variety of hybrid arrangements. While much of this literature is concerned with describing the impact of home and host country effects, Elger and Smith (2005: 362) note that the notion of hybridization can also be applied effectively to 'the emergence of distinctive configurations that may depart from both home-based templates and local practices'. At the level of the firm, IR and labour process scholars suggest that most organizations are hybrids that combine elements of different models: since management styles are always embedded in a particular context, the change process will entail the pursuit of new initiatives alongside the continuation of established practices; the devolution of managerial authority, combined with technological and strategic factors, will tend to produce different management styles within the same organization; and given the variation in skills and bargaining power among employees, different management styles are likely to be applied to different segments of the workforce (Friedman 2000; Salamon 1998).

While hybridization is a pervasive phenomenon across and within national capitalisms, the hybridization thesis should not be reduced to the claim that organizational variety is purely a product of the way employers have modified the guiding principles of HRM in response to the requirements of the local institutional context. A significant part of the variety within and between firms is a product of managerial efforts to draw on local institutional and normative resources in ways that offer distinct compromises between conflicting interests in the workplace. Research on 'hybridization' has frequently deployed it in an undifferentiated, mechanical fashion that impedes multi-scalar analysis and conceptual bricolage (Gamble 2010; Meardi and Tóth 2006). The constitution and institutional bases of hybridization are empirical questions that require detailed historical evidence of the processes of institutional diffusion, borrowing, clashes, and complementarity. Broad generalized categories are inadequate to explore the complex dynamics and diverse patterns of hybridization. This clearly suggests that the binary opposition between hard and soft HRM is a poor reflection of the variety in managerial practices. Even hybrid models, however, often fail to account for conditions and practices that are not captured by the basic models, which they rely on as evidence of hybridization. That is, the notion of 'hybridization' presupposes an underlying coherence and rationality within prevailing typologies of managerial practice. Variations in managerial practice could also be interpreted as proof of the deficiencies of extant taxonomic categories and the inherent heterogeneity, disjointedness, and contingency of actual managerial practices. The tensions between interpretations of difference as hybridization of ideal types or as evidence of the limitations of prevailing typologies presuppose contrasting conceptions of the articulation of scales of governance, the spatio-temporal dynamics of capitalist economic development, and the institutional and normative foundations of diversity in work and employment relations.

Labour Regulation: Scales of Governance, Uneven Development, and the Foundations of Diversity

The complex dialectic between accumulation and regulation unfolds in a variety of different ways as reflected in the diversity of modes of regulation. Since social structures of accumulation and regulation are relatively autonomous, yet bound together dialectically in an essential or necessary relation, the causal liabilities with which they are endowed will be realized in different ways at different times and places, depending on contingent circumstances (Jessop et al. 2008). Modes of regulation are formed through indeterminate socio-political struggles and the contingent institutional mediation of capitalist accumulation. Regulationists emphasize the conjunctural determination of economic development and insist that the societal variability of the forms taken by the employment relationship is a product of 'the multiple levels that play a significant role in the structuring of the system and that reflect the heterogeneity of economic and social space' (Michon 1992: 227). For regulationists, the different levels of governance are characterized by relations of emergence—that is, lower levels are emergent from, yet irreducible to, higher levels. Labour regulation, for example, would be impossible in the absence of wider processes and structures of social regulation such as the state, the family, schools, and prisons. As a site of regulation, however, the workplace is ontologically constituted by sets of relations that cannot simply be reduced to wider processes of social reproduction.

The concepts of 'rootedness' and 'emergence' allow for a move away from both functionalist notions of context and reductionist accounts of the interaction between the various scales of governance. As against atomism and holism, Bhaskar's (2008) theory of emergence enables us to conceive of real, irreducible wholes that are both composed of parts that are themselves real irreducible wholes, and are in turn parts of larger wholes, with each level of this hierarchy of composition having its own peculiar mechanisms and emergent powers. The diverse national growth paths of capitalist societies are attributable to variations in factors such as institutional frameworks, industrial profiles, political alliances, and the balance of class forces. There is thus considerable scope for incongruence between the structural forms of Fordism and their expression in strategic patterns and institutional forms, as well as for significant national and local variations (Jessop 1994). Local institutional variability should be understood as 'part and parcel of a wider process of *spatially uneven development*' (Peck 1996: 102). The issue is not simply which levels are becoming more or less significant, but changing *relations* within and between levels.

Labour regulation, as the mediation of power relations, takes place at multiple levels or scales. In the regulation approach, as Peck (2000: 68) notes, there is 'nothing theoretically pre-ordained or fixed... about the scale at which regulatory functions are sited'. The sites of regulation are heterogeneous, follow diverse logics, draw on divergent resources, cover varying aspects of the employment relationship, and mobilize and rely on different tools of legitimation. Crucially, there can be no guarantees that the complex and dialectical interaction between the various scales of governance will be coherent or functional for work and employment relations. Comprehending local modes of labour regulation requires a careful consideration of emergent complex, concrete regulatory systems as well as their manifestation via specific regulatory forms and mechanisms that operate in and through a variety of spatial scales. Peck and Tickell (1992, 1994) argue that a local mode of regulation is not to be understood as a microcosm of a national mode, merely relaying a national agenda unproblematically. However, they also insist that a local mode of regulation does not indicate the domain of exclusively local regulatory practices. While regulatory functions may be anchored at the local level, a local regulatory system is defined largely by its mode of integration into wider structures, while the latter are simultaneously partly constituted of, and by, local systems. The focus is on local agencies and mechanisms that comprise the medium though which regulatory practices are articulated, interpreted, and instantiated.

A meso-level theorization of the local labour market is an indispensable component of any explanation of the disjuncture between general processes of labour regulation and the variety of local outcomes. By combining a critical realist interpretation of the relationship between labour market processes and space with a regulationist interpretation of the distinctive ways in which labour markets and their regulatory institutions interrelate at the local level, Peck (1996) demonstrates how local labour markets are both constructed (in terms of the concrete working out of generative mechanisms underpinning them) and socially regulated (in terms of the distinctive 'regulatory milieux' formed in and round them) in locally specific ways. This is also implied in the distinction drawn by French regulation theorists between: (a) the *rapport salarial*—the general configuration of the employment relationship in relation to the exchange, utilization, and reproduction of the labour force; and (b) the *fait salarial*—the specific institutional form exhibited by the employment relationship in particular industries, regions, and countries. Concrete research on local forms of labour regulation must therefore consider the intersection of a localized *fait salarial* with the broader processes of uneven development in the *rapport salarial*. If each local labour market represents a unique geographic conjuncture of regulatory processes, it follows that the institutional form of the employment relationship (the *fait salarial*) will also take on a locally distinctive character.

Integrating an analysis of macroeconomic forces with a methodological sensitivity to uneven development, according to Peck (1996: 102–5), allows us to conceive the relationship between labour regulation and uneven development at three levels of abstraction. First, uneven development must itself be regulated in that a regulatory regime must be capable of containing the geographic contradictions of the prevailing mode of growth. While regimes of accumulation typically contain a distinctive spatial 'core' and 'periphery', each national variant displays a specific form of uneven spatial development. Second, national regulation produces uneven geographic effects both intentionally and incidentally. Intentionally, some policies are designed explicitly as spatially targeted interventions. Incidentally, even policies that appear to be non-spatial inevitably produce uneven spatial effects because of the uneven geographic distribution of the affected phenomena. A third aspect of the relationship between social regulation and uneven development concerns the 'interaction effects' resulting from the interplay between regulatory processes and historically prior uses of space. While a particular policy programme may possess immanent tendencies, whether and how those tendencies are realized as empirical outcomes will vary from place to place depending on their interaction with pre-existing institutional and economic structures and with the particular configuration of labour–capital–state relationships at the local level.

Given the complex relationship between governance and uneven development, there can be no universal functions and effects of labour regulation. The latter inevitably vary from place to place. Although it is certainly permissible to make general statements about national models of labour regulation, emphasis needs to be placed on the fact that national systems are internally differentiated along a myriad of fault lines. 'The geographical anatomy of labour regulatory systems results not only from their internal tendencies and causal liabilities, but also from the complex and indeterminate ways in which these are reconciled with other, simultaneously unfolding social processes and in contingent interactions with prior institutional uses and space' (Peck 1996: 105). A logical conclusion is that a range of localized institutional forms underpins the geographically distinctive ways in which labour markets are regulated. There is scope for local agency, but it is bound by a broader set of structural parameters that relate to state policies, product market conditions, and so on. The local configuration of opportunities and constraints for regulatory functions, according to Peck (1996: 109), should be conceived not so much as a locally organized regime or system, but more as a set of regulatory/institutional dialectics articulated at the local level.

The conceptual tools of regulation theory allow us to explain how IR projects emerge, interact, and combine to produce particular workplace regimes and, once produced, how they are vulnerable to the basic contradictions, crisis tendencies, and conflicts inherent in the employment relationship and to struggles for the dominance or hegemony of rival IR projects. The focus is therefore not only on how different configurations of institutional forms can be stabilized, but also on different patterns of conflict and compromise and the relative, precarious and contingent success of strategic interventions. In short, regulationists regard institutional integration as deeply problematic. According to Jessop (2002: 34–6), particular institutional forms are 'always constituted in and through action, always tendential and always in need of stabilization... [and] never wholly constrain actions'. Any form of stability that does arise in work and employment relations is therefore socially constructed, politically mediated and institutionally embedded. Hyman (1994: 7–10) underlines the value of regulation theory for making sense of the relative stabilization of IR in developed countries during the mid-twentieth century and its subsequent instability and change (see also Friedman 2000; Lucio and MacKenzie 2004; Vidal 2011). That is, tendencies towards the stabilization of IR through the institutionalization of conflict are neither linear nor irreversible, but rather historically conditioned and contingent concomitants of a distinct phase of economic evolution.

Labour's fictive commodity status and the inherently open-ended nature of the employment contract provide the basic impulse for labour regulation. A contract of employment empowers the employer to utilize an employee's capacity for a specified period and typically in a specified range of tasks, but the exact content and pace of work or initiative to be displayed by the employee cannot be predetermined contractually (Edwards 1995). The contract of employment is thus a social contract, endowed with implied expectations and embedded in extra-contractual relations of trust and reciprocity (Streeck 1992: 46). The notion of an 'incomplete contract' is a defining feature of capitalism and has major implications for its overall dynamic. Since an employment contract cannot specify the precise relationship between income and performance and cost control must be continuously emphasized and achieved, the detail of the wage–effort bargain is subject to continuous and usually tacit negotiation. This indeterminacy provides the formal conditions under which employers hire and utilize labour power and implies a model of the employment relationship as essentially a power relationship, qualitatively different from a 'pure' exchange relationship. It follows that labour regulation plays the role that it does because the employment relationship is structured in the way that it is.

Labour regulation is geared towards the mediation of conflicting objectives and the management of antagonistic social forces. It is characterized by a complex and contingent amalgam of regulatory mechanisms, which comprise variegated bundles of rights and obligations, opportunities and constraints, takes place at more or less mutually coordinated levels, and is comprised of more or less mutually integrated forms. However, no regulatory system comprises a stable, unified, functionally integrated totality, but always reflects the antagonistic and contradictory logic of the employment relationship. Under capitalism there is a perpetual tension between treating workers as commodities to be hired and fired, and harnessing their ingenuity and cooperativeness. For a system of labour regulation to provide a stable foundation for collaboration in the workplace, it must maintain an institutional and normative framework capable of sustaining an (always partial and unstable) compromise between the employer's need for efficiency and the employee's need for equity. Market relations cannot perform this intricate and fundamentally social task, and there can be no stable or long-term solutions in the context of a structured antagonism between capital and labour. The extra-economic factors that are required to 'resolve' this regulatory dilemma contribute to the intrinsically politicized nature of managerial practices.

The framework that gives a particular employment system its coherence and functionality, and tempers the outright exercise of economic power, is best viewed as 'a form of micro-political regulation, as a social constitution' (Jones 1996: 127). Reproducing and regularizing the employment relationship therefore involves a 'social fix' that compensates for the constitutive incompleteness of the labour contract and gives it a specific dynamic through the articulation of its economic and extra-economic elements. This social fix, which includes the imposition of various 'spatio-temporal fixes', helps to secure a relatively durable structural coherence by containing, displacing, or deferring the contradictions and dilemmas inherent in the employment relationship so that different forms, institutions, and practices tend to be mutually reinforcing (Jessop 2002). Spatio-temporal fixes facilitate the institutionalized compromises on which accumulation and regulation depend by delimiting the boundaries within which structural coherence is secured, and externalizing certain costs of securing this coherence beyond and within these boundaries. This may involve

> super-exploitation of internal or external spaces outside the compromise, super-exploitation of nature or inherited social resources, deferral of problems into an indefinite future and, of course, the exploitation and/or oppression of specific classes, strata or other social categories... The primary scales and temporal horizons

around which such fixes are built and the extent of their coherence vary considerably over time... As part of a given spatio-temporal fix, different institutions, apparatuses or agencies may specialize primarily in one or other horn of a dilemma, deal with it over different temporal horizons, or address different aspects at different times. (Jessop 2002: 49–50)

As labour regulation develops, different institutions tend to emerge to express different moments of its dilemmas and tensions and these may then interact to compensate for the indeterminacy of labour potential within the framework of specific spatio-temporal fixes and institutionalized class compromises. The variability of regulatory dilemmas and tensions suggests a corresponding variability in viable institutional responses. It follows that there is no single best solution to the regularization of the employment relationship and the overall course of IR will depend on how different solutions complement or clash with each other. Moreover, there are always 'interstitial, residual, marginal, irrelevant, recalcitrant and plain contradictory elements that escape subordination to any given principle of [social organization] and, indeed, serve as reservoirs of flexibility and innovation as well as actual or potential sources of disorder' (Jessop 2002: 22). The regulatory dilemmas arising from the incorporation, allocation, control, and reproduction of labour are systemic and ultimately 'resolvable' only in terms of temporary and partial institutional containment. Hence, the institutional framework of the employment relationship, while necessary for its continued reproduction, does not fully resolve its underlying contradictions. Institutional responses, as Peck (1996: 26) explains, rarely if ever provide unconditional solutions to regulatory dilemmas. Rather, the process of labour regulation is continuous and imperfect, and any social fix is always contingent on the simultaneous operation of a range of other mediation mechanisms.

The binary contrast in the HRM literature between low discretion, hierarchical forms of control and high discretion, decentralized forms of control is incapable of shedding light on the diversity of managerial practices that fall between these extremes. The taxonomic approach of HRM tends to underestimate both the 'tremendous variations' in how the 'detailed control' of work is exercised (Thompson and McHugh 1990: 147) and the extent to which different configurations of product and labour market pressures are likely to give rise to distinctive strategies for regulating the employment relationship (Tsoukas 2000: 41). Moreover, control cannot be adequately conceived in terms of 'discrete management systems that embody a single organizational logic; bureaucracy coexists with decentralization rooted in opposing organizational logics' (Gottfried 1994: 121). Hakim's (1990) research shows that employers rely on a blend of HRM policies with few sharp distinctions and considerable overlap between types, and some ambiguity and variation within types. There is thus no single, clear division between strategies, but rather many gradations. Hence, it is necessary to move down a level of abstraction in order to consider the more concrete dynamics of labour regulation. Descending from the abstract level of analysis means coming to grips with the complexity and indeterminacy of institutional restructuring (Peck and Theodore 2007). Empirically, strategies may be combined, and the particularities of each case will reflect institutional legacies, conjunctural conditions, the balance of class forces, and so on. In their efforts to convert labour power into actual work performance, managers are confronted by a complex amalgam of constraints and opportunities, and have (differential) access to various mechanisms of control and coordination. As Edwards (1986: 41) argues,

> [f]irms will develop their practices of labour control with whatever materials they have available. They are unlikely to have explicit strategies and more likely to react to particular circumstances as best they can. Even when they have fairly clear goals they are unlikely to follow a policy which conforms to an ideal-type: they will proceed according to their own needs. In particular, they are likely to use a variety of means of controlling the labour process and tying workers to the firm.

Typologies of managerial practices must reflect endogenous as well as exogenous opportunities and constraints as mediated through prevailing normative and institutional frameworks, discursive apparatuses, organizational structures, and regulatory mechanisms. The recurrent tendencies towards instability, which continually threaten to undermine the equilibrating effects of regulation, are rooted in a tension in the very purpose of managerial control: namely, that managers require workers to be 'both dependable and disposable' (Hyman 1987: 43). Distinct regulatory frameworks reflect, in part, the manner in which a particular distribution of the costs and rewards of production is institutionalized. The notion of a 'frontier of control' allows for a range of possible tactics by management, with the degree of discretion conceded to workers being dependent on (among others) the levels of worker resistance and competitive market pressures. A frontier of control signifies the fact there is no one best way to manage the workplace, 'only different routes to partial failure' (Hyman 1987: 30). The dialectical interplay of control and autonomy generates a force that shapes the nature of the regulatory system itself. The frontier of control is therefore a crystallization of the balance of powers at a given time and place. As such, it is conditional, unstable, always open to renegotiation and reflects the imprecise limits of managerial authority and employee compliance. Instead of positing simple dichotomies, a retroductive analysis of the socio-political, institutional, and normative context that makes particular managerial practices possible will yield a deeper appreciation of the variegated and contingent realization of the management function. The wider institutional and cultural milieu in which systems of labour regulation are embedded is so dynamic and varied that grand models of managerial practices are bound to be static and reductionist. Robust efficiency–equity couplings are chance discoveries emanating from resistance and accommodation between management and labour, which in turn generate a specific strategic terrain on and through which subsequent interaction between the parties will take place.

Conclusion

The epistemological and ontological principles that inform regulationist accounts suggest that science proceeds by uncovering the underlying structures which generate surface-level appearances, and that social reality is intrinsically dynamic and complexly structured, consisting in human agency, structures, and contexts of action, each presupposing the other without being reducible to any other (James 2009; Lawson 1997). In line with these principles, research should be focused on the working out of causal processes in different contexts and locating managerial practices in terms of wider patterns of uneven development and the forms of conflict and accommodation at various scales (Peck 1996). In contrast to the functionalist implications of some institutional approaches, regulated outcomes are conceived as potentially conflict-ridden and destructive of the reproduction of the regulatory system itself. The contested nature of national institutional complexes is easily overlooked in taxonomic approaches with an overriding concern for internal coherence and systemic continuity (Jessop 2011). In contrast to the voluntaristic undertones of strategic choice models, the emphasis on the structural determination of choice accentuates the need to explore the conditions of possibility for different types of change.

If we are to avoid emptying social structures of their context-related or essential content, we need to take seriously the fact that the general coherence of an IR system takes on a variety of different institutional forms and spatio-temporal modalities. In addition, since work and employment relations are not infinitely malleable and vary in their amenability to different types and degrees of control, the various forms of regulation yield different levels and kinds of power according to the nature of the activities concerned (Sayer 1995). In the real world, there are only conjuncturally specific forms of regulation involving definite objects of regulation constituted in and through distinct modes of regulation (Jessop 1990). Understanding the variable effects and differential reach of regulatory mechanisms involves, among others, exploring the different conditions under which these mechanisms may be activated to regulate struggles in the workplace and beyond. Accordingly, a description of the generic forms, functions, and outcomes of managerial practices falls short of a genuinely explanatory account of the actual tendencies, powers, and liabilities of a particular mode of labour regulation.

The nature of labour power is such that the market for labour is shot through with contradictions, tensions, and dilemmas of regulation. Pressures for regulation do not necessarily result in effective institutional mediation. The claim that the labour market's inherent capacity for self-destruction necessitates social regulation should not be confused with either a crude functionalism in which appropriate regulatory responses are somehow always materialized or institutionalist perspectives that regard the dilemmas of labour regulation as somehow soluble in an absolute sense once an 'appropriate' institutional framework is established. The necessity for extra-market regulation of the employment relationship does not imply a particular institutional response, nor can the effects of institutional interventions be guaranteed. Moreover, once it is accepted that there are no institutional guarantees that class struggles will be confined within the boundaries of a given form, it becomes possible to explore how these struggles can both reproduce and transform the dominance of specific forms (Jessop 1988: 151). The approach defended here, which Peck (1996: 42) describes as 'regulatory necessity but institutional indeterminacy', is not rooted in naive faith in the efficacy and rationality of extra-market interventions, but rather in the strength of the case for systemic labour market failure. Institutional formation and articulation invariably produce unanticipated consequences as the behaviour of labour market actors is adjusted in complex, dynamic, and contingent ways to the changing regulatory framework. Once established, labour market institutions acquire their own bureaucratic and political impetus, which only fortuitously will happen to coincide with the shifting regulatory requirements of the employment relationship. This approach allows us to proceed beyond mere taxonomies of managerial practices to explore their conditions of possibility, emergent properties, contradictions, reproduction, and propensity for transformation.

Attempts to impose the logic of HRM on the changes unfolding in the workplace rests on the questionable assumption that ostensibly similar features (e.g. team working and employee involvement) in different work and employment relations systems can be regarded as analogous, comparable outside their contexts, and hence open to similar interpretations. Although the dominant regulatory forms tend to place limits on the patterns of the work and employment relations, there are no a priori rules dictating how diverse regulatory mechanisms will be coordinated in a specific empirical context. This is partly a product of the differential interaction across time and space between the institutional processes associated with production, reproduction, and social regulation. Furthermore, variations in systems of labour regulation rarely amount to a simple extension or restriction of the role of institutional regulation to the benefit or detriment of market mechanisms (Deakin and Reed 2000; Lucio and MacKenzie 2004; Regini 2000). Given the variety of levels at which the employment relationship may be coordinated and the non-zero-sum articulation of markets and institutions, it is misleading to classify managerial practices in terms of a simple contrast between the relative influence of markets and institutions. The forms that regulation assumes and the dynamics that it displays are determined in large measure by the structures and propensities of the object that is to be regulated. The employment relationship is dependent on numerous mechanisms of reproduction, regularization, and governance capable of generating the social rules and conventions necessary for its cohesion and durability. As a complex and contingently realized 'fit' between institutional mediation and capital accumulation, labour regulation is patterned by prevailing institutional frameworks; unevenly realized across space, time, and scales; and inherently unstable and conflict-ridden. A search for coherent regulatory modes is misguided: regulation is always emergent and tendential rather than being achieved (Painter and Goodwin 1995). In other words, the reality of local regulatory dialectics is incompatible with the idea of a standard set of solutions that can be applied independently of local contexts.

Since management of the production process can potentially 'degenerate into a power capable of destroying the labour force it has subjugated...capitalism must be hemmed in by constraining structures' (Aglietta 1998: 50). Regulation is therefore fundamentally concerned with placing limits on capital's boundless desire to accumulate profits. Since neo-liberalism aims to dislocate or dilute these limits, its predominance as a global economic policy framework is bound to have profound institutional and normative implications. Insofar as its policy prescriptions are reflected in the competitive downgrading of regulatory norms through the increasing prominence of market-based forms of regulation, flexibilization of the labour market, and the casualization of employment, neo-liberalism is deeply implicated in the contested, unstable and fractional nature of labour regulation. Accordingly, Brenner et al.'s (2010: 331–2) analysis of neo-liberalization provides crucial insights into the processes of regulation:

> The uneven development of neoliberalization results, on the one hand, from the continuous collision between contextually specific, constantly evolving neoliberalization projects and inherited politico-institutional arrangements, whether at global, national, or local scales. At the same time, through this collision, neoliberalization processes rework inherited forms of regulatory and spatial organization, including those of state institutions themselves, to produce new forms of geo-institutional differentiation... [N]eoliberalization processes... should not be viewed as representing a totality encompassing all aspects of regulatory restructuring in any context, site, or scale. Rather, neoliberalization is one among several competing processes of regulatory restructuring that have been articulated... Neoliberalization is never manifested in a pure form, as a comprehensive or encompassing regulatory whole. Instead, neoliberalization tendencies can only be articulated in incomplete, hybrid modalities, which may crystallize in certain regulatory formations, but which are nevertheless continually and eclectically reworked in context-specific ways. Consequently, empirical evidence underscoring the stalled, incomplete, discontinuous, or differentiated character of projects to impose market rule, or their coexistence alongside potentially antagonistic projects... does not provide a sufficient basis for questioning their neoliberalized, neoliberalizing dimensions... Crucially, however, as unevenly as neoliberalization processes have been articulated, they have not entailed a haphazard 'piling up' of disconnected, contextually contained regulatory experiments. Rather, processes of neoliberalization have generated significant, markedly patterned, cumulative effects upon the geo-regulatory configuration of capitalism.

The recurrent realignment of the local and the global and the continuously shifting balance between social equity and economic efficiency are best captured by a view of regulatory articulation as multi-faceted, variable, incomplete, faltering, unstable, and conflict-ridden. Locating uneven development at the heart of regulatory processes provides a basis for rethinking their 'discontinuous, wave-like historical ascendancy, their mottled, polymorphic and striated geographies, their associated contradictions and crisis-tendencies, and their contemporary limits' (Brenner et al. 2009: 217). While managers differ significantly in the ways in which they recruit, deploy, develop, control, and reward employees, it does not follow that their practices are entirely random or untrammelled. The path-dependency of the processes of labour regulation—stemming from their rootedness in diverse contexts, their co-evolution with opposing modes of coordination and their (partially) regularized forms of articulation and institutionalization—suggests that they are conjuncturally specific phenomena, which only coalesce under certain spatio-temporal conditions, and that a determinate variegation is one of their necessary and persistent features.

References

Ackers, P. and Wilkinson, A. (2005). 'British Industrial Relations Paradigm: A Critical Outline, History and Prognosis', *Journal of Industrial Relations*, 47(4): 443–56.

Adeleye, I. (2011). 'Theorising Human Resource Management in Africa: Beyond Cultural Relativism', *African Journal of Business Management*, 5(6): 2028–39.

Aglietta, M. (1998). 'Capitalism at the Turn of the Century: Regulation Theory and the Challenge of Social Change', *New Left Review*, 232: 41–90.

Almond, P. (2011). 'Re-visiting Country of Origin Effects on HRM in Multinational Corporations', *Human Resource Management Journal*, 21(3): 258–71.

Amable, B. (2003). *The Diversity of Modern Capitalism*. Oxford and New York: Oxford University Press.

Bhaskar, R. (1998). *The Possibility of Naturalism: A Philosophical Critique of the Contemporary Human Sciences*, 3rd edn. Sussex: Harvester.

—— (2008). *A Realist Theory of Science*, 2nd edn. Sussex: Harvester.

Boselie, P., Dietz, G., and Boon, C. (2005). 'Commonalities and Contradictions in HRM and Performance Research', *Human Resource Management Journal*, 15(3): 67–94.

Boyer, R. (1993). 'The Economics of Job Protection and Emerging New Capital–Labor Relations', in C. F. Buechtemann (ed.), *Employment Security and Labor Market Behavior*. Ithaca: ILR Press, 69–125.

—— (1994). 'Labour Institutions and Economic Growth: A Survey and a "Regulationist" Approach', *Labour*, 7(1): 25–72.

—— (2011). 'Are There Laws of Motion of Capitalism?', *Socio-Economic Review* 9(1): 59–81.

Boyer, R., Charron, E., Jürgens, U., and Tolliday, S. (eds.) (1998). *Between Imitation and Innovation: The Transfer and Hybridization of Productive Models in the International Automobile Industry*. Oxford and New York: Oxford University Press.

Boyer, R. and Saillard, Y. (eds.) (2002). *Régulation Theory: The State of the Art*. London: Routledge.

Brenner, N., Peck, J., and Theodore, N. (2009). 'Variegated Neoliberalization: Geographies, Modalities, Pathways', *Global Networks*, 10(2): 182–222.

—— (2010). 'After Neoliberalization?', *Globalizations*, 7(3): 327–45.

Brewster, C., Wood, G., and Brookes, M. (2008). 'Similarity, Isomorphism or Duality? Recent Survey Evidence on the Human Resource Management Policies of Multinational Corporations', *British Journal of Management*, 19(4): 320–42.

Brewster, C., Wood, G., Brookes, M., and Van Ommeren, J. (2006). 'What Determines the Size of the HR Function? A Crossnational Analysis', *Human Resource Management*, 45(1): 3–21.

Brooks, M., Croucher, R., Fenton-O'Creevy, M., and Gooderham, P. (2011). 'Measuring Competing Explanations of Human Resource Management Practices through the Cranet Survey: Cultural versus Institutional Explanations', *Human Resource Management Review*, 21(2): 68–79.

Brown, W. and Nolan, P. (1988). 'Wages and Labour Productivity: The Contribution of Industrial Relations Research to an Understanding of Pay Determination', *British Journal of Industrial Relations*, 26(3): 339–61.

Cappelli, P. (1995). 'Rethinking Employment', *British Journal of Industrial Relations*, 33(4): 563–602.

Deakin, S. and Reed, H. (2000). *The Contested Meaning of Labour Market Flexibility: Economic Theory and the Discourse of European Integration*. Working Paper No. 162, Cambridge: ESRC Centre for Business Research, University of Cambridge.

Ebner, A. and Beck, N. (eds.) (2008). *The Institutions of the Market: Organizations, Social Systems and Governance*. Oxford and New York: Oxford University Press.

Edwards, P. (1995). 'The Employment Relationship', in Edwards (ed.), *Industrial Relations: Theory and Practice in Britain*. Oxford: Blackwell, 1–36.

—— (2005). 'The Challenging but Promising Future of Industrial Relations: Developing Theory and Method in Context-Sensitive Research', *Industrial Relations Journal* 36(4): 264–82.

Edwards, P. K. (1986). *Conflict at Work: A Materialist Analysis of Workplace Relations*. Oxford: Blackwell.

Elger, T. and Edwards, P. (2002). 'National States and the Regulation of Labour in the Global Economy: An Introduction', in J. Kelly (ed.), *Industrial Relations: Critical Perspectives on Business and Management*, vol. III. London: Routledge, 182–225.

Elger, T. and Smith, C. (2005). *Assembling Work: Remaking Factory Regimes in Japanese Multinationals in Britain*. Oxford and New York: Oxford University Press.

Esping-Andersen, G. and Regini, M. (eds.) (2000). *Why Deregulate Labour Markets?* Oxford and New York: Oxford University Press.

Ferner, A., Almond, P., and Colling, T. (2005). 'Institutional Theory and the Cross-National Transfer of Employment Policy: The Case of "Workforce Diversity" in US Multinationals', *Journal of International Business Studies*, 36(3): 304–21.

Fleetwood, S. and Hesketh, A. (2008). 'Theorising Under-Theorisation in Research on the HRM–Performance Link', *Personnel Review*, 37(2): 126–44.

Frenkel, S. (1994). 'Patterns of Workplace Relations in the Global Corporation: Towards Convergence?', in J. Bélanger, P. K. Edwards, and L. Haiven (eds.), *Workplace Industrial Relations and the Global Challenge*. Ithaca: ILR Press, 210–74.

Friedman, A. L. (2000). 'Microregulation and Post-Fordism: Critique and Development of Regulation Theory', *New Political Economy*, 5(1): 59–76.

Gamble, J. (2010). 'Transferring Organizational Practices and the Dynamics of Hybridization: Japanese Retail Multinationals in China', *Journal of Management Studies*, 47(4): 705–29.

Gill, C. (1999). *Use of Hard and Soft Models of HRM to Illustrate the Gap between Rhetoric and Reality in Workforce Management*. Working Paper Series 99/13, Melbourne: RMIT Business, School of Management.

Gottfried, H. (1994). 'Learning the Score: The Duality of Control and Everyday Resistance in the Temporary-Help Service Industry', in J. M. Jermier, D. Knights, and W. R. Nord (eds.), *Resistance and Power in Organizations*. London: Routledge, 102–27.

Hakim, C. (1990). 'Workforce Restructuring in Europe in the 1980s', *International Journal of Comparative Labour Law and Industrial Relations*, 5(4): 167–203.

Hall, P. A. and Soskice, D. (eds.) (2001). *Varieties of Capitalism: The Institutional Foundations of Comparative Advantage*. Oxford and New York: Oxford University Press.

Hesketh, A. and Fleetwood, S. (2006). 'Beyond Measuring the Human Resources Management–Organizational Performance Link: Applying Critical Realist Meta-Theory', *Organization*, 13(5): 677–99.

Hollingsworth, J. R. and Boyer, R. (eds.) (1997). *Contemporary Capitalism: The Embeddedness of Institutions*. Cambridge: Cambridge University Press.

Hyman, R. (1987). 'Strategy or Structure: Capital, Labour and Control', *Work, Employment & Society*, 1(1): 25–56.

—— (1989). *The Political Economy of Industrial Relations: Theory and Practice in a Cold Climate*. London: Macmillan.

—— (1994). 'Industrial Relations in Western Europe: An Era of Ambiguity?', *Industrial Relations*, 33(1): 1–23.

—— (2003). 'Varieties of Capitalism, National Industrial Relations Systems and Transnational Challenges', in A. Harzing and J. Van Ruysseveldt (eds.), *International Human Resource Management: An Integrated Approach*. London: Sage, 411–32.

James, T. S. (2009). 'Whatever Happened to Régulation Theory? The Régulation Approach and Local Government Revisited', *Policy Studies*, 30(2): 181–201.

Jessop, B. (1988). 'Regulation Theory, Post Fordism and the State: More Than a Reply to Werner Bonefeld', *Capital & Class*, 12(1): 147–68.

—— (1990). 'Regulation Theories in Retrospect and Prospect', *Economy and Society*, 19(2): 153–216.

—— (1994). 'Post-Fordism and the State', in A. Amin (ed.), *Post-Fordism: A Reader*. Oxford: Blackwell, 251–79.

—— (2002). *The Future of the Capitalist State*. Cambridge: Polity Press.

—— (2011). 'Rethinking the Diversity and Variability of Capitalism: On Variegated Capitalism in the World Market', in C. Lane and G. Wood (eds.), *Capitalist Diversity and Diversity within Capitalism*. London: Routledge, 209–37.

Jessop, B., Brenner, N., and Jones, M. (2008). 'Theorizing Sociospatial Relations', *Environment and Planning D: Society and Space*, 26: 389–401.

Jessop, B. and Sum, N.-L. (2006). *Beyond the Regulation Approach: Putting Capitalist Economies in their Place*. Cheltenham: Edward Elgar.

Jones, B. (1996). 'The Social Constitution of Labour Markets: Why Skills Cannot be Commodities', in R. Crompton, D. Gallie, and K. Purcell (eds.), *Changing Forms of Employment: Organisations, Skills and Gender*. London: Routledge, 109–32.

Kahancova, M. (2007). 'One Company, Four Factories: Coordinating Employment Flexibility Practices with Local Unions', *European Journal of Industrial Relations*, 13(1): 67–88.

Kaufman, B. E. (2004). 'Employment Relations and the Employment Relations System: A Guide to Theorizing', in B. E. Kaufman (ed.), *Theoretical Perspectives on Work and the Employment Relationship*. Champaign, IL: Industrial Relations Research Association, 321–66.

—— (2008). 'Paradigms in Industrial Relations: Original, Modern and Versions In-Between', *British Journal of Industrial Relations*, 46(2): 314–39.

—— (2010). 'SHRM Theory in the Post-Huselid Era: Why it is Fundamentally Misspecified', *Industrial Relations*, 49(2): 286–313.

Keegan, A. and Boselie, P. (2006). 'The Lack of Impact of Dissensus Inspired Analysis on Developments in the Field of Human Resource Management', *Journal of Management Studies*, 43(7): 1491–1511.

Keenoy, T. (1997). 'Review article: HRMism and the Languages of Re-presentation', *Journal of Management Studies*, 34(5): 825–41.

Kim, S. and Wright, P. M. (2010). 'Putting Strategic Human Resource Management in Context: A Contextualized Model of High Commitment Work Systems and its Implications in China', *Management and Organization Review*, 7(1): 153–74.

Lane, C. and Wood, G. (2009). 'Capitalist Diversity and Diversity within Capitalism', *Economy and Society*, 38: 531–51.

Lawson, C., Peacock, M., and Pratten, S. (1996). 'Realism, Underlabouring and Institutions', *Cambridge Journal of Economics*, 20: 137–51.

Lawson, T. (1997). *Economics and Reality*. London: Routledge.

Legge, K. (1978). *Power, Innovation and Problem Solving in Personnel Management*. Maidenhead: McGraw-Hill.

—— (1995). *Human Resource Management: Rhetorics and Realities*. Basingstoke: Macmillan.

Lipietz, A. (1986). 'New Tendencies in the International Division of Labour: Regimes of Accumulation and Modes of Regulation', in A. J. Scott and M. Storper (eds.), *Production, Work, Territory*. Boston: Allen & Unwin, 16–40.

—— (1988). 'Accumulation, Crises, and Ways Out: Some Methodological Reflections on the Concept of "Regulation"', *International Journal of Political Economy*, 18(2): 10–43.

Lucio, M. M. and MacKenzie, R. (2004). '"Unstable boundaries?" Evaluating the "New Regulation" within Employment Relations', *Economy and Society*, 33(1): 77–97.

McGregor, D. (1960). *The Human Side of Enterprise*. New York: McGraw-Hill.

Marsden, D. (1999). *A Theory of Employment Systems: Micro-Foundations of Societal Diversity*. Oxford and New York: Oxford University Press.

—— (2004). 'Employment Systems: Workplace HRM Strategies and Labor Institutions', in B. E. Kaufman (ed.), *Theoretical Perspectives on Work and the Employment Relationship*. Champaign, IL: Industrial Relations Research Association, 77–103.

Martin, R. and Bamber, G. J. (2004). 'International Comparative Employment Relations Theory: Developing the Political Economy Perspective', in B. E. Kaufman (ed.), *Theoretical Perspectives on Work and the Employment Relationship*. Champaign, IL: Industrial Relations Research Association, 293–320.

Meardi, G. and Tóth, A. (2006). 'Who is Hybridising What? Insights on MNCs' Employment Practices in Central Europe', in A. Ferner, J. Quintanilla, and C. Sánchez-Runde (eds.), *Multinationals and the Construction of Transnational Practices: Convergence and Diversity in the Global Economy*. Basingstoke: Palgrave Macmillan, 155–83.

Michon, F. (1992). 'The Institutional Forms of Work and Employment: Towards the Construction of an International, Historical and Comparative Approach', in A. Castro, P. Méhaut, and J. Rubery (eds.), *International Integration and Labour Market Organisation*. London: Academic Press, 222–43.

Moule, C. (1998). 'Regulation of Work in Small Firms: A View from the Inside', *Work, Employment & Society*, 12(4): 635–53.

Nielsen, K. (1991). 'Towards a Flexible Future: Theories and Politics', in B. Jessop, K. Nielsen, H. Kastendiek, and O. K. Pedersen (eds.), *The Politics of Flexibility: Restructuring State and Industry in Britain, Germany and Scandinavia*. Cheltenham: Edward Elgar, 3–30.

Paauwe, J. (2009). 'HRM and Performance: Achievements, Methodological Issues and Prospects', *Journal of Management Studies*, 46(1): 129–42.

Paauwe, J. and Boselie, P. (2003). 'Challenging "Strategic HRM" and the Relevance of the Institutional Setting', *Human Resource Management Journal*, 13(3): 56–70.

Pache, A. (2010). *Inside the Hybrid Organization: An Organizational Level View of Responses to Conflicting Institutional Demands*. ESSEC Working Paper 11001, Cergy-Pontoise: ESSEC Business School.

Painter, J. and Goodwin, M. (1995). 'Local Governance and Concrete Research: Investigating the Uneven Development of Regulation', *Economy and Society*, 24(3): 334–56.

Peck, J. (1996). *Work-place: The Social Regulation of Labor Markets*. New York: Guilford Press.

—— (2000). 'Doing Regulation', in G. L. Clark, M. P. Feldman, and M. S. Gertler (eds.), *The Oxford Handbook of Economic Geography*. Oxford and New York: Oxford University Press, 61–83.

Peck, J. and Theodore, N. (2007). 'Variegated Capitalism', *Progress in Human Geography*, 31(6): 731–72.

Peck, J. and Tickell, A. (1992). 'Local Modes of Social Regulation? Regulation Theory, Thatcherism and Uneven Development', *Geoforum*, 23: 347–63.

—— (1994). 'Searching for a New Institutional Fix: The *After*-Fordist Crisis and the Global-Local Disorder', in A. Amin (ed.), *Post-Fordism: A Reader*. Oxford: Blackwell, 280–315.

Pudelko, M. (2006). 'A Comparison of HRM Systems in the USA, Japan and Germany in their Socio-Economic Context', *Human Resource Management Journal*, 16(2): 123–53.

Ram, M., Edwards, P., Gilman, M., and Arrowsmith, J. (2001). 'The Dynamics of Informality: Employment Relations in Small Firms and the Effects of Regulatory Change', *Work, Employment & Society*, 15(4): 845–61.

Rees, C. and Edwards, T. (2009). 'Management Strategy and HR in International Mergers: Choice, Constraint and Pragmatism', *Human Resource Management Journal*, 19(1): 24–39.

Regini, M. (2000). 'The Dilemmas of Labour Market Regulation', in G. Esping-Andersen and Regini (eds.), *Why Deregulate Labour Markets?* Oxford and New York: Oxford University Press, 11–29.

Rubery, J. and Grimshaw, D. (2003). *The Organization of Employment: An International Perspective*. Basingstoke: Palgrave Macmillan.

Salamon, M. (1998). *Industrial Relations: Theory and Practice*. Hemel Hempstead: Prentice-Hall.

Sayer, A. (1995). *Radical Political Economy: A Critique*. Oxford: Blackwell.

Schuler, R. S. and Jackson, S. E. (2007). 'Human Resource Management in Context', in R. Blanpain (ed.), *Comparative Labour Law and Industrial Relations in Industrialized Market Economies*. The Hague: Kluwer Law International, 95–133.

Spencer, D. A. (2000). 'The Demise of Radical Political Economics? An Essay on the Evolution of a Theory of Capitalist Production', *Cambridge Journal of Economics*, 24: 543–64.

Storey, J. (1992). *Developments in the Management of Human Resources: An Analytical Review*. Oxford: Blackwell.

Streeck, W. (1992). *Social Institutions and Economic Performance: Studies of Industrial Relations in Advanced Capitalist Economies*. London: Sage.

Streeck, W. and Thelen, K. (eds.) (2005). *Beyond Continuity: Institutional Change in Advanced Political Economies*. Oxford and New York: Oxford University Press.

Thatcher, M. (2007). *Internationalisation and Economic Institutions: Comparing Economic Experiences*. Oxford and New York: Oxford University Press.

Thompson, P. (2011). 'The Trouble with HRM', *Human Resource Management Journal*, 21(4): 355–67.

Thompson, P. and McHugh, D. (1990). *Work Organisations: A Critical Introduction*. London: Macmillan.

Thompson, P. and Vincent, S. (2010). 'Beyond the Boundary: Labour Process Theory and Critical Realism', in P. Thompson and C. Smith (eds.), *Working Life: Renewing Labour Process Analysis*. Basingstoke: Palgrave Macmillan, 47–69.

Tregaskis, O., Heraty, N., and Morley, M. (2001). 'HRD in Multinationals: The Global/Local Mix', *Human Resource Management Journal*, 11(2): 34–56.

Truss, C., Gratton, L., Hope-Hailey, V., McGovern, P., and Stiles, P. (1997). 'Soft and Hard Models of Human Resource Management: A Reappraisal', *Journal of Management Studies*, 34(1): 53–73.

Tsoukas, H. (2000). 'What is Management? An Outline of a Metatheory', in S. Ackroyd and S. Fleetwood (eds.), *Realist Perspectives on Management and Organisations*. London: Routledge, 26–44.

Vidal, M. (2011). 'Reworking Postfordism: Labor Process versus Employment Relations', *Sociology Compass*, 5(4): 273–86.

Watson, T. J. (2004). 'HRM and Critical Social Science Analysis', *Journal of Management Studies*, 41(3): 447–67.

Whitley, R. (1999). *Divergent Capitalisms: The Social Structuring and Change of Business Systems*. Oxford and New York: Oxford University Press.

Whitley, R. and Kristensen, P. H. (eds.) (1997). *Governance at Work: The Social Regulation of Economic Relations*. Oxford and New York: Oxford University Press.

Whitley, R., Morgan, G., and Moen, E. (eds.) (2005). *Changing Capitalisms?* Oxford and New York: Oxford University Press.

Wood, G. and Lane, C. (2011). 'Institutions, Change, and Diversity', in Lane and Wood (eds.), *Capitalist Diversity and Diversity within Capitalism*. London: Routledge, 1–31.

CHAPTER 30

NEW ACTORS IN EMPLOYMENT RELATIONS

FANG LEE COOKE AND GEOFFREY WOOD

THERE has been a growing recognition that, whatever national institutional particularities are at play, there has been a general weakening of the relative position of employees worldwide (Jessop 2012). Again, the formal espoused differences of political parties notwithstanding, there has been a growing consensus among political elites as to the desirability of labour market deregulation (Streeck 2009). Indeed, it can be argued that, within many national settings, the principal political parties have been captured by economic interests, to the detriment of workers and other segments of society (Wright 2012). A reversal of this position is contingent on social power, which, in turn, depends on the interaction of a range of actors, including those additional to the normal three parties that form the centre of attention in the traditional industrial relations literature. Indeed, the growing inadequacy of the traditional institutional actors (e.g. the state and national unions) in defending workers' rights has created both the space and the need for 'new' actors to fill the gap. Examples of these actors include: civil society organizations, employment agencies, counsellors, chaplains, health advisers/trainers, citizens' advice bureaux, global union federations, employment arbitrators, grassroots activists and social movements, and so forth. Some of the actors are not necessarily new but are playing a stronger or taking on new role in (re)shaping employment relations at the workplace level (Cooke and Wood 2011). In some contexts, these actors interact and permeate each other's sites and spatial boundaries in recognition of and to complement each other's resource/capacity constraints (Cooke 2011).

Despite operating largely outside the workplaces or cross-organizational boundaries, these actors and their interactions play an important role in shaping employment relations at the workplace level. The emerging role of the new actors, in individual and/or institutional capacity, has been documented in a number of studies (e.g. Abbott 2006; Heery and Frege 2006; Michelson et al. 2008) in response to Bellemare's (2000) call for widening the scope of analysis of institutional actors in industrial relations (IR).

The majority of the existing studies of new actors have focused on the role of these actors in representing the workers/members vis-à-vis government legislative changes and employer strategies/practices. However, while the recapturing of the social domain, and, hence, the direction of state policy is dependent on broad-based coalitions, it cannot be assumed that all new actors in employment relations are progressive. Relatively few studies have examined the negative impact of the new actors in the labour process as well as employment outcomes of the workers in an increasingly fragmented and precarious labour market. This chapter aims to provide a more balanced coverage of the various roles of the new actors. In doing so, we review the types of new actors that have emerged in different national contexts and their respective functions and impacts, drawing particular attention to those that have been relatively under-explored in the less developed world. Yet, within the developing world, institutions' arrangements tend to be relatively more fluid, and it is likely that new actors will have greater impact. This chapter seeks to redress this lacuna.

The Context within which New Actors are Emerging

The emergence of various forms of workers' representational and organizing bodies in various nations in recent years is in large part an outcome of the globalization of production and the declining strength of the traditional actors, such as the trade unions, in representing workers (e.g. Heckscher and Carré 2006; Heery and Frege 2006; Osterman 2006; Michelson et al. 2008). It is also associated with the significant changes in the workplace and the workforce in industrialized economies such as the UK, USA, Canada, and Australia. These changes are often a result of heightened competition in the business sector and/or changes in legislation and public policies that have a knock-on effect on the workers in the public sector and the end-users of public services. The withdrawal of direct state intervention in the employment sphere, the growing international mobility of migrant workers, and the increasing use of (transnational) subcontracting arrangements have led to the fragmentation of the labour markets, new forms of employments, and new classes of workers. In some cases, the coexistence of both the 'native' core group of workers and the migrant peripheral group of workers who may be performing highly skilled tasks undermines each other's terms and conditions due to the differentiated labour regulation protection and the willingness of the latter to accept lower offers. An example of this is Lillie's (2012) study of the shipbuilding and construction industries in Finland.

As new services are generated and new types of workers created, so do new IR issues emerge and new actors form, consisting of, for example, new users/customers, international pressure groups, and social movement organizers. Where union presence has faded, this vacuum may have been filled, if only partially and temporarily, by other bodies whose existence is often closely linked to the special interests that underpin their campaigning, advocacy, advisory, and service-providing functions (e.g. Heery and Frege 2006; Osterman 2006). In less developed countries like China, new actors have emerged to fill a gap that trade unions or other formal bodies have failed to reach (e.g. Murdoch and Gould 2004; Kessler 2008). They may also emerge to facilitate local governments and employers to fulfil their economic agenda (Cooke 2012a).

The emergence of new actors has 'opened up possibilities for new alliances and new forms of voice within the workplace and within the public domain' (Hicks et al. 2009: 166). It has also led to the growing interests in the study of the roles of these new actors, in different parts of the world, who have been marginal to the mainstream IR systems and academic debates (Heery and Frege 2006; Michelson et al. 2008; Cooke and Wood 2011). Led by Bellemare's (2000) seminal piece on end-users of the public transport in Canada as new actors in IR, a central argument of the studies of emergent actors in IR since the 2000s has been the critique of Dunlop's (1958) narrow definition of IR actors, namely: the state, the employer, and the trade union. Continuity of influence and participation at all levels were the main criteria of being qualified as an IR actor in the traditional studies of the IR systems (Bellemare 2000). Not only are the traditional IR system and its actors inadequate in representing groups of workers peripheral to the labour market, but also the traditional IR studies tend to assume the boundaries of IR systems are somewhat static (Legault and Bellemare 2008), and recognize the important role emergent actors may play in a new economic and institutional context (Michelson et al. 2008). By allowing for the episodic intervention of the actors who may emerge in relation to specific issues and events and in specific locations and sectors (Michelson et al. 2008), IR studies can be more inclusive and IR theories enriched. In this perspective, who is or is not an IR actor becomes an empirical matter that is 'context sensitive or space-time sensitive: one can be an actor in a particular case and not in another case' (Legault and Bellemare 2008: 746).

In the next section, we examine the types of new actors that have emerged and their main functions.

TYPES OF ACTORS, MOTIVATIONS, AND FUNCTIONS

A number of new actors have been identified by researchers on the topic in different countries (see Table 30.1). These actors have emerged in the context of dynamic changes in legislation, economy, and the IR system of respective nations. They are located outside the traditional IR framework (Michelson et al. 2008). They can be state agencies playing roles different to that which such bodies commonly played in the past, employer agencies, workers' agencies or agencies who straddle the state, workers, and employers. Likewise, they may be operating at a local, regional, national, or supranational/

Table 30.1 Examples of 'old' actors in new roles and emerging actors in employment relations

Level	Actors and initiatives	Main functions	Characteristics	Engagement with other actors
National, local, and inter-organizational	State agencies, e.g.: Employment arbitrators in USA (Seeber and Lipsky 2006) Australian Fair Pay Commission (Waring et al. 2008)	Servicing Maintaining social justice	Public agencies Actors as, or part of, an institution Interests- and rights-based Individual and group-oriented Operating mainly outside workplaces	State, employers, workers
	Employer agencies, e.g. Employer pressure groups in China (Cooke 2012a)	Campaigning for more autonomous employment environment (against legislative restriction)	Semi-public agencies Loosely formed Interest-based Group-oriented	State, employers
	Workers' agencies, e.g.: Civil society organizations (e.g. British Citizens' Advice Bureau (Abbott, 2006)) Churches in Australia (Hicks et al. 2009) Church-based organization in South Korea (Michelson 2009) Workplace chaplains in Australia (Michelson 2006) Community groups and employment agencies in the USA (Osterman 2006)	Servicing individuals Organizing interest groups Mobilizing stakeholders and political influence, e.g. lobbying/ campaigning for political/ legislative change	Independent, private agencies Interests- and rights-based Individual and/or group oriented Operating outside and within workplaces, community-based	Workers, employers, state

Example	Function	Characteristics	Stakeholders
Agencies between the state, employer, and workers, e.g.: End-users of public services in the UK (Kessler and Bach 2011) and Canada (Bellemare 2000)	Monitoring labour process and influencing working conditions	Mobilization of social power via public discourse Actors may not be an institution or lack institutional influence	General public, communities, interest groups (e.g. families of those receiving the social services)
— Employment agencies in China (Cooke 2011)	— Providing employment opportunities Facilitating employers to keep employment cost down	— Private agencies but maybe government-connected Conflicting role of being an employer and a labour market regulator	— Local government, employers, workers
— Cross-organizational, e.g.: Corporate client firms in Canada (Legault and Bellemare 2008) Inter-organizational project teams in Canada (Legault and Bellemare 2008)	— Monitoring labour process Influencing working conditions and longer-term employment prospects	— Private agencies Operating within workplaces but across organizational boundaries Individual as well as group based	— Client firms, employers, workers, industrial and professional communities
Supranational International International agencies, e.g.: International Framework of Agreements	Organizing, mobilizing, and servicing to raise labour standards	Sectoral orientation Actors as emerging and private institutions	Governments, trade unions, employers, consumers, other agencies, workers
— Home country government of MNCs (e.g. the influence of Chinese government in other developing countries in Asia and Africa) (Cooke and Lin 2012)	— Facilitating MNCs to develop business in host countries through political lobbying and diplomacy	— New role whose impact is contingent upon the political relationships with host country governments	— Host country government, MNCs

international level. Some of them rise from the higher level and take a top-down approach, whereas others have emerged from the grassroots. Some of them are part of, or are closely connected to, the existing formal institutions with clear organizational forms and governance structures, whereas others are more loosely constituted and rely on alliances with other actors/social groups to gain influence. As such, they vary significantly in their functions, resources they have, processes and ways of involving those they seek to represent, impacts and levels of embeddedness (e.g. Heckscher and Carré 2006). In the international context, the legitimacy and impact of these actors are underpinned by their political status and reception by other actors in the host countries. In the text that follows, we review a number of studies to illustrate the specific features of a variety of new actors.

State Agencies

Seeber and Lipsky's (2006) study of employment arbitrators in the USA has highlighted the fact that transferring the government function of interpreting and applying labour laws from the courts to the private and independent arbitrators through subcontracting arrangements has meant that these arbitrators have become, or at least should be considered, new actors in the IR system.

In Australia, the frequent changes in employment regulations have given rise to a number of government agencies, such as the Australian Fair Pay Commission, to oversee legislative implementation (e.g. Waring et al. 2008). These extended state-based agencies, albeit some of them being relatively transient, were created to represent and give voice to those who were previously unrepresented or under-represented. They work alongside some of the existing state agencies and may reinforce or replace some of the activities of traditional actors (Michelson et al. 2008).

In transitional South Africa, the establishment of NEDLAC (National Economic Development and Labour Advisory Council) provided a forum for employers, employees, and key political players to engage in a process of dialogue, which resulted in a series of mutually acceptable reforms to South Africa's labour relations legislation. However, a more ambitious neo-corporatist settlement has proved elusive. Indeed, renewed economic growth and political stability may have removed the sense of urgency from the parties, leaving the problem of chronically high unemployment unresolved. Again, in Mozambique, attempts to promote greater tripartite dialogue through the establishment of new forums have made little real progress, in this case, probably due to chronic institutional weakness, making the enforcement of any deal very difficult.

A very different new form of state agency has been sovereign wealth funds (SWFs), that is, government investment funds, which are managed very differently to the way forex reserves have been (Jen 2007). Typically, SWFs are rather more aggressive in terms of seeking higher returns and/or in securing access to key resources (Jen 2007). While they have been around for many years, they have assumed considerably higher prominence in the 2000s. Moreover, the domain is no longer dominated by petro-states;

Asian exporting nations have attained greater prominence in recent years. While SWFs have traditionally favoured highly liquid markets, they have recently moved into the wholesale acquisition of agricultural land and mineral resources in Africa. Indeed, it can be argued that SWFs represent the new role of the state in the twenty-first century (Johnson 2007). Traditionally, within industrial relations, the state played three roles: as a major employer, a mediator, and as the promoter of perceived best practice, the latter determined by the political ideology of the government of the day. SWFs add a fourth dimension: a state which leverages its financial resources to acquire assets abroad either to gain enhanced revenue opportunities and/or to serve some or other strategic objectives. This has far-reaching implications for workers worldwide. If they are purely revenue seeking, then they will add to the pool of speculative financial players that are likely to seek short-term returns regardless of the consequences for employment or employee well-being. Indeed, through investing overseas, SWFs can ruthlessly maximize revenue while externalizing the costs; for example, the problems associated with job losses are borne by society in the country in which the investment has been made, while the benefits accrue at home. If their primary motivation is to gain access to strategic resources, then there may be little concern with workers and peasants in target countries. For example, Middle Eastern SWFs have bought up large areas of prime agricultural land, inter alia, in western Ethiopia, which has allegedly led to the wholesale dispossession of the peasantry. SWFs tend to be highly opaque, and their ultimate agendas are often obscure (Truman 2007). On the one hand, it could be argued that SWFs investing in such areas are themselves naive: they assume that property rights are immutable, and that it is unlikely that a popular backlash will lead to peasant reoccupations and/or official expropriations. On the other hand, the success of 'vulture funds' in litigating against highly impoverished Third World countries in UK courts would suggest that SWFs do have some means of recourse. And, there the possibility of outright military intervention to support SWF assets has already been the subject of strategic military planning in at least one country with a large SWF. Of course, not all SWFs are predatory. For example, the Norwegian SWF is committed to ethical investments, which may encourage firms seeking investment to adopt better labour standards.

Employer Agencies

Employer associations in many developing nations, such as China, are relatively new and under-developed institutional actors in employment relations, compared with their counterparts in industrialized economies which are well-established, provide a range of services to their employer members, and form pressure groups to influence government policy and legislation. In the case of China, the China Enterprise Confederation (CEC) is the only official employer association that the state recognizes at the national level as the sole representative of employers' interests. The state forms some kind of unequal partnership with these organizations, which often act on behalf of the state and help implement government policies (see Unger and Chan 1995). The subordination to state control means that the CEC has limited autonomy beyond state-sanctioned activities. This has given rise to the employer pressure groups which were formed outside the CEC to exert pressure on the government at the national level if forthcoming regulations and policies are perceived to have a significant negative impact on their business environment. The approval process of the Labour Contract Law (enacted in 2008) is an example of their episodic interventions—the final version was watered down from the draft version as a result of employers' lobbying. Employer pressure groups continued to lobby for the amendment of the Labour Contract Law soon after its enactment. For example, individual entrepreneurs/business leaders took advantage of their role as representatives on the National People's Congress and the National People's Political Consultative Conference, the two highest forums for consultation and decision-making in China's politics, to request amendments (Ma 2008). As business owners/leaders make up a far higher proportion in these forums and are much better networked with other institutional actors than the ordinary workers, the voice of employers is more likely to be heard and their demands acted upon than that of the workers (Cooke 2011).

Workers' Agencies

A significant proportion of the studies of new actors, often loosely classified as civil society organizations, fall within this category (e.g. Heery et al. 2012). They reveal the diversity of these organizations in terms of their modes of representation (i.e. servicing, organizing, and/or mobilizing) and sites of operation (i.e. within and/or outside workplaces). For example, in their study of employment rights organizations in the USA, Heckscher and Carré (2006) identified three major categories of what they described as 'quasi-unions'. One was community-based organizations whose 'goals were information sharing (about employers, basic rights, etc.), leadership development and advocacy' (Heckscher and Carré 2006: 608).

Osterman's (2006: 643) study of the Industrial Areas Foundation (IAF), a national network of community organizations, identified four key elements in the IAF organizing model: community-based (attaching to neighbourhood institutions), broad-based (wide range of issues and interest groups), grassroots leadership development (capacity building), and labour market concerns as part of their agenda. A strategic aspect of this all-encompassing approach is the political power building through coalitions that connect and represent a broad base of constituency.

Michelson's (2006) study of industrial chaplains in Australian workplaces demonstrated that the chaplains, as neutral actors, played an important and independent role by providing assistance and counselling services to workers. Their perceived neutrality, where managed, has also been used to address a range of workplace problems and 'help achieve the interests of both management and trade unions' (Michelson 2006: 677). The counselling services provided by the workplace chaplains are different from the employee assistance programmes offered by firms to address the rising level of workplace stress associated with work intensification and job insecurity, as the former are seen to be more independent. Such independence has the potential of creating a more sustained opportunity for the chaplains to play the role traditionally performed by the trade unions through workplace visiting and pastoral care and support (Michelson 2006).

If the chaplains in Australian workplaces operate in a comparatively individualized, local, discrete, and peaceful manner (Michelson 2006), then Michelson's (2009) study of the urban industrial mission (UIM) as a non-traditional actor in South Korean employment relations from the early 1960s to the 2000s revealed a far more radical organizing agenda within a politically difficult environment. It showed how one church-based organization in Seoul, Yong Dong Po (YDP)-UIM, was able to impact the state and employers and struggle against the suppression of labour rights and worker voice, particularly in the period up to 1987. The influence of YDP-UIM in Korean industrial relations, however, began to decline from the late 1980s as the country was moving towards greater democracy. Based on this evidence, Michelson (2009: 163) argued that 'in the absence of alliances or coalitions with established actors', pursuing orthodox economic goals is a key means that gives new and non-traditional actors enduring influence in a country's IR system.

Within apartheid South Africa, various attempts to organize African workers up until the 1970s foundered owing to state repression and an over-reliance on a few key activists (Buhlungu et al. 2008). In the early years of that decade, a cluster of worker service organizations sprang up. These included mutual aid groupings, such as funeral benefits (General Factory Workers Benefit Fund), worker advice bureaus (e.g. Western Province Workers Advice Bureau), and religious groupings (Young Christian Workers). All these bodies soon turned to organizing black workers, and ultimately transformed themselves into fully fledged trade unions. Their original purpose, however, provided them with much needed political cover, and established their legitimacy in the eyes of the workers (Maree 1987).

A key distinction between these new actors, as Heckscher and Carré (2006) argued, is their strategic orientation, i.e. service versus advocacy, and subsequently their political stance and mode of actions. According to Heckscher and Carré (2006: 610), advocacy-oriented organizations are required to be more confrontational and militant, whereas service-oriented ones 'focus more pragmatically on demonstrating competency and achieving power through market [...] or other means'. While many agencies tend to combine the two roles, most will lean towards one more than the other (Heckscher and Carré 2006). For example, Osterman's (2006: 630) study of IAF revealed that the network was not only effective in its labour market strategies, but also offered a model for 'addressing key internal challenges that have historically confronted social movement organizations such as trade unions'. The adoption of a 'particular approach to internal leadership development and training' was considered instrumental to its success (Osterman 2006: 630). Members were trained to develop their capacity and sense of agency. An adversarial culture was built in the organization to enable members to 'exercise their new skills and attitudes' through strong voice (Osterman 2006: 642).

Agencies between the State, Employer, and Workers

Not all employment agencies are on the workers' side. Nor is their role in the labour market always positive. The functioning of employment agencies in China is a case in point. Despite being in existence for over two decades, employment agencies represent a relatively new institutional actor in employment relations in China. The majority of employment agencies and job centres have been set up by, or under the auspices of, the local governments since the mid-to-late 1990s to provide services at the lower end of the labour market. Throughout the 2000s, the sector experienced significant growth as a response to the large-scale downsizing in the state sector, the continuous inflow of rural migrant workers to urban areas to seek employment, and the growing number of unemployed school leavers and college graduates (Cooke 2012a). Employment agencies are supposed to play a transitional role to facilitate the government transitioning its function through the marketization of employment services. In reality, the relationship between the employment agencies, local governments, and employers are intricate. They are governed mainly by administrative regulations issued at the local level and implemented with considerable discretion (Cooke 2012a).

It was anticipated (by the state) that the enactment of the Labour Contract Law in 2008 would see the reduction of those hired by employment agencies promoting a more direct and stable employment relationship between the worker and the firm. The reality so far has been a stark contrast. To pre-empt the negative impact of the new law on employment cost, an increasing number of employers dismissed their long-serving workers and rehired them as agency workers through employment agencies. As a result, employment agencies have prospered and the number of workers registered with employment agencies is growing. Agency workers often receive lower wages and much less social security protection than employees of the user firms. The partial compliance of the labour laws enables firms to drive down their employment cost and make a profit. With the implicit protection of the local governments and the rising demand from user organizations, employment agencies are set to become a more institutionalized actor in employment relations. And agency employment will be a thriving form of labour deployment, contrary to the objective of the Labour Contract Law (Cooke 2012a).

End-users/clients of public services are another new actor whose multiple roles and actions, intentionally and unintentionally, affect both the service they receive and the working conditions of those who deliver the services (e.g. Bellemare 2000; Kessler and Bach 2011). In their study of social care work in the UK, Kessler and Bach (2011) described the end-users as a legitimate actor of employment relations of the British public sector services. Underpinning this role is 'the notion of citizenship within the context of public service provision' promoted by New Labour governments who proclaimed: 'we will deliver public services to meet the needs of citizens, not the convenience of service providers (Cabinet Office 1999: 13)' (Kessler and Bach 2011: 81). The empowerment of end-users through the emphasis on end-user choice, voice, and control over the ways in which their needs are met has brought about significant changes in work organization, including flexible working practices, among those who deliver the services (Kessler and Bach 2011).

In the private business sector, the concept of co-designing and co-production between corporate client and supplier firms has similarly created spaces for users/receivers of the services to act as co-supervisors of the work both in an individual capacity and collectively, for example, via involvements in committees. The more complex the service, the greater level of user involvement may be required/imposed (Legault and Bellemare 2008). For instance, Legault and Bellemare's (2008) study of IT services on the client sites revealed that both the clients and the project teams have a strong role to play in shaping the organization of work and the future employment prospect of the IT professionals in a globalized and competitive market. As they observed, the professionals' performance affects the client's satisfaction which in turn secures their organization's competitive position in the market and the professionals' employment prospect (Legault and Bellemare 2008). It is clear that market competition has given corporate clients an enormous amount of power to demand, and in some cases dictate, services (Legault and Bellemare 2008).

Legault and Bellemare's (2008: 761) study further showed that, in addition to the decisive role of the clients, the project team also has the capacity to marginalize a professional by 'keeping him from participating in projects that might be gratifying in terms of money, learning, and reputation, and, most of all, of reducing his employability by tarnishing his reputation'. This is largely because the industry is more regulated by the clients' regulatory framework in practice than by the national labour regulations. So much so that an individual's reputation, and consequently future earning prospect, are beholden to the corporate clients as well as to their professional peers in an industry where 'reputation is at the heart of the sector-based regulation of professional work' (Legault and Bellemare 2008: 761).

Extant literature on emerging/new actors in employment relations has focused primarily on those that have emerged to advance the workers' rights and interest. Much less attention has been paid to those that have emerged to advance the interests of other actors, often with detrimental effects on the workers. Empirical studies reported above have provided useful insights into the intricate relationships of multiple actors and their interactive outcomes in an increasingly complex world of work.

Agencies at the International Level

At the international level, labour movement activists and consumer groups have been active in promoting a range of international voluntary initiatives in the corporate world, including for instance, the International Framework Agreements (IFAs) (cf. Niforou 2012). The concept of global value chain (GVC) governance is central to these initiatives (see Riisgaard and Hammer 2011). They are attempts to 'regulate work, employment and labour relations at the international level' (Riisgaard and Hammer 2011: 169) by introducing 'labour standards in the agenda of multinational corporations' (Niforou 2012: 352). Their primary objective is to promote a greater level of corporate social responsibility (CSR) in the context of global production and sourcing. They rely largely on the good will and ethical stance of Western multinational corporations (MNCs) to govern their business activities that involve workers from some of the poorest countries in the developing world at the bottom of the global value chain. As 'emerging private institutions of global industrial relations governance', most of these agreements operate on a voluntary basis with limited compliance enforceability (Niforou 2012: 352).

For example, Cooke's (2012a) study of private manufacturing firms in China that are export-oriented revealed two scenarios. Those who operate at the lower end of the product market reported that they had not received any pressure from their foreign client firms on CSR issues, including labour standards. By contrast, those who operate at the upper end of the product market by producing brand-named products admitted that compliance to CSR requirements, including the labour laws and other business regulations of China, is paramount for securing business contracts with foreign clients. This evidence suggests that foreign MNCs and international non-governmental organizations (NGOs) are playing an indispensable role in ensuring compliance of domestic laws. Nevertheless, the cost of compliance is largely borne by the Chinese manufacturers. As remarked by an owner CEO of a computer speakers manufacturing firm: 'The foreign client firms all come to inspect the factory when they negotiate new contracts. They demand top quality products and world-class labour standards from us but are only prepared to pay pedlars' price for it.' Cooke's (2012a) study further revealed the challenge facing both overseas NGOs and those domestic NGOs reliant on overseas support in gaining wider political recognition and operational legitimacy from the Chinese governments at various levels.

Despite operational constraints and localized impacts, these emerging transnational actors of labour movement present a challenge where national unions have either lost power (Croucher and Cotton 2009) or never acquired it. They illustrate how the emergence of these new actors has created space for labour organizing and rights movements by mobilizing the power of consumers where the power of workers at the production point is absent and where national regulatory capacity has been weakened vis-à-vis the power of foreign capital investment. As such, the GVC concept and related initiatives not only help restructure capital–labour relations through the creation of a new power base or redistribution of power, but also transcend the organizational and institutional boundaries where an array of (emergent) actors may influence the labour process and employment outcomes at various points and across industrial sectors (Riisgaard and Hammer 2011). While it may be over-optimistic to believe that these initiatives, where incorporated into corporate codes of conduct, may represent an institutionalized form of labour regulation, their existence and adoption, however, do provide the much needed momentum for capacity and network building among various actors and create an international platform for collective representation.

Again, the role of such agencies is not necessarily benign. For example, a range of CIA-front organizations have supported and abetted bosses' trade unions in Venezuela, which, under the cover of representing skilled workers, seek to overturn progressive reforms, and return power to the old oligarchy. A similar process has been at work in many countries of Central America, most notoriously in Honduras, where a democratically elected government was deposed in favour of one representing a handful of privileged families and foreign investors.

Emergent actors in the international labour relations arena do not consist solely of labour movement organizations. Nor are they all from the independent and non-for-profit sector. The role of MNCs as power political actors in shaping the employment relations environment of the host country has been well argued. MNCs may adopt a range of strategies towards host countries. When they seek to access the particular advantages conferred by a specific local production regime, and/or gain access to particularly lucrative markets, they may seek to fit in with existing local ways of doing things (Morgan 2012). In cases where they seek access to very cheap labour, it is likely that they will work together with local elites that share similar interests to aggressively promote labour market deregulation. This may even take the form of physical attacks on trade unionists. For example, there have been widespread allegations that a number of major US multinationals have developed close ties with right-wing death squads in Colombia, which have led to a wave of assassinations of trade unionists. Where multinationals seek to access natural resources, human—and indeed, environmental— interests may be completely subordinated. For example, within the criminal state of Equatorial Guinea, a number of major oil and gas companies have forged close ties to the ruling family, relying on the latter to provide and discipline unskilled labour, while making use of expatriates for all but the most menial positions (Wood 2004). Similar examples can be encountered elsewhere in Central Africa and in Central Asia.

A further issue is the role of the parent country government of the MNCs that underpins the national development agenda of the developing nations and the labour strategy of MNCs. For instance, the role of the Chinese government has been crucial in the internationalization of Chinese firms in key industrial sectors where the government has a key stake or perceives itself to have national strategic significance, such as the IT/telecom, natural resources, and construction industries (e.g. Cooke 2012b, Cooke and Lin 2012). As Arden and Davies (2006) argued, the Chinese MNCs' competitive advantage may have derived from the political advantage endowed upon them due to the diplomatic relationship between the Chinese government and the host country government in Africa. In some labour-intensive sectors, such as mining and construction, Chinese firms are beginning to import Chinese workers instead of employing local labour to avoid management problems and dealing with the local trade unions. The financial dependence of the host country governments on the Chinese government circumvents the capacity of the local actors to sanction Chinese firms' management decisions and hold them accountable.

IMPACTS AND CONSTRAINTS OF THE
NEW ACTORS

It is clear that the roles performed by new actors are diverse, ranging from the counselling role for the well-being of individual workers and labour market brokering to fighting for workplace rights and a basic living wage. The impact of emerging actors therefore differs due to their varying levels of strength and capacity, and relatedly the environment within which they operate. As touched upon in the above discussion, the interactions and relationships among actors, new or old, may create space as well as impose constraints on new actors, especially where powerful political actors are involved. At the international level, the host country environment is crucial for transnational actors and/or supranational initiatives to work. For instance, compared with China, South Africa has a relatively strong professional legal system, a well-developed civil society and an independent media industry. These institutional actors are increasingly involved in industrial relations through political alliances. By contrast, in China, civil society organizations operate within a relatively tight political environment and the role of the government continues to dominate.

At the national level, political discourse remains a vital dimension for actors to mobilize social groups through public campaigns. In particular, political opportunity proves crucial in that it not only creates legitimacy and strategic space but also provides resources for these actors to function. Their efficacy is contingent upon the perceived legitimacy from those they seek to represent and the willingness to cooperate from those they seek to influence. For example, Kessler and Bach (2011) observed that the political context (e.g. changes in the public policy and the underpinning ideology), the nature of the service providers (e.g. source of funding and ownership), and the characteristics of the end-users and the ability to influence are key factors in determining the likely impact of the end-users as actors in public service employment relations. By contrast, without political legitimacy, the sustainability of new actors is called into question. For instance, Michelson's (2009) study of the Christian church organization revealed persistent political obstructions exerted by the authoritarian Korean government on the organization, including surveillance, arrest, imprisonment, the use of the mass media, terminations of employment for YDP-UIM trained activists and so forth that were aimed to sabotage its work in order to clear all obstacles for the country's economic development.

A distinct feature of the community-based grassroots actors is that they are relatively small organizations with highly dedicated staff and a loose structure and fluctuating membership (e.g. Heckscher and Carré 2006). Their role in IR is largely discontinuous and peripheral (Hicks et al. 2009). Nevertheless, a common argument of authors on new actors is that, disregarding the level of their operation, the episodic or intermittent involvement of these actors may 'produce durable and significant change in patterns of job regulation or powerfully shape the behaviour of other actors' (Heery et al. 2012: 49).

Operating in different organizing modes from those conventionally adopted by trade unions, these new actors have widened the scope of representation in both the categories of workers they represent and the issues they seek to address. And operating largely outside the workplaces, much of the new actors' missions, particularly those waged by the civil society organizations, are targeted directly at the state. Collective bargaining is not the mechanism they tend to adopt. Rather, they 'formulate standards of labour management that they seek to have adopted by employers on the basis of the legitimacy of their claims and appeals to self-interest, reinforced by the risk of non-compliance with employment law' (Heery et al. 2012: 70). As such, these actors are unlikely to replace the trade unions 'as the primary means of representation' (Heckscher and Carré 2006: 605). Where the primary function of the new actors is to provide services, a key challenge they face may be the ability of those whom they seek to serve to access their services for various reasons (e.g. Pollert 2008).

Not all the actions of new actors, as noted earlier, will result in the improved terms and conditions of the workers. If the role of the foreign governments may have, on occasions, eroded the employment outcomes and prospects of those in the poorest countries, then the direct involvement of end-users and clients in the service provision in more affluent societies not only enables them to monitor the work workers do at a close range but may also change the rules that govern the way in which they work at a higher level with wider implications.

Conclusions

Social power—be it that of traditional players such as unions and political parties, or emergent ones, such as community groupings—can provide the basis for effective bargaining by social forces mediating economic power and impacting on state policy (Wright 2012: 392). However, other new actors in the domain of employment relations— such as SWFs—may primarily wield economic power that, it can be argued, requires mediation by social forces and the state. Only when the state and economic power is subordinated to social power, is it possible to both have democracy and to effectively regulate capital (Wright 2012: 392).

On the one hand, a constellation of new actors has emerged in search of new strategies and new organizing forms to better represent workers' rights and interests. The groupings neither constitute a coherent whole, nor are they mutually supportive. These include, for example, government-related commissions, consumer/end-user groups, bargaining agents, independent arbitrators, interest-lobbying groups, and forums that seek to enhance international labour standards through a greater level of corporate social responsibility (e.g. Michelson et al. 2008; Osterman 2006). In some countries, new actors have also emerged that serve primarily the interests of the state and employers, in the name of economic development, or the end-users, in the name of client-oriented services as the kite mark of service quality.

On the other hand, while domestic government has always been a main actor in IR, the emergence of foreign governments as a new actor is to a large extent a result of the globalization of capital investment and production, a notable example being SWFs, whose role is at best ambivalent. It is also important to note that while some actors, e.g. employer associations, may have long existed in certain countries as main actors, they may only start to emerge with embryonic function in other countries.

Empirical evidence discussed in this chapter (and elsewhere) highlights important points for a number of non-conventional industrial relations actors operating in the transnational, national, and industrial/sectoral contexts in different parts of the world. One is that there is increasing scope for the emergence of new actors, whose presence is generally beneficial to those whom they seek to organize and represent, against a universal trend of deteriorating employment security and workforce well-being. The other point is that the growth and operations of these new actors is contingent upon a number of factors, from their institutional legitimacy to resources acquisition. As such, the prospect of their becoming an independent and powerful force in shaping the labour process and employment outcomes of individuals remains less than optimistic without forming alliances with the more powerful mainstream actors to complement each other's resources and capacities (Cooke and Wood 2011). Equally, not all new actors' involvement will lead to enhanced workers' conditions. Instead, they may weaken the regulatory capacity of host governments, and indeed lead to the dispossession of peasants and the erosion of the bargaining power of workers.

The study of new actors and their interactions is now an important and integral part of the studies and theorization of employment relations, albeit that much more work needs to be done. As Murray (2010: 21) argued, the analysis of the multiple interfaces between private and public institutions and the construction of new and revival of old institutions helps 'elucidate how the development of actors, processes of regulation and institutions will enable them to contend with the changes that they are experiencing'.

References

Abbott, B. (2006). 'Determining the Significance of the Citizens' Advice Bureau as an Industrial Relations Actor', *Employee Relations*, 28(5): 435–48.

Bellemare, G. (2000). 'End Users: Actors in the Industrial Relations System?', *British Journal of Industrial Relations*, 38(3): 383–405.

Buhlungu, S., Wood, G., and Brookes, M. (2008). 'Trade Unions and Democracy in South Africa: Union Organizational Challenges and Solidarities in a Time of Transformation', *British Journal of Industrial Relations*, 46(3): 439–68.

Cooke, F. L. (2011). 'The Enactment of Three New Labour Laws in China: Unintended Consequences and the Emergence of "New" Actors in Employment Relations', in S. Lee and D. McCann (eds.), *Regulating for Decent Work: New Directions in Labour Market Regulation*. Basingstoke: Palgrave Macmillan and Geneva: International Labour Organization, 180–205.

—— (2012a). *Human Resource Management in China: New Trends and Practices*. London: Routledge.

—— (2012b). 'The Globalization of Chinese Telecom Corporations: Strategy, Challenges and HR Implications for Host Countries', *International Journal of Human Resource Management*, 23(9): 1832–52.

Cooke, F. L. and Lin, Z. H. (2012). 'Chinese Firms in Vietnam: Investment Motives, Institutional Environment and Human Resource Challenges', *Asia-Pacific Journal of Human Resources*, 50(2): 205–26.

Cooke, F. L. and Wood, G. (2011). 'New Actors and Employment Relations in Emerging Economies', *Relations Industrielles/Industrial Relations*, 66(1): 7–10.

Croucher, R. and Cotton, E. (2009). *Global Unions, Global Business: Global Union Federations and International Business*. London: Middlesex University Press.

Dunlop, J. T. (1958). *Industrial Relations Systems*. New York: Henry Holt.

Heckscher, C. and Carré, F. (2006). 'Strength in Networks: Employment Rights Organizations and the Problem of Co-Ordination', *British Journal of Industrial Relations*, 44(4): 605–28.

Heery, E., Abbott, B., and Williams, S. (2012). 'The Involvement of Civil Society Organizations in British Industrial Relations: Extent, Origins and Significance', *British Journal of Industrial Relations*, 50(1): 47–72.

Heery, E. and Frege, C. (2006). 'New Actors in Industrial Relations', *British Journal of Industrial Relations*, 44(4): 601–4.

Hicks, J., Sappey, R. B., and Basu, P. K. (2009). 'Australian Christian Churches and "New" Actors in Industrial Relations Theory', *International Journal of Employment Studies*, 17(1): 164–88.

Jen, S. (2007). 'Sovereign Wealth Funds: What They Are and What Is Happening', *World Economics*, 8(4): 1–7.

Jessop, B. (2012). 'Rethinking the Diversity and Variability of Capitalism: On Variegated Capitalism in the World Market', in C. Lane and G. Wood (eds.), *Capitalist Diversity and Diversity within Capitalism*. London: Routledge, 209–37.

Kessler, D. (2008). 'Business Struggles with Worker Participation and Its Consequences for the Role of NGOs', paper presented at the International Conference 'Breaking Down Chinese Walls: The Changing Faces of Labor and Employment in China', Cornell University, 26–28 September, Ithaca, New York.

Kessler, I. and Bach, S. (2011). 'The Citizen-Consumer as Industrial Relations Actor: New Ways of Working and the End-User in Social Care', *British Journal of Industrial Relations*, 49(1): 80–102.

Legault, M. and Bellemare, G. (2008). 'Theoretical Issues with New Actors and Emergent Modes of Labour Regulation', *Relations Industrielles/Industrial Relations*, 63(4): 742–68.

Lillie, N. (2012). 'Subcontracting, Posted Migrants and Labour Market Segmentation in Finland', *British Journal of Industrial Relations*, 50(1): 148–67.

Maree, J. (1987). 'Overview: The Emergence of the Independent Trade Unions', in Maree (ed.), *The Independent Trade Unions*. Johannesburg: Ravan, 1–11.

Michelson, G. (2006). 'The Role of Workplace Chaplains in Industrial Relations: Evidence from Australia', *British Journal of Industrial Relations*, 44(4): 677–96.

—— (2009). 'The Dynamic Evolution of Urban Industrial Mission in Korea', *Indian Journal of Industrial Relations*, 45(2): 163–80.

Michelson, G., Jamieson, S., and Burgess, J. (eds.) (2008). *New Employment Actors: Developments from Australia*. Bern: Peter Lang.

Morgan, G. (2012). 'International Business, Multinationals and National Business Systems', in G. Wood and M. Demirbag (eds.), *Handbook of Institutional Approaches to International Business*. Cheltenham: Edward Elgar, 18–40.

Murdoch, H. and Gould, D. (2004). *Corporate Social Responsibility in China: Mapping the Environment*. London: Global Alliance for Workers and Communities Publication Series.

Niforou, C. (2011). 'International Framework Agreements and Industrial Relations Governance: Global Rhetoric versus Local Realities', *British Journal of Industrial Relations*, 50(2): 352–73.

Osterman, P. (2006). 'Community Organizing and Employee Representation', *British Journal of Industrial Relations*, 44(4): 629–49.

Pollert, A. (2008). 'Injustice at Work: How Britain's Low-Paid Non-Unionised Employees Experience Workplace Problems', *Journal of Workplace Rights*, 13(3): 223–44.

Riisgaard, L. and Hammer, N. (2011). 'Prospects for Labour in Global Value Chains: Labour Standards in the Cut Flower and Banana Industries', *British Journal of Industrial Relations*, 49(1): 168–90.

Seeber, R. L. and Lipsky, D. B. (2006). 'The Ascendancy of Employment Arbitrators in US Employment Relations: A New Actor in the American System?', *British Journal of Industrial Relations*, 44(4): 719–56.

Streeck, W. (2009). *Reforming Capitalism: Institutional Change in the German Political Economy*. Oxford and New York: Oxford University Press.

Truman, S. (2007). *Sovereign Wealth Funds: The Need for Greater Accountability and Transparency*. Washington, DC: Petersen Institute.

Unger, J. and Chan, A. (1995). 'China, Corporatism, and the East Asian Model', *Australian Journal of Chinese Affairs*, 33: 29–53.

Waring, P., de Ruyter, A., and Burgess, J. (2008). 'The Australian Fair Pay Commission: A New Actor Performing an Old Function', in G. Michelson, S. Jamieson, and Burgess (eds.), *New Employment Actors: Developments from Australia*. Bern: Peter Lang, 43–66.

Wood, G. (2004). 'Business and Politics in a Criminal State: The Case of Equatorial Guinea', *African Affairs*, 103: 547–67.

Wright, E. O. (2012). 'Taking the Social in Socialism Seriously', *Socio-Economic Review*, 10(2): 386–402.

CHAPTER 31

THE FUTURE OF EMPLOYMENT RELATIONS IN ADVANCED CAPITALISM

Inexorable Decline?

SABINA AVDAGIC AND LUCIO BACCARO

INTRODUCTION

WHAT will be the likely future of the regulatory regime known as 'collective employment relations', a regime in which trade unions and collective bargaining (including political bargaining of the corporatist kind) play a crucial role in the determination of wage and working conditions, as well as in the definition of various forms of public policy?

In this chapter we seek to answer this question by extrapolating from recent historical trends. We consider the aggregate macro evidence for 25 capitalist countries between 1990 and the current period, looking at the evolution of both institutional features and socio-economic outcomes. Our conclusion is pessimistic: employment relations are in crisis everywhere, not just in liberal market economies (LMEs) and former communist countries from Central and Eastern Europe (CEE), where they have been traditionally less institutionalized than elsewhere, but in coordinated market economies (CMEs) and Scandinavian countries, too. The decline is more advanced, and hence more visible, in some countries and less in others, but the trajectory of decline is present everywhere.

In LME and CEE countries organized employment relations apply to a small portion of the labour market. In continental European countries employment relations are still numerically important, but the weakening of organized actors and the slow hollowing out of formally unchanged institutions of collective bargaining and corporatist policy-making are clear signs of decline. In some cases, this decline resembles an institutional drift (Hacker 2004), whereby changes in the operation or effect of institutions occur without significant changes in formal institutional structures. In these countries, embattled trade unions engage in a strenuous defence of their key constituencies, which in turn contributes to a growing labour market dualism between insiders and outsiders. In Scandinavian countries the decline is in its early stages. However, even in these countries centralized institutions have been changed from the inside to accommodate growing workplace diversity, and institutional changes are undermining the institutional basis of union power.

It is important to say right at the outset that we are not making an argument for institutional convergence in any crude sense. The precise features of employment relations crisis are shaped by different institutional environments and different mobilization capacities of collective actors (Locke and Thelen 1995). There is no convergence everywhere on the same institutional model, say on the prototypical LME model in which trade unions are weak and marginalized, economically and politically, and collective bargaining decentralized or irrelevant, although there are certain signs pointing in this direction. Trade unions are still remarkably strong in some countries; the industry level is still the main level of bargaining in most continental European countries; and workers' and employers' associations continue to play an important role in economic policy-making. Nonetheless, we argue that the direction of change is approximately the same everywhere and manifests itself more clearly as a generalized decline in trade unions' organizational fortunes, a tendency for collective bargaining to become more differentiated and to accommodate firm-level diversity even when the main level of bargaining remains unchanged, and a tendency for peak-level corporatist bargaining to become increasingly concessionary and/or ceremonial (Baccaro and Howell 2011). Employment relations are not likely to disappear from one day to the next. Unions will still be important regulatory agents and a force to be reckoned with in some countries for quite some time. However, the current trends point to a decrease in their relevance everywhere, albeit to a different extent and at a different pace.

In addition, we do not see any credible signs of reversal in the near future, and this more for political than for purely economic reasons. There is nothing 'natural' in employment relations decline. It is a political phenomenon and as such it could in principle be redressed by political intervention. This would require, however, a fundamental shift in public policy at the national and supranational level. The state would need to acknowledge that employment relations produce positive 'externalities' for society and be ready to intervene to permit and facilitate their development though appropriate incentives and organizational support. We believe, to put it shortly, that such a shift is unlikely, and we articulate below the reasons for our scepticism. In addition, we doubt that reversing the decline could simply be the result of organizational reforms by the trade unions themselves. However necessary such reforms may be, they are unlikely to be sufficient.

The remainder of this chapter is organized in three sections. The next section documents the extent of labour's decline by examining changes in employment relations institutions and in terms and conditions of employment. The following section discusses the reasons why a renaissance of employment relations seems unlikely. The concluding section summarizes both the empirical evidence and our interpretation of it.

LABOUR'S DECLINE IN THE LAST
TWO DECADES

One of the arguments we make in this chapter is that the fortunes of employment relations were tightly linked to the Fordist accumulation regime. We discuss the mode of functioning of this regime later in the chapter. For the time being, it suffices to say that by the early 1980s, it became obvious that Fordism was facing a crisis. Its central pillars, including trade unions, collective bargaining, and employment protection, came to be seen as rigidities that undermine economic performance, not just by employers and their political allies, but sometimes even by left-leaning actors and commentators. Consequently, the more recent decades have witnessed significant efforts on the part of employers and a majority of policy-makers to increase labour market and workplace flexibility. These developments have had a profound impact on employment relations, leading to their erosion in most contemporary capitalisms. This section assesses these developments by examining a range of indicators of employment relations in 25 countries during 1990–2008. Our sample of countries covers different capitalist models or varieties: coordinated market economies (Austria, Belgium, Germany, Netherlands, and Switzerland), liberal market economies (Australia, Canada, Ireland, UK, and the USA), mixed Mediterranean countries (France, Greece, Italy, Portugal, and Spain), Scandinavian countries (Denmark, Finland, Iceland, Norway, and Sweden), and CEE economies (Czech Republic, Hungary, Poland, Slovakia, and Slovenia). We focus on the 1990–2008 period for two reasons: first, to keep the analysis within manageable proportions and, second, in order to isolate factors which characterize specifically the more recent period of historical development, particularly economic globalization (whose effects are most clearly visible from the 1990s on) (Frieden 2006) and European integration (run-up to monetary unification, transition to the euro, and enlargement to the former countries of the Soviet bloc). This is not to say that the phenomena we analyse here are peculiar to the post-1990 period. Some of them begin well before then, but most trends we focus on are more clearly visible since the onset of the 1990s.

We analyse two sets of aggregate, country-level indicators of labour's position. The first focuses on institutional characteristics, namely trends in union density, collective bargaining, and corporatist-style policy-making. The second concerns the terms and conditions of employment, including indicators such as wages and their distribution, labour's share in national income, employment protection and the associated changes in the structure of employment. Taken together, these indicators offer a sufficiently clear picture of the state of employment relations in contemporary capitalism.

Institutional Features

To a large part, the state of employment relations is defined by three sets of institutions: trade unions, collective bargaining, and corporatist policy-making. The existence of collective organization of economic actors, in particular trade unions, is a precondition for an effective relationship between employers and workers' organizations. Collective bargaining and corporatist policy-making are the outcomes of this relationship. Thus, trends in the main indicators of these institutions offer a good indication of the direction of change in employment relations. In all three cases data for 1990–2008 suggest a clear deterioration of employment relations.

Union Density

The general decline in union density that was clearly visible already during the 1980s continued during the 1990 and 2000s. Table 31.1 presents data on average union density in 1990–94 and 2004–2008 as well as the percentage change between the two periods (Visser 2011). Union density declined everywhere, albeit to a different extent in different countries. The largest declines occurred in Hungary (–79% of the unionization rate in 1990–94), Slovak Republic (–69%), Czech Republic (–67%), Slovenia (–51%), Australia (–47%), and Poland (–45%). There was a steep drop in the first few years of the post-communist transition in Central and Eastern European countries (on average 2.3 percentage points per year during 1990–95), which largely reflects the end of compulsory union membership. However, the unionization rate in CEE has continued declining even after the mid-1990s on average by 1.39 percentage points each year.

The lowest declines are to be found in Belgium (–3%) and Spain (–5%). In Spain, however, unionization was already low in the early 1990s. In Scandinavian countries union decline began later than elsewhere—in the mid-1990s in Sweden and Finland; in the early 2000s in Denmark and Iceland. Consequently losses are more limited than elsewhere. The 2000s have seen an attempt by governments in Denmark, Finland, and Sweden to weaken trade unions by reforming the Ghent system of unemployment insurance that de facto links access to benefits to membership in trade unions and thus provides a powerful selective incentive for affiliation (Andersen 2011; Lind 2009; Rothstein 1992). Recent institutional reforms do not bode well for trade unions in Scandinavian countries.

Determining the causes of the decline in unionization is beyond the scope of this chapter. Previous research has identified several factors that may be related to this decline. Business cycle conditions, such as declining inflation (Checchi and Visser 2005; but see Sano and Williamson 2008) and rising unemployment (Ebbinghaus and Visser 1999; Checchi and Visser 2005), and especially changes in political-economic institutions, such as the decline in centralized collective bargaining or corporatism (Wallerstein and Western 2000; Western 1995; Ebbinghaus and Visser 1999) are among the most emphasized factors. Increasing economic openness (Western 1995; Swank 1998; Scruggs and Lange 2002), the decline in strikes (Checchi and Visser 2005), and

Table 31.1 Trends in union density, bargaining centralization, and coverage by collective agreements

	Union density (0–100)			Bargaining centralization (1–5)			Bargaining coverage (0–100)		
	1990–94	2004–08	change	1990–94	2004–08	change	1990–94	2004–08	change
Australia	37.76	20.00	−47.03%	2.80	1.60	−42.86%	76.67	42.50	−44.57%
Austria	44.26	31.48	−28.87%	3.00	2.40	−20.00%	98.00	99.00	1.02%
Belgium	54.44	52.98	−2.68%	3.60	3.40	−5.56%	96.00	96.00	0.00%
Canada	35.08	29.68	−15.39%	1.00	1.00	0.00%	38.42	31.68	−17.54%
Czech Rep	57.95	18.94	−67.32%	2.80	2.00	−28.57%	63.30	44.18	−30.21%
Denmark	76.34	69.90	−8.44%	3.00	2.60	−13.33%	84.00	80.90	−3.69%
Finland	77.46	71.04	−8.29%	4.20	3.80	−9.52%	81.60	90.00	10.29%
France	9.54	7.68	−19.50%	2.00	2.00	0.00%	91.60	90.00	−1.75%
Germany	32.66	20.72	−36.56%	3.00	2.40	−20.00%	71.20	63.28	−11.12%
Greece	35.30	24.46	−30.71%	3.60	3.60	0.00%	68.00	65.00	−4.41%
Hungary	83.10	17.02	−79.52%	2.00	2.00	0.00%	–	35.63	–
Iceland	86.95	79.40	−8.68%	–	–	–	60.00	46.54	−22.43%
Ireland	56.04	36.02	−35.72%	4.80	4.00	−16.67%	92.85	88.23	−4.97%
Italy	38.86	33.56	−13.64%	3.00	3.00	0.00%	82.40	80.00	−2.91%
Netherlands	24.82	20.46	−17.57%	3.40	3.20	−5.88%	83.67	83.96	0.35%
Norway	58.10	54.36	−6.44%	4.20	3.60	−14.29%	71.00	73.37	3.33%
Poland	31.62	17.26	−45.41%	1.00	1.00	0.00%	–	38.13	–
Portugal	26.86	20.94	−22.04%	2.80	2.80	0.00%	75.00	59.08	−21.23%
Slovak Rep	67.30	20.60	−69.39%	2.20	1.60	−27.27%	–	43.00	–
Slovenia	61.10	29.70	−51.39%	2.40	4.00	66.67%	100.00	96.40	−3.60%
Spain	15.86	15.12	−4.67%	3.00	3.00	0.00%	84.38	86.25	2.22%
Sweden	84.76	73.54	−13.24%	3.60	2.40	−33.33%	89.00	92.50	3.93%
Switzerland	22.82	18.90	−17.18%	2.00	2.00	0.00%	48.00	48.00	0.00%
UK	37.62	28.48	−24.30%	1.00	1.00	0.00%	47.00	34.22	−27.19%
USA	15.22	11.80	−22.47%	1.00	1.00	0.00%	17.90	13.52	−24.47%

Source: Visser (2011). Union density rate is net union membership as a proportion of wage and salary earners in employment. Bargaining centralization index captures the main level at which wage bargaining is taking place. Bargaining coverage refers to employees covered by wage bargaining agreements as a proportion of all wage and salary earners in employment with the right to bargaining.

broader social and demographic factors (Visser 2002; Machin 2004) have also been identified as possible causes of union decline.[1] Regardless of what is causing it, the data suggest that union decline is a truly general phenomenon, which is not just limited to the CEE or LME countries, but involves the CME countries as well, with Austria and Germany experiencing larger percentage falls than the UK and the USA.

Collective Bargaining

Centralized collective bargaining is commonly assumed to raise unionization by extending union agreements to non-unionized companies, thereby indirectly reducing employer opposition to the expansion of union membership. Centralization also reduces inter-union competition and enhances coordination among union affiliates (Wallerstein and Western 2000). In addition, collective bargaining centralization is associated with more equal distribution of wages (Rueda and Pontusson 2000); Wallerstein 1999).[2] According to available data, collective bargaining has displayed greater resilience than unionization. The index of collective bargaining centralization displayed in Table 31.1 (with higher numbers indicating a higher level of centralization) shows that the main level of bargaining did not change in 11 countries for which data are available out of 24, while bargaining was decentralized in 12 countries, with Australia (−43%), Sweden (−33%), Czech Republic (−29%), Slovak Republic (−27%), Germany and Austria (−20%) experiencing the greatest changes. Only in Slovenia, which is commonly depicted as the only corporatist or coordinated market economy in CEE, was there a recentralization of collective bargaining (+67%) (Visser 2011).

It has to be noted though that the greater resilience of collective bargaining may just be a feature of the indicator used. This refers to the main level of bargaining and as such, may underestimate the extent of bargaining decentralization that has occurred in countries where industry and national bargaining have remained formally the main level, but an increasing number of regulatory issues have been dealt with at the company level.

Germany seems a case in point. The German collective bargaining system has undergone significant erosion in the last several years, visible in declining membership in trade unions and employer associations, decline of works council coverage, a growing low-wage sector, increased diffusion of atypical forms of employment, and declining stringency of industry-level contracts (Addison et al. 2007; Hassel 1999, 2007; Kinderman 2005; Streeck 2009; Streeck and Hassel 2004). A shift seems to have occurred in the internal power balance between trade unions and works councils, with the latter increasing their influence over bargaining outcomes at the expense of the former (French 2001; Raess and Burgoon 2006; Whittall 2005). The works council's first priority is often employment security. To obtain it, they are willing to make more concessions than industrial unions would. There is also evidence of employers trying to exploit union weakness by demanding opt-out clauses from higher level collective agreements or sometimes striking deals with unions to pay new entrants less than stipulated by collective agreements (Hassel and Schulten 1998; Kinderman 2005; Streeck 2009).

Similarly, in Sweden since the mid-1990s collective agreements have become more minimalist, giving employers wide discretion at the firm level. This decentralization and individualization of bargaining has gone hand in hand with considerable degree of continuity of formal institutions of coordinated bargaining (Baccaro and Howell 2011). These changes therefore introduce creeping liberalization that makes collective bargaining less constraining for employers but remains largely undetected by indicators that focus on the main level of bargaining.

Parallel to this trend, coverage by collective bargaining (the proportion of workers whose wages are determined by collective agreements) has declined in a majority of countries for which data are available (14 out of 22), even though this decline has been generally less pronounced than the decline in union density. As Table 31.1 shows, this decline was the largest and most obvious in LMEs and CEE countries, but several countries where employment relations have traditionally played more of a central role have not been immune to this trend either. Among these the decline was particularly sharp in Iceland (−22%), Portugal (−21%), and Germany (−11%).

Countries that have escaped this trend are facing a different problem, namely the growing uncoupling of union representation and collective bargaining coverage, especially in continental European countries. Collective bargaining coverage has declined much less than union density rates and in some cases it has even increased (Visser 2011). In countries such as Spain, France, Italy, Austria, Slovenia, Belgium, and others, a much higher proportion of workers are covered by collective bargaining agreements than are represented by trade unions, largely as a result of automatic extension clauses. On the one hand, this is a reassuring sign of resilience: it means that employment relations are highly institutionalized in some contexts and their impact on working conditions is partially independent from the organizational fortunes of class actors. On the other hand, it is a worrisome sign of disconnect: trade unions that directly represent only a minority of the workforce are increasingly called upon to negotiate the working conditions of a much larger proportion of workers. In so doing, they may privilege the interests of those groups they are still able to organize (the insiders) at the expense of other categories (young, women, workers on precarious or atypical contracts) that are outside their sphere of influence (Boeri et al. 2001; Lindbeck and Snower 1988; Rueda 2005, 2007; Saint-Paul 2002). This insider/outsider dialectic contributes to delegitimizing the unions and to casting them as defenders of special interests which stand in the way of a more equitable, as well as efficient, organization of the labour market.

Taken together, this evidence of collective bargaining decentralization, declining bargaining coverage, a hollowing out of formally stable institutions and the growing divisions between labour market insiders and outsiders signals the increasingly problematic status of collective bargaining in a majority of countries, even though the problem manifests itself differently in different countries.

Corporatist Policy-Making

As far as corporatist policy-making and social pacts are concerned (Table 31.2), data provided by Visser (2011) show that in 15 out of 24 countries there was no social pact either at the beginning or the end of the period under consideration.[3] In other countries there was a decline in social pact activity (Australia, Czech Republic, Norway, Poland,

Table 31.2 Trends in social pacts, conflict, and employment protection

	Social pact applies			Conflict rate			EPL regular workers		
	1990–94	2004–08	change	1990–94	2004–08	change	1990–94	04–08	change
Australia	0.6	0	–100.00%	130.87	19.60	–85.02%	0.99	0.96	–3.33%
Austria	0	0	.	5.92	0.01	–99.84%	3.59	2.84	–20.81%
Belgium	0	0	.	26.59	62.08	133.50%	1.50	1.50	0.00%
Canada	0	0	.	198.23	218.67	10.31%	1.30	1.30	0.00%
Czech Rep	0.8	0	–100.00%	.	.	.	3.63	3.29	–9.45%
Denmark	0	0	.	32.46	27.95	–13.89%	1.93	2.01	4.29%
Finland	0.8	0.6	–25.00%	173.81	75.77	–56.41%	2.79	2.59	–7.13%
France	0	0	.	21.73	.	.	2.48	2.48	0.00%
Germany	0	0	.	16.43	4.91	–70.13%	2.74	2.77	1.03%
Greece	0	0	.	1857.17	.	.	3.07	3.05	–0.84%
Hungary	0	0	.	.	.	.	2.05	1.92	–6.12%
Iceland	.	.	.	147.43	899.40	510.05%	.	.	.
Ireland	1.0	1.0	0.00%	101.27	6.75	–93.34%	1.88	1.69	–10.13%
Italy	0	0	.	169.85	33.66	–80.19%	2.25	2.33	3.66%
Netherlands	0.2	0.4	100.00%	14.97	6.38	–57.41%	2.66	1.34	–49.65%
Norway	0.4	0	–100.00%	64.45	31.31	–51.42%	1.71	1.71	0.00%
Poland	0.2	0	–100.00%	.	.	.	1.95	1.98	1.54%
Portugal	0.4	0.6	50.00%	28.16	7.24	–74.29%	4.57	4.02	–12.15%
Slovak Rep	0.4	0.2	–50.00%	.	.	.	3.47	2.87	–17.18%
Slovenia	0.2	0.8	300.00%	.	.	.	3.33	2.97	–10.87%
Spain	0	0	.	348.31	96.24	–72.37%	3.73	2.25	–39.68%
Sweden	0	0	.	48.92	6.10	–87.54%	3.22	3.08	–4.40%
Switzerland	0	0	.	0.98	3.24	231.09%	1.77	1.77	0.00%
UK	0	0	.	31.56	25.68	–18.63%	2.28	2.53	10.84%
USA	0	0	.	39.28	11.51	–70.71%	0.08	0.08	0.00%

Source: Social pact data (Visser 2011) indicate whether a wage clause in a pact applies in a given year. Each year in which a pact applies is coded as 1, and 0 otherwise. Strike rate indicates the total number of working days lost due to strikes and lockouts per 1000 employees normalized by civilian employment. ILO Laboursta database for conflict data (Variable 9C) and OECD.stat database (both accessed January 11, 2012) for civilian employment data. The EPL index (Allard 2010 for advanced economies; Avdagic 2011 for CEE countries), devised originally by the OECD, measures the strictness of employment protection legislation on a scale from 0 to 6, where higher numbers indicate stronger job protection.

Slovak Republic, and Finland); while in three countries (Portugal, Netherlands, and above all Slovenia) there was an increase. In Ireland, the incidence of social pacts was stable during this period. However, in 2009 the 20-year-long Irish social partnership was unceremoniously jettisoned by the government which responded to the financial crisis of 2009 with unilateral measures (Regan 2011; Roche 2011). At first sight it may be surprising that corporatist bargaining did not decline more given plummeting unionization and bargaining decentralization. However, as we discussed elsewhere, the new forms of corporatist bargaining that have emerged from the late 1980s–early 1990s on bear little resemblance to 'classic' corporatism as most policy reforms introduced by recent corporatist deals are market-conforming, facilitating liberalization of macroeconomic, welfare, and labour policies (Avdagic et al. 2011; Baccaro and Howell 2011).

Finally, it is worthwhile considering the incidence of industrial conflict as a related indicator of collective employment relations. The conflict rate has been declining dramatically for most countries for which data are available (see Table 31.2). The extent of decline is greater than 80% in Austria, Ireland, Sweden, Australia, and Italy. Exceptions to the common trend are Canada, Belgium, Switzerland, and Iceland, in which the incidence of industrial conflict has grown, starting however from very low levels in the case of Switzerland. It is well known that data on industrial conflicts are difficult to interpret. A low level of conflict may be a sign of trade union strength if the sheer threat of a strike leads the counterpart to cave in, or it may signal demobilization. However, given current circumstances the decline in conflict rates is almost certainly not a sign of trade union strength.

Overall, the aggregate evidence on institutional and organizational trends points to a generalized decline in the organizational fortunes of labour across different capitalist varieties. Union density is falling everywhere. This is combined with a decline in industrial conflict (with very few exceptions), a tendency for bargaining to become more differentiated and to accommodate firm-level diversity even when the main level of bargaining remains formally unchanged, and a tendency for peak-level corporatist bargaining either to disappear or to become increasingly ceremonial and/or concessionary.

Terms and Conditions of Employment

In addition to the institutional indicators, different indicators of the terms and conditions of employment reflect the state of employment relations. Formal and perceived job security, the structure of employment, labour's share of national income, and wage inequality are the most obvious choices. In the Fordist accumulation regime, in which employment relations played a central role, job security was high, the proportion of temporary and precarious jobs was low, labour's share of income matched productivity increases, and relative wage equality was secured through strong unions and/or centralized bargaining. Thus, a deterioration of these outcomes signals not only changes in the specific policies, but a broader decline of employment relations. The remainder of this section examines the trends in these outcomes over the last two decades.

Employment Protection

Not surprisingly, the decline of employment relations institutions overlaps tempo-rally (and perhaps causally as well) with a relaxation of employment protection rules. Apart from liberal market economies where employment protection was low to start with, employment protection has generally declined. During 1990–2007 EU countries alone have adopted 105 liberalizing reforms in this area (Avdagic 2012).[4] Most of these reforms (around three-quarters) have affected primarily those on the margins of the labour market, such as temporary employees (Boeri and Garibaldi 2007). However, many countries have seen a reduction in regulations for standard employment as well. As Table 31.2 shows, the largest declines—40–50%—have occurred in the Netherlands and Spain. Austria, the Slovak Republic, Portugal, Slovenia, and Ireland have also seen considerable declines. Liberalizing reforms were much more common and comprehensive than regulatory reforms. Only six countries increased protection for regular work-ers and they did this only to a very limited degree. For reasons of space, we cannot show data on employment protection for temporary workers. Here, extensive liberalization occurred in the Netherlands (where the EPL index for temporary contracts declined by 55%), the Slovak Republic (–54%), Italy (–50%), Germany (–44%), and Spain (–42%) (Allard 2010). Among advanced economies only two saw a considerable increase in the EPL index for temporary contracts—Ireland (from 0.25 to 0.63) and Belgium (from 1.73 to 3). Apart from these countries only CEE economies, which had very liberal rules gov-erning temporary employment throughout the 1990s, have strengthened protection for temporary workers. These regulatory reforms, however, reflect primarily adoption of various EU Directives that seek to improve the terms and conditions of employment for non-standard workers (Avdagic 2012).

Countries that adopted significant reforms affecting temporary employment but left rules for regular employment largely untouched have experienced increasing dualiza-tion in the labour market. One of the key examples of this trend is Germany where tem-porary agency work has become a major source of highly flexible but low-paid work in manufacturing and some services (Palier and Thelen 2010; Eichhorst 2011). The upshot of this is increasing divisions between relatively well-protected 'insiders' with regular employment contracts and the more vulnerable 'outsiders' subject to non-standard forms of employment.

Another sign of the general trend of the declining employment protection comes from survey data, which indicate a decrease in perceived employment security in many OECD countries. Interestingly, the rise in perceived insecurity was evident even in the absence of significantly higher labour turnover rates (OECD 1997). Unsurprisingly, temporary jobholders and low-skilled workers feel less secure than highly skilled work-ers and holders of permanent (in particular public sector) jobs (Clark and Postel-Vinay 2005; Maurin and Postel-Vinay 2005; de Bustillo and de Pedraza 2010). An OECD study examining the impact of an intensification of foreign competition on job stability con-firms these perceptions: the growing integration of national economies increases the probability of job separations, while low-tenure and low-skill workers tend to experience the biggest increase in transitions out of employment (OECD 2007).

It is well known that perceived job security has important consequences for a range of socio-economic outcomes, such as individuals' well-being and fertility (Böckerman 2004; Bernardi et al. 2006). However, job security perceptions may also affect the very institutions that govern employment relations. Recent research has shown, for example, that an increase in job insecurity may lead to reduced union loyalty and withdrawal from union membership (Sverke and Goslinga 2003). It is therefore plausible to argue that changes in employment protection affect broader institutional outcomes, such as the level of union membership, and consequently the nature and quality of collective bargaining and corporatist policy-making.

Changes in the Structure of Employment

The broad trends of deindustrialization and a rising share of employment in services that started during the 1970s continued, albeit at a slower pace, during the last two decades. In addition, atypical forms of employment, such as fixed-term and part-time employment, have become more prevalent.

Part-time employment (persons working usually less than 30 hours per week in their main job) has been on the rise in most OECD countries during the last two decades. The Netherlands, Italy, Spain, Ireland, and Germany have seen the largest increases. Due to the prevailing division of family and care labour across genders, this form of employment has been much more prevalent among women than men. Currently, the largest gender gap is visible in the Netherlands where almost 60% of women in employment work part-time, compared to 17% of men (OECD 2010). This gap is smallest in CEE countries, which also have the lowest rates of part-time employment overall. While most part-time work is voluntary according to the available statistics, in several countries considerable portions of part-time workers would prefer to work full time. Data on involuntary part-time employment, however, are rather patchy, so it is difficult to identify clear trends across countries and over time. Nonetheless, it is clear that the Mediterranean countries have all experienced an increase in involuntary part-time employment over the last two decades, with particularly large increases in Portugal (from 14% of total part-time employment to 53%), Italy (from 11% to 31%), and Greece (from 17% to 29%). Among continental European countries Germany has seen the largest increase: in 1990 less than 5% of part-time employment was involuntary, while in 2008 one in five part-time workers would have preferred to work full time.[5] While part-time work enables a better work–life balance and has been associated with better health and safety outcomes, this form of employment carries a number of penalties. Recent survey data show that in almost all OECD countries part-time workers have lower hourly wages than their full-time counterparts. They also participate less in training and have lower promotion prospects. In addition, these workers are less likely to be union members and tend to have less job security (both formal and perceived) than full-time workers (OECD 2010). Given these penalties a general increase in part-time employment can be seen as one indicator of labour's weakening position.

Temporary employment (defined as fixed-term or employment of specified duration) has also grown in several countries during 1990–2008. While most continental and Mediterranean countries have experienced an increase in temporary employment in this period, this trend was most pronounced in the Netherlands, Italy, Germany, and Portugal where temporary employment increased by 5–10 percentage points. The sharpest increase was seen in Poland where temporary employment increased from 11% to 27% during 2001–2008. In terms of the levels, however, the highest proportion of temporary jobs can be still found in Spain where roughly 30% of dependent employees have temporary jobs. While temporary employees are a diverse group, young or less educated workers fill most temporary jobs. In comparison to permanent jobs, these jobs have lower pay, less training, and less access to paid vacations and unemployment insurance and other fringe benefits. Temporary jobs are also associated with lower job satisfaction. In addition, temporary workers enjoy less job security. An OECD study found that during the 1990s about a quarter of temporary workers became unemployed, while an even larger share remained in temporary jobs (OECD 2002). Low mobility into permanent jobs, in turn, increases labour market dualism, which undermines labour unity and collective bargaining power.

Labour Share of National Income

During the last two decades the share of national income received by labour has decreased in all advanced OECD countries (IILS 2008).[6] This general trend is generally attributed to market forces. For example, recent research by the IMF has argued that the growth of the effective global labour force, which increased fourfold during this period, causes labour share decline by lowering its price (IMF 2007). A by-product of the changing global labour supply is the increase of imports from developing countries. These are typically intensive in unskilled labour and thus tend to have a depressing effect on unskilled wages. A similar depressing effect can be attributed to the offshoring of the production of intermediaries. IMF research argues that much of the decline in the labour shares in advanced economies can be attributed to the fall in unskilled sectors associated with the increasingly globalized markets (IMF 2007). This decline has been much more pronounced in Europe than in the Anglo-Saxon countries, and the UK and the USA in particular. The latter, the IMF study argues, have been able to avoid large declines in labour share because they were champions of deregulation, in particular with respect to taxes on labour and unemployment benefits.

There are several problems with this argument. First, the Anglo-Saxon countries started at significantly lower levels of labour income shares (with roughly 65% of GDP compared to 73% of GDP for continental Europe in 1980) (IMF 2007). Second, as Glyn (2007) argued, overvalued currencies and especially a dramatic rise in the share of the very top 'wage earners' such as CEOs may be a more plausible explanation for the slower decline of labour share in the UK and the USA. In addition, there seems to be a positive statistical association, displayed in Fig. 31.1, between union density and labour shares: the greater the decline in union density in a given country, the higher the decline in the labour share in the same country on average. This relationship is weak in the case

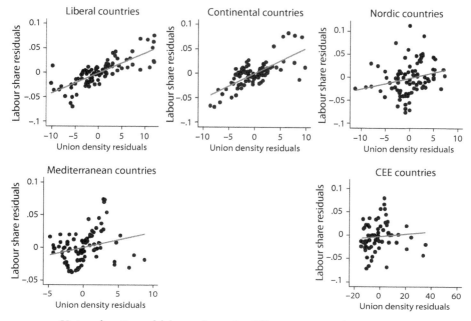

FIGURE 31.1 Union density and labour shares in different groups of countries

On the y-axis are the residuals from a regression of labour share of GDP on country fixed effects; on the x-axis the residuals from a regression of union density on country fixed effects. The straight line is a linear fit, which is clearly inappropriate for some graphs but useful to identify the trends.

Sources: Visser (2011) for union density data and OECD.Stat (accessed 11 January 2012) for labour share data.

of the CEE countries, due to the shocks mentioned above, but considerably stronger for the two purest models of capitalism, the liberal and continental (also known as CME) (Hall and Soskice 2001). It may be a spurious statistical relationship, i.e. there could be other factors that explain both union decline and declining labour shares. If it is indeed a causal relationship, it would suggest that the decline in labour share is due to the reduced ability of trade unions to push for wage increases equalling productivity increases.

In fact, the average annual wage has increased in all countries but on average less than the increase in productivity—which explains the declining wage share. In addition, there is clear evidence that wage volatility has increased as employers have become less willing to insulate wages, particularly of low-skilled and low-tenure workers, from adverse market conditions (OECD 2007). Growth in labour compensation in unskilled sectors has been particularly slow in the USA, which has caused the earnings gap between the skilled and unskilled sectors to widen by 25% since 1980. The earnings gap between the sectors has remained smaller in Europe, but employment in unskilled sectors has declined substantially (IMF 2007). The latter has been a consequence of technical progress favouring skilled workers, increased imports from developing countries,

and generally weaker labour demand, which allowed employers to recruit better qualified workers for jobs that were previously reserved for the low-skilled (Glyn 2006).

Wage Inequality

Wage inequality is also an important indicator of changes in employment relations.
It is well known that the changing economic environment over the last two decades
has caused the wage distribution to become more unequal in most OECD countries.
However, if we disaggregate the overall trend and examine separately the evolution of
inequality in the upper and the lower halves of the distribution, it becomes clear that the
increase in inequality since 1990 has occurred primarily in the top half of the earning
distribution (Atkinson 2008). The rise in inequality in the top half of the earnings distribution (d9/d5) has been particularly pronounced in liberal economies, such as the USA
and the UK, where the very top earners have benefited enormously. Recent research has
shown that the income share of the top 0.1% of the income distribution, which was in
decline for most of the twentieth century, has increased dramatically in these countries
since 1990 (Piketty and Saez 2006). Most other countries examined here have also not
been immune from the general trend of rising inequality in the top half of the earning
distribution, even though in many of them inequality may have increased by a more
modest amount. Particularly steep increases have occurred in Switzerland, Denmark,
Hungary, and the Netherlands.[7] By contrast, the measure of earnings inequality in the
bottom half (d5/d1) does not show a significant increase, apart from Denmark and
Norway. The fact that inequality has not increased significantly in the bottom half of
the distribution suggests that import competition from developing countries is not the
key culprit (OECD 2007) and that domestic policies and institutional features, such as
unionization levels and collective bargaining arrangements, play a more decisive role in
shaping the trends in wage distribution.

Trade union density and centralized (or coordinated) collective bargaining have
traditionally been considered key determinants of more egalitarian wage and income
distributions (Blau and Kahn 1996; Bradley et al. 2003; Freeman 1988; Hicks and
Kenworthy 1998; OECD 2009; Pontusson et al. 2003; Rowthorn 1992; Rueda and
Pontusson 2000; Wallerstein 1999). Thus, the weakening of these institutions may
contribute to explain the generalized increase in inequality. However, recent literature
suggests a more nuanced and worrisome interpretation. Baccaro (2011) has argued
that the inequality-reducing effect of industrial relations institutions has largely disappeared since the early 1990s. Similarly, Golden and Wallerstein (2011) argue that centralized collective bargaining no longer has egalitarian effects. This research suggests that
(within-country) variation in employment relations institutions is no longer robustly
associated with (within-country) variation in distributional outcomes. There may be
different interpretations for this phenomenon: on the one hand, changing economic
conditions (more elastic labour and product demands) may hinder the ability of unions
to impose outcomes that differ significantly from those compatible with a market equilibrium (Baccaro 2011). On the other hand, the unions themselves may have changed as
political economic actors. Due to trade union decline, these organizations may currently

predominantly represent relatively more skilled workers, and as such be less interested in redistribution than they once were. If this is true, union decline would contribute to growing inequality indirectly by altering the internal composition of trade unions. While the data needed to test this interpretation are not available, supportive evidence along this line has recently been provided by Becher and Pontusson (2011).

Overall, different indicators suggest a generalized deterioration of the terms and conditions of employment for most workers (growing inequality, declining wage share, growing precariousness, etc.). Combined with the institutional developments discussed above, these trends paint a rather gloomy picture of the future of employment relations, an issue we discuss in more detail in the next section.

WHAT PROSPECTS FOR EMPLOYMENT RELATIONS?

It is not at all clear that one should try to predict future developments by extrapolating from past trends. To paraphrase Shakespeare, there are more things in heaven and earth than we can dream of in our philosophy. Furthermore, the employment relations field is probably not the best one for historical extrapolation. It is not the first time social scientists predict fundamental changes in this domain. They have been proven wrong before, for example when they anticipated the withering away of strikes just a few years before a true and proper explosion of strikes in most if not all advanced countries (Crouch and Pizzorno 1978; Dahrendorf 1959; Kerr et al. 1962). Nonetheless, our 'philosophy' is all we have to try to peer into the future. It leads us to formulate deeply pessimistic conclusions about the future of employment relations.

The evidence outlined in the previous sections indicates that the key actors of an employment relations system—namely trade unions—are in crisis everywhere. In addition, a crucial employment relations institution, centralized or multi-employer bargaining, is also changing, although in more subtle ways: even in countries (like the continental European and the Scandinavian ones) where the main locus of bargaining remains at the sectoral level, multi-employer bargaining is increasingly unable to impose standard conditions of employment across different firms. Although corporatist policy-making and social pacts experienced a surprising re-emergence in various countries in the 1990s, they have become less prevalent afterwards. In addition, they are very different from the corporatist pacts of the 1970s: they contribute to mobilize support and legitimacy for market-conforming reforms of the labour market and the welfare state, and for competitiveness-enhancing wage policies (Avdagic et al. 2011; Baccaro and Howell 2011).

All of this signals a clear decline in labour's bargaining power. Trends in the terms and conditions of employment point to the same conclusion: employment protection is declining everywhere, although in non-liberal countries the decline predominantly affects non-standard workers. A sense of precariousness is on the rise in many countries for which data are available. There is a generalized decline in the labour share of GDP, which in liberal and continental countries seems to correlate well with the decline in union density. Wage inequality is increasing, particularly in the upper half of the distribution. Although some countries provide exceptions on specific dimensions, these trends cut across different models of capitalism. Given these developments, how likely is it that the balance of power will shift back to employees, and under what circumstances may employment relations experience a renaissance?

Although we do not think there is anything natural in labour's decline, we believe that redressing it would require a shift of such proportion as to make it not very probable. Essentially, the state should step in—as it once did (Howell 1992; Howell 2005)—and promote unionization and collective bargaining because of their positive externalities. We surmise that employment relations do have beneficial consequences for a capitalist economy as they promote 'balanced growth', i.e. growth in which wages augment at the same rate as productivity increases, and in so doing allow for a more equitable distribution of the returns to technological progress, one which benefits the 'middle class' as opposed to the top 1 or even 0.1% (Levy and Kochan 2011; Levy and Temin 2007).

Despite this positive contribution, the revitalization of employment relations seems an unlikely event for several reasons. First, it assumes that the national state still has the capacity to intervene decisively in the economy—an assumption that clashes with the current reality of economic globalization. Second, it presupposes that there are partisan actors that would be interested in strengthening unions and collective bargaining. This presupposition, too, is doubtful seeing the ideological changes that have occurred within centre-left parties and their 'divorce' from national labour movements (Giddens 1994; Kitschelt 1994; Simoni 2007). Third, it would involve the return to a Fordist-type accumulation regime at a time in which Fordism has disappeared everywhere (Boyer 2004).

Fordism was a system in which employment relations played a central role in stabilizing a capitalist economy by providing an institutional link between productivity increases and aggregate demand formation. It promoted the growth of consumption demand by, on the one hand, tightly linking wages and labour productivity and, on the other, relying on the welfare state to protect demand from business cycle fluctuations. Unionization and collective bargaining, as the central pillars of employment relations, served to ensure the transmission of productivity increases to disposable income increases, which in turn induced increases in demand for mass-produced consumer goods. Steadily increasing demand allowed for the economies of scale needed for productivity increases. In addition raising wages decreased the relative cost of capital and therefore stimulated technological and organizational innovation. The institutionalization of employment relations and wage-productivity bargaining underpinned by strong unions, rather than market-driven variation in wages and profit, was instrumental in ensuring macroeconomic balance (Grahl and Teague 2000). The social compromises of the Fordist era were thus based on the premise that a stable portion of the fruits of economic growth was going to be distributed to employees. The central role of the unions and wage bargaining coupled with the redistributive efforts on the part of the state worked to produce a relatively egalitarian distribution of earnings and income. The latter in turn supported an accumulation system based on the wage–productivity nexus and aimed at mass consumption. In short, employment relations ensured the viability of the whole accumulation regime that was at work until the 1970s in advanced industrial democracies.

This is of course a highly stylized representation, which overemphasizes the functionalist coupling of institutions and underplays the politics that undergirded them. In reality, Fordism was always internally contested. As Streeck (2011) has argued, the Fordist era may have been exceptionally successful, but democratic capitalism is inherently conflictual and 'ruled by an endemic conflict between capitalist markets and democratic politics' (Streeck 2011: 6). Be that as it may, the Fordist system is no longer dominant, even though in many countries the precise contours of a new system are somewhat unclear and not easy to define. What seems clear, however, is that the regulatory system that has replaced Fordism is very different insofar as the wage compromise no longer plays the same central role. Rather than the wage–labour nexus, it is finance that assumes the central role in the new regime (Boyer 2000). While the engine of growth is still linked to domestic consumption, the latter is no longer secured through real wage increases, but in many cases it increasingly relies on the stock market (wealth effect) and the expansion of credit. An increasing portion of wage earners has access to financial gains, mostly via pension fund intermediaries but sometimes also via direct equity holdings. As a consequence, the situation of financial markets increasingly has an influence on the households' decision to spend or save. The wealth effect of increasing asset values and growing indebtedness made possible by easy access to credit are increasingly eroding the importance of the wage–labour nexus. Rather than wages and productivity, the key variables in this system are profitability and capital gains.

The above characterization captures well the situation of countries like the USA and the UK in which the process of financialization has proceeded furthest (Crouch 2009). However, even in countries like Germany and other CMEs, in which manufacturing remains very important, the main driver of growth is not domestic consumption as in the Fordist regime of accumulation, but exports (Iversen and Soskice 2012). Germany has always been an export-driven economy, but its share of exports as percentage of GDP has increased dramatically from the Fordist era, and especially from 2000 on.

In export-oriented economies, employment relations institutions have a dual role: on the one hand, they ensure the institutional resources needed for the production and reproduction of industry-specific skills, which are very important for manufacturing success (Soskice 1999). On the other hand, by redistributing productivity increases they may have a detrimental impact on export competitiveness, which depends on relative unit labour costs. Hence, employment relations in these economies are increasingly dualistic: on the one hand the old compromise between capital and labour is maintained for a shrinking portion of core workers; on the other hand, a growing army of non-core workers is created through the use of atypical contracts (Berger and Piore 1980; Palier and Thelen 2010). In these conditions the public at large no longer perceives unions as contributing to reconciling efficiency and equity but as catering to the narrow interests of a well-organized and relatively well-protected, albeit numerically declining, constituency—which adds to the unions' woes.

All this does not bode well for the prospect of employment relations renaissance. Our interpretation of developments is that the current state of decline of employment relations will not be reversed unless there is a return to an accumulation regime in which domestic demand growth through real wage growth is the key driver. This 'back-to-the-future' type of scenario seems unlikely due to the political power wielded by the financial industry, which is sure to fiercely resist any change to the status quo (Johnson and Kwak 2010).

A possible response to the decline of employment relations is related to the dynamics of union growth. A common argument is that 'union revitalization' is the answer to employment relations troubles: if unions invested more heavily and smartly in organizing the unorganized, they would be able to wield the power necessary to promote more employment relations friendly institutions as well. While much scholarly work has been devoted to identifying mechanisms and strategies for union revitalization in different countries (Baccaro et al. 2003; Frege and Kelly 2003; Milkman 2006; Murray and Waddington 2005), there has been little evidence of union revitalization (measured as growing density rates) occurring on a large scale anywhere. In addition, the literature suggests that union growth tends to happen in 'spurts' during relatively short periods of time characterized by both functional problems of capitalist reproduction (as evident in inflation, unemployment and other business cycle variables) and 'fundamental unrest' or mobilizational offensive (Barnett 1916; Dunlop 1949; Bain and Elshelkh 1976; Bain and Price 1980; Freeman 1998). The current conjuncture does not seem of the kind conducive to rapid union growth. While functional problems of capitalist reproduction have been abundantly present for a few years now as a consequence of the global economic and financial crisis, the mobilizational potential seems absent, in part because the actors on whose legs mobilization should walk (unions and social democratic parties) have been either weakened or changed by the very developments they are supposed to undo.

Still another response to the crisis of employment relations concerns the transnational level. This argument complements the former in various respects. Trade unions should shift their focus beyond the nation state and exploit the (thin) institutional supports provided by European institutions, such as European Works Councils or European Social Dialogue (see for example Erne 2008). Although we acknowledge that the Europeanization of employment relations is possible and certainly desirable, we are not persuaded that reconstituting employment relations at the European, let alone transnational, level is a realistic option, just as we are not persuaded that a voluntaristic project of union revitalization is a real possibility either. First, what remains of workers' solidarities remains firmly anchored at the national level. Second, although there are certainly cases of cross-country cooperation, they remain isolated examples and do not seem to generate a critical mass. Third, as Streeck and Schmitter (1991) argued after the introduction of the Single European Act, the European project was conceived essentially as a deal between national states and capital from which labour was excluded. Twenty years after, we see no reason to alter their assessment. On the contrary, at the time of writing the countries of the eurozone are in the midst of a 'sovereign debt crisis' and Europe is responding by promoting austerity policies and structural reforms which are likely to negatively affect unions and collective bargaining (Armingeon and Baccaro 2012). In other words recent European developments make us believe that when it comes to the resurgence of employment relations, Europe is more a part of the problem than a part of the solution.

Conclusion

In this chapter we have provided an analysis of the available quantitative evidence about institutional developments and the evolution of terms and conditions of employment. On this basis we have argued that employment relations are on a declining trend every-where and that a renaissance is unlikely. The main problem, we have argued, is the crisis of Fordism, an accumulation regime in which employment relations institutions (primarily trade unions and collective bargaining) played a central role in stabilizing a capitalist economy by both enabling productivity growth (by expanding the market and by stimulating technological and organizational upgrading) and by ensuring the smooth transition of productivity increases into aggregate demand.

Although no clear alternatives to the Fordist accumulation regime have emerged, both in the finance-based regime that prevailed in the USA and the UK before the global financial crisis, and in the export-based regime that has dominated in Germany for much of its post-war history and at least since the late 1990s, employment relations institutions are more a liability than an asset. In the finance-based model employment relations institutions are perceived as a liability because they impair productivity and capital gains, which are the true drivers of accumulation. In an export-based regime the impact of employment relations is more nuanced. On the one hand these institutions are needed to ensure the reproduction of skills needed for manufacturing export prowess. On the other hand, there is a concern among employers that they may compromise relative cost competitiveness. Therefore, in this system employment relations institutions apply only to a shrinking core portion of the economy and generate dualistic labour market outcomes.

We have argued that employment relations renaissance is unlikely to come from voluntaristic strategies aimed to relaunch union organizing or promoting cross-national cooperation across national union movements, although both would be important elements of a global strategy. We believe instead that it would require a fundamental shift in public policy at the national and supranational level. The revival of employment relations has a chance only if the state accepts that employment relations produce positive 'externalities' for society and is willing to intervene to facilitate their development. The most important of these externalities is that the transmission of productivity increases to domestic demand is not automatic, as suggested by the generalized decline of the labour share of GDP, but requires actors, such as trade unions, and institutions, such as collective bargaining, that make it happen. However, this strategy for renaissance assumes the state would be able to provide such support if asked to—an assumption that clashes with current realities of economic globalization. Furthermore, the crisis of Fordism and the emergence of alternative accumulation regimes in which employment relations institutions are no longer crucial for the overall stability of the system make it very difficult for trade unions to credibly demand and obtain state support. The credibility of unions is further undermined by the fact that they are often blamed for labour market dualization and for catering to the narrow interests of their steadily declining constituency.

The kind of shift in public policy that would be required for employment relations renaissance is unlikely to happen, as it would imply large-scale changes in the institutional infrastructure of contemporary capitalism. It would require a coordinated international effort to reduce the weight of the financial sector and correct macroeconomic imbalances (primarily by countering the tendency of some countries to run systematic current account surpluses), and a renewed effort to ensure once again 'balanced growth', i.e. growth in which productivity increases are transferred to wages and lead to greater aggregate demand. The financial crisis of 2008–2009 provided a window of opportunity both for a drastic reform of finance and for introducing a more hospitable regulatory framework for employment relations (Baccaro et al. 2009). Five years after the beginning of the crisis and with no end to it in sight yet, it seems fair to say that the opportunity has been missed.

Notes

1. It should be noted, however, that the direction of causality here is not entirely clear since several of these factors may be both a cause and a consequence of union decline.
2. While the positive impact of collective bargaining centralization on unionization and wage equality is widely accepted, its impact on macroeconomic performance, and in particular unemployment, is a more disputed issue. See, for example, the discussion in Wallerstein and Western (2000: 373–4).
3. Social pacts are a form of corporatist-style policy-making that spread through many traditionally non-corporatist European countries during the 1990s. They involve formal or informal agreements between unions, employers, and the state on issues such as incomes policy, labour market, and welfare state reforms.
4. These data refer to all current EU countries apart from Cyprus and Malta.
5. Online OECD Employment database, accessed on 6 January 2012.
6. An exception is CEE countries, where the labour share increased in the early to mid-1990s. The reversed trend in CEE is most likely due to the fact that GDP had experienced much larger drops than wages during the early period of post-communist transition.
7. Data on earnings inequality are not available for all our countries and all periods. Data for CEE countries are particularly patchy. However, other sources and the literature on

individual CEE countries suggest that the rise of inequality has been a uniform phenomenon in transition economies, and it is likely that both halves of distribution were affected.

REFERENCES

Addison, J. T., Schnabel, C., and Wagner, J. (2007). 'The (Parlous) State of German Unions',
Journal of Labor Research, 28: 3–18.

Allard, G. (2010). 'The Employment Protection Index in OECD Countries, 1950–2008'.
Unpublished data. Madrid: IE Business School.

Andersen, J. G. (2011). *Activation of Social and Labour Market Policies in the Nordic Countries,
1990–2010*. Centre for Comparative Welfare Studies (CCWS), Aalborg University Working
Paper 2011-71.

Armingeon, K. and Baccaro, L. (2012). 'The Sorrows of Young Euro: Policy Responses to the
Sovereign Debt Crisis', in N. Bermeo and J. Pontusson (eds.), *Coping with Crisis: Government
Responses to the Great Recession*. New York: Russell Sage Foundation, 162–98.

Atkinson, A. B. (2008). *The Changing Distribution of Earnings in OECD Countries*. Oxford and
New York: Oxford University Press.

Avdagic, S. (2011). Database on Employment Protection Legislation (EPL) Index in Central and
Eastern Europe. ESRC Data Store. Available at <http://store.data-archive.ac.uk:80/store/
collectionEdit.jsp?collectionPID=archive:598>.

—— (2012). 'Partisanship, Political Constraints and Employment Protection Reforms in an Era
of Austerity', *European Political Science Review*, 5(3): 431–55.

Avdagic, S., Rhodes, M., and Visser, J. (eds.) (2011). *Social Pacts in Europe: Emergence, Evolution
and Institutionalization*. Oxford and New York: Oxford University Press.

Baccaro, L. (2011). 'Labor, Globalization, and Inequality: Are Trade Unions Still Redistributive?',
Research in the Sociology of Work, 22: 213–85.

Baccaro, L., Boyer, R., Crouch, C., Regini, M., Marginson, P., Hyman, R., Gumbrell-McCormick,
R., and Milkman, R. (2009). 'Labour and the Global Financial Crisis', *Socio-Economic
Review*, 8(2): 341–76.

Baccaro, L., Hamann, K., and Turner, L. (2003). 'The Politics of Labour Movement
Revitalization: The Need for a Revitalized Perspective', *European Journal of Industrial
Relations*, 9(1): 119–33.

Baccaro, L. and Howell, C. (2011). 'A Common Neoliberal Trajectory: The Transformation of
Industrial Relations in Advanced Capitalism', *Politics & Society*, 39(4): 521–63.

Bain, G. S. and Elshelkh, F. (1976). *Union Growth and the Business Cycle*. Oxford: Blackwell.

Bain, G. S. and Price, R. (1980). *Profiles of Union Growth: A Comparative Statistical Portrait of
Eight Countries*. Oxford: Blackwell.

Barnett, G. E. (1916). 'Growth of Labor Organization in the United States, 1897–1914', *Quarterly
Journal of Economics*, 30: 780–95.

Becher, M. and Pontusson, J. (2011). 'Whose Interests Do Unions Represent? Unionization by
Income in Western Europe', *Research in the Sociology of Work*, 22: 181–211.

Berger, S. and Piore, M. J. (1980). *Dualism and Discontinuity in Industrial Societies*.
New York: Cambridge University Press.

Bernardi, L., Klärner, A., and von der Lippe, H. (2006). *Perceptions of Job Instability and the
Prospects of Parenthood: A Comparison between Eastern and Western Germany*. Max Planck
Institute for Demographic Research Working Paper 2006-017. Rostock: MPIDR.

Blau, F. D. and Kahn, L. M. (1996). 'International Differences in Male Wage Inequality: Institutions versus Market Forces', *Journal of Political Economy*, 104: 791–837.

Böckerman, P. (2004). 'Perception of Job Instability in Europe', *Social Indicators Research*, 67: 283–314.

Boeri, T., Brugiavini, A., and Calmfors, L. (2001). *The Role of Trade Unions in the Twenty-First Century: A Study for the Fondazione Rodolfo Debenedetti*. Oxford and New York: Oxford University Press.

Boeri, T. and Garibaldi, P. (2007). 'Two Tier Reforms of Employment Protection: A Honeymoon Effect?', *The Economic Journal*, 117: F357–F385.

Boyer, R. (2000). 'Is a Finance-Led Growth Regime a Viable Alternative to Fordism? A Preliminary Analysis', *Economy and Society*, 29(1): 111–45.

—— (2004). *Théorie de la Régulation, 1. Les Fondamentaux*. Paris: La découverte.

Bradley, D., Huber, E., Moller, S., Nielsen, F., and Stephens, J. D. (2003). 'Distribution and Redistribution in Postindustrial Democracies', *World Politics*, 55: 193–228.

Checchi, D. and Visser, J. (2005). 'Pattern Persistence in European Trade Union Density: A Longitudinal Analysis 1950–1996', *European Sociological Review*, 21(1): 1–21.

Clark, C. and Postel-Vinay, F. (2005). *Job Security and Job Protection*. IZA Discussion Paper 1489. Bonn: Institute for the Study of Labor.

Crouch, C. (2009). 'Privatised Keynesianism: An Unacknowledged Policy Regime', *British Journal of Politics and International Relations*, 11: 382–99.

Crouch, C. and Pizzorno, A. (eds.) (1978). *The Resurgence of Class Conflict in Western Europe since 1968*. London: Macmillan.

Dahrendorf, R. (1959). *Class and Class Conflict in Industrial Society*. Stanford: Stanford University Press.

De Bustillo, R. M. and de Pedraza, P. (2010). 'Determinants of Job Insecurity in 5 European Countries', *European Journal of Industrial Relations*, 16(1): 5–20.

Dunlop, J. T. (1949). 'The Development of Labor Organization: A Theoretical Framework', in R. A. Lester and J. Shister (eds.), *Insights into Labor Issues*. New York: Macmillan, 163–93.

Ebbinghaus, B. and Visser, J. (1999). 'When Institutions Matter: Union Growth and Decline in Western Europe, 1950–1995', *European Sociological Review*, 15(2): 135–58.

Erne, R. (2008). *European Unions: Labor Quest for a Transnational Democracy*. Ithaca: Cornell University Press.

Freeman, R. (1998). 'Spurts in Union Growth: Defining Moments and Social Processes', in M. D. Bordo, C. Goldin, and E. N. White (eds.), *The Defining Moment: The Great Depression and the American Economy in the Twentieth Century*. Chicago: University of Chicago Press, 265–95.

Freeman, R. B. (1988). 'Labour Market Institutions and Economic Performance', *Economic Policy*, 3: 63–80.

Frege, C. and Kelly, J. (2003). 'Union Revitalization Strategies in Comparative Perspective', *European Journal of Industrial Relations*, 9(1): 7–24.

French, S. (2001). 'Works Councils in Unified Germany: Still Loyal to the Trade Unions?', *International Journal of Manpower*, 22: 560–78.

Frieden, J. A. (2006). *Global Capitalism: Its Fall and Rise in the Twentieth Century*. New York: Norton.

Giddens, A. (1994). *Beyond Left and Right: The Future of Radical Politics*. Cambridge: Polity Press.

Glyn, A. (2006). *Capitalism Unleashed: Finance, Globalization, and Welfare*. Oxford and New York: Oxford University Press.

—— (2007). *Explaining Labor's Declining Share of National Income*. G-24 Policy Brief No. 4.

Golden, M. and Wallerstein, M. (2011). 'Domestic and International Causes for the Rise of Pay Inequality in OECD Nations between 1980 and 2000'. Unpublished manuscript.

Grahl, J. and Teague, P. (2000). 'The Régulation School, the Employment Relation, and Financialization', *Economy and Society*, 29(1): 160–78.

Hacker, J. S. (2004). 'Privatizing Risk without Privatizing the Welfare State: The Hidden Politics of Social Retrenchment in the United States', *American Political Science Review*, 98(2): 243–60.

Hall, P. A. and Soskice, D. (eds.) (2001). *Varieties of Capitalism: The Institutional Foundations of Comparative Advantage*. Oxford and New York: Oxford University Press.

Hassel, A. (1999). 'The Erosion of the German System of Industrial Relations', *British Journal of Industrial Relations*, 37: 483–505.

—— (2007). 'The Curse of Institutional Security: The Erosion of German Trade Unionism', *Industrielle Beziehungen*, 14: 176–91.

Hassel, A. and Schulten, T. (1998). Globalization and the Future of Central Collective Bargaining: The Example of the German Metal Industry', *Economy and Society*, 27: 486–522.

Hicks, A. and Kenworthy, L. (1998). 'Cooperation and Political Economic Performance in Affluent Democratic Capitalism', *American Journal of Sociology*, 103: 1631–72.

Howell, C. (1992). *Regulating Labor: The State and Industrial Relations Reform in Postwar France*. Princeton: Princeton University Press.

—— (2005). *Trade Unions and the State: The Construction of Industrial Relations Institutions in Britain, 1890–2000*. Princeton: Princeton University Press.

IILS (2008). *World of Work Report 2008: Income Inequalities in the Age of Financial Globalization*. Geneva: International Institute for Labour Studies.

IMF (2007). *IMF World Economic Outlook*. Washington, DC: International Monetary Fund.

Iversen, T. and Soskice, D. (2012). 'Modern Capitalism and the Advanced Nation State: Understanding the Causes of the Crisis', in N. Bermeo and J. Pontusson (eds.), *Coping with Crisis: Government Responses to the Great Recession*. New York: Russell Sage Foundation, 35–64.

Johnson, S. and Kwak, J. (2010). *13 Bankers: The Wall Street Takeover and the Next Financial Meltdown*. New York: Pantheon Books.

Kerr, C., Dunlop, J. T., Harbison, F., and Myers, C. A. (1962). *Industrialism and Industrial Man: The Problems of Labor and Management in Economic Growth*. London: Heinemann.

Kinderman, D. (2005). 'Pressure from Without, Subversion from Within: The Two-Pronged German Employer Offensive', *Comparative European Politics*, 3: 432–63.

Kitschelt, H. (1994). *The Transformation of European Social Democracy*. New York: Cambridge University Press.

Levy, F. and Kochan, T. (2011). 'Addressing the Problem of Stagnant Wages'. MIT IWER Unpublished Working Paper.

Levy, F. and Temin, P. (2007). *Inequality and Institutions in 20th Century America*. MIT Industrial Performance Center Working Paper Series MIT-IPC-07-002.

Lind, J. (2009). 'The End of the Ghent System as Trade Union Recruitment Machinery?', *Industrial Relations Journal*, 40: 510–23.

Lindbeck, A. and Snower, D. (1988). *The Insider-Outsider Theory of Employment and Unemployment*. Cambridge, MA: MIT Press.

Locke, R. M. and Thelen, K. (1995). 'Apples and Oranges Revisited: Contextualized Comparisons and the Study of Comparative Labor Politics', *Politics & Society*, 23: 337–68.

Machin, S. (2004). 'Factors of Convergence and Divergence in Union Membership', *British Journal of Industrial Relations*, 42(3): 423–38.

Maurin, E. and Postel-Vinay, F. (2005). 'The European Job Security Gap', *Work and Occupations*, 32(2): 229–52.

Milkman, R. (2006). *L.A. Story: Immigrant Workers and the Future of the U.S. Labor Movement*. New York: Russell Sage Foundation.

Murray, G. and Waddington, J. (2005). 'Innovations for Union Renewal', *Transfer*, 11(4): 489–95.

OECD (1997). *OECD Employment Outlook*. Paris: OECD.

—— (2002). *OECD Employment Outlook*. Paris: OECD.

—— (2007). *OECD Employment Outlook*. Paris: OECD.

—— (2009). *Growing Unequal? Income Distribution and Poverty in OECD Countries*. Paris: OECD.

—— (2010). *OECD Employment Outlook*. Paris: OECD.

Palier, B. and Thelen, K. (2010). 'Institutionalizing Dualism: Complementarities and Change in France and Germany', *Politics & Society*, 38(1): 119–48.

Piketty, T. and Saez, E. (2006). 'The Evolution of Top Incomes: A Historical and International Perspective', *American Economic Review, Papers and Proceedings*, 96(2): 200–5.

Pontusson, J., Rueda, D., and Way, C. R. (2003). 'Comparative Political Economy of Wage Distribution: The Role of Partisanship and Labour Market Institutions', *British Journal of Political Science*, 32: 281–308.

Raess, D. and Burgoon, B. (2006). 'The Dogs that Sometimes Bark: Globalization and Works Council Bargaining in Germany', *European Journal of Industrial Relations*, 12: 287–309.

Regan, A. (2011). 'The Rise and Fall of Irish Social Partnership: Euro-Irish Trade Unionism in Crisis?' Unpublished manuscript, University College Dublin.

Roche, W. (2011). 'The Breakdown of Social Partnership', *Administration*, 59: 23–37.

Rothstein, B. (1992). 'Labour-Market Institutions and Working-Cass Strength', in S. Steinmo, K. A. Thelen, and F. H. Longstreth (eds.), *Structuring Politics: Historical Institutionalism in Comparative Analysis*. New York: Cambridge University Press, 33–56.

Rowthorn, B. (1992). 'Corporatism and Labour Market Performance', in J. Pekkarinen, M. Pohjola, and B. Rowthorn (eds.), *Social Corporatism: A Superior Economic System?* Oxford: Clarendon Press, 82–131.

Rueda, D. (2005). 'Insider–Outsider Politics in Industrialized Democracies: The Challenge to Social Democratic Parties', *American Political Science Review*, 99: 61–74.

—— (2007). *Social Democracy Inside Out: Partisanship and Labor Market Policy in Industrialized Democracies*. Oxford and New York: Oxford University Press.

Rueda, D. and Pontusson, J. (2000). 'Wage Inequality and Varieties of Capitalism', *World Politics*, 52: 350–83.

Saint-Paul, G. (2002). 'The Political Economy of Employment Protection', *Journal of Political Economy*, 110: 672–704.

Sano, J. and Williamson, J. B. (2008). 'Factors Affecting Union Decline in 18 OECD Countries and their Implications for Labor Movement Reform', *International Journal of Comparative Sociology*, 49(6): 479–500.

Scruggs, L. and Lange, P. (2002). 'Where Have all the Members Gone? Globalizations, Institutions, and Union Density', *Journal of Politics*, 64(1): 126–53.

Simoni, M. (2007). 'The Renegotiated Alliance between the Left and Organised Labour in Western Europe'. Ph.D. dissertation, London School of Economics and Political Science.

Soskice, D. (1999). 'Divergent Production Regimes: Coordinated and Uncoordinated Market Economies in the 1980s and 1990s', in H. Kitschelt, P. Lange, G. Marks, and J. D. Stephens (eds.), *Continuity and Change in Contemporary Capitalism*. Cambridge: Cambridge University Press, 101–34.

Streeck, W. (2009). *Re-Forming Capitalism: Institutional Change in the German Political Economy*. Oxford and New York: Oxford University Press.

—— (2011). 'The Crises of Democratic Capitalism', *New Left Review*, 71: 5–29.

Streeck, W. and Hassel, A. (2004). 'The Crumbling Pillars of Social Partnership', *West European Politics*, 26(4): 101–24.

Streeck, W. and Schmitter, P. C. (1991). 'From National Corporatism to Transnational Pluralism: Organized Interests in the Single European Market', *Politics & Society*, 19: 133–64.

Sverke, M. and Goslinga, S. (2003). 'The Consequences of Job Insecurity for Employers and Unions: Exit, Voice, and Loyalty', *Economic and Industrial Democracy*, 24: 241–70.

Swank, D. (1998). 'Funding the Welfare State: Globalization and the Taxation of Business in Advanced Market Economies', *Political Studies*, 46(4): 671–92.

Visser, J. (2002). 'Why Fewer Workers Join Unions in Europe: A Social Custom Explanation of Membership Trends', *British Journal of Industrial Relations*, 40(3): 403–30.

—— (2011). The ICTWSS Database: Database on Institutional Characteristics of Trade Unions, Wage Setting, State Intervention and Social Pacts in 34 countries between 1960 and 2007, Version 2. Amsterdam: Amsterdam Institute for Advanced Labour Studies AIAS, University of Amsterdam.

Wallerstein, M. (1999). 'Wage-Setting Institutions and Pay Inequality in Advanced Industrial Societies', *American Journal of Political Science*, 43: 649–80.

Wallerstein, M. and Western, B. (2000). 'Unions in Decline? What Has Changed and Why?', *Annual Review of Political Science*, 3: 355–77.

Western, B. (1995). 'A Comparative Study of Working-Class Disorganization: Union Decline in Eighteen Advanced Capitalist Countries', *American Sociological Review*, 60(2): 179–201.

Whittall, M. (2005). 'Modell Deutschland under Pressure: The Growing Tensions between Works Councils and Trade Unions', *Economic and Industrial Democracy*, 26: 569–92.

Name Index

SUBJECT INDEX